Places in the United States of America mentioned in the text

One Flight Too Many

Roy and Pat Leach

With very best wishes for
your own history of 16 Squadron

Yours ever,

Jimmy

24.5.12

One Flight Too Many

The unusual saga of a young photographic Spitfire pilot in WW2 – and its aftermath

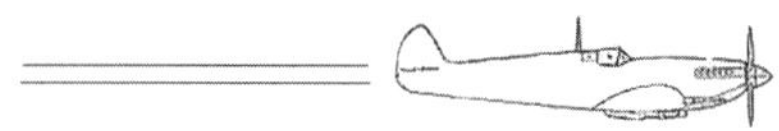

by

Jimmy Taylor

Foreword by

H.R.H. The Duke of Edinburgh, KG, KT

Published by Greystones Publishing

A CIP catalogue record for this book is available from the British Library.

ISBN 978-0-9572210-0-0

Design and layout by Barry Perks

Prepared and printed by:
York Publishing Services Ltd
64 Hallfield Road
Layerthorpe
York YO31 7ZQ
UK
Telephone: 01904 431213
Website: www.yps-publishing.co.uk

Dedication

Dedicated to the ever-living memory of my friends in 16 Squadron in 1944
who were killed on operations:

P/O Hew Colgate 31.8.44

F/O Jimmy Wallace 9.9.44

F/L Tony Gibb 18.9.44

F/O John Brodby 21.9.44

W/O Donald ('Jolly') Jolliffe 1.10.44

F/O Clyde Heath 18.11.44
posthumous DFC

and of the four Dutchmen whom I never knew who, following my landing in 't Hesseler
on 19th November 1944, were executed by the Germans:

Jan Vonk 19.11.44

Jan Boomkamp 25.11.44

Piet van Dijk 25.11.44

Hendrik Roetgerink 25.11.44

"Goodnight, sweet Prince, may flights of angels guard Thee to Thy rest."
Shakespeare

"Lord God of Hosts, be with us yet, lest we forget – lest we forget."
Kipling

Foreword

BUCKINGHAM PALACE

For six years during the Second World War, life changed dramatically for every inhabitant of these islands. Those who joined the services gave up quiet risk-free jobs, or left school, and found themselves training for and then taking part in about the most dangerous occupations in every part of the world. Jimmy Taylor and I were at school together in the '30s, but then our lives took different paths.

'One Flight Too Many' is one man's account of his experiences in that war, and the consequences of his involvement in photographic reconnaissance. For many, the end of the conflict enabled them to start a new life, but none of us could quite make a clean break with our lives during the war. Jimmy Taylor's crash started a sequence of events that came to dominate his post-war life.

This book is not a history, but it is the sort of book from which history is written.

Philip

Introduction

This is a wartime flying story but, unlike most others, it is concerned not with savage air-battles and dogged bombing-raids, but with the quieter and little-publicised business of photographic reconnaissance. I was one of the pilots of the Spitfires that flew alone and unarmed over enemy territory to photograph targets of importance to all three Services in the prosecution of the war but, in the case of my Squadron, mainly for Montgomery's 21st Army Group in Europe.

Because I am frequently asked how we managed to find our way, often over thick cloud-cover, to photograph a dot or a line on our maps and return with the vital pictures, I devote several chapters to describing our cameras and equipment and our methods of using them, our navigational procedures with just our maps, a compass and a clock, and what happened to the films on our return.

I try to present the reality of my own small number of sorties by quoting the official records of each of them and then adding my very personal account from the diary that I wrote-up soon after the event. My good friend and colleague, Michael Horsfall, did the same and also took a large number of brilliant photographs, a few in colour, many of which he has generously allowed me to use in the earlier pages of this book.

The human factor was also important, involving both our Squadron commander at the top and the airmen mechanics and photographers st the bottom, whose skill and devotion to duty ensured that the airframe and engine were in peak condition, that we went out and returned safely, and that the photographs came out clearly.

The fact that my engine failed proved, later, to be no one's fault, but it brought misfortune to me and tragedy to a small Dutch community. It also led, from 1990 to the present-day, to my visiting the small town of Borne and the hamlet of 't Hesseler, not far from the German frontier, every year and forming warm relationships with the families of the victims and other inhabitants. It also led to my close friendship with the town's archivist, Hennie Noordhuis, who organises all my visits and has opened the way to my many rich and unusual experiences in both Holland and Germany. As a result, I have included a chapter called "Dutch Voices", which is mainly in Dutch, with some translations into English. Hennie also is an excellent photographer and deserves my deep thanks for letting me use many of his pictures in the later part of this story.

I also owe a special debt of gratitude to H.R.H. The Duke of Edinburgh, KG, KT, for the extremely perceptive and understanding Foreword that he has so kindly written. Our paths certainly divided after he left Cheam School, but they have crossed occasionally in the last two decades, as I have mentioned in this book. As a distinguished veteran of WW2 himself, his wise words are a great encouragement to me and will, I hope, find an echo in the hearts and minds of my readers.

Jimmy Taylor
Leeds 2011

Contents

		Page
Foreword by H.R.H. The Duke of Edinburgh, KG, KT		v
Introduction		vi
	Prelude	
Chapter 1	Boyhood – Pre-war	1
Chapter 2	Schoolboy in Wartime	23
Chapter 3	Early Days in the RAF	30
Chapter 4	Aviation Cadet in America	41
Chapter 5	The Other Side of the Joystick	61
Chapter 6	In Limbo in Britain	78
Chapter 7	Bound for Bomber Command?	86
Chapter 8	Fulfilment	98
Chapter 9	16 Squadron	124
Chapter 10	The Spitfire in Blue and in Pink	144
Chapter 11	Planning a Sortie	152
Chapter 12	Flying a Sortie	167
Chapter 13	My Operations – the Full Story	180
	Downfall	
Chapter 14	Bale-out and Evasion	283
Chapter 15	Capture and Interrogation	301
	Interlude	
Chapter 16	The Passing Years	319
	The Aftermath	
Chapter 17	Shock! Horror! Was I the Missing Pilot?	336
Chapter 18	Return to 't Hesseler	346
Chapter 19	Exit 16 Squadron – Enter a Musician	367
Chapter 20	Wind, Helmets and Museums	372

Chapter 21	Beyond the Ignorance	383
Chapter 22	My Spitfire Unearthed	388
Chapter 23	Reunion with the Relics	396
Chapter 24	Schoolchildren and a Sovereign	406
Chapter 25	Fun with F-16s	414
Chapter 26	Return of the Veterans	418
Chapter 27	"Aliquippa" – Bentelo – 'Little Peter'	430
Chapter 28	Investigating My Engine Failure	437
Chapter 29	Silent Flights and Noisy Reunions	447
Chapter 30	Enter a 17th-Century Jesuit	470
Chapter 31	Happy Returns to Holland	476
Chapter 32	Reviving My Memories – Improving My Know-how in UK	492
Chapter 33	Return to the Air over Holland	513
Chapter 34	Forging Closer Links with the Dutch	523
Chapter 35	Focus on Arnhem	533
Chapter 36	Saluting Those Who Did Not Return	547
Chapter 37	Return to Rheine	568
Chapter 38	More Flights – Real and Simulated	578
Chapter 39	Tying-up the Ends of 16 Squadron's Part in 'Market Garden'	591
Chapter 40	The Rhine Crossing	612
Chapter 41	The Battle of the Twente Canal – the Liberation of Borne	626
Chapter 42	Journey's End	638
Chapter 43	Full Circle	647
Dutch Voices		664
The Epilogue		726
Appendices		728
Bibliography		742
Acknowledgements		746

Prelude

CHAPTER 1

Boyhood – Pre-War

My love-affair with flying began, I suppose, when I was about eight years old. Before that, I was determined to join the Navy, an ambition that horrified my peace-loving parents. My father, Rev H.M.S. Taylor, had been a chaplain in the Great War and had won an OBE for bringing in wounded soldiers from No-Man's-Land; but he had ministered to so many dead and dying, had read the Burial Service so often, and had written so many sad letters to bereaved families, that he regarded the war as obscene and would never talk about it. After it, he felt the need to try to restore the values of the stable world he had known before 1914; so he became a schoolmaster and, in 1921, bought Cheam School near Sutton in Surrey, a long-established preparatory school for boys, which badly needed a young and energetic Headmaster with a good war-record. The fact that he had no money was a drawback, but he managed to borrow enough to rent the School for the first five years from Arthur Tabor, the previous Headmaster.

One of the School's former pupils commanded a submarine at Portsmouth so, in the summer of 1930, my father took my brother Gerald, born 18 months before me, and myself to visit him on this submersible boat; my father was sure the experience would make me change my mind about choosing a Naval career.

He was quite right: at the end of our visit, I regarded life on a submarine as cramped, noisy, smelly, and highly dangerous – in short, horrendous. Almost on the spot, I decided to make my future in the Royal Air Force! My poor parents were too stunned to resist and, to give them their due, they never once complained about my choice. From then on, my mind focused on aviation in all the forms open to an eight-year-old, and most of my pocket-money went on model aeroplanes, 'Biggles' books, and pulp-fiction magazines, commonly called 'comics', containing the dramatic adventures of clean-cut heroic characters, based on the pilots of the Great War and drawn with skill and technical accuracy in a continuous picture-sequence. It was the absence of reading matter (except for 'balloons' of speech emerging from the mouths of the participants) that raised the ire of my parents and teachers and provoked their condemnation, obliging me to read such inspiring stuff under the bed-sheets.

Saro London flying-boat, similar to the one that gave me my rather unappreciated first flight in 1934

My fixation on flying did not preclude an abiding interest in all forms of transport, especially in the record-breakers of their day. My awareness of the sea was kept alive by a much-loved uncle, who was a respected figure in Southampton and delighted in taking his nephews to see the great ships in the docks there. This was the hey-day of steamships as the carriers of passengers and freight around the world, before they were challenged by the pre-war flying-boats and supplanted by the post-war land-planes. In January 1933, we saw the Cunard "Berengaria", the third largest ship in the world, went aboard the White Star "Georgic", saw her two sister-ships "Olympic" and "Homeric", also seven other great liners and twelve smaller ones, two warships in dry-dock, and ten submarines – and we walked on a huge recumbent bronze propeller of the "Majestic", a work of art in its own right. On another visit the

Cheam School, Surrey, with the main building (left) and the Chapel and the private garden in front

Cheam School, Surrey, with the asphalt playground in front and (1-r) the Chapel, connecting corridor, main building, classroom blocks, and fives courts on extreme right

following year, we were taken to the RAF base at Calshot and shown over a Saro Lerwick flying-boat, whose two engines looked inadequate to get its great hull airborne. I was then given a flight in another Saro flying-boat, a twin-engined biplane London; I sat in the fuselage without much of a view, but I remember vividly the loud crashing noise, like ball-bearings falling on a tin tray, when the metal hull hit the water on landing.

Gerald (left) and I in our primitive pedal-cars in the fine asphalt playground of Cheam School in 1928

I had another brother, Christopher, 2½ years younger and plagued with Hodgkin's Disease, which threatened him with an early death. Our childhood was blissful, highly privileged in many ways, except that we never had much money; we learned to make do with very little, though, and to create our own amusements. A boarding-school was a perfect environment for three active boys to grow up in, especially in the holidays, when all the facilities and grounds were at our disposal. We had our own bedrooms on the top of the third floor and an adjacent nursery, from which we could see the great 'Hannibal' biplane airliners taking-off and landing at Croydon Airport, ten miles away; the Big Schoolroom and a Long Corridor gave us space indoors for the launching of home-made paper gliders of our own design, even 15"-wingspan triplanes; the large tarmac-covered outdoor playground was ideal for roller-skating and for careering about in our wooden pedal-cars; and beyond this lay the extensive playing-fields for flying kites and model aeroplanes.

In those days, the latter were made of wire or thin strips of birch-wood and covered with silk, their wooden propellers being driven by the unwinding of long strands of elastic. Solid scale-models came in boxed kits of roughly-cut hardwood, which had to be laboriously filed and sand-papered to shape; struts and undercarriage legs would be clipped from a coil of brass wire, while propellers, wheels and machine-guns were lead castings. These kits were manufactured by 'Skybirds' and were really too difficult for a small boy to construct; the slow-drying 'Seccotine' glue and glossy enamel paints made the job even harder, while cutting-out the paper insignia and sticking it on with 'Gripfix' paste added a final untidy element to the messy end-product. Nevertheless, it was an absorbing hobby and I became more proficient as time went on.

Cheam School, Surrey, domestic staff c.1927

Back row:	**?**	**Donald**	**Mr Elson**	**Mr Williams**	**Fraser**		
		odd-job man	*head-gardener*	*carpentry teacher*	*gardener*		
Front row:	**?**	**Albert**	**'Mrs' Sawyer**	**'Mrs' Lamb**	**Mr Golding**	**Jane Fraser**	**? ?**
		footman	*cook*	*housekeeper*	*butler*	*dormitory maid*	

Cheam School, Surrey, boys and staff in Summer 1933
Gerald is 4th from the left in the back row; I am 4th from the right in the row below; Prince Philip is on the right at the end of the next row; my father and mother are in the centre of the row below: to the left are Miss Morgan-Brown, B.E.H. Elwin, W.J. Malden, and C.H.M. Pearson; to the right are R.B. Meredith, W.J. Lock, C.M. Gubbin, and Miss Heelis (matron)

Our parents seemed to be always occupied in term-time, with 70 boys to look after, together with ten or so teachers, a dozen domestic servants and half-a-dozen outdoor staff; but even in the holidays there were activities for them to supervise, potential parents to entertain, and the business of running the estate to attend to. This did not matter much to us, as we had many friendly allies among the domestic and outdoor staff: the butler – first Mr Golding and then Mr Law – was almost a father-figure, although we kept him waiting endlessly at meal-times until we had finished our particular projects.

Albert, the footman, and his brother Donald, the odd-job man (both former boys from Dr Barnardo's Homes), were drawn into our activities and experiments, and helped to work or repair our clockwork toys and steam-engines; and Mr Williams, the carpentry teacher and estate handyman, who came from Osborne Naval College when this closed in 1920, was our sternest critic, but with a twinkle not far from his eye; he was an exemplary craftsman and set the highest standards in woodwork: boys could progress onto the sharper tools in his workshop only after we had shown ourselves proficient at straight sawing, smooth planing, and making accurate joints. Perhaps more than any of his academic colleagues, he earned the gratitude of his pupils in later life, when we found he had given us the skills to meet the challenges of DIY in our homes.

My parents were liberal in many ways, but still believed strongly in the value of a classical education. At the age of six I attended Miss Brown's Academy on the outskirts of Cheam village. Donald took me there and back on the cross-bar of his bicycle. Here I learned the rudiments of French and Latin, as well as English, Maths, Geography and History, and copper-plate handwriting along ruled lines, correctly spelled and punctuated – no creative writing scribbled across a page, no play with sand and water, no paints brushed over large sheets of paper, no modelling with clay or plasticene, although our numbers were small enough for us all to be seated round one large table. Good behaviour was the watchword. Were we naughty? Sometimes. Did we suffer from this regime? I doubt it.

With the need to economise all the time, it made sense to my father (although, in retrospect, I think it was rather unfair on us) to give all three of his sons their preparatory school education, from the age of 8 to 13, at Cheam. In fact, Miss Brown had done her work so well that I was ready to join the bottom class at 7½. The curriculum was little different from hers, although I added Greek in my fourth year. There was, of course, in keeping with the tradition of 'a healthy mind in a healthy body', great emphasis on physical activity: compulsory games of cricket, soccer, and rugby, and swimming; optional fives in the four outdoor courts, and hockey in the indoor playground; boxing and fencing as paid extras, along with music; roller-skating and practice cricket in the big playgound; Scouting in the grounds and on Banstead Downs; keeping individual gardens, which could be converted into race-tracks for wind-up cars; and ice-skating in severe winters on ponds in Nonsuch Park and Wimbledon Common. When to these are added the plain cooking (the same menu every week of the year), straw mattresses (called 'biscuits') on iron bedsteads, open windows at night, even in winter, in the unheated dormitories, and corporal punishment on the bottom from my father (*"This hurts me more than it hurts you"*), it is clear that, at Cheam School, either we were being given an early antidote to a future of comfortable and carefree living or we were being prepared for the worst privations that life might have in store for us. For me, it was the latter.

Boarding-schools can be very self-contained worlds, with matches against other schools the only reason for going outside their boundaries. My father aimed to extend our range of experience by inviting speakers from varied backgrounds to give talks on Saturday evenings, usually accompanied with lantern slides, on all manner of subjects, from Polar exploration to motor-racing, the latter given by his wartime friend, George Eyston, the holder of several records; similarly, sermons in Chapel were given by visiting clergymen, but often by missionaries and representatives of charities. He also continued the long-established Cheam tradition of a whole-day outing of the School to the wooded expanse of Box Hill, where we could climb trees and wander off on our own, even to a ruined castle, with rusty chains in the dungeon to feed our imaginations. My father also organised visits to the daylight rehearsals of, in my time, the Aldershot Tattoo in 1933, 1934 and 1935, the Royal Tournament in 1930, and the Hendon Air Pageant in 1931 and 1932, when we watched in awe as parachutists were pulled off the wings of ancient Vickers Virginia bombers, Bristol Bulldogs looped the loop tied together with elastic rope, and an 'Arab fortress' or a mock-up battleship was bombed by Armstrong-Whitworth Atlases. Boys' ambitions, including mine, could be given a lasting stimulus by such occasions.

One of the set-piece scenes at the Aldershot Tattoo rehearsal in 1935

From an early age, we spent the long summer holidays by the seaside, eventually fixing on Praa Sands in Cornwall, a few miles from Penzance, as the ideal situation. Here my parents had a small bungalow built on land running down to the sea (cost: £800!), and here we lived a gloriously free outdoor life and got to know my father and mother as ordinary loving parents.

Gerald (right) and I in extremely well-used green overcoats in Cornwall c.1929

From 1929-1935 Sir Alan Cobham, the great pioneer of airline routes, set out to make Britain more air-minded by establishing National Aviation Day throughout the summer at about 200 locations outside towns and villages. Here, just for a day in some suitable field, he would bring an 'aerial circus' of aircraft, which gave displays of intrepid flying and offered short joy-rides to the public at 5/- (5 shillings) a flight.

On 30th August 1933, the fleet arrived at a field near Penzance and we persuaded my father to take us there. I clearly remember our apprehension as we watched Geoffrey Tyson pick-up a handkerchief on the ground with a spike on the wingtip of his Tiger Moth, and the fun of seeing a 'fugitive' being pelted with flour-bombs from a Gipsy Moth. We begged my father to let us go up in an Avro 504N with the rear cockpit enlarged to hold four passengers, but he said he would take a flight first to see if it was safe. Unwisely, he chose a moment when he was the only passenger – and he was petrified throughout the flight: he kept his eyes fixed on the floor of the cockpit, not daring to look out over the edge. After he was helped out, white-faced, he was adamant that we could not follow him into the air; so we had a rather glum journey home.

Two years later, though, on 26th August 1935, we were allowed to attend the Cobham Air Display again at Penzance and, this time, my father agreed that we would all together take the 7/6d final formation flight of the day in the 'Giant Airliner', the Handley Page W10. So, wildly excited, we raced into the fabric-covered fuselage and sat down in the rows of wicker armchairs, from where I experienced the ecstatic pleasure of my first fully-aware flight. I don't remember my precise sensations, except that the horizon tilted at a strange angle whenever we turned; but I can see, even now, the rest of the aircraft stretching out in a Vee behind us: two Airspeed Ferrys, two Fox Moths, two Tiger Moths, and a Cierva Autogyro, bobbing up and down in the warm summer air. Even my father enjoyed this flight, so this time the journey home was full of excited chatter.

Sir Alan Cobham's Handley Page W10 in which my brothers and I had our first flight in 1935

My father's conversion was completed when, during an Easter holiday in Cornwall in 1938, he and my mother decided to take us all to the Scilly Isles, and to fly us there rather than travel all day by the slow-moving "Scillonian" steamship. So we drove to the small grass field, not far from Lands End,

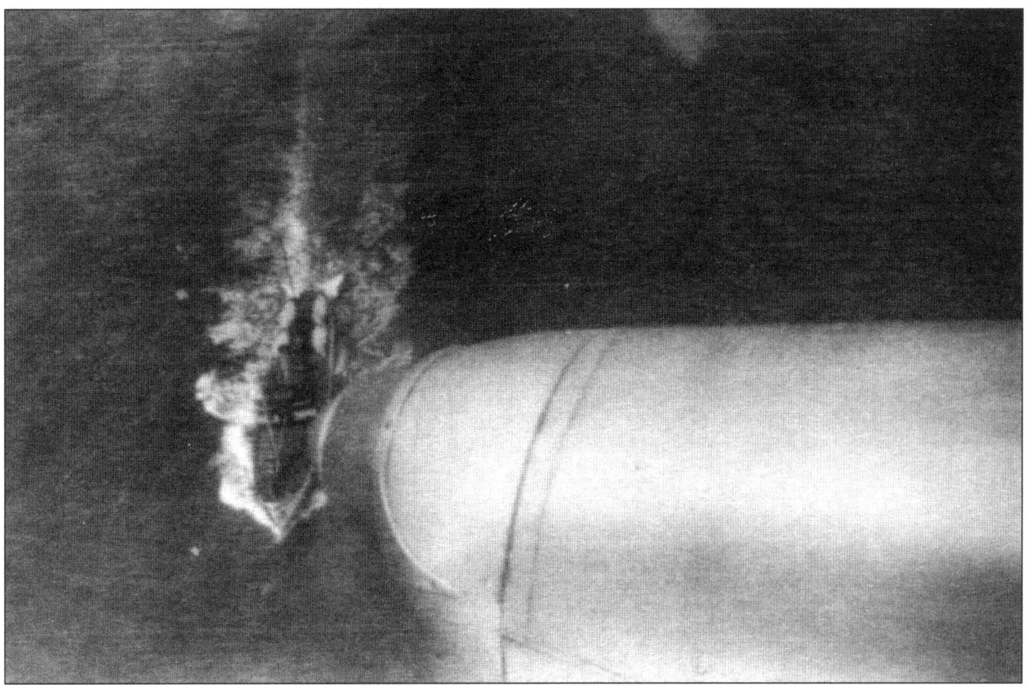

Flying to the Scilly Isles in 1938 in a DH Dragon we pass over the returning SS "Scillonian". This is my first aerial photograph.

which called itself an airport, and boarded a de Havilland Dragon for the flight of a mere 20 minutes. On our way we actually passed the returning "Scillonian" and felt very superior, in spite of the noise and bumpiness of our flight. We landed on the golf-course near St Mary's, the capital of the islands – and here I made the first of the many faults of judgement in the environment of an airfield that dotted my future flying career. I had a small camera, bought in three separate parts (at 6d each) at Woolworths. I wanted a good photograph of the Dragon coming in to land so, at the end of our visit while we were waiting for its arrival, I ran out onto the golf-course and hid behind a gorse bush. Then, when the Dragon was almost on top of me, I popped up and clicked my camera. I went back to the group feeling very satisfied. But my smile soon disappeared when a very irate pilot strode over to me and shouted, "What the hell do you think you were doing! You nearly made me crash with your idiotic behaviour! Where's your father?" He then subjected my poor father to a diatribe about controlling children on airfields, etc, etc. Obviously, I have never forgotten this occasion, which somewhat blighted our carefree day-out on the Scilly Isles.

My photograph, which infuriated the pilot, of the DH Dragon landing on the golf-course of St Mary's on the Scilly Isles

In 1934, the tentacles of London's suburbia were stretching ever further out into the gentle Surrey countryside. Cheam village was not immune and the local council decided to widen the High Street by removing 40 feet of frontage from the School, which would expose it directly to the traffic. My father was already suffering from a drying-up of new parents, who wanted a country environment for their sons' upbringing, so he had little alternative but to move the School to a more attractive situation. After searching, with my mother, in every spare moment for about two months, they found Beenham Court, a neo-Georgian mansion set in 350 acres of parkland and woodland in Headley, on the Hampshire-Berkshire border, four miles from Newbury. There was little demand for large estates at this time, in the aftermath of the 1929 'slump', so Beenham Court was relatively cheap, which was just as well, as my father had to build a classroom wing onto one side of the house and convert many of the rooms into dormitories and a dining-hall. On the other hand, the buildings and grounds of the School at Cheam fetched a good price from a developer, who built a large block of flats ('Tabor Court') and a hundred houses on the site, leaving only the Chapel to become a Roman Catholic church.

The move came at just the right time, not only for the School, but also for the adolescent development of my brothers and myself. Despite the five years' age-difference between them, Gerald and Christopher were united by their common interest in technical and scientific apparatus and machinery. Gerald first explored a subject, and Christopher picked it up from him; they then developed it together. Thus they covered electricity, magnetism, chemistry, photography, wireless, aeronautics, steam-engines, petrol-engines, and explosives – they proved photographic flash-powder to be as effective as gunpowder – later, they took up acoustics, music and geology. Gerald had a workshop near the stables, which eventually became a 'ham-shack', or amateur transmitting and receiving station with its own international call-sign. He also set up a darkroom in one of the attics, where he developed films and made increasingly effective prints. Christopher followed suit and even I tried my hand, but stuck at an elementary stage. My father had no understanding of what two of his sons were doing and could only voice his astonishment when he happened to catch sight of their activities.

Cheam School, Headley c.1936
The mansion and garden of Beenham Court (centre) with my father's classroom wing on the right

Aerial view of Cheam School, Headley c.1939
The garden (left), tennis court and start of the long drive (top left), classroom wing (right), and outbuildings (in trees)

My younger brother Christopher at the age of 12

Aeroplanes, in every manifestation open to us, filled much of our time. In December 1934 Edward Appleby, the chief exponent in Britain of the 'Flying Flea', brought one of these controversial little single-seater home-built machines to a field near Newbury as part of his sales-drive. Its 40hp Carden-Ford engine could hardly get it off the muddy field and the onlookers held their breath as it just cleared the surrounding trees. It was lively enough in the air, but we were not persuaded that it had a future; not long afterwards, its Certificate of Airworthiness was revoked.

My father had a cousin who was married to a very handsome RAF officer, Bill Pearson-Rogers, who in the summer of 1937 was a Wing Commander and Operations Officer at Duxford aerodrome. He was aware of our interest in aviation and invited the family to visit him at the Station; here we examined silver-coloured Gloster Gladiator biplanes lined up on the grass and watched them perform in the air for us; but what really impressed us was a drably-camouflaged Fairey Battle, which was there to be evaluated, one of the first all-metal low-wing monoplane light-bombers, with a retractable undercarriage, a Rolls-Royce Merlin engine and a variable-pitch propeller, to enter service with the RAF. To us, it was a huge machine straining to get airborne: we felt sure it was invincible. Others must have thought so, too, as ten squadrons were sent to France in 1939, only to be slaughtered, six months later, by German flak and Messerschmitts.

A Fairey Battle – impressive in 1937, but obsolete by 1940

Building model aeroplanes had been revolutionised by the arrival in Britain of balsa-wood; lightweight structures could be glued together with quick-drying cement and covered with thin but strong tissue, made airtight and waterproof with aircraft dope, exuding the pleasant smell of peardrops. Our flights could now be measured in minutes rather than seconds and kits of the Wakefield Cup winners were available from the distributors. The catalogues of Messrs F.P.Sweeten of Blackpool, S.Smith of

Warrington, and Model Supply Stores of Manchester took up space in my bedroom, along with copies of "Aeromodeller." From the ceiling hung, literally, my biggest disappointment: a high-wing monoplane of 5-foot wingspan, impressive when covered but with too few spars and ribs in its structure; when I began to wind-up the elastic, the whole fuselage twisted and it was clear that there would never be enough power to carry the monster into the air. So it became a somewhat forlorn bedroom ornament.

My brother Christopher's photograph of me with a 'Baby Gnome' in 1937

As I became older I received more pocket-money and more generous gifts of cash at birthdays and Christmas; so I could afford to join the Aviation Book Club, which published special editions of books, such as the history of aviation and the memoirs and biographies of famous airmen, especially of the 'aces' of the Great War and the pilots of record-breaking flights, for only 3/6d per volume. I took the first issues of W.E.Johns's "Popular Flying", and I collected Player's sets of 50 aviation cigarette-cards, first of RAF planes and then of civil ones, which could be pasted into free well-presented albums. All these increased my knowledge and enthusiasm for flying. I also started collections of picture-postcards of aeroplanes, and kept scrap-books illustrating all the stages of the development of aviation, from the pioneering days, through the biplane era, to the 'modern' monoplanes produced by F.G.Miles, Edgar Percival and de Havilland, whose DH Comet, made of plywood and balsa-wood, won the 1934 England-Australia air race and was the precursor of the 'Wooden Wonder' of the war years, the Mosquito.

The 'Baby Gnome', a typical balsa-wood and tissue, elastic-driven flyer

And I 'doodled' aeroplanes everywhere: in my school note-books and textbooks, on score-cards and writing-pads, on backs of envelopes and margins of newspapers; planes of all kinds, vintage, modern and futuristic appeared, but I never managed to make them look quite right. This tiresome habit remains with me still today: you can measure my attention to a lecture or a committee meeting by the density of drawings scribbled half-consciously on whatever paper is provided; the subjects have remained the same over the years: twisted skeletal early machines; asymmetrical biplanes incapable of flight; and streamlined monoplanes that look like Spitfires but lack the elegant lines of the original. A psychiatrist would, no doubt, claim to find a perpetual adolescent behind this helpless artistry.

The downside of my brothers' talented lives was that neither of them could hit a ball in the air or kick one on the ground; they had no interest in physical games and took no exercise, except for swimming and bicycling when necessary. They were anti-social, much preferring their own company and interests to meeting other people and making conversation with them.

I was virtually their opposite: I had no feeling for science or technology and was a mere onlooker to most of their activities. I had quite a good eye for a ball, enjoyed organised games, tennis and squash, and learned the ways of nature in the acres of woodland on the estate, which boasted a lethargic old gamekeeper. My father kept a fine 16-hand horse and hunted regularly, and my mother had a fat little pony, which she seldom rode and which became more-or-less mine by default; I rode it a good deal,

Boys enjoying a Meet of the Craven Hunt at Cheam School in 1935. My father is at the top of the steps on the right facing the camera.

Boys chosen as 'beaters' ready for a rough shoot in the woods with Jack Malden (left rear), my father (right rear), Kneller, the gamekeeper, (on his right)

but I was not attracted to hunting, even though the Craven Hunt twice met at the School. My father gave me a 12-bore shotgun, and the games master, Jack Maiden, who lived nearby on Greenham Common, taught me to shoot wild duck, pheasant and pigeon: the latter were the bane of the local farmers, as large flocks could devour a sizeable proportion of a cornfield. We could receive free cartridges in return for shooting them, and I learned to steal silently into a wood to pick them off as they flew in to roost. Occasionally, in the winter terms, my father would organise a shoot of local farmers and residents, with the senior boys, including myself, acting as 'beaters', but the 'bags' would rarely reach double-figures.

Jack Malden kept in touch with the world of flying and had an RAF friend who would arrive for a weekend by landing his Hawker Tomtit, a small biplane trainer, in a field next to Malden's cottage. He would sometimes fly round the School as he left. To me, this was a thrilling event, one which brought flying very close to everyday living.

New Cheam, as we called Beenham Court, had grass and hard tennis-courts, an open-air swimming-pool at the end of the beautiful garden, and even a golf-course which, after one term as a nine-hole nursery, was soon turned into a first-class cricket-ground. I was only a modest cricketer and barely made the first XI in my last year. At football, I started as a hopeless wing-forward, as revealed by the following extract from an account, written by Jack Maiden – in caustic mood – in the "Cheam School Chronicle", of a 2nd XI match against Banstead 2nd XI on 15th October 1932. It was my first appearance for the School and I was overcome with nerves:

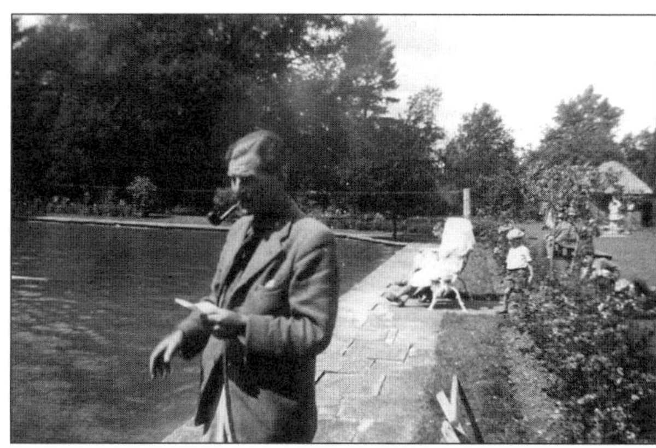

Jack Malden, games master and one of the long-serving staff 1929-59, by the swimming-pool of Cheam School, Headley

> *"Cheam did most of the attacking during the second half, and would have scored many goals if it had not been for Taylor and Worth, who need not have been on the field for all the work they did. Taylor was really pathetic, not even trying to get to the ball when it came his way. He got his toe once to the ball and scored Cheam's third goal. Philip* (Prince Philip of Greece, now HRH The Duke of Edinburgh) *played a very good game at centre-half, and was the outstanding player on the field."*

I was gradually moved back down the field until I found my forte as a goalkeeper, in which position I eventually captained the XI.

Cheam School Cricket XI summer 1935
(with those killed in action (k.i.a) during the war or decorated for valour).
Back row 1-r: Anthony Ellwood Timothy Lewis Robin Worth (k.i.a) William Edwards (k.i.a)
Middle: John Wynne (DFC) Brian Bland Benjamin Rodwell (k.i.a) Henry Radice Llewellyn Evans (k.i.a)
Front: Richard Norton (MC) Jimmy Taylor

As a 12-year-old, I was tall and lanky, with prominent front teeth, which prevented me closing my mouth. Partly for this reason, I was hopelessly shy and, although my instinct was to be sociable, I usually joined my brothers in hiding in the shrubberies whenever visitors or other children called in the hope of seeing us or playing with us. Like them, I had an inquiring mind, but mine was channelled into the humanities, such as history and art and, later, architecture and archaeology. Under my father's tutelage, I was writing both Latin and Greek verse, more as an intellectual exercise than from an understanding of poetry. It was part of the preparation for trying for a scholarship to Eton but, although we both invested much time and effort for a year in the process, I failed to reach the required standard. I ended my years at the School by becoming Head Boy; my father agonised over the decision because of its shades of nepotism, but eventually the masters persuaded him that I was the leading candidate. It probably gave me some self-confidence at Cheam, but it was all knocked away again at Eton.

I had no wish to go there: one of my best friends had gone to Blundell's School, a small but thriving public school in Devon, and I was very keen to join him. But my father considered Eton the best place and was prepared to scrape together the money (£100 per term) to send all three of us there in due course. Unfortunately, he chose, or had chosen for him, the worst-but-one out of the 24 boarding Houses, which meant the weakest Housemaster. Two-thirds of a boy's life at Eton was spent in or controlled by his House, and the House was run by the senior boys under the supposedly watchful eye of the Housemaster. Mine saw and did absolutely nothing, and the older and bigger boys behaved little better than thugs. Gerald had been there 18 months before I arrived and was bullied mercilessly every night by a group of mindless, heartless lay-abouts, who forced him to do their homework for them, leaving him no time to deal with his own. Gerald never recovered from the experience and henceforth hated Public Schools: he joined the RAF in 1940, went into radar, despised the officer-class, refused a commission, and became an ardent Socialist, happy only in the company of fellow 'boffins' in the ranks. Fortunately, he made his post-war career in Marconis, where he became fulfilled as the successful Sales Manager of the Radar Division, setting-up radars at airports in Saudi Arabia and China – and even voicing Conservative opinions. He died of Alzheimer's Disease on 7th November 2000.

I was more fortunate: I was good enough at games to be encouraged rather than picked on, but I saw what happened to Gerald. The tradition of 'stiff upper lip' prevented our saying anything of this either to the Housemaster or to our parents; but when, four years later, I became Captain of the House, I told the Housemaster what had gone on in those earlier days and he gave me permission to use the

Three brothers at Eton together in 1938 – I'm on the left

cane to deal with any manifestation of bullying from then on. At least, by the time I left, my House was a more civilised place than when I entered it; but, because of Gerald's ordeals and the element of fear that prevailed in my earlier years, I felt no affection for it.

Eton was not the place for us: it was still a school mainly for the sons of landed gentry and aristocrats, rich industrialists and businessmen, and highly-successful professional people: the boys would one day inherit titles, fine estates, or places on the boards of important companies. It was not 'done' to talk about money. The shop-keepers in Eton High Street were despised for being in 'trade', yet among my contemporaries were a Wills, a Vickers, and a Horlick, scions of prosperous trading families who had risen up the social ladder. Professionalism was equally despised: the ideal was 'the gifted amateur'; a good athlete in my House was ostracised for practising running before breakfast – regarded as 'unsporting'! This was still the day of the "Gentlemen vs the Players (professionals)" cricket match at Lords. The most important person at home might well be your game-keeper.

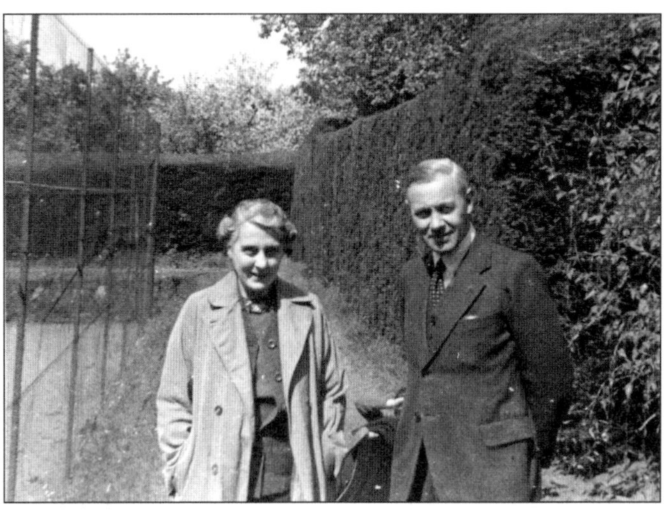

My father and mother near the kitchen garden in 1947, the year of their retirement from Cheam School

This was not the right atmosphere for the sons of a middle-class schoolmaster, who had to count every penny (he claimed one discount off the school-fees because he was a clergyman, and another because he had two, and later three, sons at the school at the same time).

Christopher, however, arriving nearly five years after Gerald, went to a different House, run by a cultured and understanding Housemaster, and had a wonderful time, making many friends whom he kept till the end of his tragically short life – he died in January 1950. But I am sure that Gerald and I would have been much happier in the less exalted community of a school like Blundell's.

Of course, Eton was not all doom and gloom for an active adolescent; it had its in-built advantages: every boy had his own study-bedroom, so my aero-modelling could proceed in leisure moments, especially with the new-fangled kits of Frog 'Penguin' models, made of detailed moulded plastic, glued together with quick-drying cement, painted with matt or glossy enamel, and adorned with authentic insignia on transfers that dried integral with the surface. Far less labour and skill were now needed to make a satisfactory 1/72nd-scale model, and I gradually produced a whole fleet of the most significant machines, from Hawker Fury to Spitfire I, and Cierva Autogyro to Vickers Wellington.

Frog Penguin Hawker Hart with Frog hangars behind

After passing School Certificate in 1938, I could more-or-less choose my own curriculum in the two years of the Upper Fifth Form, as Eton regarded the Higher School Certificate as unnecessary. In addition to small classes for lessons, senior boys had individual tutoring at a high-grade level, when almost any subject valued by the tutor could be discussed for an hour twice a week. I was blessed with Geoffrey Agnew as a tutor; he was a director of his family firm of art-dealers in Bond Street and had tried to enlist in the RAF as an air-gunner, but his bad eye-sight had let him down. He therefore came to Eton to help replace the younger staff who were being called-up. For two years he attempted to enlighten me on the history and appreciation of art; it was hard going for both of us, but my wits were sharpened and my viewpoint broadened by long debates with Geoffrey on topics extending over the whole range of human activity. As a result of such tuition, many school-leavers in those days did not go on to university but moved straight into affluent jobs in the City or into traditional family regiments in the Army; in their minds, 'the Old School Tie' was better than a degree as a passport to entry into positions of future power and influence.

A low-flying Messerschmitt 109 ?
Actually a Frog Penguin plastic model
hanging by a thread from my window

The funeral procession of George V
inside Windsor Castle on its way to St George's Chapel on 28th January 1936. Among the double ranks of soldiers lining the route were the members of the Eton College OTC, of whom I was one.

After a year as a Classics General specialist, I switched to History General, with German, Art and General Science as extra subjects. The latter included visits to various factories in Slough: the manufacturers of 'Aspro', the 'Speedway' motor-cycle company, a paint works, and the Tipsy Aircraft Company. Here we saw the production process of these delightful little wood-and-fabric single- and two-seater low-wing monoplanes, which might have become the Austin Sevens of the air.

In my first year at School, I joined the Officers' Training Corps (OTC), when I put on the distinctive Eton mulberry-coloured uniform, with breeches and puttees, and found myself, on a cold and wet January day in 1936, standing over my reversed rifle in an inner courtyard of Windsor Castle, as part of the guard of honour for the funeral cortege of King George V. Peering from under my peaked cap, I watched a procession of kings and princes pass by, the like of which would never be seen again.

Young boys do not usually take much interest in matters of State, but we could not ignore the later publicity accorded to Edward VIII's affair with the twice-divorced Mrs Simpson. On 10th December 1936, we crowded into the private room of M'Dame (the House-matron) to hear the King announce on the wireless – in his upper-class English accent with strange German, American and Cockney interferences – that he was abdicating the Throne in order to "marry the woman I love". We were deeply shocked, as we had hardly recovered from the death of his much-respected father; but we soon became aware of the country's good fortune in exchanging the mercurial, wilful Edward for his reluctant brother George VI with his solid family virtues.

In addition to Field Days, when we pretended to be attackers or defenders out in the Berkshire countryside, with umpires telling us whether we were alive or dead, I attended two Summer Camps under canvas, one at Tidworth, the other at Aldershot; at the latter in August 1938, I had my first ride on a tank and saw my first Spitfire, a Mark I, which dived down on the camp at awesome speed.

My first sight of a Spitfire at the OTC camp at Aldershot in 1938

In December 1938 I scraped a Pass in Certificate 'A', which involved taking a written examination and a test of leadership ability in a TEWT – tactical exercise without troops – on a sand-table. This entitled me to quit the infantry and join the small but, to us, exclusive Air Section. We wore the same Boer War uniform, but had a striped light-blue, dark-blue and red arm-band to identify our special unit. Instead of weekly drills, we had lectures on theory of flight, engines, armament, navigation, and airmanship, learned the Morse Code, and practised aircraft recognition. On Field Days, we visited RAF airfields, where I enjoyed flights in an Avro Tutor and a Miles Magister.

The highlight of the year, and of my life till then, was the Air Section Camp, held with about 200 other Air Cadets and housed in tents near Selsey Bill in Sussex in August 1939. This was a wonderful week: we had two squadrons of Avro Ansons allotted to us for flights to and from a series of RAF Stations, where we were given talks and demonstrations, examined aircraft and equipment, and were treated to informal flying displays. Thus I experienced the delights of plodding along in an early Anson and helping to wind the undercarriage up or down with 132 turns of an awkward handle. The greatest joy was to climb into the primitive midships gun-turret and observe the formation of 31 other Ansons gently rising and falling all around me. In this stately way, we descended on Tangmere, Hornchurch, Gosport, Calshot, and Southampton.

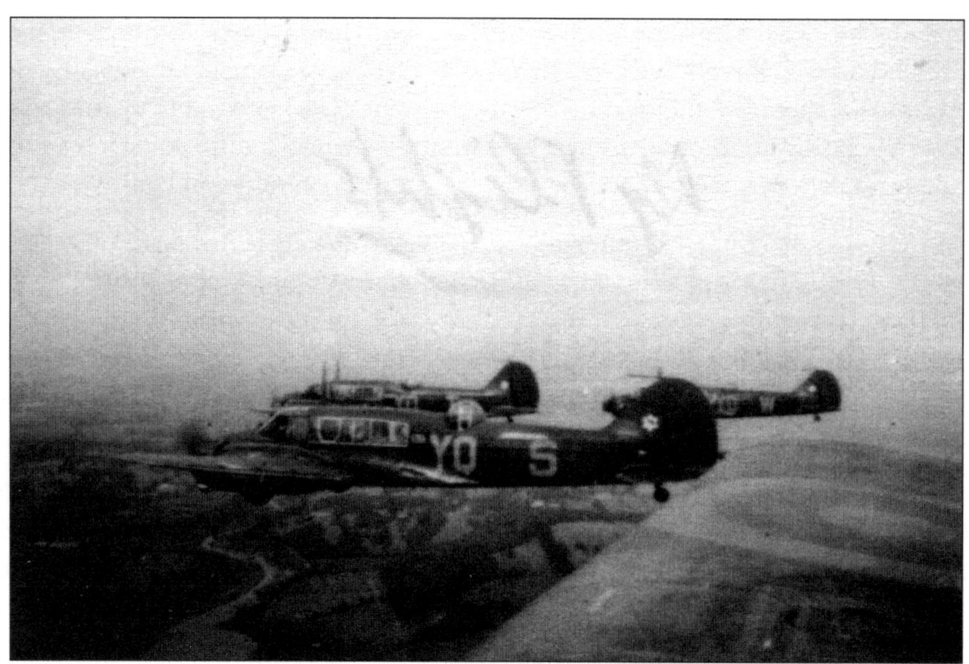

Avro Ansons at the Air Section Camp in 1939
taken from the midships gun-turret

On one of our flights we had to carry-out a reconnaissance mission and fill-in a Form 228 message-slip 'for use in the air only':

"Date: 4th August. Aircraft: Avro Anson 7994. Unit; 4 Squadron. Pilot: F/0 Welsh,
Passengers: 4 Cadets.
Height: 1900'-2000'.
Conditions: bumpy, with poor visibility.
Over Portsmouth and Southampton harbours: HMS Hood, 4 cruisers, 6-7 destroyers, 12 steam-yachts, an Empire flying-boat, a 10,000-ton cargo-liner, and 22 other ships.
Over Wimborne Minster Aerodrome: Fairey Battles, Avro Ansons, Avro Tutors."

At Hornchurch, I glimpsed live rounds in the four guns in the belly of a Blenheim I fighter and was told, *"We're on constant stand-by."* I then remembered the Munich Crisis of the previous summer, when we had sandbagged the windows of my House's dining-room as a forlorn attempt at an air-raid shelter, and I had gone with some other boys to welcome Chamberlain back from his meeting with Hitler on 30th September; I had helped to push his car out of Heston Airport after he had waved a piece of paper at the crowd and declared, *"I believe this means peace for our time!"* – to be followed only three months later by Hitler's invasion of Czechoslovakia. I felt relieved to think that we were not to be caught napping again. Alas, one month later, the Blenheims were shown to be useless against Messerschmitts.

Just as Eton forced my growing-up, so the holidays expanded my horizons, although I was still a skinny youth and pitifully shy. Gerald introduced a new element into my life when together we bought a 1927 Morris Oxford open two-seater, with a 'dickie' seat behind for two spare passengers. Gerald was a member of the School of Mechanics at Eton, which was a workshop, with power tools, materials and instruction on an almost industrial scale, available at a small extra fee. Another boy had bought the Morris to renovate it, but ran out of money by the time he had finished; so he sold it to Gerald for £3.10s.0d. – of which I contributed the 10/-. My father drove over from Headley and towed the car back on a rope, with Donald steering – no mean achievement. We had a 1½-mile gravel drive through the woods at New Cheam and it was here that Gerald and I learned to drive the Morris, which we named the 'Tadpole', and painted a large white image of one on each door. The multiple garage in the courtyard at Cheam had a pit with removable wooden 'sleepers', which enabled us to get underneath a car. Here we maintained and repaired the Morris, and even learned to remove the sump, disconnect a connecting-rod, withdraw a piston and fit a new piston-ring, for instance, long before we were old enough to drive on the roads.

Whenever relations or adult friends came to the School, we would beg sixpence off them and cycle up to the village garage to buy half-a-gallon of petrol in our old tin can (with a hole in the bottom!). We would then rush back (one finger over the hole), pour the petrol into the 'Tadpole', put the donors into the 'dickie', and give them a fearsome ride down the drive and back, charging round blind corners, horn blaring to scare off walkers or other drivers coming in the opposite direction, and flinging up dust and stones from the pot-holes. Our passengers never asked for a second ride.

More importantly for Gerald, the car contributed to his wireless experiments. He and Christopher had gradually developed a rudimentary walkie-talkie with, at first, a very limited range. One set, manned by Christopher, would be based in the workshop, while the mobile one would be fitted into the 'dickie' with Gerald sitting alongside; it was a cumbersome affair and needed heavy acid batteries. I would now steer slowly down the drive until reception failed. Gerald would then return to the workshop for further technical modifications until, after many trials and much frustration, he managed to talk to Christopher from the end of the drive. He refined the sets sufficiently to be allowed to use them for communicating messages on OTC Field Days, although he still needed another boy to carry the batteries. The Berkshire countryside, however, was full of ditches and rabbit-holes, which too often caused sudden breaks in transmission by the Wireless Section, and – to tell the truth – the commanders found it quicker to send their messages by runner! Nevertheless, when the war came and all transmitters were confiscated, the Army found that Gerald's walkie-talkie was more efficient than their own.

I also bought my first motor-bike, for 10/- from a local farmer. It was a 500cc BSA, so heavy and powerful that I could hardly turn the engine over on the kick-starter. I painted it orange and called it 'Thunderguts', a very appropriate name. It nearly killed me, and I still carry a scar on my hand when it fell on me on the gravel drive. It featured in an early 8mm film that Gerald made with a second-hand cine-camera, after which I sold it for £5.0.0 and bought a little 250cc machine via "Exchange and Mart" for £21.0.0. This was a mistake: it was so lacking in power that it would hardly climb the hill to Newbury when, at the age of 16, I was allowed to take it on the road. I then tried to build my own car and designed a three-wheeler: I found the front wheels and steering mechanism for an Amilcar on a scrap-heap and sent up to Gamages, in Holborn, for a 98cc engine, in its original wooden box, for £3.0.0. I bench-tested this with a bicycle sprocket and chain, and was delighted with the horrible noise it made without a silencer. I constructed a vee-shaped framework from 5"x2" pine-wood, fitted the Amilcar wheels at the front, and a small bicycle wheel, with a chain-drive to the engine, at the rear. An embryonic instrument-panel and a seat completed the vehicle. My brothers and Donald gave me a hearty push down a suitable slope under the yew trees – there was a rending crash, the framework broke in half, and I sat down heavily on my backside on the ground! The engine had not even fired. After this, we bought a bicycle with a similar engine already

On my 500cc BSA motor-bike 'Thunderguts' at speed down the drive at Cheam School

fitted in front of the pedals, so that it could be pedal-assisted up hills. It was marketed as an 'Autocycle' and was a good-natured little machine, which we used as a very economical (120 mpg) local runabout. On the estate, we had an original Ford van, with belt-driven pedal-operated gears, for carrying grass-cuttings, logs, and loads of all kinds. It was usually driven by Donald, but Gerald soon mastered the peculiar footwork needed to change gear on this vintage wagon, but I never did.

We still had the cottage in Cornwall, but my parents now looked at Europe for more ambitious family holidays. My father had a 22hp Ford V-8 saloon and decided that, by staying in small hotels and guest-houses, we could spend a month touring the Continent as cheaply as staying in England. Hitler was steadily building up Germany as a Nazi state with a militant foreign policy to acquire 'lebensraum' (living-space) in Eastern Europe; but he badly needed foreign currency to purchase raw materials. He therefore encouraged tourists to visit Germany by relaxing the 'Guns Before Butter' policy under which ordinary Germans had their economic lives strictly controlled by ration cards: he offered a good rate of exchange, petrol coupons in greater quantity and at a lower price than his own motorists were allowed, and more coupons and better food than the German housewife received. So, in the summer of 1936, we set out for Germany en route to Alt Aussee, our destination in Austria, aware that we were probably entering a hostile rather than a friendly country.

The Taylor family starting on a holiday in their 22hp Ford V-8 in 1938 – I'm on the right

Our last meal in England was taken at the 'Wattle and Daub' café near Dover, so we decided to take precautions by referring to Hitler as 'Mr Wattle', to the Hitler Youth as 'Wattle Minors', and to the rash of long red banners adorned with the swastika, which we had seen on news-reels, as 'daub'. We were probably being too cautious, as we met no animosity from anyone and, indeed, were welcomed wherever we stayed. The 'autobahnen' were fast and impressive, making the narrow English roads seem very out-of-date. The only signs of military activity that we came upon were the Labour Battalions marching out in the early morning with polished spades carried on their shoulders, and a Dornier Wal flying-boat parked outside a museum in Munich. Austria was a great contrast: a sad little fragment of the vast Austro-Hungarian Empire, which had been dismantled by the Treaty of Versailles 17 years before. The people were delightfully friendly and cheerful, even though their beautiful capital of Vienna could hardly be supported by their impoverished rural economy. Little did they know that they were fated, two years later, to be locked into the embrace of Nazi Germany.

Malcolm Campbell's speedboat 'Bluebird" en route to Lake Maggiore in 1937

In 1937 our itinerary took us to the battlefields of the Great War at Chateau Thierry and Vimy Ridge, to the Rhone glacier in Switzerland, to Venice and Pisa in Italy, and to the Paris Exhibition. Mussolini's Fascist state was very similar to Hitler's: the frontier guards and Customs officials were courteous and efficient; the 'autostrada' made motoring a pleasure, the Italians we met were easy-going and helpful, and the gorgeously-uniformed Carbonieri seemed to belong more to a comic opera than to a police-state that posed a serious threat to Western democracy. On our way home, we stopped to admire Malcolm Campbell's 'Bluebird' speed-boat on a lorry on its way to make an attack on the World Water Speed Record on Lake Maggiore.

In 1938 we visited Stockholm and Gotland in Sweden, Berlin in Germany, Interlaken in Switzerland, and Rheims and Chartres in France. Germany was more forbidding this time and we were glad to get out of it; but one incident is imprinted in my memory: we joined a crowd lining the famous Unten den Linden to watch Admiral Horthy, Regent of Hungary, drive along it on his way to meet Hitler, to negotiate peaceful co-existence. I had a small camera, but my view was blocked by a row of well-built Stormtroopers. Seeing my frustration, one of them stepped aside and placed me in front of him. I still have the resultant photograph and a warm spot for that soldier, whatever his future role in the Army.

Unter den Linden in Berlin in 1938 with Nazi banners replacing the lime-trees and soldiers lining the route for Admiral Horthy

August 1939 saw us driving to Hendaye, close to the Atlantic border of France and Spain, with the Pyrenees rising spectacularly behind. This was a seaside holiday, but we took a bus-trip to San Sebastian in Franco's Spain, where the bitter Civil War had only recently ended. We visited a Nationalist war museum and found a Bristol Bulldog, complete but stripped of fabric, standing amidst a profusion of mediaeval torture instruments, which were said to have been employed by the Communists against their prisoners during the conflict.

Our peace was shattered by the war-drums that started beating at the end of August: Hitler stated that his patience was exhausted and massed his troops and aircraft on the Polish border. The other tourists soon left our hotel, whereupon the manager closed it down, forcing us to leave, too. As we drove north at speed, we saw French reservists being called up on general mobilisation and horses being rounded up everywhere for service with the Army. At St Malo we found crowds of English holidaymakers desperately trying to get on any ferry sailing for Britain. We booked in with the AA and went off to visit the wondrous castle of Mont St Michel. On 1st September, the day that Hitler invaded Poland, our number came up and we sailed for Portsmouth, although we had to leave the car behind; we assumed it would be commandeered by the French. It was, therefore, a most pleasant surprise to receive a phone-call from the AA next day to say that it was waiting for us on the quayside at Southampton.

At 11.0am on 3rd September, my father gathered the family and all the domestic staff round the primitive, small-screen, black-and-white television-set in the large lounge at Cheam, to hear Chamberlain regretfully announce:

"I have received no reply from Herr Hitler to my ultimatum and therefore this country is at war with Germany."

The air-raid sirens in London sounded immediately in the background, presaging – fortunately falsely – the expected aerial onslaught on the capital. Our lives were to be changed for ever, mine amongst them.

Mont St Michel looking splendidly defiant on 31st August 1939

CHAPTER 2

Schoolboy in Wartime

The six months after the declaration of war became known as "The Phoney War" because, contrary to all expectations, nothing very startling happened. We now know that Hitler still hoped to come to a peaceful agreement with Britain, whereby he would let us continue to enjoy our Empire in return for giving him a free hand in Europe. We sent an Expeditionary Force to France, but our Whitleys, Hampdens and Wellingtons dropped mines and leaflets rather than bombs, and both sides concentrated their aggressive actions against shipping rather than against each other's frontier defences.

Civilian life gradually moved on to a war footing, with the introduction of rationing and conscription, and shortages slowly began to be felt as imports declined and industry changed over to the production of armaments. Blacking-out all the windows at Cheam was a major undertaking, but the extensive cellars were easily adaptable as an air-raid shelter; the addition of bunks, later on, enabled the boys to sleep down there, if necessary.

An incident in December 1939 had ironic overtones for the family. My father was never willing to allow the war to interfere too much with his own occupations and interests; for instance, he felt he had an absolute right to drive his car and so did his best to ignore petrol-rationing, managing to use a 1000-gallon tank in the garage courtyard for quite some time before officialdom caught up with him and it was recorded. On this occasion, he decided we needed a breath of sea air and so drove the family down to Weymouth. On the way, we stopped by the boundary of Andover aerodrome while I photographed a Blenheim I taking-off and, later, I took a barrage balloon on the ground near Weymouth harbour. We stayed in a small hotel and found ourselves observing a foreign-looking gentleman with broken English, who spent much of his time poring over maps in the sitting-room. Eventually, we decided he was a spy and told the police, who came and took him away.

After a few days we returned home, and next day were surprised when our local policeman (who rented his house from my father) arrived on the doorstep and very apologetically told my father that he had only just prevented him being arrested for spying! The policeman said, *"I told my superior that I knew the reverend gentleman well and I was quite sure he was no spy!"* My father, of course, was very shocked and asked what had occasioned this charge. *"Someone saw your car stopped by Andover aerodrome and a person taking photographs, so he took down the number of your car and reported it. And, again, near Weymouth harbour, your car's number was reported for taking photographs."* Naturally, I owned up straightaway, whereupon the constable said, *"I'm afraid I must ask you to hand over the photographs."* Fortunately, Gerald had developed and printed them as soon as we returned home, so we gave the prints to the policeman, who was most grateful, apologised for all the trouble he had caused, and left us with conflicting feelings. My father, of course, was annoyed with me, but Gerald collapsed into a chair, laughing: *"He's got the prints, but I've still*

A print of the Barrage Balloon near Weymouth that escaped the hands of our village policeman

got the negatives!" And I still have the duplicate prints he made of the Blenheim and the barrage balloon. We often wondered what happened to our 'German spy'.

The German 'blitzkrieg' in Northern Europe in April and May 1940 changed everything. The Home Guard, originally Local Defence Volunteers (LDV), was formed and my father became a Captain commanding the Headley Platoon, with Headquarters at the School. Parades were held on the front drive and exercises on the playing-fields. The main fear was of German paratroops descending on the extensive downs south of Kingsclere; here the Home Guard established a lookout post in a shepherd's hut on wheels, with six men in pairs on two-hour shifts patrolling the grassland from dusk till dawn. Gerald rigged up an Aldis lamp, which was sighted on a tent in the kitchen garden of the School, where two other men kept watch. With a series of simple messages translated into Morse Code placed beside the lamp, the guards on the downs could signal "All Clear" – it was fortunately never anything more threatening – at intervals throughout the night.

My father in early LDV battle-dress

The Home Guard carried ancient American .300 rifles, with six rounds handed out to the men when they were on duty. We spent much of our time making 'Molotov Cocktails': bottles filled with petrol, with a piece of cotton-wool wired to the neck. This would be lit before the bottle was thrown at an enemy vehicle, so that the petrol exploded when the bottle burst on impact. We also had a primitive cannon, a piece of drain-pipe on wheels, which would fire a mortar-bomb dropped down its throat. I always felt it was more likely to burst the drain-pipe and damage our own side rather than the enemy.

**Headley Platoon of the Home Guard outside the west door of Cheam School.
Capt. The Rev. H.M.S. Taylor is seated in the centre with a stick; behind him is Mr Tilley, the head gardener, while Lawrence, a groundsman, is third on my father's left**

People laugh at "Dad's Army", but we all felt very confident of 'giving Jerry a bloody nose' if he invaded. True, he had overwhelmed Holland, Belgium and France in ten days, but none of them had its population organised and armed for resistance in towns and villages throughout the country, with each man willing to die in the effort to hold-up the enemy's advance. We knew every hedge and ditch, every lane and culvert, and we were up to every trick of concealment and deception. We held occasional exercises with regular troops stationed in the neighbourhood – and we always won, by 'cheating', as the opposition claimed: hiding men on carts under straw or potatoes, attacking before dawn, sabotaging their transport, cutting their telephone wires, or kidnapping their commander.

A near-disaster occurred one summer evening when a report came through that paratroops had been seen in a clearing in our woods bordering the main Newbury-Basingstoke road. I rushed round the village on our Autocycle, calling-out the men who were available and telling them to report at the School. Guns and ammunition were issued and two squads were formed, who crept uphill towards the clearing from two directions. At the first sight of greyish figures spotted on the crest in the dusky twilight, rifles were cocked and cries of *"Hands-up!"* echoed – but from both sides of the clearing! Understanding then dawned, followed by embarrassment, and then dismay: *"What if...?"* Various theories were aired about the alert: *"the 'paratroops' were thistledown descending in the evening haze"*, or they were *"two gipsy-women searching for kindling in the clearing"*. It was good practice, but also a salutary warning for the Home Guard.

On 16th September 1940, however, the real thing happened. Throughout that brilliant summer, we had watched the contrails forming mighty doodles in the sky as our fighter-pilots sought to deny to the Luftwaffe the air superiority that Hitler needed for his invasion. Now, all the Home Guard units in the Southern Counties were called out, church bells were rung, and we waited expectantly for news of where the enemy had landed. At Cheam, the Home Guard gathered in full force – although one over-excited member, who ran up and down the road with his loaded rifle demanding the pass-word from each new arrival, thereby holding up the assembly process, had to be taken back to his family. After 'falling-out' from the parade, the men stood around in groups discussing the possibilities of the situation. From the roof, we could see bombs and anti-aircraft shells lighting up the sky over Southampton. By 11.0pm no "Stand down" had been ordered, so the platoon took over the boys' dormitories – luckily, they were still on holiday – and went to bed.

At 4.0am my father was met by a deputation of uniformed cow-men: *"Please, Sir, can we go and milk our cows – they won't wait for Hitler!"* As the sky brightened, more anxieties about work were expressed until, at about 12 o'clock, the order came through to dismiss the men. They departed with a certain air of disappointment that we hadn't been allowed to 'have a go at Jerry', after all.

Was it real or another fantasy? At the time, we heard that underwater pipe-lines carrying petrol, part of our beach defences, had set the sea on fire and caught the German invasion barges as they tried to come ashore at night; the proof lay in the scorched bodies of German soldiers washed-up on the beaches. Later, this story was replaced by a more likely explanation: that a flotilla of our motor-torpedo boats was returning from a sortie in the Channel when it ran into a group of similar German boats looking for trouble off the South Coast. A running fight ensued, boats were set on fire, petrol spilled onto the sea, which caught fire and burned the German sailors who fell into it, and their bodies were subsequently washed ashore. Whatever the cause, it was certainly a night to remember.

Another excitement in this period, although not connected with our Home Guard, was the crash-landing of a Heinkel 111 bomber onto farmland near Highclere. After hopes of invasion had faded, the Germans turned to the night bombing of London, the ports and industrial cities. The typical unsynchronised beat of their two engines distinguished the German bombers from our own aircraft, and Newbury lay roughly on the route from the South Coast to Birmingham and Liverpool. Coventry was raided heavily and with great destruction on the night of 14th November 1940, and the Heinkel forced-landed on its way home from this operation.

The news spread quickly by word-of-mouth and, next morning, I bicycled over and found a crowd round the recognisable wreck of the machine, which was closely guarded by the Army. There were too many people around, so I waited a few days and then returned to the scene. The wreckage had been removed and there was no one about. By diligent searching in the nearby grass and undergrowth I discovered the front sight of a machine-gun, the deviation card of a compass, the magnifying-glass of some small instrument, and a handful of live rounds of ammunition, whose charge I removed at home. These were a fine addition to my collection of aeronautica, which included control wires from an SE5a (whose rotted wings languished behind a shed at Eton) and the roundel on fabric from a Short Singapore, presented to me at Calshot.

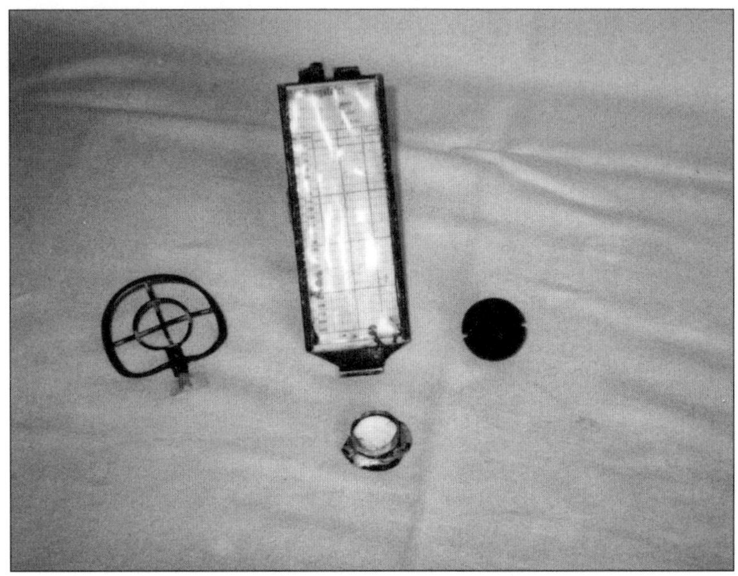

Relics from the Heinkel 111 that crashed near Highclere on 14th November 1940: an air-gunner's front sight, the compass deviation card, a magnifying-lens, and the plastic ball of a toggle

A few bombs landed near Newbury, probably dropped at random from aircraft in trouble. Two fell on open ground near Basingstoke, where trial drilling for oil had taken place before the war. The site was actually marked on Ordnance Survey maps as 'oil-well', so our local pundits announced knowingly that, of course, the Germans must have been aiming at it!

One also fell near Cheam School: it hit the edge of the small sewage-plant that worked untended near the stream that ran through the grounds; the damage was limited and soon repaired, but the blast cracked a pane of glass in a window in the lounge, which was not replaced for many years. Much more serious was the worry that this, and the possibility of many more and worse incidents, caused my parents, with their responsibility for the safety of the sons of sixty families. Cumulatively, the burden of trying to maintain the normal activities of the School during six years of wartime danger and restrictions resulted in their early retirement from Cheam in 1947.

At Eton, the war interfered considerably with our schooling, although it also broadened my education by the wider experiences it introduced. Two air-raid shelters were built in the garden of my House; windows were taped over; the black-out, a particular headache with carefree and careless boys about, was strictly enforced; gas-masks had to be carried to lessons and into Eton High Street, but top-hats were discarded for the duration.

After Dunkirk, when the Home Guard was formed, the senior boys in the OTC automatically found themselves enrolled, keeping watch at night on the Slough-Windsor railway line, the Slough water-works, and the many playing-fields on Agar's Plough. A master would go out with a section, which would patrol for four hours or so; we would then be excused Early School (before breakfast) next morning. At least one master, as I experienced, was not above sharing his hip-flask of whisky with the boys in his charge – very welcome in the freezing cold of a winter's night on a railway embankment. Considering that we were comparative youngsters, usually considered irresponsible, and were marching around with loaded rifles, it is surprising that I can recollect only one dangerous incident: this was when a boy pressed the trigger before unloading his rifle; fortunately, he was pointing it at the ceiling of the Orderly Room in New Court. The noise of the shot indoors was shattering: the bullet whizzed through the ceiling into the classroom above – and was never found.

As with the Home Guard at Cheam, we also had occasional exercises with the troops stationed at Windsor Castle – and, again, used every trick to outwit them. On one occasion, we were defending the streets between the Houses at Eton against the Household Cavalry, who were attacking in their Bren-gun carriers. We quickly climbed to the top floors and, as the open-topped carriers passed beneath the windows, poured buckets of coal into their immaculately-painted carriers. Their Commanding Officer was furious: he telephoned our CO to say that we had spoiled the paint-work of his carriers and, if we used such tactics again, he would not play war-games with us any more!

After calling-off their invasion, the Germans started their night-bombing campaign in the autumn of 1940; air raids on the area round Slough and Windsor took place sporadically until the spring of 1941, with only a small number of aircraft involved. Anti-aircraft guns were sited round Windsor Castle especially, including what we believed was a particularly heavy naval gun, whose firing made a thunder-ous noise, audible in every study-bedroom in Eton. There were no reports of German aircraft being shot down in the vicinity, but the steel splinters from the exploding AA shells fell all over the School, slicing through the branches of the trees and clattering down onto the roads and pavements. Boys, of course, were forbidden to leave their Houses at night when the air-raid sirens sounded, but occasionally I would be leaving a tutor's house in the dark when the gunfire started and would run the gauntlet of returning to my House, which happened to be at the most distant end of Eton, through this dangerous but most exciting fusillade.

More prosaically, on Wednesday afternoons, instead of playing organised games, the older boys would go out to local farms, to assist in the war effort by hoeing potatoes and helping to gather in the harvest, or by cutting and stacking pit-props in Windsor Great Park. We soon discovered that these everyday rural activities were much more demanding on our physical energy and will-power than commonly supposed.

The reality of bombing struck home in November 1940, when Eton was showered with incendiary bombs all over the place. Fortunately, the ground was soft and damp, causing many of these small pro-jectiles to fizzle out innocuously. One fell through the roof of my House and landed on the armchair in a boy's room, burning his Eton tails and trousers. Another dropped onto a flat roof and cut-out a perfect circle of lead, with the imprint of the maker's specification, which was stamped into its base, accurately reproduced in negative. Yet another that fell through the roof lay unnoticed in the attic until a damp patch appeared on a boy's ceiling – the rain had kindly extinguished the bomb. Walking to les-sons next morning, I saw a finned tail protruding above the surface of a piece of waste land; returning at dusk, I climbed over the fence and retrieved the unburnt half of an incendiary bomb – one more item to be added to my collection.

The most serious incident, however, happened in the night of 4th December. Two boys were on fire-watch on the tower of the New Court classrooms, overlooking the Slough-Eton road; there was a wild

Damage to Upper School at Eton caused by a delayed-action bomb dropped in the night of 4th December 1940.

whooshing sound and two 5001b bombs hurtled over their heads and slammed into the buildings on the other side of the road, part of the old College precincts and Upper School, bordering School Yard. The Music Precentor' s house was completely demolished, but Dr Ley and his wife, amazingly, emerged shaken but uninjured. In the confusion that reigned round this scene of destruction, that could easily have embraced the whole of College with the 70 resident Collegers, the second bomb was forgotten until the next morning, when the School Clerk entered his office under Upper School and almost fell down a hole in the floor. At the bottom lay a delayed-action bomb, too awkardly placed and too delicate to be de-fused. The whole area was evacuated, with anxious crowds behind the barriers staring at the historic buildings of Upper School, reputedly designed by Wren, and the 15th-century Chapel. It was difficult to concentrate on lessons when the wretched thing was liable to explode at any moment.

In the early evening, with a tremendous roar heard all over the School, the bomb went off. It destroyed the end of Upper School and its roof, it blew out all the windows of the Chapel on that side of School Yard, and it hurled a great lump of masonry right over the four storeys of Lupton's Tower (built in 1521) on the opposite side of the Yard. The 15th-century College wing adjacent to Upper School remained sturdily in place. Fortunately, no lives were lost; but the war came very close to Eton that day.

The Air Section of the OTC had been 'stood down' when invasion threatened, but it was re-formed when it became clear that the RAF was going to be the only service to be able to hit the Germans in Occupied Europe and in their homeland. I became the Cadet Sergeant in charge of the Section, under one of the masters, Acting Pilot Officer 'Cub' Hartley – so-called because of his youthful appearance. He was friendly and enthusiastic, but he could never remember the words of command to use when we paraded with the rest of the OTC, numbering nearly 500 boys. I therefore had to stand close behind him and tell him, in a loud whisper, what to say! We were destined to meet each other again in May 1945 in remarkably different circumstances.

The Air Section's activities were undertaken with greater urgency as boys left the School to join the RAF and valued whatever grounding they could be given in the basic subjects, especially Morse Code and aircraft recognition. In my final year I was allowed a bicycle and used to pedal over to White Waltham airfield to watch the Tiger Moths and Miles Magisters performing endless 'circuits and bumps' with embryonic pilots under tuition, interrupted every now and then by an Anson or Airspeed Oxford of the Air Transport Auxiliary (ATA) taking-off or landing with a load of civilian pilots – many of them women – to ferry operational aircraft of all kinds from the factories to the squadrons.

By the beginning of 1941, many of my friends had left to join up in one or other service: Arthur Schofield, who was younger than me and my closest colleague in the Air Section, left early to enter the RAF, and 'Bunty' Rodwell, a delightful contemporary at Cheam, had already been killed on operations with the RAF. I was 18 and badly wanted to leave, too, but my parents persuaded me that the war would last a long time and that I would benefit greatly from staying-on another term, to be Captain of my House and in the top ten boys in VI Form, with some authority in the School. They were probably right, but I felt very frustrated and my conscience kept pricking me. Things came to a head when

I was given twenty lines of some tedious poem to learn by heart: this seemed to me to be a total waste of my time and I told the master so. The result was that I had to appear before the Headmaster – quite an intimidating experience. He gave me a stark choice: conform or quit. Not wishing to hurt my parents, I agreed to conform.

At the end of March, I handed-in my last essay – on "Statesmanship". I was elected to 'Pop' (the select Eton Society), but only because more eligible candidates had already gone off to the war; and I left Eton with no regrets and, I'm afraid to say, with little feeling of gratitude, except to a few perceptive masters who I recognised had helped to further my development as an individual. My strongest feeling was relief that I was now free to join the war properly.

CHAPTER 3

Early Days in the RAF

The war news was bad: Greece and Crete had fallen to the Germans; Yugoslavia was partitioned between them and the Italians; Malta was under daily aerial bombardment; in North Africa, Rommel was intent on capturing Tobruk; and in June the Russians were reeling from the German invasion. There was no doubt in anyone's mind that we would win in the end, but it was obvious that we were in for a long haul. I took a short holiday at home, exercised with the Home Guard, and tried my hand at teaching some lessons at Cheam, notably 3rd Year Maths under Jack Malden's tutelage. I found it came easily to me – as long as I knew more than my pupils! Nevertheless, I was itching to get into the RAF, but concerned about the effect on my parents of their second son joining his brother on active service.

Conscription had not yet reached down to 18-year-olds, but I felt it was better to volunteer and be given my choice of service than to wait to be called-up and be pushed into whatever arm was in need of new recruits. So on 29th May 1941, two days before my 19th birthday, when my parents had gone out for the day, I straddled my under-powered motor-bike and phut-phutted the 16 miles to the Recruiting Centre in Reading. This was housed in a run-down school-building, with a series of uniformed clerks at desks trying to cope with a crowd of like-minded young men. Nothing much happened: I was registered as an applicant for aircrew training in the RAFVR (Volunteer Reserve) and told to wait at home for a call to the Aircrew Medical Board at Oxford. I told my parents what I had done, and my mother said, *"I knew you would"* – which was a relief.

A few days later, I was called to Oxford and endured a very intensive medical inspection, at the end of which I was told that I had a hydrocele (a swollen testicle), which would need an operation before I could be accepted for flying. I had had this condition for several years, but was much too embarrassed to call anyone's attention to it. It was equally embarrassing in Newbury General Hospital to have this intimate organ operated on, being prepared and later tended by a series of pretty nurses, for whom, of course, this was just another routine case. It required six weeks' convalescence, which meant lazing in the enchanting garden at Cheam, surrounded by flowers, ponds, butterflies, bees and dragonflies, and trying to concentrate on Frank Kermode's beautifully-written "Theory of Flight", the essential manual for all budding aviators, still in vogue today, I believe.

That summer remained an idyllic memory throughout the war, but I was glad when I was recalled to Oxford on 8th August and, after a short inspection, was passed as fit for aircrew.

A strange little episode occurred when I visited the toilet: I was surprised to find a stocky young man hiding fully-dressed in one of the compartments. I asked him what he was doing:

> *"Well, you see, my eyes aren't very good, so I've given my papers to somebody else and he's going through the eye-test for me. He'll come back here and hand me back my papers, all signed up. Quite simple, actually, but don't tell anyone."*

It did indeed work out as he said, and he and I took the oath of allegiance to King George VI standing side-by-side. It was then I learned his name was Peter Thorne, and we stayed together for nearly a year. His story became a sad one and, ultimately, a tragic one, which I learned about in Holland fifty years later. This will appear in due course.

After two days' leave at home, I reported to the Aircrew Reception Centre at Lord's Cricket Ground in London on 11th August, along with hundreds of other aircrew recruits in every variety of civilian

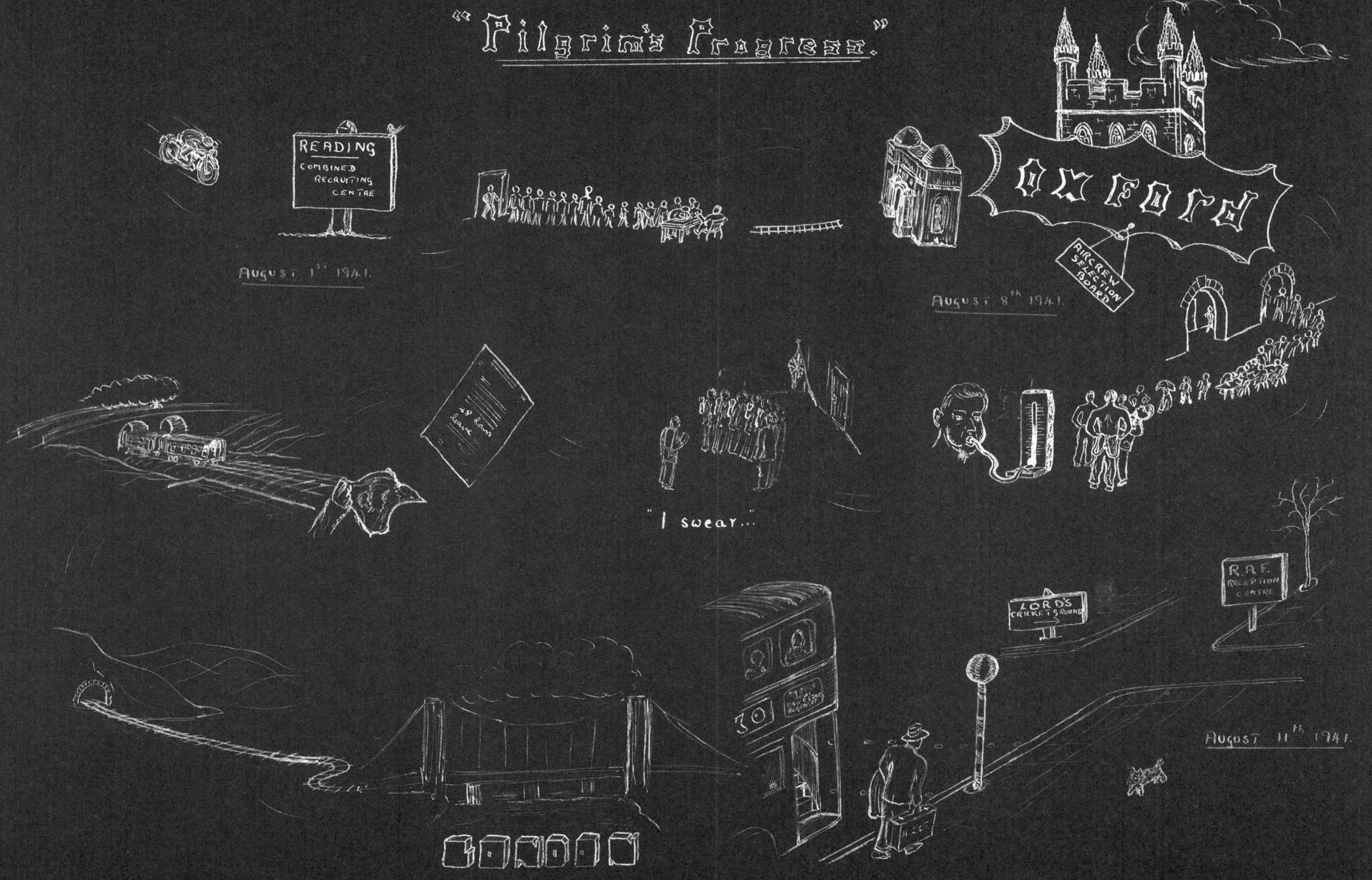

"Pilgrim's Progress."

READING
COMBINED
RECRUITING
CENTRE

August 1st 1941.

OXFORD

AIRCREW
SELECTION
BOARD

August 8th 1941.

48 hours
leave

"I swear..."

LORDS
CRICKET GROUND

R.A.F.
RECEPTION
CENTRE

30

August 11th 1941.

LONDON

clothes, all carrying suitcases. Here we waited for hours, with a low-class cricket match arranged to keep us entertained, until we had filled-in a pile of forms and I found myself the recipient of a sacred number, '1323278', my RAF identity from now on. Later that evening, Peter Thorne and I were allotted to a room in St James's Close, a former luxury apartment overlooking Regent's Park. Here, with three others, we were each given a space on the floor, two square 'biscuit' mattresses, and four blankets. We were already a long way from home.

We spent ten days being 'processed' in the adjoining buildings and discovering a little about Service life. We were divided up into squads and given some elementary drill. We marched, or rather shambled, to the stores, where a tailor with an expert eye looked us up and down and called out some numbers, whereupon an underling produced a jacket and trousers of rough blue serge which, amazingly, were not too bad a fit; the snag was that the jacket was equipped with a brass buckle and buttons which, together with a pair of black boots, became the centre of attention of the various corporals who had charge of us, and we spent hours cleaning and polishing the wretched things. We also learned to keep our living-quarters in a condition to satisfy the most demanding housewife, mopping and dusting meticulously, folding our blankets 'square' on our mattresses, and putting our regulation knife, fork and spoon at the right angle in our mug on our blankets. 'Bullshit' was the name of this game, usually shortened to 'bull'; it extended to adding whitening to the white felt 'flash' which we wore in our 'split-arse' caps, to signify that we were not just plain AC2s, the lowest form of life in the RAF, but aircrew cadets, hopefully heading for higher things one day.

Our meals were taken in the restaurant of the Regent's Park Zoo: 3000 of us formed an immense queue, which snaked in continual 'Ss', so that we passed and re-passed the same men on each side of us time and again, engaging in schoolboy banter as we seemed never to get any nearer to the promised land. However, we had free entertainment from the animals and birds in the Zoo: the mountain goats cavorted on their terraces, giraffes' heads appeared suddenly over high walls, and the antics of the monkeys and their explorations of their own and each other's bodies produced raucous laughter from the hundreds of hungry men in the apparently never-ending lines. All this was against a background of hoots, screams and whistles from a variety of exotic birds.

Eventually, we reached the doorway, where two burly sergeants kept watch against any queue-jumping and tried to spot any miscreants attempting to get a second meal. But no sooner were we in than other sergeants rushed us along with a *"Hurry up, there!"* and *"Wash your 'irons' under the tap as you leave!"* before we had even found a place to sit and eat the 'meat and two veg' and suet pudding and custard plonked onto our plates. Ordinary visitors to the Zoo, passing by, found our behaviour just as fascinating as that of the other animals!

Medical matters formed part of our induction: we marched into the Odeon Cinema for a talk on the necessity for health care and the avoidance of infectious diseases. Slides showing the results of sexual promiscuity were deliberately scarifying and produced white faces among some of the more active members of the audience. Injections against typhoid and tetanus followed, involving more queues with rolled-up sleeves and causing several strong-looking fellows to pass out before they even reached the needles.

Finally, we experienced the pleasure of our first pay parade. Once again we were seated in our hundreds in Lord's Cricket Ground, with a boring game played out in front of us. We eventually found ourselves performing what was to become a fortnightly ritual:

"AC2 Taylor, H.J.S.!" I approach the desk of the admin. officer. *"Sir, '278!"* A snappy salute, an outstretched hand, 30/- in coins and notes, a signature on a sheet of paper, a step back, another salute, a smart about-turn, and I march away, smiling sheepishly as I rejoin my colleagues.

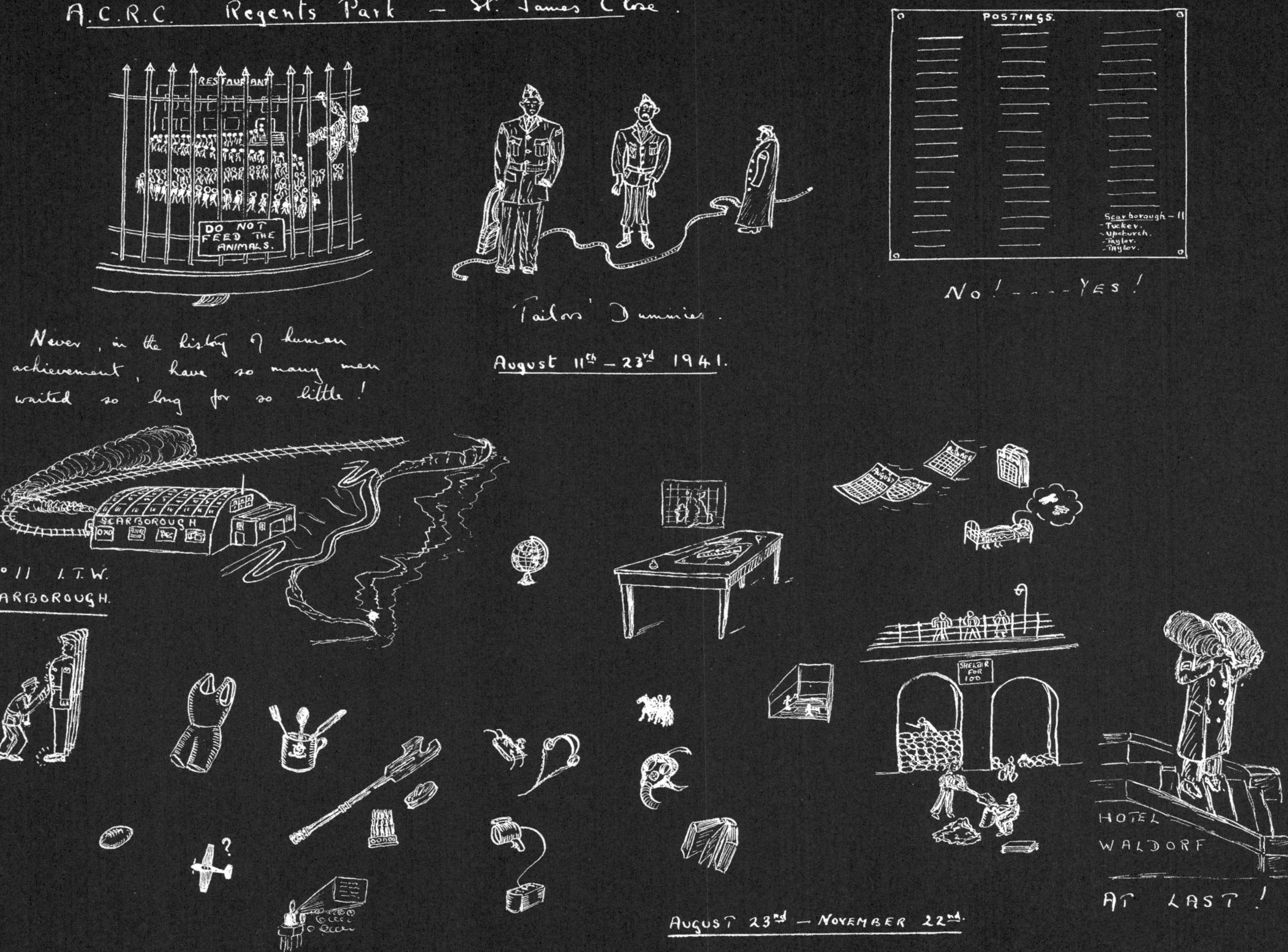
A.C.R.C. Regents Park – St. James Close.
RESTAURANT
DO NOT FEED THE ANIMALS.
POSTINGS.
Scarborough – 11
- Tucker.
- Upchurch.
- Taylor.
- Taylor.
Never, in the history of human achievement, have so many men waited so long for so little!
Tailors' Dummies.
August 11th – 23rd 1941.
No! - - - - YES!
SCARBOROUGH
No 11 I.T.W.
SCARBOROUGH.
SHELTER FOR 100
HOTEL WALDORF
AT LAST!
AUGUST 23rd – NOVEMBER 22nd.

On 22nd August, the posting list went up and I found I was destined for No 11 Initial Training Wing (ITW) at Scarborough. My parents and my younger brother Christopher came up to Town and we had dinner in the Cumberland Hotel and then went to see "Fantasia", the latest Disney creation, which offered a delightful escape from a war-torn world.

The next day, I entrained from King's Cross station with the rest of the Scarborough detachment for my first visit to the north of England. Several seaside resorts had been virtually taken over by the RAF for the Initial Training of aircrew entrants, and here I found myself in the Prince of Wales Hotel on the sea-front, sharing a room with three others. We were put into Flights of 50, in our case under a Corporal Beal, a leather-faced individual with a voice like a fog-horn, an eye trained to see hitherto invisible specks of dust, a ripe command of the saltier words in the English language – and a heart of gold beneath it all. He wanted us to be the best Flight in everything and, once we discovered what a caring chap he really was, we tried our hardest to reach his standards.

Drill, drill and yet more drill in the open spaces of Scarborough, until we could do five minutes of 'continuity drill' without a word of command; daily PT and weekly games of rugger, soccer and tennis ensured that we became remarkably fit.

The eight-week course had been reduced to six weeks, so the academic work was intense. It covered theory of flight, maths, navigation, meteorology, armament, Morse Code, aircraft recognition, law, administration, hygiene, making camp, and first aid. We were taught in a row of summer houses along the cliff overlooking the sea – which made steady concentration rather difficult. I had heard that a deep knowledge of maths was vital for aircrew selection but, in the event, little more than elementary skills were expected.

Over the weeks, we changed gradually from carefree civilians to well-setup service-men, proud to show that we were in the RAF. The level of 'bull' increased with the need to whiten our already distinctive white belts; our buttons gleamed, our boots shone. We thought as a Flight or a team, we covered up the deficiencies of our friends, and we tried to behave well in our time-off in Scarborough.

Most of the boys enjoyed the pubs and dance-halls in the evenings, or strolling along the promenades and piers at the weekends in the hope of meeting the local girls. Peter Thorne and I weren't yet

My course at No 4 I.T.W., Scarborough.
Cpl Beal is 4th on the right of the front row;
I am in the centre of the back row.

interested in these activities: we might go to the cinema or music-hall in an evening, but at the weekends we spent our pay on hiring horses to ride out on the North Yorkshire moors. The others thought we were daft, but we found great relaxation and a bracing change of air and scenery in this activity.

Another source of pleasure lay in finding Arthur Schofield on the same Course 44, but in a different Squadron and Flight and so in another hotel. He and I were certainly the only Old Etonians in Scarborough and, for all I know, the only ex-Public School boys. Life on 11 ITW had opened my eyes to a startling and humbling truth: heretofore, I had assumed that my upbringing at Cheam and expensive boarding-education at Eton had given me certain advantages over my less privileged contemporaries, that I had acquired certain values not shared by them. It was therefore a deep shock to find that my room-mates and fellow-members of D Flight, who had mostly been to day Grammar Schools, had exactly the same attitudes as I had: they were honest, truthful, loyal, well-mannered, modest, sensible, and brave; they could talk intelligently, discuss objectively, work as a team, and take initiatives without becoming loudmouthed or arrogant. In short, if I were a gentleman, so were they. This realisation coloured my outlook from that time to the present day, not only on education, but also on politics and the class-structure of our society.

At the end of the course we were asked to choose a Home or Overseas posting. Arthur chose the latter and disappeared onto a Grading Course. I chose Home and found myself stranded in Scarborough and going round the curriculum again for another six weeks, interspersed with heavy shifts of sandbag-filling. I don't think I have ever felt so bored and frustrated – and there was absolutely nothing I could do about it.

However, even penal servitude comes to an end and, on 22nd November, Peter and I, along with about 80 others, were posted to No 4 EFTS (Elementary Flying Training School) at Brough, six miles outside Hull. This was the home of the Blackburn Aircraft Company, whose works occupied one side of the grass airfield and whose twin-engined Bothas were continually being air-tested in the midst of our Tiger Moths.

We were on a Grading Course, which meant that, in spite of our first choice, we would be trained overseas. This course took us up to solo standard to make sure that we had the necessary ability to learn to fly fully, and we would not waste public money and effort by proving later to lack one or more of the necessary skills.

We were divided into two Flights, one flying in the morning and having ground-school in the afternoon, and the other 'widdyshins' (as they say in Yorkshire!). I found the flying wonderful. I had several instructors, but mainly weatherbeaten patient F/Lt Woods. My main difficulty was in taking-off: he told me to fix my eye on a point on the horizon and keep

We learned to fly a Tiger Moth, like this one, up to solo standard on No 1 Grading Course at No 4 E.F.T.S. at Brough, Yorkshire, 22nd November to 12th December 1941.

heading towards it. The trouble was that he sat in front and his head was in the way forward, so I would choose a tree to one side. Heading towards it meant that I traced a curving path over the ground – not to Mr Woods's liking. Once we had sorted this out, I had no real trouble.

I found 'circuits and bumps' a continual challenge (as they did throughout my flying career, even on gliders), so I am happy to quote from the notes I made at the time of how they should have been done in a Tiger Moth in November 1941:

"Taxi out to the desired position in a slightly zig-zag fashion, owing to the poor forward visibility, and set her at right-angles to the take-off path in order to have a good view of incoming aircraft and to allow them to see you easily.

Carry out the cockpit-checks: check the petrol amount, fuel taps, ignition, tail-trimmer, throttle-nut, oil pressure, altimeter, and slots. Make sure nothing is hanging outside the cockpit.

Look around for other aircraft; when the coast is clear, rev up and turn 90°. Take another quick look round and set-off.

Increase throttle smoothly and ease stick forward, raising tail and machine into flying position and improving forward view. Keep left rudder on pressure to counteract torque under full throttle. Keep your eyes fixed on some object in front and, by gentle anticipatory pressure, keep the nose dead into wind.

At about 45mph the speed of the machine should give it sufficient lift to rise off the ground. Keep her at about 20 feet off the ground until 65mph is reached, and then keep her climbing at that speed.

Keep her climbing until 1000ft, then throttle down to 1900 revs and do a Rate 1 turn to the left: left bank and rudder to get her into the turn, slight top rudder and stick centralised and back to hold her in, and then right stick and forward and right rudder to roll her out.

Repeat twice more, with wing-tip tracing aerodrome boundary. Then, when ½-way across wind, cut engine, trimmer forward, and glide at 90° to landing-path, applying right rudder to counteract loss of torque.

Choose landing-path and, when at 500ft opposite to it, do left-hand gliding turn and aim at path. Aim to cross boundary at 20 feet and level-out. Hold her there until wheels are about 5 feet off ground then, as she sinks in stall, draw stick back until eventually wheels and skid touch down together at about 35mph. Q.E.D.

There's no doubt that this requires a lot of judgement and concentration and is intensely satisfying when successfully completed."

I flew for about 3 hours in the first week, hardly at all in the next owing to fog, and for 3 hours 55 minutes in the last. My instructor then said I was ready to go solo, so that was the end of the course for me.

A few memories stand out. We had the usual drill and PT, but here the drill was for aerodrome defence against invaders: broomsticks with bayonets lashed to one end! All the mechanics were women. The Tiger Moths were parked all round the field; when we wanted to start, an old man or a boy used to spring out of the surrounding bushes and swing the propeller.

The great thing about life at Brough, though, was the friendly relations we had with the instructors, on the ground as well as in the air, and the relaxed atmosphere that prevailed during our three weeks. The RAF's attitude to flying training was that it was a demanding activity and that we should be as relaxed as possible on the ground in order to concentrate fully in the air. There was minimal 'bull' and just one

No 4 E.F.T.S., BROUGH, HULL, YORKSHIRE.

No 1 GRADING COURSE.

22nd November – 12th December 1941.

Patience is rewarded – we become fledglings.

"wonderful weather we're having!"

CREW ROOM.

7 hours flying in 3 weeks.

A last look at home – EMBARKATION LEAVE. DEC. 12th – 27th.

Christmas 1941 was spent at home.
"Eat, drink and be merry, for tomorrow..."

Mr and Mrs Hornby – cold supper and a hot water bottle.

A.C.D.C.
HEATON PARK,
MANCHESTER.
DEC. 27th – JAN 6th 1942.
Fog – snow – rain – ice – waiting.

BONNIE SCOTLAND

GREENOCK

church parade, when the officers seemed to be even less familiar with the drill than we were. In spite of its many drawbacks, Brough contrived to be a happy Station.

Hull was bombed periodically because of its docks and was badly damaged. To ensure that we had at least one good night's sleep in two, half of our number were taken by bus to Selby, 15 miles away, where we slept either in a YMCA canteen or in a little old church. I always chose the church. The disadvantage was that it had no washing facilities and the barest toilets. Returning to the aerodrome for breakfast, we soon tired of the perpetual sausage and mash – but this was wartime rationing. More to our liking were the squash-courts, where Peter Thorne and I played almost every evening, and a nearby stables, which gave us some pleasant riding in the local countryside.

Ten of our course were regarded as below standard, but five of them continued onto the next course and passed; the other five became navigators. Our previous choice of a Home posting regardless, we were now heading overseas, with Manchester as our next destination.

Before this, however, we were granted 14 days' embarkation leave. Saddled with two heavy kitbags, I reached London from Hull at 9.30pm on 12th December, and caught a train to Reading, which arrived at 11.30pm, but went no further. There were no more trains and everywhere was blacked-out, but I managed to hitch-hike to Newbury on a couple of trucks. A kindly policeman took me to a bakery, where I was able to leave my kitbags. I then walked the four miles home along the road across Greenham Common and reached Cheam School at 4.0am.

We had a lively Christmas, with my elder brother Gerald also on leave and several uncles and aunts visiting. On Christmas Eve, Jack Malden took me out shooting duck against a glorious sunset and I managed to bag a brace – my first and last. But all good things come to an end, and on 27th I journeyed back north and reported to the Aircrew Departure Centre at Heaton Park, outside Manchester.

Here we were accommodated in private billets. My hosts were Mr and Mrs Hornby, living with their sweet little 2½-year-old daughter in a semi-detached house in the suburbs. If a householder had a spare room, he was virtually obliged to offer it as a billet to the military if they needed it; he was paid a rent and for any meals, so he could gain a little from the arrangement. Mr Hornby was an Auxiliary Fireman and was out nearly all the time; he and his wife were willing hosts and made me very comfortable in my first experience of suburban living. Unfortunately, there was either heavy rain or dense fog for each of the nine days I was in Manchester, giving me a poor view of the place, both literally and figuratively. We attended a few lectures, drew some more kit, and spent most of the time in the canteen or in the cinemas. Security on the movement of ships was extremely tight because of the submarine menace, so we still did not know when or where we were going.

On 5th January 1942, we were told we were entraining at 10.0pm. Peter Thorne and I went to the Midland Hotel, the best in Manchester, and had a slap-up dinner that cost us 15/- each. We then joined the parade at the station and left at 2.0am. The moon shone brightly on snow-covered hills, and then we knew we were headed for Scotland, with the probability that we'd be sailing from the west coast port of Greenock. Rumours flourished as to our ultimate destination: Rhodesia, South Africa, Australia, New Zealand, Canada or America. Still ignorant, we detrained on the dockside and climbed the gangway onto the SS "Montcalm", re-named HM Troopship "Wolfe", at 11.0am.

This was a superannuated passenger liner converted into a troopship. She had a straight bow, a single funnel, and three or four decks, and displaced about 10,000 tons. Single cabins now held three or four men, hammocks were slung over the mess tables along the decks, and the holds were filled with scaffolding supporting three-tier bunks, reached by vertical steel ladders. I was one of the hundreds so incarcerated, well below the water-line: if a torpedo had hit us, we would not have stood a chance of getting out.

We had two meals a day and a canteen that provided cigarettes and chocolate for the permanent queue of hundreds of impatient airmen; its stocks ran out before the voyage ended.

We moved slowly down the Clyde and out into the Atlantic, escorted by two destroyers. The betting now was that we were heading for either Quebec or New York. All was plain sailing for the first day or two. We had PT and life-boat drill on the upper decks, although it was clear to me that there were not enough life-boats for the thousands of men on board. Otherwise, we read, played cards, walked the decks, or leaned on the rail chatting.

However, this was the Atlantic in January: as soon as we reached deep water, we began to pitch and roll. The peaks of the waves grew higher and the troughs deeper, and our old tub started shipping tons of water over the bows, so that the look-out men had to be withdrawn and we had to reduce speed; the wind whistled through the rigging and churned-up the surface of the sea into a sheet of foam; our escorts could be seen with their sterns lifted high out of the water before they disappeared out of sight in the valleys of the waves. Eventually, after 48 hours of this, their signal-lamps winked a message and they turned back for home. We were left to plod onwards on our own; we had a comforting communique that, if we were attacked, HMS "King George V" was somewhere off Iceland, 200 miles to the north, and could steam to our rescue! The majority of the passengers were now in the grip of sea-sickness, meals were sparsely attended, and the stench down below was appalling, contributing greatly to prolonging the sickness. To make matters worse, because of the danger of people being swept overboard, we were forbidden to go up on deck, where we might have gained some relief. I was fortunate in being appointed a submarine look-out; this meant that I had to spend several hours a day standing in one of the outposts of the bridge overhanging the ship's side, peering through the mist and spray for the sight of a submarine's periscope. With the sea's surface streaked with white foam, there was no chance whatever that I should spot the wash of a periscope, but I was glad to have some connection with the running of the ship and to have an escape from the hellhole below decks.

THE NORTH ATLANTIC. Jan. 6th – 19th 1942.

Sailors win our respect, but not our envy.

" .... and, behold, there arose a great tempest in the sea, insomuch that the ship was covered with the waves .... "

H.M. Transport 'WOLFE', ex-S.S. 'MONTCALM'.

CHAPTER 4

Aviation Cadet in America

The voyage seemed interminable, but after ten days the sea became a little calmer and people recovered their spirits and their balance. On the twelfth day there was great excitement as lights appeared on the horizon. After the wartime black-out of Britain, this seemed all wrong, almost treachery. It was probably Newfoundland, for we turned to port and followed the coastline south. Then we headed for the shore and entered the large harbour of Halifax in the evening of the 19th January. We blinked at the floodlights illuminating the scene and at the sight of large stems of bananas being paraded on the dockside by some enterprising merchant – they were quite unobtainable in Britain. Our envy turned to cheers when one of our number found a rope, slid down the side of the ship, ran up to the banana-merchant, somehow acquired a whole stem of bananas, and ran along the dockside brandishing it with whoops of glee! Not for long, though: two sturdy policemen strode up to him, removed the bananas to the accompaniment of our jeers and catcalls, and frog-marched the brave fellow up the gang-plank which connected us to the quay.

Next morning, we entrained for the Aircrew Reception Centre at Moncton, New Brunswick. There was deep snow on the ground, but it was crisp and the air was dry; we wore our greatcoats and gloves, but the barrack-blocks, where we spent two nights, were centrally-heated and wonderfully warm and overcame the need for thick clothes indoors. Indeed, we were so hot that we opened the double-glazed windows, earning instant rebukes from our Canadian corporals that we would cause the hot pipes to burst if the cold air reached them.

We then discovered that we were not to stay in Canada, but would be leaving by Canadian Pacific Railway next day and travelling for over a thousand miles all down the Atlantic coast and into Georgia, the heart of the Deep South of the United States. We had arrived on the Arnold Scheme, an arrangement made before the Americans entered the war after Pearl Harbour on 7th December 1941; under this, 10,000 British pilot trainees would be taught alongside American cadets in the US Army Air Corps. Arthur Schofield, who had left Scarborough two months before me, had found himself on the same Scheme and had written to me about it just before I went to Manchester; he had not been very impressed by his introduction to the American scene, but I went with an open mind.

The journey was an exciting experience. We travelled in what, to us, was extreme luxury: the coaches were open, but divided into shallow compartments, with comfortable seats and a table, on which our meals were served. At night – and we spent two on board – the seats and their backs formed one bed, and the curved ceiling was pulled down on a hinge to become the base of a second bed, complete with sheets and blankets. At first we had White attendants to look after us, but when we crossed the border into USA we were treated to our first encounter with Black ones. This came as a shock, and the further south we travelled the more upset we were by what we saw of the treatment of the Blacks in their segregated condition, no different in practice from the apartheid practised by the Nationalists in South Africa.

For the rest, it was fascinating to get a train's-eye view of the east side of America: Boston, New York, Philadelphia, Washington, sky-scrapers, industrial centres, small towns with the railway running down the main street, mountains, rivers, forests, farms, rolling grasslands and cotton-fields. The sheer size of things American began to impinge on us: the distances, the monuments, the railway wagons, the cars (now to be called autos), the T-bone steaks, the stadiums, the supermarkets (not yet seen in Britain), the newspapers with their multiple sections, and so on.

Our destination was Turner Field, outside the sleepy town of Albany, Georgia. We were to be given a one-month Acclimatisation Course to enable us to settle comfortably into the US Army Air Corps and to understand the basis of American life. As Churchill put it, *"We are two countries divided by a common language"*.

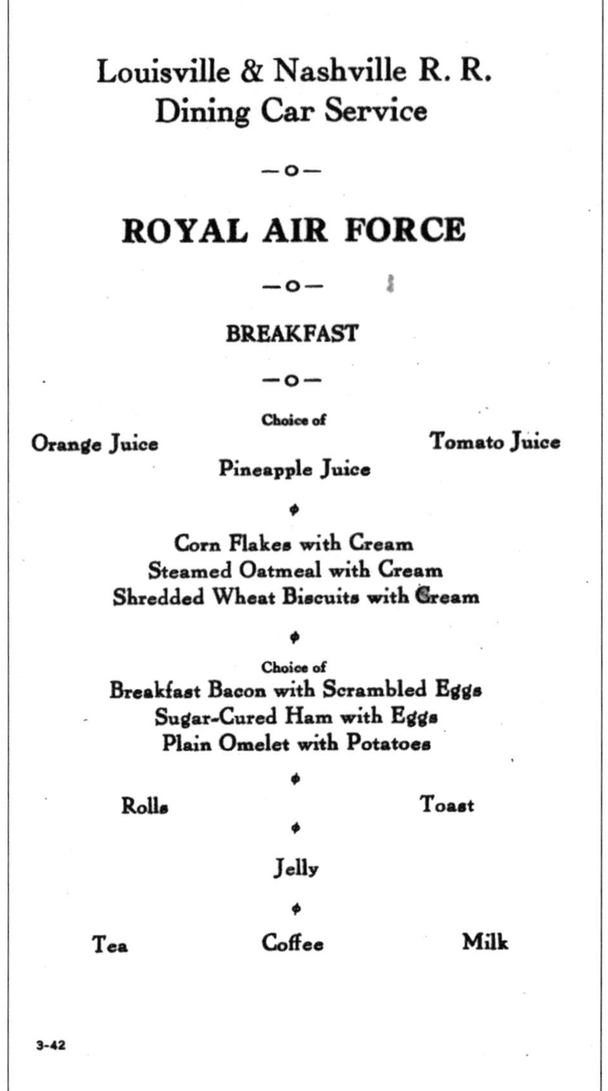

Louisville & Nashville R. R.
Dining Car Service

—o—

ROYAL AIR FORCE

—o—

BREAKFAST

—o—

Choice of

Orange Juice — Pineapple Juice — Tomato Juice

Corn Flakes with Cream
Steamed Oatmeal with Cream
Shredded Wheat Biscuits with Cream

Choice of
Breakfast Bacon with Scrambled Eggs
Sugar-Cured Ham with Eggs
Plain Omelet with Potatoes

Rolls — Toast

Jelly

Tea — Coffee — Milk

3-42

Luxury Travel: Moncton, Canada, to Georgia, USA, 22nd-24th January 1942

In effect, at Turner we became aviation cadets in the Air Corps, but there was one vital difference between American cadets and ourselves, which was not acknowledged by those who framed the Arnold Scheme: the Americans were mainly college graduates being trained to be officers as well as pilots, whereas we would finish only as sergeant-pilots. Discipline was harsh, based on the Army's West Point – the American equivalent of Sandhurst – and the elimination rate was high: 50%-60% overall. This weeded out the Americans who showed they were not officer material, but it was unfair and totally unnecessary for us, who had only to reach the required standard of flying.

The Americans had the 'Honor System', which directly contradicted the RAF ethos that we had absorbed at Scarborough and Brough. The RAF had NCOs to discipline the cadets; the Air Corps appointed 'cadet officers' to control their colleagues: *"You have no friends now"*, they were told. The RAF encouraged a team spirit, for future crew and squadron solidarity, so that we stood by our friends and covered up for their faults, such as lateness on parade; the Air Corps required us to report them to our cadet officer – and even to report ourselves! The RAF encouraged us to relax when we were not flying; the Air Corps filled our day with activity and made us move everywhere 'at the double'. The RAF respected our dignity and believed in our common-sense: if we committed some offence, we were expected to offer an explanation, even to invent one; the Air Corps allowed no such initiative: *"No excuse, Sir"* was the stock answer to any accusation. The Air Corps believed that cadets would become swollen-headed with any success, so they were deliberately humiliated, and other cadets were expected to mock those humiliated. Thus a bad landing could be punished at one base with a dumb-bell hung round the offender's neck until someone else made an equal mistake; at another, it was a chamber-pot; at a third a notice proclaiming *"I am a dumb cluck"*. But we sympathised with the victim and cursed the system.

Worst of all was the Upper Class/Lower Class division: new entrants could be harassed and bullied by the senior class, made to answer insulting questions, run errands, do any number of press-ups, by any Upper Class man who happened to pass them: *"Hit a brace, mister!"* was a typical order. After a month of this 'hazing', the seniors would move on and the Lower Class men became the Upper Class, enjoying the right, in turn, to revenge themselves on the new intake.

These were obvious grounds for misunderstanding and disliking each other right from the start, as such practices were basically unacceptable to British young men. In fact, we had a rebellion at one base, with senior RAF liaison officers arriving from Washington to calm us down. Their remedy was simple;

> *"Don't upset our American allies: we're dependent on them for so much. Show them you can take it – it won't last long, anyway."*

Small comfort to us.

The factual elements of our indoctrination caused no problems: learning about the history, geography, government, politics, administration, education, public services, and media of the USA, and the history and structure of the Air Corps. We were also introduced to the differences in terminology used by the two Services: 'airplane' for aeroplane, 'air base' for airfield, 'gas' for petrol or throttle, 'radio' for wireless, and so on.

We were woken up by a band marching round the camp at 6.0am, even in the dark with snow on the ground; we then had an hour's calisthenics (PT) before returning to wash, dress and form up to march to breakfast. The food was lavish: a pint of milk, white bread, fruit, and piles of eggs, bacon, and sausages. We marched back to our barracks, made our rooms spick and span (*"If you can't be disciplined on the ground, you can't be disciplined in the air"*, so ran the Air Corps code), and went out on parade for the flag-raising. This was full of 'bull', but the RAF could put on a show; their marching, with arms swinging to the horizontal, in contrast with the slight movements made by the Americans, impressed onlookers. At the evening flag-down ceremony, the local people would come out onto the Base to watch the RAF boys in their blue uniforms, so much so that eventually the Commandant had a flagpost erected on the far side of the airfield and banished our parades to that deserted spot!

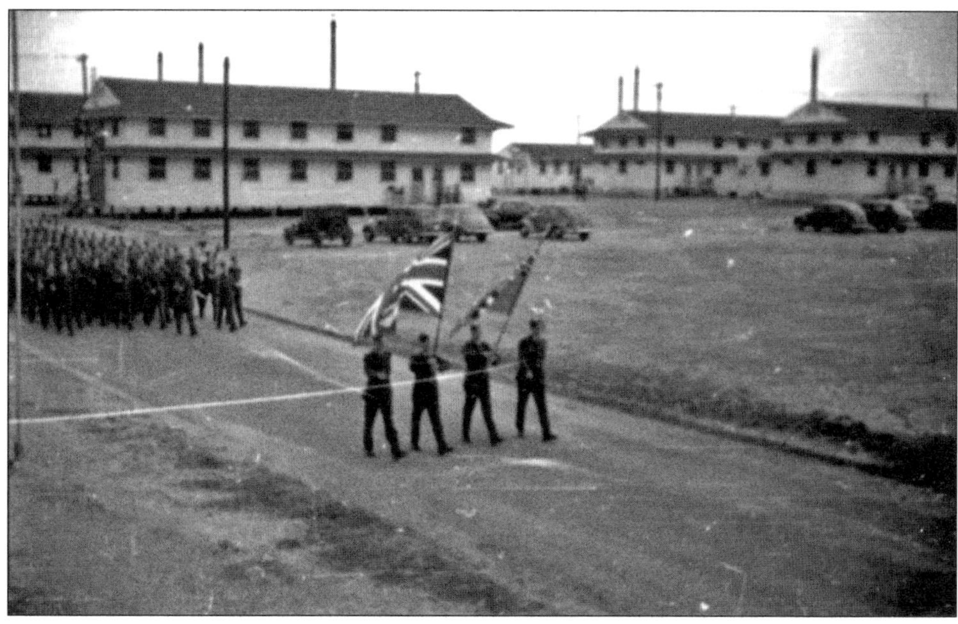

Orientation Course, Turner Field, Albany, Georgia.
RAF Cadets march to the Flag-raising ceremony.

Although Turner Field was an Advanced Flying School for twin-engine pilots, we rarely had occasion to meet the American cadets. Nevertheless, we were subjected to their disciplinary treatment. We each had a card with a number of locations on the camp printed on it; whenever we went to one of these, we had to put a paper-clip against it on the card and place it in the centre of our bed. Woe betide anyone who was found to be elsewhere than where indicated on his card! Equally, a dirty wash-basin, or a bed whose blankets were not tight enough to bounce back a coin dropped on them by the inspecting officer, resulted in the offender 'walking tours' for so many hours. We were allowed out of camp on Saturday afternoons and Sundays, but 'walking tours' meant marching up and down with white gloves and a rifle for however many 'tours' we had been awarded.

The other thing the Americans prized was uniformity, in contrast to the RAF's preference for individuality and initiative. We used to go out on route marches into the countryside and, in typical RAF style, would start to sing to keep us going, until everyone was joining in a rousing chorus. This did not suit the Air Corps. On our next outing, we found ourselves diverted into an empty hangar and supplied with song-sheets, printed out with all our favourites and several of the Air Corps' virtual anthems. To our astonishment, we were made to sing every song on the sheet to the Major's satisfaction and were told to learn them by heart.

On the next route march, we were on our way back when the officer called out, *"All right, men, we'll now sing the Air Corps song!"* By some strange mutual understanding, with one accord we all burst out with the warm-hearted RAF protest, *"Why did we join, why did we join, why did we join this bloody Air Force?" "Stop! Stop! Stop!"* yelled the officer and his minions, running up and down our ranks. But we went on remorselessly until we had finished. We were never told to sing again!

These were the hardships and the sometimes ludicrous moments of our American experience but, of course, there were many good things, even wonderful interludes in our time at Turner Field and the other locations where we trained. Chief among these was the sheer material wealth in American life, compared with the run-down civilian economy of Britain at war; everything we dreamed of, and saw in Hollywood's films, was available: elegant houses on open grassy lawns (no walls or fences to divide them); huge cars everywhere and cheap petrol; Black servants to do the menial jobs; drug-stores that sold all kinds of drinks and useful items and acted as focal points for social contacts and gossip; supermarkets overflowing with food and clothing; open-air drive-in cinemas where you watched films from your car; football and baseball stadiums where everyone cheered on the local High School team; churches attended by the majority of the population, where newcomers such as ourselves would be invited back home for a meal and even encouraged to take the daughter out for a drive in the car; local radio stations and newspapers, which featured every little incident to ensure that no one in the community was overlooked. This was the atmosphere in Albany, Georgia, typical of small-town life in America, quite distinct from the much less friendly spirit of the big cities. Of course, the Blacks did not share in this semi-paradise, nor did the poor Whites, or 'White-trash', who lived, literally, on the wrong side of the railway tracks. Among these folk, drink was the only solace and violence was commonplace, someone being murdered every weekend.

For all their comfortable lives, ordinary people had an underlying insecurity: the postman and the laundryman carried pistols in their belts; most drivers had a revolver or an automatic in the dashboard pocket of their car. When I asked why, the answer always was, *"Just in case... You never know..."* I felt that not very far down in American society was a layer of people given to violence, which generated fear in the peace-loving majority and that this contributed to the gun-culture that exerted (and still exerts) a powerful influence in the political arena.

The drawback for us in all this rich life-style was that we had virtually no money. As Leading Aircraftsmen, with overseas allowances and, later, a flying allowance, we received $25 a month, whereas the lowest American enlisted man was paid $50, and aviation cadets $150. Unless we had private means, we could hardly afford even to go out at weekends. Fortunately, we were rescued by one of the best features of American society: the extraordinary hospitality and generosity extended towards strangers by American families and social organisations: this included us RAF boys in our unfamiliar uniforms and also their own servicemen from other States, some of whom were as far away from home as we were. The

Servicemen's Club in town was a welcoming address for food, facilities and friendship and held dances to introduce new arrivals to the local girls.

I had my 'home from home' with Billy and Betty Rothwell. Billy was a Yorkshireman, whose forbears probably originated from the town of Rothwell, and had been an Observer and Air-Gunner in the First World War – his fingernails were all bashed-in from firing his Lewis guns. He ran a private photographic studio and was married to Betty, a sweet-natured American lady; they had no children, but they had come upon Pilot Officer Guy Pease, an Old Etonian a year senior to me, who had been on Class 42A and, after graduating, had been posted as a check-pilot and liaison officer to Darr-Aero-Tech, the local Primary Flying Training School.

Billy and Betty Rothwell in their home in Albany, Georgia

Betty Rothwell with her 'family' of Old Etonians wearing our summer uniforms (1-r) JT Peter Wallace Guy Pease (check pilot) Jeremy Wilson

He had heard of my arrival and introduced me to Billy and Betty. Later, two more Etonians whom I knew, Peter Wallace and Jeremy Wilson, arrived in Albany and joined the 'family', with another one, Vanbergen, coming in occasionally. Betty kept 'open house' for us and we could call in at any time or spend our leaves with them; Billy let us take their car, an old Studebaker sedan with a 'dickie' seat behind, whenever we wanted. They had several girl friends and there were always lively discussions and occasional outings for our benefit. Their presence was a godsend, and I stayed in touch with Billy and Betty for long after the war, until our correspondence faded away in their old age and death.

So much for Turner Field; it served its purpose in introducing us to some of the highs and lows of life in America and in the US Army Air Corps. We left it without regret on 22nd February 1942, when our Class 42H was distributed to several different Primary Flying Training Schools and I found myself moving not very far to Darr-Aero-Tech, just down the road, as it were.

After Turner, Darr was a treat. It was a civilian airfield, with civilian instructors, and we lived in what had been the flying club, with a few additional buildings. Rows of Stearman PT-17s, with 225 hp Continental 7-cylinder radial engines, stood parked outside the hangars. The airfield was grass, with a 'Tee' in the middle to indicate the direction of take-off and landing (into the wind); there were two traffic patterns, left-hand and right-hand, each side of the 'Tee', so a good number of aircraft could take-off and land at the same time. In fact, at meal times, the air was thick with Stearmans all jostling to get down beside, in front of, or behind each other in the minimum time.

'Gassing-up" 28 Stearman PT-17s at Darr-Aero-Tech
Primary Flying Training School, Albany, Georgia

I had several instructors at the start, mainly middle-aged, patient, and experienced men, friendly and quiet on the ground but quite short-tempered and loud-voiced in the air. They each had charge of five of us. The instructor sat in front and talked down a speaking-tube, but we had no means of replying or making queries. We flew half the day and had ground-school or recreation the other half. There was an open-air swimming-pool right under the flight-path and, lying out in the sun, we could often hear the instructors 'bawling out' their pupils: *"Get on the ball, mister!"*, *"Pour on the coal, mister!"*,

Pupil (in the back) under instruction in a PT-17 (colour print)

"Give 'er the gun, mister!", "Where're we goin' now, mister?", "Jeez, mister, get the ants outa yore pants!", etc, etc. Not so funny if we were on the receiving end.

The main principle in the flying was accuracy: exact heights and speeds were prescribed for flying in the circuit; for doing figures-of-eight over cross-roads, making perfect circles over the ground in spite of a steady side-wind; for doing chandelles – going up vertically almost into a stall, turning 180° at the top, then diving down again and up the other side – and for all our loops, rolls and spins. We became precision pilots, good for peacetime, but not necessarily the best preparation for war.

The Stearman was a big, strong, roomy machine, twice the power and weight of the Tiger Moth, pleasant to fly as long as we kept it under control, but a beast if it ran away with us. There were 32 numbered flying exercises, from Air Experience to Pylon 8s. We were all expected to progress at the same rate: if you fell behind, you went for a check-ride with another instructor; if you failed this, you went for a ride with a check-pilot in what we bitterly called 'the washing machine'. Failure meant returning to Canada and, usually, re-mustering to navigator, bomb-aimer or air gunner. In addition, we had automatic check-rides after 20, 40 and 60 hours' flying, and these also could lead to elimination. The elimination rate at Darr was 40%-52% of our Course, which was scandalous, considering that we had all gone up to solo-standard in UK to prevent elimination and that Britain in 1942 was still in desperate need of trained pilots to fly the planes in the steadily enlarging theatres of war.

As a result, the prevailing feeling at Darr was not of enthusiasm, as it should and could have been, but of fear of being 'washed-out'. I was worried because 1 took 9 hours to go solo, just over the average. I was more than worried, I was prostrated when, with nearly 40 hours in my log-book, I was engaged in spot-landings by the 'Tee', with the instructors bunched together watching their pupils' performance. I came in too fast, bounced, dropped a wing, swung towards the 'Tee', gave her the gun, swept over the heads of the instructors, who flattened themselves on the grass, staggered back into the air and brought her back to earth further down the field. I taxied slowly back to the 'Tee' with my heart in my boots: I had committed a crime worthy of a check-ride in the 'washing-machine'. Mr Naylor, my instructor, climbed into the front seat morosely. *"Take me back to the Flight Line"*, he said. I taxied in and waited. *"Go and see the Medical Officer for a check-up"*. This was the routine procedure after any incident or accident; I walked dismally to the MO – and he found I had mumps! Glory be! I spent three weeks in hospital and, when I came out, my class-mates had moved on and everyone had forgotten about me. I had to join the next Class, 42I, and fly only a small amount each day. I had a friendly new instructor, Mr Reed, who taught me mainly aerobatics; I passed my 40-hour and 60-hour checks with Army pilots, and completed the course on 27th May.

Far less fortunate was my good friend Peter Thorne: his poor eyesight caught him out: he could not manage the landings properly and was 'washed-out'. He became thoroughly depressed, as his one aim in life was to fight the Germans, and he had been foiled. He had ten days before being sent back to Canada to re-train as a navigator, so I asked Betty if he could come to them and be 'mothered'. She and

My final instructor, Mr Reed, and his pupils
Bob Ford N.M.R. Edwards David Irvine JT

Betty Rothwell with Peter Thorne (right) and JT

Billy did wonders for his morale and he set off for Canada, if not in high spirits, at least in a philosophical state of mind. In fact, his elimination as a pilot was a blessing in disguise: if he had become a multi-engine pilot, with a crew depending on him for their survival, and he really could not see properly, it would have been unpardonable for him to have been allowed or enabled to complete pilot-training. As it was, I was fated to come across Peter again in even more tragic circumstances.

In spite of its reputation for good flying weather, the Deep South had its share of hazards, both from the terrain and from its proximity to the Gulf of Mexico. This was the breeding-ground for violent changes in the weather, some of which we experienced at Darr-Aero-Tech. In April and May, we could see huge piles of cumulus building-up to the south-west and, at night, electrical storms lit-up the far horizon. For us, the danger came in line-squalls, emanating from solid rows of cumulo-nimbus, with high winds whirling round their base and sweeping the dirt and sand into 'dust-devils' and sandstorms that blotted out the airfield. We had no radios on the Stearmans so, on these occasions, a red flag would be hoisted and the instructors would fly out to try to round-up any solo students who had not the sense to return before they were caught out. I vividly remember, when the landing-ground was virtually invisible, running out onto it in pairs when we heard an aircraft overhead hanging almost motionless against a 50-mph wind; we would reach up to the wing-tips and literally pull it down to earth, and then guide it back to the flight-line. We did this several times on a particularly stormy occasion.

Another hazard was the Everglade swamps of Florida. Contrary to popular belief that Florida is a Garden of Eden for retired millionaires, more than half the State is virgin jungle standing in swamp water and infested with alligators and deadly water-moccasin snakes. It was impenetrable in those days and we flew over it only on authorised cross-country exercises. A nasty warning in my time was the sight of a Stearman that sat spread-eagled on top of the trees after a forced-landing, from which the student-pilot could not be rescued. At least, I avoided that fate.

The hot weather meant that we changed into American summer uniform of khaki shirt and trousers, but we kept our RAF black tie, black shoes and blue cap, producing a rather incongruous effect: off the Air Base, we were asked, *"Are you a bell-hop in a hotel?"* or *"Which High School uniform is that?"* Only little negro boys in New Orleans knew: they ran alongside us once, shouting *"English pilots in the RAF! English pilots in the RAF!"*

So Darr ended for me as a generally happy experience, one that I came to look back on with increasing fondness as I encountered the harshness of our next stage of training.

In the RAF, students progressed direct from Tiger Moths to Harvards; that is, from 120-hp wood-and-fabric biplanes to 650-hp metal monoplanes, which had all the features found on operational aircraft. The USAAF, by contrast, inserted an intermediate stage labelled Basic, which was flown on a metal monoplane called the Vultee BT-13a, with a wider wingspan than a Harvard, but with a smaller 450-hp engine, a fixed undercarriage, a two-pitch propeller, and manually-operated flaps.- It was therefore slower and less manoeuvrable than a Harvard, but it could take rougher handling from student-pilots and was therefore a useful stepping-stone between the Stearman and the Harvard (AT6 in USAAF terminology); this was by no means an essential one, however, especially as the Stearman was already a heavier and more powerful trainer than the Tiger Moth – but we had no choice in the matter.

The 42I contingent from Darr was distributed to three Basic Flying Schools, most of us being sent to Cochran Field, outside Macon, another town in Georgia, the size of Albany. Cochran was run by the Army Air Corps and I was lucky in having an excellent instructor in 1st Lt Boyers, a friendly young man with an encouraging manner. The flying was fine and I found the BT-13a to be a reasonable step-up from the Stearman, not too complex and with no unpleasant vices. What made Cochran a hell-hole was the application of the full West Point disciplinary regime and harassment by the American Upper Class

Flaps down, a BT-13a approaches to land.

men. It was resentment and frustration caused by this, rather than a lack of flying ability, that resulted in another 10% of our number being 'washed-out'.

1st Lt Boyers, my very courteous instructor

The Administrative Officer at Cochran was Captain Knight, a true product of West Point. He had the impression that all cadets coming up from Primary training with their 60-hours' flying experience were swollen-headed, cocky, self-styled 'hot-pilots'. This may have been true of some Americans, but certainly could not be applied to any of the RAF boys, who knew well that learning to fly was a difficult and dangerous business, with grim fighting ahead of us once we had gained our 'wings'. Nevertheless, the moment we stepped out of our coaches on 2nd June, we were told to put our kitbags and suitcases on the ground and we were subjected to an hour's drill in the boiling sun – the South is semi-tropical, with high temperatures and strong humidity. After being taken to our barracks, we were marched to the Stores and fitted with mechanics' overalls which, in spite of the heat, had to be zipped up to the neck and down to the wrists and ankles. We then moved to the Barber's shop, where we had most of our hair shaved off, leaving us looking like convicts. All this was designed to humiliate us, to show us that we were the lowest form of life on the Base and that we had nothing to be proud of.

After this initial debasement, we were harried by the American Upper Class whenever we were at leisure: they could stop us, ask us rude or stupid questions and demand a straight-faced answer, however idiotic or embarrassing. They could force us to do press-ups there and then, or run errands, sometimes useful, sometimes deliberately trivial. It was sheer bullying, sanctioned by the system, and we objected to it – but without redress.

The worst manifestation of the system was at meal-times. The food was, as usual, bountiful and nutritious, but the circumstances in which it was eaten were degrading. We marched to every meal behind a military band; we climbed the steps into the mess-hall and stood at attention behind our

Basic Flying Training School, Cochran Field, Macon, Georgia, busy with Vultee BT-13as

chairs, with an American Upper Class man at the head of the table. On the command *"Seats!"*, we sat down, not to eat but to sit at attention on the edge of our chairs. On the command *"Rest!"*, we had to pass the food dishes to the Upper Class man and only when he was satisfied could we serve ourselves. Then, out of the blue, came the order, *"Attention!"* Regardless of where we were in the meal, we had to lay down our utensils and return to sitting bolt upright on the edge of our chairs. The orders for the day would then be given by the officer in charge and any mail would be distributed; he would then call out, *"Dismiss!"* We then stood up, filed out of the mess-hall, formed up on parade, and marched back to our barracks. Prison inmates have more freedom at meal-times than we had.

All the time, the 'Honor System' was strictly enforced, cadets being expected to report on the peccadillos of their friends or, as cadet officers or NCOs, to enforce quite unnecessary levels of discipline on them. This reached such a pitch that we wrote up in large letters on our notice-board, *"It is obvious that 'Honor' is totally different from 'Honour'"*. It did not remain there for long.

There was a camp cinema, a well-stocked PX (equivalent to a NAAFI), various shops, a swimming-pool and tennis courts as well as a gymnasium, so we had little cause to go into Macon. In any case, most of us accumulated so many 'tours' that we spent much of the weekends parading uselessly up and down for several hours. Even the ground-school lectures, which featured subjects of importance to us such as airframes, engines, armament, radio, navigation, and meteorology, were spoiled for us by the weekly examinations in them. These took the form of multiple-choice 'quizzes', in which we ticked one of four answers to a large number of questions, which tested information only and encouraged guess-work; they did not really involve us in a proper knowledge of the subject, so we disapproved generally of this method of instruction.

The flying, as usual, was different and exciting: we learned day and night cross-country work; navigation by using the radio beams transmitted by the numerous beacons for the airlines; instrument-flying under a hood in the back seat, relying solely on the instruments; formation-flying with two aircraft behind or beside our instructor, putting on a tight show especially when coming back over the airfield; and urging the under-powered 'Vultee Vibrator' into aerobatics by the use of considerable muscle-

Place under bedding

ABSENCE CARD
(see par. 202, Flying Cadet Orders)

____ON LIMITS. (This entry is defined in Flying Cadet Orders and on the reverse side and will be made during Call to Quarters when no other entry is accurate).

____FLYING CADET OFFICER OF THE DAY.

____FLYING CADET IN CHARGE OF QUARTERS.

____HOSPITAL.

____LEAVE or SPECIAL PASS.

____OPEN POST (This entry will be removed or changed immediately upon returning from open post privileges.)

I certify that the above entry is correct.

H.J.S.Taylor.
H.J.S. TAYLOR.

R.D.-76

ON LIMITS DEFINED

(See Sect. 8, Call to Quarters, and Sect. 18, Limits, Flying Cadet Orders)

"On Limits" for the lower class shall include the following:

1. Class formations or duties scheduled or ordered by proper authority.
2. Barber shop as authorized.
3. Latrine or drinking fountain.
4. Squadron bulletin board.
5. Link Trainer when scheduled.
6. Night flying when scheduled.
7. Office of the F.C.O.D. for a proper purpose.
8. Phone booth to answer a call.
9. Another room in barracks for the purpose of study and academic coaching only.
10. Authorized committee meeting.
11. Tactical Officer's Conference Room.
12. Wherever ordered by an officer or member of the flying cadet guard.

"On Limits" for the upper class shall include all the above plus the following:

1. Bowling alley.
2. Night flying even though not scheduled to fly.
3. Post Exchange for authorized purpose.
4. Swimming pool in season.
5. Tennis courts.
6. First show at Post Theater.

The sort of 'bull' we endured at Cochran Field:
we had to put the paper-clip against our situation and place the card precisely at the top of the blanket

It is rumoured that a certain mechanic from Pennsylvania has been issued with a blue flying suit to make him feel more at home. Squadron Ten will suffer a sad loss when he is transferred. Good luck to a friend who was only "happy" when he was working for us.

A robust Instructor of the same Squadron has designed a new type trainer especially for night flying. It has no flaps and climbs at 100 MPH.

"I OVERHEARD-----"

NIGHT FLYING:

"And after I had bounced I set up a 90 mph glide and made a perfect three-pointer."

ON THE BEAM:

"Can you see the cone of silence, yet?"

ONFORMATION:
"Come up 420 you are too low......"
"Not nearly as low as you, Sir!"

Institution of a novel decoration created by the Flight Commander has aroused keen competition among Squadron Ten cadets. His ingenuity must have been the result of some very "heavy" thinking.

FAMOUS LAST WORDS

The Squadron Leader told me .....

I am going to shake my instructor on combat today.

I said to the Flight Sergeant, "Definitely No."

I am sure this is the right light line.

* * * * * *

The cadets of Training Sqdn. Eight are undecided as to how far they have to pull Lt. Wylie's periodic inspections.

We hear that Captain Woodyard has had a nightmare, he dreamed that one of his cadets has ground looped.

Congratulations to Cpl......on his promotion to the rank of Sergeant. Celebrations are forthcoming (we hope).

* * * * * *

Some aspects of flying and life at Cochran Field seen through the pen of the students' newspaper: note the 'dumb bell' punishment

We are introduced to night flying.

power and careful coordination. We also did short landings, coming in over a tape held up between two poles, with full power on the engine, nose-high, and flaps wound right down. There was great rivalry for the shortest run; one chap overdid it: he hit the ground on all three points with a tremendous crash, the engine fell off and the aircraft ran over it – like a headless chicken! Yes, there were times, even at Cochran, when we could laugh and this was one of them. But we reckoned that if we could survive Cochran, we could survive anything. So, maybe, it had its value – but we could have done without it.

Our next posting, to Napier Advanced Flying Training School, near Dothan, Alabama, was a refreshing contrast. First, all the cadets there were British, so we had no nonsense with Upper and Lower Classes; secondly, many of the instructors were RAF officers, so there were no cruel or childish rituals to humiliate us; thirdly, 1 had a first-class instructor in P/O Gallagher, a cool quiet person, who knew how to pass on his own ability and confidence to his students; and, fourthly, we now moved up to the AT-6 or Harvard, with a 650hp engine, a constant-speed propeller, retractable undercarriage, hydraulic flaps, and a performance that was equivalent to that of a pre-war fighter. It had to be treated with respect and handled with good flying techniques, especially on landing; it then became a responsive and reliable machine and a delight to fly.

Quite a daunting array of instruments for the pupil in the BT-13a

The course was not much different from our training at Cochran Field, but it was more intensive and almost every flight ended in aerobatics. We engaged in mock combats, as well as in plenty of formation flying, instrument flying, and day and night cross-countrys. Our training was completed with a

In formation with a North American AT-6 (Harvard in the RAF) at the Advanced Flying Training School, Napier Field, Dothan, Alabama

gunnery course, for which we journeyed south to Eglin Field, in Florida. Here our AT-6s were fitted with a single machine-gun in the nose and we aimed mostly at targets on the ground, but we also had three opportunities to shoot at a cloth target towed by another plane. My scores on the ground targets were not high, but on the aerial ones I scored 8 hits from 100 shots, 47 from 200, and 7 from 200. Unknown to me then, this period from 22nd September to 2nd October was the only time in five years of war when I fired a gun!

Of course, we had our incidents: one chap came back with a bullet-hole in his propeller, when the interrupter-gear failed. Someone else was sitting in his plane when the gun suddenly went off and emptied the whole magazine, fortunately without hitting anyone. Eglin was memorable also for another reason: there was no fence round the Base, but no one walked out except through the main entrance; it was surrounded by dense jungle and we could hear the sound of rattlesnakes by day and night!

Before we went to Eglin, a Commissioning Board, consisting of three RAF officers, arrived at Dothan to interview any candidates who were willing to stay behind in America for another year to instruct American cadets in flying. The US Army Air Corps was expanding rapidly and aiming to produce 100,000 aircrew per year. Because General Arnold, initiator of the Arnold Scheme, had offered 10,000 places to British cadets, he now asked that 10% of the survivors, the same proportion as US cadets, be kept back to help train the new intakes of Americans. Not many of 42I wanted to remain, either for family reasons or because they had had enough of the US Army Air Corps. I felt I needed to improve my flying skills and experience, as I considered that the war was bound to continue for several more years; so I was very pleased when I was one of the 20 or so selected from 42I at Napier. The interview is perhaps worth recording:

Officer 1: *"Who cleaned your belt-buckle this morning, Taylor?"*

JT: *"I did, Sir."*

Officer 2: *"Do you shoot, Taylor?"*

September 22nd – October 2nd 1942.

EGLIN FIELD, FLORIDA.

Gunnery Course.

Comfort in travel.
Jimmy Dunn, Beveridge, Davies.

Jungle, thick, uninhabited, savage, untamed, infested jungle; compare with regular Florida adverts.

This wonderful Florida landscape.

ground gunnery.

Lost – 200 yards from the camp!

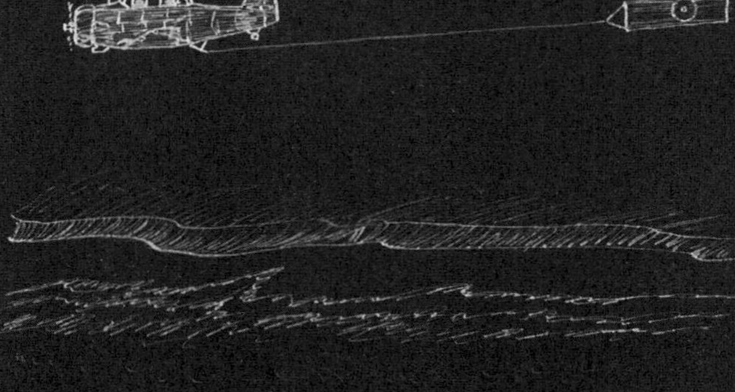

aerial gunnery.

JT: *"Yes, Sir."*

Officer 3: *"Do you use your own gun?"*

JT: *"Yes, Sir."*

Officer 2: *"Who cleans it?"*

JT: *"I do, Sir."*

Officer 3: *"Thank you, Taylor. That will be all."*

They must have been desperate for volunteers to stay behind in USA!

Arthur Schofield, my best Eton friend, had finished his course on Class 42F and invited me to join him with his American 'family' in Montgomery, the capital of Alabama. Here I met Mrs Dimmick, an elderly widow, and her companion, Miss Spann. They lived in a large white Southern mansion, with palm-trees looming over extensive lawns. One room was kept like a mausoleum, curtained-off in darkness, just as it was on the day that Mr Dimmick died, thirty years before. Arthur and I reclined at ease in comfortable chairs on the grass and were served ice-cold 'Tom Collins' by the two ladies; in fact, we were very spoiled for 24 hours. Then we had to say good-bye to them and to each other. This was the last time I saw Arthur.

He returned to Britain, trained on Oxfords and Blenheims, and joined 272 Squadron on 8th May 1943, flying Beaufighters on anti-shipping strikes from Ta Kali airfield on Malta. Just two weeks later, on 22nd May, with Sergeant Lavin as his observer, in company with three other aircraft, he was flying on an armed reconnaissance 30 miles from the west coast of Sicily when they were attacked by five Me 109s; two Beaufighters were shot down into the sea, one of them being Sgt Arthur Schofield's. He was desperate to get into the war and upbraided me for staying in the States. Underneath all his self-

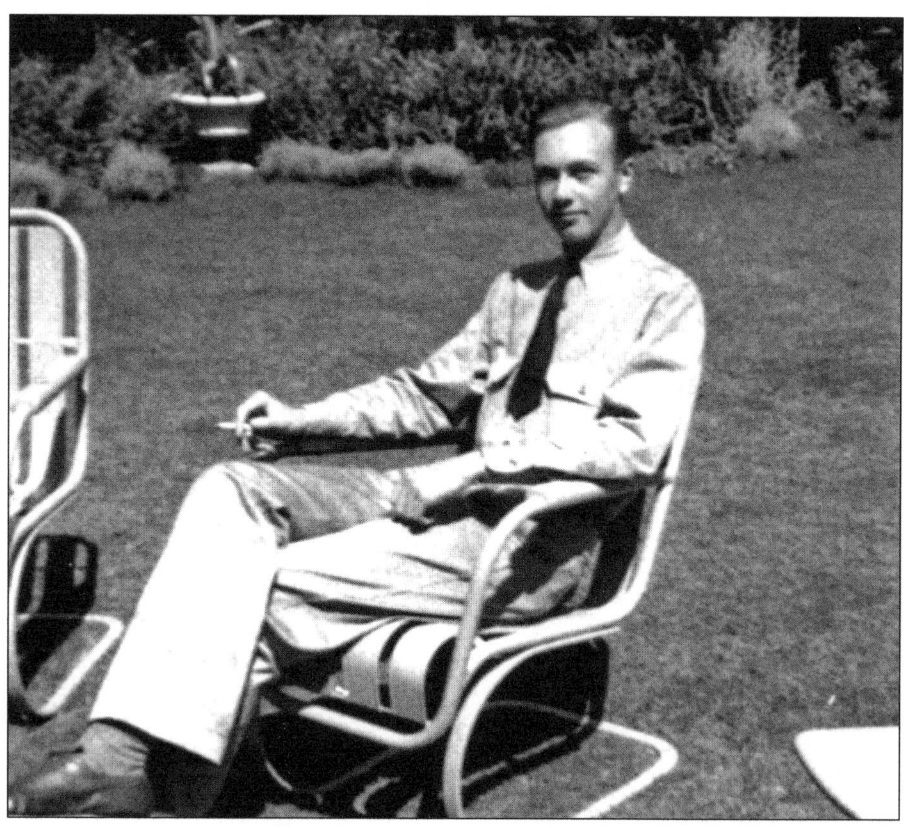

My last photograph of Arthur Schofield in Mrs Dimmick's garden in Montgomery, Alabama

confidence, however, I have my doubts, perhaps unfairly, about whether he was really ready for such dangerous operations. We shared so much in the flying world at Eton and afterwards that I feel his loss keenly to this day.

One thing that the Americans were very good at was publicity, which both impressed us, because the RAF did so little of it, and depressed us, because we thought they went too far into sentimentality. For example, each Course at Cochran Field had a hard-back album of photographs and text describing in great detail the history of the Army Air Corps and the training of pilots, followed by individual passport photos of every member of the Base, from Commanding Officer down to the lowliest Black mess-waiter, including the flying instructors, the ground instructors, the Upper Class 42H of American cadets and the Lower Class 42I of British, the ground staff and mechanics, the meteorologists, the medical corps, the military police, the military band, and so on – a valued glossy souvenir, but giving no indication of the harsh disciplinary system that governed the lives of the cadets.

Equally, our Graduation Ceremony at Napier Field was similar to a university's: families, friends and sweethearts attended and filled the chapel, which was adorned with a platform, flags and flowers. In our thick RAF LAC's blue uniform, we marched in behind the band and listened patiently to speeches from the 'top brass'; then watched as, first, the 46 American cadets were individually presented with their 'wings' and graduation scrolls to general applause, and then it was the turn of the 190 British cadets

Blind Flight

SOUTHEAST AIR CORPS TRAINING CENTER
NAPIER FIELD, ALABAMA

This is to Certify that embryo Pilot H. J. S. Taylor has satisfactorily completed a course of Instrument flying, on this 9 Day of October 1942, in "The Jeep" without Peeping.

Capt. A.C.
INSTRUMENT OFFICER

A light-hearted Certificate granted on our completion of the course on the Link Trainer at Napier Field, USA

From LACs to F/Sgts!
Don – JT Raymond Picot

of 42I: we each climbed up onto the platform, the Director of Training pinned our pewter American 'wings', inscribed on the back "USA Napier Field Oct 9th 1942", onto our tunics and the CO handed us our scrolls, to the vigorous clapping of our friends. At home in Britain, we would probably have found our cloth RAF 'wings' on our plate at breakfast!

The really big difference between our training with the US Army Air Corps in America and what would have happened to us if we had stayed in England and continued our flying training in the RAF was the 'wash-out' rate. In England, perhaps 10% of the Course would have been failed early on at the Elementary stage, with a possible further 5% at the Advanced level. On the Arnold Scheme, of the 7500 British cadets who went over to the USA, after a Grading Course in Britain to ensure they could fly, 3000 were 'washed-out' as unsuitable to be pilots. For the Air Corps this was a peacetime figure and, of course, for them it was partly officer-training as well as pilot-training. Nevertheless, at a time when Britain was fighting for her life and needed pilots desperately, it was, in my opinion, too high a price to pay for the 4500 who did graduate successfully. It would have been better if we had all joined the many thousands of others who trained under the RCAF in Canada under the Empire Air Training Scheme. Survival, under the Air Corps, was a matter of resilience under stress plus a degree of luck, as evidenced by my good fortune in falling ill at a critical moment. The RAF, by contrast, believed in removing the stress from learning to fly and encouraged a relaxed attitude whenever possible. However, I shouldn't complain: I was now a Pilot Officer on probation, with my American 'wings', which I could wear in the United States, but which I had to exchange for RAF ones in Britain and elsewhere.

I might add that there were six British Flying Training Schools (BFTSs) in the USA – in Oklahoma, California, Arizona, Texas, and Florida – which were run by the RAF, but with American civilian instructors; they produced 7000 pilots from 1941-45, who had the best of both worlds: the RAF' s relaxed approach to learning to fly and its low wash-out rate, coupled with American weather, food and hospitality. All these cadets, unlike those of us on the Arnold Scheme, maintain that they had a wonderful time.

Army Air Forces

Be it known that

UK CADET HAROLD JAMES STRICKLAND TAYLOR

has satisfactorily completed the course of instruction prescribed for

PILOT TRAINING

at the ARMY AIR FORCES ADVANCED FLYING *School.*

In testimony whereof and by virtue of vested authority I do confer upon him this

Given at NAPIER FIELD, ALABAMA *this* NINTH *day of* OCTOBER *in the year of our Lord one thousand nine hundred and* FORTY-TWO.

Attest

HERMAN L. HARRIS,
Major, Air Corps,
Adjutant.

JAMES L. DANIEL, JR.,
Colonel, Air Corps,
Commanding.

U. S. GOVERNMENT PRINTING OFFICE : 1942—O—446650

The Diploma that we received with our Air Corps 'Wings' when we completed Flying Training on the Arnold Scheme

CHAPTER 5

The Other Side of the Joystick

After receiving the visible rewards for our endeavours, we packed our kit that same afternoon and boarded a train to Atlanta. Here we joined a special train for all the 421 graduates from the five Advanced Flying Training Schools in the Arnold Scheme and proceeded north to Canada. After New York, while our classmates went on to Moncton and UK, those of us who were commissioned were put together in one coach and attached to a train bound for Toronto. Here we were to spend ten days getting fitted with officers' uniforms before returning to the Deep South. We were accommodated in the former 'hog-pens' in the Exhibition grounds and were well looked after by the Canadians while we waited for our uniforms to be made by private tailors. Toronto was an extraordinarily pro-British city, filled with goods made in Britain for export to raise dollar currency, such as biscuits, china, linen, and clothing, but not for sale within UK. Visits to a munitions factory, to the University, and to Niagara Falls were arranged for us in the daytime, and parties and dances were held in the evening. We left on 18th October, my uniform being delivered to me with just half-an-hour to spare.

Keeping dry in the "Maid of the Mist" below the Niagara Falls while we wait for our uniforms to be made

We arrived next day at Maxwell Field, Alabama, the HQ of the South-East Army Air Corps, where we expected to take a Flying Instructors' course; but there was no room for us, and we were distributed to the various Flying Schools where we would actually be instructing. The 20 of us bound for Greenville Army Air Base in Mississippi looked out with deepening dismay on this State, with its Black majority in the population, and rated only above its neighbour Arkansas as the poorest in the United States; it was just beginning to emerge from its economic depression through the awarding of wartime contracts for new armament and equipment factories for the vastly expanding American Army and Navy.

In fact, Greenville turned out to be a pleasant small town, protected from the great Mississippi River by a high 'bund', surrounded by cotton-fields, through which ran Mississippi State Highway Number 1 – a strip of concrete, wide enough for one car, with a dirt shoulder each side. Passing cars drove half on the concrete and half on the dirt: the ditches were filled with the wrecks of cars that came to grief with drunken drivers every weekend.

"The Cup Overfloweth."

'The thundering torrent o'er the rapids flowed ...

... guided by no hand but God's.'

"MAID OF THE MIST."

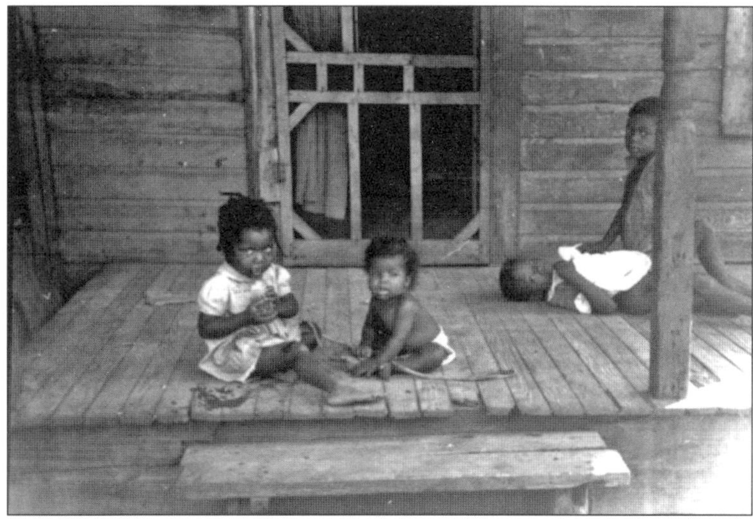

The RAF cadets never became used to the Racial Segregation we saw and experienced in Georgia, Alabama and Mississippi in the 1940's.

The Air Base was spacious and well-organised. We each had a large room in a timber barrack-block, and belonged to the comfortable Officers' Club – the equivalent of an RAF Officers' Mess – which on Wednesday afternoons was turned over to the wives and families and barred to us. The other difference from the RAF was that we had to pay the commercial rate for our accommodation and food, so that our lowly LAC's pay, including flying allowance of $25 a month, shot up to $240 per month, getting close to what the American officers received. For once, we had just enough money to enjoy life, to travel on Greyhound buses, and even, for some, to purchase a car, an old second-hand jalopy, which some kind Black might be happy to buy from us afterwards.

131017 P/O H.J.S.Taylor, RAFVR

Photo: Billy Rothwell

Greenville was a Basic Flying Training School holding about 200 Vultee BT-13as. Our Instructors' Course was mounted by the School and lasted just ten days, during which time we learned to fly the aircraft from the back seat and to go through all the manoeuvres we would have to teach our students. These were listed in order on a sheet of paper, but there was no set 'patter' or approved language for teaching each manoeuvre, as there was in the RAF, so we used our own initiative on this. Back-seat flying was not too difficult, although the forward view was almost totally blocked by the student in front. The most frightening part of the course was learning to land at night, when we flew in pairs, one piloting from the back, the other monitoring from the front. Allowing your colleague to fly almost blind into the ground at night required plenty of trust and cool nerves. Surprisingly, we had near-misses but no accidents during the course.

The flying side of the Air Base was divided into six Squadrons and the British instructors were distributed among them. I was put into No 1 Squadron with six other British Pilot Officers and 13 American instructors. The latter were very tolerant of us and we all got on well together. What the American cadets thought when they found themselves with a 'Limey' instructor, I don't know; but I think that they appreciated the fact that we avoided 'bull' as much as possible, did not 'bawl them out' when they

Certificate of Graduation

Instructor's School

Greenville Army Flying School Greenville Mississippi

This is to Certify that:

P/O H. J. Taylor

HAS SATISFACTORILY COMPLETED THE COURSE PRESCRIBED FOR INSTRUCTORS BY THE SOUTH EAST ARMY AIR FORCES TRAINING CENTER, THIS 10th DAY OF Nov. , NINETEEN HUNDRED FORTY Two.

A.V. Santangini
1st LT. A. C.
INSTRUCTOR

R B Blackledge
R. B. BLACKLEDGE, CAPT. A. C.
COMMANDING
INSTRUCTORS SCHOOL

W. M. Brown
W. M. BROWN, LT. COL., A. C.
DIRECTOR OF TRAINING

The Certificate we received after a mere 10-day Course to turn us into Flying Instructors on the BT-13a

made mistakes, and did our best to encourage them, especially if they had problems. All I required was that they should bring a bottle of 'Coke' (Coca-Cola) to me in the rear cockpit while two students changed over in the front! Above all, we had no time for either the Upper Class/Lower Class syndrome or for the 'Honor Code'; as a result, perhaps, these abuses seemed much less evident at Greenville – and perhaps also on other Bases. The masses of new recruits for pilot-training in 1943 came from a lower and broader level of American society than the previous ones; perhaps they resisted the system as strongly as we did and there were fewer West Pointers to enforce it.

The instructor's forward view from the back seat of a BT-13a

After a ten-day course I was now an instructor on the BT-13a at Greenville Army Air Base in Mississippi.

My first group of Aviation Cadets from Class 43C (November 1942 – January 1943)
1-r: P.L.Hartman K.Hindersinn H.W.Dorland W.F.Hicks C.F.Heil

There were about 70 cadets in each Squadron; their day was divided between flying and ground-school, so that we flew in either the mornings or the afternoons, but not both. The hours were quite long, though, starting at 6.30am for the morning shift and at 12.30pm for the afternoon one.

When Class 43C arrived on 17th November 1942, we were each given five cadets: mine were Hartman, Heil, Hicks, Hindersinn, and Hodgson, all bigger and older than me and two were married. I was completely tongue-tied with shyness and could only mutter, *"Come out and look at the aircraft."* Here I was on my own ground: I knew the BT-13a inside-out, while to them she was a strange, huge, metal monoplane with all kinds of unfamiliar mechanisms. Showing them round and explaining the workings and procedures to these five apprehensive young Americans did wonders for me: I knew about flying this machine and they knew nothing; in the next two months I would transfer my knowledge and skill to them. In those first few minutes together, I lost my shyness and felt a self-confidence that I had never experienced before.

I had four Classes altogether: 43C, 43E, 43G, and 43I, and covered more or less the same syllabus with them as we had received at Cochran Field. The emphasis gradually moved away from precision flying for its own sake to encouraging initiative and developing skills which would ultimately be more useful to operational pilots. Thus we provided plenty of aerobatics and low flying and more cross-country flights by both day and night; we also practised more formation flying.

Perhaps because we had already been at war for three years, I think the RAF instructors were more enterprising and less inhibited than our American colleagues. The latter seemed to prefer a quiet life and rarely talked about moving out of training into a combat unit. One event illustrated this: a new model of BT-13a with a rear fuselage of composite materials (to save metal) arrived, and the rumour went about that the tail might fall off in a spin. The Americans thereupon refused to give their students

Very apt cartoon of a typical American cadet's impressions of the Basic course at Greenville Army Air Base

Unheard of! – Greenville Army Air Base under snow in January 1943

Instructors of No 1 (The Wabbit) Squadron (1st May 1943)
Back row: Lts Koestler Brown Bohannon Robertson Kennedy Turner Black Witcomb
Middle: F/Os Jimmy Holloway JT Leslie McCracken Jimmy King Don White Geoff Kinsey Lee Hodge
Front Row: Lt Bressler Capt Cobb Capt Frisbie Capt Schonenberg Lt Graham

instruction in spinning. The RAF were unmoved and continued to train their students with 3-turn spins. I went further: on a dual flight, I would tell my student to climb up to 10,000 feet and then to put the aircraft into a spin, holding back the stick and applying full rudder; he had to count the number of turns up to 13, then let go the stick and rudder and I would raise my hands to show him I had done the same – the BT would then come out of the spin on its own! I did not publicise this approach in case it was banned, but I am sure that my students from then on had no fear of spinning.

There was a great single-span bridge over the Mississippi not far from Greenville and most of the RAF boys succumbed to the temptation of flying under it. I never did, as I saw no particular point in doing so and the risk of being caught and being sent back to UK as a punishment was too great. In night-flying, though, we would carry out 'bombing' missions on the large barges that had the

Temptation: the bridge over the Mississippi River near Greenville – but I never succumbed

misfortune to be cruising up or down the river while we were flying overhead. We carried empty 'Coke' bottles, which made a horrid whistling sound as they fell from several hundred feet. They certainly frightened the bargees, and one of my friends returned to the Air Base with his tailplane riddled with pellets from an irate bargee's shotgun – good shooting at night-time!

Instructors Three and the Vultee 'Vibrator'
JT Jimmy King Don White

On solo night cross-countrys, we would have all the students going out alone to fly a triangular or quadrangular course at intervals, so they would be lined-up for take-off behind each other. One student had his head in the cockpit studying his maps and failed to notice that his Vultee was creeping forward until, with a nasty churning noise, his propeller cut into the tail of the one in front and slowly moved up the fuselage. The student was too shocked to act quickly and, although the Control Tower and several instructors yelled at him on the radio, he switched off the engine only when his propeller was inches behind the other pilot's head. He had a tough time on the course after this.

On these occasions, the students had to check-in by radio at each turning-point: an instructor would be circling high above each point to acknowledge their calls and to check-off their safe arrival so far. When I had this duty, I found it rather tedious to circle round the same spot at night for two or three hours. I could tune into a local radio station to listen to dance music, but I might miss a student's call. More amusing was to switch on my landing-lights and do loops and rolls with these two great beams shining out in front in the dark, especially if there were clouds around which could be illuminated. Best of all was to do a loop with the lights on inside a cloud – an almost surreal experience.

Another thrill was formation-flying, particularly when we had trained our students to fly correctly each side of us. We had a satellite field some distance away, bounded by a small wood on each side. It required nice judgement for me, flying the lead ship, to bring my wing-men round and down into the field without getting them too close to the trees. The students would have their eyes fixed rigidly on the star-roundels on my wings and would not know where they were or what they were doing until they levelled-off for a formation landing. We might then stop our engines, climb out, and quench our thirst with some juicy water-melons stolen from an adjacent field. We would then start-up and do a formation take-off. If they were good enough, I would lead them back over the Air Base at 1200 feet, the lowest height allowed, with their wing-tips closely tucked-in behind mine, and hope that people on the ground would look up at the roar of three 450hp Pratt and Whitney engines and admire our precision – rather than criticise the lack of it.

The 800 more flying hours that I accumulated in my extra nine months in America certainly provided the additional experience that I hoped to gain by staying longer; and, of course, they were not lacking in incidents and mishaps on the ground and in the air. Strangely, the ones that are etched on my memory occurred not while I was instructing from the rear seat, but while I was flying from the front seat, with a student who was to practise flying by the flight instruments alone; for this, he would pull a hood over his cockpit so that he could not see out, while I monitored his flying.

An instructor (in the back seat) leading his pupils in formation flying (colour print)

The earliest incident happened just after I had finished the Instructors' Course at Greenville, but before I began teaching my own students. In the interval, I was given the job of taking other people's cadets on instrument-flying – a not very demanding business. I was to fly the plane until we reached sufficient height for the student to take over and continue the flight under the hood. I did my take-off checks: Throttle, Mixture, Pitch, Fuel, Flaps, Gyros, and Instruments, wound the elevator-trimmer wheel back a little, lined-up on the runway, gradually opened the throttle fully, and let the BT-13a rise into the air. But the plane did not start a gentle climb as I expected: it lifted its nose and continued lifting it at an increasingly steep angle. I pushed forward hard on the joystick to bring the nose down, but the stick would not move. I wound the trim-wheel fully forward, but it made no difference. By now we were 100 feet up, on the point of stalling and falling to the ground. There was only one thing to do: I pulled back the throttle, cutting the engine, and letting its weight pull the nose down. We had passed the end of the runway, but I kicked hard on the rudder and forced the plane round 90° to stay over the grass. It swooped down, gained speed, and tried to go up again in a stall. I was struggling to move the joy-stick but, just as we were level with the ground, all three wheels struck it at the same moment. There was a mighty crash, but the undercarriage took the strain and the plane stayed on the ground in one piece. *"Well done, Sir"*, cried the student, who had sat still throughout this ordeal. I taxied back to the flight-line, convinced that someone had, literally, 'left a spanner in the works' and jammed the controls. I asked for the machine to be stripped down but, later, the mechanics reported that they had found nothing wrong. True to tradition, we were given another plane immediately and took off again, this time for a successful flight.

The second occasion was less dramatic, but more expensive. Again, I was in the front seat, with one of my own students in the back, going out for an instrument flight. As we moved away from the flight-line, another BT, in the hands of a solo student, suddenly taxied straight across my path. I jammed on the brakes – and my plane toppled onto its nose. With a crunching sound on the concrete, the propeller blades bent back; the aircraft then recovered its balance and fell back on the tail-wheel, with the sad-looking blades still revolving and the engine vibrating unhappily. *"Turn that damned engine off!"*, yelled a voice on the radio just as I was switching it off. The engine stopped and peace reigned. Of course, there was an inquiry into how Government Property, to wit one engine and propeller, had been damaged. The student was said to be at fault for not keeping a proper look-out, but I received the major part of the blame because *"An instructor must always expect the unexpected!"* Nothing happened to either of us, which was generous, but I have never forgotten those words which, I still feel, were extremely wise and capable of universal application – and not just to flying.

On the third occasion, the student concerned was already under the hood and flying quite steadily on instruments alone. A nice large cumulus cloud appeared in front of us, so I thought it would be a good opportunity for the student to fold back the hood and do some real instrument-flying inside the cloud. So we flew into the cloud but, very soon and before he had emerged from the hood, we started to climb. *"Hold your altitude,"* I said to the student. *"I'm trying to, Sir,"* he replied. The altimeter continued rising, so I told him to push the stick forward. I watched my stick move in unison, the speed increased from 140 mph to 160 mph, but we continued to climb. I realised something peculiar was happening. *"OK, I've got control,"* I said. *"You can come out of the hood."* I pushed the stick forward more: we were now doing 200 mph, but the altimeter was still rising. I remembered stories of aircraft getting caught in the up-draughts of large cumulus clouds and being broken-up by the force of the air-currents. At 240 mph and still going up, I realised there was only one way out – and that was back! We turned round and rushed back the way we had come. It was a great relief to emerge into clear air, but 4000 feet higher than when we went in. As is said in the magazines: *"I learned about flying from that!"* Clouds near the Gulf Coast – or anywhere else, for that matter – need to be treated with the greatest respect.

Altogether, I never tired of instructing these American cadets, cushioned perhaps by the knowledge that we would be going back to Britain in nine months' time – or less, as the days passed by. I enjoyed the company of my students and learned a great deal indirectly from them about the United States and its immense variety of people: none of my cadets had been to university or college and none came from any of the major cities; they were all very ordinary, well-balanced young Americans, eager to serve their country even if their parents were recent immigrants with little or no English.

Consequently, I completely rejected the ruling we were given about the final assessment of their performance, which was based on a theoretical formula called the 'Bell Curve'. This was a prediction of the psychologists and sociologists that, in any group of students, 5% would be outstanding, 20% above average, 50% average, 20% below average, and 5% useless. This might have been true of a group of 100 people or more; but when we were told at the beginning of a Course that, out of our five students, one would be above average, three would be average, and one would be 'washed-out', I rebelled instinctively. I knew that if a cadet really wanted to fly, given time he would learn; I also knew that not everyone learned at the same rate. So, although on paper I gave each of my students the same number of hours of instruction, in the air I took time off my better ones and gave it to my weaker ones – with the result that all of them passed. Whether, in their later flying, some of them proved inadequate, I don't know, but I am proud to this day that I never 'washed-out' any of them.

I could have done so: there was the thick-headed one who 'froze' on the controls in a spin and whom I had to prod on the shoulder with my own joystick before he would let go! At the other extreme was a high-spirited student of French extraction who gave me a real scare: we had practised formation-flying, which then broke up into a tail-chase. After several minutes of this, I called them back into formation and waited for them to draw up each side of me. One did so, but the other one dived underneath us, pulled up right in front, and did a 'chandelle' – a 180°– turn at the top of a stall – and dived back underneath us in the opposite direction! What could I do? If I reprimanded him on the radio, the officers in the Control Tower would hear me and certainly have him thrown off the Course. All I could say was, *"Rejoin the formation!"*; but when we were back on the ground, I gave him the biggest tongue-lashing I ever gave anyone. The trouble was that he was too emotional, too carried away by the joy of

My next group of cadets of Class 43-E (January-March 1943)
Back row: (1-r) C.L.Gallagher J.Gervan M.H.Fryman
Front: A.R.Gallucio H.L.Grainger

My third group of cadets of Class 43-G (April-May 1943)
Back row: (1-r) J.Nesnick H.H.Newman
Front: F.J.Mousseau R.C.Watterson E.L.Dodder

Unfortunately, the photograph of my last group of cadets of Class 43-I (June-July 1943) has been mislaid
1-r: J.H.Carr P.Cavallo E.M.Davis A.J.Deak W.C.Hopkins

flying, yet he undoubtedly had a flair for it. I thought he was good, but I also knew that, metaphorically rather than literally, he needed to be brought down to earth. I hope he learned to control his enthusiasm, gained his 'wings', and went on to become a successful fighter pilot. One day, I must try to find out what happened to all my boys when they left me.

At one time, the instructors at Greenville were allowed to take an aircraft away on a private trip once a month; but, as the American economy became increasingly geared into the war, this was reduced to one flight of up to 1000 miles a year. Don White and I decided to take advantage of this and selected Colorado Springs as a suitable destination, just 950 miles away and near the Rocky Mountains, which we both wanted to see. It was a simple matter to draw a straight line on the map from Greenville to Colorado Springs, passing nowhere of any importance except Oklahoma City, about half-way along our route, where we could refuel. We each packed a small bag of night things, as the Vultee cruised at only 140mph, so this trip would take nearly seven hours. We had to do our usual instructing in the morning of 3rd July, so we set off in the afternoon. I sat in the front cockpit on the flight out and did most of the very undemanding flying – just holding a steady compass course. The scenery was quite interesting for the first half, with towns and villages and cultivated fields, mainly of cotton. But after Oklahoma City it was virtual desert, endless miles of it, as we flew out of Oklahoma State into part of Kansas and then into Colorado, with only an occasional curving river, straight railroad or roadway as useful visible features. In fact, we crossed only one river and, as it was easy to find the exact point on the map, this was the only navigation check we needed in hundreds of miles. The monotony was relieved for a time by a small hillock that appeared in front but was not marked on the map. In the flat landscape it was difficult to judge how far away or how big it was until we were almost on top of it, when it turned out to be a rocky outcrop no more than 200 feet high. We flew at 3000ft but, to our surprise, the ground appeared to be getting gradually closer; we then realised that the desert was rising slowly up towards the Rocky Mountains; so we too had to climb gradually up to keep to our height above it: the military airfield outside Colorado Springs where we landed was 6000ft above sea-level. From 100 miles away, we could see the outline of the Rocky Mountains on the horizon, but the sun was setting behind them and an evening haze was rising from the desert, so that they were neither clear nor very impressive. Much more arresting was Pike's Peak, a great lump of a mountain 14,110ft high, a few miles to the west of Colorado Springs. This was certainly something we had to see close-up next day.

The town itself was pleasant enough, with nothing distinguished about it except for its wonderful setting, with a fine bridge over a gorge with a rushing river and waterfall and a vista of peaks reaching up to the distant Rockies. We found a quiet hotel and dined and slept well, then walked over the bridge after breakfast and admired the view. We took a taxi out to the airfield, where our sturdy Vultee had been re-fuelled and well serviced by the mechanics. Having signed all the appropriate papers, we took off with Don in front on the controls. We had reached 500 feet and were turning out of the circuit when we were horrified to discover that the airspeed indicator was showing zero mph! This was a nasty situation. At first we thought that the instrument had failed; but then we looked out along the left wing and there, to our dismay, sticking out into the airflow was the pitot head – which fed air into the instrument – still wrapped in the cover that protected it from dust while on the ground! It was our duty to have checked that all

JT in Colorado Springs with Pike's Peak behind

the night-time covers had been removed before we climbed into the cockpits. Now, however humiliatingly, we had to radio the Base that we had an emergency and needed immediate clearance to land; Don then had the difficult task of nursing the aircraft back to the runway, with no means of knowing the vital airspeed except from the attitude of the plane, the noise of the slipstream, and his experience as a pilot. He naturally kept on the safe side by flying and landing faster than usual, and fortunately without further incident. We stopped by the Control Tower, reported rather shamefacedly what had happened, removed the offending cover, and took off again with the airspeed indicator in full working order. Breathing a sigh of relief, we climbed up and slowly circled Pike's Peak, levelling-off at 12,000ft, beyond which we would have needed oxygen. It was a fine sight: a mass of small craggy peaks and valleys gradually rising to a rocky point, with several roads winding their way up. From our height we could make-out many more peaks in the distance, and we could truthfully say we'd seen the Rockies – but not the deep canyons that cut into them.

Holiday on the Gulf Coast
Back row (l-r): Straker Hodge Holloway JT
Front row: Wilkinson Kennedy Hicks White

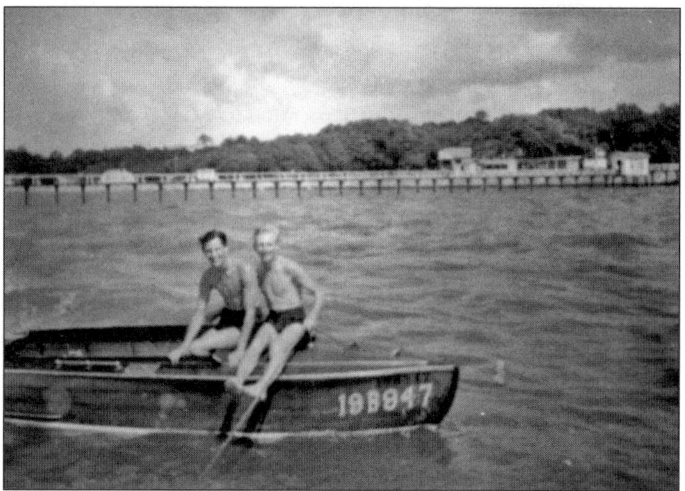

Reggie Hicks and JT in the Gulf of Mexico

The return flight was a repeat of the outward one, made more tedious by our knowing what lay ahead; however, we flew gradually 'downhill' this time until Oklahoma City, and so arrived back at Greenville after 6 1/2 hours, twenty minutes less than our outward time. It had been an interesting trip, revealing the huge size and great distances of the United States, and a useful experience, not least for its warning to us pilots about the necessity of checking the aeroplane properly before each flight.

Don White (on right) and JT in Washington

We had a Farewell Dinner in the Officers' Club, then eight of us – Reggie Hicks, Lee Hodge, Jimmy Holloway, John Kennedy, Bill Straker, Don White, David Wilkinson, and myself – in two cars drove down to a pair of cabins on the coast outside Gulfport and spent a totally relaxed week, 21st–27th July 1943, on the beach and in the sea, before returning to Greenville, handing in our flying gear, packing our possessions, and heading independently back to Moncton in Canada. Tom Adams, Don White and I teamed up and spent a few days in Washington, being taken round the sights by a friendly Army officer called – of all names – Gustav Stalin, whom we met in the Officers' Club. The monuments to Presidents Jefferson and Abraham Lincoln were awe-inspiring, the White House was remarkably visible from a public footpath, and the Smithsonian Museum held a marvellous collection of historic aircraft.

I had an introduction to a US Army Colonel and a date with his daughter, brought about by the anxious sister of Mrs Dimmick, who was married to the Colonel. She had telephoned me at Greenville to beg me to take out her 18-year-old elder daughter in Washington as she was depressed by the fact that her younger sister had just become engaged and she was feeling 'left on the shelf'! Such were the competitive social pressures on teen-age boys and girls in the States in 1943, unknown in Britain at the time, but crossing the Atlantic 20 years later, like so many other features of American life. She was a sweet, rather shy girl, and I enjoyed her company on a wet and windy day. Next day, I took Tom and Don with me to the Pentagon, where we met the Colonel and had a most interesting tour of this vast five-sided structure, with five concentric rings of five-storey buildings stretching out from an open space in the centre. The higher and closer to the centre we walked, the grander became the carpets and fittings in the corridors, giving a fine visual indication of the rank and importance of each officer and his post – our Colonel, on the inner circuit, was clearly doing quite well!

Don and I also spent a week in New York, likewise seeing all the sights, but we found the city cold, impersonal and expensive. The reason perhaps was that, although we stayed at the friendly Wings Club, we didn't know anyone and we failed to find the usual American hospitality. Nevertheless, we reached the top of the Empire State Building – then the highest in the world – by express elevator (lift), climbed up inside the Statue of Liberty and looked out of the windows set into her crown, and visited Wall Street, the Rockefeller Center, and Coney Island. We were well primed about shortages in Britain, so we spent our remaining dollars on cosmetics, silk stockings, pencil-leads, lighter-flints, razor-blades, and films, as well as on the usual cigarettes and whisky.

Waiting for our transport home
Johnny Passmore Philip Back JT

Arrived at Moncton, we found thousands of aircrew awaiting transport to Britain, spending the time amusing themselves in every possible way: football and cricket matches, athletic competitions, swimming parties on the beach, dances and visits to the cinema.

One incident led to a meeting of considerable influence on my outlook on life: a little airman stepped off the pavement one evening and saluted as he passed me. I looked at him and burst out, *"Stephen!"* It was Stephen Catto, who had been in my House at Eton and, in fact, succeeded me as House Captain. He had just arrived in Canada for pilot-training. *"This is extraordinary,"* he said. *"I know only two people in Canada: you and Philip Back."* The name rang a slight bell with me. *"Philip Back? Is he fair-haired, with slightly protruding front teeth?" "Yes"*, replied Stephen. *"Good Lord!"* I said, *"He stands next to me on parade!"* We had one parade a day, just for a roll-call and possible movement orders, and I had heard this name without thinking any more about it. At our next parade I mentioned Stephen's name to Philip and introduced myself; from then on we became close friends – until his sad death in 2006.

Philip was a great enthusiast for an exciting life: extrovert and uninhibited, he despised doing the mundane thing and always sought out a more adventurous approach. He was on his way back after getting his 'wings' in Canada, and now decided that a group of us should spend a weekend on Prince Edward Island, a kind of local Isle of Wight. We crossed over by ferry, but Philip insisted that we should travel with the captain on the bridge and pay a visit to the engine-room. On the island, we had to take a train to reach our destination; but not for me the comfort of a coach: Philip required me to make the journey with him on the foot-plate of the engine, from which we emerged with grimy faces and me with a piece of grit in my eye. Such was life with Philip Back, and eventually I found myself adopting a little of his outlook.

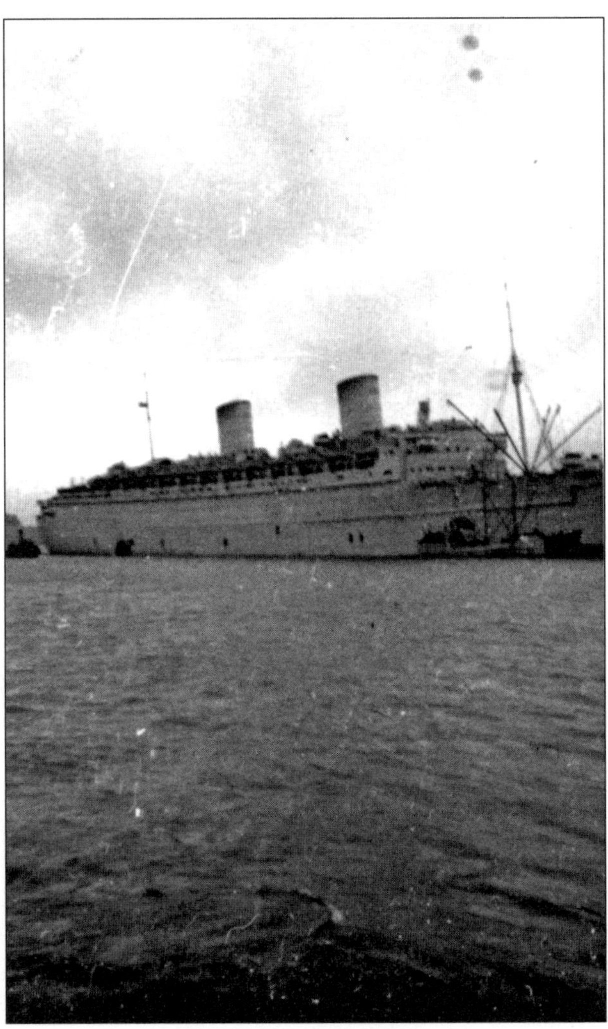

The "Queen Elizabeth" (a severely illicit photograph)

At last, after five frustrating weeks at Moneton, we boarded the "Queen Elizabeth", the largest passenger liner in the world, now converted to carry 12,000 troops. Twelve of us shared a state-room, its fittings all boarded-up, and we had meals only at 8.50am and 6.0pm – but what meals! They contained four lavish beautifully-cooked courses served by attentive waiters. It was, indeed, a luxury trip compared with our outward crossing, and lasted just seven days. The great ship steamed, unescorted, at 30 knots, zig-zagging all the way in a sea that remained remarkably calm. Each day, at about noon, an aircraft would drop magically out of the clouds overhead, even in mid-Atlantic: a Liberator, a Hudson, a Catalina. When a Spitfire turned up and circled the ship, we realised we were getting close to land.

Philip, of course, knew his way about the ship, having crossed over in her nine months earlier. He led me down into the bowels of the huge vessel to the crew's quarters, and then through a door into the foot of the hollow steel mast; here there was a vertical ladder which led, after an interminable climb, into the 'crow's nest', the look-out position frighteningly high above the decks and funnels, with the whole panorama of the ship laid-out beneath us, and the sea stretching away to the far horizon. Trust Philip!

Soon a Customs launch drew alongside and a team of officers came aboard to collect the duty on our goods purchased overseas. Immediately, as if on cue, hundreds of kitbags, bulging with contraband, could be seen suspended from portholes all down the opposite side of the ship, and the poor officers raised only some token revenue from the wide-awake RAF personnel. I disembarked at Greenock on 20th September 1943, having been away from Britain for three months less than two years.

It had been a great experience in the USA: I was a little more mature and a great deal more confident; and, most importantly, I had 1000 hours and 45 minutes flying time in my log-book, which would greatly affect my future. I looked forward to getting onto operational flying as soon as possible, but the first priority now was two weeks' leave at home.

CHAPTER 6

In Limbo in Britain

My brother Gerald on a radar site in the Faroe Islands

My leave was blissful: my brothers Gerald and Christopher both managed to come home for a few days, Gerald from a radar station 'somewhere in Britain' and Christopher from Initial Training for aircrew (which never progressed any further). Everything at home was much as it was when I left: my parents were straining to keep the School going as normally as possible; younger staff had been called-up and replaced with older men; the cellars had been fitted up with bunks for boys to sleep during air-raid alerts, but these had now lost their frequency; food was in short supply, but rationing actually made catering for almost 100 people a little easier than for a small household, and the large kitchen garden and a chicken-run helped to make the School self-sufficient in eggs and vegetables.

In Britain generally, after the great distances and open spaces of America, everything seemed on a very small scale, especially cars and railway carriages and trucks. People, too, were more closed-up than the talkative Americans. Here, a glance round one's fellow-travellers in a railway compartment would establish their occupations, from their clothes, their newspapers, and their accents; whereas, in America, people had a more uniform appearance and could satisfy their curiosity about each other only by talking about themselves and their home-town and showing photographs of their family, who were

I spend time hay-making with a converted Essex saloon.

Home on Leave
Crowning the Headley National Savings Queen
on the tennis lawn outside the west front of Cheam School

always 'the prettiest' or 'the finest', until all identities were known. In America, there were no walls or fences between neighbouring gardens: people led more open lives, which was reflected in their abundant generosity. Here, I felt we were more cramped by greater numbers in a smaller space, and so needed to create and maintain our privacy tenaciously. Conditioned by my experience in USA, I too began to talk to strangers in public places.

The treatment of Blacks by Whites, which had upset us in the Southern States, also caused friction between the American soldiers, 'over-paid, over-sexed, and over here' while I was away, and the villagers of Hampshire and Berkshire. The Blacks were polite and well-behaved and became more popular as neighbours than the Whites, who were infuriated at the sight of English girls going out with or dancing with Black soldiers. This eventually led to the 'Battle of Kingsclere', two miles from the School, when White soldiers cleared the Blacks out of a pub; the Blacks went back to their base, broke into the armoury, returned with rifles, crouched behind the wall facing the pub, and shot several White soldiers as they came out. The Whites returned fire with their side-arms until, as I was told, 'the gutters ran with blood'. After this, the Blacks and Whites were put into bases in separate parts of the locality. However, with the war on, there was no publicity about any of this, just gossip and rumour.

My leave was over far too soon and, on 6th October, I arrived at No 7 Personnel Reception Centre at Harrogate, a residential spa town in Yorkshire. With three others, I shared a room in the Queen's Hotel, with a bathroom and a batwoman, who cleaned the room and polished our shoes and buttons – luxury indeed. We found ourselves part of a throng of thousands of aircrew trained in Canada, USA and Rhodesia, all longing for a posting to an Operational Training Unit as the preliminary to getting onto an operational squadron. Every month a thousand more would arrive, but only four hundred would be posted away. Anyone not earmarked for single-engined aircraft went into Bomber Command, after waiting at Harrogate for only a few weeks. Those who had already done one operational tour or who had been instructors were allowed to choose which branch of the Service they would go into: those who chose or were nominated for fighters formed the longest queue, with little or no movement in months.

The thousand hours in my log-book were treated as the equivalent of an operational tour, so I was given my choice; but by the time I was interviewed only night-fighters or a return to instructing was available – so I opted for night-fighting. I was happy with this, as I liked the idea of flying alone on individual sorties, rather than as part of a squadron or larger group. Also, the queue appeared to be moving and I might get out of Harrogate quicker.

After two months, though, this movement had ceased, presumably because German night-bombing had declined considerably and there had been few casualties among the defenders. I then heard, from some source, that the Photographic Reconnaissance (PR) queue was moving. I felt immediately that this would suit me admirably and applied to have my name transferred to this list. Once again, however, postings came to a virtual halt and, after the first month, the days dragged by in dull and increasingly cold succession.

The authorities did their best to make our time useful for our hoped-for future participation in the air war. Except for the few weeks we had spent on our Grading Course, in my case on Tiger Moths at Brough, most of us had little experience of flying over the English countryside, with its small fields and many villages and towns, under grey European skies, with all the features looking very much the same, or invisible in total blackout at night. Equally unfamiliar were the British aeroplanes and engines, with controls and instruments different from our training planes, with guns and gun-sights, bombs and bomb-sights, and unaccustomed radio, signalling, and night-time lighting systems. These important subjects were presented to us in an intensive programme of lectures and demonstrations lasting a month. Recognition of our own and enemy aircraft and ships was another vital matter, as was learning and using the Morse Code, at which we had to become reasonably proficient, capable of receiving and sending at least ten words per minute.

Our afternoons were usually spent in more physical activities, among which clay-pigeon shooting sharpened our eyesight and coordination, while dinghy drill in an indoor swimming-bath would prove, we were aware, a real life-saver for some of us. In fact, I found this quite a frightening exercise: in overalls, with a dinghy-pack strapped to my backside, I had to jump into the water from the highest diving-board in the baths. It probably wasn't any great height, but to me it looked and felt like sixty feet: it required real nerve to launch myself into the air and hit the water with a resounding splash. Releasing the dinghy, inflating it, climbing into it, and starting to paddle to a 'distant shore' was quite fun after my fear both of the jump and of the others seeing me quaking.

Another valuable activity was keeping up our instrument-flying on the Link Trainer, the original flight-simulator, in which we sat in a dark mock-up fuselage with no view out and obeyed orders from the instructor; the machine responded, through mechanical jacks, to our movement of the controls and a 'crab' left a trace on paper on the instructor's table-top. It was quite an ordeal, from which I usually emerged in a sweat! But it was a welcome approximation to real flying in cloud or at night. I also spent

A Link Trainer in action
A pupil is 'flying' it (not under the hood) while the instructor watches the 'crab' tracing his path on the paper on the table.

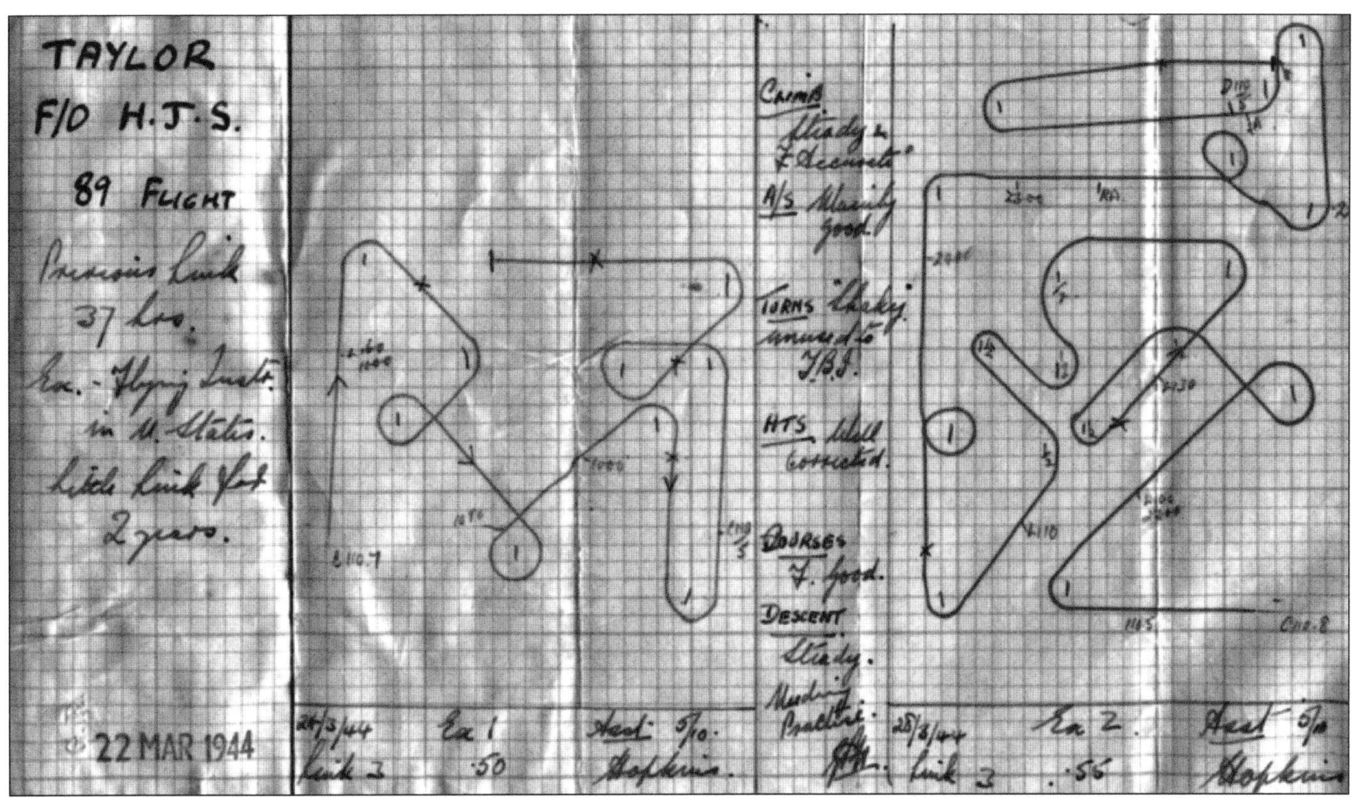

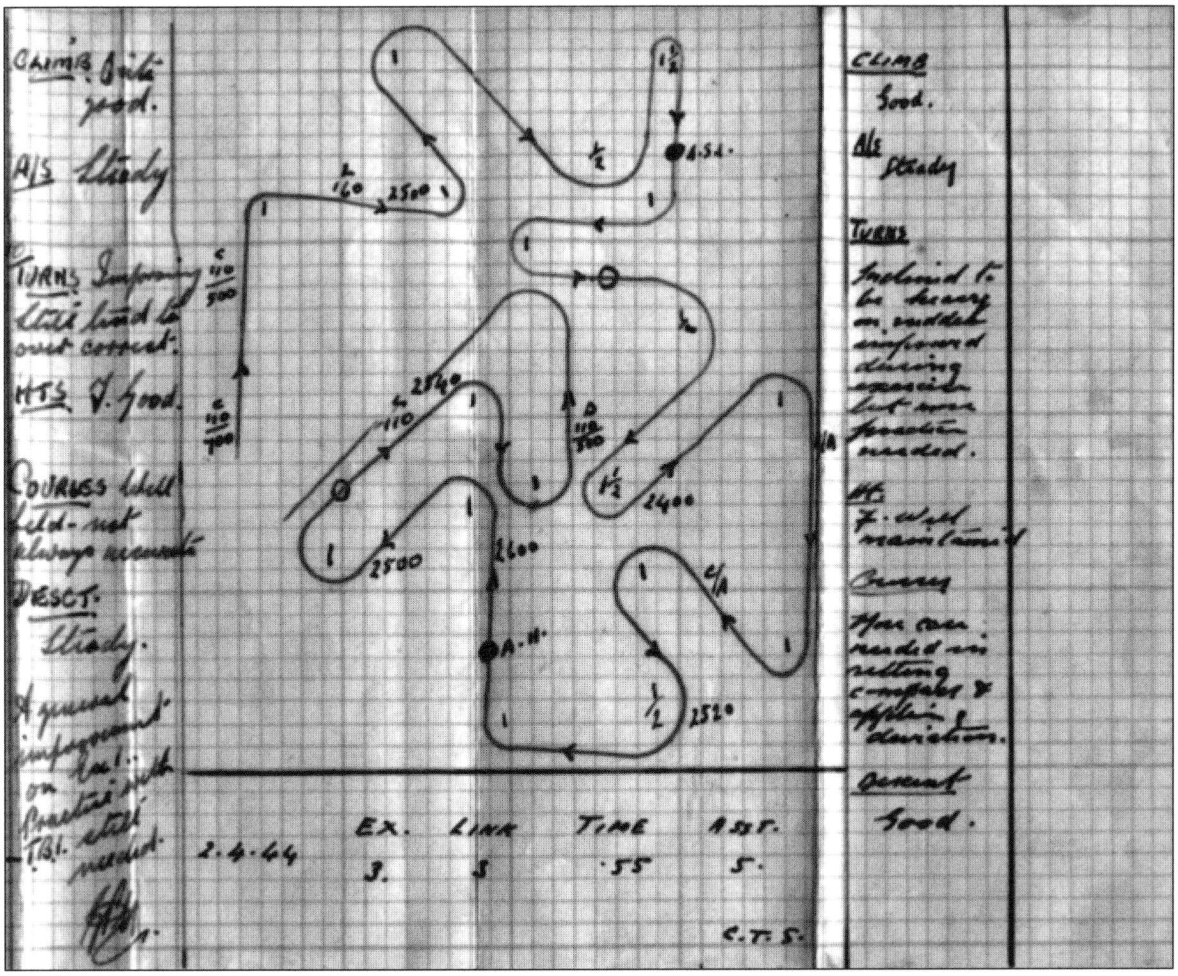

Some of the 'traces' the 'crab' made on the Instructor's chart when I tried to carry-out his orders on the Link Trainer at Harrogate.

a good number of afternoons practising my embryonic golfing skills on the links outside Harrogate. I could drive the ball quite a long way, but spent most of the time looking for it in the long grass or trying to get it out of a bunker, while my putting was not much better than my efforts on the Link!

All this mental and physical activity was useful and enjoyable first time round but, after a short leave, much less interesting when we had to go round the programme again in a second month; after this, there seemed little prospect of our leaving Harrogate at all, and the staff were getting as tired of seeing us around as we were of being there. The easiest way of avoiding us was to give us generous amounts of leave, which was better than hanging around Harrogate, but not what we really wanted. Even then, 'red tape' prevailed at Christmas-time, and many of us were refused leave to go home. I spent the day with C.H.M. Pearson, a master at Cheam, who had been in my father's artillery battery in WW1 and whom the boys naturally nicknamed 'Chump'. He was an easy-going bachelor, who lived in Harrogate, and he had somehow recruited four ATS girls for a pleasant, but unromantic Christmas.

On 18th January, 3 months after arriving in Harrogate, I at last received a message to report for interview at RAF Benson, the home base of PR, ten miles south of Oxford. I hurried there by train and found myself accommodated in the very comfortable Officers' Mess of a spacious pre-war Station. Next day, I presented myself at the Headquarters building and was told to report to the 'Wing Commander Air'. After a good deal of searching and questioning, I eventually found the door with this name on, knocked and was invited in by a middle-aged Wing Commander. Still under the influence of US Army Air Corps procedures, I was very ignorant of RAF positions and styles of address, so I assumed his name was Air. It was only much later that I discovered that "Wing Commander Air" was a title equivalent to "Wing Commander Flying", and therefore I never learned the actual name of my interviewer!

He questioned me in detail about my flying experience and my reasons for wanting to join the Photographic Reconnaissance Unit (PRU). He told me that, in fact, there was a PRU in each theatre of the war and that, at Benson, there were two squadrons of Spitfires and two of Mosquitos in what had been 1 PRU but was now 106 Group, which included four American PR squadrons on Lightnings at nearby Mount Farm. In spite of this, flying on PR in any squadron was still known generally as 'flying on PRU'. He then told me that the Spitfire was being phased out and all the work was going to be done by Mosquitos. How many hours did I have on twin-engined aircraft? When I said *"None"*, he replied, *"In that case you'll have to learn to fly them. I shall recommend that you are sent to Little Rissington, not far from here, to fly Oxfords, and then, if you do all right, you'll go to the PRU OTU at Dyce, near Aberdeen. How would this suit you?"*

I had hoped to fly Spitfires, but Mosquitos would be nearly as good and, in any case, the posting would get me out of horrible Harrogate. I said it would make me very happy and I thanked him effusively. I put on my cap, saluted him and walked out – and felt like dancing a jig in the corridor!

The weekend was coming, so I hitch-hiked home, only 30 miles away, returning to Benson on the Monday for a Decompression Chamber test to check that I was fit for high-level flying. With several others, I entered a large metal tube, sealed at one end and with an airtight door at the other, with seats along each side and a window or two for us to be observed. By reducing the pressure inside, the operator could simulate the air condition at 20,000 feet and higher. We were given oxygen-masks and a plentiful supply of oxygen. No one suffered any ill-effects, so we were told to remove the masks and to try to draw certain figures and write our names. We soon began to feel lightheaded, we lost our hand-eye coordination, our drawings became child-like and our names mis-spelled. However, when we were told to replace the masks, the oxygen quickly restored our natural abilities, The attendant doctor told us we had just experienced the symptoms of oxygen starvation, which could kill us in a few minutes unless we recognised what was happening and took quick action, such as checking our oxygen supply or descending to 10,000 feet or lower.

Wellington 1A bombers similar to those at RAF Gamston
From the painting by Edmund Miller

Back at Harrogate, I now had something concrete to look forward to, but the emptiness of our lives was no less frustrating. The authorities, however, had devised a new scheme, theoretically a useful one: this was to send us out in groups of three or four to airfields all over the country to learn the job of Airfield Controlling. To young men who had no other ambitions, this would have been a worthy, even absorbing, occupation; and to us, who had been accustomed to very different procedures in our training overseas, it should have been a worthwhile experience. But to young qualified pilots itching to get back into the air and into action, it was a total bore, which even turned into another form of detention when it became clear that the real Airfield Controllers had no intention of letting unprofessional people like us share in any of their responsibilities.

On 19th February 1944, therefore, now more than four months after arriving at Harrogate, I set out for RAF Gamston, an Operational Training Unit outside East Retford in Lincolnshire, for what turned out to be the most depressing posting of my RAF career. East Retford appeared to consist of rows of terrace houses in a totally flat landscape, with no redeeming feature whatever: I can't remember ever seeing any shops, but there must have been a street of them; with a few pubs and a cinema. The airfield was some miles away and even bleaker. The sole activity was getting fleets of Wellingtons into the air, with 'browned-off' instructors ('on rest' from operations) teaching student-pilots how to fly the aeroplane, by day and by night, on 'circuits and bumps' and on cross-countrys. I went up into the Control Tower and was given a guided tour and allowed to watch the proceedings, after which it became clear that I was not required to do anything more, and it became the routine for the four of us to report to the Tower each morning and then spend most of our time reading the newspapers and magazines in the Officers' Mess, or playing squash.

The only relief was a sudden message from Philip Back that he would come to see me on one of my otherwise empty Sundays. A main road ran alongside the airfield; I was standing beside it at the appointed hour when a lorry stopped next to me and out stepped an immaculate Philip, wearing a

Philip Back, Pathfinder DFC in 1946

Pathfinder emblem on his tunic and smiling all over his face. He had good reason: he had a relation, a Group Captain of considerable influence, who had plucked him out of Harrogate after only a few days, had put him through a Mosquito OTU, and then had him posted to a Pathfinder Squadron. He was already half-way through his tour and was enjoying it immensely. In fact, he had finished his tour and been awarded a DFC before I had left the clutches of Harrogate/Gamston!

After lunch in the Officers' Mess, we debated what to do: Philip decided that the only choice was to go to Newark, the nearest sizeable town. We could hitch-hike there, but only on lorries – Philip's principles ruled out private cars. We were lucky to find a truck that took us into the town centre. Everywhere was shut and Newark was dead on a Sunday afternoon in wartime. However, the cathedral had to be open, so there we went. After looking around, Philip spotted some stone steps leading into the tower. Up we climbed for a fine view of the river flowing below into the leaden Lincolnshire countryside. Philip's keen eye then lighted on a ladder leading up to a small wooden door. Of course, he had to go up and give the door a push, whereupon it swung open with a creak. We could see timbers illuminated vaguely by the light from some small dormer windows. *"Come on!"* he called, and so we crawled up more ladders into the mediaeval woodwork, festooned with mediaeval cobwebs and smelling of 20th-century Rentokil. Halfway up, a locked trapdoor blocked further progress, which was just as well for me: the wind was lapping round the spire, soughing gently in the angles of the stone cladding: I was sure I could feel it rocking in the stronger puffs. *"Built-in elasticity"*, said Philip authoritatively. *"Those old builders knew their stuff. Come on, let's go down."* This was harder than going up, but we eventually emerged onto the floor of the tower, covered in dust and spiders' webs. Philip was grinning happily: curiosity and honour – being adventurous, at all costs – were satisfied.

We walked slowly along the street when, to our surprise, we saw a small general store that was open. The following conversation then ensued:

Philip: *"I say, I wonder if he's got any chocolate biscuits."*

Me: *"Don't be silly. There's a war on and you can't buy any."*

Philip: *"Let's try, anyway."*

We enter the shop.

Philip: *"Good afternoon. Have you any chocolate biscuits, please?"*

Shopkeeper: *"I dunno if I've got any left. I'll have a look."*

He rummages under the counter and pulls out a zinc-coloured tin.

Shopkeeper: *"Ah, you're in luck: I seem to have some. How many do you want?"*

Philip: *"Oh, half a pound, please."*

The shopkeeper puts a half-pound weight on his scales and doles out exactly the right amount, down to the last biscuit. He empties the scoop into a paper bag and twirls it tight.

Shopkeeper: *"Will that be all, sir?"*

Philip, *"Oh, yes, thank you."*

Shopkeeper: *"That will be two and sixpence, please, and sixteen points."*

Philip finds half-a-crown, puts it into the shopkeeper's hand and stretches out for the biscuits.

Shopkeeper: *"And the sixteen points, please, sir."*

Philip: *"Points? What are points?"*

Shopkeeper, patiently: *"Points are in your ration book, sir; you need them for most sugary things – sweets, jam, cakes, and the like."*

Philip: *"But we don't have ration books: we're in the RAF, you see, and we eat all our meals in the Mess."*

Shopkeeper: *"I'm sorry, sir, but the regulations say you can only buy biscuits on points."*

Philip: *"Yes, but if we don't have any ration books, we're not the same as other people, so the regulations don't apply."*

Shopkeeper scratches the back of his head: *"Well, I dunno; regulations are regulations – and what will my other customers say?"*

Philip: *"Oh, never mind them. After all, we're in the RAF."*

Shopkeeper, unsure, but a true patriot: *"Oh, well, just this time, then, for you young gentlemen. But don't you go telling anyone else about this."*

Philip: *"Oh, of course not: mum's the word. You're most kind. Thank you very much."*

We shake him by the hand in real gratitude and step out into the street, leaving the poor man still scratching his head. I chided Philip for having bullied the shop-keeper, but he replied, *"Most people are probably too short of points to buy chocolate biscuits, so perhaps we were doing him a favour!"*

I returned to the purgatory of Gamston, but relieved the monotony by getting two flights in a Wellington. They were each at night and involved a pupil-pilot being trained in take-offs and landings; I stood behind the instructor and pupil and watched the whole proceedings: it was interesting, but what I saw, heard and felt convinced me that I was temperamentally quite unsuited to fly a multi-engined aircraft with a crew in Bomber Command. Yet, a few days later, I found myself pointed forcefully in this direction.

CHAPTER 7

Training for Bomber Command?

On 19th March 1944, a posting came through for me to report directly to No 6 Advanced Flying School at Little Rissington in Oxfordshire. With a huge sigh of relief and gratitude to the anonymous Wing Commander Air of Benson, I packed my kitbag and arrived eventually at this smart pre-war RAF Station. Among others reporting was Tim Fanning, who had been at Darr and Cochran Field with me and had also instructed on BT-13as, but at Waco in Texas.

Our first meeting was to hear the Commanding Officer telling us in no uncertain way that his sole duty was to train pilots for Bomber Command – anyone with a different idea could forget it! I crossed my fingers and vowed to keep my mouth shut. Because of overcrowding at Rissington, we were then transported to the satellite grass airfield of Windrush, conveniently sited beside the Witney-Oxford road. Here we were told that the course would last for nine weeks of flying by day and night, including a week away on Beam Approach training. There would also be an intensive programme of ground-school: besides repeating all the subjects I had studied twice at Harrogate, this would include the Airspeed Oxford and the 350hp Armstrong-Siddeley Cheetah engine and its systems; coping with fire, abandoning the aircraft, and more dinghy drill; meteorology, including the hazard of icing; gun turrets and sights, bombs and bomb-sights, the Sten gun and hand-grenades; radio sets, channels, beacons, and 'homing' procedures; navigation, maps, the Dalton Computer (actually a clever calculator), and compass-swinging; more practice in instrument-flying on the Link Trainer; and work on the Bombing Trainer, a tall tower with a bomb-sight at the top and a moving landscape projected on the ground below, marked with a target on which we would try to drop a bomb.

Oxfords were parked all round the airfield, behind which were masses of standard one-storey, flat-roofed RAF huts for a variety of purposes and rows of Nissen huts with semi-circular roofs of corrugated iron for sleeping accommodation. 13 of us were in one hut, with a round potbellied iron stove in the centre, which worked well when it could be stoked red-hot. We had to wash in the Officers' Mess situated in one of the buildings four hundred yards away, while the flight-line was about half-a-mile further on. Our hut was right alongside the main road, which meant it was very convenient for hitch-hiking to Oxford, then to Newbury, and then home – on a lucky day I reached home in less than two hours. There was a good deal of rain during my two-month stay at Windrush, and the grass field frequently became waterlogged. Flying would then be cancelled and we would be given short leaves. On one of my several visits home, I brought back my bicycle by train, which made it much easier to get about the camp and also to explore the local countryside and visit the churches. The back of my notebook contains a list of the Kings and Queens of England with their dates, a plan of the layout of a church, and a description of the different styles of Gothic architecture – which reveals that, after flying, my next major interest lay in history.

Windrush, in fact, turned out to be a happy place: out of sight of the formality of Little Rissington, there was relaxed discipline, little or no 'bull', and very friendly relations between instructors and students. I was allocated to F/0 Hansen, a little Canadian, but he was away on a course, so I spent the first two weeks as a passenger with a variety of instructors, who flew me cross-country to orientate me or showed me landings with sodium flares or on the radio beam. Eventually, F/0 Hansen returned and I started my instruction proper.

I found the Oxford a very pleasant aircraft, a low-winged cabin monoplane of wooden construction, with two Cheetah engines, fixed wooden propellers and retractable undercarriage. From the cockpit, with dual controls, there was a wonderful view forward (compared to a single-engined aircraft) and it rattled along at about 130mph cruising speed. Starting-up the engines was the only difficult procedure: each engine had to be cranked round with a geared handle, which was inserted into the nacelle. We had WAAF mechanics, and the poor girls had to kneel on the wing, prime the cylinders, and then use all their strength to turn the engine over. We shouted *"Contact!"* and switched the engine 'on', with our hand on the throttle, when we thought the girl was rotating the handle fast enough to cause the engine to fire. It usually did, but the little WAAF would then be half-blown off the wing by the slipstream while she struggled to remove the handle from its socket. On a cold day, the engine would be more reluctant and a beefy male mechanic might have to come to the rescue. Yes, those WAAF mechanics at Windrush were truly heroic.

My diary records 6th April as the day of my first efforts at flying a twin-engined plane:

"The engines were already running when I got in, followed by a Flight Engineer, under

Airspeed Oxford in unauthorised formation, up from Windrush satellite airfield of No 6 Advanced Flying Unit, Little Rissington, May 1944

training also, who was going to take notes. Hansen came along, we chatted a bit, and then he taxied out. A moment later, he let me take her but, unaccustomed to turning with the engines rather than with the rudder, I soon got an uncontrollable swing on and went off the perimeter-track. Hansen rescued me, put me straight, and let me go again, only for the same thing to happen again a little later. However, we eventually reached the marshalling-point, where we stopped and I checked TMPFFGI (Throttle, Mixture, propeller Pitch (although ours were fixed), Fuel, Flaps, Gyros, and Instruments). Then, after an intermittent 'green' from the Aldis in the Airfield Control Post (ACP), I taxied out onto the grass and contrived to line-up with the little placards placed down the centre of the field. Then, with a steady 'green' from the ACP, I eased open the throttles and we staggered across the field. I managed to get the throttles fully open before too much of a swing developed and we left the ground at 65mph. I held her down till about 85mph, then eased back the stick, raised the undercart, reached 300ft, put the mixture to 'normal' and boost to 'zero', trimmed her up, and climbed up at 110mph. The view ahead was perfect and it felt funny not to make climbing turns as we ascended.

We levelled-off at 5000ft and I tried to synchronise the engines, without much success as it has to be done by ear and mine was not attuned. Hansen then took-over and I tried to find our whereabouts, but was rather hopelessly out. He then did three types of stalls – one with wheels and flaps down and engine off, another with just flaps down, and the third with wheels and flaps down but only approaching the stall before recovery. I then tried my hand and she seemed to recover very simply, just by pushing the stick forward and closing the throttles.

Quite a lot of time had passed by now and we started back to the field, descending at 110mph with 20° of flap at 500 ft per min. We flew over the landing leg at 2000ft and got down to 1000ft on the downwind leg, where I did BUMPF (Brakes, Undercarriage, Mixture, Pitch, Flaps), then onto the base leg, and finally onto the approach, with full flaps, 1400rpm and 85mph. We came in over the boundary quite nicely, I cut the throttles, stick right back – and she dropped like a brick, bounced right up, and settled again. I don't think Hansen helped me and I felt quite pleased with myself, not having flown since July and this being my first time up on a twin. Rather to my surprise, Hansen said, *"Tomorrow we'll do some circuits and bumps"*. Heck, I hardly know the airwork!"

In fact, the weather closed in and I didn't fly again till 9th April. Back to my diary:

"In the afternoon we were flying again; the front had passed, with an improvement in the weather. Hansen and I took-off and I gave him a circuit; then we went out of the circuit and flew up to 2000ft, where he demonstrated single-engine flying, turns and recoveries. I then tried my hand and found an awful lot of opposite rudder was needed to hold her straight and, of course, I forgot the drill of CASTE (which remains forgotten!). We then came back to the field, entered the circuit, and he showed me a single-engine landing. I then took-off and, at about 500ft, he cut one engine and I flew around on the other, cut the other at 400ft on the approach, and glided-in the rest of the way. We then taxied back to the flight area; he asked me if I had any questions, said he'd go and get another instructor, smiled and departed.

About 15 minutes later, F/0 Poole arrived to give me my solo test. I thought I'd put up a 'black' when I found I couldn't move the aircraft out. Poole had a try and, fortunately, he too couldn't move it, so he hopped out and had a look at the undercart. Nothing was wrong except that the ground was soggy, so he hopped in and managed to get us out. I then took off and, most unexpectedly, although Hansen had warned me, he cut an engine on me. However, I did the right thing this time and he soon gave me back the engine. We then did an overshoot and one landing, which wasn't too bad.

Leaving the engines running, I got out and signed an authorisation form for solo, and then found I had to sign a chit in my log-book, which was back in the hut. So, onto my bike and furious pedalling while Government petrol burnt in the engines – until finally all the forms were signed and I got in, checked-up, and taxied out on my own. I didn't feel at all excited, just determined to be careful, as I had had only 3 hours 20 minutes dual and about six landings; in spite of this, I felt fully confident.

The first circuit was uneventful but, in the second, I found plenty of drift and decided to overshoot, as I'd been told to practise one. Accordingly, I flicked on a landing-light and, giving full throttle, enjoyed a healthy roar from the engines. Next time around, I came in a bit high and had to throttle back almost entirely to get in. About 50ft from the ground, I found I was drifting badly and, at the same time, I felt I was falling like a stone. Not liking it a bit, I gave it some throttle, thought of landing, decided it was too risky, and went around again. Next time, I landed OK and, though my time was up, decided to make one more landing, and finished-up OK. All the time, I hadn't been able to get a thing on the radio and should never really have taken-off but, wickedly, decided to chance it."

Windrush was not just flying training and ground-school: those of us who were officers also had occasional routine duties to perform. In my case, as American flying officers never issued orders or went on parade, I had absolutely no experience of being in authority over anyone except my flight cadets. So, after being told that I was to be Orderly Officer on 13th April, I felt acutely aware that I might make a total fool of myself before senior NCOs and other long-serving personnel. My diary recorded the day:

"At 8.30 I reported to the Adjutant as Orderly Officer and got an armband and a list of duties. I then went to the Clerk of Works and told him the lights had failed in our hut. He rather shook me, by saying, *"If people will use electric fires, etc....,"* as Cookie has one such!

At 9.30 I signed the book at the Guard Room and inspected non-existent prisoners, and at 10.30 I had a look at the Sergeants' Mess. I was surprised how roomy and comfortable it was. Afterwards, I cycled in the rain through the village of Windrush to inspect the dechlorination plant. Here we filled a test-tube with chlorinated water and made sure, by a colour test, that it had the correct proportion. On the way back, I took the opportunity to have a look at the little church.

At 12.0 I went to the Airmen's Mess with the Orderly Sergeant, whom I didn't recognise as the Link instructor. I heard him call out, *"Orderly Officer, any complaints?"* and, as everyone seemed happy, went on to inspect the food – and jolly good it looked, too, with mutton and about five varieties of vegetable, though I noticed the cook gave an extra large portion to the next man – for my benefit.

After lunch, I went flying with Hansen. I was late for Link after that. When I came out, flying had been 'scrubbed', so I helped taxi the 'kites' (aircraft) back to the picket lines. I then took my parachute along to the Parachute Section.

At 7.0pm I went down to the Guard Room, stopping on the way to object to the Clerk of Works about his not mending our fuse. Arrived there, I watched 10 rounds of ammunition being issued to each of the six men of the guard picquet, and had the pleasure of hearing, *"Officer on parade, to the right, dismiss!"* addressed to myself, for a change. At 10.0 I went back there again to check-up on all the keys issued, and at 11.0 I inspected the night-flyers' supper. And so to bed after a well-filled day."

Pride comes before a fall, though, as my diary now relates:

"On Thursday I gave myself my first shock and nearly killed myself. It happened that I was doing an overshoot and, with wheels and flaps down, gave it the throttle in the approved style. At 100ft I pulled up the wheels and continued to climb up at 80mph. I tried to increase the speed but found I couldn't and, as I couldn't see ahead for the sun glaring in my eyes, I made a turn at 300ft, still at 80mph. As she was still climbing with difficulty, I suddenly realised that I must have forgotten to raise the flaps – no wonder she only just staggered around that turn. Never again!"

The course continued with cross-countrys and instrument-flying, and I had my first experience of day 'night-flying' with F/Sgt Epworth, as my diary shows:

"It consisted of taking him over to Akeman Street (airfield), doing a circuit with stress laid on 'vital actions' (landing procedures and checks), then him doing a circuit, then me doing a couple wearing dark glasses. These keep out most light, so the instruments are lit with sodium lights, and sodium floodlights are laid along the runway. You can see a fair amount in the circuit but, once you're on the approach, there's very little difference between light and shade, and only the vertical interval between the lights tells you whether you're high or low. I found that I didn't really see the ground till I hit it but, by pushing forward on the stick, I managed to hold it down fairly well. In fact, I made better landings like that than I did without the glasses! At any rate, Epworth complimented me by saying that I was the first he'd known who didn't need 1½ hours vital actions drill before using the sodium."

On 25th April a group of us went by train to Worcester to spend a week at RAF Pershore to do a Beam Approach Training (BAT) course. This was basically the pre-war German Lorenz system used by several European airlines and equivalent to that used by all internal airlines in USA. In fact, the Americans asked me frequently why the RAF didn't bomb Berlin 'on the beam'. The Germans certainly bombed British cities, Coventry in particular, by using long-range beams; eventually Bomber Command was equipped with 'Gee,' which used a radio 'grid' from three ground-stations, and 'Oboe', which worked with radar pulses from two ground-stations rather than a beam. For our purposes, the Beam Approach was a means of enabling an aircraft to land at an airfield, known or unfamiliar, in conditions

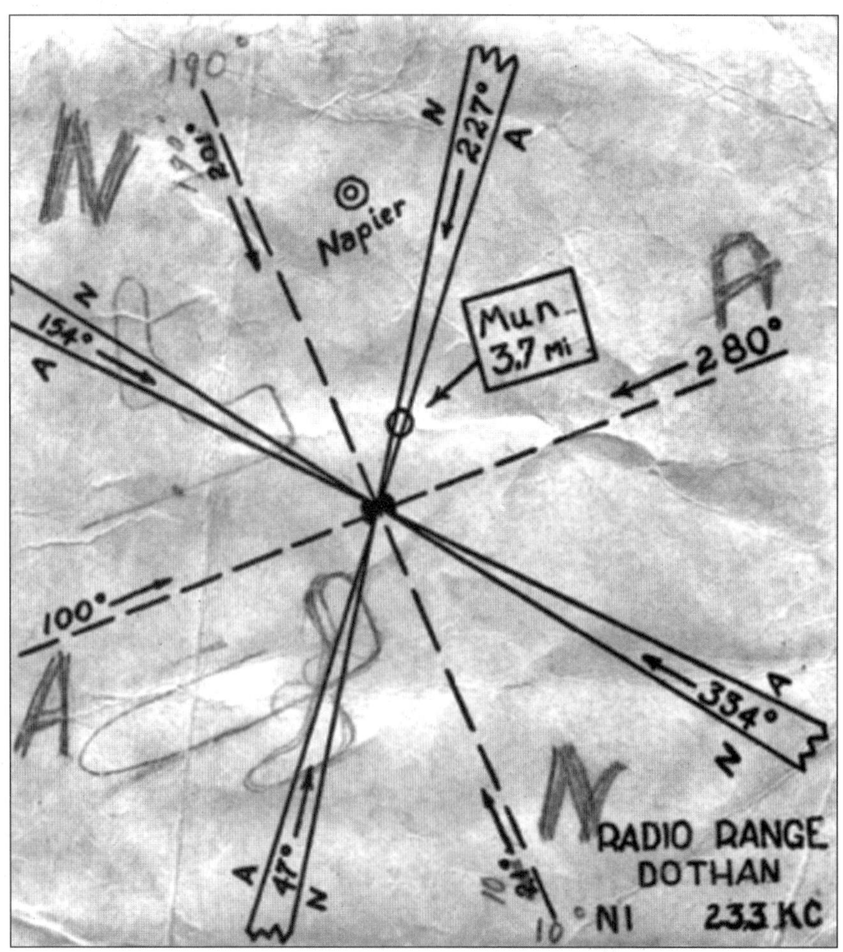

Diagram of the pattern of radio beams at Napier Field (with my annotations), in situ at all US airfields, adopted by the RAF, and taught on the BAT course at Pershore

of thick cloud down to about 100 feet. There was a strict procedure for bringing the aircraft in along a path identified by a steady note in the pilot's headphones: if he strayed off it in one direction, he received dots, and if in the other, he received dashes. He would then correct his course till they merged into the steady note again; he made his turns and lost height at an accurate set rate. The whole procedure depended on the pilot's prompt obedience to commands from the ground and on his very precise instrument-flying, for which our hours on the Link Trainer were a valuable preparation.

F/O 'Foxy' Fox, RCAF, at the controls of an Oxford

The course demanded close concentration, but my instructor was F/Sgt Doak, another old friend from Darr and Cochran Field days, which eased the strain. The Mess was very comfortable and the food was plentiful. On two evenings I went to the Riding Club and enjoyed my first jumps on an old plodder of a horse, to the amusement of the onlookers; I also rode a beautiful thoroughbred mare, but she refused to canter round the field.

We returned, very satisfied, to Windrush and, next day, I went over to the low-flying area with Hansen; but we had a student Flight

Oxford cockpit, with three blind-flying instruments visible: gyro artificial horizon just above F/O Fox's right hand; to the right, rate of ascent/descent; below, turn-and-bank indicator

Engineer on board, which I didn't like, especially when Hansen made me fly really low. I hated the feeling of having someone else's life dependent on my flying ability. Passing on my skills to a student-pilot was a different matter: they might save his life one day.

My next flight, on 3rd May, proved to be another humiliating experience, recorded in detail in my diary:

"Then I went up for a momentous 2-hour solo trip. First, I decided I'd try to get home again (I'd flown there once before), so set course vaguely South, as there was a fierce wind blowing, and eventually found Harwell after a bit of searching. Soon reached Newbury and buzzed past the house at about 1000 ft, opening and closing the throttles. This produced Law (the School butler), and a second time round produced Mum, waving handkerchiefs. The garden was a riot of colour and I wish I could have stayed, but it was too risky to hang around too long, so I stooged off and returned to Oxford.

Arrived there, I climbed up above the clouds and flew around them, working-in a few stalls and single-engine flying. All the time, I thought I was within distance of Oxford so, at about 12.30, turn roughly West to fly back to Windrush. After about five minutes, cannot recognise road, so circle round to find a pin-point. Eventually find a place with a small railway terminal, which might be Woodstock, but doesn't seem quite right. However, set course roughly West again, keeping eyes well open for Rissington. Pass lots of airfields, but recognise none of them, so eventually turn South to come down on Windrush from the North. After further ten minutes or so, am rather shaken to come across a large railway which shouldn't be there. Fly down it to try to identify it, but fail and decide that, unless I can recognise the next town, I'm lost.

Next town comes up and proves to have weird conglomeration of railway lines running through it. Look all over the map to find it, but nearest approach is Stratford, but no river Avon visible on ground. Give up then, see a small airfield beneath, and go in and land. Ask a WAAF mechanic where we are and she says *"Andover"* – Andover!

Report to Control office, get them to phone through to prevent search-party going out, and take-off twenty minutes later for West. Have to wait for six Lightnings to land and they all disappear into valley – this airfield is worse than Windrush.

Arrived back at 2.30 and greeted with highly ironical jeers. Report to Flight Commander, but he seems quite acquainted with such occurrences and rather amused. Hansen, grinning all over his face, asks me what the hell I've been doing – and mentions proximity of Andover to Newbury – yet I got lost from Oxford. Expected various rockets and strips, but doesn't look as if anything more will happen, unless someone thinks I was low-flying over home; then I will be in the soup, though I never came below 500ft. At any rate, now have a map of the district, so shouldn't get lost again."

The next major event was night-flying which, strangely, I found easier than day-flying, at least insofar as it was more difficult to get lost. My diary explains why:

"I got in a couple of hours sleeping before supper and then reported to our Navigation briefing-room for a lecture on night-flying. Here Mr Green, the Flying Control type, gave us the gen on radio, pundits and occults (flashing beacons), and procedures in general, and then the rest of the blokes trooped in and we got briefed for the night. First, a sergeant gave us the weather – a ridge of high pressure moving SW, with winds very slight from that direction. Clear night with full moon at 12.0 and probability of haze or radiation fog at dawn. Then Green asked a few questions to make sure everyone knew what they were meant to know. Then the officer in charge of night-flying gave us the colours of the period, and the challenge and replies. Finally we new boys were shown a chart of the circuit with the positions of the various lights.

We then went out to the Flight Room, where I found I was to fly with F/Lt Genth on a W/T (wireless telegraphy using Morse Code) cross-country – that is, a navigational trip via beacons and occults, with a wireless operator to give us any radio assistance. Genth took-off and put us on course, then I took over. There was quite a lot of haze and no horizon, and I had to fly entirely by instruments; but the red pundits and white occults were easily visible, while there was a surprising number of airfield lighting systems all over the place. Occasionally, a brilliant flash around a triangle of lights indicated a bombing-range, and there were quite a lot of other kites flitting about; but, on the whole, navigation was very easy and very similar to that in the States. Provided you kept to your courses and ETAs (Estimated Times of Arrival), you shouldn't go far wrong.

We came back and he landed; then, about half-an-hour later, I went up dual with F/0 Brand, my night instructor. A mechanic using two blue torches got us out of the pickets and we taxied over to the take-off point – a red-and-green light on a post. Here, a mechanic inspected the tailplane, we did our vital actions, then flashed our recognition letter to the ACP. He replied with a 'green' Aldis, which we answered by leaving our light on. We took-off, turned the light off at 300ft, and did a normal circuit, flashing our light again on the downwind leg to get permission to land. Halfway along the base leg, we could see the angle-of-approach indicators, which should be green on the left and red on the right on the approach. On the last 100ft, you ignore them and concentrate on making a wheel landing with the runway markers alone.

He did one, then I did one; then I did a 600ft circuit followed by an overshoot. Then two more landings, and we stopped at the marshalling-point – three blue lights – and Brand got out and I did two landings solo. My third landing with Brand was quite good, no bounce at all, but my first solo one was a real old bouncer, though my second was somewhat better.

I left the kite at the marshalling-point and went for a meal at 2.30am in the Airmen's Mess. I got to bed about 3.0 and didn't get up till 12.0 next morning, thinking this night-flying wasn't at all a bad deal.

Night-flying continued till 19th May, with circuits varying with cross-countrys. The first time I did a solo W/T x-c, I was somewhat shattered to find I had a navigator as well as a wireless/op, and the thought of a crew with me put me off for quite a long time. But my first solo R/T cross-country (radio-telephone using voice), which was truly solo, was the nearest approach to death I've ever been. The whole trip seems to have been infected with finger-trouble or 'gremlins' (mischievous little green men!).

First of all, I thought my R/T was u/s (unusable) and sent for a mechanic, only to find I hadn't plugged-in my connection. I then took-off and forgot to turn off my downward recognition light and flew round the whole course with it on. (I was therefore visible and German 'intruders' were known to lurk over our training airfields, looking for victims.) The only bright thing I did after I'd completed the course: I flew around a pundit flashing my light and 'Q', and got a reply in red and a Tee (for landing) illuminated.

I returned to the field and, after calling for a QFE (barometric pressure to set on my altimeter), forgot to put my set to 'receive'. I then lost height rapidly to 1600ft, going about 160mph. At 1500ft I looked twice at my altimeter and found it was 500ft – surprise! I then came into the circuit and, getting onto the approach, found I was in both ambers (too high). I promptly put down full flaps, closed the throttles, and dropped quickly. A moment later I glanced at the altimeter and saw it read 300ft when it should have been 600ft – and realised the lights had been red (too low) all the time! I guess I must have been born lucky.

Actually, I found navigating at night easier than in the daytime: everything is jet black except for the Drem circuit systems and the flashing beacons, so that it's hard to go wrong. On the ground, nothing is recognisable from their lights except the marshalling-point."

By now it was clear that I was being put through a course that was training me to fly bombers, with a crew and especially at night, albeit pretty incompetently. The CO at Little Rissington had told us this on our first arrival, but I hadn't really accepted it as applying to me. Now, people on other courses were being posted away to OTUs to fly twin-engined Wellingtons (commonly called Wimpeys) as the prelude to moving onto four-engined bombers, such as Stirlings, Halifaxes and Lancasters. I began to feel panicky that Benson's offer would not be realised and that I was losing all chance of getting onto PRU. I decided that the only thing to do was to go back to Benson and remind them of my situation, in the hope that they would apply with greater urgency for my posting to the OTU at Dyce.

Accordingly, on Sunday 21st May, I went to Oxford and caught the 12.30 bus to Benson. My diary records my experience:

"I had a wonderful lunch at the KCB cafe in Benson village and walked onto the aerodrome, despite barbed-wire, at 2.0. I reached HQ at 2.30, and there the dilemma began, as I didn't know the name of anyone there. However, I went to the door of the room where I'd been interviewed before, and found Wing Commander Watts's name on it. I hung around outside, but there was no one in, though a conference seemed to be going on with the CO next door. I waited for a horrible hour for someone to come out and, eventually, the Air Officer Commanding, an Air Commodore, came out. A few minutes later, the CO, a Group Captain, followed suit. I then toddled along, but found no one left in the room. I decided, therefore, to take the bull by the horns and risk my reputation and my neck by asking some-one. So I went up to an oldish Wing Commander passing by and asked him where Wing Commander Watts was. He told me he'd be in Operations but, after making my way there, I found he wasn't there. I was told he might be in Briefing, but he wasn't. But, eventually, I ran him to earth in Met.

While I was pondering how best to approach him, he saw me through the door and asked me who I wanted. I stammered rather that he wasn't quite the man I thought, as he certainly hadn't interviewed me. But he was very helpful and suggested he might have been the man, but now Flight Lieutenant Cussons of 106 Group, on the other side of the field, had taken over.

I thanked him warmly: at last, I'd got help and I hadn't been chewed up for working independently – not even by the Wing Commander. I was very lucky to be put into an official car with a smart WAAF driver, who took me over to the HQ of the Group, told me where to find Cussons (in a red-brick farm-house), and waited for my return.

I found the Flight Lieutenant to be quite a young chap. After I'd told him my story and asked if he could help me at all, he said he could promise me nothing, but he was quite pally with the posting civilian at the Air Ministry; that he would write to him with my name and particulars, as he had done with others; that it was useful my having been to an AFU; that I didn't have enough twin-engine time and, in any case, single-engined machines were now back in demand, so did I think I could fly a Spitfire after half-an-hour in a Miles Master?

Did I think...? Oh, boy! My spirits rose and I could have kissed the fellow! However, he could prom-ise nothing, so now I am waiting in hope, not knowing which it will be – towing gliders (the fate of failed bomber pilots) or Spits – but content, at least, in knowing that I have done everything I could to get the desire of my heart – and, boy, do I hope!"

I returned to Windrush walking on air, finished my night-flying, and was assigned to a new instruc-tor, F/0 Herbert. I discovered he'd been in Class 42G in America and had become an instructor at

I signed to fellow-student F/Sgt Roberts to put the wheels down.

Columbus, Mississippi, so we had several friends in common. He introduced me to formation-flying in the Oxford, as related by my diary:

"We flew with our wingtip roughly opposite the roundel on the leader's fuselage and on the same level. I found it fairly easy, but I was rather rusty and at odd times I would suddenly get left behind or in too close and have to adjust everything quickly. I also found that the divisions of the windscreen exactly interfered with vision, while the look-out was none too good, anyhow, when we were on the leader's left, owing to my having to look out across the instructor.

I then went up solo in formation with F/Sgt Roberts, an Australian. I had arranged with Tim Fanning to meet at a certain height and time for a purpose. [This was to take photographs, but I didn't say this in my diary in case it fell into the hands of authority: photography and diaries were strictly forbidden in wartime!]. Although Tim flew with us for a bit, he had to go home early, so I had to use Roberts (with gestures and hand-signals), which actually turned out quite successfully.

F/Sgt Roberts peels off at the end of our illicit photo-shoot.

Next day, we were fortunate in having a high ceiling and could do 'camera obscura'. This consisted of flying over a hut – the target – with a hole in the roof containing the lens. The shadow of the plane was thrown onto a sheet of paper, on which its track was plotted; at the moment of bombing, a magnesium flash bulb was set off, which showed on the silhouette and was marked on the sheet. Allowance was made for height and airspeed and it was worked out as a 'hit' or a 'miss', whichever it was.

I went up as pilot to Cook, after Fox and Mac had done it and, apart from a horrible smell of burning when I let off the Very cartridge to indicate a 'dummy run', our four runs were uneventful. When we got down, we discovered that Cookie had an average of 89-yards miss, which was very good; yet, considering one of the lamps had failed to flash, but four almost direct hits had been scored, we 'smelt', but did not complain of, 'a rat'!

In the afternoon, the clouds formed and we were only just allowed to fly, as 5000ft was the minimum ceiling, but we did it at 3500ft. It was not exactly reassuring to look down through the bomb-aimer's panel and realise how little separated you from the outer air, nor was it exactly comfortable to lie full-length for half-an-hour. I had to find a wind by twiddling various knobs and, though I got one, I felt it was wrong and altered it slightly for the better. All my runs seemed to be bang-on, with the target in the apex of the pointers each time, even though it didn't travel down the drift-wires as it should. I was somewhat surprised, then, to find that I had a 189-yard average miss, which constituted a failure although, to tell the truth, I was not disappointed, as I never had any desire to be a bomb-aimer. I soon 'fixed' it, however, and remained quiet about it.

On 24th May I did my last cross-country, as navigator with Tim Fanning, but next day old Goulding, the Flight Commander, was keen for us to do more local map-reading. The cloud ceiling was very low at 800ft, but I flew to Moreton-in-the-Marsh, then across the hills to Cheltenham, along the railway to Swindon and then Oxford, and so to Newbury and over home, then back to Oxford and Blenheim Palace, arriving back at Windrush after what, I hoped, was my last flight in an Oxford."

Next day, those of us who had finished the course had to clear out of Windrush and were given leave; I said goodbye to Goulding, Hansen, Genth, Brand and Herbert, and went home for ten enjoyable days, shooting a few rabbits and pigeon for the pot, and trying my hand at developing and printing my films and enlarging the prints. I found my brother Gerald there, back from the Hebrides after only a weekend on a radar post, and now on a course at Yatesbury. On 4th June, a sort of Commemoration Day, I went back to Eton and saw my old masters and tutors and a few of my school-friends – and was saddened by finding too many others, in all three Services, had already gone missing or been killed in action. On Tuesday 6th June, I was lying in the bath at 10.30 in the morning, when a knock came on the door and my father's voice said, *"It's happened – last night!"* He meant, of course, D-Day, the start of the Invasion of Europe, which we had been awaiting for weeks past. But now that it had occurred, we all felt rather sober, realising the immensity of the task before us. As I finished my bath, I thought of those men who must, even now, be dying over there, and wondered at the fortunes of war.

I went back to Little Rissington that night, meeting 'Foxy' Fox on the train. He was a Canadian, who had been in England since 1939 and had instructed on Oxfords for two years, and then on Tiger Moths, Magisters and Masters. While learning to fly Oxfords, he had had an unhappy experience which contradicted the received wisdom: coming in to land at night with an instructor, he went too low and hit a tree-top on the airfield boundary; Foxy (for some reason) was not strapped-in and was thrown out through the windscreen, sustaining only a broken arm. His instructor was strapped-in and was sadly killed in the crash. What lesson do we learn from this?

Next day, about ten of us found that we had been placed in Reserve Flight and were expected to continue flying. That day I flew to Windrush and collected my kit and my bicycle, but I found that somebody had borrowed it and bent the front forks into the frame; it collapsed when I tried to ride it.

The following day, the CO assembled in one of the hangars all of us who had finished our training and preceded to read out our names and postings; without exception, they were all to either Bomber Command or Transport Command OTUs – until he came to my name:

"F/0 Taylor, No 8 OTU. Where's this, Taylor? I've never heard of it."

"I don't know, Sir."

"What are you going to do there, Taylor?"

"I don't know, Sir."

"Well, it all seems highly irregular to me. I'll have to see about it."

"Yessir. Thank you, Sir."

My diary records my feelings:

"Gee, was I relieved, and was I grateful to Flight Lieutenant Cussons! When I told them at home, they said that they had mentioned it to someone (actually, Air Marshal Sir William Welsh, who had a son at the School), but I hardly feel that this could have had much effect. At the same time, a new fear overtook me: that I wouldn't be able to make it on Mossies or Spits and I'd be slung out of Dyce on my ear. However, my feelings were as nothing compared to poor old Tim's, who was bound for Wimpeys; Foxy and Ellis were happy enough as they were going to Bramcote on Transport Command, but everyone else, to all intents, had Wimps and heavy bombers.

On Sunday, I found I was down for another navigational flight with Tim Fanning and we tried to get to Wales, but the cloud-base was too low to allow us to fly over the hills, so we turned back at Ludlow and stooged round his home to fill in the time. I should have finished by now, but F/Lt Barnes, our Flight Commander, decided I had to fly once more. So, for the third time, I took-off 'for the last time', hoping it really would be my last flight in an Oxford – and possibly in a twin. The ceiling was down to 1000ft, but I flew home and found it at 400ft. Accordingly, I felt justified in flying low over the house, blipping the throttles for the last time for several months. I then returned to Rissie and made quite a good landing, which I discovered really was my last one."

My log-book showed that I had flown 32 hours dual with instructors, including 11 hours on the BAT course and 6 hours at night; I had another 32 hours solo or as 1st pilot, including 14 hours at night, and I had done 20 hours on the Link Trainer. I was assessed as 'Average' on the Oxford, which I felt was as much as I deserved. I was very much at ease now flying the Oxford, but I knew I should have done better after my experience as an instructor in the States – on the other hand, if I had shown more expertise, I might have been press-ganged into flying four-engined aircraft. So I was really very satisfied.

CHAPTER 8

Fulfilment

On Monday, 12th June, I said good-bye to Tim Fanning, whom I discovered playing the piano in a manner very reminiscent of a scene from "Dangerous Moonlight": in this a Polish pianist-pilot is persuaded to fly a Spitfire out of doomed Warsaw in order to give concerts in America to publicise the agony of Nazi-occupied Europe; it remains one of my favourite films. I felt very sorry for Tim, but he was bearing up well. I left Windrush and reached Edinburgh, via Paddington and King's Cross, at 6.45am after a sleepless night on the train. Two more train journeys via Aberdeen and at 3.40pm I found myself standing on the little platform of Dyce Station on the eve of my big adventure.

From now on, because I confided all my feelings to my diary, I shall quote from it at length – at the risk of a little tedium:

"Got transport to the Mess and saw those sleek Spits and Mossies. First person I met was an Australian with NAAFI gong [colloquialism for the British Home Defence medal ribbon], who had also just arrived, destined for Spits. Reported to Training Wing Adjutant, who told me to come back at 9.30am next day. Told me I was on Course 45, but I forgot to ask whether I was on twins or singles, so all that day I didn't know what I was destined for, until I met up with the four others on the Course, and then I realised.

Discovered Joe Selka here, but didn't find Dicky Goodwin [a fellow-instructor at Greenville, Mississippi], which surprised me. Poor old Joe is on Mossies and not coping very well, and seems to find them rather fast near the ground.

After tea, piled into a truck and, with a policeman, was taken to my billet, all of us being billetted in Dyce. One Australian drove his own Austin 7 £15 Special. Found myself at a small farm on the edge of the village. Very kindly buxom Scotswoman, with a dour sensible husband and a big son. Very comfortable room, with good furniture but no electric light. Obviously quite a prosperous family, with another son in the Middle East. Surprised to find Robin Sinclair [an Eton contemporary, son of Sir Archibald Sinclair, the Air Minister] had been billeted here, now out in India.

Returned to the Mess for dinner and chatted with Joe. Came back early to sleep, but could get little of it owing to feverish imagination trying to convert to Masters, then to Spits, and thinking of all the drills, settings, and controls, and fearful of failing – in fact, a terrible day-dream, from which I eventually dropped off, despairing of a solution.

Got up next day at 6.30am (!) and walked to the Mess, which took ¾ hour. Met up with the other boys and started pumping them for knowledge. Discovered Leagh-Murray – an Australian, 600 Hurricane hours, 60 Typhoon hours, 60 Spit hours, ex-ops type and obvious PRU choice. Hozy – a Canadian, ex-instructor on Masters at Tern Hill, with 40 hours on Hurricanes. Aldworth – another Canadian, also ex-Tern Hill, but only 6 hours on Hurries. Cadan – Australian, ex-target tower on Masters, 800 hours, rather apprehensive of Spits, feeling the junior of the party. Finally, myself – no Master hours, no Hurricane hours, obviously the weakest of the five. Shaky do, altogether!

9.30. Wing Commander Chief Flying Instructor (CFI) said a few words to us; told us masses were waiting for our jobs, so up to us to make the grade. Chief Ground Instructor (CGI) then said the same thing – obviously very interesting course, only 6 weeks, with 44 flying hours. Heck! 144 wouldn't be enough for me!

Had our photo taken, then went around to get various people's signatures on things and talked a lot more 'shop', picking the others' brains. Looked into a Spit and was amazed how simple it all looks inside and how few controls, many less than an Oxford. Hope begins to grow a little.

After lunch, collect a bicycle – absolutely essential if billetted out – and have our picture taken again as the first one is duff. Then collect parachutes, dinghys, Mae Wests [life-saving jackets]. Gee! I've simply got to get through now that I've got all this – and my personal property, too, all signed for. Also, collect new oxygen-mask, and am very happy at getting it fitted to my old original helmet (an out-of-date model), to which I am greatly attached. New type aertex helmets being issued for coolness, but think I'll start off with as many accustomed things as possible. God knows, I shall have enough new things to deal with on Saturday.

Apparently, we do ground-school two days, then a flying day, twice a week with one day off. Ground-school consists of: Navigation, Met, Signals, Engines, Photography, Intelligence, Dinghy Drill, PT, and a few other odd subjects such as Aircraft and Ship Recognition.

After tea, went with Joe to the sun-ray room and had six minutes' treatment. Hope I'll be able to keep it up as it will do my spotty back good, besides providing a sun-tan, which the present weather doesn't seem capable of doing. Ceiling about 2000ft, but shower clouds continually roll up over the hills. The camp is a civil Station, but all huts are wood and temporary. Food is good in the Mess and we get our 1/2 pint of milk. Altogether, I think good Station, an interesting course, and a nice crowd of fellows. Please God, I can stay with them all ; but I can quite see I shall have to work like a black, especially flying.

Stole into a Master on my way to bed and spent an instructive 10 minutes. Once again, the lay-out seems simple, with nothing complicated or illogical about it. Here's hoping I get a nice understanding instructor.

Thursday. Started ground-school today with a Signals lecture, followed by Navigation. We also went down to 'B' Flight and had a short gen talk from the Squadron Leader, who seemed quite friendly. Lectures were very interesting, with competent and human instructors and a full but not overworked schedule.

We started off on Friday with PT, which wasn't so much of a bind as I thought it might be, and we went down to the Flight afterwards to have another talk on operation of the Spit. In the afternoon, we had a Met lecture and a talk on the Intelligence Library by one of the Intelligence Officers, who also seemed a good sort. It obviously pays to work hard during our six weeks as we have an exam on each subject and also a PT test, and I wouldn't like to fail any of them.

Tonight I went to Aberdeen after tea and, after a very good dinner at the Caledonian Hotel, saw a film, "A Guy Called Joe". It included a short shot of a BT-13a with RAF markings, taken at Shaw Field, and also some shots reminiscent of our Greenville days; but an otherwise good story was spoiled by a girl bombing Japan in a Lightning (a single-seater)!

Saturday. Well, today the great day dawned and I actually felt quite confident, though poor old Joe Selka told me he hadn't made the grade and had washed-out on Mossies. He had no idea what was going to happen to him now.

We went down to 'B' Flight at 8.30am, but it wasn't till 9.30 that anyone made a move and I didn't go up in a Master till 11.0. Refuelling takes a long time, and it surprised me that a Master has an endurance of only 1½ hours.

To simulate a Spitfire's handling more exactly, we flew from the back seat, used only 25° of flap, and came in on a long curve of an approach at 105mph, crossing the boundary at 95. She climbs at 135, and flies straight-and-level at about 150.

I had a very young DFC Flight Lieutenant taking me up, who put me into my seat and strapped me in like a valet. I was sitting on my dinghy-pack and, added to that, the fact that the seat has only two positions meant that I found myself perched right up, only just able to reach the rudder-pedals and getting very little protection from the slipstream.

He took it round first of all, and the power and rush of air past me was something I had never experienced before. On take-off, I was pressed back in my seat as if by an invisible hand and I had the horrible thought that it would run away from me. In fact, when I took over and then took-off, I had only a very hazy idea of what I was doing and found myself in the air with only half-throttle. The landings I found were easy enough, but I took a bit of time catching on to the curving approach, and it took quite a lot of judgement to make the correct sort of turn. The actual operating was very simple, with less to do than in an Oxford, although the speed ran away with me on the downwind leg and very quickly mounted up to 160 or 170mph unless I pulled the throttle right back. But quite the worst part was the horrible buffeting I received, and the fact that I was reaching down for the stick and could only just touch the rudder pedals.

A Master II Advanced Trainer

After the flight, he said I'd done fair enough and would be OK for a Spit, except that I'd need to be checked by another instructor.

Accordingly, after I'd spent most of the afternoon lying out in the grass, I went up with another F/Lt at 4.0pm. My first circuit was OK but, on my second landing, I would have landed on the grass before the runway; from then on, I went from bad to worse, misjudging the approach and coming in at 100mph. He told me afterwards that I'd deteriorated; I hope that it won't make any difference to my taking a Spit up the next time we fly, on Tuesday; but I think part of the reason was the fact that the front windscreen was very dirty and I was wearing dark goggles to keep the wind out of my eyes. At any rate, I hope that was the cause, otherwise I may yet find myself 'up a creek'.

My general feeling at the end of the day was happiness that I'd found so little difficulty after my apprehension, but a little disappointment at the fact that I didn't keep up my good beginning.

Sunday. Another day of work, starting with PT in the morning and including all the usual ground-school subjects. In the evening before going to bed, I watched my host and hostess playing solo with another farmer et sa femme – both without collars; they played rapidly and skillfully and with money that was specially kept for the purpose – with true Scottish thrift.

Monday. We went down to Aberdeen baths for dinghy drill in the morning. It's a beautiful place, indirectly lighted, with marble paving and polished wood panels and a 30ft-deep pool. I was lucky, or unlucky, to get a Mae West and dinghy-pack first, but felt horribly frightened at having to jump from a 15-ft board. However, I took the plunge and, after an agonising drop, hit the water quite softly and erected my little dinghy without much trouble. I was glad I'd got the practice, but hoped I'd never need it.

We had the rest of the day off, so four of us repaired to the George for drinks and, later, I took Hozy and Leagh-Murray to the Caledonian for dinner. They left soon after to continue drinking but, as that was hardly my line, I wandered off by myself, but could find little to do or see in Aberdeen and was not very impressed by it.

Tuesday, 20th June. Our second flying day and I managed to get in half-an-hour solo in the Master. I don't think anyone realised it was my first solo, or that I'd never sat in the front seat before – and I was in no hurry to disillusion them!

I clambered in with assumed confidence, but was rather put-out when the engine stopped just as I was about to taxy out. However, I managed to get it going without a crowd forming and did three circuits and quite reasonable landings. It's got a beautiful acceleration on the ground at take-off, flies really well, and is very simple to land.

However, as I taxied back, regardless of the throttle I gave it, the engine just wouldn't 'take' and nearly gave-up; then I found the left brake wouldn't work and forced me onto the grass. I extricated myself, only for the engine to peter-out again and I found myself quite bogged. Fortunately, some mechanics rescued me and, on putting the prop into 'fine' pitch, the engine and the brakes seemed to work OK – but altogether it was rather a shaky do, and I was glad all the instructors had gone to lunch at the time.

Incidentally, I feel that everybody has far more interest in a rough game of cricket than in flying and, certainly, no one seems to exert themselves to get us into the air.

At 2.30pm, I was given the momentous news: *"Take up 918 for an hour"*! At last, I was to fly a Spit [a Spitfire V but, with cameras, called a PRIV] – though why 'at last' when I had done only 1½ hours on a Master, I don't know.

I went out with a F/Lt to see me off the ground, and found considerable difficulty in getting into the seat. And when I did get in, the buckles of my Mae West, of my parachute, and of the safety-harness so compressed me that I could hardly breathe, much less move. I checked all the controls, the F/Lt re-checked them, and then he left me in the cockpit.

"Contact!" – I pressed the starter, the prop turned, I primed – nothing happened; then a burst of flame from the exhaust, a puff of smoke, and 1515hp[1] was turning-over in front of me!

I wasted little time in taxying out, checking the drill before take-off; then, after waiting for an Oxford to land, took-off down the runway. Then my troubles started! The throttle-nut wasn't tight enough, so I couldn't let go of the throttle to move my left hand onto the stick while my right hand moved to the undercarriage lever on the right-hand side to select "wheels up". The result was that we climbed a little but barely sufficient to get over the hills. Every time I let go the throttle, the vibration moved it back, cutting out the engine. At the same time, the wheels still hanging below blocked-out the radiator and would soon cause the engine to boil! I struggled to tighten the nut before I could raise the wheels.

Eventually I did it, then reached up to close the canopy. I was doing 200mph by then and, on putting my hand back, I found the nose dropped sharply. Eventually, after much wrestling, I managed to close it and reached the base of the clouds at 1000ft.

I now had time to settle down, check the instruments, and close the radiator a bit. I then flew up the coast to Peterhead and tried to get the 'feel' of the kite: she was awfully delicate on the ailerons and the slightest pressure would bank her over, and she was nearly as touchy on the elevators; the rudder needed a little more strength, but was nonetheless effective in its action.

After about 20 minutes, I returned to the field and set about coming in to land, and then overshooting as I'd been ordered. I opened the hood – and again my troubles started: the wind got under my helmet and almost blew it off and my oxygen-mask flapped all around in the breeze. Perforce, I had to beetle off, close the hood, and put everything in order.

I came in for my approach much too fast at 120mph instead of 105 and overshot before reaching the runway. I opened the throttle, pulled up the undercarriage, and then tried to close the hood. But the locking device was too strong and, try as I might, I couldn't do it. Eventually, by using both hands, while the kite dashed all over the place, I managed to close it, and then found I'd hardly climbed at all and could get only 160mph when she should have been doing at least 180. I flew on and on without gaining height, when suddenly I remembered "Flaps!", whipped them up, and we shot up again.

20 minutes later I came in again for a real landing – and not without trepidation. After opening the hood, I opened the radiator - downwind leg 140mph, undercart 'down', pitch 'forward', 110...110, too fast, getting too far out, turn... turn, line-up with the runway, too early, get speed down, 95... should be 90, there's the hedge, here's the ground, hold her off gently, back on the stick, not too far – was that the tail-wheel touching? – back... then a soft feeling, and we were down – not too bad!

I taxied in, switched-off, then sat looking at the instruments, wondering which switch I'd forgotten to turn off.

I got back to the Flight Office and was told; *"Slow in getting your wheels up, approach much too long, but landing very nice."*

Tonight I shall celebrate the dismissal of my fears of being unable to cope and of the horrid thought of flying 'heavies'. I was also glad to see Dicky Goodwin's face in the Mess; after three times valiantly resisting postings to Wimpeys and Whitleys, he's eventually arrived here on Mossies.

Small talk. As I walked out to the kite earlier, the F/Lt disclosed that he'd been to a BFTS [British Flying Training School] in Oklahoma. He looked at my feet as I got in and asked me if I'd like to buy a

[1] The Merlin 45 was rated at 1185hp at take-off and 1515hp at height.

pair of shoes! He told me that on his first landing in a Spitfire he was given a red light – he'd forgotten to put down his wheels!"

Having passed the hurdle of my first solo in a Spitfire, I think it may be useful to digress for a moment from the immediacy of my diary, which was usually written-up before I went to sleep, and certainly within 24 hours of the events described.

It will have become clear by now, I think, that although I might eventually become a reasonably average pilot, I was slow to learn and perhaps reluctant to leave familiar territory for the unknown. Thus, in the matter of the shape of a circuit, in America we had always flown a rectangular pattern in the Stearman, the BT-13a, and the AT-6 or Harvard. All these machines had a good view from the front cockpit and an adequate one from the rear seat; the Oxford also, like all two- and four-engined aircraft, had an excellent view forward, so that a rectangular circuit and a long straight approach were quite acceptable. The trouble with high-performance, single-engined aircraft, such as the Spitfire, Hurricane and Mustang, was that the long nose obstructed the view forward and, in a three-point landing, the runway disappeared from sight altogether. The only solution was to make a slow curving approach from the end of the downwind leg, with a quick levelling of the wings just before touching-down on the runway. My F/Lt instructor had shown me this on my preliminary flight in the Master, which had a short nose, so he had made me fly it from the rear cockpit. I soloed it, however, from the front seat and did my usual long approach without anyone checking me. So, when it came to flying the Spitfire, my dislike of too many innovations at one time, as noted in my diary, kept me to my familiar approach and took me later to the edge of disaster.

Another important element has been missing from my diary so far and does not feature very much in the future: the RAF pilot's traditional involvement with girls. The war, of course, brought many changes, including the recruitment of young men from backgrounds often very different from those of pre-war fliers. In my case, I had no sisters and both my boarding-schools were single-sex; the only girls I saw, at a distance or in chapel at a Sunday service, were the sisters of fellow-pupils, and my innate shyness made any approach unthinkable. Also, although my father was a gregarious sportsman and my mother was an extrovert artist with a liking for a scandalous story, and they both smoked and drank moderately, my father was a clergyman Headmaster and basically puritanical: so girl-friends and sex were never discussed either with them or with my brothers, thus ensuring that, as well as being a late developer, I would remain a sexual innocent. There was a further inhibition: nice girls did not sleep with men outside marriage; so, when I thought of girls at all, I was looking for someone marriageable. But, as it was possible that I might succeed my father as Headmaster, it was important that the girl I chose could cope with the social and domestic demands that a fine building, extensive gardens and grounds, a large staff, and many well-to-do parents, would make on her. At the same time, these conditions might attract a girl who thought they made me a good 'catch' – which put me off getting too friendly with any girl whom I didn't judge suitable for such a life. Finally, as I was getting closer to operations, I had no great optimism that I would survive the war, and so there seemed to be no future and much possible heartache in allowing myself to fall in love with anyone, or even starting on the slippery slope. However, as my diary shows, I did make an advance to a strange girl in Aberdeen, but with the ultimate objective, not of bedding her, but of getting her to teach me to dance, which in those days was a social necessity. She happened to be a very attractive girl, who had just been let down by another pilot on a course at Dyce (he had been posted away without telling her), so she clearly regarded me as a useful replacement; she certainly expected me to be interested in her physically, and perhaps romantically. If so, she must have been sadly disappointed, as I was undoubtedly a 'cold fish', unwilling to go beyond a chaste kiss. However, at the farewell dance at the end of my course, she drifted off happily into the arms of a newcomer – an expert dancer!

A third subject that has not been elaborated on in the diary is the technical side of aerial photography. We received much of this in lectures at Dyce, but we were told very little about the ultimate objective of PR, which was not just to take photographs of enemy targets, but to take them in a particular way to satisfy the operational needs of the Commands that required them. There was, in addition, the great value of aerial photography to the Photo-Interpreters (PIs), whose work in keeping a continual visual check on the German war effort was a form of Intelligence-gathering equivalent to the efforts of the decoders of Enigma at Bletchley Park in reading all-important German communications. In this sense, PR aircraft were indeed "spies in the sky", flying alone over enemy territory, faced with the determined reaction of the Germans – who were fully aware of the strategic importance of PR missions and opposed them with radar-guided flak and fighters – and subjected to the vagaries of the weather over Britain and Europe at all times of the year.

To achieve these long flights, lasting up to 5 hours, the Spitfire XI carried 218 gallons of fuel: the guns had been taken out, so 66½ gallons were stored in the leading-edge of each wing, together with 85 gallons in a tank in front of the pilot. The safety of the pilot depended on the aircraft's high speed and great manoeuvrability, helped by its small size, which rendered it less visible on the German radar screens and, with its 'PR Blue' camouflage, difficult to see with the naked eye.

These last qualities were not important to us at 8 OTU at Dyce, as we stayed within the bounds of friendly Britain and usually flew elderly Spitfire PRIVs, long retired from front-line service. Nevertheless, they gave us good experience of our role before we moved onto the higher performance of the XI.

On operations, the Spitfire XI could be fitted with two F52 cameras mounted one behind the other and pointing down vertically through two glassed-in portholes in the underside of the fuselage. For flying at the ideal height of 30,000ft in a clear sky with no clouds in the way, the cameras would be fitted with 36" focal-length lenses, which would provide a scale of 1:12,000 to satisfy the PIs, as they could spot a man on a bicycle on the 8½"x 7" prints from the 500 exposures contained in the magazine.

l-r: Three F24 cameras with 14" lenses and two F52s with 36" lenses waiting to be fitted into the PR Mosquito behind

A Spitfire PRXI reveals the portholes for the two vertical F52 cameras mounted in the fuselage.

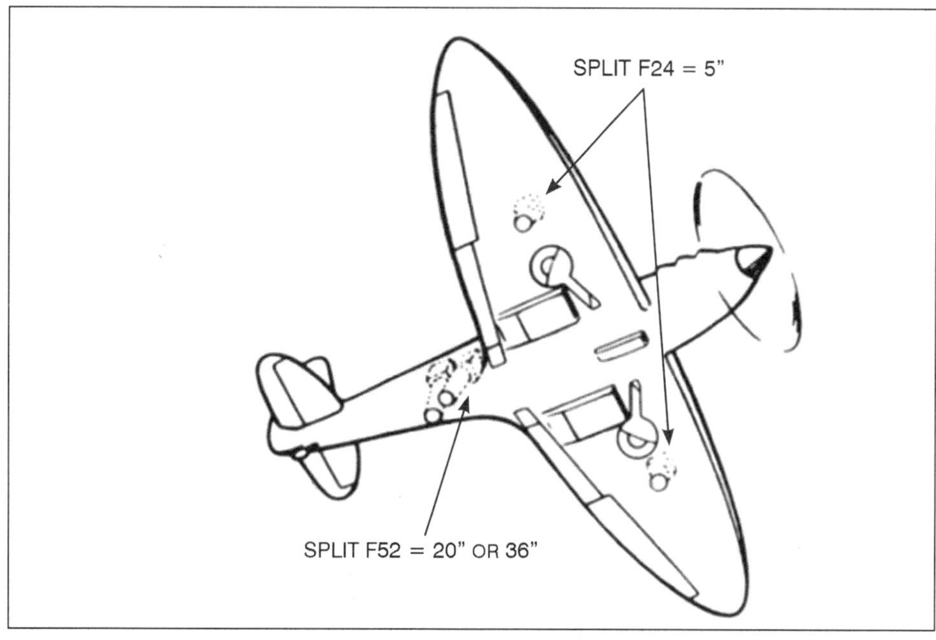

Camera installation in a PR Spitfire

Diagram: Wally Rouse "Born Again – Spitfire PS915"

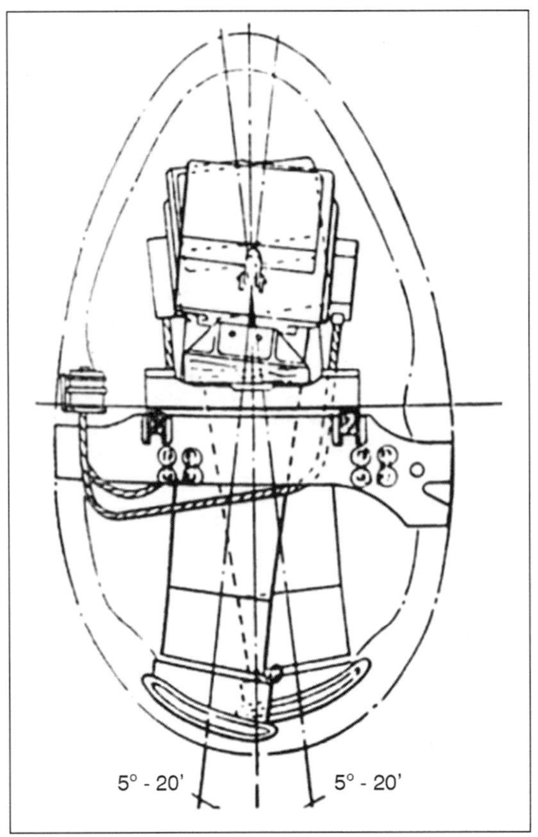

A cross-section view of two F52 cameras mounted in line and angled to provide 10° side-by-side overlap

Diagram: Col. Roy Stanley "WW2 Photo Intelligence"

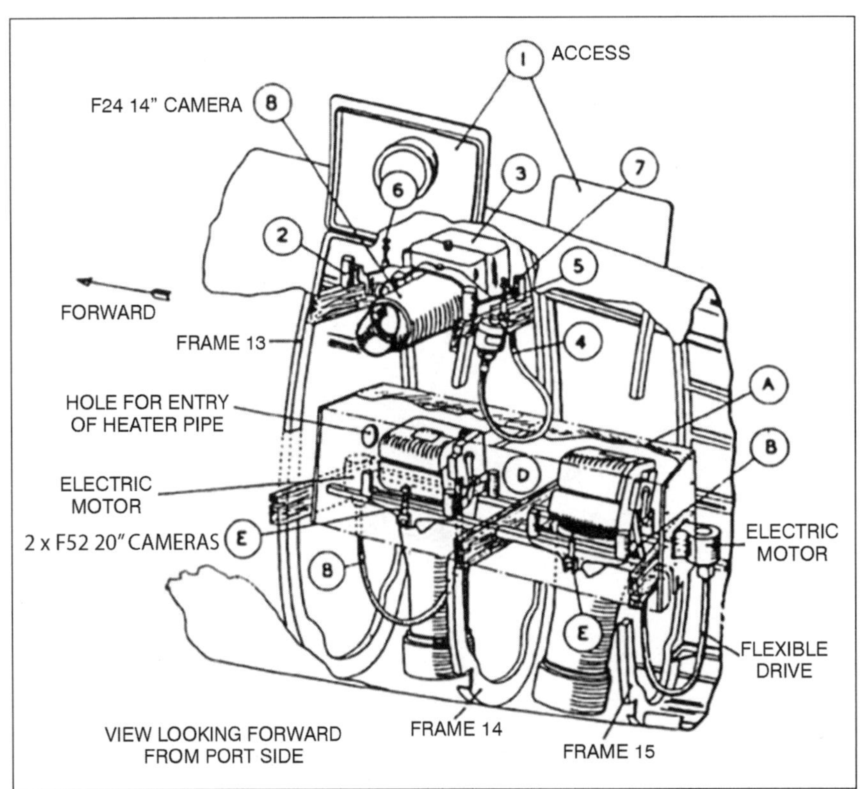

Diagram to show an F24 oblique camera with a 14" lens above a split pair of F52s with 20" lenses

Diagram: Hugh Smallwood "Spitfire in Blue"

To do this, however, they needed the pictures taken consecutively to overlap each other fore-and-aft by 60% so that the common area could be viewed in 3D through simple stereoscopes. This involved the pilots in quite complex calculations before the flight, which I explain in detail in Chapter 11.

The area coverage of the 36" lens was 2-3 miles, but it decreased if the aircraft had to descend from the high altitude of 30,000ft to about 20,000ft, when the coverage became too small; it was then replaced with a 20" lens for photography at a medium-height where it still provided a scale of 1:12,000. Lower still, st 5,000ft or less, the F52s were usually replaced with smaller F24 cameras fitted with 5" wide-angle lenses. The disadvantage of the F24, however, was that its negatives were only 5"x 5" and its magazine held only 250 exposures. The choice of cameras and lenses was governed almost entirely by the weather over the target predicted by the meteorologists (Met.). This was no easy task when the information was difficult to obtain from Occupied Europe and Germany. Very often, therefore, the Spitfire would carry two types of cameras and lenses: F52s in the fuselage with 36" or 20" lenses, and an F24 with a 5" lens in each wing. The pilot had a camera selector-box on the left of the fuselage and could switch-on whichever type of camera he needed for the weather conditions he found over his target.

Besides these vertically-mounted cameras, a single F24 with a 14" lens could be mounted horizontally behind the pilot and above the F52s, provided these had lenses of 20" or less. The camera pointed out of the left side of the fuselage, behind a glassed-in porthole near the top-left of the roundel and took oblique photographs from 5,000ft, or often from much lower altitude, on dangerous sorties nicknamed 'dicers' ('dicing with death'). The pilot sighted it by lining-up a ring on his canopy and a line on the left-hand aileron with the target. He could take single photos by pressing a button on his joy-stick.

The selected cameras were operated by the pilot working the Type 35 camera control-box mounted in front of him in place of a gun-sight. This contained a push-pull knob for starting and stopping the cameras – not easy to do with gloves on; a turn-knob for setting the interval between exposures; a press-button in the middle of it for making single exposures; a small curved window to show the number of exposures that had been made; another knob for re-setting this counter to zero; and two small lights: a red one to warn that an exposure would be made in 4 seconds' time, and a green one to show that an exposure was taking place.

James Marett with an F24 camera with a 20" lens

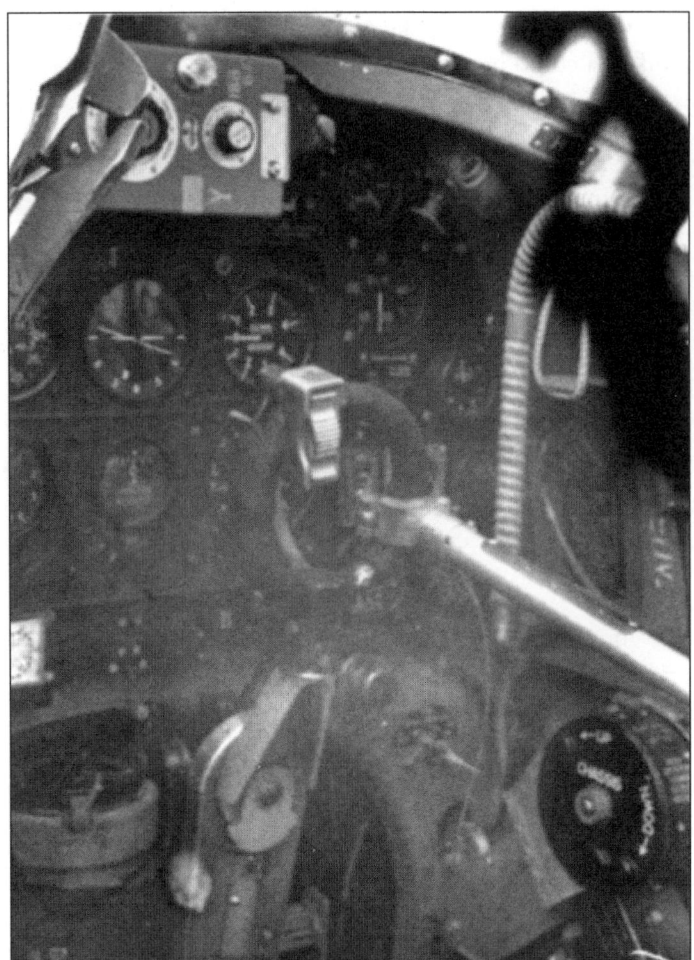

Spitfire XI cockpit with camera-control box (top), undercarriage/ chassis lever (bottom right), and control column locking-arm in place
Photo: Michael Horsfall

T35 Camera Control-Box on a Spitfire XI
1-r: green and red lights, interval selection knob with single-shot button in middle, start-stop knob (top), exposure counter (centre), counter re-set knob (right)
Camera Control Box and Photo: Lewis Deal

Taken together, all these procedures may appear complicated; but many of them related only to operational sorties; at Dyce, we had just a single vertical or oblique F24 camera in use. We needed to operate the Type 35 control-box, but we were not concerned with PIs and stereoscopic pictures. Our instructors were interested only in whether our small 5"x 5" photos revealed that we had found the target and that we had placed it well in the picture. However, there were three types of aerial photography that we had to master, depending on the nature of the target: these were a single feature called a 'pinpoint', such as a bridge, a building, a light-house, etc., which needed only one good picture, but of which we usually made several to be on the safe side; a continuous strip of photographs known as a 'line-overlap', which followed the course of a road, railway, canal, river, coastline, etc.; and a 'mosaic', which required the coverage of an area of ground, such as a town, harbour, airfield, etc. and needed several 'runs' up and down, like a farmer ploughing a field. This was a difficult procedure, especially for 3D viewing of the photographs, as the wind affected the ground-speed differently depending on whether we were flying upwind or downwind; so if we were flying at 300mph against a 50mph wind, our ground-speed would be 250mph and we might need an interval of 8 seconds between exposures to obtain the required 60% overlap between successive photos; but downwind it would be 350mph, which would need a shorter exposure-interval of perhaps 4 seconds. We had a mathematical card to give us these figures in graph form.

The real drawback in the Spitfire was that it had no window or periscope for looking underneath us; so, if we were following the course of a river, we had no means of checking that we were following it accurately except by turning the aircraft on its side and peering down through the canopy in the few seconds available between exposures. A further complication lay in our two compasses disliking being upset and spinning round, or 'toppling', with the magnetic one not returning to its correct heading for about 15 seconds. We therefore needed some landmark or cloud in front of us to keep us straight until we could re-set the gyro and proceed until another check was needed.

The flying programme at Dyce was certainly valuable in training us to navigate over long distances in unhelpful weather, to find and photograph our targets, whether as pinpoints, line-overlaps, or mosaics, and to use our initiative if things went wrong – as they often did with me! What was, to me, surprising was that we had this wonderful Spitfire and the latest cameras, yet our navigation to important targets was dependent entirely on relatively primitive means: our maps, our knee-pads with our pre-planned courses, heights and exposure intervals, our compasses, and the clock on our instrument-panel – no different from those used by WW1 pilots in their slow-moving, wood-and-fabric biplanes! The only modern advantage we possessed was our radio, with which we could contact direction-finding ground-stations to give us a 'homing' to our base or to the nearest airfield – it was a very valuable lifeline.

Now let us return to my diary and see how I fared in flying the Spitfire and in taking photographs.

"Wednesday, 21st. June. Started off the morning with a Commando exercise. Guess what? Just walked up a hill overlooking the field, nattered for an hour, and walked down again – morning's work! Usual ground-school: Photography, Met, Nav. Played squash with Scotty Cadan in the evening: very good games, but he won all but one of them.

Thursday. PT first thing, followed by usual ground-school all day. Interesting lecture on types of Photography and Assessing. Squash again in the evening.

Friday. Flew again this morning, doing an oxygen climb. Had a shocking bad kite, which couldn't reach more than 24,500ft and must have had something wrong with it. [It was probably a tired ex-operational machine]. Stayed up an hour and came in on a QGA [radio direction] quite successfully.

A typical 8 ½" x 7 " print taken by an F52 camera with a 36" lens
In this case, I was trying to photograph the contrail of a V2 rising through the clouds, by tilting my Spitfire into its side and shooting horizontally with the vertical cameras (in vain).

After landing – too far down the field – I was told to have an early lunch as taking-off at 1.30pm for local photography. Got given all the gen, but rather anxious about the sighting business, which seems to me to be very haphazard.

Clambered in complete with all the paraphernalia and flying-boots, knee-pad and map. Had an excellent kite, which reached 25,000ft quite quickly, and started trying to photograph. But soon found it awfully hard to line-up a target which I hadn't seen for the last 30 secs. Took photos of Leuchars[1], Dunino, Tay Bridge, and Montrose but, after 2nd hour, felt rather fed-up with whole show, as I had little confidence in my judgement. Got down and found I had forgotten to note number of exposures per picture, direction of turn, and time, and had to fill-out a map and a log, giving all details.

Somewhat deflated over Spits – glamour is all in the imagination, not in the actual flying. Went into town and had a few drinks with the boys and MacKay, but not very impressed with Aberdeen.

Saturday. This being our day off, I got up at 9.30am and put on the old 'flannel bags' and cycled off into the hills. Had a very pleasant day visiting Kemnay and Alford and had some very good meals in pubs. Noted a nice hotel with a good hill for next weekend.

Sunday. PT again in the morning, an excellent PTI, who makes us do things which few would imagine us capable of or enthusiastic about. Did Signals and then saw an assessment of the films I took on Friday. First one was an absolute beauty – smack-on 10/10, but, of the others, the majority were off the picture and very disappointing – only 41%. Found I was drifting to the right and starting too early.

Monday. Got up at 5.0 this morning for an early start on a high-level X-C at 7.30. But the weather was exceedingly duff and, after being briefed, we sat in the kites for half-an-hour before the mist cleared off the field, and then the only cloudless patch was over the field. However, climbed up and soon found myself over 10/10ths cloud. Tested camera and found nothing working. Thought frantically of all that could be wrong and finally changed all the fuses. Then went back and changed them one-by-one - still no joy. Eventually pressed button on throttle and found camera worked, so decided to continue, as it seemed unlikely the clouds would clear and, anyway, I could use the button, if necessary.

The first leg was to Stranraer and lasted an hour, but at the end of that time I could see nothing, so decided to fly on for 10 mins and then turn back. At the end, suddenly spotted the glint of water and, realising I was somewhere over the Irish Channel, turned back and then pin-pointed a small island through a gap. Using this gap, I managed to find the coast and, following its

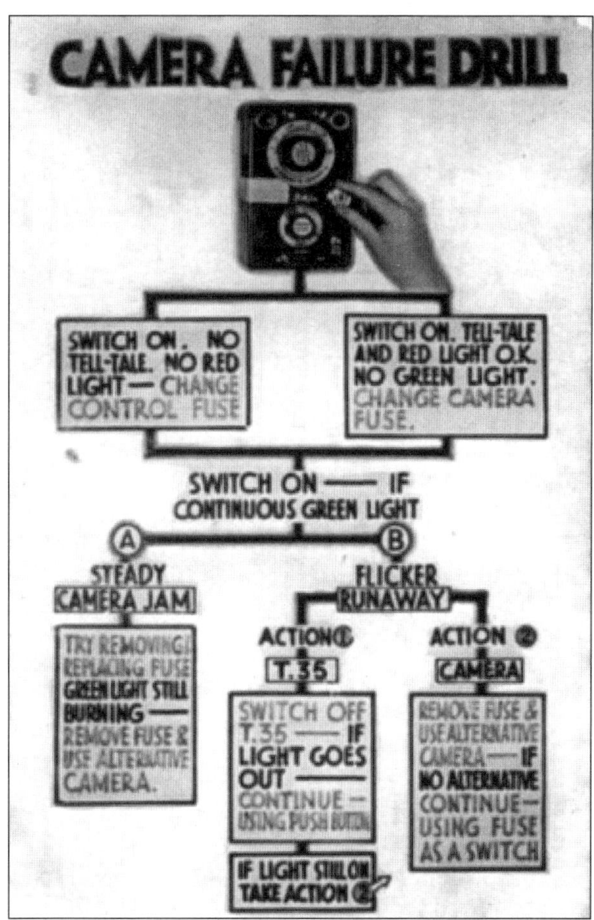

Complicated remedies for camera problems: the fuses were down by the rudder-pedals!

[1]All the places in the text can be found on the map in the end papers.

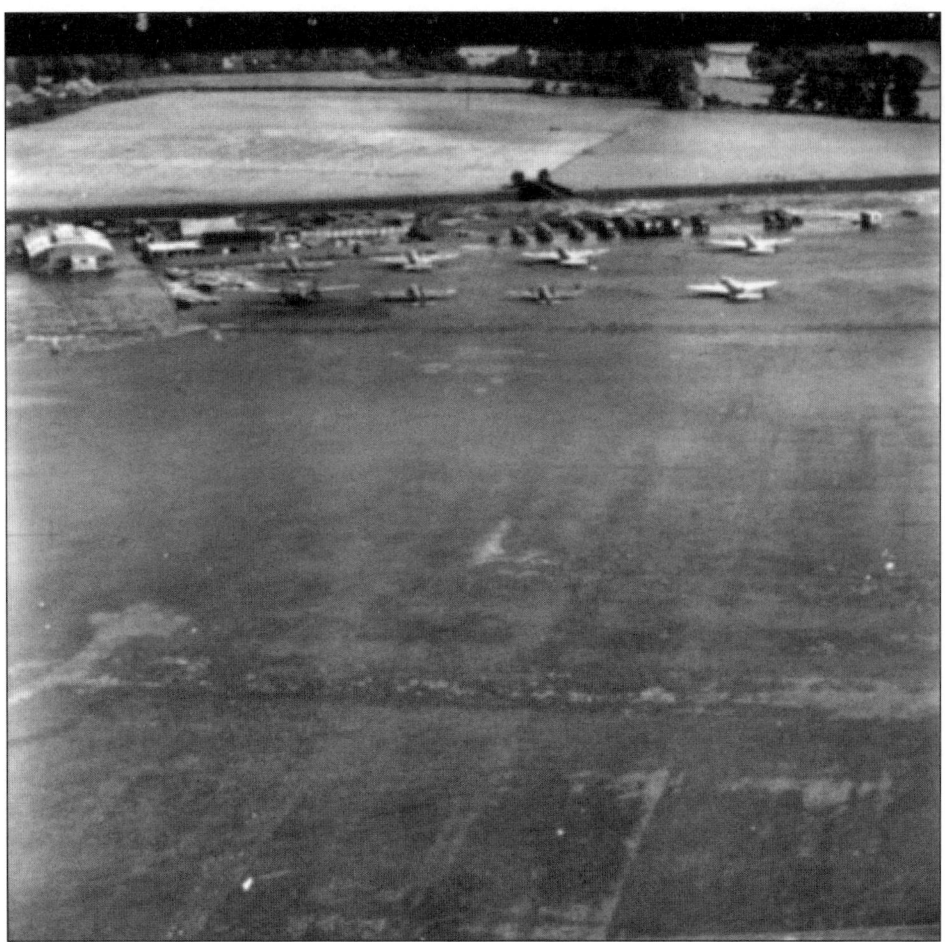

A typical 5" x 5" F24 print taken by me on a practice sortie in a pink Spitfire FRIX with an F24 oblique camera on 2nd September 1944

progress, took about 80 photos of an airfield and harbour with the button, until eventually it clouded over again.

Set course for home and, while still 150 miles away, asked for and received a 'homing', which brought me back in a very short time. While circling the field, saw a Spit lying on the grass and wondered who'd pranged. I then came in for a landing and, after floating nearly all down the runway, tried to land 10 feet off the ground. She dropped in with an awful crash, but fortunately did not ground-loop. Got a strip torn off for the landing, but felt more sorry for poor Scotty, who'd undershot, hit the tarmac edge, ripped a wheel off, and collapsed on one wing.

Had an early lunch and took-off for a low-level oblique trip after a very cursory briefing and not even a line drawn on the map. Had rather a shaky take-off and found clouds at 2500ft. Flew on the course determined, but soon found that hills sticking into the clouds necessitated frequent changes. Soon I had little idea of where I was; I couldn't climb to look around because of the clouds, and could only move forward by flying up valleys. After 40 minutes, got a bit apprehensive, as I thought I should have reached the sea by now, while the clouds were much lower and it was raining. I couldn't see my way clear ahead and I felt quite sure I'd never find it back again. The only alternative to going on blindly was to climb up through the clouds and get a 'homing' back to base. Decided to go on, though was too occupied to think of taking many pictures and spent most of my time failing to find myself on the map. Finally, just when I was about to give up hope of reaching anything, I came across a lough [loch] which had features recognisable from the map. From then on, the trip became quite enjoyable and I buzzed around, photographing anything I could see at any height – and quite legally, too.

I realised the only way home would be through the Caledonian Canal and, though I had quite a job finding it in the rain, had a very pleasant run through, with hills above on each side. Castles, houses, towers, lighthouses, boats and farms all passed before the lens and, if they come out, should be quite good. After leaving Inverness, followed the coastline back and met up with George Hozy for a short while. Eventually got back after 3 hours after taking another 70 individual photos. And then my troubles really began...

'Pipkin' (call-sign of Dyce) kept calling-up, wanting to know my position and when I was going to land, and I realised that after this morning's effort the 'Gestapo' were out. Came in a bit high on the approach and floated some way, but only dropped a little; but then she started surging back and forth and swinging to the left. We still seemed to be going remarkably fast and, in spite of full right brake, she left the runway and clattered over the ground some distance before I could get her back on. Horribly shaky do – and I certainly put my foot in it with a vengeance. Lord knows what will happen now: I shall probably get a check in the Master but, even if I pass that, I shall be watched like a hawk. Oh, gee! I certainly boobed with a vengeance. But I'll show 'em next time that it was only a day off. I hope to hell it was!

Dicky Goodwin very happy at soloing the Mossie. But Scotty and I are plunged in gloom, both mad with ourselves. Got a letter from Joy Wynne [old family friend married to an actor] asking me to be her son's god-parent. Very flattered.

Tuesday morning was another Commando training day but, as it was raining, we all beetled off and Scotty and I went to Aberdeen and did some shopping, returning for lunch. In the afternoon, the Station Sports were held, so spent some of the time watching them, as ground-school was cancelled. Most amusing race was the toddlers, many of whom collapsed, bawling.

Wednesday was ground-school again and I had my photos assessed. The morning's work wasn't too bad: I got 63%, as compared with 41% on my first attempt; but I got 82% for the low-level, which amazed me by the fact that most of them were bang-on and extraordinarily clearly defined. In the evening, I went to town with Scotty to see "Phantom of the Opera" for the second time, and enjoyed it as much as before.

Thursday, we reported down to Ops again at 6.30am and were airborne by 8.0. We crossed the sea to Holy Island; and went inland to Bishops Auckland, then back to Falkirk, and then on to targets up to Frazerburgh on the north coast. In fact, there was thick cloud till we reached Holy Island; though I saw Newcastle,

F/O 'Scotty' Cadan, RAAF
Photo: Michael Horsfall

I couldn't identify Bishops Auckland. Falkirk was also cloud-covered, so contented myself with the Tay Bridge, Montrose, and an aerodrome and a railway junction. I was up for nearly four hours, but didn't feel too fatigued.

Realising I had still to land and knowing how the 'Gestapo' would be out in force after my last efforts, I went inland a bit and did a spot of low-flying and also a practice landing on a large field. I then returned to the airfield and, by flying 200ft low, to prevent overshooting, and making a fairly good approach, I pulled off quite a respectable landing, much to my relief.

When the photographer took the magazine out, he discovered it wasn't winding on correctly, and I had grave doubts whether any of the exposures would turn out. Actually, only half of each picture came out, but it was sufficient for the purpose of marking and they actually gave me 81% for them. Unfortunately, I had lost my pencil on the way out and, on the way back – almost more importantly – my chocolate ration! So I had to make out my photographic report and trace from memory.

We had little time for lunch, as we had to report back for more photos from high-level, but in the local area. I soon found myself above cloud and, as my kite hadn't got any radio, it didn't look too good. However, there was a break over the coast east of Inverness and I managed to make some quite ambitious runs over aerodromes, harbours and towns around there. Coming back, I went inland down low over the mountains and followed the way I'd cycled the week before, also shooting-up the castle I broke into. On returning, I made rather a bumpy landing, but nobody commented. The pictures this time were even better and I got 82%, which I think is about as much as we can expect from Spits. I went into town and saw "The Divorce of Lady X", quite an amusing comedy.

Friday was our day off, so I stayed in bed later, and then decided I'd better clear-up all my duties on the Station, so I did 1½ hours Link, had a hair-cut, collected first-aid kit, and collected cheque-money. In the afternoon, I decided at last I must learn to dance, so found addresses of dance-schools from YMCA and went round looking at the places in Aberdeen. I wasn't very impressed, but decided to telephone, only couldn't find tuppence [two pence]. Then nerve failed at last moment and retired to Caledonian for tea. Got talking to a girl there, and eventually we went off to the Palais and bought tickets for the dance that night. Went there from 9.0pm to 1.0am and seemed to do all sorts of dances from eightsome reels to foxtrots. Very confused about it all, but just started to cope. Took girl home at 1.0 and taxied back at 2.0, arriving at 2.45, hoping Mrs D. wasn't awakened. Bloke I shared the taxi with was assaulted by drunk Canadian sailor and, after picking himself up, laid out his assailant and another on the floor! His girl was very peeved with him. Saw Scotty on the floor, but he fell asleep in the house he had taken his girl home to and fled at 7.0am without waking anyone!

Saturday was a thick clamp all day, with mist right on the ground. Ground-schooled and had a hectic game of squash and sun treatment with Scotty.

Sunday, 2nd July. Got up at 5.0am to fly, but found clamp still present. Reached Mess at 6.0 for breakfast and found flying had been cancelled – somewhat cheesing! Three others turned up, but Leagh-Murray stayed in bed, sensible fellow. Filled-in form for electoral register and did Link in morning and saw a few films and read papers in afternoon. Saw Dicky Goodwin's wife as I came back (she lived on a cotton plantation in Mississippi and they were married while he was an instructor at Greenville), and was surprised at her Southern drawl, which I hadn't noticed there, but now seemed fearfully pronounced. Apparently London is pretty hellish with flying-bombs – or 'doodle-bugs' – and she was glad to get away.

Monday, we did the usual ground-school, but on Tuesday I went to the dentist instead of going swimming in Aberdeen and, accordingly, had a long lie in bed in the morning.

Wednesday was another flying day and I forgot to get up at 5.0am and didn't reach the Mess till 6.15, with briefing at 6.30. Met said everywhere would be overcast except over the Wash, so our cross-country took us there. After being told the targets – aerodromes, towns and railways – we collected our Very pistols, chocolate rations, and radio flimsies and pedalled down to the Flights, where we proceeded to draw-in tracks, measure distances, and work-out courses. This took about 45 mins, then we grabbed on our Mae Wests, long stockings, flying-boots, helmets and oxygen-masks, made sure we had our maps, notebooks, rations, cartridges, and gloves with us, then shouldering our dinghy-packs and parachutes, we staggered to the planes, and eventually got settled in, straps adjusted, oxygen tested, camera tested, headset plugged-in, and everything put in its place in the cockpit. Then tail and rudder trim adjusted, throttle-nut tightened, throttle just opened, pitch in 'fine', flaps 'up', fuel cocks 'on', radiator 'open', electrical switch 'on', ignition switch 'on', camera heater 'on', followed by 7 or 8 primes, a press on the starter and booster switches, *"Contact!"* from the ground-crew, prop revolves, she fires, smoke pours out, engine picks-up, she purrs smoothly, radio 'on', warm her up, then test prop control, full revs, then switches, then taxy out to take-off as soon as possible before engine over-heats and boils over. Green lights from ACP, then we're off, full throttle, change hands, right hand on u/c lever; when I feel we're off the ground, up with the wheels, then a struggle to find the handle and close the hood; then back with the throttle and pitch and settle down on course to a steady climb.

I soon enter and pass through cloud, up and up, calling 'Roseglow' to test radio, taking a couple of exposures to test camera, up and up, increasing oxygen, checking engine instruments. Oil temp. gets high, reduce rpm, up and up through the cloud, 6000ft above the cloud. Spot George alongside me, but he soon draws away and disappears. Up and up, noting clouds and weather on notepad: above is a layer of cirrus and, below, a solid eiderdown of cloud stretching in all directions. I don't think we'll get many pictures today.

F/O ('Leagh') Leagh-Murray, RAAF
Photo: Michael Horsfall

After 25 minutes, I reach 25,000ft and by previous calculation should be just crossing the coast preparatory to going inland. Change course slightly to head for Doncaster and settle down to a steady cruise at 190mph indicated airspeed, but actually 280 true airspeed (because of the thinner air at this altitude). 47 minutes later, my time is up and I can see ground through a break in the clouds. But it is very hazy and hard to distinguish details, but I think I can see a large town. At least, the haze proves I am over the Midlands.

I decide to call-up an aerodrome and ask them for my position, but I can get little satisfaction from them – and then another station butts in to say I am 25 miles west of them but, as I don't know where they are, it isn't much help. All the time, the gap in the clouds has been enlarging, but all I can see are numerous large towns and masses of railway-lines connecting smaller towns. I give up trying to guess my position and strike off as if I was over Doncaster, heading in what I hope is the direction of the Wash. 20 mins later I am overjoyed to see the sea and, a minute later, to recognise the Wash, which – praise be to Met! – is quite clear of cloud.

I get over there and spend the next hour photographing towns, a canal, aerodromes, and a railway-line. I feel I've shot most of the targets, but am not awfully optimistic about them all. Finally, at 11.0, decide it's time to go back, and set course for Doncaster again. I am still fairly warm, though my behind is very uncomfortable, and I cannot be bothered to open my rations. I've seen quite a lot of the others over the targets, hurtling along at what looks like an incredible speed, but now demoralisation sets in with the knowledge that I have an hour's more flying to do and, today particularly, nature is calling me – and in a Spit there is no relief.

I turn over what I hope is Doncaster and head back to St Abb's Head, 150 miles away. I just sit there, all crumpled-up, not daring to move too much in case I find a harder position, praying for a chance to relieve myself, and just leaning gently on the stick, keeping to the course. I feel no physical discomfort at 25,000ft, but my left arm is rather numb and heavy all the time up here. On and on, a few breaks in the cloud, but I cannot be bothered to see if I can recognise anything through them. On and on – then suddenly alarm: the sea! But the sea isn't due for another 12 minutes. A hasty look all round: I can just identify the coast, so turn slightly and continue along it. The engine splutters, coughs – gosh, the fuel! A quick change (to another tank), then she picks-up with a roar – good! 1½ hours more fuel: should be ample.

I think I recognise a bay, a headland, through the clouds and decide to alter course for home, anyway. Already I can hear other chaps calling-up base on the radio and getting 'homings' and, after a while, I too get a course from them, which isn't far off the one I'm already steering.

But nature won't be denied, and I feel if I don't get back as soon as possible, I shall burst. So down with the nose, back on the throttle, and soon we are into cloud, 260mph, down, down, and on, on, going like a meteor through the cloud, down, down, 2000ft, 5000ft, 8000ft, 10,000ft – Gee, what a cloud! When's it going to end? Concentrate all the time on the instruments, 12,000ft, still in cloud – then, 500ft later, out I shoot and find myself well over the sea. Call up again and am told to continue on course; on and on, and still down and down until, at 3000ft, I realise I'm just passing Aberdeen. I call-up again and ask if I can come straight in. They ask, am I in trouble? I answer, no, but nature's calling urgently. No answer to that, so I let down to 500ft, below the low cloud blowing in from the sea and fly inland to the field. I'm circling round preparatory to landing, and all fears of landing are gone with the urgency of my situation, when I hear a voice over the radio saying, *"My port wheel won't come down!"*, and see old George stooging round with his right wheel down, but his left one only half-down. He has shaken it and levered it again and again, to no avail, and now the right wheel is blocking-up the radiator and the engine will soon overheat, so he must come down.

Then they tell him to shake the kite – and, *"Boy, it worked!"* he shouts over the air, then comes in and lands. I follow him and make a reasonable landing, though partly on one wheel. I taxy in, unbuckle everything, and practically fall out of the kite and stagger away, all doubled up – then what a relief! But oh, what pains in my posterior! I seem to have put creases into it: 4½ hours on a dinghy-pack is certainly no rest-cure – very much the opposite. A kindly 'erk' [mechanic] has brought in the parachute and dinghy, but I have to go back to collect the rest of the equipment and make sure all switches are turned 'off'. Never again will I drink anything before flying!

In the afternoon, we go off on another low-level show and have great fun again, shooting-up the countryside. This time, I decide to go round the other way from last time but, while I'm in the middle of the Caledonian Canal, with clouds sitting on the hills each side, I see a wicked-looking storm in front and decide that discretion is the better part of valour and start to turn back. It's then I realise that my turning-circle is too great and I am too close to the clouds: I cannot go forwards, I cannot go up quick enough, and I cannot go round. Horrible thoughts flash in front of me... I open up everything to maximum, change my mind about the direction of turn, just scrape over a hill-crest and slip down thankfully back into the Canal again.

My mistake: George's incident was on my return this afternoon, not in this morning's episode. After making-out a recce report on this morning's and this afternoon's work, go back, get spruced up, then go out to dinner with Helen and continue my dancing-lessons at the Palais.

Thursday, 6th July, should have been our day off, but we're working today, flying on Friday, and having Saturday off, as we're so far behind; though not so very far, really, as I have 23 hours in already. Go for a run with Scotty for PT, very pleasant as it's a beautiful morning, for a change. Find I got 76% for yesterday's vertical shots and 79% for the obliques. But they missed out 5 overlapping exposures on the morning's work, so I've been gypped!

Got a letter from Dad saying Chris is home on leave, not looking very well, and may go to South Africa and India, while they have no idea where Gerald is – he may be in France! Poor show all-round – I seem to be the only one enjoying himself. At least, now I can hold up my head in a Mess as I am flying an ops kite – before, I always felt somewhat of a fraud, though of course it was no fault of my own.

Friday, 7th – Tuesday, 18th. Flying and ground-school continue as usual, with the weather as bad as ever. We were lucky if we found any gaps for photography, and I was more fortunate than the others in finding targets. At the moment, I seem to have taken 300 more pictures than anyone else, though my score must be second-lowest; 71% average. My furthest flight so far has included Swansea, and it took only a little over an hour to get back from there. Navigation, to date, has been extremely lucky guesswork, with pin-points appearing at the critical moments, if not on track, at least recognisable.

Strange things occur with high-altitude flying:

1. I had to climb 22,000ft through cloud to get above it: from 8000-29,500.
2. I tried to talk over the R/T [radio], but couldn't produce enough air to produce gutturals.
3. Difficulty in sucking: no palate to mouth, apparently; coughs are hollow, and sneezes produce agonised exhausted feeling in face and lungs.
4. Windscreen in front freezes completely over, blocking vision.
5. Bags of snow-flakes appear in cockpit in quick descent. I thought once the dinghy had started to inflate, so I detached oxygen and prepared to bale out! False alarm, fortunately.
6. The plane is extremely touchy and unbalanced – ⅛" movement of stick produces a steep bank or dive. It's very unstable and tends to increase the bank and tighten-up in turns, and increase climbs and dives in the fore-and-aft direction.

Everyone except me (touch wood!) seems to have had an emergency, for some reason:

Louie lobbed down at some place with no oil-pressure. Leagh had to come back from oil leaking into the cockpit. George had trouble getting his wheels down. Scotty had no oil-pressure on his last leg home, came in much too fast, overshot, and had to spin round at the end of the runway. Louie called-up with cylinder temperature showing 40°. Louie had both-'up' and 'down' showing on his u/c lights!

Aberdeen Views in 1944

Great Man: William Wallace
Scottish leader 1297 – 1305

Poor Men: Open-air Draughts

Today, Wednesday, we did our first 'mosaics', Leagh and I, of an island called Barra, with runs up and down. That was how we were meant to do it but, on my second run, the camera green light [showing a picture was being taken] failed to go on and I wasted about 20 exposures trying to make it work, changed all the fuses, and tried the push-button. Thought the green light might just have fused, and continued, but didn't like the thought of it all possibly being a waste of time. However, I shall see from the result.

Dancing instructions from Helen have been progressing quite well and, on Friday, took her to the 'Northern Aid for France' dance. Quite good fun, but got caught out in a hellish downpour of rain. Didn't get to bed till 2.15am and set alarm for 5.50, as we had to be in Ops by 6.50. At 6.20 woke up, Ops 6.50 , in air 8.0 , down 12.50pm, then breakfast – pretty good show, what!

Making quite good landings now, but shocking approaches, much too low and fast. Am also failing to check whether u/c wheels are down, and am bound to run into trouble over this if I don't wake up about it.

Bill Webber suddenly arrived yesterday, having at last got out of Rissie after 6 months. Doesn't seem to have wangled anything, and I guess he's just plumb lucky.

Bit of a flap the other day as some devil (known!) pinched my flimsy with Met gen on it and Very cartridges, and I couldn't produce them – court-martial offence! However, said devil produced them next day, to my relief.

Thursday 20th-24th July. Can't remember much happening recently, except for the following incident. Mosaic turned out not too good and not too bad, really. The film ran out before I could do the run across, but I wasn't too disappointed; they gave me 71% for it, which was no worse than some of the Mossie boys (who have a navigator in the nose looking through a bomb-sight).

Weather was shocking all the rest of the week and it wasn't till next Tuesday that we flew again. On Friday, we had a Mess Dance, to which Helen came, but it wasn't as good as the previous one, or so I thought. I had to get up early next morning, but was glad we didn't fly.

And now for the story of the following Tuesday, 25th. We didn't get up early, as we'd done so the day before and Met said the weather wouldn't clear before 8.0am. The clouds eventually lifted a little and at 10.50 we were all set to go: 5 in Spit Vs and George and I in the new Spit XIs for the first time. [The XI had a more powerful Merlin engine of 1280hp (at take-off), a four-bladed propeller, a bigger, pointed rudder, and two under-wing radiators; it climbed faster, and had a higher top speed of 406mph, but its endurance was slightly less than the Mark V.] Of course, just before we left, they discovered the compasses hadn't been swung, so we didn't take-off till 1.0pm after an early lunch. I had only two more hours to go, so this would be my last flight.

We were soon over cloud and climbed steadily to 30,000ft, the XI going up very fast and the supercharger coming-in at 20,000ft. For over an hour I flew above cloud, turning on ETA at Harrogate and eventually arrived within a few minutes of Ipswich. Realising there was no future in trying to photograph above clouds – especially as I had found thick cumulus at 30,000ft – I descended beneath it to 22,000 and found the air was fairly clear but very hazy. There seemed to be a lot of rivers and canals and, eventually, I thought I recognised Downham Market. I circled round for a bit, but couldn't be sure, so carried on till I came to a big wood, which I knew to be on track. From here I could make-out Ipswich, so headed there and made three runs over the town, realising though that I had turned-off the camera a bit late.

Leaving there, set out for Woburn, our next point, switching-on the supercharger again – I had switched-off to save fuel – and started to climb. But, just before I got there, I realised everything around would be covered with cloud; so using, as I thought, my initiative, but actually unwisely, I turned back to the area where I knew it was clear and proceeded to photograph Colchester. I then flew up the coast some way and took Lowestoft and Great Yarmouth, finishing my run with a great strip of coast of 30 exposures. The reason for this was that my wing-tanks had given out and I realised I'd better start getting back before it was too late.

By rough-and-ready calculations, I discovered it was a very close thing, so I headed back home the way I had come, heading first for Feltwell to avoid flying over the Wash. Leaving there, I altered course for Harrogate and saw land for the last time as a thick roll of cloud obscured it from me. I then called-up any station on Channel C to let them know my route back, but got no response, so gave it up.

I arrived at Harrogate – or where I thought Harrogate would be – and set course for base, which I should have reached in 33 minutes. But now I checked my fuel and found only 37 gallons (the Spit XI used about 40 gallons an hour) and, further, I wasn't too sure whether my airspeed was the same as it should have been (as my true airspeed varied with my different heights). I decided, therefore, it wasn't worth risking not getting back, as it might be touch-and-go and I had no desire to prang a new kite on my first flight.

I therefore called-up Acklington, which was the nearest field this side of the Firth of Forth, and tried to get a 'homing'. But, again, I could hear nothing; so I tried any ground-station with, again, no result. I learned later that many stations had heard me, but had been unable to contact me, as my receiver must have been u/s. I was in rather a quandary now, as I didn't like to come below the clouds in case I couldn't find an airfield in time, and yet I couldn't get any help from the radio. Finally, I decided to call 'Rainbow' to let them know I couldn't make it, and changed to Channel B; but although I could hear voices, I could distinguish nothing.

And then the miracle happened: 'Chapman' in Northern Ireland piped up and asked if he could be of any assistance. I replied that I was trying to get to Acklington with half-an-hour's fuel left – could he help? He told me to stand-by and, a little later, gave me a course to steer in a southerly direction and, although this meant going back, I wasn't going to argue at this stage. Eventually, he got me going south-west and then handed me over to another station, which at first couldn't believe I was at 22,000ft, but brought me in to their field. I could see quite well at 6000ft, but at 1000ft vis [visibility] was very poor and I didn't make too good a landing, but was glad at least to be on the ground again.

I hadn't the vaguest idea where I was and, as a swarm of Yanks flocked around, I thought it must be an American station, but soon realised they were just visiting. [It was Woodvale]. Went over to the Mess for tea while the kite was being refuelled, then returned about 5.15 to take-off for Dyce. But meanwhile the weather had closed-in there and I couldn't leave, so I was ordered to stay the night. I had a bed in a large house given over to sleeping officers, and found the three other occupants were all Naval pilots.

Next day, I telephoned early – no good, *"Call again at 10.0."* At 10.0 it was *"12.30"*, then again at 4.0, and again at 6.0 – still no good. God, I felt cheesed! So went to Southport and saw "The Halfway House" again. Next day, fog at Dyce again but, in the evening, at Woodvale it was lovely and Dyce said 2000ft ceiling – but still they wouldn't let me go; so I retired to a bath and a bed for the third night – in a dudgeon.

I was fortunate in borrowing a cap and shoes (I couldn't go about everywhere in flying-boots) from quite a decent bloke, and I also borrowed a razor, towel, etc from the RN types, but my clothes were getting filthy and I felt awfully shabby. I met Buckley, an instructor from Rissie, there on a night-fighter course, and also some very pleasant ground-wallahs. They [the airfield] seemed to have Bisleys from Grantham, Naval Hurries [Hurricanes] and Defiants, ops Spits and Beaus [Beaufighters], and Hurries on odd jobs.

My Dreams Come True
A classic photograph of Spitfire XI EN654
which served on 16 Squadron from October 1943. I flew it from A12 airstrip
to Amiens-Glisy airfield on 9th September 1944, just before it returned to UK.
Photo: Charles E. Brown Collection, RAF Museum, Hendon

Eventually, on Friday 28th July, I managed to get away, but the ceiling was 100ft and they forbade me to go above the clouds. I had to go over to the east coast through the Tyne gap and nearly lost my way, while at St Abb's Head the clouds were right on the cliffs and I had to fly below them to know where I was going.

Eventually I landed and reported to F/0 Platts, who didn't seem to take too poor a view, which gave me hope for the future. The kite was u/s though, as one of the cowling-nuts had loosened and fallen out, hitting the prop and taking out a strip 2" x ¼" near the hub; the cowling had bulged out a bit and the spinner had chewed into it a little. Also, the coolant cap had not been put on correctly and it had been leaking out all the way. One of those irresponsible Yanks had jettisoned the hood, too, but I had put that right before leaving.

No one else seemed to want to see me so, after a late lunch and ringing-up Helen, I went to the Aircraft Recognition room and did the test, passing with 90%. I was lucky in exchanging the seats at the theatre I had booked for Tuesday night for chairs in the aisle, and afterwards we went on to the Officers' Club for a bit of dancing. I tried to get a taxi around 2.0am, but eventually walked home just for the heck of it, getting to bed at about 4.0am.

I was up again at 8.30 on Saturday and first of all saw my film, for which I was given 81%, then had a practical camera test, and then I was summoned to see S/Ldr Glaister. I expected to have a fearful strip torn off, but after I admitted that I spent too long taking photographs, it seemed to spike his guns and he was quite pleasant. He wasn't as pleased with my Airmanship exam, for which I managed 43% – damn good, considering the stinking nature of the questions. But I left him with a feeling of relief and went off to see S/Ldr Mason, the Navigation Officer, to tell him my story. He gave me a mild reproof, and then I went to the PTI to do my Physical Training test: I managed to beat the record of 97 'sit-ups' with 103 and, by doing 10 'pull-ups' and running 5 laps of 60yds in 50 sees, got an average of 70% – the Course as a whole establishing a new record of 62%.

In the afternoon, I filled-in my log-book: 48.55 hours on the Course, and in the evening went to a pub with George and Leagh just to be sociable. I'm still hoping not to have to see the CFI, and I should be able to get some leave on Monday – good show!"

This section of my diary ends here, so I can pause to reflect on my time at Dyce. They gave me another "Average" assessment as a pilot, which I was perfectly happy with. In fact, considering all my difficulties in handling the Spitfire, I reckon I was quite lucky to complete the course. *"We can't have pilots here who break up our aeroplanes"* said the CFI to me after my worst landing from 10ft high, so the threat of dismissal hung over me all along. Taking-off and flying the machine was no problem; the headache lay in the landing. The Spitfire was as light as a butterfly and responded to exact piloting: come in a little too fast and she would float down the runway, subject to updraughts, downdraughts, and crosswinds. The undercarriage was much too narrow and she would tilt easily to one side or the other until she was fully down on all three wheels and her weight kept her to the runway; even then, she could veer left or right and needed a quick push on the rudder-bar and perhaps a stab of brake to make her run straight. So my landings were always somewhat unpredictable, especially after a long trip at a high altitude, when my concentration would be at its weakest.

Consequently, although the course was intended for experienced pilots to learn the skills of aerial photography, in my case I was learning the skills of flying the Spitfire and leaving the business of photography to more-or-less look after itself. Fortunately, my efforts here were reasonably successful and were not subjected to major criticism.

Navigation, also, was obviously of great importance, especially as we had to do it unaided in the cockpit. On the course, we were so dogged with bad weather that we spent much of the time flying above cloud; our only resource was Dead Reckoning – flying by accurate compass-heading and time – and hoping that Met's wind forecasts held true. To take photographs, we had to be in the clear, so when we emerged from the clouds, everything depended on finding on the ground what was on our map, or finding on our map what we saw on the ground. In this respect, eye-sight, recognition, and readiness to change one's mind about the reality, were vital, but a large part also was played by luck, insofar as the weather conditions, especially the visibility, were outside our control. Even the manner of descending through cloud was open to debate: should we come down in a straight line from a distance, maintaining our heading? Or should we arrive overhead on ETA and then spiral down, hopefully over the target? What was the wind doing during our descent through the cloud? At 30,000ft it might be 100mph from one direction, whereas at 5000ft it could be 20mph from another. And if, later, on operations we were faced with enemy flak or challenged by fighters and had to alter course abruptly, and then try to reach the target from a different angle, good luck was almost as important as good judgement in achieving success – at least, it was with me.

As for the rest of the course, it was satisfactory, without being brilliant. Because PRU was put under Coastal Command (since Bomber Command and the Army each wanted it under their control), we spent an inordinate amount of time studying Ship Recognition, which would have been of value in some PRU work, but I never once had to report on or photograph a ship. More importantly, looking back from experience on operations in Europe, I am aware that I didn't understand enough about what was done by our flight mechanics and photographers. What I needed was, not more lectures, but practical hands-on experience of the Merlin engine, or at least to examine a cutaway version of one, and become fully acquainted with its working. Equally, I ought to have handled different cameras, learned about their components, and become familiar with their working. I should also have liked to witness the processing of the films and to understand, for example, how the photographers could improve, in the dark-room, photographs taken in poor light over the target. Of course, I am aware that active young men were probably guilty of under-estimating the value of ground-school at the time – and my doodles in my notebook bear witness to my lack of concentration – only to regret their lack of knowledge when the opportunity to study was no longer available to them. But more hours in practical workshops and fewer in lecture-rooms could have been the means of catching my attention during the learning phase at Dyce.

The most serious omission, in my opinion, resulted from our being assessed only on the accuracy of our photographs, with no interest shown in the information they might contain. This ignored the existence of the photo-interpreters, who were not part of the staff at Dyce, and we received no clear statement on the vital importance of their role both in informing our senior officers of enemy targets to be photographed – and possibly bombed – and of extracting priceless information from the photographs after we had taken them. We may have been the "eyes in the sky", but the brains lay on the ground with the PIs. We discovered this for ourselves only when we joined our squadrons.

For the rest, I was delighted to have realised my dream of flying a Spitfire, and I hoped that my navigation and photography were good enough to enable me to play some small part in defeating Hitler.

CHAPTER 9

16 Squadron

**The 16 Squadron crest and motto:
"What is Hidden shall be Revealed"**

16 Squadron had been associated with the Army from its formation at St Omer, in France, in February 1915. During the next three years, it flew dangerous reconnaissance and artillery-spotting missions over and behind the German lines in flimsy, slow-moving BE2c and RE8 biplanes with devastating losses. Disbanded in 1919, it was re-formed at Old Sarum in 1924 flying Bristol Fighters in Army Cooperation Command, many of its pilots being seconded from the Army. It continued to do almost the same kind of work as in WW1, with little change when, over the next 15 years, it received in turn the Armstrong-Whitworth Atlas, the Hawker Audax, and the Westland Lysander,

The Squadron went to France again in April 1940 with the latter obsolete aircraft, which fell easy prey to the Me109s when the Germans started their 'blitzkrieg' on 10th May. The surviving Lysanders escaped to Lympne, in Kent, while the ground-staff managed to drive to Cherbourg and take ship from there. Thereafter, the Squadron was based at Weston Zoyland in Somerset, and flew anti-invasion and air-sea rescue patrols along the South Coast. This was uninspiring work for a front-line squadron and it had a bad effect on the pilots' morale. However, in April 1942, the Squadron exchanged its Lysanders for Mustang Is, which had six machine-guns and an oblique camera pointing out of the left side behind the pilot; with this high-performance aircraft, 16 Squadron became a Tactical Reconnaissance (TacR) unit, still with the Army, but also engaging in fighter sweeps over Northern France.

On 30th June 1943, Army Cooperation Command was disbanded and re-formed as the Second Tactical Air Force (2nd TAF) for the Allied return to the Continent. 16 Squadron went to Hartford Bridge in Hampshire (now Blackbushe Airport) where it joined 140 Squadron, which had been doing photo-reconnaissance (PR) work over Europe for the Army in Spitfire PRIV and Ventura aircraft. The two squadrons together formed 34 PR Wing, in which 16 Squadron now found itself adapting to high-level PR work. It took over 140 Squadron's tired Spitfire PRIVs, while 140 converted to the Mosquito PRXVI, which had almost the same top speed as the Spitfire, but a considerably longer range of 2,500 miles; its 'A' Flight made daytime sorties, while 'B' Flight engaged in night-photography.

Aircraft flown on operations by 16 Squadron:
Top left: Lysander 1938-1942 **Top right: Spitfire XIX 1945**
Lower left: Mustang 1942-1943 **Lower right: Spitfire XI 1944-1945**

In December 1943, 16 Squadron received the much more effective Spitfire PRXI and, in May 1944, 34 Wing moved to Northolt, outside London. From here it participated in the intensive photographic surveys of the French coast and hinterland, in all kinds of weather and at all heights of the tides, required for the production of hundreds of thousands of up-to-date charts, maps, and photographs for the Invasion on 6th June.

Also in May 1944, 34 Wing was completed by the arrival of 69 Squadron, newly posted from Malta, where it had been looking for and bombing Axis shipping. It was freshly equipped with Wellington XIIIs, stripped of their bombing equipment and front turrets, and fitted with cameras and flash-bombs for night-photography. Their sorties, however, were very different from 'B' Flight's of 140 Squadron. Because the Germans' troop movements by day were under constant attack by Allied fighters and fighter-bombers, they had taken to moving their tanks, guns, men, and supplies by night. 69 Squadron's task, therefore, was to fly at 800 feet over the German lines and supply routes, dropping flash-bombs at regular intervals over selected areas and photographing whatever military targets they found. The flares, of course, revealed their presence to the Germans and they were subjected to intense flak and ground-fire; they retained their rear turrets, however, which enabled them to shoot back at the searchlights and batteries that harassed them. Nevertheless, they often returned riddled with bullets and shrapnel, some of which fortunately passed straight through their fabric-covered geodetic structure. Even so, they suffered grave losses, and we considered all their crews to be heroes. We rarely met them, though, even in the Mess, as they were usually on duty when we were off, and their aircraft were located on a different part of the airfield from ours.

Besides 34 Wing, there were two other Reconnaissance Wings in 2nd TAF: 35 Wing comprised two Mustang I squadrons doing TacR and No 4 Squadron flying Spitfire XIs on longer-distance PR; the Wing was part of 84 Group, which worked directly for 1st Canadian Army. 39 (RCAF) Wing was similar, with three Mustang TacR squadrons and No 400 PR Squadron with Spitfire XIs, in 83 Group, which worked with 2nd British Army. The two armies were part of 21st Army Group under General Montgomery (Field Marshal in August 1944). The odd circumstance of an RAF unit working with the Canadians, while an RCAF unit worked with the British, proved strangely satisfactory to both parties.

A Mosquito PRXVI of 140 Squadron at Melsbroek airfield

Colour Photo: Arthur Kirk-Waring

69 Squadron flew Wellington XIIIs on night photo-sorties, similar to these Mark 1s, but minus the nose-turret; the rear turret was kept to shoot-up German searchlights and flak batteries.

Christmas card from the late James Marett

34 Wing on Parade
G/C R.J.M Bowen, DFC, successor to G/C Ogilvie as CO 34 Wing, with three officers in front of a Wellington XIII of 69 Squadron, a Spitfire XI of 16 Squadron, and a Mosquito XVI of 140 Squadron
Photo: Hugh Smallwood "Spitfire in Blue"

34 Wing, however, did not belong to any Group and worked directly for the HQ of 21st Army Group and for the Supreme Headquarters of the Allied Expeditionary Force (SHAEF) under General Eisenhower. It also received requests for photography from the HQ of 2nd TAF and occasionally from Bomber Command. The Wing needed to be near these HQs, which was the reason for its moves to Northolt before the Invasion and, at the end of August, to A12 airstrip near Bayeux; to Amiens-Glisy a week later; to Melsbroek, outside Brussels, on 27th September; and to Eindhoven, in Holland, in April 1945.

In general, whereas the other two Wings worked close to their armies, 34 Wing went much further afield: my own most distant trip was to Gardelegen, about 100 miles from Berlin, while 140 Squadron's Mosquitos could reach into Austria, Czecho-Slovakia and Poland. For SHAEF and 21st Army Group, we would photograph the areas where they would next expect the Allied forces to attack, with special interest in the German defences, natural obstacles such as high ground, rivers and canals, and the road and railway systems, which might help or hinder the advance. Their chief concern, though, was that their maps too often were out-of-date, and they needed good photographic coverage of the next battle-grounds in time for new, corrected, maps to be made and issued to the troops. 2nd TAF, on the other hand, required photographs of the targets of its medium-bombers before a raid, and afterwards for damage assessment; the targets were related especially to the transport and supply of German troops: railways, stations, marshalling yards, bridges, tunnels, canals, locks, cross-roads, airfields, strong-points, ammunition dumps, headquarters, barracks, factories, and so on. Bomber Command, working from UK, would have bigger targets, such as towns, harbours, the much-used Dortmund-Ems canal, and districts of the Ruhr which, for PR sorties, might be nearer to us in France, Belgium or Holland than to 1 PRU at Benson. Requests from these HQs kept us extremely busy; the bad weather which so often interrupted photography in the autumn and winter of 1944-45 served only to increase the pressure in the good days, when some pilots were required to fly two long sorties.

With three quite different squadrons in 34 Wing, the administration of the Wing had to be very efficient to ensure that all their needs were satisfied. As a rule, whatever elements or activities were common to all three units were the responsibility of the Wing, while their separate interests remained the concern of each squadron individually.

Operations were supervised by the Wing Commander Operations, and other flights came under the Wing Commander Flying. Common areas with their own Senior Officers were Intelligence, Meteorology, Signals, Airfield Control, Stores and Supplies, Transport (including ambulances, fuel bowsers, and the trucks for moving the whole Wing to a new base), Fire-fighting, Medical and Dental services, Catering, Accommodation, the Chaplaincy, RAF Police, and Airfield Defence (by the RAF Regiment).

The Men behind the Machines
F/O Edgar Quested, the Engineering Officer (hands crossed), with l-r: F/Ms Sharpe, Littler and Nicholls
Photo: Hugh Smallwood "Spitfire in Blue"

16 Squadron's 6016 Servicing Echelon, as written on the wall behind them

Two other Sections were of direct importance to ail three squadrons. Before joining 34 Wing, each of them had its own Engineering Section and Photographic Section. Now, all the main repair work on the aircraft was undertaken by the Wing Repair and Inspection Section, including engine and propeller changes. This left just the daily inspections (DIs) and routine maintenance of our Spitfires for our own ground-crews, now named 6016 Servicing Echelon. F/0 Edgar Quested – 'Mr Q' to the Flight Mechanics (FMs) – our own very talented Engineering Officer, always lamented the loss of much of his little kingdom, over which he reigned with skill and fairness through his very professional and responsible NCOs.

The men in the Photographic Section of 16 Squadron underwent quite a different change from the Flight Mechanics when 34 Wing was formed: they joined the 60 Photographers of 140 Squadron, who were very experienced and well-equipped, and became No 7 Mobile Field Photographic Section (MFPS); this was a self-contained unit which, in most respects, looked after itself. Some of the Photographers worked on the aircraft in the field, fitting the cameras and ancillary equipment into them before a sortie, and removing the film magazines for processing as soon as they landed. Others worked in the mobile trailers on the processing, printing and enlarging of the photographs. Still others did similar work in No 1 MFPS, which concentrated on making prints and enlargements from negatives already processed and stored. The Photographers in both MFPSs cooperated closely with each other; so, if a flight of aircraft were detached temporarily to another base, it was possible to send a fully-equipped MFPS to go with-them to look after their photographic needs.

Each MFPS was housed in several long, air-conditioned, motorised trailers: one contained an office and dining-room (7 MFPS had its own two cooks), another a store-room and equipment for mixing the chemicals; a third was a film-processing room, and two others were for the mass-production of prints and selected enlargements. Each MFPS had its own electricity generator and water pump. Each trailer

16 Squadron Photographic Section: Ron Miller standing 3rd from right.

Photo: Ron Miller

A 2nd TAF Mobile Field Photographic Section on the road: 60 men under 3 NCOs and a F/Lt
Photo: Ron Parnell

Photographers at work in an MFPS vehicle
Photo: Col. Roy Stanley (USAF): "WW2 Photo Intelligence"

was manned by eight Photographers, divided into two teams, each working a 12-hour shift, seven days a week; they could, however, be relieved by some of the field Photographers and by their colleagues in the other MFPS. The four men in each team chose to stay together for the whole two years of the MFPSs' existence and became highly skilled in their work, making clear prints from badly-exposed negatives or from negatives of targets only partially lit by night-time flash-bombs.

The F52 camera carried a film-magazine holding 500 exposures, and the F24 held 250; so, with three squadrons taking photographs by day and night, it was possible for 40,000 negatives to be processed by No 7 MFPS alone in one 24-hour period; with up to eight copies needed of each photograph, it could produce 130,000 prints in the same period.

Working very closely with the MFPSs were the Photographic Interpreters (PIs), a group of highly-trained and experienced officers belonging either to the RAF or to the Army Photographic Interpretation Section (APIS). These experts were called-in at an early stage, often to view the negatives before the prints had been made; this could be because of the urgency of the situation for which a PR sortie had been ordered, and the resultant photos had to be checked for their accuracy, otherwise another sortie might have to be flown; or a particular photograph, or set of photographs, might reveal something of special interest to the PIs in the prosecution of the war. In fact, when we had finished a sortie and were on our way back, we were also encouraged to let the cameras run over the landscape until the films were finished, just in case the PIs found something worthy of further investigation. All this was called Stage 1 of photo-interpretation and was done on the Wing. It was expected that any photographs that showed an immediate need for offensive action by forward troops or by fighters or fighter-bombers should be in the hands of the responsible commanders within 24 hours.

The decision about the number of prints would often be made by the Senior PI, Squadron Leader Michael Spender, a brother of the poet Stephen Spender and of the artist Humphrey Spender. He was one of the pioneers of photo-interpretation and was recruited by Sidney Cotton in 1939 from a commercial firm engaged in aerial surveying in 1939. He did a great deal of the early work on the huge Swiss Wild machine, which enabled stereo photographs to be seen in 3-D, to be enlarged up to nine times, and to have measurements taken to establish the size of, for example, buildings and ships. 34 Wing was extremely fortunate in gaining his appointment, and it was a totally unnecessary tragedy that he was killed in an Anson that stalled and crashed on take-off from an airstrip in Germany, probably because its load (of captured German photographic equipment) was placed too far back towards the tail of the aircraft – just three days before the war ended.

Photo-Interpreter Extraordinary
S/Ldr Michael Spender, pioneer interpreter, killed in a plane crash 3.5.45
Photo: Constance Babington-Smith "Evidence in Camera"

In Britain, all the RAF's strategic PR was done by two squadrons of Spitfires and two of Mosquitos based at RAF Benson, in Oxfordshire; at the nearby American base at Mount Farm, the USAAF's 7th Photo Group, consisting of several squadrons of Lightning F5 and F7 aircraft, did the same for their forces. In May 1944, these two organisations were combined into 106 Group, which also included the Allied Central Interpretation Unit (ACIU) at Medmenham, close by on the Thames. After Phase 1 interpretation had been done on the bases of all the PR Wings in UK and 2nd TAF, most of the prints were sent to Medmenham for Phase 2, a more detailed examination by their PIs for potential targets to be attacked in the near future; this was followed by Phase 3, a continuous in-depth survey by hundreds of specialised PIs of German production of every kind of war material, from synthetic oil to new breeds of submarines, with the aim of telling the Allied Command when production had reached the stage for the most effective bombing raid.

RAF Medmenham on the Thames, the Central Interpretation Unit, showing the many huts in the grounds for the hundreds of PIs

A group of PIs at work in one of the rooms at Medmenham – now a hotel

16 Squadron at Northolt in April 1944
(l-r) Back row: F/O Kemp F/O Davies F/O Spring F/O Murphy F/O Suttor F/O Armstrong F/O Bastow F/O Martin F/O Winter F/O Wetz F/O Tibbits
Front: F/O Godfrey F/L Petrie F/L Pughe S/L Goodale F/L Sampson F/L McGilligan, F/L Ransley
Sitting in front: F/Sgt Brodby

Photo: Douglas Petrie

One other body came directly under 34 Wing, but it did not move with it. This was the Wing Support Unit (WSU), which was based at Northolt for much of 1944. New aircraft went from the factories to Benson, where they were fitted with their camera equipment; they were then flown to the WSU and kept, together with a large store of spare parts, until they were required by the squadrons in 34 Wing. New pilots were posted first to the WSU and then to the squadrons when the appropriate vacancy occurred; tour-expired pilots were often sent there 'on rest', rather than to units in UK, as they could test-fly new or repaired aircraft and ferry them to the squadrons; they could also be recruited for occasional operational sorties.

Although I had many dealings with 34 Wing personnel, from the Intelligence Officers who briefed us for our sorties, and the Photo Interpreters who told us whether our photography had been successful, to the Dental Officer who pulled out a tooth that caused agony on a high flight, and they did a good job, I didn't have any strong sense of 'belonging' to the Wing: they lived in the world of Headquarters, a place where I never felt at ease. After nearly two years in America, I was more tuned-in to the Air Corps' way of doing things than I was to the RAF's. At Greenville, I belonged to the Officers' Club and paid the commercial rate for my accommodation and meals which absorbed half my monthly pay of $240 per month. On Wednesday afternoons, the Club became the Ladies' Club, when we were unable to enter – a situation inconceivable in the RAF. Here, the Officers' Mess was almost sacred ground: we saluted or stood to attention and nodded when we entered the foyer, where portraits of the King and Queen were always hanging. My Mess bills for my room, meals, and drinks at the bar were ridiculously small, about £5 per month; but, then, our pay was only about £1 a day. A batman or batwoman also looked after the rooms and uniforms of three or four officers in UK. On operations in Europe, sleeping in tents and eating and relaxing in marquees, life was naturally much more informal: the only orderly we saw shook us awake and gave us a mug of hot tea if we were due for a sortie early in the morning.

**16 Squadron at Eindhoven in May 1945 on a Spitfire XIX, probably PS 853, currently with Rolls-Royce Corporate Heritage
1-r: F/L Barker F/L Stutchbury F/L Quested, MBE (Eng. Off) F/L Godfrey, DFC, CdeG
F/L Jones F/L Thompson S/L Davis, DFC, CO (standing) F/L Martin, DFC (sitting) Lt Estaria
F/L De Mestre F/L Snell F/L Müller F/L Cadan F/L Wheeler F/O Williams (Adj.) F/L Wetz, DFC**
Photo: Basil Jackson

The focus of my short operational life was very much on 16 Squadron. Making good friends with Mike Horsfall on my very first day, when he invited me into his tent, was a pleasant introduction. F/0 Jimmy Wallace, a relative newcomer like us, was a cheerful third tent-mate on A12 and at Amiens-Glisy until he, sadly, crashed to his death on 9th September, probably from oxygen-failure. P/0 John Brodby, a long-serving member of the Squadron, took his place in our tent but, on 20th September, he was shot down by flak near Nijmegen and killed in the air or in the crash. At Melsbroek, we invited the Adjutant, P/0 Don Williams, the peace-time Town Clerk of Pontardawe in Wales, to share our room in a brick bungalow built originally for the Germans. He was happy to join us, as he said that Mike and I were "indestructible". He was, unfortunately, quite mistaken: I went missing on 19th November, and Mike on 14th January 1945, both of us becoming POWs. Poor Don thenceforward refused to share the room with anyone!

The other 18 or so pilots, with for me only one exception, were all friendly and helpful but, as we were briefed and flew our sorties individually, there was little collaboration in our operations, unless we asked for help in working out our navigation or photography calculations. Our main meeting-place was in the Mess at meal-times; we also got to know each other a little better when we went in small groups into Amiens or Brussels. We might meet the two-man crews of 140 Squadron's Mosquitos in the Mess but, as they flew individually like us, neither side did much to make friends; as for 69 Squadron's Wellington crews, they flew only at night, so we rarely saw them.

One jarring note, for me, was the treatment of our several NCO pilots, who were exactly like the rest of us – and often better pilots – and were treated entirely as equals when flying; yet they lived apart from us, ate in the Sergeants' Mess and, officially, could not socialise with us in pubs and restaurants – idiotic rules which we disregarded on all possible occasions. In my opinion, all pilots should have received a commission at the end of their training. On 16 Squadron, our NCOs were nearly all commissioned within six months, half of them received DFCs, and at least one became a Squadron Leader – proof of the unfair nature of the arbitrary RAF system.

F/Sgt 'Jolly' Jolliffe, JT, and the 'Two Rons' at Melsbroek:
F/M Ron Parnell (Airframes) and F/M Ron Abrahams (Engines),
with Spitfire MB953 'H' showing 68 'camera ops' painted by Ron Parnell
Photo: Michael Horsfall

It was not as if the officer pilots had a weight of responsibility towards the airmen: quite the opposite. I personally never gave an order to anyone during my time on the Squadron. It was divided into two Flights, 'A' and 'B', and everyone was meant to belong to one or the other, although I never knew which one was mine. The airmen, however, needed to have papers of various kinds, such as leave passes or travel warrants, signed by their Flight Commander, who would be one of the senior pilots. The rest of us had no official duties, except helping the Adjutant to censor the airmen's letters, which was a chore nobody liked. When Don Williams shared our room at Melsbroek, Mike Horsfall and I felt obliged to do more than our fair share of this; but that was all. We had no drills or parades and no reason to march anywhere.

We wore whatever clothes we preferred for sorties: some people dressed up in wool or leather, but I found the Spitfire's cockpit quite warm enough and wore no more than my blue battle-dress, leather flying-boots and silk under-gloves. The same casual approach to dress was common on the ground: the airmen, working out-of-doors most of the time, tended to wear a leather jerkin topped with a woolly hat. White polo-neck sweaters were popular with the pilots, although our CO, Squadron Leader Tony Davis, DFC, looked on them with disfavour. I incurred his wrath in all innocence: my mother had knitted me one in blue wool but, not having enough wool of that colour, added the polo-neck in grey wool. When Tony saw me wearing this, he blew up, complaining loudly of *"officers who wore dirty-neck sweaters!"* I couldn't disown my mother's handiwork, but I had to wear it discreetly after this.

Morale on the Squadron depended largely on the quality of leadership shown by the Commanding Officer. We were extremely lucky to have Squadron Leader Tony Davis, DFC as our CO from mid-August 1944 till after the end of hostilities in June 1945. His appointment came about, however, only because of a tragic accident to his predecessor who, on his first day on the Squadron, walked in front of a Spitfire taxying along the narrow perimeter track at Northolt and was beheaded most horribly. Tony, who had already served a tour on the Squadron, arrived so shortly afterwards and made his mark so quickly that this terrible incident of war was soon forgotten. He was a rather shy man, with a short fuse before 10.0am, when it was unwise to argue with him. I was 22 and should have known better, but perhaps a cheeky schoolboy still lurked within me. As may have become clear, we were not a particularly well-disciplined bunch on the ground in France – living in tents was close to camping-out. If we weren't due for a sortie, we took our time in getting-up and going in to breakfast in the mess-tent. One day, Tony admonished us that it wasn't fair on the mess-staff to keep them waiting for us. *"I've given orders"*, he said, *"that any officer coming in to breakfast after 8.30am is not to be served."* So, next morning, we were all seated in the mess-tent before 8.30. Five minutes after that time, in came Tony; most unwisely, I stretched out my arm and ostentatiously looked at my watch. All hell broke loose! Tony went red, then white in the face. *"Dumb insolence!"* he shouted. *"Get out of the Mess!"* I tried to apologise, but he wasn't having any. *"Out! Out!"*, he cried, and I crept out while the rest looked on in deathly silence. But by 12.00 it had all blown over, and Tony and I were chatting and smiling as if it was all a bad dream. This is what made us so fond of Tony: he never bore a grudge. After the war, we met at Cambridge: he was doing a short Russian course before going to Moscow as our Air Attaché, and I was on a degree course in History. Tony came to tea in my digs, with a pile of books and a gown under his arm. Halfway through, he looked at his watch, jumped up, and announced, *"I'm sorry, Jeems* (my nickname on the Squadron), *I've got to dash: I've got a tutorial!"* He grabbed his books and gown and ran out of the room – much more like a 19-year-old under-graduate than the distinguished former CO of our great Squadron!

Tony led from the front, taking the most dangerous or difficult sorties himself, without telling any of us; we only learned of his trips when we saw him come back. He expected the best from us – and we tried to fulfil his expectation.

Squadron Leader A.N. (Tony) Davis, DFC CO of 16 Squadron August 1944-June 1945. He was awarded a DSO in July 1945 for his leadership.

Photo: Michael Horsfall

Flying an unarmed aircraft alone, with no wing-man or formation to accompany us, for several hours over enemy territory, taking photographs and returning safely, required and attracted pilots with a relatively 'loner' mentality. When a unit contained a score or so of such individuals, in the easy-going atmosphere of an operational squadron in the field, living in tented or improvised accommodation, it needed a strong personality to hold it together and give it cohesion. This was Tony's great contribution, which he achieved not by being a martinet or keeping a cold distance from us, but through the deep respect that we held for him as a pilot and as a person, which amounted almost to devotion.

Just as he kept a shrewd eye on our performance, occasionally inviting one or two experienced pilots to accompany him on a special photographic mission, so he gauged the mood of his 'boys' and, on the Continent, knew when to fill his official station-wagon with pilots and take us off to a cheerful meal in a cafe in Bayeux or Amiens or elsewhere. He showed his concern for his pilots in other ways also: he made widespread inquiries and started his own search when any of us went missing. Flying from Amiens, one pilot had his radio fail on his way back from a sortie and landed at the first Allied airfield, which happened to be Melsbroek, outside Brussels. Communication between the two airfields failed, so Tony took off and, later, radioed back that he'd found the pilot in a hotel in Brussels! In my own case, when I went missing, he even flew back to UK to visit my parents and give them whatever information he had about my chances of being alive. Indeed, whereas in his official capacity he acted with quiet authority, in his less public actions he behaved as a father-figure to us; with his strong features and dark, bristling moustache, we took him to be in early middle-age – in fact, he was just 26! He was awarded a DSO at the end of the war for his distinguished leadership of what he moulded into a very successful Squadron.

As for the pilots, several of them received immediate DFCs for outstanding achievements in carrying out difficult or dangerous tasks, and many others received DFCs on completion of a tour of 60 operational sorties. This would have taken between six months and a year, depending on the weather and the number of pilots on the Squadron. The autumn and winter of 1944 were particularly severe, with several periods of four or five consecutive days when virtually no photography was possible. In my three months on the Squadron, I did 16 operational sorties, which doesn't sound very many; but the Squadron Operations Record Book shows that this was more than anyone else during those months. No 1 PRU at RAF Benson was the elite PR unit, but their pilots' average of sorties per month was even lower than ours.

I had no interest in decorations: they would never be within my reach. For me, the knowledge that I was flying the fastest and most beautiful aeroplane in service in the RAF, behind the wonderful Merlin engine, with everything geared to enable me to fulfil a wartime role whose usefulness I could see for myself if I came back with the required photographs – this was quite sufficient reward for some-one who loved flying for its own sake. Add to this the knowledge that I wasn't trying to shoot anyone or drop a bomb on anyone, yet I was doing my little bit to eradicate the evil of Hitler – this was immensely satisfying, and made me feel sorry for the other aircrew who were flying through hell night after night, for the men in tanks and submarines who could be blasted to eternity by a single shot or depth-charge, and for the deprived civilians at home, living on their nerves as V1s and V2s dropped at random around them, blowing homes and people to smithereens. Yes, indeed, I felt I was extremely lucky.

This is not to say that we didn't suffer casualties and, considering our individual flights, relatively heavy ones. In our Spitfire XI era, from January 1944 to May 1945, we lost ten pilots killed and three taken prisoner. In spite of the fact that four of those killed were good friends of mine, I held to the belief, common to most pilots, that "Whatever happens to other people, it can't happen to me!" This mental illusion saved us from fear and depression when even experienced pilots failed to return, At the same time, in direct contradiction to this, if anyone asked me what I intended to do after the war, I always said I didn't know, because I couldn't envisage an 'after the war' – I really didn't think I would get through to the end; but, as I lived for the present, the far-off prospect of oblivion didn't bother me.

Because we flew alone, and few people were interested in our individual take-offs and landings, it was only when someone was overdue that we began to worry about him; after 24 hours, he would be posted as 'missing'; but we had no means of knowing what might have happened to him unless a report came in that he had been found in or near the wreck of his plane on our side of the lines. There were a number of possible causes of the crash: he could have become disoriented on entering cloud and lost control; or flown into high ground in cloud; suffered oxygen failure or engine failure; run out of fuel; or baled out too low and his parachute didn't open in time. If the crash occurred in German-occupied territory, it might have resulted from the same causes, with the additional possibility that he had been shot down by enemy fighters or flak; in this case the pilot would continue to be posted as 'missing' until the Allied armies advanced into that area and found the local grave and could question possible eye-witnesses. Some pilots were never found: their names are recorded on the impressive RAF Memorial at Runnymede, beside the Thames.

The most distinguished of these unresolved casualties was the 34 Wing CO, Group Captain Pat Ogilvie, DSO, DFC. He was originally a bomber pilot, but was early persuaded of the value of PR and was made CO of No 3 PRU when Bomber Command demanded its own PR unit in 1940. His Spitfire PRIVs flew all over NW Germany, photographing targets before and after bombing. He soon became aware of how few of the plodding twin-engined bombers reached their targets and how even fewer managed to drop their bombs anywhere near them. He instigated the mounting of a camera in the bombers, and the training of the crews to drop a flash-bomb and take a photograph just before the bombs hit the ground. He flew the first sortie by a Spitfire to photograph Berlin, and followed it a few nights later with a similar flight in a camera-equipped Wellington – achievements for which he was awarded the DSO.

It was common practice for members of the 34 Wing Staff to borrow a 16 Squadron Spitfire to keep themselves in flying practice. On 11th December 1944, G/C Ogilvie took-off from Melsbroek, outside Brussels, in a pink Spitfire IX to make, as he said, a Met. flight over the North Sea – he never returned. In spite of a line-abreast search by the aircraft of 16 and 140 Squadrons, no trace of either him or his aeroplane was ever found. His death remains a tragic unsolved mystery.

Group Captain P.D.D. Ogilvie, DSO, DFC, CO of 34 Wing. Missing from a Met. Flight 12th December 1944
After the oil painting by Raeburn Dobson

We were at the sharp end of operations, but for every pilot there were at least fifteen airmen and NCOs. Indeed, the success of a sortie depended as much on the work of the Flight Mechanics and Photographers and other specialist 'tradesmen', such as Electricians and Instrument Repairers, in ensuring that our Spitfires and their camera equipment were in first-class condition as it did on our piloting skills. Yet I never knew any of these dedicated airmen personally, and it is only in recent times that I have made friends with a number of the survivors and discovered what intelligent, reliable and highly-skilled people they were. The fault was partly mine: I had little or no technical understanding; the numerous lectures I attended on engines, for example, never stimulated me to take an interest in them; all I wanted to do was to pilot the plane, and I took it for granted that everything under the cowlings was in perfect working order.

The main fault, however, lay in the change of organisation when 16 Squadron joined 34 Wing as part of 2nd TAF: previously, a pilot had more-or-less his own aircraft and ground-crew and they worked together as a team; but, when 34 Wing took over the main engineering functions, 16 Squadron's Flight Mechanics were re-classified as 6016 Servicing Echelon and allotted in pairs to several aircraft, under the eye of an NCO. When the Squadron Engineering Officer was told the requirements of a sortie, he ordered a particular Spitfire to be prepared. The same arrangement applied to the Photographers, who had to fit the specified cameras into that aircraft.

The pilot was chosen according to the system devised, early on, by 1 PRU at Benson: the names of all the pilots available to fly were listed vertically on a 'ladder'; the one at the top took the next sortie, whatever it was; when he came back, his name went to the bottom of the 'ladder' and climbed again,

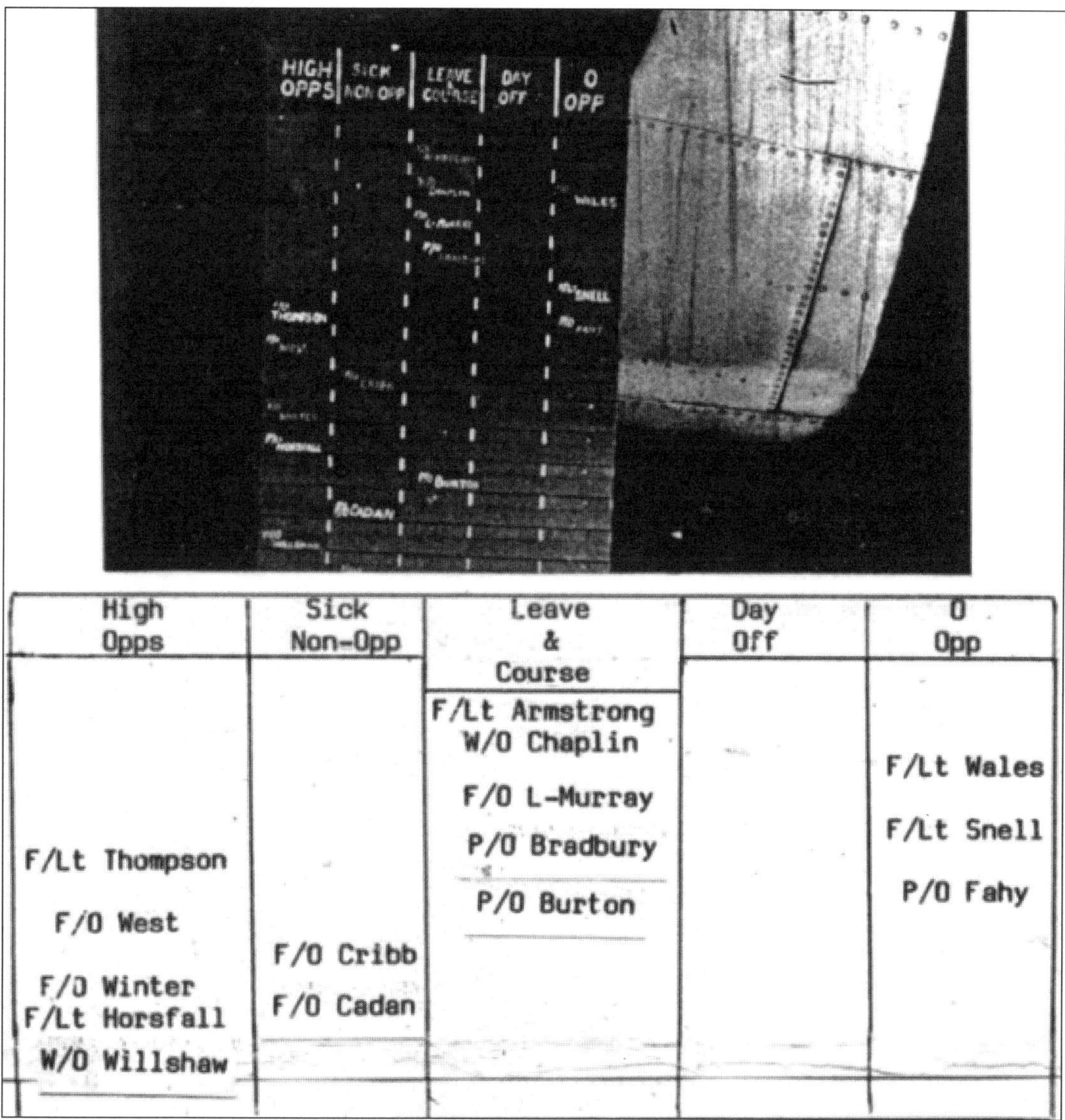

High Opps	Sick Non-Opp	Leave & Course	Day Off	0 Opp
		F/Lt Armstrong		
		W/O Chaplin		F/Lt Wales
		F/O L-Murray		F/Lt Snell
F/Lt Thompson		P/O Bradbury		P/O Fahy
F/O West		P/O Burton		
	F/O Cribb			
F/O Winter	F/O Cadan			
F/Lt Horsfall				
W/O Willshaw				

The 16 Squadron Pilots' 'Ladder'
F/Lt Thompson, at the top of the left-hand column, would take the next sortie – and go to the bottom on his return.

Photo: Michael Horsfall

Some of 16 Squadron Signals Section at Melsbroek December 1944
Front (1-r): Eric Phillips George Norman Harry Martin Ernie Sellars
Back: Arthur Legge F/Lt Hartley
Photo: Eric Phillips

fast or slowly depending on the demand for sorties. Thus the selection of a pilot was entirely random: he walked out to the designated Spitfire and found the Flight Mechanics waiting for him, the Photographers having already done their part in preparing the aircraft. Under these conditions, there was little time to get to know these ground-crew and, for our next sortie, we might well have a different Spitfire with other personnel preparing it. In fact, in my 16 operational sorties, I flew 14 different Spitfires; so that I never learned the names of any Flight Mechanics or Photographers.

Airmen's Rest
A hut built from packing-cases where some airmen preferred to live rather than in the former German barracks at Melsbroek
Photo: Ken Holloway

Nor did I know anything about their lives, on or off the airfield. I presumed that, like us, they lived in tents on A12 airstrip and at Amiens-Glisy; but, at Melsbroek, the officers were accommodated in brick bungalows, with a fine Mess and well-designed administration offices, all built by Belgian labour under German supervision. The airmen were accommodated in another part of the large airfield; but it is only recently that I learned that some of them built their own living-quarters out of empty packing-cases rather than stay in their official accommodation of former German barracks.

One question Mike Horsfall and I still ask ourselves is, What did we do when the weather was unfit for flying? There were always a few chores to be done, such as taxying a Spitfire round to where the Engineering Officer had set-up a workshop for

16 Squadron Instrument Section at rest
'Bill' Bull (with woollen hat), others unknown
Photo: 'Dakota', Melsbroek

Dreaming!
F/M (Engines) Ken Holloway in the cockpit,
dressed up but not going anywhere
Photo: Ken Holloway

minor repairs. Another was flying an air test on an aircraft if the local weather was adequate. I always enjoyed doing this, as I could finish with a high-speed dive up to 400mph – if the skin on the wings started to wrinkle, I could report a fault in the aircraft! Another alternative was taking the Squadron Auster, a 'hack' aircraft used for fetching spare parts, giving flights to the airmen, visiting friends in other units, or other forms of pleasure-flying. In Normandy, Bayeux was about 10 miles away and offered few diversions except the Cathedral with its replica "Tapestry"; Amiens was badly knocked-about throughout the war, but also had a fine Cathedral, and some reasonable cafés and bars, but no night-life at all. Melsbroek, however, was a paradise by comparison, as the tramline between Brussels and Louvain went right past the airfield, and Brussels was full of the peacetime attractions of a capital city. There were a very comfortable Officers' Club, and Malcolm Clubs for the Other Ranks with regular ENSA entertainment and dances.

Fortunately for me, at Northolt I shared a tent with Mike Horsfall and we struck-up an immediate friendship – which continues to this day. He was two years older than me and already a veteran: he had joined the Army in 1938, gone to Sandhurst, and been commissioned into the Royal Irish Fusiliers; he went to France in 1939, and was lucky to get out via Dunkirk in May 1940. He then transferred into the RAF, learned to fly Hurricanes, and joined 241 Squadron just before it sailed to Tunisia. He was involved in the North African campaign until he baled out of an aircraft whose engine caught fire while he was ferrying it back to Egypt. He broke his back on landing in the desert, was brought in by the Arabs, and invalided back to Britain. On recovering, he was posted to the PR OTU at Dyce, as PR was considered 'a soft option', and so to 16 Squadron at Northolt.

We found we both enjoyed fairly simple pleasures, among which was walking round the airfields at Amiens-Glisy and Melsbroek and taking photographs with our forbidden cameras of the aircraft that the Germans had abandoned after rendering them unserviceable. They had been pretty well vandalised by Allied troops and other squadrons, usually of Typhoons, who preceded us in occupation; but we found that the small, very powerful electric motors that controlled the all-flying elevators of the Fw 190s could be removed with the aid of a pair of pliers and a screw-driver. We also took to going to the Officers' Club in Brussels, where we knew one of the attractive hostesses, Denise Henri-Jean and her friends. She eventually invited us to her very pleasant home where, somehow, the other pilots gradually joined us until it seemed that the whole Squadron was sitting on the floor in the evenings, enjoying ourselves and drinking her father's excellent liqueurs. We would then clamber aboard an ancient tram and persuade the driver, as we were then often the only passengers, to let us drive it and ring the bell until we arrived boisterously at the entrance to our quarters.

Before we left England for Normandy, I determined to carry with me a book that would take time to read and that reminded me of the countryside I was so fond of. I therefore went to Foyle's great bookshop in Charing Cross Road, an untidy treasure-store of books with no simple classification system. After several hours, I chanced upon "Hillingdon Hall", written by R.S.Surtees in 1844, and re-published by Methuen in 1917, with a 4th Edition in 1944. It is one of a trilogy of books describing the efforts of John Jorrocks, a retired Cockney merchant, to set himself up as a country squire in a typically feudal and snobbish semi-aristocratic community, with hunting as its main pastime. I derived enormous pleasure from the misadventures of Mr Jorrocks and the attempts of the designing mothers to marry off their unattractive daughters to the titled young blades. This book, so full of nostalgia for a long-past life-style, passed round the Squadron and resulted in several pilots being nicknamed after characters in the novel. Two of them stuck: mine was and still is 'Jeems', the name given to James, the son of the Duke of Donkeytown; and Derek Wales, an experienced pilot and delightful colleague, was labelled 'Squire', perhaps for no other reason except that his handsome features were just the opposite of fat, red-faced Mr Jorrocks's.

Derek survived the war, and joined the detachment of six Spitfires and pilots from 16 Squadron that helped to form the Air Delivery Letter Service (ADLS); this flew important military and diplomatic mail, in converted drop-tanks, between the capital cities of a grimly disorganised Europe. In August 1945, Derek took off from Berlin in bad weather at night to fly along the Allied Corridor through the Russian Zone, perhaps to Brussels; he crashed in that Zone from unknown causes. No information was given about what happened to him after that: in those tense early days of the Cold War, the Russians gave nothing away. My well-thumbed little red-covered book remains as a sorrowful memorial to our good friend, 'Squire' Wales.

An example of the friendly relations prevailing between pilots and ground-crew in 16 Squadron. Derek Wales (killed in August 1945 flying mail from Berlin) discusses tactics with 'Scotty' Cadan (in the cockpit) in the presence of l-r: Flight Mechanics Rae, 'Jock' Pate and Ron Parnell

Photo: Michael Horsfall

CHAPTER 10

The Spitfire in Blue and in Pink

Let us pause for a moment and consider how the beautiful, powerful, willing Spitfire XI came to be one of the two main workhorses of the PR squadrons.

Between the wars, the RAF took little interest in the development of photographic reconnaissance (PR) aircraft. By 1939, the high-wing Lysander was the standard Army Cooperation aircraft, with a glass panel in the bottom of the observer's cockpit through which he could take vertical 5"x5" photographs with an F24 camera. The Bristol Blenheim light bomber could also be fitted with an F24 camera for photographic missions at a longer range. The early days of the war, however, soon showed that neither of these aircraft was capable of reaching its targets and returning without disastrous losses to German flak and fighters; and the few pictures they secured were lacking in suitable size and quality. This situation became even more obvious when the Germans launched their 'blitzkrieg' on Holland, Belgium and France on 10th May 1940, shot down many of the Lysanders, Blenheims and Battles of the RAF's Advanced Air Striking Force, which included 16 Squadron, and swept the survivors out of France – all within a fortnight.

Fortunately, Sidney Cotton, a masterful entrepreneur, who had been a pilot in WW1 and invented the 'Sidcot' flying-suit, supported by Wing Commander 'Fred' Winterbotham, an RAF Intelligence Officer, advocated an alternative policy for PR: the use of fast, high-flying single-seater fighter aircraft, stripped of their armament and given extra fuel-tanks. Just before the war, in a twin-engined Lockheed 12, Cotton had taken secret photographs of German harbours, airfields, and defences, and of Italian bases in Libya, Eritrea and Somalia. The Lockheed was fitted with a 'fan' of one vertical and two oblique F24 cameras in the fuselage controlled from the cockpit; with extra fuel-tanks, painted a duck-egg green and flying at 20,000ft, nearly invisible, it enabled Cotton to impress senior officers in the RAF with his photographs of German targets taken only 24 hours earlier; these supported his arguments on the need not only for specialised PR aircraft, but also for rapid film-processing facilities, and expert photo-interpreters.

Sidney Cotton

Immediately after war was declared on 3rd September 1939, Cotton was asked by the Air Staff to take-over the RAF's PR operations; he was granted the rank of Wing Commander in charge of a handful of aircraft and two pilots based at Heston airport, their purpose disguised by the name, 'The Heston Flight'. Cotton thereupon persuaded Fighter Command to 'lend' him two Spitfires; he took out the guns, put in extra fuel tanks, fitted an F24 camera in each wing, angled to take slightly overlapping side-by-side vertical photographs, and painted them his shade of green. He sent one to France in November 1939 (keeping the other as a spare) with his two pilots; in two months they made 15 sorties from 30,000ft without loss and took more photographs of the dispositions of the German forces than all seven Blenheim squadrons put together, who suffered considerable casualties.

Sidney Cotton had proved his case; but he was a difficult individualist, who ignored official channels and upset many of his colleagues and superiors. In June 1940, he was given an OBE and removed from the RAF; he was replaced by Wing Commander Geoffrey Tuttle, with the Photographic Development Unit integrated into Coastal Command; a month later, this was re-named the Photographic

Reconnaissance Unit. In January 1941, it moved to RAF Benson, in Oxfordshire, only an hour by road from the various HQs in London; in March it was re-titled No 1 PRU when No 2 was formed in Egypt to cover the Middle East, one Flight being established on Malta. No 3 PRU was formed originally for Bomber Command in December 1940, but was disbanded six months later and re-formed in India, operating over Burma; while No 5 provided PR for the rest of the Far East campaign. No 4 was formed at Gibraltar in November 1942 for the Allied landings in North Africa. Thereafter, Nos 2 and 4 were split up into their respective squadrons, each of which, together with the Americans and South Africans, was allocated to a specific part of the Mediterranean theatre. As we have seen, the three PR Wings in 2nd TAF in Europe, Nos 34, 35 and 39, were not allocated to any PRU. Thus Cotton's vision resulted in the creation of five entirely new organisations in the RAF, which became the essential 'eyes of intelligence' for all three Services.

The early PR Spitfires were Mark Is and these were gradually improved with more powerful Merlin II engines of 1310hp, extra fuel tanks, and cameras mounted in the fuselage. When the PRID was reached, its Mark was revised to PRIV, which was, against all reason, the PR development of the Spitfire V. It had a Merlin 45 engine of 1515hp; two fuel tanks in front of the pilot holding 85 gallons, and one with 66½ gallons in the leading-edge of each wing, providing a total of 218 gallons; a 'split' pair of F8 cameras with 20" lenses or F24 cameras with 14" lenses, or one F52 (introduced in January 1942) with a 36" lens, mounted vertically in the fuselage; an F24 camera optionally fitted above the vertical cameras to take obliques out of the left-hand side of the fuselage; heating of the cockpit and cameras by hot air and an overall camouflage scheme of matt 'PR Blue'. The F8 and F24 cameras had film magazines holding 250 exposures, while the F52 held 500 exposures. This was the very efficient standard PRU aircraft until the arrival of the aggressive German Fw190 and the upgraded Me109G fighters in 1942. These outclassed the Spitfire V, but were countered by the Spitfire IX, whose PR development was the PRXI – the mount of 16 Squadron pilots in 1944-45. The PRIVs were relegated to No 8 OTU, the PR operational training unit at Dyce, in Scotland, where I cut my teeth on Spitfires and had a slightly unhappy experience when, near the end of my course, I was allowed to make my first flight on a PRXI – as described earlier.

Externally, the two Marks of Spitfire looked quite similar: both were very beautiful machines, with the fine lines R.J.Mitchell had given the original prototype; the curved leading-edge of their wings was unbroken by cannon or machine-guns, and their sky-blue finish, lovingly polished by the mechanics for a few extra mph, made them appear more like an exotic bird than a weapon of war. Both Marks had the same rounded, single-piece windscreen, which provided an exceptionally clear field of view, and was topped by a rear-view mirror – vital for checking that we weren't leaving a give-away contrail behind us, and that no 'bandit' was 'jumping' us from the rear. The Rolls-Royce V-12 Merlin engine of 27 litres capacity was an inspired design, capable of steady development throughout the war and even afterwards.

Profile of Spitfire XI PM151 on 400 Squadron in February 1945, similar to 16 Squadron's but for the extra-vision 'blisters' on the canopy

Coloured drawing: Peter Celis

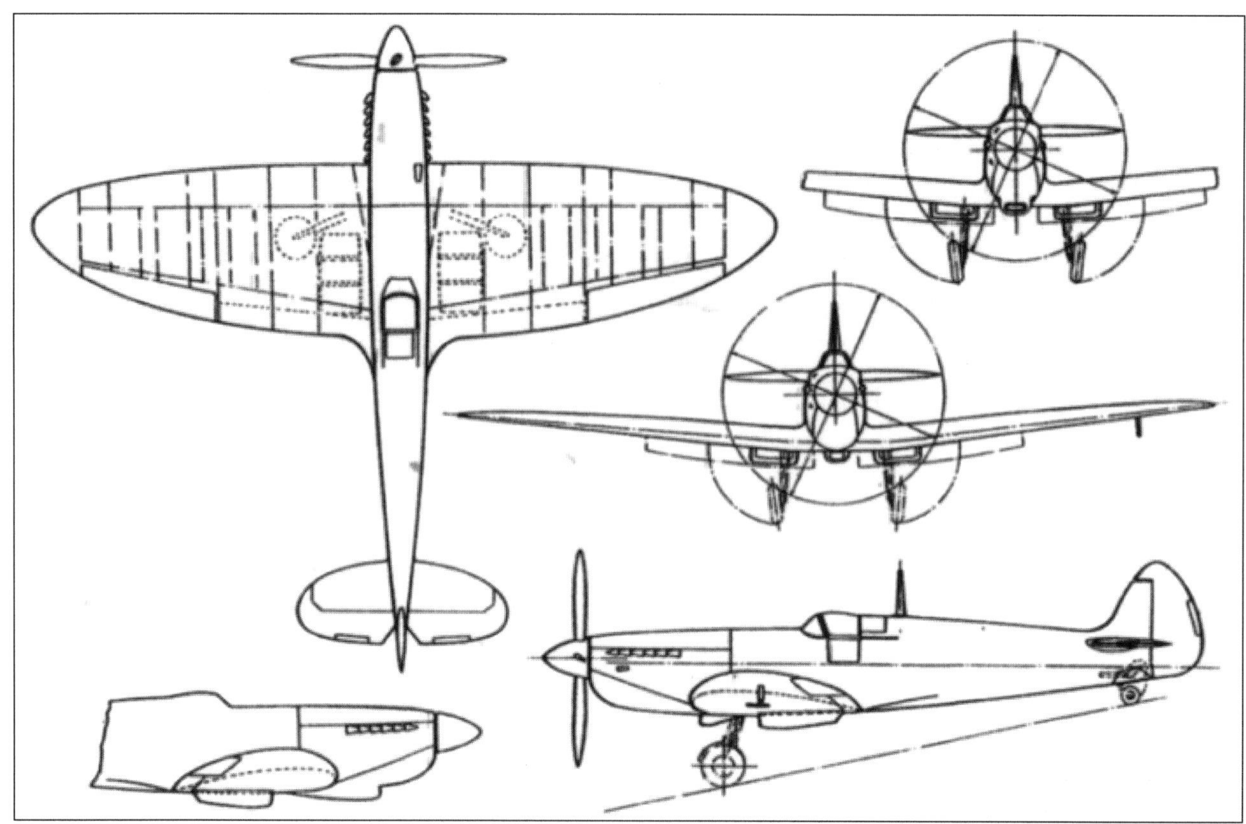

Three-view drawings of Spitfire XI

Drawings: Morgan and Shacklady "Spitfire – the History"

The visible differences between the two Marks were the four-bladed propeller, needed to absorb the greater power of the Merlin 63 of 1710hp, or the Merlin 70 of 1665hp, which gave more power at high altitude; two large coolant radiators under the wings, thermostatically controlled, replaced the single manually-operated radiator of the PRIV, while the latter's small oil-cooler was incorporated into one of the PRXI's coolant radiators; the XI had a deeper 'chin' under the nose to make room for a bigger oil-tank; a broader- chord rudder, with a pointed tip, replaced the smaller, more rounded one of the PRIV; and a retractable tail-wheel added several more mph to the XI.

Underneath the cowling, two major changes gave the XI its superior performance: a two-stage supercharger, whose second stage came in at 18,000ft, granted a considerable extra boost to the climbing-speed and maximum altitude of the XI – and also often took me by surprise with its sudden 'thump' and kick in the back when it cut in automatically on the way up. The second innovation was a Bendix-Stromberg carburettor that did not cut-out during negative-g manoeuvres, giving greater confidence to the pilots. As a result of these improvements, the PRXI could reach 20,000ft in five minutes, and had a service ceiling of 44,000ft, a maximum speed of 422mph at 27,000ft, and an official range of 1350 miles.

In practice, we seldom reached these figures. Our preferred cruising speed and height were 360mph at 30,000ft, but we were always conscious of the need to keep plenty of fuel in hand in case we had to spend time waiting for cloud to clear from a target, or were obliged by bad weather at base to divert to a clear airfield, or were chased by enemy aircraft and used-up fuel in flying at full throttle. I was probably more economically-minded in this respect than most of the other pilots: the recommended cruising settings were 1850rpm (set by the propeller-pitch control) and +7lbs of boost (set by the throttle); but I sneaked along at 1750rpm and +4 boost – which ran the risk of oiling-up the sparking-plugs unless I speeded-up the engine occasionally to clear them, something I usually forgot to do, with potentially serious results. These reduced settings had little effect on our cruising-speed, but substantially affected our petrol consumption, increasing our duration to over 5 hours and our range to beyond 1500 miles.

The Full Specification of my Spitfire XI MB957

Ordered on 12th May 1942 as one of the 426 Spitfire Vc's, later amended to PR XI
Delivered to Chattis Hill
Delivered to 16 Squadron 5th November 1943
Flying Accident Category AC 27th September 1944
412 Repair and Servicing Unit
34 Wing Support Unit (which supplied 16 Squadron and the other two in the Wing) 12th October 1944
Flown by H.J.S. Taylor: 12th September 1944
12th October 1944
14th November 1944
19th November 1944
Failed to Return 19th November 1944

(Information from "Spitfire – the History" by Morgan & Shacklady Key Pub. Ltd, Stamford 1987 and my log-book)

Wingspan	36' 10"		
Length	31' 4½"		
Height	12' 7¾"		
Wing Area	242 sq ft		
Weight	empty	5575 lbs	
	take-off	7721 lbs	
Engine	Merlin 63 1710 hp		
	The Merlin 63 was rated at 1280 hp at take-off and 1710 hp at height		
Fuel	100 octane		
	capacity	upper fuselage tank	48 gallons
		lower " "	37 gallons
		wing leading-edge	2 x 66½ gallons = 133 gallons
		total	218 gallons
	consumption at cruising speed		40 gallons per hour
Endurance	5½ hours		
Oil	14.4 gallons		
Coolant	70% water 30% glycol		
Reduction Gear	.477:1		
Supercharger	2-stage + intercooler		
	impeller diameter	1st stage 11.5"	
		2nd stage 10.1"	
	impeller gears	1st stage 6.39:1	
		2nd stage 8.03:1	
Carburettor	AVI 44/201 or 215, with R.A.E anti-G device		
Propeller	Rotol R12/4F5/4 Hydulignum (= wooden blades)		
	pitch range 35° – 22°20'		
Radio	IR 1133		
Cameras	2x F52 36" focal length 5°20' from vertical each side of fuselage		
	1x F24 14" focal length oblique behind pilot		
	2x F24 5" focal length under each wing		
Performance	Climb up to 20000 ft 5 mins (We usually climbed more slowly than this)		
	Cruising speed at 30000 ft	360 mph	
	Max. Speed at 24000 ft	417 mph	

(Information from "The Merlin in Perspective" by Alec Harvey-Bailey Rolls-Royce Heritage Trust 4th Edition 1995)

Spitfire XI from below, showing the twin camera-ports in the lower fuselage within the Invasion recognition-stripes
Photo: Alfred Price "Spitfire at War 2"

The major advance in the XI's photographic capability lay in its cameras; a 'split pair' of F52s with 36" lenses could be mounted in the fuselage for high-level vertical photos, which enabled twice the area of ground to be covered by each exposure; in addition, an F24 with a 5" lens could be fitted into each wing for low-level verticals. If F52s, or K17s, with a 20" or shorter focal-length lenses were carried, there was room for an F24 with a 14" lens to be mounted above them to take oblique photos out of a port-hole on the left side of the fuselage.

On our sorties, we rarely carried this full complement of five cameras; the cloud conditions expected in the region of the one or more targets of a sortie usually decided the likely height of the photography and therefore the size of the lenses and cameras, in that order: high-level F52s with 36" lenses, medium-level K17s with 20" lenses, and low-level F24s with 5" lenses; fitting a combination of two of these would cover most variations of cloud-base or the requirement for different heights of photography for two or more targets on a sortie. The oblique camera was generally employed at low-level, so it was usually accompanied by 5" verticals in the wings; this was the choice of Wing Commander 'Sandy' Webb, DFC, when he took his famous low-level photos, from a 16 Squadron Spitfire, of the parachute-drops at Arnhem and of the bridge littered with wrecked German vehicles.

The only weakness in the Mark XI was the lack of vision vertically beneath it; this was partially overcome by the provision on some squadrons – but not on 16 Squadron – of perspex 'blisters' fitted into the sides of the canopy. For me, also, the narrow undercarriage could too easily lead my landings astray. Otherwise, the Spitfire XI was a wonderful aircraft, eagerly responsive, highly manoeuvrable, and superbly fit for the purpose of PR.

In addition to its 20 or so Mark XIs, in May 1944 16 Squadron received half-a-dozen Spitfire LFIXs, still fitted with their 20mm cannon and machine-guns and with an F24 camera pointing out over the left wing from behind the pilot's head. They were painted pink, as the best form of camouflage against

One of the oblique photos taken by Wing Commander 'Sandy' Webb, DFC, of the bridge at Arnhem littered with wrecked German vehicles.

a background of low clouds. Because of their guns, which some pilots used, although I was never given any ammunition – it was more important to bring the photographs back than to get involved in a dog-fight – these Spitfires had to be serviced by 69 Squadron's ground-crews, as they included armourers for the guns. As a result, these pink Spitfires were not so visible on our part of the airfield and some members of the 16 Squadron ground-crews even denied we ever had any! They were withdrawn in December 1944, as the fact that the XIs could be fitted with an F24 oblique camera rendered the IXs virtually superfluous; apart from message-dropping in Operation 'Market Garden' they saw little operational use.

I was not alone in 16 Squadron in regarding the Spitfire IX as a relatively rough-running aircraft compared with the smooth performance of the XI.

Profile of Spitfire FRIX MK716 'X' on 16 Squadron August-October 1944

Coloured drawing: Peter Celis

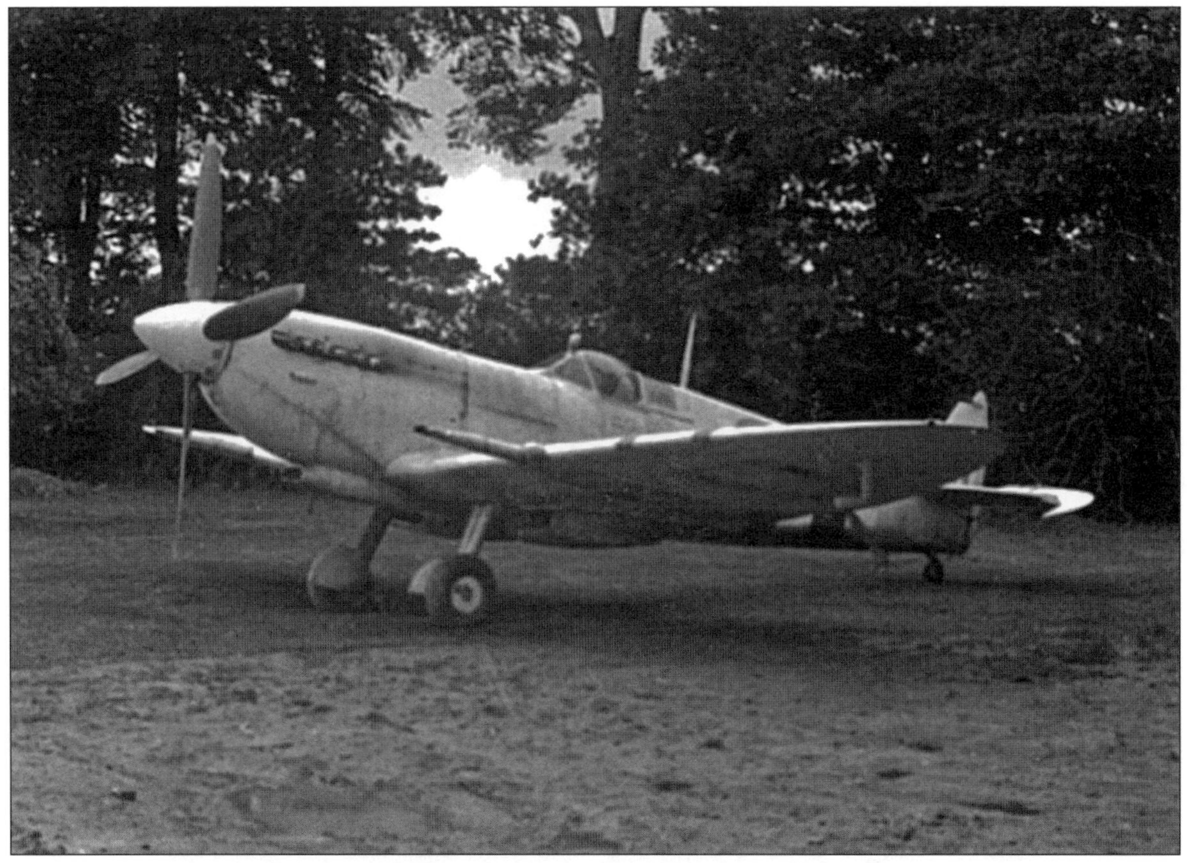

Spitfire FRIX MK716 'X' at A12 airstrip in September 1944

Photo: Michael Horsfall

Two elevations of Spitfire FRIX MK915 'V' on 16 Squadron May-October 1944

Coloured Drawings: Alfred Price "The Spitfire Story"

Four pink Spitfire IXs outside an ex-German hangar, camouflaged to look like a large house, on Melsbroek airfield in October 1944. The objects in the doorway are German drop-tanks.

Photo: Michael Horsfall

CHAPTER 11

Planning a Sortie

Because PR sorties were substantially different from the work of fighters, bombers and Coastal Command, it may be helpful to put the organisation of a sortie first into simple diagrammatic form to reveal who was involved and how the order reached them:

Target

- Decided by the HQ of SHAEF, 21st Army Group, 2nd TAF, Air Staff, or Bomber Command
- Request passed down to 34 Wing HQ
- Order passed to 34 Wing Intelligence Officers, Briefing Officers, Met. Officers, and Photo Interpreters
- Order passed to 16 Squadron Office
- Order passed to Engineering Officer, Flight Mechanics, and 'Tradesmen'
- Order passed to Photographic Section
- Aircraft prepared for Sortie
- Order passed to Pilot in Briefing
- Pilot prepares Flight Plan
- Pilot carries out Sortie
- Films processed by 7 MFPS
- Prints assessed by Photo Interpreters
- Prints despatched to relevant HQ and perhaps to subordinate units
- Prints sent to the Allied Central Interpretation Unit, Medmenham, for Phase 2 and 3 interpretation

The planning of sorties was greatly facilitated during the six months, October 1944-April 1945, that 34 Wing was based at Melsbroek, north-east of Brussels, where the HQs of 21st Army Group and of 2nd TAF were both situated. The 34 Wing Staff and the Squadron COs often met the HQ Staffs and came to know each other personally, frequently meeting over coffee. We used to see Tony Davis driving off to Brussels, but we were never told the purpose of his visits.

The original request for photography would state the location and nature of the target, with an indication of its tactical or strategic importance; the type of photographs required: whether vertical and capable of stereo viewing, or oblique, which usually meant from 5000ft or lower. For vertical photos, the scale required would be stated, usually 1:12000; an F52 camera with a 36" lens would provide prints 8½" x 7" to this scale from 30,000ft; the K17 camera with 20" lens produced 9" x 9" prints to the same scale from 20,000ft; and the F24 camera with 5" lens made prints 5" x 5" to this scale from 5000ft. As the safety of the pilot and aircraft were of prime importance in taking the photographs and getting them back to base, the preferred height was 30,000ft., which was why our Spitfires were painted in 'PR Blue' to match the sky.

However, as weather conditions in NW Europe in the autumn and winter of 1944 were generally cloudy, it was necessary to fit cameras with lenses of different focal lengths into our Spitfires, one pair in the fuselage and one pair in the wings. For oblique photos at low-level, an F24 with 14" lens could be fitted, pointing left from behind the pilot; and the six pink Spitfire IXs with their oblique camera were also available, although little used on operations. During Operation "Market Garden", however, as will be explained later, they dropped messages from Montgmery's HQ in Brussels to Lt. General Browning, the commander of the 1st Allied Airborne Corps, who was waiting near Nijmegen for XXX Corps to progress up "Hell's Highway" from Eindhoven, under constant German intervention, in its vain effort to relieve the Airborne troops valiantly holding the northern end of the bridge over the Rhine at Arnhem. From 20th – 30th September 1944 this was the pink Spitfires' most notable contribution during their six-months service in 16 Squadron.

Many requests were to provide photos of targets to be attacked later by the medium-bombers of 2nd TAF; these might require single pinpoints of individual buildings or line-overlaps of continuous subjects such as roads or railways. 21st Army Group frequently requested pictures to update their maps of the ground over which they planned to advance at a later date; these required us to fly steadily at a given height to produce the correct scale for the maps, and usually involved line-overlaps of transport and communication routes, or mosaics for coverage of a wide area. We might thus find ourselves taking photographs of a seemingly bare landscape, which would nevertheless be of significant value to the troops later. Shadows could be of importance in determining the terrain, so the time of day might be specified in the request.

Once the request from HQ was received at 34 Wing HO, discussions would take place between the CO of the Wing, the Wing Commander Operations, the Wing Commander Flying, the COs of the three Squadrons, the Chief Engineer, the Senior Intelligence Officer, the Senior Army Liaison Officer, the Officer in charge of 7 MFPS, the Senior Photo Interpreter, the Senior Met. Officer, and the Transport Officer – all of those whose duties were most closely connected with operational procedures.

The Senior Intelligence Officer was almost certainly the secret recipient of information that came via a small undercover unit which received ULTRA messages emanating from Bletchley Park in Britain; these resulted from the interception and transcription of German radio messages encoded by their Enigma machines into what they thought was an unbreakable code. No one else on the Wing knew about ULTRA and I certainly never heard of it at any time during the war. However, two of our experienced pilots, who were friendly with Michael Spender, were impressed by the accuracy of the intelligence at their briefings and asked him if he had a secret source of information. Spender immediately stood up, red in the face, and told them that if ever they breathed a word of this again to him or to anyone else, he would have them arrested and sent home to Britain for court-martial! So they were right.

The 34 Wing HQ staff had to decide which Squadron should undertake the sortie: 49 Squadron specialised in low-level night-photography over the German forward areas; 'B' Flight of 140 Squadron also did night-photography, but from a higher altitude and further back into support areas; 'A' Flight undertook day-sorties similar to those of 16 Squadron, but especially the ones beyond the usual range of our Spitfires. However, the arrival of the Me262 jet-fighters in August 1944, with their high speed and heavy armament, put the Mosquitos at risk and 'A' Flight was gradually converted to night-photography, leaving the daytime work to 16 Squadron. Being smaller and more manoeuvrable, a Spitfire was less visible on the German radar and could out-turn an Me262 until the latter ran out of fuel and had to return to its base. The availability of aircraft could also be a deciding issue, either because of losses and the need for repairs and inspections, or because good weather had caused all the available aircraft to take-off on sorties; so another squadron might be asked to do the job. These were some of the factors that affected the choice of Squadron for a sortie. If the requirements of the sortie affected other Sections of the Wing, they would be fully discussed at this meeting.

If 16 Squadron had been selected for the sortie, the order would arrive through Tony Davis in person or by telephone to the Adjutant. The Squadron Engineering Officer would choose the particular

The two Rons
F/M (E) Ron Abrahams (left) and F/M (A) Ron Parnell, MiD, the 16 Squadron artist, in front of a Spitfire XI with a 'Devil' painted on it – the only example of nose-art on a 16 Squadron plane.
Photo: Michael Horsfall

Spitfire and alert the Flight Mechanics (F/Ms) and specialist 'tradesmen' – such as the Electrical Section, the Instrument Repairers, and the Radio Mechanics – to get the aircraft fully prepared and ready for take-off at the specified time.

The F/Ms usually worked on an aircraft in pairs: an F/M (Airframes) with an F/M (Engines). Distinctive on the Squadron were "the Two Rons": F/M (A) Ron Parnell and his close friend F/M (E) Ron Abrahams; for the excellence of his work, including being the chief wielder of a paintbrush, and for maintaining the morale of his colleagues by running his own tea-bar on the airfield, Ron Parnell received a Mention in Despatches (MiD), of which he was justifiably proud.

The F/M (A) would examine the whole aircraft, both on the outside and inside the cockpit, looking for any kind of damage to the structure and tyres caused by enemy action, stones, or an accident. He would check the free working of the flying controls, the movement of the sliding canopy, and the adjustments to the pilot's seat and rudder-pedals, ensure that all the detachable panels were fully secured and all caps screwed-on and locked, and note any signs of leaking fluid for the F/M (E)'s attention. He would make a special point of cleaning the windscreen and canopy – a speck of dirt might look like an enemy fighter in the distance – and, in any time remaining, he would polish the skin of the aircraft to gain a few extra miles-an-hour.

Meanwhile, the F/M (E) would inspect the engine and all the systems that fed it or were dependent on it, for anything broken or damaged; he would top-up the coolant glycol for the radiators, the oil for the engine and the hydraulics, and the battery for the radio, lights, and emergency starter; he would check and, if necessary, replace the compressed-air bottles for operating the brakes and flaps, and the oxygen bottles for the pilot's breathing above 10,000ft; and he would check the fuel in the 87-gallon fuselage tank and the 66½-gallon tanks in the leading-edge of each wing: if necessary, he would call-in the petrol bowser to fill the tanks to the brim.

He and the F/M (A) would then bring up a 'trolley acc.' (a trolley loaded with 12-volt batteries), the F/M (A) would plug the cable into the engine socket, and the F/M (E) would start the 1710hp Merlin

Starting-up a Spitfire XI: the centre F/M has just unplugged the 'trolley-acc'
Photo: Eric Martin

Signals Selection personnel working on the radio of Spitfire XI PL823 'O'
Photo: Eric Phillips

engine. He would run it up to its operating temperatures and pressures and check that everything was working perfectly, including all the instruments, gauges, and lights. If it was, he would run the engine at full throttle and check the operation of the constant-speed propeller mechanism; he would then reduce the power and measure the efficiency of each of the two magnetos separately: a small drop of 150 rpm was acceptable. If anything was defective and repairable or replaceable, the F/Ms would summon the appropriate 'tradesman'. In any case, the Signals Section would have already checked that the correct crystals were in the radio: Channel A for airfield control; Channel B for sector control and providing a 'homing', with the call-sign "Penman"; Channel C for more distant warnings and providing a 'fix' of the aircraft's position, with the call-sign "Kenway"; and Channel D for emergencies. They would also check that the IFF (Identification, Friend or Foe) set was working properly. The Electrical Section and the Instrument Section would be on call for any faults, especially if the warning lights for the undercarriage 'up' or 'down', the cockpit lights, the navigation lights, or the landing lights proved to be faulty, or if any instrument failed to give a true reading. The Section involved would make a quick repair or replace the defective item, and the F/M (E) would then have to check that the fault had been corrected. If the defect was serious and could not be repaired, the F/Ms would report it to the NCO in charge, who would order another aircraft to be prepared. When the two F/Ms were fully satisfied with the condition of the aircraft, they would report to the NCO and enter on the Form 700 – the record of the aircraft's flying life – the condition of the aircraft and any faults they had found and put right. They would then sign to certify that, as far as their responsibilities were concerned, the aircraft was fit to fly the sortie.

In a similar fashion, the NCO in charge of the Photographic Section would select two Photographers and tell them what cameras to fit to the aircraft and what aperture and exposure to set for the weather conditions expected over the target. The two men would fetch the required cameras and film-magazines and fit two F52 cameras side-by-side vertically onto their mountings in the fuselage for high-level photography, or two K17s for medium-level. They would set the aperture and exposure on the cameras, usually f8 and 1/100th second, and connect up the electrical cables and leads for the drives to the motors and to the camera control-unit in the cockpit. They would follow the same procedure when fitting an F24 camera with a 5" lens into each wing, near the tip, for vertical wide-angle photographs at low-level. The Photographers would then check that the whole system worked effectively from the pilot's control-box, mounted below the windscreen, by running a few exposures through the cameras.

An F/M checks-out Spitfire XI PL892 'H' at Melsbroek in late 1944.

Photographers installing an F24 camera in the fuselage of a Spitfire XI

Photo from TV: Ron Nobes

F/Ms and Photographers preparing Spitfire XI PL830 'G' for a sortie at Melsbroek. Note the F52 camera with 36" lens on the ground.

Photo: Michael Horsfall

They would take particular care that all the lenses and glasses in the cameras and in the port-holes in the bottom of the fuselage and wings were scrupulously clean. They would then also enter what they had done on the Form 700. The members of 7 MFPS would be warned to expect the delivery of the film-magazines for processing shortly after the estimated time of arrival (ETA) of the aircraft's return.

I have detailed the work of these Flight Mechanics and Photographers at some length as, if they failed in their duty in even one respect, the whole sortie might be put at risk and vital information denied to the HQ that requested it. They had to take infinite pains to ensure accuracy: for example, the camera mountings had to be precisely lined-up, by the use of a spirit-level, with the horizontal line of the aircraft in level flight; equally, the two vertical cameras, in the fuselage and wings, had to be angled towards each other by 5° to ensure a 10° side-by-side overlap of the resulting photographs. Working to such fine measurements was little different – except for the time factor – from the pilot maintaining an accurate compass course, yet these intelligent ground-crew received almost no recognition of their skill and devotion when the resultant photographs were despatched to the HQ that requested them.

The early morning light was inadequate for good photography so, if we were the pilot whose name was at the top of the 'ladder', we would not have been called from our sleep until 6.50am or later. We would have had a good breakfast including eggs, and a chocolate bar to take with us, and then reported to the Operations Room at a stated time or to find out when we would be needed. The Briefing Officer, either an RAF Intelligence Officer or an Army Air Liaison Officer, would tell us the target and show its location on a 1:1,000,000 wallchart; we would mark it on our own 1:250,000 map in blue wax-pencil. We were often given two or three targets on a mission if they were within 100 miles or so of each other, and they might involve all three types of photography: perhaps a pin-point, a line-overlap, and a mosaic. We would be given enough indication of a target's importance to motivate us for the sortie, but the less we knew, the better for us if we were captured and interrogated by the Germans. We would also be told of any special dangers on the route out and back: the sites of known flak batteries and fighter airfields, or the presence of other Allied aircraft flying in the same vicinity.

From this target briefing, we would move on to the Met. Officer, who would tell us of the weather to be expected in flying to the target, at the target itself, on the return flight, and at base on our return. In the autumn and early winter of 1944, it was unusual to have a day of clear blue sky, suitable for photography from 30,000ft; layers of high cirrus or lower stratus clouds or the presence of large or smaller cumulus clouds were more likely, forcing us to descend beneath them to get our photographs. Hence the need to have cameras with lenses of different focal-length fitted to our Spitfires. Sometimes, we would be told we could fly out to the target in blue sky over a thick sheet of stratus below us obscuring the ground, but that there would be a fortunate hole in the clouds through which we could take our photographs. More often than not, Met's forecast was right, although we might have to fly around for a frustratingly long time waiting for the hole to drift into place over the target, or for a particular cloud to move out of the way.

Besides the cloud-cover and height of the cloud-base, the other vital information that Met. would give us was the direction and speed of the wind; this would vary at ground-level, at medium height 5000-15,000ft, and at high-level 20,000-30,000ft, where it could be as much as 100mph. We needed to know the average wind-speed as we climbed to our operational height, the speed at that height, and the likely speed over the target. Considering that the only aids Met. had for forecasting the weather over Occupied Europe or Germany were their own recording instruments and balloons, their knowledge of the UK weather, the reports of returning aircrews, and perhaps the intercepted transmissions of German weather stations, it was astonishing how accurate their predictions usually were.

Armed with this knowledge of the target and the weather, we would call in at the Squadron Office, empty our pockets of all items that might identify our squadron, aircraft, or base, if we were captured –

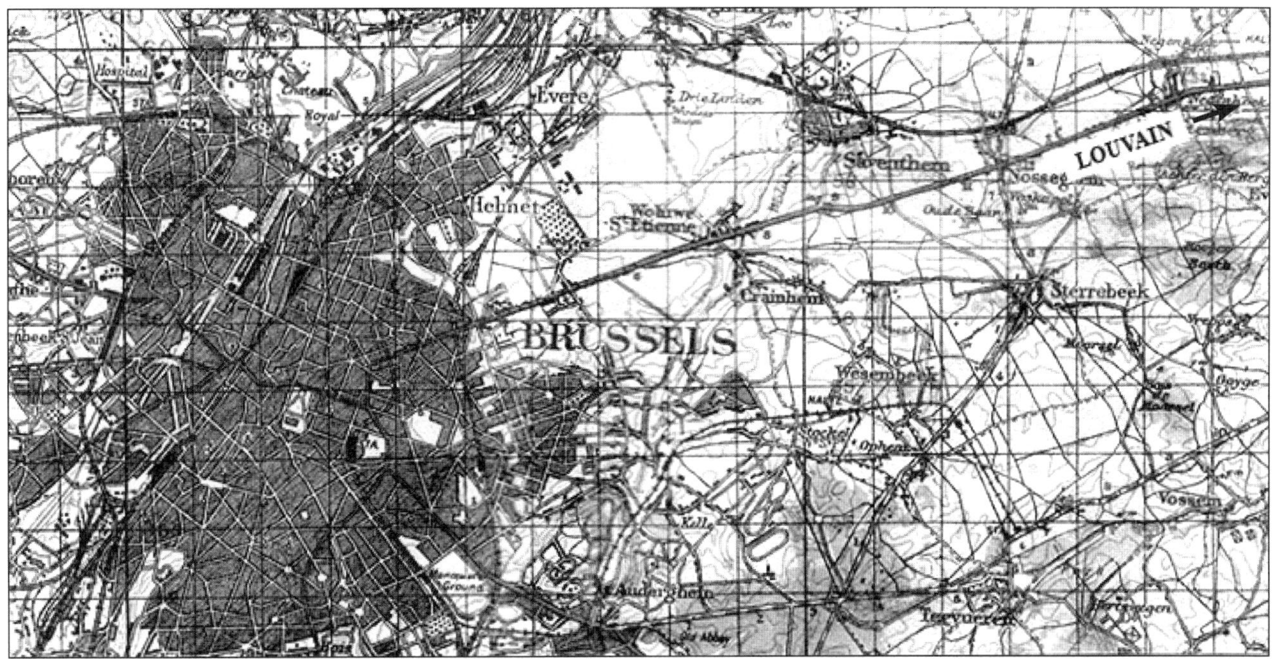

Scale: 1:100,000 Brussels-Louvain 16 miles = 9½", for pin-pointing small targets

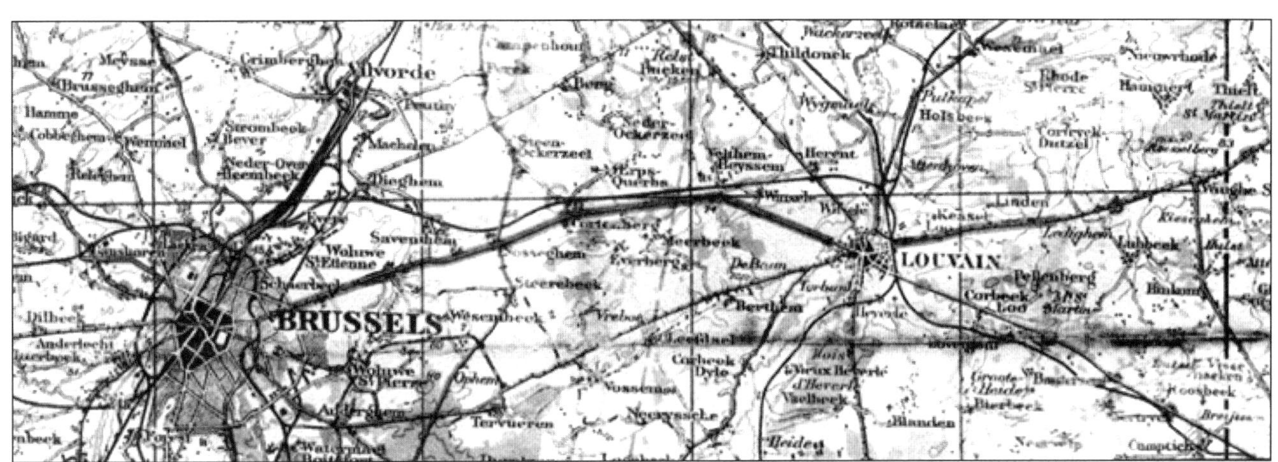

Scale: 1:250,000 Brussels-Louvain 16 miles = 3⅞", for mid-distance navigation

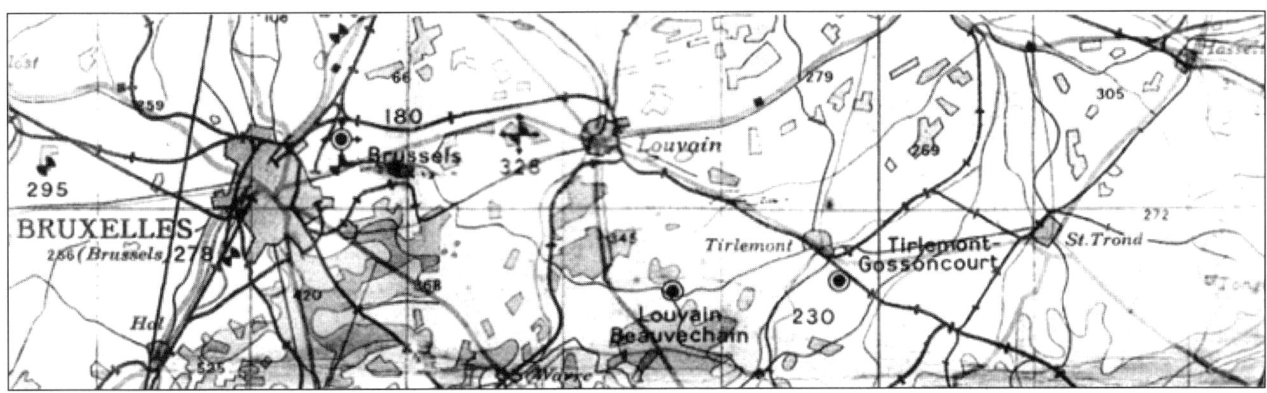

Scale: 1:500,000 Brussels-Louvain 16 miles = 1⅞", for long-distance navigation

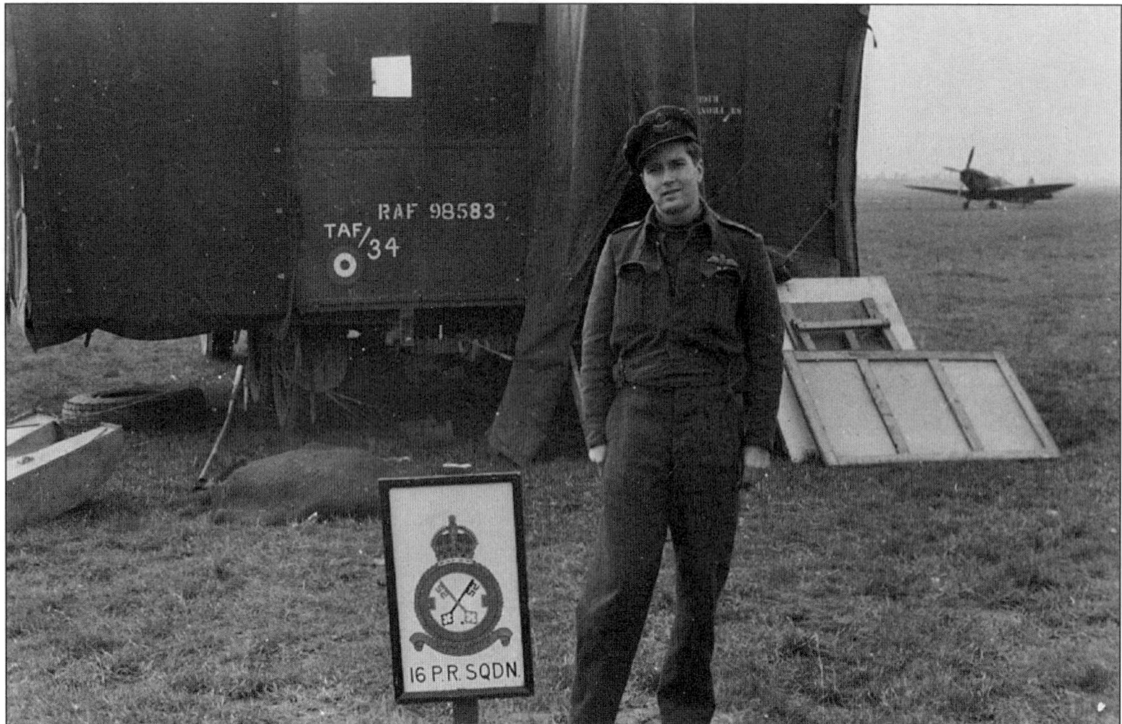

F/Lt Derek Wales in front of 16 Squadron's Operations Trailer at Melsbroek, Belgium, October 1944
Photo: Michael Horsfall

letters, bills, receipts, tickets, money, etc. – and collect any other maps that we needed and an escape-kit: a plastic box containing essential survival material for us if we found ourselves evading capture.

From here we would go to the Squadron Crew Room, which was either a comfortable room with tables or, on the airfield, a room in a large trailer with canvas-sided extensions, to work-out the all-important navigation courses and times and the photographic procedures. This was a complicated business, as we had no electronic navigational aids to help us; so we had to rely entirely on our magnetic compass, a gyro compass (that needed continual re-setting to the magnetic compass), a cockpit watch, our maps, and our reading of the landscape as we passed over it – provided we could see it.

The first move was to draw a line on the map between our base and the target, which would be our 'track', and measure its direction. We then opened up a helpful instrument called a "Dalton Computor". This was not at all a modern computer, but a clever manual calculator, consisting of a circle of transparent plastic, with a rotatable metal rim marked with 360° and the points of the compass; beneath this was a sheet of graph-paper, marked with mph, which could be wound forward or back according to the speed. We would turn the rim to point in the direction of our track, and draw a pencil line along it from the centre of the plastic for the length of our speed; we would then turn the rim to the direction of the wind and draw another, much shorter, line from the centre to represent the speed of the wind. By joining the ends of the two lines and turning the rim till it pointed in the direction of this new line, we could read-off the 'course' we had to steer and, by measuring its length, we would determine our 'ground-speed' (speed over the ground, taking account of the wind). By dividing the distance of the target from our base by our ground-speed, we could learn how long this part of the flight would take.

In fact, we had to make two measurements: the first for our climb from take-off to our operational height (hopefully, 30,000ft) at climbing-speed (180mph), with an average wind-speed between ground-level and 30,000ft; we usually aimed to be at the latter height before crossing into enemy territory. The second measurement was for the rest of our outward flight at our operational height and cruising-speed (360mph). If we had to cover two or three other targets, we would have to make similar calculations for each course; and we also had to work-out our course for our return flight to base.

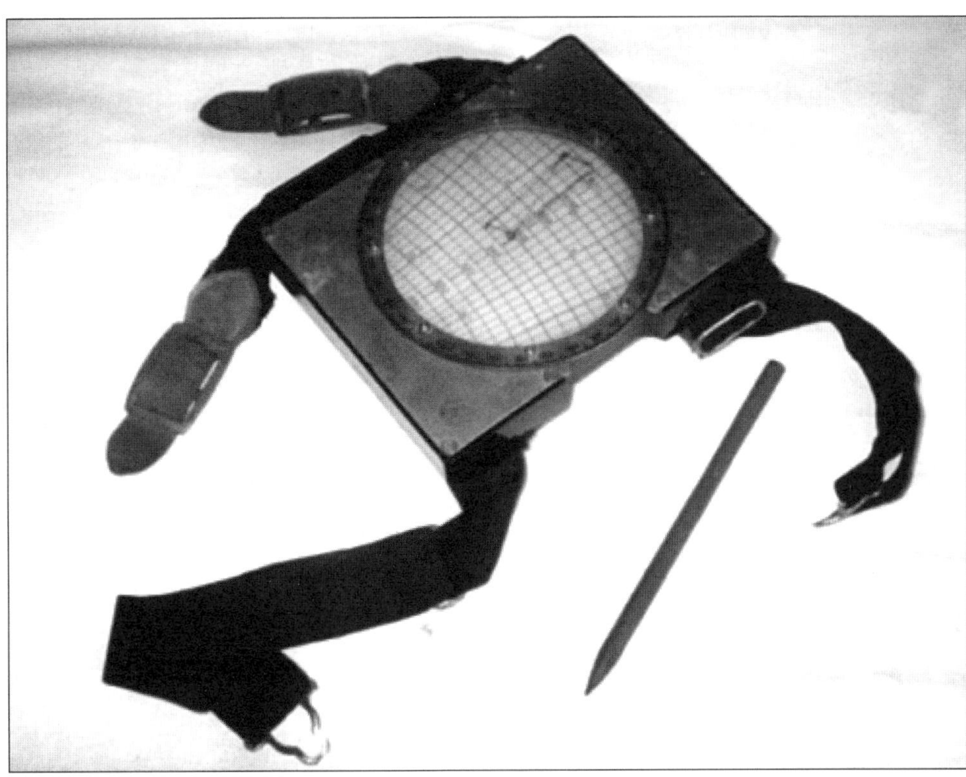

A Dalton 'computor' (calculator) with the lid open, showing the rotatable plastic disc for calculating directions, and the moveable graph-paper underneath for speeds; the straps enable the pilot to take it into the cockpit with him.

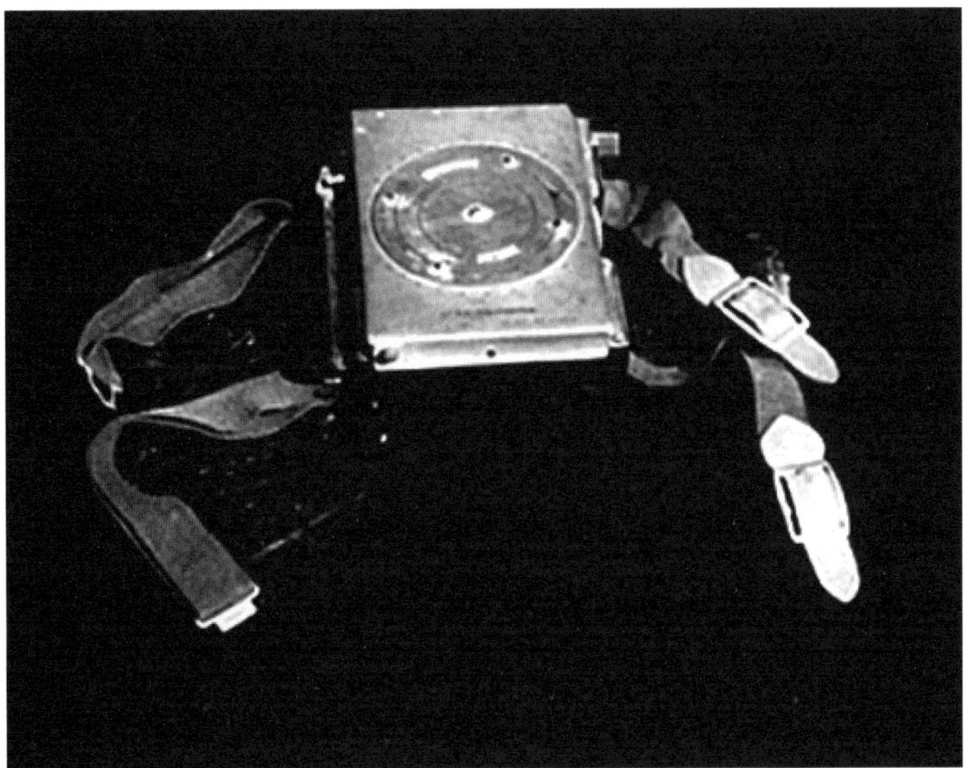

The Dalton 'Computor' with the lid closed, showing the rotatable top disc for setting the height and temperature, and thereby enabling the True Airspeed to be calculated from the Indicated Airspeed, and the True Altitude from the Indicated Altitude.

The directions on the map were headed from True North, but our cockpit compass worked on Magnetic North, so we had to subtract Variation (about 10° in NW Europe) from the courses we had worked-out to adapt them to the magnetic compass in the cockpit. In addition, the metal in the aircraft had its own effect on the compass, called Deviation, which influenced each heading by a few degrees. A Deviation Card was kept in the cockpit of each aircraft to show the Deviation on the compass of that particular aircraft, which we had to allow for.

I must confess here that I could never hold a steady course within a degree or two, as my colleagues claimed; we could trim the rudder and elevator controls to take off any undue pressure on the joy-stick, but not the ailerons: we had to keep the wings balanced by switching from one wing-tank to the other; the weather conditions, with 'bumps' and 'air pockets', could move us around; the steady gyro-compass slowly processed from the course we set on it and needed regular checking and adjustment to the magnetic compass; and we had to spend so much of our time with our head out of the cockpit on the look-out for trouble that the compasses could drift off course to one side or the other before we glanced down again to check them. For all these reasons, I don't think I could maintain a course within less than five or six degrees of my intended one. This perhaps made me even more careful in my navigation calculations – I couldn't afford two sets of errors!

Another concern was that the higher we went, the thinner the air became. Since our Air Speed Indicator worked from the air blowing into it, its readings of our Indicated Air Speed (IAS) would gradually drop below our True Air Speed (TAS). Our Dalton Computor, therefore, had two overlapping circular discs on its cover, which could be rotated to show the TAS from the IAS, or vice versa; thus, at 30,000ft, our TAS of 360mph was shown as only 210mph IAS. Likewise, the outside temperature affected the reading of the Altimeter; so, if the outside air was – 20°, the Indicated Height of 30,000ft was actually 33,000ft of True Altitude. However, our instrument panel contained no air temperature gauge, so there was no means of finding a reliable figure to enable this difference to be calculated on the Computor. In practice, I – and, I suspect, other pilots – ignored this adjustment and relied on the height shown on the Altimeter.

The Dalton Computor had knee straps so that we could use it in the cockpit; but, after one attempt, I found it took up too much room and required too much concentration and fiddling with the knobs to justify taking it with me on a sortie.

We would now draw our track on the map, or maps, from base to target, and mark it with crosses at 20-mile intervals: at 360mph (six miles a minute) each stretch would take us a little over 3 minutes; our ground-speed might, of course, be more or less than 360mph, but it would serve as a rough guide. We would take a close look at the landscape each side and mark particular landmarks and danger-points: towns, airfields, high ground, rivers, the shape of lakes and large woods. From 30,000ft, a road or railway was only a hair's breadth on the ground beneath us but, on a clear day, we could pick out the light shapes of water, the dark shapes of woods, and the smoke of towns a long way away and so check our navigation.

Our photography also required preparation in our Flight Planning. Taking pictures of a single pin-point target – for example, a bridge – should have been simple enough, but we had no window in the bottom of our Spitfires and therefore could not see vertically downwards. So it was wise to let the cameras run for several exposures to ensure that the target was well covered. However, for stereoscopic (3-D) viewing by the photo-interpreters, we had to provide them with a 60% overlap fore-and-aft of successive photos. This required an interval between exposures of several seconds, depending on our height and ground-speed: the higher we were, the longer the interval would be; but the faster we flew, the shorter it would be. If the wind at 30,000ft was 100mph, our ground-speed flying against the wind would be 260mph, requiring a longer interval than when flying downwind at 460mph. Fortunately,

F.52. CAMERA DATA CARD 36" LENS.											
HEIGHT in FEET	SCALE	GROUND COVERED in YARDS	TIME INTERVAL IN SECONDS FOR 60% OVERLAP AT GROUND SPEEDS. M.P.H.								
			240	260	280	300	320	[illegible]	360	380	400
15000	1/5000	972	3	3	3	2	2	2	2	[illegible]	[illegible]
16000	1/5333	1030	3	3	3	2	2	2	2	2	2
17000	1/5666	1102	4	3	3	3	2	2	2	2	2
18000	1/6000	1166	4	3	3	3	3	3	2	2	2
19000	1/6333	1231	4	4	3	3	3	3	2	2	2
20000	1/6666	1298	4	4	4	3	3	3	3	3	2
21000	1/7000	1361	5	4	4	3	3	3	3	3	3
22000	1/7333	1426	5	4	4	4	3	3	3	3	3
23000	1/7666	1490	5	4	4	4	4	3	3	3	3
24000	1/8000	1555	5	5	4	4	4	4	3	3	3
25000	1/8333	1620	5	5	5	4	4	4	3	3	3
26000	1/8666	1688	6	5	5	4	4	4	4	3	3
27000	1/9000	1750	6	5	5	5	4	4	4	3	3
28000	1/9333	1815	6	6	5	5	5	4	4	4	4
29000	1/9666	1880	6	6	5	5	5	4	4	4	4
30000	1/10000	1944	7	6	6	5	5	5	4	4	4
31000	1/10333	2009	7	6	6	5	5	5	4	4	4
32000	1/10666	2074	7	7	6	6	5	5	4	4	4
33000	1/11000	2140	7	7	6	6	5	5	5	4	4
34000	1/11333	2203	7	7	6	6	6	5	5	5	4
35000	1/11666	2268	8	7	7	6	6	5	5	5	5
36000	1/12000	2333	8	8	7	6	6	5	5	5	5

Camera Card for calculating exposure-intervals and area coverage at different heights

Card: Gordon Bellerby

we had mathematical cards for each type of camera, each card showing the exposure interval for one particular focal-length lens, according to the height and ground-speed; it also showed, at each height, the area covered by the camera with this lens and the scale of the photographs. It was a primitive aid, but extremely useful. If we had to photograph a stretch of road, railway, canal, river or coastline, a single long 'run' was usually sufficient; the same 60% overlap was needed in this 'line-overlap' and we would make the same calculations as above for the exposure interval. We had, therefore, to measure the direction and distance of the 'run' on the map and use our Dalton Computor again to learn our heading and ground-speed. The 'run' might be ten or more miles long; so, after setting the exposure interval on the camera control unit in the cockpit, we might need to keep the cameras working for several minutes.

A 'mosaic' required several parallel 'runs' upwind and downwind until we had covered the whole area, so we would need two sets of calculations of the intervals, one for upwind and the other for downwind, and re-set the relevant interval at the beginning of each 'run'. This would mean more work with the Computor to establish our heading, ground-speed and duration in each direction.

Our memory would be quite unable to cope with the mass of figures resulting from all these calculations for our navigation and photography, so we would be careful to write them down on our knee-pad, which we carried with us into the cockpit. The more preparations we made beforehand for accurate navigation and photography, the less distracted we would be from the business of flying our unarmed Spitfire for several hours to the target and back. For this, we needed to keep checking the instruments ate 3.9.44 Aeroplane .... Pilot ....

WIND			NOTES
HEIGHT	FROM °T	SPEED	310/70 320/110

FROM	TO	T.A.S.	Height	True Track	Mag Course	Distance	G/S	Time
BASE	SELSEY			195	222	60	240	15
SELSEY	Port en B			187	210	93	424	13
Beach-head				281	302	30	268	7
Port en B	SELSEY			007	005	93	280	20
SELSEY	BASE			015	013	60	200	18
								73

Time	Observation	E.T.A.
1005	S/c	
1020	Selsey	
1045	Strip 1-95	
	~~St A s M~~ Port en B 96-115	
	St A s M 116-0	
	P de P 26000 1-11	
	15000 12-37	
1115	out	
1132	in	

166355r. Wt. 5436. 20,000. 10/43. W. & S. Ltd. 51-8886. FORM 433 A.

A time-worn example of my knee-pad entries for an early sortie to the Normandy beach-head, which did not count as an operation. 'G/S' means ground-speed.

for our accurate course, speed and height; for boost and rpm; for oil-pressure, glycol temperature, electrical output, oxygen supply, and fuel position, changing wing-tanks every 20 minutes to keep the wings balanced – all the while keeping a sharp look-out for enemy, fighters or bursts of hostile flak. Our eyes would swivel continually from the rear-view mirror (were we leaving a contrail?), to the left horizon, to ahead, to above us, to the right, and down to the instrument panel from right to left, then back to the mirror and round again. Any unplanned change in the wind or the weather, in our height or our speed, and any interruption caused by enemy interference, would send all our plans awry and necessitate our making quick mental calculations of fresh courses or exposure intervals to meet the new situation. However, we had enough real issues to consider on each flight without worrying about those that might be forced on us if the conditions of the sortie changed.

Thus, we hoped, thoroughly prepared for the sortie, we would relieve ourselves physically as, although there was a relief-tube under the seat in the cockpit, it was a demanding and distracting job to use it, even though an over-full bladder had a detrimental effect on our concentration on our flying.

We would then collect our parachute, which had a dinghy-pack attached above the parachute-pack in case we had to bale out over water – but it made for an uncomfortable seat. With a chocolate bar stuffed into a pocket and clutching our maps and knee-pad, we would stagger out to our designated Spitfire, grateful if one of the F/Ms came forward to relieve us of the weight of the parachute and spread it out on the cockpit seat, ready to be sat on. We would walk round the aircraft, looking carefully at all the surfaces, checking especially that the small cover had been removed from the airspeed pitot-head. We would exchange a few words of reassurance with the Flight Mechanics, and one of them would climb up on the wing behind us to help to strap us in and do up the connections of the radio and oxygen. He would then join the other F/M by the trolley acc. ready to start our waiting engine.

F/Ms ready to start-up the engine of a Spitfire XI at Amiens-Glisy; note the trolley-acc on the left.

Colour Photo: Michael Horsfall

A Good Send-off for Michael Horsfall on 14th January 1945 surrounded by (1-r) Cpl Hayward and F/Ms Forster, Holloway, Jacques, Pate, Beamish and Last. Unfortunately, Michael was shot down on this sortie by an FW190 and became a POW.

Photo: Hugh Smallwood "Spitfire in Blue"

CHAPTER 12

Flying a Sortie

Some account of how we handled the Spitfire XI may be relevant here, as the next section on 'Operations' does not feature our procedures for getting into the air and coming back to earth – yet they contained the seeds of a successful sortie or, for me, the risk of an unhappy ending.

We were last left in the cockpit of our Spitfire, ready to start the engine. Let's give her the Squadron letter 'P' and call-sign 'Peter One'. We would have checked that there were chocks in front of the wheels while we walked round the aircraft, and our first move now is to see that the undercarriage lever is fully back and locked in its gate and to apply the brakes. We put on our flying-helmet, pushing the goggles above our forehead and checking that the oxygen-mask fits snugly when we clip it across our face. We take the bayonet-plug dangling from the cable that runs to our ear-pieces and microphone and insert it into the radio socket, and we connect the tube of the oxygen-mask to the supply-line from the oxygen-bottle behind us in the fuselage. We turn on the tap, check the contents on the gauge, and hear the comforting hiss of the oxygen flowing into our mask. We turn it off and leave our face open so that we can communicate with the F/Ms.

Even though the F/Ms have already done a thorough Daily Inspection on the aircraft, we leave nothing to chance and do our own careful check in the cockpit. We turn on the electrical master-switch and check that the undercarriage indicator-lights show 'green' (meaning 'down'); if they showed 'red', when we taxied out, the aircraft would gently subside onto the grass and wreck the propeller and, perhaps, the engine! We adjust the seat to a convenient height and the rudder-pedals to suit our length of leg. We move the joystick forward, back and sideways, looking out to see that the elevators and ailerons respond correctly, and do the same with the rudder. We press the button on the fuel-gauge and check the contents of the main tanks and wing-tanks, and turn the handle of the fuel-cock to the main tanks for starting-up. We loosen slightly the friction-nut on the throttle-quadrant, and pull the throttle lever right back, then open it just an inch: we push the lever of the propeller pitch-control fully forward into 'fine' pitch (when it turns with less air resistance), and we put the supercharger switch into the 'Auto/Normal' position. We are now ready to start the engine.

The two F/Ms go up to the propeller and one of them calls out, "*Switches off!*" We check that the ignition-switches are in fact 'off' to avoid any possibility of a sudden, unwanted start when the F/Ms turn the big propeller by hand to free-up the engine oil, and reply, "*Switches off!*" They pull the propeller over several revolutions, then return to the trolley acc. and plug the cable into the socket in the engine-cowling. We unlock the priming-pump on the instrument panel and give five or six pumps until we feel resistance. We call out, "*Switches on!*" and raise the two ignition-switches. Then "*Contact!*" They switch-on the trolley acc. and we press the booster-coil and starter buttons on the panel. The propeller turns once, the engine coughs, and emits a puff of blue smoke from the exhausts. We give another prime, press the buttons again, two revolutions, two coughs, and more smoke. We prime once more, the engine catches and gives a roar, with smoke billowing back, then settles down to a steady throb. We adjust the throttle to 1000rpm and allow the engine to warm-up. The F/Ms battle against the slipstream to unplug the trolley acc. and wheel it away.

We continue our check of the working of all the systems. We turn on the cameras and test that the camera control-box is working: the red light comes on 4 seconds before the exposure occurs; when the green light shows, it has been taken; we take two or three exposures in succession, then re-set the exposure-counter to zero. We uncage the gyro-controlled artificial horizon and the gyro compass, let them settle down to steady indications, then set the latter to the heading of the magnetic compass beneath the instrument-panel. We glance at the Deviation Card to see whether we have to add or subtract any significant number of degrees. We turn on the radio and check its working by calling-up Airfield Control:

"*Airfield Control from Peter One, how do you read me? Over.*"

"*Peter One from Airfield Control, loud and clear. Over.*"

"*Airfield Control from Peter One, Roger. Thank you. Out.*"

We set on the altimeter the height of the airfield above sea-level, as all the heights on our maps are shown 'above sea-level'; the altimeter has a slot in its face to show the barometric pressure at this moment – which may have altered by the time we return.

By now the oil-pressure has reached 40lbs/sq in and its temperature 20°C, the coolant temperature is hovering around 50°C, the pneumatic pressure is showing 2201bs/sq in, and the brake-pressure 80lbs/sq in, so we test the operation of the pneumatic wing-flaps and radiator-flaps; an F/M gives us a 'thumbs up' to signal they are working. The volt-meter indicates that the generator is charging properly. So everything is functioning correctly. We switch-on the heater on the pitot-head to ensure that it doesn't freeze-up and deny us our airspeed-indicator. We now have only to check the engine and its controls.

We throttle up to 0lbs boost and move the pitch-lever from 'fine' to 'coarse' and back again, twice, and listen to the change in the engine-note, which goes deeper in 'coarse' pitch. We press the test button on the two-stage supercharger and note that the red light comes on and the boost increases significantly at the "Fast Speed' setting; releasing the button returns the supercharger to 'Medium Speed'. We then signal to the F/Ms and the poor chaps go to the tailplane and lie over it, facing backwards to keep the tail down with their weight, while we hold the stick right back and steadily run the engine up to full-throttle power at 16lbs boost and 3000rpm. 1710 horsepower produces an unholy bellow; grass, dust and debris are hurled back behind the aircraft, and the gale of slipstream tugs at the F/Ms' clothing; in the winter, it feels like an arctic blizzard. We throttle back enough to release the men and test the two magnetos by switching one off and checking that the other continues with a drop of no more than 150rpm. We let the engine tick-over while one of the F/Ms climbs up on the wing and hands us the Form 700; we sign it to show that we accept the Spitfire as fully fit for the sortie, and smile our thanks to the F/M as we hand it back. He shouts "*Good luck!*" as he closes the cockpit flap and jumps down. We check the sliding of the hood, then strap our oxygen mask over our face and turn on the tap: it's wise to start acclimatising ourselves by breathing oxygen from ground-level.

We call-up for permission to taxy out:

"*Airfield Control from Peter One, permission to taxy out, please. Over.*"

"*Peter One from Airfield Control, permission granted. Taxy out to Runway 20 (= 200° direction) and wait for a 'green'. Acknowledge when airborne. Over.*"

"*Airfield Control from Peter One, taxying out to Runway 20. Wilco* (= Will comply). *Out.*"

We raise the seat to its full height, to give us the best view out, and slip our feet to the top of the rudder pedals. We look around to make sure no other aircraft or personnel is in our way, then signal for the chocks to be removed; pulling on the ropes, the F/Ms drag them from the wheels and wave the 'all clear' to us. We release the brakes, give a burst of throttle, and get the aircraft moving over the grass; we are careful not to apply the brakes harshly as, with its heavy engine in its long nose, the Spitfire can tip up easily onto its propeller. The long nose also prevents us seeing ahead, so we have to swing it from side to side, especially when we trundle onto the narrow perimeter track that will take us to the end of the runway in use. We mustn't hurry, but we can't taxy for too long, as the Merlin engine overheats if it stays ticking over on the ground for more than a few minutes.

We stop near the beginning of Runway 20, at an angle so that we can see any aircraft coming in to land, and do our take-off checks: TTPFFGH. We tighten the Throttle-nut; move the elevator Trim to slightly nose-down and the rudder trim to full right; check that the propeller Pitch is in full 'fine', that the Flaps are up, and that the Fuel-cock is on the main tanks; we set the Gyro-compass by the magnetic one, tighten our Harness, and lower our seat to a comfortable position for flying; we jot down the time of take-off on our knee-pad. We keep our cockpit canopy open – a personal choice: it's easier to get out if we have an accident on take-off. We don't spend long over these checks, and call-up Airfield Control:

"*Airfield Control from Peter One, ready for take-off.*"

Fortunately, no one else is in the circuit; the controller in his caravan by the end of the runway has heard us on the radio and gives us a 'green' on his signal-lamp. We taxy forward onto the runway, blast the tail round with a touch of throttle to line ourselves up properly on the centre, open the throttle gradually, kicking on the rudder to keep her straight, and throttle up to +9 boost and 2850rpm, sufficient to get us racing smoothly, tail lifted, down the runway. We're on our way on another sortie.

At 90mph she lifts off almost by herself and we help her up by raising the undercarriage as soon as possible. This is easier said than done, as the undercarriage lever is on the right-hand side of the cockpit, yet our left hand is on the throttle and our right hand is holding the joy-stick. We have, therefore, to leave the throttle alone – which is why we ensured the throttle-nut was tight before we started to take-off – and change hands on the stick. With our right hand we can now reach down and push the lever sideways out of the bottom gate, then up, fully forward and into the top gate. As the wheels come up, we apply the brakes to stop them spinning and vibrating in the wheel-wells, and watch the undercarriage-position lights change from 'green' to 'red'. In practice, we take pride in changing hands rapidly immediately after take-off and whipping the wheels up before we reach the end of the runway. Indeed, if we leave the undercarriage down too long, the legs will cover up the radiators sufficiently for the coolant to boil within a matter of minutes, so it pays to do the job quickly.

A Spitfire XI takes to the air at Amiens-Glisy September 1944.

Photo: Michael Horsfall

On its way: a Spitfire XI in flight

At 500ft, we close the hood and start a wide climbing turn to the left and, as the speed increases to 180mph, we throttle back to +6 boost and reduce the revs to 2650rpm. We call-up Airfield Control:

"*Peter One, airborne. Out.*"

We change the radio to Channel B, the sector watch frequency. At 2000ft, we come back over the centre of the airfield, point our nose precisely in the direction of our first compass course, check that the gyro agrees exactly with the magnetic compass, note the time on our knee-pad, and fly accurately on our course at our climbing speed of 180mph (= 3 miles a minute) to our first landmark at 20 miles on the map.

It is vital that here we check whether we have drifted off to one side or the other of our intended track, as it will reveal whether Met's forecast of the strength and direction of the wind is reliable. If we are, say, a mile to the right of our track, we can judge we have been blown 5° off our course in 6½ minutes. We therefore turn 10° left and hold this course for another 6 minutes, then turn back to 5° to the left of our original course to counteract the increased strength of the wind from that side. We'll bear this in mind for the rest of the sortie.

The next chapter gives some idea of the actual progress of my sorties onwards from this early stage of a flight, so let us just take a look at how the flight might end.

Let's assume that a good deal of cloud has developed, but we've managed to take our photographs either through holes or by going underneath the cloud-base. We find our return course on our knee-pad and turn 'P' Peter onto it. If we're a long way from home, it may pay us to climb back to 30,000ft through and over the cloud and travel back at speed. If, however, the cloud has forced us down to about 5000ft and we're not too far from base, we're better off flying back in the safety of cloud, relying on our blind-flying instruments. These are grouped together in the centre of the instrument-panel in two rows: top-left is the airspeed indicator, with the altimeter below it; in the middle is the artificial horizon, with the gyro compass beneath it; and on the right is the rate-of-climb or -descent indicator, with the turn-and-bank indicator underneath it. I did a one-week course on instrument-flying before going to the PR OTU, so I feel quite happy trusting the instruments rather than the-seat-of-my-pants when flying blind in cloud. We've checked that there isn't any high ground on the way back, so we climb up to 6000ft and settle down to a moderate cruise of +4 boost and 2000 rpm, which will give us 240mph: at 4 miles a minute, we should be back in just over an hour. We re-set the gyro compass, change our wing-tanks and check all the gauges carefully. The Merlin engine roars steadily and reassuringly beneath the long nose in front of us, worn and polished to the grey undercoat. We stay on oxygen, in case we have to climb up again for some reason. Unlike the bomber pilots, we have no auto-pilot, so our hands and feet are kept busy keeping the aircraft straight and level on our course at our altitude. The Germans can see us on their radar, but they can't do much about us, wrapped in our cloud. The only other danger is from the weather: if we run into dark cumulo-nimbus cloud, with strong vertical currents containing hail and even ice, we can be pitched up and down most unpleasantly and have ice coating the wings and windscreen, forcing us to descend quickly to get out of it. The wind speed and direction may also change significantly from Met's forecast, so we may be driven a long way off course; this doesn't matter too much, though, as when we get within about 50 miles of base, we can get a 'homing' from 'Penman' on Channel B.

Replica instrument panel of a Spitfire XI PL965 built by MAPS, now in the Manston Battle of Britain Memorial Building, Kent, showing the six blind-flying instruments grouped on a panel below the camera control box.

Photo: Lewis Deal

On this trip, the cloud seems to extend all the way home; we could go down beneath it and hope to find landmarks to navigate back to base. But we feel a bit lazy and we'd rather use our height to get help from 'Penman'; so we call up this invaluable radio direction-finding station:

"*Penman from Peter One, do you read me? Over.*"

"*Peter One from Penman, loud and clear. Over.*"

"*Penman from Peter One, request a homing to base, please. Over.*"

"*Peter One from Penman, transmit for ten seconds. Over.*"

"*Penman from Peter One, one, two, three, four, five, six, seven, eight, nine, ten. Over.*"

"*Peter One from Penman, steer 235° for 30 miles. Over.*"

"*Penman from Peter One, 235° for 30 miles. Wilco. Thank you. Out.*"

We realise we've done quite well and are not so far from base. We turn onto 235° and note the time. After five minutes (=20 miles), we change to our main fuel tanks, switch-off the oxygen, and call-up base on Channel A:

"*Airfield Control from Peter One, do you read me? Over.*"

"*Peter One from Airfield Control, loud and clear. Over.*"

"*Airfield Control from Peter One, please give me QFE (the barometric pressure at the airfield) and cloud-base. Over.*"

"*Peter One, QFE 998. Cloud-base 2000ft. Call when overhead. Over.*"

"*Airfield Control from Peter One, QFE 998. Cloud-base 2000ft. Wilco. Out.*"

We set 998 mbs on our altimeter, which now gives us our exact height over the airfield, then reduce the throttle, lower the nose, re-trim the aircraft, and start descending while maintaining our course. Two minutes later, the cloud begins to thin: we flick through patches of lighter and darker grey, then the fields and woods define themselves clearly on the dull-green landscape. We level-off at 1800ft, increase the throttle and keep a sharp look-out for other aircraft. We soon spot the grassland, runways, hangars, huts and buildings of our base – 'Penman' has done a good job, as usual.

"Airfield Control from Peter One, overhead. Landing instructions, please. Over."

"Peter One from Airfield Control, Runway 20. Left-hand circuit. Wind from 270°, 15mph. Call when on the ground. Over."

"Airfield Control from Peter One, Runway 20. Left-hand circuit. Wilco. Out."

Radio Direction-Finding Unit
From a short transmission by a pilot to its call-sign 'Penman', and within a range of 30 – 100 miles depending on the aircraft's height, the operator could give him the course and distance to his base – the only navigational aid available to us. The operators were very efficient and much appreciated.

We swing to the right over the airfield, throttle back and turn gradually to the left, joining the circuit at 1000ft on the down-wind leg at 160mph. We carry-out our landing-checks: BUPFGH: we apply the Brakes (to stop the wheels spinning from the airflow in the wells); pull the Undercarriage lever out of its gate and down towards us, and wait for the two little 'thumps' and the indicator lights to turn from 'red' to 'green'; push the propeller Pitch lever forward into fully 'fine'; check that the Fuel is on the main tanks; in bad weather we would set the Gyro compass to 20°, the reverse of the runway heading, but there is no need to do so today; and slide open the Hood. We turn left onto the base-leg and throttle back to 110mph; we flip down the little lever on the instrument-panel that lowers the flaps, with a hiss of compressed air, to 60° – no more or less: they're either 'up' or 'down'. The nose drops a little; we re-trim and, to the accompaniment of the Spitfire's familiar 'popping' sounds, reduce throttle to go down to 700ft. We then start a slow curving descent to the left, keeping the end of the runway in view and reducing speed to 90mph as we cross the threshold of the runway. When we're almost on the runway, we level the

End of a Sortie
W/O 'Charlie' Chaplin lands a Spitfire XI at Amiens-Glisy September 1944.

wings, ease the throttle right back, and hold the stick back as she drops gently onto the ground with, we hope, the wheels and tail-wheel making contact simultaneously in a 'three-point' landing.

A Spitfire, however, is as delicate as a butterfly and can be quickly disturbed by a puff of cross-wind; one wing can be uplifted and she can be easily unbalanced on her narrowly-spaced undercarriage legs. On the other hand, she responds willingly to movements of the ailerons and rudder, and a touch of brake can stop an incipient ground-loop. We concentrate hard on keeping her rolling straight ahead while she slows down; when she's at walking-speed, we turn off the runway, raise the flaps (to protect them from stones thrown up), and call-up on, the radio:

"*Airfield Control from Peter One, landed and clear of runway. Out.*"

We loosen the throttle-nut, raise our seat, and taxy back towards Dispersal, weaving from side to side, until we see an F/M waving his arms, ready to marshal us into our parking-place. With bursts of throttle and heavy use of one or other brake, we bring 'P' Peter near enough to the spot to satisfy him. We apply the brakes, run the engine up to half-throttle and back, bring the pitch-lever right back to 'coarse', and pull out the 'cut-out' ring on the instrument-panel; the faithful engine clanks to a stop, taking the propeller with it. We turn the ignition-switches down to 'off', switch-off the pitot-head heater and the main electrics, and turn-off the fuel. The F/Ms place the chocks in front of the wheels, while the photographers are already at work removing the precious film-magazines from the cameras and carrying them over to a waiting jeep for delivery to the MFPS.

We unclip our oxygen-mask and disconnect the tube, remove the radio plug from its socket, release our cockpit harness by removing the pin from the top of the retaining stud, undo our parachute straps by turning the top of the quick-release box, sit back and relax for a moment after the flight, while our sturdy Merlin engine gives-off gentle 'ticks' as the hot metal slowly cools. We open the side-flap of the cockpit, haul ourselves out onto the wing, reach back for the parachute, collect our maps from the metal case inside the cockpit, and jump down onto the good earth.

We walk to the Squadron trailer and leave our parachute, dinghy pack, helmet and goggles on their rack. We take the opportunity to relieve ourselves. We get a lift to the Operations Room and meet the Intelligence Officer, who wishes to know about anything of interest on the flight; the Met man also is

Journey's End
Spitfire XI PL965 being marshalled into the Dispersal at Eindhoven in April 1945, with Cpl Ron Coleman holding the wing-tip. This is the only known wartime photograph of PL965, currently on the display circuit in the UK, owned and flown by Peter Teichman.
Photo: Hugh Smallwood "Spitfire in Blue"

keen to learn whether his forecasts proved correct. We hand back our escape-kit to the Adjutant's office and sit down to write our report of the sortie in the Line Book. This is a handwritten record in our own words, as long or as short as we see fit; by writing it so soon after landing, there's a good chance that it will be reasonably accurate. This is important, as the clerks will type it up into the Squadron Operations Record Book and some items may feature in the Adjutant's Monthly Summary, a compilation of the events of each day. Later on, we'll go over to No 7 MFPS to have a look at our photographs, to see whether we actually took the targets which were the objective of the sortie; we may be disappointed to find we missed a bend in a road, or that the overlap was not the 60° that we planned, or that there was too much cloud over the target to get a clear image; if our navigation was out, we may even find we took a bridge as briefed, but it was not the right one. The photo-interpreters, however, are very human and realise that we operate under quite taxing conditions. But we kick ourselves if we've missed part of a line-overlap or mosaic and someone else has to fill-in this gap on another sortie. If the PIs greet us with smiles, though, we know that we have done a satisfactory job and can relax until our name reaches the top of the 'ladder' again.

Meanwhile, our mission completed, the camera magazines containing the precious films have become the centre of attention. A motor-cyclist rushes them to No 7 Mobile Field Photographic Section, where they are developed and printed in huge numbers: the film in each of the two F52 magazines holds 500 exposures, so mass-production machines are used whenever possible.

Amid this flood of prints, one problem is a means of enabling each one to be easily identified. The solution is for the details of the particular sortie to be hand-written at the top or bottom of the relevant negative so that it is reproduced on every print. This caption is called the 'titling' and contains the following information, reading from left to right:

The exposure number; the squadron number; the sortie number; the date; the focal length of the lens; the number of the camera; and sometimes the aeroplane's height. Different processing units may vary the position of these items a little and some may add the name of the pilot.

A broader form of identification is used to show whether a photograph has been taken by an aircraft belonging to the RAF or to the USAF. For this purpose, during the manufacture of an RAF camera, a small long-stemmed cross was etched into the middle of each side of the register glass at the top of the camera mechanism; they would thus appear on every RAF negative and print. The Americans used the same system, but their symbol was half a black arrow-head in the middle of each side. These signs are known as 'register collimation marks' (RCMs).

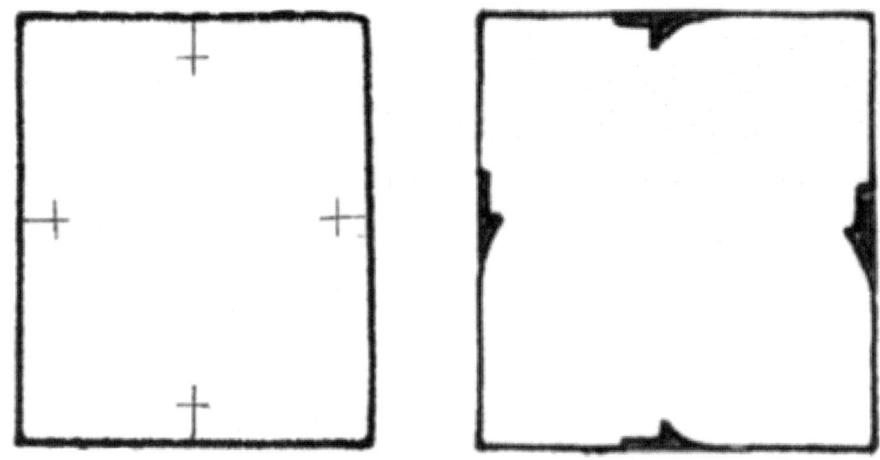

Register Collimation Marks: RAF (left) and USAF (right)

A Continuous Film Processor and Dryer at RAF Medmenham

Photo: Roy Nesbit "Eyes of the RAF"

A Multi-printer at RAF Medmenham; note the prints passing underneath.

Photo: Roy Nesbit "Eyes of the RAF"

A low-level oblique of a house standing isolated among polders in Holland flooded probably by the Germans. On the original print, RAF RCMs can be seen in the middle of the top and each side. The titling along the bottom reads: Exposure No 0002 P (unknown) 16 Squadron Sortie No 1493 17th December 1944 14" focal-length lens camera No M14.

Unfortunately, many publishers of WW2 books reproducing aerial photos consider the titling and collimation marks 'spoil' the pictures and cut them off or 'crop' them, thereby making it virtually impossible to discover anything about the origin of the pictures or the conditions under which they were taken.

As I have mentioned earlier, 34 Wing had its own PIs, who looked at our photos from the point of view of initiating immediate action against the targets. This was Stage 1 of the interpretation process. For the longer-term assessment of the pictures, they were sent to the Allied Central Interpretation Unit (ACIU) at RAF Medmenham, on the Thames a few miles from RAF Benson and 1 PRU (in mid-1944, integrated with the American 7th Photo Group at nearby Mount Farm and re-named 106 Group). Here hundreds of specialist PIs, viewing the 60% overlap of two adjacent photos through simple stereoscopes, examined them in 3D, which revealed every detail with remarkable clarity. Scale-models of the targets of particular importance could be made from these images and used in briefing aircrews for punitive operations against them.

To assist in the speedy retrieval of photos covering targets of particular interest, the PIs drew on a map the exact area covered by each exposure – usually in pairs from split-pair vertical cameras – and gave each one the relevant exposure number on the titling of the print. They followed the track of the

This is a vertical photograph of the River Rhine flowing past Arnhem from right to left under the road bridge on the right. Two USAF RCMs can be seen, one in the middle of each side, and the titling is printed on the bottom of the black frame used by the USAF. It reads:
Exposure No 3096 U S 7 Group (=RAF Wing) Sortie No 3356 18th September 1944
24" focal length (altitude) 15-20,000ft 27 Squadron.

aircraft taking the photos and so built-up a 'plot' of the pictures taken during a 'run'. Quite often, for simplicity, they showed only the numbers of the exposures starting and finishing a 'run', connecting them with a line each side but leaving blank the intervening exposures.

The resultant numbered 'plot' was a valuable reference sheet of a sortie and was accompanied with a card which contained full information of value to the PIs. It contained:

> the pilot's name; his squadron; the sortie number; the task number; the start and finish exposure numbers of each of the pair of cameras (port and starboard); the time of photography; the date; the focal length of the lenses; the height; the scale; and the relevant map references.

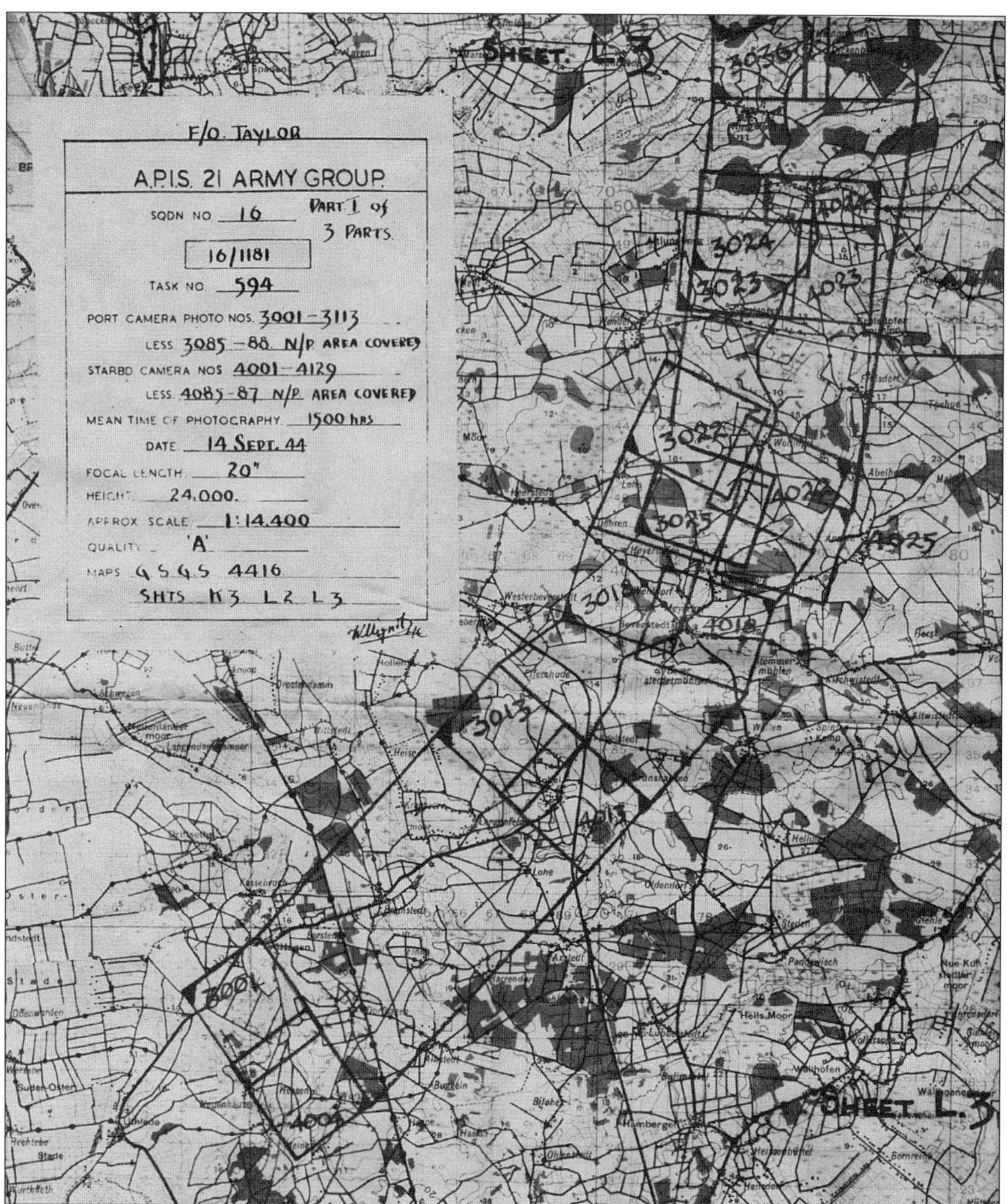

The PIs' 'plot' of the photographs I took on the 14th September 1944 with a split-pair of F52 cameras with 20" lenses from 24,000ft; I was on my way back from taking roads north of Bremen and let the camera run over this countryside and then over Wilhelmshaven. The 'plot' made it easy for the PIs to pick out the prints of a particular location.

Plot: DotKa, Holland

So, at the request of several different HQs, we flew our sorties as one part of intelligence gathering, supported by the 600 or so ground-personnel of 16 Squadron and 34 Wing who fitted the cameras and enabled the 20 pilots to fly and take photographs and those who processed, printed, copied, and distributed the resultant images. A wide variety of similar operations was undertaken by the other two PR Wings in 2nd TAF, by the British and American squadrons in 106 Group, and by the five PRUs in the other theatres of the war.

The second part of intelligence gathering was achieved by the PIs, both in the field and at ACIU at RAF Medmenham, who for five years elucidated the details of every aspect of the German war effort – and probably had a better understanding of it than the Germans themselves.

The two groups formed an essential partnership, in which every member played a particular role and which made an invaluable, largely unpublicised, contribution to the winning of the war by the Allies.

A WAAF Photo-interpreter at work on a stereo pair of photographs

Photo: from TV: Ron Nobes

CHAPTER 13

My Operations: the Full Story

Introduction

Except for the comments in the left-hand margin of each page, the contents of this Chapter have all been taken from contemporary 1944 documents: the 16 Squadron Operations Record Book (SORB), containing the Daily Summary by the Adjutant; the entries in my flying Log Book, signed each month by the CO of 16 Squadron; my entries in the 16 Squadron Line Book, written within hours of landing by the pilot of each sortie and later copied into SORB by a clerk in the Adjutant's office; and my Diary, written-up in the evening within 48 hours of the events it describes.

Diaries and cameras, officially, were not allowed to be kept by Service personnel for reasons of security in case they and their contents fell into the hands of the enemy; it is clear, however, that this regulation was widely disregarded by both officers and enlisted men. I was well aware, though, that my Diary might reach the hands of the wrong people, British or German; so I tried to conceal the items that breached security by hiding them in a code, using first letters for place-names, such as "A" for Amiens-Glisy, and distractors, such as "mess-tin" for camera; I have explained these in the margins.

Every occupation has its own special language or 'jargon' and RAF jargon in 1944 may be unfamiliar to some readers; thus an aeroplane was commonly called a "kite", and the ground-crew were "erks" or "bods"(= bodies). There were also many acronyms in use, such as "E.T.A." (with full-stops) or "ETA" (without them) for Estimated Time of Arrival. I have explained each of these in the margins as it occurs with a numeral reference. We didn't call the Germans by the First World War epithet of "Huns", but usually referred to them as "Jerry"; in writing, however, they were generally called "the enemy".

This is an autobiography rather than a history of 16 Squadron, so I have introduced the SORB entries only when my name appears or when I was involved in the sorties or incidents described by the Adjutant. The large number of entries about other sorties and Squadron events have therefore been passed over. Equally, my Diary recorded only the events that interested me or involved me personally. I did not include any gossip and rarely wrote anything disparaging of other people; this was more for my protection if the Diary was discovered rather than to suggest that personnel of 16 Squadron or 34 Wing were saints or heroes.

Ranks and decorations are those held at the time. In SORB, the language and any mistakes are those of the Adjutant or his clerks. In the Line Book, brackets round serial letters or numbers indicate they were added post-war to identify the aircraft more fully.

Finally, the reader who has followed my career thus will far will be well aware that, at the age of 22, I was by no means an accomplished pilot, even though I was capable of flying the superb Spitfire XI: only one of the several official ratings written in my Log Book covering my three years of flying to date said I was more than "Average". In the Diary, I frankly admitted my difficulties, mistakes and failings; but I draw comfort today from the knowledge that Wing Commander Adrian Warburton, the ace photographic pilot in the Mediterranean theatre with two DSOs, three DFCs, and an American DFC, was notorious for his unreliable take-offs and landings.

Indicates an operational sortie

Indicates a non-operational flight

Diary

1st-26th August

I left Dyce on August 1st before the other boys had finished owing to the bad weather, and came home[1] for a fortnight's leave. I had a very good time, with a Youth Club Conference for a week, a Women's Institute garden fête and cricket match, swimming and tennis, and some glorious weather – almost the first this year. I also bought a 1930 Singer for £5, which I drove home from Whitchurch unlicensed and uninsured at 50 mph I.A.S.[2], and on whose rejuvenation I spent some considerable time.

[1] Cheam School was open in the holidays

[2] Indicated Air Speed

The day before I was due back I got a telegram from Dyce reminding me, so on the 14th I set off and, after standing from London to York, arrived at Aberdeen at 1.30 am. Not wishing to disturb my billetors[3] at Dyce, I eventually managed to find a bed with 3 others in Aberdeen and went to the Mess about 10.0 next morning. Here I discovered that Leagh and Scotty[4] had been posted immediately on completing the course to a place[5] in Hants, and Aldworth had been sent straight to a squadron in France. George Hozy, the only one left besides myself, was still on leave.

[3] on a farm

[4] Scotty Cadan and Leagh-Murray, both Australians

[5] Hartford Bridge

I spent the next three days in the Mess or in my billet or picknicking with the Goodwins[6] and getting increasingly bored, as there were only two other Mossie[7] crews in the pool and they had nothing organised for us.

[6] Dicky had trained and instructed with me in USA; he flew [7]Mosquitos

On Friday night we had a Station dance and Helen[8] came along to it, although not feeling very well. But the ludicrous thing was that, just before it started, Peter Walker – one of the instructors – came to me and said, *"Hey, you're posted!"* and the next minute George Hozy calls in from leave and says, *"What, haven't you gone yet?"* And then the sorry tale unfolds itself. Apparently, I was posted with 5 others on Monday and they left on Monday evening. A telegram was sent recalling me but, as no one had a very clear idea of who this Taylor was, they thought I was a Canadian; the fellow[9] in charge of the draft says, *"Oh, he'll turn up"*, takes my warrant and clearance, and departs with me supposedly with them – while my name stinks for not signing all the departure forms. I turn up on Tuesday morning, not realising that my telegram was actually a misdated immediate recall, and hang around, till someone thinks I must have returned to sign my papers and uncovers the whole affair. Well, I wasn't worried: there was nothing I could do about it, so I said Goodbye to Helen and Dicky and, next day, spent most of it getting signatures on my clearance to the accompaniment of an enormous amount of red tape.

[8] a local girl who taught me how to dance

[9] Michael Horsfall (Mike)

Eventually I departed on the 6.0 pm and reached K.X.[10] at 8.0 next morning, having met a great friend of Van B's[11] on the train, just going onto Lancs.[12] We had an excellent bath and breakfast in the K.X. Hotel, to the accompaniment of an almost coincident siren. I then took the train and had to wait an hour at Ealing. In that time distinct bumps were heard, and when I felt the whole sky reverberating over my head and the carriage windows shaking with my head, I realised I was scared stiff of doodle-bugs[13]. However, I forced myself to continue with my X-word instead of rolling into the nearest gutter, and was relieved to hear it explode a bit beyond.

[10] King's Cross

[11] Vanbergen, a school friend who was also in USA with me

[12] Lancasters

[13] V1 flying bombs

F/Lt Michael (Mike) Horsfall
Photo: Hugh Rigby Collection

F/Sgt 'Jolly' Jolliffe
Photo: Michael Horsfall

I eventually reached the main gates of Northolt at 1.0pm and thought what an excellent place this was going to be. I enquired for 34 W.S.U.[1] and got hold of a truck to take me and my luggage there.

[1] Wing Support Unit

Shock No 1 came when we passed the hangars and brick buildings and headed out for the open country. *"Oh no, Sir, we all live in tents."* And, by George, he was right! I reported to the Adjutant in a tent and he kindly told me to get some lunch; so I went to the Mess – another tent – got a tin plate full of dinner and sat down at a trestle table to eat it – shock No 2. It seemed incredible that here we were only 5 mins. out of civilisation, yet living and eating like Boy Scouts. I got talking to a Captain[2] and discovered that the Wing contained three squadrons of different types, all living as a mobile unit doing reconnaissance work.

[2] one of the Army Liaison Officers

When I got outside I found it had started to rain and I had my third shock – mud – and everything was soon churned to a shiny sticky quagmire. After filling-out arrival forms, I got a truck to take me to Wing stores and drew a camp kit, then went out to a camp site, selected a tent which had only two occupants, and erected the contents of my kit: one bed, chair, wash-basin, bath-tub, 3 blankets, pillow and a ground-sheet – very comprehensive.

I discovered I knew Horsfall and Scovill, so we were quite a happy party. Next day I went down to the W.S.U. – a sort of pool – but soon left to have my photo taken and go to stores. In the afternoon it clamped[3], so we didn't do much then either. On Tuesday we heard we might be going overseas, so we asked and got permission to take home our excess luggage. I got home at about 5.0 pm with a suitcase of dressing-gown, civvies, and my spare blues, and left again with Goop[4] at 7.30. I got in about 1.0 am and slept quite well in my blankets. I was beginning to get quite acclimatised to this kind of life.

[3] low cloud and rain

[4] our nickname for the owner of the local garage and taxi

Wednesday, it clamped all morning, but in the afternoon it cleared for Horsfall and Jimmy Wallace to go to Odiham to collect a couple of kites[5]. I was meant to take up an XI in the afternoon, but I had a tooth out – a bit of a bore – and didn't feel like it. Instead, I set off for home again as we were told the next day was our day off. I got a lift with the C.O. and he told me I was lucky to be the only Spit type. I informed him there were 4 of us, at which he said two had been posted. I said on the contrary: we had all been to 16 Sq. the day before and been told we were not wanted and would not be going overseas. *"Ho!"*, says he, *"I'll see about that!"* But it didn't affect my day off and I got home to find Helen[6] there, though Mum and Dad were still on holiday.

[5] aeroplanes

[6] my cousin, married to Grey-Smith, a pilot and now a POW

Coming back, my wretched train was late and I got stranded and spent the night on a sofa in the K.G.Club[7] in Piccadilly. Got out at 9.0 am and was told all four – that is, 3 and Jolliffe[8] – were going to 16 Sqdn. that day, but all non-flying personnel of 34 Wing were going overseas, starting tomorrow. We'd be following at a later date.

[7] King George

[8] F/Sgt 'Jolly' Jolliffe

Accordingly spent all day packing-up luggage and kit, moving flying stuff to 16 Sqdn's hut, and luggage to a house in Cavendish Avenue, where we'd be sleeping. We had our last meal at 5.0 pm out-of-doors as the tent had gone, and then took up our quarters in someone else's filthy rooms in the house.

* entered 18.9.95

YEAR 1944 MONTH	DATE	AIRCRAFT Type	No.	PILOT, OR 1ST PILOT	2ND PILOT, PUPIL OR PASSENGER	DUTY (INCLUDING RESULTS AND REMARKS)
16 Sqdn.		Northolt *	—	—	—	— TOTALS BROUGHT FORWARD
Aug.	26.	SPITFIRE XI	PL 834 Q834	SELF	–	LOCAL.
"	26	"	MB 954 K954	SELF	– 1.	A/F: BEACHHEAD : BAYEUX - CAEN 18000'.
Aug.	31	SPITFIRE XI	PA 933 J 933	SELF	– 2.	DUMPS : LILLE - LE CATEAU - VALENCIENNES 23000'.
SEPT.	2.	SPITFIRE IX	E 632	SELF	–	PRACTICE: L.L.O. SALISBURY - SWINDON.
SEPT	3	SPITFIRE XI	PL 830 PL Q830	SELF.	–	BEACHHEAD: 'MULBERRYS'. 30,000'.
"	"	SPITFIRE XI	PL 795 P 795	"	– 3.	DUMP: LE CATEAU, A/F: CHIMAY. 5000'
SEPT.	5	WELLINGTON	HZ 883	F/O BROADLEY	SELF (pass)	NORTHOLT - A12, FRANCE: LIGNEROLLES.
SEPT.	8.	SPITFIRE XI	MB 958 M958	SELF.	– 4.	VILLAGE S. of NANCY - NO PHOTOS. (first flak) 1200'.
SEPT.	9.	SPITFIRE XI	EN 654 F 654	SELF	–	A12 - GLISSY A/F, AMIENS.
SEPT.	11.	SPITFIRE IX	D	SELF.	–	GLISSY - NORTHOLT and RETURN.
SEPT.	12th.	SPITFIRE XI	MB 957 L957	SELF.	– 5.	ANTWERP & AREA NORTH MOSAIC 30000'. (First sighting of launching of V2?)
SEPT.	14th.	SPITFIRE XI	PA 869 T869	SELF.	– 6.	ROADS N. of BREMEN: CUXHAVEN, WILHELMSHAVEN 24000'.
SEPT.	18th.	SPITFIRE XI	MB 953 H953	SELF.	– 7.	IJMUIDEN : COASTAL GUNS, 24000'. (150' ceiling on return.)

GRAND TOTAL [Cols. (1) to (10)] 1166 Hrs. 20 Mins. — TOTALS CARRIED FORWARD

The page from my Log Book with my first seven sorties

Scotty and Leagh were already in the Squadron – they'd been posted to the place it had left months ago[1], of course – and we joined the Squadron with the minimum of formality. No one seemed to know whether we were really in it, but they were all quite glad as it would mean less work for them. We also drew filthy old battledress[2] to wear in France.

[1] 16 Squadron was based at Hartford Bridge, June 1943 – April 1944

[2] khaki, because RAF blue was too like German grey, but I preferred to wear it

The Adjutant's Summary in the Squadron Operations Record Book (S.O.R.B.)

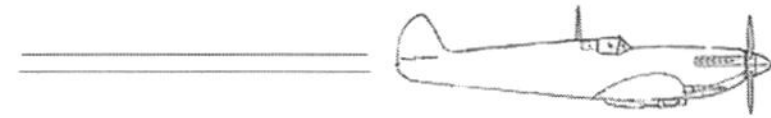

Northolt

26.8.44 Seven operational sorties were despatched to-day. Five of these were successful, two were abortive due to technical trouble. There were six non-operational flights. Four new pilots to the flight [Squadron] each did an operational sortie today. Three were successful in their missions. Main party of the Squadron moved over to France this morning at 0800 hrs. The Squadron was stood down in the afternoon, except for four pilots who were standing by.

Log Book*

Aug 26	SPITFIRE XI	Q[3] (PL)834[4]	LOCAL	1.20[5]
26	SPITFIRE XI	K (MB)954	1.[6] A/F:[7] BEACHHEAD: BAYEUX – CAEN. 18000'	2.10

[3] its identity letter

[4] its serial number

[5] duration of flight

[6] my first sortie

[7] airfields

Line Book

26.8.44	F/0 TAYLOR	SPIT XI	1500[8]	A/F Bridgehead.
	S/20"[9]	K 954	1715	Photos.
	18000' & 26000'.			
	16/[10]			

A/B[11] 1500. Out Selsey 26000' beneath cirrus 1519; in Port au Basin 1540. Photos 18000' beneath Cs.[12] Out P. au Basin 1635. In Selsey 1650. Landed 1715. No incidents.

HJS Taylor F/0.

[8] time of take-off and landing

[9] split-pair of F52s with 20" lenses

[10] 16 is the Squadron number/ the sortie number is missing

[11] airborne

[12] cirrus

Diary

26/8

Next day was the day of my first op., but I had better begin at the beginning. We reported at 9.0 am and, of course, were told to clean-up the hut[13]. The M.T.[14] of the troops moving out drove by at intervals and we waved them on. Then Mike and Jimmy were told there was a nice job for them photographing airfields in France, so they set off while Jolly and I hung around the hut.

At 1.30 pm Jolly took off for his first flight in an XI, and at 12.0 pm I managed to get a local flight to renew my acquaintance with the Spit and to look around the area. I was given a pink-coloured XI[15] used for dicing and, after rather a ropey take-off, I had a look at the extremely impressive balloon-barrage south of London and then flew on home. Here I managed to attract attention and saw people waving, though I couldn't stay long as too much

[13] the Squadron flight hut for parachutes, etc. and for waiting

[14] Motor Transport

[15] it must have been a IX, used for low-level sorties

*See Appendix F pp. 738-741 for the actual entries of my sorties in my Log Book, and the End Papers for a map of all my sorties.

Date 26 . 8 . 44 Aeroplane .... Pilot ....

WIND			NOTES
HEIGHT	FROM °T	SPEED	220/30 climb 220/45 ht

FROM	TO	T.A.S.	Height	True Track	Mag Course	Distance	G/S	Time
BASE	SELSEY	220	climb	194	208°	60	193	19
SELSEY	Port en Bessin	380	30000	174	190	103	338	18
Port en B	SELSEY	380	30000	355	000	103	400	15½
SELSEY	BASE	230	3000	015	023	60	242	15
								67½

Time	Observation	E.T.A.
1500	S/c SELSEY 21000′	
1519	S. S/c Pen B.	
	26,000 cirrus C/s 23500′	
1540	enemy coast.	
	C 24000 1–5, 1–10 21000′	
	B17 20000 – 18500 11–20 150°	
	18000 21–26 250°	
	B16 18500 26·32 150°	
	B10 18000 33–41 330	
	B4 18000 42–46 0	
	B5 18000 47–52 S	
	14 18000. 53·59 W	
	B3 18000 60–65 030	
	B9 18000 66–72 080	
1635	S/c SELSEY	
1650	cross coast.	
1716	pancake	

s/c = set course to

pancake = landed

165910M. Wt. 7492. 37,000. 12/42. W. & S. Ltd. 91-4224. FORM 433 A.

My knee-pad for my first operational sortie. The lower letters and figures are the titles of the airstrips, followed by my height, the exposure numbers on my counter, and my heading with my times at the bottom.

attention was obviously unpleasant[1]. I landed at 1.20 pm and got back to the flights at 1.45, to be told there was a job waiting for me – photographing airfields – take-off 2.45.

[1] if I was reported by a policeman

I didn't like the idea too much at first, but I was advised to take it as easy jobs didn't often come our way and it would be a good starter. So I piled into a truck and drove to the Ops. room. Here I filled-out an ops. form, handed-in my personal possessions, received an escape-kit and money, and was briefed by an Army officer. I was given a map with lots of airstrips shown on it, but 10 of them were marked as requiring to be photographed. I was warned there might be low cirrus and was given a small-scale map for navigating. I then returned to the flight hut and prepared my flight plan – the chaps being very helpful, one of them working-out the computer[2] for me. Having signed the authorisation book, I donned boots and Mae West[3] and took my 'chute, dinghy and helmet to the kite. Leaving the mechanics to fix it up, I went over and signed the 700[4], then returned and climbed in, as all was ready.

[2] the Dalton Computor was a manual calculator for working-out course and ground-speed

[3] inflatable life-jacket

[4] an authorisation form

Thankful for the fact that I had become familiar with the field from my previous flight, I started up, tested switches, supercharger, prop and radiators, taxied out, and took-off at 3.0 pm. After doing a half-circle, I set course, determined to fly as accurately as possible. I checked all the gauges, changed onto wing-tanks, and settled down for the climb.

Up till now I had been so hurried I hadn't had time to think of anything and just had confidence in my ability to cope; but ordinarily my imagination would have had full play and I would probably have been a nervous wreck when the time came. Now, however, when I realised I was really off on my first op. – albeit all over friendly territory – in imagination I had already finished this trip, then five trips, then a tour, before I had reached the coast, and had to tell myself severely it wasn't going to be such a piece of cake as all that and, anyway, anything might go wrong in the next two hours.

Guildford seemed to be in the right place, so I concentrated just on maintaining the same course and was quite happy when I saw Selsey Bill ahead and realised I was dead on track. I crossed the coast at 21000' and altered course slightly towards the French coast. Over to the right, in Southampton Water, I could see the sea speckled with ships over practically the whole area between the Isle of Wight and the shore. The cliffs on the Isle stood out white in the sun, and I noted them for the return journey. The Channel seemed to have little traffic on it today, though I saw occasional aircraft pass far beneath.

After 15 minutes I could see the coastline ahead, though only dimly owing to the haze. I could make out the outline of the Cherbourg peninsula and I tried to identify the curve of the coastline at Port-en-Bessin, where I expected to make a landfall.

It didn't take long to materialise and I was soon over a broad stretch of coast, anxiously trying to pick out my position from the map. At three points great piers seemed to run out into the water, and masses of shipping – dark outlines, like minnows in a pond – clustered around them. Then I realised that they weren't piers, but ships anchored bow-to-stern[5] and surrounded by lighters and barges – a hive of humanity.

[5] part of the Mulberry artificial harbour

**Caen Airfield in Normandy – my first operational photograph, taken on 26th August 1944.
The presence of British Army trucks confirmed that it was in Allied hands.
Note the aircraft (circled) at the end of the runway.**

Inland, the airfield strips I was meant to photograph stood out very plainly: sandy strips with dispersal points running out like arteries, but so many of them that I couldn't see how I was going to identify them. All along the coast bomb and shell craters stood out very markedly, at times forming lines, at times pitting whole areas, but everywhere giving evidence of colossal bombardments. But, from up here, it all looked serenely peaceful and it was hard or impossible to imagine that each crater told a story of blast and noise and destruction.

I could see two or three big towns along the coast and then a river mouth which, according to the map, must be the Orne. I had a large-scale map and the distances seemed quite big, but on the ground it seemed a very short way along the coast.

Tearing myself away from the role of an interested spectator, I realised I had a job to do, so I set about trying to identify the first airfield. But everywhere was so pitted with holes and the roads had been so messed-up with tank tracks that I despaired of doing it and, furthermore, the clouds were low, making it necessary to go below 20000'. After vainly looking at woods and rivers and relative positions, I gave it up and went along to the river mouth and decided to start from there and work backwards. Here I managed to recognise the right field and took some photos, but ran into cloud, so I went down to 18000' and made another run.

The next one was up the river in an angle of two roads leading into Caen. I had a look at the city as I passed over, but it was so battered it was hardly recognisable as a town. From above, it looked like an area of grey concrete with a few honeycombs at each end. On closer inspection, the honeycombs turned out to be the remaining walls of houses, but I couldn't see a roof anywhere. The concrete areas were just a mass of debris and rubble, and I understood suddenly why some of the French were bitter.

However, this was no time for day-dreaming, so I photographed the airfield, which was pitted with little holes from what I imagined were anti-personnel bombs, and then photographed strips as and when I recognised them.

About halfway through, my perspicacity seemed to crystallise and I grasped the layout of the ground beneath me: instead of being a confused picture of roads and strips and woods and more strips, I suddenly realised the interrelation of the roads, the lines of the trees and the location of the strips. From then on, recognition was no difficulty, though I wasted some time at pretty poor attempts at photography. However, eventually I'd done them all and, not without relief as I was beginning to get hungry, I crossed over the coast again and set course for home.

I had kept a vague lookout for other planes but had seen nothing at my level any of the time.. Below, I had seen odd formations returning to our lines, but never a sign of a puff of smoke or a flash of an explosion to indicate the thousands of men toiling beneath. Looking up the coast towards Calais and Boulogne, I told myself it was Hunland – but it failed to stir me at all. I wasn't concerned with anybody and a '190[1] could have shot me down with impunity.

[1] Fw190

S/L Tony Davis, DFC CO
Photo: Eric Martin

F/O Peter Cribb
Photo: Hugh Rigby Collection

F/O Michael (Mike) Wetz
Photo: Hugh Rigby Collection

P/O Peter Fahy
Photo: Peter Fahy

JT
Photo: Hugh Rigby Collection

Losing height all the way, I was glad to see old England again and to cross it where I'd aimed for. A string of barges was beating its way towards Southampton, and masses of light bombers were winging their way out over the sea, but I was more concerned with the fact that I could get no reply out of the radio. However, I didn't worry, but returned to Northolt and landed at 5.20 pm.

I went straight over to Ops, handed back my stuff, and made a trace of my movements and activities. They then remarked that they were starting to worry about me, as a Station had heard me call up but could only get the words *"I've had it!"*[1] I swore I'd never said such a thing, but I could see they were amused and unconvinced.

[1] this means "I've been shot down!"

Two hours later I had a look at the results and found the targets were quite nicely in the picture. But I also found I'd left one out altogether and never realised it, but no one seemed to mind. They were so busy that if a fellow failed to get a target, it just meant that someone else had to go out to get it, but they never had time to look it up and work out who had failed to get what. But I think, if I continue as I started, they shouldn't have any complaints to make about anything.

So ended my first op. and I have now got 79 more. I must say that it's a really good job and the cleanest way of fighting a war – and there's no doubt that it's a most important phase of the fighting, though you wouldn't think so from the casual attitude everyone has to the way the Squadron's organised. But I can see I shall have to find something to pass the time away while we are waiting for a trip, otherwise I shall be a nervous wreck, not from flying, but from sitting on the ground unoccupied all day.

Sunday 27th Aug. – Sunday 3rd Sept.

The day after my first op. I went home and was fortunate in being there to keep Chris[2] company on his '48.

[2] my younger brother who joined the RAF in 1944; he was on a 48-hour pass

The next few days were of a poor quality and, as we now had a full Squadron, few sorties were flown and I personally became pretty cheesed off. I got to know the boys on the Squadron by name, and also hoofed around getting odd things from stores.

On 31st, I had my second trip, when all four of us newcomers were up early at 5.45 am, breakfasted and were in the Ops. room at 7.0 am. My particular job was to photograph dumps at various places near Lille, Le Cateau and Valenciennes. I probably wouldn't see anything, I was told, but I was meant to just cover the area. Perhaps I'd better explain that, the night before, we'd had a Squadron party in a pub, but Mike and I left early knowing that we were due for a call in the morning.

S.O.R.B.

31.8.44

Eleven operational sorties were despatched over France, Belgium and Holland. Eight were successful and two unsuccessful due to weather conditions. One aircraft P/0. H.E.W. Colgate failed to return from an operation over Lille area, nothing is known of him.

Major Hugh Rigby, Oxs and Bucks Regiment,
Senior Air Liaison Officer of 34 Wing
Photo: Hugh Rigby Collection

Captain 'Bill' Bailey
one of several Air Liaison Officers
from the Army and RAF
Photo: Eric Martin

Log Book

Aug 31 SPITFIRE XI J (PA)933 2.[1] DUMPS: LILLE – LE CATEAU – VALENCIENNES 23000' 2.55

[1] Sortie number

Line Book

31.8.44	F/0 TAYLOR	SPIT XI	0805	DUMPS AT YPRES,
	16/1099	(PA933)	1100	LILLE, LE CATEAU,
	23000'.			VALENCIENNES (2),
	36"			ECHEUX.
				Photos.

A/B 0810. Out BEACHY 0830, in BOULOGNE 0838. Cloud ceiling of cirrus at 24000'. YPRES area unidentifiable due to cloud. One run made over Lille dump before cloud covered area. Clear areas at Le Cateau and Valenciennes. Overcast at Echeux. Out Boulogne 1030 In Dungeness 1038 Landed 1100 No incidents.

HJS Taylor F/0.

Diary

31/8

I set off O.K. and reached Boulogne via Beachy Head, but then had to fly over a sheet of cloud. At E.T.A.[2] a gap appeared, so I circled over it trying to find Ypres. It was my first experience of a Continental landscape from the air and it is quite horrible for identification. Everywhere, you can see nothing but fields, with straight roads, railways and rivers all running towards towns in a very orderly and therefore highly confusing fashion. At any rate, I spent twenty minutes now circling a spot, now darting off to have a look at a town, now trying to follow on a map the winds of a river. I know, at one point, I was at the Dutch frontier in my efforts. But finally I realised it was quite useless, so turned to go home or something – I hated to give up.

[2] Estimated Time of Arrival

Then, just as I turned, I spotted the haze of what could only be a large industrial town hidden under the clouds. I buzzed over quickly, praying it would be Lille and, thanks be, it was. From then on, it was comparatively easy going and I took a run over the nearby aerodrome before the clouds closed over it. From there I went to Le Cateau and made three runs over a dump in a wood – of which more anon. The other targets were obviously covered in cloud, so I made three more runs over an area near Valenciennes.

In my efforts to identify these targets, I had been twisting and turning a lot and the air was getting quite bumpy. While I was identifying my last target I felt suddenly cold and sweaty. Fearing a lack of oxygen, I turned it on full but got no relief. However, I continued and was halfway through the run when I felt suddenly sick. I snatched off my mask and vomited all over my clothes and the inside of the kite. I didn't feel particularly miserable, but I'd had quite enough and set course for home, and couldn't bother even to look at the map. However, I got back O.K., but my uniform was in a pretty mess. Later, I went to see the results and thought I'd covered two of the areas alright, but events afterwards proved me wrong.

Cheam School, near Newbury, taken from pink Spitfire IX 'E' 632 on my practice flight from Northholt on 2nd September 1944

Sailsbury Cathedral in a rain-storm on the same flight

From then on, the Squadron was expecting to move daily, but each day we were still there. But, eventually, on Friday the 1st of Sept. half of the boys flew off in the Spits and landed on the airfield[1] which our advance party had prepared a week ago.

[1]A12 airstrip near Balleroy, Normandy

S.O.R.B.

2.9.44

Only three operational sorties were despatched during the day, all of which proved to be successful. In addition to operational flying, seven non-operational flights were carried out. P/0. N. Bradbury landed at A. 12 in the morning and gave the news to the Adjutant regarding P/0. H.E.W. Colgate who was reported missing from operations on 31.8.44.

Log Book

Sept 2 SPITFIRE IX E 632 PRACTICE: L.L.O[2] SALISBURY – SWINDON 1.15

[2] Low-level Op

Diary

2/9

On Saturday there were very few ops, but I took a IX up to do a low-level x-c[3] with photos. The weather was very bad, with 800' ceiling, and I was almost lost in a storm before I started. But, eventually, I recognised Basingstoke, so flew to Kingsclere and took some pictures of home. Then I flew on to Salisbury, shooting trains and railway sidings on the way and a couple of shots of the Cathedral. It was just as well this was so conspicuous as I'd lost my way again en route and just glimpsed the spire in time. From there I went to Swindon, low down over Salisbury Plain, all over various prohibited bombing-ranges. At Swindon I took lots of railway yards, then flew a compass course to base, which ended up at Reading – well off track.

[3] cross-country

I was taking the yards there, concentrating on sighting over the side[4] and, for some unknown reason, looked ahead for a moment. I must have been losing height for there, right close in front of me was a whacking great line of high-tension cables! I just heaved back on the stick and thanked my lucky stars all in one gasp. From there I flew on to Eton and also to Windsor photographing both but, unfortunately, I later discovered I'd run out of film before this and hadn't taken either, though the ones of home came out very well.

[4] we sighted the oblique camera by looking over the left wing-tip

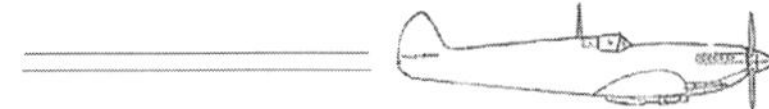

S.O.R.B.

3.9.44

Not very good flying weather to-day, only two operational sorties were carried out, and they managed to take photos.

A12 airstrip, near Balleroy, about 10 miles from Bayeux

16 Squadron Auster coming in to land on A12 in September 1944

Photo: Mike Horsfall

Log Book

Sept 3 SPITFIRE XI G (PL)830 BEACHHEAD: 'MULBERRYS' 30000' 1.45

.. .. SPITFIRE XI P (PL)795 3. DUMP: Le CATEAU; A/F CHIMAY. 5000' 2.30

Line Book

3.9.44 F/0 TAYLOR SPIT XI 1700 DUMP – Le Cateau
16/1118 P 1930 A/F – Chimay.
20" & 5"[1] Photos.

A/B 1700 out BEACHY 1715 in BOULOGNE 1733 30000' Cloudy overcast – broke cloud 19000' over DENAIN over 7/10 cumulus. Below cloud at 5000' for photos at Le CATEAU and CHIMAY. Returned in cloud at 20000' Out NIEUPORT 1900 in NORTH FORELAND 1920 Landed 1930.
No incidents.

HJS Taylor. F/0.

[1] two F52s with 20" lenses in the fuselage and an F24 with a 5" lens in each wing

Diary

Sunday was a particularly full day. After waiting around for a couple of hours, a call came through for a new bod to do an especially easy job. I wasn't exactly new but, as I was top of the ops. list, I took it and discovered the Navy wanted a view of the coast from Caen to Isigny to get an idea of the congestion and disposition of the shipping.

It was a gorgeous day and I quite enjoyed myself and hoped I'd done a good run along the coast. But to get to one 'Mulberry'[2], I had to go down to 15000', below the cloud and, while coming down, clocked 360 I.A.S.[3] On working it out later, I found that at 20000' this was equivalent to 500 mph, and at 25000' to 550 mph – the fastest I've ever been.

[2] concrete floating harbour

[3] Indicated Air Speed under-reads at height

I got back about 1.30 pm and, after lunch, returned to the flight and at 3.0 pm was told there was an op. for me. Apparently my morning's effort was hardly considered one and, anyway, I was quite keen to go; so I went down to Ops. and found that one of my targets was the same dump near Le Cateau I'd thought I'd photographed before, while the other was an aerodrome hidden in the forests near Chimay. S/L Davis[4] was also going to the same area, so we went to the Met. office together and were told that the weather would probably be clear over there, but it would be raining on our return.

[4] S/L Tony Davis, DFC was our much-respected C.O.

At 5.0 pm I took-off and climbed through about 15000' of cloud and reached Beachy at 26000', turning on ETA as it was quite invisible. I levelled off at 30000' and reached Boulogne in 8 mins. This too was under cloud, so I altered course on ETA and set off for Le Cateau, where I was due in 20 mins. About 5 mins. before ETA I decided it was time to go down below the cloud, although I could see a lessening of the cloud some way further off in the distance.

I broke cloud at 19000' and started anxiously scanning the landscape for a pinpoint. It took me a good ten minutes before I could identify all the roads, railways and canals as the country round Denain and Douai. Leaving there, I followed a railway to Le Cateau, but the atmosphere was so hazy and there was such a large amount of cumulus that I realised that I'd have to go much lower to get a clear picture.

Roadside Graves
Sad Evidence of the Normandy Fighting

140 Squadron Mosquito PRXVI parked on A12

The front-line was rumoured to be quite close, but no one knew exactly where the Americans or the Germans were. Accordingly, I felt quite excited and determined to crack down as fast as I could and beetle off again. The clouds were just above 5000', so I stayed in them as much as possible and just dropped down to check-up on my position. Then the moment came: I winged over and dived down over the wood, spotted the dumps, rolled onto course, switched on the cameras and held her steady, wondering what the flak[1] would look like. I still don't know. I did two runs then darted back into the cloud and headed for Chimay.

[1] German anti-aircraft fire

This was well into the forests and I had a job deciding whether or not I was over the right area. Eventually, I pinpointed a small town and set course from there. Three minutes later I should have been over the airfield. I scanned the woods and fields, but could see nothing. Then suddenly I noticed a country lane which had a kink in it for no apparent reason and which, on closer inspection, looked much broader than it should have been. One or two tracks led off into the woods and, for lack of anything else, I decided this must be the airfield – and a very cunningly concealed one. I made three screaming runs over it, but it seemed to be deserted and I found no incidents.

A little town lay nearby, but there were no trucks in the sidings and only one occasional lorry in the streets The roads on which the poplars cast their shadows showed no signs of life.

I decided to come back in cloud for safety, so climbed to 20000' and remained in cloud till I'd about reached England. Then I was called up on the radio and told that base was u/s[2] and I was to land at an unintelligible place. They gave me a course to steer, but later said Northolt was O.K. and, after a very bumpy and roundabout journey, during which I remember feeling remarkably happy, I landed – a very poor, almost ground-loop[3] effort – at 7.30 pm.

[2] unservicable

[3] one wing-tip touches the ground and pulls the aircraft around

Two days previously we lost Hugh Colgate. I was despatching officer and was almost the last to see him alive. He went to the Lille area – and just did not come back. I still hope he may not have been killed.

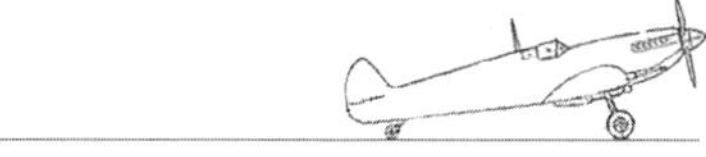

A. 12.[4]

[4] A = built by the Americans
B = built by the British

S.O.R.B.

5.9.44

Seven operational sorties were despatched during the day. The targets were based in Holland, France and Rhine districts in Germany. Five were successful and the two failures were caused by very bad cloud conditions in the target area. Early in the day when F/0's C. Leagh-Murray and Armstrong set off, conditions at base were particularly bad, after lunch there was an improvement. The C.O.[5] and F/0's M. Wetz and G. Cribb and P/0. P.E. Fahy after lunch went to the Rhine and the trip was successful. Quite a lot of flak was encountered here and a considerable balloon barrage was evidenced at Wesel. One non-operational sortie was flown by F/Lt. A.P.G. Holden who went to Dreux. All but two of the Squadron have now arrived at A.12. F/Lt A.G. Gibb and P/0. J.R. Brodby are expected tomorrow. This incidentally was the first day the Squadron became

[5] in an unusual 4-ship sortie, the pilots divided the Rhine between Arnhem and Wesel into 2 stretches and each took low-level obliques of one bank of a stretch.

l-r: F/Sgt 'Jolly' Jolliffe, F/O Jimmy Wallace and JT on A12 in September 1944
Photo: Michael Horsfall

P/O John Brodby with the 16 Squadron Auster on A12
Photo: Michael Horsfall

operational from its new base in France. During the period of change-over, a number of 'old hands' have left the Squadron namely F/Lt. J.B. Suttor whom we congratulate on receiving the D.F.C., F/Lt. G.H. Bastow, F/Lt M. Murphy and F/0 S.B. Spring. New pilots who joined the Squadron just before we left England were F/Lt J.M. Coldwell-Horsfall, F/0's J. Wallace, H.J.S. Taylor and F/Sgt. D.W. Jolliffe.

Log Book

Sept 5 WELLINGTON HZ885 F/0 BROADLEY SELF (pass.)[1]
NORTHOLT – A12,
FRANCE; LIGNEROLLES. 1.15

[1] passenger

Diary

On Monday I was told to prepare to leave by 1.30 pm, so got all packed up ready to go. In the morning the remaining Spit boys left and shot[2] the place up quite nicely. But an hour later they returned as the weather wasn't good enough. And after we'd chased around with the luggage, looking for our kite among the wrong Dakotas – amid general confusion and the lack of anyone in authority – we were told they weren't coming, so come back tomorrow! That night Mike, Brodby and I took two of the M.T. drivers out and saw a very good play called "Bird in Hand", had dinner at Frascatis, and slept at the Wings Club.

[2] dived down on it or 'beat it up'

Next day the Spits took-off again, but the Dakotas never came and we were told they might not be here for 2 or 3 days. Then essential personnel were informed that Wimpeys[3] of the W.S.U. would take them in the afternoon, but at 11.30 am I was told in the Mess that one was waiting now to take-off and I could go on it.

[3] Wellingtons

After ringing in vain for the truck with the Squadron luggage, I seized a motorcycle combination and, at great risk, rode it to the flight, discovered the truck, rode back to the Wimpeys, and put some of it on board, making sure that mine at least went. Brodby was to organise the rest of the luggage, then follow in the Anson.

I sat in the blacked-out midships of the Wimp, but got a real bird's-eye view through the flare-hatch. The trip was a bit bumpy, but I was fairly comfortable on the commode and read some of the time. After 1¼ hours we reached A12 and landed in France about 1.0 pm.

I saw my first Frenchman as I went in a truck down the odd mile or so of muddy road to the Mess. He wore the usual blue smock affair but otherwise appeared normal. The Mess looked identical to the tents at Northolt and there was no real indication of our being in France. Our tents were pitched near a blackberry hedge in an orchard with an old horse tethered nearby. Operations were quite close by, but the flight tent was a good 15 mins. walk down the road.

The field consisted of a strip of waterproof material overlaid with wire mesh, with a perimeter track round about. Our kites were littered around a detour of the perimeter track, with the Mossies next to us and the Wimpeys the other side of the field.

The first evening I spent erecting my camp kit and talking to various types. A few sorties had already set off from here, but most of the chaps had only arrived

Pink Spitfire IXs parked either side of the runway of A12

Pink and Blue Spitfires on A12

that morning. Next morning my name appeared near the top of the ops. list, so I had to stand-by at the flights. The next day the same thing happened again and the four of us who were waiting were getting distinctly cheesed off. The rest of the boys were meanwhile enjoying themselves by hitchhiking to Bayeux, Caen and the Falaise Gap and seeing the results of war at close quarters.

From my first day, there had been rumours that we were going to move again and, on the second day, the C.O. told us officially that we were leaving early Saturday morning, going to A[1] en route to B[1].

[1] my code for Amiens and Brussels

This move required quite a lot of organisation and our tents and not-vital luggage had to be ready by Wednesday evening; so we spent that afternoon packing up after staying just one night in the orchard. We then hunted around for a place to sleep, some of the boys going to the flight tent and others preferring to sleep under the trees or under a hedge. Mike, Jimmy and I decided that neither would suit us and, eventually, I discovered a barn with the majority of the roof intact but possibilities of lice or animal fleas. However, we decided to risk it and made ourselves comfortable, and soon Jerry Winter and Peter Fahy joined us. The Mess had also half departed and we ate rather scruffily on bully-beef stews, etc.

On Thursday night, the four of us decided we'd had enough of waiting for ops. that did not materialise and asked for the next day off. The C.O. okayed it, and Mike and I agreed to fly down to St Malo in the Auster. Of course, as luck would have it, an op. came through, so I cancelled my trip with Mike and went to bed early for an early rise.

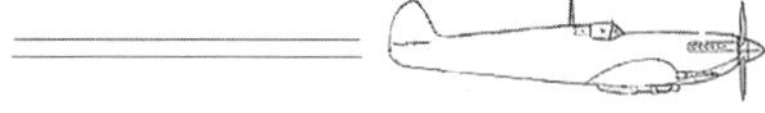

S.O.R.B.
8.9.44

No entry

Log Book
Sept 8 SPITFIRE XI M (MB)958 4. VILLAGE S. of NANCY – NO PHOTOS.
(first flak) 1200'. 3.30

Line Book

8.9.44	F/0 TAYLOR	SPIT XI	0830	Village of Nemoxy
	16/	M	1200	S. of Nancy.
	S/36", 5".			No Photos.
	30000'			

A/B 0830 Started letting down through cloud at 32000' 10 mins before E.T.A. broke cloud 1500' indicated. Pinpointed apparently at JOINVILLE, but low cloud and heavy rain prevented accurate observation. Followed railway for 5 mins and unexpectedly met red flak at junction. Made detour in cloud but never managed to identify landscape. After 30 mins fruitless stooging returned to base landing at 1200 hrs.

HJS Taylor. F/0.

Diary

Next morning I was up before dawn and, after a bit of bread and a cup of tea from our improvised Mess, I was briefed and took-off at 8.30 to photograph

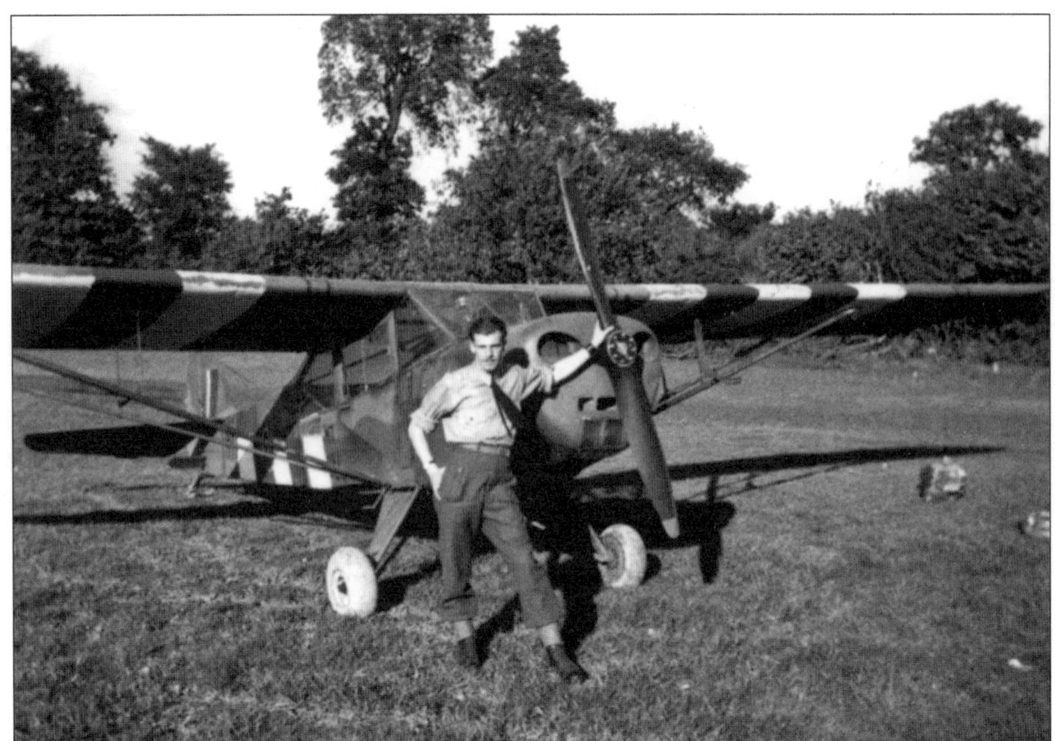

F/O 'Gerry' Winter with the 16 Squadron Auster on A12

Members of 34 Wing outside the Ops. tent on A12
l-r: ? P/O John Brodby ? ? ? F/O 'Scotty' Cadan (behind) F/O Leagh-Murray
Photo: Michael Horsfall

a small village near Nancy, a photo of which was needed to prove that some Mosquitos had pranged[1] it. I was meant to take-off at 8.0, but various causes, such as a case of Normandy tummy, a lack of bods[2], the wrong oxygen fitting, and the unreadiness of the kite, delayed me.

I passed over Paris at 30000' with a clear blue sky and was sorely tempted to take a photo of the Eiffel Tower, Arc de Triomphe and Notre Dame with a 5"[3]. However, I thought I'd better press on, but soon arrived over some cirrus. When I got within 5 mins. of Neuf Chatel, I decided it was time to come below the cirrus to pinpoint myself. I went down – but it wasn't cirrus but thick stratus[4] all the way to 2000'. Here I thought I was getting too low, but went on to 1500', when I was glad to spot the earth through a break.

The clouds were only about 700' above the terrain and it began to rain after a while, so that it took me at least 10 minutes to find myself, I think, at Joinville. From here I set course for the village, but the vis.[5] was so bad that I returned and started off again, this time following a railway. I went on quite well until I came to a junction which, however, had a large canal which, from the map, wasn't so conspicuous. I throttled back while I looked at the map again to check-up on this. When I looked up again – I was flying at 1200' – I noticed red Very[6] lights shooting up underneath me. Thinking I must be over the front-line, I was about to turn back when I realised startlingly that they were being fired at me and were not Verys but tracer or flaming onions[7] – I don't yet know which. This demanded action, so I poured on the coal and shot up into the clouds, still pursued by flak. They must have been rotten shots, as I could see a liberal spray passing underneath, yet I was only going about 200 mph at 1200' at the time.

I then made a detour round the hostile region, but failed to find anything to pinpoint. Eventually I did discover a railway tunnel, but it failed to correspond with the only one on the map. Then I tried going down over a village and reading the signposts and though, by flying below the church steeple, I managed to read the names, I couldn't tell the distances, so that it wasn't really much use. After spending more than 30 mins. in this useless fashion I decided conditions were against me and set course roughly for home

After flying for about 30 mins., the ceiling lifted until I was flying under a clear sky and I knew that I must be in the Paris region. Accordingly, I started to follow a broad road, on the assumption that all roads led to Paris; but when it turned due north I decided against it. I then started to climb to increase my area of visibility, but could see no identifiable object.

An hour had now gone by and I should have been almost home, but I hadn't the vaguest idea where I was. Being at 10000', I called up on the radio on both channels, but got no reply. Later, I tried again and this time Penman[8] replied that they could hear me very faintly. Eventually I got a homing from them, but the fact that I flew NW for nearly 30 mins. showed that I must have been about 50 miles south of Paris, which meant pretty poor navigation.

That afternoon I went to Bayeux with Gerry Winter and found it rather a picturesque place with narrow streets, but only a few civilians among the throngs of troops. The shops had a certain amount in the windows but not much

[1] bombed

[2] airmen

[3] 2 wide-angle cameras in the wings

[4] cloud layer

[5] visibility

[6] signal flares

[7] an incandescent form of flak

[8] call-sign of our base radio, which could give us a compass course to bring us home

Bayeux Cathedral, Normandy
with a French policeman and a British Army truck

The 'monastery' I photographed with my own camera on my way to Amiens-Glisy
in Spitfire XI EN654 (on the front cover of this book)

selection, though there seemed to be plenty of meat. The Cathedral was a fine upstanding building, with two steeples and a domed tower made up from various periods, starting apparently from Norman times. The Tapestry had been removed for safety, but a very crudely painted reproduction gave promise of a feast of interest for the original. The roads were crowded with transport, among which 'ducks'[1] loaded with crates stood out rather incongruously.

[1] amphibious vehicles

We got back to find that our camp kits had to be packed by 6.0 am next day and that we were leaving around 9.0 am.

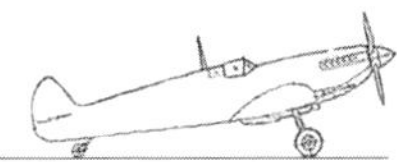

Amiens/Glisy B48

S.O.R.B.

9.9.44

Only two sorties were flown during the day. These were despatched to Holland and Germany. The one to Germany was successful but only partially. W/0. W.J. Willshaw managed to take photographs of the mouth of the Elbe. F/0. James Wallace who only recently joined the Squadron from 34 W.S.U. failed to return from his sortie. Communication being not up to scratch just yet, we have great hopes that Jimmy is O.K. These two sorties flown to-day were our first from Amiens, our pilots and aircraft only arrived here this morning from A.12.

Log Book

Sept 9	SPITFIRE XI	F	(EN)654	A12 – GLISSY A/F, AMIENS	1.00

Diary

Saturday, 9th September

Having arisen at 5.0 am and got everything ready, we breakfasted off bacon sandwiches and saw the kites leaving at 8.0 in good order, and hoped they'd be at A in time for us that night. Mike and I decided to leave together and do a spot of sightseeing as he had no map, but a spot of bother arose over flat accs.[2] and he left before me.

[2] accumulators

I first flew to Caen and had a good look at it and took some pictures[3], and then went on to Falaise and Argentan. Here the ground was pitted with bomb and shell holes everywhere, but I couldn't see any sign of wrecked transport. Falaise itself was practically flat, Lisieux was rather similar, but a large cream-coloured monastery seemed to have been mostly spared.

[3] with my personal camera

Villages along the Seine were rather battered, but I noticed that at Rouen a temporary bridge had already been built on the foundations of a former one. The Cathedral seemed to face clear ground, but whether it was the result of bombing or intended I could not tell. I reached Amiens[4] without trouble, but made the most awful landing, which rather disappointed me as my previous one had been quite smooth.

[4] Amiens-Glissy airfield. I seem to have forgotten about security

Most of the other chaps had arrived and were putting up the tents. The flight was only about 5 mins. walk from the Mess and our tents about 100 yds from there, so the situation was quite favourable. After lunch on the floor of the Mess tent, Mike and I walked around the airfield.

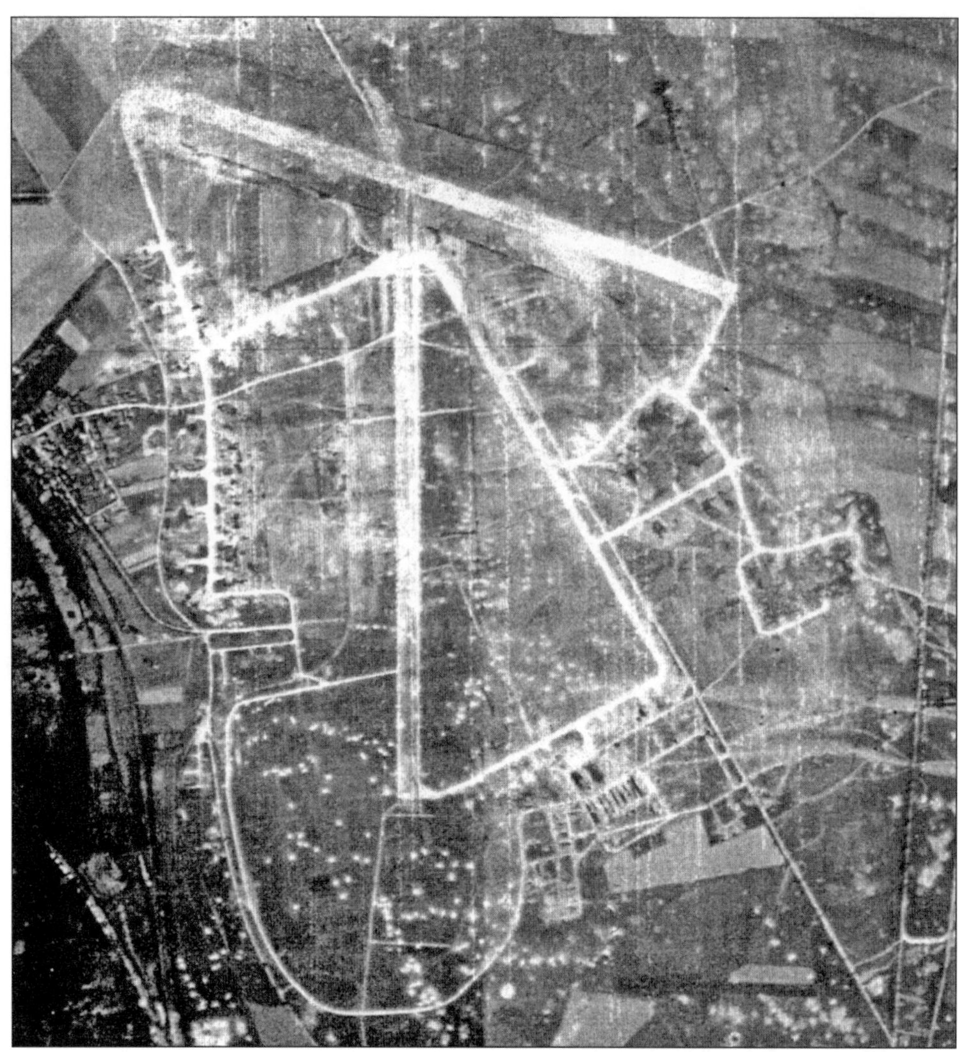

B48 Amiens-Glisy airfield

Photo: Hugh Rigby Collection

**Camouflaged German hangars on Amiens-Glisy airfield.
Note the netting reaching the ground from the adjacent roof.**

It was a large 'drome with two runways only, only one of which had been made serviceable for us. On three sides were wooden hangars, very skillfully camouflaged as houses by a painstaking Jerry, but as conscientiously blown up and rendered useless before he left. Remains of a dummy Ju88 and some Me 109's were also visible but, otherwise, absolutely nothing of any use had been left behind. On the far side we were picked up by the Padre in a truck and he took us on to a deserted village, which had been extended by dummy houses to cover up the presence of hangars. All the cottages and the church were absolutely bare[1], stripped in a most thorough fashion.

[1] we had been preceded by soldiers and another squadron

When we got back, we found Jimmy Wallace had already gone off on an op. but was a bit late in returning, and there was still no news of him next morning.

We'd settled into our tents quite comfortably, though most of us were almost frozen that first night. Unlike A12, here we really knew there was a war on. There were no guards on the field, but the FFI[2] were everywhere – young men with armlets and rifles, who wandered around and had caught five German snipers in the woods the night before. Everywhere, too, were civilians, wives and children, who came and went as they pleased. Odd German bombs lay around, and we pinned up a picture of the Fuehrer near the tents. The wrecked hangars provided a copious supply of wood for tent furniture and, as Amiens was only a few miles away, we felt quite comfortable, only hoping that the rear party would hurry up, to make the Mess and food more palatable.

[2] Free French Insurgents

In the morning, Bill Burton pranged a Spitty when the u/c[3] collapsed on landing.

[3] undercarriage

Saturday - Saturday 16th

During this time, we got settled in and really felt quite satisfied. The food in the Mess wasn't too good, as it all seemed to come out of a tin – sausage meat for breakfast and bully-beef stew for dinner and supper.

The saddest news was that Jimmy Wallace was found dead near his kite after, apparently, spinning down from a great height before even crossing into enemy territory. Our theory is that he failed to see to his oxygen properly; but, whatever it was, it was a very poor show. Mike spent the next day or two packing up his kit and, though I felt very impersonal about it most of the time, I must say I felt a bit shaken when the Adj. gave me his ring and lighter to pack up, and showed me the Certificate of Burial.

Mike and I went to Amiens one afternoon, but except for the Cathedral, which we found really beautiful, we found little of interest in the town. The railway station was wrecked out of all recognition and so were the streets round about, but we learned that most of the damage in the town itself was done by the Germans in 1940. The shops were not very showy and had little except what was displayed in the windows. The styles were often very up-to-date, but the quality of the material was not very high.

One big store we entered had a wonderful display on view, and some of the cutlery and toys were of very good quality, but the obvious effort to impress was almost pathetic. We had some beer and red wine at a couple of cafés, but left

Remains of dummy Me109s on the airfield

A dummy Ju88 on the airfield

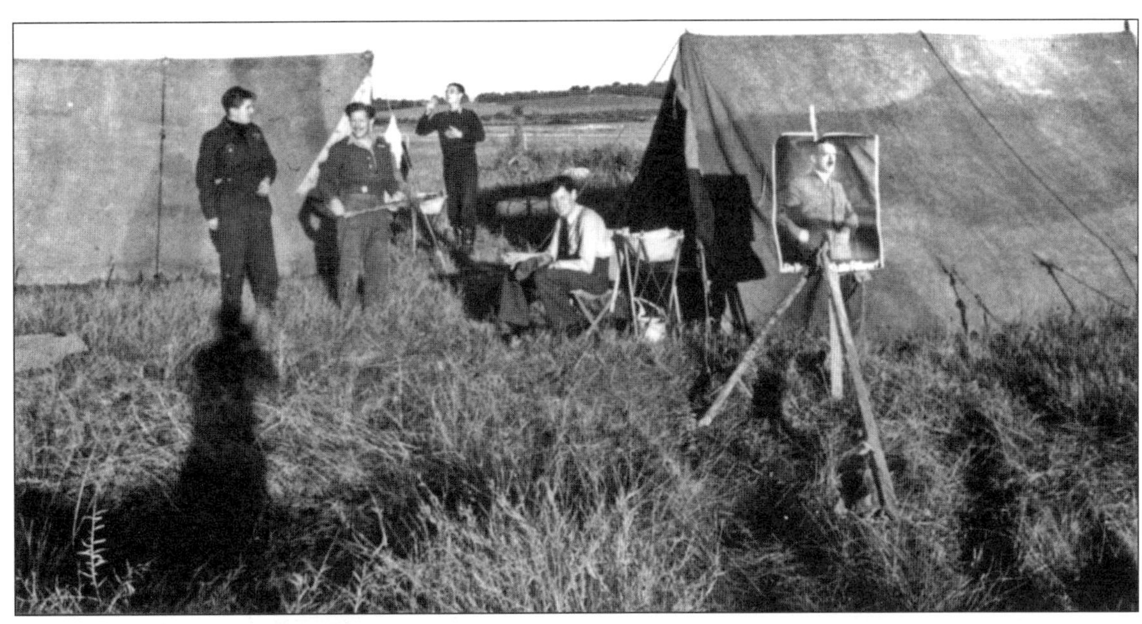

Roughing it with Hitler at Amiens-Glisy in September 1944
l-r: F/L Derek Wales, F/O 'Scotty' Cadan, RAAF, F/O Leagh-Murray, RAAF, and JT
Photo: Michael Horsfall

Larking-about at Amiens-Glisy
Some airmen out shooting rabbits had just captured two German soldiers in a nearby wood.
1-r: F/L Derek Wales, JT, P/O Peter Fahy, F/O 'Gerry' Winter, and F/L 'Tommy' Thompson, RCAF
Photo: Michael Horsfall

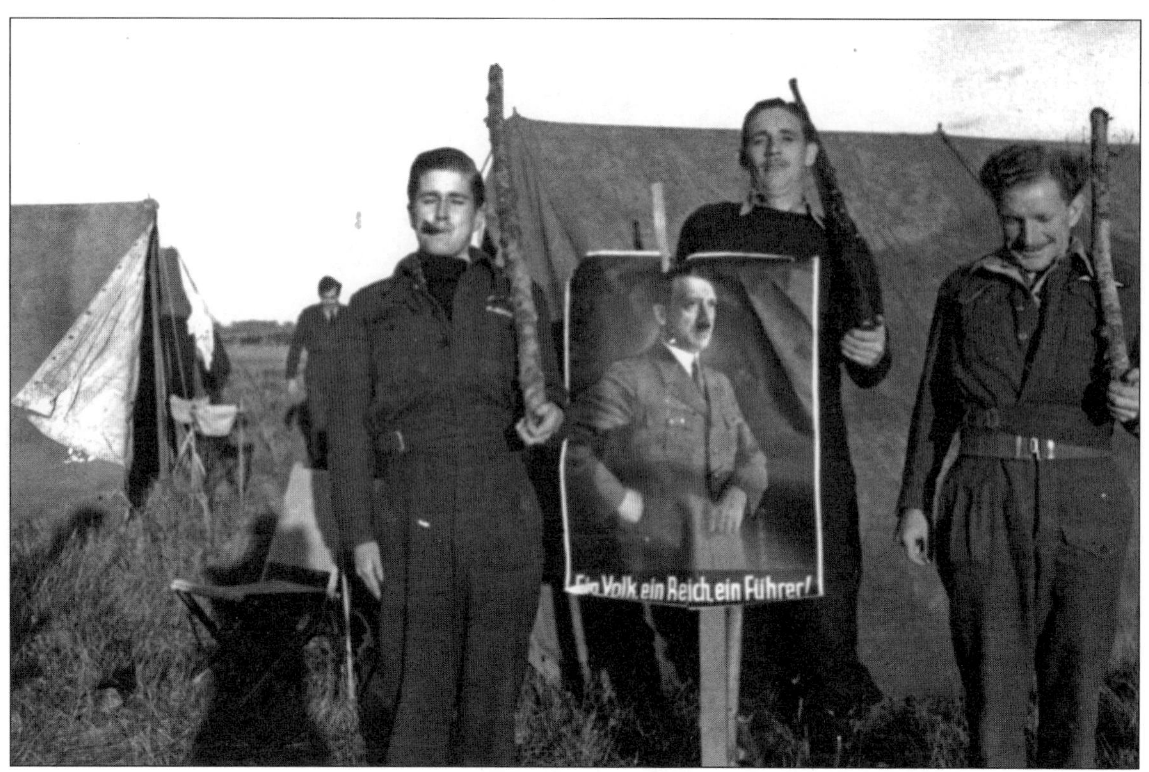

More tomfoolery at Amiens-Glisy
1-r: F/Lt Derek Wales, F/O Leagh-Murray, and F/O 'Scotty' Cadan
Note the canvas chair and wash-basin behind them.

Photo: Michael Horsfall

The 34 WSU Anson, flown by F/Lt 'Pete' Petrie, DFC,
landing at Amiens-Glisy in September 1944

quite early as we saw no cinemas or other forms of entertainment. We left in state, hitching a ride with a farmer on his trap. Later on in the week, 7 of the boys went to Paris by car, but Mike and I were unlucky and contented ourselves with a walk to a nearby village. The children were very friendly and insisted on shaking hands with us, and surprised us by taking English money, but refusing French.

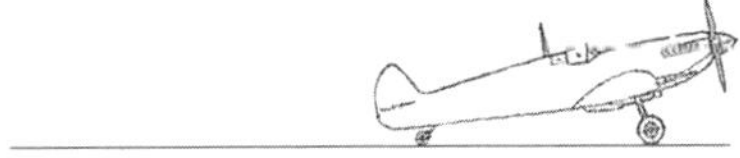

S.O.R.B.

11.9.44

Nine operational sorties were despatched over Germany and Holland. Of these seven were successful, one partially and the other abortive. F/0. Cadan's trip was abortive due to engine trouble. He returned to base abandoning his task. Quite a number of incidents were reported. F/0. Leagh-Murray saw what he believed to be 4 M.E. 410's. F/0. M. Wetz was disturbed by an unidentified aircraft in the Ghent area. Flak was reported by another pilot in the Cuxhaven Estuary. F/Lt. A.P.G. Holden saw many fires at Breskens and noticed ships ferrying between Breskens and Flushing. Sad news received to-day that F/0. James Wallace for whose safety we entertained great hopes has been killed near Douai.

Log Book

Sept 11 SPITFIRE IX D GLISSY – NORTHOLT and RETURN. 1.40

Diary

I did two ops. in the period, neither of them without incident. but I had a little trip to England the night before the first one. I was Orderly Officer that day – the first at Amiens – but tried to go on an op. about 4.30 pm. But Wales[1] on two occasions took my kite as his own was u/s, so that I never took-off, though crowds of civilians milled around waiting to see me go.

Feeling rather cheesed, I offered to take a message to England from the C.O., recalling two of our boys[2] who had been sent to Northolt to stand-by while we moved. Actually, there were three of them, but Louie Hill had had a nervous breakdown and been grounded. I got there alright, but almost missed Northolt altogether as there was a terrific haze and I couldn't see a thing.

It was getting dark when I left and I had to go down to 500' before I reached Amiens, but I got in O.K. That night, I got up at 2.0 am to inspect the guard – what little I could find of them – and then was up at 6.0 for my op. at 8.30 am.

[1] F/Lt Derek Wales, killed in 1946 flying mail from Berlin in a Spitfire

[2] Scotty Cadan and John Brodby

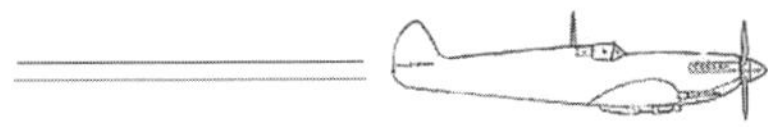

S.O.R.B.

12.9.44

Eight operational sorties were despatched over Germany and Holland during the day. Six trips were successful and the other two were abortive due to cloud conditions over task area. F/Lt. D.W.H. Wales saw large fires at Breskens. F/O. H.J.S. Taylor saw strange vertical contrails 20 miles N. of the approaches to Ghent, they

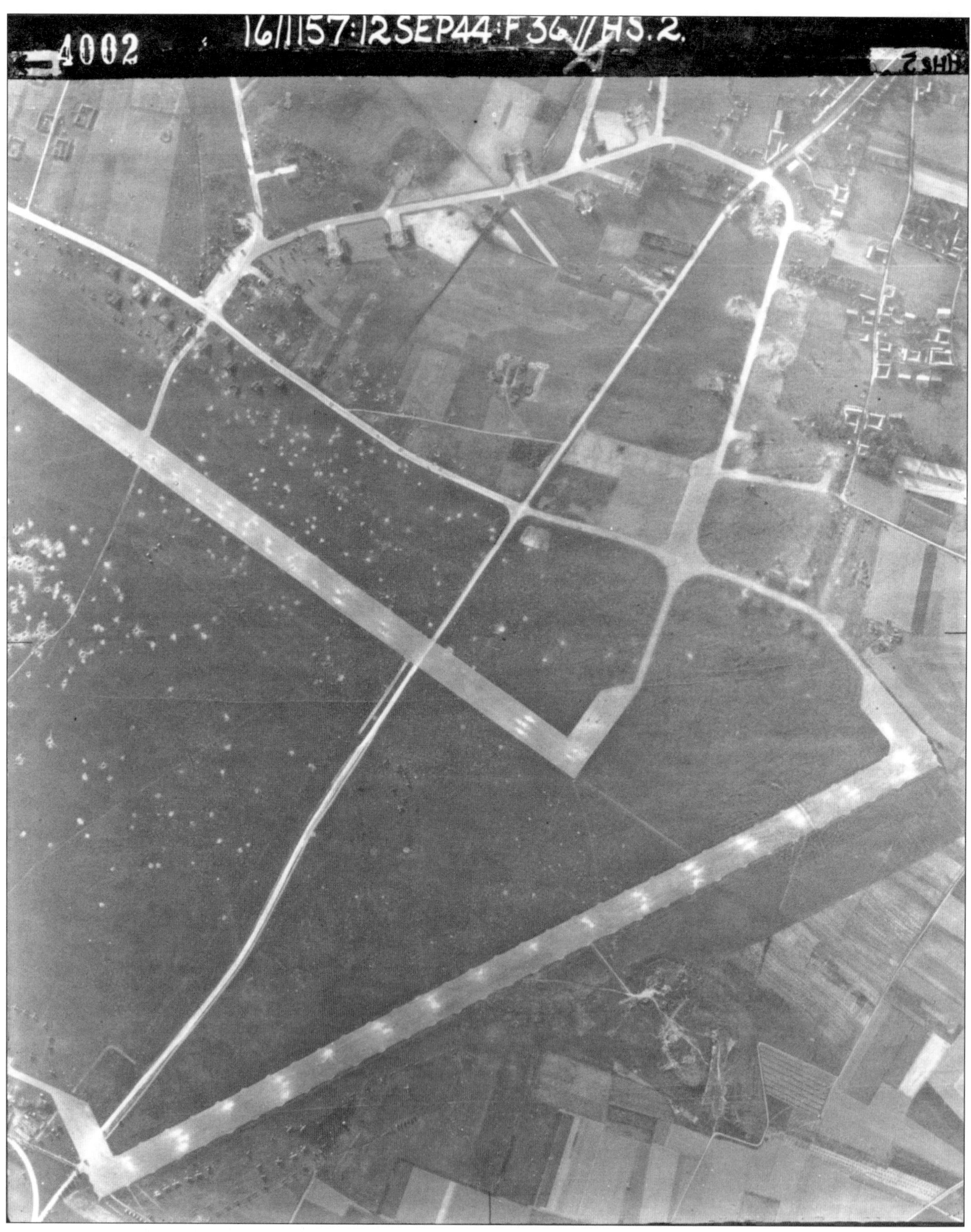

Photo of Lille-Valenciennes airfield on my sortie of 12th September when I failed to catch the vertical contrail of a V2 rising through the clouds.

ascended to apparently 45,000'. F/0. G. Cribb corroborated observation of the visions. W/0. W.J. Willshaw saw heavy bombers over the Ruhr meeting concentrated flak. F/Lt. G.H. Bastow and F/0. S.B. Spring, two of the old brigade now with W.S.U., brought a couple of Spitfires to us from Northolt. They stayed to tea and we were all pleased to see them.

Log Book

Sept 12th SPITFIRE XI L (MB)957 5. ANTWERP & AREA NORTH MOSAIC 30000' 1.50
(First sighting of launching of V2?)

Line Book

12.9.44	F/0 TAYLOR	SPIT XI	0825	Antwerp.
	16/1157	L 957	1015	Area Bergen – Antwerp.
	36"			Photos.
	30000'			

A/B 0825 Photos 0930. Landed 1016.
Saw strange vertical con. trail not less than 20 miles N. of my position when approaching Ghent. Trail started at 30000' and ascended rapidly to apparently 45000' when it stopped, but course may have continued higher. I was making short dispersable trails at the time. F/0. Cribb corroborated observation of 'the vision'. Portent of V2?

HJS Taylor. F/0.

Diary

It was quite a pleasant little trip to Antwerp and an area north of it, and I think it would have been successful but for the fact that one of my cameras went u/s without my knowing. On the way, though, I saw a strange contrail going vertically from 30000' to about 45000'. At first I thought it was a plane coming down, but then I realised it was going up and decided it must be one of those rocket planes[1]. Then I realised it was going up much too fast for a human being, and made up my mind that it was an experimental rocket. I reported it when I got back – and Peter Cribb corroborated it – and I soon found I'd started quite a flap, as a large explosion had occurred in London, suspected of being a V2[2] – in which case, as the times agreed, my trail was a V2 starting into its initial flight.

[1] Messerschmitt 163

[2] the first V2 fell on Chiswick on 8th September; mine fell at Keston in Kent

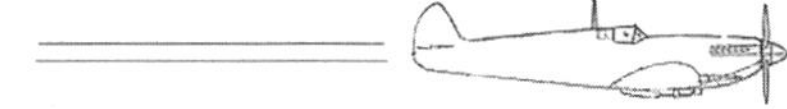

S.O.R.B.

14.9.44

Six operational sorties were despatched over Holland and Germany during the day. Of these four were successful. Two were failures because of cloud conditions over the task area. A number of incidents were reported. F/Lt. J.M. Horsfall being intercepted by an unidentified aircraft which climbed to attack, it was then lost sight of. Another pilot, F/Lt. A.P.G. Holden reported heavy and accurate flak over Cuxhaven. One burst tipping his aircraft violently. He got away without mishap fortunately. F/Lt A.G. Gibb had to abandon his sortie, his engine showed lack of power when he climbed. Some non-operational flying was accomplished, mainly local and air tests.

Michael Horsfall sitting on a blown-up bridge over the Somme during one of our walks in September

Riding in a horse-drawn cart through Amiens city with Allied trucks in convoy

F/O Michael Wetz (right) and F/Lt Norman Godfrey
Photo: Norman Godfrey

W/O 'Willy' Willshaw
Photo: Hugh Smallwood "Spitfire in Blue"

l-r: F/Sgt Harry Simkins, P/O Peter Fahy, F/Sgt 'Jolly' Jolliffe, and P/O Norman Bradbury outside administration tents at Amiens-Glisy
Photo: Peter Fahy

Wilhelmshaven harbour: 6 exposures with 60% overlap, part of a line-overlap taken from 24,000ft on 14th September 1944 when I was returning from a sortie. The white smudges are a smoke-screen started-up because of my arrival overhead.

Log Book

Sept 14th SPITFIRE XI T (PA)869 6. ROADS N. of BREMEN:
CUXHAVEN, WILHELMSHAVEN
24000' 3.25

Line Book

14.9.44	F/0 TAYLOR	SPIT XI	1325	Roads N. of Bremen.
	S/20"	T 894	1650	Photos.
	20000'			
	16/1181			

A/B 1325. Over 10/10 cloud from ANTWERP onwards. Descended to 19000' 5 mins before E.T.A. and pinpointed OSNABRUCK. Altered course to BREMEN and photographed road at 24000'. Finished run and then discovered it was wrong road. Wasted time looking for the right roads and photographed another. On leaving target area let cameras run over CUXHAVEN and WILHELMSHAVEN. Landed 1650 rather short of fuel. Discovered first run was unwittingly along another road required. No incidents.

HJS Taylor. F/0.

Diary

My other flight was my first over Germany, to Bremen to take some .secondary roads. I had a job getting there as it was over 10/10[1] most of the way and, after my first run, I discovered I'd taken the wrong road. The road was very curving and, after each exposure, I had to tip the plane onto its wing to make sure I was following the road along alright. I was pretty mad at this mistake, but managed to find the right road, only to have excessive finger trouble in failing to switch-on the cameras properly and in getting confused over the roads again.

[1] 100% cloud cover

Eventually, I had to leave before I'd finished and, on the way home, let my cameras run over Cuxhaven and Wilhelmshaven[2]. These should have been hot-spots and I was prepared for any sort of trouble, but fortunately nothing happened. The petrol situation was touch-and-go, but I managed to get in with 10 gallons, after a lot of worrying and radioing en route.

[2] the photos revealed a smoke screen set off on my approach

Later, from my plot I was delighted to find my original run followed exactly the second road I should have taken and that, in fact, I had covered every single yard of my allotted target.

Saturday 16th - Tuesday 19th

Little happened on Saturday. We sat around all morning and, in the afternoon, Mike and I walked to a nearby village, gathering blackberries from a marshy area of the Somme. We also came across a well blown-up little bridge. In the village we found the children quite charming, very keen on shaking hands and holding them while we walked down the street. One lot surprised us by refusing to look at French money, though they were begging for English money. I noticed that one of the little devils had at least 1/6d before they asked us!

In the evening we fraternised with the photo-interpretation types, whom we find very friendly and cooperative.

Sunday was very similar, except that I walked over to a Harrow[3] and had a look at it. Grand old lady.

[3] an obsolete transport

Part of my mosaic of Ijmuiden taken on 18th September 1944 from 24,000ft by one of 2 F52s with 36" lenses

Photos: DotKa, Holland

S.O.R.B.
18.9.44

To-day proved to be a black day in the Squadron's history. Two Flight Commanders F/Lt. A.G. Gibb and F/Lt. A.P.G. Holden are casualties. F/Lt. Gibb we know for certain has been killed. He crashed a very short time after taking off from base. F/Lt. Holden is reported missing, we are more than hopeful that we shall get good news of him very soon. The Squadron feels these losses sustained very deeply and quite a gloom has been cast over us all. Altogether nine sorties were despatched. In addition to the mentioned tragedies, F/Lt. D. Wales came back to base – safely we are glad to say – with engine trouble. Two other trips were abortive due to cloud conditions over the task area. Four pilots were successful in taking photographs. Conditions at base when pilots returned were shocking, but they all made wizard landings. There was no non-operational flying and in the afternoon the Squadron stood-down.

Log Book

Sept 18th SPITFIRE XI H (MB)953 7. IJMUIDEN: COASTAL GUNS
(150' ceiling on return) 2.10

Line Book

18.9.44	F/0 TAYLOR	SPIT XI	1045	Area N. and S.
	S/36"	H 953	1255	of IJMUIDEN.
	24000'			Photos.
	16/1203			

A/B 1045. 10/10 cleared at AMSTERDAM enabling 3 runs over target to be taken and 2 over harbour. Descended through cloud S. of Ghent and returned at 300', landing at 1255. No incidents.

HJS Taylor. F/0.

Diary

Monday was full of bitterness and remorse, and was one of the worst days I've lived through. There were 6 early take-offs but, as I was 7th on the list, I wasn't troubled. But the weather was duff, with a thick clamp and very bad vis. At 8.30 am I looked in at Ops. and found four of the pilots with the C.O. and G/C[1] debating the situation. The G/C was urging them on, but Holden, Gibby[2] and Wales were remonstrating that, with the long distance they had to go – about 400-odd miles each way – they would have no margin for detouring round or under the cu.nimbus that was forecast en route. Furthermore, conditions at base would not improve, while there was no advantage in going down at Brussels as there was no radio contact.

However, eventually they went off and, not long afterwards, Peter Cribb, Bradbury and self were briefed for trips to Holland, where it was expected to be clear. I took-off at 10.45 am, leaving Gibby still on the ground, looking very depressed and obviously not keen on going. I found myself in cloud practically immediately after take-off, but I was surprised at emerging into blue sky at 8000'. I continued to climb to 24000' – my operational height – but when my ETA was reached, I was still over 10/10 and no gaps to be seen in any direction.

[1] Group Captain Pat Ogilvie, DSO, DFC, CO of 34 Wing

[2] F/Lt Tony Gibb

Low-level view of Amiens and its Cathedral on a postcard

Amiens Cathedral from the Squadron Auster

Giving a mental raspberry to Met., I thought I'd go on and see just where the clouds ended, for Met's information. Accordingly, I flew for another 15 mins. before I came to the edge of the front. Then I was surprised to see some islands in front – must be the Frisians[1]. Flying on a bit more, I suddenly saw a large town, which must have been Amsterdam, not far from my target. Thanking my lucky stars, I continued on and did two runs over Ijmuiden, with two more over the harbour and one more for luck, to cover up any holes.

[1] more likely, inland lakes south of the Zuider Zee

Coming back, the clouds started very soon, so when I got over about Flushing, I began to let down to get below them over country that was almost at sea-level. At this time I could hear various of our other kites calling in for homings and, as their need was obviously greater than mine, I kept off the air and decided to go down to the deck early. I calculated I was just south of Ghent when I got out of cloud at five hundred feet – a bit low. I then flew for quite a time on my course, but failed to recognise any of the country from the map. I then started to call Penman, but could get no reply – which didn't surprise me as I was very low. Eventually I heard them answering someone else, so I called again and established contact. Here I got a homing and continued on, concentrating on avoiding the hills, which were only just below the clouds, while vis., especially in showers, remained very poor.

I must have been about 20 miles from the field when another Spitty dashed into view and I had to take evasive action to avoid a collision. He flew up alongside and I thought it was Peter Cribb – though actually it was Bradbury, who'd changed kites.

After one more course, I suddenly saw Amiens church-spire in front and roared low over the town. I didn't know what direction to take from there, but decided I could do no worse then go on; so I went on, followed the railway, and found myself over the field, with the clouds down to 150'. I circled once, but couldn't keep it in sight, owing to the clouds, and couldn't recognise the runway when I could see it. However, somehow I managed to find it again, lowered my wheels and flaps, and then did another semicircle.

Again, I couldn't see the runway, but the ACP[2] started shooting up Verys, which enabled me to see it. But it was too late and, though I banked hard, I couldn't get round in time, and when I got straight with the runway I was skidding all over the place. I tried to get her down but, fearing to land in such a crabwise condition, I gave her the gun and went round again. This time I knew what to expect, got lined up earlier, and managed to make my best wheel-landing to date. A moment later I was told to keep rolling and old Burton landed just behind me, with 7 gallons left. Others came dribbling in until only two were unaccounted for out of the 9 sent out. But then I heard the sad news that someone, presumed to be Gibby, had crashed soon after take-off, and by evening Bunny Holden was still unheard of.

[2] Airfield Control Post by the runway

That night, the whole Squadron was in the Mess drinking and charging manslaughter against people who sent pilots out in such weather for targets which could wait for the morrow. Everyone was feeling embittered, but I don't think they were drinking to forget. I know I felt I was drinking to the memory of poor

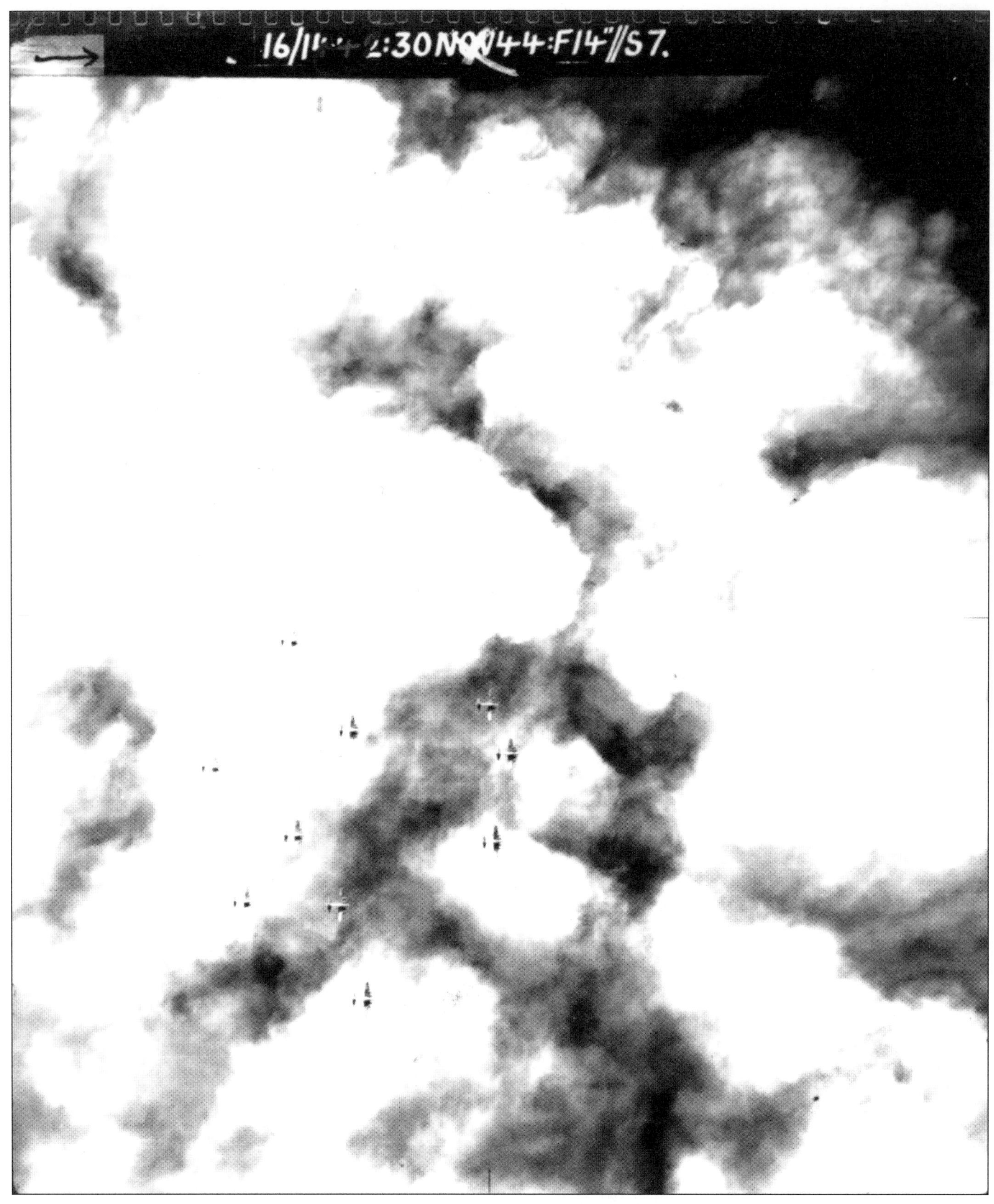

Ray Dutt's operational photo of B-17s on their way into Germany on 30th November 1944

Photo: Ray Dutt

old Gibby, one of the finest men in the Squadron, with an extremely level head, a slow smile, and experiences which enabled him to give advice to everyone. We all felt he knew it was coming, as he hated cloud-flying and his last words to the Adj. were that, if anything happened, he was going to bale out.

Two flight commanders in one day – we hoped that someone would learn a lesson. The one redeeming feature was the excellent way Flying Control handled the situation and brought people back dead over the field. Most of us went over and personally thanked the D/F[1] people for their efficiency.

[1] direction-finding from radio trans-missions from the aircraft

S.O.R.B.

19.9.44

Five sorties were sent to Holland and Germany. Four pilots took photographs, one sortie was abortive, the task area being covered by 10/10ths stratus. P/0. P.E. Fahy was fired at by heavy A.A. over Flushing and also observed a lot of aerial activity in that area. P/0. W.C. Heath saw formations of Fortresses in the same area, England bound. P/0. Moody saw allied gliders on the ground at Arnhem[2]. At Venlo he observed four F.W. 190's below him, flying in an Easterly direction. The only flying of a non-operational character was two air tests. Late in the evening we received the wonderful news that F/Lt. Holden was safe, he had landed at Brussels. Owing to poor communication he was unable to inform us of his whereabouts. The C.O. went to Brussels on another mission and returned with the grand news.

[2] first mention of 'Market Garden'

Diary

Next day was very similar but improving and, in the afternoon, the C.O. went over to Brussels to see how Wetz and Willshaw had got on with their message-dropping[3] to our advanced forces. In the meanwhile, the largest parachute force had been dropped in Holland and we imagined their job was something to do with that.

The C.O. brought back the glad news that he had found Bunny. Apparently his wireless failed, and then at 30000' his oxygen tube broke. From what I've heard, he held it together with his hand and completed his mission – but that has still to be verified. At any rate, it's a relief to know he got down alright.

The C.O. also congratulated me on my mosaic, which turned out very well, especially as it was one of the few sorties that day that achieved any results.

[3] in pink Spitfire IXs to Gen. Browning's Airborne Corps HQ near Nijmegen in connection with 'Market Garden'

S.O.R.B.

20.9.44

A completely duff day. Only one sortie was flown and that was a Met Recce by F/Sgt. H. Simkins to Hanover. During the afternoon the whole Squadron stood-down. Every member of the Squadron went to F/Lt. Gibb's funeral, Gibby was buried with full military honours in the cemetery of the 25th General British Hospital in Amiens. In addition to his Squadron's comrades, W/Cdr. P. Stansfeld, S/Ldr. Beer, Capt. Wickes came to pay tribute. During the evening F/Lt. Holden returned from Brussels, we were all delighted to see him again safe and well.

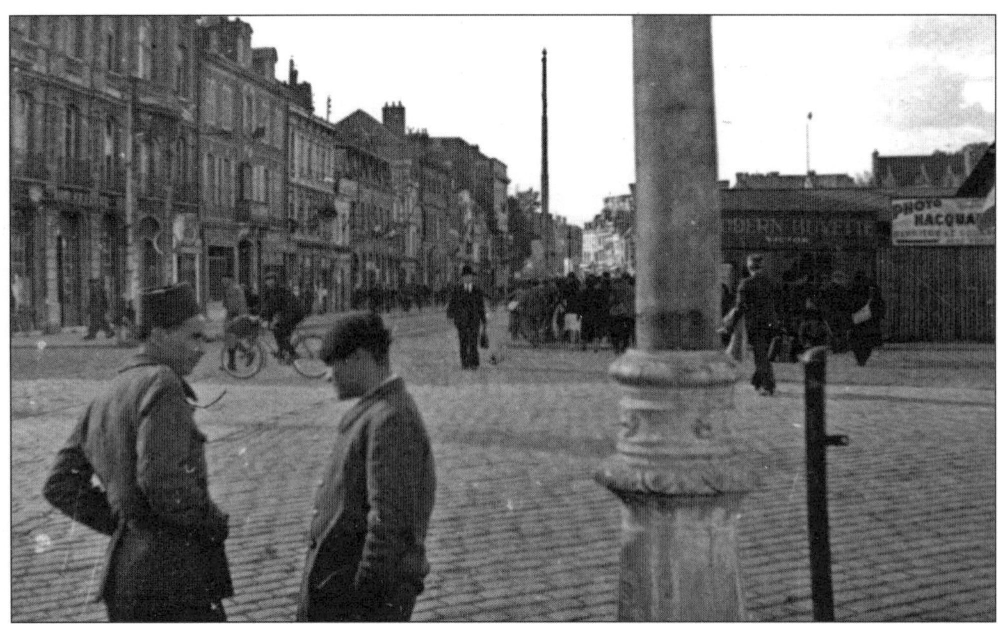

Street-scene in Amiens in September 1944
two French-Moroccan soldiers in the foreground

16 Squadron pilots in battered Amiens
l-r: JT, F/Lt 'Bunny' Holden, F/Lt Derek Wales, and P/O Don Burton
Don is wearing khaki battle-dress and carrying a pistol on his belt.
Photo: Michael Horsfall

Diary

Wed. 20th-Fri. 22nd

This morning, like the last, was foggy and damp and the mist remained most of the day; so at 2.0 pm the Squadron was stood-down and we all tidied ourselves up and put on our best blues for Gibby's funeral at 4.30. There were about a dozen pilots, about 6 of the ground-staff, an Ops. representative, and F/L Pollitt (Polly)[1] present. We drove out to the cemetery in the grounds of Amiens hospital and took part in a very simple but sincere ceremony.

[1] of 140 Squadron

First came the Padre, then the four pall-bearers, followed by the firing-party. We were all lined up at the foot of the grave, the firing-party stood at either side, the Padre at the head, and a party of soldiers lowered the remains, draped in the Union Jack, into the hole in the ground. The "Last Post" was then sounded on a bugle, three volleys were fired by the firing-party, then "Reveille" on the bugle, the Padre uttered a few words, and a soldier sprinkled a handful of symbolic earth into the grave. We then in turn paid our last respects to Gibby by stepping up to the grave and saluting.

Previously, Mike had suggested having a Squadron booze after the ceremony, but I had objected on principle. But now the eight of us in the C.O.'s car decided to stay in town for a little and meet again at 6.0 pm. Five of us went to a cafe and had a beer, then went into another and had some white wine, at 22 francs a glass. After three rounds, we found we could get some food there, so went to a table and ordered dinner. A little later, the C.O. and the other two turned up and ordered dinner. This was a very good meal, considering, starting off with tomatoes and cucumber in vinegar, followed by fish or rabbit and potatoes – and those who had fish found themselves treated to rabbit, as well – then finished up with peaches and apples. In spite of the fact that we had two rounds of wine, it only cost us 500 francs in all.

We then adjourned to the bar and had a round or two of cognac. Then Madame very graciously put out champagne glasses and treated us to two bottles on the house. It was well past six by now and everyone was pretty well oiled, but round after round of cognac followed and, though I refused the last three, I know I wasn't the least affected of them. It surprised me that the C.O. drove us back quite safely at 7.30.

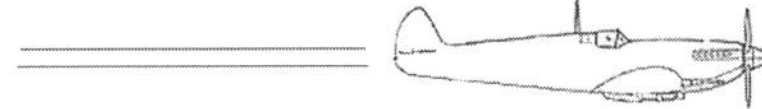

S.O.R.B.

21.9.44

Four operational sorties were despatched to Holland and Germany during the day. Three of these sorties were partially successful, the fourth being abortive owing to 10/10ths cloud. F/0. H.J.S. Taylor when N.W. of Gardelegen was pursued by an enemy aircraft from 23000' to 29000'[2] [39000']. At this height enemy aircraft broke off the pursuit. No other incidents were reported by any other pilots. Very little local flying was accomplished except a few air tests. We have once more received bad news P/0. J.R. Brodby[3], who for a few days past has been operating from Northolt, is reported missing. We trust soon to hear that he is alright.

[2] a clerk's misprint for 39,000' – perhaps he couldn't believe it!

[3] one of the pilots detached to cover 'Market Garden'

Photograph taken by one of my F52 cameras with 20" lenses of the grass airfield near Salzwedel, with 4 aircraft circled, before I was driven off by a then unknown jet.

Log Book

Sept 21st	SPITFIRE XI	O (PA)899	8. ROADS N. of GARDELEGEN Nr BRUNSWICK
			22000' 4.00
			(first encounter with E/A:- 22-39000' T.E.)

Line Book

21.9.44	F/0 TAYLOR	SPIT XI	1050	Roads W and NW of
	S/20"	O	1450	GARDELEGEN no photos.
	16/1215			Road N of GARDELEGEN
	30000'			photos.

A/B 1050. 10/10 cloud ended just short of target. Took road N. of GARDELEGEN beneath cirrus at 22000' then turned to take road NW of town when EA passed beneath leaving trails. I was then at 23000' and EA, an unidentified twin-engine, passed 3000' lower. EA proceeded to follow in an offensive manner forcing me to climb to 39000'. EA moved very much faster but was slower in rate of climb. After 10 mins., during which EA never came within range, he was about 2000' lower and 3000' behind, when he broke off the pursuit. Landed 1450 hrs.

HJS Taylor. F/0.

Diary

Next day, they expected fog on the ground so there were no early calls, but we were at Ops. at 9.0 am. A gap was expected round Hanover at 12.0 pm, after the mist had dispersed and before the cu. started to form. Six of us were sent off – 4 Spits and two Mossies – taking roads round that area. Apparently, they wanted a mosaic of practically the whole of NE[1] Germany but, time being short, they had compromised by requiring all the principal roads.

I took-off at 10.50 am and soon found myself in cloud. I'd switched on my pitot-head[2] heater before, but I got rather a shock when the ASI faltered, then dropped down to zero. I thought it might have frozen, but after a while it didn't improve and, as I had fortunately broken cloud, I started fiddling around with the fuses. But, just as suddenly, it started picking up again and I realised the heater must be just starting to take effect.

I flew on steadily over solid cloud, but over the Ruhr there were a few gaps, with a very hazy earth visible beneath. Railways, towns and rivers were all confused, but I decided I must be roughly on course and settled down to my heading as a continuous stretch of cloud appeared in front. It happened I was flying a kite with the pitch-control linked with the throttle so that, if you opened the throttle, the revs. automatically increased. This was all very well, but in our job you wanted high boost and low revs. to keep down the petrol consumption; so that I wasn't too happy at finding I couldn't get less than 2200 revs. and then at only –2 boost. However, I went on, but determined to come home the moment my wing-tanks ran out.

At exactly ETA, just when I was thinking my trip would be abortive, the cloud finished and I could see a large area of ground: woods everywhere and little towns

[1] NE, that is, from Amiens; actually NW Germany

[2] the pitot-head connected with the Air-Speed Indicator

Date 21.9.44 Aeroplane Longbow Pilot D C B

WIND			NOTES
HEIGHT	FROM °T	SPEED	Kenway
			250/15
			230/25
			428 − 77 = 351
			428

FROM	TO	T.A.S.	Height	True Track	Mag Course	Distance	G/S	Time
BASE	OPS HT.	220	Climb	063	071	77	235	20
OPS HT	GARDELEGEN	340	30000'	065	072	351	365	58
RUN		340	"	355	357	40	355	7
GARDEL-	BASE	340	"	245	250	428	315	82
DANNENB	BASE	340	"	239	246	437	315	84
	[BRUSSELS					328		60]

Time	Observation	E.T.A.
1050	S/C	
	24000 8 Salzwedel	
	21500 6	
	Chased 1315 – 1325 (?)	
	3 strange smoke(?) marks	
	28000	
50	3 ... P 1 5 2 3 1350	
	1400 ... 1410 ... A.	

165910M. Wt. 7092. 37,000. 12/42. W. & S. Ltd. 91-4224. FORM 433 A.

My knee-pad for my flight on 21st September with navigational data in the top half, a sketch of the unidentified jet that chased me from 24,000 – 39,000ft, and stretches of presumed smoke markers

and, to the right, a stretch of water. I had already been flying 1 hr 20 mins, for I was well into Germany, yet I had to waste 15 precious minutes trying in vain to locate my whereabouts. Eventually, I decided to fly over to the water, fly down it and, if I came to some marshes, then I knew it would be the Ems Canal[1]. Accordingly, I flew over there and proceeded to fly alongside it when, after a few minutes, I suddenly realised that a medium-sized town corresponded with one on the map. It was Gardelegen, the starting-point of one of my roads. Thinking that I wouldn't be able to spend long over the target, I picked out the longest run and proceeded to follow it up, taking it as I went. Unfortunately, the clear gap finished just over there and I had to go down to 24000' to get under the cirrus. As I went on, I had to descend to 21500' to stay beneath and, even so, it was so hazy I doubted if the pictures would come out.

At first, I had a time-interval[2] of 8 secs., which gave me time to roll over and have a look between each shot, to ensure I was still over the road. But later I reduced it to 6 secs. and found myself still rolling out when the cameras clicked. In those cases, I had to switch the cameras off, do a complete circle, and come round over the same spot and start again.

By the time I'd finished 40 miles of road, I was getting distinctly cheesed and, as the coverage at 21000' isn't very great, I was much afraid I'd missed one or two bends in the road. I was still running on my wing-tanks, so I decided to do a little stretch of road just east of Salzwedel. As this was in the clear area, I started to climb up to get better coverage.

It was then that, looking up from my map, I saw a double contrail disappearing under the nose about 2000' below. I followed it up and saw a twin-engine plane speeding away to my right. I assumed straightaway that he was an enemy and, keeping him in view, hoped he hadn't seen me. But no, he turned back in a big circle – and I decided that this is where young James starts for home.

As I said before, this area was clear and the clouds were a good 20 miles in front, so I had no choice but to climb up as fast as possible and hope to hold him off in this way. The EA[3] started climbing up in pursuit, making large S-turns presumably to avoid getting in front of me. As for me, I felt a horrible dread in my stomach when I imagined the cannon and m/guns[4] he obviously packed in his nose and, opening the throttle wide, climbed at the fastest rate possible.

The situation resolved itself like this, with me climbing up straight, heading for distant France and using up precious gallons every minute, while Joe swept from side-to-side, now beneath, now away to one side, but never really dropping far below. And so it went on for five minutes.

Then came an awful 30 secs. when my wing-tanks ran out and the engine stopped. Frantically I turned onto mains – and it seemed ages before the old Merlin picked up again. Then on I went, scared to find old Joe getting closer behind. At 37000' I levelled-off and turned slightly to see how Joe was coping. But the devil was still coming on, so I had no alternative but to go on climbing and found myself at 39000'. Here I levelled-off again, not thinking that Joe could make it, for it was devilish high and I'd turned my oxygen on full. I was too excited to feel or notice any ill-effects, but I got a shock when I turned to look for Joe.

[1] Dortmund-Ems Canal

[2] between exposures

[3] enemy aircraft

[4] machine guns

An Arado 234 single-seater jet reconnaissance/bomber
This successful jet plane, fortunately produced too late in the war, had Junkers Jumo 004B engines and carried fuel for two hours flight. 9 of them were based on Rheine airfield in September 1944, making regular photographic sorties over Allied-held Europe and Britain. It was probably one of these aircraft that pursued me – for fun? – on 21st September; I was not to know that, like the Mosquito PRXVI, it carried no armament. The swept-wings which I put into my sketch were caused by my seeing it only from above and in front. The Ar234 was not known at this time and was not reported officially seen in the air until 21st November.

Photo: Ethell and Price "The German Jets in Combat".

Occasionally he had skulked beneath the plane, where I couldn't see him, but now he looked most menacing, being just underneath my tail about 1000 yds behind, but still fortunately 2000' beneath. I continued to watch him, and he must have levelled-out too, for his speed brought him level with me. Then he turned to the right and made off into the distance. I expected him to come back again, as usual, but the last I saw of him he had put his nose down and was losing height, soon becoming a speck and then invisible. I suspected a trap – it was too good to be true – but, though I searched the sky in all directions, I could see no sign of him or any compatriots.

But I still had to get home. I didn't know where I was, I knew I'd been heading vaguely on the right course, and I had 57 gallons left. My time-table allowed for 82 mins. flying, but that had gone to pot. The only thing to do was to take up a course, reduce revs. as low as possible, and just hope to make our lines. And so for the next hour I continued, over cloud all the way and not caring to try to identify anything I might see in the few gaps I did pass over. The only good thing was that, somehow, my wing-tanks had lasted 2½ hours and I might get a similar low consumption on my mains. With luck, I considered I should be able to make Brussels.

Accordingly, after an approximate hour, I called up Kenway[1] and asked for a fix and approximate position, and I was overjoyed when they said I was about 30 miles N. of Brussels. I then had 37 gallons left and realised the prospects looked brighter. I then called up Penman and asked for a homing, and was pleased to find it was almost identical with the course I was then steering. After another ten minutes or so, I called up Kenway again and was told I was 40 miles S. of Brussels. This left only 60 miles to go and I still had 25 gallons. So I continued on and started letting down to the top of the clouds and arrived over the field, which I was lucky to see through a gap at 1400'.

[1] call-sign for the long-distance D/F station

I thought I'd earned it, so I treated the flight to a beat-up, roaring down at 300+ mph from about five miles away and, I hope, impressing the 'erks[2], whom I could see all lined-up at the NAAFI[3] wagon. Vanity of vanities – all is vanity! I had been up 4 hrs, yet I still had 15 gallons. My appreciation of 'O' Oboe[4] was 100%.

[2] mechanics

[3] welfare agency

[4] the Squadron letter of my aircraft

I spent a lot of time trying to identify the enemy machine[5], to which I hadn't given much thought; but, to date, it is still unidentifable and a report went through about it. My plot of the road, I was glad to find, was bang-on, so I think it pays to under-estimate the coverage of the cameras.

[5] almost certainly a jet Arado 234 on an unarmed reconnaissance or training flight

S.O.R.B.

22.9.44

A very poor day for flying and only two operational trips were flown. One was a Met Recce to Hanover and Rotterdam which proved abortive because the aircraft's wireless became U.S. The other trip was a success, although conditions in the target area were far from favourable. Four non-operational sorties were flown. F/0. Taylor and P/0. Fahy flew to England. P/O. Moody returned from Antwerp and W/0. Willshaw flew from Brussels.

I was flying Spitfire IX MK915 'V' when I took these photos with my own (illicit) camera of P/O Peter Fahy flying another IX to RAF Ford on 22 September 1944 to pick up extra drop-tanks for the messages dropped by 16 Squadron pilots near Nijmegen.

Log Book

Sept 22nd SPITFIRE IX V AMIENS - FORD (BOGNOR!) and RETURN 1.30

Diary

That night ENSA[1] presented a show: 3 musicians, a pianist, and two song-and-dance girls. A very good effort, considering, and a very welcome change; but I felt sorry for the girls in their bare legs in the cold and holey hangar. They were afterwards entertained in the Mess. Next morning, I rather Bolshiely stayed in bed till 10.0 am and then had the nearest approach to a bath from my canvas basin, and showed myself at the flights for an odd hour.

[1] Entertainment Agency

Leagh and Armstrong had already gone on leave, Willshaw and Wetz were still at Brussels on their mission[2], Winter was sick and Gibby was dead, and Brodby and Cadan were at Northolt[3], so we only had a dozen on the ops. list. It had also been decided that those with 30 or more ops. before coming to France need only do 60 instead of 80 for a tour, so Bradbury and one or two others had nearly finished and about 70% of the Squadron would be finished in about a month.

[2] dropping messages to the Airborne troops near Nijmegen

[3] on detachment to photograph 'Market Garden'

In the afternoon, the C.O. told Fahy and myself to go to Ford in England in IX's and bring back a drop-tank each[4], which the Brussels pair needed for their trips. Accordingly, we set off at 2.45 pm and I flew alongside Pete all the way, using my mess-tin[5]. About 5 miles from the coast we ran into very low cloud, with very poor vis. beneath, but we made a landfall alright and found ourselves bang over a field. But Pete said, *"Can't be Ford – it's got runways"*, so we stooged off down the coast a little and came to another grass field. Pete told me to go ahead and, though the vis. was almost impossible, I did a very low circuit and made quite a nice landing, taxied off the track, switched off, got out and went over to Pete. It was then that we discovered it wasn't Ford, but Bognor! We were right first time.

[4] they were needed to hold messages

[5] my code for my personal camera (illegal)

Nothing for it but to take-off and go there, which we did, though neither of us saw the other en route till we were circling Ford. Vis. was bloody awful. I followed Pete in, turned onto the runway at the very last moment, tried to get rid of my drift, failed, touched down and carted onto one wheel. I applied full brake and gave a burst of throttle and fortunately slewed her round before the wing touched the ground. We then taxied round to where we saw other Spits, quite blind to an enormous sign saying "Visiting Aircraft" at the opposite end of the field.

After a trip to Flying Control and the CTO[6], we arranged for the tanks to be fitted; but afterwards, when I came to taxy round, I found an air-lock in the fuel-pipe and she would only run on the primer. It took 1½-hr's work to clear that out, then we went over to the Aircrew Mess and had tea. Peter phoned his wife up and I rang home, but unfortunately Mum and Dad were out, but I felt gratified at having spoken to Law[7]. It seemed ridiculous that in half-an-hour such distances could be taken away – and then put back again. Poor Law, he asked me for a number to ring back, and I had to tell him there was no point as I'd be back in France in an hour's time.

[6] Chief Technical Officer

[7] the butler at Cheam School

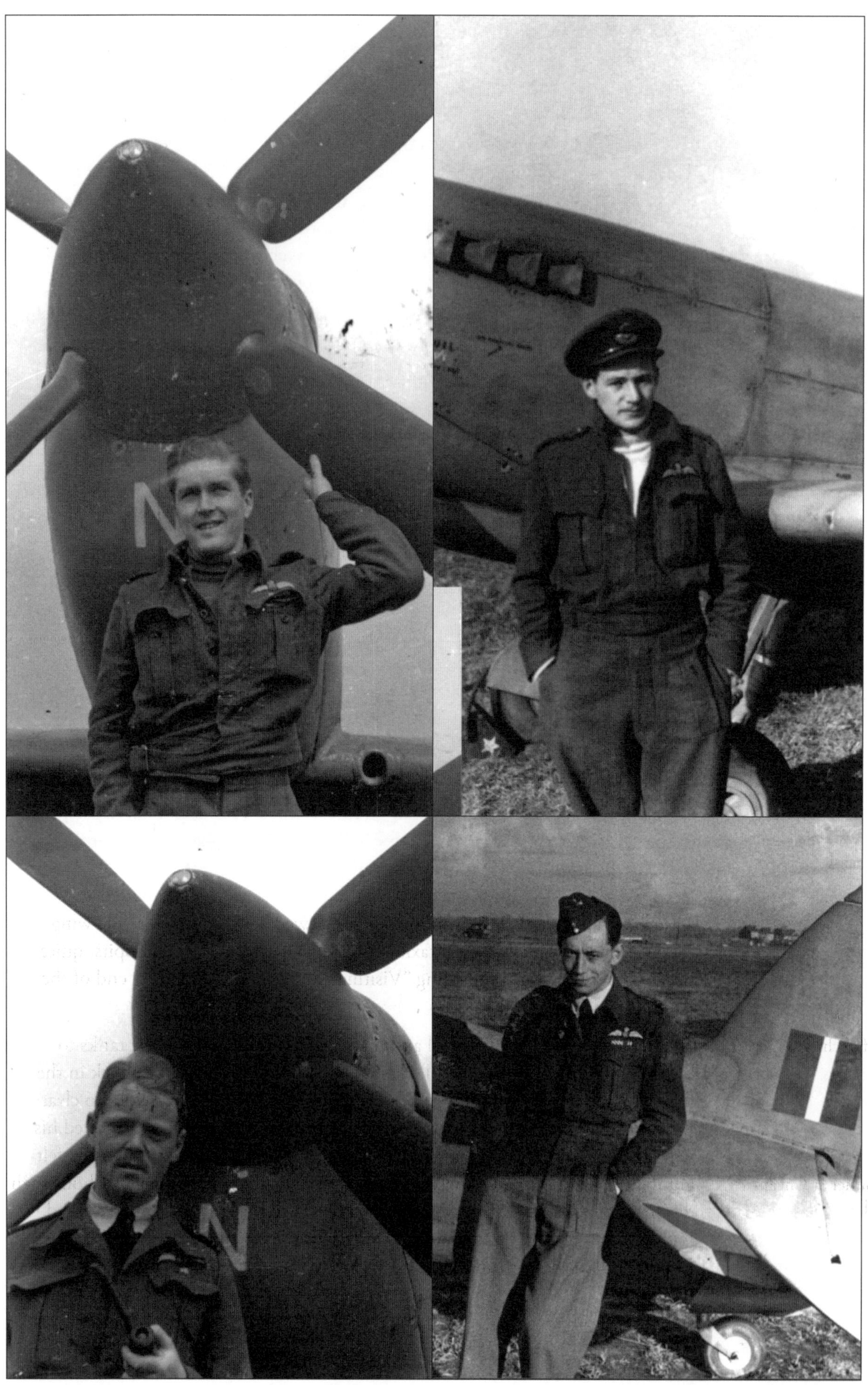

l-r, top-bottom: F/Lt Derek Wales P/O Trevor Moody F/Lt Michael Horsfall F/Lt Ray Dutt, AFC

All Photos: Michael Horsfall

We took off at 6.0 pm in formation owing to the poor vis., but I lost Pete as I struggled to close my canopy. However, the weather cleared up in mid-Channel and we made a good landfall. I closed-up for a beat-up on arrival over the field and, apparently, it was a very good one, so much so that F/Control radioed up to tell us they were forbidden – *"Roger!"*[1] Typical of the unexpectedness of things, I came in and made, for me, a very nice wheeler. After losing speed, I let the tail down and she immediately swerved to the left and tried to leave the runway. I had to give her full brake and a burst of throttle, and saw a row of bods waiting to cross the runway running for their lives.

[1] "message received"

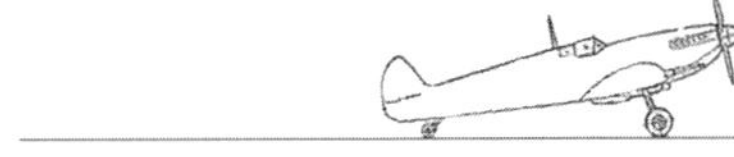

S.O.R.B.

23.9.44

Only one operational sortie was flown during the day and that was to Holland. F/0. Winter was the pilot and the trip was a successful one. He had no incidents of any kind to report. There were however a number of non-operational sorties. The C.O. flew to Brussels and from there to Northolt, and back. The G.C. did a local flight.

Log Book

Sept 23rd	AUSTER	MT854	F/Lt WALES, F/Lt HORSFALL, SELF (Pass)	AMIENS – ST OMER and RETURN 2.15

Diary

Mike had bartered 4 bars of chocolate and 60 fags for 11 eggs – good show. I was also asked to pack-up Brodby's kit. He left Northolt two days ago for a low-level over Holland and was last heard of saying he was lost over the radio. Poor show – and, though I've never been very keen on him, I always thought he was quite capable of looking after himself. Bad show, though – that's the fourth loss since we joined the Squadron, and the second out of our tent – must be a hoodoo somewhere.

The finale is all about a little flight on the 23rd Sept. in an Auster with two others. F/Lt Wales wanted to go to St Omer to see a friend, so Mike and I piled in too and, in spite of very low cloud and misty visibility, we took-off at 2.45 pm and flew first of all to the Cathedral at Amiens.

The first impression I got was of the colossal damage to the railway yards outside the city – the way the platforms and roofs had been devastated to the level of the line, and the flat clear spaces where everything material had been blasted away. The same scene of destruction was evident round the Cathedral, but here it was not the painful necessity meted out by the Allies, but the wanton demolitions carried out by the Germans in 1940. The Cathedral itself was fortunately spared and its Gothic outline stood up like a rock, graceful in its tracery and steadfast in its position, as if almost aloof from the petty squabbles of this tiresome Twentieth-Century civilisation.

From the air: Amiens railway-station truly pranged by Allied bombers

Photo: Michael Horsfall

From the ground: the scene of destruction at Amiens railway-station

The same characteristic impressed me as I surveyed the sorry spectacle of the countryside between Amiens and St Omer. Everywhere were bomb-craters and shell-holes, but the stoic French farmers had either filled them in and were ploughing over them, or else were conscientiously ploughing round them, making use of every available plot to draw a furrow, trying to make up by their industry for what other men in their madness had tried to destroy.

Some parts of England have suffered from bombing, and pretty awful they look and infinite suffering has been caused; but what I saw in these sixty miles overshadowed by far anything I've seen in England. Everywhere you look you can see craters, some older and grass-grown, others with the brown earth quite freshly disturbed. When I first saw these craters, I looked around for any possible target – and, at first, I couldn't find any. And then, after a time, you would realise what you were looking for – not targets as we know them over here, but anything that could be used for covering or transporting Germans. Dug-outs, gun-positions, slit-trenches, were liberally sprinkled, but the worst sufferers were the railways and airfields. Little one-track railways would suddenly end in a vast crater; a little bridge over a road would have collapsed; and the little local railway stations, in which at home we take some personal pride, would be blasted off the face of the earth. Airfields were just pockmarked with holes, added to by others obviously made by the Germans before they cleared out.

But what hurt one most was not the damage to these military objectives, but the awful toll taken of the farms, villages and chateaux that were so unfortunate as to be in the vicinity. Chateaux, once the pride of some wealthy owner, stood in their vegetable-covered gardens – a sign of the times – desolate, with one wing shattered; or, like a sleeping giant, with all their shutters closed, except maybe for a servant's window at the top, waiting for the return of the master who had deserted them. Farms had suffered likewise, but here could be seen the efforts of the farmer to repair the damage and continue earning his living. New red tiles stood out prominently on the roofs, and cattle grazed peacefully round the craters; but I wondered at the toll that must have been taken of the livestock, and the harrowing effect on the country-people, young and old, who lived around.

But most pathetic of all were the villages – as disorderly as our own, but displaying horrible whitened wounds: a shell for a church, a row of rubble for streets, and cracked and spattered walls and roofs. The railway station, of course, would be demolished with little trucks tumbled over each other, a signal-gantry sagging in the middle, and the repair shops – the pride of the station-master – just gutted casemates and girders. I hated to think of the awful awakening to the war these places must have had and the price they must have paid, for months and even years, before they were finally liberated.

But perhaps what awed me most was the clear evidence of the most systematic and thorough destruction of everything that could possibly be of use to the Huns, and the attention paid to the smallest detail as much as to the more obviously important. To the Germans, it must have appeared uncanny, the way they were sought out and harried hither and thither; and what mortification and defeat they must have felt as they saw each utensil snatched out of their hands and dashed to pieces just when they needed it most.

**V1 launch-ramp pointing at London,
blown-up by the Germans themselves**

Cheerful visit to the V1 launch-site from Amiens-Glisy
l-r: F/Lt 'Tommy' Thompson F/O 'Jock' West P/O Peter Fahy F/Lt Derek Wales,
F/Sgt 'Jolly' Jolliffe W/O 'Willy' Willshaw JT

Photo: Michael Horsfall

Sat. 24th Sept. – 2nd Oct.

Nothing much happened after our trip to St Omer as the weather was uniformly duff. We made a slight expedition to a flying-bomb site outside Amiens and were duly impressed with the launching ramp and the adjacent flak battery. From there we went back to Amiens, but I left the party and walked to the railway, spending a couple of hours rummaging round the trucks and trying – and failing – to scrounge something of interest left behind by Jerry.

Little of interest happened thereafter except that, one evening, we had another sortie into town with the C.O. It wasn't as spirited as the first one and we stayed in one cafe – an Officers' Club – all the time.

Next day, Tuesday 26th, we heard officially that Brodby and Gerry Bastow[1], who'd finished his tour and was now attached to the W.S.U., were both missing from a low-level over the Rhine. Scotty Cadan[2], who'd gone to England to operate from there, said he'd heard Brod calling up saying he was lost, but from then nothing more has been heard from him. As he was in our tent, the Adj. asked me to pack his kit up, so I had the unenviable job. Actually, I didn't feel bad about it, as Brod was so good at taking care of himself that I believed I was packing it up for him on his return, rather than for his people.

[1] Gerry Bastow was helped by the Dutch Resistance and came back a month later. See Chapter 39 for details.

[2] Scotty must have returned and given this second report already noted.

The same day, the advance party left A for B and we found ourselves reduced to half of everything in the Mess. Next day, we were told we were leaving before lunch, so we had to get our kits and tents packed early so that they might arrive at B in time for us the same night. We then pulled down the flight tent and gradually got off the ground.

The day before, the C.O. had very nobly scrounged a Mustang which had been left behind ever since we'd arrived. It was in perfect condition, with guns loaded, so Jerry Winter flew it to B. Unfortunately two days after arriving at B, another Mustang with the same markings arrived and parked alongside, and next day ours was gone – we heard to 35 Wing, where it was being used on ops. Peter Cribb and Michael Wetz, the artful scroungers, had somehow managed to possess themselves of an Auster, so this too came to B with us.

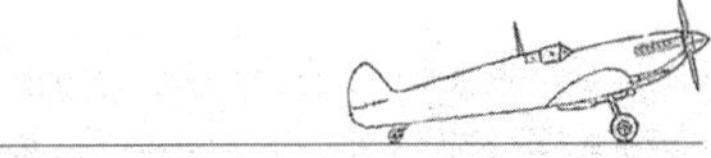

S.O.R.B.

27.9.44

There was no operational flying at all. Today the Squadron pilots flew all our Spitfires from Amiens to Melsbroek, in Belgium. Five of the pilots returned by Wellington to Amiens and did a second trip, the reason being that at the moment we have more aircraft than pilots. A number of our pilots being on leave just now. The advance party of the Squadron arrived at our new Station at 5 p.m. the night before. They travelled by road bringing with them the bulk of the Squadron equipment. The night before the advance party left Amiens two new pilots arrived from W.S.U., namely F/Lt. J.M. Thompson a Canadian, and F/O . J. West AFC. They came to replace F/Lt Gibb and P/O Brodby.

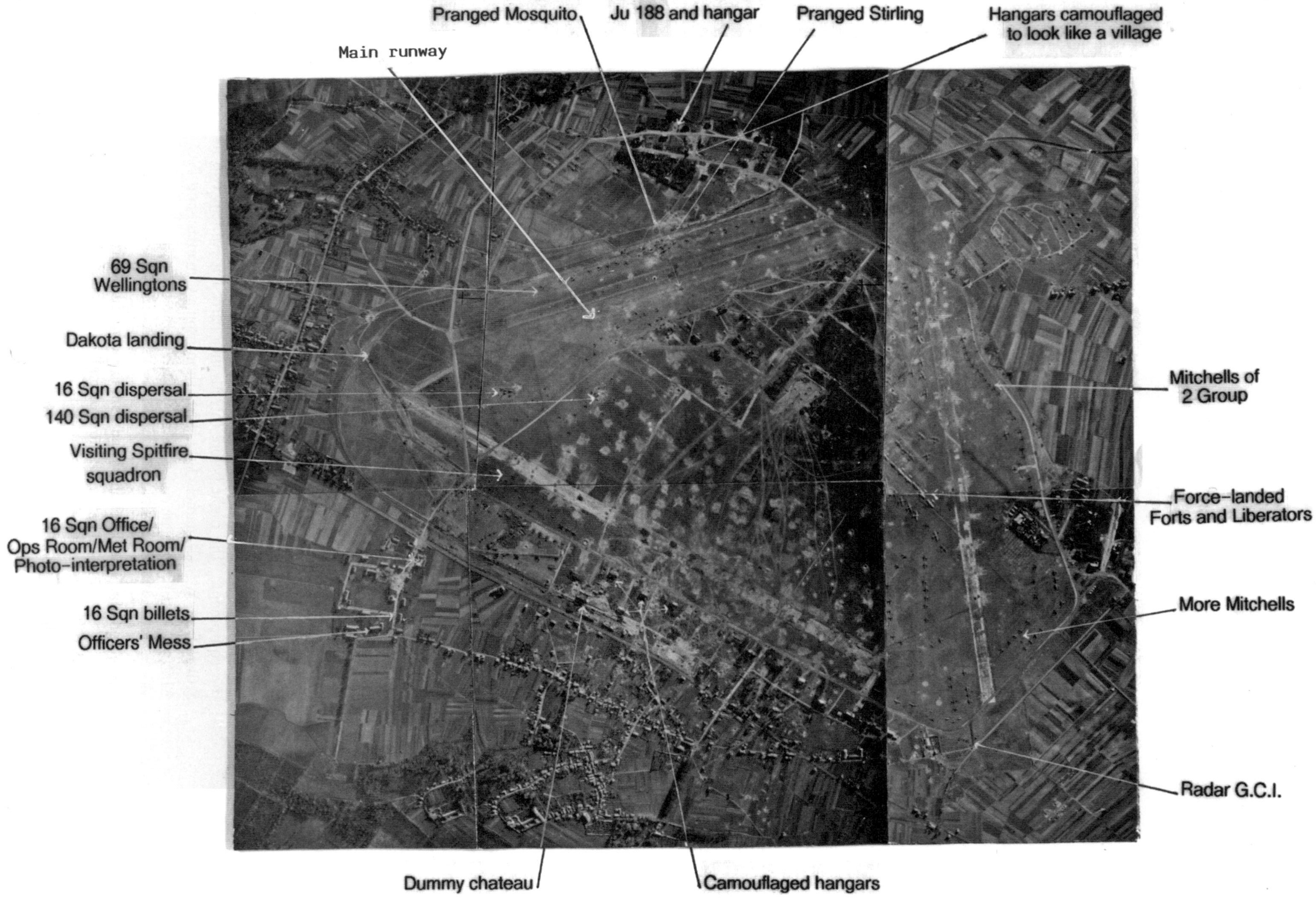

B58 Melsbroek airfield, outside Brussels, heavily bombed before capture: a mosaic of six prints made by my wing F24s with 5" lenses from 3000'

Log Book

Sept 27th AUSTER MT 854 AMIENS – MELSBROEK, BRUSSELS 1.40

Diary

I thought I'd fly our Auster for a change, so I loaded it up with my kit and Mike's and some office equipment, and took-off after all the others had gone. The trip was uneventful but quite fun. I followed roads all the way and went via Charleroi and Mons. I arrived at B at 1.44 pm and had quite a job getting in, as the circuit was crowded with Halifaxes, Marauders and Wimpeys.

We found ourselves quartered in the former German barracks, which were built in a high-gabled Flemish style by the Germans themselves. The furniture was still in the Mess, with very comfortable chairs and sofas and carpets. Our kits arrived late that night so, after blocking-up the holes in our windows, we spent quite a sheltered night. The electricity and water mains had not been repaired, and the smell in some of the rooms and drains was terrible, but this was put right fairly soon. The food in the Mess wasn't very good, but after a few days we got quite well organised. The lights came on; water ran; bread, cheese and fruit appeared on the tables; and Flemish girls took over as waitresses. They could speak no English or French, and took great delight in challenging everybody with "Suppe" or "Sweet", as the fancy took them. I went into a room with Mike and Don Williams, the Adj., and after a day or two we settled down quite well, with a stove and home-made furniture. Mail came in quite regularly, only taking three days to arrive.

That first afternoon, Mike and I wandered around to see what we could scrounge. It was a vast airfield, with the most intricately camouflaged hangars – whole villages and one great chateau, all false and complete down to advertisements on the walls and knobs on the doors. Jerry had obviously left in a hurry as 1 complete Ju188 and one under repair had been left behind, also 2 '190's[1] – one on its nose – 1 Do17[2], 1 '109, and the remains of an '88, '110[3], and lots of engines. Unfortunately, another squadron had preceded us and everything of value had been pinched.

[1] Fw190s

[2] Dornier Do17

[3] Me109, Ju88, Me110

Next day, the various offices and Ops. room were organised in different buildings, and we took a caravan down to the flights and sited it as our crew-room, which was a great improvement on tents. Next day, 5 of the boys went on leave. This had become quite well organised by now and, as the hours of daylight became shorter, we could afford to have fewer people on the ops. list. At the moment, we should get a week's leave about every five weeks.

I spent most of the morning taxying kites about, and in the afternoon went into B with Mike, Don, Jock West, Leagh and Bunny. We found B a gay, crowded city, apparently little affected by the war. Shops had an indecent amount to sell and at not unreasonable prices: grapes at 20 fr a kilo, peaches and all sorts of fruit, ices, glass-ware, tools, etc, and clothes were of good quality but rationed. The girls were well dressed and made-up, and everywhere were flags and patriotic emblems.

The German-built Officers' Mess at Melsbroek
Photo: Michael Horsfall

Built with Belgian forced labour, the bungalow where Mike Horsfall, Don Williams, and I lived in one of the rooms in Autumn 1944.
Photo: Michael Horsfall

Part of the Officers' Mess, as left by the Germans

"Getsum Inn" – the bar of the Officers' Mess

P/O Don Williams, 16 Squadron Adjutant and former Town Clerk of Pontardawe, seen against the background "16 Squadron Bayeux Tapestry" frieze depicting the Squadron's experiences in France and Belgium, painted by Mike Horsfall: a steamship can be seen on the left, and a figure waving two flags enthusiastically behind Don's right shoulder.

Photo: Michael Horsfall

First Sight of Brussels
The Palais de Justice as seen from the Auster

Trams ran regularly and, though the black-out was enforced, at dusk the shops and streets were a blaze of light. Beer and wines were cheap and plentiful, and the cafés and restaurants were crowded out, and nearly all boasted a band.

First, I went with Mike and had a bath in Bunny's hotel, which he was still putting down on TAF's[1] bill; then we went to a big store, Au Bon Marché, where we had ice creams and 'maurangs'. Here I bought a file, a saw[2] and a photo album, all unobtainable in England. We then drove around a bit and stopped at a café for a couple of drinks. Then we went to TAF Main[3], which we entered under false pretences, and had some more drinks and dinner. The magnificence of the place drew all sorts of caustic comments from us and made a rather disgusting distinction between the living conditions of the staff and those of the operating personnel. We were all a bit cheesed by now, so we came home after dinner, leaving Bunny to spend the night in town.

[1] 2nd Tactical Air Force

[2] I had scrounged a small, broken wooden German propeller

[3] 2nd TAF HQ

I spent several other afternoons in Brussels on shopping expeditions, but have yet to look into the night-life – that will come.

As far as the flying went, the weather was very cloudy, which prevented many trips. I did a couple of air-tests, which consisted of climbing to 10000', doing a stall, and then diving down at 400 I.A.S, and watching how much the ailerons bent up. On the second occasion, I reached 420 indicated, the fastest I've been, to date.

Melsbroek

S.O.R.B.

28.9.44

Eight operational sorties were flown over Holland and Germany. Every flight was a success. The C.O. had quite an eventful trip, his cockpit heater froze and he was almost frozen as a result, he almost encountered a met balloon, and to add to his troubles he was chased home by two unidentified S/E[4] aircraft leaving contrails above and astern of him. P/0 Moody received a bandit[5] warning from the C.O. but saw nothing hostile, he returned to base with a glycol leak. F/Lt. J.M. Thompson had three bursts of flak in the Frisian Islands area. F/Lt. A.P.G. Holden and P/0. G. Cribb went to Nijmegen on a special mission which they accomplished without mishap. To-day F/Lt. J.M. Thompson and F/0. J. West AFC our new pilots accomplished their first operational sorties. This evening at 6 p.m. the rear party of our Squadron arrived bringing the remainder of our gear.

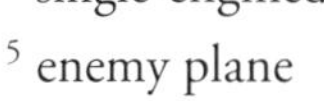

[4] single-engined

[5] enemy plane

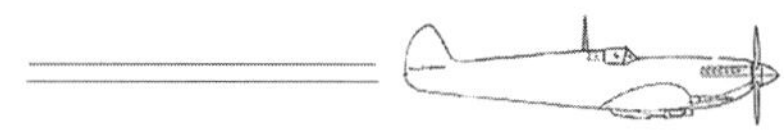

S.O.R.B.

29.9.44

Three operational flights were flown to Holland and Germany, all pilots successfully accomplished their tasks. F/Lt. Horsfall and F/0. Taylor were on photographic sorties, F/0. G. Winter went on a message dropping mission to our forward troops at Nijmegen. F/0. H. Taylor had trouble with his electrical equipment which became u/s at 29000'. Owing to 10/10 cloud he landed at 1st airfield he identified as ours which was Florennes, 60 miles S. of base. He arrived back at base without further mishap. No further incidents were reported. 1st aircraft airborne 0750 hrs, last one down 1800 hrs.

German hangar at Melsbroek camouflaged as a farm-house with an abandoned Ju188 painted to represent a burnt-out building

The above Ju188 in its unusual camouflage

The Ju188 seen above, vandalised by the first Allied troops to occupy the airfield

An Fw190 abandoned at Melsbroek attracting Michael Horsfall (l) and colleague

The German control tower at Melsbroek camouflaged as a school
Photo: Col. Jo Huybens, 'Dakota', Belgium

Another remarkably detailed camouflaged German hangar at Melsbroek

Log Book

Sept 29th SPITFIRE XI A (PL)770 9. BRUSSELS: NIENSBURG, ROTEBURG – roads 2.50

Electrical failure. Landed FLORENNES. .25

Line Book

29.9.44	SPIT XI	F/0 TAYLOR	0750 } 1140	Roads near NIENBURG,
	A 770			ROTEBURG, STADE
	S/20"		1405 } 1430	and BREMEN
				Photos.

A/B 0750 First target was covered with cloud but managed to take three others in clear but very hazy areas, Bremen being under cloud. About 100 miles from base, all electrical equipment became u/s at 29000' over 10/10, so landed at first airfield I identified as ours – FLORENNES 60 miles S. of base. Refuelled and re-started on a jeep battery, arriving back at base at 1430 hrs. No incidents.

HJS Taylor. F/0.

Diary

I did a trip to the Bremen area on the 29th Sept., soon after we'd arrived at B, and found my targets after a prolonged search due to the thick early-morning haze. I didn't take them all owing to cloud, and one was dubious, as two roads of identical size appeared on the ground yet only one was marked on the map. The last target was a silly little strip of a secondary road and, while I was looking for it, my wing-tanks gave out, showing I had a little less than two hours juice left.

However, I found a road that might have been it, did a run, then set course for home. There was a layer of cirrus at 27000' so, to save myself the trouble of looking around for Jerries, I went into it and flew back on instruments. I was soon over 10/10 cloud, so there wouldn't have been any advantage in staying out of it and, when I was about 100 miles from base, I called up and asked for a homing. I got the reply, which entailed a change of about 10° in course, and then my radio faded away. I continued to talk a bit to let them know my position[1], as I thought it might only be my receiver which had gone u/s. But, on checking-up, I found I was only getting 3.5 volts, which meant my whole electrical system had failed – radio, lights and petrol gauges.

[1] the D/F station needed to receive a continuing transmission

I knew I had enough fuel to get home on, but not enough to look around very much once I got below the clouds. Accordingly, 5 mins. before I was due back, I started down to the top of the clouds, then through them to 3000' before I got through, and then there was a lot of haze and scraps of cloud floating around. I looked around hard and, eventually, found a largish river flowing roughly in my direction. I looked on the map and, at first, couldn't find a river at all; and then I did, on the edge of the map, but there was no telling on which part I'd come out. Then I spotted an aerodrome and decided, if it was ours, to go in and land directly.

But, first, I went back under the cloud and flew towards and then over the field, and breathed relief when I recognised Liberators parked on one of the runways.

16 Squadron's Spitfire XIs dispersed on Melsbroek airfield in 1944: Operations caravans in centre; shot-up Halifax crash-landed at top; transport Dakotas on disused runway at bottom.

Photo: Michael Wetz

The front-line is rather close to B round here and, if you don't know where you are, it's 50/50 whose side you're on. I went in and landed and, after bags of taxying, found a place where I could leave the kite.

The first people I spoke to had no idea where they were, either! I then walked over to the Flying Control truck, but had to wait half-an-hour while they landed three squadrons of Lightnings. I then discovered there were no facilities for refuelling or for communicating with B. Seeing I'd have to organise it myself, I walked over to a dispersal and discovered a bowser trying to pull a Lightning out of the mud. A Major standing by agreed to let me use the bowser afterwards and took me over to a hangar for lunch. He turned out to be the C.O. of a squadron and they'd only arrived the day before, with the resultant disorganisation. He said they were mainly on fighter-bomber work and saw very few Jerries, though they wouldn't mind seeing more. He also told me that Liberators came into the field at the rate of one every 6 mins. bringing petrol day and night for the 2nd Army. He then took me down to the kite, now surrounded by curious Yanks, and saw it refuelled, then had to go off for a meeting of his pilots.

I soon realised that it was going to need more than petrol to start her up, as the batteries also were flat. Eventually, a couple of boys managed to organise a Jeep battery and a couple of lengths of wire – but it had no effect. After further searching, they managed to find a new one and, with this and my fingers crossed, she started up and I took off not long after.

The weather wasn't too good, but I got back in 15 mins., having a look at the mound of Waterloo on the way. Having landed, I found everyone very relieved at my return, as they'd heard nothing from me after giving me the course to steer, and had listed me as overdue, believed missing.

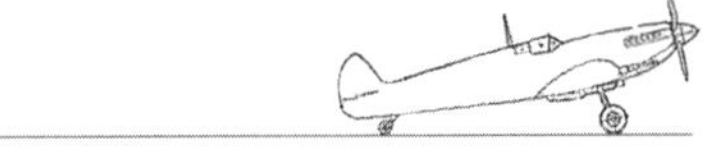

S.O.R.B.

1944

1/10

Three operational sorties were despatched during the day to Holland and Germany. One flight only was successful. P/0. W.C. Heath had an eventful trip, he received bags of red tracer at Bewrath. In following the Rhine Southwards he was fired at any time he showed his nose. On completion of a run over the target, his port wing tip was blown off. Fortunately he got back to base without further mishap. Despite all this opposition he secured photographs. P/0. Moody met such a terrific concentration of flak at Nijmegen that he had to abandon his sortie[1]. F/Sgt D.W. Jolliffe has failed to return from his sortie. We have great hopes that he may be alive and well, perhaps in hiding, or may be a prisoner of war. We know that he was going to bale out. Had he arrived on our side of the lines, we most certainly would have heard something by this time.

[1] the last (unsuccessful) message-dropping sortie

Log Book

Oct. 1st	SPITFIRE IX	V (MK915)	AIR TEST	.20

Best Blues in Brussels – with Gloves
l-r: F/Lt 'Bunny' Holden F/O Leagh-Murray P/O Don Williams F/O Jock West, AFC JT
Photo: Michael Horsfall

One of the Bright Lights of Brussels

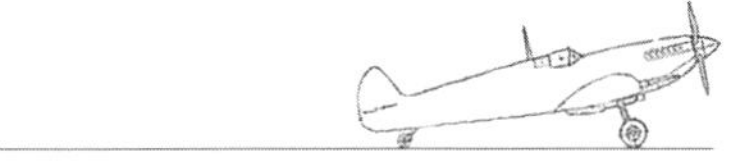

S.O.R.B.
3/10

A completely duff day and as a result there was no flying. During the afternoon the Squadron was stood down.

Log Book

Oct. 3rd SPITFIRE XI P (PL912) AIR TEST .20

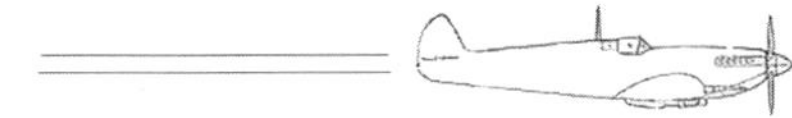

S.O.R.B.
5/10

Six operational sorties were despatched during the day over Holland and Germany. Of these, four trips were successful, the two others only partially so. P/0. W.C.Heath observed a vertical trail presumably from V.2, in the Stavoren area. A number of pilots reported great allied aerial activity, and a considerable amount of interference. Another new pilot has now joined the Squadron from 34 W.S.U., namely F/Lt. R. Dutt, A.F.C.

Log Book

Oct 5th SPITFIRE XI F (PA854) 10. MOSAIC HOOK OF HOLLAND
5" 32000'. 2.20
(60% abortive due to haze)

Line Book

5.10.44	SPIT XI	F/0 TAYLOR	1615	Mosaic HAGUE – AMSTERDAM
	F	16/1250	1835	– DEN HELDER
	S/5"			

A/B 1615 Started photography 27500' under cirrus. Later cleared and continued at 30000' rising to 32000' but extreme haze made navigation difficult and photography impossible, 60% of mission turning out to be abortive. Vertical contrail seen at 1740 in the direction of Den Helder. No further incidents. Landed 1835.

HJS Taylor. F/0.

Diary

My other trip wasn't so eventful. The Squadron had been stood-down, but I happened to be at the flight at 3.30 pm when Ops. decided that the weather was good enough for a 5" cover[1] of the Hook of Holland, to estimate the area of flooding[2]. Accordingly, I took off at 4.15 and started on my mosaic O.K.

[1] a 5" lens was wide-angle

[2] the Germans had opened the dykes

But, after a bit, it got so hazy I couldn't see the ground except by turning right up on my wing-tip and looking vertically down. All I could do was to turn onto my pre-arranged courses and hold them – 65 miles being the longest one.

About halfway through, I saw another V2 contrail – I'd seen two on my last trip – and tried to photograph it by banking up vertically. But when I tried to

The new menace: the Me 262 jet fighter
It could fly at 540mph and was armed with 4 x 30mm cannon. However, it had a short duration and was vulnerable during take-off and landing, when it suffered heavy losses from Allied fighters patrolling over its airfields round Rheine.
Photo: Ethell and Price "The German Jets in Combat"

This badly shot-up Halifax made a good forced-landing at night.

get back on course, my gyro[1] had toppled and the air had become so bumpy I couldn't re-set it. Nor could I see ahead to set course visually. Eventually, I did my mouths[2], but 5 mins. later found myself over the sea – not at all according to plan. I switched off and looked around, eventually locating Amsterdam. I tried again from there and managed to reach the tip of Holland, and broke off my last run to fill-in the bit I'd missed before.

[1] the ordinary compass took time to settle down

[2] of the Maas estuary

But it was so dark I knew I couldn't have succeeded in penetrating the haze and, what with that and the bumpiness and the fact that my fingers froze up and I couldn't switch the cameras off, made me feel pretty disgruntled. I came back on a homing and found it almost black as I came down through the clouds. I also experienced horrid pains in my left nostril and sinus and, finally, as I came in at dusk, they switched off the red light at the end of the runway, so that I couldn't see till almost too late, and then I finished up with a horrible bounce. Altogether, a most unsatisfactory sortie and, as I'd expected, only 40% of the prints were plottable.

I discovered the cause of my pain in descent was a cold, and I spent next morning in bed trying to cure it, but without effect. It actually grounded me for 6 days, as it was useless attempting to fly at altitude with a cold – just asking for trouble - though it was the first time a cold had caused me any dislocation of life. The next day was one of the best days we'd had, but there were so many on leave or sick that there were only 11 on the ops. list, and two of them had to fly two sorties. It made me feel rather bad, but I couldn't help it. On that day, we finished all the outstanding demands and, for the next five days, didn't send off more than ten sorties, one of the days being at an absolute standstill.

Various incidents happened, to interest us; but usually people went into Brussels[3] in the evening or the afternoon.

It was on the busy day that we had six different sightings of these jet-planes[4], which were just coming into the news by operating over the Arnhem front. Ray Dutt was accompanied by one for about half-an-hour, but it appears not to have seen him any of the time. Ray Armstrong and Trevor Moody were both intercepted by Mustangs and Thunderbolts and had to. give up their task because of them; and there are grave fears that one of the Mosquito boys was shot down by a couple of 'Bolts. Anyway, a Yank claimed to have shot down a Mossie with Jerry markings and they're having a Court of Enquiry about it. But these jets seem to be becoming quite a menace, though fortunately they give away their presence by a thick trail of black smoke.

[3] again, I seem to have forgotten security

[4] Messerschmitt 262s

Another incident was the arrival and departure of about 140 Dakotas, interspersed with shot-up Liberators and Forts, who rarely came in with more than three engines and sometimes with less. However, there were no serious prangs.

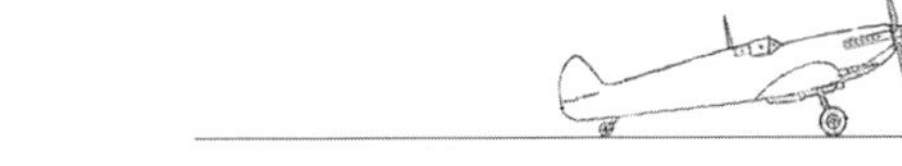

S.O.R.B.

12/10

Three operational sorties were despatched during the day to Holland and Germany. Two of these sorties were successful, the third was abortive due to

The Chateau de Perck not far from Melsbroek

The aristocratic owner of the Chateau de Perck entertaining a group of 16 Squadron pilots in March 1945:
1-r: F/Lt 'Tommy' Thompson, RCAF F/Lt Joe Renier (Belgium)
Lt André Estaria (Free French) F/L David Stutchbury

a huge patch of stratus over Hamburg. It was quite a busy day as far as non-operational flying was concerned, six local practice flights were flown by our pilots and Wg/Cdr Hardiman of T.A.F. did a local flight also. F/Lt. J.M. Coldwell-Horsfall flew to Eindhoven and back, and F/0. Taylor did an air test.

Log Book

Oct 12th SPITFIRE XI L (MB)957 AIR TEST. .50

Diary

Derek Wales and Trevor Moody went off, another day, on a publicity stunt to photograph some of the 5000 kites which were pranging the front. We saw streams of Lancs. coming back, but the other two saw nothing at all over their area and came back clueless.

Mike and I spent some time scrounging, and I managed to get hold of a couple of midget electric motors and gadgets from a Lorentz beam-approach set. While Mike was battling with the throttle lever of a '190, I opened up the tail and found the electric motor that drives the stabiliser unit. We found another one on the tail-end of another kite and today, the 11th, I took over a third one for Mike. They're wizard little jobs – very fast and geared down to be immensely powerful.

We also had to change all notes of over 100 francs into the new currency designed to put a stop to the inflation in the country. The money has been printed in England, and each Belgian gets 2000 francs down and about 40% of his savings while the manner of his making it is investigated – to hit at the black marketeers.

The other afternoon, I decided to walk over to a chateau I'd seen from the air and not far from the Mess. I eventually trespassed into the grounds and found myself opposite a charming place surrounded by water. The owner came out – a dear old man – welcomed me and chatted for a while about how the Germans wouldn't sleep there for fear the water would be too great a landmark, how the only bomb that hit it was a German one, and how the Germans were always trying to shoot his tame ducks, but he used to clap them away before the Jerries arrived.

S.O.R.B.

14/10

One operational sortie only was flown, the task area being Utrecht and Amersfoort in Holland. F/0. Taylor was the pilot, the only incident he had to report was a vertical contrail in approximate area of Rotterdam.

Log Book

Oct 14th SPITFIRE XI D (PL)851 11. 36" Marshalling yards:
UTRECHT, AMERSFOORT
31000'.
Area ALPEN – HOMBORN
in the RUHR
25500'. 2.00

The Solitude of the Long-Distance Photographic Pilot

Line Book

14.10.44	F/0 TAYLOR	SPIT XI	1445	Marshalling Yards at Utrecht and
	S/36" S/5"	D 851	1645	Amersfoort. Run alongside river
	29000'			towards the Ruhr.
	16/1277			

A/B 1445 Made two runs over Utrecht over 3/10 cloud, and two over Amersfoort, followed by two more at a lower and clearer altitude. Returned to Utrecht and took a nearby A/F while waiting for cloud to move over. Made another run and went onto area between Alpen and Homborn. Cirrus at 27000' so made two runs at 26000'. Observed vertical contrail in approximate area of Rotterdam on way back. No other incidents. Landed 1645.

HJS Taylor. F/0.

Diary

Friday 13th October – 23rd October

Stood-by all day for the third day, but next day went off in the afternoon on a trip on the offchance of catching a break in the clouds. There were two marshalling-yards, at Utrecht and Amersfoort, to be done for bomb-damage assessment and, at the last minute, they threw in a couple of areas near the Ruhr, needed to complete a mosaic.

Met. was quite right and I found the breaks, though at Utrecht a little blob of cumulus was most annoying in its persistence over the area. However, I made two runs and then went off to Amersfoort, where I made another two. I then found myself in haze, so decided to do two more for a clearer picture. But, when I switched off, I found I had only just reached the centre of the area, owing to my not allowing for the strong head-wind. I tried again – and suddenly realised I'd almost fallen asleep. I switched off the cameras and turned the oxygen on full and looked around for something wrong with the tube, but could find nothing. I then did that run again and went back to Utrecht, hoping it would be clear. But a large area of cu. had now arrived, so I went over to a large aerodrome and photographed that in the interval. The yards were in sunlight when I returned, so I made a run and decided to go on down the Rhine and hoped it would be clear.

However, there was a large sheet of strat.cu.[1] all the way and, when it broke, I had some difficulty in recognising which part of the river I was over. However, I identified Wesel and found the turning-on point. Unfortunately, there was cirrus at 26000' and I had to stay below that, so I knew the coverage would not be very great. I decided therefore to do two runs, but found it hard to make out where they ended. There was a lot of smoke in front coming from Duisburg and I thought it must be a smoke-screen put up in my honour.

On my second run, I saw a contrail some way away to my left, and I continued to watch it while I finished my run. On my way home I stayed beneath 'trail height, determined not to give away my presence. Of course, I had to see my old friend V2 again and I tried to photograph the 'trail, but the results showed I didn't turn up on my side enough.[2]

I got quite a welcome from the Ops. room when I returned and they were very pleased that the sortie was successful. I was pleased, too, as it meant that now I was bottom of the ops. list and could take a kite to Rouen to try to see Gerald.[3]

[1] strato-cumulus

[2] to use my vertical cameras

[3] my elder brother who was on an RAF radar site, directing night fighters

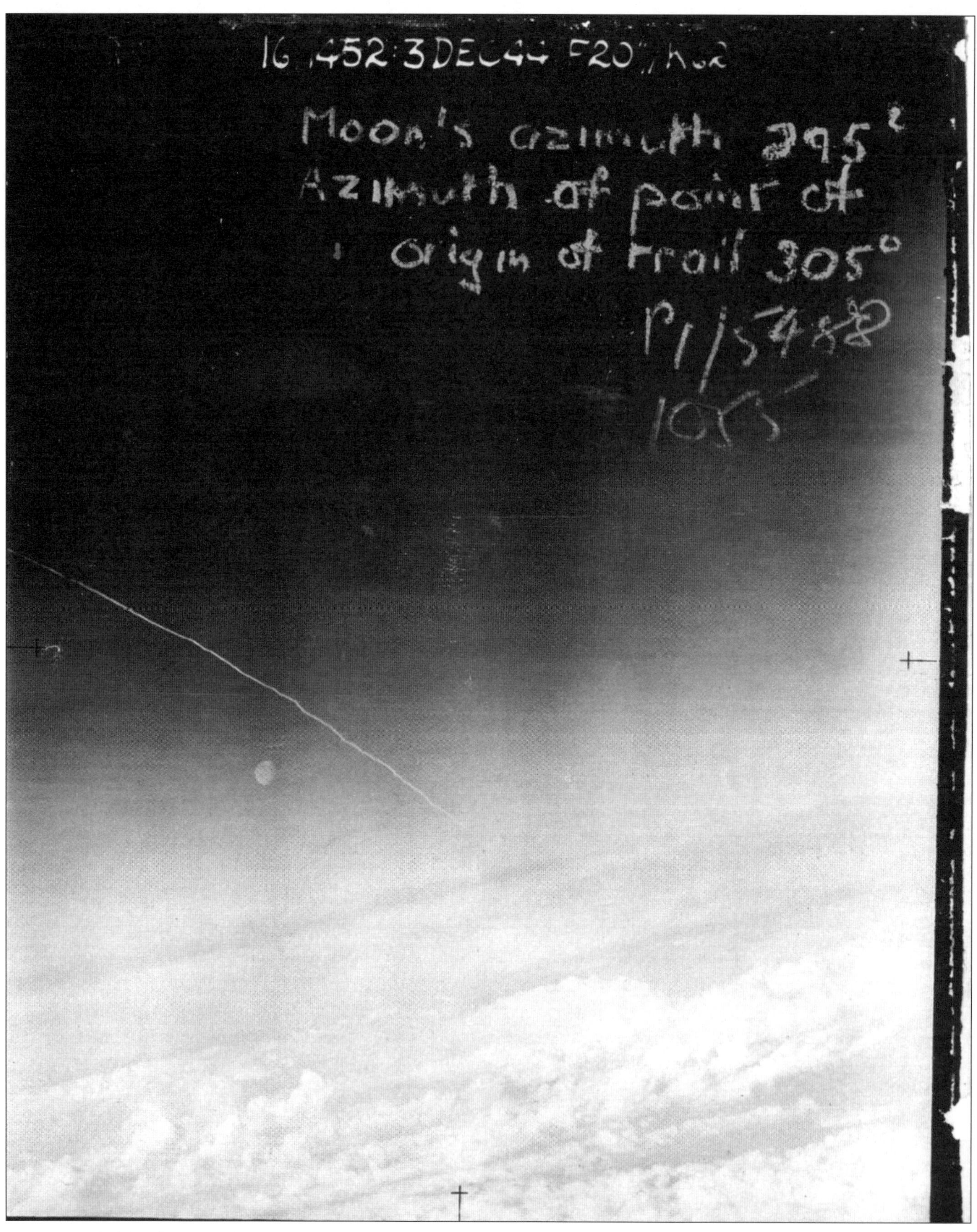

Remarkable photograph, taken by F/Lt Ken Snell of 16 Squadron on 3rd December 1944, of the trail of a V2 curving up over the daytime moon. Efforts to calculate the launch-point have been scrawled over the print by photographer James Marett.

Photo via Michael Horsfall

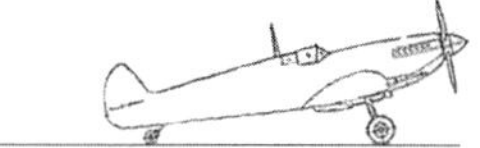

S.O.R.B.

15/10

Three operational sorties were despatched during the day to Germany. One was successful, one partially, and a third abortive due to 10/10ths cloud cover. F/0. Leagh-Murray saw a heavy Fortress raid on Ruhr, and got a burst of flak, accurate as to height but off to port. F/Lt J.M. Thompson and P/0. M.T. Moody also received bursts of flak at Wesel and Wilhelmshaven respectively.

Log Book

Oct 15th SPITFIRE G (PL)830 BRUSSELS – ROUEN and Return (abortive) 2.10

Diary

Next morning[1] it was pretty clear, so I got a kite ready and also got an oblique camera fitted, as I decided to take advantage of the trip to fly around various places, such as Paris, and take some photos.

[1] my diary has missed a day: it was now 15th October

My take-off was delayed by streams of Forts and Libs, which came back from a raid on Duisburg. Their Mustang escort also arrived in strength. One Fort gave us a scare, as he had an enormous chunk out of his left wing, which prevented him flying straight and level. He came in all the way on a gradual right-hand turn but, when he straightened out before touching-down, his left wing went down until he was almost on his side just above the runway. Somehow, I don't know how, he managed to bring that wing up and landed right down the runway; but he left us all weak at the knees and muttering our relief and admiration for the pilot.

I took-off just after, but ran into a front just around Douai. Amiens was almost invisible but, by steering an accurate course and getting right down onto the deck, I managed to reach Rouen. The ground is much higher there, though, and I kept having to go into the cloud, then letting down through it again, with my fingers crossed, hoping I wasn't over a hill.

At Rouen, I managed to find a field with a tee[2] on it, but I could see no other kites there and it looked waterlogged, so I made no effort to land there, though I saw a few 'erks dashing around in the rain. I then went off to look for the other field, on top of a hill; but the latter was in cloud and, after risking my neck getting up there, I decided it wasn't worth it – and, anyway, they probably wouldn't allow me to take-off again. So I called it a day and came home again. The electrical supply had failed, so I couldn't have taken any photos, anyway.

[2] showing direction of landing

I discovered that my trip the day before was fairly successful, the yards being well covered; but I hadn't gone quite far enough on my run to complete the target. I also found out that Duisburg had just been pranged by 1500 Lanes, so I was rather annoyed at not having gone on and taken some on-the-spot photos.

The rest of the morning I spent packing-up my Jerry prop and the motors we'd scrounged, and organising our leave.

The ubiquitous Dakota: this one was used for dropping paratroops at Arnhem.

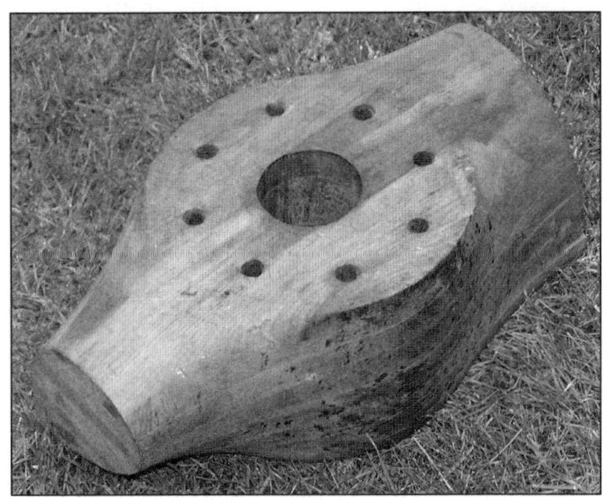

The German wooden propeller – probably from a Fieseler-Storch, equivalent to an Auster – whose broken blades I sawed off

My younger brother Christopher, who sadly died in 1950

My Singer Nine, purchased for £5 off an ash-heap with a hen's nest on the back seat

[1] Mike Horsfall and I

Next morning, Monday 16th October, we[1] got to Evère early and took-off for Antwerp just after 9.0 am in a Dakota. The weather wasn't too good this side and it was reported to be on the deck on the other, so our chances of getting over looked rather slim. At Antwerp, we were told it was definitely u/s, so we waited 2½ hours, hoping that at least we'd be able to go back to Brussels for the night. At 12.30 pm the pilot said there was a chance we might be able to get over between two fronts and, accordingly, we took-off without delay. The ceiling was pretty low, with bags of low cloud, but there was quite 300' over the Hog's Back[2]. We arrived at Northolt in pouring rain after they'd experienced hail, thunder and lightning.

[2] a hill-top road in Surrey

We found no trouble with the Customs, which was a relief, and we only hoped the grapes and peaches we'd brought hadn't been squashed in transit. We were taken to a place in the Haymarket[3] by bus, where we signed-in and were told our leave began at 12.0 am on Tuesday and we had to report back at the same time on the following Tuesday. At Paddington, I found complete chaos, due to the derailing of the Cornish Riviera, and I didn't reach Newbury till 10.30 pm.

[3] near Piccadilly Circus in London

I had a very pleasant leave, which seems to have been occupied principally with getting the old car on the road, doing a lot of developing and printing, and going over to Leamington Spa to do some shooting with Mike.

We had a good day in spite of the rain that poured all the time, Jimmy Reid being there and Colin and Mary, Mike's b. and s.[4] I left at 5.0 pm to get back on Friday night, and the old bus ran perfectly till I hit a kerb outside Oxford. For five hours I walked, taxied, heaved, pulled, scrounged tools, stopped cars, and entered caravans in an effort to get the wheel off. Eventually, I spent the night in the back of the car. Driving back, the radiator would boil over about every 10 miles and I had to stop four times to fill it up. When I did get back, I tried to repair it – with the result I ruined it altogether!

[4] brother and sister

I did a lot of printing and got some very good results with some paper I bought in Brussels, though I spoiled some by not letting the hypo fix them properly. Dad and I walked round with Kneller on Monday and I managed to get an old cock[5] right at the end.

[5] Cheam School had 350 acres of woodland, a game-keeper and some pheasants

24th October - 8th November

Next day I left fairly early and signed-in at the Haymarket. We boarded a Dak at 2.0 pm, took off at 2.15, and landed at Eindhoven before continuing and landing at Melsbroek at 5.0.

Here we found a rather changed situation. A Spit Wing had arrived – shelled out of Eindhoven – and so had the flying-bombs, which had fallen one on our M.F.P.S.[6] and two or three in the village. 4 airmen had been seriously hurt and quite a few civilians killed. The glass and slates had been blown out of our quarters and from the Mess and, altogether, there had been quite a lot of excitements.

[6] Mobile Field Photographic Section

I also found that I was, even now, only 7th on the list, as they hadn't sent out more than 10 since we'd left. There were indications, too, that we were going to do Tac/R[7] work during the winter months, when High-Level would mostly be impossible.

[7] Tactical Reconnaissance

Impressive photo of a sleek Spitfire XI at Melsbroek

Photo: Michael Horsfall

Jolliffe was now reported as killed, and Derek Wales was off ops. for three months because of his arm. I had a letter from Don White[1], who was now in Holland, and we found carpets on the floor of our room, also a cupboard and a few other scrounged articles. I also found I'd left my battle-dress at the cleaners in Newbury, and khaki was going to be withdrawn.

[1] he trained and instructed with me in the USA

Log Book

Oct. 16th	DAKOTA	KG934	P/0 ANON	SELF (pass.)	MELSBROEK – NORTHOLT via ANTWERP	2.30
Oct. 24th	DAKOTA	693	W/0 ANON	SELF (pass.)	NORTHOLT – MELSBROEK via EINDHOVEN	2.30

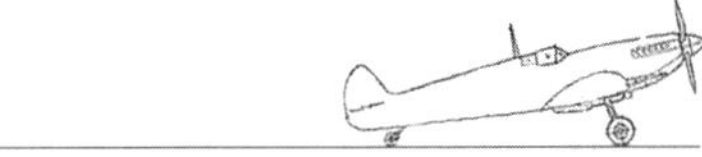

S.O.R.B.

16/10

The Squadron stood down with the exception of F/0. J. West and P/0. W.C. Heath who stood by in case of eventualities. Nothing materialised, the day being completely non-operational. There was a little practice flying.

Diary

Wednesday, we were stood-down, except for two, before lunch.

Thursday, we were stood-down again by 12.0 pm. I went into town and had tea at the Officers' Club with three other boys and a couple of quite pleasant girls.

On Friday I again had tea at the Club, and was invited to her home next night by one of the girls. Accordingly, after warning Mike I didn't know what we were letting ourselves in for, we took a tram out some distance and arrived at a large house with a bell in the gate. We pressed it and got the shock of our lives when a voice said, "Qui est la?" from a microphone also on the gate. Not knowing what to answer, we said nothing and an elderly maid let us in.

We were introduced by the two girls to their mother and two sisters, and then went downstairs to one of the most palatial rooms ever. It seemed to take up the whole ground-floor and was segmented with half-walls and pillars into a lounge, dining-room and bar. Indirect lighting was achieved by lamps buried in urns placed on pillars, and the whole place was done-up in white stucco, with white leather furniture – very fine.

An army lieutenant arrived later, followed by an aunt and two cousins; then a Belgian solicitor, who was called The Communist because of his high-flown ideas, and finally a colonel. The Communist was great fun, though I didn't realise that that was not his avocation till I had been talking with him for about ten minutes.

After about an hour and a half we drifted to the bar – a beautiful little piece of work – and toasted Monsieur et Madame Baliseaux in champagne, followed by the RAF and the King. We then sat down to dinner at three different tables and, though they told us they'd had nothing to eat the week before, they gave us a three-course meal with roast beef. Mike and I had to leave early to catch our tram and were lucky in getting a lift that enabled us to make it.

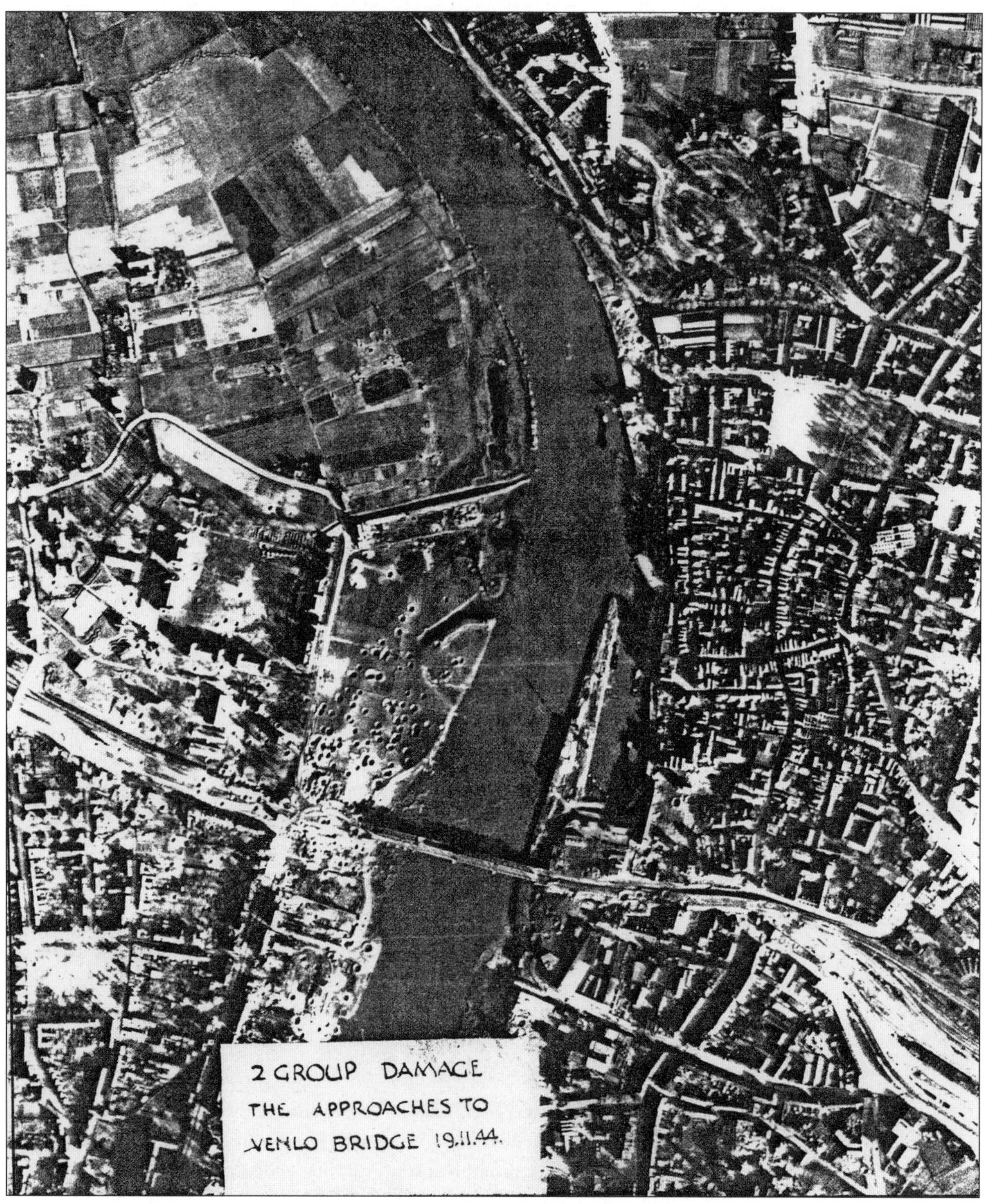

The Bridges over the Maas at Venlo
On a vital supply route for the Germans, they were attacked frequently, but fruitlessly, by the Mitchells of 2 Group, each time requiring a damage-assessment sortie by a pilot of 16 Squadron.
Photo: "34 Wing – an Unofficial Account"

S.O.R.B.

29/10

Another good day. Eight sorties being despatched to Holland and Germany. Six were a success, two others being abortive. One pilot sighted a F.W. 190 over the Ruhr Valley, but was not attacked. Two other pilots reported the encountering of light flak. Nothing else of interest to report.

Log Book

Oct. 29th	SPITFIRE XI	0 (MB)950	12. BRIDGES at VENLO and ROERMOND 4500'. 1.45

Line Book

29.10.44	F/0 TAYLOR	SPIT XI	0915	Bridges at VENLO and
	5"	0	1100	ROERMOND
	4500'			

A/B 0915 Circled EINDHOVEN for 45 mins. before receiving instructions to cover the bridges. Made one run over each at 4500', encountering one burst of light flak at start of first run. Landed 1100 with no further incident.

HJS Taylor. F/0.

Diary

I was told I wouldn't be needed for flying early next morning, but at ten to 8.0 am Willie[1] woke me up and told me to go down to Ops. straightaway, without breakfast. Damning that, I dressed quickly and had a hasty meal and reported to Ops.

[1] W/O Willshaw

Apparently, the Mitchells[2] had pranged a bridge[3] at Venlo and another at Roermond, and a Mossie was being sent over high to take the pictures. But, in case cloud-cover interfered, I was to circle round Eindhoven and, if necessary, go over and take the bridges from low level – at any rate, not above 4500'.

[2] of 139 Wing, also based at Melsbroek

[3] at Venlo there were a road bridge and a rail bridge side-by-side, usually called 'Venlo Bridge'

Accordingly, I took-off at 9.15 am and flew to Eindhoven and circled for a solid hour before the message came through. In that time, I flew over to the bridges and discovered that they were under about half cloud and informed base of it. However, the Mossie's message came through, at last, to say he'd taken 'A' bridge, but not 'B' and 'C' – so those were my marching orders.

I flew over to Venlo above cloud and let down rapidly before the bridge, calling out 'Tally ho!' on the way, just to encourage myself. I saw three black puffs appear behind and then concentrated on making a good run. After passing the target, I pulled up steeply and proceeded up the river, turning and twisting, to Roermond, where I again dived down and made a run over the bridge. I then made off for home.

On the way, I passed over a wood with a surprisingly distinct straight shadow-line. Thinking it must be an underground hangar, I made a run over it for interest but, to my chagrin, I found on development that it was only an overgrown slag-heap. I also made a run over the field[4] on my return, for interest.

[4] I made a 'mosaic' of the airfield: see p242

Rouen and its cathedral taken from the air on my trip there on 29th October

Rouen Cathedral taken from the ground on the same occasion

Log Book

Oct. 29th SPITFIRE XI B (PA)944 MELSBROEK – ROUEN and RETURN. 2.00

Diary

Now came an incident which was personally of importance – and that was my second flight to Rouen, on the same day as my Venlo dicer.

This time the weather was good and I got to Rouen by 3.0 pm. But the field looked hopelessly small – just a grass square full of puddles and wheel-tracks, extended in one direction in the form of a narrow runway on chalk. I began to come in once and put my wheels down, then thought I'd better take a close look at the surface, so pulled them up again and did two slow low circuits, trying to make up my mind.

However, having got so far I determined to have a smack at it and came in to land. But I found the runway was too narrow to allow me to position myself properly and, having got quite close to the ground, I was not lined-up with it, so gave it the gun and went round again. Next time, I flew on a straight approach and tried to drop her just over the boundary. But I was going too fast and I was well down the runway when I eventually touched the ground. But the latter was very rough and it was in the balance whether I'd hit my wing-tip before my tail-wheel. She did settle, though, but while I was still going fast, I saw the far end of the strip looming up. I braked hard all the way and managed to stop right at the very end.

As I taxied back, scores of little kids emerged from the woods waving a greeting. I looked around the place and realised how terribly small it was – also that there were no other kites around. A naval seaman ushered me in, and I prayed she'd start-up easily as I switched her off.

On getting out, I found two naval officers and one RAF type, who welcomed me. It turned out to be an F.A.A.[1] station, with one officer and 6 bods! And they had no idea of any radar station. But, most fortunately, the RAF type had enquired of an RAF type he'd met in Rouen as to where he was, and the latter said, "On the Paris road, about 15 miles out." At this my heart sank but, to cut a long story short, this fellow said he'd take me there in his truck. It was now 3.30 and, after I'd rung up the Garrison Intelligence for further gen.[2] and he'd done his business, we set off at 3.50.

[1] Fleet Air Arm

[2] information

At 4.15 we reached the HQ chateau, and further enquiries elicited that Gerald was on the site ½-mile away. I accordingly borrowed the truck and, with a motorcyclist leading the way, I did my first solo down a wretched lane. We found the unit at the end of it – and Gerald turned up just as I arrived.

We talked for about 10 mins. and then I had to leave, as I wanted to get off by 5.0 to be home before dark at 6.0. But, of course, I got stuck in the Mess over a cup of tea with the very decent C.O., a S/Ldr, and his three subordinates.

Eventually, I left at 5.20, after bags of civvies had gathered to watch. Fortunately, she started-up O.K. and, by using full throttle, I got off about half-way down the runway. I climbed up and dived down low, just to give them their

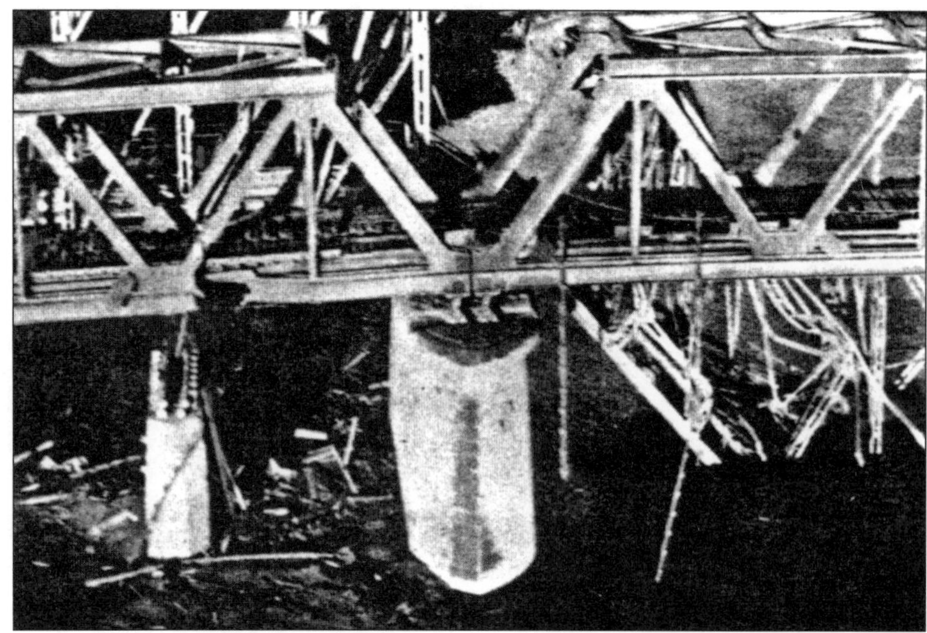

P/O Clyde Heath's very low-level close-up of the Venlo bridges, which survived numerous bombing raids and required damage-assessment sorties by PR aircraft afterwards.

Photo: "34 Wing – An Unofficial Account"

The destroyed bridge at Roermond: low-level oblique taken by F/Lt A.S. Baker of 34 Wing staff in Spitfire PL765 of 16 Squadron on 28th October. Baker succeeded Tony Davis as CO of 16 Squadron in June 1945.

money's worth. I then went over to Gerald's place and beat them up a couple of times as a farewell[1].

I then set off hotfoot for home, and the darker it got the more I increased speed – until I was doing 270 mph indicated. I got off course a bit near Amiens and, eventually, had to ask for a homing. I got back at 6.0 and it was quite dark when, just as I was rounding the circuit, I saw bags of flak going up – right in my direction. I took another look to make sure, called up on the radio, and was told to shove off! I left the circuit and, by looking closely, could distinguish the glow that gave away the presence of a doodle-bug. Keeping a safe distance, I circled slowly till it had passed over the field, then came in and, with the assistance of the moon, made quite a nice landing.

The chief event of interest, from the operational point of view, was the continual sorties we flew to photograph the bridge at Venlo[2] after continual abortive attacks by Mitchells. Each time they went, they met a hotter reception – and our boys got the full dose of it when they followed-in 30 mins. or so afterwards.

Burton got hit twice at 15000' so, next time, Clyde Heath went in on the deck all the way and brought back close-up shots of a child in a gutter, a dog, and a buttress of the bridge, on which you could almost count the splinters on the sleepers. I don't think the bridge was ever demolished, but it was eventually decided that it had been rendered impassable[3].

[1] He said I nearly carried away their radar aerial!

[2] it was a main route for German supplies and reinforcements

[3] the Germans blew it up after they had retreated over it

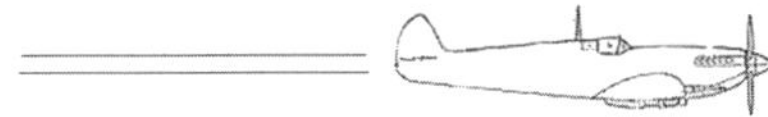

S.O.R.B.
4/11

An improvement all round, six trips were made, targets being in Holland and Germany. Four pilots took photographs, two sorties being abortive owing to heavy cloud cover in target area. F/0. C.D. Burton ran into a lot of trouble, his target was the bridge at Venlo. He experienced very intense and accurate light flak. On his first run his aircraft was hit and turned over on its back, but he finished his run as best he could. He left area until the cloud cleared, then came back to do another run, this time flak was even more intense and accurate and once again he was turned over on his back, he managed to finish-the run and then "beat it" as fast as he could. No other incidents of note were reported.

Log Book

Nov. 4th	SPITFIRE XI D (PL)851	13. FRISIAN ISLE – COASTLINE: DEEPEN – SCHILLIG 20000'. 2.15

Line Book

4.11.44	F/0 TAYLOR S/36" 20000' 16/1327	SPIT XI D 851	1455 1710	FRISIAN ISLE S. of JUIST. Coastline NORDEN – SCHILLIG.

A/B 1455. Island clear of cu. but only two-thirds of coastline uncovered. Cirrus at 21000' so made two runs at 20000', but towards the end light was failing. Landed 1710. No incidents.

HJS Taylor F/0.

Typical strato-cumuls weather, with an occasional gap

'Tommy' Thompson all dressed up for a high-level sortie, with a 'Mae West' life-jacket on top
Photo: Michael Horsfall

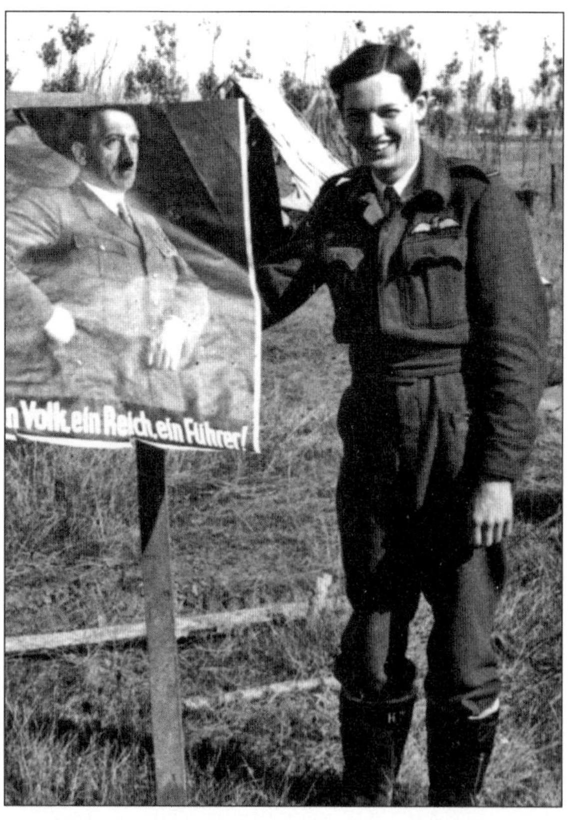

I found the Spitfire XI cockpit quite warm and wore this battle-dress with wool-lined 'escape' boots and silk under-gloves – by a Hitler poster at Amiens-Glisy.
Photo: Michael Horsfall

Diary

Nothing else seems to have happened till my next sortie on the 4th. This was to the coastline south of the Frisians, to determine coastal gun-batteries and the height of the tide. It also included a small island.

After a bad start, because 5" had not been fitted and my transmission on the ground was very weak, I had quite a nice flight to the target – though my heart went to my mouth once when, happening to look behind, I saw two kites very close in, just banking away from me. Fortunately, I recognised them from their outline and markings as Spits, but they could easily have been Jerries, and I wondered what they were doing so far away, up near Emden.

Everything was covered with cloud, except that it was rolled back a little way inland of the coast I was meant to take. But the island was clear, so I took that first and then made my run along the coast. Unfortunately, there was cirrus down to 20000', so I had to stay below that height, where I knew the ground coverage was not very great. This meant that I had to be bang over the right place and, after experimenting, I found the only way was to take separate pictures and roll over onto my side between each.

In this way I progressed along the coast, till the presence of cloud prevented me. I then flew on, hoping for another gap, and then changed course for Wilhelmshaven – but this, too, was under cloud, so I returned the way I'd come and went back along the coast, taking pictures as I went. I'd spotted a radio station on the way, but the time was 4.25 pm, past last light, and though I made an extra run over, I felt uncertain of the result – which turned out later to be too dark. I then flew home without incident.

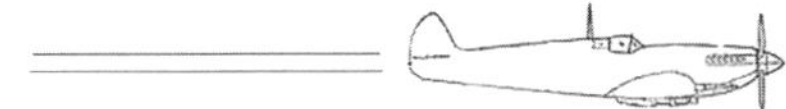

S.O.R.B.

8/11

A slight improvement in conditions today. Two sorties were flown over Germany. Only one was successful, the other was abortive due to cloud obscurity. F/0. H.J.S. Taylor had a trying trip, he experienced heavy and accurate flak each time he emerged from cloud. No other incidents were reported. Some local flying was done.

Log Book

Nov. 8th SPITFIRE XI O (MB)950[1] 14. "DORTMUND – EMS CANAL". (TWENTHE CANAL) 3500' 1.40

[1] an example of the not unusual wartime confusion of entries

Line Book

8.11.44	F/0 TAYLOR	SPIT XI	1555	JUNCTION of
	20" 5"	O 823[1]	1705	DORTMUND – EMS CANAL.
	3500'.	(PL)		Near RHEINE.

A/B 1525 Stayed above 6/10 low cloud and below 10/10 medium cloud at 10000'. After EINDHOVEN over 10/10 low cloud and let down through it on E.T.A. Photographed junction in vicinity of what I presumed to be RHEINE,

A section of the Dortmund – Ems Canal re-routed and rebuilt after suffering heavy damage from a Bomber Command raid

Operational photo taken by 'Scotty' Cadan

but being dubious of the correct location followed canal Northwards and took another junction which seemed more likely. Experienced heavy and fairly accurate flak each time I emerged from cloud, and found severe icing in cu. nimbs on return journey. Landed 1705 without further incident.

HJS Taylor F/0.

Diary

The weather continued duff but, on the 8th, Ops. thought there might be a chance of getting a Priority One target, which was to see, photographically or visually, whether a portion of the Dortmund-Ems canal near Rheine had been broken open on their[1] last prang. I was given 20" cameras to take it from about 12000' but, in case cloud interfered – and they expected there'd be about 3/10 – I had 5" for a low-level effort.

[1] presumably by Lancs

I realised the weather was going to be sticky, so I concentrated on flying an accurate course and reached Eindhoven in 12 mins, which gave me a ground-speed of 300 mph. I worked out an exact ETA for Rheine from this, but soon found myself underneath a canopy of cloud at 9000', with 9/10 below me. Eventually, just before my time came up, I decided it was time to go down through but, on breaking cloud, I found there were no recognisable features.

But, a minute later, I saw a town in front, with a river or canal flowing past it on this side. Reference to the map showed it should be Rheine, with the canal beyond. There was a large cu. nimb. over the town, so I flew through a hole – and got rather a shock when I found no canal on the other side. I searched the map for a similar town, but could find none; so I went back through the cloud to have another look at the canal.

Then I discovered another large town on my left, or downstream, and that had me completely foxed, as Osnabruck was the nearest feature like that, but it only resembled it superficially.

Then I spotted a junction of waters and decided that must be it so I nipped into the cloud, flew over, and nipped out again for my runs. I made a run over each branch of the canal and was rather surprised to encounter no flak, as I had been warned there were a good 6 batteries around.

On my last run, I took time to look around and was in doubt about the situation of the bridges, which crossed over in the right places but failed to continue according to the map. I looked all over the map for any other junction that I might be over, with a big town nearby. Finding none, I decided I could hardly be north of the target, so followed the canal along intending to have a look north of where I was. Eventually, a river joined us[2] at the right position as if we were going towards Rheine, and I was checking-up on the map – when flak started bursting all around.

[2] this was the junction of the Twenthe Canal with the River Ijssel just north of Zutphen (Twente is the post-war spelling)

I immediately made for the cloud, but it seemed like ages before I reached its sanctuary, and those horrible little streaks of tracer continued to follow me even inside it. This, I decided, was the real thing so, keeping just in the cloud, I positioned myself then turned down over one leg. I immediately met intense flak of all descriptions – tracer, self-destroying 20 mm stuff, black puffs of Bofors, and

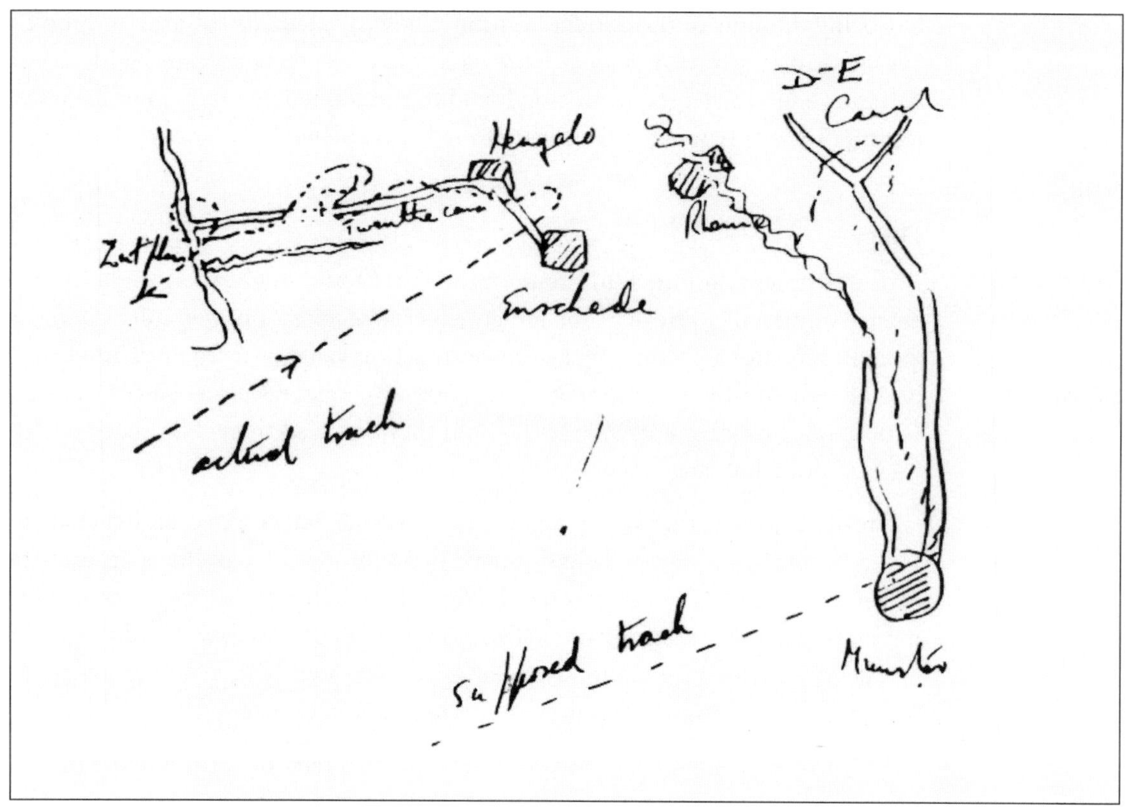

My 1944 sketch to try and work out where I had been; the junction with the Almelo Canal (not drawn) was the basis of the loop after Hengelo and the cause of my confusing it with the Dortmund-Ems Canal.

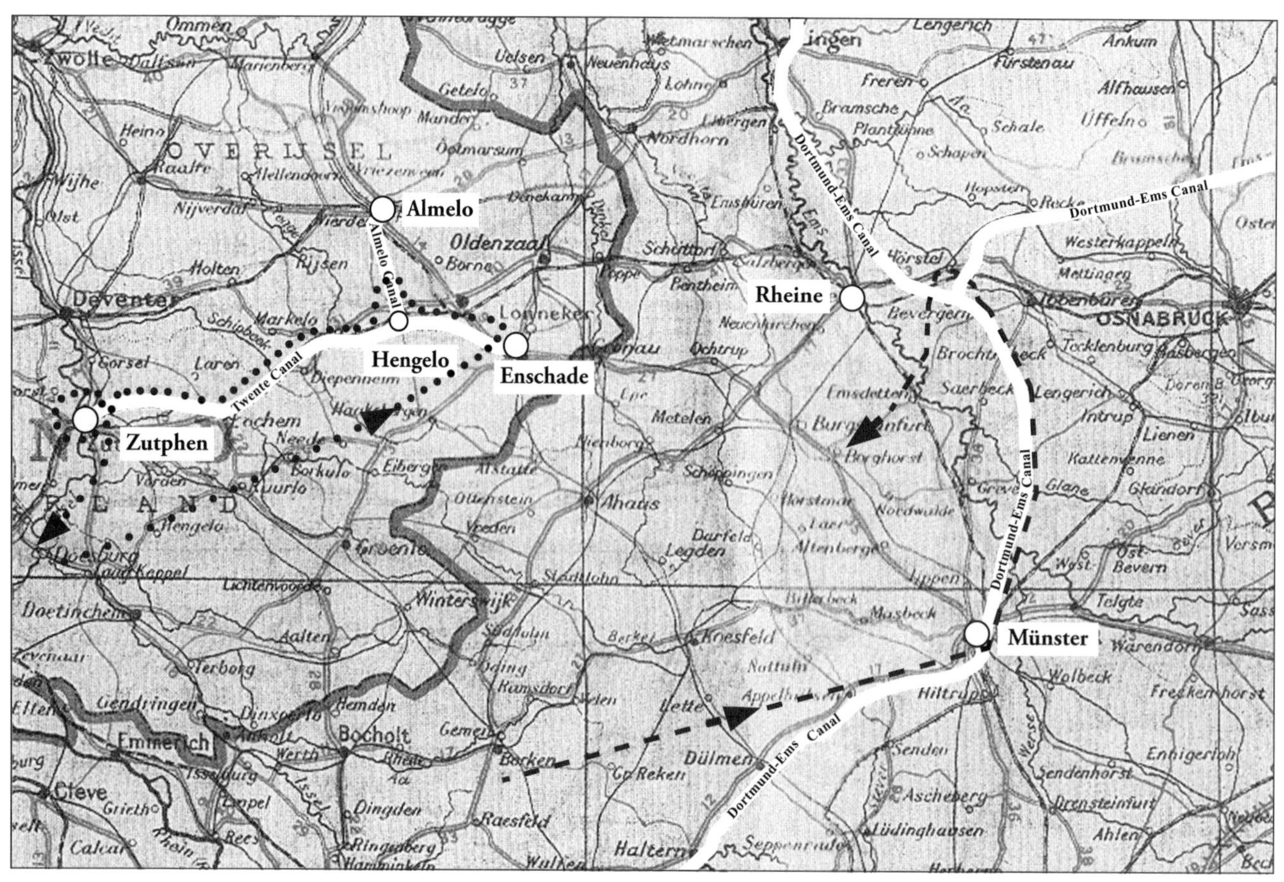

Map of the area showing my supposed track and target — — — and actual track and target • • • • •

great red blobs that seemed to crawl up to me with deceptive slowness. However, I made one run, then whistled back into cloud, flew on a bit, then made another, with less interference

On the third leg, I could see a lock with water flowing through it, so I decided that was a good thing to take. I concentrated on flying directly over it, as I was now down to 2500', and failed to notice any flak directed at me. I then climbed up into the cloud and set course for home in its protection.

I emerged just short of a river that looked like the Rhine, so I photographed a temporary bridge that had been erected and the trenches that had been dug around it, though the failing light made a successful picture doubtful.

On continuing, I found a solid wall of cumulus in front of me but, hoping it was only a thin one, I started to fly through it. The next moment my windscreen iced over completely and I realised it would be suicide to go on, as it was probably a cu.nimb. I turned so sharply that I toppled my artificial horizon and, at the same time, my compass started spinning and the speed increased alarmingly. Anxiously I peered at the turn-and-bank indicator and, resisting the impulse to keep pulling back on the stick, I remembered to roll out of the turn and concentrate on maintaining my height. A moment later, I heard Penman calling me, so I told them I couldn't get through and they dog-legged[1] me back via Antwerp.

[1] indirect routeing

I told Ops. I didn't know where I'd been, but I rather thought I'd got it on the second attempt; but I had a bitter disappointment later that evening when I helped the APIS [2] plotters to work out what I'd photographed. For I'd never reached Rheine – I'd hit a town N. of my position and photographed a canal which wasn't marked on the map. Then, instead of flying north as I'd thought, I'd followed the canal S.E.[3] and taken a junction 30 miles from Rheine.

[2] Army Photographic Interpretation Section

[3] I should have written S.W., as I actually flew Enschede-Zutphen

God, was I annoyed and chagrined – more especially as it was a No. 1 target and it was unlikely the weather would allow another sortie for some time. I felt awfully bad about the whole thing, but everybody was very sympathetic and, finally, Groupie[4] did the job himself two days later – but I certainly learned a few lessons from it.

[4] Group Captain Ogilvie, lost on a Met. flight 11th December 1944

The Diary ends abruptly at the end of this 14th operation. We had a period of bad weather which affected our operations and it was a week before I went out on another mission. I probably had little interest in recording my leisure activities, and perhaps my sorties were beginning to feel routine.

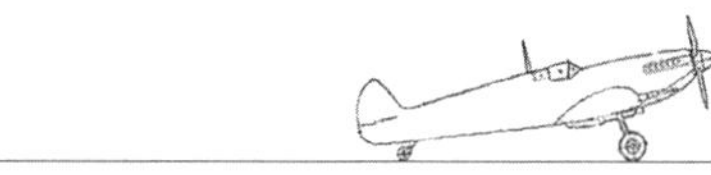

S.O.R.B.

14/11

Hardly any better to-day, only one sortie was despatched and this was a Met Recce to Germany. The pilot reported 10/10ths cloud at various levels up to 32000', he had the unpleasant experience of being engaged by our own A.A. North of base.

P/O W.C. Heath (left)
He was promoted to F/O posthumously
and awarded the DFC.
Photo: Hugh Rigby Collection

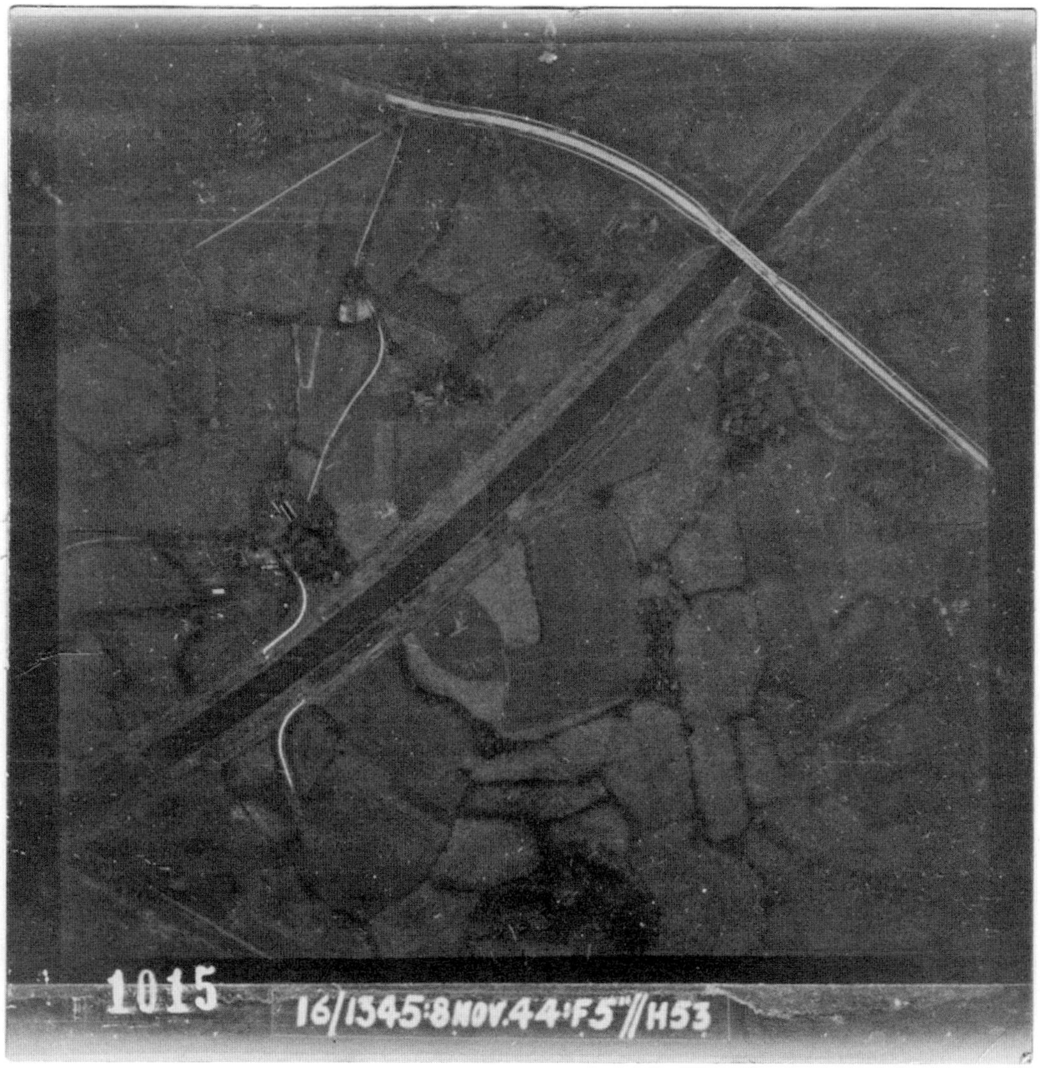

1015 16/1345:8NOV.44:F5"//H53

One of my F24 5" photographs of the Twente Canal (presumed Dortmund-Ems) taken in conditions of very poor light

Log Book

Nov. 14th SPITFIRE XI L (MB)957 BRUSSELS – EINDHOVEN – BRUSSELS 1.00

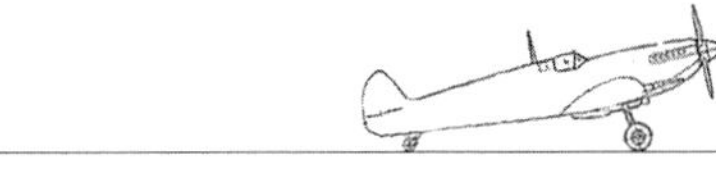

S.O.R.B.

15/11

Once more a duff day operationally, but eight short trips of a non-operational nature were flown.

Log Book

Nov. 14th SPITFIRE XI W 959 (PA949?) AIR TEST. .30

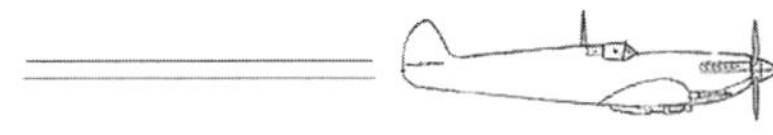

S.O.R.B.

18/11

Seven operational sorties were despatched to-day to Holland and Germany. Five of these trips were successful, four being photo recce's and one a Met Recce. One trip was abortive due to cloud conditions and the seventh was brought about by the non-return of P/0. W.C. Heath. Clyde went on a dicer to Venlo in the late afternoon, and so far has failed to return, we all earnestly hope that he managed to get back to our own lines; and that communication difficulties may be the reason for his silence, The sad news was received to-day that P/0. J.R. Brodby is dead. His grave has now been located at Wychen in Holland. He was reported missing on 20.9.44 whilst on detachment at Northolt on special duties. He will be greatly missed, because John had been with the Squadron a long time, both as an N.C.O. and commissioned officer.

Log Book

Nov. 18th AUSTER MT854 F/L SNELL SELF (pass.) CIRCUIT. .20

" " MT854 SELF L.A.C. ANON AIR TEST. .30

" SPITFIRE XI S (PL)905 15. R.R. at VIERSEN – KEMPEN – KREFELD – DULKEN 24000' 2.40

Line Book

18.11.44 F/Lt.[1] TAYLOR S/36" SPIT XI S 905 13.05 15.45 VIERSEN – KEMPEN – WESEL

[1] my promotion two years after being commissioned

A/B 1305. Took VIERSEN as ordered, other targets cloud covered. Took further pictures of VIERSEN and KEMPEN at intervals but could see no signs of pranging. Took other marshalling yards and bridges while hanging around. Landed 1545. No incidents.

HJS Taylor F/Lt.

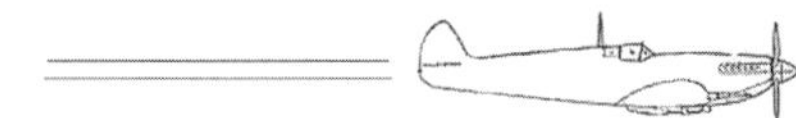

S.O.R.B.

19/11

The biggest "press on" day for about six months. Twenty-one (21) operational sorties were despatched to Holland and Germany. It was an excellent day for flying and 19 trips were successful. The remaining two sorties were abortive. Weather conditions in target area were responsible for one failure, and the other through the failure of F/Lt. H.J.S. Taylor to return to base. F/Lt. H.J.S. Taylor we regret to say has now been reported missing. Quite a gloom has been cast over the Squadron, because Jimmy is the second of our pilots reported missing within the space of 24 hours. We all earnestly hope that we shall receive re-assuring news of both F/Lt. Taylor and P/0. Heath very soon.

During the other 19 operations, five of the pilots reported sighting V.2 trails, one pilot managed to take a photograph. F/0. G.A. Winter reported activity by our own and enemy a/c over the Ruhr, he came into land with his tail wheel retracted, but made it without mishap. F/0. G. Cribb encountered red tracer which was very accurate at Venlo, but luckily was not hit. His R/T became U/S and he was lost for a while, but eventually made base quite safely at dusk.

Log Book (completed by F/Lt Michael Horsfall)

Nov. 19th SPITFIRE XI L (MB)957 16. AIRFIELDS IN RHEINE AREA.

MISSING FROM THIS OPERATION.

(See Appendix F for the entries in my Log Book of all my flights in 16 Squadron)

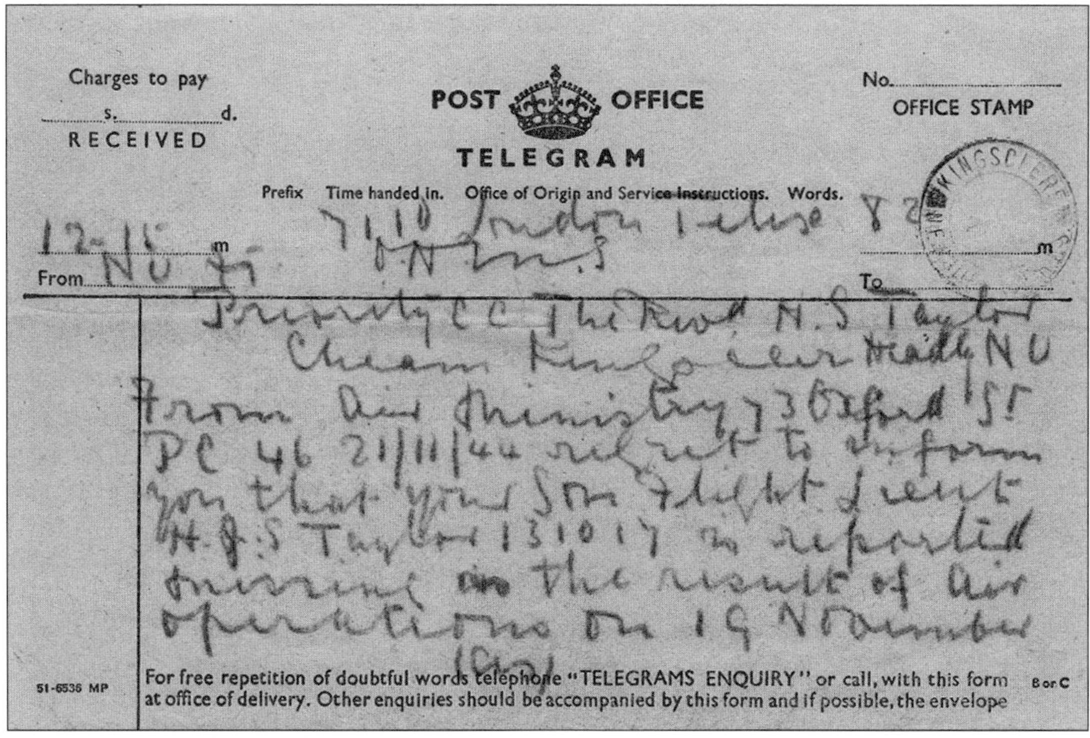

Charges to pay
s. d.
RECEIVED

POST OFFICE
TELEGRAM

No.
OFFICE STAMP

Prefix Time handed in. Office of Origin and Service Instructions. Words.

12-15 m
From NU

Priority CC The Revd H.S. Taylor
Cheam Kingsclere Heath NU
From Air Ministry 73 Oxford St
PC 46 21/11/44 regret to inform
you that your son Flight Lieut
H.J.S. Taylor 131017 is reported
missing as the result of air
operations on 19 November

For free repetition of doubtful words telephone "TELEGRAMS ENQUIRY" or call, with this form at office of delivery. Other enquiries should be accompanied by this form and if possible, the envelope

51-6536 MP B or C

The official telegram, dreaded by all next-of-kin, telling my parents that I was missing on operations on 19 November 1944. This one was written out at the local telegraph office in Kingsclere.

Downfall

CHAPTER 14

Bale-out and Evasion*

My next flight was certainly the most memorable of my life. Sunday, 19th November, was a fine clear day, very welcome after a week of low cloud and rain. All the aircraft were sent out on missions except for two, one of which was rather worn-out and ready for overhaul. Another pilot and I spun a coin to decide which of us should take this one – and I lost the toss. However, I'd flown MB957 to Rouen and was not at all worried about its condition.

This could have been me making an unwelcome contrail on my way to Rheine.
Photo: Alfred Price "Supermarine Spitfire"

I took off at about 11.0am and set course for Rheine, a base for the German jets, and other airfields near Münster. At 24000', I found my exhaust was leaving a white 'contrail' across the sky, so I stayed just below this height and began taking my photographs. Suddenly, while I was in the middle of a 'run', there was a loud 'bang' from the engine, it stopped momentarily and then tried to continue, but clouds of smoke filled with oil came out of the exhausts, followed by a sheet of flame. I switched-off my cameras and juggled with the controls to try to get the engine to run properly, but the smoke continued to pour out and my windscreen was soon covered in oil, so that I had to open the hood to see out. I called up Melsbroek on the radio and reported that I had an engine-failure; they told me to try to get back by gliding at 140 mph on a course of 230°, although the wind of 60 mph at my height was against me and reduced my speed over the ground by that amount.

I was leaving a trail of dirty grey smoke behind me in the sky, which would soon attract the Germans' attention. There was an 87-gallon petrol tank between me and the engine; so, when smoke began to come up from the floor of the cockpit, I felt that the whole plane might explode at any moment and decided to bale out before I was blown out. I made careful preparations and told Melsbroek what I was doing; then, when the radio cut-out at about 14000', I turned the aircraft upside-down, released my harness and dropped out.

Unfortunately, either I hit the tail, or the wing or tail struck me. I felt as if I had been cut in half and lost consciousness. I was woken up by a small voice urging me, "Pull the rip-cord! Pull the rip-cord!" I did so and saw the parachute begin to open, then I lost interest in the proceedings. I came-to again over a large sheet of water (possibly the junction of the Twente and Almelo Canals) and feared, feebly, I might drown. Then I passed over a man on a bicycle, who didn't look up, and I thought, "Silly fellow, can't see me." The next moment, the ground rushed up, the same voice called, "Knees together! Knees together!" and I rolled over onto wet grass.

*See "Dutch Voices" p. 669 for a translation into Dutch of this account.

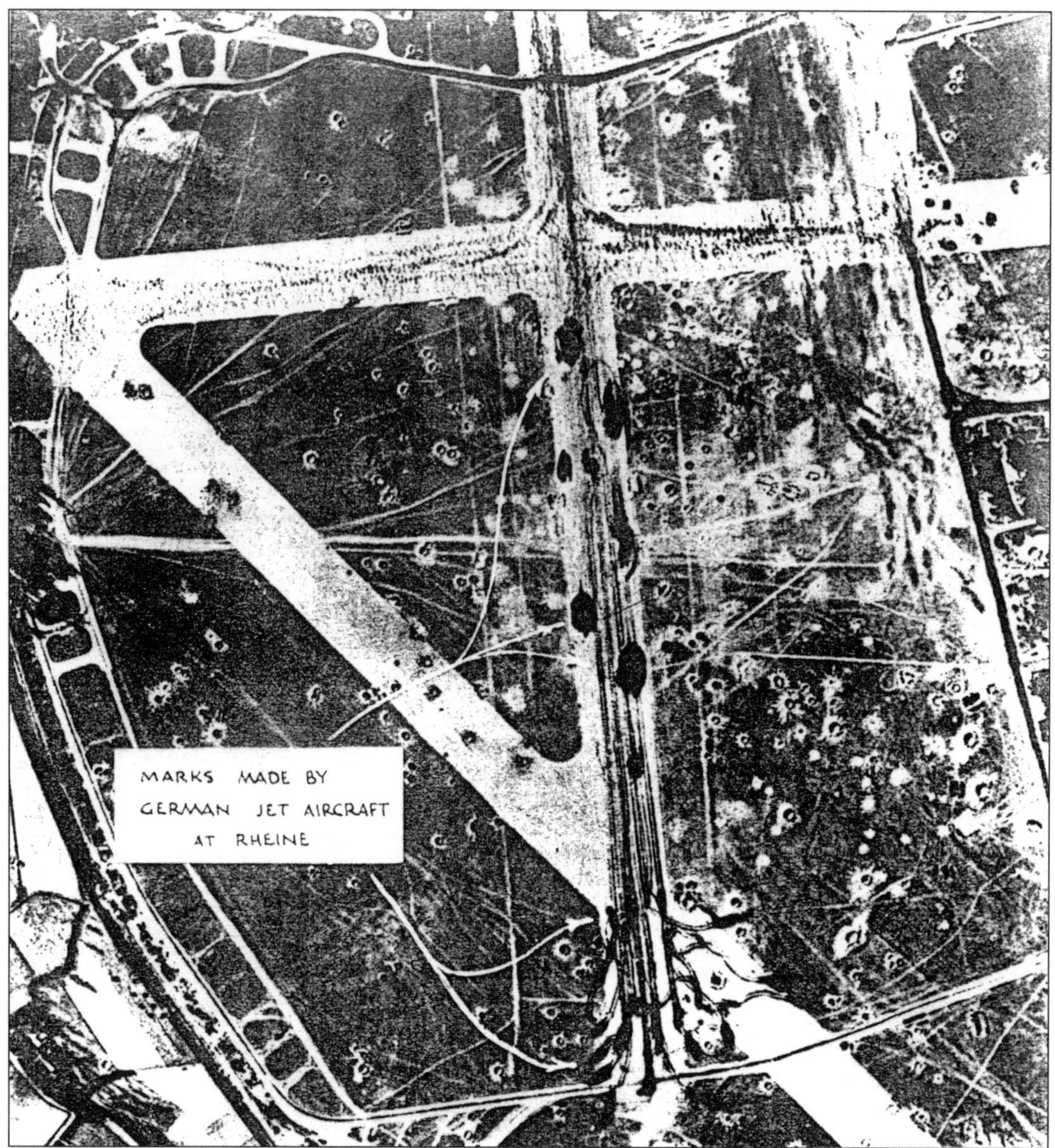

Much enlarged print of Rheine airfield, heavily bombed and with the runways showing scorch-marks from German jet-planes

Photo: "34 Wing – An Unofficial Account"

When I woke up, there was a circle of men in long black overcoats standing round me; but when I released my parachute and the wind blew it away into a tree, they all ran after it. Assuming they were Germans, I struggled to my feet, pulled off and dropped my helmet and goggles, and limped away in the opposite direction, bent over because of the pain in my stomach. I saw a wood about fifty yards in front of me and crawled under the wire into it. I sat there for a short time and then moved further into it. But I realised this would be an obvious choice for the Germans to think of as my hiding-place, so I walked to one side where it bordered a large open field. A drainage ditch ran through this into the wood, so I decided to crawl along it into the centre of the field; I would then be able to see anyone coming in my direction before they were likely to spot my head among the grasses on the top of the ditch. Not long afterwards I saw soldiers on bicycles, with rifles on their backs, pedalling along a lane at the far end of my field; but I felt pretty sure they would not bother to search for me in a large open meadow.

I now took stock of my situation: I had an escape-kit, a plastic box tucked into my battle-dress blouse; it contained 24 Horlicks tablets, some biscuits and chocolate, a plastic bag and water-purification tablets, a box of matches, a razor, a needle and thread, and two buttons which, placed one on top of the other, behaved like a compass, with a dot of luminous paint pointing to North. I calculated that, as I was fit and had eaten a good breakfast, I could survive for a week on one-seventh of these rations a day and plenty of purified water. My Spitfire was well-heated, so I was wearing my ordinary blue battle-dress, with no flying-jacket, and leather, wool-lined, 'escape' flying-boots, whose tops could be torn off to leave plain-looking shoes. I ripped the tops together and wrapped them round me as a waistcoat, since this November was unusually cold. I cut off my RAF 'wings', which were very conspicuous, and put them in my pocket, and I rubbed mud over my blue Flight Lieutenant's tapes on my shoulder-straps so that, if I were captured, I would be treated as an officer. I had lost my watch somehow in my bale-out, which was a serious blow; henceforth, all the times in this account are my own approximate calculations.

My situation at about noon on 19th November 1944

I had no idea where I was. After the explosion of my engine, I had no time to navigate and, in any case, the ground was half-obscured by small cumulus clouds. My maps, which I had stuffed into my boots, had fallen out during my descent, and there were no maps or European money in my escape-kit, as there should have been. I felt it was wiser to assume I was still in Germany. I could tell the approximate direction for me to travel by the winter sun, now approaching the horizon. I had a vague idea that the German border with Holland ran a long way to the south; so, if I went south, I might be staying inside Germany unnecessarily. It would be better to go west for a good distance, perhaps 100 miles, possibly to Utrecht in Holland, and then turn south to the Rhine. Here I thought I might find an abandoned Dutch house, perhaps with bottled fruit and other food in the cellar, where I could lie up and wait for the Allied armies to arrive. The Arnhem disaster had taken place two months earlier, but I thought our troops would soon cross the Rhine and I would emerge from my cellar and be taken back to 16 Squadron. This was Sunday and I had a date with a girl in

Congratulations . . .

It is indeed a pleasure to welcome you as a member of the Caterpillar Club.

As is customary, we have had the official insignia of the Club made and engraved especially for you, which you will find attached, together with your membership certificate.

We have pleasure in sending these to you with our compliments and best wishes, in recognition of the emergency parachute jump which you made.

CATERPILLAR CLUB.

The Irvin Air Chute Co. kindly organised the Caterpillar Club for airmen who had baled out successfully.

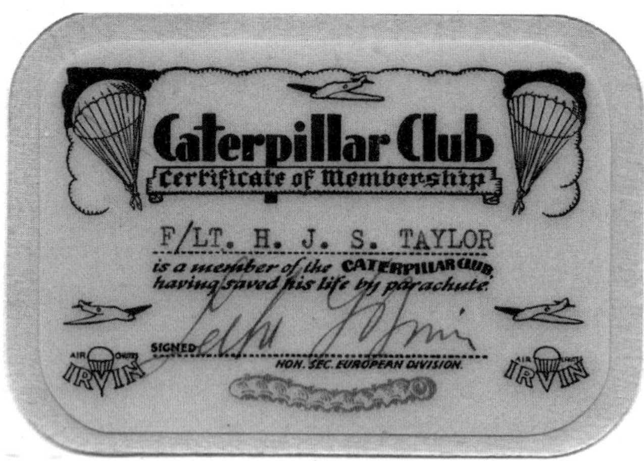

Caterpillar Club
Certificate of Membership
F/LT. H. J. S. TAYLOR
is a member of the CATERPILLAR CLUB,
having saved his life by parachute.
SIGNED
HON. SEC. EUROPEAN DIVISION.
IRVIN

A gold silkworm brooch came with this certificate.

1954 photograph of the scattered hamlet of 't Hesseler, a mile south of Borne, where I landed on 19th November.

Photo via Harry Leuveld

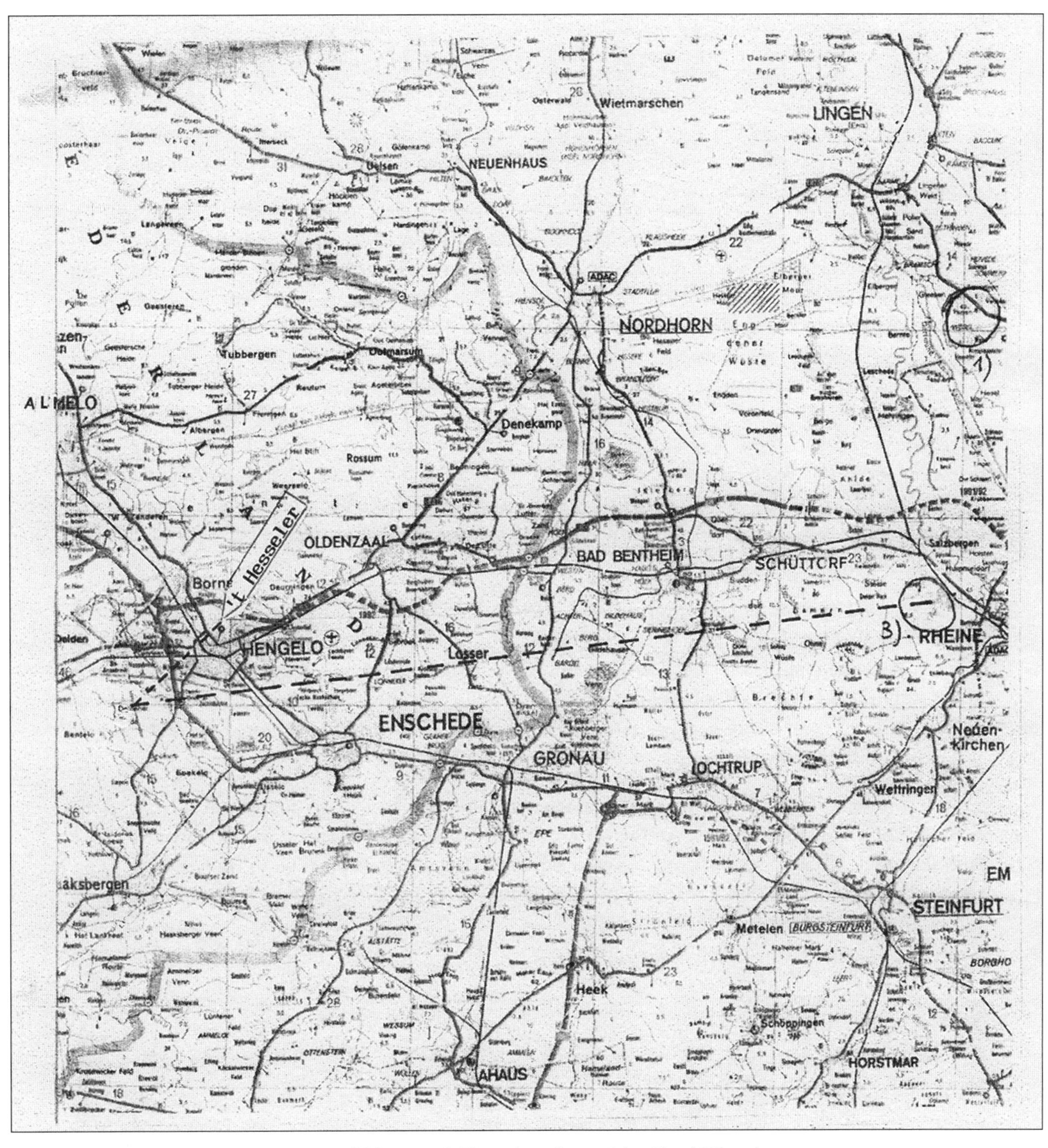

Map of Rheine – 't Hesseler, about 34 miles (55kms).
Circles with numbers indicate German jet-plane bases.
— — — — — — glide-path of my Spitfire
- - - - - - - - - - - - my parachuting path

Map supplied by Dr. Thomas Giessmann, Archivist of Rheine

Brussels on the Wednesday, so I felt a slight spur of urgency to get back without delay, before someone else took her over! (In fact, the Allies did not cross the Rhine in Holland until March 1945, so my simple plan would have back-fired badly.)

I had a scare at about 4.0pm, when a large herd of cows, driven by a farm-hand, came across the field in my direction, no doubt to be milked. However, they crossed my ditch further down and the herdsman never even glanced in my direction.

At night-fall, I felt it was safe to leave my ditch and started walking west across the fields towards where the sun had set; but I soon found that every field was surrounded by barbed wire, beyond which was a water-filled ditch. In the dark, I was caught on the wire and soon drenched from falling into the ditches. It was most unpleasant and very cold, so I changed my mind and walked along the lanes, even though these did not necessarily run west and held the danger of my meeting Germans. I avoided houses and villages by going round them through the fields, but this meant my progress was very slow. By accident, I found myself on a footpath beside a tarmac road, with cars passing occasionally. I knew there would be a curfew in Germany and the sight of a single pedestrian in the headlights would be suspicious, so I took refuge in the roadside ditch whenever I saw a vehicle's lights approaching. Near one of these I found a mile-stone and managed to read on it "Hengelo to Zutphen". These names were familiar from the map, but I couldn't remember where they were; at least, from them I concluded that I must be in Holland.[1]

This gave me food for thought. In Brussels, we had heard that many Dutch people were sympathetic to the Germans – in fact, a Dutch division had fought, without much effect, against the British at Arnhem – so I had decided that, if ever I were on the run in Holland, I would not risk knocking on a Dutch door for help, in case I was unlucky in my choice. In any event, I had been a Boy Scout and felt quite confident of my ability to move across the country in an unobtrusive manner, walking at night and hiding to sleep in the daytime.

Things turned out rather differently. Following the footpath, I suddenly found it had become the pavement of a small town. In spite of the black-out, I could see a curving street with shop-windows on both sides of it. I didn't like this at all, and even less when I heard the tramp of boots walking in step and coming towards me. I guessed this was a military patrol and quickly moved aside into a space between two buildings until the soldiers had passed.

I wanted to get out of this place (which was most probably Delden) quickly, but there were still streets with houses and, at one point, I crossed a railway-line. The houses became farms, and then the road ran down to a bridge over a canal (the Twente Canal). I could hear guards pacing about on it, so I knew there was no hope of walking over the bridge.

I decided to look for another crossing and walked a mile up and down the tow-path that ran beside

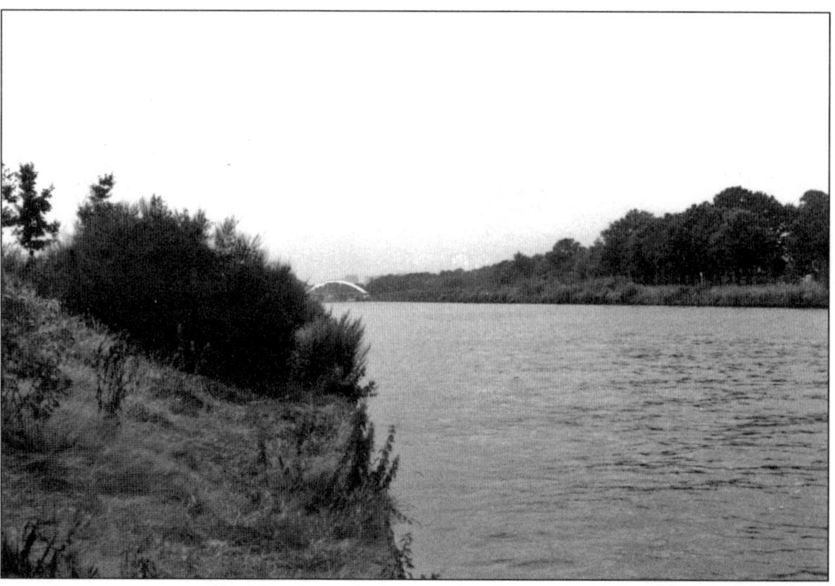

The Twente Canal, which runs between Enschede and Zutphen with several locks, a distance of about 28 miles (45 kms).

[1]See End Papers for the map of my evasion route.

the canal each side of the bridge – but without success. This wasn't a very thorough search, as I couldn't see too much in the dark. The only thing to do was to wait for light in the early morning. I found a small wood near the tow-path and snatched a few hours of cold, broken sleep under the trees.

The St Anna bridge taking the road from Delden over the Twente Canal

Next morning it was drizzling with rain. I didn't mind this as it meant that fewer people would be around and the guards on the bridge would probably be sheltering. I walked for miles along the tow-path in both directions from the bridge, now hoping to find a small boat on the bank rather than another bridge. But I found nothing – which was dispiriting. I realised now that the only way over the canal was to swim across it at night. I spent the rest of the day in the shelter of a hut beside some disused tennis-courts.

When it grew dark enough, sitting under the bridge, where the guards couldn't see me and I was out of the rain, I took off all my clothes except my under-pants and tied them in a bundle on the back of my neck. Then I lowered myself gently into the water and struck out with a breast-stroke. But the water was freezing and took my breath away: after three or four strokes I knew I'd never be able to continue. I turned round and climbed back up the canal bank. Here I sat shivering, wondering what to do. I told myself I was stupid: I was a good swimmer: of course I could swim across this canal. So I lowered myself into the water again, took two or three strokes – and the cold defeated me: I knew I could never swim across. I hardly had the strength to turn round, swim back and climb out again.

Now I really was in trouble: I felt I was going to catch pneumonia – and that would be the end of me. I thought I'd better give myself up to the guards above me – but what would happen to me then? I wouldn't get any sympathetic treatment: I'd be thrown into a cold cell and probably die of pneumonia there. What I needed more than anything was a hot fire to dry my clothes, which were sopping wet, and to warm me up. How could I achieve this?

I walked back half-naked and barefoot up the road I had used and looked into a farm-yard that I passed, hoping to find a barn with a pile of hay. What I saw first was a low mound that looked like a potato-clamp. As I walked past it, I noticed an opening at one end, leading down to a small room with an earth floor, its walls and roof made of branches, with straw everywhere and potatoes lying on the floor. Casting all caution aside, I made a small fire, lit it from my box of matches, and suspended my clothes on sticks on three sides of it. The fire blazed up well and its glare could have been seen through the entrance, but I didn't care: they could arrest me provided I'd first dried my clothes. I rolled two potatoes into the embers and, two hours later my clothes were dry and I had eaten two excellent baked potatoes; my morale had recovered and I felt ready for anything.

I dressed, stamped out my fire, looked out cautiously, then walked out of the farmyard and up the road towards the town. I thought I had been walking more or less westwards in the dark, in which case the canal ran north and south; it was still a major obstacle to my progress. I remembered the railway-line I had crossed earlier and decided that it must go over the canal somewhere, and this might enable me to get across also. So when I reached the railway-line, I turned left onto it and walked steadily along it. It wasn't all easy going, though. The sleepers should have made for pleasant walking, but they were just too far apart for comfort; the alternative was to walk on the ballast stones around them, but these were uneven and, in the dark, tripped me up. In the end, I switched from one to the other for the sake of variety.

As dawn was breaking, I saw a pine wood on my right and turned off into it. I took refuge under a large tree, whose brown fallen needles made a comfortable bed, and hoped to get some sleep. But as it grew lighter, I found that all the trees had no branches near the ground and I could see, and be seen by, anyone coming through the wood. Worse still, I heard voices and laughter and, peering round my tree, saw a man pushing a bicycle and a woman with a child in a pram coming too close for comfort. As soon as they had passed, I crawled out of the wood and decided I was better off in the open as I had been on my first day. The sun was shining and I found a grassy bank overlooking some rough ground, with the railway line and more trees and fields beyond. I don't think I slept at all, but I dozed on and off, with my ears alert for trouble. It came in a surprising but harmless manner. I suddenly noticed an object shining in the blue sky, travelling more or less parallel to the railway-line and going upwards at about 30° to the horizon. It looked like a shell, but I couldn't hear anything, so it was obviously bigger but further away. Because it was shining in the sunlight, I thought it must be a V2 at an early stage in its launch: I didn't know how this was actually done. I thought it couldn't be a V1 as these were always painted a matt dark-green and wouldn't reflect the light. An hour later I saw another, and another. I tried to work-out where they were coming from, so that I could tell our Intelligence people when I returned to Melsbroek. (I learned afterwards that they were V1s launched probably from near Borne against Antwerp or Brussels).

I ate my small rations of three Horlicks tablets, a biscuit and a square of chocolate slowly during the day and washed them down with plenty of purified water from a puddle. I tried to nibble raw potatoes and turnips picked up from a field, but they were hard and totally inedible.

The railway-line from Delden to Zutphen along which I walked for two nights

The type of closed wagon in which I spent a night

When darkness came, quite early of course in mid-November, I went back to the railway-line and resumed my walking. I don't remember passing through any stations and I met no trains, so perhaps the line was no longer in use. Dogs barked occasionally, suggesting some sort of habitation nearby, but my walk was quite uneventful until, after several hours, I saw the curved outline of a large bridge against the night-sky. This is what I had expected, but my railway-line was now joined by more and more lines, and then by trucks of all kinds parked on them. I realised I had stumbled into a marshalling-yard, which seemed to cover a large area. I didn't like to go further until I could make a reconnaissance in daylight; so I found a covered wagon with a half-open door, climbed in, shut the door, and fell asleep on the floor.

I intended to wake up at dawn, but I over-slept and it was broad daylight when I opened the door. This worried me, as I foresaw railwaymen working in the yard and finding me among the trucks. I went forward carefully and took a look at the bridge and found there were two side-by-side: one with a curved top for the road and another, flatter one, for the railway. But as the canal was still running parallel to the railway-line, I guessed the bridges were crossing something else. Moving as close as I dared, I saw the banks of a wide river and realised that this was the obstacle that I now had to cross.

To my left I could see the domed spire of a large church and guessed a good-sized town lay beneath it. (It was Zutphen; but, of course, I had no idea of this.) I realised that I had to go north to investigate a means of crossing this river.

I made my way stealthily out of the goods-yard and found a lane that led gradually towards the river. I turned a corner and suddenly found myself walking into a farm-yard full of German soldiers washing and grooming their horses! What to do? No one seemed to notice me, but if I stopped or turned round, they would look round and wonder at this blue-clad figure, young, unshaven, with uncombed hair, walking into their yard. There was no alternative: stooping over, eyes down and not looking around, I shuffled between the men and horses, muttering *"Morgen"* when I got too close to a soldier – and nobody bothered to look round at me. The lane continued and I passed out of their sight, mightily relieved.

It now started to rain again, which I welcomed, as it reduced visibility and would keep the local people indoors. I reached the river bank eventually and found another tow-path. I walked up this several miles, looking for a boat, but all I found was a huge raft about 30 feet square, perhaps for ferrying farm animals and vehicles across. It was chained up and there was a large pole lying across it. I managed to undo the chain and lift the pole into the water, but the wind and rain were blowing hard in my face and it proved quite impossible to shift this heavy thing from the bank. Somewhat forlornly, I gave up, my spirits dampened as much as my clothing. I wandered back along the tow-path until I came to a row of houses, each with a long garden ending with a chicken-hut. I needed to dry-out somewhere and decided to join the chickens in one of the huts. They squawked noisily when I entered their pen and crawled into their hut, but nobody seemed to hear and I spent the afternoon in reasonable comfort while I planned my next move. Finding me harmless but unable to feed them, the chickens calmed down and accepted me as one of themselves.

It was obvious now that the only way over the river was by one or other bridge and, as they would both be guarded closely, the only choice was the railway one. The best plan seemed to be to get into a

The bank of the River Ijssel, which I walked up and down in the rain

covered wagon on a train that was about to cross over and jump out at the right moment. Accordingly, as the grey day changed to twilight, I walked back into the marshalling-yard and found a line of wagons that were waiting not far from the bridge. I opened the door of an empty one and sat down on the floor, expectantly. Two hours later, nothing had happened; I realised that this was too speculative: I might sit here for a week. The answer now was to stand by the track leading over the bridge and jump onto a flat truck of a train already on its way to crossing it. A bit risky, perhaps, but better than waiting in a wagon that didn't move.

So I made my way to the correct track and stood beside it, about 100 yards before the bridge. It was quite dark, but I could see enough to know what I had to do. The first train came past me much too fast; I realised I needed one that wasn't moving much faster than I could run. The next one was a passenger train. The third one was going slower: it had probably started from the marshalling yard. The first trucks were all wagons, but the later ones were empty flat-beds. Summoning up my strength and courage, I ran alongside and tried to get on; but the stanchions on the trucks swept me aside. I was still running when the last truck drew near; I threw myself over the side and dug my fingernails into the floor-boards. Half of me was on, but my backside and legs were hanging down over the edge. The train was gathering speed and, a few seconds later, it was rumbling over the bridge. Guards with torches were standing on each side, shining their light on the passing trucks. The first ones saw a strange shape hanging from the last truck and started shouting and waving their lamps towards their colleagues at the far end of the bridge. The train gathered more speed – the guards at the far end, forewarned, waved their lamps and shouted – I could feel myself slipping – we sped past the frustrated guards – I held on desperately, but when I could do so no longer, I let go – I ducked my head, and rolled down the embankment.

I picked myself up, felt all over my body for any breaks or bruises, and breathed a sigh of relief that I'd got away with it. Feeling much happier, I climbed back up the embankment and continued walking along the line.

Ten minutes later, I bumped into my flat-bed truck! The train had stopped, no doubt because of the noise on the bridge, and was sitting there, probably waiting for someone to explain the disturbance. I sat on my truck, ready to jump off and disappear if necessary; but, after ten more minutes, the train

The railway line on the bridge over the River Ijssel,
which enabled me to cross the river at night.

The type of flat-bed truck on which I crossed the bridge

moved on at a fair speed. I was feeling the cold, but I was delighted that we seemed to be travelling more-or-less westwards. We passed over some more bridges and each time the guards would spot me, wave their lamps and shout, but too late for the engine-driver and crew to hear. However, there must have been a telephone-call at some point because the train stopped and I saw men walking along the line flashing their torches onto and under the trucks. Without waiting for them, I slipped off my flat-bed and ran back down the line into the darkness. The men gathered round the end of the train, obviously discussing the fact that they had found nothing, and started walking back to the engine. I ran back up the line, climbed onto my truck, and off we went again.

I had seen that there was a guard's van about five trucks ahead of mine and no one had come out of it or gone back into it. I thought this would be better for me than sitting out in the cold, so I walked along the flat-beds, climbed up into the guard's van, opened the door, felt around the interior, and lay down on the lino-covered floor. My hand felt something soft, so I picked it up, sniffed it, and decided it was a crust of bread. I was over-joyed, felt around and found some more – pure bliss! They were a bit leathery, but manna from heaven after my self-imposed survival diet. The train rumbled on and I fell asleep.

I woke up, too late again, and found my train surrounded by goods-trains on either side and beyond. I noticed there was a bill-of-lading attached to each wagon and, when I climbed down to inspect one, I read the name "Utrecht". I couldn't believe it and inspected several other wagons: their bills-of-lading all read "Utrecht". This was wonderful – I had arrived at my first objective in just four nights.

However, I knew Utrecht was a big place and I would have difficulty in getting out of it. But the railway-line had brought me in, so I reckoned it would lead me out. It was daylight, though, and I was doubtful of my chances of walking through the goods-yard and the suburbs without being challenged by some guard or official. Nevertheless, there was no alternative and I adopted my former pose of a rather stupid tramp and struck out along the railway-line.

Fortune favoured me again: I came to the end of the houses, which gave way to a river and fields. But I was now walking on the top of a high embankment, feeling very exposed and conspicuous. I also knew I had to stop going west and start moving south towards the Rhine. So when the railway crossed over a motorway, I slid down the embankment and joined a throng of Dutch workers, all dressed in blue denim, making their way to work along a wide footpath. Cars with German officers on board were passing continually, but no one, Dutch or German, gave me a second glance – I seemed to merge into the crowd.

My fellow-pedestrians gradually turned away to work in local industrial or commercial buildings until I was walking virtually alone and feeling rather too visible. So I turned to the right off the motorway and onto a minor road. This led me to a large village, with too many soldiers walking about for my comfort. It also started to rain heavily, so I thought it time I found some shelter. I happened to pass a fair-sized orchard and saw, in the centre, a small wooden hut. This seemed just right for me, so I entered the orchard and approached the hut. I was surprised to find the door fastened with a peculiar criss-cross of string. However, I undid it and stepped inside. There were four or five stools made from sawn-off tree-trunks grouped round an old iron stove; on the floor was a basketful of apples. It seemed to be partly inhabited, but I felt safe as long as it kept raining outside. I ate one of the apples and tried to light a fire in the stove, but without success.

I was sitting quite peaceably, thinking of my next move, when I heard a sound outside and saw the door slowly opening. Caught unawares, with no escape, I could only stare at the door, where three small faces suddenly appeared, wide-eyed with apprehension. I immediately realised that these were the children whose play-hut I was occupying. *"Come in, come in!"* I said in English, then changed into my schoolboy German, *"Komm herein!"* They came forward and stood in the doorway, not at all sure who this stranger was. They were good-looking boys in shorts or knickerbockers, aged between about 8 and 12. I tried to reassure them and win their confidence and support. I told them in my simple German, not too different from Dutch, that I was an English flier and showed them my RAF 'wings'. I asked them if they were good Dutch boys, and they nodded vigorously. I then asked if their father was at home, whereupon they all left me without a word.

The three van Hengstum boys: Piet, Ben and Henk
Photo: Ben van Hengstum

Ten minutes later, a little man, whom I took to be a farmer, entered the hut with two of the boys. He was highly suspicious of me. He spoke no English, but in my German and his Dutch we could make ourselves understood to each other. After I had repeated that I was an RAF pilot and showed him my 'wings', he believed me and sent the boys back into the house. He said he had German soldiers billetted in his house at the end of the orchard, so he could not bring me there. He offered to take me to a friend's house, but I said I wanted to get back to my squadron. He told me that Rhenen, a town on this side of the Rhine, was in the hands of the British. The boys then came back with a big bowl of steaming mashed potatoes. I ate greedily as we talked.

He said his name was Piet van Hengstum and that the village was Houten. He gave me a small map, a page torn from a school atlas. He also gave me a very small overcoat, which I took to be one of his children's: the sleeves came halfway up my arms and I could do up only two buttons. He went back to

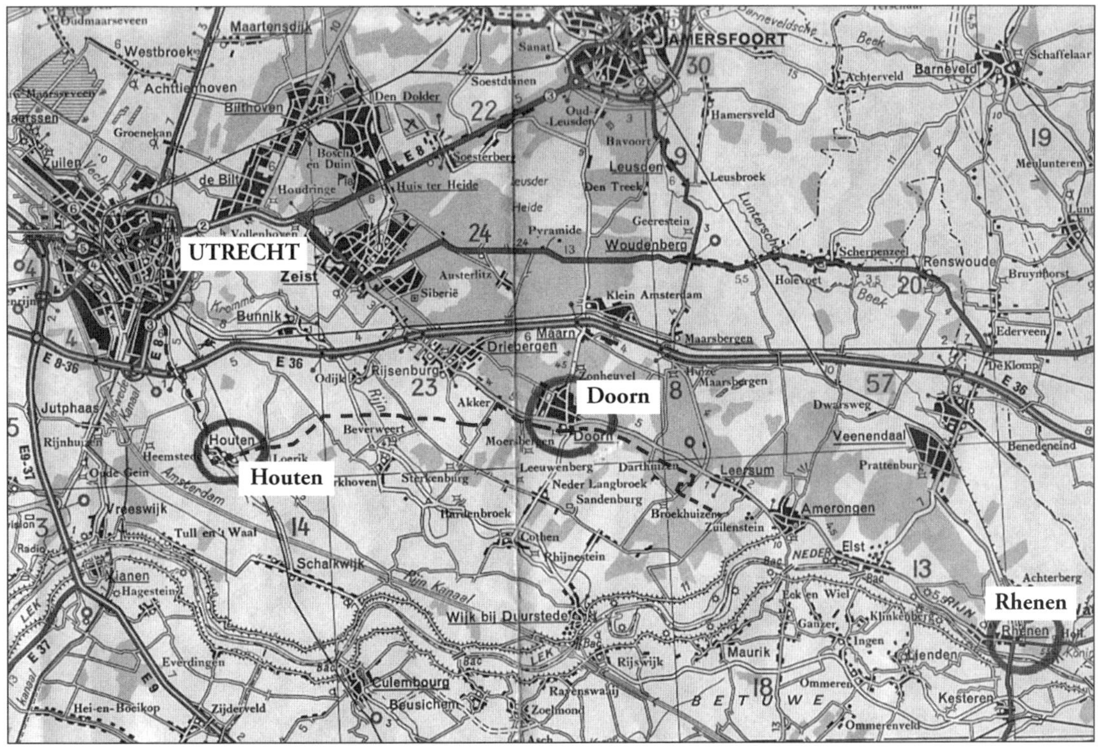

Map of the area in which I left the train in Utrecht station, walked to Houten, cycled to the entry to Doorn, and walked to a lane within sight of the Rhine
Map: Michelin 1968

his house, but returned half-an-hour later. He then outlined a plan for me: when it was dark, two of his sons on a bicycle would lead me, on another bicycle, over the dykes and polders onto the main road to Doorn, which was on the road to Rhenen. I would keep about 50 yards behind the boys, so that if I was stopped by anyone, they would not be involved. At this point, I would give my bicycle to one of the sons, and they would ride them back to Houten.

I thought this was a very brave and self-sacrificing move by this small family and I thanked him profusely. My aim, all along, was not to get close to the Dutch, both for my security, but also because I didn't want anyone to risk their lives for me – the Germans would have them shot without mercy. However, this plan seemed unlikely to incriminate this little man and his very mature young children.

When it was dark, I was taken to the roadway outside the orchard and given my bicycle; it had no tyres, just a strip of rubber round the rim of each wheel. A number of neighbours had come to see me and wish me luck. The boys started off, one standing on the back-axle with his hands on his brother's shoulders. I ran alongside my bike, put one foot on a pedal and swung the other over the cross-bar to reach the other pedal. The bike and I fell to the ground with a crash on the cobbles! The Dutch scattered in all directions. I waited, but nobody came to find out what was going on. I picked myself up and everyone emerged from hiding and started laughing – I hadn't been told that the bike had a back-pedalling brake, which applied itself automatically when I tried to mount in my fashion. I had to straddle the bike with both feet on the ground before starting to pedal and mount at the same time.

I said a fond farewell to Mr and Mrs van Hengstum and to the neighbours, then pedalled off after the boys. They led me over trackways and footpaths, along the tops of dykes and even across the fields. The ride lasted almost an hour, but we passed no one. There were touches of frost on the ground and I was glad of the little coat I'd been given. Eventually, we came to a major road with a signpost pointing to Doorn, and I had to hand back my bike and say good-bye to these gallant young boys.

I walked on, but my feet were now very painful; they had been in my wet, wool-lined shoes for so long that they had become swollen and raw, and every step made them worse. It was therefore quite a relief when I came upon a single-decker bus lying, apparently abandoned, in a ditch. I pulled open the door at the front and started to climb the steps. But then I heard a sound from the back, a sort of rustling: it was too dark to see. I stood there undecided, but when the rustling became louder and suggested feet and clothing in motion, I realised at least one other person was already on board, perhaps two, and felt it was not a safe place. So I backed down, shut the door and walked on.

Not long afterwards, I found a deep pine-wood in front of me on both sides of the road. Having experienced a comfortable bed in one earlier in my travels, I thought this would be the place to spend the night. I walked into the wood on my right, picking my way carefully through the trees in the dark. It was then that I heard a twig snap. My ears were always alert to any unexpected sound and this was one. I stopped and listened. Nothing. I took another step on the dry pine-needles and I heard another twig snap. In fact, every time I took a step, I heard someone else do the same ahead of me. Once again, I felt that this was not the place for me, so I turned round and tip-toed out of the wood. I walked further along the footpath, then crossed the road and entered the wood on the other side. Here I found some bigger trees, perhaps oaks, on a sloping bank, pulled some leaves together and went to sleep without any more disturbances.

Next morning, when I woke up, I could see people walking to work in both directions along the footpath. I felt quite happy now in daylight if there were other people on the move. I joined them and knew that I was approaching Doorn, the former home of the exiled Kaiser Wilhelm. It was no great surprise when I passed an opening in the wood on the right and saw a German soldier on guard at each side of it and rows of German trucks parked inside. The footsteps I had encountered the previous night were obviously from one of the other sentries posted round the outside of this transport park.

The well-wooded road into Doorn in 1997

I plodded on and was relieved when the road skirted the town; its condition deteriorated, worn down perhaps by tanks and other vehicles. Later, the woods re-appeared, stretching away on each side. As before, though, the other pedestrians gradually moved off to their work-places, leaving me conspicuous on my own. Fortunately, at the approach to a largish village, a minor road turned off to the right and I followed it cheerfully. I then came upon a sign in the middle of the road, "Kampfzone" ("War Zone") – "Keep Out!", clearly intended to prevent civilians entering. But the sight of Dutch people here and there ignoring the sign encouraged me to continue.

I could now hear thuds and bangs in the distance, which made sense of the German warning. However, Rhenen was at least 20 miles further on and I felt I should get nearer to it. My spirits were rising and I was building castles in the air about how soon I might be back with 16 Squadron. At the same time, my senses were alert to any eventuality, and I felt that discretion, rather than a 'press-on' attitude, would be more sensible in the circumstances. So I reduced my already slow walking-pace and allowed an old man trundling a laden wheel-barrow, accompanied by his wife and small son, to overtake me; I then followed behind them, keeping to the other side of the road: if there was trouble ahead, they would encounter it first and give me time to consider my own plan of action.

So we progressed, on this fine Friday, with the weather feeling quite mild and the countryside looking quite peaceable, except for the increasing number of German uniforms and the growing intensity of the gunfire. The road went up a slight rise, then made a turn to the left and there below, only a mile or so away, flowed a broad river, which I knew to be the Rhine – the second objective of my journey.

The noise of battle was getting clearer and I could see puffs of smoke rising up on the far side beyond the river, which I guessed were shells bursting on the Allied lines. The road ran roughly parallel to the river and, rounding a gradual corner, I suddenly found myself looking at a battery of 88mm guns, with their muzzles depressed for horizontal shooting. The crews were standing-by at the ready and there was much searching of the battle-scene through binoculars. Some soldiers looked at me curiously for a moment – my little coat was pretty ridiculous – but odd civilians must have been a fairly common sight, even in this war-zone. I glanced once or twice at the battery – to try to take it all in for later Intelligence information – but I didn't want to be caught showing interest in it, so I shuffled past with eyes down.

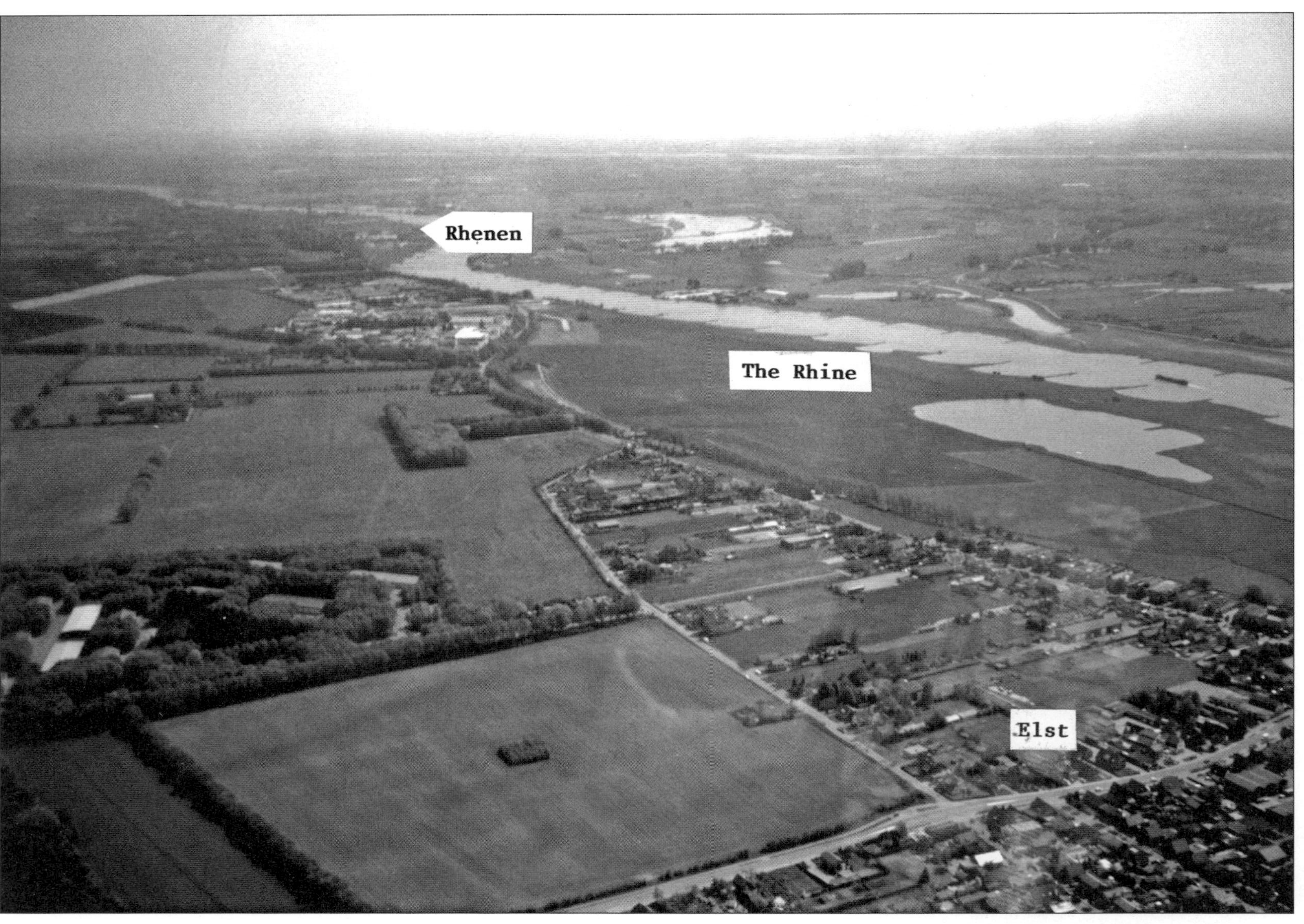

Aerial view of the Rhine, looking south across it, with the lane where I was captured somewhere in the foreground or off to the right.

I had been walking on the left side of the lane, but now an officer appeared walking towards me, probably the commander of the battery. He ignored the old man and his family, but stopped me and asked me in German where I was going. I hadn't prepared a story for such an emergency, as I knew it would have to be very flexible to suit the circumstances. So I said I was going to Rhenen. He then asked where I came from, so I told him *"Doorn"*. He then said that Rhenen was *"kaput"*, so I expressed my concern. He went on, *"Don't you know there's a battle going on and there's a good chance of your being killed?"* I said I realised this and I would leave the area as quickly as possible. He agreed and said the sooner the better; so I thanked him very much and continued on my way.

But I then did something very foolish. I felt the officer was very suspicious of me so, after about fifty yards, I turned round to look back at him. He had stopped and also turned round to look at me. Our eyes met at this distance and I sensed instinctively, in that moment, that the game was up!

However, I had no alternative but to keep on walking, while I looked desperately for a turning to the left that would take me out of this dangerous situation. There was nothing, and I caught up with my old couple, who had been stopped by a soldier with a rifle standing across the road. He was obviously asking them for their pass to proceed further. I hung around behind them, and saw some more civilians cycle up, produce their passes, and pedal on, while my old dears were still arguing with the sentry. To appear authentic, I felt I had to join in, so I added my voice to theirs, asking why we couldn't go on.

Just then, I felt a hand on my shoulder and a voice said, *"Komm mit mir!"* I turned round and there was a soldier on a bicycle, with a tommy-gun slung round his neck, and a grim look on his face. He repeated his order, *"Come with me!" "Why?"* I said, playing dumb. *"Just come,"* he replied and moved his gun. There was no answer to this so, trying to look as down-trodden as possible, I walked back with him. He asked me whether I was German or Dutch. I obviously could not be German, so I said I was Dutch. *"Why don't you speak Dutch?"* was his response. There was no answer to this, so I kept quiet.

We came to a pub filled with soldiers and my guard inquired if the Hauptmann (Captain) was there. Not finding him, he mentioned that he'd picked up a Dutchman who couldn't speak Dutch. A thin-faced civilian came up, whom I took to be a 'quisling', and they talked together for a time, while I looked around cautiously to see if there was any way of escaping. I saw no chance while all these soldiers were looking at me as a curious specimen of some unknown kind.

After a few minutes, we left the pub and continued down the road in search of the Hauptmann. We stopped opposite the battery, but no one knew where he was, although they expected him back any minute. Three or four men then strolled over and, in collusion with the guard, started asking me very awkward questions. *"Where were you going?" "To Rhenen." "Why?" "To fetch my family's possessions, which we had to leave behind when we moved to Doorn." "Where are you going now?" "Back to Doorn." "What do you do?" "I'm a labourer." "Show me your hands!"* I showed him my filthy dirty hands. *"Ach, those are no labourer's hands!" "What part of Holland do you come from?"* Here I was stuck: I didn't know the name of any Dutch province. Then I had an inspiration: *"I'm a Walloon,"* I said. This mystified them a bit, and I heard the word *"Flemish"* used several times, perhaps to explain my non-existent Dutch. *"So where is your home?"* Oh dear, this was beyond me; so in desperation I offered, *"In Walloonland."* Strangely, this seemed to satisfy them. (I've since found that there really is a region of Holland called Walloonland!).

They were getting more suspicious and I was getting more annoyed that this idle questioning was incriminating me more than anything that had gone before. However, there was no help for it and more was to follow, for they looked at my clothing and wanted to investigate it. *"Take off your coat!"* I unbuttoned it slowly, but left it on. Immediately, my blue battle-dress was revealed. *"What's this uniform?" "My working clothes." "Where did you get it?" "From the Germans,"* I said; then, to substantiate it, I went on, *"There were twenty of us brought from Walloonland by the Germans and they gave us this uniform."*

They then spotted something black under my battle-dress. I had to open my jacket and they hauled out the waistcoat I had made from the tops of my leather flying-boots. *"What's this?"* they asked. *"I don't know,"* I replied, feeling despair. *"I found it in a ditch."* Delving further into my battle-dress, they came up with the remains of my escape-kit. *"What's this?"* they exclaimed, in surprise. *"I don't know,"* I said. *"I found it with the leather things."*

By now, I was feeling desperate and knew that the less I said the better. One of the soldiers pulled from my pocket a sandwich that the van Hengstums had given me for my journey and, to show how boorish I was, when he dropped it on the ground, I picked it up and started eating it. With a full mouth, I could only mumble replies; when I'd finished the sandwich, I started on an apple – the van Hengstums had filled my pockets – which effectively kept my mouth shut. But they were getting too close to the truth: from *"Parlez-vous francais?"* they moved to *"Do you speak English?"* The arrival of the Hauptmann was actually quite a relief.

He was shown everything they had found and then, at the bidding of the tommy-gun, I was made to walk in front of them a short way to a house, and then into a room, which I took to be Platoon Headquarters. A few soldiers were sitting around in chairs, but I was taken to an inner room where an officer was sitting at a desk with a pistol placed on it pointing in my direction. On my right, half-a-dozen NCOs were lounging in chairs and looking at me. They made me take-off my old coat, whereupon they spotted my Flight Lieutenant's tapes and I knew that any further bluffing was useless. A number of satisfied *"Ahs!"* and *"Sos!"* went round the room, and then a voice drawled in perfect English, *"Bad luck, old man! You nearly made it!"*

CHAPTER 15

Capture and Interrogation

The English voice turned out to belong to an affable young man of about 30, who had been a traveller for Lipton's Tea before the war and visited England many times. He told me that the Hauptmann had sent the tommy-gun soldier after me so, in their view, my number was up as soon as he had stopped me. They gave me something to eat – corned-beef and potatoes, bread and a couple of apples – and we discussed the war in general and in particular. They were all members of the flak-battery and claimed that their group had shot down 64 Stirlings and Dakotas at Arnhem. I think they imagined I was a Typhoon pilot, as they said that the rockets made a lot of noise but did little damage. They wanted to know what I thought of German flak: I told them that it was very intense, but not very accurate – which they received in silence. (I think this was true of all anti-aircraft fire, except in the special case of Arnhem, when the glider-tugs and transport aircraft had to drop parachutists and supplies from a very low altitude. But it was a great deterrent and forced hostile aircraft to fly higher than they would have done otherwise.)

At about 1.0pm, after more discussion, they gave me back all my possessions but, not wishing to be hindered in my eventual escape – for I was sure the opportunity would present itself – I purposely left behind my leather boot-tops. I was taken to another house and another room while they telephoned around and wrote a report of my capture. I thought of making a bolt for the door, but I saw that it jammed easily and I would have looked very foolish struggling to open it: it would also have put them on their guard against my making any more attempts to escape, I also left behind the little overcoat, which I knew would lead to awkward questions.

Eventually, the Lipton's man asked me if I could ride a bicycle. I decided to be an awkward prisoner, so I said *"No."* *"In that case"*, he replied, *"you'll have to walk."* *"In that case,"* I answered, *"I'll ride a bike!"* So we rode forth to our next destination, about twenty minutes' ride away. Unfortunately, I was sandwiched between Lipton and Tommy-gun and their vigilance never relaxed. Except for this, we might have been out for an afternoon's ride through the lanes of England, as the sun was shining, the air was almost warm, and we conversed in English.

Moreover, reaction to the nervous strain of the last few days was setting in, and I felt a kind of relief that my fate was now settled and I didn't have to jump every time a twig cracked or a heavy footfall sounded in the dark. I was on my guard to confine my conversation to generalities but, otherwise, I saw no reason why I shouldn't get in some propaganda whenever opportunity offered. I decided that my attitude should be respectful to superior officers, and affable but not helpful to any others; my own situation might be unfortunate, but I would express total confidence in the final result of the war.

We arrived at a town peopled entirely by soldiers, and dismounted at what I presumed was an HQ of some sort. I said *"Auf Wiedersehen"* to Lipton and was taken into an Orderly Room. I was asked if I had eaten, so I naturally said *"No"* and was treated to a large plateful of potatoes and gravy. I then wandered round the room looking with great interest at old maps, although I couldn't recognise any of the present landscape. This infuriated the senior NCO, who went round the room rolling up the maps; then told me to sit on a stool and called-in a soldier to watch over me.

After a while, a door to an inner sanctum opened and I was invited to go in. I found myself in a large panelled room, with elegant heavy curtains drawn over the windows, and a long, polished table in the centre. On this places were set with glasses, jugs of water, sheets of paper and pencils. Standing round were a number of officers, captains and lieutenants, but the central figure was the Herr Major, a short, stocky, little man in a perfectly-fitting uniform, adorned with the Iron Cross. He motioned everyone to sit down and I did so at the other end of the table from him. An officer next to him held a pen and wrote down everything that was said, which began with my name, rank and number. I showed them my identity discs as proof of this information. The Major then asked me in English, *"What plane were you flying?"* I answered, *"I'm sorry, Sir, but I can't tell you."* He then asked, *"Where were you flying from?"* And again I said, *"I'm sorry, I can't tell you."* A third question, *"What was your objective?"* received the same answer. Controlling himself quite well, the Major asked, *"Aren't you going to tell us anything?"* My reply was firm but respectful, *"If you were in my position, Sir, what would you do?"* He thought for a moment before replying candidly, *"The same as you."* There ensued some minutes of chatter, then he shrugged his shoulders and left the room, and I was taken back to the Orderly Room.

A particularly stolid-looking soldier led me to the guard-room, with a table in the middle and double-tiered bunks all around. At the suggestion of one of the guards, I lay down on one of the beds and dozed for a while. I was still hopeful of escaping – the books all say it's much easier in the early stages of being captured – so I asked to go to the lavatory. I stood on the seat to look out of the window and found there was a path beneath leading into a garden, which might have been a useful way out; but the guard who showed me to the lavatory was standing in a doorway, watching the window and path. I gave up my idea, used the lavatory, tore up the school map, which had the name of one of the Dutch boys on it, flushed the toilet, and returned to my bunk. Half-an-hour later, nature asserted herself again, but this second request met with great suspicion and I had to leave the door open.

At length, as it was growing dark, I was brought out of the guard-room and taken to another building down the road. Here I was put into a window-less cell, but it was quite warm and a mattress was put on the floor for me to sleep on. Again I was asked if I had eaten and, this time, I was given a plateful of potatoes and pink sauerkraut – which I didn't take long to consume. When I took off my shoes, I found my feet were quite black and heavily blistered. I requested a bowl of water to soak them in and was pleasantly surprised to be given some salts to add to it.

In fact, the German soldiers were quite friendly. Half-a-dozen of them gathered in the doorway while I was eating my supper and bathing my feet. I told them about all the good things still available in England. Only one of them spoke English, although the others appeared to understand it. This one, who said he had been a marine, stated that the whole of the South of England was in flames. I replied that, on the contrary, I had taken-off from there the day before and there was nothing wrong anywhere; furthermore, I'd had an excellent meal in a restaurant without giving any coupons. The bit about the coupons seemed to impress him. I asked him if he thought the Germans could still win the war. He replied that V1 and V2 were highly successful and that Hitler had promised them even more secret weapons, which would drive the Allies back into the sea. The others all nodded their heads in agreement with this opinion – which must have been one of the reasons why the Germans fought so tenaciously right up to the news of Hitler's death.

About 9.30pm I took off my clothes for the first time for five days and, as the room was heated, soon fell into an exhausted sleep in my underclothes.

I was roughly awakened from this, about half-an-hour later, by shouts of *"Heraus!"* and found the room full of soldiery urging me to dress. I did so by the light of a lantern, but not hurrying particularly. I had no idea of the time, but it was pitch-black outside as I fumbled my way out of the door and into the back of a truck. I was still dozey and just scrambled on until I hit an obstruction and sat down on it. I soon regretted this when my seat turned out to be a sack of hard coal. Three guards climbed in after me and sat by the flap, throwing the light of a torch onto me, but never uttering so much as a syllable.

It was bitterly cold as we rattled through the deserted countryside for a considerable time. Our way seemed to follow a devious route along secondary dirt roads, punctuated with continual stops, harangues in German, reverses, and continuations in some other direction.

I was still hoping for a chance to slip out, and let my arm slide down between the outside of the truck and the tarpaulin cover; I found there might just be room for me to squeeze between them once I got my body over the side. The guards, however, were very alert and flashed a torch on me whenever I stirred. Only once did I have the vestige of a chance, when the truck gave a great lurch and stopped. The guards were thrown to the floor and I almost fell on top of them. But we must all have recovered at about the same time for, even as I thought of nipping out and running for it, one of them fixed me with a torch and held his tommy-gun at the ready while his comrades sorted themselves out. Thenceforward, I lost interest in the proceedings and dozed off on my sack of coal.

I was awakened by the cry of *"Heraus!"* and stumbled out of the truck into the night. A large block of buildings was just visible. I was led up a couple of steps, through a door, through a dark room, round some corners, down a corridor, and into a room. The guard swung his lantern towards a table, a chair, and then a bed; he turned to the door, went out, locked the door, and left me to myself in the darkness.

I felt around the bed and found it was a flat wooden shelf, raised about two feet off the floor, with one end inclined at a slight angle to form a head-board. Tired out, I clambered onto it, pulled the solitary blanket over me and fell asleep. Thus ended Friday, 24th November, my first day of captivity.

Next morning I was awakened at dawn, about 8.0am, and given my breakfast: two slices of bread and margarine and a cup of 'ersatz' coffee. I ate them ravenously and then looked around me. My cell was quite bare, except for the things I've mentioned already, and possessed one window at about shoulder-height. The prospect through this was not reassuring: a strip of dry earth bounded by a high brick wall, beyond which I could see the tip of a wire fence and a thick fir belt stretching to the horizon. The window was barred with five iron rods, well cemented into place. The floor, the walls and the door were equally solid. The latter had a little spy-hole consisting of a small round window, with a flap covering it on the outside. I wondered what kind of prison I was in, and concluded it was most likely a local punishment centre for civilian criminals and military delinquents.

I then sat down and made an inventory of my possessions. They were very few: my knife, comb, handkerchief, identity discs, and the remains of my escape-kit. I also still had a couple of apples. I decided to make the best use of my time by sewing into the lining of my jacket my ten guilders from van Hengstum, the two buttons that formed a compass, and my matches inside the plastic water container. That done, I proceeded to sew up the worst rents in my clothing.

This all took some time and, while I was still engaged, an officer and a guard came in and gave me quite a thorough search, but without finding any of the things I had so fortuitously sewn away. However, they relieved me of my penknife, sewing-kit, nail-file, and razor, leaving me with only my comb, handkerchief, and a stub pencil. Much against my will and despite my protests, they also took one of my two identity discs, which they said they needed, at the same time assuring me that I would get everything back eventually.

Lunch then arrived in the shape of a bowl of soup and a slice of bread, after which I was left to myself, with nothing to do. Then, and for the next 24 hours, the anti-climax set in and I realised the helplessness of my position. Now, for the first time, I understood the full implications of being a prisoner, and felt full of regret and self-pity. I reviewed all the events leading up to my capture and tried to pinpoint where I had gone wrong: what I shouldn't have done and what I ought to have done – but it was all quite pointless now. All the castles in the air, about getting back to my Squadron, that had buoyed me up, had collapsed. My empty cell reflected the bleakness of my present condition and future expectations. I could have cried – but this also was pointless.

This account of my downfall is based mainly on the record I made later in prison-camp. But I omitted anything that might lead the Germans back to where I had landed, or that might incriminate the van Hengstums in any way, directly or indirectly. I kept my notes in my mattress, but our rooms were subject to sudden searches by the German 'ferrets' – when they could tear everything apart – so it was better to be cautious.

As food was the main preoccupation of most prisoners, I also added a list of the first or last meals I had eaten between leaving Melsbroek on 19th November 1944 and arriving in Britain on 13th May 1945, together with the date and name of the relevant place. From this, I discovered recently that the German soldiers gave me my first meal on 24th November at Wegen, which must be between Doorn and Rhenen; but this Punishment Cell has no location given it during my stay from 24th-27th November.

There was, in fact, nothing noteworthy about the place and I have virtually no memory of my time there, not even whether I was allowed to wash or shave or shower. But I do remember the toilet arrangements, which gave me acute embarrassment. The latrine was a trench dug in a piece of open ground, with a pole supported at each end about two feet above the trench and overhanging the length of it. A guard would take me out to this wintry spot and stand over me while I lowered my trousers, hung my backside over the pole, and tried to perform in front of him. The only undignified position that came anywhere near this in my experience was on my first visit to the toilet in the barrack-block on my arrival at Turner Field, Georgia, USA, and finding all the twelve 'Johns' were spread openly round the room and we all performed in front of each other! But that was in a heated room with friendly, equally embarrassed, fellow-cadets. Now it was out-of-doors in a freezing winter under the unfriendly gaze of a German soldier. Of course, I looked around for a chance to escape, but this fellow with his rifle put it out of the question. The wire fence, not always visible, that ran round the prison, also constituted another obstacle.

Passing the time was the main problem: the meals were small and disappeared too quickly. I was not allowed out for any exercise. I didn't reveal that I could understand and speak a little German, but the guards gave me some old German newspapers and magazines to read, no doubt thinking they might have some propaganda effect on me. It was interesting to see what Dr Goebbels, the Minister for Information, allowed the German people to know about the war. The approved news was, of course, concerned mainly with German successes in defending the Reich, and the bravery shown by various units of the Services and by individuals; it did not exclude photos of the results of the Allied bombing campaign, but talked up the horrors inflicted by the "terrorfliegers" and the revenge being taken by the V1 and V2 guided missiles, as well as the courage of the civilians and the increasing production of war weapons from the factories. All this was predictable, but struggling with the German language at least helped to pass the time.

Fortunately, my stay in this unpleasant place was quite short as, on the 27th, I was taken out and put in a truck with guards for another long cross-country journey. I have no recollection of this and I thought, for many years, that it finished in Deventer. But my meals list shows that from 27th November to 6th December I was held in a converted factory in "Enschiede", my attempt to reproduce the "Enschede" that I must have heard.

This was a large two-storey building from which all machinery and equipment had been removed, leaving a spacious room on each floor, with a machine-gun protected by barbed-wire installed at the end of each. Straw had been spread all round the edge of each room and here about 50 Airborne troops, picked up by the Germans after the Arnhem debacle in September, sat around in the daytime and slept at night. A group of about six NCOs sat together in one corner and called me over as soon as I was led into the ground-floor. Their spokesman told me that, as I was the only officer present, I had to be the Senior British Officer and represent the prisoners to the German Commandant!

This was an unexpected responsibility for me, but I could not duck it. In fact, I found great pleasure in exercising it. We had no meals in the factory but, twice a day, we marched under guard down a slight slope to a dining-hall, where we were served lunch and supper, with a diet little different from the one I had experienced in the previous days. The German civilians had little enough to eat at this stage in the war; the front-line troops, as I had seen, were well-enough fed, but the home defence soldiers and the men employed on such duties as our guards fared little better than the civilians. However, I felt that my main role as a prisoner was to be a nuisance to the Germans, and that our food served as one legitimate cause of complaint to the Commandant.

Accordingly, I asked a guard to take me to him and I was ushered into his office on my second day. He was an elderly, red-faced Hauptmann, who found it very difficult to accept that I, a dirty, scruffy, young Flight Lieutenant, held the same rank as himself. He spoke no English, so I had to draw on all my schoolboy knowledge of German to present my case. It is extraordinary, though, how fluent one becomes when one's emotions are stirred in an argument!

I asked for jam on our bread and margarine and, surprisingly, he agreed eventually. On another occasion I complained about the rats that ran across the room at night and even over our bodies, but he said he couldn't do anything about them. On a third occasion I said the Geneva Convention required us to have a daily exercise period; but he said he had no guards available to take us outside. We actually became quite friendly in the course of these exchanges, which certainly gave me a break from the boredom of our existence on the straw.

These Airborne boys were the first British fighting-men I had met close-up during the war and I felt an intense admiration for them. They came mainly from paratroop and glider-borne units and were tough, seasoned campaigners, who each had a vivid story to tell of the battles they had fought at Arnhem. Their NCOs were even more impressive, in fact quite outstanding. Somehow they knew the best way to handle the men in the conditions of a prison, and how to relate to the Germans. They kept the

The factory in Enschede used as a POW cage, where I spent from 28th November to 6th December 1944.

men under firm discipline and watched over them as if they were in a barracks back at home. They held an exercise period of physical training every morning, and required each man to look as smart as possible and keep his sleeping space tidy. We marched down to meals and we marched back: the NCOs were determined to show the guards and any passing civilians that the spirit of the British was unbroken. Anyone could raise any subject with the NCOs, but no one was allowed to moan for long. The men were forbidden to speak to the guards, but the NCOs were able to communicate with them in one way or another and sometimes bargain for something 'under the counter' from one or other of them. As a result of this remarkable understanding of man-management under difficult circumstances, the morale of the prisoners in this factory was extraordinary high. Their motto could have been: "There is no defeatism in this house."

On Sunday, they asked me to hold a simple church service. This was far outside my competence; but I agreed, provided it was voluntary. Together we wrote down the first verses of hymns with familiar tunes, and I recollected the words of some of my father's favourite prayers. I am not religious, but I found it a very moving experience to lead these proud men, all of whom attended in a semi-circle, in prayers for their families and loved ones, for their King and country, for the Allies' speedy victory and for our own release.

After about five days, half the men were taken away, presumably to a prison-camp, and I was moved upstairs, which was no different from the ground floor – except perhaps that there were fewer rats! Two or three days later, a large group of us were taken to the railway station; but then we went separate ways: the soldiers moved off to one or other prison-camp, while I was bound for Dulag Luft, the Luftwaffe Interrogation Centre outside Frankfurt-am-Main. I said good-bye to the NCOs and men with genuine regret – my life had been enhanced by contact with these magnificent unsung heroes.

Two guards with rifles took me through the large crowds of passengers swarming in the station and onto our platform; people looked at me with curiosity, but without overt hostility. When the train arrived, there were signs of envy when we three entered a reserved compartment. The guards were not unfriendly, but I decided not to let them know I could understand a little German by not speaking to them. They took turns to cat-nap, while one of them kept his eye on me. We had to change trains at some point, and I was given a bowl of soup and a slice of bread by the German Red Cross women, who ran a canteen on the platform. At other times, the guards gave me a share of their bread and 'wurst' sausage. My 'meals list' shows the journey lasted two days, which suggests the train travelled slowly, with stops no doubt for air raid alarms. We were perhaps lucky not to be strafed by Allied fighter-bombers on the prowl.

The idea of trying to escape passed through my mind, but I did not consider it feasible: it was bitterly cold outside; I had no rations to survive on; we were now well into Germany; and I had no map and no chance of receiving any help from anyone. It was better to save my energy for the next challenge.

We arrived at Frankfurt in the evening and drove by truck to Dulag Luft. Here I was 'welcomed' by a German officer who said, *"I'm sorry, old man, you've just missed our evening meal, but you'll get breakfast at 7.0am."* He then took me along a corridor, opened a door and beckoned me into a room with a bench and a table and chair. I sat there for a while, then a man in a suit with a Red Cross armband came in and sat down at the table. He was holding a form with a red cross at the top and introduced himself as the representative of the Red Cross. He said that when I had answered the questions, he would send in the form and my family would learn that I was a prisoner-of-war (POW). We smiled at each other and he started reading the questions.

"Name?" "Rank?" "Number?" "Next-of-kin?" "Address?" No problem as he filled them in. Then *"Squadron Number?" "Squadron Number?"*, I said. *"Surely, you don't need that." "Oh, yes, we do,"* he said: *"and the base you flew from? Type of aircraft? Call-sign?"* I stopped him and said, *"This is*

ridiculous: the Red Cross has nothing to do with all this." "Oh, yes," he replied, *"we need all these details before we can inform your parents." "Well,"* I said, *"this Red Cross is nothing like ours. I don't think you're Red Cross at all."* He became very angry and said, *"If I don't fill-in this form about you, your parents will never hear that you are a POW." "Too bad"*, I replied; *"they'll just have to go without."* He then stood up and stalked out of the room. One up to me, I thought.

In fact, my parents never heard, and never received any of the letters I wrote from Stalag Luft 1 – they were all found, with thousands of others, piled up in a room in the administrative block when we were liberated. But Tony Davis, my wonderful 16 Squadron CO, flew over to England to see my father and mother and told them that I had radioed that I was going to bale out, so there was a good chance that I had become a POW.

A guard then took me to one of the cells in the corridor and locked me in. I now felt myself really to be a prisoner-of-war.

The room was about 12 feet by 6, filled mainly with a wooden bed, on which was a straw mattress and a single blanket. Beside it was a small table with a tin mug on it. The ceiling was high and at the end of the room was a window, through which I could see only the sky; below it, fixed to the wall, was an electric radiator, consisting of two short, horizontal metal planks, one above the other; this was on for two hours in the morning and three hours in the evening; I huddled under my blanket for the rest of the time. On the wall beside the door was a handle: when pulled, it allowed a signal-arm to drop down into the corridor and, in his own good time, a guard would come and ask what I wanted. Breakfast was two slices of black bread with a smear of 'ersatz' raspberry jam inside and a mug of 'ersatz' tea; lunch was a bowl of watery soup with, perhaps, a few grains of meat at the bottom; supper was two slices of bread with a smear of margarine inside and a mug of 'ersatz' coffee. I told myself I could survive for a month on this diet, after which I knew nothing of such importance to the Germans that would warrant my dying of starvation by holding it back.

There were scratches on the wall indicating the days and weeks passed by one or two other prisoners, with none showing more than a month. I started my own row of scratch-marks, which reached twenty, eventually.

There was nothing whatever to do all day or night. Only when the 'meals' came round did the guards unlock a few doors and we could stand in the doorway and perhaps exchange a few quick words with our neighbours. From them I learned that if you asked for a shower, especially if you said you had lice, you would be taken to an interrogator, who could authorise you to be led to the showers: the Germans, fortunately, were obsessed with the danger of lice spreading through the prison. Otherwise, the only way out of the cell was to make your signal and ask to go to the toilet; but the guard accompanied you and, if you chanced to meet another prisoner on the way, it was rarely that you could snatch a sentence with him.

I assumed an interrogator would call me in when he wanted me, and I filled the first week by recalling all the things I had once memorised at home or at school: nursery rhymes, the nonsense verse of Lewis Carroll and Edward Lear, and poems I'd been forced to learn by heart; the declensions of Latin and Greek verbs and Greek and German articles; counting the numbers in these languages and French; reciting the alphabet and numbers in reverse, and so on.

After a week, I decided I needed a shower and was taken to see Captain Schwarz. He was a slim, pleasant-looking man of about 40, with perfect English and courteous manners. He asked me all the expected questions about my aircraft, base and mission, but I told him I could tell him only my name, rank and number. He sighed and said he was sorry, but I would be kept in this inhospitable place until I told him something more. He asked me where I'd been to school and I was quite happy to have a

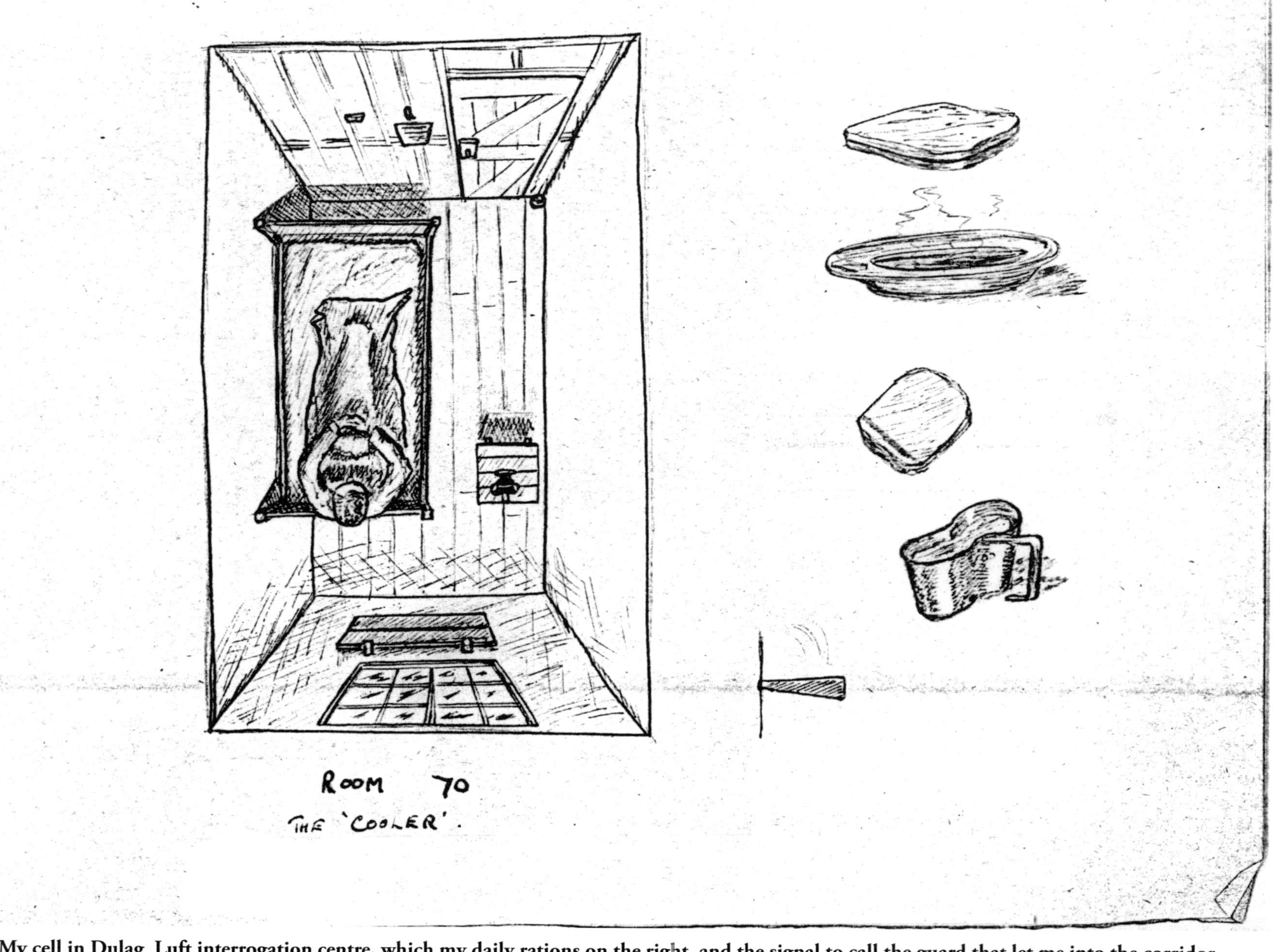

My cell in Dulag Luft interrogation centre, which my daily rations on the right, and the signal to call the guard that let me into the corridor. Drawn from memory in Stalag Luft 1.

noncommittal conversation about Eton and similar civilian subjects. We also got onto the progress of the war: when I said the German position was hopeless, he replied that the Fuehrer had promised that the V1 and V2 and their jet aircraft would drive the Allies out of Europe and their new submarines would win control of the Atlantic again. He then called a guard and told him to take me to the showers.

This was a real luxury, added to which I found an old American magazine high up on a window-ledge. Now I had something to read, and when I'd finished it several times, I could count the number of words and letters on a page and note the commonest ones. Later, I persuaded an old guard to lend me a pencil and we chatted while I quickly made a pack of cards by writing their values on patches of blank paper torn from my magazine. Unfortunately, we got into an argument about who was winning the war and, in anger, he snatched back his pencil, tore up my pseudo playing-cards, and marched out in a huff. I was sad at losing my 'cards', but I felt that I, a powerless prisoner, had scored a moral victory.

A week later, my morale had fallen quite far and I felt I had to talk to someone, even an interrogator. So I signalled for another shower and was taken, after a long wait, to a new interrogator. He turned out to be very different from the courteous Schwarz: he was short, thick-set and red-faced, and immediately started shouting at me, telling me I was a spy or a saboteur, and that if I didn't answer all his questions, I'd be sent to the Gestapo, who would know how to deal with me. I protested that if I told him anything it would be giving information to the enemy, which was against the Geneva Convention. He replied that until I told him who I was, I wasn't covered by the Geneva Convention. All this was shouted at me with thumps on his desk. At this point, a door behind me opened, and a grey-haired officer in immaculate riding-breeches, probably the Colonel in charge, stepped in and said in English, *"What's all this noise about?"* The interrogator was now standing up. I said to the Colonel, *"It's this man, he's shouting at me and making threats, and it's no use." "Oh, dear"*, said the Colonel, *"We can't have this sort of thing."* and addressing the interrogator, he continued, *"You mustn't treat Taylor in this way: he's a gentleman."* Then, turning back to me, he said, *"I see you've been to Eton. I'm most interested in the English Public Schools. You must come and talk to me about them."* (The Nazis always took an inordinate interest in what they thought was the English method of producing leaders.) I replied, *"If you'll invite me to dinner, Sir, I'll tell you anything you want to know about them!"* He smiled, brought his stick up in a mock salute, nodded to the interrogator, and went back through his door, The interrogator looked a little subdued, called in a guard, ordered him to take me to the showers, and I was led away.

Later, I felt something hard in the straw of my bed and found a length of electric cable from someone's heated flying-suit. This was a godsend. I unravelled it carefully until I had a number of separate strands of thin copper wire, and I then proceeded to fashion a little bowl, by making a wire frame, and then winding more wire round it. I made two of these bowls and persuaded a guard to give me half a loaf of bread in exchange for one of them. The other I kept and gave it to my mother on my return home; I still have it in my possession.

I was a little confused by my treatment, as I was not then aware that a common interrogation technique was to soften-up a prisoner with a 'kind' interrogator and then pass him on to a 'harsh' one; if this failed, he could be 'rescued' by a senior officer – psychological moves to encourage the prisoner to talk.

In my case, "Name, rank, and number" was my watchword, the official line of our Armed Forces and of the Geneva Convention. In addition to this, I didn't know how much the Luftwaffe knew of PR techniques. I imagined that they might well think that we carried the latest technology for navigation and photography and they would naturally want to know all about it. In fact, we were operating with virtually the same equipment as was used in WW1, with the addition of our being able to get a 'homing' for the last 20-50 miles back to base. My secret, therefore, was that we had no secrets! But just what did the Germans know about us? There were plenty of PR pilots who had been taken prisoner before me, and the Germans would certainly have examined every scrap of their aircraft's wreckage. But what did they know about me? Almost certainly, nothing. It was four weeks since I had landed in the field in 't Hesseler, and I'd been picked up near the Rhine about 100 miles from there. Even if they'd found the remains of my blue Spitfire, there was little likelihood that they would connect them with this pilot who had arrived a month later at Dulag Luft from Enschede. The only clue as to my occupation was that I appeared not to be worried about any fellow-crew member, so they could presume I was not flying a bomber. But all else was a blank.

After two weeks of this prison regime, I was getting increasingly frustrated. I could hear American airmen entering the cell on one side of me, being interrogated briefly – I couldn't make out what was said – and leaving next day. It seemed as if they were talking quite freely. On the other side of me was an RAF bomb-aimer, whom I'd been able to contact by shouting through the wall. He was very unhappy: he was a bombing leader and was using the latest equipment and systems; the Germans obviously knew about his role and he didn't think he could hold out much longer against their questions and threats. I tried to encourage him, and he said he had fashioned a small crucifix, which gave him hope. The guards interrupted our noisy conversations by banging on our doors; so we could communicate for only a few minutes and not very often. There were plenty of punishments available if we persisted.

I was a little surprised, after another three days, to be called-in by my original interrogator, Captain Schwarz. Any conversation was better than none, and the prospect of talking to a German immediately restored my morale and my determination not to give away anything of operational value.

Captain Schwarz was as pleasant as before and commiserated with me when I complained of the brutish way the other interrogator had treated me, *"Well, we all have our different approaches, you know"*, he said in a soothing voice. He went on, "*I like you, Taylor, and I want to get you out of here and into a prison-camp, where you'll have plenty to eat and find good friends. But you must help me. Look, here's the form I have to fill-in about you, with a lot of questions. Now, I'll cross out all these ones"*, scoring lines through almost the whole document, *"and you'll only have to tell me your squadron number, your base, and your call-sign. I can't do more for you than this. Oh, and by the way, don't call me Captain Schwarz – my friends call me Blackie."*

"That's awfully good of you, Blackie," I said. *"but, you know, I can't tell you anything: whatever I say will be information, and I can't do it."*

"You're wrong," he replied. *"It's not information, it's identification. We know all about a pilot called Taylor, who you say you are. All you have to do is to tell us about yourself so that we can identify you as this pilot, and then you can go to a prison-camp."* He paused, went to a drawer and pulled out a small address-book, *"I've had dozens of pilots through here"*, he said, *"some of them very distinguished, and they've thanked me for helping to get them out of here."* He opened the book and showed me a number of grateful remarks signed by a British or American airman. One, in particular, I noted because the name was unusual; it read, "Many thanks, Blackie, for your understanding treatment", signed "Hubert Zemke, Col. USAAF."

This was another step in softening me up, but it had no effect on me at all, as I assumed it was a book of faked messages to try to overcome a prisoner's natural reluctance to talk to his interrogator. This entry, however, recurred to me in Stalag Luft 1, as Colonel Zemke, a highly-decorated American fighter leader, was Senior American Officer in the camp, but not a very effective one. A few years ago, I requested Roger Freeman, a leading British aviation historian who knew Zemke well, to ask him if he ever wrote anything in a book for his interrogator while in Dulag Luft. Zemke replied, not surprisingly, that he never had. They have both died since then.

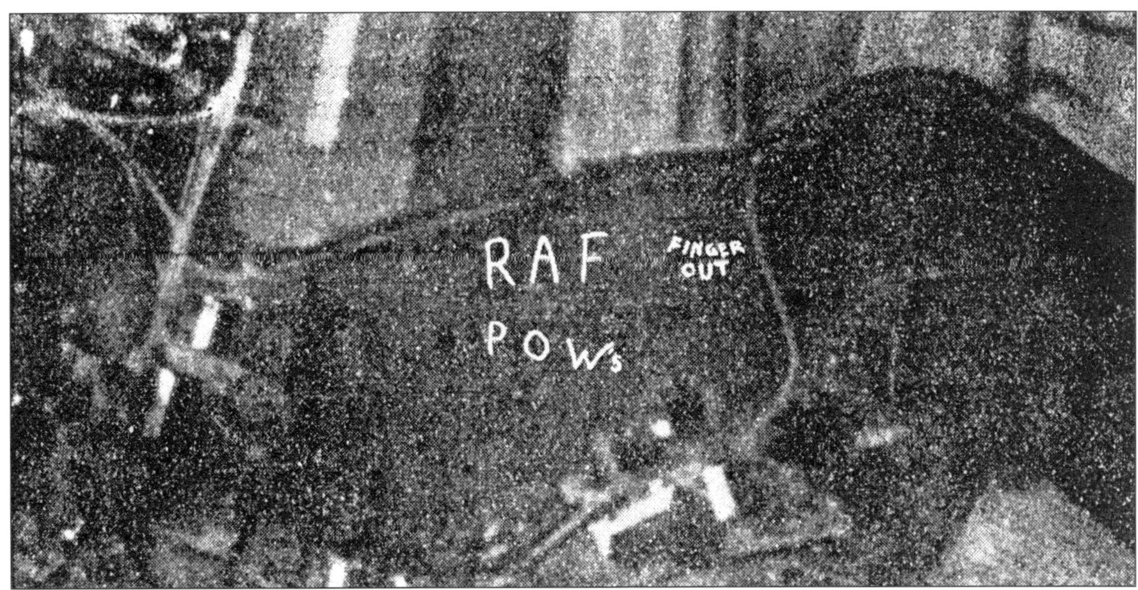

Not my Camp
POWs wrote this message on their roof to warn-off RAF bombers, who might have taken it for a German troop barracks. Photographed by 16 Squadron's F/O David Stutchbury on 28th April 1945
Photo: 34 Wing's short-lived post-war magazine "Wingspan"

"I can't agree with you, Blackie," I said. "You know nothing about me, so whatever I tell you has to be information."

"You're wrong", he replied. *"We know much more than you think. Look at this"*, and he pulled down a fat volume from a shelf full of similar books. *"This is the American 8th Air Force."* He opened the book at random. *"Here's a typical squadron,"* and he showed me a coloured illustration of a Boeing B-17, with a red-painted fin and rudder. All the markings were visible, with lists of names, including ranks and nicknames, details about the unit's history and present base, the names of the local pub and barmaids and, no doubt, any other items of interest gleaned from the interrogations of members of the crews. Now I understood how it was possible for the American airmen to be processed so quickly in the cell next to mine: the Germans knew more about their squadron and aircraft than many of them would know themselves, especially if they were fairly new arrivals on the unit. On the page I was shown, were a number of question-marks; it was easy to imagine how the interrogator would talk to a prisoner about his squadron and casually introduce, say, his aircraft number, but get one numeral wrong, whereupon the unthinking airman would instantly correct him – and one more question-mark would disappear from the page.

"Well", I said, *"that's amazing, really impressive; I'd no idea you knew so much about the Americans. But it doesn't alter the fact that you know nothing at all about me."*

"You're wrong again", he replied. *"How do you like being in photographic reconnaissance?"*

This was a real body-blow, and I hoped I hadn't shown by the blink of an eye-lid what a shock he had given me. *"Why should I like photo-reconnaissance any more than any other activity?"* I asked, rather lamely.

"Well", said he, *"let's assume that this was your job"*. He went back to the shelf and produced a rather smaller volume and opened it, without showing it to me. *"Now, here we have No 34 Wing, and in this Wing are No 40, No 260 and No 400 Squadrons. So, you see, we know a great deal."*

This was an extraordinary situation: he'd named my Wing correctly, but in it he had put three totally different squadrons, and he hadn't mentioned my own squadron, No 16, at all. What was he doing?

Did he really know the facts and was he just playing with me, waiting for my reaction? Or was he really ignorant? Either way, one thing was absolutely clear, any mention of 16 Squadron was impossible – apparently, that really would be information. I decided to stall.

"Well, I must say, you know an awful lot already, Blackie. You might as well let me go now."

"Ah, but you haven't identified yourself yet."

"But I can't, Blackie. I really can't."

"In that case you will just have to stay here very uncomfortably until you change your mind. I'm sorry about it. Go away and think about it." He called a guard and dismissed me from the room.

So back I went to my solitary cell and the debilitating diet. Three days later, he called me back again.

"Well, have you thought about it? What's your answer?"

"Blackie, you know me, you know my background, you know I can't give you information."

"All right. I understand. You've been here long enough; I want you out of here and in a prison-camp for Christmas. I'll tell you what I'll do: I won't fill-in any forms about you, I won't write anything about you. You just tell me your squadron number and I'll check it against our records and, if it's all right, I'll go to the Colonel and tell him 'Taylor's all right', and you'll be out of here next day."

I suddenly realised that with this concession Blackie had provided me with a possible opening to satisfy him without telling him the truth: I could give him a false squadron number. On the other hand, if he really knew as much about me as he claimed, he would immediately realise my deception and I would assuredly be handed over to the Gestapo. I've never been much good at telling lies, and now my face grew red and my hand began to shake as I tried to steel myself for a big one and, at the same time, to think of a squadron number that was realistic, ie one that was operating in Europe and not, for example, in Italy or Burma. Unfortunately, I'd never taken much interest in what went on outside 34 Wing and 16 Squadron, so my choice of a number was going to be a huge gamble.

Blackie saw my symptoms and misinterpreted them. *"Don't worry"*, he said; *"I know what you're going through: you have your honour as a Public Schoolboy. But you needn't be afraid: I promise you, no one will ever know what you've told me. Come, let's have a drink. Let's drink to the end of the war."* He went to a cupboard and took out a bottle of red wine and a wine-glass. He filled the glass for me and poured some wine into an inkwell for himself. *"Here's to the end of the war, whatever happens,"* he said. *"To the end of the war"*, I repeated.

The wine, of course, made my face even redder and my hands were still trembling. Seeing this, Blackie said, *"Now, Taylor, I'll make it even easier for you: you needn't tell me anything. Here's a piece of paper and a pencil. Just write down your squadron number. I'll look at it, tear up the paper, check our records, go to the Colonel and say you're all right. And you'll be out tomorrow."*

This was my only chance and I had to take it. I knew very little about other PR squadrons, but somewhere someone had mentioned No 4 Squadron in some context. I picked up the pencil and wrote '4' on the paper.

Thoroughly nervous, I stood up and stammered to Blackie, *"You promise that I'll be out of here tomorrow?"*

"Yes, I promise," he replied. We shook hands and I couldn't wait to get out of the room. All the rest of that day and throughout the night, I listened to the sound of boots along the corridor: if they passed

without stopping, I breathed a sigh of relief and my heart ceased its accelerated pumping. If they had stopped, I knew I'd be for the high jump for trying to deceive my interrogator.

Eventually, next morning after breakfast, my door was unlocked and I was led along the corridor into the courtyard outside, where a line of prisoners was already drawn up. And now occurred something very unexpected.

I was standing behind the man in front of me and I suddenly recognised his extremely straight back. I tapped him on the shoulder and said, *"I know you - you're Whitamore."* He turned round, *"How the hell d'you know my name?"* I laughed and said, *"We were at school together, but we never knew each other."* At Eton, the 1000-plus boys lived very much in their boarding Houses, of which there were 25, and met other boys only in lessons and games. From that moment onwards, Tony Whitamore and I became firm friends, and remained so, with our families closely connected, until he died in 2007.

It was 24th December. We were taken to the Transit Camp at Wetzlar, not far from the Dulag and run by prisoners under German supervision. Here we were kitted out with whatever we needed, in my case long-john underclothes, shirts, socks, boots, an RAF fore-and-aft uniform cap, a razor and blades, soap, a toothbrush and dentifrice, some letter-cards, and a wind-cheater jacket, with "USA" and "POW" scrawled across the chest in red paint. I packed all these items, which came through the Red Cross, into the small fibre suit-case which we were also given – and which I still have.

There was some suspicion about the prisoners running this camp, that they were living a good life from the pile of Red Cross food parcels which they stored. On Christmas Day, however, we had no complaints as we sat down to the best dinner we'd had for weeks, mostly provided by those providential Red Cross parcels: 'Spam' and corned beef, German cabbage, bread and potatoes, tinned fruit salad and 'Klim' powdered milk, biscuits and cheese, coffee and 'D-bar' chocolate. We weren't too worried that the men serving us were pink-faced, clean, well-dressed, and clearly well-fed.

Two days later, on 27th December, we left Wetzlar in a whole train-load of POWs being taken to Stalag Luft 1 and possibly on to other Stalags. We were searched before we left the camp and I found a dinner-knife with a wooden handle lying under a seat; someone had obviously got rid of it before being searched. I tucked it into the lining of my hat and it survived the inspection. We were given a Red Cross parcel between two men for the journey, so Tony and I shared one. My knife proved invaluable in opening tins which had no key; the blade became jagged with this use and thus equally useful for slicing German bread and Red Cross corned-beef and cheese.

The journey to Barthe, on the Baltic coast, took five days and was tedious in the extreme. The German transport system was in chaos from constant bombing and strafing: the train was held-up continually by repair-work on the line; if we were waiting in a station and the air-raid sirens sounded by day or night, the train would steam out a few miles and stop in the countryside until the 'All Clear' was announced. We slept wherever we could find a space: I used our seat, while Tony, who was smaller, occupied the luggage-rack above. The train also stopped periodically to allow the prisoners to go to the toilet beside the track. Needless to say, our guards were especially watchful at these times.

Eventually, on New Year's Eve, we walked in a motley bunch through the old town of Barthe and along two miles of road until we came to the tall watch-towers and barbed-wire fences of Stalag Luft 1, a camp of 10,000 American airmen and 5000 British. Old 'kriegies' came up to the wire and scanned the faces of the new arrivals, looking for familiar ones, or asking for news of their units or about the latest progress of the war. So we entered my home for the next four-and-a-half months.

However, I didn't feel entirely safe from the long arm of Dulag Luft, which had been known to claw prisoners back for further interrogation. But even if Blackie realised he had been fooled, there were many more airmen for him to deal with and he would probably not have wished to admit to the Colonel that he had virtually allowed me to get out unchecked. On the other hand, it's just possible he really was a nice man, or he knew the Germans were losing the war, and deliberately did me a good turn. In my bones, I feel this is unlikely – but who knows?

As there was not much about flying in my four-months' incarceration in Stalag Luft 1, I shall say little about it. The only direct connection we had with the war was the sight of the flak-training school just 200 yards beyond our barbed-wire fences. The trainees were all women, not surprisingly, perhaps, after Germany's five years of total war. They were kitted out in field-grey caps and long grey overcoats. Several of them had blonde locks hanging over their collars, and these always attracted a line of sex-starved 'kriegies' along the wire, some of whom had been 'in the bag' from the early days of the war, who couldn't take their eyes off these tantalising alien figures. The only aeroplane to be seen was an ancient Junkers monoplane, which patrolled monotonously up and down, giving the girls practice in range-finding. The Germans blew the school up on the day they left.

Stalag Luft 1, near Barthe, North Germany: I had no such concept of the layout of the camp except that it was near an inlet of the Baltic and Barthe.

Stalag Luft 1, near Barthe, North Germany: beyond the barbed-wire to the Baltic inlet

Sketch by JT March 1945

Name: Taylor
Vorname: Harold James Strickland
Dienstgrad: F/Lt.
Erk.-Marke: 8688 St.L.1 8888
Serv.-Nr.: 131 017
Nationalität: Brite
Baracke: 5
Raum: 16
131017
131017
K. Liebig-Sagan

My German POW Identity Card found in the Admin block after liberation

Collecting coal-bricks in an upturned bench: one of the daily chores

Every variety of clothing was worn by POWs to keep warm.
Fortunately, I had the Camp Education Officer in my room, who gave me paper and crayons.

We were liberated eventually by the Russians on 3rd May, and their first order was that the 10,000 Americans and 5,000 British should all leave the camp, beat up the German men and rape the women, just as they were doing. Some of the Americans grabbed the opportunity to get out, but the British were under strict orders to stay in camp, on pain of court-martial on return home: here we were safe and known, whereas outside was total chaos, with Russian troops, panic-stricken Germans, deserters from different armies, escaping or liberated slave labourers, and many others, all milling about looking for food or anything of value and holding life very cheaply.

We heard about V-E Day on 8th May on our secret BBC radio, but the Russians were now keeping us in camp for Stalin to use as a bargaining counter to get the Allies to send all Soviet-born men back to Russia, regardless of whether they were willing to go or not. Those who had been captured, as well as the deserters and men like the Cossacks in Yugoslavia, had no wish whatever to return, as they knew that they would be shot on arrival in Russia. I feel guilty that my freedom, and with it my life, was traded against theirs – and they lost theirs.

Eventually, the Senior British Officer escaped to the Allied front-line 70 miles away and thence to England, where moves were set in train to rescue us. On 12th May, several squadrons of B-17s landed at the nearby Barthe airfield and took off the sick and wounded under the watchful eyes of the Russians – but they made no move to interfere. Next day, the rest of us marched up to the airfield and climbed into lines of B-17s. With two others I crammed into the tail-turret of one of them, and we were treated to a low-level tour of blitzed German cities and the wreckage of Rotterdam. We all felt the Germans had brought destruction on themselves and we were very relieved to be getting out of Europe.

We landed at RAF Ford, in Sussex, and the Station Commander stood by the steps to greet us. I was astonished to recognise him as 'Cub' Hartley, the OC of the Air Section at Eton, whom I, as the NCO in charge, had stood behind on parade and whispered the orders he had to give us! Here he was, a Group Captain; I regretted I had no chance to ask him what he had done to achieve such rank, while I was still a humble Flight Lieutenant. We were quickly transported to RAF Cosford in Shropshire, where a well-run organisation had been put in place to process the flood of returning prisoners, de-briefing us on our experiences, examining us medically, fitting us out with the necessary clothes, ration books, and railway warrants, and sending us home on extended leave within 24 hours.

If meeting 'Cub' Hartley was one surprise, an even greater one was to find a note from Mike Horsfall, saying that he had been shot down on 14th January 1945 and had spent time in hospital before going to a prison-camp near Munich. He came to fetch me next day in his rakish green MG sports-car, took me to his home in Leamington to meet his family, and then drove me to Cheam School, near Newbury; here we were met with a large banner strung across the front of the building, reading "Welcome home, Jimmy". It was great to be home and there was much to enjoy, even though the basics of civilian life continued to be rationed on a war footing for many months, even years, to come.

Michael Horsfall at the wheel of his MG, with his sister Rosemary and brother Colin

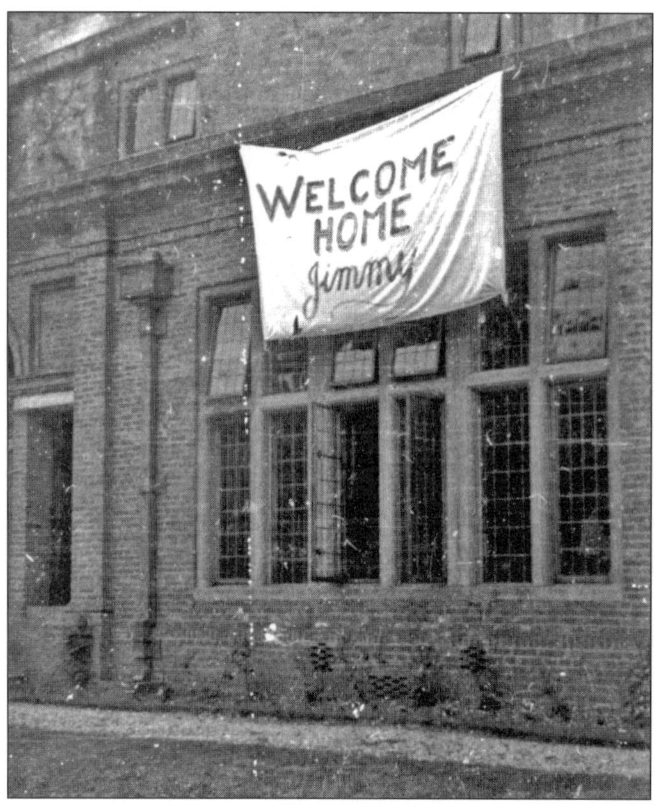

It was good to be back at Cheam School on 15th May 1945.

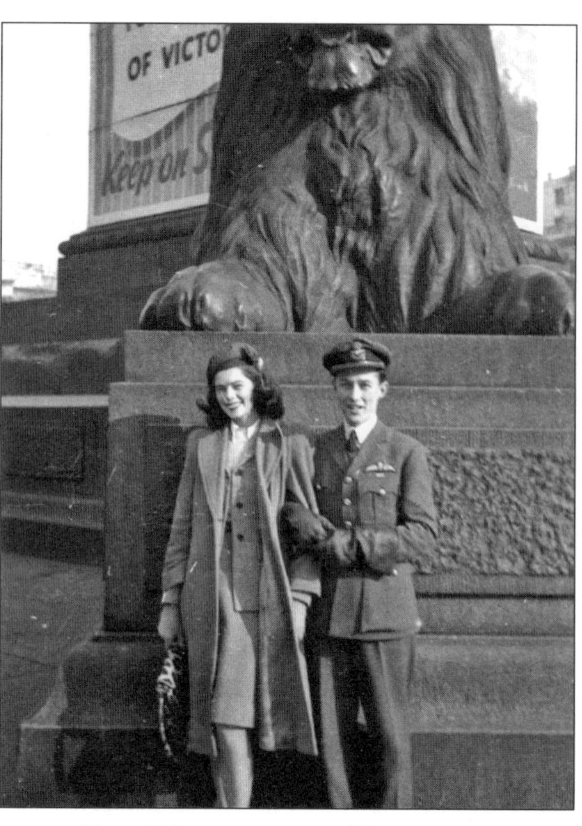

Tony Whitamore in Trafalgar Square with Paddy Dean, his future wife

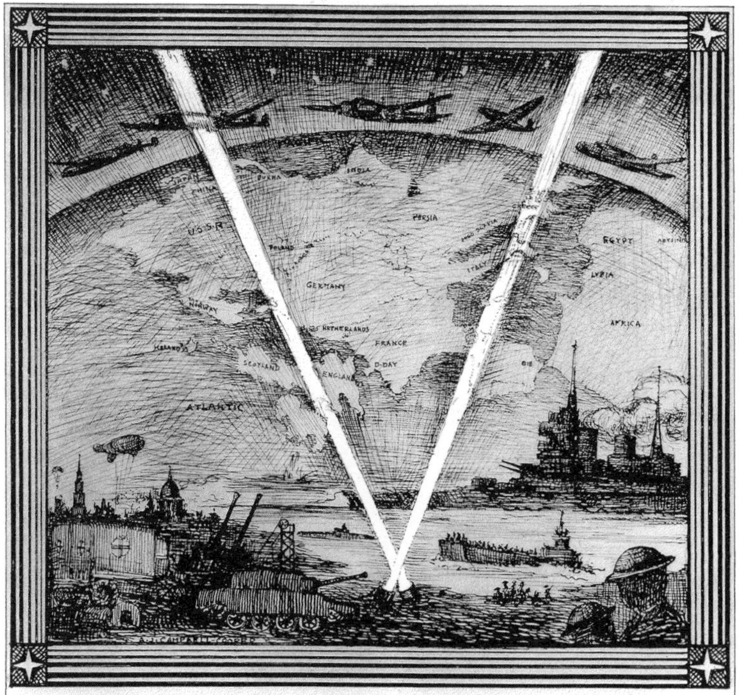

THE PEOPLE OF
HEADLEY WOODLANDS
GIVE YOU THEIR GRATEFUL AND
HEARTFELT THANKS FOR YOUR
SERVICES DURING THE WAR YEARS
1939–1945
H·J·S·TAYLOR·

Interlude

CHAPTER 16

The Passing Years

Mike and I made a short cycle-tour of Wales to try to get fit again, and managed to get a flight to Eindhoven from Hartford Bridge in a Warwick on 12th June to see 16 Squadron. Many of the personnel, however, had changed since our days and no one seemed very interested in two returned POWs. Mike persuaded his friend 'Polly' Pollitt of 140 Squadron to fly us in a Mosquito to Brussels. We stayed here for three nights, principally to enable Mike to become engaged to Denise Henri-Jean, whom he had last seen in the Officers' Club. They were married the following year in a union that has proved remarkably happy and prolific, with seven children and twenty-two grandchildren to date. We flew back to Hartford Bridge on 16th June in a Mosquito that David Stutchbury, who had transferred from 140 to 16 Squadron at the end of 1944, had been allowed by Tony Davis to bring from Eindhoven to Brussels for this purpose. Mike sat beside David, while I was squashed under the instrument panel and a third passenger, Lord Ossulton, lay prone in the nose. Considering he was gravely out of practice on Mosquitos, David did a praiseworthy job in bringing us all back to England without any kind of hitch.

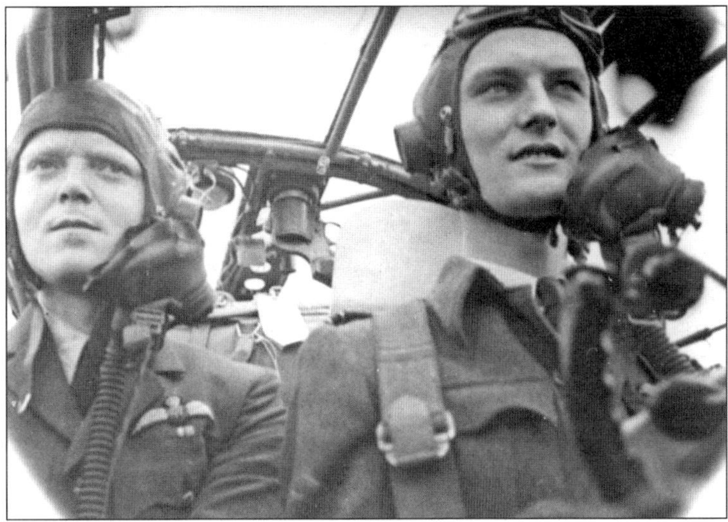

David Stutchbury (r) at the controls of a Mosquito with Michael Horsfall beside him, Lord Ossulton in the nose and JT under the instrument panel flying from Melsbroek 16th June 1945

My wedding present to Tony Davis in January 1947 a tile I made in a pottery based on Michael Horsfall's Melsbroek 'tapestry'; he and I were invited to France as 'témoins' (witnesses), but I was unable to attend.

On 7th July I reported back to Cosford for a full medical, when I was given A/B – whatever that signified. I was also asked to state what I wanted to do in my remaining time in the RAF before being demobilised. The choice was actually quite limited: either a ground-job or a return to instructing. As my only reason for being in the RAF was to fly, I had no hesitation in requesting the latter. However, they refused to accept my

800 hours of instructing in America and, although I told them I would be out of the RAF in May next year, they insisted I should go on a normal RAF instructor's course at No 7 Flying Instructors' School at Upavon, in Wiltshire. This was a historic grass airfield, where the first RFC pilots were trained in 1912, and here I learned to teach RAF cadets to fly the Harvard.

It was a very pleasant aircraft to fly and was an excellent advanced trainer; but I was subjected to the most frightening experience of my life as a pupil or instructor during the four-month course. We were all former operational pilots on the course and I had two decorated Battle of Britain veterans in my particular flight. Some of the time, we had to work in pairs, as simulated pupil and instructor. I found, to my dismay, that these two, a Wing Commander and a Squadron Leader, had no idea of handling the controls in a smoothly coordinated manner; instead, they hurled the Harvard about as if they were ham-fisted rugby-players – which they had both been. Perhaps they each owed their survival in the war to the fact that they slipped and skidded their aircraft round the sky so much that no German pilot could hold them in his sights – their aircraft didn't fly in the direction in which its nose was pointing! Flying in a Harvard in the day-time with either of these veterans was uncomfortable and frightening enough; but coming in to the airfield at night, with one or other of them trying to land from the back seat, was absolutely hair-raising! I pitied the poor pupils who would later find themselves placed in the care of either of these two misfits.

I finished the course on 28th April without blotting my copybook and was posted to No 3 Service Flying Training School (SFTS) at South Cerney, in Gloucestershire. Here budding pilots were taught to fly the Harvard and were awarded their 'wings' when they had fully mastered it. But I found confusion and demoralisation on the Station, brought about by the steady progress of demobilisation, which everybody wanted, but which ensured that all the senior and experienced NCOs, the backbone of the servicing, repair, and inspection of the aircraft, left the Service before the later, less experienced entrants – unless an NCO had signed on to stay in the RAF for a number of years. The result was that when a Harvard was due for an inspection, it disappeared into the hangars and stayed there for several months; consequently, there was a shortage of aircraft, and flying time had to be strictly rationed.

Another indication of the limited flying was that junior officers were given administrative jobs in addition to their instructional duties. I was made Fire Officer and found myself in charge of an experienced Corporal, two airmen who lived off the Station and seldom appeared, and a handsome fire-engine. This was the only time I commanded anyone or anything in the RAF, and it reinforced my impatience to be demobilised. I was baffled by the chemical constituents of the liquids, sprays and powders designed for fighting different kinds of aircraft fires; but, fortunately, the Corporal knew all the procedures and had rescued the crew from a burning aircraft in Canada. My first act was to put him up for promotion to Sergeant – as a reward for his devotion to duty, and I felt I couldn't let my Fire Brigade be run by a mere Corporal! Nevertheless, his third stripe hadn't arrived by the time I left.

I used to visit the Fire Section every morning, look around vaguely, have a chat with the Corporal, and discuss the whereabouts of the airmen. After a time, the Station Commander called me in and said, *"Well, Taylor, you've had a couple of weeks to settle in. I intend to hold a Fire Practice in the near future, so you'd better be on your toes."* With a nervous *"Yessir"*, I scuttled out of his presence – senior officers always frightened me.

A few days later, I was sitting on the fire-engine while the Corporal was warming-up the engine, his usual morning routine, when the Fire Alarm sounded all over the Station. We glanced at the Alarm Board, saw which alarm was sounding, and proceeded at high speed to the location. When we got there, we saw the glass door of the fire-alarm open and the Group Captain kneeling on the grass nearby, just about to light a pile of paper and sticks – but we had arrived before he had time to do so! Looking somewhat crestfallen, he could only congratulate me on our efficiency – and he never called another Fire Practice during my time.

PER ARDUA AD ASTRA
No. 87 F.I. COURSE (7 F.I.S.), R.A.F. UPAVON. NOV.—MARCH. 1946
Front Row.—F/Lt. W. A. Wooden, F/Lt. B. P. Mugford, F/Lt. A. E. Ballam, A.F.C., A.F.M., S/Ldr. E. J. B. Langhorne, W/Cmdr. J. L. Waters, A.F.C., G/Capt. E. A. C. Britton, D.F.C., F/Lt. A. J. Picknett, D.F.C., F/Lt. R. F. Herbert, F/Lt. J. H. A. Prichard, F/O. R. H. Burgess, F/O. K. R. H. Cowell.
Centre Row.—P/O. R. S. Jones, P/O. J. M. Heald, F/Lt. P. W. Racey, F/Lt. H. J. S. Taylor, F/Lt. R. S. Royston, S/Ldr. P. D. F. Mitchell, D.F.C., F/Sgt. Hooper, F/Sgt. Kerr. Sgt. Smith, F/Lt. A. Griffiths, S/Ldr. D. Forde, D.F.C., F/Lt. G. T. Dunger.
Back Row.—P/O. J. Morgan, F/O. J. J. Morgan, F/O. E. Linter, F/O. J. Walker, F/O. J. S. Madgett, F/O. A. L. Bryant, F/Sgt. Riddoch, F/Sgt. Carter, F/O. C. Horn, F/Lt. G. H. Pilbrow, F/Lt. H. R. Hall, P/O. P. C. Lowthian.

At No 7 Flying Instructors School, RAF Upavon November 1945-April 1946

F/Lt Roy Royston with Billy, his unpopular squadron mascot: it ate all papers in reach.

Category 'C' instructor

Harvard in the snow at Upavon

A few weeks later, the Station held an Open Day on St Dunstan's Day – the equivalent then of Battle of Britain Day. I was having tea out-of-doors with my girl-friend, by chance next to the CO with his wife and family. Suddenly, the Fire Alarm sounded. I looked across at the Group Captain, and said, *"I presume this is a false alarm. Sir?" "No, it damned well isn't!"* he shouted. *"Get moving!"* Excusing myself to my girl, I raced across to the Fire Station and found the Corporal gazing at the board. *"I don't know where the fire is, Sir,"* he said, *"there's nothing on the board." "Well,"* I replied, *"we'd better drive round the peri track and look for smoke somewhere."* We stopped at every alarm-point, but not one had a broken glass. We returned to look again at the board, but nothing was showing. We went round again – in vain, while the fire-bells continued to disturb the peace. Then my clever Corporal announced, *"I know what it is, Sir: the sun's expanded the glass and pressed a button somewhere!"* We drove round again, examining every alarm-point until we came to one glass which was pressed tight against the button. We opened the offending window, which released the little button, and the all-pervasive alarm-bells ceased. I returned to the CO. *"It was a false alarm, Sir,"* I said, barely hiding a smirk. *"The sun did it."* He stared at me hard. I saluted and went back to tea with my girl.

My biggest worry was when No 5 SFTS moved to RAF Feltwell in Norfolk and I had to cover, with only one fire-engine, the departure of the Harvards from South Cerney and their arrival at Feltwell. I decided that an accident was more likely to happen on landing than on take-off, and ordered the Corporal to drive the fire-engine to Feltwell with one airman, while I stayed behind with a jeep, the other airman and a few fire-extinguishers. Fortunately, all went well with the Harvards and our services were not required at either end.

It took several weeks before, as an instructor, I was given five students, who had a woeful tale to tell. They had been training at an RAF base in California – far more congenial than my Arnold Scheme – and were just about to get their 'wings' on the AT6 (the original American designation of the Harvard) when the war ended and all flying stopped. A bankrupt Britain hurried them back home, where they were made to start flying-training again on Tiger Moths at Brough, near Hull. They eventually arrived at South Cerney, where their time was filled with doing menial work about the Station: cutting the CO's lawn, polishing the Officers' Mess silver, and so on, until they were told to report to me. I felt very sorry for them and tried to get them into the air as much as possible. Knowing that there were now

My first and last group of RAF cadets
1-r: Les Hollis Johnny Douche Ray Bailey Ian Macdonald
at Feltwell on 4th June 1946

only three weeks remaining before I left Feltwell for demobilisation, and concerned about what would happen to these eager young men when I had gone – they might be left with no instructor or with one who took them back to the beginning again – I managed to give them each nine flights and, on my last day in the RAF, I sent them all off solo! Fortunately for me, and for them, they acquitted themselves well and I was delighted when, on 19th February 1947, they invited me to their long-delayed Graduation Dinner and Dance.

Sadly, this was not the last I heard of two of them. Johnny Douche was an outstanding pilot and became an instructor on Meteors at the Central Flying School at Little Rissington. His natural talent brought him into the CFS Aerobatic Team, one of the precursors of the Red Arrows; but he died when his Meteor crashed on a training flight. Ray Bailey was a reliable pilot and joined the Auxiliary Air Force when he finished his time with the RAF. He flew at weekends and one day, for no obvious cause, stalled and spun in on the approach when landing his Spitfire, and was killed in the crash. Did I fail them in some way? I hope not. They both loved flying.

I had tried to get the Air Force to release me early so that I could go up to Trinity College, Cambridge, in 1945, but it wasn't possible. Now I went there in October 1946. I was aged 24, among a host of similar young men and women, old beyond our years, with war service behind us and an uncertain future ahead. I fell in love with the romantic atmosphere of the Cambridge colleges, symbolised by King's College Chapel towering majestically over well-manicured lawns, while the placid river carried punts and canoes beneath the graceful arches of 18th-century bridges. But I had lost five years of my life and needed a professional qualification to earn my living. So I worked seriously hard – perhaps missing out on many of Cambridge's delights – and took a degree in History in two years (allowed by special

Farewell from a Harvard on 6th June 1946 after five happy years in the RAF

Three years of study at Cambridge 1946-1949

Returning to the air: in a Slingsby Prefect in the University Gliding Club during the summer of 1949

Holding my unearned MA (left) in 1953 beside John Lloyd, whose father was at Trinity College with mine wartime sanction) and a Diploma in Education in my third year. My father had been at Trinity before the First War, while Gerald, demobilised from radar in the RAF in the same year as myself, also came up in 1946, and Christopher, invalided out of the RAF with a resurgence of his Hodgkin's Disease, joined us in 1948, making an unusual trio of brothers up at Trinity together.

While my instinct for education came probably from my school-master father, my mother was a good amateur artist and perhaps was responsible for my strong desire to have some means of expressing myself creatively. I knew I didn't want to be a proper artist, but I decided to take out a year from my earning life by going to an Art School. I managed to persuade the Principal of Chelsea School of Art – who thought I would be a steadying influence on his younger students – to accept me for September 1949. To pay for the experience, I went to work as a temporary clerk in the Education Department of Dorset County Council. I lived with my parents, who had retired from Cheam School in 1947 and settled into an attractive cottage in the tiny hamlet of Little Stinsford, a mile outside Dorchester.

I was placed in the Further Education Department and part of my work involved drawing up a formula that enabled my boss to award County Bursaries and Scholarships to deserving young people in Dorset who wanted a wide variety of training courses, but had very different qualifications. Among them, I noticed two who were going to art schools; so I asked my boss if I qualified for an award. He said I'd saved the County a lot of money with my new formula, and he was agreeable. So I sent myself a form, filled it in, returned it to myself, filed my application, called myself up for interview, and my boss awarded me £100! As I paid only £1.00 a week for a large bed-sitter in Chelsea, a few yards from the Art School, this meant I was not dependent on my parents for support – not even in London – in 1949-50.

The Art School was very traditional at this time and, in their first year, students were restricted to Pencil Drawing, Design, Lettering, and Art History. However, I was in a hurry to learn as much as possible: I found the Sculpture room and spent one morning a week with the masterly Willi Soukop; I joined adult evening classes and studied Oil Painting: and I argued with the Lettering teacher about shapes, so he invited me to come to his studio in Hampstead Garden Suburb Institute on Saturdays to learn about Pottery. Thus, after ten months, I had a fairly well-rounded introduction to Art and, without being able to practise it, I had a reasonable idea of what artists were trying to do and of some of the media and techniques they used to achieve it. I have always benefitted from the insights this mini-training gave me.

I now had to find a job. I went to the London County Council and told them that, in direct contrast with the privileged education I had received, I wished to teach ordinary urban children. The Chief Inspector was friendly and put me on 'Supply', to fill gaps in school staffs. I spent two terms teaching English to the younger boys in a Junior Technical School (no longer in the school system), and was then sent to a run-down ex-Elementary School, in the back-streets of Ladbroke Grove behind Notting Hill Gate, re-named a Secondary Modern School after the 1944

One of my classes at St.John's Secondary Modern School, near Ladbroke Grove, London 1953

Education Act. The boys and girls came from slum homes, with parents who usually scorned education – yet education was the only avenue that offered these children a way out of the slums. I ended-up with a class of illiterate 14-year-old boys and girls, whom I taught every day in nearly every lesson; I enjoyed designing projects to involve these otherwise defeated youngsters in practical learning tasks. My heart bled for them yet, after 2 years, I felt I had to move on or stay there, as some teachers did, for ever.

David and Goliath
My compact little Austin Seven nestles under an Avro Tudor at Blackbushe Airport (yes, you could drive onto it in 1953!).

As it happened, just at that time, my eye was caught by an advertisement by the Iraqi Ministry of Education, asking for teachers of English in Boys' Secondary Schools in Baghdad. My sense of history was still strong, but I knew I should never be able to afford to travel to the Middle East, the land of T.E.Lawrence, Crusader castles, Graeco-Roman cities in the desert, and the remains of even older civilisations. However, here was the opportunity not only to live there, but to be paid to do so!

I flew out to Baghdad in a propeller-driven BOAC Argonaut, and became very excited at my first view through the window of endless sand: I asked my neighbour to tell me about the countries of Lebanon and Jordan that we were passing over: he replied rather gruffly. We stopped to refuel (from a pile of tins) in the desert at Maffraq, in Jordan, and I was surprised to see a guard-of-honour of the Arab Legion standing by the aeroplane's steps. My neighbour left the aircraft and the guard presented arms: he was our High Commissioner to Jordan, returning from leave in UK!

We were served cold drinks under a canopy while we waited for the flight to continue. I had to shade my eyes from the scorching glare to see how the refuelling was proceeding. We took-off eventually, and followed the furrow drawn over the desert by a plough to guide to Baghdad the slow-moving biplanes of 30 years before, military transports initially, and early airliners in the 1920's.

So I changed from trying to educate street-arabs in Ladbroke Grove to teaching real Arabs in Baghdad – except that most of the boys were thoroughly urbanised. The teaching was very formal: Arabic lessons were chanted in chorus, and everyone knew that learning the textbooks by heart was the key to success in the examinations, which was the purpose of education. In my school there was no assembly hall and no assemblies; no dining-room and no school meals; no science laboratory; no library which the boys could enter, no browsing therefore, only a hatchway through which they could receive a book they asked for; no playing-fields or organised games; no woodwork or hobbies; no stage or drama; no music or orchestra; no societies or effort to develop boys' interests or personalities. School was a mini-university: the teachers had no chair and were not allowed to sit down; they were expected, more or less, to lecture the boys.

When the boys demonstrated politically in the street outside (adults were not allowed by law to meet in groups of more than ten), the Principal, a huge man named Naji Abdul Amir, asked me what was wrong with his school: *"I love my boys – why don't they come into my school?" "Why do you ask me?"* I said. *"I've only just come here." "Because you're an Englishman,"* he replied. *"You know everything."* So I wrote him 20 pages, translated later into Arabic, describing an effective school, concerned with character-development as well as with learning.

As I knew no Arabic, I had to teach the first class from scratch to learn English not by translation from the textbook, but by communicating with me. All the orders I had to give in the classroom or the requests they needed to make to me I had to teach specifically step by step, with plenty of gestures, miming and pictures. The boys were bright and gave no trouble – so unlike Ladbroke Grove! At the end of the year, the Principal said I was a very good teacher. I told him I wasn't; but my classes had to learn to listen and speak English in order to understand anything, while the other teachers of English spent most of the time speaking in Arabic, even for the most simple instructions. As a result, when the Principal was promoted to the Primary Teachers' Training College, he asked me to come with him as Head of the English Department. As a history graduate who had never been in a Primary School, I felt it would be a challenge, but I couldn't refuse.

So started one of the happiest periods of my life, 1954-57. I returned to London by desert bus, boat, and train to get married to Susan Hendrie; for our honeymoon, we drove back to Baghdad in a second-hand Ford station-wagon, with a bed behind the back seat and stores on board for two weeks. The roads across the Balkans and Greece were primitive, and in Turkey and Syria they were gravel, with only one petrol-pump somewhere in the towns, which took some finding. We rented a small house, with date-palms in the garden, in a pleasant suburb of Baghdad, and had friends among the Iraqi artists trained in Europe; the adults to whom I taught English in the evenings in the British Council; the ten other English teachers and their wives; the staff of the British Council and some of the British Embassy; and the temporary and permanent residents of the YMCA, which was preferred to the single, expensive, European-style hotel by the international engineers, archaeologists, and travellers, and by the airmen on leave from the great RAF base at Habbaniyah, 50 miles north of Baghdad, and Shaibah outside Basra in the south.

The work in the College was fascinating: the students were mainly village boys with two years' secondary education; they came to the College for a course of two years, long enough to experience an urban standard of living without being seduced by it; it included agriculture, plumbing and hygiene, as well as the usual subjects and English, as they were expected to return to their villages as the main agents to introduce fertilisers, pumped water and drainage. Considering what a responsibility was placed on their immature shoulders, these students were one of the success-stories in 1950's Iraq.

Baghdad was peaceful then: the young King Faisal was on the throne, tolerated rather than loved by his people; the oil revenues went into the Iraq Development Fund, which built up the infrastructure of the country by financing roads, hospitals, dams and irrigation schemes to harness the waters of the

A group of students at the Primary Teachers Training College, Baghdad, in 1957

Tigris and Euphrates. The British Ambassador exerted subtle influence on the Government, and the Prime Minister made long summer visits to England and held talks with the Foreign Office. Iraq was administered centrally by the Civil Service, which followed the slow-moving methods of administration inherited from the Indian Civil Service, which ran the country under the British Mandate of 1920-1932; while the regions were subject to provincial governors, and the desert to tribal sheikhs. The British business-community flourished in Baghdad, closing the office doors to Iraqis at 5.0pm or earlier and retiring to their two exclusive clubs, which provided a virtual English environment. In contrast, the British Council and the British teachers in Iraqi schools and colleges enjoyed the company of Iraqis and encouraged them to develop their culture and economy by gaining knowledge and experience, especially through learning English: its classes in their Institutes were always full, and the British Council libraries were a much-used source of information and ideas. Little were any of us aware of the nationalist storm that was brewing that would sweep the British out of Iraq in 1958.

In the long hot summer vacations, we were able to travel all over the Middle East in our old, wooden-bodied car, visiting most of the historical sites which I had read about in England and which had inspired me to come out to Baghdad: Jerash and Petra in Jordan; Aleppo and Palmyra in Syria; Baalbek and Byblos in Lebanon; Istanbul, Pammukkale, Kayseri and Bogazkoy in Turkey; Isfahan, Persepolis, and the Caspian Sea in Iran; and, of course, Babylon, Ur, Nimrud, Nineveh and Kurdistan in Iraq. This was the time before cheap air travel and package tours existed: there were virtually no good roads

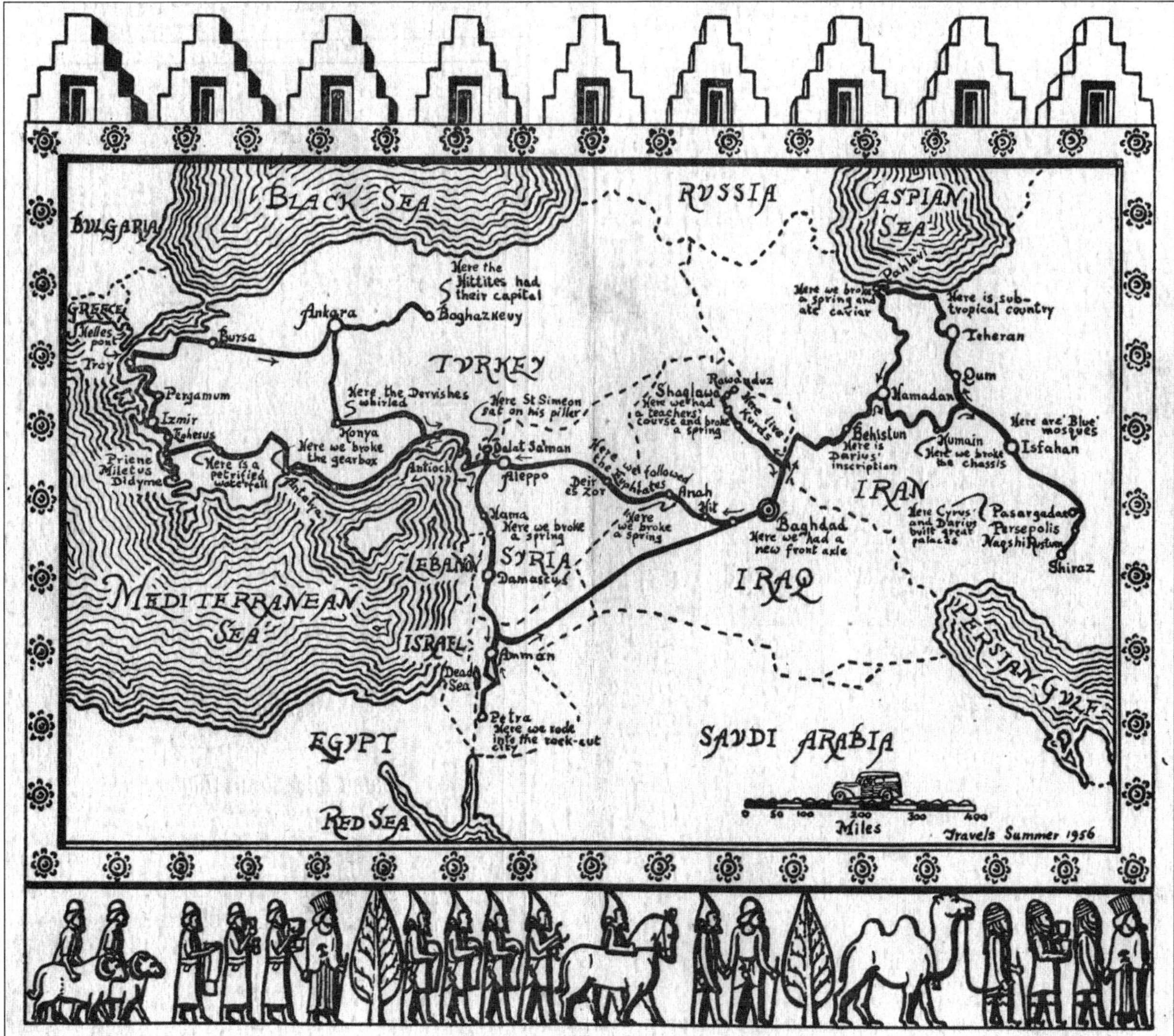

My Christmas card of 1956 shows our travels in the Middle East, accompanied with punctures and breakdowns.

One of the fascinations of Iraq: a huge human-headed Assyrian bull excavated in a gateway of ancient Nineveh outside Mosul

or European hotels near these historical sites; and we were able to walk round them at sunset, eat and sleep in our car, and view the ruins again in the morning light. We did indeed feast on the remains of ancient civilisations.

There was, however, a price to be paid: the atrocious roads wrought havoc with the tyres and springs of our old car (the Ford had just two large transverse springs), causing a puncture or breakdown every 200 miles or so. With few garages available, we had to undertake our own repairs: I had a kit that would weld a patch onto an inner tube in fifteen minutes, and we carried a spare spring, two jacks, and some short planks, and were able to replace a complete spring in a couple of hours. Fortunately, time was not at a premium and the only limitation was the length of our visa for each country.

Cool relief in an Auster Autocraft of the Iraqi Flying Club at Baghdad Airport

These holidays provided adventure enough, but I was also able to fly as much as I wanted or could afford. The Iraqi Flying Club was situated at Baghdad Airport and owned half-a-dozen Auster Autocars and Autocrats; these were comfortable, easy-to-fly, four-seater, high-wing monoplanes, far removed from the utility Mark 1 military Auster that we used as a 'hack' aircraft on 16 Squadron. The mechanics were Iraqis, but the controlling genius was an Englishman, who was Club Manager, Chief Instructor, Chief Pilot, and Chief Engineer all-in-one. He checked me out for my Pilot's Licence, and thereafter I could ring-up at any time and he would have a plane ready for me when I arrived at the Club. The first attraction of flying was to climb above the heat of the city, and the second was to view historic buildings from the air, such as the Shia mosque of Khazimain with its two golden domes (which infidels could not enter), the great 5th-century AD, brick-built arch of Ctesiphon, and the spiral minaret of Samarra, one of the earliest in Islam. It was a pleasure to give our friends such joy-rides. Unfortunately, in my last year, the Iraqis sacked the Englishman: he was too good and showed up the inefficiency of the Iraqis; so, as I couldn't trust myself to their maintenance of the Austers, I also quit flying.

I would have stayed longer in Iraq than my four years, but my wife wanted children and Baghdad, in her opinion, did not have adequate facilities for the safe delivery of a baby or for the treatment of mother or child in the event of an emergency. So, in June 1957, I said good-bye to the Principal, my good friend Naji Abdul Amir, whose parting words were, *"Mr Taylor, I still read your 20 pages!"* We drove our broken-down car, stuffed with our possessions, across the desert road to Jordan – where we were stoned because of Suez when we stopped for petrol, slept under the stars that night, and early next day arrived in Beirut. Here we shipped the car to Genoa, from where we drove through France to Le Touquet; we were surprised to find we could drive straight onto a Bristol Freighter and drive off at Gatwick for little more than the cost of a sea crossing.

The next year, a group of Army Colonels rose in revolt, murdered the King and his uncle, who had been the Regent during his boyhood, and Nuri Said, the Prime Minister (who had fought the Turks alongside T.E. Lawrence in 1916-1918), and proclaimed the full independence of Iraq. From then on, the country went steadily downhill, culminating in Saddam Hussain and the disaster of the invasion by America and Britain, setting fundamental Islam against the West and the Shias against the Sunnis, with terrible loss of life and no end in sight at the time of writing.

I spent the next three years in the British Council's London Overseas Students' Centre, teaching English to some of the 27,000 foreign students who came to study in one or other of our many colleges and universities. We also organised weekend programmes of general interest for them, ranging from talks and debates to Political Forums of MPs, and from discos and film-shows to ballet dancing by some of the Royal Ballet's young stars.

However, after three years, the Council required that I should take up a post in one of their Institutes overseas, but my wife and I had had a beautiful daughter, Jennifer, in 1958 and now wanted another child. So I left the Council with regret, and found a satisfying job teaching English to British boys in Woolverstone Hall, a Boarding Grammar School run by the London County Council in an 18th-century mansion on the banks of the River Orwell in Suffolk! Here we bought a cottage near the school and produced a brother for Jennifer, a sturdy son called Jonathan.

Half the 360 pupils at Woolverstone Hall were bright boys, usually from large families in the East End of London, whose intellectual development was being held back by their home environment: they needed a boarding school to provide them with the academic, athletic and social training to enable them to realise their potential in higher education. The other half were boys from families who accompanied the father in his work overseas in one of the Services, or in an agency of HM Government, or on some engineering or business contract. The family might have moved with the father from one country to another at the expense of the boy's education so, at 13, he would need five steady years in the same school in order to acquire 'O' and 'A' Level qualifications. Woolverstone Hall provided these at very reasonable cost, on a means-tested basis, a second son being educated free of charge.

Surprisingly, the mixing of clever, but mis-understood, Cockney boys with relatively sophisticated, but under-educated, sons from families overseas worked very well: new boys soon accepted Woolverstone's special ethos and even adopted its particular accent. There were several Quakers on the staff and, from its establishment in 1951, the school's aim was not to try to emulate the Public Schools, but to find the best approach to boarding education through liberal principles, applied with a good deal of trial and error. Nevertheless, when I joined the school in 1960, it felt very like a minor Public School – but with two big exceptions. In my time at Eton, sporting prowess was far more highly regarded than scholar-

Woolverstone Hall Boarding Grammar School for Boys, near Ipswich, Suffolk.
A brave effort by the London County Council, but they closed it after 30 years.

ship; but at Woolverstone they, and the arts, were regarded as of equal importance. A classic example was a boy who was a first-class fly-half in the School Rugby XV, which won the Public Schools' Championship in 1961; he also played the flute and conducted the School Orchestra, sometimes straight off the rugby pitch; and he won an Open Scholarship to Oxford. He was by no means the only one to shine in all three areas, and all the boys benefitted from this all-rounder atmosphere.

The other great advance over my own education was that whereas, in the absence of girls at Eton, older boys could be attracted to younger ones, at Woolverstone girls played a significant part in the lives of the older boys. Girls from local schools were invited by the music master to join the various orchestras, bands and choirs on special occasions, and they came up by bus from Ipswich to enjoy the discos put on by the boys in the school's painted-up cellars. Senior boys were allowed occasional visits to Ipswich, and prefects went there on the look-out for junior boys breaking the rules. Altogether, it was a backward boy who could not find himself a date for a School Dance. The school also put on an opera every year, which was a black-tie affair for the adults in the audience, which included personalities from the local communities, after an excellent buffet supper. I have a recording made by the BBC of Brecht's "Mother Courage" sung by boys and some girls, with music played by the School Orchestra conducted by the Head Boy. The part of Mother Courage was taken by a boy with a very 'bolshie' attitude to life in the school, but who underwent a complete change of outlook as a result of the rich applause he received for his dramatic performance. Altogether, Woolverstone Hall, with only 360 boys, was a remarkable school, and I feel very privileged to have spent three years there.

However, my degree in History was a drawback when teaching English in a Grammar School, and the kindly Headmaster, G.H.Bailey, advised me to move to somewhere where I had better prospects. Sadly, the LCC, a Socialist body in those days, discovered too late that it was producing an expensively-educated elite at Woolverstone and lost interest in this most successful project. It was gradually run down from 1980 onwards, until it held just 25 Special Needs children; in 1990, it was sold to Ipswich Girls' High School. Old Boys have done well in the professions and some have become known nationally as politicians, journalists, musicians, actors, and policemen. They continue to meet at Reunions in London and regale each other with lurid tales of derring-do in all manner of activities. They have even bought a race-horse to wear Woolverstone's colours!

Meanwhile, I had answered an advertisement for a Lecturer to set up a new course in the (then) Institute of Education in the University of Leeds in the Teaching of English as a Second or Foreign Language. More for the experience of having an interview at university level than with any hope of being given the job, I applied and was taken aback when, of the three candidates. I was called back and offered the appointment. Thus began twenty-four very happy years in a most congenial post, lecturing and tutoring groups of mature teachers from Third World countries, who came to learn the latest and best approaches to teaching English to their Primary and Secondary children; in time, their ranks included Training College lecturers, head-teachers, inspectors, examiners, and textbook writers, and they came from over 80 countries. I was soon joined by specialists in the fields of linguistics, phonetics, literature, and Secondary teaching, while I concentrated on Primary methodology and visual aids. I also started an illustrated Newsletter for former students, which still continues after 50 years. As teachers of English should know something of British life, they visited many institutions and historical places and, together with overseas students on other courses in the Institute, spent a week in the country, experiencing life in the Yorkshire Dales – in great contrast to the urban scene they were familiar with in Leeds.

In the vacations, the British Council invited me to participate in or run Summer Schools for the many hundreds of teachers in Third World countries who would never be able to come on a course in Britain. In this way, I spent two or three weeks at a time in, ultimately, over 20 different countries, from Denmark to Singapore and from Nigeria to Chile. The greatest challenge was working with Black teachers and lecturers in South Africa under the appalling 'apartheid' regime. At one time, Mrs

JT, top left, with a group of overseas teachers from the University of Leeds in 1976
Photo: Calderdale Teachers Centre

Running a summer school for Junior Secondary Teachers in the State of Jos in Northern Nigeria for the British Council in 1989

Thatcher was supporting the White Government, which was deliberately restricting the education of Blacks; while the British Council was doing its best to educate Blacks so that they would be ready to take over senior posts in education and other areas of government when the time came! Running courses there, and also in Czecho-Slovakia while it was still under Communist rule, was a most interesting, exciting, and even emotional experience. For ten years, I also directed a Summer School in Bristol for 60-80 Dutch teachers of English, and went to Holland to judge its effects on their work. One element in the Bristol course was a day in a local Comprehensive School; there was an outstanding one at nearby Gordano, which had individual 'Houses' for every 50 pupils, so that no one felt lost in a 1000+ pupil environment. The curriculum was equally remarkable, with boys making jewellery and girls building glass-fibre canoes. The engineering department bought old cars, which the pupils had to repair, and then learned to drive in the school grounds. At the end of one day there, I asked the visitors what they thought of the school. One Dutch teacher reflected the generally conservative attitude of Dutch schools at that time with the surprising answer: *"Too much education and not enough teaching!"*

In 1987 I retired after many extremely satisfying years in a University that was typically 'red-brick', but was very much part of Leeds City and was still growing and developing. A much-valued component of the student-body, who contributed both financially and culturally to the University, was the 10% from overseas. The number of such students in the (now) School of Education has risen from the 24 when I started to the 100+ today. In my time, they received Certificates or Diplomas; now it's Master's Degrees or Doctorates!

Unfortunately, my wife and I had domestic problems and divorced when our children left home, Jennifer taking a degree in Art at Leicester Polytechnic and Jonathan graduating in Business Studies at Aston University in Birmingham. I was very lucky to fall in love with a delightful Malaysian Chinese girl and we married in 1983. Margaret joined me in what had become the School of Education and became a very experienced Student Support Officer, the editor of the Newsletter, and a University Accommodation Officer – a career in which I take great pleasure.[1]

On my retirement from the University in 1987, I knew that one of my activities would be on the water in some kind of boat. Perhaps because of childhood holidays spent at Praa Sands in Cornwall, where the cottage my parents had built was in the middle of a grassy strip above a mile-long stretch of golden sand between two rocky headlands, I have always loved the sea, and I wanted very much to have a small yacht to fulfil my dreams. Michael Horsfall had built his own 25-foot boat after the war, and I had a memorable sail with him and my 11-year-old goddaughter Annie from Southampton to Weymouth in which, as a complete novice, I did most of the work under Annie's tuition, while Michael spent the whole voyage in the cabin, working-out courses. Margaret and I drove to virtually every harbour and marina from Berwick-on-Tweed, all round the coast of England and Wales, up to Whitehaven in Cumbria, following-up advertisements in the nautical magazines for the sort of small second-hand yacht that would fit my limited purse. Eventually, we found a 17-foot, two-berth trailer-sailer in Romsey, miles from the sea in Hampshire, and towed it back to Leeds. It was a wood Lysander, which I christened "Amadeus", and it had everything I wanted, except for the horrible overall yellow paintwork. A white re-paint soon changed this and, when the cabin, mast and spars had all been re-varnished, we had a very smart little boat. To equip myself with the necessary skills, I went down to Dartmouth and, together with a young New Zealand couple, took an excellent week-long course under an instructor on a well-equipped 27-foot yacht, which certified the three of us as Day Skippers; this gave me the basics of sailing by day and night and the ability and confidence to handle my own boat. It then turned out that Margaret didn't like the water at all, so I started to change over the rig and rigging for single-handed sailing.

It looked as if I was all set for a very contented retirement, enjoying Margaret's excellent cooking and her refreshingly different views from my own traditional English ones; taking up a few occasional consultancies abroad on English teaching – we went to Thailand on two British Executive Service Overseas (BESO) assignments in 1987 and 1988; doing much DIY work maintaining our old 19th-century house in Leeds and trying to control its over-large garden; trailing "Amadeus" to beautiful inland lakes within 100 miles, such as Ullswater in the Lake District, Kielder Dam in Cumbria, and Rutland Water in the south; delighting in visits to and from my children and grandchildren, although our homes are 200 miles or more apart; and taking holidays in idyllic Mediterranean islands such as Cyprus, Rhodes, Crete, Corfu, Corsica and Sardinia, awash with historical reminders of Greek, Roman, Crusader, Venetian, Turkish and British occupations.

But cruel fate decreed otherwise: in 1990, the tragic aftermath of the events of 19th November 1944 in 't Hesseler burst into my tranquil life and completely overturned it.

[1] Margaret retired from the University in 2011.

The Aftermath

CHAPTER 17

Shock! Horror! Was I the Missing Pilot?

WANTED.

IN BORNE, HOLLAND.

Flt Lt James Strickland Taylor (131017) bailed out of Spitfire FR.IX PL957 19.11.44. taken PoW; and Sgt Roy Bernard Fernie (1530183) bailed out of Halifax W 1108 of 158 Sqn 15.10.42. taken PoW, please contact: H. Noordhuis, Postbox 200, 7620 AE Borne, Netherlands.

In March 1990, Mr Hennie Noordhuis, the archivist of Borne, a small town in eastern Holland about 20 miles from the German border, put an advertisement in the Spring issue of "Air Mail", the journal of the RAF Association, asking for information about me.

I don't belong to the RAF Association, so I didn't see this notice at the time. However, on 4th May 1990, Margaret and I set out from London with a coachful of former members of 16 Squadron to travel to RAF Laarbruch, in Germany, to celebrate the 75th Anniversary of the Squadron. We stopped en route to visit St Omer aerodrome, where 16 Squadron was formed on 10th February 1915, and where the Mayor gave a reception for us in the Town Hall. The following day, there was a fine Anniversary Parade of the Squadron, after which we were free to examine a Tornado GR1A, which equipped the Squadron from 1984 to 1991. This was followed by a Formal Dinner in the Officers' Mess and, next day, by a trip up the Rhine to Arnhem; on the morning afterwards, we said our goodbyes and returned to London.

Ron Parnell, with (behind 1-r) David Greville-Heygate, 'Bunny' Holden, Denise and Michael Horsfall, and a Tornado GRIA with the 'Crossed Keys' crest of 16 Squadron, at its 75th Anniversary in 1990 at RAF Laarbruch

It was while we were in the hangar that I was approached by Ron Parnell, a wartime fitter awarded a Mention in Despatches for his dedicated work on the Squadron. I knew him only as a Flight Mechanic in 1944, and had had no further contact with him until this moment; but he was a member of the RAF Association and showed me the cutting, with the words, *"I think you should answer this."*

On our return, therefore, I sat down and wrote a reply to Mr Noordhuis, giving a brief account of my baling-out and evasion on 19th November 1944, culminating in my capture on the Rhine on 24th. A few days later, I received a phone-call from Holland in a voice which I was to get to know very well, that of Hennie Noordhuis. He said, *"Congratulations on being alive! But did you know that three Dutchmen were executed after you landed by parachute in a field in the village of 't Hesseler, outside Borne?"*

I must have stuttered out my immediate reactions of sorrow for the victims and their families, but also of incredulity that such a tragedy could have resulted from my baling-out 46 years earlier.

In truth, I felt absolutely shattered: the war had been a great adventure for me, the realisation of boyhood dreams; I had flown a most wonderful aeroplane and I had not been required to hurt anyone; I had survived an engine-failure, a bale-out, an unpleasant but short-lived captivity, and a brush with the Russians. I had nothing about which to reproach myself – but now I'm told I caused the deaths of three innocent Dutch people.

I felt sick at the thought. And then I realised it might not be true, it could not be true. I needed reassurance: two houses away from ours lived Ronnie Hardy, a very friendly former Wing Commander in Bomber Command and his wife Sheila. I rushed round to them and blurted out the dreadful news I had just heard. What did they think? Ronnie tried to calm me down: he agreed that it might all be a mistake – after all, what proof was there that I was the pilot? But, in any case, if it was true, it couldn't be my fault, it was just bad luck.

This cool analysis helped me a lot; nevertheless, I did something that I very rarely do and only under strong emotion: I took a sheet of paper and, almost without thinking, allowed my stream of thought to evolve into a poem, quite a long one, in just an hour.[1] In this way, I exorcised the worst effects of Hennie Noordhuis's news on my mental balance, but I have never recovered from the destruction of my former peace of mind that it caused.

Hennie followed-up his phone-call with a copy, in Dutch, of the chapter[2] he had written in the history of Borne during the war, which he had edited in 1990. As the very active archivist of a small town of 15,000 inhabitants, he was well equipped to record the stories that he was told by a wide range of people over the course of several years. Mine was not the only flight to terminate near Borne: a Halifax in 1942 was mentioned in Hennie's appeal in "Air Mail"; a Wellington crashed near Bornerbroek on 26th April 1943; an American B-17 forced-landed near Bornerbroek on 11th December 1943; and an American Lightning crashed near Hengelo on 10th June 1944.

I received this account on 21st June 1990 and had it translated by a Dutch lecturer in the University of Leeds and by the Dutch mother of a member of the Photographic Department of the University, I checked these two translations against each other and occasionally tidied up their English.

Chapter 11 "The Missing Pilot"

Sunday, 19th November

Many people in our town will never forget what happened between 19th and 25th November 1944 in the area of 't Hesseler, just over the municipal border with Weerselo, which has been part of Borne since 1971 as the result of a border change.

[1] See Appendix A for this poem "Requiem for 't Hesseler", and "Dutch Voices" pp. 690-691 for the Dutch translation.
[2] See "Dutch Voices" pp. 665-667 for the original chapter in Dutch.

On Sunday 19th November around midday, Mrs Roetgerink-Hudepohl was standing in front of her house getting water from the pump. At that moment above her head a furious air-battle developed between an English and a German fighter-plane. The unfolding of this spectacular duel, with the screaming of the engines and the rattling of the guns, was watched by many other people in Borne and its environs.

The English machine was fatally hit, and its flight was followed in suspense by anxious eyes looking for the opening of a parachute. They did not have long to wait, as the pilot managed to leave his stricken plane. His parachute broke out and he descended slowly towards the earth, landing a short distance from Mrs R-H in the field of "Knipp'n Mulder", next to the present nursery of Mr van J.Boomkamp beside the Hesseler Road.

The members of the family of the astonished woman saw the man, after landing, get out of his parachute, which was hanging in a tree, and take off his flying-helmet. With gesticulations and a few words of English, the unexpected visitor from the sky asked the growing crowd of onlookers to keep silent while he made off.

In doing so, he must have passed some of the Germans who were coming in from all directions. 500 men detached from a parachute regiment stationed in Borne immediately closed the surrounding area and began to search it. The bystanders and locals were threatened harshly and interrogated in a brutal way. The search, however, did not produce any clues that might have led to the capture of the pilot.

The Germans then became so angry that they took hostage six men at random: G.J.Boomkamp, H.F.Roetgerink, J.H.Roetgerink, J.A.Klaaskate, J.A.Kotte, and H.Smit. The first three lived in the immediate surroundings of the landing-place, while the others had followed the pilot during his descent out of curiosity. The men were taken to the police-station in Hengelo at about 4.30pm, via the Military Police Headquarters in Borne, which was at that time in the Town Hall. In the evening, the Security Police in Enschede also arrested Mr P.A.van Dijk, the 56-year-old father of Piet van Dijk, a civil servant who was in the Resistance Movement.

That same day, the German authorities declared the municipality of Borne responsible for what had happened and issued an ultimatum that, if the parachutist was not found, the hostages would be shot at 7.0am next morning. The protest of the Mayor, Mr van den Toren, that Borne could hardly be held responsible for what took place in another town, was dismissed by the Security Police in Enschede with the accusation that Borne was "a large pig-sty" full of terrorists and collaborators with the enemy. However, the zonal commander of the Military Police in Oldenzaal managed to arrange a delay in the execution until 10.0am next morning.

After working all day without getting any result, the Germans' anger reached boiling-point and a youth from Borne, Jan Vonk, became a victim of it [he was in prison in Almelo, suspected of smuggling Dutch forced-labourers out of Germany on forged passports]: he was shot that night beside the Town Hall.

Monday, 20th November

The start of a week with a lot of insecurity for the hostages and their families. Through the good offices of Military Policeman De Hair, who worked at the police-station in Hengelo and lived temporarily with a family in 't Hesseler, the families were kept informed of the situation of their loved ones and had the opportunity of sending something to them every now and then.

Discussion with the Germans led to delaying the execution till 5.0pm. It also became clear that the case had been put in the hands of Wilheim Karl Rudolf Hadler, a 40-year-old officer in the infamous Knop Commando, which had ended up doing Security work in Enschede after being driven out of France by the swift moves of the Allied armies in September 1944. His boss, Erwin Knop, took over command from Karl Alfred Schöber, who had been in charge of the Security Police in Enschede since 1942.

**The tragic aftermath of my landing in 't Hesseler on 19th November 1944.
The hostages were taken in the afternoon: Jan Vonk was shot the same day,
the three others on the 25th. RIP.**

Photos: Noordhuis, ter Braak and Kienhuis
"In Suffering, Resistance and Freedom 1940-1945" (Borne during the war)

That morning, under the supervision of the divisional commander of the Military Police in Oldenzaal, a reconstruction of events took place in the presence of the group commander of the Military Police in Borne and the Mayor, Mr van den Toren, and it was here decided that the hostages could not have seen the pilot run away. This conclusion, however, did not satisfy Hadler, who came to the Town Hall in the afternoon with the prisoners seated in a darkened car. When he discovered that the investigation had not made any progress, he left the Mayor's office announcing *"Then the rifles will speak"*.

The Mayor ran after Hadler and tried to convince him of the unreasonableness of his demand that the missing airman should be handed over, and of the injustice and inhumanity of executing innocent people. Hadler did not appear to be amenable to reason; nevertheless, that night the Town Council received the message that the execution had been suspended till 3.0pm next day, and that the prisoners Klaaskate and Kotte had been released. This was probably also the work of the Mayor, who had earlier approached Schöber to help in the matter. In exchange for the released men, Knop demanded the handing-over of the "terrorist". Schöber had taken the opportunity of the events of 19th November to arrest the father of Piet van Dijk in the evening, in revenge for his son's liberation by the Resistance from the prison of Almelo on 22nd March 1944 – he had been imprisoned by Schöber on 14th March. Perhaps it was this arrest of the older van Dijk that led, one day later, to the release of Klaaskate and Kotte.

Tuesday, 21st November

The Germans now formulated a condition for the release of the hostages: they needed to know the direction in which the flier had disappeared. In this connection, the Mayor arranged meetings with the Town Council of Weerselo and with the farmers who lived round the place of landing and those in Deurningen and Borne, whom he met in the Café Bos and in the farm of Hassels Mönning respectively.

As a result, that afternoon three witnesses were heard who had seen the pilot: G.H.Leuverink, M.Post, and D.Bosman. Two of them gave a nearly identical description: a slim person, about six foot tall, dark blond, wearing an overall flying-jacket and a white jersey. What was also conspicuous was that the man had a bit of a limp – obviously he had hurt himself with the impact of his landing.

The report that was made in Dutch and German about these findings convinced the Military Police in Hengelo of the hostages' innocence; whereas the Security Police in Enschede would go no further than again allowing a delay in the execution. When the message arrived that night that the planned execution would not be carried out, it looked as if the Army had beaten the Security Police in making the final decision. But the five hostages had to stay in custody until the missing man was found and arrested.

Wednesday, 22nd November

A feeling of relief swept over all those involved because of the good news from Hengelo. Marie, the sister of the brothers Jan and Hendrik Roetgerink, cycled to Hengelo in the morning to try to tell it to them. Although the cells were at the back of the police-station, she managed to pass the message to them by means of sign-language. To show that he had understood, Hendrik put his hand through the bars of their cell. This was the last sign of life that his sister would have of him, for on Saturday, 25th November, the Germans put a seal on all hopes of a happy ending in a merciless way. As so often before during the war, the word of the Occupying Power would turn out to be worthless.

Saturday, 25th November

Towards noon, the door of the cell of the Roetgerink brothers was unlocked and Jan was summoned to go with the Germans. Assuming that they had come to shoot him, he said farewell to his brother

Hendrik and gave him some small personal items. To his surprise and relief, however, he was told that he was a free man: he could not suspect what fate was awaiting his brother. Mr Kotte was also released that afternoon.

At 3.30pm Hadler arrived at the police-station, accompanied by an SS commando and some soldiers. Before this, thanks to Military Policeman De Hair, Mrs Boomkamp had had a short talk with her husband – they had been married for only six weeks. Boomkamp, Roetgerink and van Dijk were taken out of their cells and had to get into separate places in waiting vehicles, in which the soldiers of the execution squad were already seated. With a saloon car in the lead containing Hadler of the Security Police and an Army officer, the procession left in the direction of Weerselo.

At 3.40pm, Mayor van den Toren was told by the Security Police of the impending execution. His objection that a decision had been made not to execute the prisoners because of the convincing nature of the evidence of their innocence was not accepted, with the remark that this was none of their concern.

In a last all-or-nothing attempt, van den Toren then tried to persuade other German people to use their influence to stop the executions. But both the local commander in Hengelo, the highest German representative in Borne, and the Army commander in Enschede declared that they had nothing to do with the case. The duty officer of the Security Police in Enschede said he had no authority in the matter. Because of poor telephone communications, the Mayor could not reach the Army commander in Zwolle. The local German government representative in Delden, who had been posted there after "Mad Tuesday" in September 1944 [when the Germans fled in panic from the swift Allied advance through France and Belgium], absolved himself from any responsibility, but promised to phone the Security Police. As a result of this call, van den Toren was told that the verdict had been carried out, which was confirmed shortly afterwards when he arrived at the place of execution.

The convoy from Hengelo had reached it at 3.50pm. From the first vehicle emerged Boomkamp, from the second Hendrik Roetgerink, and from the third van Dijk, all three accompanied by a number of German soldiers.

Family friends and acquaintances who had gathered together saw the Germans lead their victims to a field not far from the spot where the flier had landed a week before. Boomkamp and Roetgerink walked in front, supporting each other in these last minutes. The watchers saw the execution squad fill the bodies of the hostages with bullets. They were further shocked at the disgusting way the drunken German soldiers said good-bye to their victims: singing and swaying, unable to stand up. For them, forgiveness will be virtually impossible.[1]

It may be assumed that Hadler acted on orders from his boss Knop, with the approval of the Head of the Security Police, Dr Eberhardt Knoop, who had taken the place of Rauter and had also taken over the synagogue in Enschede. It is a pity that Knop, Hadler and Knoop were not available for a full account of this case: shortly after the war they were condemned to hang [for this and other similar crimes] by the Allied court in Burgsteinfurt.

One point of our investigation concentrated on the identity of the flier and his plane. This was not easy as, initially, there was no data about it. In all the relevant documents an English pilot is mentioned, whilst eye-witnesses remember having recognised an English plane.

A starting-point was found when an inhabitant of Hengelo showed us the goggles that he had picked-up near the landing-place on 19th November. It was even more surprising that on the band of the goggles was written "H.J.S. Taylor". Experts from the Royal Netherlands Air Force recognised the goggles as a late-type worn by fighter-pilots of the American Air Force. However, goggles were often exchanged with the British because they were more attractive or fitted better, so we cannot exclude the possibility that English fighter-pilots wore such goggles.

[1] See "Dutch Voices" pp. 674-689 for Obituaries of the Victims.

My goggles, with my name on the strap, were picked up on the landing-field by a Mr ter Borg; his son handed them in to a War Exhibition organised by Hennie Noordhuis in 1988.

From the air scene of 19th November 1944, when nine planes were lost by the RAF: 6 Typhoons, 1 Mitchell and 2 Spitfires, and a Thunderbolt 390 by the Americans, we can finally deduce the solution of our problem.

The name we found has led us to a Spitfire of 16 Squadron of the RAF which disappeared that day. The plane, FRIX PL957, was flown by Harold James Strickland Taylor and was never found. Unfortunately, we have not yet succeeded in tracking down Mr Taylor, who left the RAF in 1946, despite the efforts of the English Air Force authorities during the last few years. Nor have we found his helmet."

Hennie Noordhuis also sent me a photograph, taken in 't Hesseler on the 4th May 1988, of Mr Maarten Vunderink, the Burgomaster of Borne, dedicating the Memorial to the three hostages executed on 25th November 1944. It is a Crucifix, beautifully carved by the brother-in-law of one of the victims, which stands by a simple country lane, on the edge of the field of execution and opposite the place of my landing. Hennie also enclosed a photo of the critical goggles, with my name on the strap.

This was a dreadful tragedy, and I felt the deepest sympathy for the families of the victims and, indeed, for the whole small community of 't Hesseler. To compound the atrocity, I had already been captured beside the Rhine on 24th November, the day before the executions; however, there was no reason for the Germans there to have heard of "The Missing Pilot" of Borne, or to connect me with him, or to communicate with the Security Police in Enschede. The executions, therefore, were even more pointless than the Mayor had asserted and with whose view some Germans had, in fact, agreed.

At the same time it was plain to me, from the description of the air-battle and of the pilot who was seen running away, that this was a different situation from the one in which I had been involved, and that, clearly, there must have been two events ending in bale-outs in the general region of Borne on 19th November 1944.

I therefore wrote a lengthy letter to Hennie Noordhuis, enclosing an account of that day that I had written previously, entitled "The Last Flight of H.J.S.Taylor 19th-24th November 1944", a copy of my log-book entry for 19.11.44, and some photographs of a Spitfire XI and of myself. My letter included the following extracts:

"From a comparison of these two accounts, it is clear to me, as I think it will also appear to you, that by an amazing coincidence of date, time and place, two airmen baled out in the neighbourhood of Borne-Weerselo at about midday on Sunday, 19th November 1944. The evidence for this is considerable:

The Memorial to the 't Hesseler victims dedicated by Maarten Vunderink, the Burgomaster of Borne, on 4th May 1988

Photo via Hennie Noordhuis

1. Pilot X was seen to bale-out during a dog-fight with a German fighter over the Borne-Weerselo area.

   Spitfire XIs had no guns (as the photographs show) – they were full of cameras (5) and fuel-tanks for a 1500-mile range. (Spitfire IXs did have guns, but ours were painted pink and were used only for low-level sorties – mine was a high-level one.)

   I was not involved in any fight and saw no other plane at any time.

2. Pilot X is described as 6 foot tall, slim and dark blond.

   I am 5 foot 10 inches tall, slim, and was very black-haired at that time (see the photographs), although I am now quite grey.

3. Pilot X is described as wearing a white jersey under an overall flying-jacket.

   I was wearing an RAF blue battle-dress with no jersey or flying-jacket: our cockpits were well heated.

4. I started descending when my engine caught fire at 24,000 feet somewhere near Rheine. I baled out at 10,000 feet, which could have been after 10-15 minutes. My plane would have gone down nearly vertically from there – probably over Holland, but not necessarily. It would have taken me about 10 minutes to float down from 10,000 feet. My diary says I did so at midday, so I must have landed at about 12.10 to 12.20pm.

5. Pilot X was seen flying, baling out and landing at about midday.

   His aircraft is reported as never being found, which is very strange when so many people, both Dutch and German, witnessed the air-fight and his parachute descent.

   Because the Germans picked me up near Doorn five days later, they never connected me with the wreckage of any aircraft. In fact, they never knew anything about me, except that my interrogator in Frankfurt suggested that I was flying on Photographic Reconnaissance work – he probably deduced this from the fact that a bomber pilot would have been anxious about his crew, and a fighter pilot would have been seen going down by the pilots of other aircraft.

6. No one claimed to have seen two parachutes landing on 19th November, so it is clear that I landed well away from Pilot X, and therefore from his section of the Borne-Weerselo area.

7. The only firm piece of evidence that I landed in your area is the finding of my goggles – but not my helmet, to which the goggles were usually attached by three small buttoned straps. They might have been torn off during my bale-out, or fallen off during my descent, or become detached during the landing. Or they might have been separated by the original finder, or finders: if two people were together, they might have shared them. (Incidentally, I'm afraid your experts are quite wrong: these were regular RAF issue to all pilots, certainly from when I started flying in 1941 until I finished in 1946. The Americans wore a quite different type, and very often preferred sun-glasses.)

   The major questions are: Where exactly were they found? Is the present owner the original owner? Did the person who showed them to you actually find them himself?

   My guess must be that they were picked up in a field at least one, if not two miles away from Pilot X's landing-place, possibly even five, and that they could have arrived in that field any time from my original bale-out until my actual landing.

   So, although they solve a number of problems and are the fortunate cause of your finding me and of my writing my account and this letter, they don't resolve the final one and they leave some more questions to be answered.

8. I should also like to try to identify Pilot X: he must have been flying either the other Spitfire lost that day or one of the six Typhoons. The former were still being used for Tactical Reconnaissance with the forward troops; the latter for shooting-up all forms of transport in the back-areas, including barges on the canals. If Pilot X were doing this, one would have expected him to have had comrades who would have reported him missing over a particular area and while doing a particular job. This report would be in one of the Typhoon squadrons' records and still available somewhere. If he were the other Spitfire pilot, there must be a record of his Squadron number and personal details of him, of the same nature as you have been able to find out about me."

Having thus presented Hennie Noordhuis with all the arguments against my being "The Missing Pilot", I set about finding Pilot X. I wrote to the President of the 16 Squadron Association, Air Vice-Marshal David Cousins, AFC (now retired as Air Chief Marshal Sir David Cousins, KCB, AFC), for help in locating this person, and he forwarded my letter to the Air Historical Branch (AHB) of the Ministry of Defence. On 12th October 1990, Mr G.Day, of Room 308 of AHB, sent me a reply indicating that the only other pilot to bale out over Holland on 19th November 1944 was F/Lt E.F.Ashdown of 430 Squadron; he was flying Mustang AG664 on Tactical Reconnaissance near Venlo when he was shot down, crash-landed and was captured. Mr Day kindly wrote again three weeks later to send me a brief history of 430 Squadron, which showed that it was based at Eindhoven in November 1944, and to tell me about the facilities for finding documents in the Public Record Office at Kew, outside London (now the National Archive).

From all this I was happy to draw the conclusion that, like me, F/Lt Ashdown was flying alone; but, as the Mustang was fully armed with six machine-guns, he returned fire when he was attacked near Venlo and a dog-fight ensued. In the course of this, the combatants must have drifted over to the Borne area, where Ashdown was shot down in front of the 't Hesseler eye-witnesses. Dutch civilians would have recognised an English plane, but would not necessarily have been able to identify the type, whether a Spitfire or a Mustang. The only remaining problem was how my goggles reached Borne: I was quite sure that they could have been picked up miles away and passed through several hands in the intervening years before being handed to Hennie Noordhuis.

On 16th May 1991, however, I visited the Public Record Office and looked at 430 Squadron's Operations Record Book on microfilm. To my dismay, I found the following entry for 19th November 1944:

Operations Record Book of 430 Squadron, RCAF				
Date	Aircraft Type & Number	Crew	Duty	Time Up Down
19.11.44	Mustang I AM237 B	F/0 M.J.Geddes Can. 3.24152	Tac/R	1535 1635
	AG664 H	F/L E.F.Ashdown Can. J.12093	Cover	1535
Details of Sortie or Flight				
Venlo area. 3/10's cloud at 5000'. Visibility 15 miles. 50+ closed trucks marshalling yards A.0808. 150+ trucks marshalling yard at Krefeld, also 3 engines. 1 MET A.135035. 1 MET F.031199. New diggings in area. F/L Ashdown's aircraft hit by flak and broke into flames. Pilot baled out landing at E.8708. Intense accurate light and heavy flak Venlo E.8503.				

From this it was clear that F/Lt Ashdown was the wing-man of a pair of Mustangs, that he was hit by flak and baled out while still in the Venlo area. This was witnessed and reported by his leader. There was therefore no chance that F/Lt Ashdown could be "The Missing Pilot" of 't Hesseler. The only realistic candidate for this unwanted role had to be myself. I was now forced to accept Hennie Noordhuis's firm conviction that I was the leading player in the tragic drama that unfolded after my landing on 19th November 1944.

CHAPTER 18

Return to 't Hesseler

In spite of the contradictory evidence of the eye-witnesses – one of whom even had me riding away on a white horse! – the absence of any other pilot baling out near 't Hesseler on 19th November 1944 and the finding of my goggles on the landing-place persuaded me that Hennie Noordhuis was justified in identifying me as the "The Missing Pilot". Yet my acceptance of my innocent role in the ensuing tragedy was to be disturbed, even shaken, by several conflicting situations that arose later on. For the present, however, I was determined to do everything possible to show my sorrow and sympathy for the families of the victims: this was made possible by Hennie Noordhuis's invitation to Margaret and me to come to Borne at the end of August, staying with the Burgomaster and his wife, and laying a wreath on the Memorial in 't Hesseler to the victims. Hennie also told me that my flying-helmet had been found: it had been picked up on the landing-place and worn by the finder for motorcycling for 40 years; this was further evidence of my identification although, when Hennie sent me a photograph of this helmet, it was so shapeless that I couldn't recognise it as mine.

My flying-helmet was picked up on the landing-field by a Mr Bruggink, who wore it on his motor-cycle for 40 years: his son handed it in to the War Exhibition.
Photo: Hennie Noordhuis

On 21st May 1991, I wrote to Air Vice-Marshal Cousins, outlining the course of events and saying I would be going to Borne in August to lay a wreath on the 't Hesseler Memorial. I then offered my opinion that, as I was a member of 16 Squadron in 1944, it would be fitting if someone came as a representative of the present Squadron and laid a wreath on its behalf. I went further and suggested that this ceremony was bigger than just in memory of the hostages shot at 't Hesseler: it could be seen as commemorating the suffering of all Dutch people under the German Occupation, the defiance of the Dutch Resistance Movement, and the role of the RAF in the liberation of these brave people. In this wider context, it would be a diplomatic move to send a 16 Squadron aircraft to over-fly the Memorial at the moment of wreath-laying.

David Cousins approved of these suggestions and contacted Wing Commander Ian Travers Smith, the CO of 16 Squadron, who had just been awarded a DSO for his leadership of the Typhoon echelon in the First Gulf War. W/C Travers Smith sent me a very supportive letter, stating that he would send a Squadron representative to the ceremony and that he had gained permission from the Commander-in-Chief of the RAF in Germany to provide a fly-past by a formation of three Tornados at the appropriate moment. He also gave me the sad news that 16 Squadron was leaving Laarbruch and disbanding in September, so I had communicated with him just in time. I was most grateful and suggested he contacted Hennie Noordhuis for all aspects of the arrangements, especially as Hennie was already in touch with the Commandant of the Royal Netherlands Air Force (RNLAF) base at Twente, quite close to Borne, who would also participate in the ceremony. Hennie was enthusiastic about these developments, and I was delighted that, by this fly-past, the RAF was both saluting the innocent victims of 't Hesseler and paying its highest tribute to the courage and endurance of our Dutch ally throughout five years of German occupation, oppression and terror.

It was, therefore, an unpleasant shock and a huge disappointment when, just a week later, Hennie telephoned to say that the villagers of 't Hesseler had expressed their disapproval of a fly-past: it would be too militaristic at a ceremony which they wished to be quiet and peaceful. I immediately acquainted David Cousins and Ian Travers Smith with this unfortunate news; it turned out to be more difficult to cancel the fly-past than it had been to arrange it in the first place.

Hennie now came up with an alternative suggestion: that I should unveil a plaque on the Memorial. I immediately accepted this as an inspired idea. He also gave the date as 28th August, and stated that the RNLAF would send a representative and a band, and that there would be a Reception after the ceremony for the families of the victims, for leaders of the 't Hesseler community and Borne municipality, and for the representatives of the RAF, the RNLAF, the wartime Resistance Movement round Borne, and the local Press. I felt that events were now moving into top-gear and that, whatever my personal feelings, I had a central part to play in them.

First, I had to design a plaque and get it suitably produced. I tried various engravers and found the up-to-date firm of J.H.Thompson situated in a carefully renovated building in the early industrial part of Leeds beside the 18th-century Leeds-Liverpool canal. We agreed on an etched bronze plate, with white enamelled lettering and with the crests of the RAF and 16 Squadron embossed on separate small square plates, to be attached to the left and right top corners respectively. I was reassured about the quality of the work when I visited a nearby cemetery and saw how well a similar plaque made by the firm had weathered over the years, I circulated the design and wording to David Cousins, Ian Travers Smith and Hennie Noordhuis, and was relieved when they not only gave their approval, but 16 Squadron contributed £100 and the 16 Squadron Association £50 towards the cost of £580.

I also felt I should make some tangible acknowledgement of the sufferings of the victims' families by presenting them with a small token of my appreciation; I therefore visited a coin merchant in Leeds and bought six attractively-boxed silver-gilt Churchill Commemorative Crown coins of 1965, the year of his death, with Elizabeth II on the obverse, for the brothers of Jan Boomkamp and sisters of Hendrik Roeterink; I had one also for the daughter-in-law of Piet van Dijk, although Hennie told me that she was not well enough to attend at this time.

Mr ter Borg who, as a 7-year-old, was with his father on 19th November 1944 when the latter picked up my goggles, and Mr Herman Bruggink, whose father had picked up my helmet and worn it for forty years, both wished to hand back these personal items to me at the Reception. I therefore bought them each a brass figurine of an airman in full flying-kit with a parachute, with another one for Hennie Noordhuis.

Thus burdened and with the precious plaque also in my luggage, on 26th August, Margaret and I boarded a plane from Leeds-Bradford airport and landed at Amsterdam's airport of Schiphol, to be greeted by Hennie and Joke Noordhuis. Rather to my surprise, Hennie turned out to be a youthful 40-year-old, and they both spoke excellent English. We had a great deal to talk about, much information to exchange, and many facts to digest on the drive back to Borne, mostly on the A1 motorway to Germany.

My greatest pleasure lay in getting to know Hennie and in finding that, unlikely as it might seem, we held remarkably similar views on nearly everything connected with the tragedy of 't Hesseler and, in the following years, on many other aspects of life, in both war and peace.

Hennie is a tall, well-built man with fair hair and a long face, that can look serious when involved in a professional discussion, but quickly breaks into a broad smile when he finds humour in a situation –

Hennie and Joke Noordhuis meet my wife Margaret (centre) and me at Schipol Airport on 26th August 1991.

which is frequently. As the Archivist of Borne, he has a profound knowledge of every event that has had an effect on the historical development of Borne; at the same time, since the demolition of any building and the construction of any new one has to be reported and registered with his department, he is the best-informed person in Borne and the surrounding district and an excellent guide for me.

The 1939-1945 war, which brought very great suffering to the whole Dutch population, inflicted on them by their close neighbours the Germans, is still embedded in the national psyche, and not least in Hennie's. Every Allied soldier who fought in Holland is regarded as a 'liberator', and all those who died are commemorated on 4th May, the Day of National Commemoration, when school-children place flowers on every Memorial. When I pointed to a posy on a paving-stone in one town, Hennie told me an Allied soldier was killed on that spot in 1945. Hennie supervises the arrangements for the ceremony at each of eight Monuments in and around Borne: he ensures it is properly organised by the leader of the local community, that Scouts are positioned each side of the Memorial, and that a small band is at hand to play the National Anthem and appropriate music. Here his own love of music comes to the fore; he plays the trumpet and his delightful wife Joke teaches the piano (and also runs marathons in a group for charity); he is devoted to Brass Bands and he and Joke travel to London every autumn to attend the final of the Brass Band Competition in the Albert Hall. To cap it all, Hennie for many years has broadcast a weekly programme on the local radio station, reviewing the latest releases of Brass Band recordings. These are just a few of the qualities of the man who has masterminded a vital part of my life for the last twenty-one years – and will continue to do so indefinitely.

Our first move in Borne was to drive out to 't Hesseler, a bare mile to the south-east of Borne, to view the field where I had landed and to pay our respects at the Memorial to the three men so needlessly shot on 25th November 1944. In fact, only two of them were from 't Hesseler: Piet van Dijk was included by the Germans in reprisal for the freeing of his son from prison by the Resistance. The fourth man, Jan Vonk, who was shot outside the Town Hall of Borne on 19th November, is commemorated by a white cross in a garden beside the Town Hall. As he had no connection with 't Hesseler, I did not appreciate till some time later that his death was so closely related to my landing; I had therefore made no provision to meet his relatives on this visit.

The lane in 't Hesseler leading towards Borne. The Memorial is on the left, with the Field of Execution behind and my landing-field in front on the right.

The Memorial to the 't Hesseler victims with the Field of Execution behind

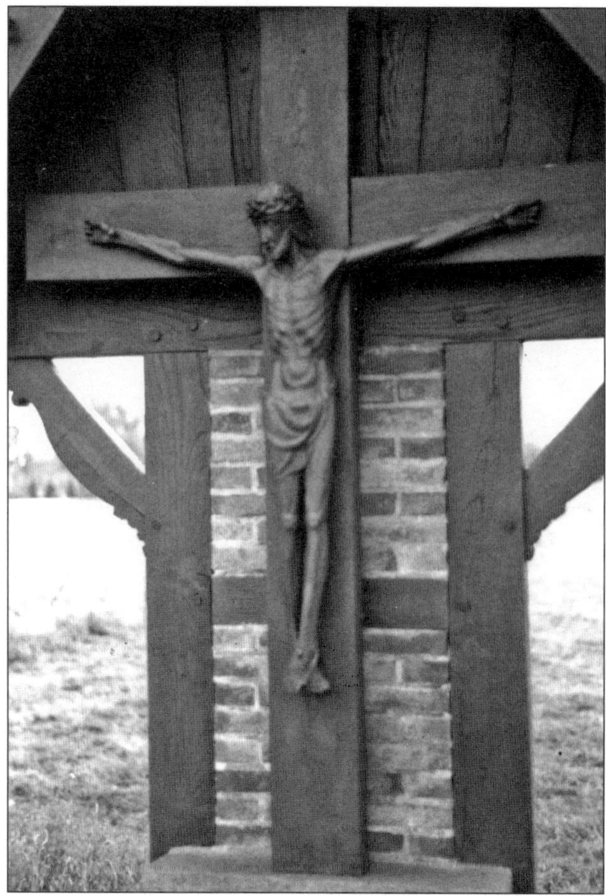

The Cruicifix, carved by Mr Leuveld,
husband of Marie Leuveld-Roetgerink

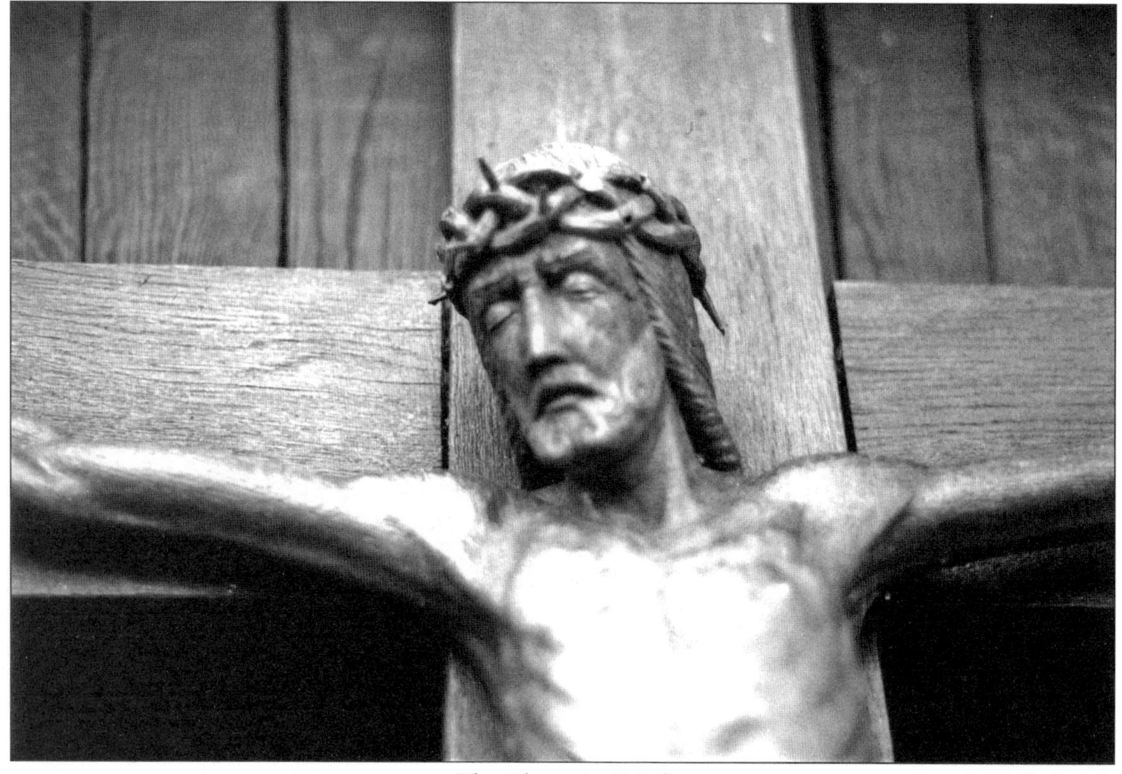

The Christ in Grief

't Hesseler is a scattering of about twenty farms and houses extending perhaps half-a-mile in all directions; it has no shop or post office, no school or community centre. Three lanes run south-east out of Borne, diverging gradually as they pass through 't Hesseler; they are crossed transversely by a single lane running roughly north-east. At the crossroads where the middle lane meets the transverse one is the only focal point in the hamlet; the Memorial stands beside the middle lane, a hundred yards or so towards Borne from the cross-roads.

A group of villagers, who are all staunch Catholics, was walking back along this lane from the Roman Catholic church on this side of Borne on 19th November 1944, when I sailed over their heads and fell into the field on their left. It was the men from this group, wearing long dark overcoats, who came up and surrounded me and whom I assumed were Germans; but then they ran after my parachute when I released it and it blew away into a tree; so this was the signal for me to disappear in the opposite direction.

As Hennie walks with us from the crossroads, a row of trees lines the left side of the lane, which is raised up a little above the fields on each side. The Memorial is a beautifully carved Crucifix of a grieving Christ, protected from the weather by a simple gabled roof and standing on a low rectangular base of roughly-hewn stones. The grass in front is where I landed; the grass behind is the Field of Execution. Now all is calm and peaceful: only the gentle wind ruffles my hair and sighs faintly through the branches overhead. I have a lump in my throat.

I take out the plaque and we examine the base of the Memorial to see what needs to be done to nail and cement it permanently in place. We then climb back into the car and drive to the Burgomaster's official house, close to the Town Hall, where he and his wife are waiting to welcome us.

Maarten Vunderink is of average height, grey-haired, with regular features. He was a six-year-old living with his parents in the Dutch East Indies when the Japanese struck in 1941 and he spent the next four years in a civilian detention centre; we therefore already had a certain amount in common, and I found him a very pleasant and sociable person. His wife Jeanette is attractive and smartly-dressed and proved an attentive hostess, looking after Margaret especially and making us feel very much at home over the next three days. It helped greatly that, like most of the people I met, they spoke fluent English.

The following morning, Hennie drove Margaret and me about ten miles to the RNLAF air base of Twente, which also serves as a commercial airport for the region of Twente. The airfield has a somewhat chequered history: opened in 1921 for private flying, it was enlarged in 1931 as a civil airport for the nearby town of Enschede (population 145,000), with strong support from KLM for direct flights to Schiphol. In 1940 it was occupied by the Germans, who developed it into a large-scale base, although it was used operationally only for their Ardennes Offensive in December 1944. It features in the 16 Squadron Operations Record Book as a target that we photographed on several occasions, and it was heavily bombed and wrecked by B-17s in March 1945, just before the Germans were driven out of this part of Holland by the British and Canadian armies. The RAF quickly moved into the airfield, which was coded B106; in April, 15 squadrons of Spitfires, Mustangs, Typhoons and Tempests occupied it variously for six weeks; in May three squadrons of Mosquitos stayed for eleven weeks; and, in September, three Tempest squadrons dropped in for just two days. After the war, it became a major RNLAF air base, hosting two or three fighter squadrons and playing a vital part in the NATO early warning and European defence system.

Hennie had arranged our visit well in advance and we were welcomed by Colonel Vogelpoel, the Commandant of the Base. He kindly gave us an extended tour of all the facilities, and I was privileged to sit in the cockpit of a single-seater F-16, the current fighter equipping the Dutch squadrons, and had all the switches and dials explained to me. The instrumentation was a far cry from the simple lay-out of

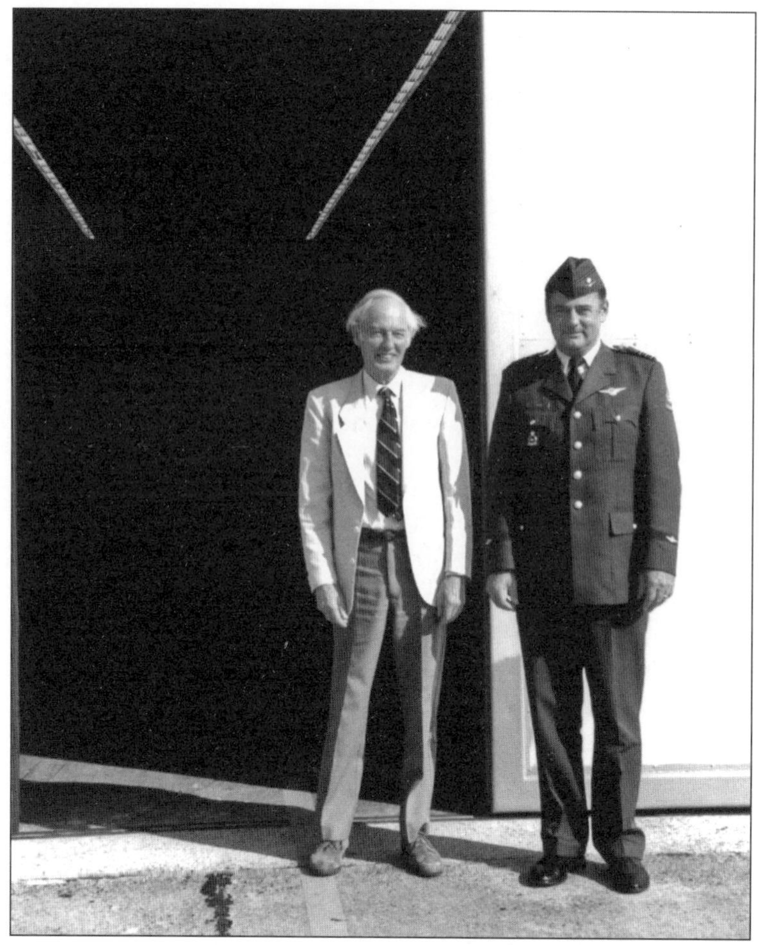

JT with Colonel Buffard, Deputy Commandant of Twente Air Base
Photo: Hennie Noordhuis

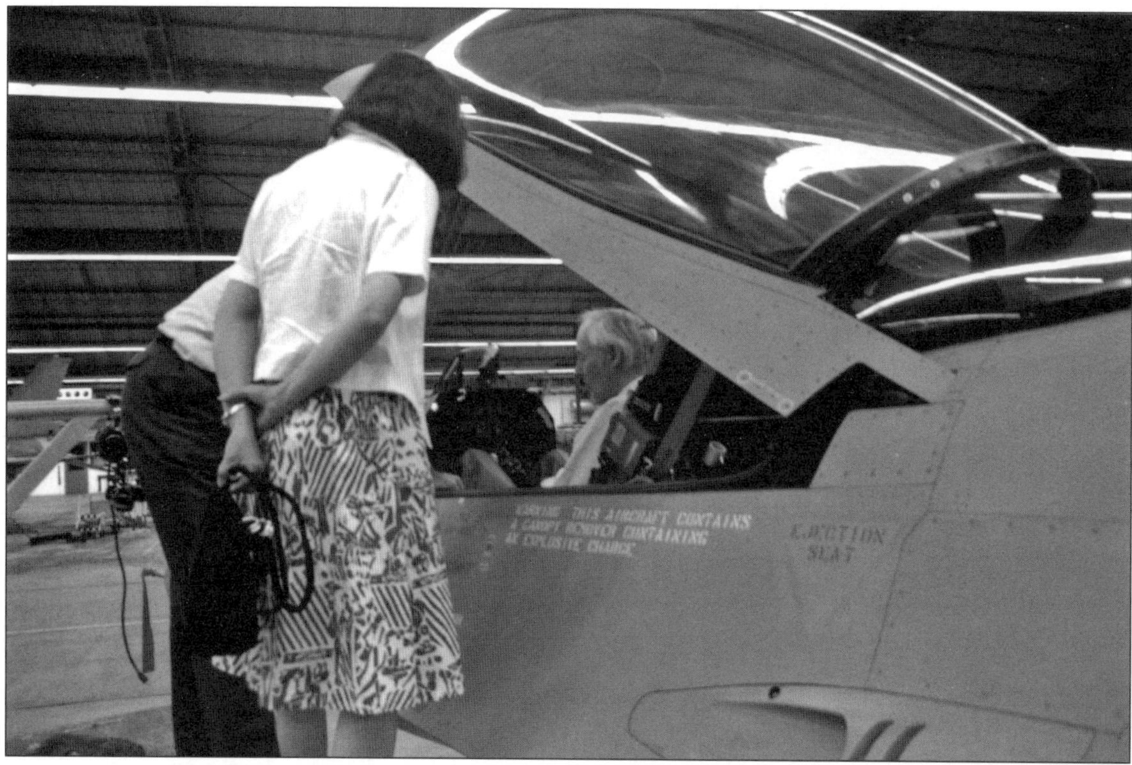

JT in the cockpit of an F-16 at Twente Air Base, watched by Margaret
Photo: Hennie Noordhuis

a Spitfire's cockpit; yet with one hand on the throttle and the other on the side-mounted control-stick, my feet on the rudder-bar, and a superb view ahead, I felt I could probably get it up in the air and bring it down in one piece – if some emergency compelled me!

After an excellent lunch, we returned to Borne, where Jeanette was waiting to show Margaret this little town, which has an old quarter with wooden buildings, as well as modern shops and a very up-to-date Town Hall, while Hennie took me off to 't Hesseler to retrace my steps of 19th November 1944.

Starting at the landing-field, he wisely let me work out the direction I had taken to run away, the wood I had entered, and the ditch cutting into a large field that I had found refuge in for the rest of that day; from here I had seen soldiers with rifles on their backs cycling along a distant lane, watched with some apprehension a farmer driving his cows across the field for milking; and waited for the winter sun to set before leaving my ditch and setting off towards the west in the dark on the first stage of my journey to the Rhine.

To reach the wood, we had to pass through a farm-yard and, walking back, we met the farmer, Harry Leuveld and his wife Gertie, and discussed my quest with them. I was a little put out to learn that the farm was here in 1944, although I had not seen it then, and that the poplar trees, into which I was sure my parachute had blown on 19th November, were not there at that time. Harry kindly gave me a photograph of 't Hesseler taken from a helicopter in about 1955, which showed the fields and lanes and the small Garden Centre which had now expanded and taken over much of the ground. This was the property of Jan Boomkamp, nephew of the victim Jan Boomkamp, whose business expertise had already made him the local millionaire.

Hennie then told me that my recollections did not agree at all with what the eye-witnesses claimed to have seen of my moves after landing! We walked along the transverse lane and came to two houses, on opposite sides of the cross-roads with the Memorial lane. We found Mrs Veenhuis-Weghorst and her husband, the owners of one, in their garden and, after introducing me, Hennie asked her where I had run to in November 1944. She immediately pointed north-east, over one or two fields, to a wood of small trees some distance away, I told Hennie that this was too far away, that I could not have run there in my weakened condition from the blow I had received from the aircraft, which was not improved when I hit the ground.

We spent a short time chatting with Mrs Veenhuis-Weghorst (who died in 2003) in her very pleasant house, then moved across the road to visit Mr Hennie Roetgerink, who also was working in his garden.

Here I'd better pause to explain that, as in many other small communities, the inhabitants of 't Hesseler had inter-married quite widely, so that the same names cropped up continually, the Dutch practice of the wife hyphenating her own maiden name to her husband's surname adding to the confusion, while the seemingly arbitrary choice of the order of the two surnames further complicated the issue. The principal families were Boomkamp, Roetgerink and Leuveld: I will limit my description to just those members whose names appear at some point in this narrative.

The victim Jan Boomkamp had three brothers: Bernard, Herman and Hendrik;

Bernard has a daughter, Josine, who married Hans Wools, a teacher, and they have two children.

Herman (d. 1998) had a son, Jan Boomkamp, who owns the Garden Centre and is married to Lydi, with two sons Dirk and Joost. Another son is Harry, who lives in 't Hesseler, where he makes cheese on a large scale.

Harry Leuveld, nephew-by marriage of the victims Jan Boomkamp and Hendrik Roeterink, with his wife Gertie and son (l)

Photo: Hennie Noordhuis

Herman also had a daughter, Ria, who married Jan Bovenmars, also a teacher, and they have two daughters Anne and Helen and a son Bram. Josine and Ria are therefore cousins, and their husbands Hans and Jan are close friends.

Hendrik, the surviving brother, married Diny, and they have three grown-up children: Maria, Henk and Gerard.

The victim Hendrik (Hennie) Roetgerink had an elder brother whose wife became Mrs Roetgerink-Hudepohl; their son is Hennie Roetgerink, whom we have just met and who is married to Miny, and a daughter, who is Mrs Riet Sanders-Roetgerink

Hendrik's sister was Marie, who married a Leuveld, the sculptor of the impressive Crucifix on the Memorial; she became Mrs Leuveld-Roetgerink (d. 1997), the aunt of Hennie and prominent in my story; their son is Ger Leuveld, married to Ria, with three children.

The victim Jan Boomkamp had an elder sister who married the elder Leuveld's brother; their son was Harry Leuveld, the farmer we have already met, with his wife Gertie and their two sons.

This is the web of relationships between these three families in 't Hesseler as far as I have understood it, but I can give no guarantee as to its accuracy.

Hennie Roetgerink took us into his house and introduced us to his mother, 91-year-old Mrs Roetgerink-Hudepohl, and to his sister, who was the only one to speak English; she was keen to tell me how vindictive the Germans in Borne were towards the Resistance and would execute them on any pretext, especially Mr Piet van Dijk, whose son was one of the leaders.

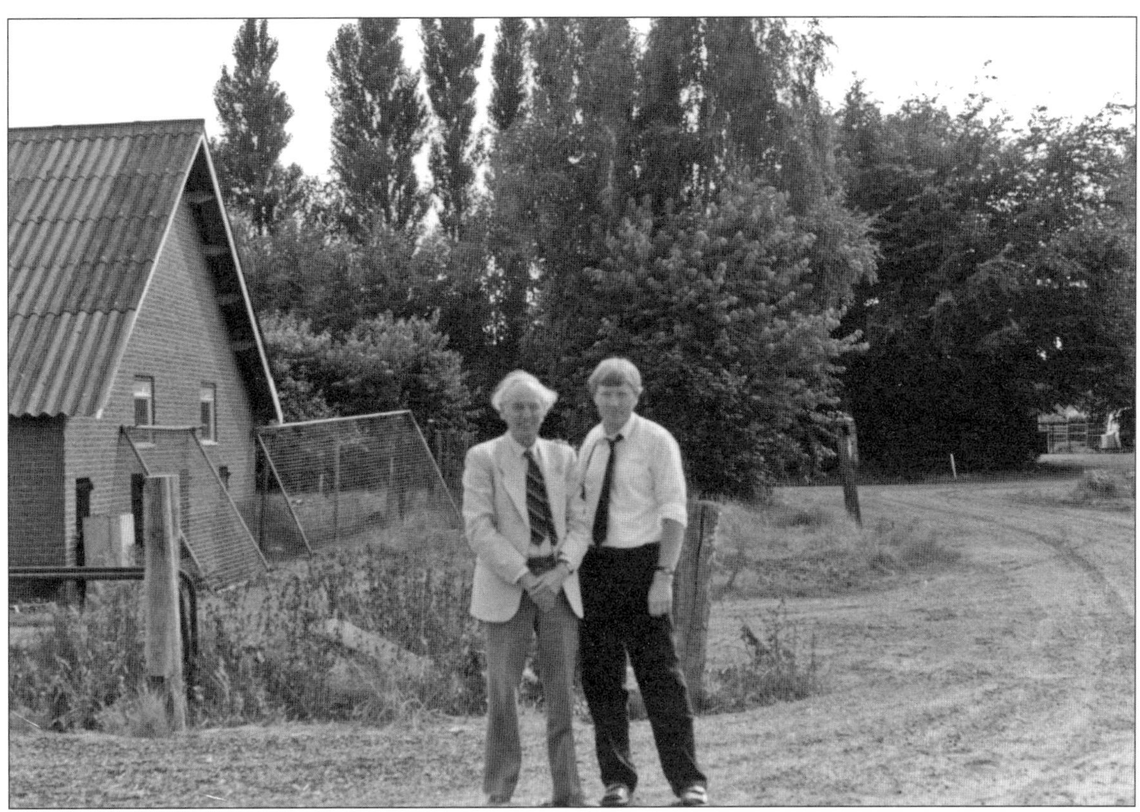

Hennie Noordhuis and JT in Harry Leuveld's farm

Photo: Harry Leuveld

Hennie Roetgerink was another of those who claimed to have seen my landing. He pointed to the same distant group of trees identified by Mrs Veenhuis-Weghorst, and then took us onto the landing-field to indicate the tree into which he said my parachute had blown. Hennie clearly agreed with the versions of these two witnesses. They also told me that the wood to the north-east was much larger in 1944 and extended to nearer the cross-roads. Nevertheless, it was a long way from the wood which I had shown Hennie earlier, beyond Harry Leuveld's farm, where the ditch felt very familiar as soon as I saw it. There was now also a problem of the tree into which my parachute had blown, and therefore about the direction I had taken when the villagers ran after it to grab the precious silk. All these issues led me to wonder, once again, whether I really was "The Missing Pilot"; but the present was not the time or occasion to voice such doubts, and perhaps I would make other discoveries that would counteract them.

In the evening, after a convivial dinner with Maarten and Jeanette, we were relaxing in the sitting-room and discussing the programme for the Ceremony and Reception next day, when we learned that some of the villagers were doubtful about meeting me: they still thought that I had been hidden by the Resistance in 1944 and that I should have given myself up to the Germans to save the lives of the hostages.

The Resistance was very strong around Borne, sabotaging work for the Germans in the local factories and the trains on the railway. They could certainly not have let me give myself up even if I had wanted to: I would have known too much about their personnel and organisation, which the Germans would have extracted from me under torture. As it was, of course, the Resistance hadn't hidden me; but the problem was how to convince people of this in the short time available.

After much discussion of various alternatives, it was decided to print copies of my story, which had already been translated into Dutch as "De laaste vlucht van H.J.S. Taylor 19.11.44 – 28.8.01"[1], and distribute them to the villagers early next morning. This solution was greeted with great relief and proved to be most effective.

[1] See "Dutch Voices" p. 669 for this translation.

Mrs Roetgerink-Hudepohl was a witness of my landing in 't Hesseler on 19th November 1944 and points to the field in 1990.

Photo: Hennie Noordhuis

Margaret and I meet Mrs Veenhuis-Weghorst and her husband at her house in 't Hesseler, with Hennie Noordhuis (left).

Hennie Roetgerink – nephew of the victim Roetgerink – who saw my landing, points out the spot to Hennie Noordhuis.

Hennie Roetgerink stands with his back to the wood, which was much bigger in 1944, into which he said I ran.

The next morning, Hennie and I decided to try to retrace the more accessible part of my evasion route. This was easier said than done, as the special maps printed on silk were somehow missing from my escape-kit in 1944, and I had really no idea where I was when I landed and when I set off westwards on the night of the 19th November to try to reach the Rhine. I knew that I would be well inside Holland if I could reach Utrecht, and then turn south for the river. Not until I chanced on a roadside milestone that read "Hengelo – Zutphen", was I convinced that I was actually in Holland.

I had started by trekking cross-country but, in the dark, I had been caught on so many barbed-wire fences and fallen into so many wet ditches that I gave it up and took to the lanes, even though their direction varied considerably, eventually leading me into a small town. It was therefore impossible for us now to follow my early route.

The only feature that I remembered of this town was that I walked beside what seemed to be a curving line of shops, before an approaching German patrol made me hide in an adjacent alley-way. After the noise of their boots had died away, I continued through the town, over a single railway-line that crossed the road and, for about half a mile, passed houses that gradually changed into farms and fields. The road then unexpectedly arrived at a canal, which it crossed over by a bridge with a high arched span and with sentries stamping up and down at each end. This was the obvious place to start our journey, but confusion arose because we were faced with more ambiguity.

The trouble was that if, in November 1944, I had walked westwards on that first night, the only canal I would have met was the Almelo Canal, which runs south from Almelo midway into the Twente Canal. The latter goes more or less west-to-east between Zutphen and Enschede, roughly parallel to my intended track. In 1944, the canal lay close to a town and formed just another obstacle that I had to deal with. I had slept fitfully under some trees till early daylight, when I had walked a mile or so along the canal-bank in each direction to try to find a smaller bridge, perhaps, or an untended boat. But there was nothing, and I had been forced to try to swim across under the bridge at night in the rain.

Now Hennie and I consulted my 1950's road-map and saw that there was no town anywhere near the Almelo Canal; the only ones that fitted this situation were Delden and Goor beside the Twente Canal. Our conclusion had to be that, walking in the dark, I had strayed 90° to the south and struck this canal outside Delden. or perhaps Goor about five miles further to the west.

When we drove into Delden, about the same size as Borne, I was disappointed not to find 'my' curving street of shops (in fact, Borne happens to have just such a feature); but I may have entered by a different route in 1944, and the road to the canal seemed longer now than I remembered. The bridge was a typical modern Dutch road-bridge, with the roadway supported by a steel round-arched span overhead and by a concrete buttress at each end underneath. The ground here sloped down to the canal, with the bank lined with cut blocks of stone.

This was exactly as I remembered it from 1944, when I had undressed under the bridge, which sheltered me from the rain although I could hear the guards overhead, tied my clothes in a bundle behind my neck, and tried several times to swim across the freezing water – in vain. I had sat on the stone edge of the canal, naked and shivering, with my sodden clothes in my lap, wondering whether it would do me any good to give myself up to the guards! My memories came flooding back, making our search so far so good.

We then walked back towards the town, looking for the farm-yard on the right, where I had found a small hut buried in one end of a potato-clamp and, despite the risks, had dried my clothes round an open fire. We did, in fact, find a large yard, with nearby buildings, which Hennie said had been a food storage depot during the war; it was most unlikely that 'my' potato-clamp would have been maintained for 47 years, but there were several piles of bricks and rubble lying around which, to some extent, simulated it.

This was a good start, but I was dismayed to think that I had veered so far from my intended track so soon after I had started out: I had lost my watch during my bale-out, but I calculated I had been walking for over five hours when I reached the canal, yet this was only about six miles from 't Hesseler.

Hennie then said that Goor, about five miles further west, had a similar road-bridge over the canal, so we decided to have a look at it. We drove out along the road that connects Delden with Zutphen to the west and Hengelo to the east – which may have been where I saw my "Hengelo – Zutphen" milestone in the dark. The road runs roughly parallel to the Twente Canal and to the railway, at a varying distance from them. It also took us over the Almelo Canal, on another arched-span bridge, but I felt no connection from 1944 with either the road or the bridge.

The bridge near Goor turned out to be identical in every respect to the one outside Delden, with a similar bank sloping down to the water beneath it; but the road leading back to the small town did not look the same to me, nor could we find a yard that might have accommodated 'my' potato-clamp. We therefore returned to Delden and decided to look for the next landmark – the railway-line.

My memory was very clear that, as I left 'my' German-patrolled town, I had walked across a single-track railway-line set in the surface of the road. After I had dried my clothes and recovered my morale, I had realised that the railway might lead me to crossing the canal further on and, in any case, as it seemed to go west, it would be better to walk along it at night than to continue on lanes and roads that had already led me astray. However, Hennie and I could not find 'my' simple road-rail crossing and we had to make our way to the station to gain access to the line.

To the west, this ran straight as far as the eye could see and looked very familiar to me. The sleepers were the same awkward distance apart, too close for an ordinary stride; I had tried to walk on the clinker surrounding them, but this offered an uncomfortably rough and uneven surface to my feet. My solution had been to walk on the sleepers and clinker alternately.

Satisfied that the railway-line fitted my recollection, we drove out on the road to Goor to try to spot the pine-wood beside the line in which I had intended to lie-up during the daytime, but had been disturbed by women and children passing nearby. I had moved into open, sloping ground facing south and containing a few bushes; lying down behind these I could probably spot any dangerous individuals approaching before they noticed me. From here, I saw strange gleaming missiles crossing the sky at about 30° to the horizon, which I took to be V2s. Hennie now told me that they were V1s, launched against Brussels or Antwerp from a site some distance away, as I could hear no sound of a rocket engine. We found several woods along the line that might have qualified as mine, but there was nothing to indicate 'my' particular one.

We returned to Borne after a morning that had been both satisfying and rather disturbing. We had found a town, a canal, a bridge, a potato-yard, and a railway-line that conformed to my memories; but I was a little upset to discover how wayward my navigation at night had been: in six hours or so, instead of keeping west, I had apparently wandered south-west to the Twente Canal. If this was true, it raised the question of where I had started from in 't Hesseler: the wood to the north-east identified by the witnesses, from where I could have reached Delden without too much interruption; or 'my' wood to the north, beyond the Leuvelds' farm, from where I might have found myself in Borne – with its curving street of shops, but a long way from any canal before I diverged towards Delden to the south-west. This was a problem to which I had not found a satisfying answer.

We called in at the Town Hall and were delighted and relieved to learn that a number of messages had been received from the villagers of 't Hesseler indicating that they had been reassured by my story and would be attending the Ceremony and Reception. Several others, notably from the many Boomkamp relatives, stated they would be glad to welcome me into their homes. Kick van den Akker, a former Air

Force Captain was looking after F/Lt Mark Roberts, the representative of 16 Squadron, who had driven over from Laarbruch, in Germany, about seventy miles to the south, and who would take Margaret and me back to the Squadron with him next day.

After lunch, we went to 't Hesseler and checked that the plaque had been attached correctly to the Memorial, where it was now draped in the Dutch flag. We then visited the Garden Centre, which was being steadily expanded by the younger Jan Boomkamp; the land which could have been part of the witnesses' wood 47 years ago was now being excavated for a large car-park.

From there we went round to No 42 Deurningerweg, one of several houses opposite the Leuvelds' farm. Here live the Bovenmars family, consisting of Ria, daughter of Herman Boomkamp and married to Jan Bovenmars, a tall bearded English teacher in a school in Delden and the leader of the small 't Hesseler community. They were in the garden with a group of young children, among them their eldest child Anne, aged 10, and her cousin Dirk, the 12-year-old son of Jan Boomkamp. Anne has a sister Helen and a younger brother Bram.

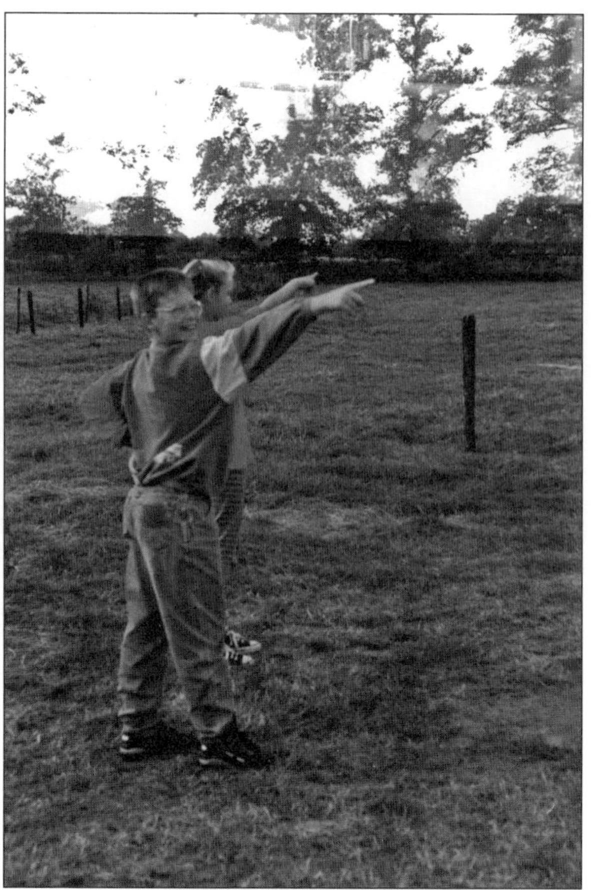

"Over here, Taylor!", but Dirk Bookamp and Anne Bovenmars, cousins, seem a little uncertain about which tree my parachute blew into on 19th November 1944.

The end of the garden was adjacent to the landing-field, but the Garden Centre was fast encroaching on the latter and would soon engulf the whole area. We started to discuss which tree on the landing-field my parachute had blown into when Anne, brimming with vivacity, called out, *"This way, Taylor, here's where your parachute went!"* She and Dirk then ran ahead of us, dancing up and down and pointing to the middle tree. I stood and looked at this tree, perhaps a species of elm, whose location so strongly contradicted my own memory; but, truth to tell, I was more diverted by these two bright children, who spoke perfect English and wanted to know everything I could tell them about my landing on this field, now Boomkamp property.

Anne, in fact, the following year wrote a project, in Dutch, about it all for her Primary School, with drawings and photographs, a description of me and of the setting, a narrative of the events, and her own opinion of my feelings; she gave me a bound copy, complete with her teacher's complimentary remarks – a gift that I treasure.[1]

Later in the day, we returned to the Town Hall to meet two people who, all unknowingly, were mainly responsible for my coming to Borne. In 1988, Hennie Noordhuis had organised an exhibition about the war in the district round Borne and had asked people to lend any artefacts that they had in their possession from those days. As a result, Mr ter Borg came forward with the goggles that he, as a small boy, with his father had picked up on the landing-field on 19th November 1944; it was my initials and name on the strap that had enabled Hennie to trace me to Leeds. Hennie had now persuaded him that he should return the goggles to me.

[1] See "Dutch Voices" pp. 696-707 for this essay.

The second man was Mr Herman Bruggink, a physio-therapist, who happened by chance to be treating Mrs Marie Leuveld-Roetgerink. On 19th November 1944, his father was cycling near 't Hesseler when he saw me descending by parachute; he hurried to the landing-spot, picked up my helmet, and bicycled quickly away with it. He then used the helmet on his motor-bike until his death in 1986, when Herman's brother-in-law, a passionate collector of WW2 memorabilia, took possession of it. He too had lent it to Hennie's exhibition, but it was Herman who was now going to give it back to me.

The Press was also present in the shape of journalists from the local papers "Tubantia" and "Twentsche Courant", both with very reliable reporters who asked me all the right questions.[1] They took photographs of the two men with me and the goggles and helmet, but this was just a preliminary meeting before the actual handing-over at the Reception later in the evening. I told Hennie I would like them to retain these things, which they had kept for so long; but he said they wanted me to take them back with me to England. I was also interviewed by a reporter from Radio East, the regional radio station; he later recorded the ceremony at the Memorial, and the tape was broadcast that evening; they kindly gave me a copy and I found the music especially moving. The broadcast and the accounts in the newspaper all presented the occasion truthfully and sympathetically.

At 7.0pm, we all assembled at the crossroads: the Burgomaster and Jeanette; Colonel Vogelpoel, the Commandant of Twente Air Base; F/Lt Mark Roberts; the leader of the local Resistance Movement during the war; the three Boomkamp brothers: Bernard, Herman, and Hendrik with his wife Diny; Marie Leuveld-Roetgerink in a wheel-chair, and about sixty other relations, friends, villagers, and journalists.

Maarten Vunderink and I led the procession along the lane to the Memorial, which was flanked by flagposts flying the Dutch national flag and the Union Jack, to the strains of a small silver band playing "Abide With Me". This tune has haunted me ever since and brings tears to my eyes whenever I hear it, because of its association with this simple little rural ceremony for the victims of a wartime atrocity.

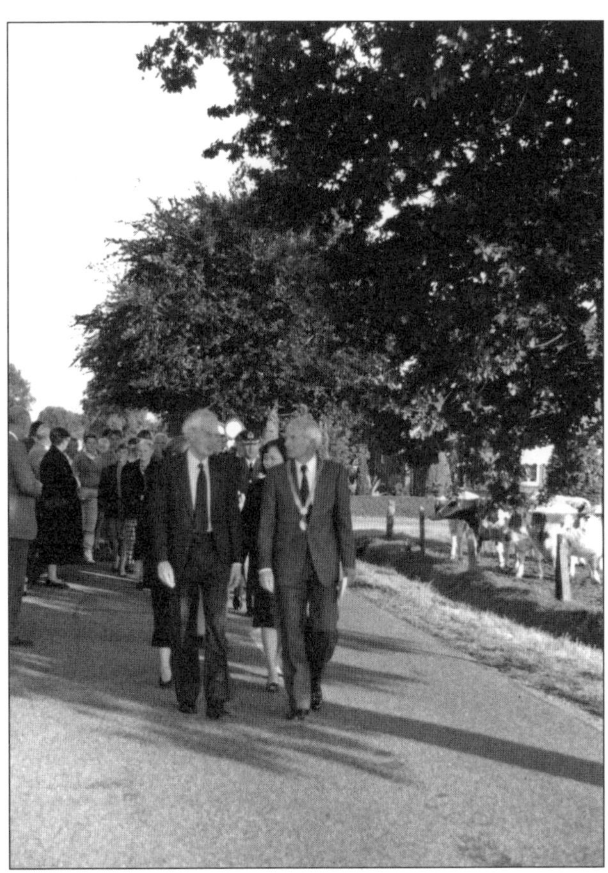

The Burgomaster and I lead the procession up the lane to the Memorial to the victims on 28th August 1991.
Photo: Hennie Noordhuis

The Burgomaster gave a short but discerning address, embracing my landing, sympathy for the victims and their families, the contribution of 16 Squadron and the RAF in the liberation of the Netherlands, and gratitude to the Allied Forces today for preventing another war breaking out in Europe. I then unveiled the plaque on the Memorial, Mark Roberts laid 16 Squadron's wreath, many other wreaths were laid by representatives and individuals, the two National Anthems were played, and we walked slowly back to the cross-roads, accompanied by more music, performed under the watchful eye of Hennie, who had organised the whole ceremony.[2]

[1] These newspapers merged in 1996.
[2] See "Dutch Voices" p. 692 for the Burgomaster's Address, and pp. 693-694 for Press Reports of the Unveiling.

At the Memorial (l-r): Margaret, JT, the Burgomaster, the leader of the local Resistance, the Commandant of Twente Air Base, and F/Lt Mark Roberts, representing 16 Squadron

Photo: D. Doornbos

I unveil the Plaque.

Photo: D. Doornbos

The Burgomaster and his wife lay a wreath on behalf of Borne Municipality.
Photo: D Doornbos

F/Lt Mark Roberts lays a wreath from 16 Squadron.
Photo: D Doornbos

IN EVERLASTING MEMORY
OF
J.G. BOOMKAMP
P.A. VAN DIJK
H.F. ROETGERINK
MUCH LOVED MEN OF 't HESSELER
TAKEN HOSTAGE AND EXECUTED BY THE GERMANS
25th NOVEMBER 1944
THIS PLAQUE WAS PRESENTED BY
16 SQUADRON RAF AND 16 SQUADRON ASSOCIATION
AND DEDICATED BY F/Lt H.J.S. TAYLOR THE 'MISSING PILOT'
WHO ON 19th NOVEMBER 1944 LANDED BY PARACHUTE NEAR THIS SPOT
28th AUGUST 1991
"At the going down of the sun and in the morning we will remember them"

The Plaque

He and I and Mark Roberts were disappointed at the absence of the 16 Squadron Tornados, whose fly-past would have underlined the Burgomaster's words as well as paying a supreme tribute to the victims. On the other hand, in that peaceful country lane, by the golden light of the setting sun, with the flowers surrounding the base of the sorrowful Cross that bears the names of three innocent men, who walked their last along this lane in 1944 – perhaps the villagers were right.

All the representatives and many of the villagers met up again in a large room in the Town Hall and, after light refreshments, were welcomed by the Burgomaster, with another excellent address in Dutch and English. He then introduced me and, as my story had already been published in the Dutch circular, I read out my poem, which Hennie translated into Dutch line-by-line. It was warmly applauded, but what impact it really made I cannot say.

Mr ter Borg was then introduced, and he showed my goggles and described how he and his father had found them. He then presented them to me, and Hennie related how valuable they were in enabling him to find me. He was followed by Mr Herman Bruggink, who produced the helmet but, before handing it to me, he read out an address in very good English that he had composed for the occasion[1], in which he described how his father had picked up and used the helmet; he added how glad he was that the mystery had been resolved about what had happened to me after my landing. He then handed over the helmet to me. I expressed my gratitude to both these kind people for their generosity and told them how much I valued the return of these very personal wartime possessions.

In fact, the helmet looked quite unlike mine. Herman Bruggink's father had used macassar hair-oil liberally on his head and, after 40 years, the helmet was saturated with it and it was now a hard, flat slab of compressed leather. Furthermore, mine was an early wartime model, with rubber ear-pads encased in zip-fastened leather covers stitched onto the helmet. There were no such pads or covers on this specimen, although round pieces of leather had been sewn over the ear-holes. However, on a public platform, I had to accept it with the same enthusiasm as I had shown over being given the goggles.

I receive my goggles, with my name on the strap, from Mr ter Borg (r) and my flying helmet from Mr Herman Bruggink.

Photo: D Doornbos

[1] Printed in full in "Dutch Voices" p. 695

The Churchill Coins (front and obverse) for the Relatives

I had brought the Churchill coins with me, and I now went round the room presenting them to each of the close relations of the victims Jan Boomkamp and Hendrik Roetgerink. I then called up Messrs ter Borg and Bruggink and gave them each a figurine of an airman and a framed photograph of me wearing a helmet and goggles in the cockpit of an aircraft. Finally, I turned to Hennie and praised him for all he had done, first in discovering me, and then in becoming such a wonderful organiser, guide, companion and friend; in my gratitude, I presented him with a larger brass figure of an airman. Maarten Vunderink then closed the proceedings by making me a present of the official tie of Gemeente Borne (Borne Town Council), which I am very proud to wear on special occasions.

Figurines of Airmen (wearing helmets and goggles) for the Finders

The following morning, we said a heartfelt goodbye to Hennie Noordhuis and Joke at the Town Hall; it was more an 'au revoir', as I knew I would be returning next year on 4th May, the day of National Commemoration in Holland. We collected our luggage from the Vunderinks' house and made our farewells to Maarten and Jeanette. As a thank-you present, we gave them a pair of goblets engraved with the coat-of-arms of the City of Leeds, the most appropriate gift we could find for the Burgomaster of this friendly, well-run Dutch town.

Hennie Noordhuis shows his airman figurine to Marie Leuveld-Roetgerink, sister of the victim Hendrik Roetgarink, with her daughter (l) and Margaret looking on.

Mark Roberts then arrived in his car and took us first to pay a last visit to the Memorial in 't Hesseler, now surrounded by wreaths and flowers, with tributes to the victims written by families or friends. We were pleased to find Hendrik and Diny Boomkamp and Hennie and Miny Roetgerink also engaged on the same mission, and it seemed very fitting that they were still standing by the Memorial to Jan Boomkamp and Hendrik Roetgerink as we drove away. It had been a remarkable three days and I felt that, by great good fortune, I had been accepted into a circle of people with whom I shared a tragic experience that started when the engine of my Spitfire blew up on 19th November 1944 and which continues most happily to this day.

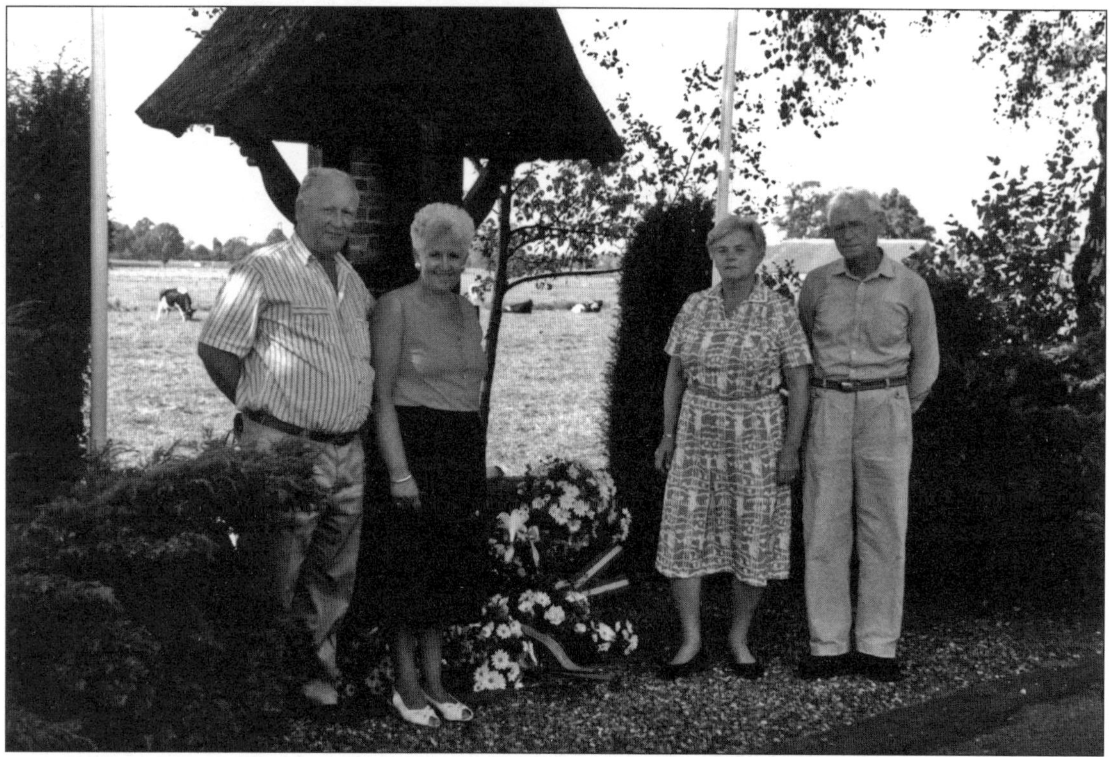

Hennie and Miny Roetgerink (l) with Hendrik and Diny Boomkamp at the Memorial

CHAPTER 19

Exit 16 Squadron – Enter a Musician

I persuaded Mark to drive us to Laarbruch via Zutphen, where I wished to see whether it really was the location of the marshalling-yard and the railway-bridge which had enabled me to cross 'my' canal in 1944. On our way in, we stopped by the railway line and I could see that the goods-yard, with its wide expanse of lines, covered wagons, and flat-bed trucks, agreed closely with my memories. The bridge, however, surprised me greatly as there were two bridges side-by-side, an arch-spanned one for the road and a flat one, built of many transverse girders, for the railway; and they crossed, not the canal but the River Ijssel, which flows from south to north through the town. The Twente Canal joins this river a mile or two north of the bridges, and the road and railway-line from Delden cross it before they enter Zutphen. Somehow, I had not noticed this crossing as I walked along the line in the dark on 21st November 1944. But the river I now saw from the road-bridge looked just like the one that I had spent the next, rainy day trying to find a way across, until I decided that I could do so only by being carried on a train, first by trusting to a stationary covered wagon but, when this proved a vain hope, by jumping on an already-moving truck – a precarious but successful tactic.

Wing Commander Ian Travers Smith, DSO, CO of 16 Squadron; he led the RAF's Tornado echelon in the 1st Gulf War.

During the rest of the journey, I chatted to Mark about his part in the 1990/91 Gulf War, in which the 16 Squadron detachment flew the greatest number of Tornado sorties, and he flew the most in the Squadron; I was impressed – and it came as no great surprise, in 2007, to learn that Mark had risen to be a Group Captain and a Station Commander.

On arrival at Laarbruch, I paid our respects to Wing Commander Ian Travers Smith, DSO, the CO of 16 Squadron, who made us very welcome, even though he was busy preparing for the Disbandment of the Squadron a week later. However, it would be reformed immediately at Lossiemouth in Scotland, replacing 226 Operational Conversion Unit as the training squadron for the Jaguar single-seater fighter-bomber. This was a sad affair in one sense, as most of the personnel would be dispersed to other units; on the other hand, 16 Squadron's number, name, Standard, archives, silver, and memorabilia would be transferred to Lossiemouth, where its history and traditions would be continued in its new role and aircraft. To show its vitality, as the fly-past over 't Hesseler on 28th August had been cancelled, the CO led a Diamond-Nine formation of Tornados at 250 feet over all the RAF bases in Germany in a noisy farewell.

16 Squadron's Farewell 'Diamond Nine' Flight

Unfortunately, our night was disturbed by some members of the RAF Regiment celebrating their return from a night exercise by downing a few beers and behaving rather boisterously in the corridor outside our room. They woke us up and spoiled Margaret's sleep, especially; she thenceforth held a low opinion of all RAF personnel – but, of course, this was her first experience of life in the Services and we should not have been put into the Regiment's barrack-block.

I soon forgot all about it, as the CO put me in the hands of F/0 Mike Read, a young Tornado pilot, and his navigator, F/0 Mal Craghill, who gave me a wonderful introduction to their impressive aircraft. They let me sit in both the cockpits of the Tornado they were about to fly, and showed me how everything worked, and then allowed me to watch and photograph them as they made ready for their practice sortie. It took a long time, half an hour at least, to get all the systems into efficient working mode – and then, just as they were about to taxy out, they had a malfunction and had to abandon the use of that aircraft, transfer to another, and start all over again! However, this gave me time to walk from the dispersal onto the airfield and watch them taxy out and roar off down the runway into the blue – lucky chaps. They flew to the Lake District in England, dropped some practice bombs, and returned to Laarbruch, all within two hours, a vivid example of the performance of modern jet aircraft compared to our wartime Spitfires – but, remember, we were nearer in time to Bleriot, who took 27 minutes to cross the Channel in 1909, than to the Tornado, which truly lives up to its name.

Margaret, meanwhile, had been put in the care of the senior WAAF officer and given a close-up view of the WAAFs at work on the Station; but she was not as enthusiastic about her experiences as I was about mine. We took several trains to get back to Amsterdam, where we spent a very pleasant evening, and flew home to Leeds next day.

Flying Officers Mike Read (r) and Mal Cragill of 16 Squadron explain the Tornado to me at RAF Laarbruch in August 1991.

F/Os Mike Read and Mal Cragill ready to go on a practice sortie to the Lake District in a Tornado GR1A in Gulf War colour

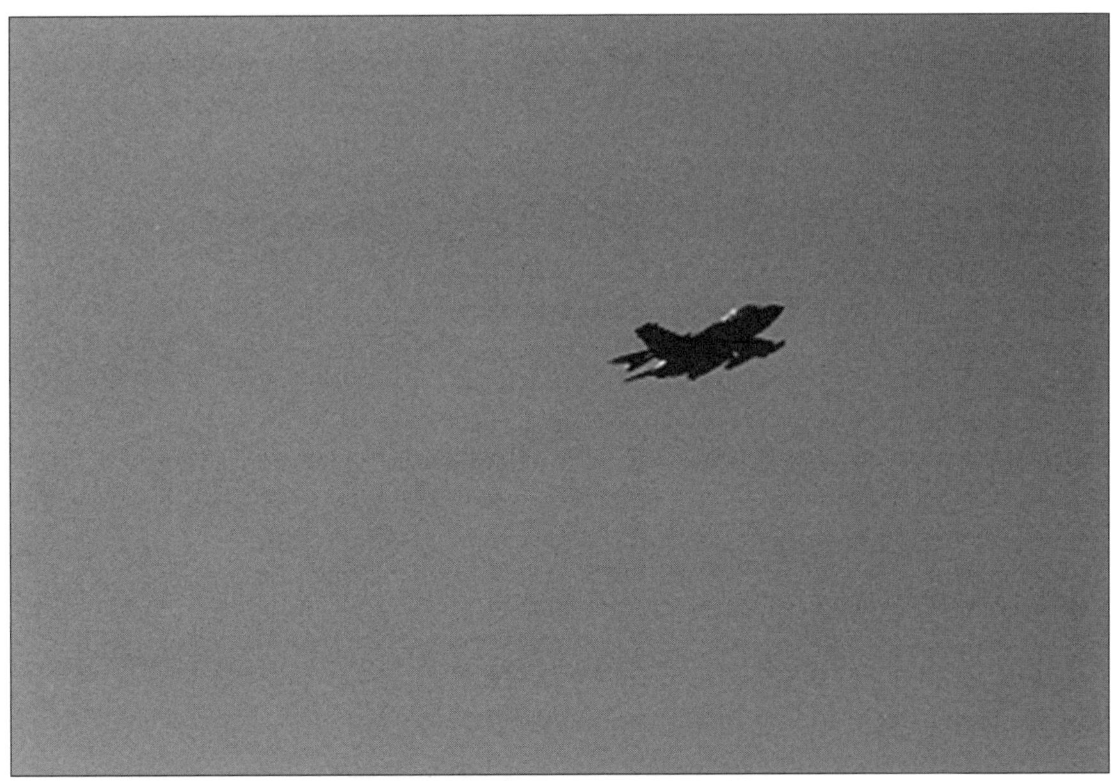

Mike and Mal on their way – lucky fellows!

16 Squadron's Disbandment Parade at RAF Laarbruch on 11th September 1991

Ten days later, I was back at Laarbruch for the Disbandment Parade of 16 Squadron on 11th September 1991, before its transfer to Lossiemouth, with a slight loss of class in becoming a Reserve Squadron training Jaguar pilots. The Parade was a very impressive ceremony in a large hangar, with the salute taken by Air Marshal Sir John Wilson, C-in-C RAF Germany. This was followed by a Squadron Fete for the benefit of all the families, and an All Ranks Dinner and Dance in a local hotel. As a result, what could have been a rather depressed ending of a significant period in the Squadron's life became more of a celebration of its distinguished history, especially its involvement in the two World Wars and the First Gulf War and, later, in peace-keeping operations over the Balkans and Iraq.

On my train journey back to Schiphol, an event occurred that had no connection with RAF Laarbruch, but was of considerable significance in the continuing saga of the aftermath of the tragedy in 't Hesseler. Sitting opposite me in the train was a young Dutchman, who was spending the time composing some kind of musical score. I was so intrigued that I asked him if he spoke English and, when he said he did, I questioned him further about what he was doing. He said he was writing a cantata but, although he played the trumpet and enjoyed composing, he was at present studying to be a conductor at the Conservatoire in Rotterdam; it was an intensive five-year course, which he had started the previous year. He had just come back from a Summer School at Dartington Hall, a well-known musical centre in Devon.

Air Marshal Sir Andrew Wilson, C-in-C RAF Germany, takes the salute.

He then turned the subject onto me and questioned me about why I was travelling on this train; so I told him about my attendance at the 16 Squadron Disbandment Parade. When he then asked if I'd been to Holland before, I described the ceremony at the Memorial in 't Hesseler the previous month. This led to more questions, until I had related all the events in November 1944. I showed him a few photographs and our conversation lasted all the way to the outskirts of Utrecht, where he was changing trains to Rotterdam. Just before we parted, on the spur of the moment I had an inspiration and said to him:

"You're a young Dutchman who had no personal experience of the war. But you know a good deal about it, and you've heard my story. I should be very glad if, as a composer, you would write down your feelings about my story in the form of a piece of music. This would be entirely your own reaction to what you've heard from me. Would you like to do it?"

"Yes, I would," he replied. *"But it will take a long time. My course requires all my concentration, so it would be at least three years before I could complete such a composition. Would that be all right?"*

"Of course," I said. *"That would be wonderful. We'll keep in touch and I'll remind you as the years go by. Excellent."*

We then exchanged our names and addresses and shook hands as he left the train at Utrecht. He was Lukas Groen, who looked about 24 years old and was clearly a serious young man, strongly motivated towards a successful musical career, whether as a conductor or a composer or both.

Perhaps it was a sight with some kind of symbolism but, as the train moved on from Utrecht, I looked out of the window and saw, in a siding, a flat-bed truck just like the one on which I had arrived stealthily in this same station in November 1944.

Lukas Groen was composing music on the train like this when we fell into a significant conversation.

CHAPTER 20

Winds, Helmets, and Museums

Back home, my mind continued to revolve over all the events that had taken place during those three emotion-charged days in 't Hesseler, Borne and the district of Twente. I realised there were still a number of questions that had to be answered satisfactorily before I could really feel peace of mind about my part in the events that followed my involuntary landing in 't Hesseler in 1944:

Which direction did I land in?

Did my parachute actually blow into the tree the witnesses indicated?

Which wood did I run into and which ditch did I hide in?

If the railway-bridge in Zutphen crossed the River Ijssel, how did I cross the Twente Canal?

A final long shot: was it even possible that I had gone west, after all, and arrived at Utrecht via Almelo, crossing that canal near the town and not going near Zutphen?

This last possibility seemed remote, but it was a little disturbing, as it meant that the Delden-Zutphen route had to be very well substantiated in order to negative the very idea. My midnight sighting of the Hengelo-Zutphen milestone, the very likely location of 'my' potato-clamp as outside Delden, and the probable identification of the marshalling-yard and the railway-bridge over the river as being at Zutphen were the strongest evidence for the Delden-Zutphen route, but I was still in doubt about my movements immediately after my landing. The solution to this seemed to lie clearly in my discovering the prevailing direction and strength of the wind in that part of Holland on 19th November 1944.

On 15th November 1991, therefore, I wrote to the Meteorological Office in Bracknell asking – without a great deal of hope – whether they could give me this information. I was amazed and delighted when Mr M.J.Wood, the Archive Manager, not only told me the basic facts, but also included a copy of the German synoptic chart for north-west Europe on that day. He told me that the probable surface wind was from 200° at 15 knots, and at 2000ft the wind had veered to 240° at 35 knots. The Germans' chart disagreed slightly with this: their forecast came from a station that appeared to be quite close to Borne and gave the wind as coming from about 185° at 18-22 knots, with a visibility of more than 1000 yards. Considering that the Germans had to rely on one or two weather ships in the Atlantic and a few daily Met. flights over the sea, it was surprising that their forecast came so close to ours. I would, nevertheless, take Mr Wood's figures, especially because he gave them for the winds both on the ground and at 2000ft.

The wind he gave at 2000ft was blowing from south-west to north-east at slightly over 35mph; at ground-level, this backed a little and decreased in speed to just over 15mph. When I transferred these figures to a map of Borne and 't Hesseler, it became clear that I would have crossed almost at right-angles to the lane along which the church-goers were coming back from Borne. When I landed in the field and released my parachute, it would have been blown in the same direction and, most likely, into the middle tree, to which Anne and Dirk had pointed so enthusiastically the previous August.

This evidence, which was quite irrefutable, made it impossible for the parachute to have been blown into the poplar trees opposite the Leuvelds' farm, which I had identified on my first day with Hennie.

What about the course I had taken when I ran "in the opposite direction" to the men in long coats chasing my parachute? If I had really done this, I must have double-backed across the lane near the site

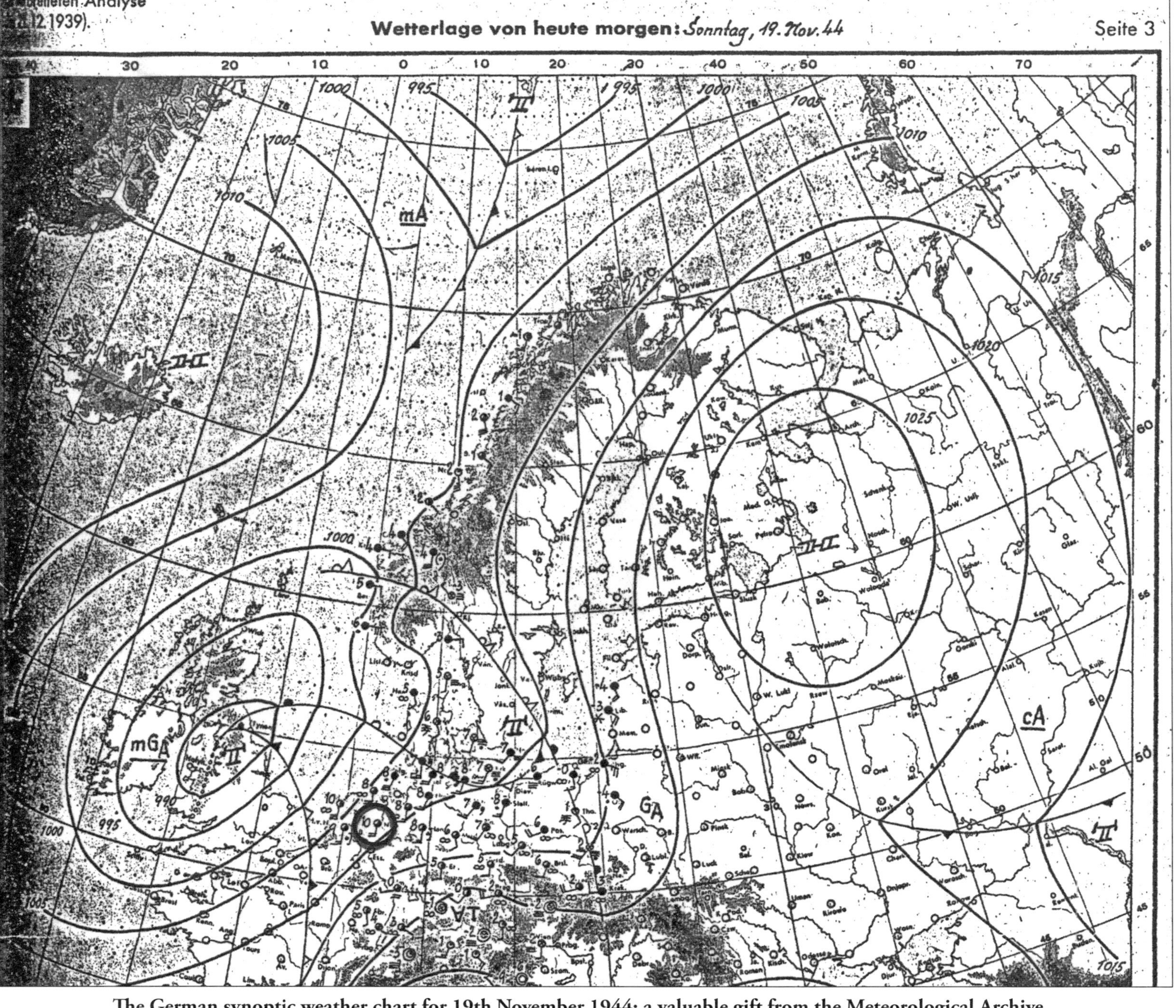

The German synoptic weather chart for 19th November 1944: a valuable gift from the Meteorological Archive
The German weather-station near Borne (circled) with its forecast

of the later Memorial; but I have no recollection of crossing any lane or road in my first movements, and there is no indication that there was a wood of any kind in that direction.

Could I have reached the wood beyond Harry Leuveld's farm? It seemed much less likely now, as I would have had to run in the same direction as the men pursuing the parachute. The only alternative that now seemed possible was that I had disappeared at an angle to the right or left of the path the long-coated men had taken. Therefore I now needed to find a wood on either side of the landing-spot and not more than 100 yards distant from it – the limit of my strength in my battered condition, The trouble was, and still is, that the only wood that might qualify is today too far away; this is the one identified by the witnesses, but only if it came much closer to the cross-roads in 1944 than it did in 1991.

Although my memory and sentiment still felt attached to my first, comforting choice of wood and ditch, the logic of the wind direction now agreed with the choice made by everyone else. I determined that, when I returned to 't Hesseler in 1992, I would make a very thorough examination of the witnesses' wood and its adjoining fields.

Having settled the first two questions for the time being, the problem of the helmet now arose. I had taken a strong dislike to the object that I had received from Herman Bruggink, even though he was a very charming man; I had put it away in a trunk containing other pieces of my wartime equipment. At the same time, I felt that the helmet and goggles belonged to the people who had found them, or at least to the local community, and therefore the best place for them would be the Twente Air Base Museum, which already contained a good collection of artefacts from before, during, and after the Second World War. I therefore wrote to Hennie and suggested that one of the activities next year should be my presentation of these two objects to the Museum. Hennie agreed with this and began making the arrangements in the New Year.

Meanwhile, I felt that I ought to do something to improve the condition of this helmet; it looked repulsive, not unlike the shrivelled skin of the Neolithic Iceman that had recently been found in an Alpine glacier. Round pieces of leather had been stitched over the holes where the ear-phones had been attached. I wrote to the RAF Museum at Hendon to ask how to restore it, and Mr A.E.Cormack, of the Aircraft Department, suggested I should try using ordinary dry-cleaning fluid on it. However, I managed to get some trichlor-ethylene, useful for cleaning antique ceramics, and dipped the helmet in this for a few seconds. When the colour began to come off, I drained the fluid and found half a centimeter of oil floating on the surface. I washed the helmet thoroughly in soap and water and it became soft and flexible. I mounted it on a big red inverted flower-pot and took some photographs of it.

As I looked at it in its rejuvenated state, it slowly began to appear more familiar. Threads of memory struggled to the surface and took my mind back to my first days' flying in the RAF. When I arrived at No 4 Elementary Flying Training School at Brough, outside Hull, in November 1941, to take a Grading Course before going to the USA for my real training, I was issued with a Type B flying-helmet and goggles. The helmet had round sponge-rubber muffs over each ear-hole, held in place by a circular leather cover; this had a zip-fastener down the middle to allow the ear-phone to be inserted inside the rubber. There was a long horizontal strap round the back of the neck, with a buckle for adjustment, and a short vertical strap to hold the middle of the long strap in place. We used to loop our goggles under this little strap to keep them with the helmet, although they would dangle rather dangerously when we carried the helmet or hung it on a coat-hook.

There were two studs each side of the front of the helmet to hold on our oxygen-mask and the microphone built into the end of the mask. We usually undid the studs on the left side, but kept those on the right pressed in so that we could carry the helmet with the mask attached. When we put the helmet on, the mask would swing to the right and we could talk normally to the ground-crew; but, of course, we had to fit the mask across our face by pressing together the studs on the left side when we were ready to start up, use the radio, and draw our first breaths of oxygen while still on the ground.

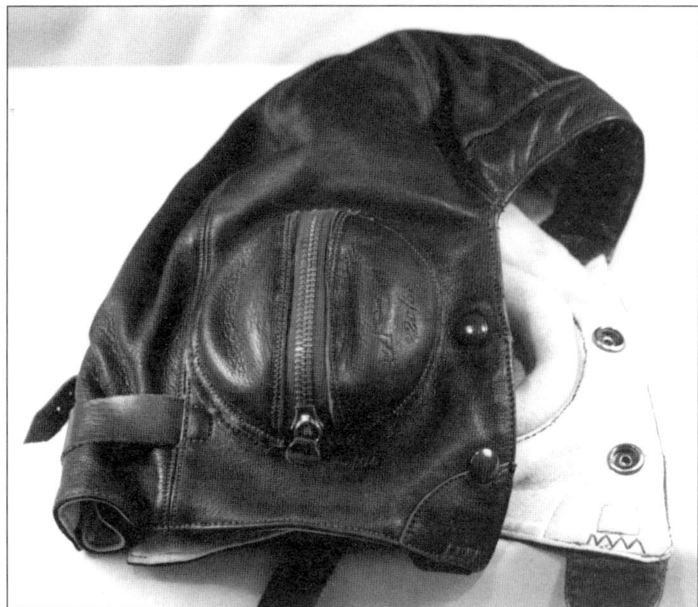

A Type 'B' flying-helmet of the type I was wearing on the 19th November 1944. Note the padded zip-fastened ear-muff to contain a headphone.
Photo: RAF Museum Hendon

Thinking back to 1943, when I returned from the USA (where the USAAF wore a quite different style of helmet), I remembered that I took to wearing my original helmet, even though it had been superseded by a later model, Type E, F or G; this replaced the sponge-rubber muffs and zip-fastened covers with hard rubber rings, which protruded about 1" each side of the helmet and into which the ear-phones could be easily fitted. Nevertheless, I had become so fond of my old helmet that I took it with me to 16 Squadron and had two extra studs added to each side to hold my new-style oxygen-mask and microphone. Was it possible that the mutilated object handed to me by Mr Bruggink, now restored to something like its former appearance, could be my old friend, after all?

My helmet, picked up by Mr Bruggink senior, with the ear-muff unstitched and replaced with a round leather patch

I took a magnifying-glass and examined the whole surface minutely, especially near the ear-patches sewn on by Mr Bruggink senior. Sure enough, I found a circle of tiny holes, measuring a little over 5" in diameter, round each one. I took photographs of them and of every detail of the helmet inside and out, including the 1941 label (which was still legible), and sent them to Mr Cormack in .the RAF Museum for identification.

He replied at length, confirming that "the item is indeed a Type B Helmet. I am most interested to read that you retained yours long after its obsolescence date because you found it comfortable. One of the principal reasons for the introduction of the Type E was that it was supposed to be more comfortable than its predecessor!" He very kindly enclosed photographs of a Type B helmet complete with ear-muffs and zip-fasteners.

So the mystery of the helmet was resolved: it had needed these original little stitch-holes to identify it and remind me of my somewhat eccentric sentimental action in continuing to use an obsolete piece of personal equipment. Perhaps I was the only RAF pilot operating over Europe in 1944 who was still wearing a Type B flying-helmet! And this unique helmet was the one that Mr Bruggink senior happened to pick up in a Dutch field on a cold November day in 1944.

More importantly for me, the helmet could now join the goggles as the major means of identifying me as "the missing pilot", whose arrival by parachute on the landing-field had precipitated the sequence of events that ended in the tragedy of 't Hesseler six days later. I now felt even more strongly that their proper place lay in the Twente Air Base Museum, where they could be put on display and remind local people and other visitors of the story behind the Memorial in 't Hesseler, with which they were so intimately connected.

I had a strong desire to return to Borne for 4th May 1992, the Dutch Day of Commemoration, in order to join the 't Hesseler families in the ceremony at the Memorial, which now bore my plaque. I also hoped to get to know them better and to become more familiar with Borne itself, which had given me such a good welcome. Another, closely connected objective, as I have already explained, was to give my helmet and goggles to the Museum. In addition, to come to a firm conclusion about my own movements after landing, I needed to explore fully the topography of 't Hesseler and that of the northern part of Zutphen. As in 1991, I would need Hennie Noordhuis's help and organisation; and, as before, these were forthcoming in abundance.

I was very busy at home preparing to leave for Serbia on 9th May to spend a month lecturing on 'Teaching English as a Foreign Language' at the University of Novi Sad, as part of the Tempus Project; so I had to fly out to Schiphol on 4th May itself and took a train to Hengelo, as Hennie was very busy with the arrangements for the ceremonies at eleven separate Memorials. I was picked up by Joop, one of his colleagues, and taken to "The Ship", a pleasant little hotel on the edge of Borne. I had a good walk round the old part of Borne, looking at its well-preserved 17th and 18th century former farm buildings, before Joop appeared, with a wreath for me provided by Hennie, and drove me to 't Hesseler at 6.45pm. At the cross-roads, I received a warm welcome from all those I knew: the elderly Bookamp brothers; Bernard, Herman, and Hendrik with Diny; Jan and Ria Bovenmars with Anne; Hennie and Miny Roetgerink; Harry and Gertie Leuveld; Marie Leuveld-Roetgerink was not strong enough to attend, but Ger and Ria were there. Other villagers included Mrs Veenhuis-Weghorst, while Herman Bruggink came from Borne with his wife Bernadette; there were nearly fifty others, including a good number of children.

Some of the family of the victim Jan Bookamp at the cross-roads:
(l) his brothers Herman, Hendrik with Diny, and Bernard (2nd on rt), Herman's daughter Ria with husband Jan Bovenmars, and JT (on rt)

Photo: Hennie Noordhuis

Maarten and Jeanette Vunderink then arrived and we proceeded together up the lane to the Memorial, with the little band providing a solemn accompaniment. The ceremony followed closely the pattern of 1991, with Maarten giving a short address, in which he thanked me for coming, before he led the way in laying his wreath. I laid mine next, followed by many others, including children. We stood in silence for two minutes; then the Dutch National Anthem was played and Martin and I led the way back up the lane.

We returned to the cross-roads, where I met a few more villagers. Maarten then took me to the Town Hall, where coffee and rolls were being served to the councillors and staff and wartime Resistance leaders. Hennie then appeared and presented me with a huge wreath with my name on, and we all walked into the square outside the Old Town Hall. The War Memorial was at one side, flanked by flags flying and backed by a row of Scouts. A large band, under Hennie's supervision, was playing "Nimrod" while we stood in silence or spoke in whispers until 8.0pm pealed out from the church clock. A bugler then sounded the "Last Post" from the balcony of the Old Town Hall, which was followed by a two-minutes' silence. It was ended, as at the Cenotaph in London, by the clear notes of "Reveille" from the bugle, after which the Burgomaster led the way in placing his wreath on a stand in front of the Memorial. I followed suit, feeling a little like an outsider. The officials did the same, and then members of the public laid their wreaths and posies, followed by husbands and wives, mothers and children, placing a single rose amongst the mass of flowers. The band then struck up the Dutch National Anthem, sung with patriotic fervour by the crowd, while their flag fluttered in the breeze. I felt very privileged to be present at this very Dutch occasion. The people slowly dispersed, and the traffic moved again. We retired into the Town Hall for some more refreshment.

Afterwards, Hennie showed me the Memorial to Jan Vonk, the young man of 24 years old, who saw himself as a sort of Scarlet Pimpernel during the war, making friends and drinking with the Germans, then stealing their pistols and documents, forging passports, entering Germany and bringing back rescued Dutch slave labourers. Eventually, he aroused the suspicions of both the Resistance and the Germans, and the Germans locked him up in Almelo prison and then moved him to Enschede, where they tortured him. My disappearance in 't Hesseler on 19th November 1944 was sufficient excuse for them to bring him to Borne and shoot him outside the Town Hall. When a Dutch policeman asked the soldiers why they had done so, he was told, "To show you people what happens to you if you hide Allied pilots." Jan's grave is elsewhere, but beside the Town Hall is a small plot with a marble cross and an inscription commemorating his death. Poor boy, he was extremely brave, but to take on the enemy single-handed was an enterprise doomed to failure.[1]

The Memorial to Jan Vonk, executed on the 19th November 1944, beside the Old Town Hall in Borne

Hennie and I then drove to 't Hesseler to visit the Roetgerinks in their home by the cross-roads: 91-year-old Mrs Hudepohl-Roetgerink, Hennie and Miny, and their two daughters, who spoke better English than the others. Mrs Hudepohl-Roetgerink was a sister-in-law of Marie Leuveld-Roetgerink and I gave her the Churchill Commemorative Coin that she would have received if she had attended the Reception in the Town Hall in 1991. We stayed chatting for a time, and then moved

[1] See his Obituary on pp. 682-683 of "Dutch Voices".

on to Jan and Ria Bovenmars' house and into their large sitting-room with deep armchairs and sofas.

Two of the grandchildren of the victim Jan Boomkamp: Dirk Boomkamp, a keen modeller, son of Jan Bookamp junior and Lidy, and Anne Bovenmars, daughter of Ria and Jan. In 1991 they pointed out the tree my parachute had blown into.

Photo: Hennie Noordhuis

Here were gathered nearly the full Boomkamp family: all the ones I had seen at the ceremony, with the addition of Bernard's partner Annie, and young Dirk, who gave me a fine book on Dutch aircraft. He had brought the plastic model Spitfire that I had given him last year, now completed; he was going to Schiphol plane-spotting next day. Anne also had brought her model, but a friend had made it for her. Helen brought in some pet rabbits.

We had the fine Bornsche Bier, made from wheat, and large cubes of cheese, a Boomkamp side-line, produced in and distributed from an adjacent barn. The talk turned to how the Boomkamps lived so long. I suggested that it was because they lived on the land; but it turned out that only Herman had taken on the family farm; Bernard had worked in a marine valve factory in Hengelo, while Hendrik had been an engineer employed by the local Water Board. Bernard's great passion was 'hunting', the Continental word for shooting, everything from rabbits anywhere to grouse in Scotland and wild boar in Poland. Altogether, it was a lovely evening, which didn't end till midnight; I felt very much at home with such a warm and friendly family.

Mrs Van Dijk-Kopkamp, daughter-in-law of the victim Piet van Dijk, with her son Piet and his wife Ineke, talking to Hennie Noordhuis

The next morning, Hennie arrived at my hotel, closely followed by Mrs Piet van Dijk, the widow of the younger Piet van Dijk, who had died in 1986. His father was the Piet van Dijk who had been executed beside Jan Boomkamp and Hendrik Roetgerink – in reprisal for his son's escape from prison. She had driven from her home in Voorschoten, just south of Leiden, with her son, another Piet, who worked in the International Office of the Ministry of Education, and her daughter-in-law Ineke. a Montessori teacher, with one child and another on the way. We had a most interesting time discussing many aspects of life under German Occupation, especially the activities of the Resistance, and looking at photographs. She was a very sensible and dignified lady, not too weighed down by the past, but keeping it all in sad perspective. I presented her with my last Churchill Coin, for which she was very grateful. We had lunch together and then accompanied them to the Memorial, which they had never seen. We parted good friends, and I was very pleased to have met the nearest relation of the victim Piet van Dijk and, through her and his grandson, paid him my respects.

The following day, Hennie drove me to Arnhem, a place of strong emotions for the bravery of the forlorn Airborne troops and the suffering of the local population, forced to leave the city after the help and encouragement they had given the British and Polish forces. I had spent ten days in the company of some of these courageous fellows and their highly-disciplined NCOs, cooped up in a converted factory in Enschede, before I was transported to Dulag Luft, the aircrew interrogation centre. But I knew nothing of the Battle of Arnhem or of the fighting that took place in the other sectors of Operation 'Market Garden', where the Americans were eminently successful, whereas the relieving British XXX Corps failed to perform with any real distinction. So, to me, Arnhem presented a rather blurred picture of great gallantry in a very confused and desperate military situation, coupled with huge incompetence by the, at that time, faceless men who planned, but failed to execute, a risky combined air and land operation.

The Oosterbeek Museum in the former Hartenstein Hotel, the HQ of the 1st British Airborne Division, housed a truly comprehensive display of maps, photographs, weapons, vehicles, uniforms, and other artefacts, as well as well-designed dioramas of typical situations and critical moments during the eight days' fighting. I could now visualise the scope and ferocity of the battle, but the day-to-day sequence of events, in the air as well as on the ground, still eluded me.

We came back via Zutphen and saw both closed wagons and flat-bed trucks in the marshalling-yard. We couldn't go in and so were unable to discover the lane which I had followed that led me through the farmyard full of German soldiers washing their horses. We did, however, find a small road that took us to the river-bank, and this certainly looked the same as the one beside which, in pouring rain, I had struggled to launch a large raft tied up on the bank and pinned there by the strong wind. A widespread industrial estate now filled the area between us and Zutphen, preventing any approach along the river-bank to the shed which I had shared with some indignant chickens until it grew dark; but I'd seen enough to convince me that this was 'my' river. Unfortunately, I forgot to look for the whereabouts of the Twente Canal, so we failed to resolve this particular question, which had some relevance for me in establishing my actual evasion route in 1944.

In search of further proof, we crossed over the River Ijssel by the road-bridge and walked as close as possible to the railway-line, where we saw the embankment which looked just like the one down which I had rolled when I had to let go my grip on the flat-bed truck as the train gathered speed. I now felt certain that Zutphen had been the starting-point of the rail-journey that, by great good fortune, had landed me in Utrecht.

On our way back to Borne, we passed the T-shaped junction of the Almelo Canal with the Twente Canal; this covered quite a large area of water and was the most likely location of the 'lake' that I had seen during my parachute descent, and where I thought, in my semi-conscious, detached state, that I might drown.

The junction of the Almelo Canal (foreground) with the Twente Canal, perhaps what I took to be a lake during my dazed parachute descent

In the evening, we visited Mrs Marie Leuveld-Roetgerink and her family, her son Ger and his wife Ria and their two children. She was very frail but, as I knelt beside her wheel-chair, she whispered one sentence to me in Dutch which, when translated, raised my spirits more than anything else that anyone had said to me: *"It was not your fault."* Others had said the same thing, but for the sister of the victim Hendrik Roetgerink to acquit me of any responsibility was the most effective absolution that I could have received.

The following morning, I walked from my hotel to 't Hesseler and conducted a thorough search of the fields round the Garden Centre, looking for a wood and ditch that might correspond with my memories. I have to admit that I could find nothing convincing: the transverse road, the Hesselerweg, had to be crossed and there were houses in sight, whereas I had no recollection of seeing either; there was no big field and, although there were several ditches, none of them resembled 'mine'. Worst of all, perhaps, none of the fields outside the remaining wood looked west towards where the sun would have set. One of my strongest memories was of waiting impatiently for it to do so, and it was a marker that enabled me to set off in the right direction for my hoped-for objective of Utrecht. So, although I accepted that my own choice of wood and ditch was unrealistic, I wasn't persuaded that the witnesses' suggested replacement was the obvious alternative, even though it appeared at present to be the only one. What I really needed was a 1944 map of the topography of 't Hesseler that showed the shape and location of every wood at the time of my landing. Thus the question of where I had hidden on the first afternoon still awaits a convincing solution.

As I walked back to Borne, a car stopped beside me with Herman Bruggink at the wheel; as a physiotherapist, he was treating all three of the elderly ladies in 't Hesseler, Mrs Leuveld-Roetgerink, Mrs Hudepohl-Roetgerink, and Mrs Veenhuis-Weghorst. What a small world I had entered! He gave me a lift to my hotel.

From here I walked to the Town Hall, where I had coffee with Hennie and then visited his archivist's department: six friendly people in airy offices, with a large archive stored in a very up-to-date retrieval

Marie Leuveld-Roetgerink, sister of victim Hendrik Roetgerink and widow of Leuveld, the sculptor of the Memorial, with her daughter Ria and son-in-law Ger (r) and their children.
Photo: Hennie Noordhuis

system. We then paid a visit to the Leuveld's farm; Harry wanted to show me some photographs taken forty or more years before and gave me one shot from a helicopter over the Garden Centre in the 1950s. Gertie was suffering from cancer but was surprisingly cheerful; fortunately, it was detected early and responded well to treatment so that she was out of danger by the following year. I gave them my own Churchill Coin. Their two sons came in to greet me and join in coffee and cake. The family was typical of the kind, hospitable people I kept meeting in 't Hesseler: what happened in 1944 was a brutal tragedy, but what I found on all my visits from 1991 onwards was a warm-hearted little community, who displayed the very best traits of any nation, Dutch or English.

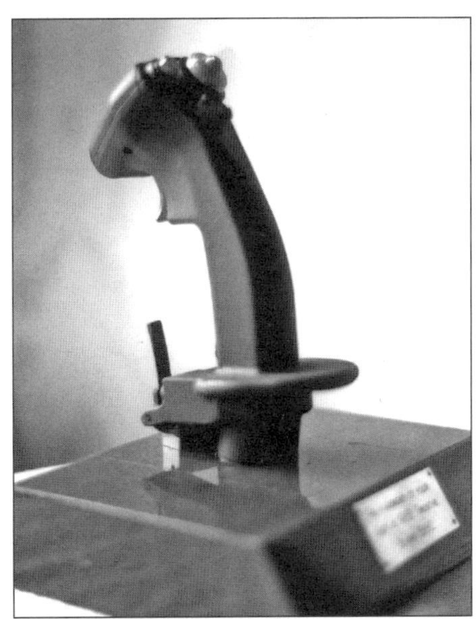

Replica F-16 control-stick kindly presented to me by the Air Base Museum, inscribed: "In Memory of your visit to A/B Twenthe 6 May 1992"

After lunch, Hennie took me to the Twente Air Base to hand over my helmet and goggles. We were met by Colonel Vogelpoel who, in 1991, had promised me a flight in a two-seater F-16. He now wanted me to fly the F-16 Simulator, but the air-conditioning had failed, so this was not possible. He gave me a book recording the history of flying in Holland, and I responded with a first draft of my "One Flight Too Many" and a copy of the RAF annual "Royal Air Force 1992", for which I was the proof-reader. Colonel van der Broek, Chairman of the Air Museum Committee, then took us to the Museum, on another part of the airfield, and introduced us to the Curator, Mr Adri van der Laan. We moved into the ground-floor, full of exhibits from World War 2, and here I presented the Colonel with my flying-helmet and goggles, and photographs of a Spitfire XI and myself. In return, he gave me a beautiful fibreglass model of an F-16's control-stick, mounted on a wooden

Lt Col van der Broek, Chairman of the Twente Air Base Museum, waits at the entrance with Hennie Noordhuis to receive my helmet and goggles.

base with an inscribed brass plate. He left us with the Curator, who gave us a very full tour of all the exhibits on two floors, from the 1920s down to the post-war period. We then moved to an adjacent hall, where there were several full-sized aircraft, including a British two-seater Meteor jet trainer and an American F-104 single-seat jet fighter. Outside was parked a Spitfire Mark IX in Dutch markings, beside a German 88mm flak-gun, one of their most successful weapons. I collected some photos and booklets in Dutch for Dirk, and we then went to the Officers' Mess.

We were introduced to the Mess President, who asked me to say a few words to the 30 or so officers present, so I told them why I had come to Borne. They then celebrated the promotion of five of their number with a traditional ritual: starting from each other's shoulders, they had to climb up to one or other of the large wooden 'cartwheel' chandeliers hanging from the ceiling and sit there; their shoes were then removed and thrown outside. All rather childish, perhaps, but things no doubt became rather rougher once we had left. English is the language of the Dutch Air Force, so perhaps it is not surprising that they have copied some of the morale-building celebrations of an RAF aircrew's Mess.

I had decided to fly to Schiphol from the little airport which shared space with the Air Base. I said my warm goodbyes to the two Colonels, and drove with Hennie to the terminal building on the other side of the airfield. I gave him my heartfelt thanks for all he had done for me, and then walked out to board the little Cessna 200 twin-engined plane. The nine seats were already taken by passengers so, very fortunately, I had to sit beside the pilot. This gave me a fine view as we took off from the former German airfield, and I could see the whole lay-out of the hangars, dispersals and squadron offices. It was a very pleasant flight, skirting Amsterdam, and I was in good time to catch my somewhat larger airliner back to Leeds.

I felt I had done all I could to trace my evasion route and I had made many good friends among the inhabitants of 't Hesseler and Borne; so, when 1993 arrived, I didn't think that another visit was necessary. When the 4th May actually arrived though, I had very strong feelings of regret that I was not there, honouring those poor victims alongside their relatives and neighbours. I felt I had neglected my duty and I vowed I would go back every year from now on, as long as I was physically capable. Hennie also wrote to me later that it was my presence that would ensure that the ceremony at the Memorial would continue for the foreseeable future – I therefore really had no choice in the matter. However, a significant event cropped-up in 'my' part of Holland in November 1994, which replaced my intention to return for 4th May.

CHAPTER 21

Beyond the Ignorance

In April 1994, I received from Lukas Groen a copy of his newly-composed score of "Pro Borne" inscribed:

"Hereby I dedicate this piano piece "Pro Borne",
composed February 1993,
to you H.J.S.Taylor.
Yours sincerely, L.S.Groen"

The first page of the Score for "Pro Borne", the cantata for piano composed by Lukas Groen after hearing my story

With it was a tape-recording. I am no musician and I don't really appreciate modern music. This is a piece of contemporary abstract music, deliberately non-representational, appealing entirely to the emotions. I cannot pretend that I understand it, but I am delighted that this is a sincere and deeply-felt response to my story by a serious and sensitive young Dutchman. Lukas orchestrated it soon after, and it received its first public performance at the Rotterdam Conservatory on 18th May 1994. I badly wanted to attend but, at the last minute, I was unable to leave Leeds.

Hennie Noordhuis had expressed his feelings, earlier in the year, that the story should be made into a television programme. He persuaded me to try the BBC, but my heart wasn't in it and I was not sorry when Lawrence Rees turned it down for 'Timewatch'. I was convinced that it was a Dutch tragedy, which should centre round the relatives of the victims, and that this could be handled much better by Dutch broadcasters and viewed by a Dutch audience.

So it was not such a great surprise when, in July 1994, I received a letter from Ellen van Helsdingen, the 28-year-old producer of short regional documentaries for NOS, one of the Dutch national TV companies. Ellen had been in touch with Hennie and proposed making a 15-minute feature to be included in the weekly half-hour regional programme "From Region to Region". Some time later, I asked her why she had decided to cover this particular story when so many other similar, and worse, atrocities had been committed by the Germans during their 1940-1945 Occupation of her country. She replied that what distinguished this story from the others was the music of Lukas Groen! She had been in touch with him and had gone to Rotterdam to record him conducting the orchestrated version.

This came as quite a surprise, but a very pleasant one, as it showed that Ellen shared my sentiments when I first approached Lukas on the train with the suggestion of a composition. She intended to use "Pro Borne" as the theme music, linking together interviews with him, with the Boomkamp brothers and the Roetgerink sister, with Hennie Noordhuis, and with myself.

On 13th November, Margaret and I set out for Holland, but from Amsterdam we took a train to The Hague. The purpose was not in connection with the events round Borne, but because I had spent several years researching Adriaen Hanneman, a 17th-century Dutch artist, one of whose portraits had been bought by my grandfather in about 1910 and, in my life-time, had always hung in our dining-

The serious business of re-enacting my 1991 conversation with Lukas Groen (l)
Photo: Hennie Noordhuis

On location within sight of the bridges over the River Ijssel at Zutphen

Photo: Hennie Noordhuis

rooms. It was known only as "Portrait of a Jesuit 1661", but why my father and his father, both Church of England clergymen, should have valued this picture of a severe-looking Jesuit, remains a mystery. I had decided to try to trace this unknown sitter and, by close liaison with Jesuit historians and archivists in England, France, Belgium and Holland, I had discovered that he was Father Roeland de Pottere, SJ, Head of the Jesuit Station in Delft 1630-1662. In order to establish more about the life and art of Hanneman, I was actively looking for other paintings of his, and there were several in the Mauritshuis, the world-famous art museum in The Hague. Strangely, in a tale based on flying, Adriaen Hanneman and Roeland de Pottere feature in it several times more.

We stayed in Borne as the guests of the municipality, and I spent the next two days in the company of Ellen van Helsdingen, her cameraman Hans de Ruiter, a veteran of wars in Vietnam, Israel, Biafra and San Salvador, the sound-recordist Roelof Dijkman, and Hennie Noordhuis.

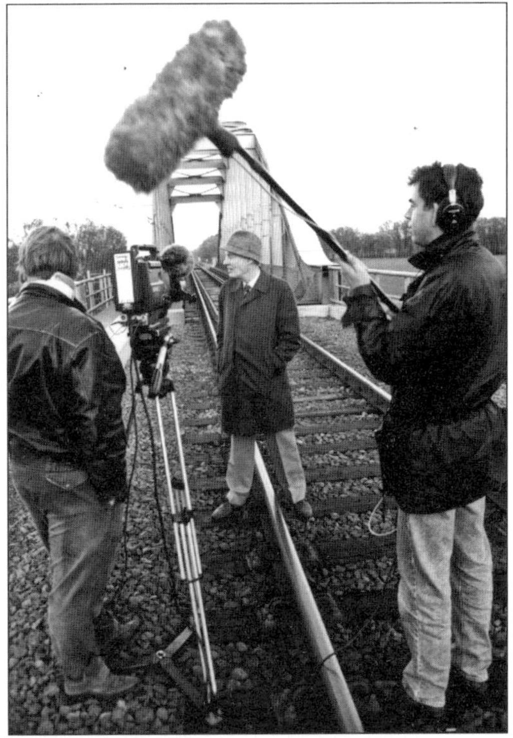

A pause in the filming on the bridge over the Almelo Canal; fortunately, Ellen did not need me to repeat my train-hopping escapade.

Photo: Hennie Noordhuis

The story was filmed in reverse order: first, Lukas Groen and I were shown meeting on a train going to Utrecht; then I was interviewed on the banks of the River Ijssel outside Zutphen, near the bridge that I had crossed at night on a flat-bed truck; after this, Ellen questioned me on the railway-line between Delden and Zutphen, along which I had walked for two nights. On each occasion, Ellen asked me what my feelings were when I found myself back at these places – I could tell her only what they were at the time when I reached them.

Next day, in 't Hesseler, we had a moving meeting with Bernard, Herman and Hendrik Boomkamp and Marie Leuveld-Roetgerink, who were filmed walking slowly along the lane to the Memorial to the victims, with Herman pushing Marie in her wheel-chair. The camera-crew took pictures from many different angles, but we gradually lost our awareness of them: the situation had become very emotional for us: a cold, windy, November day; the stark outline of the trees etched against the grey clouds scudding overhead; the simple Christ-figure on the Cross, at peace after an agonising death, beautifully carved by Marie's husband in memory of the three men butchered so needlessly fifty years before; we, survivors, standing bare-headed close to the spot where I had landed and where the victims were shot – a choice of place that reflected the methodical cruelty of the Germans in the manner of their revenge; and, finally, the three brothers of one victim walking away beside me, with the sister of another between us in her wheel-chair. Later, Ellen went to talk to Marie in her house; I saw her come out – crying.

Herman Boomkamp welcomed everyone to his home, shared with Jan and Ria Bovenmars and their three children, now tall teenagers – I called them 'my giraffes'. Hot soup, bread and cheese on a long, polished, solid oak table were most welcome, after which Ellen interviewed the three Boomkamp brothers in Dutch, of course. She then took me back to the landing-site for my final interview. But the field

Gathering at the 't Hesseler Memorial
l-r: Hennie Noordhuis Bernard, Herman and Hendrik Boomkamp
Marie Leuveld-Roetgerink (sitting) Ellen van Helsdingen Roelof Dijkman Hans de Ruiter

Sombre Memories for Bernard, Herman and Hendrik Boomkamp,
Marie Leuveld-Roetgerink and JT

Photo: Hennie Noordhuis

had now been incorporated by the younger Jan Boomkamp into his expanding Garden Centre and was becoming unrecognisable. However, Ellen and I stood on the edge of the lane and she asked me some leading questions about my feelings about being traced by Hennie Noordhuis.

"Were you glad he found you?"

"At that time, between just him and me, I wish he hadn't. But I've had such a wonderful welcome in 't Hesseler by the relatives of the victims, and we have such a warm relationship, and I feel I belong to this little village and these are my family now, that I am very happy to be involved with this community, after the war, after all this has happened.

But it still fills me with regret that my days of innocence, of ignorance, were destroyed by Hennie's message.

So I have two feelings."

We then moved off to the Town Hall in Borne, where Hennie was subjected to the last round of Ellen's perceptive interviewing.

"Have you ever had any doubts about whether it was a good idea to search for the missing pilot?"

"What happened was this. I sensed that, among the relatives, there was a belief until two years ago that Taylor had been kept in prison in Borne.

And I also heard some slight reproaches against the Resistance Movement in Borne: 'If they had handed him over, we should have kept our loved ones.'

As long as I didn't know the answers to these questions, I thought to myself, I need to know the facts.

That's why I decided to bring the case of Taylor to its true conclusion."

Finally, after nightfall, the filming was finished; it was now Ellen's task to reduce about five hours of recording on videotape to a coherent 15-minute programme – an unenviable task which I didn't think could be done to the satisfaction of any of the participants – much less of all of us.

The programme was broadcast on two successive nights, 25th and 26th November 1994, exactly 50 years after the executions had taken place. Ellen's title was very subtle: it took me some time to work it out: the Germans' ignorance of what had happened to me after my landing; their ignorance of my capture the day before they executed the victims; and my ignorance for 46 years of what had happened in 't Hesseler after I had run away. It showed how sympathetically Ellen had reconstructed the story from her researches and from the answers to her penetrating questions.

I was astonished at how much she had been able to include in such a short programme, and I felt humbled to learn for the first time of the events as actually witnessed and described by Marie Leuveld-Roetgerink and the Boomkamp brothers – I could not, of course, understand their answers in Dutch until Ellen had transcribed and translated them for me. I congratulated Ellen on her achievement, and I was very pleased when she told me that she did, in fact, consider that this was the best programme she had ever made.[1]

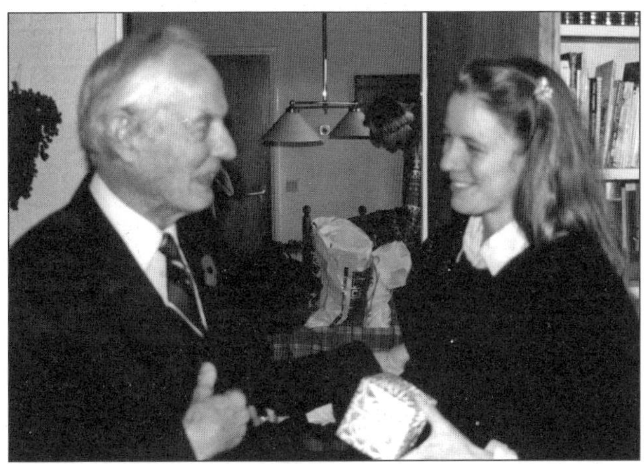

Many thanks to our charming and perceptive producer:
JT and Ellen van Helsdingen
Photo: Hennie Noordhuis

[1] See Appendix B pp. 730-733 for the complete Transcript.

CHAPTER 22

My Spitfire Unearthed

I had baled out, landed, and run away in 1944 without speaking to anyone on the ground – indeed, I assumed that I was in Germany – and for 46 years I thought I was the only person to have suffered from my misfortune. Now that I had been made aware of the tragedy that had followed my landing, Marie Leuveld-Roetgerink had absolved me of any blame, yet it was obvious that my landing in 't Hesseler had triggered the German reprisals; so, indirectly and in all innocence, I had caused the tragedy.

The kindness and hospitality of the Boomkamps, Bovenmars, and Roetgerinks had gone far to dispel this feeling. On 4th May 1994, in my absence from 't Hesseler, Anne and Dirk became my willing representatives and laid a wreath on the Memorial on my behalf. In 1995, Bernard and Hendrik Boomkamp effectually eradicated my sensitivity to my past role: they announced that they wanted to come to Leeds "to see your house!"

This was a great occasion for Margaret and me. They arrived on 3rd March 1995, bringing with them as their interpreter Hans Wools, who was married to Bernard's daughter Josine and was a teacher of history in Borne and a fluent English speaker. I found them a small hotel near our house, where they were given a huge English breakfast and where they spent the evenings till past midnight playing a form of whist over glasses of whisky. I took them to see the glories of York, and out to the wilder, more remote parts of the Yorkshire dales and moors, where the sun was shining on the snow still lying on the top of Pen-y-ghent . Surprisingly, in spite of the relative flatness of the land around Borne, Bernard was no stranger to hilly country: he had already been to the Scottish Highlands in his pursuit of shooting game, but his lack of English meant he couldn't tell me about it. They came to dinner on their last evening and, through Hans, we were able to hear the full details of that awful week in November 1944 that culminated in the wanton shooting of their brother Jan, his neighbour Hendrik Roetgerink, and Piet van Dijk. Hearing these two kindly, down-to-earth Dutch countrymen answering my questions was as close to the truth as I was ever likely to get.

't Hesseler comes to Yorkshire 3rd-7th March 1995
JT, Bernard and Hendrik Boomkamp warm up in front of snow-capped Pen-y-ghent.

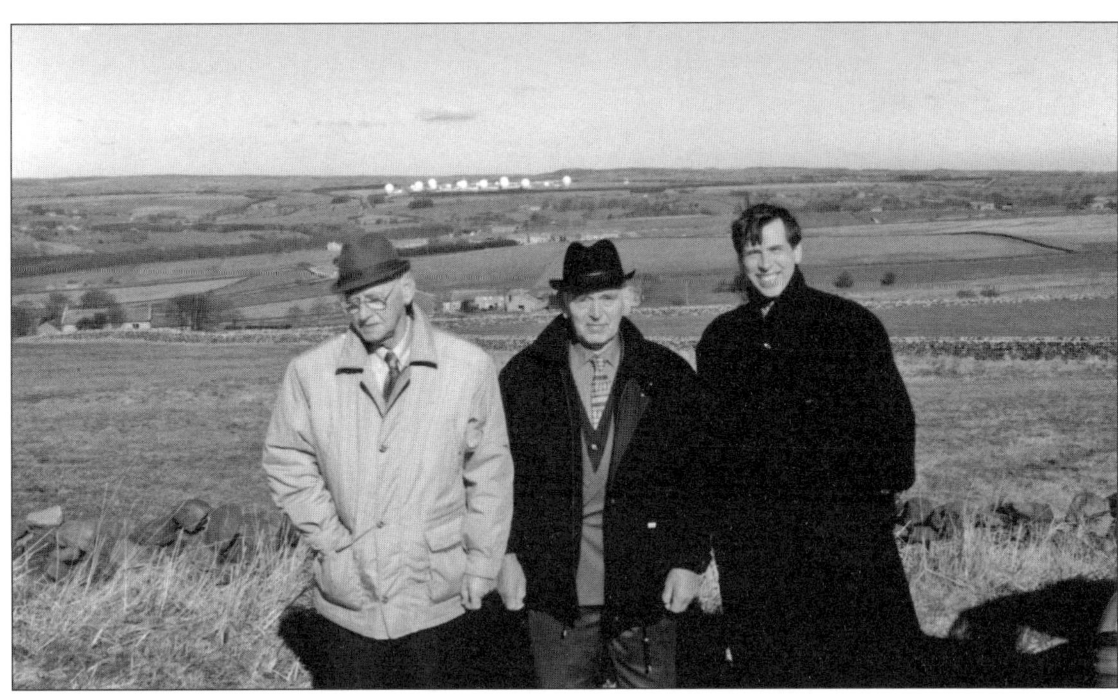

Hendrik and Bernard Boomkamp and Hans Wools with the 'golf-ball' dishes of the US listening-post at Menwith Hill behind them

Borne is the administrative centre of the district of Twente, an area of about 30 miles square in the province of Overijssel. It bulges into Germany, leading towards Osnabruck, Münster and the Ruhr, and lay more or less directly on the route of Bomber Command and US 8th Air Force aircraft attacking these industrial centres from their bases in Yorkshire and East Anglia. As a result, the Twente region saw hundreds of British, American and German aircraft fall out of the sky or crash-land on its soil. After D-Day, with the advance of Allied troops across France, Belgium and Holland, the area also became an arena for tactical bombers, fighter-bombers and fighters, with considerable losses being suffered by both sides – including myself. In fact, over 700 aircraft found their last resting-place in this small region of Holland.

Hennie Noordhuis, as a professional archivist, kept in close touch with several teams of aviation archaeologists busily engaged in locating, digging-up and identifying the remains of buried aircraft; this was especially important when they lay near towns or building-sites and were thought to be carrying unexploded bombs, rockets or cannon-shells.

Aware of all this activity, Hennie had long told me of his ambition to find my Spitfire. I thought that this was a very long shot, but I was able to give him a fairly good clue as to its likely whereabouts. A parachutist falls at about 1000ft per minute so, assuming I didn't pull the rip-cord immediately, I could assume that my descent took about 10 minutes. Now that I knew from the Met. Office the direction and strength of the wind on 19th November 1944 as being at an average speed (from 14,000ft to the ground) of about 35mph, I would have been blown about 6 miles in those 10 minutes. The wind-direction from 240° is approximately from the south-west; this meant that, if I drew a line from 't Hesseler towards the south-west for six miles, it would indicate a spot vertically underneath the point where I had baled out. Provided the aircraft fell vertically from that point – and there was no reason why it should have done so, but equally no reason why not – then the crash-site was possibly in the fields between one and two miles south-west of Delden.

Now, as a result of seeing the television programme on 25th November 1994, three men telephoned Hennie Noordhuis claiming to have seen or heard my machine falling out of the sky. One of them

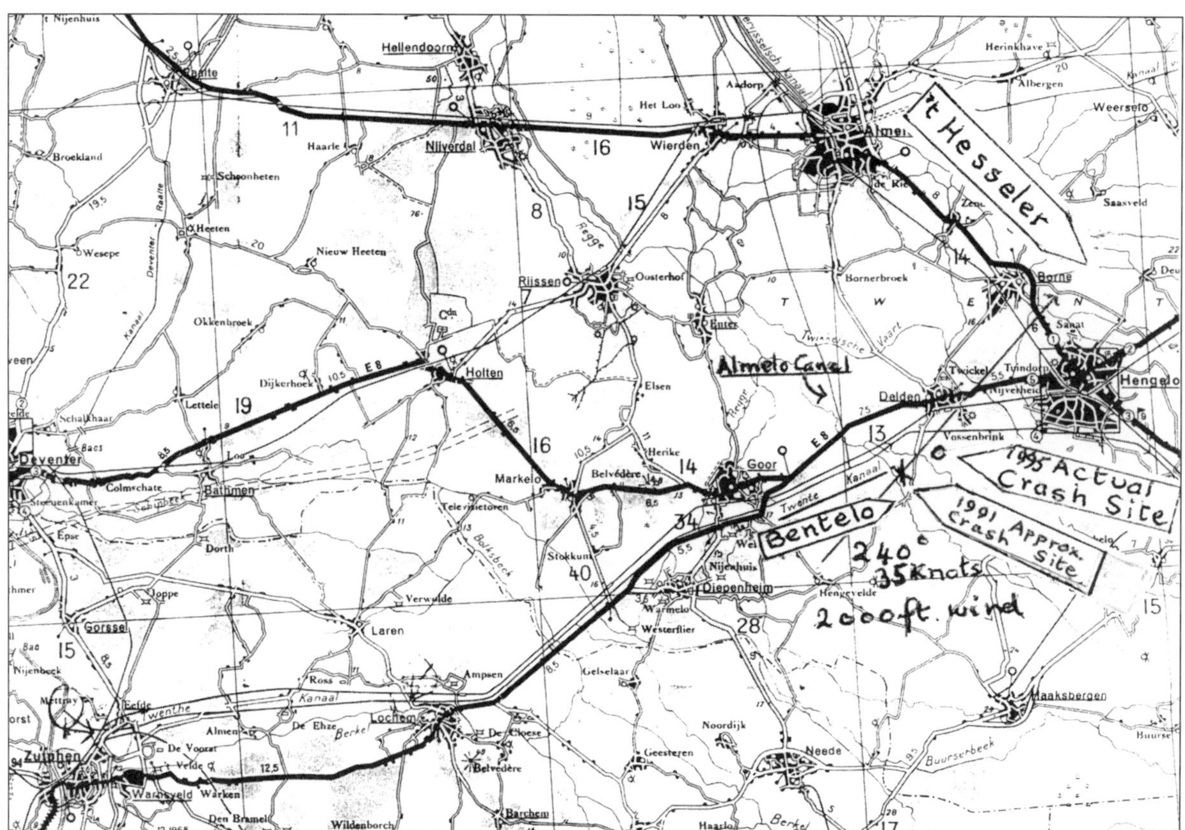

My sketch-map predicting where my Spitfire could have crashed.

claimed also to have seen me coming down in my parachute, while another said he had burned his fingers when he touched the hot metal of the wreckage.

The first witness was Joop Roetgerink – no relation of the 't Hesseler family – who telephoned Hennie on 10th January 1995 to say he was cycling past a church in Delden when he looked up and saw my parachute in the sky; he also saw my Spitfire coming down, but was too far away to see the actual crash. He told Hennie the rough area where he thought it had hit the ground, so Hennie went there with a team of metal-detectors, but failed to find anything. Personally, I doubt if his witness is credible: as I have described earlier, the aeroplane would have come down fast, even without the engine running, and would have hit the ground while I and my parachute were still at least 7,000ft up and invisible to the naked eye. As we have discovered from the eye-witnesses of my landing in 't Hesseler, people's imagination can lead them far astray, even to 'seeing' a non-existent white horse. Joop was a lovely, friendly man and, sadly, died of cancer a few years after this.

Joop Roetgerink points to where he saw my Spitfire coming down to earth in the sky above this church in Delden.

Later, on 20th February, Hennie telephoned me to say that two brothers, Marinus and Jan Timmerman, had come forward with further evidence. In 1944, their father was the owner of a restaurant, "De Rustende Jager" ("The Resting Hunter"), beside the road between Delden and the large village of Bentelo. They were teenagers who heard the noise of an aircraft screaming overhead and ran outside, to see it crash into the edge of one of their fields, about 200 yards from the restaurant. Marinus

The young Timmermans in 1946
l-r: Marinus (youngest, in RNLAF uniform), Betsie and Jan (on the right)
Photo: Betsie Timmerman

went up to the wreckage and burned his fingers when he touched the hot metal, but Jan was frightened the Germans would arrest them if they went near it. Their sister, Betsie, also heard the crash, but remained indoors. The Germans were soon on the scene and requisitioned a farm-cart to take away the remains of the fuselage, wings and tail, which lay close to the surface. A local farmer had carried off the wheels to make a trolley, but the Germans made him hand them over. They were not interested in digging down into the hole for more remains.

The brothers now took Hennie to the field and he quickly picked up a small piece of duralumin, about six inches square, with a patch of blue paint still on it. This was very exciting and suggested that the field really was the correct location.

Hennie then organised another team of metal-detectors, but they were unable to get any reaction from the field. He then appealed to the Dutch Air Force at the Twente Air Base and they eventually provided him with much more sophisticated equipment. With this they soon received a strong response but, when they dug down with a small excavator belonging to Hennie Egberink, a large-scale contractor in Borne, they found only the remains of metal fence-posts set in concrete.

"The Resting Hunter" restaurant on the road from Bentelo (r) to Delden (l)

They persevered, however, and late in March the detectors gave a good reading on the side of a ditch under a line of trees bordering the field. As soon as they started digging, they found grey, oily mud filled with bits of metal and other materials: fragments of duralumin 'skin' and aluminium castings; small, much-mangled parts of hydraulic and electrical fittings; pipes and wires of different shapes and sizes; strips of rubber; bits of items from the cockpit that had been flung forward by the impact; and – giving the biggest surprise to the excavators – pieces of shattered wood from the four-bladed propeller, raising doubts about the type of aeroplane they had dug up.

The crash-site in 1995 in the sandy patch on the bank under the trees

Excavation in progress, with a mound of oily sludge

Photo: Hennie Noordhuis

The propeller-hub with the big reduction-gearwheel emerging from the sludge of 51 years
Photo: Hennie Noordhuis

Hennie telephoned me again about this and I was able to tell him that most Spitfires carried Rotol propellers made of wood with a covering of composite material that gave them the appearance of metal. I was also able to reassure him that there were no guns, ammunition or bombs on the aircraft.

The excavators could not dig down into the bank of the ditch more than six feet before they reached the water-level of the ditch – they could not let the water flow into their hole; nor, for environmental health reasons, could they allow the oil to flow into the water of the ditch. Nevertheless, it was here, on 2nd April, that they found their prize exhibits: the propeller hub containing the four stubs of wood that were the roots of the propeller-blades with the massive cast-iron gear-wheel of the reduction-gear still attached to it, and the smaller gear-wheel, broken off from the engine-shaft, embedded nearby. These gear-wheels, with a ratio of .477:1, reduced the speed of the propeller to a little less than half that of the engine.

From these fragments, it seems clear that the machine hit the edge of the field in only a slightly nose-down attitude, but travelling very fast. The propeller, gear-wheels and front two cylinders of the Rolls-Royce Merlin engine broke off from the rest six feet down, while the impact shattered the whole of the aeroplane: as the heavy engine carried it into the earth, the wings and tail would have been torn off the fuselage and the cameras and the contents of the cockpit reduced to rubble.

There were enough clues, however, to inform any German investigators that this Spitfire was not a fighter: they would have found no guns or ammunition, no grey and green camouflage paint, and no unit markings on the fuselage, instead, they would have noticed the overall blue colour, the holes for camera lenses in the bottom of the fuselage and under the wings, and the single letter beside the fuselage roundel. These would have identified it as a photographic reconnaissance machine even if there was nothing left of the cameras, their lenses or the camera control-box.

Hennie Egberink took all the bits and pieces coated with oily sludge, however small, to his contractor's yard and washed off all the mud with high-pressure jets, then covered everything with a film of fine preservative. Because of the sludge, the pieces were in remarkably good condition. He laid out the bigger ones on planks on the ground, and left the smaller fragments in the old bath in which he had washed them. Hennie Egberink had done a wonderful job and was entitled to regard himself as the caretaker of the relics. Many visitors came to admire his handiwork and they were free to take away whatever took their fancy. The two Hennies had achieved something that was of great significance to me, but which I had never thought possible, and I was deeply grateful to them both.

Hennie Noordhuis triumphant over the main prize!

Photo: Hennie Noordhuis

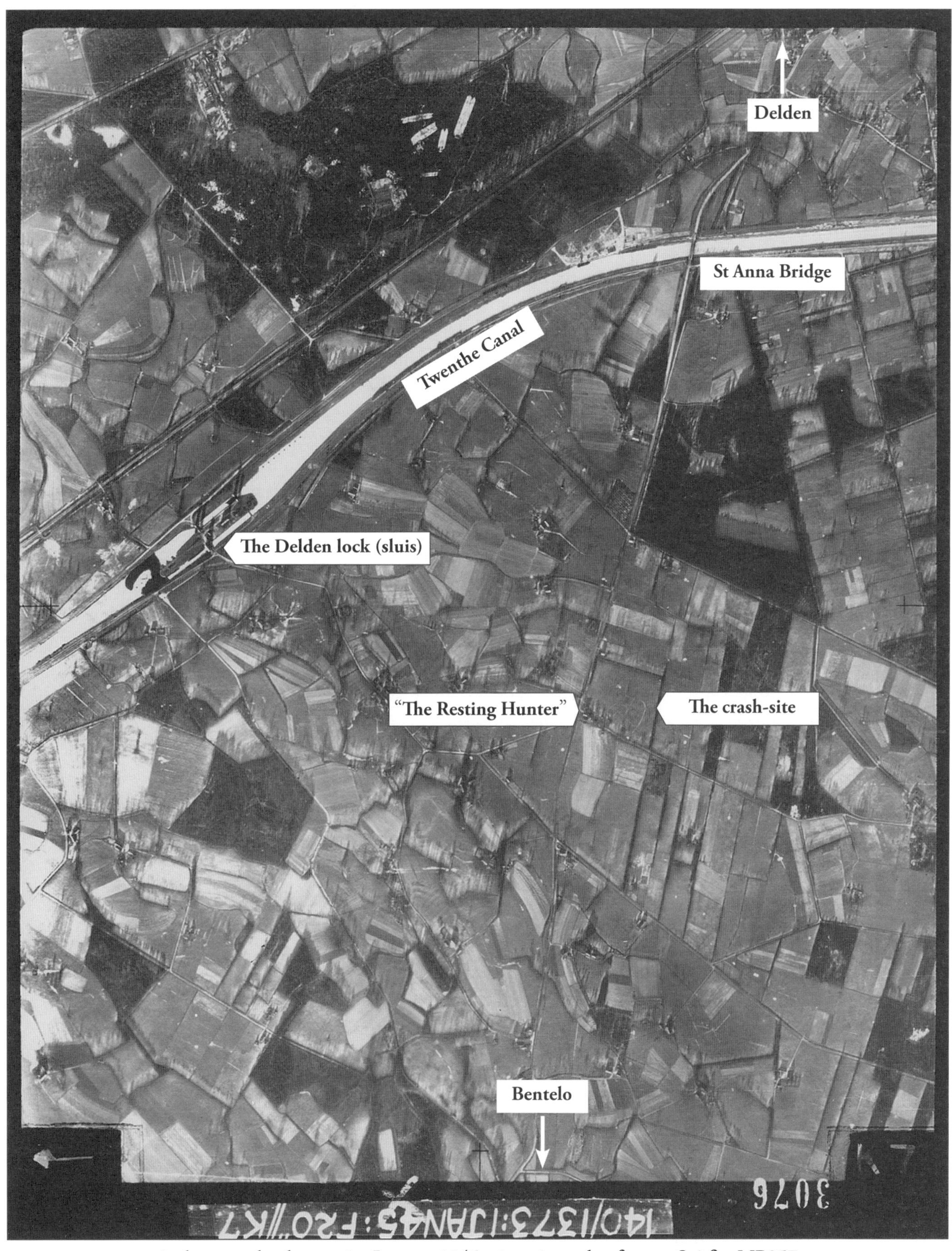

A photograph taken on 1st January 1945 – just six weeks after my Spitfire MB957 crashed into the Timmermans' field – by a Mosquito of 140 Squadron of 34 Wing engaged on an operational sortie, which happened by chance to include the crash-site.

Photo: DotKa, Holland

CHAPTER 23

Reunion with the Relics

4th May is the Day of Commemoration in Holland, followed on the 5th by the Day of National Liberation. 1995 proved to be a special year, as it was the 50th Anniversary of the Liberation, after five years of horrendous German Occupation, of the greater part of the country by the 2nd British and 1st Canadian Armies, aided of course by the Air Forces of all the Allies. Every town would have a particular date to remember and Borne was no exception, but the pattern of Liberation was by no means regular: the Twente Canal was a well-defended obstacle, so that Enschede was freed on 1st April, Twente airfield on the 2nd, Hengelo and Borne on 3rd, and Delden on 4th; whereas Goor, a few miles west of Delden on the north bank of the Canal, not until 8th. The Germans were finally driven out of Borne on 3rd April 1945 by battalions of the Dorset Regiment and the Canadian Grenadier Guards, Like every other town enjoying Liberation, Borne's citizens went wild with excitement and delight that their long agony was over. Now, in 1995, they were determined to celebrate the 50th Anniversary with the biggest festival they could afford, on a scale that would never be repeated, since those survivors who had shared in the suffering and participated in the victory would not be around for the 100th Anniversary.

Borne's Town Council set up a Liberation Committee 1945-1995, of which Hennie Noordhuis, as the principal archivist of the town, was a very prominent and energetic member. This Committee devised a full programme of social, cultural and military activities covering the period 30th April to 8th May. Several hundred veterans of the Dorsets and Canadian Grenadiers were invited, together with the crew of an American B-17 that had crash-landed near Bornerbroek in 1943, the Canadian pilot of an Auster spotter-plane who had been active in the locality, and myself. I protested to Hennie that I was not a Liberator – indeed, I had been liberated by the Russians – so I should have no place in these celebrations. But he countered that all Allied aircrews had contributed to the defeat of the Germans and therefore to the Liberation of the Occupied Countries, so I had every right to be included amongst the honoured guests.

In fact, I was involved more than most people, as I was invited to visit Primary Schools in and around Borne to talk about the war in the week before the beginning of the main events. I therefore arrived at Schiphol on 23rd April, to be met by Hennie and Joke and taken to the home where I was to be accommodated. All the veterans were being put up by the residents of Borne, with their interests matched, where possible, to their hosts'. In my case, Hennie had selected an ideal family for me, with whom I passed a delightful fortnight.

This was in an old restored farm-house, close to the centre of Borne, with a large garden and a small self-contained apartment, consisting of a bed-sitter and a kitchen, in a separate annexe on one side of the garden. This enabled me to join with the family or keep to myself according to my own inclination, but I spent most of my time with the family. The owner was Captain Tye Verf, RNLAF, a flight commander on 315 Squadron, flying F-16s at Twente Air Base. He was a tall, good-looking man, with an easy-going manner and perfect English – the language of the Dutch Air Force. His wife, Chantal, was a French-Canadian, with a warm, out-going personality and much involved with the local community, especially as she managed a factory employing seventy disabled people. They had two children: Trystan, a lively ten-year-old with a quick-silver mind, which sometimes spurred him on to actions that strained the patience of his teachers at school and his parents at home. I found him an exciting child, full of curiosity and very quick on the uptake, with whom I had an excellent relationship – but I was in the privileged position of being a newcomer who enjoyed exchanging ideas with him. His sister was Justine, a pretty little five-year-old, just breaking through the reading-barrier, and having to put up with alternate petting and teasing by her volatile brother. To help look after them was Cathleen, an attractive au pair girl coming, rather surprisingly, from South Africa.

My generous hosts: the Verf family
l-r: Tye JT Justine Chantal Trystan

The Verfs were the soul of hospitality, fed me wonderfully, and catered to my every whim. This meant that the busy programme Hennie had arranged for me became even fuller, as various other opportunities arose which they were willing to satisfy. The weather also made its own contribution: contrary to expectations, Borne was warm, sunny and dry throughout the fourteen days I was there, a great blessing for the organisers, participants and spectators of the commemorative events.

Without allowing me even to unpack, Hennie whisked me off to attend to the first priority of my visit: to see the crash-site and the collected remains of my Spitfire, so astonishingly located and retrieved more than fifty years after I had turned the burning machine upside down and dropped out of it – with no idea of the consequences except that I hoped it would save my life.

We drove about two miles to Hennie Egberink's contractor's yard, which was full of large trucks and earth-moving equipment. Hennie himself was a member of the Liberation Committee and came out to welcome us. There, on a few planks on the ground, was a large mass of identifiable metal while, in an old bath, were innumerable unrecognisable scraps of all the different kinds of materials that made-up the once-familiar shape of a photo-reconnaissance Spitfire.

In Hennie Egberink's yard in April 1995
l-r: Hennie Egberink Joop Roetgerink Hennie Noordhuis Joop de Melker Worms

This was my Spitfire – thanks to the two Hennies.

I didn't feel any strong emotion at the sight. Bomber crews and fighter pilots usually had their own or a favourite aircraft, to which they became almost superstitiously attached. On 16 Squadron, however, when we reached the top of the 'ops. ladder', we took the machine that had already been prepared with the appropriate cameras and lenses for that particular sortie; in fact, I rarely flew the same aeroplane twice. So, although I loved flying Spitfires, I had no emotional feelings for any one aircraft – and certainly not for this one, which had let me down and caused such a disaster on the ground near Borne.

Now I was looking at a scatter of debris that in no way resembled the machine I had jumped out of, but I couldn't really blame it fully, as I had an uncomfortable nagging feeling that I might have contributed to the engine failure by not handling it properly in flight. I was always very economically-minded, and cruised at the lowest efficient engine settings in order to conserve fuel in case I met with an emergency situation. There was always a risk, though, that low throttle settings and low rpm could cause leading-up of the sparking-plugs, with consequent engine-failure – but I never paid much attention to this possibility. Seeing the wreckage now brought back this notion and with it the doubt: was I the cause of my own downfall?

So I looked through the remains quite dispassionately and thought, first, of trying to find something which had a human connection, such as a warning or instruction plate; then, an item which identified the wreckage as belonging to a photographic machine, such as a scrap of metal with blue paint on it; and, thirdly, a part that might offer evidence of the cause of the engine-failure, such as a fire-blackened piece of metal. I found samples of all three types: a piece of plastic with part of a notice of how to lower the undercarriage in an emergency; half-a-dozen scraps of twisted duralumin 'skin', with patches of grey-blue paint visible in the folds; and a variety of small shattered chunks of cast aluminium, one with a bent valve and valve-spring still attached, most with at least one face blackened either by the regular cylinder firing or by the fire. All these relatively significant bits I put into a plastic bag.

The thermostat for the two under-wing radiators originally thought to be the constant-speed unit for the propeller

The propeller-hub, showing the roots of the wooden blades and the lesser gear wheel on the right

There were masses of longer pieces which had no value for me: electric wiring, high-tension cables, hydraulic piping, coolant tubing, strip-rubber sealing, bent and twisted control-rods, and all kinds of other scraps whose function I couldn't even guess at. However, I kept a few slivers of wood which obviously came from the propeller, the top of a pump, the knurled brass cap of some filler-tank, and a broken-toothed cog-wheel from one of the instruments. The most complete and recognisable small object was a six-inch-long cylindrical metal casing with a brass spring-loaded mechanism inside it; it looked to me like the constant-speed unit that controlled the pitch of the propeller-blades. I was reluctant to take this away, but I decided to do so to prevent anyone else removing it as a souvenir.

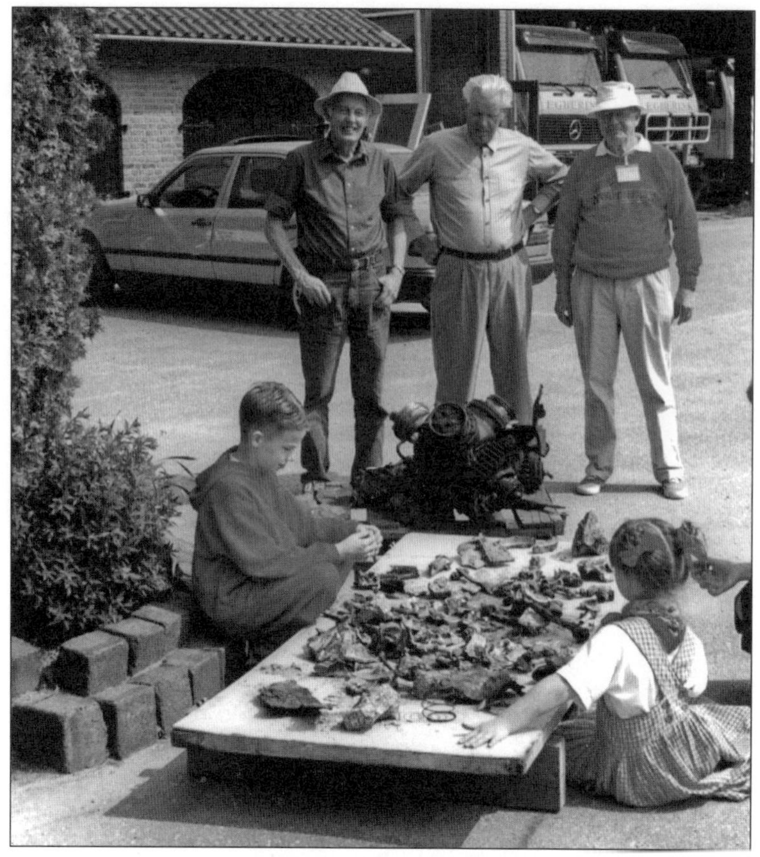

A prize for Young and Old
JT, Hennie Egberink and Alan Blyth (Canada) take pleasure in watching Trystan and Justine pick over the bits.

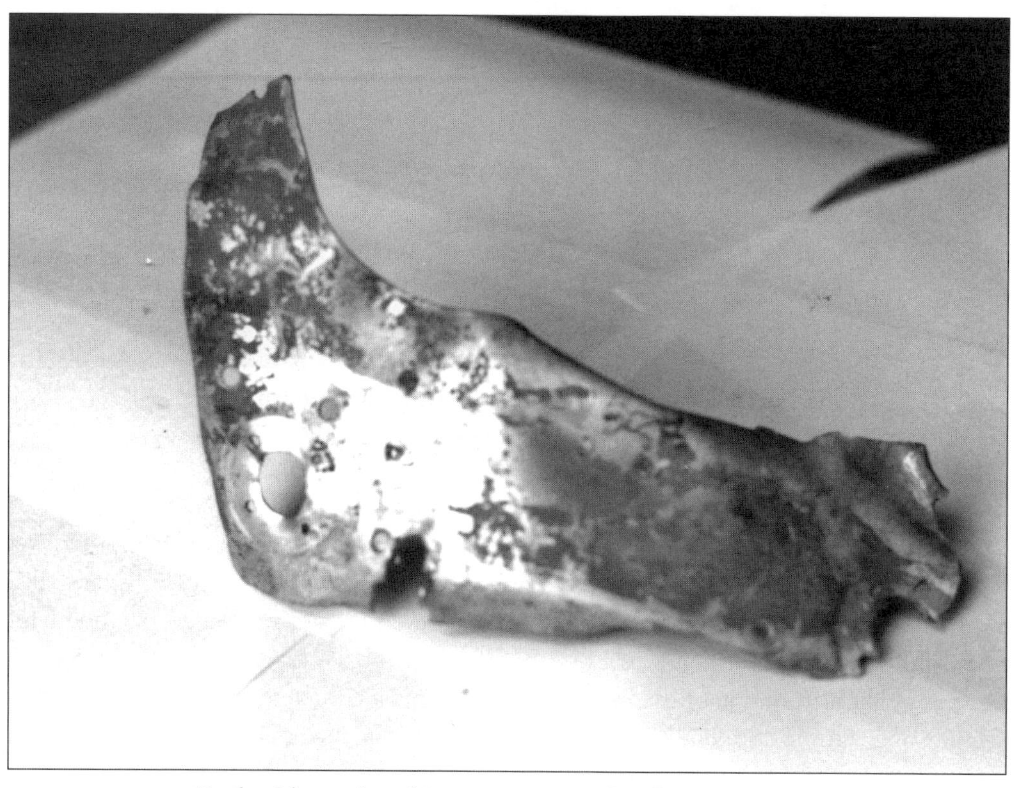

Real evidence that this is, or was, my Spitfire XI MB957: a piece of duralumin 'skin' with blue paint still adhering.

The prize exhibits definitely were the propeller-hub with the broken-off stumps of the wooden blades, and the two massive reduction gear-wheels, now cleaned of all the oily mud in which they had been embedded. I had not seen these before – I had never examined a stripped-down Merlin engine during my training or in a hangar – and was amazed at their size and weight.

The question, of course, arose as to what was to be done with these relics. I was quite clear in my own mind that they belonged, not to me or to anyone in Britain, but to the community in whose fate in 1944 they had played a part. This meant that, after they had finished being displayed in Hennie Egberink's yard, they should join my helmet and goggles in the Twente Air Base Museum. The propeller-hub and gear-wheels would make interesting exhibits, while all the other fragments could be collected in bags and stored in the Museum, available for anyone who wished to do research on such relics. The two Hennies agreed with this and carried it out later in the year.

A few days later, I showed what I assumed to be the constant-speed unit to Tye and a fellow-pilot, Captain Monk, sitting in the Verfs' garden. They were both in their 30s, had both flown operationally over Bosnia, and were both aware that, because of their age, their time as fighter-pilots was coming to an end. They were therefore intent on leaving the RNLAF and were preparing to take very demanding examinations in order to be accepted by KLM to fly airliners. *"Ah, yes,"* said Tye, *"I'm just studying piston-engines: this is definitely the constant-speed unit."* Captain Monk voiced his agreement. On 4th May, in the afternoon, Chantal took Trystan and me to the Twente Air Base Museum, where I presented this identified relic to the curator, Sergeant Hennie Oude Hilbert. Trystan had a field-day racing round all the exhibits, after which Hennie opened the hall next door and allowed him to sit in the cockpits of the E-104 Starfighter and the Gloster Meteor – Trystan was in his seventh heaven! On my return to Britain, flight-mechanics at Duxford Airfield identified this so-called constant-speed unit as the thermostat that operated the two under-wing radiators on my Spitfire! I can't recall whether I let Tye know of this professional verdict – but he passed his exams without this knowledge: KLM doesn't fly piston-engined airliners.

Recognisable fragments: an inlet valve complete with its spring and a broken-off exhaust valve

The 'big-end' of a piston-rod (top right) with its lining 'shells' (bottom) and a 'little end' (l)

On 23rd April, the day of my first visit to Egberink's yard, Hennie Noordhuis had made appointments for me at the crash-site, so we had to move on, but I vowed to return as often as possible. In fact, I returned three more times, including once with Tye Verf and, another time, with Chantal, Trystan, Justine and Cathleen, when Chantal presented me with a sparking-plug she had found among the debris in the bath.

I had by now come to realise that I should retrieve any part of the engine that might indicate the cause of its breakdown. Thus, on my four visits to the yard, I picked out several pieces of 'skin' with blackened or heat-crinkled paintwork, an inlet and an exhaust valve, a tappet, a camshaft bearing, two sets of main-bearing 'shells', and bits of cylinder-block, cylinder-walls, and the sump. The most emotive piece was a fragment of the camshaft cover with 'CE' moulded into it – the ending of 'ROLLS-ROYCE', which would have been imprinted along both sides of the cover. I hoped it might be possible, on my return to England, to subject these bits to metallurgical analysis.

For all these relics I was totally indebted to the two Hennies: Noordhuis for pursuing and finally realising his dream of finding the remains of my aircraft and reuniting me with them; and Egberink for volunteering his professional skills and equipment for use in excavating, retrieving, transporting, cleaning and displaying every single item, from the massive propeller-hub and gear-wheels to the smallest clip or piece of 'skin'. I had brought a few presents with me, but they were mere tokens when set against the scale of their achievements: a brass scale-model Spitfire XI for Noordhuis, and a colour print of Frank Wootton's wondrous painting of a Spitfire XI circling at 30,000ft over a coast-line for Egberink. They deserved much more.

Hennie Noordhuis now drove me through the outskirts of Delden, only two or three miles from Borne, and over the Twente Canal by a bridge that was a replacement for the wartime one, blown-up by the retreating Germans in April 1945. This was probably the one under which I had sheltered when I tried to swim across the canal in the night of 20th November 1944. A mile or so further along the road to the village of Bentelo, between green fields and copses of small trees, we turned off the road and followed a lane for about a hundred yards, and stopped by a grassy meadow. Hennie pointed to two earthy patches on the edge of the field under a line of trees: the nearer patch was the site of their first, unsuccessful excavation; the further one was where they had discovered the remains of my Spitfire XI.

Men of the Moment
l-r: Joop Roetgerink Hennie Egberink Jan Timmerman Hennie Noordhuis Marinus Timmerman

Hans Bellert and Hans Meyer (of TV Oost) Hennie Noordhuis Jan Timmerman Joop Roetgerink

As we stood by the side of the lane, looking and talking at a distance from the patches, more cars arrived until quite a crowd of people had collected: Marinus and Jan Timmerman, who had run out of the "The Resting Hunter" restaurant in 1944 and seen the Spitfire crash; Joop Roetgerink, who claimed to have seen both the aircraft and my parachute descending; Hennie Egberink, the excavator; Joop de Melker Worms, Hennie's chief assistant in the Town Hall; René Schabos, a journalist from the "Twentsche Courant", a local newspaper, with a photographer; several wives and various children – too many people for me to identify on my first day in Twente, but they were all very friendly.

We trooped over the meadow to the further patch of earth, where the hole had been filled in by the excavators rather hurriedly, as there were fears of pollution from the oily sludge. The patch was quite large and passed under a loose barbed-wire fence that ran along the top of the bank under the trees; the earth then sloped steeply down to a ditch filled with rust-coloured water. Fear of the water entering the hole prevented the excavators digging down more than six feet, so there might still be some further pieces of wreckage lower down.

I had trimmed the Spitfire to glide before I turned it upside-down to fall out of the cockpit: there was no knowing, therefore, what attitude it might have adopted in its subsequent descent. But it appeared to have hit the ground fairly flat at high speed: the trees probably knocked off the wings at the same time as the wings knocked down some of the trees; the ones we saw now were of later growth. After the Germans had removed the surface remains, the earth was filled-in, the grass returned, and the meadow reverted to its role of a horse and cattle pasture for the next fifty-one years. Hennie was fortunate to have found the scrap of duralumin lying in the grass that provided the definite evidence of this being the crash-site.

The photographer now took control and posed us in various groups and situations; meanwhile, the children scoured around the undergrowth and came up with further scraps of the Spitfire. Everyone spoke English, so there was no problem of discussing the events of fifty years ago with these eye-witnesses, who had clear memories of the event and were as interested in meeting the pilot as I was in questioning them; we quickly established a warm relationship.

Marinus Timmerman had been a serving airman: he had joined the Dutch Air Force in 1946 and been sent to England to learn the trade of instrument technician at RAF Langham in Norfolk. He worked on the Spitfires of the Dutch 322 Squadron at Twente Air Base from late 1946 to 1947, so he might well have come to know PL965, the former 16 Squadron Spitfire XI that was sold to the Dutch on 10th July 1947 and spent until 22nd at Twente before moving, with five other ex-RAF Spitfires, to Deelen Technical School as instructional airframes. We shall meet it again in this story. Marinus was due to go out to Indonesia at the end of 1947 to fight the 'rebels', but was found to have 'sweaty feet' and was medically discharged!

Having seen all that was visible at the crash-site, we repaired to "The Resting Hunter", just 200 yards away, for a cup of coffee. The restaurant was now managed by Henk Timmerman, the son of the eldest of the four Timmerman brothers, who had died some years before. Henk was out but, while we were waiting for our coffee, I was interviewed at some length by René Schabos, who wrote a very sound article for his newspaper. This contrasted well with a report in another journal, written by a reporter whom I did not meet, which was full of inaccuracies, as it was based on Hennie Noordhuis's original speculative account in the 1990 first edition of his book, long before he found me. On the way back, Joop Roetgerink stopped to show me where he was standing with his bicycle near a church in Delden when, he claimed, he saw both my plane and my parachute coming down. I'm afraid this still strains my credibility.

I didn't sleep much that night: my head was alive with memories of 19th November 1944 and its aftermath: my engine-failure, my poorly-executed bale-out and landing, my somewhat erratic journey to the Rhine over five days, my bitter frustration at being taken prisoner, the tragedy of the unfortunate Jan Vonk and the three hostages caught up in the Germans' brutal and senseless reprisals, now seeing the remains of my Spitfire, and meeting the people who had witnessed its crash – all this left little room for sleep.

The following afternoon, Hennie and I returned to the crash-site, where Hans Bellert and Hans Meyer from TV Oost (East) were waiting with Marinus Timmerman, Joop Roetgerink and Hennie

Henk Timmerman makes me a present of my Spitfire's hole in his field.

Egberink to film a re-enactment of yesterday's meeting. Afterwards, I met Henk Timmerman when he opened the restaurant to give us coffee. He was a delightful person, with twinkling eyes and a laughing mouth. He said he wanted to commemorate the crash in some way – and then declared that the hole in his field was mine to keep!

We moved from there to Egberink's yard for more filming, and then to the landing-place in 't Hesseler, where I was dismayed to find that Jan Boomkamp had extended the Garden Centre to cover the whole field. It did not seem at all appropriate to be interviewed again amongst displays of flowers, shrubs and garden ornaments. We found a secluded corner, but it was not the same. That evening, at the Verfs, I saw myself on television – in several hours' exposure to the camera reduced to a brief two-minute news item – and was distinctly unimpressed: my face had a cobweb of lines that I had never seen in the mirror – maybe, the shape of things to come. I join Max Beerbohm in complaining (long before television): "Few people look like themselves!"

The next time I visited the crash-site was with Tye Verf who, as a present-day fighter pilot, could look on everything with a professional eye. We walked over the site with Henk Timmerman and unearthed a scrap of metal for Tye. We then drove to Egberink's yard, where Tye was able to identify several pieces, in particular a very corroded exhaust-valve, which I thought might hold some significance for the engine-failure.

At the yard we met Alan Blyth, a Canadian computer consultant who was staying with the Egberinks as their house-guest, together with his son. In 1945, Alan was an observer in a 'Bird-dog', an Auster-type spotter plane, flying low over the front-line to pick out targets for the guns of the Canadian 52nd Regiment of Artillery – German tanks, guns, infantry, fuel-dumps, etc, – and then radioing where their shells were falling until the targets were wiped out. This was a dangerous game for the crew of the spotter plane – equivalent to the work of the 'line squadrons' on the Western Front in WW1; they operated from any convenient field and did their own maintenance of the aircraft. They moved forward so continually with the artillery that Alan had only a slight memory of flying over the Delden-Borne area in April 1945, but he remembered using a field quite close to Hennie Egberink's yard.

My final visit to the crash-site and yard was on my last full day in Borne, when Chantal drove me there with the children and Cathleen. Trystan and Jasmine were thrilled to be allowed to take whatever caught their eye and, in the yard, they became so dirty that we had to ask Mrs Egberink to allow them into her house to get clean! At the crash-site, their sharp eyes spotted bits that everyone else had missed.

At "The Resting Hunter", Henk Timmerman's charming wife Ans introduced herself and her teenage daughter Frederika, and then provided tea for us in their extensive garden. Here we were joined by Jan Timmerman and his sister Betsie and by Harry, the head chef of the restaurant. Betsie had also been inside on the 19th November 1944 and had heard the sound of the crash, but she did not go out to see the wreckage for fear the Germans would arrest her. Later, she sent me a detailed plan of the area of Bentelo, where the restaurant and the field are located, because the village is so unremarkable that it does not feature on smaller-scale maps. She accompanied it with a photograph of herself with her four brothers – Marinus in RNLAF uniform – taken in 1946. These are members of yet another Dutch family with whom I have formed close links as the result of my Spitfire falling out of the sky by chance into their field.

CHAPTER 24

Schoolchildren and a Sovereign

Holland has the misfortune to be a close neighbour of Germany, and the district of Twente lies next to the border, straddling the main highway that runs from the Ruhr to Amsterdam in the west and to Brussels in the south-west. It was therefore among the first to feel the cruel weight of German Occupation in May 1940, and was one of the last areas to be liberated five years later. We in Britain, having suffered no lasting invasion since 1066, have little idea of what it was like for the people of Occupied Europe to live virtually as slave states, especially when the occupier was infused with the fanatical Nazi creed of racial superiority, including the extermination of the Jews, and their entire economies – their industry, agriculture, transportation, and manpower – were devoted to the maintenance of the German war-machine. Hitler's maniacal dream, that the single country of Germany could hold down and control almost the whole of Europe, from the Arctic Circle to the Pyrenees, and much of Russia from the Baltic to the Caspian Sea, could be realised only by one means – the use of terror, re-enacting every day in every corner of this subject empire the kind of atrocity that the villagers of 't Hesseler experienced on 25th November 1944.

The Dutch, of course, cannot forget the Occupation although, for the sake of peace and trade and harmonious relations with the remorseful next generations of their powerful neighbour, they keep the awful suffering of their war years to the back of their minds. On an occasion such as the 50th Anniversary of their Liberation, however, they let their memories flood out and they wanted their children and grandchildren, especially, to know what had happened and why, and to learn what kind of relationships are needed between the countries of Europe to avoid a similar catastrophe in the future.

I was not therefore surprised, although I was very flattered, to receive a letter in January 1995 from Maarten Haalboom, a leading teacher in Borne, written no doubt in collusion with Hennie Noordhuis, inviting me to participate in a project on "Freedom", which would involve all the Primary Schools in Borne and lead into the week of the 50th Anniversary celebrations. He asked me to visit the schools to talk about my war experiences to the children and answer the questions which they would have prepared for me after being given an outline of my story. All this would be in English, and teachers would be on hand to interpret, if necessary.

This was an unusual and intriguing invitation, which I was delighted to accept. I had a particular interest in doing so as, for nine years from 1968-1976, I had run a three-week Summer School in Bristol for up to a hundred Dutch Teachers of English in Secondary Schools; this was arranged by the British Council and the Dutch Ministry of Education and gave me some understanding of the Dutch educational system, which differs markedly from our own, yet produces, from my short experience of it, very well-rounded children.

They start English in Primary School, but I didn't expect that they could follow a talk by an Englishman about the war; so I had about twenty slides and OHP transparencies made from my wartime photo album, and brought with me a plastic model Spitfire XI, painted blue with an electric-powered propeller, and some relics of my aircraft that could be handed round the class. I also had colour photo-copies made of Frank Wootton's evocative painting of a Spitfire XI leaving a contrail as it circles at 30,000ft in an azure sky, as a souvenir of my visit for each school.

Thus equipped – and, as it turned out, too well equipped – I was driven by Hennie Noordhuis, at 8.45am on a Monday morning, to the first school, de Hooiberg Primary, which happened to be where his wife, Joke, was a music teacher. Here were two classes, of 10- and 11-year-olds, sitting in a semi-circle, with the headteacher and several of the staff. Each class had prepared a list of questions in English but, by the time I had told my story with all my visual aids, there were only a few minutes left for them – and some brave children were already putting up their hands to ask more immediate questions. So, in this connection, my talk did not fulfil all the expectations, but I was very impressed with the children's degree of understanding: only once or twice did the teachers have to interpret my words for them. They were very attentive and responsive and showed a good sense of humour – in English. In return for their Frank Wootton picture, they gave me a bag of Dutch bon-bons.

The next school was Molenkamp Primary, where Maarten Haalboom himself was the teacher of a slightly older class. Waiting here, in addition to the children, were a group of student-teachers and the film-crew from TV Oost. Maarten was concerned that the theme of "Freedom" should be adequately addressed, so the children read out their views and we discussed them, in English, before I was asked to give my talk. One boy, especially, came forward to show me his plaster sculpture, which he explained to me in good English symbolised "Freedom"; there were also drawings and press-cuttings about the war pinned up on a large screen. The TV people had a field-day, and I received a fine bouquet of flowers in return for my Spitfire picture.

Next day, I visited Stella Maris, a Roman Catholic school, equivalent to a Secondary Modern in England. Here I spoke to two classes together of 11-year-olds, three of 12-year-olds, and three of 15-year-olds. In one class was the daughter of Hans Wools, who had come to Leeds with the two Boomkamp brothers in February; in another was a junior member of the Boomkamp family; and, during a break, my young friend Dirk Boomkamp, who in 1991 had pointed-out the tree which my parachute had blown into in 1944, came up and introduced himself, already grown up unrecognisably since that first meeting. The school presented me with a substantial Travel Diary, which has proved invaluable to me for recording my visits from then on, with every space now filled, both backwards as well as forwards and even upside-down.

Molemkamp Primary School: Maarten Haalboom (centre) JT

The boy with his sculpture representing 'Freedom'

I received a pleasant surprise here: the teacher in charge of the third group of pupils happened to mention that he had visited a Comprehensive school in England in 1973; when he added that it was near Bristol, I realised that he had been one of the 80 Dutch teachers on my Summer School that year. He was Hans Eppink, but we hadn't recognised each other from those rather distant days. Later, outside a telephone kiosk in Borne, I was able indirectly to assess his teaching skills when I chided two girls for gossiping in the kiosk while I waited outside. One of them spoke delightful English, the other daren't open her mouth – the first one turned out to have been in one of Hans Eppink's classes at Stella Maris. Whether the Bristol Summer School can claim any responsibility for this achievement remains an open question.

On Wednesday morning, it was the turn of De Rank Primary School, where the class was joined by another that had walked over from the nearby Casimir Primary. After my talk, the De Rank teacher gave me a school-child's haversack in return for my Spitfire picture. The Casimir teacher thereupon asked for one for his school, a request I couldn't refuse although it depleted my stock. The next school was Flora Primary, where I found two classes of very lively and appreciative children, who were reluctant to let me go and escorted me to the school gates. As a result, I was late for my last visit: to two schools on one campus – Regenboog and Temenschelf. Here, over a hundred children were patiently waiting in one room, and they were disappointed when there was not enough time for all their questions to be answered.

These two schools took my last Spitfire pictures and I was faced with the problem of getting more made in Borne and finding suitable card mounts. After much searching, I discovered an art-shop and discussed my difficulties with the owner. When he saw the Spitfire picture, he exclaimed, "*You must be Jimmy Taylor!*" It turned out that his son was in one of the classes that I had addressed. He offered to get more copies made in the bigger town of Hengelo and to cut the mounts himself. This was a great relief but, although I gave him one of the pictures, he still charged me four times as much as the original mounts had cost in Leeds!

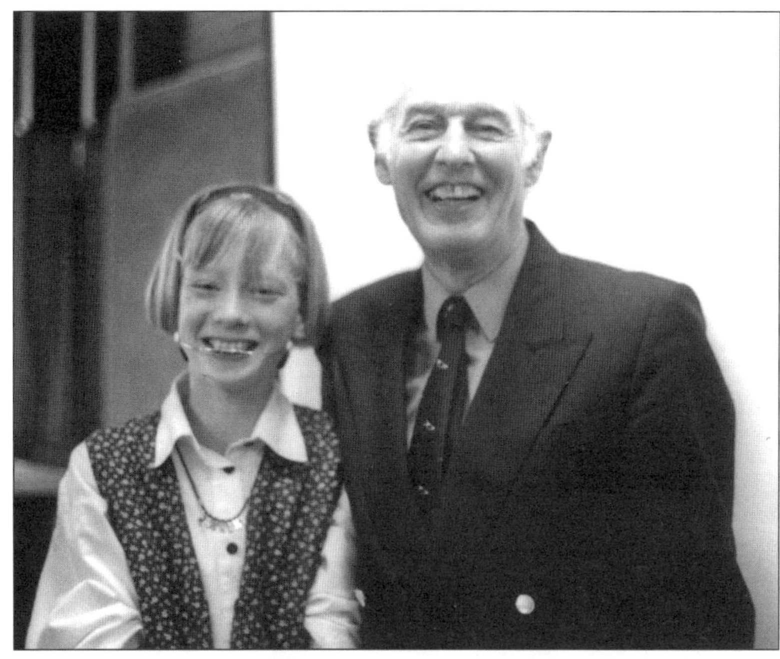

With Janneke Bruggink, granddaughter of the man who had picked up my helmet on 19th November 1944

Thursday started with a talk at Wheele Primary, followed by another at Olthof Primary, where two classes were joined by a third from Jan Ligthart School. Here at Olthof[1] they had set up their own exhibition of WW2 memorabilia, including some pieces from my aircraft contributed by Hennie Noordhuis. I was a little dismayed when one of the audience, after my talk, announced herself as a parent and a journalist on "Bornse Courant" and "Dagblad Tubantia" – she was not particularly friendly, but I never learned whether she wrote anything about my talk. One of the pupils also came up and introduced herself as Janneke Bruggink, the grand-daughter of the man who had picked up my flying-helmet at 't Hesseler in 1944 and wore it on his motor-cycle for forty years. His son Herman, this girl's father, had given it back to me in 1991. Later, I was to meet the mother, and then all the family in their home.

For lunch, I grabbed a quick sandwich at the Verfs, after which Hans Beld, the handyman at the Town Hall, who had been acting as my pleasant and efficient chauffeur, fetched me for my last school-visits, this time outside Borne itself. The first one was to St Stephanus Primary School in Bornerbroek where I had only one class to face, which felt quite small compared with most of the others. Even so, I misjudged the time again and arrived late at my last stop. This was another St Stephanus, this time at Zenderen, where the class had been joined by another from the neighbouring Aegidius Primary. In addition to the two headteachers and two teachers, there was also in the audience a member of the local Liberation Committee. We had a lively session, after which each headmaster presented me with a bottle of red wine and a card signed by all his pupils.

Friday took the "Freedom" theme a stage further, when Lukas Groen arrived from Rotterdam to involve the children in his composition "Pro Borne" and to explain his motivation in writing it. Hennie Noordhuis, who with his family is very musical, had originally suggested that a youth orchestra should play it, but this proved too complicated to arrange and a pianist, Jeroen Liedorp, had come with Lukas instead. All the schools had been invited to send classes to the Music Centre in Borne but, in the end, only three managed to do so; they attended in two separate sessions.

Maarten Haalboom presided over each of these; he began by interviewing Lukas and me, and asking how we had met and why Lukas had agreed to write a sonata. After leading the children to consider and discuss abstract music, he asked them to suggest a variety of emotions; after each one, Jeroen Liedorp expressed it in different bars on the piano. This opened the way for him to give a careful rendering of "Pro Borne", after which the children were invited to describe their reactions.

[1]See "Dutch Voices" p. 712 for a Press Report.

Jeroen Liedorp plays 'Pro Borne' to school-children while Lukas Groen sits on the left.

On both occasions the children were excellent: very attentive and willing to express their views – in Dutch, this time. Maarten's exposition, and his sensitivity both to the music and to the difficulties the children had in understanding it, were admirable; even I felt that I had reached a better appreciation of Lukas's composition! I presented Lukas with a bronze figurine of an airman; in return, he gave me a copy of his new orchestral composition, "Sacrifices for a Picture", and a tape-recording of it – yet another example of a clever Dutch title. I am still sorry, though, that we didn't experience a youth orchestra playing "Pro Borne".

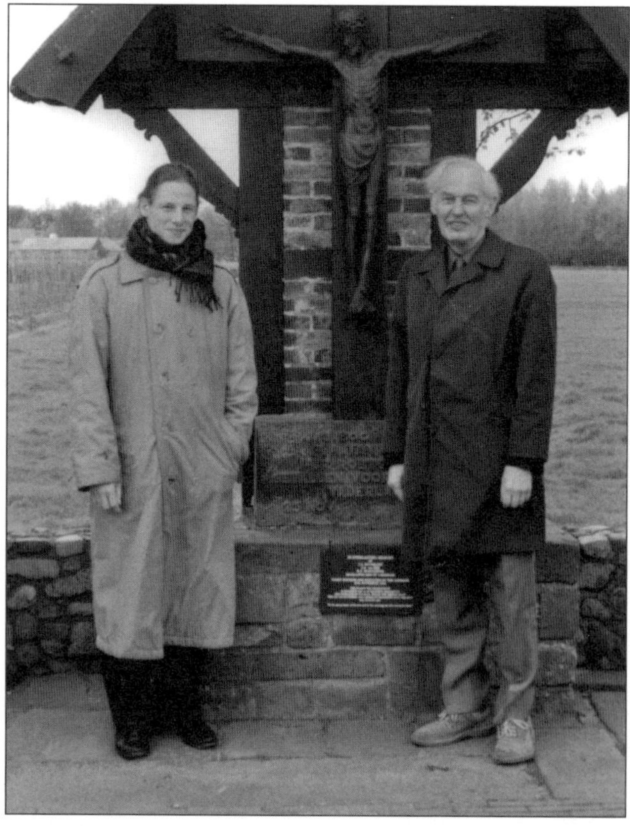

Lukas Groen and JT at the 't Hesseler Memorial

Hennie then took Lukas and me out to lunch in a Borne restaurant, where we were pleasantly surprised to find the journalist, René Schabos, at the next table. We introduced Lukas to him and he was soon subjecting Lukas to an interview which, if it later appeared in print, would have given Lukas's career as a budding composer and conductor a useful boost.

Before he took the train back to Rotterdam, I was keen that Lukas should visit 't Hesseler and the site of the landing, the executions, and the Memorial. First we visited Jan Vonk's memorial beside the Town Hall; then we

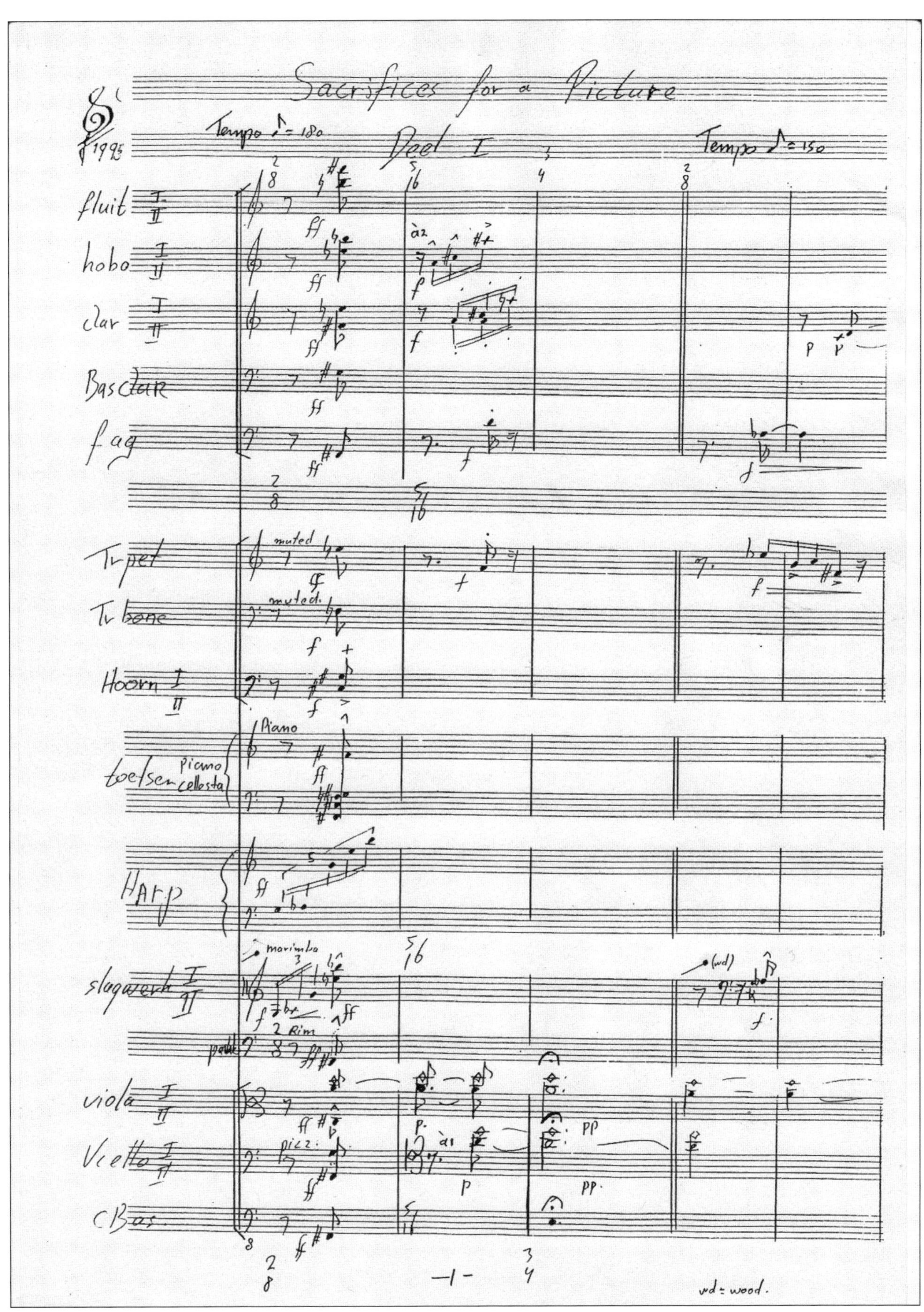

Extract from Lukas Groen's orchestral composition, 'Sacrifices for a Picture', his second cantata on the theme of my story

Farewell from Flora School

hailed a taxi but, when the lady-driver learned our destination, she looked at me and said, *"You're Jimmy Taylor!"* and refused to let us pay any fare; she also took a photograph of Lukas and me standing together at the Memorial. Such are the good people of Borne!

My final appearance on a platform took place that evening, when Hennie and I went to the Twickel Community Centre, which was actually the hall of a large Secondary school. About 40 adults and school-children were divided into groups to discuss "War and Freedom", but there was not much interaction between the young and old, and they preferred to listen to Hennie and me giving our versions of the 't Hesseler story. The evening ended with Bernadette Bruggink, Herman's wife, leading a short ceremony for Peace, then everyone received a long-stemmed yellow rose as they left for home.

I had greatly enjoyed these visits to schools, even though the time was usually too short and included the minutes it took Hans to drive me from one school to the next; I was especially impressed by the interest and friendliness of the children and their ability to communicate in English – a foreign language to them. As I have said earlier, Dutch children are brought up to value their freedom and to venerate those who died in giving it to them. The intention is not to encourage morbid sentiments, but to imbue them with the resolve to preserve that freedom at all costs. I don't know whether I contributed anything towards achieving this objective – I was more concerned to utilise my visual aids to the full; but afterwards I found myself being greeted continually in the streets of Borne by children who recognised me from my talks. *"Hello, Taylor!"*, they would call out in their friendly Dutch way as they cycled past, and twice I was stopped by a boy or girl and introduced to their parents, all with big smiles and kind words. The little town of Borne is the only place where this has happened to me – or is ever likely to happen.

In the warm evenings of this first week when work had finished, Hennie Noordhuis, ever-mindful of my interests, took me out to various places connected with the war. The first was to a small exhibition, which he had helped to arrange, in the village of Bornerbroek. Here was a lively display of military and civilian artefacts of all kinds, the most interesting for me being a child's dress made from the silk of a parachute – it might just possibly have been from mine!

The next evening, Hennie drove me to the nearby town of Enschede, which was the place where, long after the war I discovered from an entry in my POW diary, I had been incarcerated for ten days in a converted factory alongside about 40 Airborne troops, picked up after the debacle at Arnhem. Now

Bronze sculpture of a mother holding a dead baby.

Hennie showed me a variety of life-size bronze figures, standing in a spread-out group in a corner of a public park. They represented ordinary people suffering the horrors and traumas of the Second World War: a trio of gaunt displaced persons; a homeless mother and child; a soldier looking up fearfully into the sky; a forlorn bombed-out family group; a mother holding a dead baby; a proud figure standing alone, upright and defiant; and several more. Each was easily recognisable by its bold treatment and its pathos; their massive castings will still be standing there, warning the spectators of the barbarity of war, when the original people have long passed away. Public art can keep alive awareness not only of great achievements but also of great suffering.

It was about 10.0pm when we came back from this excursion; nevertheless Hennie made for the Town Museum in Borne, formerly the Jewish Rabbi's house, where two of the voluntary curators were waiting for me: Fred Bakker, an artist and gallery owner, and Jaap Grootenboer, a photographer and local historian. They showed me over the building, which held a fascinating exhibition of life under the German Occupation and during the Liberation. Upstairs, part of the floor had been removed to reveal a hideaway, the sort of concealed space where an Allied evader, or a Dutch absconder from deportation as a slave worker, or a local Jew escaping being rounded-up, could be given refuge until they were moved on to another 'safe house', or were betrayed to the Germans by an informer, or were given their freedom by the advancing Allies. At the top of the house was a different kind of exhibit: a series of rooms furnished in the post-war austerity style imposed by the scarcity of goods for the civilian market – very nostalgic for those who remembered those cheerless days, and a considerable surprise for the younger generation, to whom 'making do' or 'going without' something pleasant is inconceivable.

I stayed with Fred and Jaap till after midnight, drinking good Kruidenbitter and discussing the realities of life under the Germans and the events surrounding their departure from Borne. I was especially honoured by being asked to sign my name in the Visitors' Book on the page next to the signature of Queen Beatrix.

This was not the end of my connection with either Fred Bakker or Jaap Grootenboer. A few days later, I met Jaap by chance in the road outside his home; he invited me in to meet his partner, Ine, and have some coffee and cake. He showed me his photographic archive of wartime Borne, including the excavation of several aircraft that had crashed in the surrounding district – but not including mine. We then fell to discussing history in general, from which we moved into the history of art, about which Jaap was particularly knowledgeable – but he had never heard of Adriaen Hanneman.

Hennie's last invitation to me, before the arrival of the veterans from Britain and Canada and the start of the Commemoration programme on Sunday, 30th April, was to attend the final meeting of the Liberation Committee Borne 1945-1995 in the Town Hall. This was a special privilege: my presence was acknowledged and everyone was very friendly, making the effort to speak to me in English; I found it a little embarrassing that, after the introductions, I had difficulty remembering the names and roles of the twenty members either then or when I met them later at various events in the coming week. They had all worked together admirably as a team for the past year, organising the many activities on the programme that gave the veterans such an unforgettable time, while providing the residents of Borne, including the children, with numerous occasions to ponder the past and to celebrate the ultimate victory.

CHAPTER 25

Fun with F-16s

Tye Verf was a most interesting and satisfying host for me. I indicated to him one day that I would value a visit to his Squadron at the Air Base above most other pleasures, and he was kind enough to arrange this on 2nd May. Hennie Noordhuis agreed that going with Tye would be most rewarding for me, especially as it was he who had fixed up my staying with the Verfs, in the first place.

So, after an early start, Tye and I arrived at 315 Squadron's operational centre at the Twente Air Base, an airfield which had been well equipped by the Germans, but not used by them for active operations. I had, however, flown over and photographed it at least once in 1944, as it was one of the many German airfields that we kept under regular photographic survey, bringing back pictures that our photo-interpreters pored over with their stereoscopes, looking for any fresh developments. Some of the hangars and other buildings were still being used by the RNLAF.

Tye introduced me to some of the pilots, who all spoke excellent English. They were several years younger than their British counterparts whom I had met on 16 Squadron at Laarbruch and Lossiemouth. The Dutch policy was to take them straight from school and train them in two years. The RAF preferred to recruit graduates or to send intending aircrew to university, on the principle that these young men would be flying expensive aircraft with nuclear capability and would need to exercise mature judgement and be totally reliable, when they held such power literally at their finger-tips. The Dutch, however, told me that their young men had all the qualities – they were not given nuclear weapons – although it was becoming more difficult to get recruits of the same high calibre; clearly, men of Tye's age and experience were invaluable role-models for their more junior colleagues.

Thanks to Tye, I was allowed to attend the briefing for the Squadron before they set off for an operational training exercise. It was held in Dutch, but appeared remarkably similar to one I had joined at Lossiemouth the year before. One difference, though, was that at the end of it a quiz was held on aircraft recognition – an important subject when modern fighters might have only a split second to check on the identity of another aircraft: friend or foe. A more substantial difference – although it is not really fair to compare 16 Squadron's role of training Jaguar pilots with that of a fully operational Dutch F-16 squadron – lay in the physical environment: here, there were banks of computers and information retrieval systems, with several clerks keeping in touch with every other department on the Base and with those outside. These enabled constant updates to be made on the weather, the serviceability of the aircraft, the provision of suitable armament, liaison with other units such as for in-flight refuelling and electronic counter-measures, and information concerning the enemy, real or simulated, the disposition of his fighters and anti-aircraft

An F-16 taxies noisily past the crew-room of 315 Squadron.

Squadron pilots watch their friends returning.

missile batteries, and all the related matters that come under the heading of 'Intelligence'.

In 1944, we needed the same kind of information at our briefings, but it was all provided by word-of-mouth from the Army or RAF briefing officer, who might have learned it via the telephone or a despatch-rider, and the only display was the targets and German flak-batteries and airfields marked on a map in blue wax-pencil. We now know that Bletchley Park distributed, only to a hand-picked group of senior officers, top-secret information known as 'ULTRA', derived from the breaking of the German orders, reports and messages encoded through their 'Enigma' machine. But we had no inkling of this source at the time. What I saw at the Air Base was the application of modern media, electronic and digital, to the purveyance of Air Force intelligence.

Tye left me in a comfortable crew-room, with a coffee-bar and a choice of sitting inside or outside under the trees, right next to the perimeter-track. It was not long before a high-pitched whine could be heard from the left, heralding a procession of four F-16s taxying past at a fast pace, two pilots waving to their buddies around me, who were sipping their coffee and reading the newspapers in the sunshine. The noise became deafening and several of my neighbours put their fingers in their ears; a groundsman sweeping up leaves nearby wore ear-mufflers all the time. The F-16s were grey, sleek and purposeful – the design did not look 25 years old.

A few minutes later, they took off in pairs and we could see them rising above the line of fir trees that separated the operations building from the main runways. Soon afterwards, more whistling, turning to whining and then to shrieking, announced the arrival and passing of a second flight of F-16s. More waves from the cockpits – perhaps at me, standing up with my camera focussed on them – as they taxied past and, minutes later, they too were climbing into the sky.

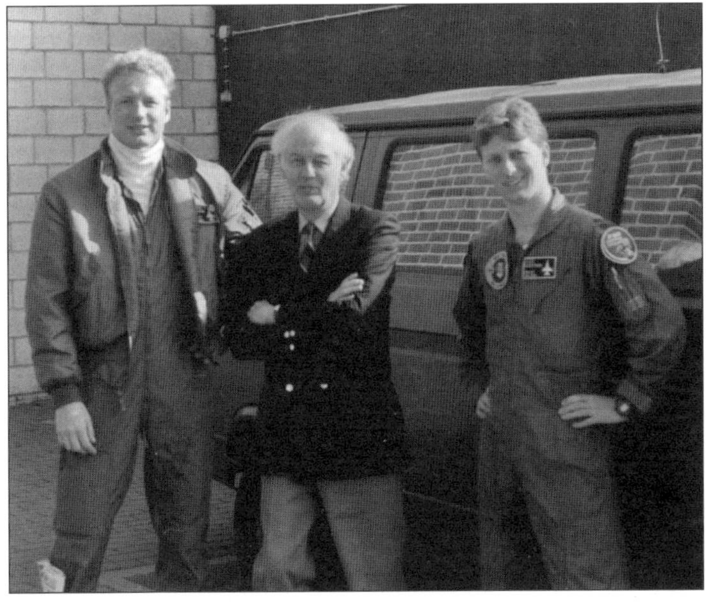

JT with 'Bark' and 'Ditch',
pilots of 315 Squadron RNLAF at Twente Air Base

Tye had assigned two young pilots, nicknamed 'Ditch' and 'Bark', to look after me; 'Ditch' had earned his soubriquet from a forced immersion, but I did not learn the origin of 'Bark' or of his other name 'Paint'. They now took me in a minibus to one of the 'hardened shelters' to look over an F-16. I had sat in one on my 1991 visit to the Air Base, and I was very happy to do so again and to have the whole fantastic array of instruments, switches, buttons, screens, and controls, with their manifold functions, explained in all their complexity by my knowledgeable young guides. The most extraordinary parts were the control-stick and the

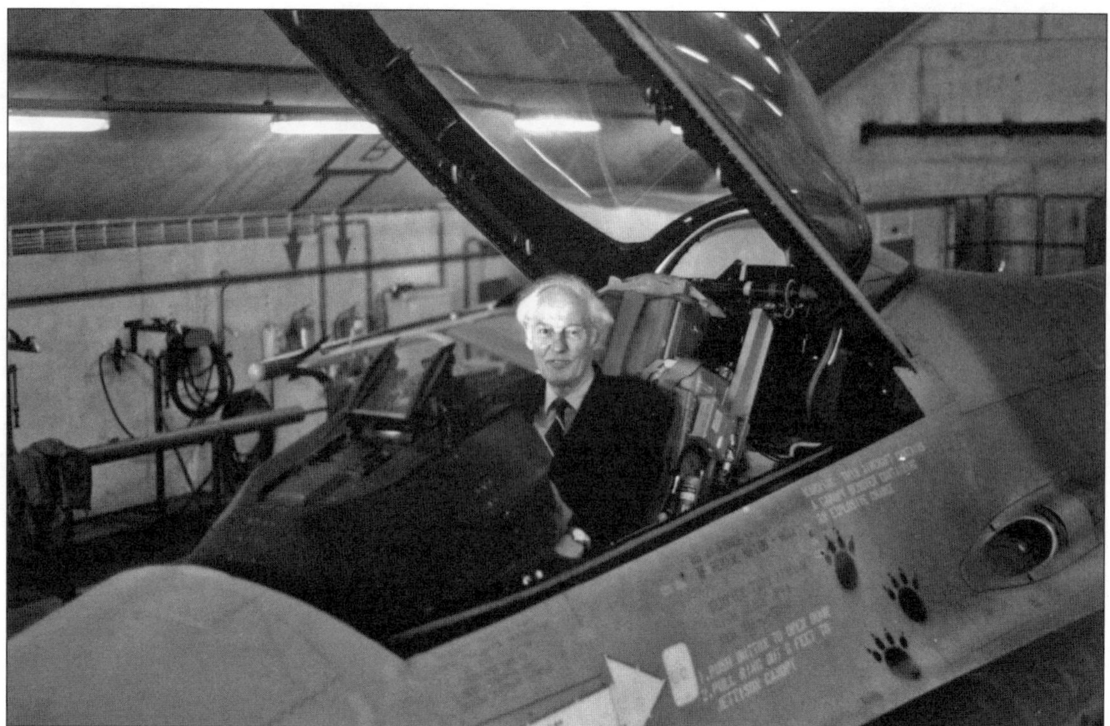

Pleasant Dreams in the cockpit of an F-16

throttle-arm, both of which have a number of buttons within finger-tip reach that enable the pilot to operate virtually every system on the aircraft with the minimum of effort; he is, as it were, playing a tune on a flute with both hands, while the score – all the information he needs to fly, navigate, shoot, bomb, and avoid danger – is displayed on the windscreen in front of him. Miraculous!

My escorts took me to the Officers' Mess for an excellent lunch, then I returned to the Squadron crew-room to await Tye, who was busily engaged as the Operations Officer for the day. Eventually the F-16s returned from their sorties and I watched them peel-off overhead to enter the circuit and land in quick succession. When Tye had checked them all in and de-briefed them on their mission, he was free to take me over to the Simulator Centre.

Here was the 1990s' counterpart of the wartime Link Trainer, which was used to teach us to fly by the cockpit instruments alone, without looking out and without leaving the ground! But this was a far more sophisticated piece of electronic gadgetry, costing £30 million, that could reproduce any normal condition of flight – and a great number of abnormal ones. Even experienced pilots could be seen staggering out of the cockpit with the perspiration running down their face. In one room was an F-16 cockpit, half-hidden by a pile of 'magic boxes'; nearby was a long desk where two controllers sat, with a battery of multi-coloured screens in front of them: these displayed the position of all the systems and controls in the cockpit and the readings of the instruments. On another screen to the side was a replica of the pilot's view of the windscreen, with the 'head-up' display of his instruments projected onto it. Next door, another room was completely filled with stacks of computers – the brain of the Simulator. Modern military aircraft are so expensive to build or buy, to fly and to maintain, that the pilots spend as much time in the Simulator as they do in the air, and the training they are given in operational procedures and emergency situations is so effective that the Simulator very soon pays for itself just in terms of accidents avoided.

Tye went into the cockpit first and did half-an-hour of advanced flying exercises, with a full dose of emergencies thrown at him by the cheerfully challenging controllers – from which he emerged cool and calm. Then I was given fifteen minutes – and made a mess of almost everything! The control-stick was incredibly sensitive: it needed the slightest nudge to bank in one direction but, if I held it over for a second, the aircraft made a complete rotation; similarly, if I held back-pressure on the control-stick for a fraction too long, the machine looped the loop! In fact, of course, it did no such thing; but that is what the view out of the cockpit and the readings of the instruments seemed to be telling me – and that is what it felt like. Eventually, I had Tye on one side and a controller on the other, peering through the 'windscreen' (which was actually a video projected onto it), and telling me what to do, so that I was able to use my guided missiles to 'shoot down' enemy aircraft quite successfully. However, when it came to the approach and landing, the super-sensitivity of the controls meant that, on my first attempt, I landed several feet under the ground; on my next, I was far off to the side of the runway; and, on the third, although I landed all right, I couldn't stop the aircraft turning a complete circle on the runway. I don't know how much my fifteen minutes cost the Dutch Air Force but, if it had been for real, I should certainly have destroyed at least one F-16 valued at £10 million!

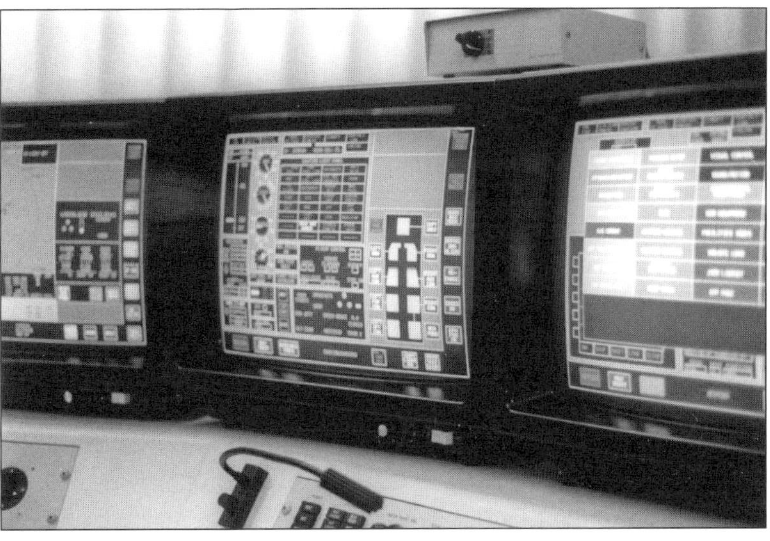

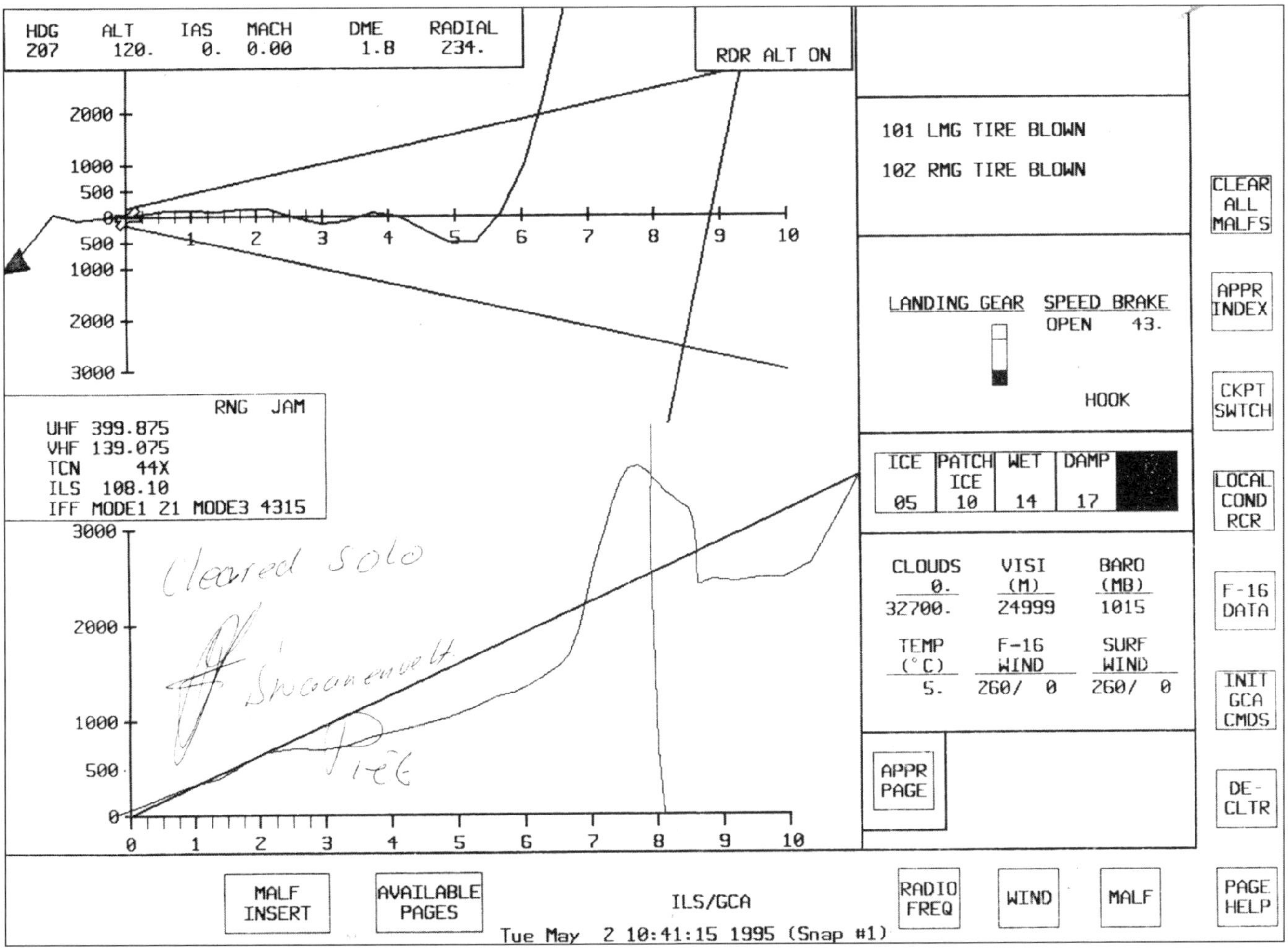

The Instructor's Panel of the F-16 Simulator

HDG 207 ALT 120. IAS 0. MACH 0.00 DME 1.8 RADIAL 234.

RDR ALT ON

101 LMG TIRE BLOWN

102 RMG TIRE BLOWN

LANDING GEAR SPEED BRAKE OPEN 43.

HOOK

RNG JAM

UHF 399.875
VHF 139.075
TCN 44X
ILS 108.10
IFF MODE1 21 MODE3 4315

ICE	PATCH ICE	WET	DAMP
05	10	14	17

CLOUDS	VISI (M)	BARO (MB)
0.		
32700.	24999	1015

TEMP (°C)	F-16 WIND	SURF WIND
5.	260/ 0	260/ 0

Cleared solo

APPR PAGE

CLEAR ALL MALFS · APPR INDEX · CKPT SWTCH · LOCAL COND RCR · F-16 DATA · INIT GCA CMDS · DE-CLTR · PAGE HELP

MALF INSERT · AVAILABLE PAGES · ILS/GCA · RADIO FREQ · WIND · MALF

Tue May 2 10:41:15 1995 (Snap #1)

The 'trace' of my 3rd attempt at landing, inscribed "cleared solo"!

CHAPTER 26

Return of the Veterans

The real heroes of the Liberation arrived in Borne on Sunday, 30th April 1995: representatives of the British and Canadian tank-crews, gunners, signallers, transport drivers, and long-suffering infantry, who had travelled in tanks, in trucks or on foot, all the way to Borne from the landing-beaches of Normandy.

The British had fought their way across France and Belgium into the south of Holland, then into Germany and over the Rhine between Kleve and Wesel, after which they veered left, back into Holland, to attack the Twente area. The 1st Canadian Army had advanced more directly, but with equally bitter fighting, along the Channel coast, clearing the ports one by one of their tenacious German defenders, and having a prolonged struggle to free the island of Walcheren and capture the Scheldt Estuary; they then spread north and east to join the British 2nd Army in liberating the rest of Holland. These warriors ate from field-kitchens, slept in slit-trenches or ditches, rarely took their clothes off, endured continual shelling, sniping, and booby-trapping, and had no sooner cleared the Germans out of one line of defences than they had to evict them again from the next. No wonder the girls in each town and village they entered, hugged and kissed these brave men, muddy and battle-stained as they were, climbed onto their tanks and put flowers down the muzzles of their guns.

"Dagblad Tubantia" and "Twentsche Courant" published a special edition for the 50th Anniversary, which was translated into English and given the title "Liberated". This contained a panoramic map showing the disposition of all the Allied troops and the dates on which they entered the towns of Twente.

Now the veterans were coming back fifty years later, some with their wives, as civilians in their Regimental Associations, but wearing a uniform of dark-blue blazers, grey trousers and berets of various colours, medals glinting on their chests, and marching erect behind their Associations' standards. There were altogether in Borne that week about a hundred British and Canadians, with a sprinkling of Americans, including at least one shot-down aircrew. In Borne, there was no doubt that the heroes of the hour were the Dorset Regiment and the Canadian 52nd Regiment of Grenadier Guards, and the seven-day programme of events to commemorate their achievement revealed the depth of the people's gratitude to their Liberators.

The starting-point on Sunday was a drive in a procession of horse-drawn carriages from the Town Hall, round half the town, to the White House, a beautiful mansion, which had been the headquarters of the Canadian Grenadier Guards. Before the war, it was the home of the Spaniaards, a Jewish family; the son was arrested by the Germans in September 1941 and sent to Mauthausen concentration camp in Austria, where he died two

The Farm Wagon in which I travelled

weeks later. The father was taken away in January 1944, but survived the war. The house is now a study and conference centre.

Crowds in Borne lining the streets to watch the carriage procession

I was urged into the first carriage by a Committee member and found myself sitting in a typical Twente covered farm-wagon with a number of Dorsets and their wives. The seats were wooden planks and we could scarcely see out because of the low semi-circular awning which hung down on all sides. The wagon was drawn by a sturdy cart-horse and driven by two local farmers. The other vehicles were all one- or two-horse carriages, some of them smartly turned-out in full dressage, with appropriately-costumed drivers. The inhabitants of Borne lined the route of our procession, waving cheerfully and exchanging pleasantries with the veterans.

Outside the White House, there were a Sherman tank standing aggressively on the lawn, a smartly-uniformed local band, and a large crowd to watch the arrivals. The Burgomaster, Maarten Vunderink, greeted each of us at the entrance and we were taken inside into a grand reception room. However, we now had to wait a while, as our carriages had to go back to bring the second group of veterans from the Town Hall. Unfortunately for them, the bystanders were not aware of this repeat procession, so only a few people remained to cheer them on their way. Then we heard that the Canadian contingent, who had flown direct from Canada to Schiphol Airport, were late and would not arrive in their coach for another hour.

A carriage, a Sherman tank, and a band await our arrival at the White House.

Veterans, Families, Friends and Citizens in front of the White House

In spite of the Dorsets' friendliness and the fact that I had lived in Dorset for several years, I did not feel that I really belonged in their company, who all knew each other well in the British Legion and were accustomed to attending functions of this kind together. So, when I saw a group of men not wearing the blue blazers and grey trousers of the Dorsets, I went over and introduced myself to them. To my delight, I found that they were some of the American crew of the "Aliquippa", a B-17 Flying Fortress that had crash-landed between Delden and Bornerbroek in December 1943. They had returned to Borne in 1990, and Hennie Noordhuis had often talked about them. When they discovered that I had trained in the 'States in 1942 and instructed American cadets in flying in 1943, we became immediate friends or, I should say, 'buddies'. They told me the circumstances of their crash (see later) and their individual experiences before they all eventually became POWs. I also met up again with Alan Biyth, the Canadian spotter-plane observer; so, by the time the Canadian veterans arrived, the six of us from the flying world had formed our own small group. We were served an excellent meal and were then given an official welcome by the Burgomaster and other speakers.

The following afternoon we were taken on a coach-tour of the Twente district, driving through the beautiful woods and avenues of tall trees that distinguish this part of Holland and make it a tourist attraction to both Dutch and German visitors. At Denekamp, we came very close to the German border, which confirmed for me the logic of my reasoning in November 1944 in assuming I had landed in Germany.

I spent Tuesday with Tye Verf at Twente Air Base, while the others were taken on a day-trip to Amsterdam, with a boat-ride on the canals and a visit to a cheese factory. In the evening, there was a Commemorative Concert in a church, where a packed audience much appreciated the playing and singing of a Dutch orchestra and choir; this was followed by a 100-strong Canadian High School band and choir, whose repertoire ranged from Elgar to Glenn Miller. Walking back along a darkened footpath, I overtook a lady being pushed in a wheelchair and was taken' aback when she looked up at me and said, *"Hello, Jimmy Taylor!"* When I asked her how on earth she had recognised me, she simply said, *"I'm a Roetgerink"* – which, in a way, explained it all!

Memorial to 117 civilians executed on 8th March 1945 for the wounding by the Resistance of SS Officer Reuter, Head of the Police in the Netherlands

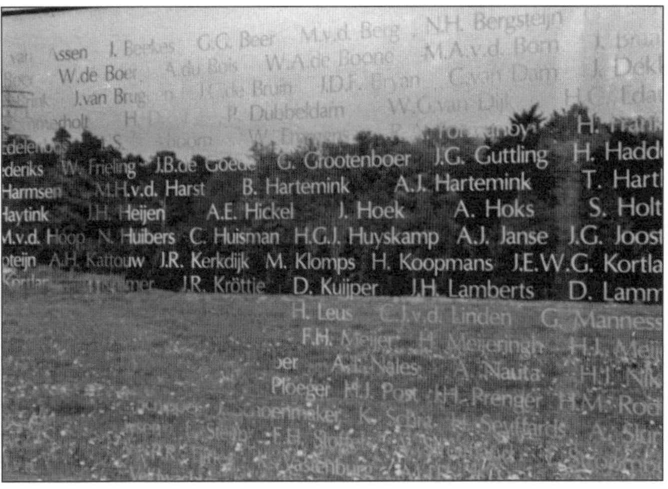

Wednesday saw me joining the Dorsets for a visit to Arnhem. On the way, we stopped by a striking metal, glass and stone Memorial, with the names of over a hundred people etched on the glass and easily read against the sky. They were local people rounded up and shot when the Resistance tried, and failed, to assassinate a high-ranking German officer travelling by car. It showed me that the Germans committed some much worse atrocities than the one at 't Hesseler – but an atrocity on any scale is still an atrocity.

We visited the fine Airborne Museum in what had been the Hartenstein Hotel in Oosterbeek, a suburb of Arnhem; it was taken over as Major-General Urquhart's headquarters during the ten days of Operation 'Market Garden', 17th-26th September 1944. This was doomed to failure even before it started by the planners' refusal to accept the evidence of Intelligence about the strength of German forces in the area, their misguided assumption of the Germans' low morale after their defeat in Normandy, and their failure to recognise the difficulties resulting from landing lightly-armed Airborne troops six miles from their objective – the bridge over the Rhine in the built-up area of Arnhem. The Germans' quick reaction to the landings of gliders and paratroops soon had the Airborne troops encircled in Oosterbeek, but the resistance of the steadily decreasing number of survivors was so fierce that the surrounding Germans called it "the Cauldron", where even their Tiger tanks were at risk from the heroism of the defenders. 2400 of these were able to be evacuated across the Rhine in pouring rain in the night of 25th/26th September.

We also visited the Old Church in Oosterbeek, which was on the southern edge of the enclave; here the Airborne Light Artillery was situated, dropping shells on the Germans besieging the bridge until the remnants of Lt Colonel Frost's 500-strong 2nd Parachute Battalion were forced to withdraw on 21st September. The church itself was extensively damaged, but has been restored, a new Communion Table and Font being presented by the 1st British Airborne Division and the 1st Polish Parachute Brigade. The sadly impressive Airborne Cemetery at Oosterbeek, with its 1705 Commonwealth graves and 51 Polish, reveals the intensity of the fighting. The Dorsets held a short ceremony at the central Cross of Sacrifice and laid a wreath on the grave of a colleague who fell in the battle.

The Dorsets' Standard at the Cross of Sacrifice

Of the many monuments and plaques to the Allied formations that fought and died in the battle, the latest is the Memorial unveiled in 2006 to the Allied Aircrews who lost their lives while flying various aircraft involved in Operation 'Market Garden' : the

Some of the 1700 graves in the Arnhem Commonwealth Cemetery

The Aircrew Memorial at Arnhem;
it includes F/O John Brodby on its register

bombers that softened-up the defences before the landings; the gliders and tugs that brought in the Airborne troops; the transports that dropped the paratroops and, later, the supplies; and the fighters that escorted these aircraft when the weather made it possible. Included in the casualty list is my friend F/0 John Brodby of 16 Squadron, shot down and killed while on a photographic sortie over Nijmegen on 20th September.

We British, conscious of our own losses, forget too easily the huge sacrifices made by the 100,000 Dutch inhabitants of Arnhem, who not only suffered casualties from both sides during the fighting, but were all forced by the Germans to evacuate their homes and leave Arnhem at a moment's notice, as their punishment for having welcomed the Airborne troops and given them every support and encouragement during the battle. Most of them trudged with their minimal possessions to Apeldoorn, 16 miles away, while the Germans systematically looted their houses. How many Memorials have they been given? Only the Ceremonial Sword, in a case in the central Provincial House in Arnhem, engraved with the badges of all the participating Allies. It was presented by General Urquhart, on behalf of the 1st British Airborne Division and the 1st Polish Parachute Brigade, to the people of Arnhem for their self-sacrifice and assistance during the battle, and afterwards in helping some of those left behind after the withdrawal to escape across the Rhine.

That evening, there was a large-scale Dinner and Dance arranged for all the veterans and their hosts, in a community centre artfully decorated to look like somewhere much more sophisticated. A wonderful buffet was laid out for the 300 guests, and a Big Band in 1944 American uniform played through-

A Monument to the Enforced Evacuation of the people of Arnhem and other communities by the Germans in reprisal for their support of the Airborne troops

out the evening, attracting old and young onto the dance-floor. The Verfs, of course, were with me and we managed to chat to an unending stream of friends, old and new, including my lady in a wheel-chair of the night before. Tributes were paid to the Dorsets, the Canadian Grenadier Guards, and the crew of the "Aliquippa", and each of us was presented with a handsome enamelled commemorative medal and a photograph of the whole group outside the White House.

4th May is the Day of National Commemoration in Holland and I went to get a small wreath from a flower-shop in Borne. In the afternoon, I visited the Air Base Museum with Chantal and Trystan, as I have mentioned. On my return, I was picked up by Jan Bovenmars and Anne and taken to their home in 't Hesseler, where there was a full family get-together in the garden. Jan's wife Ria was the daughter of Herman Boomkamp, who lived with them; he sadly died on 4th May 1998. I had previously met his son Jan, the dynamic owner of the spreading Garden Centre; he had taken me on a tour of his estate, including the horses he bred and exported all over the world, the land he had bought to re-sell to the expanding town of Hengelo, and the houses that he had already built to satisfy the increasing demand – it was not surprising that he was a millionaire, but a most unassuming one. After a delightfully friendly meal, at 7.0pm we all gathered at the cross-roads for the ceremony at the Memorial.

With the Boomkamps and Bovenmars
l-r: Village Council leader and wife Diny and Hendrik Boomkamp JT
Bram, Helen and Anne Bovenmars Bernard and Herman Boomkamp Ria Bovenmars

This was a major occasion, but I was surprised to see the bandsmen of the Royal Tank Regiment arriving in a coach; they led our procession along the lane, with Maarten Vunderink, other officials and myself following, and the Boomkamp and Roetgerink families and many other people behind. The band played at the simple wreath-laying – but, really, it was too big and loud, out of keeping with the simple rural environment; I preferred the gentler strains of Hennie Noordhuis's small group of local musicians who had accompanied the ceremony on former occasions.

Jan Boomkamp generously provided tea in the refreshment room of the Garden Centre for everyone, after which many of us drove to the Old Church in Borne for a Service of Commemoration, attended by a large congregation including all the veterans. It was held in Dutch and English and was both sombre and uplifting, a fitting prelude to the Silent Walk through the old streets of Borne that followed.

The Royal Tank Regiment Band leads the procession at 't Hesseler.

Three Red-Coated Drummers head the Silent Walk through Borne.

The start of the ceremony at the Old Town Hall in Borne

This was most impressive, for the silence as much as for the walk. It was headed by three drummers, followed by the Burgomaster and officials and then by the veterans, each of us carrying a single rose; any bystanders who felt like it could join in, and many did.

The walk ended in the square outside the Old Town Hall (superseded by a modern building next to it); here the Royal Tank Regiment Band and a Canadian Scottish Pipe Band were already playing solemn music, together with Boy and Girl Scouts standing each side of the Municipal War Memorial, under the flags of all the Allied countries. The square and adjacent roadways were filled with hundreds of people drawn from Borne and the surrounding villages. At precisely 8.0pm, signalled by the chimes of the clock on the Old Church, the 'Last Post' was sounded on a bugle, followed by Two Minutes' Silence, and then 'Reveille'; after this, wreaths and flowers were laid on and around the War Memorial by the Burgomaster and many groups and individuals, including veterans with their roses; the ceremony ended with the National Anthems of the Dutch, British, Canadians and Americans.

Afterwards, I was invited into the Town Hall, where I met two charming elderly ladies, Joanna Pouwer-Vonk and Hermine Vonk, the sisters of Jan Vonk, the first victim of the Germans' reprisals on 19th November 1944. I was relieved to find that they were very realistic about their brother's activities in the war, that "he was playing with fire" and "running great risks" in trying to take-on the Germans single-handedly. They took me to an old house in Borne, the 'Pastoria' (vicarage), where I met the owners, Harry and Nel Rientjes, and their family; Hennie Noordhuis joined us later. Harry had been a radio and radar operator in the Dutch Air Force 1954-56 and his children, Toon and Colette, were both at Technical Colleges, so we had a very interesting and convivial evening. I was much helped by the fact that Jan Vonk's sisters would not allow the tragedy to cast a shadow over the occasion.

Tributes to the Fallen:
Dutch, British, and Canadian
The children have a strong place in the Borne Ceremony.

Hermine Vonk (l) and her sister Joanna Pouwer-Vonk

Hennie had asked me, several months earlier, whether it was possible to arrange for a Spitfire to give a display over Borne. I had therefore contacted the late Mark Hanna, with his father Ray the manager of the Old Flying Machine Company at Duxford Airfield, which maintains a large collection of WW2 aircraft in airworthy condition, including at one time Spitfire XI PL965, which flew on operations in 16 Squadron from January to May 1945; but Mark's price was too high for the Liberation Committee's budget. However, later, Hennie was able to book the Spitfire IX of the Dutch Historic Aircraft Flight. He also told me that there would be a fly-past over Borne by other aircraft at some time.

It was therefore quite by chance, at midday on Friday, when Hennie was driving me to Borne's Town Cemetery to pay my respects at the tragic joint grave of the three 't Hesseler victims, that I glanced out of the car's window and saw a formation of three aircraft passing nearly overhead at about 2000ft. We jumped out and watched the flight of a B-25 Mitchell leading a Spitfire IX on one side and a P-51 Mustang on the other. They didn't deviate from their course and I guessed that they were covering a large number of towns and cities in their fly-over. Some weeks later, at Duxford, I gave a copy of my photograph of the formation to Mark Hanna, who was actually flying the Spitfire; he said that the whole formation had come from Duxford, booked by the Dutch Government, but he had no idea of his whereabouts over Holland – he was just concentrating on keeping good formation on the Mitchell!

The afternoon was devoted to a Grand Cavalcade of military vehicles and 'floats' designed and produced by the residents of each street in Borne or by the nearby villages. A viewing stand had been erected at the junction of two main streets in the town, with seats reserved for the veterans. I sat down to await events on a wonderfully sunny afternoon, when a Committee member came up and said a place was being kept for me on a tank! I followed him into a back-street, where I saw a row of trucks, two of which were being filled with veterans, but no sign of a tank. I hunted around, but in vain; I decided that, in any case, I would rather watch the procession than take part in it; so I returned to my seat, where chatting with a Dutch student-teacher on one side and a Canadian couple on the other helped to pass the two hours we had to wait before the Cavalcade came into sight – moving, as in a traffic jam, by fits and starts.

Every conceivable military vehicle of WW2 was represented in the 100 or more that passed before us, flying Dutch, British and Canadian flags. All of them were privately owned and many had crossed over from Britain to take part in several such parades in Holland. Jeeps, trucks, staff-cars and motor-cycles proliferated, but most impressive were the huge mobile workshops and recovery vehicles, an amphibi-

A Sherman tank (its tracks covered) makes itself felt in the Cavalcade as it might have done on 3rd April 1945.

ous DUKW, and a massive Sherman tank. The scene in the street, hung with flags and bunting, with the crowds, waving, laughing and pushing forward, must have been a close reflection of what it was like when the first Allied tanks and jeeps entered Borne on 3rd April 1945.

In contrast, the parade of civilian 'floats' represented themes typical of Borne today: some industrial and commercial, some cultural and sporting, others historical and educational, many of them broadly humorous. The crowd applauded each one generously, especially when children participated. 't Hesseler showed a true incident at the end of the war: a chicken-coop full of German soldiers, locked in and guarded by angry farmers. The Verf family appeared with their street's contribution: a small-scale replica of the Canadian war cemetery, for which they won 5th Prize – although Chantal claimed they should have been placed higher!

't Hesseler's 'Chicken-shed full of Germans 1945' float

The veterans had disembarked from their trucks to take their seats on the stand. Various groups stopped to sing or dance in front of them, while others presented them with samples of local food or drink, miniature Dutch clogs, and bunches of yellow tulips. A nearby TV camera recorded everything and the commentator interviewed several of the veterans, coming to me at the end of the day. I had to answer several questions about

The Spitfire IX of the Dutch Historical Flight performs over the Tattoo.

my experiences, but I was given no opportunity to express my appreciation and gratitude to the organisers and the good people of Borne – which, to my regret, was the one element missing from the finished video, a copy of which I received from the ever-generous Hennie.

The Committee chairman passed by and gave me a ticket to join the party that evening for all the performers in a vast marquee erected next to the Town Hall. When I entered, it looked as if most of Borne was crammed inside, while the noise of amplified pop-music was quite deafening. I met several people I knew, including Trystan and Justine Verf, and then I was greeted by a totally unrecognisable black face – which turned out to belong to Colette of the previous evening!

The day ended at Hennie Noordhuis's house, where he and Joke were entertaining the four Americans and Alan Blyth and various other guests. Hennie gave each of us a revised edition of his book on Borne during the war, and I presented him with a brass model of a Spitfire XI – a very small return for all the special treatment that I had received from him during these intensive two weeks.

Saturday saw the last event of the official programme: an Evening Tattoo on the local sports field, which all the inhabitants of Borne seemed to be attending. I found all the veterans sitting in a covered stand, including the Americans, and I ran into Tye Verf's F-16 colleague, Captain Monk, and his son. I missed the display of flying model aeroplanes, but the Dutch Spitfire came over and performed a few manoeuvres, although it stayed too high to make much of an impression. However, I was able to tease Walter Sybo, the American Flight Engineer, by calling to him, above me in the stand, that this was a real aeroplane compared to his B-17!

The Tattoo took the form of several marching bands from neighbouring towns putting on lively performances, and a battery of field-guns going through the procedure of moving into action and then firing blank rounds. It ended with a superb firework display, culminating in a grand set-piece, which spelled out in fiery letters:

THANK YOU LIBERATORS!

I was treated to a last example of the extraordinary warmth shown by the people of Borne towards the veterans when I was walking back from the Tattoo in the dark. A man on a bicycle overtook me and, as he passed, turned round and called out, *"Well done, young man!"* I felt 50 years fall away.

Borne had excelled itself in every way and the Liberation Committee Borne 1945-1995 deserved the warmest tributes. Such a week-long programme of events can never be repeated on this scale, I am sure; but then we hope that there will never again be such a terrible experience as the Second World War to require its ending to be commemorated so fervently and dramatically.

CHAPTER 27

"Aliquippa" – Bentelo – 'Little Peter'

In the early morning of 22nd December 1943, B-17 Flying Fortress 423184, bearing the name "Aliquippa" (origin unknown) on its nose and the code-letters 'PY-Q' on each side of the fuselage, took-off from Poddington airfield in Norfolk on a mission to bomb the mashalling-yards at Osnabruck, about 90 miles into Germany due east of Borne. The 10-man crew consisted of 1st Lt Henry Roeber, 1st pilot and captain; 2nd Lt Casimir Paulinski, 2nd pilot; 2nd Lt Donald McPhee, navigator; 2nd Lt George Sokolsky, bombardier; Staff Sgt Walter Sybo, engineer; Staff Sgt Clayton Verlo, ball-turret gunner; Staff Sgt Royce McGillvary, mid-ships gunner; Sgt Seymour Wolfson, mid-ships gunner; Staff Sgt Irvin Sumpter, tail-gunner; and Staff Sgt Hubert O'Neill, radio operator.

After the "Aliquippa" had dropped its bombs on Osnabruck and turned 90° right, it was hit by flak, although the Germans claimed it was by one of their fighters. Smoke poured from No 4 engine and the other engines lost power. The aircraft dropped out of the formation and quickly began to lose height. The crew fired off two green Very Lights, which attracted the attention of the escorting Lightnings and Thunderbolts, some of which closed in to protect the crippled bomber. At about 2.30pm and 9000ft, the "Aliquippa" entered cloud. Steadily losing height, it emerged still over Germany and Roeber began looking for a field for a forced-landing. Before they reached Holland, however, he gave the order to bale out. This took some crew-members longer than others: MacPhee, Sokolsky, Wolfson and O'Neill jumped and were captured in the region of Itterbeck, in Germany; from there, they were taken to Dulag Luft, the interrogation centre near Frankfurt-am-Main, and to a POW camp.

Sumpter and McGillvary landed between Delden and Bornerbroek and were picked up by local Dutch people; they were taken on bicycles to a school and on the way, saw the "Aliquippa" lying in a field. The Resistance brought them to Antwerp via Utrecht and Echt; but there they were captured and were sent eventually to Stalag Luft IV, then moved to XII, and finally sent to VIIA at Moosburg, in southern Germany.

Verlo landed a mile to the east of Vriezenveen, in Holland, and was given refuge by a lawyer, Mr. C.J.M. Kruisinga. Through a lack of caution, however, he was arrested by the Gestapo on 24th December and taken to Zwolle. In January 1944, he was brought to Dulag Luft and then sent to Stalag XVIIB at Krems, in Austria.

Sybo and Paulinski remained in the aircraft with Roeber. With only one engine working properly, the "Aliquippa" slowly came down in the neighbourhood of Borne; Roeber cut the engines and made a successful belly-landing in a meadow belonging to farmer Bolscher, not far from the border between Azelo, in the district of Delden, and Bornerbroek. Sybo and Paulinski stepped out unhurt with Roeber and reached Goor, where they were arrested in a restaurant by the Gestapo on 24th December and became POWs. Like all the rest of the crew in their different camps, they were liberated by the Americans in April 1945.

Now, in May 1995, I met four of these men, fifty years older: Walter Sybo, engineer, short, rotund, pink-faced, smiling and always ready with a wise-crack; Hubert O'Neill, radio operator, tall, lanky, well-educated and serious; Irvin 'Sarge' Sumpter, tail-gunner, small and rather quiet; and Clayton Verlo, ball-turret gunner, also small, but with his own agenda and I saw little of him. They told me that Henry Roeber was still alive, but had no interest in re-living their wartime experiences and they had lost contact with him.

The Crew of the B-17 "Aliquippa" December 1943
Standing l-r: Walter Sybo Clayton Verlo Lawrence Anderson Hubert O'Neill
Seymour Wolfson Irvin Sumpter
In front: Henry Roeber Casimir Paulinski George Sokolsky Donald MacPhee
Lawrence Anderson was killed on 11th December; Royce McGillvary replaced him.
Photo: Noordhuis, ter Braak and Kienhuis "In Suffering, Resistance and Freedom 1940 – 1945"

Belly-landing of the B-17 on the boundary Delden-Bornerbroek 22nd December 1943
Photo: Noordhuis, ter Braak and Kienhuis "In Suffering, Resistance and Freedom 1940 – 1945"

Young Bart and JT raise the Union Jack at the opening of the Liberation Exhibition in Bentelo Town Hall, under the eyes of the Burgomaster, Mr Van Der Vegt.

Walter Sybo, Hubert O'Neill, 'Sarge' Sumpter and I came together on the 5th May because of an invitation we received from the Burgomaster of Bentelo, a village between Delden and Bornerbroek which, nevertheless, boasted a Town Hall, of not much more than bungalow dimensions.

Bentelo was severely damaged during the 1945 fighting, and it had never forgotten the bravery and suffering of those who had freed it from the Germans; now, like Borne, on this 50th Anniversary it was determined to honour the Allies, and their Liberation on 1st April 1945 of Bentelo, on the biggest scale that it could afford. It therefore mounted an exhibition filling most of the rooms in the Town Hall, and invited representatives of the British, Canadians, Americans, and Dutch to open the exhibition by raising their national flags on four large masts specially erected outside. Why I should have been chosen to represent the British rather than one of the many veteran soldiers, remains a mystery; but it may be that both the Americans and I were selected because our aircraft crashed or forced-landed within the wider boundaries of Bentelo.

So, at 8.30am on the last Friday, I was picked up from the Verfs by Hennie Noordhuis, with Hubert O'Neill and 'Sarge' Sumpter already in the car. We arrived in Bentelo to find the Burgomaster and a small crowd waiting outside, together with Walter Sybo and Marinus and Henk Timmerman. (Clayton Verlo had failed to return from some mission of his own.) The Dutch never fail to involve the younger generation in these events; so, after general introductions had been made, we were each given a young assistant, a boy or girl, to help us raise our flag. I received Bart, a very pleasant 10-year-old, to assist me, and we stood by our flagpole as the Dutch National Anthem was played and their flag was hoisted. Then I let Bart do most of the work of raising the Union Jack, while the strains of "God Save The Queen" floated over Bentelo – and Henk Timmerman took photographs with my camera.

Everyone then filtered into the main assembly room of the Town Hall, where we were served coffee and cake; after this, the Burgomaster made a long speech in Dutch, no doubt recalling the hectic days of the fighting for the Twente Canal. We were each then called up to the platform and presented with a book (in Dutch) about the history of Bentelo, a large copy of an old map of the meadows and ditches of the village, and a document (also in Dutch) explaining the significance of the map.

Realising that this was the end of the formal proceedings, I returned to the platform and asked a friendly official to be my interpreter. Speaking on behalf of the Americans as well as myself, I expressed our gratitude to the Burgomaster and township of Bentelo for our welcome and our presents, and then said that I wanted to give them something in return. I had brought with me the last of my reproductions of Frank Wootton's "Photographic Spitfire" pictures and, when I saw Jan Timmerman among the officials – he lived in Bentelo – I told the audience that I felt it very fitting to present the picture to him,

Survivors of the Crew of the B-17 "Aliquippa" in Bentelo Town Hall
l-r: Walter Sybo, flight engineer   Hubert O'Neill, radio engineer   'Sarge' Sumpter, ball-turret gunner

since he was one of the people closest to the events that brought me there: he had seen my machine descending in circles, trailing smoke. I suggested that the picture should be hung in the exhibition. When I was asked to recount the story, including how Marinus had burnt his fingers on the hot cowling of my crashed plane, I said it was better for Jan to tell it in Dutch – and so he did. In this way, I felt we gave a little back to the people of Bentelo for all the efforts they had made to put on a show for us.

From here, we slowly circulated round the exhibition. The centre-piece was a large panoramic model of the village as it appeared in April 1945, with every house and barn shown in its condition, damaged or destroyed, and the positions of the Allied tanks, guns and infantry, and arrows indicating the development of the battle. I should like to have had more time to examine this brilliant reconstruction in more detail, or at least to have had a photograph of it, to clear up some of the confusion I have mentioned earlier.

The rest of the exhibition was devoted to weapons and equipment from the battlefield, with Hennie Noordhuis's helping hand again in evidence. An excavated piece of my Spitfire was one of the items on display, and a video screen replayed my interview with TV Oost on the crash-site. There seemed to be nothing retrieved from the "Aliquippa", but the Americans had made a good belly-landing in December 1943 and the Germans had, no doubt, dismantled the B-17 carefully and taken away all the components on special low-loaders for close examination, leaving nothing behind for the Dutch to preserve – a rather different scenario from the removal of the shattered remnants of my Spitfire on a farm-cart!

Bentelo had done itself proud, and we left with real affection for this little community that had suffered so much fifty years ago and recovered with such vigour and enterprise.

Saturday I spent packing, taking Chantal and the children to the crash-site and Hennie Egberink's yard, and enjoying the Evening Tattoo. On Sunday, I stuffed about 50 scraps of my aircraft into an old bag lent me by Chantal and said farewell to the family. They had given me a wonderful home back-ground and it had been fun to mix with the children, encouraging Trystan to take time in building a plastic model Spitfire that I gave him. Not long afterwards, Tye passed his examinations for a commercial pilot's licence and left the Air Force to train with KLM. I was fortunate to have met him just in time to benefit from his last few days as a fighter-pilot on the potent F-16 in 315 Squadron RNLAF. Very sadly, some time after this, the Verfs separated: Chantal took the children back to Canada, while Tye continued flying with Martinair.

Hennie Noordhuis took me to his home for a light lunch with Joke and their daughters, Judith and Mijke. He then drove me to Hengelo to catch the train direct to Schiphol. He had been a fantastic organiser and friend, always around in the background or foreground, showing the same enjoyment as the rest of us in the activities or performances that he had worked so hard to arrange. Borne is very fortunate in having an Archivist who is motivated, by his very acute sense of history, to relate the past to the present, and has the practical ability to offer it to the public in a most attractive form, while keeping close touch with the human factor. I owe him everything I have experienced in Holland since 1991.

So this fortnight in Borne was like no other in my life. I have never been the recipient of so much friendliness and hospitality by so many people in such a short time, and I have never felt so much at home in a town in England as I did in Borne. This made 1995 one of the most significant and memorable years in my life, so I was pleased and flattered when I was asked to write a letter of thanks from the veterans to the members of the Liberation Committee of Borne. I paid tribute to the wonderful programme and to the great welcome and hospitality we had received, and congratulated the Dutch on their courage and fortitude during the war, and on their efforts today to make their children aware of what they owed to the Liberation by the Allies in 1945.[1]

The Tragedy of Warrant Officer Peter S.C.Thorne, MiD 1923-1945

Quite by chance, in early 1994 I was looking through Hennie Noordhuis's fine book, in Dutch, on Borne during the war, when I came upon a photograph of a face I recognised as that of Peter Thorne, a young man whom I'd first met in bizarre circumstances in 1941. I can't read Dutch, but I could make out sufficiently from the text that 'Little Peter' had been shot down over Germany on 28th July 1943 and taken prisoner, but had escaped and was hidden by the Resistance based near Borne; he was recaptured eventually and was being taken back by train to Germany when he was killed trying to escape on 2nd February 1945.

Peter Thorne: 'Little Peter' in Hennie Noordhuis's book "In Suffering, Resistance and Freedom 1940-1945"

This was not only a tragic end for my friend, but also one that might have been the result of an atrocity: 'shot while trying to escape' was a common cover-up for the illegal killing of a difficult or continually escaping prisoner. I wanted to know more. I had the article translated by a Dutch lecturer at Leeds University and learned that Peter was serving as a navigator on 102 Squadron in Bomber Command, and had been shot down in Halifax JB864 on a bombing-raid on Hamburg on 28th July 1943 and been taken prisoner. He had escaped, however, and reached Holland, being hidden in Enschede and Hengelo through the agency of the Resistance near Borne, where it was especially strong and well-organised. However, he was betrayed and recaptured on 2nd November 1944. He jumped off the train taking him back to Germany, but was killed; he was buried in the cemetery at Doetinchem.

[1] See Appendix C p. 734 for the full text.

When I returned to Borne in November 1994 for the filming of "Beyond the Ignorance", I asked Hennie to take me to this cemetery, where we found Peter's grave in a section established by the British War Graves Commission, with its usual immaculate layout and maintenance. The inscription said he had died on 2nd February 1945. At the bottom were two lines subscribed, no doubt, by his family:

"For of all sad words of tongue or pen,
The saddest are these, 'It might have been.'"

After this, I put an advertisement in "Air Mail", the magazine of the RAF Association, asking any of Peter's next-of-kin to contact me if they wanted to know any more about him. I received two replies: the first came from Tom Wingham, Secretary of No 102 (Ceylon) Squadron Association, in May 1995; he gave me Peter's story in greater detail. This was followed by a letter with yet more details and a photograph of his grave from Karl Lusink, a Dutch air-historian, who was in touch with another Dutch historian "who wanted to know everything about Peter Thorne". I wrote to Mrs Susan Dickinson, in the Air Historical Branch of the Ministry of Defence, and she gave me further facts about Peter. Then, in 2004, I bought a book called "Footprints on the Sands of Time", by Oliver Clutton-Brock (published by Grub Street in 2003); this is a masterly account of the experiences of all the members of Bomber Command who became POWs, with descriptions of their Camps and of their eventual liberation. The author recounts many remarkable stories, including that of F/Sgt Peter Whittaker, DFM, a fellow-POW in Stalag IVB at Mühlberg, whose escape route from the camp crossed several times with Peter Thorne's, who receives several mentions. And I had a letter from John Slater, in South Africa. What follows now is a compilation of the information from all the above sources, to whose authors I am greatly indebted.

After qualifying as a navigator in Canada in 1943, F/Sgt Peter Thorne flew on anti-submarine patrols in Whitleys with P/0 John Slater as an air-gunner; they dropped depth-charges on two submarines, which they damaged. Later in the same year, he and Slater joined No 102 (Ceylon) Squadron flying Halifax IIs from Pocklington, in Yorkshire. On the night of 27th/28th July, as part of a force of 786 aircraft, Peter navigated Halifax JB864 on a heavy raid on Hamburg, when strips of foil called 'Window' were dropped for the first time and brought confusion to the radars of the German flak batteries and night-fighters and enabled the bombers to destroy much of the port and city for the loss of only 17 aircraft.

One of these was JB864, which was hit by flak (according to Lusink), or by a night-fighter (Slater). Four members of the crew were killed, probably by the ensuing crash at Keekekamp; Peter, Slater and the bomb-aimer, F/0 E.W.Slipp, baled out and were picked up by the Germans; they met in the guardroom of Hamburg's Fühlsbüttel Airport. The three were taken to the Dulag Luft interrogation centre, from where the two officers were sent to Stalag Luft III, while Peter went to an NCOs' Camp at Stalag IVB, becoming POW No 222444.

From what I knew of Peter, I was not surprised to learn that he made four attempts to escape from this camp – in vain; but on his fifth, in May 1944 with five others, he hoped to catch a train to Switzerland; however, they were locked into a goods train going west by a friendly French forced-labourer. Three days later, half-starving, they cut a hole in the floor and dropped out, finding themselves in Holland, where they were hidden by the Dutch Resistance at Nijverdal, a large country town about 10 miles west of Almelo and just inside Twente district. Here they joined Peter Whittaker and a group of other escapers on a farm; they remained on the run for several months, finally being sheltered in Hengelo and Enschede by the Resistance centred near Borne when, no doubt, Peter acquired the nickname of 'Little Peter'.

Eventually, on 1st November, they were betrayed to the Landwacht – a Home Guard of Dutchmen under German officers – and taken first to Laren and then to the German SD (Security Police, akin to the Gestapo) prison in the Landwacht HQ in Deventer. Here, for a week, 24 men were crammed into a cell 18ft x 8½ft; later, he was in a cell 12ft x 6ft with 13 men. One of the Dutch Landwachten, Rottenführer Kuehne, managed to bring them extra food to eke out their minimal rations. In December, Peter was moved to Oxelhoft prison in Deventer, and in January 1945 to the SD prison in Doetinchem. Here the conditions were awful, with beatings and torture and little food.

On 1st February 1945, a total of about 94 British and Dutch prisoners were put into two covered goods-wagons en route to Hamburg. The journey would take six days and they were each given a loaf of bread as their rations. Peter Thorne, Peter Whittaker and fifteen others were convinced that they would be executed on arrival, so they determined to escape. They ate their loaves for strength, then hacked their way through a small ventilator and five of them dropped out that night, while the train was moving at about 25mph. The guards spotted them and opened fire, but missed in the dark. The others, on arrival in Hamburg, were sent to the concentration camp at Wobelin, where many of them died.

Whittaker landed successfully and was given refuge by two Dutch farmers until, on 31st March, he heard the sound of gunfire and met the approaching British troops next day. Peter, however, smashed his arm by landing on a points-lever and lost a great deal of blood. He was found by the Germans and taken to the Parachutists' Hospital in Doetinchem, where he was given a blood-transfusion. He was then transferred to St Josef's Roman Catholic Hospital in the same town, where his arm was amputated, but he died from loss of blood. He was buried in the military section of Doetinchem General Cemetery, maintained by the Commonwealth War Graves Commission. In June 1946, he was awarded a Mention in Dispatches.

So unfortunate was my friend Peter Thorne, a persistent little fighter to the end. It was strange that Peter and I both became POWs, that we both jumped from a train at night, and that a vital part of our lives centred round Borne in the strongly Resistant district of Twente, where he now rests in peace. Peter was 21 years old.

Peter's headstone in the CWGC cemetery of Doetinchem

CHAPTER 28

Investigating My Engine Failure

I had selected many bits of my Spitfire from the hundreds in Hennie Egberink's yard in the hope of having them analysed metallurgically by the appropriate experts in England; from this, they might be able to deduce the likely cause of the engine's blowing-up on 19th November 1944. I had therefore concentrated on those parts of the engine which might hold useful clues: an inlet and an exhaust valve, a spark-plug, a main bearing and shells, a tappet, a camshaft bearing, and a solitary roller from a roller-bearing; also some broken-off parts of aluminium castings from the crankcase and the camshaft cover, the latter including a romantic fragment bearing the letters "CE", the ending of "ROLLS-ROYCE.". Other items were more sentimental: bits of 'skin' still bearing traces of blue PR paint, and portions of cockpit labels and control instructions; but nothing from the cameras and no pieces of perspex from the canopy – they must have been near the surface and taken away by the Germans. All the other remnants were collected-up later and delivered to the Twente Air Base Museum.

In 1994, I had visited the Imperial War Museum's Duxford Airfield, outside Cambridge, to see Spitfire XI PL965, which had arrived on 16 Squadron in January 1945 and flown on PR operations till the end of the war; it had been sold to the Royal Netherlands Air Force in 1947, but had been bought back by Nick Grace and Chris Horsley in 1987 and restored by the Medway Aircraft Preservation Society under its Managing Director, Lewis Deal, MBE. It flew again in the hands of the late Mark Hanna in December 1992, and thereafter was maintained at Duxford by him and his father, Ray, co-owners of the Old Flying Machine Company (OFMC). I had spoken to Ray Caller, their head mechanic, so now my first thought was to take my bits to Duxford and get the opinion of OFMC.

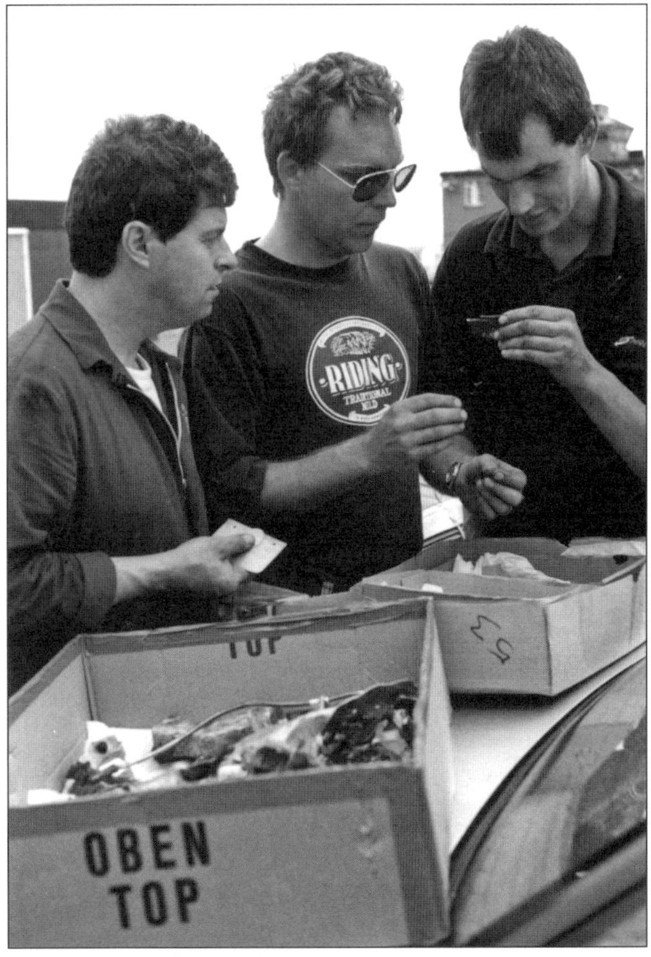

Mechanics of the Old Flying Machine Company at Duxford examine and identify scraps of my Spitfire retrieved from the Timmermans' field:
l-r: Tim Fane Steve Kingman Ray Caller

On 29th May 1995, I arrived with three well-filled cardboard boxes and was directed to The Fighter Collection's hangar, where PL965 was sitting with its cowlings removed, as one of its systems was giving trouble. This suited me fine, as I could try to match some of my pieces with what I could see of the engine. A friendly mechanic was working nearby and he was very helpful, but we succeeded in identifying only half-a-dozen of my bits.

After lunching with Philip Back, an old friend and former Mosquito Pathfinder pilot, who arrived in his own Cessna, I returned to the OFMC office where I was fortunate to run into Ray Caller. He came out to look at my relics in the boot of my car, which I had parked in front of one of the two surviving TSR-2s, a world-beating fighter-bomber scrapped by the politicians twenty years earlier. Here we were joined by two other OFMC mechanics, Tim Fane and Steve Kingman, and soon all three were very happily going through my boxes, picking up every piece and, between them, trying to identify it. As a result, I was able to label more than half the items, confident that these dedicated technicians, who were used to keeping at least three Merlin engines in running order, were the best-qualified people I could find for my purpose. However, they could not offer any opinion as to the cause of my engine-failure and they did not know anyone who could.

Being somewhat obsessed with PL965, I was keen to find out if anyone was likely to record, on film or video, the sequence of a pilot – preferably, a master such as Mark Hanna – walking out to the aircraft, settling himself into the cockpit, starting the engine, taxying out, taking-off and giving an immaculate display of this supreme WW2 machine; then joining the circuit, producing that iconic 'popping' noise of a Merlin being throttled back on the approach, landing, returning to the apron, parking, shutting-off the engine, and listening to the gentle 'tinkling' sound of hot metal cooling-down. I therefore contacted the Imperial War Museum's press officer at Duxford; he gave me the name of Tod Nichol, a local producer of films for TV, who often recorded the flying displays at the airfield. When I telephoned him, he held out some hope that PL965 might be featured one day in the future. More importantly, however, when I mentioned my search for an expert able to analyse my bits of engine, he suggested David Birch, of the Rolls-Royce Heritage Trust, in Derby.

I therefore wrote to David Birch, describing at some length the circumstances in which my engine failed on 19th November 1944, and the excavation of the remains on 2nd April 1995, and enclosing photographs of all the most relevant engine parts. I asked him whether the Rolls-Royce Heritage Trust or the Rolls Royce Company itself could make an analysis of the actual pieces to determine the cause of the failure.

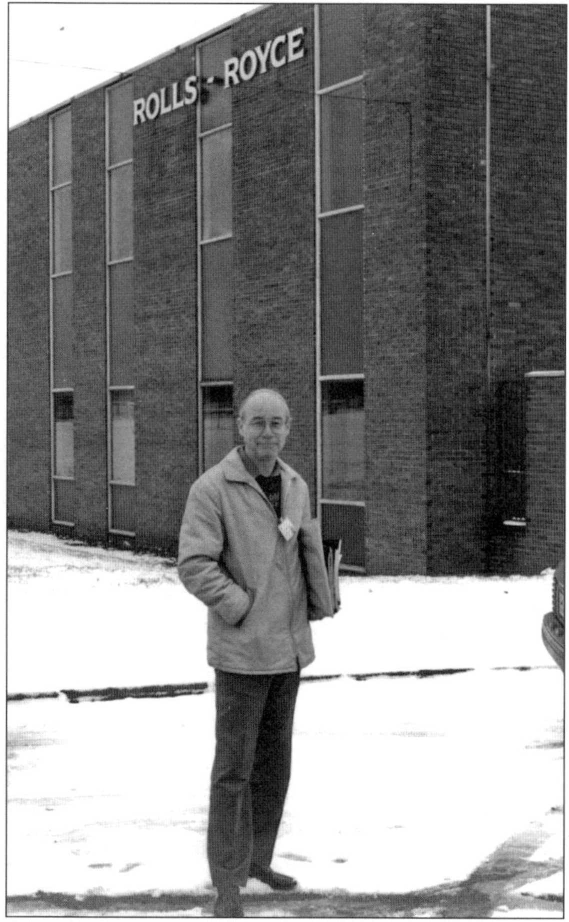

David Birch, excellent Rolls-Royce historian and my guide

David Birch replied on 18th August, saying that he had consulted Alec Harvey-Bailey, who was the most knowledgeable person concerning Merlin and, later, Griffon engines. His father, R.W.Harvey-Bailey, had joined Rolls-Royce in 1910 and designed the excellent Eagle and Falcon engines that powered many British aircraft in WW1; afterwards, he became Chief Technical Production Engineer and a senior executive of the Company. Alec grew up with virtually the run of the workshops and, at an early age, was test-driving some of the prototype cars. Unfortunately, he crashed one of these and lost an eye, putting paid to any hope of a career in flying. When WW2 came, as he was fully conversant with the production of the Merlin engine, his father put him in charge of a new small specialist department in the Derby works, the Engine Failure Investigation Section: any engine whose failure defied the efforts of the engineering officer of a squadron or maintenance unit, would be sent to this Section, where it would be stripped down and worked on until the fault was identified. If it was economically feasible, Alec would recommend a change in the production line or tell engineering officers in the field to alter

Alec Harvey-Bailey visiting an airfield in 1945
Photo: Rolls Royce Heritage Trust

Alec Harvey-Bailey in later life with a Merlin engine
Photo: The Daily Telegraph

their maintenance schedule in some way; in a few cases, no remedial action was worthwhile and occasional failures had to be accepted.

Alec had a wonderful memory, which made him the ideal person, when he retired in 1981, to record the history of the development of many Rolls-Royce products. Sadly, he had recently suffered a crippling heart attack and stroke, which left him unfit to receive visitors. David Birch considered that it was beneficial for him to be given something to exercise his mind on, and my request had therefore come at an appropriate moment.

As Alec Harvey-Bailey was unable to write, David Birch passed on his thoughts in a letter to me of 18th August. In this he postulated three causes of oil entering the combustion area of the cylinder-head: piston-failure, valve-failure, and piston-ring gumming. The first and second were rare occurrences, but the third was not uncommon: the piston-rings became glued to their grooves and did not spring out to seal against the cylinder wall, allowing lubricating oil to force its way past into the combustion space and starting a fire when it ignited. Ring-gumming was the result of running the engine for long periods at low rpm.

This conclusion reflected my own personal assumption that I had caused the sparking-plugs or the valves to foul-up by my flying for too long at low economical rpm. It was ever-present in my mind during a sortie that I might be 'bounced' by a German fighter or face some other emergency that would require full throttle and plenty of fuel. We were aware of the danger of 'ring-gumming' and were advised to open the throttle every ten minutes or so to clear the plugs. I was not very good at keeping to this principle and I recognised that I might have contributed to my own downfall. Bearing in mind the tragic consequences of this to the Dutch people, my faulty airmanship had long rested uneasily on my conscience. Now Alec Harvey-Bailey, without actually pointing his finger at me, had confirmed that my neglect was the most likely cause of the engine-failure. This did not make me feel any happier.

On 30th August, however, David Birch wrote again to say that Alec, who was a very sick man, had reconsidered his previous verdict and now wished me to tell him in more detail what I could remember of what happened when the engine began to fail. The ring-gumming answer was valid only if smoke was emitted from just one exhaust-port, as the condition was not likely to occur in more than one cylinder at a time. If the smoke came from all the ports together, then the fault lay elsewhere, either in the supercharger, or in one or more of the sparking-plugs, when it would lead to piston-failure. Alec was also surprised by my mention of oil covering my windscreen: oil ejected from the exhausts was usually blown down the side of the fuselage by the slipstream; if it sprayed over the windscreen of a Merlin-engined aircraft, it usually indicated a leak in the casing of the propeller reduction-gear.

This unexpected turn of the inquiry required me to search my memory of the sortie on 19th November 1944 with great stringency: I had to imagine myself back in the cockpit of my Spitfire and endeavour to recall the details and exact sequence of events on that fateful occasion.

My reply to Alec included the following:

"I remember clearly the engine 'hiccoughing', i.e. losing revs all at once, and then trying to 'pick itself up again', rather like a horse that stumbles and tries to stagger on. The smoke came out almost immediately, and then the gobs of black oil that quickly covered the windscreen. I can't remember how long this process took – whether it happened before or while I was juggling with the throttle. I know I first closed the throttle, but the smoke continued to come out; and then I opened it fully, having heard that this was one way of blowing-out a carburettor fire. But neither action made any difference, and the rough running with the throttle open didn't seem the answer at all.

With the throttle closed and the propeller windmilling, smoke (and perhaps oil, I can't recall) was still coming out and I remember, as I slowly descended, being concerned about the great trail of dirty smoke that I was leaving behind me, which was sure to attract the attention of the Germans. In fact, I kept my head turning constantly on the look-out for unfriendly fighters.

My recollection is strong of a lot of smoke and oil from the right-hand side – and I would say from more than one port; but I don't recall the left side so clearly. But I am right-handed and tend to think and look right in preference to left, so left always gets a little bit neglected.

You can't normally see the exhaust-ports from the cockpit of a Spit XI, so it's difficult for me to say whether the smoke and oil came from one port or many. The extent of it has never suggested to me that only one port was responsible. If I shut my eyes and think back, it looks like a lot coming from the right side, and I would guess from many ports rather than just one.

As for the airflow blowing it over the windscreen, I reduced speed to 140mph and started to lose height quite soon after the outbreak; so the aircraft would have been in a slight nose-down attitude after, say, two or three minutes and, with the prop windmilling, the airflow would have been more upward than usual. I must leave the rest of the puzzle to you."

David Birch delivered this to Harvey-Bailey, probably by reading it to him because of his illness; Alec chose to reply by recording his answer on tape, which was addressed to David, who sent it on to me. It was quite long, about 20 minutes, and filled 2 A4 pages when transcribed. The contents proved to be of historic importance as, in addition to describing in detail the bearings of the Merlin's two-stage supercharger and the working of the intercooler, Alec also recounted the wartime operation of his Engine Failure Investigation Section. I have picked out what I feel were his most significant observations on my particular case:

"First of all, I do not think I was right in assuming that it was ring-gumming. On a fighter, it is generally possible to detect ring-gumming by increased oil-consumption and the like, possibly increased engine-breathing and this does not appear to have taken place.

However, the relatively sudden nature of the symptoms that occurred indicates to me that it is more likely to be involved in the supercharger.

The two-stage Merlin in that particular Mark of Spitfire had the conventional rotor-shaft, with a ball-bearing front-bearing location, and a tail-bearing having a floating bronze bush and a floating steel bush running in a fixed bronze bush.

It seems likely, in this case, that there was a defect in the front-bearing and we did have a few ball-bearing failures in that position. It is quite a heavy-duty operation, running at high speeds – over 20,000rpm – and, although the bearing was not short of capacity, we did have the odd failure. The damage was so severe that it was difficult to point to a particular cause.

The symptoms described by Mr Taylor, of the engine hiccoughing and losing revs, all at once and then trying to pick itself up again, are quite symptomatic of supercharger trouble, and the smoke would come, I think, from the tail-bearing, because the tail-bearing would suffer if the front-bearing failed. I do not think I could be more definite than that."

After describing the working of his Engine Failure Investigation Section and the efforts his father who, during the war, was Chief Quality Engineer of the Aero-engine Division, made to maintain quality control and to investigate problems, Alec continued:

"The practices established on the Merlin during the war years have continued since then, and the investigation of problems is still a key issue with the Company.

So, on that note, I will close. It has been interesting to think back over those eventful years with the Merlin during the war, and I hope what I have said has been useful.

Goodbye,
Alec."[1]

[1]See Appendix D pp. 735-736 for the full transcript of Alec Harvey-Bailey's tape.

I expected this to be Alec Harvey-Bailey's last communication to me but, surprisingly, it wasn't. After our Duxford Reunion, I sent him a Christmas card with seven pilots and three ground-staff of 16 Squadron 1939-1945 sitting in front of 'our' Spitfire XI PL965, adding, of course, our very best wishes for his recovery. In reply, he managed to write from the Burton Clinic, in Burton-on-Trent, in scrawled capital letters, no doubt with great effort, the following charming letter:

"4.1.97

Dear Jimmy,

Nothing has given me greater pleasure than to receive your 16 Squadron card. It reached me in the middle of my fifth week in hospital following a massive heart failure at the end of a year which saw the death of my wife after 53 years of marriage.

There is something so heartwarming in the picture – the veterans of 1939-1945 with one of their Spitfires, still a wonderful fighter and they were people who added to the lustre of Mitchell's great basic design.

It was an honour to work with such people and such a brilliant aircraft. It was most kind of you to search me out and has helped on my road to recovery. Please give my best wishes to your Associates, the picture will be a treasured possession.

Happy New Year,

Alec Harvey-Bailey
Please excuse the dreadful writing"

Sad to say, shortly after this fine tribute, Alec succumbed to cancer.

The photo that impressed Alec Harvey-Bailey:
(l-r) Back row: Peter Fahy Ron Abrahams Michael Horsfall Ken Holloway JT
Front: Michael Wetz Ron Parnell Edgar Quested Norman Godfrey Douglas Petrie
with ex-16 Squadron Spitfire XI PL965 at Duxford in 1996

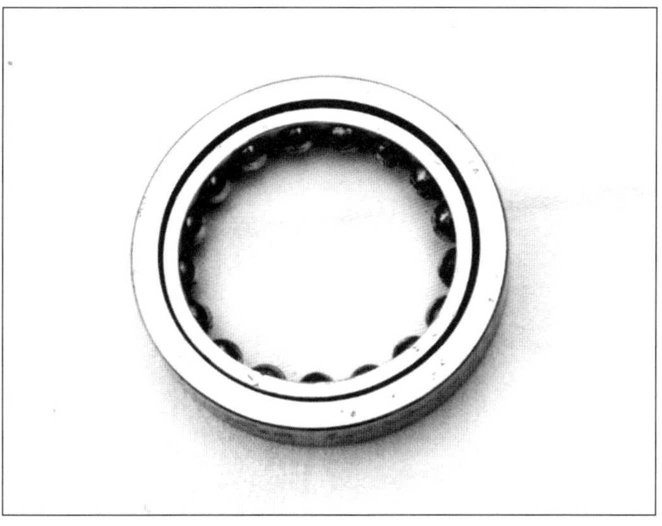

A bearing from crashed Spitfire IX NH523, similar to the one that caused the engine-failure on JT's Spitfire XI MB957 on 19th November 1944

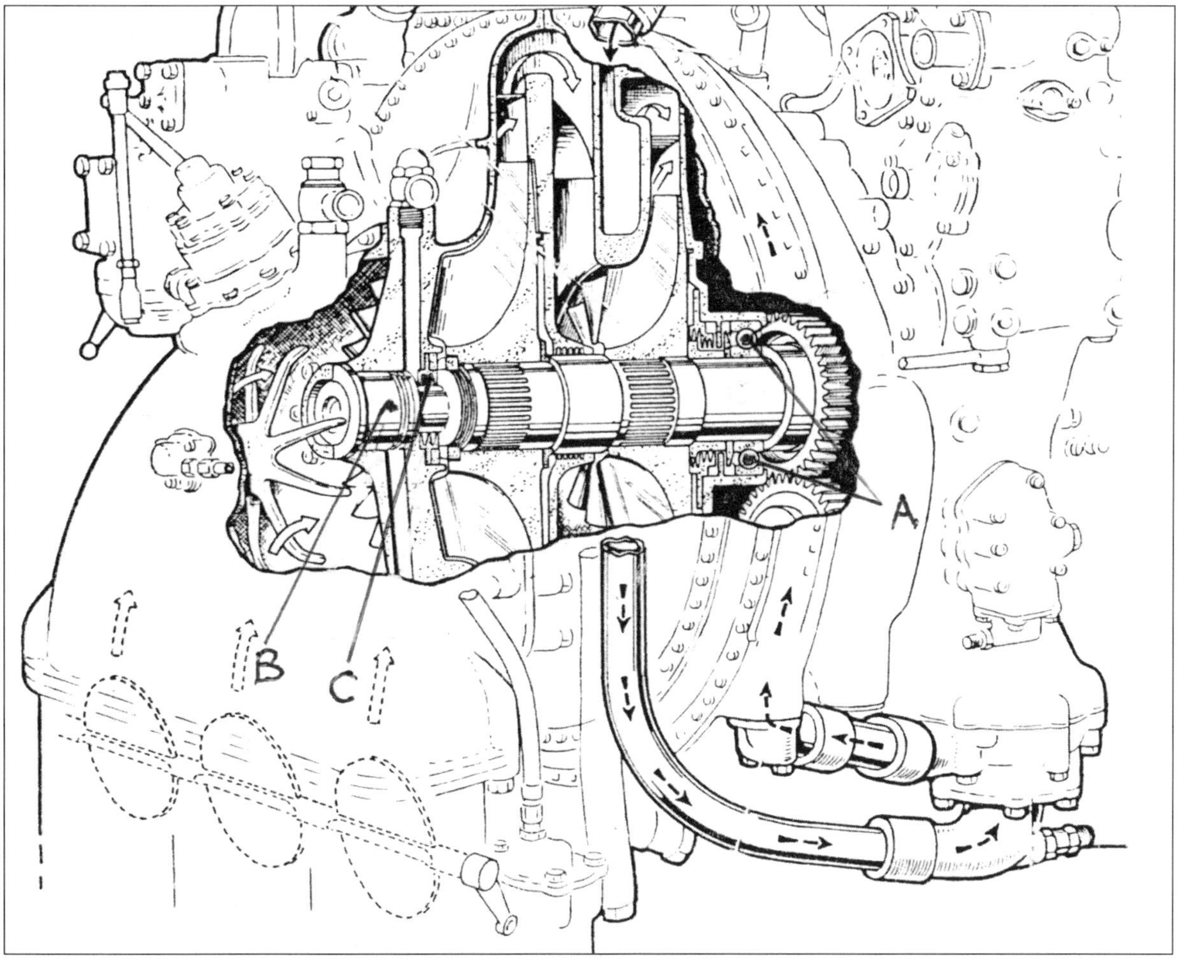

Diagram of supercharger and rotor-shaft
A: front ball-bearing B: rear plain-bearing C: sealing

Diagram: David Birch

I was most fortunate, through David Birch's kind offices, to receive the benefit of Alec's unsurpassed knowledge and experience of the Merlin engine, and thereby to gain an invaluable reprieve from the guilt I had felt previously that Dutch lives were lost near Borne through my own careless handling of my Spitfire's engine.

A few days after I had received Alec's remarkable tape, which David Birch asked me to return to him for Rolls-Royce's own archives when I had made a copy, David most thoughtfully sent me a valuable complement to it in the shape of diagrams and notes describing and illustrating the working of the Merlin's and Griffon's supercharger. These enabled me to visualise the position and function of the front bearing, and to imagine the destruction wrought on the rest of the engine if this disintegrated at 20,000 or so rpm. They also served to raise my interest in examining an actual Merlin engine and seeing these vital components at first-hand.

I therefore wrote to David and asked if I could visit the Rolls-Royce Heritage Trust to see their museum and workshop. He kindly agreed, so in due course, on 7th February 1996, I drove into the Rolls-Royce works at Hucknall, outside Nottingham, one of the centres of Rolls-Royce engine development and production, with an airfield much used for the test-flying of aircraft fitted with their world-famous power-units.

In the workshop of the Heritage Trust I found a friendly group of retired Rolls-Royce employees, who met there every Wednesday to discuss past and present Rolls-Royce achievements and to work on repairing and restoring Merlin and Griffon piston-engines for restored WW2 warplanes, and early types of Rolls-Royce jet engines for later military and civil aircraft.

David Birch turned out to be one of the younger members, who had taken early retirement to become the Trust's historian. He had been a pipe-fitter on both piston and jet engines, and very soon showed that he had an expert knowledge of the production and working of every type of Rolls-Royce aero-engine. He let me wander round the displays of photographs and aeroplane models, and helped me to choose the books most appropriate for my interests from those written by Alec Harvey-Bailey and published by the Heritage Trust.

We then went downstairs into the workshop, where there were several rows of engines, including a Merlin 100, a sectioned Griffon, an early Whittle-type centrifugal jet, a sectioned axial-flow jet, and many others. One engine was being hoisted up for work to be done on it in the interests of restoration and preservation.

David was able to show me on the Griffon – which was a scaled-up version of the Merlin, from 27.0 to 36.7 litres capacity – exactly what the interior of the supercharger looked like and where the front bearing was located, and we speculated on the sequence of destruction inside the engine if it failed. I learned, for the first time, about the technicalities of the two-stage two-speed supercharger, which enabled our Mark XI Spitfires to get increased power to take us up easily from 18,000ft to 35,000ft

An intact Merlin engine at the Rolls-Royce Museum in Derby

Ivor Purkis, Chairman of the Derby and Hucknall Branch of the Rolls-Royce Heritage Trust, presents me with a framed technical drawing of a Merlin supercharger bearing on 29th July 1998.

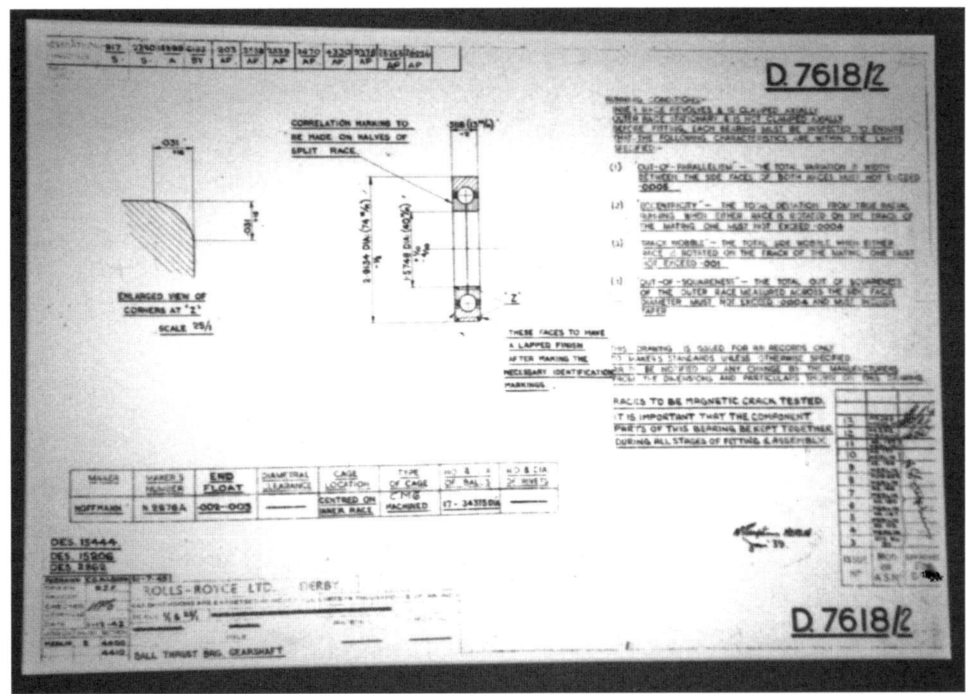

The framed technical drawing of a Merlin supercharger bearing

or even higher; and I began to understand, again for the first time, the significance of different impeller diameters and gear-ratios and the function of the intercooler.[1] We also discussed wood and metal propeller-blades, and I learned that the reduction-gears on a Merlin (like those which Hennie Noordhuis had excavated from my hole in the field near Bentelo) slowed down the propeller to less than half the speed of the engine.

I apologised to David for my ignorance of what went on under the cowlings of my aircraft. Throughout my training as a pilot, in both UK and USA, I had been given lectures on aero-engines of several different kinds but, as a young man, my mind was closed completely, even fatally, to science and technology, and I mastered only those controls that enabled me to fly the aircraft. David, however, said that Rolls-Royce realised that this was the attitude of many wartime pilots and they therefore tried to make their products more-or-less fool-proof for this very reason. I told him that I should have made this visit fifty years earlier: today's RAF pilots very often have the benefit of a university science degree before they begin their training.

Thanks to David Birch and Alec Harvey-Bailey, I had undergone a belated but invaluable initiation into the complexities of the Merlin engine, and I felt that there was now little left for me to discover about my last flight in Spitfire XI PL957. How wrong I was!

In a different context, I had also been wrong about a small but very important detail – the identity of my Spitfire. Up till this juncture, I had recorded it as PL957; but David Birch, with his historian's feeling for accuracy, had looked-up this aircraft in Morgan and Shacklady's great work, "Spitfire: the History" (Key Publishing 1987) and found that on 19th November 1944 it had been damaged on operations with 4 Squadron and been scrapped in 1947!

In my log-book I had recorded all my aircraft under their Squadron letter followed by the last three numerals of their serial number – e.g. in this case 'L' 957. I seem to have applied 'PL' quite arbitrarily; it happened to be the serial prefix of the latest model of Spitfire XI with a Rolls-Royce Merlin 70 engine of 1250hp for take-off; so it may have been wishful thinking on my part. Now, however, David discovered that it had to be MB957, which the book showed was an earlier model with a Merlin 63 engine, which was actually rated higher for take-off at 1280hp, but had a slightly lower performance at altitude. In fact, this aircraft arrived on 16 Squadron on 5th November 1943, so it was definitely due for retirement by 19th November 1944. I was and remain greatly indebted to David Birch for his two invaluable contributions to the facts about the Spitfire that ultimately let me down on my last flight.

[1]See Appendix E p. 737 for the complete diagram of the Merlin Supercharger, with David Birch's explanations.

CHAPTER 29

Silent Flights and Noisy Reunions

On my retirement from lecturing at the University of Leeds in 1987, I knew that one of my activities would be on the water in some kind of boat. Perhaps because of childhood holidays spent at Praa Sands in Cornwall, where the cottage my parents had built was in the middle of a grassy strip above a mile-long stretch of golden sand between two rocky headlands, I have always loved the sea, and I wanted very much to have a small yacht to fulfil my dreams.

Michael Horsfall had built his own 25-foot boat after the war, and I had a memorable sail with him and my 11-year-old goddaughter Annie from Southampton to Weymouth in which, as a complete novice, I did most of the work under Annie's tuition, while Michael spent the whole voyage in the cabin, working-out courses. Margaret and I drove to virtually every harbour and marina from Berwick-on-Tweed, all round the coast of England and Wales, up to Whitehaven in Cumbria, following-up advertisements in the nautical magazines for the sort of small second-hand yacht that would fit my limited purse. Eventually, we found a 17-foot trailer-sailer in Romsey, miles from the sea in Hampshire, and towed it back to Leeds. It was a wood Lysander and had everything I wanted, except for the horrible overall yellow paintwork. A white re-paint soon changed this and, when the cabin, mast and spars had all been re-varnished, we had a very smart little boat. I then went down to Dartmouth and, together with a young New Zealand couple, took an excellent week-long course, under an instructor, on a well-equipped 27-foot yacht, which certified the three of us as Day Skippers, and gave me a degree of skill and confidence in handling my own boat. It then turned put that Margaret didn't like the water at all, so I started to change over the rig and rigging for single-handed sailing.

At this point, in 1992, I saw a notice in the University that read, "Come gliding on a summer evening!" This sounded delightful, so I rang the Leeds University Union Gliding Society (LUUGS) and received a visit to my house from a Senior Lecturer, the late Dr Arthur Chadwick, who was a long-term member of the club, with his own glider and a share in a motor-glider. LUUGS was the happy associate of the Cleveland Gliding Club, one of eight clubs round the country run by the RAF Gliding and Soaring Association; it was based at Dishforth airfield, alongside the A1 just north of Boroughbridge. Except for two gliders owned by LUUGS, everything else belonged to Cleveland and was available to the University students. They were welcome to Cleveland, as they gave work to the instructors, and were also useful in moving gliders around, launching and retrieving them, driving the tractors, and keeping the log of the flight-times.

From my very first flight on 18th July 1992, I was hooked! Sitting in the front of a glass-fibre Grob Acro glider, towed up by an elderly Chipmunk, with an instructor, Dick Brisbourne, behind me doing all the flying, I was totally captivated. Released at 2000 feet, we drifted across the Yorkshire landscape at 44 knots (= 45mph), in a silent world in which we were able to chat to each other with perfect ease, accompanied only by the gentle sighing of the slip-stream through small holes in the fuselage. Dick found a thermal, an invisible column of warm air rising from ground heated by the sun, and we circled round, slowly gaining height until we ended up under a friendly dark cumulus cloud, itself supported by the rising air. He let me fly the glider and, under his directions, I tried to find another thermal; but we were out of luck and gradually returned to the airfield. He took over, flew the glider downwind parallel to the runway, then round onto the base leg, followed by a final turn onto the approach; he extended the air-brakes – strips of metal that stood up on the wings and reduced the lift – allowing him to descend more rapidly and, with a few small adjustments, as with a throttle, he landed smoothly and

Launching a K13 two-seater glider of the Cleveland Gliding Club by aero-tow behind a Chipmunk tug at Dishforth airfield

stopped exactly on our starting-point. It was a glorious experience to be free in the air once again, to look down on the cars and trucks moving on the A1, much faster than us, but infinitely inferior.

My next flight was an hour later in the same glider, but with George Brindle, a very experienced instructor; it provided me with more surprises and thrills. In the sky were rows of clouds in long cigar-shapes with straight lines across their tops: they were formed from the wind passing over the Pennine hills away to the west, blowing the air upwards until the moisture in it condensed out in the form of these rows of 'zeppelin-like' clouds at right-angles to the wind. They were known as the 'wave', spreading both vertically and horizontally, like ripples on a pond. I had never noticed them before or even heard of them in the lectures on meteorology we were given in the RAF.

We were towed up again until we were underneath and just in front of one of these clouds, pointing into the wind. To my astonishment we started to rise, in the same air that was forming the cloud. Our airspeed of 44 knots just equalled the wind-speed so that, pointing in to it, we were virtually motionless over the ground, but were gaining height at 400 feet a minute – one of our instruments was a variometer, which measured the rate of ascent and descent. This increased to 600 feet a minute as we passed above the top of the cloud and saw rows, or 'streets', of these formations stretching out beneath us. In the gaps between them, the ground was visible but rather dark, and I had no idea where we were. George let me fly the glider, still pointing into the wind; I was just sitting there, holding the joystick and rudder steady at 44 knots and still going up – a most extraordinary sensation.

We were now in clear blue sky, the sun shining brightly on the long streets of 'wave-clouds' below us, white as snow. They were not static, however, but moving slowly, coalescing together, pinching out the gaps, but letting others appear. George was watching them, and warned that if the gaps were disappearing altogether, we would have to go down in a hurry while the ground remained in sight. He took-over the controls and turned the glider to fly along the 'wave', which was still present, but invisible in the sky and now slowly decreasing in power; he proceeded to fly up and down the 'wave', stopping to turn back into the wind where the rise was greatest. In this way, we reached 8,500 feet and I felt on top of the world!

The instructor's view on tow (the student sits in front).
"Keep the wheels on the horizon" – if you can see it. The pilots of the Glider Pilot Regiment had to hold this position for nearly 3 hours as they were towed to Arnhem in September 1944.

View of an aero-tow from the ground

Dishforth airfield, a wartime bomber station, now an Army Air Corps helicopter base, with the helicopter pad in front of the hangars. The airfield was open to the Cleveland Gliding Club at the weekends.

The ascent had dropped to only 50 feet a minute and we had now virtually exhausted the 'wave'. George turned the glider downwind and we headed for the open sky near Dishforth. To have all this height in a glider was a luxury and George asked me if I'd like to do some aerobatics. Nothing would please me more, so he "cleared the sky', turning each way and ensuring there were no other aircraft beneath us; he then dived the glider down until we were doing 90 knots, heralded by the increasing noise of the slipstream; he then pulled back on the joystick progressively until we were pointing straight up, then upside down, and further back still, until we returned to the dive and the nose came up to the horizon again, when he levelled-off. I asked if I could try and it was not difficult – I just had to get up sufficient speed initially because we had no engine, and keep pulling back on the joystick to ensure we had sufficient flying-speed even at the top of the loop, so that we flew a figure more like a '6' than an '0'. George then did some 'stalled turns', which he called 'chandelles', pulling the glider up vertically and then pushing hard on the right rudder to turn the nose down at the top just before the stall; then down, up the other side, and turning the nose down again at the top to complete an oval figure pulled high at each end. So, in such pleasurable, controlled manoeuvres, we lost height and returned to the airfield, where George made the expected perfect landing. We had been up for just over an hour.

I had discovered a whole new flying scenario: 'wave-flying'. It was wonderful, but I felt it was rather mechanical: the height record in the Cleveland Club was an amazing 25,000 feet! Pilots were limited to 12,000 feet, after which they needed oxygen; this meant they had to carry an oxygen bottle and mask, and get authorisation from the Duty Instructor; they also needed a GPS navigation aid in case they were caught out by closing clouds when returning to the airfield. All this deterred, rather than encouraged me; but the aerobatics gave me huge pleasure and I felt that this was the activity that I would enjoy most.

My third flight in 1992 took place a week after the previous two and introduced me to something different again which, on my first experience, was so exciting as to be almost frightening: this was winch-launching. This time I was in LUUGS's two-seater metal, wood, and fabric-covered K7, and my instructor was Jack Clark, a little man with many years of gliding behind him. The winch was a powerful engine mounted on an old truck, with a drum and 3000 feet of wire-cable. This terminated in two small linked rings, and was pulled out by a tractor along the grass parallel to the runway in use to the launch-point, where we were waiting in the glider. At Jack's command, *"Cable on, please"*, a launch-man kneeled down and called *"Open!"* Jack pulled a yellow knob in the cockpit and the launcher attached the links to a hook in the bottom of the glider. When the launcher called *"Close!"*, Jack let go the knob and the hook closed. The launcher then stood up and pulled on the cable as hard as possible, at the same time searching the circuit for any other glider coming in to land. As there was no one approaching, he called out to Jack, *"Cable on and secure. All clear above and behind!"* He then went to a wing-tip and lifted it to level the glider for flight. He shouted *"Take-up slack!"*, at the same time waving his arm below shoulder-level; this was the signal for the time-keeper in the launch-van to flash a light slowly to the winch-driver and repeat the call *"Take-up slack!"* to him on the radio; the winch-man then gradually wound-in the cable until it was taut between the winch and our glider. Seeing this, the launcher shouted *"All out! All out!"* and waved his arm over his head; the time-keeper blinked the light faster and repeated *"All out! All out!"* on the radio; the winch-man accelerated his engine to full power; and the glider rushed forward faster and faster until we were off the ground at about 35 knots. Jack held it down until we had reached 50 knots, then he pulled back the joystick and with a whoosh! the nose went up to what felt like an angle of 80°, although it was actually only 40°. We shot up as if in a perpendicular Dodge'm car, at 65 knots to over 1000 feet in a matter of seconds. I looked over the edge of the cockpit: we seemed to have left the ground a long way below in the blink of an eye. Our climb slowed down as we came closer to being over the winch; before this happened, Jack lowered the nose and pulled the yellow knob to release us from the cable. It dropped away beneath us, and a small parachute opened to slow down its descent while the winch-man wound it in as fast as possible until it

The K13 going up on a winch-launch. The object beneath it is the parachute attached to the cable to slow its descent after the glider pilot has released it.

The side-view shows the glider going up on the winch at a modest angle.
Note the skid and single-wheel undercarriage.

was all back on the drum, except for the length with the parachute; the tractor then towed the end of the cable slowly back to the take-off point, ready for our next flight or for someone else to be launched.

Jack and I were now floating along at 44 knots at 1200 feet, which gave us just time to make a few turns in the air before starting on the downwind leg at the prescribed circuit height of 700 feet. We speeded-up to 50 knots; then at about 500 feet Jack turned 90° to the right to put us on the base-leg at 450 feet. We were flying a right-hand circuit to land back on the grass, while gliders being launched on aero-tow flew a left-hand circuit (out of our way) to land on the runway. At 350 feet, Jack turned right again onto the approach, flying now at 55 knots and putting up the air-brakes by pulling on a blue-painted lever in the cockpit. With his precise judgement, we skimmed over the grass until we lost flying speed and rumbled along the ground, the glider coming to rest almost on the spot from which we had started, within easy reach of the cable waiting for our second launch. Our flight had lasted just three minutes.

Gliding is not all flying:
JT on a tractor ready to retrieve a glider.

My second and third winch-launches followed straightaway – gradually less awesome, but still extraordinary. Jack allowed me to take-over the controls once he had released the cable and I flew most of the circuit until the final turn onto the approach. I saw that by keeping as closely as possible to the prescribed speeds and heights, it was not quite so miraculous as it had first appeared when the instructor landed virtually on the same place that we had started from – without an engine and propeller to pull him on to it. If we were too low on the approach, we had no means of regaining height; so it was better to plan to over-shoot and then apply the air-brakes to control the descent. It sounds easy, but it took me a whole year before I mastered it sufficiently to be allowed to go solo – and even after that, when I had gained a Bronze Certificate, I was never 100% certain where I would end up.

An unexpected sequel to my glider training occurred in September 1993, when Margaret and I were invited for a fascinating weekend at the RAF College at Cranwell, by the Commandant, Air Vice-Marshal David Cousins, AFC (later Air Chief Marshal Sir David, KCB, AFC), who was President of the 16 Squadron Association. He very kindly gave me a flight in a Bulldog trainer, with full flying-kit and boots laid out on my bed the night before. My instructor, a young Tornado pilot, let me do all the flying in the side-by-side aircraft; on returning to the circuit, he cut the engine for me to make a power-off landing. He couldn't believe it when I stopped exactly on the spot where we had started from. He made me take-off two more times and cut the engine at different heights, expressing his continued surprise at my precise landings on the take-off place. Of course, it was all due to my training at Dishforth. I think all trainee pilots should first learn to fly gliders – as young Germans did in the pre-war Luftwaffe – they would then be well-equipped to make accurate landings and to cope with unexpected engine-failures.

As a retired member of staff of the University, I was allowed to join any Society I wished, although I could not have any authority in it, as one purpose of all the University clubs was to enable the students to gain experience in running an organisation. Although ultimately part of the RAF, the Cleveland Club had to be self-supporting; but, by the members doing everything themselves, costs were kept to the minimum and the flying fees were very reasonable: I could learn to fly again at about two-thirds of the cost of being taught in a Cessna or a Tiger Moth. Unfortunately, I was 70 years old and found flying a glider, especially the take-off and landing, almost the opposite of flying a powered aircraft; for example, the Chipmunk tug-aircraft pulled us off the ground at about 35 knots, while it took much longer to take-off itself; so we had to fly behind it a few feet up, keeping straight and level, before it was off the ground; I found this difficult when a cross-wind blew the glider sideways. Another surprise was to find that, opposite to a powered aeroplane, a glider had to fly faster coming in to land, at 55 knots or more, because variable wind conditions required more control near the hard, unforgiving ground. The fact that, in spite of my wartime experience, I was such a slow learner didn't worry me: I just enjoyed being airborne once again, with my hand on a joystick and my feet on a rudder-bar and a set of simple instruments on the dash-board in front of me. A different kind of pleasure was participating in all the physical activities on the ground, and mixing with all the very friendly people in the Club, male and female, as young as 16 and as old as me, and with the mature University students, in whom I took a special interest. There was also the mental exercise of learning once more the principles of flight, the elements of meteorology that affected the flight of a glider, and the rules of airmanship that governed our behaviour in the air and the handling of the gliders on the ground.

All thoughts of sailing now went overboard and I laid up the Lysander in my covered car-port – where it stayed for the next fifteen years, never having been put on the water! I kept it because I didn't expect to be allowed to go on gliding for more than a few years. I went to Dishforth two or three days a month – the RAF used the airfield during the week and we flew from it at the weekends. A day out in the fresh air of Yorkshire, full of physical activity, in the company of fellow-enthusiasts, with the challenge of getting an engine-less aeroplane to go up as well as down, and the satisfaction of gradually acquiring the skills I so admired in the instructors and other members, all made for one of the most lasting pleasures of my life.

There was, however, one thing in the Club I objected to, and this was being introduced to newcomers as "our Spitfire pilot". I avoided mentioning my wartime past for as long as possible, but it slipped out eventually. The trouble was two-fold: Spitfire pilots are held in far greater veneration today than in 1944; after all, 25000 Spitfires were built and the great majority of their pilots were very ordinary people

JT in the cockpit of LUUG's K6 single-seater glider. The cockpit harness is visible above the straps of the parachute, which has to be worn because the seats are shaped to hold it. The canopy is on the ground, to be fitted before take-off.

The K21, a high-tech glass-fibre two-seater, waits to take-off on the runway while some students cluster round the cockpit of the K13 flying on the winch. On the left is the launch-van, with a windsock and two lamps for signalling to the winch-driver, who controls two cables for two consecutive launches.

Some of the cheerful, capable Cleveland members:
l-r: Roger Burghall, very knowledgeable and experienced; Henry Pantin, a long-term member (Research Fellow at the University); Jill Povall, one of my early instructors (retired teacher); Dick Cole (retired Squadron Leader and Tornado pilot), former CFI, international rally and competition pilot and examiner.

The K13 comes in for a typical landing on the grass. Note the air-brakes extended above and below the wings. The North Yorkshire Moors are visible on the skyline.

like myself, recruited as volunteers and becoming neither 'aces' nor above-average pilots. There was a natural expectation in the Club that, because of this past experience, I would quickly become a superior glider-pilot;, so there was surprise and not a little disappointment when I took a year to go solo and was liable to make mistakes at any time, both on the ground and in the air.

The other drawback was that they didn't realise the effect of my not having flown an aeroplane since I stopped flying Austers in the Iraqi Flying Club in 1956. In the intervening 40 years, I had concentrated on my teaching and lecturing career and given little thought to aviation; so I had to learn a lot of new tricks and, as everyone knows, this takes an old dog much longer. However, it was all my own decision, and I was as happy doing 'circuits and bumps' as other members were in making high-altitude flights or long cross-country ones or taking part in local and national gliding competitions, none of which attracted me.

On the other hand, I took great pleasure in climbing up inside a thermal – rising either from a relatively warm place on the ground such as a tarred road, a metal roof or even a ripe cornfield, or under a blossoming cumulus cloud – and staying up as long as possible. It became more exciting when I did so in rivalry with another glider – or with more than one. We would circle round on opposite sides of the invisible thermal, both gaining height until the better pilot or the one in the more efficient glider rose higher than the other; he could then overtake his rival and fly above him until the thermal grew weak and one or other flew away. If I was in LUUGS's old wooden K6 and found I could beat a rival in a streamlined glass-fibre machine, my morale was boosted sky-high!

Not being ambitions, I usually kept within sight of the airfield, my furthest flight being to Fountains Abbey about 20 miles away. But on a day of (for me) high wind of 40mph at 3000ft, when I thought I was over nearby Boroughbridge, I discovered I'd been blown 15 miles further east and was over Thirsk. Cruising at 42 knots (44mph), there was no hope of my getting back to Dishforth but, by putting the nose down to fly at 60mph I could make a little headway until an inevitable forced-landing in somebody's field. At 1500ft, however, I spotted the disused airfield of Topcliffe about four miles away.

Fountains Abbey (centre), taken from the K6 at sunset from 3000ft

Perfect soaring conditions under cumulus clouds over the Yorkshire landscape; the wing-tip belongs to the K6.

By increasing speed to 70mph (=30mph against the wind), I was just able to reach the very end of a runway and land almost motionlessly – when the wind started to blow the glider back. I jumped out, stuffed my parachute pack behind the wheel, and returned to my seat to hold the K6 down. Eventually, a Chipmunk came from Dishforth and towed it home, with the CFI flying it, and me in the back of the Chipmunk.

In my RAF life, aerobatics had always been a particular joy and, as an instructor, I think I taught them quite well. I had always confirmed my control of an aeroplane new to me by performing loops and rolls in it as soon as possible: I even coaxed an old, wooden, twin-engined Oxford into a loop. Now that I had learned that gliders were strong enough to do aerobatics, I determined to continue my practice after I had gone solo but, although loops were easy, I never managed to complete a roll: the K6 always fell out half-way round. However, whenever I was lucky enough to climb to 5000ft in one or more thermals, I used to reward myself by doing a couple of loops. But aerobatics needed to be authorised by the Duty Instructor, which was difficult in my case, as I never knew whether I would reach my own stipulated height, so I didn't bother with this rule. On the other hand, I made sure I was out of sight of any instructors, usually by putting a few clouds between the airfield and me.

One fine day some years later, when I had indulged my passion happily, as soon as I landed, Jim McLean, a senior member of the club who looked after the airframes of all the gliders, strode up to me and said accusingly:

"You've been doing aerobatics!"

"What do you mean by aerobatics?" I answered, prevaricating.

"You were seen," said Jim, who hadn't been a witness.

"Who says they saw me?"

"The Chief Flying Instructor." (CFI)

"But he's not here."

"That's how he saw you."

"What are you talking about?"

"He had flown to Burn and was lying on his back in the sun, looking up, when he saw a K6 looping the loop several times. He thought he recognised it as LUUGS's, so he rang up on his mobile and asked who was flying it – and it was you!"

There was no point in denying it, and I just laughed when other people came up and asked me about it. When the CFI Mark Desmond returned, he gave me a ticking-off for breaking the rules, but then added in true RAF style:

"I'd have done the same if I'd been in your position!"

Nevertheless, I didn't stretch my luck any further and did no more aerobatics until my last week in the Club in 2007, when I was being checked by an instructor, Peter Mason, and gave him a couple of loops to show him I could still do them at my age.

Gliding was full of challenges: to my flying skill, to my knowledge of meteorology, to my airmanship, to my ability to tow a glider with a tractor, and to my judgement in launching other pilots in their own or Club gliders; there were few dull moments and, because the Cleveland Club, with its basis in the RAF and with ex-RAF Squadron Leaders such as Dick Cole and Derek ('Grinner') Smith as CFIs, insisted on safety first and sensible discipline, there were no serious accidents in my 15 years with the Club. We had to wear back-parachutes, but this was more because the seats were shaped to accept them than with an expectation that we would need to use them. The only real fright I had was when I was chasing round the edge of a big white cumulus cloud, with the sun shining behind me, when another glider came out of the cloud, flying straight at me. I pulled frantically up and round and the other glider did the same! Then it suddenly disappeared – and I realised it was my own shadow inside a corona of sunlight projected onto the cloud! No wonder cloud-chasing was frowned upon by the authorities.

"Come gliding on a summer evening": the Irresistible Invitation!
A glider comes home as the sun dips below the distant Pennine foothills.

Eventually, of course, my age caught up with me: in September 2007, the instructors said my judgement and reactions were slipping, and suggested I should fly with an instructor as a safety pilot. This was not at all to my liking; it was gliding solo, making all my own decisions, that was the great attraction for me. In any case, I had reached my goal by continuing to fly until after my 85th birthday. So I decided to quit there and then, with no hard feelings of any kind – in fact, very much the opposite: I was most grateful for all the opportunities that I'd been given. My last flight was solo and my landing was a good one, with everybody watching, so I ended-up on a 'high'. I gave my gliding books to form the nucleus of a Club library, and presented an annual award, in the shape of a mounted pewter model Spitfire, for the LUUG's student making the most progress each year; the Club, in its turn, gave me a pewter beer-mug, which I hardly deserved, but value greatly.

However, although gliding was my only recreation and gave me great satisfaction, it did not take up as much of my time as a very different occupation: the organising of the survivors of the wartime 16 Squadron into a group. The event which sparked this off was the publication in May 1996 of Hugh Smallwood's brilliant book "Spitfire in Blue", a detailed study of Spitfire XI PL965 from its birth until 1995, which included a lively account of 16 Squadron from mid-1944 to mid-1945. Hugh did an impressive amount of research into both the plane and the personnel, in the course of which he wrote to me for any contributions. I sent him a few recollections and offered to do the proof-reading for him, as I had gained some experience of this when I proof-read the "RAF Magazine" for 1992 and 1993.

This came about because I wrote to the Editor, retired Squadron Leader Jake McCoughlin, to complain about the poor English and inconsistencies in spelling and punctuation in the 1991 issue: I told him, *"Anything to do with the RAF should be beyond criticism."* He replied by offering me the job of proof-reading; we became good friends through our lengthy correspondence, which eventually covered the content as well as the presentation of the material. He paid me by giving me a pair of his own RAF pilot's kid-gloves for my gliding!

This contribution to "Spitfire in Blue" brought me in touch with the whole design and layout of Hugh's book, and I shared in his anxieties when Osprey, the publishers, took their time; but what they produced finally was masterly, with a strip of a wartime map running down the edge of each page, ensuring that photo-reconnaissance was seen as the heart of all the activities of PL965 and of 16 Squadron.

On 6th May, Osprey launched "Spitfire in Blue" at Duxford, the site near Cambridge of a pre-war airfield that now also housed the aircraft collection of the Imperial War Museum (IWM). The day was doubly important for Osprey as on it they also published another new book, "Spitfire – Flying Legend" by Tony Holmes, Aviation Editor at Osprey. This was a big coffee-table book, beautifully illustrated with large close-up air-to-air shots by John Dibbs of every Mark of Spitfire. Tony asked me to write the feature about the Mark XI, which I did in about 1700 words; but he didn't tell me that it would appear in company with highly authoritative articles by a number of well-known pilots and aviation writers – otherwise I would have offered a more rounded picture of our wonderful aircraft and the work we were called on to do in it.

The day was also well chosen by Osprey as Duxford was holding a superlative air display, with 23 Spitfires on the ground, most of which flew in an impressive fly-past, to mark the 60th Anniversary of the First Flight of the Spitfire. There was thus a large attendance by the public and the likelihood of good sales of Osprey's two books about the famous aircraft.

Osprey had hired a large marquee, in an enclosure with chairs set out for viewing the air display, and invited former members of 16 Squadron to attend, with plenty of refreshments, books for sale, the author at hand to sign them, and the opportunity to meet several wartime Spitfire 'aces'. Unfortunately for them, in my opinion, only four of us took up their invitation, all being pilots: F/L Mike Wetz, DFC, F/L Gordon Bellerby, DFC, F/0 Bill Anderson, and myself. Mike Wetz was the only one I knew from my own short time, August-November 1944, on 16 Squadron, but we all fell into an easy relationship and thoroughly enjoyed looking back on the life and work of the Squadron; we discussed personalities and events, and talked about what had happened to us after those unique experiences.

This gave me the inspiration for deciding to organise a proper Reunion for former members of 16 Squadron, both ground-staff and aircrew, and covering the whole span of WW2, under the title "16 Squadron 1939-1945". Hugh Smallwood kindly gave me his list of about 60 names, 40 of them with addresses; David Lee, Deputy Director of IWM, said they would welcome our Reunion being held at Duxford and would be able to provide the catering for it at cost; Jonathan Parker, managing director of Osprey, offered the use of their marquee, which they would keep up until after our Reunion; Mark Hanna, with his father Ray, the owner of the Old Flying Machine Company, which maintained 'our' Spitfire XI PL965 at Duxford, said he would fly it for us for the relatively low price of £600; the owner, Chris Horsley, generously said he would provide this for us; and Wing Commander Brian Newby, AFC, CO of 16 Squadron at Lossiemouth, agreed to send a formation of Jaguars to overfly the event. Spitfire XIX PS853, 'our' other surviving PR Spitfire, was not certified airworthy, so there was no chance of the owner, Mrs Karen English, letting us see it; but Squadron Leader Paul Day, AFC, CO of the Battle of Britain Memorial Flight (BBMF), agreed to send another Spitfire XIX from his Flight to display for us. Our own Mike Wetz offered to supply drinks for the occasion from his family firm of Unwins, of which he was a director; and, finally, after consulting with all these people, I decided on Thursday, 19th September, as the date for the great day.

Unfortunately, from the start, we were hit by bad luck: the day dawned cold and blustery, too windy for the Spitfire XIX from BBMF to take-off; worse, PL965 was unflyable as its Certificate of Airworthiness had expired; and, to cap it all, 16 Squadron at Lossiemouth had just lost a Jaguar over the sea – fortunately without any casualties – and were holding back temporarily on all non-essential flights. Not the news to give me a happy morning!

However, Mark Hanna saved the day: he parked PL965 in a commanding position outside the marquee and placed a Messerschmitt 109G, one of our former adversaries, directly facing it. He also told me he would fly his Spitfire IX MH434 (a type which we also used in 1944 for low-level PR) for us if we paid him £400. I telephoned Chris Horsley, who turned up trumps and agreed to pay this. The Members arrived in reasonable numbers: nine pilots and four ground-staff, together with wives, adult sons and daughters, and friends; Lewis Deal, managing director of the Medway Aircraft Preservation Society, who had restored PL965 in 1987-1992, brought 15 of his members; and a dozen other people connected with either PL965, 16 Squadron, or IWM also attended. We held a short Reception in the marquee, with champagne provided by Mike Wetz and his co-director Martin Saunders, where I expressed our gratitude to the many people who had made this event possible at very low cost to ourselves. We then toasted "The Queen", "Absent Friends", "16 Squadron", "Aircraft Restorers", and "Ospreys", before sitting down to an excellent buffet lunch, with wine again supplied by Unwins.

Mark Hanna then taxied out in MH434 and proceeded to give us a spectacular exhibition of brilliant aerobatics, ending with a breath-taking grass-cutting run across the airfield. When he brought the aircraft back and climbed out of the cockpit, the veterans surged around him like excited schoolboys! Group and personal photographs followed, and the day ended with tea in the marquee, where I offered the first Associate Memberships of our group to Mark Hanna, Chris Horsley, Hugh Smallwood, and Tony Holmes. who had steered "Spitfire in Blue" through Osprey. Everyone agreed that it had been a memorable day.

It was therefore a disaster, felt by ourselves as well as by all in the aviation world, when Mark Hanna was killed on 26th September 1999 at Barcelona, landing an Me109G, which caught fire on the approach from a broken fuel-pipe; there was no way out for him at such a low level. So passed one of the greatest display pilots of the post-war generation.

Wartime Opponents face each other at the First Reunion of "16 Squadron 1939-1945", at Duxford airfield on the 19th September 1996: a Messerschmitt 109G and 16 Squadron's Spitfire XI PL965, both maintained by the Old Flying Machine Company.

Mark Hanna is the centre of attention after his brilliant display: wartime pilots David Stutchbury (l) and Douglas Petrie in discussion.

Fortunately, we could not see into this tragic future, and everyone agreed that, at £12 per head, the first Reunion of the wartime 16 Squadron had been a most enjoyable occasion and one that was well worth repeating. It set the pattern for the eight more-or-less annual Reunions that followed. We had no organisation except myself, and I determined to keep our association as simple and friendly as possible, with no distinction between pilots and ground-staff or between former officers and airmen. I also developed a set of principles which governed the organisation of the Reunions:

they had to be held at a place of aeronautical interest, either an airfield or an aviation museum;

if at all possible, one or both of 'our' Spitfires, PL965 and PS853, should be seen in the air;

other aircraft, which had some relevance to 16 Squadron, would be welcomed;

the ability of the location to provide refreshments and a buffet lunch in a room devoted to us was essential;

the day should be mid-week, to ensure that display pilots were not likely to be committed elsewhere, and to make road-travelling easier;

and, of major importance, the cost should be kept well within the means of the poorest veteran pensioners.

This last point meant that I had to trade on the wartime connection of 16 Squadron with the two Spitfires, PL965 being owned and flown by a series of private collectors – Chris Horsley, Tony Smith, and Peter Teichman – while PS865 was bought from Mrs English by Rolls-Royce in 1996 to form part of their Heritage Trust. I found all the owners and pilots were amazingly generous towards us and we never had to pay for any of the displays that were so much at the centre of our Reunions. What was equally astonishing to me was that all my arrangements were made over the telephone, in a matter of minutes, nearly always with people whom I had never met. I did, however, make a point of visiting the location three or four weeks before each Reunion, in order to discover the road approaches to it, meet the management, familiarise myself with the layout of the premises, inspect the facilities, draw up the time-table for refreshments, the menu for lunch, and the drinks to be provided, and agree on the total cost for the day. I would pay this myself, and expect to recoup it from those attending at a fixed price per head on arrival; in this way they would not need to keep putting their hands in their pockets to find money. I never covered my expenses, as I also produced a programme aimed especially at families and friends, who were unlikely to know much about 16 Squadron and the aeroplanes performing for us; and I also bought suitable thank-you presents, such as models or framed pictures of Spitfires, or figurines of airmen, for our hosts and the pilots of the displaying aircraft – but all this was my personal contribution and my pleasure. I arranged the flying programme in a general way, but left it to the pilots to agree with each other and with Flying Control the actual procedure for their displays. I thank my lucky stars that we never had an accident of any kind to cast a shadow over our gatherings.

I also very much encouraged the display pilots to join us for lunch and mix with our Members, especially if the visitors included any pilots from the contemporary 16 Squadron. I felt strongly that our veterans should be kept in touch with present-day military flying and, equally, that the young aircrews serving on the Squadron would benefit from meeting people who had maintained and developed the traditions of the Squadron in the circumstances of the Second World War. I was happy to be proved right when, in two Reunions, we had a sizeable number of pilots from the Squadron taking lunch with us, who soon became engaged in lively discussions with our Members.

Most of our Reunions were as successful as the first one, although one was almost washed-out by torrential rain all day, and another was circumscribed by official restrictions. This, in fact, was in September 1997, when we went to RAF Benson, the base from 1941 of No 1 PR Unit, which pioneered many of the techniques of photo-reconnaissance; it also fitted out our Spitfires with the cameras and controls for PR work, and was the first posting of several of our pilots before they joined 16 Squadron. It was therefore an obvious choice of location for our second Reunion.

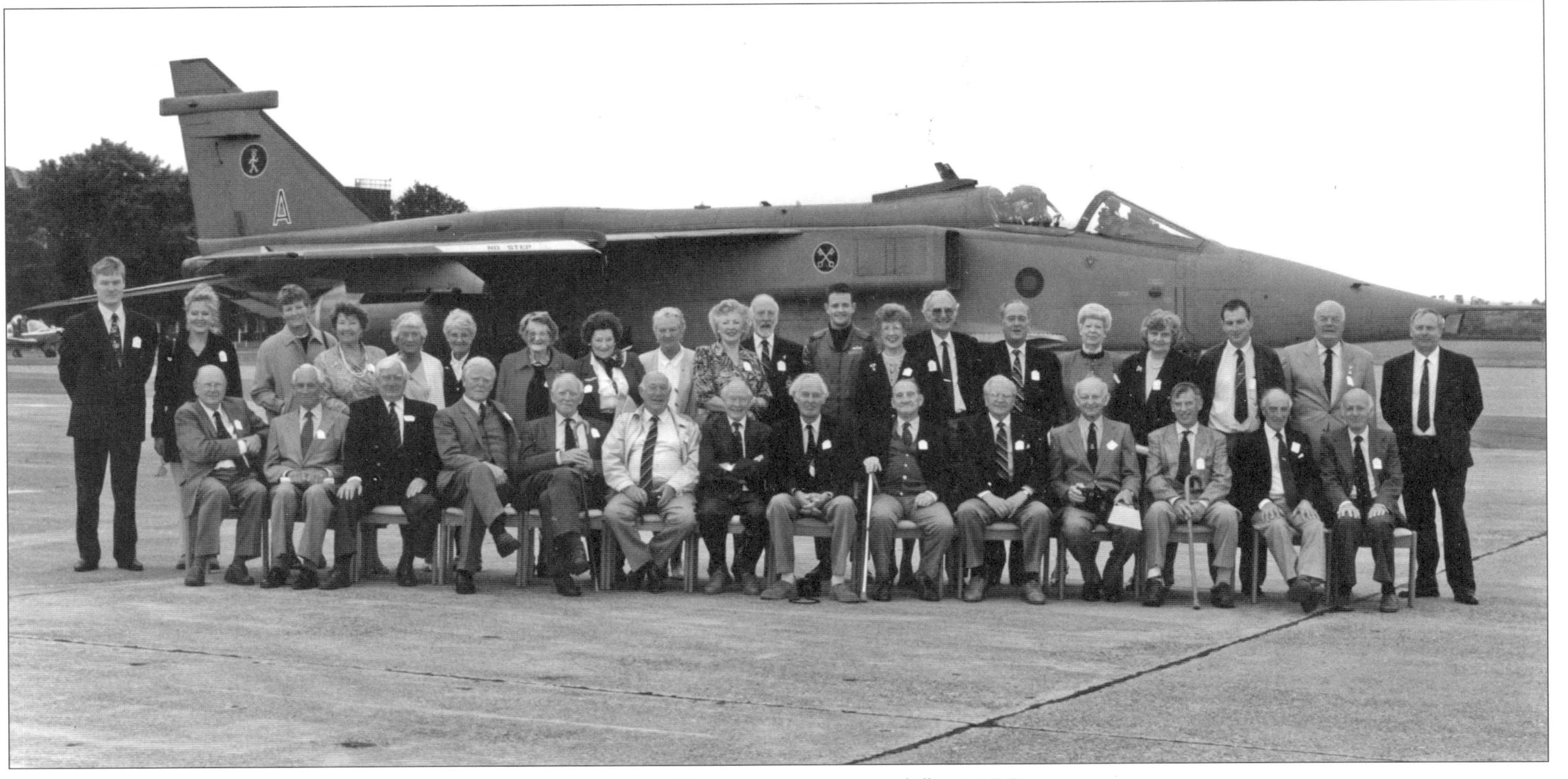

The 1997 Reunion of "16 Squadron 1939-1945" at RAF Benson
Front row l-r: wartime pilots and ground-crew with final RAF ranks and decorations:
F/L M.A.Wetz, DFC W/C E.R. Dutt, AFC S/L E.N. Godfrey, DFC, CdeG F/L J.M.C. Horsfall S/L P.D. Petrie, DFC F/O W.C. Anderson P/O H.A. Simkins, MiD F/L H.J.S. Taylor Sgt A.F. Jewell A/Sgt P.J.M. Robbins LAC J. Marett Sgt A.T. Silk LAC K. Holloway S/L P.E. Fahy, DFC, AFC
(back) families and friends; (at the back centre) F/Lt Mark Cutmore, the Jaguar Display Pilot
The Jaguar carries the 'Crossed Keys' of the 16 Squadron crest on the engine cowling, and its 'The Saint" emblem on the fin.

S/L Paul Day once again lent us his support by sending the Lancaster and Spitfire of the BBMF, together with their ground-crew in a Dakota, to overfly the airfield on their way to displaying at Jersey; and W/C Brian Newby kindly let us have a Jaguar, flown by F/L Mark Cutmore, the RAF's Jaguar Display pilot, to sit on the ground for us to examine. Unfortunately, noise restrictions over Benson village forbade Mark from displaying the aircraft in the air, and prevented Tony Smith, the new owner of PL965, from coming to Benson at all. Otherwise, we visited an exhibition, specially arranged for us, of PR cameras and other equipment, together with a display of operational photographs taken by the Benson wartime squadrons, held a short Reception, and enjoyed a fine lunch in the Officers' Mess. Afterwards, group photographs were taken in front of the replica Spitfire XI EN343 of F/0 Gerry Fray, DFC, who took the famous photographs of the water pouring out of the Moehne dam, on the morning .of 17th May 1943, after 617 Squadron had breached it the night before with Barnes Wallis's 'bouncing' bombs.

After being driven to the concrete 'apron' in front of the hangars and overlooking the airfield, we examined the sleek 16 Squadron Jaguar parked there, had more photos taken with Mark Cutmore standing in our midst, and were then served a pleasant tea from a small tent. Mark now started-up his two Rolls-Royce Adour engines and taxied almost out of sight to the end of a distant runway. We watched as the Jaguar took-off with an appropriate roar, but Mark wasn't allowed even to show-off the aircraft with a farewell circuit or upward roll as he headed for Jersey, to join the BBMF and other aircraft taking part in the island's free annual airshow.

Alongside this promotion of Reunions of 16 Squadron's wartime survivors, it soon became clear that a means of keeping Members informed and in touch with me and with each other throughout the year was also needed. In fact, the one or two letters I circulated announcing our first Reunion were the prototypes of the full newsletters that followed, starting with a report of the Duxford Reunion for the benefit of those who were not able to attend it.

Thus was born "Newsbrief", a modest publication, produced entirely by myself, with basic manual equipment and at minimum expense. I typed it out on an elderly word-processor, which fortunately had a memory and floppy discs; duplicated the pages on laser photocopiers in the Media Department of the University of Leeds (another privilege of retired members of staff); collated the pages at home and bound them with a plastic 'spine' on a simple hand-driven machine; and dispatched them by post to Members, Ex-Officio Members (former COs of 16 Squadron), Associate Members, and a few outside supporters. I wrote about half the text myself and proof-read the other half, developing my own 'house-style' in the process, based on clarity and consistency in composition, and accuracy in spelling and punctuation – shades of the "RAF Magazine."

The contents usually included an editorial; news from and about Members; reports of Reunions and other gatherings; accounts of the operations in which 16 Squadron was engaged in 1939-1945; personal reminiscences of life and work on the various airfields in UK and Europe where the Squadron was based during the war; descriptions of technical aspects of the aircraft and equipment used by the Squadron and by 34 Wing in the air and on the ground – the photographers provided especially interesting material – and news of the contemporary 16 Squadron as a Tornado unit, which participated valuably in the First Gulf War, and as a Reserve squadron in Scotland and Norfolk, training pilots on the Jaguar and taking part in patrolling Kosovo and northern Iraq.

As important as the text, in my eyes, were the illustrations, especially as 16 Squadron was busy on photographic work in 1944-45. I therefore aimed to have a page of photographs opposite almost every page of writing. This was a major task, and I scanned military and aviation books and magazines for relevant material to photocopy; I also expected contributors to include suitable personal photos, which I often copied on a shop print-to-print machine before returning them to the owners. It was surprising

16 Squadron 1939-1945 Membership April 2004

Sgt A.F.(Frank) Jewell Fitter II (Engines) 20 August 1937-Sept. 1939
A/Sgt P.J.M.(Peter) Robbins Fitter II (Airframes) October 1939-November 1940
LAC W.E.(Bob) Laws Fitter II (Engines) 1939-June 1940
F/L T.B.(Jock/Tom) Clark Wireless Operator 20 January-21 July 1940
Sgt W.J.G.G.(Maç) McIntosh Administration March 1940-October 1944
A/F/Sgt A.T.(Tom) Silk Fitter II (Engines) 24 December 1940-June 1943
W/C A.G.(Glen) Pallot, AE, AAF Pilot December 1941-October 1942
F/M(E) J.J.(Jock) Waugh Fitter II (Engines) January-December 1941
LAC W.T.(Bill) Bull Instrument Repairer 1943-September 1945
Cpl R.(Ron) Coleman, MiD Fitter II (Engines) 1943-September 1945
LAC Eric Phillips Wireless Mechanic 1943-September 1945
S/L E.N.(Norman) Godfrey, DFC, CdeG Pilot Oct.1943-Aug.1944; Mar.-Aug.1945
F/M(E) K.(Ken) Holloway Fitter II (Engines) 1943-September 1945
A/Cpl R.C.(Ron/Dusty) Miller Photographer 13 February 1944-Sept. 1945
S/L P.E.(Peter) Fahy, DFC, AFC Pilot April-November 1944
LAC D.W.(Dudley) Ford F/M(Airframes) 29 May-23 September 1944
F/L L.L.(Scotty) Cadan, MiD, US Air Medal, RAAF Pilot 4 Aug 1944-20 Sept 1945
F/L J.M.C.(Michael/Mike) Horsfall Pilot 25 August 1944-14 Jan. 1945
F/L H.J.S.(Jimmy) Taylor Pilot 26 August-19 November 1944
F/L D.(David/Dave) Stutchbury Pilot November 1944-Sept. 1945
F/O W.C.(Andy/Bill) Anderson Pilot 21 November 1944-Sept. 1945
F/L G.(Gordon) Bellerby, DFC Pilot January-May 1945

Ex-Officio Members

Air Chief Marshal Sir David Cousins, KCB, AFC, RAF (Retd) CO 16 Squadron 1977 -1980; Controller, RAF Benevolent Fund; President, 16 Squadron Association
G/C Brian Newby, AFC, RAF CO 16 (R) Squadron 1995-97
G/C Andrew Sudlow, MBE, RAF CO 16 (R) Squadron 1997-2000
W/C Peter Allan, RAF CO 16 (R) Squadron, 2000-2002
W/C Guy Stockill, RAF CO 16 (R) Squadron, RAF Coltishall, Norwich, Norfolk

Associate Members

HRH The Duke of Edinburgh, KG, KT Marshal of the Royal Air Force
Lieut. General D.L. Berlijn, Commander-in-Chief, Royal Netherlands Air Force
F/L S.(Stan) Hayward, CdeG, AEA Pilot 69 Squadron 1943-1945; 34 WSU 1945
LAC Basil Jackson Photographer 140 Squadron and 34 Wing May 1944-Sept. 1945
F/L Walter Le May, DFC Pilot 140 Squadron
S/L Mark Cutmore, RAF former 16 Squadron Jaguar Display Pilot
Peter Arnold Air Historian; early identifier of Spitfire XI PL 965 in Holland
S/L Paul Day, OBE, AFC, RAF former CO Battle of Britain Memorial Flight
Lewis Deal, MBE MD Medway Aircraft Preservation Society, restorers of PL965
Michael Evans Chairman Emeritus, Rolls-Royce Corporate Heritage
Bob Forrester ex-Rolls-Royce engineer; tested the Merlin of Spitfire XI PL965
Richard Haigh Chairman, Rolls-Royce Corporate Heritage, owners Spitfire PS853
F/Sgt M.J.(Mick/Bomber) Harris, RAF Station Historian, RAF Benson
Tony Holmes Author "Spitfire - Flying Legend"; editor for Osprey Publishers
Chris Horsley aircraft preservationist; former owner of Spitfire XI PL965
Arthur Long sheet-metal worker on Spitfire XI PL965 at Aldermaston in 1944
Stuart Marshall Airport Manager, Blackbushe Airport, venue of 1999 Reunion
Harry van der Meer Dutch aircraft preservationist; restored Spitfire XI PL965
Ron Nobes Member, Medway Aircraft Preservation Society; video producer
Ivor Purkis Chairman, Derby and Hucknall Branch, Rolls-Royce Heritage Trust
Andy Sephton Chief Pilot, Shuttleworth Trust; ex-pilot of Spitfire XIX PS853
Hugh Smallwood Author "Spitfire in Blue", the history of Spitfire XI PL965
Tony Smith owner and pilot of Spitfire XI PL965, Breighton Aerodrome, York

List of Members of "16 Squadron 1959-1945" in 2004

Two operational Spitfires of 16 Squadron fly in a unique formation at the 2000 Reunion of "16 Squadron 1939-1945" at Rolls-Royce Hucknall: Spitfire XI PL965, owned and flown by Tony Smith, leads Spitfire XIX PS853, owned by Rolls-Royce and flown by Andy Sephton.

My personal reunion with a Spitfire XI, PL965, at Duxford in 1996

to discover how many members of the Squadron, both aircrew and ground-staff, had cheerfully broken the official ban on cameras in operational areas, especially as Michael Horsfall and I thought at the time that we were the only offenders!

"Newsbrief" averaged about 50 pages and was sent to about 70 people connected with 16 Squadron and also to the RAF Museum at Hendon, the Imperial War Museum, the National Archive, and the Dakota Centre of Information at Melsbroek airfield, now part of the Brussels International Airport. Our known wartime veterans numbered about 40 in 1996, but had declined to 12 in 2008. I had the sad, but also enlightening, job of writing the Obituaries of over 30 people, some of them well-known to us in 34 Wing rather than in the Squadron. It was surprising to learn how many of them, especially from the ground-staff, had devoted themselves in their retirement to working in their community or for a church or charity. Perhaps their experience of other people's suffering in the war had made them more aware after it of the need to improve the quality of life for those less fortunate than themselves.

Most of our Associate Members were distinguished in the fields of vintage aircraft restoration, preservation and display flying, and especially of PL965 and PS853. In 1998, we were greatly honoured when the Duke of Edinburgh, whom I knew at school, sent us a very supportive message for the first of our two Reunions as the guests of Rolls-Royce at their airfield at Hucknall. I then read two biographies of the Duke and was astonished to learn that he was a highly accomplished pilot, with nearly 6000 hours flying in his log-book, the great majority of which were as First Pilot. He had gone solo in .a Chipmunk in 1952, followed by soloing a Harvard and receiving his RAF 'wings' in 1953, and flying a single-seater Turbulent in 1959. Meanwhile, he had moved on to twin-engined aircraft and, in 1956, to helicopters. Then followed night-flying and instrument-training until he was fully qualified to pilot the Andovers and, later, BAe 146s of the Queen's Flight on many of his official journeys in UK and to countries in all parts of the globe. Of course, he always had a safety pilot with him, but there was no question about who was the captain. In March 1997, the Duke drew his flying career to a close with a round-the-world flight, visiting the centres of his Duke of Edinburgh's Award Scheme and the World Wildlife Fund, of which he was the President. This involved 21 take-offs and landings, 18 of the latter being on instruments – at the age of 76.

In 2002, among the celebrations of the Queen's Golden Jubilee of her reign, and in view of the Duke's achievements in the air and his patronage and support of many aviation bodies, I persuaded the wartime Members to invite the Duke to become an Associate Member of "16 Squadron 1939-1945" – the only honour we could offer him – and we were all delighted when he accepted.

Prince Philip flying solo in Harvard KF729 over Windsor Castle in 1953

Photo: "Aeroplane"

I wrote an account of the Duke's flying activities in "Newbrief" No 21 for April 2003, for which the Duke kindly made photographs and extracts from his log-book available to me; and I submitted an expanded account of this to "Wingspan" (a new glossy aviation magazine, now sadly defunct), which was published in their Issue No 18 in September 2003.

By now, it will have become clear that from 1996-2007 my life was kept very busy with "Newsbrief", the Reunions, a great deal of correspondence, and my gliding. In fact, I knew that it was only by ceasing these activities that I would have the time and energy to consider writing this book. So I organised our last Reunion at North Weald in June 2006; I distributed the last "Newsbrief" in August of that year; and I made my last glider flight in September 2007. You are holding the result!

Peter Teichman, its current owner, taxies Spitfire XI PL965 back after an impressive performance at our Final Reunion at North Weald in 2006.

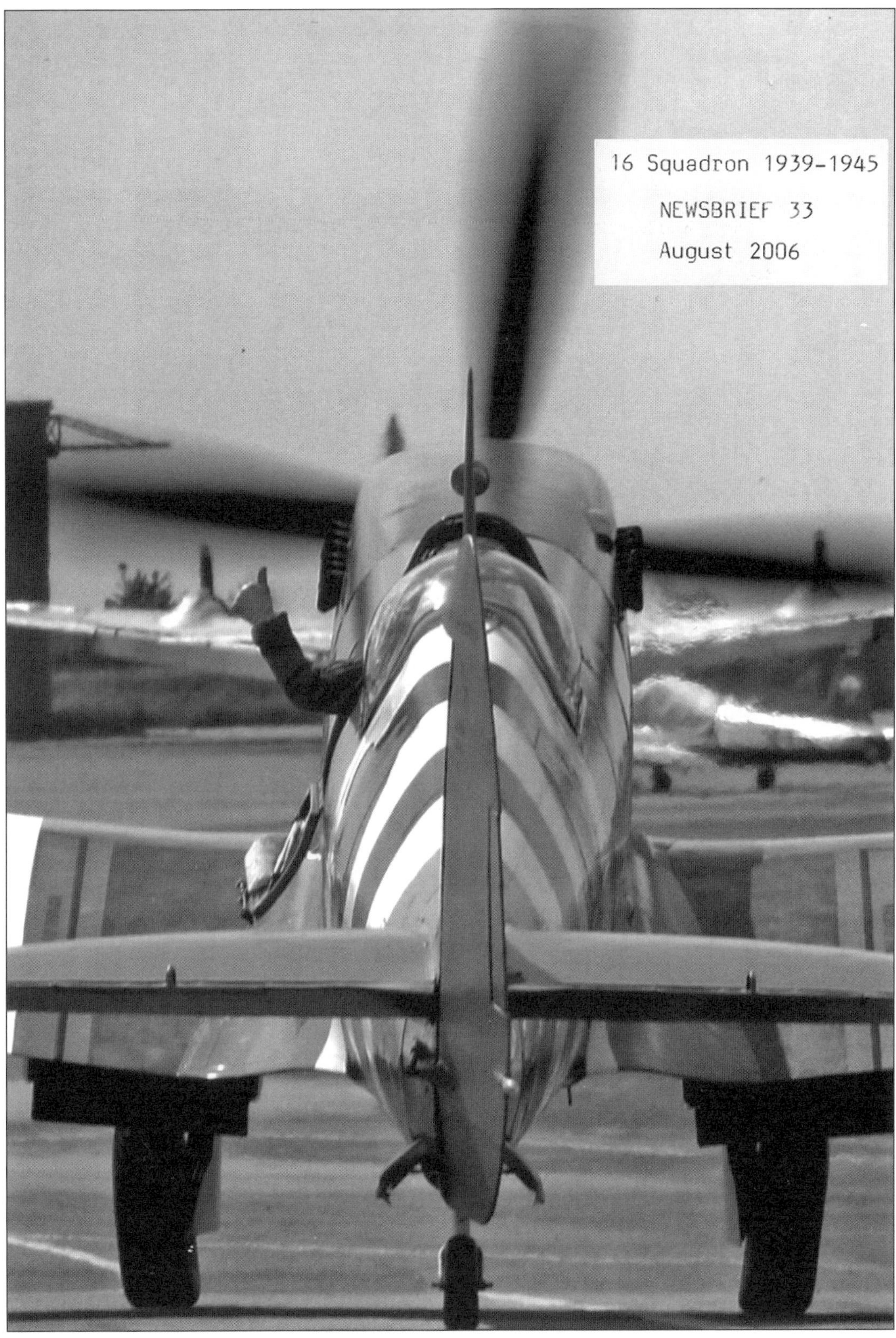

Peter Teichman bids us farewell from Spitfire XI PL965, on the cover of No 33, the last issue of "Newsbrief".

CHAPTER 30

Enter a 17th-century Jesuit

"Father Roeland de Pottere, SJ 1661"
Father Superior of the Jesuit Mission at Delft 1630 - 1662
by Adriaen Hanneman

It may seem strange that I should bring into my story the portrait of a Jesuit priest, painted by Adriaen Hanneman in 1661; but eventually it played a role of considerable relevance to my last flight on 19th November 1944.

This portrait had been in my family for at least 80 years, although I never really understood why my grandfather, a Church of England vicar, should buy a picture of a dedicated Jesuit priest, nor why my father, a schoolmaster clergyman, made a point of obtaining it from his sister, and hanging it in the dining-room of each of the three homes in turn that my parents owned. In 1974, my brother and I offered at Christie's the family pictures we didn't want, which included this portrait of a 17th-century Jesuit and other religious paintings; but the Hanneman failed to reach its reserve of £8000 and remained unsold, ending up in my own house in Leeds.

In 1991, I felt sufficiently curious about the sitter, the artist, and the picture's history to start a research that lasted for ten years and resulted in a magazine article in Holland and a booklet in England. It was one more interest that took up my time and energy, but in which I became increasingly absorbed.

My first aim was to identify the Jesuit priest, who was portrayed as an elderly man, with wispy grey hair, wearing a black clerical gown, looking rather severely at the viewer. The only possible recognisable feature was a shield in the top left-hand corner which, among other heraldic devices, contained representations of three small leather bottles, or 17th-century 'pottles'; above it was written "Aetatis 76", and below "An° 1661", followed by "Adr. Hanneman"; to the right, over part of a door, was sketched the insignia of the Jesuits.

Starting in 1991, I corresponded with the York Herald of Arms, with the English Jesuits in London; with the archivists of the Jesuit Colleges at Stonyhurst and at Liège in France; with Jesuit historians in Amsterdam and in the University of Antwerp in Belgium; with Agnew's, the art-dealer in Bond Street, and with the auction houses of Christie's and Sotheby's in London; I also spent hours in the Leeds City Art Library and Reference Library.

The result of the generous cooperation of so many knowledgeable people was that, by the end of 1994, I had learned that the sitter was Father Roeland de Pottere, SJ, (hence the play on 'pottle' in the shield), Father Superior of the Jesuit Station in Delft from 1630-1662. This was a time when the Dutch Calvinists were uniting under the Princes of Orange to try to gain their freedom from the rule of the very Catholic Spanish Crown, while the Jesuits were "the shock-troops of the Pope" in attempting to counter this rebellion and preserve Catholicism in the emerging nation of Holland. Father Roeland was a senior member of a distinguished family of ardent Catholics, many of whom served the non-Catholic House of Orange as officials in The Hague and on the royal estates. He was revered for his saintliness; but, at a time of severe persecution of the Catholics, I suspected he was more involved in the Catholic 'underground' than was revealed in the various documents in Latin that the Jesuit archivists translated for me. Father Roeland retired to Antwerp in 1662 and died there in 1675.

Adriaen Hanneman (1604 - 1671)
Self Portrait 1656

Adriaen Hanneman was a little easier to learn about, as various art encyclopaedias and art historians had something to say about him, but rarely suggested that he was a good or well-known artist. In my search, I corresponded with and visited the Heinz Archive of the National Portrait Gallery, the Witt Library in the Courtauld Institute, the Ashmolean Museum in Oxford, the Fitzwilliam Museum in Cambridge, the City Museum in York, the Print Library of the British Museum, and the Mauritshuis in The Hague. All these had fine collections of Dutch pictures of the 17th century – the Golden Age of Dutch Art. As well as maintaining contact with my previous sources, I also had valuable correspondence with the Iconographical Institute in The Hague and with the Jesuit archivists of the Flemish and Walloon Provinces of Belgium. I begged or made a photocopy of every picture I could find that was attributed to Hanneman, and ended up with over 300 portraits – his sole interest – 82 of which were dated, most of these being signed.

As a result of these investigations, by 1995 I had a reasonable outline of Hanneman's life and work. He was born into a middle-class family in The Hague in 1604, and trained as an artist under an undistinguished portraitist. His earliest picture of 1625 is a careful portrait of a woman wearing the conventional smart clothes of an affluent wife. The following year, he joined the flow of Dutch artists to England, where Charles I was trying to build up a Court that would rival those of France and Spain through his patronage of the arts. In London, Hanneman met Van Dyck and probably worked as one of the many assistants of this highly successful artist; he certainly learned Van Dyck's dramatic style of portraiture, his use of shimmering colours, the sense of movement in his poses, and the elegance that he bestowed on his sitters. By 1640, when the Civil War had closed down all Charles's patronage, Hanneman was back in Holland, introducing the new approach to portraiture; he became the favourite painter of Mary Stuart, the younger daughter of Charles I and the wife of Willem II, Prince of Orange. He painted several portraits of her and of her son, who became Willem III in 1650 and William III of England in 1688. The Royal Collection at Windsor contains six of Adriaen Hameman's portraits, which alone should have proved Hanneman's ability and gained him an effective reputation.

By the 1650s, Hanneman was prospering, running his own workshop with assistants, and accepting students. He also became active in the craftsmen's Guild of St Luke and even helped to start a new Guild for artists only. In 1661, when he painted Father Roeland's portrait, he was at the height of his powers and fame. However, in the next few years, like most artists of his time, Hanneman suffered from a change in public taste and from ill-health; he lost many customers, could no longer maintain his establishment, was declared bankrupt, and had most of his possessions auctioned off to pay his debts. He married a third time, a widow, (perhaps for her dowry), but died almost penniless in July 1671. His new Guild, Pictura, subscribed for a silver bowl in his memory; its inscription called him "the incomparable and celebrated painter"; but this reputation seems not to have survived him. Nevertheless, I developed a strong liking for Hanneman as a man, and I regard his portraits as worthy to rank him in the Top Twenty artists of the Dutch Golden Age. My several albums of photocopies of his portraits of English and Dutch men and women of substance and high standing, including Charles II and his courtiers while he was in exile in France and Holland, bear witness to this.

Hanneman's portrait of Charles II when Prince of Wales c1648

My third area of research was to try to find who commissioned this portrait of Father Roeland, what happened to it after 1661, and how it came into my grandfather's possession. My Jesuit archivists and historians were again most helpful, several of them working together. They reported that a letter written in 1889 showed that a "Mr Eyre" had bought the picture and that, in steps that I was to follow unwittingly a century later, they had identified the sitter as Father Roeland de Pottere, SJ. This name led me to visit the Westminster City Library and to find the various censuses of London's residents made in the 19th century; also to Ushaw College, a Catholic school outside Durham, whose Librarian revealed that he was Thomas Joseph Eyre, one of the four sons of a very rich Roman Catholic Count, who lived in London. T.J.Eyre seemed to have led a life of ease and luxury, marrying one of the seven daughters of the Earl of Wicklow, in Ireland, building a large mansion in that country, which he kept fully staffed but rarely visited; living in a house in Mayfair, the smart quarter of London, with eleven servants, and buying a third home at Thorpe Lee, at Egham in Surrey. In contrast, one brother became the first Catholic Archbishop of Glasgow, another was Head of the Jesuit Mission in Chelsea, and the youngest was appointed Rector of Stonyhurst College. T.J.Eyre died in 1902 and his wife in 1909; they had no children and all their possessions were auctioned at Christie's in over 170 lots; included among the pictures was Hanneman's portrait of Father Roeland de Pottere, but catalogued as "Portrait of a Gentleman (said to be Father Roland Pottre, S.J.)".

The picture then disappeared, but turned up again at Christie's in August 1916, when my grandfather decided to sell his collection of paintings, among them the Hanneman, still catalogued as in the 1909 auction. These two dates are the only clues – between 1909 and 1916 – as to when my grandfather bought the Hanneman. He died in 1919 and, by the time my father gained possession of the picture, it was known only as "Portrait of a Jesuit, aged 76" This was its title in the catalogue at the sale at Christie's in 1974 of my parents' pictures, and this was the starting-point of my own search in 1991.

While doing this research, I discovered that there were a number of Hanneman's portraits in the district of Twente; so, during my annual visit to Borne in May 1996, I asked Hennie Noordhuis to take me to see them. My first objective was Twickel Castle, a grand old house surrounded by a wide moat, a mile outside Delden. Hennie was busy, so Joke kindly drove me there; she was very familiar with the place, as her father had worked there and her home had been on the estate. In the dining-room was a strong head-and-shoulders portrait by Hanneman of Admiral Jacob van Wassenaar, a distinguished Dutch sailor, who became the commander of the Dutch fleet, but was killed in a great sea-battle off Lowestoft in 1665 during the 1st Anglo-Dutch War. The library contained a ¾-length portrait of the Admiral, attributed to Hanneman (although it may be a copy), and also a miniature copy of the head-and-shoulders portrait. In a nearby room was a similar-sized portrait of his wife, Agnes, by Hanneman, although it also may be a copy. The Admiral never lived at Twickel, but his son married the heiress and installed his father's portraits when he moved in there. Later, the family also owned another castle ten miles away at Weldam, outside Goor. They had very good copies of the portraits of the Admiral and his wife at Weldam Castle, and in both castles there were copies of the head-and-shoulders portrait engraved by distinguished contemporary print-makers. The two estates separated in 1877 and the pictures were divided between them, which accounts for the difficulty of distinguishing between the originals and the copies.

Twickel Castle is now owned by a Trust, while Weldam Castle came into the hands of a distant relative, Count Alfred Solms, an East German land-owner, whose estates were confiscated by the Russians even though he was an anti-Nazi. Hennie and I visited him next day and found an old-school aristocrat, most courteous and with perfect English: he drew aside the heavy curtains in the rooms to assist my photography. He showed us everything connected with Admiral van Wassenaar that the house possessed, including his seaman's dirk, and a naval architect's technical side-drawing of the "Arend" ("Eagle"), a 20-gun sloop, the first ship the Admiral commanded.

The third location of a Hanneman portrait was the Rijksmuseum Twente, one of the out-stations of the National Museum in Amsterdam; it was situated in the busy town of Enschede, about ten miles from Borne, and had a fine collection of art, from mediaeval to modern, comprising paintings, metal-

"Cornelis Jonson and his family 1637" by Adriaen Hanneman

work and sculpture. When Hennie and I went there, the Director took us down to the basement, where many paintings were stored vertically side-by-side in sliding carriers. He pulled out the painting we had come to see: Hanneman's large picture of "Cornelis Jonson and his Family". Jonson was a friend of Hanneman's in England, a very capable, but quieter and less ambitious artist. The family was painted in England, and the sand-dunes in the background could be in Sussex. The picture shows a relaxed family group, with Cornelis on the right with strong features; his wife, smartly dressed in a broad-brimmed hat, looking at her husband – they were married in 1622; and the curly-haired five-year-old boy, also called Cornelis and himself destined to become an artist, staring in curiosity at the painter, probably in 1628. It shows that Hanneman was at home with many kinds of sitter.

During this visit, I met Peggie Breitbarth, the editor of "Jaarboek Twente", the annual publication containing articles about events, places and personalities of historical and contemporary interest in the district of Twente. She is herself an authority on Italian art, and was surprised at how much I had discovered about Adriaen Hanneman; the result was that she asked me to write an article about his portraits in Twente. For a visitor from England, with no special art knowledge, to be invited to write about a Dutch artist, especially one living in the Golden Age of Dutch Art, was an unusual honour and very flattering. Peggie had to translate my words into Dutch, and the article, which appeared in the 1997 Yearbook, eventually ran to twelve pages and eight illustrations, including five of the portraits I have described. I hope the good people of Twente, who have been so kind to me, found it interesting. It was one more, unexpected, link in the chain of relationships that has been forged between us with each of my visits.

The following year, I brought my knowledge of Father Roeland de Pottere to completion when, on the first day of my annual visit in May, Jan Bovenmars drove me to Delft, where Father Roeland worked from 1621-62; Anne and her current boy-friend took a lift en route to The Hague. Jan and I were met by Father Dries van den Akker, SJ, one of the many Jesuits with whom I'd been corresponding. He was a teacher at the local Stanislas College and had offered to be our guide.

The Old Town of Delft is a beautiful little city, a miniature Venice, surrounded and interwoven by canals, with a huge Gothic Old Church and an equally impressive 17th-century New Church, where most of the members of the House of Orange are buried; they had a delightful palace, which is now a museum, near the fine central space of the Great Market Square.

Father Dries took us first to the 'Beguinhof' the quarter where the Catholic nuns lived and had a secret chapel; Father Roeland's assistants probably lived there also; a modern bronze statue of Father Stalpart van der Wielse, who was one of them, is a central feature. From there we walked back, past the site of the house where Vermeer was born, across the Great Square, to the new Church, near which was the site of the secret Jesuit church and of the house where Father Roeland had lived. Today, an elegant 19th-century Roman Catholic church with twin spires stands near the site, and a later building has replaced Father Roeland's house.

In 1648, the Treaty of Münster had been signed by the Spanish, bringing the fighting to an end and giving the Dutch virtually their independence. The Catholics in Delft were still proscribed and could only meet in secret; but when the Calvinist majority complained to the magistrates about their activities, the latter were more concerned to encourage trade and prosperity than to harass the Catholics: Delft was an important inland port, one of the six centres of the Dutch East India Company, and famous for its massive production of fine porcelain.

We then walked to the north-east corner of the town, where barrels of gunpowder, no longer needed against the Spanish, had been stored in a magazine; in 1654, they erupted in a huge explosion that devastated the whole area, killed hundreds of people and injured many more. Father Roeland was celebrating Mass in the secret church when a statue fell off the altar onto his head, fortunately without injuring him. The talented young artist Carel Fabritius was painting a portrait of a man: they were both killed. There is still a large empty space where the houses have never been rebuilt. A Calvinist minister declared that the explosion was punishment for the authorities' tolerating the presence of the Jesuits, but the magistrates refused to react against them; 'the common people', however, threw stones at their windows.

This is only a scanty account of an enchanting town, which retains many of its 17th-century buildings and little bridges over the canals, producing a delightfully relaxed atmosphere. I felt satisfied that I had seen something of the world in which Father Roeland de Pottere had lived for 30 years, and viewed the same reflections of the skies and buildings on the placid waters of the canals that he must have enjoyed.

Our visit ended in an open-air restaurant in the Great Square, with drinks and ice-cream shared with Father Dries and Anne and her friend, now returned from The Hague. Father Dries gave me a copy of his book on Jesuit symbols still visible on the exterior of houses in the region, and I presented him with a coffee-table book in English, "The Splendours of Flanders"; he had been a very worthy guide.

On my return to Leeds, I wrote an illustrated booklet, "Adriaen Hanneman's 1661 Portrait of Father Roeland de Pottere, SJ", containing all I knew about the artist and the sitter, including the town of Delft and describing the chequered history of the portrait. I failed to find a publisher, so I sent a photocopy to each of the historians and keepers of archives and galleries in England, Ireland, France, Belgium, and Holland who had so willingly assisted me in my researches over several years. I hoped that this would help to bring Adriaen Hanneman out of the shadows and into the prominence that I consider he well deserves. Meanwhile, the Jesuit Father Superior of Delft continued to gaze at me steadily, even accusingly, from his picture-frame in my dining-room, as if challenging me to take some action over his portrait. Eventually, I did.

CHAPTER 31

Happy Returns to Holland and Belgium

1996 was significant for me in Britain, as it brought me back into contact with my old comrades in 16 Squadron in 1944 and rekindled many memories, both fond and sad, of those momentous days. Later visits to Holland turned out to be no less important in achieving virtually the same result in that country, reminding many people besides myself of the events that followed my baling-out on 19th November 1944.

The visits started on 1st May 1997, when Hennie Noordhuis met me at Hengelo station, off the train from Schiphol Airport. Without wasting any time, we drove to the Twente Air Base Museum, where Colonel Jansen, Commandant of the Air Base, Sgt Stegeman, curator of the Museum, and A.M.Roding, a local military historian and contributor of exhibits to the Museum, were waiting to show me what they had done with the relics of my poor Spitfire since its excavation two years earlier.

The propeller hub, with the large reduction-gear attached, lay on the polished wood floor, with the smaller gear-wheel nestling up against it. Above, in a glass-topped display case, were my helmet and goggles, the strap turned outwards to show my name in faded ink, the clue which had enabled Hennie to trace my identity; there was also a copy of my story in Dutch and a model Spitfire. Nearby were interesting relics of V1s and V2s fired from Bornerbroek, near Borne. I gave the Museum the epaulettes of my 1944 battle-dress, still fitted with my original Flight Lieutenant's tapes, a 1944 photograph of myself, and a copy of Hugh Smallwood's evocative "Spitfire in Blue".

From there, Hennie took me to the woods near Twickel and Bornerbroek to show me the overgrown remains of the ruined V1 launch sites: the mossy concrete 'feet' supporting the elevated ramp of the V1s and the dark bramble-covered entrances of underground bunkers.

It was from here that the 'doodle-bugs' were launched that I had seen while resting on a grassy bank below the railway-line to Zutphen on 21st November, and which I had thought, in spite of their low trajectory, were V2s, as they glistened in the winter sun.

Relics of my Spitfire XI MB957 when in the Twente Air Base Museum: my helmet and goggles, photographs, documents and a Spitfire model

The shaft of the constant-speed unit (l) in front of the propeller-hub with the remains of the four wooden blades, and the reduction gear behind

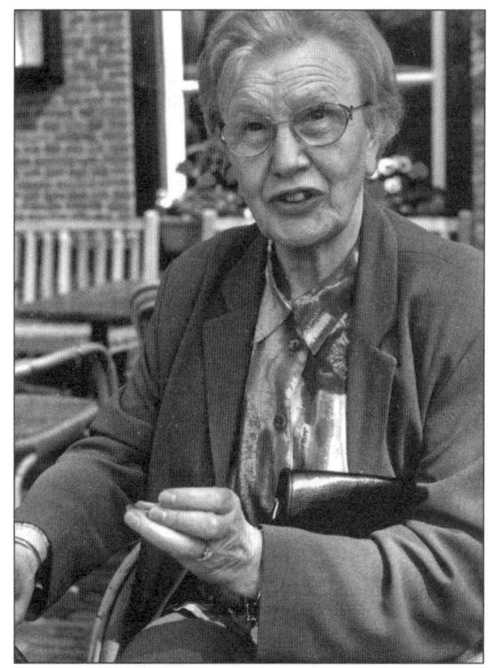

Betsie Timmerman, who first traced the van Hengstums

The following day was devoted, as I have already described, to learning more about Father Roeland de Pottere by exploring his charming town of Delft, but 3rd May was to take me back to 1944 with unusual emphasis. Betsie Timmerman-Westerink, sister of Jan and Marinus Timmerman of "The Resting Hunter", who had run a similar restaurant herself with her husband, but now lived alone in Delden, knew about my journey to the Rhine in November 1944 and determined to find the van Hengstum family again, although I had mislaid their address since my visit to them in 1947. She discovered that the name of the village was Houten, near Utrecht, but the van Hengstums had migrated to Cothen, a village near Doorn. She was frustrated, however, by finding that a large number of van Hengstums lived in that locality. Hennie Noordhuis now picked up the trail and was fortunate, when he telephoned the first van Hengstum in the directory, to talk to someone who knew them and told him that Ben, the only surviving member of the family, had moved to Rolde, in a northerly province of the Netherlands. He was able to speak to Ben, as a result of which I wrote to him about my life post-1947 and received a fascinating letter from him, translated into English by his eldest son, who was working at the University of Twente. This letter so effectively reproduces the atmosphere of those fraught days of November 1944 in Holland under the German Occupation that I quote it here in full. He wrote:

"It is very special to receive a letter after so many years. To be honest, you have never been out of my mind. For us, you were the liberator, the friend, who impressed us as small boys. I was twelve years old. I can still remember our meeting very well.

It was very bad weather that particular day. Accompanied by two boy-friends, I was hunting for rabbits and hares in the fields surrounding my parents' house. Owing to the bad weather, we decided to shelter in our shed. It must have been around twelve o'clock. We were, at the least, very surprised to encounter a complete stranger in our shed. Very soon, you showed us your RAF "wings". These made us recognise you as a "Tommy" (an Englishman). Besides these "wings", you were carrying a small bag (40 x 6cm), most likely filled with water. You told us that you put some pills in the water to disinfect it. Along with this, you showed us your boots. [These were my 'escape boots': I had ripped off the wool-lined tops and put them round my waist to keep warm; the lower parts were also wool-lined, but looked like normal shoes and were more suitable for evading, although they were horrid when wet and cold, pulling the skin off my feet.]

After the meeting with you, we hurried home to tell the breath-taking news to my parents. After we had told them the story, the family discussed how to deal with the situation. (At that time, the family consisted of my father Piet, my mother Alie, two older brothers Piet and Henk, and myself.) First, we decided to bring you some food; so I brought you a bowl of potatoes and endives. Afterwards, my father, brother Piet and I discussed with you how to proceed. Several options were considered. My father proposed helping you to hide from the Germans, but you made it clear that you didn't want to stay; you preferred to return to your comrades as soon as possible. You were very persistent in this intention.

The outcome of the discussion was that we, my brother Piet and I, should bring you by bicycle as close as possible to the front-line. [The father had told me, mistakenly, that the British had captured

The van Hengstum family in 1947: the boys l-r: Piet, Henk and Ben

Rhenen on this north bank of the Rhine.] So you got a precious bicycle, a map torn out of an atlas, and a small overcoat. To be honest, the overcoat was not one of the children's, but belonged to my father; he was a very small person and, as I remember it, you were/are much larger. The map belonged to my brother Henk; he had put his initials (H.v.H.) on it. If I'm correct, the Germans asked about these initials several times, didn't they? [I don't remember them asking about it at all, so perhaps I got rid of it before I was interrogated or searched.] Besides the map and coat, my parents gave you a hat as well, but I'm not certain about this. [No, they didn't.]

I remember well that you fell off the bike. It is one of the things I shall never forget. [It had a very unfamiliar brake: when I ran alongside and swung my leg over the frame, the brake went on and the bike toppled over with a great crash onto the cobble-stones; the family and several interested neighbours all ran off: it was dark and there was a harsh curfew every night.]

Later on, we as a family talked over this event many times. The image of a foreigner heading for an unknown destination impressed us. I also clearly remember that, when we cycled through an area flooded with water, you stepped down from your bicycle just to let a couple of persons on a cart pass you. We found that very special: we were not used to people stepping down from a bicycle into cold water.

In 1947, our family moved to Bussum, in the centre of Holland. My father died in 1972, my mother in 1976. Unfortunately, my two brothers have died as well, Henk in 1982 and Piet in 1983.

I served in the Dutch navy on an aircraft-carrier: I recorded the take-offs and landings of Fireflies and Sea Furies; very often you were at the top of my mind during this period. In the early 1960s, I attended a course on central-heating systems and have worked in this field ever since. For the past 27 years, I have worked for the Government, supervising students and companies. In August, I shall retire at the age of 65.

Ben van Hengstum and I have a joyful reunion.
Photo: Hennie Noordhuis

Perhaps you have asked yourself why I didn't contact you after the war? The reason for this is very simple: I'm not familiar with the English language, and to communicate with another person when you can't speak his language is very difficult.

I have no idea what will happen when we meet in May, but I'm certain that Mr Hennie Noordhuis will organise a perfect day."

In fact, on 3rd May we had no difficulty in communicating in my broken German and Ben's broken-English and we did have a perfect day. Hennie brought Betsie Timmerman and myself to Houten, a village I never saw in 1944, and we met Ben in a pleasant café. He and I had a joyful reunion: he was short and stocky, well-dressed, good-looking, all smiles and very friendly. He told me his father had been a small-time farmer and blacksmith, but had moved to Bussom to work in a car-assembly plant. In 1944, there were eight Germans living on the ground-floor of their house (but not taking meals), and my arrival put the family in great danger. One German, Fritz, was different: they let him listen to the BBC on their secret radio in the kitchen.

Ben and I stand on the spot where I started my bicycle journey in 1944 with a disturbing crash.
Photo: Hennie Noordhuis

We drove round to his family's former home, a well-built two-storey house that I had not seen in 1944. The orchard had disappeared, the trees now forming part of the gardens of a number of new houses. We stood in the roadway where I had tried, when night fell, to mount a solid-tyred bicycle with its back-pedalling brake and fallen off with a clatter, made louder by the silence of the curfew; everyone except me had run away, fearful of the approach of a German patrol; but they had all returned laughing two minutes later.

I got into Ben's car, with Hennie and Betsie following behind, while we retraced the cross-country route that Ben and his elder brother on one bike had taken to lead me to the Utrecht-Doorn main road. In 1944 we had no lights, of course, and I could see little in the dark; it seemed to be a footpath, partly on a dyke and partly across frozen fields, and we took about 30 minutes' hard-pedalling for the journey, with me keeping some way behind the boys in case of trouble. Now, we drove slowly in pleasant sunshine along a narrow tarred road on top of a dyke all the way, with the fields stretching out below us. As usual in Holland, there were many more cyclists than cars on this country lane, often in family groups – a very different atmosphere from the winter of 1944. The signpost at the end, though, with one arm pointing to Utrecht, the other to Doorn, looked quite familiar, and here we stopped to discuss the moment when I gave back my bicycle to the boys and they pedalled off home, leaving me to plod on, in my foot-sore state, through the outskirts of Doorn and, I hoped, to Rhenen, on this side of the Rhine, which their father had told me was in British hands.

Doorn has thick woods on at least three sides, in one of which I had a creepy experience in the dark with what was probably a German sentry guarding the transport park concealed in the wood. We took a look at the centre of this pleasant town, then drove out through more woods along the road which I had followed on 24th November 1944, my last day of freedom, in my effort to reach the Rhine. We were now looking for the lane to the right where I had found the old couple, with their barrow-load of possessions, going slowly in the same direction. I wanted to find especially the curve of the lane to the left, where I suddenly came upon the flak-battery and saw the Rhine, perhaps less than a mile away, below the hillside along which the lane was running. A short distance further along should take us to where the alert German captain stopped me and to the barrier across the road where I was finally caught.

Unfortunately, we found only one road to the right, broader than a lane, with no curve to the left, which took us directly down to the Rhine and a crossing-point for a small one-car ferry. We stopped here to admire the view along the river and to discuss the situation, deciding eventually that post-war developments in the past 55 years must have made considerable changes to the environment.

We returned to the road to Rhenen to find lunch in a small restaurant in the long, straggling village of Amerongen, after which we bade a fond farewell to Ben. He gave me a silver spoon with the crest of Houten mounted on top, and I presented him with a brass figurine of an airman – mementos of a very moving day together.

The road out of Doorn 1944 and 1997

The Rhine, from a little higher viewpoint than the one I had on 24th November 1944

Hennie, Betsie and I drove on to Rhenen, which I was curious to see after being misinformed about it by Ben's father in 1944. It had an impressive church tower, which dominated the surrounding riverside scenery, while the town climbed gradually back up the hillside. We couldn't linger, though, as we had an important date at the field near Henk Timmerman's restaurant.

Arrived there, we walked along the short lane that led to the field of my Spitfire's crash-site and found all the Timmermans and their wives and families, the Burgomaster of Bentelo, Sgt Stegeman of the Air Base Museum, Joop Roetgerink a witness of the aircraft's descent, and a small gathering of local friends, waiting for us by the end of the line of trees along one side of the field. Here Henk had erected a plaque beside the lane, now covered with a Dutch flag; the Burgomaster gave an address in Dutch and English and invited me to unveil the plaque. It held an inscription, in Dutch words composed by Hennie, recording the site of the Spitfire's crash, my name, and the tragic events that followed in 't Hesseler. I gave a short address in which I stated that, because the aircraft was empty when it hit the ground, no one was killed or injured and therefore this could be a cheerful occasion, celebrating Angle-Dutch unity during the war and continuing today; I also congratulated Henk Timmerman on his generosity, not least for giving me the hole from which Hennie Noordhuis and Hennie Egberink had excavated my Spitfire! We then retired to the garden for refreshments, followed by an excellent dinner in the restaurant.[1]

I unveil the Plaque set up by Henk Timmerman on the edge of the field in which my Spitfire crashed on 19th November 1944
l-r: the Burgomaster of Bentelo JT Jan
Henk and Marinus Timmerman
Photo: Hennie Noordhuis

[1] See "Dutch Voices" p. 714 for a Press report of the Unveiling.

Op 19 november 1944 crashte in
achterliggende bomenwal
de 'Spitfire PRXI L 957 van het 16e Squadron RAF,
die werd gevlogen door Flight-lieutenant

Harold James Strickland (Jimmy) Taylor.

Hij had het toestel boven de gemeente Borne verlaten en
kon daar na landing aan zijn parachute aan de Duitsers ontkomen.
Als gevolg hiervan werden 4 onschuldige burgers gefusilleerd.

3 mei 1997

The Plaque's inscription in Dutch
the 'L' was the Spitfire identity in 16 Squadron;
'957' was part of its RAF serial number: MB957.

Hennie drove me back to Borne on a road that took us past the field where the American B-17 "Aliquippa" had forced-landed in 1943. With engines failing, the pilot had made a good belly-landing that saved the remaining crew; but it was a gift to the Germans, who removed it completely from the field. In Borne, we found that "Tubantia" had a feature by René Schabos, based on his interview with me before we went to meet Ben van Hengstum; this was another sensitive article, which reviewed my story and described my feelings with creditable objectivity.

4th May, the Day of National Commemoration in the Netherlands, started with Hennie taking me to the studio of Radio Borghende, a local station, staffed by eight volunteers, sponsored by a bank and located on the top floor of a large Old People's Home in Borne. Matthias, the 21-year-old presenter, discussed his questions to us over coffee while he waited for a church service to finish. I was growing accustomed to the line commonly taken by the various media people in their interviews with me, that of wishing to know my feelings now about events in the past, and this young man was no exception: the subject he was most interested in was my reaction to yesterday's experiences in Houten and Bentelo. Hennie then left me with my 1995 hosts, the Verfs, who were packing up preparatory to Chantal's return to Canada with the children, leaving Tye to continue training to be a commercial pilot with Martinair,

I was questioned about my meeting with Ben van Hengstum and my unveiling of the Plaque in my interview next day on Radio Bornsche.
Photo: Hennie Noordhuis

In the afternoon, Hennie took me to lay a wreath on the Memorial beside Borne Town Hall to Jan Vonk, the would-be Scarlet Pimpernel, who was executed there by the Germans "as a lesson to you Dutch not to hide enemy airmen", on the same afternoon that I hid in the field in 't Hesseler.

We then visited the Jewish Cemetery in Borne. Before the war, there was a large and respected community of Jews in the town, who were forced to register by the Germans in 1940 and were transported to the death camps between October 1942 and January 1944. Only a handful came back after the Liberation, but a few had been hidden by courageous Gentiles and survived in terribly restricted conditions and on minimal supplies of food. I remembered the trap-door in the floor of the upper storey of the Museum, which had itself once been the home of the rabbi of Borne. The Cemetery was, to me, one of the saddest places I have visited in Holland: dark and dank, with tragic Memorials to those who never came back from Germany, and reflecting the almost unimaginable brutality and starvation experienced by old and young,, men and women and children. By comparison, the Allied War Cemeteries, all over Holland and the rest of German-occupied Europe, are places of beauty and peace, redolent of the courage and self-sacrifice of the young men of Britain and the Commonwealth who died fighting to liberate most of the people of Europe from these horrors, imposed by the crazy dreams of Adolf Hitler and his 'everlasting' Third Reich.

The evening followed what has become almost a traditional course for me on Commemoration Day: a visit and a meal with Jan and Ria Bovenmars and whoever of their children are at home; a meeting at the crossroads in 't Hesseler with the three Boomkamp brothers and their families, with Jan and Lidy Boomkamp and Dirk and Joost; with the Roetgerinks and Leuvelds and Marie Leuveld-Roetgerink and their families, and with Mrs Veenhuis-Weghorst, the Bruggink family, and other familiar faces. At 7.0pm, Jan Bovenmars, or the lady who takes his place as community leader, and I head the procession and the rest form up loosely behind us; Hennie gives me a wreath with my name on (provided by the Borne Town Council) from the boot of his car, other people are carrying theirs for their families; the strains of "Abide with me" played by Hennie's small silver band – which always brings a lump to my throat – grow louder as we walk slowly up the lane and shuffle into position before the Memorial. The ceremony is short but heartfelt: Jan gives a brief address; I recite *"They shall not grow old...."*; we lay our wreaths; the boy and girl Scouts preserve their solemnity while the children place their flowers and posies in a smiling, self-conscious way; the two-minutes silence is long enough for my cheerful memories of my evasion on 19th November 1944 to clash with my thoughts of the agonies endured by the hostages and their families in the days that followed, culminating in the three executions on the 25th in front of their friends and loved ones; the English and Dutch National Anthems bring back a sense of pride and unity; we turn and walk slowly back up the lane to the cross-roads, where we drop our gravitas and chatter like any gathering after church. Sometimes, I go to Borne, where there is a crowd of hundreds around the Municipal War Memorial in front of the Old Town Hall, and a large band starts to play when the clock on the Old Church nearby tolls out 8.0pm. I may be given another wreath to lay beside those of the Burgomaster and the leaders of the different sections of the community, followed by many of the public – husbands and wives, whole families, children alone, and individuals, with tributes ranging from wreaths to single long-stemmed roses. It is always a moving ceremony, underlined by the 'Last Post' and 'Reveille' sounded by a bugler on the balcony. Whether I go to Borne or not, the evening ends in the Bovenmars' comfortable living-room, with members of all the Boomkamps coming in to relax with each other, drink good wines and spirits and fine Kruidenbitter, and eat local bread and cheese and cake; some talk to me in easy English, others struggle to say a few words, all of them show interest when I pass around a few photographs of my wartime flying, or of my previous visits, or of Yorkshire. People come and go at their will. Finally, the time comes for me to say *"Thank you so much"* and *"Farewell"*. I salute the ladies with the Dutch treble kiss and shake the men warmly by the hand. Hennie or a family member runs me back to the "Jachtlust" hotel, and I lie in bed, thinking over all the events of my few always-crowded days, and feeling a glow of gratitude to all these kindly Dutch people who have taken me in and treat me as one of their own. Yet my landing in their field caused four of them to die. Once again, I thank Marie Leuveld-Roetgerink from the bottom of my heart for her words of absolution:

"You were not to blame."

Sadly, 1997 saw the death of Marie on 24th May. I think the revival of memories of the awful death of her brother Hendrik Roetgerink on 25th November 1944 proved too much for her emotional state and contributed towards her final end. By chance, Herman Bruggink, who had handed me back my flying-helmet, picked up by his father on the landing-field in 't Hesseler in 1944, was her physio-therapist, who visited her regularly, and he agreed with my view. Certainly she was a central figure in the 't Hesseler tragedy, and her husband's carving of the beautiful Crucifix that forms the simple Memorial will constitute the visible reminder for future generations of the senselessness of war.

I was, naturally, delighted when Hennie and Joke accepted my invitation to visit Margaret and me in Leeds, at virtually the centre of Yorkshire. They came back with me from this 1997 trip to Borne, and I was happy to drive them round many of the historical and scenic places in this large and varied county. Of course, I included the Dales, but I like to take people into the Pennine foothills, where the narrow roads climb over the sheep-strewn grass-lands and untamed moors, above which flat-topped Ingleborough and lion-like Pen-y-ghent rise to over two thousand feet, where the call of the curlews haunts the streams in the valleys, and where it's getting crowded if we meet more than one car in any five minutes. This is the joy of living on the northern edge of Leeds – we can get out to the real beauty of Yorkshire in little more than half-an-hour.

Hennie and Joke, who were familiar with London and the Albert Hall for their band concerts, experienced the contrast to the full; they also had to see round York, with its Roman, Viking, Mediaeval, Tudor and Georgian legacies, and Leeds with its less distinguished remains of the Industrial Revolution. The Brontes in Haworth and the moors beyond were another unmissable objective; but I received a surprise when I offered to take them to the splendid Rievaulx Abbey: Hennie stated firmly that they preferred to see Eden Camp. I had heard vaguely of this former Italian POW camp, now a WW2 Museum, but I couldn't imagine it rivalling Rievaulx. I was, therefore, all the more impressed by what we found: about 25 restored wartime huts, each focusing on a particular aspect or theatre of the war, with realistic dioramas and displays, and some very atmospheric scenes, such as the London 'blitz' or the sinking of a U-Boat, where we felt included in the sights and smells and even in the fear. Altogether, I judged the experience of Eden Camp to have been remarkably evocative of WW2 from a wide range of standpoints.

The Noordhuises were not the only people from Borne and 't Hesseler to visit us in Leeds: in 1995, Bernard and Hendrik Boomkamp came with Hans Wools as their interpreter; in 1998, Jaap and Ine Grootenboer called in for the evening; and in 1999 Jan and Ria Bovenmars and Hans and Josine Wools came as a foursome; their visits enabled me to repay a fraction of the hospitality they had showered on me so generously in Borne and 't Hesseler.

Six weeks after leaving Borne I was back in Europe, attending a Reunion on 14th June at Melsbroek, 34 Wing's wartime base outside Brussels from October 1944 to April 1945. This was organised by retired Colonel Jo Huybens, Director of the 'Dakota' Information Centre and Museum, located on the airfield now occupied by the 15th Wing of the Royal Belgian Air Force, flying

Exhibit in the 'Dakota' Museum: a fully-equipped Pilot

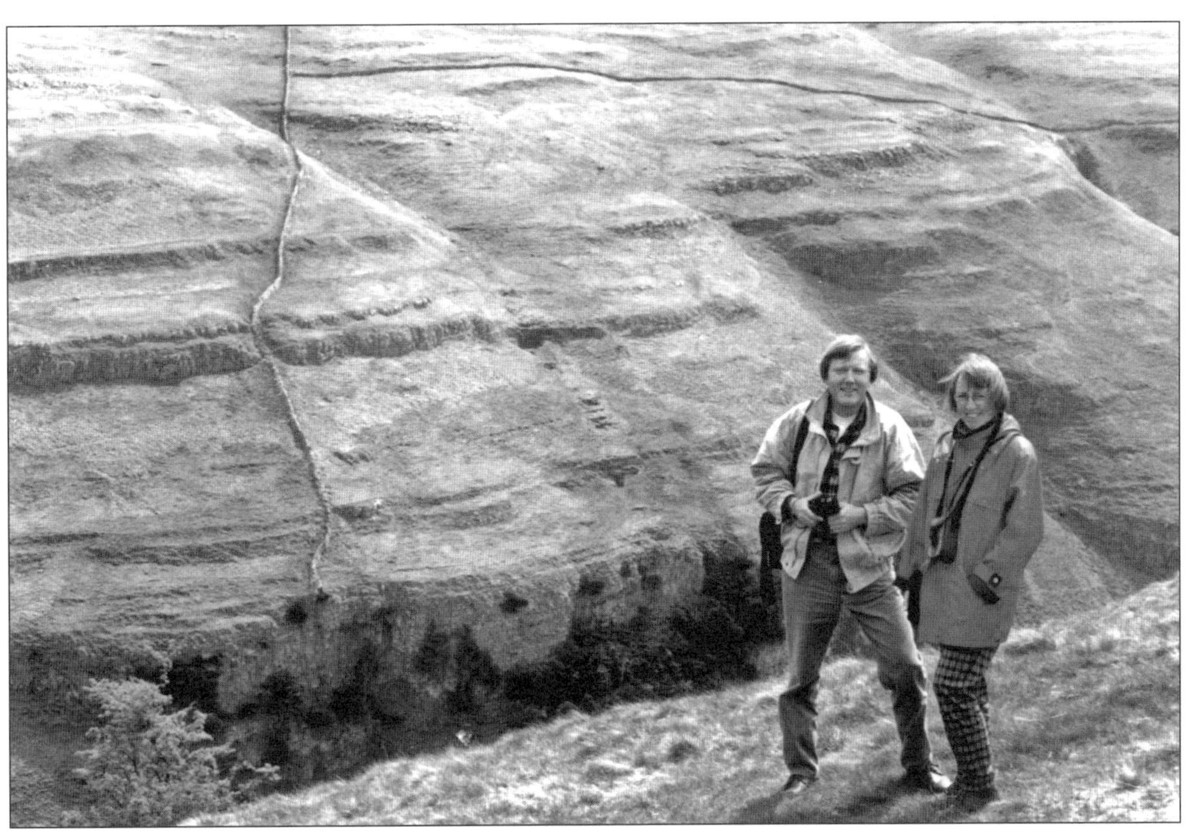

Hennie and Joke Noordhuis braving the weather on the rugged hills of Yorkshire in May 1997

Hennie and JT pose beside a replica Spitfire IX at the Eden Camp theme park near Malton in Yorkshire.
Photo: Joke Noordhuis

Hercules transport aircraft; it shares the runways with the main part of the airfield, which has become Brussels International Airport. David Stutchbury, a pilot who transferred from 140 Squadron to 16 Squadron in December 1944, Bill Bull, an instrument repairer, and I were the only representatives of 16 Squadron, but there were three from 69 Squadron, which flew Wellingtons, and five from 140 Squadron, on Mosquitos, as well as several ground-staff from 34 Wing, including 'Benny' Bennett, a self-proclaimed 'bowser wallah' (driver of a petrol bowser) and Basil Jackson, a photographer in No 7 Mobile Field Photographic Section.

It was an extraordinary feeling to be back amongst the German buildings that we had occupied in 1944, some of which were still in use by the Belgian Air Force fifty-three years later, including the Officers' Mess and bungalows for sleeping accommodation. I could not, however, identify the one that Michael Horsfall and I had shared with the Adjutant, Don Williams, the walls of which Mike had decorated with a frieze based on the Bayeux Tapestry, but depicting the activities of the Squadron in its days in France and Belgium. Other buildings, such as the large German hangars camouflaged to look like Belgian chateaux, had been converted to agricultural purposes by local farmers. The perimeter track round the airfield, which I had become very familiar with during my seven weeks at Melsbroek – including ramming my Spitfire's wing into a Belgian steam-roller – was still very much in use, and even the Nissen huts were still in place, although with very rusty roofs. The Museum held equally nostalgic souvenirs of our time in residence, with cameras, guns, and all manner of equipment on display, together with maps and photographs of people, planes and activities, not only of 34 Wing, but also of the other Allied squadrons that had occupied Melsbroek before, during and after our stay.

On the first day, besides a coach tour of the environment, we had a ceremony to mark the unveiling of a commemorative plaque on the Museum building and to remember the aircrew who had died while flying on operations from the airfield. In the evening, we were guests at a wonderful Belgian dinner – a feast by English standards – given by the officers of the 15th Wing, with appropriate speeches and many

The plaque commemorating
34 Wing's residence at Melsbroek
27th September 1944 - 14th April 1945

The Perimeter Track round the airfield, just as it was in 1944

German hangar with new front built by a local farmer

Participants in the Reunion honour those who did not return.

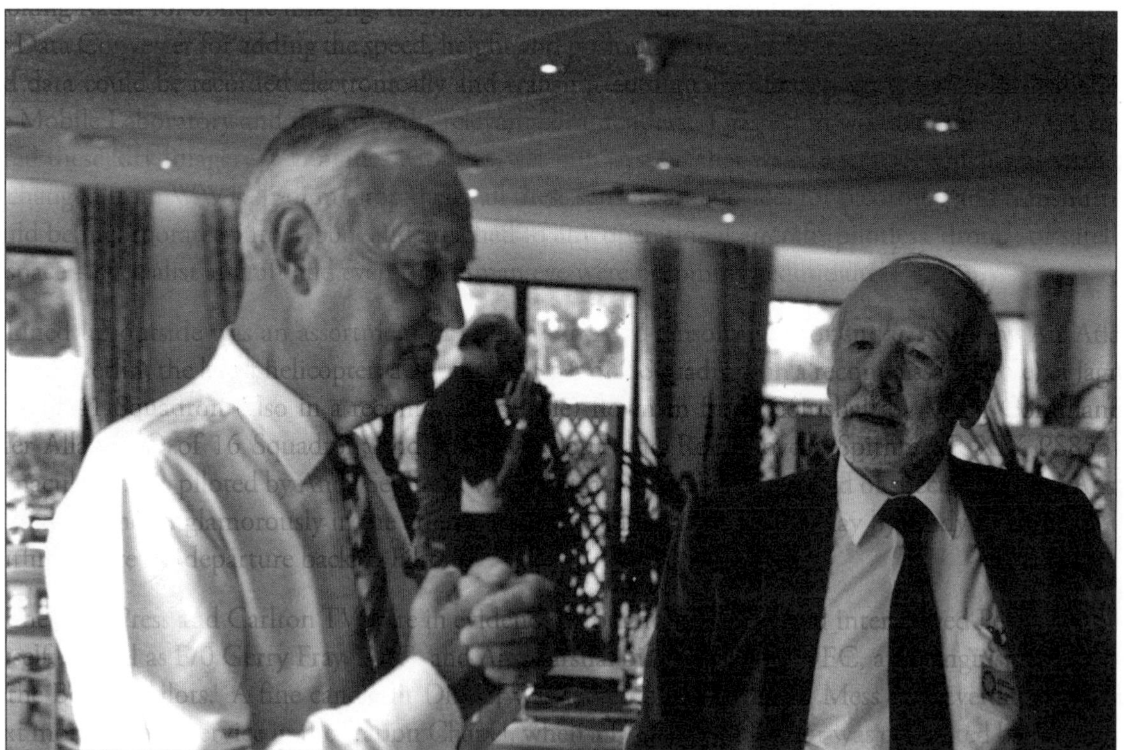

David Stutchbury (16 Squadron) and Arthur Kirk-Douglas (140 Squadron)

toasts in fine wines. The following day, we were taken to the Air Museum in Brussels, to see its large collection of aircraft, especially many unique wood-and-fabric survivors from WW1 and some rare ones from WW2, including a Battle and a Blenheim. A good lunch in the restaurant ended our visit, which had rolled back the years most poignantly, re-creating the setting from which I had taxied out on my last sad flight on 19th November 1944.

Hennie and I both wanted the tragedy of 't Hesseler to be remembered and the ceremony at the Memorial to be maintained long after all the survivors had passed away; I felt that if my family were involved, they could continue my wreath-laying visits and help to preserve the ceremony and the memories, as well as my relationship with the 't Hesseler community. I was, therefore, delighted when my daughter Jennifer (unmarried, with a partner and daughter) and son Jonathan (married, with a wife, son and daughter) showed real interest in the events of November 1944 and were keen to see the various locations and meet my good friends.

In May 1998, therefore, they joined up with Hennie and me at Schiphol Airport and drove to Borne, where the Bosch family at the "Jachtlust" hotel gave us their usual friendly welcome and comfortable accommodation. From then on, it was a matter of visiting all the places that featured in my evasion: the lane in 't Hesseler to view my landing-place, the Field of Execution, and the Memorial to the victims; the Timmermans' field to see my Spitfire's crash-site and Henk's plaque; the Twente Air Base Museum, where my helmet and goggles were on display, together with the gear-wheels of my engine and several other relics; there was also a great deal else of interest in the museum. Then to Delden, to the Twente Canal and the road-bridge over it, where I had tried to swim across the canal; to the farm-yard with the potato shed; and to the railway line that had led me to Zutphen. This was as far as we went, but we also visited Enschede to see Hanneman's "Cornelis Jonson and his Family" in the Rijksmuseum, and to look at some of the other fine 17th-century portraits there. We also walked into the town park to admire the wonderful anti-war memorial of a group of bronze figures – a soldier, fearful civilians, a slave labourer, a mother and child, and so on – each revealing the dread and suffering brought by modern war.

Guests at the 'Jimmy Taylor Says Thank You' Dinner Party in "The Resting Hunter" on 3rd May 1998
(an identification chart appears on p. 725 of Dutch Voices)

The presence of my family had motivated me to plan, along with Hennie, a great Dinner Party for all the kind people who had done so much for me since my first return to ' Hesseler in August 1991. I had therefore circulated invitation cards entitled "Jimmy Taylor Says Thank-You Dinner Party", on 3rd May, with the details in Dutch on one side and in English on the other. Henk Timmerman was, naturally, brought into it and he produced a fabulous menu for the event in "The Resting Hunter".

A family tragedy, however, marred the occasion for the most important guests: Herman Boomkamp, the second oldest brother, and father of Ria Bovenmars, who lived in his house with Jan and her family, had died a few days earlier and put all his close family into mourning, preventing their attendance. Hans Wools, however, with his wife Josine, daughter of Bernard Boomkamp, was able to represent the family. Several others also could not accept, but there were plenty who did, with their wives and grown-up children, and they formed an unlikely gathering of people, grouped together only because of their individual links to me in one way or another. They included:

Fred and Froukje Bakker, Herman Bruggink, Peggie Breitbarth, Hennie Egberink, Lukas Groen, Jaap Grootenboer, Ben van Hengstum, Joke de Leeuw, Hennie and Joke Noordhuis, Hennie Oude-Hilbert, Adrie Roding, René Schabos, Betsie Timmerman, Henk Timmerman, Jan Timmerman, Marinus Timmerman, Mrs Veenhuis-Weghorst, Maarten and Jeanette Vunderink, Hans and Josine Wools.

Altogether 43 people sat down in one of the dining-rooms in "The Resting Hunter", where they were served drinks and I made a point of identifying each person and describing their role, so that they could relate to each other. We then went out into the garden for a group photograph. We showed the video of "Beyond the Ignorance" to remind people of the events of 1944, and then sat down to a wonderful meal, to music played by Hennie's silver band. The climax of the dinner was the dessert, a creation of meringue and ice-cream, with an apparent waterfall of 'smoke' pouring down into it, and golden fireworks emitting flames all round it; it was unveiled to the sound of wartime military music, with everyone beating time and applauding the spectacle. Afterwards, in quieter mood, Jeroen Liedorp, Lukas Groen's accompanist, played his "Pro Borne" sonata, which I found mystifying, but which was received with enthusiasm. Hennie then came forward and presented me with a tall vase of thick white and black glass, to which the guests had subscribed. I promptly named it "The Twente Crystal" and said it symbolised the suffering and the liberation of the Dutch people in the war, and that it would become a family heirloom. Thus ended a memorable evening.

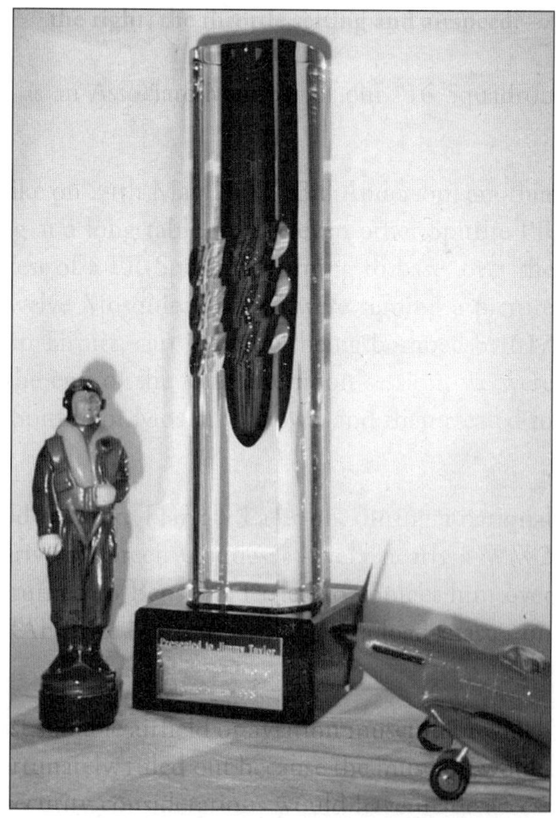

The Twente Crystal:
a constant reminder of the tragedy at 't Hesseler in November 1944

Next day, Ria Bovenmars very kindly invited Hennie and me to the funeral service and interment of her father, Herman Boomkamp; we felt it was a considerable honour to be included in the large congregation of mourners in the Roman Catholic church in Borne.

Later, at 7.0pm, Jennifer and Jonathan met at the cross-roads in 't Hesseler and then walked up the lane with the rest of us to the Memorial, although Jonathan stepped to the side to video the proceedings. It was the usual simple but moving ceremony, in which they laid their own wreath among the others at the Memorial. We then drove with Hennie to Borne, where we took part in the impressive Silent Walk through the old cobbled streets to the square outside the Old Town Hall. Here we waited with the crowd until the clock on the Old Church tolled 8.0pm, when the band struck up solemn music and the usual dignified ceremony commenced: the bugler signalled the beginning of the Two Minutes' Silence with "The Last Post", and the end with "Reveille". I was given a wreath to lay with the others at the Town War Memorial, and it was very affecting to see the many local people and children adding their posies and single flowers to the growing mass, The service ended with the singing of the Dutch National Anthem. We returned to 't Hesseler and spent the rest of the evening in the warm company of the Bovenmars family and the two remaining Boomkamp brothers, Bernard and Hendrik.

This four-day experience had a profound effect on Jennifer and Jonathan, who each maintained contact with Hennie Noordhuis. I felt this augured well for the future.

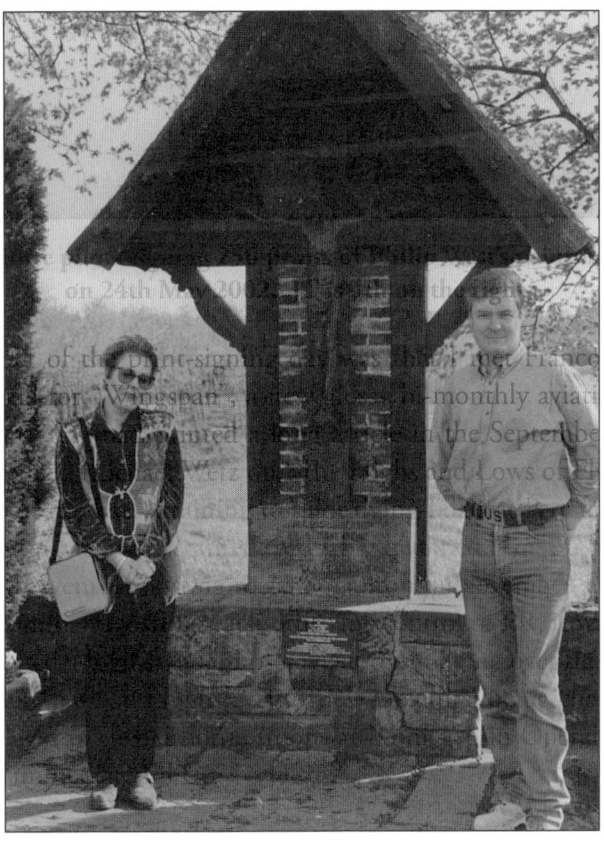

Continuing the Link:
Jennifer and Jonathan at the 't Hesseler Memorial

CHAPTER 32

Reviving My Memories – Improving My Know-how in UK

I have mentioned earlier that I was enthusiastic only about the flying in the RAF and lacked interest in nearly all the technical aspects of the business. Thus, when I joined 16 Squadron in August 1944, although my log-book showed that I was 'Above Average' as an instructor, I am quite sure I was no more than 'Average' in all other capacities. I was keen, of course, to pick up any tips or information that would help me to navigate more accurately, take better photographs, and survive encounters with German flak or fighters; but I can't say that I developed any greater understanding of what went on under my Spitfire's cowlings or inside the cameras, or what happened to my films once I had returned and the photographers had removed the magazines from my aircraft. I sometimes looked at the final end-product, the prints, with the photo-interpreters, to check on my navigation and photography, but this was the last step of an otherwise unknown process. In addition, I had paid little attention to matters above the level of 16 Squadron; I knew Tony Davis, our CO, frequently went to the HQs of 34 Wing and 21st Army Group, but I never asked what the purpose was of his visits or what kind of command structure existed among the officers on the staffs; neither did I know much about the operations of our sister-squadrons on 34 Wing: 140 Squadron with one flight of Mosquitos on day- and the other on night-photography, and 69 Squadron with Wellingtons on low-level night-photography; nor in the other Wings and squadrons engaged on PR operations similar to ours either in 2nd TAF or from RAF Benson in UK. In fact, I was always ill-at-ease in the presence of anyone of the rank of Squadron Leader or above, as I was aware of my ignorance and fearful that a senior officer would find me out. It was a case of an amateur flyer feeling very conscious of the great gap in expertise between himself and the professionals. My training and instructing in America for a year and a half probably contributed to this feeling of inferiority: as a young officer, I had not absorbed the customs and traditions observed on an RAF Station.

My last six months in the RAF, before being demobilised in June 1946, were spent on an instructor's course at Upavon and training on Harvards five sad cadets, who had been on the point of graduating in USA when the war ended and they were shipped back home; I sent them all solo on my last two days, just to give them at least this degree of satisfaction – they had gone solo already in America. Thereafter, my next forty years were spent getting a degree at Cambridge University and forging a career in education: teaching, lecturing and running courses for teachers at home and abroad. None of these activities required me to dig back into my wartime past; so my knowledge of what PR was all about, how it was organised, how our targets were selected, and so on, grew even vaguer with time. It didn't matter during my working life, as there was no great demand for such information.

However, in the 1980s, public interest in Hitler and the 1939-1945 War and the achievements of our fighting Services suddenly increased: my generation had, in general, avoided talking about the war – it wasn't 'done', and the next generation had grown up in ignorance until their curiosity got the better of them, perhaps because those who had fought in the war began to disappear from the scene – and their achievements and memories died with them.

My own introduction to this new situation occurred in 1994, when I became acquainted with Dave Tappen, who was among the people busily engaged in setting up the Yorkshire Air Museum at Elvington Airfield, outside York. One of his initiatives was to organise a monthly lecture-programme on aeronautical aspects of the war; the venue was the large canteen, which could hold 200 people. The speakers, from all levels of the different RAF Commands and even from the Luftwaffe, talked about their personal experiences, and the lectures became very popular with all ages, from wartime veterans to, for example, ATC cadets travelling in from Lancashire.

In this connection, Dave asked me to speak about PRU. Fortunately, I had my wartime photograph album and transferred many of the photos onto slides. I decided to speak to the slides as much as possible, which took me through my talk; but, when it came to questions afterwards, my limited knowledge meant that I could not give satisfactory answers to those asking about technical or wider operational issues.

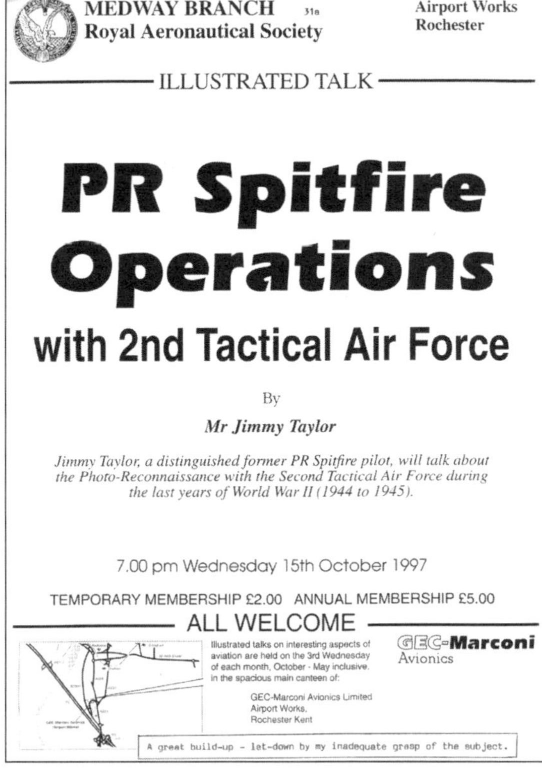

A great build-up let-down by my inadequate grasp of the subject

My embarrassment was even more in evidence in October 1997, when I was invited to address the Medway Branch of the Royal Aeronautical Society at the Rochester Airport Works of GEC-Marconi on "Spitfire Photo-Reconnaissance in 2nd TAF". The management of the electronics company kindly invited me to come early and showed me some of their latest innovations. In particular, they put me in a Tornado Simulator and placed on my head a novel helmet with a miniature TV camera built into each side; these could read the instruments and project them onto the inside of the pilot's visor; he could therefore view them or look straight through the visor as usual. I was totally bewildered by this remarkable gadget and, contrary to the expectations of the managers, who thought I would be some sort of whizz-kid, I made a mess of flying the Simulator and stumbled out of the cockpit with my head spinning.

I was then ushered into a vast hall, normally the canteen, with an audience of 400, mostly technically-skilled employees, and found, sitting in the front row, Edgar Quested, our former 16 Squadron Engineering Officer, whom I had rarely spoken to and whom, in truth, I had held in a certain amount of awe. I climbed up onto the stage and was fitted with a lapel microphone, a novelty for me; in the half-light, I turned round at the lectern to arrange my notes and became entangled in the wires, from which I had to be rescued in full view of the audience – they then let me use an ordinary desk-mike.

Edgar Quested (right) and Michael Wetz at Rochester Airport for the first post-restoration flight of PL965 December 1992
Photo: Edgar Quested

By now, I was a nervous wreck and have little memory of how I survived the lecture; certainly, question-time here was no better than at Elvington and, although Edgar Quested tried to console me by saying he'd never heard such a good talk, I left the scene with my tail very nearly visible between my legs.

This humiliating event showed me that I needed to learn much more about PR as a subject and about the place of 16 Squadron in the order of battle of 2nd TAF. Fortunately, at this same time, I realised that, if I was going to have a retirement with any worthwhile occupation, I needed to channel my various interests into one particular direction. I had done this with the Hanneman portrait of "Father Roeland de Pottere", which had taken me ten years of research in archives, libraries and galleries, and of correspondence with Jesuit historians in England, Ireland, France, Belgium and Holland; the culmination was my visit to Delft in 1997, after which I was able to write an illustrated 35-page booklet about the sitter, the artist, and the history of the picture. Although I never found a publisher, I sent copies to all the individuals and institutions that had helped me; I could therefore feel satisfied that I had added a minute fraction to the sum total of knowledge in the art world.

With this concluded, I now needed another challenge. Gliding had become one, both physical and intellectual, but I soon realised I had started too late in life to be ambitious; so, although it occupied one whole day at the weekend, it did not intrude into any of the other six days. Sailing was too akin to gliding – and both excluded Margaret – so there was no question of my adopting it as another central activity.

The field of flying, however, had been a major interest, if not an obsession of mine since the age of eight, and I had collected magazines, books, pictures and models all my life. Post-war, my brother and I both became members of the Shuttleworth Society, with its fine collection of airworthy vintage aircraft 1910-1939, and we used to meet up for family picnics on the Trust's enjoyable Air Days at its Old Warden airfield; I was also a founder-member of Northern Aeroplane Workshops (NAW) in 1970, in which a small team of volunteers, including myself for a short time, started building WW1 aircraft from the original plans and with original engines for the Shuttleworth Trust, all with distinctive shapes: the Sopwith Triplane, Bristol Monoplane, Sopwith Camel, and DH2 single-seater pusher-biplane. We also held public lectures in the University of Leeds, for educational purposes as part of our charitable status.

Northern Aeroplane Workshops' Sopwith Triplane under construction in NAW's Heckmondwike workshop

Sopwith Triplane "Dixie" looks immaculate on the grass at Old Warden.

In June 1979, the speaker was the distinguished Spitfire test-pilot Jeffrey Quill. I felt very honoured to be asked to give the vote of thanks and composed a poem entitled "In Praise of Test-Pilots" especially for the occasion. Stunned, aghast, embarrassed, or simply unused to tributes of this kind, the audience received it in total silence; in the presence of the heroic Jeffrey, I felt I was falling through space without a parachute! Not long afterwards, a totally irrelevant anti-war demonstration by a handful of students put a stop to these well-attended public lectures. I also followed the fortunes of 16 Squadron whenever it was mentioned in "RAF News", as a front-line unit on Tornados and, later, as a training squadron on Jaguars, when it provided the Display Jaguar for the RAF; if I saw it at an air display, I made a point of meeting the pilot, to bathe for a minute or two in his reflected glory.

It now dawned on me that I was slowly proceeding along a series of avenues which were pointing in one direction and occasionally crossing over each other on the way. One of these cross-connections began at the launch of "Spitfire in Blue" at Duxford in May 1996 when Steve Noujaim, an ex-RAF free-lance and display pilot, approached me and we had a long chat about my wartime activities. I thought no more about it but, two years later, I came upon him and his attractive wife walking their dogs on Dishforth Airfield: they had a house a few miles away. In September 1998, Paul Morgan brought his two preserved war-birds into Dishforth – he flew the Sea Fury and Steve Noujaim the P-51 Mustang – and parked them in a corner of our glider hangar. On 10th October, Steve had the Mustang on our flight-line, while Paul was shooting landings in the Sea Fury. Our people naturally crowded round the Mustang, so Steve offered them a flight in the jump-seat in the back for £80. A couple of our members took advantage of this, and Steve then invited me for a ride. I said I couldn't afford the money, but he replied that he wasn't going to charge me anything. I had always wanted to fly in a Mustang and compare it with a Spitfire, so I couldn't refuse such a wonderful offer: it was a flight I'd never forget.

We taxied past my assembled colleagues and took off easily on the long south-north runway. Steve turned right and held it low: I had no instruments or controls in the back, but I had my camera and clicked away as we flashed over the hills and dales of the North Yorkshire Moors at about 220mph. The highlight for me was going past the magnificent ruins of Rievaulx Abbey perched on the side of a once remote valley, dotted today with a few cottages. All too soon, we were back at Dishforth, where-

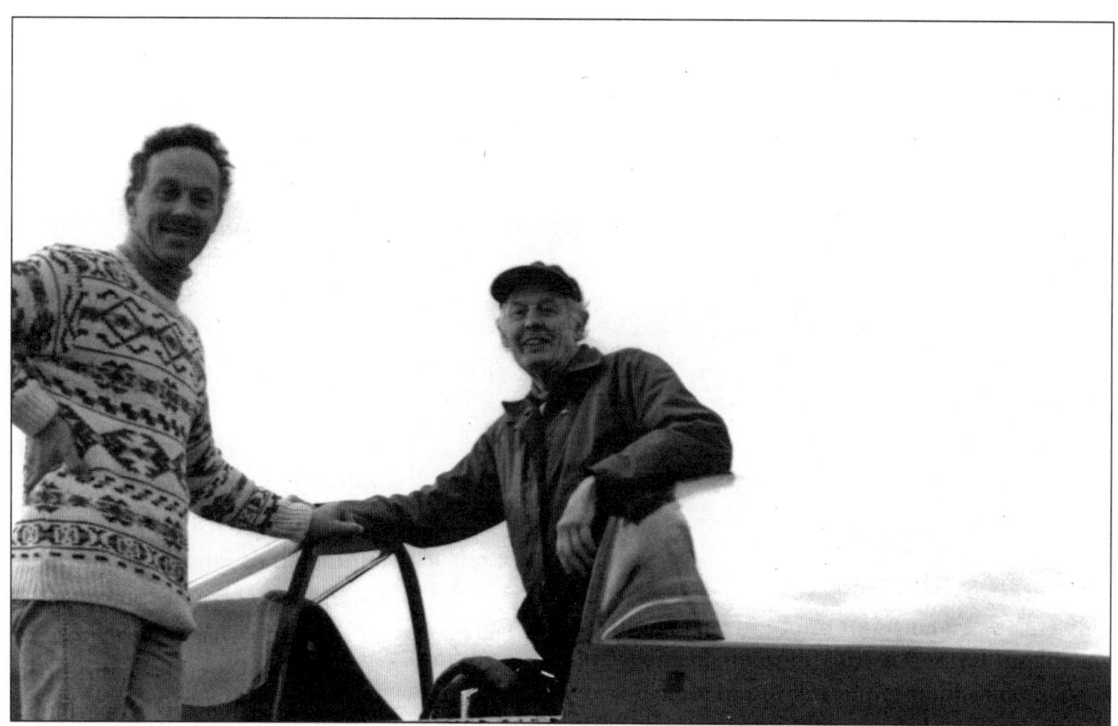

Steve Naijaim welcomes me aboard P-51 Mustang "Suzy" at Dishforth airfield in October 1997.

The elegant P-51, an aeroplane I had always wanted to have a ride in.

Warming-up "Suzy" – the huge flaps and wide undercarriage made for straightforward landings.

The wonderful 12th-century Rievaulx Abbey, cradled in the North Yorkshire Moors, slips past the P-51 and my camera pointing out of the jump-seat.

upon Steve gave me a couple of gentle loops followed by two smooth roils, which showed me the easy power of the Mustang and caused envy in my friends on the ground. Staying well clear of any gliders, Steve guided the Mustang round the circuit, lowered the huge flaps, and made a beautifully controlled approach, touching down on the wide undercarriage without a murmur. I thought back to the Spitfire's narrow little wheels and the efforts I had to make on the rudder to keep the delicate ballerina going straight ahead down the runway, and envied the pilots who could trust this masculine machine to behave as expected. I congratulated Steve and thanked him effusively for a great experience. Later, I sent him an album of the photographs I'd taken from the ground as well as from the air, and gave him one of the brass model Spitfires that I'd had modified to represent a PR XI. Sadly, a year or so afterwards, I read that Paul Morgan had landed the Sea Fury at some airfield and it had overturned, killing him instantly; I never learned the cause. Flying can be a dangerous game, and the Cleveland club's adherence to the strictest safety rules was the only way to keep the members out of trouble, even in slow-moving gliders.

A second cross-connection also started at Duxford in 1996 when Wojtek Matusiak, a Polish air historian, introduced himself to me and I showed him my wartime photograph album. He asked for copies of some of them, especially the photos of Spitfire IXs and XIs and of the German aircraft we had found on the airfield at Melsbroek, either damaged or vandalised by the British troops that had captured the base. These he reproduced later in Polish aviation magazines and monographs, which he either wrote or co-edited. The standard of publication was extremely high, on glossy paper, with many illustrations full of technical details. The last work of his that I read, in 2007, I ordered from the Midland Counties bookshop; it was titled "Merlin PR Spitfires", written in English and part of the "Classic Warbirds" series by Ventura Publications of New Zealand. Wojtek credited five of its many photographs to me, although two were actually taken by my close 16 Squadron friend Michael Horsfall.

Before this, in about 1993, Michael had called me to his home near Sutton Coldfield because Dr Alfred Price wanted to meet us; he had borrowed a number of photographs from each of us. In my case, he made great use of two air-to-air shots I had taken, with my own camera through the canopy on 22nd September 1944, of Peter Fahy flying a pink Spitfire IX when we were going together from Amiens-Glisy to Ford to pick up drop-tanks for use in message-dropping near Nijmegen during Operation 'Market Garden'. Unfortunately, Dr Price mixed up our photos and names and usually credited all our photos to 'Horsfall' – not that I minded too much, since Wojtek, for example, did the same thing in reverse to Michael.

My aircraft photographs could not, of course, stand alone on a page: they had to be put into their wartime context, which involved checking dates and facts in my log-book and in histories such as Hugh Smallwood's "Spitfire in Blue". Seeing them published gave me a degree of satisfaction, and it also stirred in me a feeling that, in spite of my dismal performances at Elvington and Rochester, I did possess certain facts and experiences in which other people had an interest. I realised that it lay within my reach to take up the relatively neglected subject of photo-reconnaissance and, in the process, to boost the reputation of 16 Squadron, which I held in splendid memory, even though I had survived only three months in its ranks.

Further strands in the rope that would pull me into writing were apparent in my contacts at Dishforth Airfield with gliders and glider pilots, my visits to active airfields and aviation museums for our Reunions, and my connection with 16 Squadron's two surviving PR Spitfires, which formed a direct link with our wartime operations.

In addition, in 1990 I was invited by Michael Cobham, son and heir of Sir Alan and a friend of mine at Cambridge, to visit the extensive works of the Flight Refuelling Group, of which he became Chairman after his father's death in 1973. My day with Michael was an eye-opening experience both of the

The late Sir Michael Cobham beside a portrait of his distinguished father, Sir Alan Cobham, at the HQ of Flight Refuelling (now Cobham) Ltd in Dorset

Group's industrial premises at Wimborne and Bournemouth Airport and of the wide range of the equipment its various companies produced for the needs of civilian and military aviation. In particular, it was running a private air force of over 50 aircraft, including 21 Dassault Falcons and 18 Hawker Hunters, to enable training to be offered to our own and allied air forces and navies in opposing hostile attacks by aircraft and missiles simulated by electronic means. Michael gained a well-deserved knighthood in 1995 but sadly died in 2006, by which time his Group had been aptly re-named Cobham Ltd.

The ultimate impetus was received when I developed the first circulars to the Members of the newly-formed "16 Squadron 1939-1945" into the formal publication of "Newsbrief", with its regular format and its own house-style. Indeed, it became authoritative enough for me to send it to the National Archive, the Imperial War Museum and the RAF Museum Hendon, and to gain their approval. It also stimulated correspondence with our Members and Associate Members and, when it spread further afield, with other historians with related interests.

For example, "Newsbrief 9", of July 1997 included an article on "Bodenplatte – the German Attack on the Airfields on 1st January 1945". Melsbroek experienced a particularly strong attack and 34 Wing suffered considerable losses: 3 Spitfires of 16 Squadron were destroyed and 3 damaged; 6 Mosquitos of 140 Squadron were destroyed; 11 Wellingtons of 69 Squadron were destroyed and 2 were damaged. In addition, among other aircraft on the airfield, 4 Mitchells of 139 Wing were destroyed and 7 damaged; 2 more Spitfires, 6 other Mitchells, 1 Boston and 1 Stirling were destroyed; of bombers that had put down in distress into Melsbroek as a forward airfield, 24 B-24 Liberators and B-17 Flying Fortresses were destroyed, along with 7 supply-carrying Harrows.

As I had just arrived in Stalag Luft 1 the night before the raid, I had to do a good deal of research for this account in "Newsbrief", and found considerable help especially in Norman Franks' excellent narrative "The Battle of the Airfields" (William Kimber 1982); I was also able to obtain eye-witness accounts from ten of our Members. It kept me busy for at least two weeks, and the ultimate article covered 19 A4-size pages, and included two full-page aerial photos of the airfield, one full-page and three half-page pictures of burning aircraft, and many anecdotes of personal experiences, all provided by our Members; this edition of "Newsbrief" was therefore of more than usual interest to outside bodies.

And so it went on. In "Newsbrief 11" next year, James Marett, a very experienced photographer who became a college lecturer in his post-war career, gave a fascinating history of No 7 Mobile Field Photographic Section, one of the two which worked for 34 Wing; he followed it up with two more long articles in "Newsbriefs 13" and "14", in the course of which he explained fully the operation of the cameras and the processes which our films went through to produce multiple copies of prints for the Commands that had ordered them. In "Newsbrief 18" he started on the, to me and no doubt to others, mysterious subject of 'titling' – putting the identifying caption onto every print. In "Newsbrief 19" he covered the use of infra-red film. Ron Miller, another photographer, who spent most of his time fitting cameras to the aircraft as required for operations and removing them before nightfall, added more detail to 'titling' in "Newsbriefs 21" and "22". Other blanks in my knowledge were filled in by periodical contributions from Edgar Quested, the Engineering Officer; Ken Holloway, Fitter II (Engines), and Eric Phillips, Wireless Mechanic. Not only did "Newsbrief" make interesting reading for our Members, Ex-Officio Members and Associate Members, it also gave me the very information that I never knew during the war and which I now absorbed fully for the development of my knowledge of PR as a literary subject.

Coming from our own wartime personnel, this was the most direct form of education I could receive but, as I suggested earlier, there were many other, less obvious sources which, nevertheless, had a cumulative effect on my post-war education. One was books about PR: the first of these, which I came upon in 1994, was Andrew Brookes's "Photo Reconnaissance – the Operational History" (Ian Allan 1975), a comprehensive survey from the early balloonists through to the Cold War, with a certain amount of technical information. The second, which was kindly sent to me, was "World War II Photo

Peter Teichman shows Ron Miller, former 16 Squadron photographer, and Harry van der Meer, Dutch aircraft preservationist, a brand-new Type 35 Camera Control Unit, in his Hangar 11 at North Weald airfield at the final Reunion of "16 Squadron 1939-1945" in 2006.

Intelligence", by Col. Roy M. Stanley, USAF (Sidgwick and Jackson 1982), a very large and detailed account, supported by full technical details, of the PR activities of the American, British, German and Japanese Air Forces. The third was, surprisingly, a remainder book in 1999, even though it had been published just the year before; this was "Allied Photo Reconnaissance of World War II" (PRC Publishing 1998), a collection of articles, edited by Chris Staerck, on the part played by PR in twelve campaigns, from our defence against the German invasion of Britain in 1940 to the liberation of Allied POW camps in 1945; this was more concerned with the strategic use of PR than the previous books. Constance Babington Smith's "Evidence in Camera" (Chatto and Windus 1958), which I could find only in the American edition and second-hand at that, revealed the early struggles to get the original PR squadrons established, their successes and losses, and the tactics and procedures they evolved. Much later, Ursula Powys-Lybbe, another former photo-interpreter, wrote a similar and slightly better account in "The Eye of Intelligence" (William Kimber 1983), which was also long out of print. Finally, of the books most useful for my purpose, Wing Commander T.F. Neil's little volume, "Spitfire" (1990), in Ian Allan's "From the Cockpit" series, gave a valuable description of what the pilot actually had to do to fly various Marks of Spitfire.

Other information came through less direct sources, although they all helped to refresh my memories of my own experiences in 1944 and to fill in the gaps in my knowledge of the wider operational field. The first was our Reunion in 1998 at Rolls-Royce's airfield of Hucknall, outside Nottingham. We were invited, on our way to the flight-line, to visit the workshops of the Hucknall and Derby Branch of the Rolls-Royce Heritage Trust (which I had visited with David Birch in 1997), where one of the senior members, Ivor Purkis – later Chairman – presented me with a framed technical drawing of the supercharger bearing that had brought about my downfall in 1944 and led, very indirectly, to the tragedy of

Together again, two thoroughbreds!
Spitfire XIX PS853 (left) and Spitfire XI PL965 both flew on photographic reconnaissance in 16 Squadron in 1945, and met again at the 1998 Reunion of "16 Squadron 1939-1945" at Rolls-Royce Hucknall.

Photo: Peter Arnold

Tony Smith watches the Battle of Britain Memorial Flight overfly our 2000 Reunion at Rolls-Royce Hucknall from the wing of Spitfire XI PL965, which he had painted pink to simulate a 16 Squadron Spitfire IX in 1944.

't Hesseler. This was an inspired choice of gift, one which both touched my heart and added a little to my very small technical understanding. The Reunion itself provided a thrill when we saw 'our' Spitfire XI PL965, owned and piloted by Tony Smith, flying in formation with 'our' Spitfire XIX PS853, now owned by Rolls-Royce and piloted by their Head of Flying, Andy Sephton. This great, and unusual, sight was repeated in 2000, when we returned to Hucknall and, in addition, I managed to get the Red Arrows, the Battle of Britain Memorial Flight, a Canberra PR7, and 16 Squadron's Display Jaguar, each to give us a fly-over en-route to displays elsewhere.

Closely related to the broken bearing of the technical drawing from Hucknall was a more national event that took place on 16th July 1998. Channel 4 TV decided to make a series of eight programmes on "Classic Aircraft", which they divided into "Bombers", "Fighters", "Trainers", "Seaplanes", "Helicopters", "Airliners", and "Sport Planes"; the eighth was "Spies", which was where PR featured. The programme started with a Bleriot monoplane of 1912 or so, moved through WW1, and arrived at WW2 with our Spitfire XIs and XIXs – in fact, it started by first showing the latter briefly in the air.

Camera and sound units came to Breighton Aerodrome, near York, where Tony Smith kept PL965 among the 30-odd privately-owned airworthy vintage planes that were hangared there. The TV people recorded a great deal of footage of Tony, wearing a period flying-jacket, helmet and goggles, getting into PL965, starting it up, taxying round to the single runway, taking off into the camera and climbing away; then, of course, returning, shooting-up the airfield, landing, taxying back, shutting-off the engine, and

Tony Smith starts-up Spitfire XI PL965 for the TV camera.

climbing out of the cockpit. As was usual with TV, he was required to do this several times. Meanwhile, Peter Fahy and I had been invited to Breighton and were each interviewed separately on the airfield while Tony was running through his flying procedures. Peter was asked about the nature and tactics of our sorties, while I was questioned quite closely on what had happened to me on 19th November 1944. My interview was interrupted while Tony roared past within a few feet – a burst tyre flashed through my mind! – on one of his take-offs. Our interviews were slotted into the section that featured PL965, which was later cut down to a mere ten minutes of the hour-long programme; this moved on to the Canberra and American U-2, and finished with space satellites.

"Spies" was broadcast on 18th December of that year. I managed to get the producer to give me some of the unused footage and, over a period of time, persuaded Ron Nobes, an Associate Member who recorded several of our Reunions and made excellent videos of them, to put together a video of my story, using material from "Beyond the Ignorance", from Jonathan's video of the 't Hesseler ceremony, and from my interview in this event at Breighton.

In 1997, when I was preparing for our Reunion at RAF Benson, the wartime base of 1 PRU, which gradually grew into 106 Group, including the American 7th Photo Group (= RAF Wing) of nearby Mount Farm, I was expecting to find on the base some interesting archives and photographs and a small museum of photographic equipment. But there was just one small room, with two cupboards containing a few papers, some random photographs, and three photo albums left behind by their owners many years ago. This was very disappointing, but it was to change with the arrival of F/Sgt Mike ("Butch") Harris, whose official job was a crew trainer for the Merlin helicopter.

Mike had a strong sense of history and had, in fact, got himself appointed Station Historian of Benson; he felt that Benson should be the national centre for PR, with a museum well-stocked with memorabilia and artefacts and including some actual aircraft – a replica of Gerry Fray's Spitfire XI was already the gate-guardian on a pedestal outside Station Headquarters. He was fortunate in having the full support of the Station Commander, Group Captain Mike Lloyd.

F/Sgt Mike Harris, Benson historian, (right) and Simon Garrett, producer of Carlton TV's feature on PRU entitled "Above and Beyond"

On 12th May 2001 they organised a Reunion for the personnel of the PR squadrons at Benson and in all the theatres of WW2, together with their wives and guests; and, to show the progress of aerial photography from then up to the present-day, Mike Harris had, by some means or other, collected a large amount of equipment and displayed it in the ante-room of the Officers' Mess: cameras, control boxes, photographs, models, log-books, calculators, helmets, uniforms and so on. In a nearby hangar was an exhibition of the work of 39 Squadron, the remaining specialist PR unit in the RAF, which was flying Canberra PR9s; they showed their range of cameras, including those for night and infra-red photography and others with Forward Movement Compensation and Automatic Exposure Control, and many examples of their work. Outside was an even more up-to-date sample of modern image-gathering technology: a van housing a Mobile Reconnaissance Exploitation Laboratory, full of computer screens and video-recorders. Here my mind began to boggle: Infra-Red Line Scan for thermal imaging and night-time imaging; Sideways-Looking Radar for oblique imaging; television cameras for video-recording in sufficient light; a Modulator Data Converter for adding the speed, height and position of the aircraft to the tape. All this imagery and data could be recorded electronically and transmitted digitally direct from the aircraft in flight to the Mobile Laboratory and thence to the relevant commanders. I gasped in wonder and envy as I compared these 'dry imagery' techniques with the 'wet film' system that we had to use, which was virtually unchanged from WW1. It didn't stop there: all these sensors and devices for recording and transmitting could be incorporated into a 'pod' and attached to any operational aircraft, pilotless 'drone', or satellite in space – specialist aircraft and even the human eye were becoming redundant!

Lined up outside was an assortment of aircraft: an Avro Anson used for survey work by Air Atlantique; a Merlin, the latest helicopter; a Tornado GR3A of 2 Squadron (in a reconnaissance role); a Jaguar GR3 of 41 Squadron (also in a reconnaissance role) flown in from Coltishall by Wing Commander Peter Allan, CO of 16 Squadron; and, above all, 'our' and Rolls-Royce's Spitfire PR XIX PS853 in immaculate blue, piloted by Andy Sephton, which attracted the biggest crowd of spectators. The Anson cruised around unglamorously in the afternoon, followed by a spirited display by Andy Sephton in the Spitfire before his departure back to Filton.

The local Press and Carlton TV were in evidence throughout the day and interviewed Peter Fahy and myself, as well as F/0 Gerry Fray, DFC, and Air Marshal Sir Alfred Ball, DFC, a distinguished survivor of the Benson pilots. A fine candle-lit Dinner was served in the Officers' Mess that evening, followed next morning by a service in the Station Chapel, when a PR Roll of Honour was dedicated by the Chaplain. I gave Mike Harris the names of the eleven losses suffered by 16 Squadron during its PR service 1944-45, for inclusion on this Roll.

The Reunion had proved a notable success, a veritable milestone in the record of aerial reconnaissance, and revealed the sort of exhibition that Mike Harris was aiming to have located permanently at Benson. For me, it helped to put into a historical perspective the aura of romance that surrounded

Wartime PR pilots
(l-r) Back row: Peter Fahy JT Peter Brearley Julian Lowe
Front: Peter Harding G/C Mike Lloyd (CO Benson) Gwyn Parry
in front of a replica of Spitfire XI EN343, in which F/O Gerry Fray photographed the breaches in the Moehne and Eder dams on 17rd May 1943 and was awarded the DFC

flying the Spitfire in 1944 and the feeling of pride, greater perhaps today than at the time, that we took in our photographic achievements.

I was back at Benson on 18th October 2001 for what should have been a print-signing session of an oil-painting by Philip West of Gerry Fray's PR sortie over the Moehne Dam on 17th May 1943. However, the horrific destruction by Al Qua'eda terrorists of the World Trade Centre in New York on 11th September put paid to that project. However, Mike Harris decided to go ahead with the invitation to the pilots and the media for the second part of the programme: a flight in a Merlin helicopter and on the Simulator.

Peter Fahy had begun his PR career at Benson and had met Joan there, a Land Girl on a local farm, before she became his wife. He therefore had a strong interest in returning to Benson; while Mike Harris knew that I supported him in his ambition to restore to Benson its central wartime PR role. So Peter and I found ourselves together again, posing for the Press with four other veterans and answering their questions under the nose of Gerry Fray's replica Spitfire XI. Later, we were introduced to the newly delivered Merlin helicopter, which would be based at Benson in squadron strength. However, neither Peter nor I had any interest in being flown around Oxfordshire while sitting in the roomy, but unexciting interior of the machine. We were, on the other hand, very keen to try our hand at flying the Simulator. Peter was actually an expert on helicopters, as he had transferred to them in the post-war RAF and had been awarded an AFC as CO of a squadron in Cyprus.

For this experience, we were led into a massive steel-and-glass building that housed three Simulators, wonderfully designed and equipped at huge expense, which the RAF rented by the hour from the private firm that built and ran them. Sitting in the pilot's seat in a complete replica cockpit and looking at a panorama of the airfield that exactly reproduced the real thing, down to individual buildings, I forgot that this was a Simulator; the operator reinforced the feeling of reality when he introduced all kinds of natural and mechanical interferences into the flight, the least of which were sound-effects, vibrations, and pitching-and-tossing in rough air.

As this was my first opportunity to take the controls of a helicopter, I wanted only to master the basic techniques of taking-off, flying a circuit, and landing; this I did several times, and soon learned how to handle the two main throttle controls: one for up and down, the other for forward motion. The only difficulty was that each time I came in for a landing, just as I levelled off to hover five feet above the ground to make a gentle descent, the down-wash from the rotor onto the ground was so great that it tipped the machine over and I landed with a crash on the runway! The only gratification was that Peter, with all his previous experience, met with exactly the same upset in the last few feet of the landing: the instructor said that this was a common phenomenon and trainee-pilots needed plenty of time to learn how to cope with it. I have never felt any affinity with helicopters, but I so much enjoyed my half-hour – at a cost of at least £1000 to the RAF – that I was half-converted to accepting them into the ranks of aeroplanes. After this generous initiative and the organising of the previous Reunion at Benson, I welcomed Mike Harris as an Associate Member of our "16 Squadron 1939-1945" group.

Rather than ride as a passenger in the real Merlin, Peter Fahy and I preferred to 'fly' the Simulator; all I needed to use to 'fly' a circuit round the very realistic 'airfield' was the display on the top screen of the instrument panel: in the centre is the artificial horizon; on the left, the torque setting (climb/descent) and altitude; on the right, the throttle setting and airspeed.

In due course, the print-signing was reinstated by Mike on 24th May 2002. Bill Anderson, another former 16 Squadron pilot, and I found ourselves sitting at a long table, with eleven other Spitfire PR pilots, signing 250 prints of a fine picture by Philip West of a PR Spitfire returning to base, over the caption "Mission Accomplished". At another table, twelve Mosquito aircrew were signing a picture of a PR Mosquito photographing the German battleship Tirpitz, capsized after being bombed by 617 Squadron, over the caption "Tirpitz Re-Visited". At the end of the long afternoon session, we were each presented with one of the prints signed by all the Spitfire or Mosquito crews, and then treated to an excellent dinner in the Officers' Mess.

This, sadly, was the last historical PR activity arranged by Mike Harris. Later on, during a national ambulance-drivers' strike, he was posted to Wales to drive a "Green Goddess" – very nearly a WW2 left-over pressed into civilian service – and he never returned to Benson. I tried to contact him over the years – in vain. However, in 2008 I found him at RAF Brize Norton, working as a load-master on TriStars and, happily, still interested in PR history.

In 2003, a serious effort was made to identify the most suitable airfield or aviation museum in which to locate a permanent PR exhibition. Benson was, unfortunately, ruled out because the museum would have been on an operational RAF helicopter base and security considerations would have made access difficult for the general public. Eventually, the Imperial War Museum's fine site at Duxford Airfield was selected as the most suitable environment in which to place a full historical record and display of Photographic Reconnaissance equipment and, I hope, aircraft.

12 former PR Spitfire pilots signing 250 prints of Philip West's painting at RAF Benson on 24th May 2002. JT is 4th on the right.

One pleasant by-product of the print-signing day was that I met Francois Prins, who was busily taking photographs of us all for "Wingspan", a new glossy bi-monthly aviation magazine that he had launched some time before. He had printed a long article in the September/October 2000 issue by 16 Squadron's very experienced Michael Wetz on "The Highs and Lows of Flying Recce Spitfires"; this was an absorbing account of Michael's training to pilot flying-boats at Pensacola Naval Base in Florida which, because of the good navigation required, probably qualified him, on his return to UK, to enter the PR OTU at Dyce, with eventual posting to 16 Squadron in November 1943. To prevent Bomber Command and Fighter Command jostling each other for control of PR, it was given to Coastal Command, who naturally expected a high standard of navigation in flying over the sea. Michael went on to relate his experiences on low-level and high-level sorties, including being chased by an Me163 rocket-plane, and dropping messages to the Airborne troops at Nijmegen in Operation 'Market Garden', for which he was awarded an immediate DFC.

With his customary generosity, Michael gave me a year's subscription to "Wingspan", which led me to offer Francois Prins to proof-read the issues for him, as the lack of such close examination of the material for textual errors was spoiling an otherwise superior publication. I thereby became friendly with Francois, who let me re-print Michael Wetz's article in "Newsbrief 21" of April 2002. It was thus that, after publishing my article on the Duke of Edinburgh's flying achievements in that same issue of "Newsbrief", I offered an expanded version to Francois, who very kindly printed it in "Wingspan" in the issue of September-October 2003 under the title "HRH Prince Philip, Duke of Edinburgh, Royal Pilot Extraordinary". He also published another article later by David Stutchbury, a contemporary of Michael Wetz's, who transferred from flying Mosquitos in 140 Squadron to 16 Squadron in December 1944 and was checked out in a Spitfire by 'Tommy' Thompson, a Canadian pilot; he did so by flying alongside David in another Spitfire for a time and then having a tail-chase with him. The trouble was that they landed on the same runway at the same time, but in opposite directions! This hair-raising experience David described in "My First Spitfire Flight – and Nearly My Last", which Francois re-printed in "Wingspan" No 32 in December 2005. Sadly, it was one of the last issues of "Wingspan", as it ceased publication unexpectedly not long afterwards, without any explanation.

Returning to 2003, 9th July saw a wonderful Reunion of "16 Squadron 1939-1945" at the RAF Museum, Cosford, in Staffordshire, which concentrates on WW2 aircraft, German rocket projectiles and guided weapons, and British experimental planes. The highlight was the appearance of five Jaguars from 16 Squadron, led by their redoubtable CO, Wing Commander Guy Stockill, who dived on the Museum buildings from all directions, with a great roar of engines, which drew out the spectators, in a thorough 'beat-up'. They then landed-on Cosford's airfield, and instructors and students joined us for a very convivial lunch in the Museum's restaurant, after which they flew back to Coltishall – no doubt, more sedately.

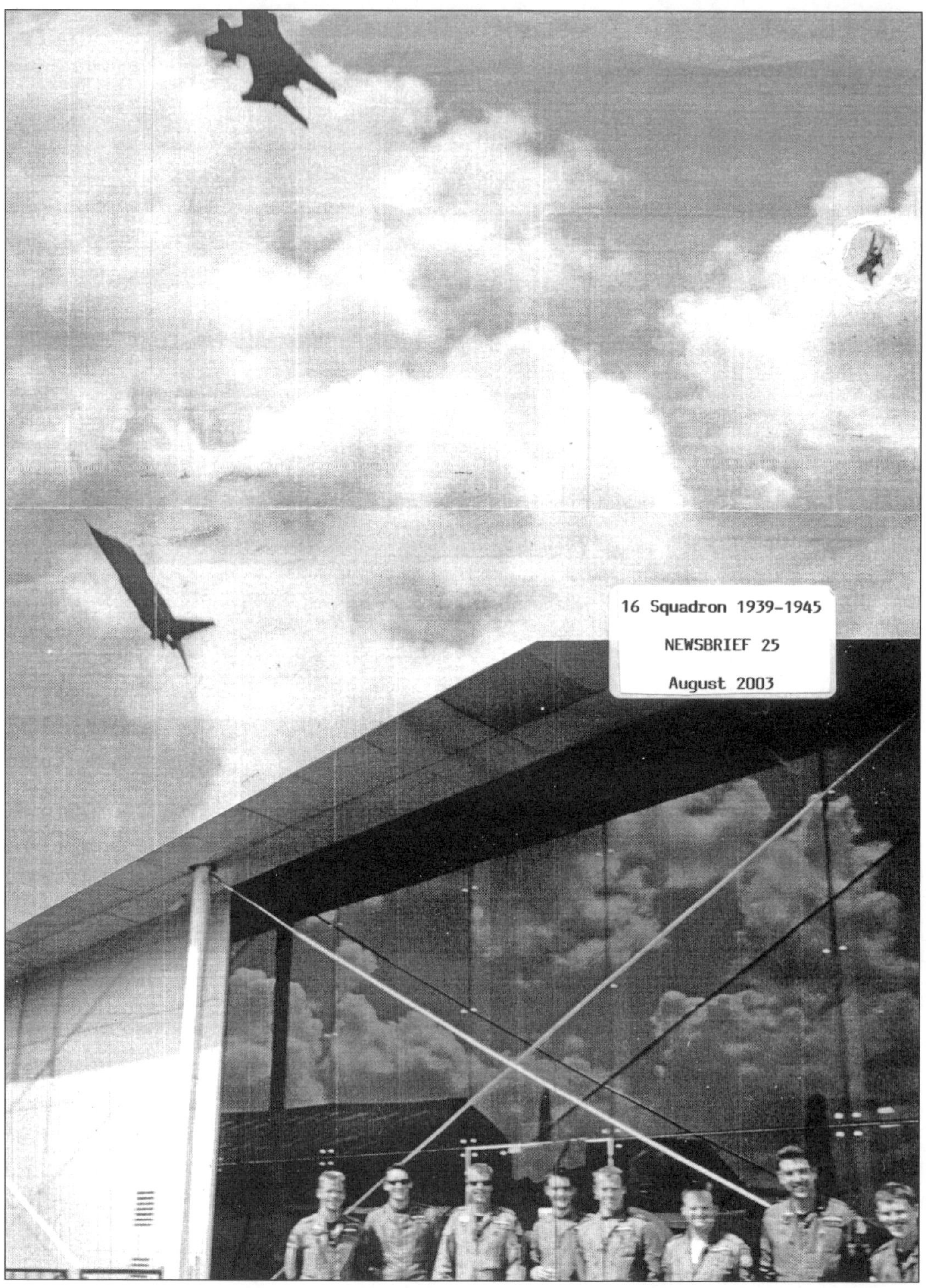

Instructors and student pilots of the 16 Squadron Jaguars which 'beat up' the RAF Museum at Cosford during our 2003 Reunion there and came for lunch. Wing Commander Guy Stockill, the then CO, is 3rd on the left. The cover of 'Newsbrief 25" managed to include both events!

Later, I was telephoned at home by the Station Commander, who demanded to know who had authorised the flight! This request to a long-retired pensioner seemed slightly laughable. I suggested he asked his Flying Control, who were bound to have discussed it with Guy beforehand. The Station Commander thought this was a good idea, and I heard no more about it. When I told Guy of this unusual conversation, he said it was a fully authorised training flight, culminating in an attack on the specified target! Later, he sent me a copy of his maps with all the courses, turning-points, distances, times, and remaining weights of fuel, marked clearly on them. It was this kind of insight into the professionalism of the young men of today's jet-propelled Royal Air Force that contrasted so strongly with the relative amateurishness of my own flying experience, and evoked my deep admiration for the Service in peace as well as in war. In fact, the instructors were being posted individually for temporary service in the Jaguar squadrons patrolling Kosovo and Northern Iraq, a peace-keeping operation, but by no means a safe one.

Related to this, in a sad way, was my awareness of how many RAF aircrew and ground-staff were killed on operations or died on active service in the course of serving their country, particularly those in 16 Squadron. At our Reunions, in remembering 'Absent Friends' we used to read out the names of all those who had died in WW2. Two of these, in succession, had shared a tent with Michael Horsfall and myself: Jimmy Wallace, on A12 airstrip, who failed to return from a sortie to Flushing, in Holland, on 9th September 1944, and John Brodby, at Amiens-Glisy, who was shot down near Nijmegen on 20th September. In the nature of PR operations, the pilots flew on their own and there was rarely a witness to their downfall. In the case of Jimmy Wallace, we had no news of him until the Army advanced through France and came upon his burial near Nord; we could only speculate that, as German fighters or flak were unlikely to be met over Northern France at that time, he could have died from any one of a number of causes, of which the likeliest was through lack of oxygen, perhaps because of a broken pipe, poor connection, or faulty gauge. John Brooby's death was better known, as the cloud-base that day was only 1000 feet and he was seen to crash in an urban area, as will be described later. A third colleague, 'Gibby' Gibb, crashed to his death five miles from the end of the runway at Amiens-Glisy on 18th September, just seconds after taking-off on a sortie, probably from becoming disoriented when he flew straight up into very low cloud. A fourth, 'Jolly' Jolliffe, a quiet friend, one of our NCO pilots, was shot down on a sortie near Antwerp on 1st October; his body, with his parachute unopened, was found lying near his crashed Spitfire: he had baled out too late. A fifth, Clyde Heath, was a popular, good-looking ex-NCO, with a beautiful Belgian girl-friend; he was shot down on 18th November, the day before my own engine-failure, while doing a low-level 'dice', photographing the vital road and rail bridges at Venlo, in southern Holland: these enabled the Germans to bring up troops, tanks, weapons and supplies across the Rhine in preparation for their unexpected offensive through the Ardennes forests in December, in an attempt to reach Antwerp or Brussels and cut the Allies' supply lines. The Mitchell light bombers of 2 Group constantly tried to destroy these vital targets and constantly failed to do so; the Germans had surrounded the bridges with heavy and light flak and knew well that, after every bombing-raid, a single PR plane would appear to record the results. This was Clyde's second sortie to Venlo – this time his luck ran out.

The loss of just these five friends of mine shows how varied the causes could be: three to German fighters or flak, one to oxygen starvation, and another to weather conditions; engine-failure, navigation error, running out of fuel, and friendly fire, were other alternatives. Fortunately, like many servicemen during the war, I was blessed with the simple philosophy of "It can't happen to me" – which suggested vaguely that "Other people might have made mistakes, but I will avoid them". At the same time, I felt quite sure that I would not survive the war – that there was no use thinking about what I would do after it ended as, by the law of averages, I couldn't survive. This pessimistic viewpoint didn't worry me in any way – it just prevented me thinking about the future.

Now, in 2003, I realised that, in editing "Newsbrief" and writing the obituaries of our Members as they gradually and inexorably "reached the end of the runway", I had a duty to produce a Roll of Honour of all the WW2 casualties of 16 Squadron, giving brief details, if possible, of how they died and where they were buried. In this project, I received immense help from Mrs Susan Dickinson, of the Air Historical Branch of the Ministry of Defence, and from Mrs Maureen Annetts and Emily Bird of the Commonwealth War Graves Commission's headquarters in Maidenhead.

I found it a saddening experience: so many good, brave, intelligent young men cut down so young and denied the pleasures of post-war life that I had enjoyed so much. What worried me especially was that death came equally to the experienced pilot and to the virtual newcomer: Group Captain Pat Ogilvie, DSO, DFC, a veteran from 1941, went missing from a simple Met. flight in December 1944, while F/Sgt Morris was shot down on his very first sortie in August 1944, but fortunately survived as a POW. I had to accept that a flak shell-fragment could miss one man by a hair's breadth, but destroy another next to him – did anything govern this choice of victim? I felt there could be no alternative but that Lady Luck stayed with the one and deserted the other. No wonder so many aircrew carried with them into the cockpit a lucky charm of some description, perhaps a little teddy bear or woolly doll; some always touched something or performed a regular action before take-off, crossing themselves, or urinating on the tail-wheel, or expecting their dog to witness their departure: they needed some kind of talisman. I never had one, but I did carry a stainless steel plate in an empty cigarette-case bearing my miniature US Army Air Corps 'wings', in my left breast-pocket, to make at least my heart bullet-proof – not for luck, but for protection.

This sense of tragic fate was with me throughout 2002 as I struggled to obtain the details of the 31 losses suffered by 16 Squadron in WW2; eventually, I managed to complete an accurate and comprehensive Roll of Honour. Of course, having achieved this and gained some experience of working with the relevant institutions, I had to turn my hand to WW1, for which also 16 Squadron had no reliable list of casualties. Here, to my surprise, I found that the RFC casualties were held in the Archive Section of the RAF Museum at Hendon. Fortunately – or unfortunately – there were 75 in 16 Squadron, so many that the Archivist decided to send me photocopies of all the 'Casualty Cards' for the Squadron, filled-out in 1915-1918, held by the Museum. At the same time, Mrs Dickinson kindly sent me a history of 16 Squadron, written in 1925 by Captain J. Morris, the then Director of the Air Historical Branch, which included a list of all the various kinds of casualties in the Squadron that he knew about.

I was also greatly helped by two books on the Great War: "Under the Guns of the Red Baron" (Caxton Editions 2000) by Norman Franks, Hal Giblin and Nigel McCrery, and "Under the Guns of the German Aces" (Grub Street 1997) by Franks and Giblin. These detailed every victory by von Richthofen and other top-ranking German pilots, with pen-portraits and photographs of their victims. Too many of these were in the slow-moving BE2cs and RE8s of 16 Squadron, patrolling the lines, spotting for the artillery, and taking photographs of enemy positions – sitting targets for the Albatrosses and Fokker triplanes of the German formations. Between February and April 1917, the Squadron lost 31 pilots and observers, twelve of them to von Richthofen himself; at least nine of the 31 were under 21 years old. It made me almost weep as I compiled these figures and looked at the photographs of these valiant young men, whose life-expectancy was just three weeks. At least, in WW2, we were spared such massacres.

I published the completed Roll of Honour in "Newbrief 24" of May 2003, and found a beautiful cover-picture in Rolls-Royce's wonderful stained-glass Memorial Window in their Derby Headquarters to 'The Few', who fought the Battle of Britain for our survival in 1940. It shows a bare-headed young pilot standing on the nose of a Spitfire, with the Rolls-Royce works spread out beneath him; a great eagle, with huge upswept wings, is perched behind him, in the eye of a flaming sun, whose rays extend over them both and in all directions. Richard Haigh, Head of Rolls-Royce Corporate Heritage, kindly gave me permission to use it. For me, it stands as a Universal Monument to the Dead Airmen of All Wars Everywhere.

Air Chief Marshal Sir David Cousins, KCB, AFC, RAF (Retd), President of the 16 Squadron RFC and RAF Association, and Wing Commander Guy Stockill, CO of 16 Squadron, had the Roll of Honour transcribed onto vellum and placed in a wooden casket, which was then entrusted to the safe-keeping of the RAF Church of St Clement Danes in The Strand, in London.

16 SQUADRON RFC AND RAF ROLL OF HONOUR 1915-2003

The cover of the Roll of Honour based on the fine stained-glass window in Rolls-Royce's HQ in Derby, by courtesy of Richard Haigh, Head of R-R Corporate Heritage

A painting of a typical scene of Photo Interpreters at work in one of the rooms at Medmenham of the Allied Central Intelligence Unit, where the more important photographs taken by 16 Squadron would have ended up.

In 2003 also, I joined the Medmenham Club as an Associate Member. Medmenham, a handsome mansion on the banks of the Thames not far from Benson, had been the Allied Central Interpretation Unit during the war. After the information of immediate value to the Command that ordered the sortie had been gleaned from the resultant films by the 34 Wing Photo Interpreters (PIs) – called Phase 1 Interpretation – the films would be sent to Medmenham for more detailed scrutiny to determine whether some action was needed quite soon against, say, a military or naval objective – Phase 2; and for further analysis by specialists of specific aspects of German war production, to assist in selecting targets for the strategic bombing campaign in due course – Phase 3.

With tens of thousands of photographs being taken and sent to Medmenham every day – six million prints for the invading armies to take with them on D-Day – the need for hundreds of PIs was urgent: the spacious grounds of Medmenham were soon covered with rows of wooden huts containing teams of PIs doing work not unlike that of the code-breakers of German radio communications at Bletchley Park. The Medmenham Club was open to all wartime PIs and also to their successors in the RAF, who were re-named Image Analysts. The Honorary Secretary, retired Wing Commander Mike Mockford, OBE, edited a Newsletter two or three times a year, with fascinating information about all aspects of PR, principally from the PIs' point-of-view, but also taking-in the aircrews' experiences. By joining, I gained access to a well-equipped museum at Chicksands, to lecture programmes, and to excursions to places of past or present significance to PR and PI.

By 2004, I felt I had gathered sufficient information about most aspects of PR in and around the wartime 16 Squadron, and I had enough confidence in my ability to state facts with some degree of authority, that I settled down to a project I had kept in mind for some time: to describe the business of PR in detail in "The Anatomy of a Sortie". This took a photographic sortie from its initial birth in an Army HQ, right through to the preparation of the selected aircraft, the actual flight with several different targets to be photographed, the processing of the films, and the dispatch of the prints to the original HQ.

I published this in "Newsbrief 27" of April 2004 it took up 55 A4 pages, half of which were devoted to illustrations of the text. It collected a few comments, some critical, others useful; but, in general, most readers seemed to accept it without protest. One, Harry van der Meer, an aircraft restorer of PL965 in 1973 when it was in Holland and a former curator of the Aviodome at Schiphol Airport, wrote, "I have read this in one run, holding my breath, and it was a feeling like I was all alone in the cockpit till the end of the sortie and stepped on the ground again. It tells us, those who have never been there, how it really was." An accolade, indeed, and it turns the story back to Holland, where several developments had taken place since 1998.

CHAPTER 33

Return to the Air over Holland

My return to Holland in May 1999 was destined to provide me with another high-light, which might have thrown some light on my capture in 1944; it was organised, as usual, by Hennie Noordhuis, but kept deliberately as a surprise for me. Before this, however, there were some other noteworthy events.

On the first day after my arrival, Hennie and Joke took me to Utrecht, where I had found myself in November 1944, in a guard's-van parked in the goods-yard on the morning of my fourth day of evading. However, although we stopped at the station, there was no point in trying to recognise anything from that day in the huge modern marshalling-yard, which we would have difficulty in even being allowed to enter. We went on therefore to the Rijksmuseum in the former St Catherine's Convent to enable me to view the fine collection of Catholic church art, especially the portraits of 17th-century Jesuit priests. I thought one or two might help me in solving some of the mysteries still connected with my portrait of Father Roeland de Pottere by Adriaen Hanneman, particularly what might have happened to it between its painting in 1661 and 1889, the earliest date I could find for its provenance, when it was in the possession of a Mr T.J.Eyre. In fact, although the museum had some fine historical pictures, I could discover no precedent in the fortunes of other Jesuit portraits that might help me in my search.

We returned along the Rhine, as Hennie and I were still keen to discover the route of my last day's walking in November 1944, and especially the spot where it had come to an inglorious end when I was confronted by the armed soldier on a bicycle. However, once again we were baffled, perhaps by the post-war changes in the landscape and by the building of new houses, which prevented my seeing the view that I had carried in my head for the past half-century.

That evening, to make up for their enforced absence from my Dinner of the previous year, I had invited the full Boomkamp family to another Dinner at "The Resting Hunter" and, to let them meet the other important family in my story, I had also invited all the Timmermans. They all came: Bernard Boomkamp, his brother Hendrik with his wife Diny, his daughter Josine with her husband Hans Wools, Ria and Jan Bovenmars with their daughter Anne; of the Timmermans, Marinus with his wife Thea, Jan with his wife Sjaan, Henk with his wife Ans and their three children; only Betsie was unfortunately ill and couldn't come. One outsider who could come was Joop Roetgerink (no relation of the 't Hesseler Roetgerinks), who claimed to have seen not only my Spitfire falling out of the sky near Bentelo, but also my parachute floating down towards 't Hesseler . (To my mind, this was visually and geographically impossible, but he assured me it was so.) We watched the video that Ron Nobes, an Associate Member of "16 Squadron 1939-1945", had compiled with great skill from all the TV programmes in Holland and England in which I had appeared; we then sat down to another delicious meal produced in Henk's extensive kitchens – he could feed 1000 people or host three separate receptions at the same time – culminating, as before, in a vivid ice-cream spectacular to the accompaniment of rousing wartime music. The two families, most of whom lived only about seven miles apart, appeared to get on very well together and, at the end, they presented me with two framed old maps of Borne and 't Hesseler, which now hang above "The Twente Crystal" in my study in Leeds.

Next day, Jan Bovenmars fulfilled an ambition of mine that linked the city of York with the German city of Aachen, the 9th-century capital of the empire of Charlemagne. The distinguished monk Alcuin of York, a great scholar and teacher, was invited to become the tutor of both the Emperor and his children, and went on to found a school in the palace in Aachen; he became the trusted friend of Charlemagne and advised him on how to bring civilisation to the Holy Roman Empire, over which he was crowned in AD 800. I had seen a photograph of Charlemagne's marble throne in the Yorkshire Museum in York, so it was quite a thrill to walk round the real thing in a gallery of his great early Romanesque church in Aachen, and look down on the richly-decorated sarcophagus in the nave below, which holds the mortal remains of the illustrious Emperor.

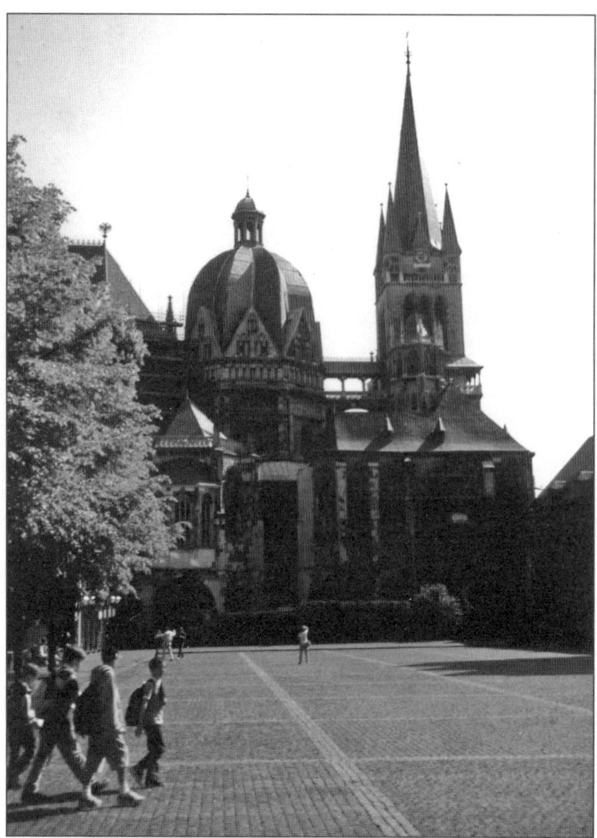

In May 1999, Jan Bovenmars took me to Aachen: Charlemangne's magnificent 9th-century Cathedral (centre). The children are walking on the site of the Palace School where Alcuin of York taught Charlemangne and his sons.

Aachen retains a strongly mediaeval flavour in its city centre, with two towers surviving from Charlemagne's palace, an impressive Gothic Rathaus (Town Hall), two fountains, one surmounted with his statue, and several other well-preserved old buildings. Our visit really brought alive for me the great man who, before this, had been little more than a shadowy figure of legend, connected with his son Roland in the troubadour's "Song of Roland".

Jan earned my deep gratitude that day, compounded further when we turned off for a meal in the equally old Dutch city of Maastricht, with its still-functioning Roman bridge and grand mediaeval Cathedral and other ancient buildings.

Charlemangne's Throne – made from marble slabs
Photo: Jan Bovenmars

Another, rather different ambition of mine, after the war, was to have a flight in a military jet-plane. I had made suggestions to various COs of 16 Squadron both when it was equipped with two-seater Tornados and, later, when it was training pilots to fly the Jaguar and had several two-seaters – but to no avail.

However, when Margaret and I had paid our initial visit to Borne in 1991, Hennie had taken us first of all to the Twente Air Base, where the Commandant, Colonel Vogelpoel, had shown us round the airfield and let me sit in the cockpit of an F-16. As we were leaving, in Hennie's presence he stated that on another occasion I could have a ride in the back-seat of a two-seater F-16. This would have been the realisation of my dream: to experience the thrill of a jet-propelled take-off, with the surge of power behind me, followed by a screaming climb high into the sky and a relaxed cross-country flight over the placid Twente landscape at 500mph or more. (This was before the present era of jet airliners, when ordinary passengers all over the world are being transported in this manner every minute of every day.) Hennie had tried several times to get the Colonel to fulfil his promise, but had failed to persuade him – in my opinion quite justifiably, in view of my age, the cost of such a flight, and the restrictions on Air Force flying imposed by the local authorities because of the noise and air pollution.

Now, on 4th May, as we drove towards the Air Base, Hennie said casually, *"You're going flying!"* I was taker aback but, thinking this would be in a passenger plane, I replied, *"You'll be coming with me, of course."* But he said, *"No, there's only room for you."* This was amazing, but when I questioned him further, he said only, *"You will see."*

Arrived at the guard-room, we were met by a very friendly Warrant Officer Wil Heregrave, a former F-16 crew-chief and now the Public Relations Officer of the Base. Over a cup of coffee, Wil told me that a Pilatus PC-7 was on its way from Hoogerheide, in the south, to give me a flight, but that I would need a medical examination. I was then taken into an adjacent room, where a highly professional lady doctor attached sensors all over my torso and made a very thorough check of my physical condition. She noted a slightly irregular heart-beat, but said it wouldn't be affected by this flight. Hennie was smiling all over his face when I came out, happy that this was a real surprise for me – and an exceedingly pleasant one.

The Pilatus PC-7 is the current initial training plane of the Dutch Air Force, a sleek, high-tech two-seater, with a jet-engine driving a four-bladed propeller, and therefore commonly called a turbo-prop. It is very similar to the RAF's initial trainer, the turbo-prop Shorts Tucano, which is a little bulkier but has a similar performance, with a top speed of 320mph at 14,000ft, quite a bit below my wartime Spitfire's and not really in the same class as a pure-jet plane. However, who was I to complain?

The next stop was the Equipment Centre, where I was kitted-out with long-johns, flying-overalls, boots and gloves, and fitted with a helmet and parachute, to the accompaniment of much banter from Hennie and the personnel, all of whom spoke excellent English, the language of the Dutch Air Force.

By then, the Pilatus had landed and I was introduced to my pilot, Captain Jeroen ('Gorby') Kloosterman, an F-16 pilot and an instructor on the Pilatus PC-7 on 131 Training Squadron. He had a distinctive birthmark over much of the left side of his face, which earned him the universal nickname of 'Gorby' (Gorbachev has a smaller mark on his forehead); it was even scrawled on the visor-cover on his helmet. He already knew some of my background and now excited me by saying he had come prepared to fly me over my route to the Rhine in 1944. I filled him in on some of the details in the Briefing Room, where we went to prepare the flight-plan for this mission. I had fortunately brought with me a 1960's map of the area, which gave a picture of the ground that was closer to what I remembered from 1944 than the modern air-map that 'Gorby' brought with him. After I had picked out on my map the landing-place in 't Hesseler , the crash-site in Bentelo, and the towns and villages between Utrecht and Rhenen, 'Gorby' ringed them in blue pencil on his map and worked-out the appropriate courses to reach them.

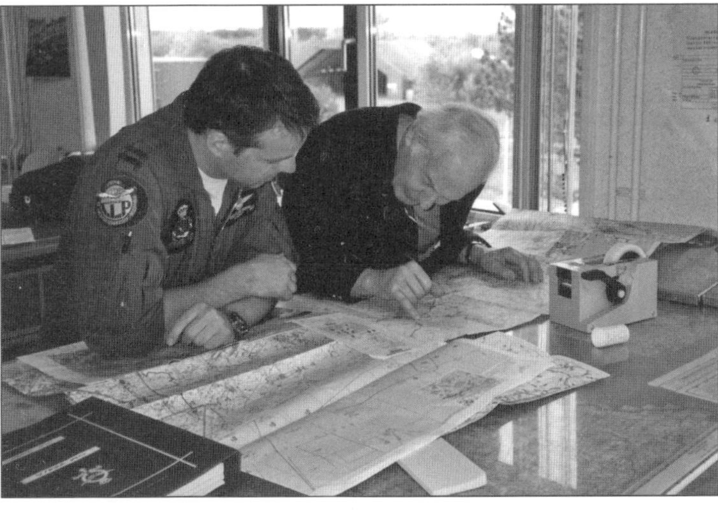

Captain Jeroen ('Gorby') Kloosterman, RNLAF, and I plan our flight to cover the route I took while evading 19th-24th November 1944.
Photo: Hennie Noordhuis

After a light lunch in the all-ranks canteen (the Dutch don't go in for

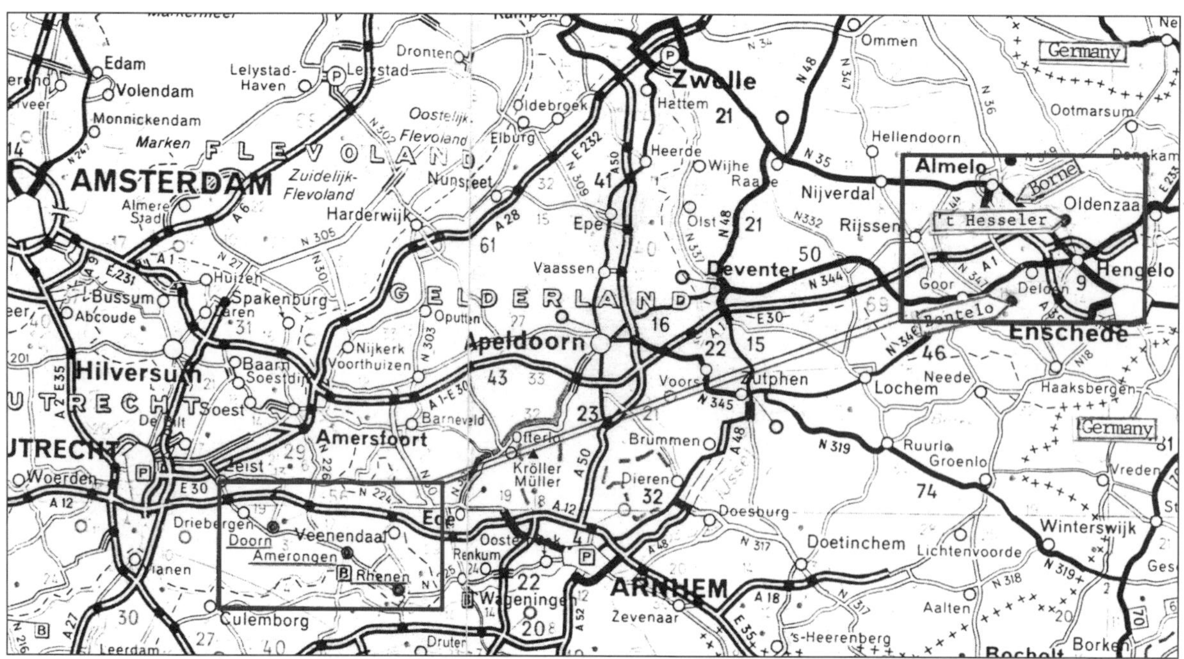

The route goes from (in the top right box) Twente Air Base, Borne, 't Hesselet, Delden and Bentelo, (along the parallel lines) to the Rhine, Rhenen and Doorn (in the bottom left box).

The Pilatus PC-7 turbo-prop trainer from 131 Training Squadron at Hoogherheide awaits me at Twente Air Base on 4th May 1999.

Officers' Messes) with 'Gorby', Hennie, and Rob Wissink, a reporter from "Twentsche Courant Tubantia", we drove out to the 'apron', where the Pilatus was standing in its bright yellow-and-red livery, the hall-mark of a trainer in the sky. As an aircraft that could fly relatively slowly, it was well-suited to my purpose of taking photographs of the significant places of my evasion – but, in the event, even this was a little too fast and a helicopter might have been better.

After donning my parachute and helmet, I was settled into the rear cockpit by 'Gorby', who carefully connected up all the straps and wires to hold me in my seat and allow me to communicate. He then explained the procedure for getting out of them all in a hurry – if required by an emergency. The photographers meanwhile were snapping away from every angle.

All strapped into the back seat ready to go!
Photo: Hennie Noordhuis

'Gorby' strapped himself into the front seat, then started-up the jet-engine. The propeller began to revolve, with only a faint whine audible through the headphones as the revolutions steadily and smoothly increased. When the gauges showed that they had reached their optimum figures and proved that all the systems were functioning properly, 'Gorby' waved away the chocks and we set off on the long trek round the taxy-path to the end of the runway in use. Cleared for take-off from the tower, he lined-up the aircraft with the centre of the runway, pushed forward the throttle, and we were in the air in no time at all.

Having been gliding for the last nine years, becoming airborne again was no novelty for me, but I was surprised to find that the ground below looked quite alien and, from 1500ft, I could see absolutely nothing that I could recognise. There was a slight mist on the ground and, at first, even 'Gorby' had a little difficulty in orientating himself. Eventually, however, we picked-out Borne and, when we flew nearer, I was able to follow the road out to the housing-estate where Hennie and Joke lived. We circled the house several times for a photograph, but the trees and neighbouring houses blocked my view from almost every angle. I managed to get one in the end, and we moved on the short distance to 't Hesseler .

Here, Jan Boomkamp's enormous and expanding Garden Centre dominated the scene and made it nearly impossible to recognise the landscape of 1944, and even of 1991. Only the Execution Field behind the Memorial remained untouched. Most of the trees had gone, and a circular garden feature appeared to have replaced the one in which my parachute had ended-up. From the air, the lanes looked very narrow, and the Memorial was almost hidden by the trees alongside it. The houses of Bernard Boomkamp and the Bovenmars family and the Leuvelds' farm were easily recognisable, but Hennie Roetgerink's house at the village crossroads had already been demolished to make way for a new road. Hengelo was expanding rapidly northwards towards Borne, and 't Hesseler and the fields between were

Airborne in the sleek-looking Pilatus
Photo: Hennie Noordhuis

'**t Hesseler, with Jan Boomkamp's Garden Centre occupying most of it: my landing place is on the right of the lane, but now unrecognisable: the Field of Execution is on the left; and the Memorial is between them.**

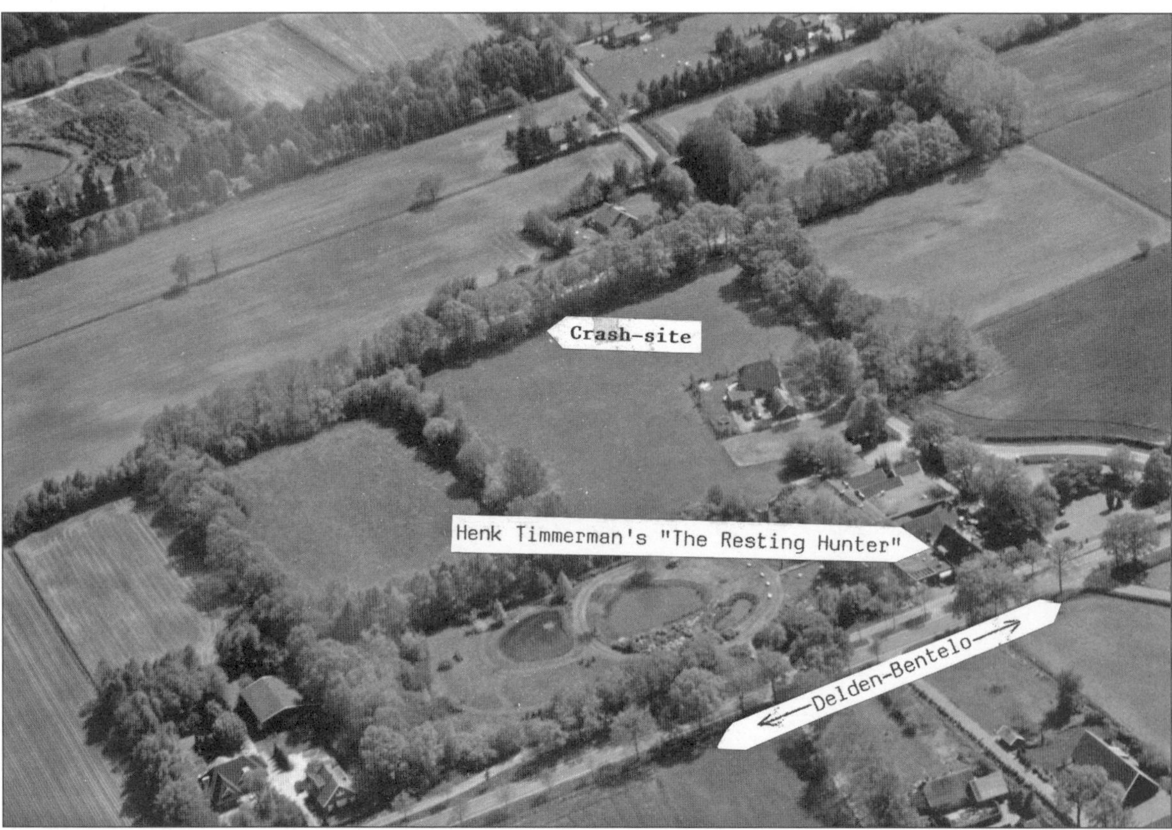

Henk Timmerman's "The Resting Hunter" restaurant lies beside the Delden-Bentelo road. In the adjacent field, my crashing Spitfire hit the ground close to the line of trees on 19th November 1944, and the remains were excavated by Hennie Noordhuis and Hennie Egberink in April 1995.

being eaten away by new housing developments – some of them promoted by the canny money-wise Jan Boomkamp himself, who knew that the land of his Garden Centre would fetch a good price from Hengelo municipality.

After I had photographed all that I wanted, we set course for the crash-site in the Timmermans' field near Bentelo. We passed over the Twente Canal and I tried to identify the bridges at Delden and Goor; but the trees and the poor visibility obscured the towns and I could not be certain about which bridge I was looking at. It was more important to recognise "The Resting Hunter", but this was rather low and dark; it was easier to distinguish the circular terrace in the large garden and follow the buildings from there. Fortunately, Henk had put out a large white sheet in the adjacent field to mark the place of the actual crash-site, so there was no problem in locating it. Again, the trees beside it made photography difficult, but 'Gorby' circled round until I was satisfied.

We then climbed to 3000ft and flew directly to Rhenen, passing Arnhem on our right. Although I could see the Rhine near there and several bridges over it, it was too hazy to determine which was the one that led to the city centre and was the objective, in September 1944, of the disastrous bid of the Airborne forces to capture it. 'Gorby' let me take the controls for a while, which I found nicely balanced; but I was more interested, on this occasion, in looking at the features on the ground and taking photographs than in flying the aeroplane.

We reached my part of the Rhine, further down below Arnhem, far more quickly than I did in my 1944 journey; after identifying Rhenen by its church-tower, we turned right along the river, while I urgently scanned the countryside on the north bank, hoping to pick-out the lane in which I had been captured.

Once again, though, trying to match the features and places on the ground to the map and vice versa – experienced though I was in doing this from my Spitfire on wartime photographic sorties – proved much more difficult than I had imagined: the Pilatus could not fly slowly enough to give me time to pinpoint our exact position while attempting all the while to identify my 1944 lane. Eventually, I

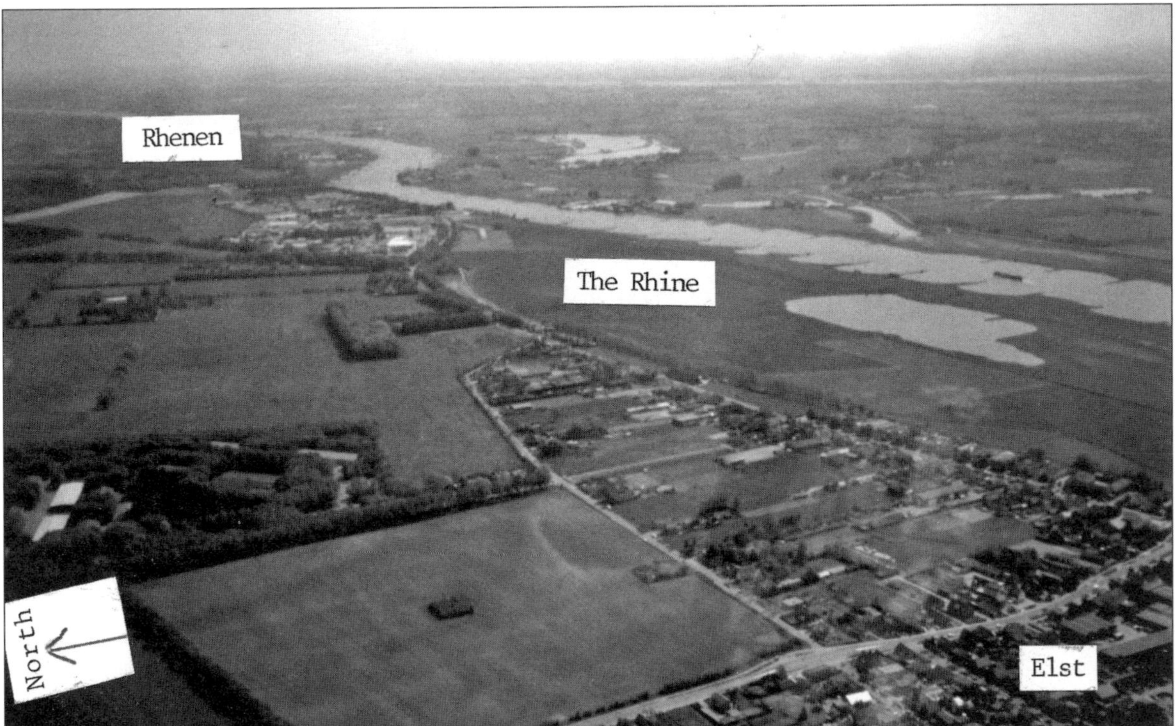

I had this sort of view of the Rhine between Doorn (behind us) and Rhenen from much lower sloping ground on 24th November 1944; but, 55 years later, on this flight I could not recognise the lane where I was captured.

contented myself with taking photographs all the way to Doorn, which had given sanctuary to the ex-Kaiser after WW1.

The town is surrounded by thick woods into which, from the air, the roads just disappeared, which made my search for the one I had followed on my way out very frustrating. The most intriguing sight was to find a transport park of the Dutch army located exactly opposite one of the openings in the woods in which, as I walked past in 1944, I had spotted German trucks concealed under the trees – showing how closely the military mind follows similar patterns of thought, irrespective of the uniform.

Time was running out, but I asked 'Gorby' to fly back to Rhenen keeping to the north of the Rhine, so that I could photograph the land sloping down to the river from roughly my 1944 viewpoint. Even then, finding on the map the villages, industrial works, and shapes of fields and woods that I saw on the ground proved no less difficult than before, and I resorted to taking more photographs for examination at my leisure later. Arrived back over Rhenen, I looked, perhaps for the last time, at this much-changed countryside that had given me so little help, and we then set course back to Twente.

Along the way, I asked 'Gorby' to do a roll in the aircraft, which he executed very smartly and smoothly, showing the power and versatility of this aircraft. I then asked him to do another and took a photograph when we were upside-down – to show that our flight wasn't all straight-and-level. With the sun behind us, Arnhem stood out more clearly this time, and I was able to identify and photograph the famous "Bridge Too Far" or, rather, its post-war successor.

In a very short time, we were back in the circuit at Twente Air Base and, by looking over his shoulder, I could see that 'Gorby' was nicely lined-up with the runway lights as he made his approach. We touched down without the slightest squeal or bump and taxied round to the apron, where Hennie and Wil were waiting for us.

'Gorby' was in a hurry to get back to Hoogerheide, for the Pilatus to be returned to its hangar by the mechanics before they went off duty for the day. So I expressed my huge gratitude to him for giving me

Upside-down in the Pilatus! I clicked the shutter in the middle of 'Gorby's smooth 'barrel roll'.

the long-desired opportunity to view from the air in tranquillity the countryside that I had tramped over, with some degree of anxiety, on my last day of freedom in 1944. We posed for a photograph, and then he was off, the aircraft looking not unlike a hunting eagle as, with its wheels retracted, it soared back into its element.

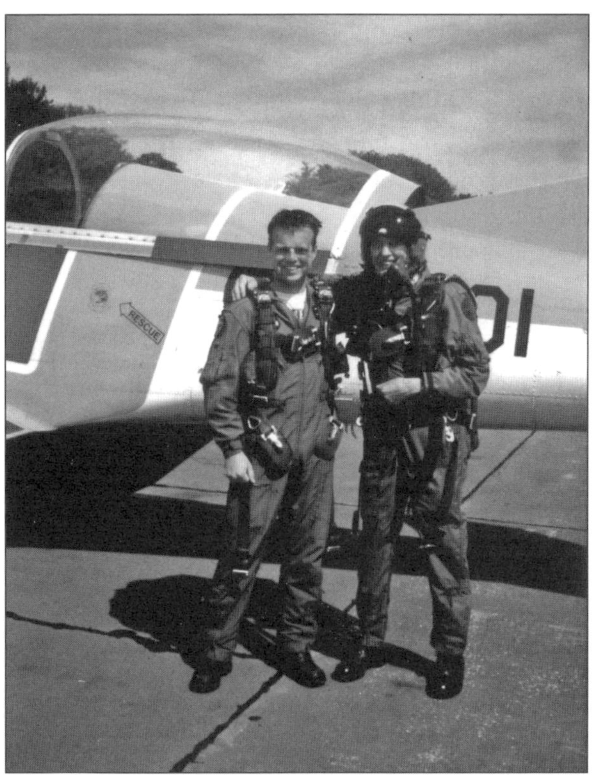

The end of a perfect flight and the start of a lifelong friendship
Photo: Hennie Noordhuis

I turned to Hennie and told him that I owed this flight and everything else in Twente to him, and I wished that he could be given a similar privilege by Colonel Jansen, the new Commandant, who had been so considerate to me. Rob 'Wissink's report on the flight appeared next day on the whole front-page of "Tubantia", with a picture of me in the cockpit in the centre, captioned in English "Ready for take-off", and three other photos, one of them of the Pilatus in flight. This was much more publicity than any such flight would have received in England.[1]

At 7.0pm, I again attended the ceremony at the Memorial in 't Hesseler, and afterwards spent the evening with all the Boomkamps, this time in Bernard's house, which was adjacent to the Bovenmars, It was such a pleasure to relax in the warmth of the friendship of these kind folk, and I was delighted when, in October, the cousins Ria Bovenmars and Josine Wools brought their husbands, Jan and Hans, to spend three days in Leeds. I found a small hotel near us for them and took great pleasure in showing them some of the historic places and scenic beauties of Yorkshire, a small and inadequate return for all the hospitality and kindnesses I had received from them.

Ria Bovenmars (l) and Hans Wools make an intrepid crossing of the River Wharfe beside the ruined Bolton Abbey.

[1] See "Dutch Voices" p. 715 for a Press report of my flight

Back in Borne, on the day of my return home, Hennie took me round to see Fred Bakker and his wife Froukje, who had recently moved into one of the oldest houses in Borne, next door to the Rientjes, another of my friendly families, Harry having served in the Dutch Air Force. Fred was a dealer in modern artwork, had provided "The Twente Crystal" and inscribed its base; the old house was now his gallery, with beautiful examples of glassware, sculptures, ceramics and paintings displayed in almost every room. Froukje was a trainer of teachers, so there was much to talk about with each of them over coffee and cake, which seem to be the traditional mid-morning refreshment in this part of Holland.

I caught the train from Hengelo to Schiphol and sat back, drained as usual by these intense few days, but also exhilarated by all that I had experienced, thanks to Hennie's selfless organisation.

So ended the 20th Century for me in Holland, the last ten years of which had put my feelings through the wringer, from the deepest sorrow for the families of 't Hesseler , robbed of their loved ones just to feed the terror rule of the German Occupation, to the great happiness of being welcomed by the kindest-hearted people in the world.

The exciting flight to the Rhine, one more manifestation of this kindness, might have marked the end of my story, whose objective could be said to reflect Hennie's answer to Ellen van Helsdingen, "I had to find out the truth". Or, more precisely in my case, to establish the full facts of every incident, big or small, relating to my unfortunate downfall on 19th November 1944 and to its aftermath. Rather to my surprise, this search continued into the next century.

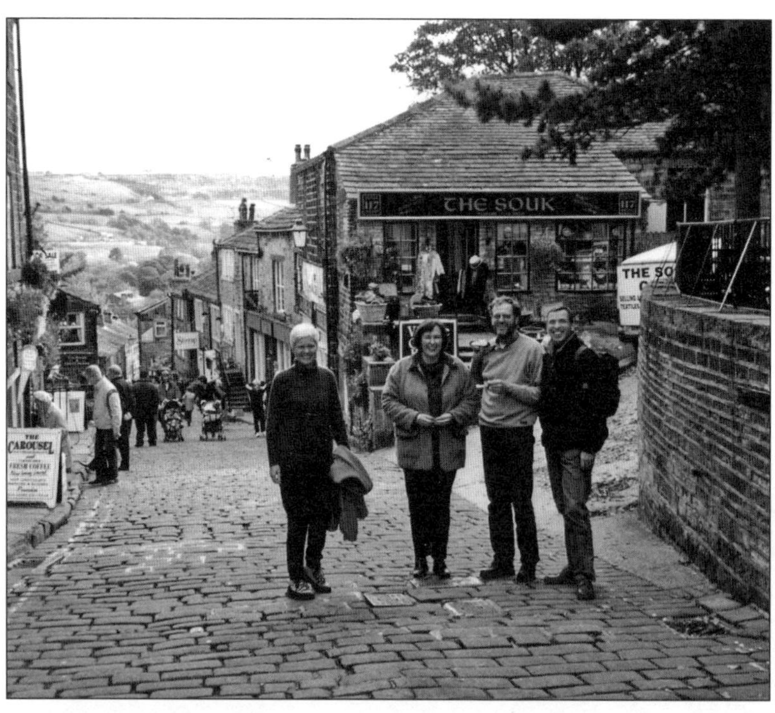

Josine Wools (l), Ria and Jan Bovenmars and Hans Wools in the Brontes' village of Haworth

CHAPTER 34

Forging Closer Links with the Dutch

My visits to Holland in this 21st Century started relatively quietly, although getting there proved quite exciting. I flew in a Fokker F50 of what was then the British Midlands KLM airline. The aircraft was a comfortable, middle-aged, high-wing, turbo-prop machine, that took an hour and a half to get to Schiphol from Leeds-Bradford. I went to the forward toilet, but found my return to my seat was blocked by the drinks trolley coming round. On an impulse, I asked a stewardess if, as a former RAF pilot, I could go and say 'Hello' to the pilots. She inquired, and said I could.

I found two very pleasant, welcoming men: the Captain was English, aged about 55, and had flown this route for five years; the 2nd Pilot was Dutch, about 35 years old, and had been on the route for two years. I plied them with questions relating to the aircraft and the radio and navigation procedures, and they were very happy to give me full answers, coming mostly from the Captain.

My friendly pilot on the flight from Leeds-Bradford to Schiphol on 2nd May 2000

He said flying on 'George', the automatic pilot, at 19,000ft at 185mph on +35° of boost (throttle), was very simple, especially as the two engines were synchronised automatically. The weather was cloudy and hazy, so the radar scope (screen) was of great value: the coast ahead appeared as a purple line, while any nearby aircraft showed-up green on an adjacent dial, with its height given underneath.

I asked if I could stay for the landing, so the stewardess pulled down the 'jump seat' behind the pilots and fixed the straps on me. Flying Control was monitoring our flight and advising us all the time on our course, speed and height, asking for position reports, making checks, confirming the checks and recording them. The Captain said that all this activity made the flights interesting, rather than boring.

The 2nd Pilot was at the controls as we neared Schiphol, with the cloud and haze persisting down to 800ft. The airfield lights leading into the runway threshold were fortunately very bright, with yellow on each side and red down the middle. The pilot made a steady approach at 130mph, levelled off about 15 feet above the ground, and lowered the nose-wheel onto the runway, making a very smooth touchdown. He reversed the propellers' pitch to assist in braking the aircraft, before swinging off the runway and taxying the long way round to the KLM parking bay, where we were picked up by an airport bus. I shook hands with the pilots, congratulating them on an untroubled flight, and thanking them warmly for letting me spend most of it in the cockpit with them.

Hennie and Joke were waiting for me as I walked out of "Nothing to declare", and took me straightaway to Bornerbroek for a Dinner with a large number of Canadian veterans, who had just arrived from Canada. With the Dorset Regiment, they had liberated Borne on 3rd April 1945. Now they had come to pay their last visit to all the towns in Holland which they had helped to free as the war drew to its close; yet it still needed much effort and sacrifice to overcome the Germans: sometimes they put up a fanatical resistance, at other times they surrendered readily to the Allies in preference to the Russians.

The Fokker F-50 cruised at 185mph with its two six-bladed propellers.

A number of my friends were there and came up to our table to greet us:

Joke de Leeuw, the Chairman of the 1995 Liberation Committee; Harry and Nell Rientjes; Hennie Egberink, excavator of my Spitfire; Joop de Melker Worms, a colleague of Hennie's; Mr F. Tjaberings, the new Burgomaster of Borne, and his wife, and several others.

D. Harrison, a former radio-operator in the Canadian Coldstream Regiment, came and chatted; learning that I came from Leeds, he told me that his great-grandfather was Lord Ingleby, owner of Ripley Castle outside Harrogate, just 20 miles from Leeds. Furthermore, he had read "Roughing it in the Bush", written in 1852 by Susanna Moodie (1803-1885), my father's aunt, (née Strickland, which is my middle name), a pioneer settler in Canada with her husband, John. They were not very successful at living the rough life of the early settlers, building a log-cabin, cutting down the forest all around them, pulling out the roots, and cultivating the resultant soil; they moved away into Belleville, one of the developing towns of Ontario, where John Moodie became the Sheriff and Susanna busied herself advising later settlers. My life is full of surprises – usually happy ones like this one.

Hennie was busy for the next two days, so I had a comparatively peaceful time with Jan and Ria Bovenmars and their family. On the first morning, 4th May, Jan took me to Delden to see the Senior Basic Comprehensive School where he was teaching, a very modern building with well-equipped classrooms for only 200 12- to 14-year-oids. In the evening, I attended the ceremony as usual in 't Hesseler and laid a wreath at the Memorial.[1] I then took part in the Silent Walk in Borne, and stood at the back of the crowd in front of the War Memorial; but Joke de Leeuw dragged me out and insisted I shared with him in the laying of his wreath. The Canadian veterans were present in force, with their own military band. I spent the evening in company with the full complement of Boomkamps.

Next day, Jan drove me round a part of Twente I had never visited, the area north of Borne that leads up to Almelo. However, we stopped so long for coffee in the pretty village of Oostmarsum, with its narrow streets and gabled houses, and in Albergen to look over its great 14th-century Augustinian monastery, now in ruins after being abandoned because of 18th-century Protestant opposition, that we had no time to do more than drive round Almelo and come home.

[1] See "Dutch Voices" p. 718 for a Press report of the 't Hessler ceremony in May 1990

A woodland road near Twickel, typical of the fine scenery in this part of Holland

This area, like the rest of Twente, is quite different from the common view of Holland: that it is flat, full of polders, canals and windmills, and is devoted to growing tulips. Here, there is gently rolling countryside, with occasional real hills, and the roads cut through many woods of tall trees, their fresh green foliage sparkling in the May sun and dappling the ground with shadows. The only real waterways are the Twente Canal and the Almelo Canal, which joins it halfway between Delden and Zutphen; the junction is quite wide, and is perhaps the 'large sheet of water' that I saw beneath me in my parachute descent and in which I had a vague, half-conscious feeling that I might drown. These are wide canals, busy with barges, but they are the only noticeable ones in Twente. The farms are numerous and large, and I was surprised at the number of horses I saw in the fields. In fact, this is tourist country, appealing especially to campers, cyclists, horseriders, and 'hunters' or, rather, shooters of game. This explains the popularity of Henk Timmerman's restaurant, well-named "The Resting Hunter", which can feed all who come. The Germans flock across the border, with its now non-existent controls and passport checks, to enjoy the scenery and holiday activities, thereby posing a moral dilemma for the Dutch; they were the first to suffer when the Germans invaded their little country in 1940, yet much of their livelihood today is dependent on welcoming them to this pleasant land and catering to their needs.

After lunch, we went into Borne to see the last parade for the WW2 veterans, with bands, floats and fifty military vehicles, including a tank and a Bren-gun carrier. We returned to the Bovenmars' family house, where Jan showed me his sheep in an extensive orchard, and the shed where many cheeses were stored and where Ria keeps the materials she needs for the flower-arranging classes she runs. I walked into the garden, where the younger generation had gathered, and found three very attractive girls sitting round the table: Anne, who as a ten-year-old had led me out in 1991 to show me the tree my parachute had blown into – calling *"This way, Taylor!"* in fluent English – now as tall as her father and working in a tourist agency in Delden; Helen, her equally tall younger sister, training to be a teacher: and Tessa Boomkamp, a grandchild of Hendrik's; each with her good-looking boyfriend; and Bram, Anne's younger brother, just as tall, but still at school. They were all eating pizzas and drinking coffee, chatting in Dutch with frequent bursts of laughter, and occasionally turning to talk to me in English. I always enjoy the company of young people – perhaps because I'm envious of their having their life still before them. These youngsters formed a delightful modern Dutch picture, worthy of a canvas, on a beautifully calm clear evening, enriched by much joyful birdsong.

Three Graces in 't Hesseler:
r-l: Anne and Helen Bovenmars with their cousin Tessa Boomkamp

Next morning, Hennie and Joke called for me at 8.30. I said goodbye to the Bosch family, who always look after me so well, and especially to old Mr Bosch, whom I would not see again, as the poor man was dying of cancer. I gave him a key-ring with RAF wings inscribed on it, and he presented Hennie and me each with a good stone bottle of Kruidenbitter. We then drove to the Concertgebouw in Amsterdam, where we listened to a Chopin Piano Concerto played with a flourish by a Chamber Orchestra. It was a short walk from there to the Rijksmuseum to see a wonderful exhibition, "The Glories of the Golden Age of Dutch Art", which contained many well-known paintings among the 200 displayed, but no sign of anything by Adriaen Hanneman. At 3.15pm Hennie and Joke left for Borne and I took an airport bus to Schiphol to return to Yorkshire.

There was no particular excitement this year, but I gained a deeper appreciation of the Dutch countryside and culture and, especially, of the Dutch character, from which I have benefitted so abundantly.

My visit to Holland in 2001 could not have been more different from the previous year's. For one thing, Michael Horsfall, my good friend from 16 Squadron days and ever since, whom I always call 'Mike', had suggested several times that he would like to see for himself the places and people in Holland that I often told him about. For another, he thought we should go there by car and boat, rather than by air, which would be an interesting change for me and would provide the transport for a valuable object.

I had completed my studies on "Father Roeland de Pottere, SJ" and distributed a copy of my booklet, "Adriaen Hanneman's 1661 Portrait of Father Roeland de Pottere SJ" to each of the galleries, auction houses, Jesuit archivists and historians who had helped me, both by way of thanking them and also in the hope that it would lead to a buyer.

After my father had died and my mother had left their London apartment, my brother and I had tried to sell at Christie's London auction house, on 6th June 1974, all the family pictures that neither he nor I wanted or had room for in our houses; Christies advised us what reserve price to put on each one, with £8000 on the Hanneman. It turned out to be one of the few that failed to reach its reserve; I therefore paid my brother half this sum and kept it in my house in Leeds. Next, I took it to the Fitzwiliiam Museum at Cambridge, the Ashmolean Museum at Oxford, and the City Art Gallery in York, each of which had a strong interest in Dutch painting and a good collection of Dutch pictures, but none of them felt sufficiently attracted to "Father Roeland de Pottere, SJ". I even got in touch with the Museum in Delft and sent them a copy of my booklet, but they said they had no money for purchases; I was asking £15,000 as a starting price – which gave me room to go lower, if necessary.

Although I had drawn a blank on a sale at a slightly up-market price, I had no inclination to let this significant picture go at a give-away figure. It had been painted by a Dutch artist, whom I think I now knew better than most living art critics and whom I respected highly; it originated in a country for whose people I now had the greatest affection; and it had strong connections with my family. I therefore decided I would make a gift of it to the people of Twente by presenting it to the Rijksmuseum (National Museum) in Enschede, a satellite of the main Rijksmuseum in Amsterdam, in a town just ten miles from 't Hesseler and Borne. It holds an excellent collection of a wide range of historical and artistic objects, including many paintings, one of which happened to be by Adriaen Hanneman of his friend and fellow-artist in England, Cornelis Jonson and his family.

This was a happy coincidence, but there was a deeper motivation: I wanted to repay in some way everything that had happened, both tragic and wonderful, to me in 't Hesseler, Borne, and Bentelo from 1944 up to that year 2001. The fact that the portrait was of a Jesuit who worked for 30 years as a prominent figure in Delft, no more than 100 miles away from Borne, made Father de Pottere almost a local figure, which was an additional reason for my dedicating the portrait to the four men – Jan Vonk, Jan Boomkamp, Hendrik Roetgerink, and Piet van Dijk – who had been executed: Jan Vonk in Borne on 19th November, and the others in 't Hesseler on the 25th, so unjustly and unnecessarily, because of my landing in a field of the village the week before. I offered it, therefore, to the Rijksmuseum as a personal restitution to the community of 't Hesseler for all that I had brought upon it and in gratitude for all that they had done for me ever since I had learned the terrible truth.

The picture was painted on wood in 1661 and was in a heavy contemporary frame under glass, so I had made a special wooden carrying-box for it, with suitable padding all round the interior. I now loaded it into the back of Mike's estate car at his home near Sutton Coldfield, outside Birmingham, and we set off at 5.45 in the morning of 2nd May to drive to Harwich to take the ferry to the Hook of Holland. The journey and the crossing were fairly painless – the ferry was a catamaran and travelled at 40 knots – but the 280 miles or so from there to Borne were more than a little tedious for people, like us, who were not familiar with the number of different motorways in the very efficient and well-signed Dutch road-system. We were therefore very pleased that Hennie was waiting for us at the Hook of Holland to guide us back to Borne; nevertheless, it was a relief to arrive at the "Jachtlust" hotel and receive a warm greeting from the Bosch family, who served us and Hennie with an excellent dinner.

The first visit next morning had to be to show Mike the landing-site and the Memorial in 't Hesseler . As we stepped out of the car, a huge bulldozer swept along the lane and stopped beside us – driven by a grinning Dirk Boomkamp, the young boy who, with Anne, had first shown me this self-same field. He was now a large, handsome, confident young man working for his father at the Garden Centre and, no doubt, learning all the about its working so as to be able to take it over from him one day. From there

Dirk Boomkamp, son of Jan Boomkamp Jnr, almost drove us off the lane with his bulldozer.

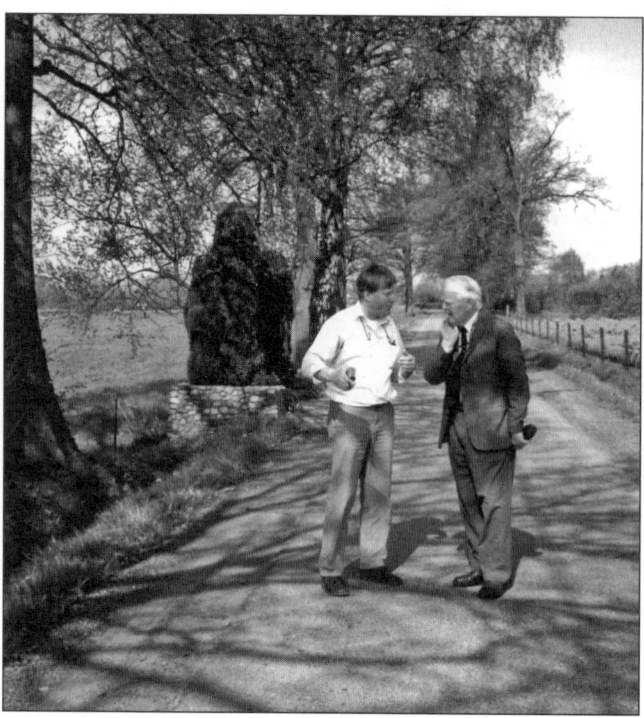

Hennie Noordhuis briefs Mike Horsfall on the events that took place on each side of the lane in November 1944.

we moved on to "The Resting Hunter", near Bentelo, to have coffee with Henk and Ans Timmerman, before Henk showed Mike the crash-site of my Spitfire and the plaque describing the event. We returned to the hotel for lunch, and picked up Jaap Grootenboer, a local historian and art-lover, before proceeding to the Rijksmusum in Enschede.

Here we met the Director, Mrs Doris Cannegieter, and were glad to see Hendrik and Diny Boomkamp and Jan and Ria Bovenmars. TV Oost and a radio journalist were present and filmed the scene as I unpacked the portrait in front of the gathering, which included the Museum staff, in a large room hung with historic Gobelin tapestries. "Father Roeland de Pottere, SJ" was placed on a large easel and subjected to a close scrutiny by everyone present, to general approval. I had put a brass plate on the frame with a dedication to the four victims of 1944 of Borne and 't Hesseler and this, I hope, gave the relatives, especially, as much satisfaction to read as it had given me to write. Hendrik and I posed each side of the painting for a photograph, and it was this that was reproduced in colour on the front page of the next day's "Tubantia". The reporter gave a good summary of Hanneman's career, of Roeland de Pottere's life, of the history of the portrait, and of the events that lay behind my presenting it to the Museum.

"Father Roeland de Pottere, SJ 1661" with some relatives of the victims commemorated on the brass plate: Hendrik and Diny Boomkamp (l) and Jan and Ria Bovenmars

He quoted me as saying, *"A significant period of my life has now been partly redeemed"*, and Mrs Cannegieter as stating, *"A splendid canvas. A special one also. We are one of the few museums that already have a Hanneman in their collection. The circumstances of this gift make it especially valuable."* [1]

However, the portrait was on probation, as it were, until the Museum's restorer had given it a microscopic examination, to determine whether it was genuine and its condition. Fortunately, a year later, I was assured that it was nearly perfect and, after being cleaned, it would take its place with the other 17th-century paintings in the Museum.

After the formalities were over and the media had finished interviewing Mrs Cannegieter and me, we repaired to the spacious restaurant overlooking a broad terrace, fronted by a long pond; this reflected the light from the sky into the restaurant, an imaginative touch typical of the design of this attractive Museum. In fact, this part of the Museum was very new as, just the year before, there had been a huge explosion at a fireworks factory in Enschede, which had killed 22 people, injured 900, and damaged the entrance of the Museum, now so well restored.

We enjoyed a pleasant tea with the guests and Museum staff, and then took a cheerful farewell of Mrs Cannegieter after a presentation that gave great satisfaction both to her and to myself. I felt that this was by far the best choice of a home for Hanneman's "Father Roeland de Pottere, SJ", and hoped that it would take its place on the pilgrimage route of any of my descendants visiting the sites in 't Hesseler and Bentelo.

What rendered it even more attractive to visit was that in the extensive, well-kept public park in Enschede there is a group of life-size bronze sculptures of typical victims of WW2 in fearful or defiant attitudes – a very moving Memorial against War, which accords closely with the spirit behind my dedication of "Father de Pottere" to the victims of 't Hesseler in 1944.

Next morning was 4th May, a working day for most people. In Borne, Mike and I ran into Hennie Egberink, excavator of my Spitfire, and had a short chat; we then joined the Burgomaster in his office for coffee and had an interesting discussion with him and three Aldermen on many subjects, especially education. In the afternoon, Joke took us to the Air Base Museum, where we met the new curator and Mike was shown the relics of my aircraft. We then drove onto the airfield and found our way to 313 Squadron, where we were greeted by a young pilot, Ian Knight, who had a Dutch father and English mother and was born in America. He took us round to the F-16 Simulator and showed us how to 'fly' it. Mike was unwilling to try his hand, but I was always eager and, having had an earlier experience with Tye Verf in 1995, I didn't find it too difficult. This Simulator, however, was much less sophisticated than the previous one, the 'cockpit' resembling a box rather than the real thing.

In the evening, we were welcomed to the Bovenmars' house and participated in the ceremony at the 't Hesseler Memorial; we then joined the Silent Walk in Borne and attended the ceremony there, returning to the home of the kindly Bovenmars and the Boomkamp families and staying until almost midnight.

The following day, Hennie had arranged for us to go to Arnhem, to be met by Henk Duinhoven, the most experienced guide, who had been awarded a British MBE for the many groups of veterans he had shown around the 'Market Garden' battlefields, memorials and cemeteries. He would give us a tour; but Mike said he had little interest and would prefer to walk from the hotel to 't Hesseler and explore the Garden Centre area. Hennie and I therefore left him to it and had a fascinating time with Henk, which I describe later. We returned to Borne, where Hennie and Joke and their daughter Judith and her boy-friend Mark invited Mike and me to dinner in the "Jachtlust", which made for a very sociable evening.

[1] See "Dutch Voices" p. 719 for this Press report and p720 for its translation into English

Mike Horsfall with the Kaiser at Doorn

Mike was always interested in the Great War, in which his father had fought in Mesopotamia, and now expressed a strong wish to visit Doorn and the house where the German Kaiser Wilhelm II, who was held responsible for starting it, had spent his years of exile, from 1920 to 1941. Hennie was busy, but Jan Bovenmars and his brother-in-law Hans Wools were willing to take us there. En route, we visited the Hotel "De World" in Wageningen where, on 5th May 1945, General von Blaskowitz surrendered the German forces in Holland to the representatives of the Allies, who included Prince Bernhard, the commander-in-chief of the Dutch military. We crossed the Rhine by ferry, drove along the minor road on top of the riverside dyke, then re-crossed the river near Amerongen. All the while, I was searching the opposite bank for a sight of the lane which witnessed the end of my 1944 evasion – but, once again, in vain.

So we motored into Doorn and found the Kaiser's 'Doorn Huis' open to the public. It turned out to be a minor palace, where he maintained a formal life-style closely resembling the one he had enjoyed while Emperor: the Dutch had allowed 22 trucks to bring all the trappings of royalty from Germany: furniture, pictures, silver, chinaware, trophies, banners, and uniforms, so much so that, although the place is now a museum, I felt sickened by the still-lingering aura of grandeur and majesty, so that the very exhibits seemed to reflect the presence of sycophantic courtiers still fawning over a despicable dethroned ruler. Mike was very satisfied, and I was glad to have come, but disturbed by the powerful reminders of the man whose monstrous envy and ambition led him to engage wilfully in a terrible conflict in order to satisfy them – only 20 years later, Adolf Hitler followed in his footsteps and started another equally disastrous European war, from which some people in German-occupied Holland have never recovered.

The house in Doorn where the exiled Kaiser Wilhelm II of Germany lived in semi-imperial state from 1920 until his death in 1941.

Photo: KLM

In the evening, Hennie and Joke drove us to "The Resting Hunter" for a reception and fine four-course dinner in Mike's honour, with a number of guests from the people who had entertained us so well in the past four days: Jan and Ria Bovenmars, Hans and Josine Wools, and all the older Timmermans, together with Fred and Froukje Bakker, and my excellent pilot 'Gorby' Kloosterman and Astrid, his delightful fiancée, to whom I felt I owed hospitality and whom, in any case, it would be interesting for Mike to meet. It was a good occasion, too, to thank Hennie for all the work he had put into organising this visit and ensuring that there were always kind people on hand to drive us around or look after us.

We set off on the drive back to Sutton Coldfield next morning, led onto the N1 motorway by Joke in her final act of kindness. She does not often appear beside Hennie in my days in Borne as she is a busy music teacher, both in a school and with private students. Mike made such good time on clear roads that he decided to go into The Hague; however, once faced with endless buildings, he changed his mind and we headed for the seaside at Schevingen, which we found very attractive. We thought "The Flying Dutchman" would be an appropriate beach restaurant for lunch, and were pleasantly surprised to find model planes hanging from the ceiling and a mass of aviation posters and memorabilia adorning the walls. We finally reached Mike's home at 10.30pm, tired after the drive and from the very busy programme in Holland, but most appreciative of the warm welcome given us by these generous Dutch people; Mike is now quite envious of the fact that I go back to Twente every year.

On the Dutch side, after getting to know me fairly well, my friends in Twente were intrigued by Mike, who looked, dressed, behaved and spoke much more like their idea of a typical Englishman. They treated him with all the hospitality and kindness which they show to me, even though he had no wartime connection with the region. The Dutch are very happy to call all Allied service-men 'Liberators', so both he and I received this honour, even though I was liberated from Stalag Luft 1 by the Russians, and Mike from Moosberg by the Americans. Whatever the basis of their feelings, my friends in 't Hesseler, Borne and Bentelo enjoyed Mike for himself; and I was especially pleased to learn that he and Hennie have maintained a correspondence since his visit – which says much for the mutual regard which they have for each other.

Not long after seeing Jan Timmerman at the Dinner on our last evening, I was saddened to be told of his death on 22nd July at the age of 83. He was a delightful person, always cheerful and full of jokes in English; but I don't think he ever really recovered from the death of his wife Sjaan the previous year.

To offset this, at Christmas I received a beautiful letter from Joanna Vonk, the sister of the young Jan Vonk, who was shot by the Germans outside the Town Hall on the day of my landing in 't Hesseler. She wrote on behalf of her sister as well as herself, and what she said convinced me that I had made the best decision about the resting-place of "Father Roeland de Pottere":

"We are very pleased and grateful for your fantastic gift to the Rijksmuseum Twenthe to commemorate our brother Jan. This gift shows us how much you still feel involved in the awful events following your crash during the war. Although we can appreciate your feelings about it, we also realise that you were only one of the many brave young men who risked their lives to fight the evils of war. Many – like our Jan – were victims in one way or another, but he was a victim of the war, not one of the heroes who tried to end it.

We are looking forward to our next trip to the region of Twente. We are sure we will visit the museum to admire your gift. It will bring back memories, not the painful ones, but the thankful ones."

Joanna Vonk's letter is an example of the way in which events which may appear apparently unrelated to my story, nevertheless throw further light on it. It was inspired, not by my last flight itself, but by my presentation of the Hanneman to the Rijksmuseum in Enschede 57 years later. Sadly she died in 2009.

This could have been the final act in the story of "One Flight Too Many"; but I continued to come to Holland to lay a wreath at the 't Hesseler Memorial each 4th May, and these visits enabled me, with the vital assistance of Hennie Noordhuis, to follow-up other interests which, although not directly relevant to my last flight and its aftermath, nevertheless contributed to building up a picture of these events as complete and in as many dimensions as possible. Hennie Noordhuis had, and still has, the same objective; which explains how it has been possible for us to work together so harmoniously for so many years.

From 1996 onwards, the significant events in this narrative were divided almost equally between Britain and the Netherlands. They were nearly all related to the war, either in retrieving memories or in searching for evidence and explanations of what had happened in 1944 that affected 16 Squadron, in particular. They also concerned the continuing development of my own flying experience and of my awareness of progress in the contemporary techniques of aerial reconnaissance. Of no less importance today are the veteran personnel of 16 Squadron, declining sadly in number year by year, and 'our' two surviving Spitfires – Mark XI PL965 and Mark XIX PS853 – maintained and flown operationally in the Squadron by some of these veterans in 1945 and still featuring regularly in aviation magazines and on the display circuit. These men and machines happily link the past to the present, and also maintain the close and valued connection between Britain and the Netherlands.

CHAPTER 35

Focus on Arnhem

During my time in 16 Squadron, we were virtually cut-off from contact with the outside world, at least while we were living under canvas on A12 airstrip and on Amiens-Glisy airfield during September 1944: I don't remember seeing a newspaper or listening to the radio. We could have tried to predict, from the targets which we were photographing for SHAEF or 21st Army Group, for example, Walcheren, Wesel, or Rheine, where the senior officers of these HQs were planning to advance at some future date; but security and the risk of being captured and having this information forced out of us made it wiser to remain ignorant.

In any case, I had no great interest in military matters: gaining my 'Certificate A' in the OTC at school – based on moving paper troops around on a sand-table – was my passport to getting into the Air Section, where I was totally satisfied and eventually became the Cadet Sergeant in charge. Consequently, although I had a notional idea of roughly where the front line was between the Allies and the Germans in Europe, I could not have drawn it on a map. On the other hand, it was ironic that, when I was behind the wire in Stalag Luft 1, one of the big attractions was a very large map, erected like a notice-board in the main compound, on which the Eastern and Western Fronts were marked-out with pins and coloured string by the prisoners and moved every day according to the news.

We had two sources of news: one was the secret radio tuned to the BBC. This was amazingly well constructed and hidden: parts, like valves, had been obtained by a few German-speaking prisoners bribing one or two guards with cigarettes and chocolate, and then blackmailing them into getting what was needed – the rest of us were forbidden ever to talk to the guards. Different people 'in the know' had responsibility for separate portions of the receiving equipment: no one knew everything about the installation, and the listener only plugged his headphones into a socket concealed in a bunk. Copies of his report were typed out and an individual came round to each hut in turn; look-outs were posted at both ends of the hut, and we gathered in the corridor to hear the BBC news.

The other source was 100% public: the Germans were keen that we should read the propaganda in their newspapers and listen to it on their radio; so a special team of POWs with fluent German would extract all the military information from these media and then reverse it: that is, a German advance would be changed to an Allied withdrawal, and a German withdrawal to an Allied advance. From experience over several years, this team could 'read between the lines' of the German communiqués and, with few German victories in autumn 1944-45 – except the Battle of Arnhem in September and the Ardennes Offensive in December 1944 – they could identify a German 'shortening of the line' as an Allied advance, although no actual German retreat had been admitted. It was this clever understanding of the likely real position that was put up on the public display map, and which always drew a crowd of prisoners, among them Tony Whitamore and myself. As a result, I was better informed about the war as a prisoner than I ever was as an operational airman! Remarkable, also, was the frequent presence of two or three German officers, equally interested in seeing for themselves our understanding of the position of the front-lines at any one time.

Returning to September 1944, I don't think I was alone in 16 Squadron in having no knowledge of Operation 'Market Garden', in which one British and two American Airborne Divisions and a Polish Parachute Brigade attempted to seize the bridges between Eindhoven and Arnhem, to enable 2nd British Army to cross the Rhine, outflank the Siegfried Line, turn right, and attack the Ruhr industrial area from the rear. Our Adjutant, Don Williams, in his day-by-day entries in his monthly Summary of

Events in the Squadron Operations Record Book (SORB) for September 1944, made no mention by name of either 'Market Garden' or Arnhem, so there was clearly a veil of secrecy surrounding the early days, at least, of the Operation, which lasted from 17th-26th September.

I was, therefore, not aware of the significance of 16 Squadron sending a detachment of four aircraft to Northolt to provide photographic cover of the Operation, even though one of the selected pilots, P/0 John Brodby, was sharing a tent with Michael Horsfall and myself. "34 Wing – an Unofficial Account", published just after the war, also managed to get it wrong: the two anonymous authors wrote a short but very confusing account:

On page 31 : "The main party of the Wing embarked for France and, having landed on 31st August, moved to A12. A small rear party, under Sandy Webb, was left at Northolt and they did not join the Wing until Sept 9th, by which time the rest of the Wing had moved to Amiens-Glisy."

On page 33 the account continues: "On Sep 7th, two Spitfires and two Mosquitos were sent to Northolt to carry out reconnaissance under Sandy Webb's direction for the Airborne Operation at ARNHEM; Sandy himself flew three outstanding sorties and the detachment met very strong opposition and had bad weather conditions over the target areas, as a result of which John Brodby and Gerry Bastow were missing."

When I first read this account in 1991, it appeared that the authors were confused and contradictory in their dates, and certainly no Mosquitos were part of the detachment to Northolt; so I did not give much credibility to their account. For the rest of the Squadron in September 1944, life and operations went on as normal, and we even took some high-level photographs of Arnhem, as one of several

W/C 'Sandy' Webb, DFC, 34 Wing Operations Officer, between (l) F/Lt 'Butch' Baker (later CO of 16 Squadron June-September 1945) and G/C Roch Lousada, OC 34 Wing June 1943-August 1944
Photo: Hugh Rigby Collection

Scotty Cadan in khaki battle-dress at Amiens-Glisy in September 1944
Photo: Michael Horsfall

targets on a sortie, without being aware that there was a battle raging beneath us. In addition, Peter Fahy and I were detailed on 22nd September to fly to RAF Ford, in Sussex, in two pink Spitfire IXs, to pick up two drop-tanks filled with beer for the airmen, as I have described earlier; but we didn't realise that the tanks were needed as extras for the aircraft dropping messages to the troops near Nijmegen every day from 20th September - 1st October; the "34 Wing" account does not mention these sorties at all.

It was against this background of ignorance and general apathy that I gradually became aware in the 1990s, helped by the book and film of Cornelius Ryan's "A Bridge Too Far", that the battle for Arnhem bridge had been a great opportunity, a great defeat, and a scene of great bravery. My interest was really stirred when I visited the Public Record Office (now the National Archive) in 1999 and photocopied, from a microfilm, 16 Squadron's Operations Record Book (SORB) for the time of my service in the Squadron, from August-November 1944. This, of course, covered the period of 'Market Garden' and so, for the first time, I read the reports of the pilots who went on the detachment to Northolt: Wing Commander 'Sandy' Webb, DFC, the OC; F/0 'Scotty' Cadan, RAAF; P/0 John Brodby; and four other pilots already at Northolt, 'on rest' in 34 Wing Support Unit (WSU) after completing a tour on 16 Squadron, who were recruited by 'Sandy' for a single sortie each: F/Lt S.B.Spring, DFC; F/Lt M.B.Murphy, DFC; F/Lt P.D.Petrie, DFC; and F/Lt G.H.Bastow, DFC. Unfortunately, John Brodby and Gerry Bastow were both shot down on 20th September: John was killed when he crashed on a suburb of Nijmegen, but Gerry was lucky to escape when his plane crash-landed near Wolfheze, a northern suburb of Arnhem; he was hidden by the Dutch Resistance for a month, and then crossed the Rhine in the company of another 140 evaders in the well-organised rescue Operation 'Pegasus' in the night of 22nd October 1944.

John Brodby (as a P/O) on A12 Airstrip in Normandy with the 16 Squadron Auster hack in September 1944
Photo: Michael Horsfall

My interest was now thoroughly awakened by discovering what an important role 16 Squadron had played in 'Market Garden', both in taking photographs of all the paratroop-dropping zones (DZs), and glider-landing zones (LZs) used by the British and American Airborne Divisions, and the main bridges they were trying to capture, and also in the quite different activity of dropping messages to Lt General 'Boy' Browning, DSO, their overall commander, on an LZ near Nijmegen. From the end of 1999 onwards, I decided to collect copies of all the aerial photographs that I could find in archives, museums and books, in the hope of being able to identify those which had been taken by my 16 Squadron. For this purpose, I visited the Public Record Office, the Photo Library of the Imperial War Museum, the Air Photo Archive at Keele University, the Museum of Army Flying, and the Airborne Forces Museum. Alan Brown, the Curator of the latter, was especially helpful: he sent me a number of acrial photos of Arnhem, including six important pictures of parachutists dropping on the DZ north-west of Arnhem and low-level obliques of the bridge itself, littered with wrecked German vehicles. I also found a large number of excellent books on Operation 'Market Garden', both on the campaign as a whole, and separately on the fighting in the different areas: the British 1st Airborne Division and the Polish 1st Parachute Brigade aiming for the Arnhem road-bridge; the capture of the road-bridge at Grave and the road- and rail-bridges at Nijmegen by the American 82nd Airborne Division and their battles with the Germans in Nijmegen

A remarkable low-level oblique by 'Sandy' Webb of Dakotas dropping paratroops on DZ 'X', NW of Arnhem, on 17th September 1944

Photo: "34 Wing – An Unofficial Account"

and with others attacking from the Reichswald, the forest to the east of the city; and the efforts of the American 101st Airborne Division to keep the 50-mile-long roadway open between Eindhoven and Nijmegen for the British XXX Corps to drive up and occupy Arnhem. The Germans reacted far more swiftly and effectively than had been expected, and all three Airborne Divisions experienced desperate fighting and heavy losses in fulfilling most of their tasks. XXX Corps, however, failed to reach the bridge at Arnhem, and the survivors of the beleaguered British troops, who had held back superior German forces for three times as long as they had been promised, had to be evacuated across the Rhine in the night of 25th/26th September.

I accumulated a small library of books on every aspect of 'Market Garden' and amassed a collection of over 100 photocopies of the aerial photographs found in them as well as from my other sources. As a result, I came to learn the broad outline of the Operation and the many causes of its ultimate failure, too numerous to discuss here, except for one particular detail which caught my attention, although it seemed to have escaped the military historians.

On the evening after their landing on 17th September, 'B' Company of Lt Colonel John Frost's 2nd Parachute Battalion was on its way to the road-bridge at Arnhem along the road nearest to the north bank of the Rhine. The railway bridge had been blown-up just as they reached it, but there was a pontoon bridge across the river a short distance before the road-bridge. Several soldiers went down the bank and saw that the centre-section, which could be removed to let boats and barges come through, was missing. They climbed back to the road and reported that the pontoon bridge was unusable because of the missing section. However, one of the photographs given me by Alan Brown was taken by

A fine low-level oblique by 'Sandy' Webb of the road bridge at Arnhem, with wrecked German vehicles at the northern end shot-up by Lt Colonel Frost's 2nd Parachute Battalion on 18th September 1944

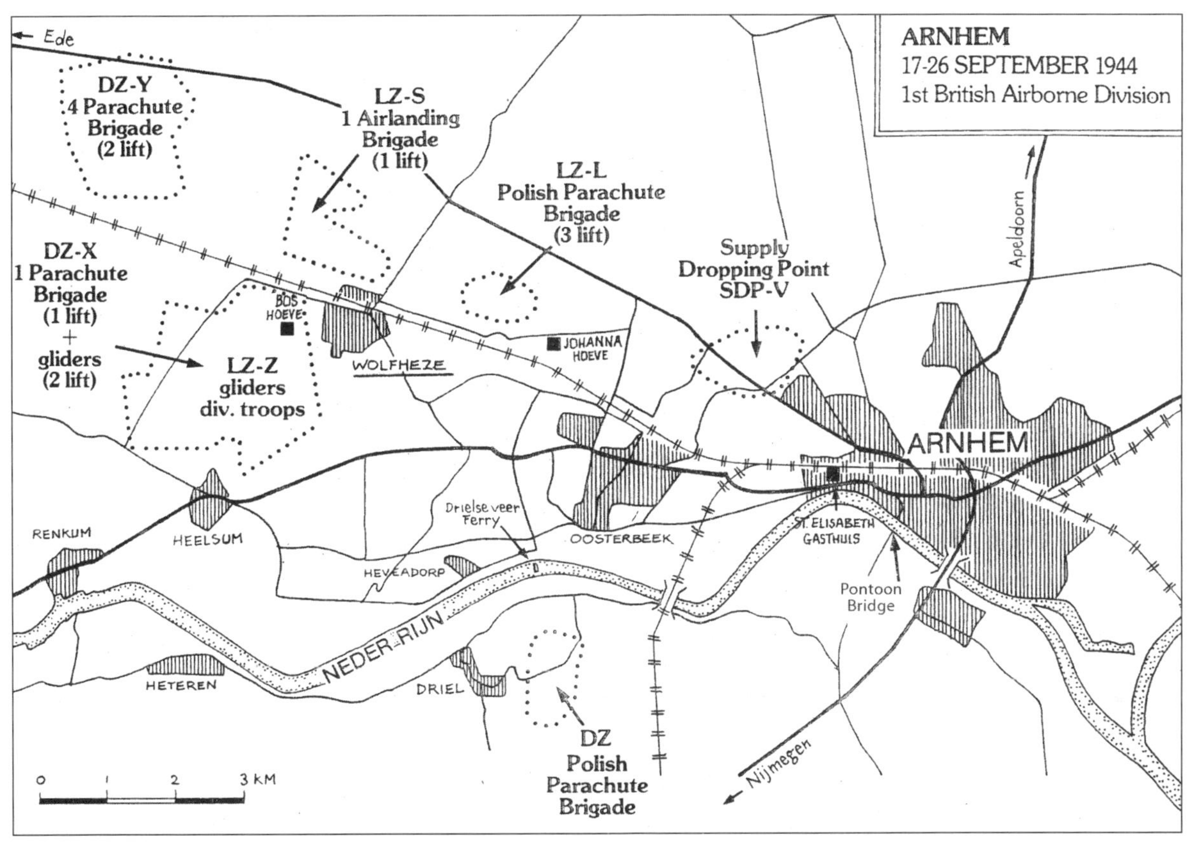

Map of Arnhem and Oosterbeek showing Wolfheze and the site of the pontoon bridge to the left of the road bridge.
Map from Altes, Margry, Thurling and Voskuil "September 1944"

an American pilot of the 27th Squadron of the USAF 7th Photo Group on 18th September and clearly showed the missing section lying-up against the north bank of the river, the same bank that the soldiers had descended the evening before. There remain two mysteries: why didn't the soldiers see the centre-section and either struggle to get it into place between the two ends, or ask the nearest inhabitants – whose welcome was so warm and hospitable that it was hindering their advance – to find the watermen to do the job for them. And, secondly, why hasn't the failure of 'B' Company to do this been identified as one of the main reasons for the British not crossing the river and capturing the southern end of the bridge – the northern end had fallen into their hands virtually unopposed – either that evening or the next morning; the Germans had not yet summoned their tanks and guns to destroy the buildings occupied by Frost's men, which eventually drove the survivors back to Oosterbeek, to join the rest of the shattered Division. The American photograph could not lie, and Frost's men could not have seen it; but their failure to spot the presence of the centre-section literally 'under their noses' on 17th September, remains unexplained to this day.

For me, this was the most poignant scene that I discovered among all the photocopies I had collected, but they also showed me that there were other squadrons taking photographs over the battle-ground besides 16 Squadron. I realised there was a value in studying them from two points of view: one was to try to understand what each picture showed, which would help the military historians to identify the aircraft, the location, the date, the soldiers involved, and the activity in which they became engaged; this was not an area of great interest to me personally, but I realised the importance such information might have in assisting an understanding of the fighting. What interested me more was to examine each print in detail for its technical data, to try to determine the size of the original negative, whether the print had been 'cropped' and/or enlarged, the camera and lens used, from what height, by what aircraft, from which Air Force, from which squadron, and even the name of the pilot. Obviously, if the 'titling' had been preserved on the photograph, this was the first source of information, giving usually the squadron number, the sortie number, the exposure number, the focal-length of the lens, the camera number, and the date; other details were more arbitrary: the height, the scale, and the processing unit. The RAF and USAAF used different 'register culmination marks', so these could identify the Air Force; they also revealed the original edges of a print and therefore its proportions; which indicated the kind of camera used; an F52 took a negative 8½" x 7", a K17 took 9"x 9", and an F24 took 5"x 5". The marks also showed whether the print had been enlarged or cut down. Orientating the print to find north was also important, as the shadows could indicate the time of day when the photo was taken, while any smoke would show the direction of the wind. One question, however, could not be answered satisfactorily: we might learn the date of the photograph, but there was no way of telling whether the gliders or parachutes had landed on that day or a day or more earlier. For this, I had to rely on the historical record.

At the end of 2000, I analysed 17 photocopies of aerial photos of the Arnhem DZs and LZs and the bridge and found that 8 of them had been taken by 'Sandy' Webb, as his entries in the Line Book revealed that he was the only member of the 16 Squadron detachment to have an F24 oblique camera with 14" lens fitted to his Spitfire XI. I published these photos and my analyses in a "Newsbrief Special" for January 2001 – without, however, stirring anyone else's interest.

In May 2001, as I've already mentioned briefly, Hennie Noordhuis and I were given a guided tour by Henk Duinhoven of the areas that were now my main concern: the LZs and DZs of the 1st British Airborne Division and the bridge at Arnhem, followed by the bridge at Nijmegen and the LZs and DZs of the 82nd American Airborne Division near Groesbeek, east of Nijmegen. Seeing these brought to life my photocopies and, especially, revealed the distances involved and the scale of the whole 'Market Garden' operation. Alan Brown added to this understanding by sending me a sequence of four oblique photographs taken by a forward-looking camera, probably on a Spitfire from Benson, of a low-level run up the Rhine eastwards, from the railway-bridge at Arnhem, over the pontoon bridge, with the

A vertical photo of the Rhine on 18th September, 1944, with the centre section of the pontoon bridge clearly lying beside the northern section (inside the brackets). The Titling shows it was taken by a K17 camera with a 24" lens from 15-20,000ft by an aircraft of 27 Squadron of the USAAF's 7th Photo Group; its records reveal the pilot was Lt Ira J Purdy flying a Lightning F-5B from Mount Farm in Oxfordshire.

The Pontoon Bridge, with the central section being moved in or out.
Low-level photo from a forward-facing oblique camera in a Spitfire flown from RAF Benson in Oxfordshire by F/Lt L.J. Scargill of 541 Squadron on 6th September 1944.
Photo via Alan Brown

centre-section just opening or closing, and then over the road-bridge – full of interesting detail for the photo-interpreters and planners before 'Market Garden' was launched. Also very useful was a large-format book: "Allied Photo Reconnaissance of World War II", edited by Chris Staerck (Parkgate Books 1998), which yielded a chapter on 'Market Garden' containing some excellent sketch-maps and a number of useful photographs, several taken by 'Sandy' Webb.

In my photocopied SORB, besides the reports of the pilots of 'Sandy' Webb's detachment, I had also found the entries of Michael Wetz and the other pilots who had dropped the messages to the Airborne troops near Groesbeek from 20th September to 1st October. During our visit to Groesbeek in May, I had seen the outline of the Reichswald Forest on the not very distant horizon, from where the Germans would have noticed Michael's pink Spitfire IX as he circled round, during the first message-dropping sortie on 20th September, looking for the markers that should have been put out by the soldiers to indicate the right dropping field. After two more such sorties, Michael was relieved by W/0 Willy Willshaw and awarded an immediate DFC. However, Michael upraided the staff at 21st Army Group in Brussels, saying that if he could fly alone to a field near Nijmegen, surely the Typhoon squadrons could be sent to support our hard-pressed Airborne troops at Arnhem. He always claimed that they gave him the DFC to keep him quiet!

The presence of six pink Spitfire IXs on 16 Squadron, and the rather bizarre circumstances in which a PR squadron dropped messages to the soldiers near Nijmegen, were still as little-known as the work that 16 Squadron did for 'Market Garden' with its detachment of blue Spitfire XIs at Northolt. The unsung nature of the two important events persuaded me that I should write an article for "Aeroplane" magazine to bring attention to these very creditable achievements of 16 Squadron in September 1944. Michael Oakey, the Editor, fortunately agreed with me and printed my article under the title of the

Willy Willshaw
Photo: Hugh Smallwood "Spitfire in Blue"

Michael Wetz (r) with Norman Godfrey. Note the camera control box in place of the gun-sight.
Photo: Hugh Smallwood "Spitfire in Blue"

Drop-tank on a Spitfire IX of a Free French squadron
Photo: Bruce Robertson "Spitfire – the Story of a Famous Fighter"

A Spitfire IX flying with a drop-tank
Photo: Bruce Robertson "Spitfire – the Story of a Famous Fighter"

Squadron's motto translated as "Hidden Things Revealed", with the sub-title "16 Squadron's Contribution to Operation 'Market Garden'"; he gave it seven pages of text and eighteen photographs, in the issue of May 2002. This made the Squadron's activities and my authorship known in the small world of military and air historians, especially in Holland and, over time, brought me into correspondence with many of them. If I had been computer-literate, I would, no doubt, have come into contact with many other interested people.

My annual visit to Borne in May that year gave me the opportunity to see more of the sites and memorials connected with 'Market Garden'. Hennie Noordhuis drove me first to the impressive nine-span road-bridge over the River Maas at Grave, captured quickly by the 504th Parachute Infantry Regiment of the American 82nd Airborne Division dropping at each end on 17th September. A fine memorial, comprising an open metal parachute canopy and lines on a polished limestone plinth, stands at the southern approach to this bridge, which was of great strategic importance in 1944. We went on to the superb "Wings of Liberation" Museum between Son and Best, in the area where some of the American 101st Airborne Division's LZs and DZs were situated. Here we met Jos Korsten, who proved to be in the same mould as Henk Duinhoven and many others I was to meet later, in being a dedicated historian of 'Market Garden'; his working life was passed as a Primary School teacher, but the rest of his time was spent helping to build up the fine collection of aeroplanes and vehicles, several of them grouped with personnel in realistic action set-pieces, together with displays of equipment and weaponry, all housed in four large buildings dispersed over the site. Other aircraft, such as two Dakotas and an F-104 Starfighter, and military vehicles including a Sherman tank were parked outside. In the nearby town of Den Dongen, Jos designed an imaginative monument called the "Silent Wings Memorial", to the tug and glider crews, some of whom landed near the town; it consists of a sheet of V-shaped metal mounted on a tall mast, with the outlines of five tugs, two of them linked to gliders, cut out of the metal and silhouetted against the changing clouds in the sky above. Later, Jos kindly sent me photocopies of aerial photos of the landing-fields used by the 101st Airborne Division during 'Market Garden'.

The vital road bridge over the River Maas at Grave captured on the 17th September by men of the 504 Parachute Infantry Regiment of the US 82nd Airborne Division and the Memorial recording this feat

An exhibit in the "Wings of Liberation" Museum near Son, showing a model blue Spitfire XI over an oblique photograph by 'Sandy' Webb of American Hadrian gliders with men of the US 101st Airborne Division landing nearby. The label reads: "Aerial photograph of landing Zone Son (behind this hall). Made by a Spitfire PR XI of 16 Squadron RAF."

After lunch, we walked round the extensive hangar-like buildings, one with a display round a reconstructed glider, another based on an artillery-spotter Auster, and a third featuring a Spitfire. I was also intrigued to find a glass case with a model blue PR Spitfire suspended over an aerial photograph of gliders landing on these same fields; it felt good to know that here, at least, our wartime work was known and understood; Jos himself was always interested in it.

At the Museum, I bought a copy of "Tugs and Gliders to Arnhem" by another Dutch historian, Arie-Jan van Hees. When I read this deeply-researched first-class book back in Leeds, I found some discrepancies in the figures, which led me to write to Arie-Jan. This started a long correspondence and friendship with him, which has been most beneficial and continues to this day. He was the first of several Dutch military historians I met who could write in English so effectively that their books sold better in Britain and English-speaking countries than in Holland.

'Sandy' Webb in a PR Blenheim when he was a Flight Commander in 140 Squadron in 1942
Photo: Graham Pitchfork

Another historian, English this time, at least with the very English name of Graham Pitchfork OBE, who specialised in recounting the stories of individual airmen in books such as "The Men Behind the Medals", responded to my article in "Aeroplane" by kindly sending me his biography of Wing Commander 'Sandy' Webb, DFC, the commander of our detachment to Northolt in September 1944. After a distinguished career as a PR pilot in 140 Squadron and as Operations Officer of 34 Wing, 'Sandy' wanted to take a more aggressive role in the war against the Germans. He therefore left 34 Wing in December and joined a Typhoon squadron, flying in close support of the Army and destroying German communications whenever possible; it was while leading his squadron in an attack on a freight-train in Germany that he was, tragically, shot down and killed in the last week of the war.

A further event connected with 16 Squadron's work over Arnhem, arising not from my article in "Aeroplane", but from its predecessor in "Newsbrief", occurred in May 2005. Harry van der Meer, the original cause of it, was another Dutchman with a historical interest, who played a significant part in locating, restoring and preserving Allied aircraft. Spitfire PR XI PL965 flew operationally on 16 Squadron from January to September 1945. Two years later it was sold to the Dutch Air Force (RNLAF) and became an instructional airframe for training their mechanics at Deelen. When Spitfires were phased out of the RNLAF in 1955, it became a gate-guardian outside the Sergeants' Mess; from there it was sold to the new museum at Overloon in 1960 and displayed out-of-doors. Considered to be a Mark IX, subjected to various paint-schemes, battered by the elements, and crawled over by children, the Spitfire was in a sorry state in 1972, when Harry van der Meer, a Spitfire enthusiast, guided by Peter Arnold, an experienced collector of Spitfires in England, sought and found its serial number, PL965, and established its identity. The following year, Harry and an assistant gave the aircraft as good a make-over as possible; in 1975, however, it was taken to RAF Brüggen, in Germany, by Len Woodgate, an RAF engineering officer, for a thorough restoration. Back at Overloon, over the years further deterioration set in and Harry, who was now Curator of the Aviodome Air Museum at Schiphol Airport, suggested that the corroded Spitfire XI be exchanged for a Mark XIV, a type operated by Dutch pilots during the war. This was done, PL965 being bought by collectors Nick Grace and Chris Horsley, and sent for restoration to flying condition by the Medway Aircraft Preservation Society at Rochester Airport in Kent, under its Managing Director, Lewis Deal. Nick was unfortunately killed in a car crash in 1989, but Chris continued as the owner, both for the first post-restoration flight in 1992 and for subsequent appearances at air displays in the skilled hands of Mark Hanna, until he sold it to Tony Smith in 1996. Tony flew PL965 from Breighton Aerodrome for eight years, and in 2000 he painted it pink, to resemble one of our wartime low-level Spitfire IXs, which made it even more eye-catching on the display circuit and on the covers of aviation magazines. Peter Teichman was forming a collection of warbirds at North Weald Airfield and bought PL965 in 2004; we saw it at our Final Reunion in 2006, back in its original blue colour with black-and-white invasion stripes, taxying past us to the familiar rumble of its Merlin engine, and showing-off its distinctive shape in the sky as Peter flew it effortlessly through its restrained repertoire of graceful aerobatics. I gave Associate Membership of our "16 Squadron 1939-1945" group to all those I have mentioned, who preserved this beautiful aeroplane for us and future generations.

Harry had read my original article in "Newsbrief Special" of January 2001, about 16 Squadron and 'Market Garden', from which he learned that F/0 'Scotty' Cadan, RAAF, one of the pilots brought to Northolt by 'Sandy' Webb from the Squadron's base at Amiens-Glisy, had flown four successful PR sorties over Eindhoven, Nijmegen and Arnhem, three of them in conditions of very low cloud and poor visibility, in one of which he was 'jumped' by an Me109. What disturbed Harry, however, was that 'Scotty' had been recommended for the award of the Dutch Bronze Cross, but it had been blocked at a higher level and he had heard no more about it. Harry now wrote to his friend, Lt General Dick Berlijn, Commander-in-Chief of the Royal Netherlands Air Force, suggesting that he might still fulfil the recommendation by awarding the Bronze Cross to 'Scotty' Cadan even at this late date. General Berlijn wrote an extremely friendly letter to 'Scotty' in Australia, regretting that it was not in his power to do so as the Government had ordained that no retrospective awards for wartime services could be considered after 1953. He went on to say, "We owe you and your squadron a huge debt of gratitude for braving the odds the way that you did above and beyond the call of duty." I was so impressed by this tribute that I immediately wrote to the General and offered him our Associate Membership, and I was delighted when he accepted.

During 2002, I collected together all my original and photocopied pictures of the bridge at Arnhem, gliders landing on the LZs, and paratroops descending on the DZs in the fields north-east of Arnhem, added my technical analysis of each one, together with a reference to the source and the caption, if any, and produced a number of copies under the title "Focus on Arnhem," I sent copies to several publishers, but they all replied equally that it was too technical and there was too small a readership – a verdict with which I totally disagreed, and still do!

Meeting with Lt General Dick Berlijn, Head of the Royal Netherlands Air Force, on 1st May 2003; Hennie Noordhuis (l) and JT

On my visit to Holland in May 2003, the first move that Hennie Noordhuis and I made on leaving Schiphol was to drive to The Hague and call on Dick Berlijn in his very smoothly-run Headquarters. We had a most interesting discussion with him about Air Force operations yesterday and today, at the end of which I gave him a copy of "Spitfire in Blue", and he presented us each with an attractive silver clock inscribed with the crest of the RNLAF. By a strange coincidence, Hennie's wife Joke was a music teacher at the school in Twente which Dick Berlijn's daughter attended – but we didn't refer to this in our conversation. In 2005, Lt General Berlijn was appointed to a new post, one perhaps specially designed with him in view: Commander-in-Chief of the Netherlands Combined Army, Navy and Air Force. We were certainly pleased to offer our distinguished Associate Member our warmest congratulations.

Another meeting arranged by Hennie had a quite different purpose but had the same friendly character. This was with two Dutch military historians: Arie-Jan van Hees, the author already mentioned, and his friend, Frans Ammerlaan, who was very well informed about all aspects of 'Market Garden'. We met in a room in the Airborne Museum at Arnhem and spent the morning discussing in detail the aerial photos of 'Market Garden' that I had collected and the analyses I had made of them. Their interest was very encouraging and motivated me to produce a proper manuscript which might, with luck, induce a publisher to put it into print. We were joined for lunch by Marinus Timmerman, of the family who owned "The Resting Hunter" restaurant, now run by his nephew Henk. Marinus lived in Arnhem and was one of the Friends of the Airborne Museum, so he also had an interest in my photographs. Arie-Jan was working on "Green On!", a follow-up to his previous book, which highlighted the splendid dedication and self-sacrifice over Arnhem of the men who mustered at the exit-doors the paratroopers jumping from the Dakotas and who too often perished if the aircraft was shot down; they also pushed out the canisters of weapons, ammunition and food on the dangerous missions to re-supply the troops surrounded in the suburb of Oosterbeek, when the flak was horrendous and 85% of their loads fell to the Germans, who continued to lay out the strips of cloth to mark the dropping areas, now in their hands. I felt almost ashamed that it was a Dutchman who recognised the devotion to their duty of the 170 members of aircrew, including the dispatchers, who were lost at Arnhem; the most famous of them was F/Lt David Lord, DFC, who was awarded the Victoria Cross for staying at the controls of his burning Dakota to enable his men to finish pushing out the containers and jump themselves, by which time he was too low to make his own escape – and he died in the inevitable crash.

After lunch, I suggested to Hennie that as we were quite near to the town of Wageningen, about ten miles west of Arnhem, it might be worth calling in at the University to see whether they would allow us to look at their archive of 90,000 wartime aerial photographs. Hennie thought it very unlikely that we could get in without an appointment; nevertheless, we made our way there, found the Department of the Environment, and were let in by a young lady, Liesbeth Missal, Keeper of the Special Collection of wartime photographs used in the work of the Department. When she learned that I had been in 16 Squadron, she disappeared and returned with twenty small original cardboard boxes, each containing about 25 5" x 5" prints, with "16 Squadron" written on the lid! Moreover, the photo catalogue listed the Sortie Numbers and usually included the names of the pilots – so someone must have had access to the 16 Squadron Operations Record Book (SORB). I scribbled down a few catalogue entries:

Cadan	16/1127	6th September 1944
Wales	1173	13th September
?	1208	19th September
West	1503	23rd December
?	1603	19th January 1945
Barker	1671	16th February
Williams	1672	16th February

We had arrived without warning, so we could not take up too much of Liesbeth Missal's time. I was able to glance through the contents of the boxes, several of which contained duplicates, but I identified only a sequence of 8½" x 7" prints going up the Rhine from Arnhem bridge; these, fortunately, retained their 'titling':

3030.. 16/1208 19SEP44 F, 36"//A27

This enabled me to match these pictures with Sortie No 1208 in the catalogue list, but the pilot was unknown. I asked Ms Missal for photocopies of these photos, which she very kindly made for me; in return, I gave her a copy of "Focus on Arnhem", together with our very warm thanks for letting us in and looking after my needs so well. It was valuable to have seen this Department, and so to have visited one more location that held PR photographs of 'Market Garden'.

After I had returned to Leeds, I looked for these sorties in my copy of the Line Book, but most of them had not been entered; this, as I have mentioned earlier, was fairly typical of those times, but they were probably typed into SORB. The only ones recorded in the Line Book, without any Sortie Numbers, were West's, Barker's and Williams's sorties. F/0 'Jock' West had quite an eventful flight, including photographing Arnhem, four days after Sortie No 1208:

"Targets: NW Arnhem, Nijmegen, E of Breda. Photos.
Climbed to 24,000ft while photographing Arnhem area, saw 5 unidentified a/c orbiting in area, and one unidentified a/c making large trail a few thousand feet higher than I was, going very fast W to E. When over Nijmegen, I was shot at with AA fire. Almost between Nijmegen and Breda at 12,000ft I passed a formation of single-engined fighters going in the opposite direction – 3 peeled off and chased me back to Eindhoven, but did not close with me. No further incidents."

The 'AA fire' was probably flak from the Germans still stationed in the Reichswald just to the east of Nijmegen; the 'fighters' were more likely to be American, who often had difficulty identifying a single Spitfire.

Back at Wageningen, there was still plenty of daylight left, so we decided to drive a few miles northwest to Deelen. This had been an important German night-fighter base and sector-control HQ, which appeared to be a threat to the Airborne forces during 'Market Garden', as it lay on the return route of the towing aircraft and transports and was well defended with anti-aircraft guns. Accordingly, Bomber Command dropped 500 tons of bombs on the airfield on the night of 3rd September, after which the airfield was partially put out of action and the Germans removed most of the flak guns.

The airfield was now a military airport, with restricted access. However, on the approach road, in the former German Under-Officers' Mess, was the Air Warfare Museum, set up by several enthusiasts in 1996, which I had read about in Major and Mrs Holt's masterly "Battlefield Guide to Operation Market Garden", which gives exhaustive coverage of every site, memorial, cemetery, and museum connected with the campaign, and describes the road access to it. Here we found a small, but very compact museum, filled with displays of interesting artefacts of all kinds – gun-turrets, engines, bombs, instruments, clothing, and so on, from all the Air Forces engaged. It is also the HQ of the Dutch Aircraft Examination Group, which excavates crashed aircraft, retrieves and identifies the bodies of any crew-members found, and traces and informs their next-of-kin. As a result, many of the exhibits in the museum were relics from the excavations. Considering that over 7000 aircraft landed on or in Dutch soil during 1939-1945, the Group will be kept busy for many years to come.

CHAPTER 36

Saluting Those Who Did Not Return

On 4th May, when Hennie was, as usual, fully occupied organising National Commemoration Day ceremonies at Borne Town Hall and at smaller Memorials such as the one at 't Hesseler, Jan Bovenmars once again acted as my chauffeur. This time he drove out about ten miles north of Borne and parked beside a large wood. We followed a narrow path through the trees until we came to a clearing where, much to my surprise, in a semi-circle, were a bronze sculpture, a white stone cross behind three white horizontal plaques, a Dutch National Flag at half-mast, another cross behind a grey stone plaque with a stone surround, and another National Flag at half-mast. The sculpture was one more example of the strength and pathos with which Dutch artists seem to be able, intuitively, to invest their proud monumental subjects; in this case a uniformed soldier was kneeling beside a woman, who supported the reclining body of a dead son, husband or lover; the whole group was mounted on a block of rough-hewn stone. On the grey plaque were three names:

Sietse Arnold Hilbrink born 1879
Coenraad Johan Hilbrink born 1915
Dirk Cornelis Ruiter born 1918
Shot during the Occupation
23rd September 1944

Of the three white plaques together, the left-hand lower one had an inscription that read:

Bote van der Wal
Born 18th March 1921
Shot during the Occupation
24th March 1945

while the right-hand lower one read:

Gerald Hood R.A.F. Aircrew
Born 25th February 1922
Shot during the Occupation
21st March 1945

After I had walked round these grim reminders of how much the Dutch had suffered under the Germans – I don't believe we should condemn only the Nazis for these atrocities – Jan explained that the Resistance in Twente was well organised and effective in sabotaging the railways and the factories producing materials for the Germans, hiding Jews and Dutchmen wanted for slave labour in Germany, rescuing Allied Service-men and helping to return them to Britain. In spite of the terrible reprisals, as I have described, taken against the innocent civilian population, the Resistance continued with its work. Yet there were many Dutch people who sympathised with the Nazi cause, and the Resistance had always to be alert for traitors and informers. Its Headquarters was in an old house deep in a wood not far from this one, where a young student, Bote van der Wal, had brought Gerald Hood, an evading airman, but where they had been betrayed to the Germans and shot. I told Jan I would find out the full story in England, if I could, and send it to him.

We returned via Enschede to visit the Rijksmuseum and see the Hanneman on display in a selective exhibition in the museum. It was gratifying to observe visitors, including children, clustering round to read the inscription on the brass plate, and to know that the names of Jan Vonk, Jan Boomkamp, Hendrik Roetgerink, and Piet van Dijk, would go down to posterity as long as the portrait of "Father Roeland de Pottere, SJ" exists.

An expressive Monument of a father grieving over his dead son

The Wood of Execution
The clearing in the wood near Almelo where F/O Gerald Hood and his young Dutch helper, Bote van der Wal, were executed by the Gestapo in March 1945. Three other Resistance workers had been shot there on 23rd September 1944.

Memorials to (top) Arnold Hilbrink (65), Conrad Hilbrink (29) and Dirk Ruiter (26); (lower l-r) Bote van der Wal (24) and Gerald Hood (23)

Gerald Hood
RAF Navigator
Born 25 February 1922
Shot by the Occupier
on 21 March 1945

The little ceremony at the 't Hesseler Memorial was as moving as ever, and it was, as usual, a pleasure to renew my acquaintance with people whose friendly faces I meet only for these few minutes each year – but they give me a bond of friendship which I do not experience in Leeds. It is, I suppose, a throw-back to the War, the Occupation, and the Liberation – and now that I have witnessed in the wood the deathly friendship between Gerald Wood and Bote van der Wal, I think I understand.

The portrait of Father de Pottere attracts attention at a later exhibition of recent acquisitions in the Museum.

Once back in England, I wrote to Mrs Susan Dickinson at the Air Historical Branch of the Ministry of Defence and asked her whether she knew anything about Gerald Hood. I enclosed a set of photographs of the clearing in the wood for her to forward to his next-of-kin, if she knew of them.

She replied that she could not normally give me any information as I was not a relative; but, since I had enclosed the photographs for his family, she had made further inquiries and could send me a full account, together with the contemporary reports of two of his surviving crew. She called it a sad but fascinating story.

F/0 Gerald Hood was the Navigator on Lancaster III LM658, coded HW-W, of 100 Squadron, based at RAF Grimsby. The other crew were:

F/Lt Harold Paston-Williams	Pilot and Captain	Saved
Sgt John Alexander Downie	Flight Engineer	Saved
F/Lt Christopher Holland	2nd Pilot	Died
P/0 Benjamin Ramsden	Bomb Aimer	Died
F/Sgt Lawrence Roy Watts	Wireless Op/Air Gunner	Died
F/Sgt Robert Stanley Williams	Mid-Upper Gunner	Died
F/0 Bruce Arnold David, RCAF	Rear Gunner	POW

On 12th August 1944, they took off at 2145hrs for a raid on Brunswick.

The report on interviews with the Captain, F/Lt Paston-Williams, on 8th April and 31st July 1945 reads:

"After being airborne for about 1hr 15mins, the navigator reported that the navigation aids for 'Gee' and 'Y' were unserviceable. As we were approaching the Dutch coast, I decided to continue. We were off course and, later, got a Position Point from the bomb-aimer and bombed our target at 0005hrs 13mins, about 8 minutes late. On the way in, we were hit twice heavily by flak, and again on our bombing run. We bombed on fires burning, seen through clouds, and turned for home.

We were hit again by flak leaving the target. We were again off course and were hit by flak S. of Hanover. Here the rear-gunner called for 'cork-screw' (an evasive manoeuvre). After 2 mins. he asked me to resume course, and barely had I straightened out than we were hit by a night-fighter's cannon-fire (Me410) from behind and below. We had been set on fire by the cross-balance pipe and inner starboard tank by the last flak hit. I saw tracer passing my head on the left and took violent evasive action to the right. The ammunition started to explode, and accumulators were also on fire and gassing us all. As I pulled the aircraft up in another 'cork-screw', the whole tail came off at circa 16,000ft.

The intercom was disconnected, but just prior to this I had signalled "Abandon aircraft!" and four of the crew jumped (bomb-aimer, 2nd pilot, wireless op, and mid-upper gunner). The aircraft dived immediately and disintegrated. Parts must have struck the four crew who had first baled out, as their bodies were found within 500ft of the aircraft, with one under the fuselage.

I baled out and came-to falling, pulled my 'chute and landed immediately, fortunately in a peat bog. I was about 15km west of BERGENTHEM on the Dutch/German border. I walked west about 6km, when I had to rest in a haystack. I was unable to move, my knees had gone completely and I had bad eyes. I crawled to an isolated farm-house and they took me in after they had satisfied themselves about my identity. They fetched a doctor and for the next four weeks I was looked after by members of the Underground in the vicinity. On 17th August Sgt Downie, my Flight Engineer, was brought to the village."

Downie's interview was recorded on 8th April 1945 after his return to UK; it reads:

"I was attempting to reach the fire with an extinguisher, but was unable to pass the navigator with his parachute on. The fire was too bad, so I turned and signalled to the second pilot and picked up my 'chute and had just clamped it (only one side fastening) when I was knocked out. I came-to falling in somersaults and blacked-out again. I came-to next falling straight and managed to reach up and open my parachute – I again blacked-out and came-to seeing the burning aircraft directly below and five flares falling, with two open parachutes underneath me, and eventually landed safely and made contact with Dutch farmers."

The report of F/Lt Paston-Williams continues:

"I think my hosts were anticipating trouble and it was arranged that we should move suddenly about the morning of 3rd September. It was arranged for me to meet Downie on a certain road, and we continued to walk until we were picked up by a biscuit-van and taken to ALMELO where we remained for a day and two nights with a man and his wife. We eventually arrived at HENGELO on the 5th September, where we remained until the district was overrun by the British Forces on 3rd April 1945. I remained in contact with Downie throughout.

About the beginning of March, the leader of the Underground asked me to instruct members in the use of small-arms and bazooka, which I did. I tried to get across the RHINE on two occasions, but it was not considered advisable to go. I was flown to the UK on 9th April."

These accounts reveal the horrors and dangers of baling out of a stricken bomber, the vital role played by the Resistance in rescuing aircrews, and the iron grip of the Germans in their Occupation of Holland, even at this late stage of the war, which necessitated these two survivors remaining in hiding from 12th August 1944 to 3rd April 1945.

About F/0 Gerald Hood we have, sadly, no such detailed information of his experiences. Mrs Dickinson, however, included the report of the War Crimes Section of the HQ of the British Army of the Rhine, dated 19th November 1945, on the trial of the four members of the Gestapo accused of murdering F/0 Hood and the Dutch civilian Bote van der Wal: Georg Otto Sandrock, Ludwig Schweinberger, Helmut Wiegner, and Franz Josef Hegemann. The report reads:

"F/0 Gerald Hood baled out of a Lancaster bomber in August 1944, apparently as a result of a collision with an Allied fighter in mid-air. He landed safely and went into hiding at the home of Mrs van der Wal. On the night of 13th/14th March 1945, the SD police (the German Security Police: the Gestapo) raided Mrs van der Wal's house in order to pick up her son Bote, who had been hiding from them. F/0 Hood and Bote van der Wal were both discovered.

On 21st March, Hegemann ordered Sandrock to execute F/0 Hood; no reason was given and, as far as can be ascertained, no trial took place. At about 10.0pm on the night of 21/22 March 1945, in a wood some 2 miles south-east of Almelo, the execution took place by a single shot through the back of the head.

On 24th March, a similar procedure took place and Bote van der Wal was executed. It would seem that the shots were fired in each case by Schweinberger.

The trial took place on 22nd November 1945 and the sentences were passed at Almelo on 26th November 1945. Sandrock and Schweinberger were sentenced to death by hanging, and Hegemann and Wiegner to 15 years' imprisonment.

On 4th August 1945, members of the Dutch Political Investigation Section, accompanied by one of the accused troopers, disinterred the body of F/0 Hood from his grave in the wood; he was buried in the cemetery at Almelo."

So my visit to the clearing in the wood on 4th May 2003 led to the re-telling to Jan Bovenmars of the story of the tragedy of F/0 Gerald Hood.

It also led to another of those happy coincidences that seem to be my good fortune: at breakfast in the "Jachtlust" hotel in May 2009 I met Mrs Sally Brown, the niece of Gerald Hood and his nearest surviving relative, as he was orphaned at the age of seven. She had come with her three daughters and a son-in-law on their first visit to Almelo. They had been given an official welcome by the Burgomaster and had been shown the Gestapo HQ building and also the former Almelo Prison, which was in the process of being converted to a hotel, with some of the cells preserved. On 4th May, National Commemoration Day, the ceremony in Almelo was held in the Town Cemetery, attended by the Burgomaster, a strong band, about 400 people, and the Press; "Tubantia" next day had a good colour photograph of Mrs Sally Brown laying her wreath on the grave of her murdered uncle. The family had also been taken into the Wood of Execution, with its fine sculpture of a mother grieving over her dead son and memorials to Gerald Hood and the other four vicitms. They said they were as impressed with the courage of the Dutch Resistance during the fearful Occupation, as they were with the warmth of the reception given to them as relatives of one of those executed – echoing my own feelings over the past nineteen years.

The story of Gerald Hood offered sombre echoes of hundreds of similar stories of the reprisals the Germans took on the civilian population, and on any other convenient victims, in the continuing struggle between the Dutch Resistance and the enemy occupying their country, in which the atrocity of 't Hesseler is only one example. The elements were the same: the immediate search for me, 'the missing pilot', by 500 paratroopers; when this failed, the automatic assumption that the Resistance were hiding me; the taking of hostages with clear indications of their ultimate fate, to force the Resistance to hand me over; the shooting of Jan Vonk outside Borne Town Hall to show they meant business; the initial efforts of some German authorities to assist the Burgomaster of Borne in finding an acceptable solution, but their eventual rejection of his pleas; the calculated callousness of the execution of the hostages by half-inebriated soldiers near the spot where I landed and in front of their families and friends; thus emphasising and publicising the ruthless nature of the measures that would always be taken by the Germans to maintain their iron grip on the Dutch people, defeated but with a handful still resisting.

The three atrocities I have recorded are just the ones that came to my knowledge through the twists of fate. For me, they underline the heroic behaviour of the Resistance in continuing the struggle by sabotaging the German war effort whenever possible, and by rescuing, hiding, and returning to Britain whatever Allied airmen and soldiers they found in German-occupied Holland, at extraordinary cost to themselves and their fellow-countrymen. Their motivation was simple: "This is the only way we can carry on the war against the Germans. The human price we pay are the casualties that all soldiers have to accept." The trial and execution after the war of a number of guilty Germans – in the case of Bote van der Wal and Gerald Hood, the hanging of Sandrock and Schweinberger; in the case of the 't Hesseler victims, the similar fate of Knop, Knoop and Hadler – were as nothing when set against the starving, deporting, torturing and killing of thousands, even hundreds of thousands, of Dutch men, women and children in the grinding five years of their government by terror.

Of course, the Dutch were not the only people to suffer under the pitiless heel of German Occupation: the Norwegians, Danes, Belgians, French, Poles, Czechs, Roumanians, Bulgarians, Yugoslavs, Greeks, Albanians, and even Italians, all suffered from the imposition of the manic Nazi belief that the Aryan Germans were the designated 'master race' of Europe – a fantasy that could be realised only through the use of unrelenting terror tactics. The small population of Holland perhaps suffered from these proportionately to the worst degree; and, certainly, it was with the plight of these kindly people that I was fated to have the closest acquaintance.

My 2004 visit to Borne started on 30th April with a round of calls on various friends, ending with the Timmermans at "The Resting Hunter", where Hennie and I admired the new practice golf nets, the putting green, and the bowling lawn, all of which would bring more customers to the restaurant.

After dinner at "Jachtlust" with Hennie, Joke and Judith, we were joined by Adrie Roding, aviation enthusiast and contributor to the Twente Air Base Museum. He gave us the news that the Airfield was being closed down as a military base and, with it, the Museum, the contents of which were to be transferred to the RNLAF Museum at Soesterbeek. As Adrie owned about a third of the exhibits at Twente, he had complained bitterly about the closure of the museum, which he felt should be kept open for local people and visitors. As a result, he had been banned from entering it! He now warned me that my relics also ran the risk of going to Soesterbeek unless I took prompt action. I therefore wrote to General Dick Berlijn, explaining the situation and asking for his help. He contacted the Air Base, with the result that, the following March, I received a letter from Major Willem Plink, saying that he had been in touch with Hennie Noordhuis, and asking me to list all my relics and memorabilia so that they could be handed over to Hennie for display in the Borne Town Museum. This was the outcome that Hennie and I wanted, so I felt very glad that we numbered General Berlijn among our Associate Members in "16 Squadron 1939-1945".

The following morning, Hennie called for me at 9.0am and we drove about 90 miles south to the town of Venlo, close to the German border and only 25 miles from the Ruhr. Its road-bridge and rail-bridge, side-by-side over the River Maas, were of great strategic importance to the Germans in 1944 for bringing reinforcements and supplies to their troops facing the Allied front-line – and especially for their secret build-up for the Ardennes Offensive in December – consequently, they became a vital target for the Mitchell medium-bombers of 2 Group, who carried out over a dozen daylight raids on them, unfortunately without putting them out of action. After each of these raids, a PR Spitfire from 16 Squadron was briefed to photograph them for bomb-damage assessment. Because of the importance of the bridges, the Germans had surrounded them with batteries of heavy and light flak-guns and knew that, following each bombing raid, a PR aircraft would appear shortly afterwards.

From mid-October, therefore, the "Venlo bridges" were a regular target for 16 Squadron and were regarded as a dangerous sortie. The briefing officer prescribed the focal-length of the camera lens and the height of the sortie, to give the required coverage and scale of the photographs, after which the pilot was free to choose whatever approach he felt would give him the greatest chance of surprise and the shortest time over the target. As the next sortie was given to the pilot who had reached the top of the Squadron 'ladder' – he went to the bottom on his return – the random nature of this selection meant that one man might find himself going twice to Venlo, while another never went there at all. I had my turn on 29th October, when I was briefed for the bridges at both Venlo and further down the river at Roermond. I was fortunate in being told to take vertical photos with the two F24 5"-lens wing-cameras from 4,500ft. Except for a burst of light flak at Venlo, my sortie passed off without incident. On 3rd November, F/Lt Michael Horsfall's tactic was to dive down from 4000ft to take oblique photographs at high-speed from 800ft. The next day, P/0 Don Burton was turned over on his back twice by the flak over Venlo, but carried on and took his pictures successfully.

P/0 Clyde Heath was a popular good-looking, quiet, slightly shy member of 16 Squadron, who had entered it as a Sergeant-Pilot in April 1944. He had met Lucille, a beautiful Belgian girl in Brussels, and they made a handsome couple. Clyde was one of those who went twice to Venlo. The first time was on 8th November, when he took oblique photographs from so close to the bridges that splinters could be seen sticking out of the railway sleepers from a near-miss, and a dog was lifting its leg against a post on the road-bridge. Unfortunately, Clyde made no entry in the Line Book about this sortie and we don't know how he planned this daring flight. On his second trip, though, his luck deserted him and he was, tragically, shot down and killed. We were still hoping to hear that he might have been picked up by the Resistance when I took-off next morning on what was to prove my own 'one flight too many'.

Now Hennie was driving me to Venlo to find Clyde's grave in the Roman Catholic church in Hout Blerick, a suburb on the west side of the city. We had the directions of the Commonwealth War Graves Commission (CWGC) on how to get there, but we decided to have a look first at the bridges; we forgot, though, that it was a Saturday until we found ourselves jammed in with dense traffic and had to take back-streets to get out to reach the western sector.

I wasn't expecting a churchyard to compare with the beautiful lay-out of the CWGC War Cemeteries; so it came as a very pleasant surprise to find that this one was spacious and well-situated in an open area, not hemmed-in by houses. Furthermore, Clyde's grave was in a special plot, his headstone flanked by those of two Dutch soldiers on each side, and with attractive shrubs and plants giving colour and a sense of life to the surroundings. When I read the inscription on his stone, I was surprised and gladdened to see that, not only had Clyde's promotion to Flying Officer come through after his death, but he had also been awarded the DFC. His citation included:

The Military Graves in the Churchyard of the Roman Catholic Church in Hout Blerick outside Venlo; Clyde Heath's is in the middle.

The only photograph of Clyde Heath, greatly admired in 16 Squadron for his bravery and modesty, and rewarded with a posthumous DFC

Clyde Heath's headstone reads:
Flying Officer W. C. Heath, DFC,
Pilot Royal Air Force
18th November 1944
Much loved by his family…
(the rest is behind the flowers)

"Throughout a large number of photographic reconnaissance sorties over France, Belgium, Holland and Germany, Flying Officer Heath has displayed a high standard of courage, initiative and determination."

This was a richly-deserved tribute and I was very pleased to have seen Clyde's grave; I could now report in "Newsbrief" to his surviving friends and colleagues that his resting-place was no less dignified than his friend John Brodby's in Jonkerbos.

On the way back, Hennie took me to the National War and Resistance Museum at Overloon, not far from Venlo. This had been the site of one of the biggest tank battles of the war in September-October 1944, when the Allies aimed to clear the stubborn Germans from the area south and west of the River Maas in preparation for the final crossing of the Rhine.

The Museum contains a fine range of armaments and vehicles of all the combatants, including of the Allies: a Sherman tank, a Churchill, a Cromwell, a Crusader, and a 'flail' tank to explode mines; plus a German Panther, and a Russian T34; there was also a 'Bailey' bridge, a German 'Wurzburg' radar, and even a German midget submarine of the kind used to try to blow-up the road-bridge at Nijmegen after the end of 'Market Garden'.

The exhibits of the Resistance Building were devoted to the rise of the Nazis, the Occupation, the Resistance;, the Dutch Nazis, the rescue of Allied airmen, the slave workers deported to Germany, and the concentration camps, several of which were in Holland. The displays and photographs were disturbing, the sculptures were lifelike and agonised, and the total impression was gruesome, so much so that this War Museum, in fact, presented a wholly persuasive argument against War.

Next day, encouraged by this visit to Overloon, Hennie and I journeyed to Soesterbeek, not far from Amersfoort on the way to Amsterdam, to visit the RNLAF Museum, the Dutch equivalent of the RAF

The Resistance Museum at Overloon:
Symbolic Figures of the Victims of the Brutal Oppression of the Nazis

The Steadfast Defence of the Dutch Resistance

Museum at Hendon. It was no less impressive, having a fine collection of aircraft featuring all the eras through which Dutch military flying has passed. Some of those I noted were: a Henri Farman pusher-biplane of pre-1914 vintage; a 1917 Fokker DVII single-seater fighter; a de Havilland Rapide, a Dornier 3-engined flying-boat, and two Harvards, of the inter-war years; two Spitfire IXs, a Spitfire XIX, and a Dakota of WW2 vintage; and a variety of postwar aircraft, such as an American Super Sabre, two Starfighters, a Thunderjet, a Delta Dagger, a Northrop A-5, a Neptune, a Phantom, an F-13 Eagle, an F-16, a Hawker Hunter, a Mig 21 and several other Migs, and a fleet of helicopters. About half of these aircraft were parked outside, looking rather weathered compared with the pristine condition of those displayed inside. Most impressive outside was a row of three deadly-looking surface-to-air guided missiles, their noses pointed aggressively skywards, completing a collection remarkable for a small country.

A manned aircraft displayed at the RNLAF Museum at Soesterbeek: an F-104 Starfighter with wing-tip drop fuel-tanks

Unmanned guided missiles at the RNLAF Museum

We came back through Markelo, a rural area with some gentle hills crowned with woods; on one of these, in a clearing, stood the Provincial Resistance Memorial. This was a huge monument made up of three tall parallel stone slabs, six feet apart, each about eight feet long, two feet wide, and twenty feet high, with a full-size human figure carved into the front: a woman in the centre and a man on each side. The lower part of each slab was deeply inscribed with the names of the men and women who had been killed fighting with the Resistance or been tortured or starved to death in captivity. I was pleased – and saddened – to find the names of Jan Vonk, shot in Borne, and Piet van Dijk, shot in 't Hesseler – the other two hostages killed on 25th November 1944 were not connected with the Resistance. The Dutch certainly know how to honour their dead heroes with very striking and thought-provoking monuments.

The names of Jan Vonk and Piet van Dijk are inscribed on the Monument.

On 3rd May, we returned to Arnhem and met Adrian Groeneweg, OBE, one of the founder-members of the Airborne Museum on the site of the Hartenstein Hotel in Oosterbeek, the western suburb of Arnhem, which had been General Urquhart's HQ during Operation 'Market Garden'. With him was Bob Gerritsen, a well-known military historian, and Marinus Timmerman, who lived in Arnhem and was a Friend of the Airborne Museum, and had distinguished himself as a teenager on 19th November 1944 by burning his fingers on the fuselage of my crashed Spitfire. They had copies of "Focus on Arnhem" and we discussed the possibility of the Museum sponsoring its publication. Adrian had access to the names of all the military units which appeared in my aerial photographs, but Bob wanted to print from the originals of my photographs and was concerned about the business and cost of obtaining copyright. As I could not satisfy him on either of these two salient points, we seemed to have reached an impasse, but I felt we might arrive at some arrangement at a later date – a forlorn hope, as it turned out.

We then went upstairs to the Archive Room, where I looked through a wide assortment of photographs in cardboard boxes, but found only a few of the DZs and LZs that were new to me. The Museum itself was stunning in its range of exhibits, especially in the full-size set-pieces, complete with guns, vehicles and the litter of the battlefield, of the most dramatic events in the Battle of Arnhem and Oosterbeek.

At 12.30pm, we found Arie-Jan van Hees, Frans Ammerlaan, and Robert Voskuil waiting for us in the hallway, and drove off with them and Marinus Timmerman to the Berg Hotel, where we had a room to ourselves and ordered a sandwich lunch. We then went through "Focus on Arnhem" page-by-page, and I enjoyed the privilege of having three of the most distinguished Dutch military historians giving their views on almost every one of my photographs and its accompanying text. What they added was mainly the identity of the paratroopers and glider-borne forces that appeared in the photos, and the way the battle was going at the time they were taken. These were features which I was not qualified to include, nor was I particularly interested in doing so. Obviously, the best way of exploiting my work was to have a partnership working on it but, although they all expressed encouraging views, I did not come to a firm agreement with anyone; so there the manuscript remained – unpublished.

The dramatic setting near Markelo of the imposing Monument to the Resistance Members of Overijsel province who were executed by the Germans

Meeting of Minds in Arnhem on 3rd May 2004
l-r: Arie-Jan van Hees Robert Voskuil JT Frans Ammerlaan Marinus Timmerman

Arie-Jan was busy finishing-off "Green On!", his vivid account of the Dispatchers fulfilling their tasks over Arnhem; while Frans gave me a set of large-scale maps of Arnhem, showing the borders of every field and wood – of great value in my attempts to locate precisely the geographical position of each of my photographs.

4th May saw me once again in the company of Jan Bovenmars, this time driving 40 miles north-east to Emmen, whose University had received 111,000 of the Canadian aerial photographs. To avoid making the same surprise call on their Department of the Environment as Hennie and I had done at Wageningen, I had been in correspondence with them from Leeds, and they were expecting us. A large friendly lady met us, but unfortunately she spoke no English. She led us into a light, spacious room, looking like a laboratory, with projectors, viewers, stereoscopes, recorders and copiers spaced around it. She showed us to a table on which were stacked about twenty plastic boxes full of photographs connected with 'Market Garden' and left us to go through them. I made a thorough search, with Jan busily re-packing the boxes after me, and found six taken by 16 Squadron and ten other useful ones. An assistant photo-copied these for me, but I was a little put-out when I had to pay 30 euros for them, even after I'd given them a copy of "Focus on Arnhem". However, we were there for 2½ hours' so I had no real cause for complaint.

We returned to Jan's house for tea and found Ria and Anne entertaining two small African boys, refugees from the Congo. Later, at the ceremony at the Memorial, my feet gave way and I had to hang on to Jan's arm for support – he never even turned his head to look down at the intrusion! Once more the wide family gathered in the sitting-room afterwards, this time with Dirk Boomkamp present, now a delightful teenager with excellent English and still making model aeroplanes. This was a fitting ending to another busy and rewarding visit.

2005 proved different but no less interesting. My third friend and colleague in 16 Squadron who had been killed in action and buried in Holland was F/Sgt Donald Jolliffe, usually called 'Jolly'. We had always thought that he was killed near Nijmegen on 1st October 1944 when he was shot down. On 1st June 2002, however, I had received a letter from Luc Cox, a Belgian military historian who took a special interest in the air war over Northern Belgium and had read my article in "Aeroplane".

He told me that 'Jolly' had been killed at Rijkevorsel on the Antwerp-Turnhout canal. After Antwerp had fallen into Allied hands on 4th September, the Germans set up strong defences in the villages north of Antwerp so no Allied shipping could travel up the River Scheldt to the city. The British 49th Division crossed the canal on 25th September and pushed forward a few miles, occupying Rijkevorsel.

He then quoted from a book "Rijkevorsel 1940-1944" by local historian Cyriel Verbist:

"Sunday October 1st. A Spitfire was hit over the Hees by flak and came down in flames. (The Hees is a heavily-wooded area 1.5 miles north-east of Rijkevorsel, where the Germans had dug themselves in. They had anti-tank guns there and apparently also AA flak guns, most likely 37mm or 22mm.) It crashed behind the farmhouse of Jan Hendrickx at the Lacijns (a hamlet, at the time in No-Man's-Land). The pilot, Sergeant Donald Jolliffe, was killed. A British patrol was sent out to bring the body back and he was buried in the garden of Mr Karel Verdonck on the Looiweg (street). According to information received from his mother, he was on a special mission and his Spitfire was equipped with a photo-camera. The barn at the farm where the Spitfire crashed was destroyed by the impact fire."

The Media Room of the University of Emmen with boxes of aerial photographs produced for my examination

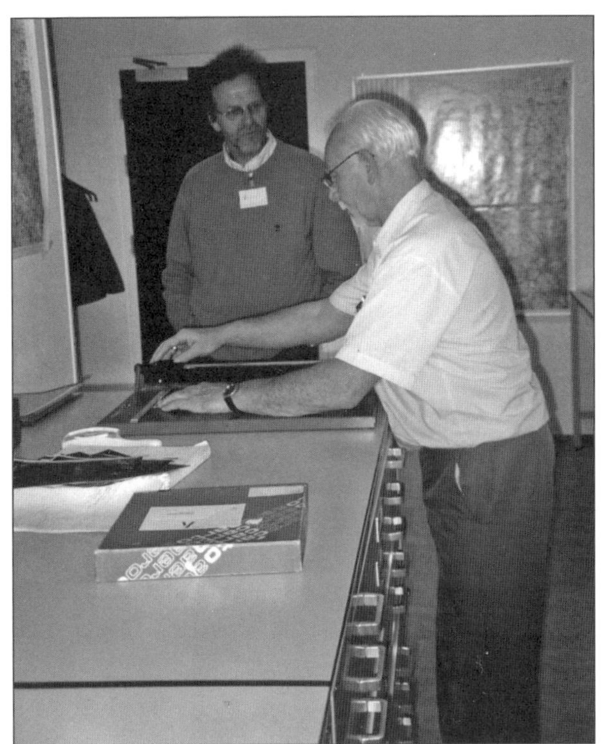

Jan Bovenmars supervises the trimming of photocopies for me.

Luc Cox went on to say that Donald was the 102nd Allied soldier to be buried at Rijkevorsel, which shows how fierce the fighting was in that sector. After the war, all the casualties were taken to CWGC burial sites; 'Jolly' was re-buried in the War Cemetery at Geel, just over the border from Holland. Luc asked for a copy of the photograph in "Aeroplane" of 'Jolly' and myself, with two Flight Mechanics, Ron Parnell and Ron Abrahams, in front of a Spitfire XI – which, of course, I was only too glad to send him in return for his invaluable information.

Luc Cox enclosed a copy of the CWGC Casualty Card with full directions on how to find Geel, so Hennie and I had no difficulty in driving there, through the unmanned border post into Belgium. We had coffee in a square in the shadow of an old church in Geel, and didn't feel we were in a town of 40,000 people. The CGWC War Cemetery was just on the edge of the town, another beautifully-designed place of peace and quiet, with a handsome little pavilion each side of the entrance, leading into what was virtually a landscaped garden. The Register of Graves gave clear directions on how to

The peaceful scene in the CWGC War Cemetery outside Geel in south-west Holland

'Jolly' Jolliffe's headstone reads:
4238969 Warrant Officer
D. W. Jolliffe
Pilot, Royal Air Force
1 October 1944 Age 22
Be Thou Faithful Unto Death And
I Will Give Thee A Crown Of Life.

Jolliffe's grave is near the white sign to the left of the brick kiosk.

JOHNSON, Private, FRED... 32. Son of Gideon and Ada Johnson, of Sherburn-in-...

JOHNSON, Lance Bombardier, JOSEPH HARRY, 1137853. 62 Anti-Tank Regt. Royal Artillery. 26th October 1944. Age 23. Son of George Thomas Henry and Alice Francis Johnson j husband of Joan Audrey Johnson, of Tooting, Surrey. III.C.12.

JOHNSTON, Captain, IAN HAMILTON, 134282. 6th Bn. King's Own Scottish Borderers. 12th September 1944. Age 29. Son of Mr. and Mrs. B. Johnston, of Kirkcaldy, Fife. B.LL. (Edin.). II.A.20.

JOLLIFFE, Warrant Officer (Pilot), DONALD WILLIAM, 1238969. 16 Sqdn. Royal Air Force Volunteer Reserve. 1st October 1944. Age 22. Son of Walter and Ruby Jolliffe, of Kinmel Bay, Denbighshire. II.C.15.

JONES, Private, CLIFFORD, 3959718. 4th Bn. Welch Regiment. 19th September 1944. Age 30. II.D.9.

JONES, Trooper, GEORGE WILLIAM, 7912738. 'A' Sqn. 22nd Dragoons, R.A.C.. 26th October 1944. Age 30. Son of George and Anne Jones, of Manchester; husband of Edith Irene Jones, of Moston, Manchester . III.B.21.

JONES, Lance Corporal, JOSEPH HARRY, 4042347. 1st Bn. The Herefordshire Regt. King's Shropshire Light Infantry. 9th September 1944. Age 23. Son of Harry and Mary Ellen Jones, of Wellington, Shropshire. II.C.9.

JONES, Private, THOMAS JOHN, 3966106. 4th Bn. Welch Regiment. 19th September 1944. Age 27. Son of Mary Jones. II.D.7.

JOPLING, Private, JOHN ROBERT, 4466182. 6th Bn. Durham Light Infantry. 10th September 1944. Age 34. Son of Ralph and Esther Jopling; husband of Hannah Jopling, of Washington Station, Co. Durham. III.A.11.

The entry for 'Jolly' Jolliffe in the register of the CWGC War Cemetery at Geel

The beautiful setting of the CWGC War Cemetery at Jonkerbos, outside Nijmegen; John Brodby's grave is on the left with the flowers.

John Brodby's headstone reads:
Flying Officer
J. R. Brodby
Pilot, Royal Air Force
20th September 1944 Age 24

find Jolly's headstone among the multitude of others on each side of the central avenue leading up to the Cross of Sacrifice. It was in the middle on the right, fronted by some verdant irises, and could have been a mirror-image of John Brodby's.

John had been buried in the beautiful CWGC cemetery at Jonkerbos, outside Nijmegen; Hennie Noordhuis had taken me there on my first visit to Arnhem and I was very impressed. We were fortunate that it was a fine Spring day, the sun shining from a blue sky dotted with light fleecy clouds. The 1600 graves were placed in a gentle curve over a rising hillside: the headstones standing out against the fresh green of the well-mown grass, with the darker greens of a small wood framing the Cross of Sacrifice in the background. A spray of white flowers grew against John's headstone. Truly, this was the most dignified and peaceful resting-place that anyone could have chosen for him.

John, aged 24, and 'Jolly', 22, are not so far away from each other, although Clyde, 21, is more distant; yet in my mind's eye it was easy to see all three together again, sitting in the Squadron trailer on an airfield, talking and laughing, lively, unworried pilots in the flower of youth. Sadly, *"They shall grow not old, as we that are left grow old."*

The Register of Graves had a remarkably vivid and concise account of the fighting to clear the River Scheldt, and I told Hennie I'd like a photocopy if we could find an office in Geel. As an archivist for the Local Authority of Borne, Hennie immediately thought of the Town Hall where, after stopping to ask the way several times, we arrived at the entrance, only to find the whole place shut up. Ever optimistic, we pressed every button on the directory by the front door, whereupon a charming lady appeared and immediately agreed to make my photocopies. Learning who we were, she refused to charge us and, instead, led us through to the back of the building and showed us the unusual Municipal War Memorial. This was a solid block of white stone, with various crests and the names of the dead on the sides; also, at intervals, black bronze hands emerged from the stone – pleading for help? for peace? for common sense? The Belgians obviously shared with the Dutch the imaginative ability to create Memorials whose poignancy and subtlety imprinted them on the mind of the beholder.

The appealing War Memorial of Geel Municipality

We took the Register back to its box in one of the pavilions, and set course to return to Borne via the "Wings of Liberation" Museum between Son and Best, in the heart of the terrain where the 101st American Airborne Division landed on 17th September 1944. The Museum was even more impressive on second viewing, and I was actually brought a cup of tea! The life-like set-piece displays were excellent, and were given their full context in a documentary film shown in one of the hangars. In gratitude to Hennie, I gave him and Joke, and their daughter Judith and her husband Mark, dinner in my hotel, always a pleasant occasion.

Next morning, we had coffee with the Timmerman family at "The Resting Hunter", then moved on to a large field a mile or so away, where a huge excavation was in progress of a Stirling bomber that had crashed here in February 1942. The bombs and machine-guns with their ammunition were still in the wreckage 40 feet under the ground, as were the bodies of four of the crew. The site was therefore being excavated very carefully by the Dutch Ministry of Defence at a cost of over £300,000. Security was very tight, and a high wire fence surrounded the whole area, with large bulldozers and cranes visible above the portakabins of the contractor's men. An open space had been left in front of the entrance and here, on long tables, were displayed many broken, and to me unrecognisable, artefacts from the wreckage; on the ground were mud-covered engines, bent propellers, and a huge wheel and struts from one of the Stirling's massive undercarriage legs. Milling around were the media: television camera-men and sound-recordists, radio reporters with microphones, and journalists with note-books. A little Welsh veteran from the Royal Engineers was also there, looking thoroughly confused by the surrounding mayhem.

Hennie had been invited to bring me there, and we assumed it was to enable me to talk to the media about the Stirling, the first of the RAF's four-engined bombers, but its slow speed and low service ceiling made it too vulnerable to German flak and night-fighters. I was prepared to describe the aircraft and the courage of the crew, flying to the heavily-defended Ruhr in this obsolescent machine. But not a bit of it: as soon as they recognised my presence, the newsmen bombarded me with questions about myself, such as *"What do you feel when you come here/ when you see this broken engine/ when you come*

The large-scale excavation of the Short Stirling bomber shot down on 27th August 1942, which crashed near Delden still with its bombs on board. A Memorial Service was held on 1st September 2006 for the British and New Zealand crew, who were all killed.

A very different excavation: post-holes of Iron Age dwellings revealed during the ground-levelling for a new estate

back to Borne?" No one asked me about the Stirling or the crew, one of whom had baled out, but died, and was buried along with two others in Delden. Hennie and I were disgusted; the only person I was willing to be interviewed by was Henk Bouweris, a colleague of René Schabos on "Tubantia"; and we left the scene immediately afterwards.[1]

On our way into Borne, we stopped to look at a very different kind of 'dig': this was an archaeological examination of the ground on the edge of Borne facing towards 't Hesseler, where 2650 new houses were scheduled to be built. Post-holes of late Iron Age huts had been found two feet below the surface, and the outlines of these were marked-in on a map shown to us by one of the archaeologists; pieces of black glazed pottery were also on display. Hennie and I agreed that this was much better than the Stirling 'dig'! I told him I thought that some part of this excavation should be preserved as the centre-piece of the new estate.

In the afternoon, we went to the Town Museum in Borne, where I presented the Curator with three pieces of equipment to be added to the relics and photographs already on display: my officer's peaked cap, an oxygen mask, and a small Dalton calculator – actually called a 'computor' by the manufacturer – that we used for working-out our courses, speeds, and flight-times while plotting our navigation to and from the targets. The oxygen mask held the microphone of the radio, so we had to hold it across our face on the ground if we wanted to talk to Flying Control. Also, although we didn't need to breathe oxygen until we reached 10,000ft, it was a good idea to start doing so even before taking-off, as it cleared our head and ensured we were mentally alert from the moment we started taxying out. I don't think anyone ever suffered any ill-effects from breathing oxygen, but we had a strong feeling that poor Jimmy Wallace had died from the lack of it.

As usual, on 4th May Hennie was busy, but Jan Bovenmars was willing to act as my chauffeur again, this time into Germany. Ever since my engine had blown up at 24,000 feet over Rheine on 19th November 1944, I had been fascinated by the very name of Rheine and had long wanted to see what it was like. On 4th May 2005, Jan Bovenmars satisfied this wish and, in doing so, started a sequence of events that ultimately involved Hennie and myself in the most bizarre situation that I had experienced in the fifteen years that I had been returning to Holland.

[1] See the Press report on p. 722 of "Dutch Voices"

CHAPTER 37

Return to Rheine

16 Squadron had been photographing Rheine or, more precisely, its airfield regularly, as it was said to be the base for the German jet-planes that were beginning to be a menace to the solitary PR Spitfires and Mosquitos, winging their way unarmed to probe the secrets of the Reich. They could be directed on to us by radar and, in theory, we should have been easy victims; the brilliant Me262 was 200mph faster than the Spitfire in level flight, it could climb more quickly, and it carried four 30mm cannon in the nose, which could blast the PR Spitfire out of the sky; but, provided we kept our eyes sweeping the skies in all directions, and especially beneath us, and spotted the approaching Me262, or rocket-propelled Me163, in good time, our superior manoeuvrability would enable us to turn into him too tightly for him to follow because of his much greater speed; we knew we could repeat this tactic continually until he ran out of fuel.

On the other hand, these aircraft could threaten the daylight bombers, making one or two high-speed dives onto a formation before the escorting fighters could intercept, or coming at the bombers head-on and destroying the pilots' cockpit with one long burst of fire. The only reason that the Germans failed to knock down more than a fraction of the attacking force was that there were not enough squadrons of them, and not enough of those available were serviceable because of the short life of only ten hours between overhauls of the Junkers Jumo 004 jet engines. Also, the jets were vulnerable during their take-off run and early climb, and again when coming down into the circuit and landing. By keeping almost constant patrols over the airfields from which they were known to be operating, it was possible for the slower, propeller-driven, long-range fighters of the Allies to inflict considerable losses on their jet-propelled opponents.

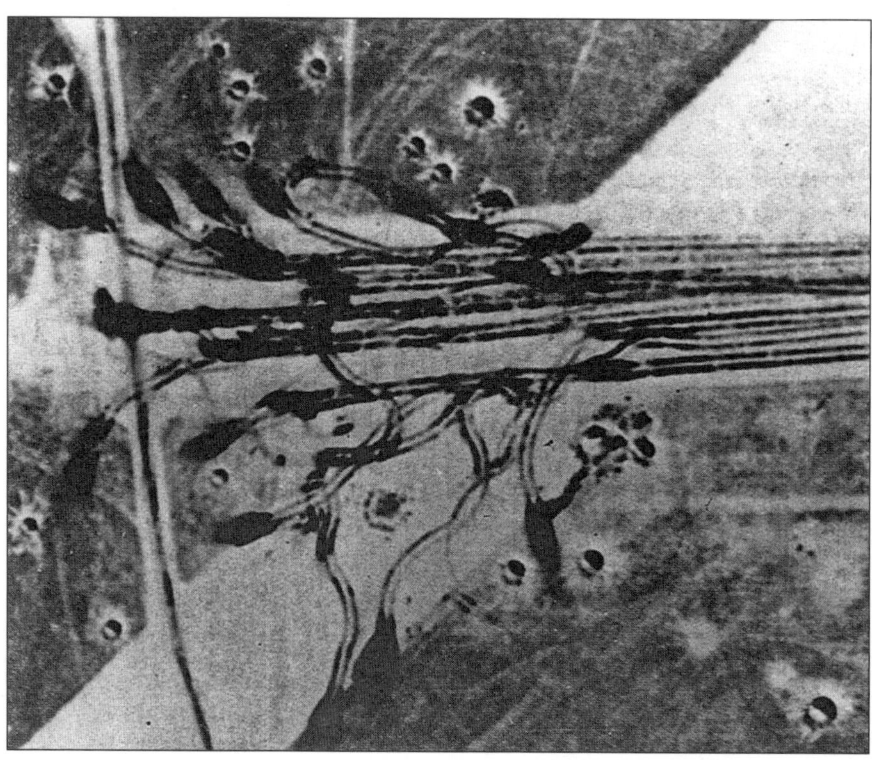

Burn-marks left on the concrete runways of Rheine by jet aircraft among the craters of Allied bombs
Photo: "34 Wing – An Unofficial Account"

On 16 Squadron, with the exception of the Arado 234 that chased me on 21st September 1944 – which we couldn't identify at the time – it was not until November that anyone else in the Squadron had the experience of being intercepted by a jet, The following reports were written in the Line Book in November and early December:

3rd November F/0 Peter Fahy: "Interception attempted by jet aircraft near Zutphen. I dived into cloud and avoided it."

12th F/Lt 'Tommy' Thompson: "Chased by jet (Me163) for 20 mins. from Antwerp area to Zwolle."

19th F/0 Michael Wetz: "Saw several aircraft in circuit at Hopsten A/F; these turned out to be Me262s (from photos)."

26th F/Sgt Bill Anderson: "Spotted probable jet job on port, but it turned away North."

3rd December F/Lt Leagh-Murray: "Crossed in at Wesel and observed 4 jets just below, flying east in a hurry."

P/0 Don Burton: "Observed 4 jets about 15,000ft flying easterly at 0955 hours."

W/0 'Willy' Willshaw: "Saw jet aircraft over Ruhr on way back."

Fortunately, we suffered no casualties from the encounters with the jets, but we heard of the losses of other units, and the Mosquito appeared particularly vulnerable; it was larger than the Spitfire, produced a bigger 'blip' on the German radar screens, was more visible in the sky, and it was less manoeuvrable. The Mosquitos of 34 Wing's 140 Squadron were being 'bounced' frequently from July 1944 onwards, so 'A' Flight was forced eventually to give up daylight PR operations and join 'B' Flight on night photography, using very bright parachute flares. Once the navigation problems had been resolved by the use of 'Rebecca' radio beacons, this became remarkably successful, as the German Army, harassed mercilessly by fighter-bombers whenever it moved in daylight, had taken to conducting most of its troop and vehicle movements at night.

Contact with the jets was being made increasingly during the autumn of 1944, with the Germans basing more and more Me262 jet fighters and fighter-bombers and Arado 234 single-seater reconnaissance-bombers on airfields in the Münster region, particularly Rheine, Hopsten, Hesepe and Achmer. From November onwards, they were photographed regularly, sometimes twice a day, and strong interest was also taken in their local transport and communication systems. Such a watch, producing photographs of the same targets taken on a daily basis over a period of time, could reveal the movements of the jet units, the arrival of new ones and departure of established ones, their numbers, and any changes in equipment or procedures. "34 Wing – an Unofficial Account" has a photograph of Rheine airfield peppered with bomb-craters, and with black scorch-marks from the jet engines on the concrete runways – tarmac melted under the heat – which gave away the presence of jet aircraft. The 'titling' had been removed, so no data about the photo is available, except that it was almost certainly taken by a 16 Squadron Spitfire. As with the sightings of jet aircraft, the Line Book reveals the extent of 16 Squadron's activity over the Münster area in November alone:

The railway station at Rheine, which supplied the jet airfields in the neighbourhood, after the devastating bombing raid of 9th March 1945.
Photo: Karl Rekers "The End of the War in our Region"

4th F/0 Peter Cribb, DFC: "Airfields Munster, Rheine."

8th F/Lt Ray Dutt, AFC: "Canal areas near Rheine.",

F/Lt Jimmy Taylor: "Junction of Dortmund and Ems Canal near Rheine."

11th P/0 Trevor Moody: "Jet airfields near Wesel and Munster."

19th F/Lt 'Bish' Bishop, DFC: "Zwolle-Rheine roads."

F/Lt Dutt: "Enschede – Rheine – Munster."

P/0 Moody: "Jet airfields in Brunswick area."

F/Lt Bishop: "Zwolle – Rheine."

S/L Tony Davis, DFC, (CO): "Airfields Munster area."

26th P/0 'Jock' West, AFC: "36inch cover Rheine area."

F/Lt Ken Snell: "Airfields in Rheine – Quakenbruck area."

28th F/0 West: "Rheine – Hanover area."

F/Lt Leagh-Murray: "Zwolle – Osnabruck – Rheine."

P/0 Moody: "Jet airfields Kassel – Halle – Baumber."

29th P/0 Moody: "Mosaic between Rheine and Enschede south."

S/L Davis: "Mapping area Munster – Hanover – Wesel."

We were by no means the only squadron busy over this region, which lay on the main bomber routes to the Ruhr and now housed these menacing jets. The Spitfires of RAF Benson and the Lightnings of the US 7th Photo Group at Mount Farm, as well as Nos 4 and 400 Squadrons in 2nd TAF, were all involved in this watch on the jet airfields.

So when, on 19th November, I was briefed to photograph "Airfields in the vicinity of Rheine" – as Michael Horsfall wrote in my log-book when I failed to return – this sortie was just one more in the on-going photographic coverage of these airfields. However, perhaps strangely, I don't remember being particularly aware of this fact. One reason was the individual nature of our flying: we didn't know, and weren't really interested in, where our colleagues were going to or had been to, especially as other sorties, besides the ones covering the Münster area, were being sent routinely to places all over Holland and Germany. So we might see another pilot collecting his parachute from the Ops trailer on the airfield, or hear an engine being started-up, or watch a Spitfire coming in to land, but we had little curiosity about where he had been or what he had photographed; it was only if the pilot had experienced trouble in one form or another or seen something unusual in the air or on the ground that he might discuss it with other people. As I've mentioned earlier, the less we knew about the purpose behind our missions, the less the Germans could learn about the likely military objectives of the Allies if we were captured. So when, on 19th November, I was briefed for this sortie, I was probably not told

The town of Rheine, with a marshalling-yard, the Dortmund-Ems Canal and a large airfield close by, was heavily bombed during the war; it was occupied by the British on 23rd March 1945; here, amid the ruins, a British soldier lends a hand to an old lady.
Photo: Karl Rekers "1945 – the End of the War in our Region"

Rheine has been largely rebuilt; these restored old houses are near the town centre.

specifically that these airfields contained jet aircraft. Certainly, although the German radar – which we could hear whining in our earphones all the time – would track my flight in the sky, I had no great apprehension that a jet would be sent up to intercept me. Even if I had felt this, by now I was becoming so accustomed to flying into Germany and out again unscathed that I was beginning to feel a sense of immunity in the cockpit of our wonderful Spitfire, that it would fly me out of any trouble I encountered. Consequently, although we scanned the dials on the instrument panel repeatedly throughout a sortie, I had never seriously considered the possibility of the failure of Rolls-Royce's remarkable Merlin.

Now, 60 years later, I was delighted when Hennie told me he had been in contact with his opposite number, the archivist in Rheine, and had arranged for Jan and me to meet him in the reception area of a shopping precinct near his office in Rheine. Hennie had told him that I wanted to find out about "the airfields round Rheine".

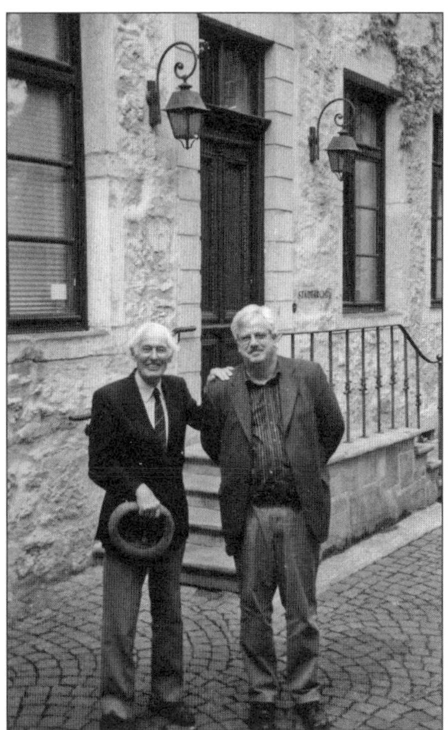

JT with Dr Thomas Giessmann, the archivist of Rheine, outside his office in May 2005

Although in 1999 Jan had driven me to Aachen, just over the border from Holland, I had little feeling then that I was back in Germany, a very hostile place in 1944. Now, driving in from 't Hesseler, on the same road that the Germans had used to invade Holland in 1940, I felt strangely aware that I was venturing into a country that had held me prisoner for six months, an experience that was still etched deeply in my memory. I leaned forward in my seat when we came to the border, but the Customs Post was deserted and we barely slowed down as we drove past. Moreover, the landscape and the houses looked exactly the same as they did in Twente, so much so that my feeling of alienation had drained away by the time we found ourselves entering Rheine.

With the exception of a few surviving traditional brick-and-timber houses, and some reconstructed high-gabled shops, the buildings, streets and squares all looked new, the people were well-dressed, and the children healthy and playful: we could still have been in Borne if we hadn't driven thirty miles east.

We found our way to our meeting-place without much trouble and a pleasant girl phoned Dr Giessmann, the archivist, to tell him of our arrival. He was a friendly, well-built, grey-haired man, whose English unfortunately was little better than my German; Jan, however, was an ever-ready interpreter. His office was situated in a stone-built 17th-century former mansion, opposite the west end of the large, mediaeval parish church. This little old corner of Rheine seemed to have survived untouched by bombs and shells and made an ideal work-place for an archivist and his staff.

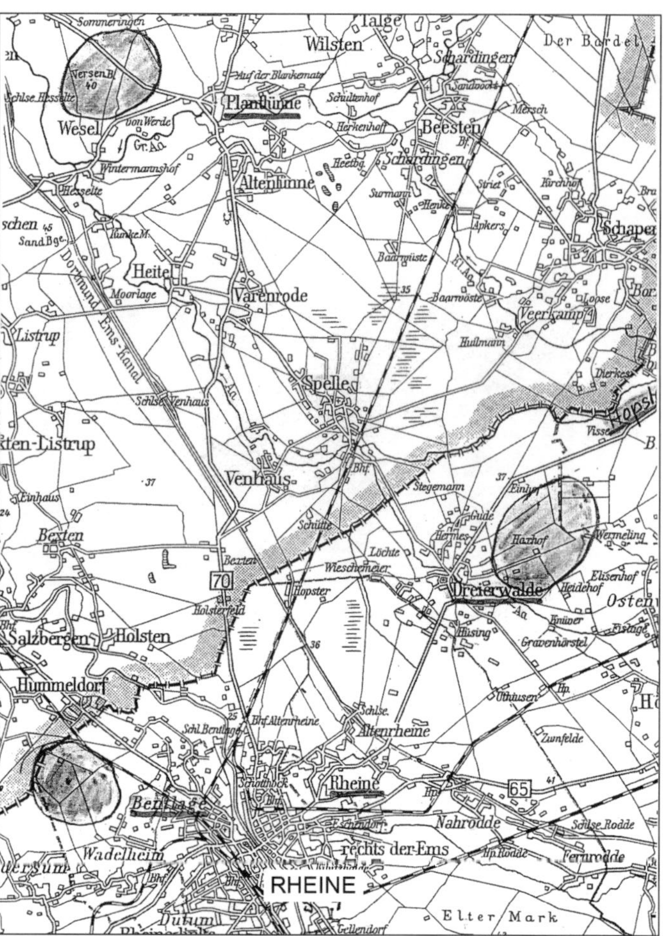

Bentlage, the airfield west of Rheine, was extended twice into Rheine 1,2, and 3; with Dreierwalde (to the east), it was one of several jet airfields near Münster. Plantlünne (to the north) was used by Me109s and Fw190s.

Dr Giessmann had maps and photographs laid out on a table and explained that there were many airfields in the area round Rheine and three in Rheine itself. He showed us photographs of the three, but I couldn't quite understand whether there were three on one airfield or three separate airfields -and I gained the impression that Dr Giessmann himself didn't really know. He made photocopies for me of several aerial photos of airfields, including the heavily-bombed one at Hopsten. He also showed us photographs of the great damage that the town of Rheine suffered as a result of its close proximity to the airfields and the usefulness of its road, rail and canal connections for supplying their fuel, armament, and spare parts, and other maintenance needs.

After a pleasant open-air lunch together, Dr Giessmann returned to his office, while Jan and I visited the massive church next door. A building on the site had been dedicated to St Dionysus in 780 AD, but this impressively tall and airy building was consecrated in 1450; we could not, however, tell how much of what we saw was mediaeval and how much might have been restored after bomb-damage in the war. It was certainly an outstanding feature of this attractive equivalent of an English market-town.

When I was back in Leeds, I wrote to Dr Giessmann and asked him if he could clarify for me the situation with regard to the single or triple airfields at Rheine. He kindly contacted Dipl.-Ing Karl Rekers, the manager of an engineering company in the nearby town of Spelle, who very generously sent me a copy of his 400-page German-language local history, "1945: the End of the War in Our Region", This was concerned more with Spelle than with Rheine, but had many illustrations of German military personnel and their activities, and of the arrival of British troops on 8th April 1945. More relevant to my interests was his listing of four airfields: Rheine-Bentlage, Hopsten, Plantlünne, and Fensterberg. Bentlage was a village just north-west of Rheine, and it now became clear that it was this airfield, with subsequent enlargements, that was the real Rheine; the other jet bases at Hopsten, Achmer, and Hesepe were quite separate, even though we might have called them loosely "the three airfields round Rheine".

One of the two factories owned by Karl Rekers in Spelle, north of Rheine; they produce all forms of paving, and the heavy machinery for making it.

I had, of course, thanked Karl Rekers warmly for his book, and this started a correspondence between us that resulted in him sending me a list of aircraft crashes in the region of Spelle, starting with a Whitley in 1941 and including many German aircraft, among them two Me262s and two Typhoons; he also gave me a wonderful invitation to come to Spelle in May 2006. He wrote:

"You will be welcome not only by me, but also by Mr Joachim Eickhoff of Bramsche, near Lingen, and Mr Gerd Schulte of Ankum, who know a lot about all the airfields near Spelle. No problem of picking you up with my car, if wanted."

This was an extraordinarily generous invitation, which seemed likely to satisfy all my curiosity about the airfields round Rheine and Münster. I quickly informed Hennie Noordhuis of this great news and he arranged with Karl Rekers that we would meet him at his works in Spelle in the morning of 2nd May.

JT with Karl Rekers in his office in May 2006; he had just retired – 50 years after starting the business.
Photo: Hennie Noordhuis

So, rather to my surprise, I found myself once again entering Germany, this time with Hennie, who was as keen as I was to discover what was in store for us. After some difficulty, we eventually drove up to a huge building, with REKERS displayed on all sides of its sky-line and international flags flying in the several car-parks. Karl was waiting for us in his spacious office; he had founded the firm 50 years ago and had just retired from managing it. He had hit on a simple everyday necessity in the rebuilding of cities after the destruction of the war – paving-slabs. From small beginnings making slabs, he had realised that towns, regions and

The grass field had been part of the wartime airfield of Plantlünne.

countries needed to make their own slabs from their own local materials. He had therefore moved into making and supplying all the machinery and equipment required for the whole process: bull-dozers to excavate the gravel and hardcore materials, concrete-mixers, pouring-machines, steel moulds, cranes, heavy-lifting vehicles, and trucks to transport the finished slabs; he also offered training in the design of pathways and in the laying of the slabs. He had clearly built up his company so successfully around this single comprehensive idea that he had broken into the international market and was exporting both his slabs and the machinery for making them all over the world, so much so that he had opened a second large works in Spelle.

Karl turned out to be a charming, silver-haired gentleman, with an excellent command of English. He told us he had been called up for the Wehrmacht, the German Army, three weeks before the war ended. He had wartime maps and photographs of the local airfields laid out on a table for us; but we were so fascinated by the tale he told us of his industrial achievements, that we spent as much time discussing what went on in his factories as identifying the airfields round Rheine.

Eventually, he warned us we would be late for our next appointment, and led us north by car for a whole hour to the small town of Bramsche; I stayed with Hennie to make sure he didn't lose sight of Karl's Mercedes guiding us. We stopped once on the way to view several grassy meadows, which Karl told us had been the site of Plantlünne airfield, a base for Fw190s and Me109s during the last stages of the war.

Joachim Eickhoff, surrounded by his collection of militaria, spends a few minutes pointing-out airfields on a map.

We arrived at a modest bungalow, with a pleasant garden decorated unexpectedly with a few aircraft relics, and were greeted by the owner, Joachim Eickhoff, a middle-aged man with fluent English and a remarkable memory for military history. He led us into the hall of the house, where we stopped, astonished at the sight of the corridor in front of us covered, on each side and on the ceiling, with swords of every shape and age: sabres, rapiers, cutlasses, scimitars, even the dress-sword of an RAF officer!

We then entered a large room, to find one wall entirely covered with rows and rows of hundreds of Iron Crosses and, below, more rows of medals of every period from other countries. The remaining walls, the floor, and various tables were festooned with uniforms, caps, helmets, rifles, pistols, bayonets, bandoliers, armour, boots, shell-cases, cartridges – you name it, Joachim had it on display!

Once again, we were distracted by our extraordinary environment, and found little time to discuss the purpose of our visit; but Joachim gave me a list of RAF losses over the area, thirteen Spitfire IXs and one XIV, and maps of 1942 date of the areas round Rheine and Münster with the airfields marked on them.

It was now one o'clock and Joachim's wife arrived with very welcome coffee and biscuits. A little later he said we must move on to our third host, who was waiting for us. We thought it would be only a short distance, but we drove for another hour into the countryside, ending up in a narrow lane that took us to a farm-house near the village of Ankum. Here we were met by Gerd Schulte, a slightly younger man with only a limited command of English, who made his living selling farming equipment, some of which lay on the ground outside his house.

He led the way to a large barn, opened a door in the side – and we stepped into a huge aircraft hangar! Inside were at least ten aeroplanes, some with their wings detached and placed alongside: four Mig-21s, an F-104 Starfighter, a Phantom, a Fiat G-50, two Macchi trainers, and a smaller Mig. Stacked all round on the floor and on shelves were a huge number of spares, including a brand-new Bristol Hercules engine and a whole clutch of propellers.

Part of the aviation Aladdin's Cave, with a Mig-21 and an F-4 Phantom

Joachim Eickhoff beside a well-preserved Mig-21

A Fiat G-52 between two other aircraft

Joachm Eickhoff, Gerd Schulte, JT and Karl Rekers
Photo: Hennie Noordhuis

Once again, all talk of wartime airfields disappeared in the presence of these modern, but no longer front-line aircraft. When I wasn't wandering around in a daze, peering above, below, behind, between these extraordinary machines, I tried to discover how two harmless-looking Germans had contrived to own a private air force! It transpired that they had bought the aircraft mainly from Poland and were renovating them to keep them in flying condition. When, in course of time, the market improved for such machines, they would sell them and make a tidy profit. That, at least, was the idea. Certainly, the condition of the aircraft and the evidence of work in progress showed that Joachim and Gerd were highly skilled mechanics and knew what they were doing – but we remained in a state of astonishment at the extent of their enterprise.

We finally said a very warm farewell to our three hosts and drove back to Borne, stopping on the way for a long-overdue lunch. We were still reeling from the way our day in Germany had turned out: nothing had gone according to plan, but our experiences were unique and quite unforgettable.

Nevertheless, I was still uncertain of the reality of "the airfields of Rheine", so I asked Michael Oakey, the Editor of "Aeroplane", who had by now become a good friend, if he knew anyone who could tell me the answer. He said he would ask his contacts in Germany and, in due course, I received their firm answer:

> Rheine itself had three runways;
>
> Rheine 1 was an additional landing-strip north-west of the runways;
>
> Rheine 2 was an additional strip next to the north-west dispersals, near Steide.

Perhaps the cameras on my last flight recorded these valuable geographical features on film but, as the film-magazines ended-up ten feet deep in Henk Timmerman's field near Bentelo, I shall never know.

CHAPTER 38

More Flights – Real and Simulated

On the way back from our visit of 3rd May 2006 to the extraordinary private air force run by Karl Rekers's two friends in Germany, Hennie Noordhuis turned to me and said:

"You'll have to get up early tomorrow morning."

"Oh, why?"

"We're going to Gilze-Rijen."

"That's a long way away, isn't it? What are we going to do there?"

"You're going flying again."

"But you're coming too, this time?"

"No, 'Gorby' wants to take you again in a Pilatus."

"Did you arrange this?"

"Well, 'Gorby' asked if you could come, so I agreed."

"Yes, but it's your turn to fly."

"No, it's for you. And the Press will be there: it will be a bit of publicity for the Air Force."

"Oh, so it's all fixed up?"

"Yes, and we've got to be there at 10.30. So we leave at 8.30!"

In fact, we reached Gilze-Rijen, not far from Breda in the south of Holland, in an hour and a half and had time for a coffee en route. We then had difficulty in finding the entrance to this huge airfield, greatly extended by the Germans, with many of their installations still in use.

My 1999 pilot and good friend Captain Jeroen ('Gorby') Kloosterman was waiting for us outside the Flight Training and Testing Centre, where he was in charge of the course in Survival Training. After exchanging greetings and the expression of my deep gratitude for this second super invitation, 'Gorby' took us into his office, gave us some more coffee, and asked me what I wanted to do in the air. With Operation 'Market Garden' still central to my researches into 16 Squadron's activities, I said I would appreciate greatly the opportunity to fly up and down 'Hell's Highway', from Eindhoven to Arnhem, taking in the bridges over the main waterways and the dropping- and landing-zones of the American 101st and 82nd Airborne Divisions; the latter would include the field where Browning landed with the 35 Horsa gliders carrying the HQ staff of the 1st Allied Airborne Corps.

'Gorby' and I went over the route together on his map, while he marked-in the salient features that I hoped to photograph along the way. He then opened the door to the camera-man and sound-recordist who would be shadowing me from now onwards. They were very pleasant professionals, who asked a few questions to establish our relations; I was quite happy to let them do what they wanted provided they didn't intrude too much into my activities.

We then drove round to the Equipment Store, where I was undressed and fully kitted into under-clothes, overalls, and boots, and fitted with a light-blue bone-dome helmet – the TV crew made sure of capturing me pulling on the white long-johns!

The next step was a medical examination. As we were going to stay quite low in a medium-performance training-plane, this should have been a formality, lasting about ten minutes. But the youngish doctor thought otherwise: maybe he'd never had such an elderly flier pass through his hands. Much

Captain 'Gorby' Kloosterman and Hennie Noordhuis, my two great benefactors, outside the Training and Testing Centre at Gilze-Rijen Airfield

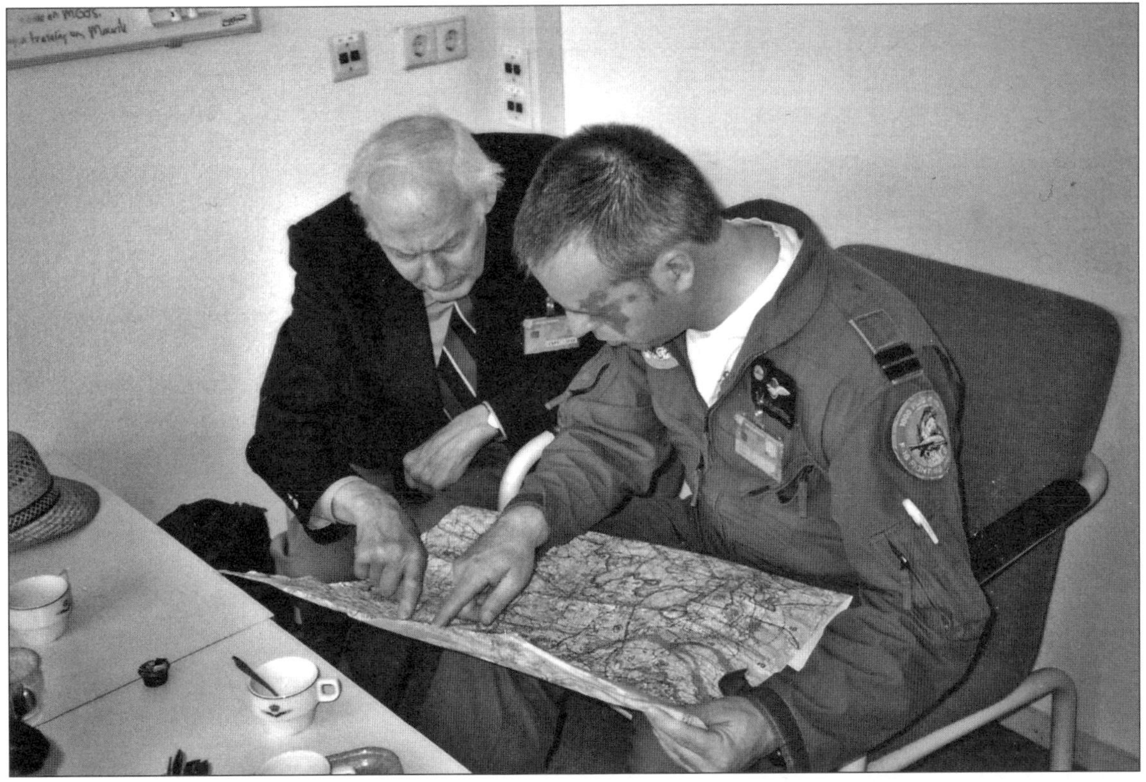

'Gorby' Kloosterman and I plot our flight along Hell's Highway from Eindhoven to Arnhem.
Photo: Hennie Noordhuis

to 'Gorby''s annoyance, who wanted to take us to lunch, the doctor gave me every imaginable test on every organ and part of my body; wires and tubes ran all over me and the proceedings lasted nearly an hour. Even the TV crew walked out after ten minutes; I wasn't bothered as long as he passed me fit to fly – which, fortunately, he did.

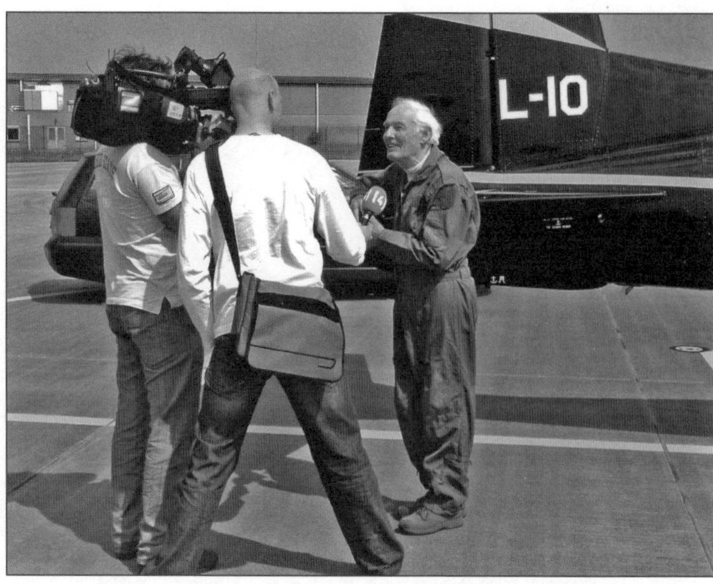

I have a pre-flight interview with the media.
Photo: 'Gorby' Kloosterman

The Dutch Air Force is more democratic than the RAF, and all ranks eat together in one large mess-hall. The food wasn't particularly wonderful, but we sat in a small side-room and I had no complaints. 'Gorby' was keen to get us out onto the airfield and, when we drove onto the wide concrete apron, I understood why: there were several cars drawn up already, the TV crew were standing-by, 'Gorby''s attractive wife Astrid and their sweet little Sophie were keeping each other amused, and the Pilatus, all-black in the current training-plane paint-scheme, was sitting silently on its tricycle undercarriage, pointing towards the runways, with its attendant mechanics.

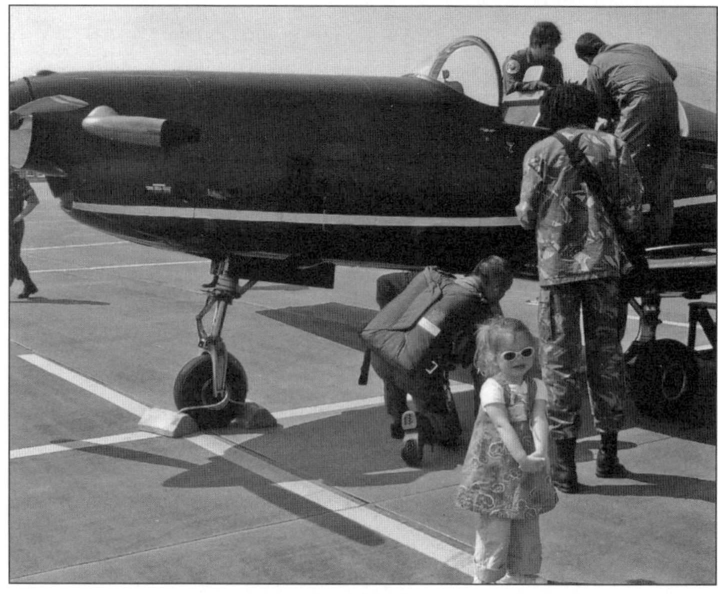

Little Sophie poses while her father checks the aircraft and the ground-crew strap me into the rear cockpit.
Photo: 'Gorby' Kloosterman

I was interviewed fully by the tail-plane – I needed to lean against something solid to keep my balance. My peripheral neuropathy had reduced my feet to little more than blocks of wood and I had become adept at finding a suitable prop whenever I had to stand still. I was asked the usual questions: What did I feel as I was about to fly over Holland again? Was this aeroplane anything like a Spitfire? What were we going to do on the flight? Duty done, they left me for more important people, quite a number of whom had gathered on the apron.

Meanwhile, 'Gorby' and the mechanics coped with the difficult task of inserting me into the rear cockpit. It wasn't all that difficult, but I had to put my feet into exactly the right places, which was made awkward by my lack of control over them. Eventually, with one man pulling me up and 'Gorby' on the other side guiding me into the cockpit, I was able to drop into the seat. I was aboard. I then had to be connected up with all the straps and wires, and shown how to operate the ejector seat – if we hit serious trouble, I had to leave the aircraft before 'Gorby'!

While 'Gorby' was settling himself into the front cockpit, Astrid brought Sophie round to enjoy the sight of the helmeted figure sitting behind her father. Eventually, 'Gorby' connected-up the inter-com and we were able to talk clearly to each other. When all was ready and the mechanics were standing-

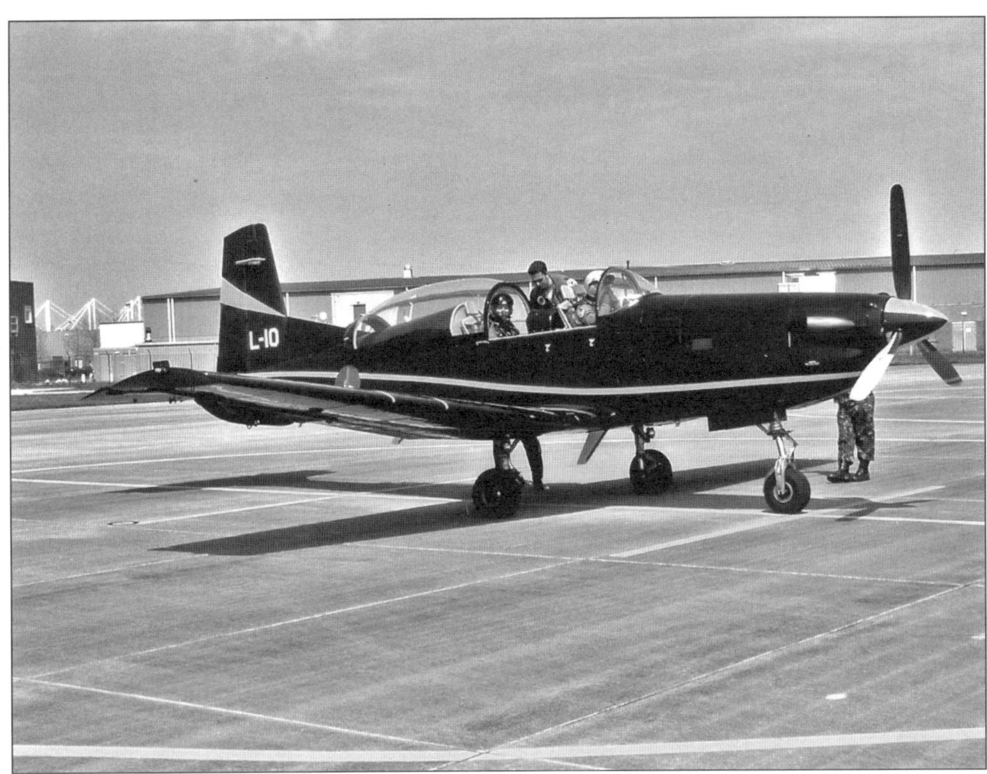

All ready for the Pilatus PC-7 to start up
Photo: 'Gorby' Kloosterman

by with fire-extinguishers, 'Gorby' pressed the right buttons and the big three-bladed propeller started to revolve, slowly gathering speed until the jet-engine was purring smoothly and steadily. This was a turbo-prop plane, which meant the jet-engine rotated a propeller; this was more economical for a trainer than if it relied for its propulsion on a torrent of air being expelled from the jet-pipe. The TV cameraman was recording all this, but he became a little impatient at the prolonged warming-up of the engine before it reached its correct operating temperatures and pressures. However, 'Gorby' was finally satisfied, waved away the chocks from in front of the wheels, released the brakes, and slowly taxied away, with much waving of hands and giving of thumbs-up between his passenger and the spectators.

The Dutch Air Force, like all of those in NATO, used English for communication, so I could keep abreast of 'Gorby''s exchanges with the Control Tower as we taxied round the long perimeter track to the end of the runway in use. He manoeuvred onto the centre-line, closed the canopy over our heads, checked with me that I was OK, and gradually opened the throttle. Almost effortlessly, within a very short distance, we were off the ground, the wheels were retracted, and we were climbing away with the greater part of the runway unused in front of us. It was a hot day and I soon noticed that the ground was covered with a light mist – not at all friendly for my photography. At the same time, the warm air was causing the aircraft to be affected by 'bumps', which threw the plane up and down to a degree not comfortable for my stomach. Meanwhile, 'Gorby' was circling the airfield at about 1500 feet, and fiddling around in the cockpit. He then turned his head and said, *"We've got an electrical problem. Can you find a switch down on your right-hand side?"* I was so strapped in that I could hardly move, and although I did my best, I couldn't see any switch down my side. When I told 'Gorby', he said he was sorry, but we'd have to go back, as the electrical fault was serious and would have to be fixed on the ground.

Actually, I didn't mind too much, as I wasn't looking forward to an hour or more of being bumped about, especially when there was little chance of being rewarded with a set of interesting photographs. Nevertheless, I felt a touch of ignominy, which I suspect was shared by 'Gorby', at having to return to terra firma so soon after leaving it in front of such an enthusiastic audience. 'Gorby' made as smooth

Part of the huge expanse of Gilze-Rijen airfield from 1500ft

'Gorby' shoots his passenger, but the flight is sadly terminated by an electrical fault.
Photo: 'Gorby' Kloosterman

a landing as at Twente seven years earlier, and we returned to the flight-line, where everyone, TV included, clustered round to find out what was wrong. The mechanics dived into the machine, but soon pronounced the fault incurable on the spot; so the whole flight had to be abandoned – a big shame from the publicity point of view. It also put paid to my last ambition with regard to 'Market Garden' – but we can't be winners all the time.

The spectators departed and I said my farewells to the TV men and to Astrid and Sophie. But 'Gorby' and Hennie had been putting their heads together and, through some wonderfully persuasive mobile-phoning, had arranged for us to visit the Royal Dutch Air Force's Historic Flight on the other side of the airfield in the early evening. Meanwhile, 'Gorby' took us to see his little kingdom in a large building which held, scattered over its floor-space, realistic reproductions of all kinds of environments found in different corners of the globe, from the arctic to the tropics, from desert to rain-forest. He explained that his course trained all kinds of personnel – aircrew, army and navy – in how to live under the most arduous conditions if they found themselves, by some mischance, fighting for survival, even on one of the many peace-keeping missions in which Dutch personnel were often engaged.

Having been duly impressed by the realism of the simulated conditions in 'Gorby's Centre, we drove round to the other side of the base and came upon a mini-airfield, with a silver Spitfire and two yellow Harvards parked on the apron, while round about were hangars and sheds and a small Control Tower.

We stopped beside a pleasant club-house, with a bar and restaurant, and a friendly man came out to welcome us. We had a much-needed cup of tea, and were then taken on a tour of the hangars, which held about 30 vintage aircraft, most of which had seen previous service with the Dutch Air Force. They included an Auster Mk III, a Beech Expediter, a Cessna Skyhawk, a de Havilland Beaver and a Tiger Moth; a Fokker Friendship, four Instructors, and a Mach-1 trainer; a North American Mitchell, six Harvards and a Yale; six Piper Cubs, a Ryan STM-2, a Stinson Sentinel, and the Supermarine Spitfire IX. Three of these were in storage and seven were being restored in the workshops, but all the rest were in airworthy condition. The Flight was financed by the Air Force, but all the members were volunteers, whether pilots, who numbered nearly fifty and had mostly both an RNLAF and commercial aviation background, or ground-crew, who included all the trades and skills that kept vintage planes flying. We saw one elderly member working on the restoration of the Tiger Moth: his proficiency was evident in the quality of his handiwork.

As the working day ended in the district, so more people turned up in the club-house. Our friend brought up a slim, keen-faced, grey-haired member and introduced him to me:

"This is your pilot, Hans Ruijgrok."

"My pilot? Am I going flying again?"

"Of course. That's why you're here!"

I looked at Hennie – but he only smiled. Well, I was born lucky.

No time was wasted on a medical or flying clothing or even a helmet. The only problem for me was that the steps on the side of a Harvard are far apart, and getting into the rear cockpit was a worse stretch than on the Pilatus. However, with one man on each side and a third to give me a good push-up on the backside, I found myself sliding into the seat. Hans handed me a pair of head-phones, tucked me in, and showed me how to get out in an emergency. My memories of flying Harvards from the back seat at Upavon, South Cerney and Feltwell from 1945-46 trickled back and I soon began to feel I was in familiar surroundings. Hans started the 650hp Pratt and Whitney engine with the winding-up of a flywheel to a high-pitched whine, and then engaged the engine, which soon responded with a few coughs, a wisp of smoke from the exhaust, and a steady rumble.

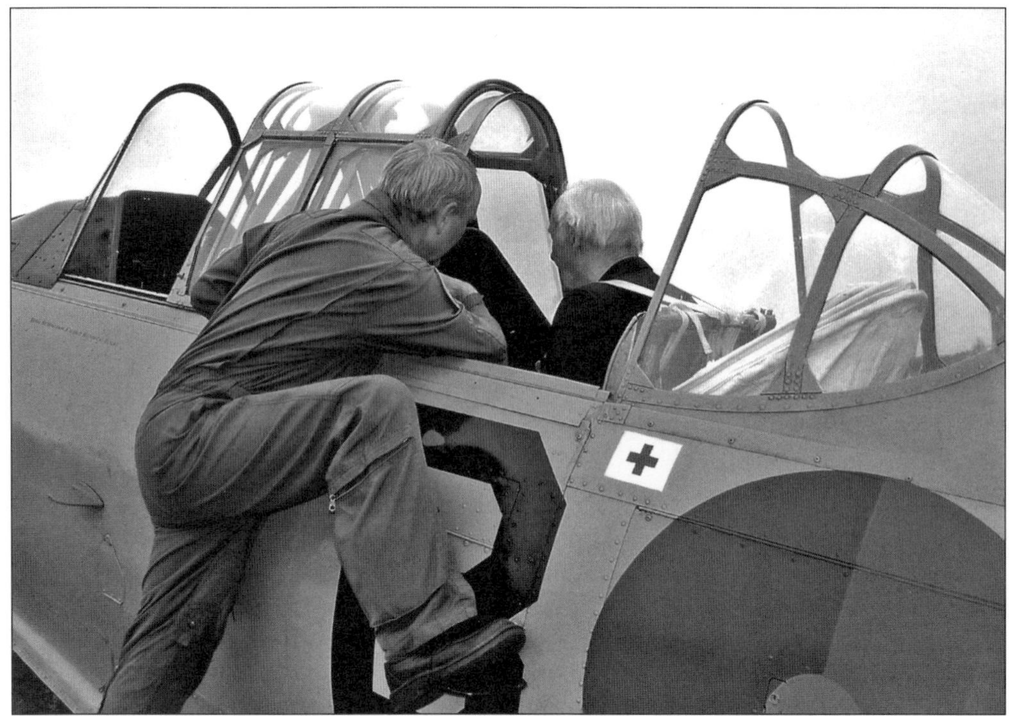

My alternative sortie with the Dutch Historic Aircraft Flight:
Hans Ruijgrok reminds me of the instruments and controls of the Harvard.
Photo: 'Gorby' Kloosterman

Hans warmed her up, then started taxying out onto the runway. I waved to 'Gorby' and Hennie, and then noticed that another Harvard, with a red engine-cowling, was following close behind us. *"Oh, yes,"* said Hans, *"he's coming with us."* As indeed he was.

We sat together in echelon on the runway, with us in the lead; then, as one, we opened the throttles and raced along till we surged smoothly into the air. Wheels up, throttle back, prop into coarser pitch, a little rattling from the canopy, and the quiet voice of Hans, *"Are you all right in the back there?"* Of course – what else could I be? Here, on a gorgeous summer evening, I was being wafted along in a beautiful aeroplane by a highly skilled pilot – Hans had been in both the Air Force and KLM – and there, opposite, was the mirror image of ourselves, flown by another veteran, with another visitor in the back seat, holding close formation, his propeller just inches behind our wing-tip – two top-gun pilots with complete confidence in each other.

Then followed half-an-hour of aerial ballet-dancing, with us leading as No 1, while No 2 changed position and flew under our tail, then appeared off our right wing, and then above and behind us. We turned steeply over the airfield, and he moved up off our right wing-tip again, but this time above us in the steep turn. Then he slid behind us, and then off our left wing- tip, while we were holding the steep bank all the time. It was exhilarating stuff. After a few minutes the prima donnas changed positions and we followed in the steps of No 2, performing the same evolutions in formation. One moment, we were tucked-in close beside him; the next, I could look up through the struts in our canopy and see him silhouetted right above us; then to the left, to the right, and below us, followed by the steep turn and the extraordinary sight of him being suspended above us as we kept position behind his lower wing-tip, followed by the reverse when we looked down on him below and slightly ahead of us, as we curved our way through the sky above Gilze-Rijen.

In truth, I saw much of these manoeuvres not directly, but through the view-finder of my camera: this was an unrepeatable experience that had to be caught on film. We returned to the lead, dropped down to 800 feet and, in close formation, roared across the airfield, the typical Harvard noise blasting out

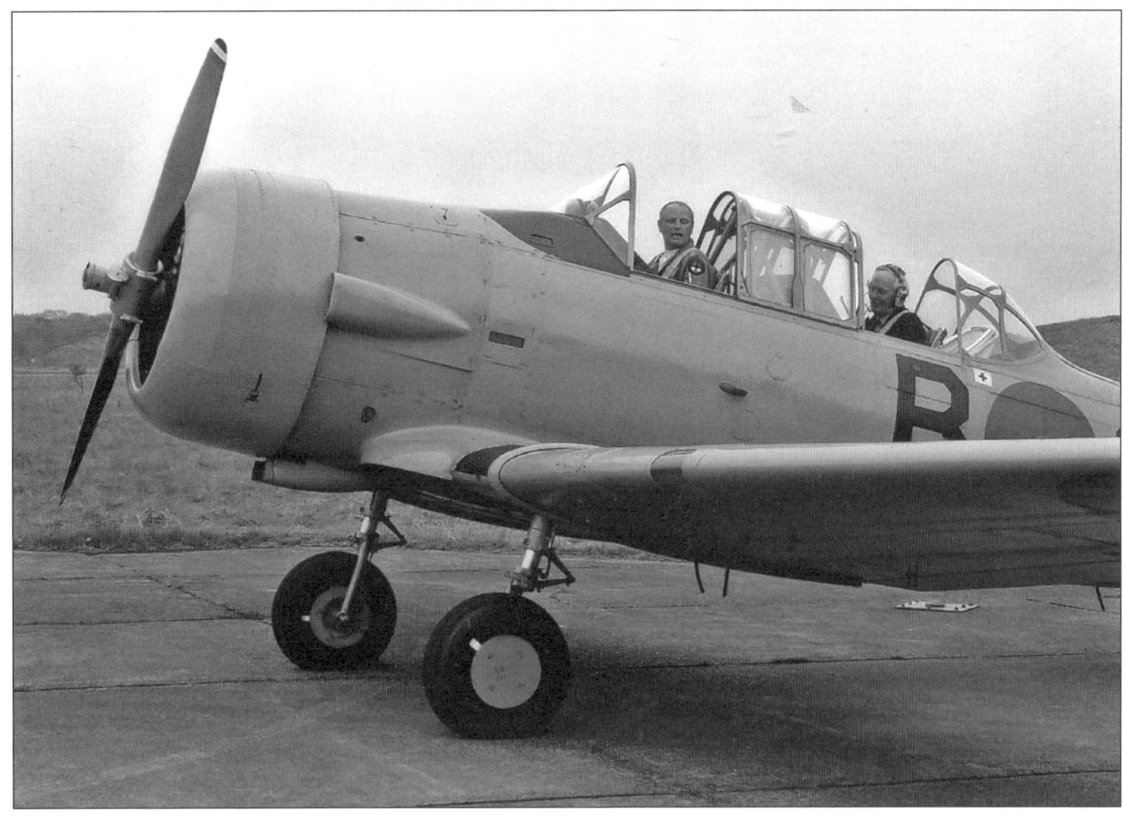

Waiting for our Number 2: the Flight has six of these rugged wartime trainers.
Photo: 'Gorby' Kloosterman

Tucked-in close: Hans Ruijgrok and another pilot practise tight formation flying.

Hans changes over from leading as number 1 to keeping station as Number 2.

Hans stays in close, even when banking in a steep turn near the airfield.

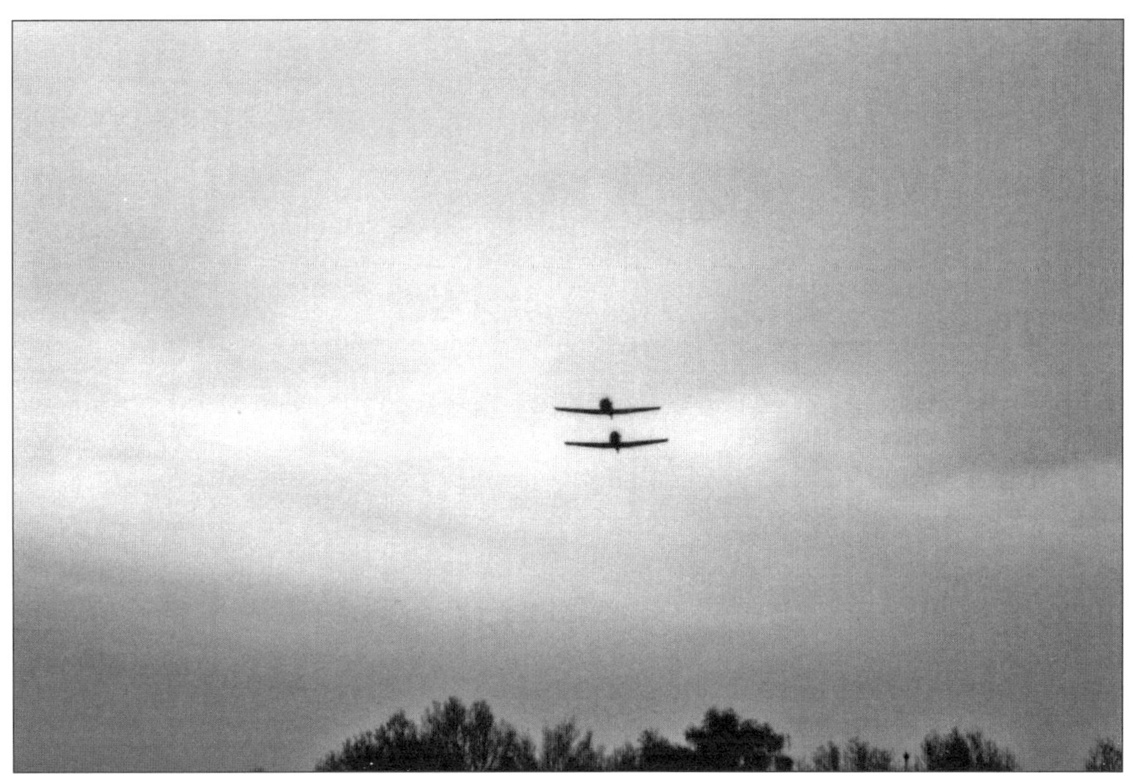

The Noisy Finale of the Aerial Ballet:
the two aircraft fly over the airfield with the typical Harvard roar.

My Two First-Class Pilots:
Hans Ruijgrok, ex-RNLAF and KLM, and Captain 'Gorby' Kloosterman, RNLAF

from the supersonic speed of the tips of two propellers, and demanding the attention of the watchers on the ground. Showing-off, maybe, but the ballerinas had to take their bow to the crescendo of the music.

No 2 peeled-off from us and we landed independently and taxied in. I congratulated Hans on his flying skill and thanked him for my glorious flight. I badly wanted the selfless Hennie to have a similar experience but, before I could propose it – whether or not Hennie would have accepted – 'Gorby' was climbing into the rear seat of No 2, as he had never flown in a Harvard, and someone else was already installed in my seat for a repeat performance with the other Harvard, after which it was too dark to consider another flight for Hennie. So my poor benefactor missed out. I gave my deep thanks to all the leading figures I could find in the club-house, and then Hennie started the long drive back to Borne after quite a day – especially for me: I may have missed seeing "Hell's Highway" from the air, but I was on "Cloud Nine" from the compensation.

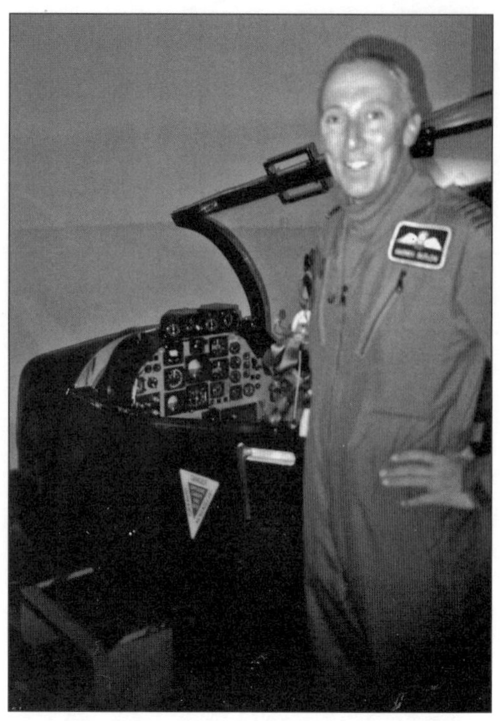

Group Captain Andy Sudlow, MBE, Station Commander of Linton, was CO of 16 Squadron 1997-2000; he had just flown the Tucano Simulator behind him.

The scene then changed to Yorkshire on 2nd August, when I paid a visit to an RAF Station which was equally interesting, but which ended with a very different result.

Group Captain (later Air Commodore) Andy Sudlow, MBE, had been CO of 16 Squadron from 1997-2000, and had famously flown a Jaguar down from Lossiemouth in Scotland in appalling weather to join our 1999 Reunion at Blackbushe Airport. He was now the Station Commander of No 1 Flying Training School at Linton-on-Ouse, which had Dishforth Airfield as a satellite landing-ground during the week, even though the Army Air Corps was in residence there with its fleet of Puma helicopters; the Cleveland Gliding Club used it at the weekends, when both the other bodies were off duty. Andy was soon to finish at Linton, so he kindly invited me to spend a day on the base and fly the Tucano Simulator.

Linton-on-Ouse was a large base built just before the war; from it flew squadrons of Whitleys, Halifaxes and Lancasters, part of the backbone of Bomber Command's relentless assault throughout the war on Germany and Occupied Europe. The valiant aircrews undoubtedly helped to shorten the war, but at an appalling cost in casualties, totalling over 55,000 for Bomber Command and 10,000 POWs. The Memorial Room at Linton is a shrine devoted to the memory of those who flew from Linton-on-Ouse.

Life was very different at Linton in 2006. Cadets did a 6-month officer-training course at Cranwell, which included 12 hours on Grob Tutors to ensure their suitability for flying; at the end of it they were directed to Fast Jets, Multi-Engines or Rotary-Wings. The Fast Jet students came to Linton and did 140 hours on the Tucano and were given their 'wings', before moving on to Advanced Training on Hawks at RAF Valley, in Anglesey. The Tucano was powered by an American Garrett turbo-prop engine of about 1100hp, which was quite a handful for a beginner. However, the training was very thorough and the drop-out rate was only about 5%; this suggested no more than one on each course of 14 students. One big surprise was to find that only 300 of the 900 personnel employed on the base were RAF regulars; the rest were civilians employed individually or engaged by civilian contractors.

After he had shown me an audio-visual presentation about the work of Linton, Andy took me to the Simulator Complex, which housed four Tucano Simulators, each in its own metal globe. I was led into

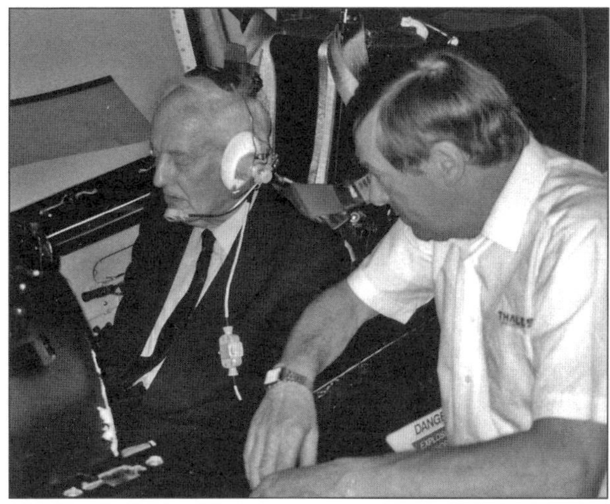

Here I am under tuition in the Simulator: I found the controls heavy to start moving, but needing swift counter-action once they began to take effect.

a fairly basic one, with no sound-effects or movements of the cockpit. The latter was extremely authentic and replicated the real Tucano exactly. An instructor explained the controls to me, and then left me to taxy out and take-off. I found the joy-stick extremely heavy to move, but once in motion, it was very sensitive. The result was I had to push hard to initiate a move, which soon became over-control, so I had to immediately pull it back again, but I pulled too hard, so that we moved too far the other way. This produced an oscillation up and down and from side to side, causing a horrid 'wallowing' which I found almost impossible to stop. As a result, my first two landings were disastrous, too high or too low, off the runway first on one side and then on the other; only after the last one could I have walked away in real life. This was humiliating, to say the least – but Andy remained very polite.

Over a drink in the bar we met the Station Chaplain and two visiting chaplains, and we all went to lunch together. They were very down-to-earth individuals and we discussed every topic of the day – except religion!

In the afternoon, I was taken over by the Linton Community Service Officer (CSO), a former Tornado navigator. He sat me down for a half-hour interview, in which he extracted my wartime career. He then took me over to the Memorial Room, which was filled with photographs, newspaper cuttings, and all manner of artefacts used in wartime bombers, some in their original boxes, and photographed

A Shorts Tucano, with its turbo-jet propeller coloured for safety, sits in a hangar of No 1 Flying Training School at Linton-on-Ouse in Yorkshire.

me with others. Many surviving aircrew returned to this, their former base, and added their stories to the Station history; while local schools paid visits on a regular basis.

It was pouring with rain outside, but we drove over to the flight-line and entered one of the hangars. It held six impressive-looking black Tucanos, with distinctive black-and-white striped propellers. I climbed up onto the wing of one and sat in the cockpit; after my time in the Simulator, it felt quite familiar: if it could be started up, I felt sure I could taxi it out and take-off – pure fantasy!

On our return to Andy's office for a cup of tea, I asked him if he thought that the workload of a Tucano wasn't too much for an embryo pilot to handle; but he said it was easier to fly than a Jaguar and gave the pilot time to attend to the various displays in the cockpit. I ended by thanking him and the CSO for giving me a stimulating and informative day. It was especially pleasant that what was probably my last visit to an RAF Station, as a former 16-Squadron pilot, should have been under the auspices of a former CO of 16 Squadron, and that it should have been to a Flying School training future generations of pilots for the RAF. A few months later, Andy left Linton-on-Ouse, where I felt he was an outstanding Station Commander, and was promoted to Air Commodore on being posted to head the Allied base on Kandahar airfield, in Afghanistan.

On 15th August, however, I received a rude shock when a neighbour phoned me to ask if I'd seen that day's "Yorkshire Post". When I looked into a copy, I was appalled to find a full-page spread under the heading:

"Former fighter pilot arrested by the Gestapo attends reunion of fellow fliers"

What followed was in the same sensational vein, such as:

"Jimmy Taylor's wartime experiences were the stuff of legend."

"... left to rot in a prisoner of war camp."

"... a joyful reunion with fellow pilots..."

"Mr Taylor's story is one of the most moving to come out of the war."

I was furious, both at the many fictions in the article and at the attempt to paint me as some sort of hero, especially when I knew it would be read by many of my friends in the Gliding Club at Dishforth. The CSO at Linton had not written the article himself, but had clearly talked to the journalist concerned and shared his notes with him. What I also objected to was that many of the visitors to Linton from the wartime Bomber Command were men who had performed courageous deeds in fearful circumstances at night, subjected to constant flak and attacks by night-fighters over Germany, and the hazards of bad weather throughout the flight and of fog over their base on their return. They were real heroes, whose stories could be told legitimately in the Press. My evasion was just an adventure compared with their nightly exposure to death and destruction. To bracket my story with theirs was to exaggerate my experiences ridiculously and to diminish theirs insultingly. I wrote to the CSO and told him so. After a very pleasant visit, this article had left me with a very sour taste in my mouth.

I was correct in my forecast: one of my friends at Dishforth commented:

"We'll have to open the hangar doors wider for you, Jimmy!"

All I could reply was that the article was *"Tosh!"*, that there were over twenty mistakes in it, and that I disowned it. It was a pity that the same Air Force in which I took so much pride should have tried to gain cheap publicity by sensationalising a story that contained tragedy for the Dutch, but no heroics by me. I complained later to Andy, but he thought I had taken the issue too seriously: it was an incident best forgotten. True – but it still rankles.

CHAPTER 39

Tying-up the Ends of 16 Squadron's Part in 'Market Garden'

Chapter 35 focussed on Arnhem and the role of 16 Squadron in sending a detachment of three pilots from Amiens-Glisy in France to RAF Northolt to provide photographic cover of Operation 'Market Garden' from 17th-23rd September 1944. It also mentioned four other pilots 'on rest' on the 34 Wing Support Unit at Northolt after completing a tour of operations on 16 Squadron, who were recruited for one sortie each by the detachment commander, Wing Commander 'Sandy' Webb, DFC, the 34 Wing Operations Officer. After the first day, the weather over UK and Holland turned increasingly hostile, with early morning mist and fog, low cloud and rain. This either delayed or cancelled aerial operations and made whatever aircraft were dispatched to Arnhem and Nijmegen easy targets for the increasingly intense German flak.

I played no part in these dramatic events but, in drawing on them in "Newsbrief" for the benefit of the wartime survivors of 16 Squadron, I found myself learning the facts and the circumstances from the memoirs of others involved, from meeting the very knowledgeable present-day historians, mainly Dutch, and from visiting the sites and the memorials. As a result, I too have become involved, to some extent, in unravelling the truth.

On 20th September, when the cloud-base was only 1200 feet, F/Lt M.B.Murphy, DFC, took-off at 0700 in 'Sandy' Webb's blue Spitfire XI PL834, equipped with an F24 14" oblique camera, but landed back at Northolt 3½ hours later without having taken any photographs because of fog over Arnhem. At 0720, P/0 John Brodby set off to cover the dropping zones near Nijmegen in PA893, but was shot down and sadly killed on this sortie. F/Lt Gerry Bastow, DFC, RCAF, took-off at 1310 to take photos of a supply-drop over Arnhem, using Webb's same PL834, but was also shot down and crash-landed next to Wolfheze, a village north-west of Arnhem. He managed to evade and was looked after by the Dutch Resistance until he joined Operation 'Pegasus', the well-organised escape across the Rhine of 140 other evaders, and returned to Northolt just over a month after being posted 'missing'. There are unusual, as well as tragic elements in both their stories.

Michael Horsfall and I knew John Brodby better than many people, as we offered him the place in our tent which had been left vacant by the loss of Jimmy Wallace on 9th September. John was quite a veteran on the Squadron, as he had joined as a Sergeant-Pilot in April, and a tour usually lasted just six or seven months. He had been commissioned, and was actually named as Flying Officer on his gravestone, although this rank had not been promulgated by 20th September. I discovered it only in May 2003 when Hennie Noordhuis and I paid a visit to his grave in the Commonwealth War Cemetery at Jonkerbos, in a beautiful setting to the east of Niijmegen.

Yet a remarkable twist was given to his story when I received a telephone call in May 2006 from Dr Nick Lambrechtsen in New Zealand; he had emigrated there from Haas, a suburb of Nijmegen, in 1958. Nick told me that, in John Brodby's final moments before crashing into the village of Haas, he had saved the lives of himself and his mother by steering his Spitfire away from their house. He was therefore a true hero, and Nick venerated him.

Unfortunately for him, the Ministry of Defence in Britain would give details of a casualty only to the immediate family; so Nick had spent the last few years contacting all the Brodbys he could trace in an effort to find John's next-of-kin and the rest of his family, to tell them of John's self-sacrifice. He had read my article in "Aeroplane" in May 2002, which mentioned John's death, so he was very pleased to speak to me, and later to write to me, as someone who knew John quite well; I sent him a photograph of John in front of the 16 Squadron Auster.

At the end of the year, Nick sent me a copy by e-mail of his summary of his researches, extracts from which I feel are worth quoting:

"My particular interest in F/0 John Robert Brodby is that he saved the lives of my late mother and me. On the day that Brodby's Spitfire had been shot, he was coming down, straight for our house in Hees. My mother and I were standing by a window at the rear of the house, on the first floor. I was nearly 10 at the time. We could see him and we thought that he could see us because, at the very last moment, he pulled up his plane sufficiently to not crash on our house. Regrettably, he did crash on the butcher's shop of Sanders, across from the St Petrus church in the village of Haas, where three people died as a result, as well as John himself. The names of the three victims were two sisters Niem and Nolda Dodemont, and Maria Satink."

"It has taken me a long time [since June 2001] to track down the hero who saved the lives of my mother and me. My mother thought that I would never succeed but, on 12th March 2002, drs Frank van der Bergh, from the Liberation Museum in Groesbeek, south-east of Nijmegen, gave me F/0 Brodby's name."

"Mr Arie-Jan van Hees suggested that I contact Mr Jimmy Taylor, who was in the same squadron as F/0 Brodby."

"Gp Capt Keith Corrans, Rhodesian Air Force and RAF (Rtd), tracked down Brodby's next of kin... a brother, Alan, ... and a sister, Anna, known as Jill. He gave me her telephone number, and I have spoken with her."

All this was very comforting for Nick, but I felt that I had to be honest with him and tell him that, in my opinion, especially on a day of low cloud, the pilot of a crashing aircraft would never notice a mother and a small boy behind a window and would have no time, even assuming he was alive and capable of moving, to steer his aircraft away from their house. Furthermore, he had killed three women in a neighbouring shop, and their families would certainly not call John a hero. Later, I spoke on the phone to John's sister Jill, and she agreed with my verdict. Nick, however, remained convinced of his facts and I saw no merit in pressing my view any further. We remained good friends, and he made several more valuable contributions to the evidence of 16 Squadron's participation in 'Market Garden', which appear later.

F/Lt Gerry Bastow's story was a happier one than John Brodby's for him personally, but equally tragic for a member of the Dutch Resistance; and it, too, had an unexpected conclusion. Arie-Jan van Hees, who had supplied my name to Nick Lambrechtsen, was equally kind to me in sending me a copy of Gerry's own account of his evasion, delivered at some time after the war to a Rotary Society in Newfoundland. I give some slightly-shortened extracts from his narrative below:

"The supply-dropping operation which I set out to photograph was laid on to try to sustain the dwindling supplies to the Arnhem bridge-head. Unfortunately, the dropping-zones, which had been previously arranged, were occupied by the Germans and the majority of the supplies fell into their hands.

Anti-aircraft fire over Arnhem was very heavy and took a severe toll of the supply aircraft. Unfortunately, they hit my Spitfire and badly damaged the engine, which seized-up shortly afterwards.

As the cloud-base was approximately 1000 feet and I had no desire to bale out, I made for a large field to the west of Arnhem and crash-landed. My first impulse was to get as far from my aircraft as possible so, using the cover of some low bushes, I ran about a quarter of a mile until I found a suitable place to hide. I knew I had been seen by the crew of an anti-aircraft battery, which was in action on the other side of the field, and that eventually they would start a search.

As soon as it was dark enough, I set out to try to get away from the area but, as I expected, sentries were posted all around the field, so I returned to my original hide-out and prepared for the inevitable search the next morning.

Why they didn't find me I'll never know – I believe they finally decided I had evaded them – for, after two days and nights in the hedge, I eventually got away during a thunder-storm on Friday night."

Gerry walked all night in a south-westerly direction but, finding himself in open country, sought help from a farm. After establishing his identity with the farmer, he was given a good breakfast, had a shave and slept for fourteen hours in a vegetable cellar. The next afternoon, the Resistance contacted him and gave him civilian clothes to wear; they took him by bicycle to another farm, where he met an American pilot, shot down the day before. They wanted to try to cross the Rhine, but learned that both banks were closely patrolled. Some days later, they were visited by a British officer in civilian clothes, who was taking a census of all the Allied personnel in hiding, with a view to organizing an escape route back to the British lines over the Rhine.

After two weeks, a German gun-crew arrived to take-over the ground-floor of the farm, forcing Gerry and his companion to leave hurriedly for another farm. Here they were joined by a second American pilot and a paratrooper and taken to a horse-drawn cart, covered with a large white canopy painted with a Red Cross. The middle-aged lady-driver told them to lie down inside and pretend to be wounded civilians from an evacuated area. In the journey of several hours they were stopped once by soldiers on the march, who looked inside but were satisfied with what they saw. At their destination they were given bicycles to ride northwards to a small farm for the night; next day they cycled on to the town of Barneveld, where they were lodged in the top of a grain elevator. From here, they watched with admiration a squadron of Typhoons attack the adjacent freight-yard. Gerry continued:

"Our host, a Mr Klooster, was in charge of the telephone and telegraph set-up in the town and used his position to good advantage, while his wife looked after the house and catered to special guests, such as ourselves. He obtained all possible information and transmitted anything of interest over an illegal radio station. His daughter, a stenographer, compiled and edited the Resistance news, and his 14-year-old son delivered the paper to the faithful.

As we'd been living on farms for the past three-and-a-half weeks, we'd been very well fed, but in the towns the situation was very different. These people were existing on two meals a day, consisting of mashed potato and apple, a piece of meat the size of a 50-cent coin per person per week, and a coloured liquid which slightly resembled coffee. Black rye bread was available on ration cards only; yet, before each meal, our host read a passage from the family Bible and gave thanks to God for the food which we were about to eat.

During our two weeks in Barneveld, we became very fond of our tireless hosts, especially Mrs Klooster, whom we called 'Mom', and we felt very low when the time came to leave.

Before setting out, we were told that the Germans were evacuating civilians from a 5-mile strip along the north bank of the Rhine, and our rendezvous was a large wood just inside the prohibited area.

We cycled there and, after hiding our bicycles in the bushes, we were led up a narrow path, which finally opened into a large clearing in the centre of the wood. As we entered, our names were checked off a list by a British paratrooper officer in full uniform. All over the clearing, paratroopers were changing into uniform from various types of civilian clothing. After searching for a short while, I found my battledress, together with the uniforms of my friends.

During the afternoon and evening, everybody pitched-in, cleaning the various weapons which the Resistance had provided and taking turns at guard duty.

We were situated about three miles from the river, and the plan decided on was to walk in single file, with an armed party at the front and rear and a Dutch farmer leading the way. Tension was high during the night and the following day – a few more stragglers were smuggled in and we formed into various units: my unit included RAF, RCAF, RAAF, and USAAF, and was assigned to the main unarmed party.

Promptly at 7.30pm we set out, walking 20 or 30 yards, stopping, lying down, up again, and so on. It took just 4 hours to cover those 3 miles. Our guide had warned us that we would possibly meet some opposition from a machine-gun position near the river and, sure enough, we were spotted just as we approached the river. Our advance guard quickly disposed of this obstacle and we moved along the bank to the crossing-point. Then, out of the darkness came rubber boats manned by Royal Engineers and, within half-an-hour, we were all safely across – 141 weary but very happy men.

Unfortunately, I was unable to return to Holland to see my friends again, but I've been in touch with them by mail. Most of them had been fairly lucky, but our kind friends in Barneveld had been caught by the Gestapo. Mr Klooster, after three months in hiding, was finally caught and shot the day before northern Holland was liberated. His wife and children had been placed in a concentration camp, from which they were released in time to bury their father.

As a member of the RAF Escaping Society, I feel I am repaying a very small part of the great debt I owe these people. This organisation was set up to assist all those people in Europe who worked, without regard for their own lives, so that victory might finally be accomplished."

Operation 'Pegasus' was planned by Brigadier Gerald Lathbury, CO of the 1st Parachute Brigade (who had escaped from hospital in Arnhem), together with other Airborne officers and leaders of the local Resistance, to locate evaders in the Arnhem area, collect them together, and get them over the Rhine to safety. Through the existing telephone line to Nijmegen, available to the Resistance, Lathbury was able to communicate with the escape organisation set up by Major Airey Neave of 2nd Army HQ. Neave arranged for uniforms and weapons to be parachuted to Lathbury's group, for paratroopers of the American 101st Airborne Division to infiltrate the German lines to protect the escapers, and for assault boats of the 43rd Wessex Division to be ready on the south bank near Randwijk to ferry the men across the river. On the night of 22nd/23rd October, the polyglot group was guided to the river and ferried over in assault boats in three trips. Last to embark were ten American paratroopers, ready to give covering fire to the end – a fine finale to a great enterprise.

This was the end of Gerry's own story, but not that of his aircraft.

In May 2007, Geoffrey Teece, an amateur historian, a Friend of the Airborne Museum at Oosterbeek and an Associate Member of the Glider Pilots Regiment, telephoned me about a review of my unpublished book "Focus on Arnhem", which he had seen in a 2004 issue of the "Eagle", the magazine of the Glider Pilots Regiment. As a result, he sent me a copy of the review, by David Brook, the Editor, and with it an oblique aerial photograph of the asylum at Wolfheze, outside Arnhem, taken on the morning of 17th September 1944, with smoke rising from the results of a bombing raid by USAAF Fortresses on the suspected German barracks and flak battery. A few days later, he sent me another Wolfheze photograph, this time of Gerry Bastow's crashed Spitfire in a half burnt-out condition. He told me the photograph was taken by Niels Bech (who could no longer be traced) and came from a detailed history of Wolfheze during the war written by a local resident, Cor Janse, whose address he also kindly enclosed.

The strange thing about this photograph was that the Spitfire did not look at all blue: either the fire – caused by the original flak, or deliberately by Gerry, or by later shelling of the wrecked aircraft – had

The Asylum in Wolfheze burning after the bombing by B-17s in the early morning of 17th September 1944. Oblique photo: (confirmed by the 'titling') by W/C 'Sandy' Webb, DFC

Photo via Geoffrey Teece

F/Lt Gerry Bastow's Spitfire XI PL834 after he was shot down near Arnhem on 20th September 1944.

Photo: Niels Bech via Cor Janse

High-level photograph of the circular road in the Wolfheze Asylum, and the wreck of Gerry Bastow's Spitfire (circled) still lying where it fell, taken by a pilot of 4 PR Squadron on 15th March 1945.

Photo: Cor Janse

turned the paint incandescent white, or the aircraft had been painted pink. Yet it was definitely an ordinary Spitfire XI serving on 16 Squadron in PRU Blue camouflage paint.

I therefore wrote to Cor Janse, explaining who I was and my interest in this photograph, and giving him an outline of how Gerry Bastow came to be flying over Wolfheze on 20th September 1944, when he was shot down. I asked him if he had a clearer picture of the burnt-out plane.

Cor replied that he had copied the photograph ten years ago from the original glass plate he had borrowed from Niels Bech, and that the latter had since disappeared. He sent me more copies of aerial photographs of Wolfheze taken on 15th March 1945, showing the defensive trenches the Germans had dug against another attack, and especially one showing the white wreck of Gerry's Spitfire, still lying where it had crashed six months before.

At this point, on a sudden whim, I looked again at the entry in the 16 Squadron Operations Record Book (SORB) for 20th September 1944 and found the following, which I had clearly not read thoroughly before:

> "F/Lt G.H.Bastow, airborne at 13.10 for the DZs and LZs near Arnhem, in pink Spitfire No PL834, with 14" oblique, to take photographs, observe and report on a big drop, did not return."

Here it was stated quite clearly that on this sortie, at least, PL834 was painted pink. The question that this posed was why, when, where, and by whom was it done.

One answer was certain: although F/Lt Murphy flew the same aircraft, PL834, to Arnhem early that morning and returned at 10.30, it was not termed 'pink' in his entry in SORB, and there would not have been time, between his landing at 10.30 and Gerry's take-off at 13.10, to change its colour from blue to pink. On the other hand, it didn't fly at all the previous day, the 19th, and the paint could have been sprayed on and dried in that time; 34 WSU, based at Northolt, possessed all the facilities and mechanics for maintaining and servicing 16 Squadron's aircraft, including re-painting those that had been repaired, and Wing Commander Webb had the authority to order virtually what he liked for his special detachment at Northolt.

My opinion is that 'Sandy' Webb, as 34 Wing's Operations Officer, knew all about the six pink Spitfires, with their guns and a single oblique F24 camera, used by 16 Squadron for low-level 'dicing' sorties under low cloud. Now, over Arnhem, he saw the same conditions and recognised that the pilots would be less at risk in an aircraft camouflaged to match the clouds overhead. He therefore had 'his' aircraft, PL834, sprayed pink, and told Murphy first, and Bastow next, to use it. Unfortunately, Gerry Bastow's pink Spitfire XI proved as vulnerable to the heavy German flak over Arnhem as John Brodby's blue one did over Nijmegen, giving a tough time for Gerry and a tragic result for John.

The only other occasion, for a far less serious reason, when a blue Spitfire XI was painted pink was in 2000-2003, when Tony Smith, the then owner and pilot of the restored Spitfire XI PL965, formerly on 16 Squadron from January-September 1945, painted it pink to make it more eye-catching on the display circuit in UK and USA. His success was shown by the aircraft's appearance on the front cover and in the centre-spread of many aviation magazines. No one then realised that he was following in 'Sandy' Webb's clever foot-prints of sixty years earlier.

It was a tragedy that 'Sandy' himself should have been shot down and killed in the last week of Nazi Germany in its death-throes.

In July 2007 Cor Jansee wrote to say that he had read my "Aeroplane" article and could help me with the story of Gerry Bastow, as he had put several pages about him into his massive history of Wolfheze during the war, "Blik Omhoog!" ("Look Up!"), covering 1200 pages in three volumes, each of 400 pages. He enclosed a map of the Wolfheze area and photocopies of three aerial photographs: one was the oblique of the asylum in Wolfheze burning after a dawn raid by USAAF B-17 Fortresses on 17th September, which I could tell from the 'titling' had been taken by 'Sandy' Webb; the second was a high-level vertical made on 15th March 1945 by a pilot of 4 Squadron, showing the whole of the asylum and a white speck which Cor identified as the wreck of Gerry Bastow's Spitfire, still lying on rough ground just outside the asylum six months after the crash; and the third was a close-up of the burnt-out aircraft taken by Niels Bech, another copy of which had already been sent to me by Geoffrey Teece. A long correspondence then ensued, resulting in our agreement to meet in May 2008.

Accordingly, on 2nd May, Hennie Noordhuis drove me to Wolfheze, where we found Cor waiting for us. He was a spare, elderly man who was 10-years old at the time of the bombing and later served in the RNLAF. He told us that Wolfheze consists entirely of the asylum, except for the railway station on the line to Arnhem and a restaurant. The central area, inside a circular roadway, contains large treat-

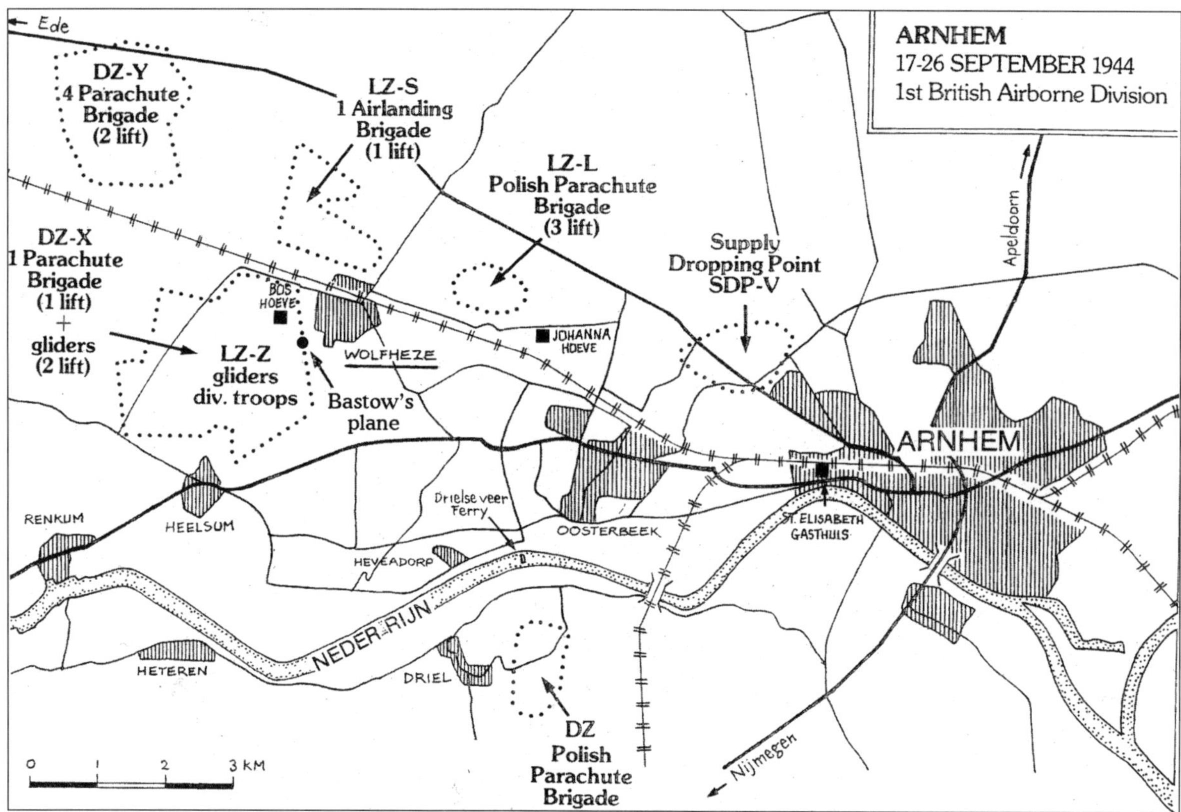

Map of Arnhem showing the western suburb of Oosterbeek, the supply dropping point that Gerry Bastow was to photograph, his crash-site between Wolfheze and LZ 'Z', and the village of Renkum near where he and 140 other evaders crossed the Rhine in Operation 'Pegasus'.

Map: Altes, Margry, Thuring and Voskuil "September 1944"

ment buildings, administrative offices and service departments; further out are rows of cottages where the patients live in groups of about six and have some public facilities; while outside the entrance but still on the estate are numerous detached houses in pleasant wooded settings inhabited by the staff.

Cor drove us slowly round this estate, where nearly all the buildings had been hit in the bombing and many destroyed. He told us unemotionally what had happened to each house and to the people who lived there. His father had been a member of the staff and Cor pointed out the house where he was born and which had been hit, but had been re-built; he no longer lives in Wolfheze. Nearby was another house, also re-built, where his uncle and two of his cousins had been killed. He then took us into the central area, where all but one of the buildings had been damaged or destroyed and needed re-building after the war.

After this extensive tour, we returned to the roadway by the cottages where Cor said the Germans had placed a large number of flak-guns – perhaps because they considered the asylum would be safe from attack. British Intelligence didn't realise that they were only parked there, and regarded them as a major threat to the gliders that were scheduled to land on the nearby fields on 17th September. The USAAF therefore agreed to bomb them before the landings took place.

It felt a little eerie to be inside this tragic area, now restored to its original use, with patients walking about freely, talking to each other and to us, just as they would have been doing on that disastrous morning of 17th September 1944.

Cor parked the car and we walked through the grounds to two mass graves under dignified Monuments: one recording the names of 50 doctors, nurses and staff who were killed in the bombing, and the other the names of the 40 patients who died with them.

The mass grave at Wolfheze of the 40 Patients killed in the bombing of the Asylum

I felt distraught at the knowledge that the asylum was known to the Allies and that the bombing had been deliberate, and I expressed my sense of shame to Cor. In fact, he replied, the American General commanding the B-17s had telephoned Major-General Urquhart, in charge of the British First Airborne Division, and asked him if he, Urquhart, would accept responsibility for any casualties caused to the inmates. Urquhart said he would, as large numbers of British gliders would be landing on LZ 'Z' in the field adjacent to the asylum, and their losses would be substantial if the flak-guns were free to shoot them down. This answer mollified me somewhat; but the whole experience of Wolfheze only added to my overall feeling that war is absolutely brutal and inhuman.

Cor brought us through the narrow strip of woodland that formed the western border of the estate and onto the rough ground, now a protected heath, between the asylum and the landing-field. It was here that Gerry Bastow had crashed on 20th September 1944, and Cor indicated the exact spot where the wreckage had lain for at least six months, surprisingly undisturbed by the Germans. It was the photo taken of it by Niels Bech, no doubt surreptitiously, that provided the clue that, although it was a Spitfire XI and normally painted PRU Blue, it had been repainted pink, almost certainly on the orders of 'Sandy' Webb.

Cor Janse stands on the spot where Gerry Bastow crash-landed his Spitfire on 20th September 1944.

We ended our visit in Cor's pleasantly roomy caravan, parked in an expansive local site as a holiday retreat, where we were warmly greeted by his wife and offered very welcome coffee and cake. Here I bought a copy of the most relevant book of Cor's three-volume history of the war in Wolfheze, all in Dutch, but with a large number of aerial photographs from British and American sources, several of them taken by 'Sandy' Webb.

Before we said our farewells, I asked Cor what he personally felt about the bombing and its tragic effects on his own family as well as on the staff and patients of the asylum. His reply was typically Dutch:

"It was part of the price we had to pay for our Liberation."

I wonder whether Gerry Bastow ever knew about the disaster that, just three days earlier, had overtaken the people in the area near where he chanced to crash. In the vicinity, nevertheless, Cor told me many Arnhem survivors were hidden until they were able to escape across the Rhine, along with Gerry, in Operation 'Pegasus'.

Also associated with 'Market Garden' was another venture of 16 Squadron, which resulted from its close relationship with the HQ of 21st Army Group: unlike the other Wings in 2nd TAF, 34 Wing belonged to no RAF Group, but worked directly for 21st Army Group, commanded by General, later Field Marshal, Bernard Montgomery. Within the Army Group were the 2nd British Army led by Lt General Sir Miles Dempsey, and the 1st Canadian Army headed by General Henry Crerar. Under Dempsey was XXX Corps, commanded by Lt General Brian Horrocks, which from 17th September had struggled to move up the 60-mile highway between Eindhoven and Arnhem to relieve the 1st British Airborne Division at Arnhem. Lt Colonel John Frost's 2nd Parachute Battalion had captured the north end of the bridge over the Rhine on 17th September, but was overwhelmed by the unexpected arrival of the tanks, guns and troops of the 9th and 10th SS Panzer Divisions, which also drove the rest of the lightly-armed Division into a gallantly defended enclave in the south-west suburb of Oosterbeek.

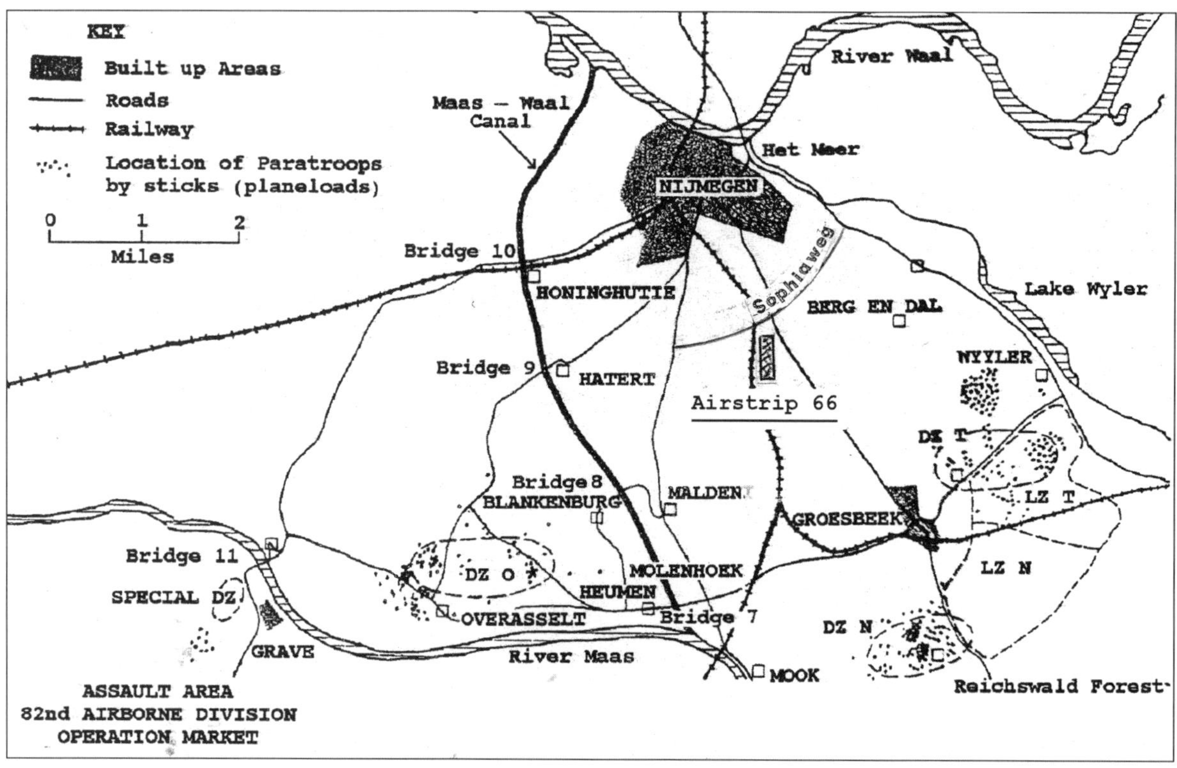

Map of Nijmegen and its environs showing LZ 'N', the Reichswald Forest, Groesbeek, Sophiaweg and Airstrip 66

Map: Chris Staerck "Allied Photo Reconnaissance of WWII"

Lt General 'Boy' Browning was the overall commander of the 1st Allied Airborne Corps, consisting of the British 1st Airborne Division and the Polish Independent Parachute Brigade at Arnhem, and two American Airborne Divisions: the 101st had landed north of Eindhoven and taken or repaired the bridges and seized control of the roadway between Eindhoven and Nijmegen, enabling the tanks of the Guards Armoured Division to reach Nijmegen on the 19th; the 82nd had arrived on fields south and east of Nijmegen and captured the great bridge over the River Maas at Grave, but had been unable to take the vital bridge over the wide River Waal in Nijmegen until they made a valiant crossing of the river on 20th September. The advance of XXX Corps then stalled, as the Germans had had time to rush reinforcements of guns and tanks covering the 10 miles of roadway leading into Arnhem and blocked any further progress.

Browning had landed, with 35 gliders (3 had been lost en route) carrying his HQ staff, on Dropping Zone 'N' (DZ 'N') used by the paratroops of the US 82nd Division near the town of Groesbeek, to the south-east of Nijmegen. Unfortunately, one of the causes of the fiasco of 'Market Garden' was the almost total failure of the Airborne radios on all the battlefields, leaving Browning in ignorance of the disastrous situation at Arnhem until it was too late for it to be restored and evacuation across the Rhine on 25/26th September was the only option available.

Meanwhile, the Germans had reacted equally quickly to the threat to their defences posed by the long columns of the 22,000 vehicles of XXX Corps bringing up the main body of troops, armour, artillery, equipment and supplies; they made unrelenting efforts to cut the 'corridor' formed 500 yards each side of the single-lane roadway by the American Airborne troops, causing frequent traffic-jams and road-blocks by their shelling and mortaring and occasional strafing attacks from the air. The road soon became known as "Hell's Highway", and despatches from Montgomery's HQ in Brussels to Browning were unlikely to reach him safely by motor-cycle; the alternative method was delivery by air.

Horrocks had 658 Squadron of Air Observation Post (AOP) Austers available for carrying messages between him and Dempsey's HQ at Bourg Leopold, 15 miles south of Eindhoven; but Brussels was too far from Nijmegen for the Austers to do the same between Montgomery and Browning.

16 Squadron, however, worked closely with Montgomery's staff and, moreover, had a long tradition of dropping messages from its Lysanders during its years in Army Cooperation Command, the predecessor of 2nd TAF; as a PR squadron, its pilots were accustomed to flying alone and being especially accurate in their navigation; the Squadron's pink Spitfire IXs carried a drop-tank, which could be loaded with the required despatches consisting, no doubt, of messages, documents, photographs and maps; the tanks could be dropped from low-level onto a pin-point target. The IX was also fast and retained its cannon and machine-guns, so it had a good chance of getting through, even if intercepted by a German fighter, as happened to at least one of them.

F/0 Mike Wetz was therefore ordered to proceed in a pink Spitfire IX from Amiens-Glisy to Evère airfield, close to 21st Army Group's HQ in Brussels, and wait for his orders. With him went Warrant Officer 'Willy' Willshaw in another Spitfire IX as a back-up pilot and aircraft. Mike made the first sortie in Spitfire IX MK362 on 20th September, and arrived at the pre-arranged dropping-point at about 1800hr, but the agreed signals had not been laid out. In the officially secret Line Book, after the heading "Message-dropping to the Airborne Troops near Nijmegen", he recorded:

> "Some trouble as Army did not show correct signals but, as it was definitely the right place and our troops were well in possession, I put it down to finger trouble and dropped the messages to them."

Mike made the next flight on the 21st at the same time with the same result:

> "Dropped messages in same place. Army still had finger in and did not put out the correct signals. Slight accurate flak near dropping-area."

Pink Spitfire IX 'V' MK915 of 16 Squadron at Melsbroek airfield in Autumn 1944, with the blue Mosquito PR34s of 140 Squadron behind
Photo: Hugh Rigby Collection

On the 22nd, he was satisfied:

> "Dropped messages, correct signs at last. Flak twice near Eindhoven, second time from airfield at Eindhoven which enemy still partially held."

At the end of these first three sorties, Mike returned to Amiens-Glisy and was awarded an immediate DFC. But, in fact, he was furious with the Army Command and berated them for not sending out the Typhoons to give fire-support to the troops on the ground. He argued that if he could fly alone to Nijmegen and return safely, surely the Typhoons could go out and strafe the Germans with bombs and rockets. As mentioned earlier, he reckoned that his criticisms had upset the Staff Officers and they had given him the DFC to keep him quiet!

'Willy' Willshaw carried out the next two message-dropping sorties from Evère, then he too returned to Amiens-Glisy; after this, the sorties became part of the Squadron's normal routine, the messages being sent first from Brussels to Amiens-Glisy. The pilots were not hand-picked, but took the sortie if they had reached the top of the Squadron 'ladder'.

The big question to which I wanted to find the answer in 2006 was: Where exactly did Mike Wetz and the subsequent pilots drop their messages? I had found no one, not even the Chief Signals Officer on Browning's staff, who had any recollection of messages being delivered by this unusual employment of pink Spitfires – and some veteran members of 16 Squadron even doubted whether we ever had any!

On 26th September, P/0 Don Burton had a particularly exciting flight, which he entered into the Line book in his own words:

> 26.9.44 Spitfire IX MK716 P/0 C.D. Burton Message dropping 1650-1810 Nijmegen
>
> "Set course Nijmegen, Weather hazy – vis. 2 miles. 5/10ths cloud at 1,500ft. Bounced by two Me109s E. of Turnhout, warning given by Kenway [ground radio controller]. Turned into the attack and opened fire as they did, but got no results, into cloud and turned west, and got thoroughly lost. Flew north until I hit the river and flew west towards Nijmegen – flak from several points up the river. Pinpointed Nijmegen and troops – dropped messages and set course base. Concentrated light flak from Veghel. Landed base 1810hrs."

Up until 27th September inclusive, the pilots used the same heading for their reports as Mike Wetz, but gave no further indication of where they dropped the tanks. Our little Welsh Adjutant, P/0 Don Williams, was even more reticent, not mentioning the first five sorties at all in his daily diary, incorporated later as his Monthly Summary in SORB, and revealing neither the task nor the name of Nijmegen in his next three entries.

I presume that the reason for Don's silence was security, and perhaps the pilots were told not to discuss their sorties in the Squadron. At Amiens-Glisy we received few newspapers and had no radios in

The top end of LZ 'N' in 2007, with the Reichswald Forest on the horizon

ex-16 Squadron Spitfire XI PL965 coming in low over Breighton Airfield, flown by Tony Smith for Channel 4 TV in 1998

our tented accommodation. I had no knowledge of why John Brodby had left our tent to go on the detachment to Northolt; and when, on 22nd September, Peter Fahy and I were sent to RAF Ford in Sussex to pick up two drop-tanks filled with beer for the airmen, it was not until long after the war that I realised that the real purpose of our mission was not to satisfy the thirst of our ground-crews, but to procure two more drop-tanks for the message-dropping sorties.

It seemed to me, because Mike Wetz referred to the troops laying out signals, made out of strips of cloth, in an agreed shape on the ground, that the pilots had dropped their tanks on a field, almost certainly at the top end of DZ 'N' near Groesbeek. By the 20th, however, the day of Mike Wetz's first drop, Browning's HQ had moved, apparently to the Primary School in Malden, a few miles south of Nijmegen. Nevertheless, it would have been easy for two or three signallers in a jeep to have driven to the top end of DZ 'N' each evening, laid out the correct cloth signals, waited for the pink Spitfire to come in low over the field, watched the tank drop, picked it up, and taken it back to be opened at their HQ.

On the 28th, however, the dropping-point changed to an airstrip, and the pilots became much more specific about it in the last three successful sorties. On the 28th, F/Lt 'Bunny' Holden reported:

> "Set course Nijmegen at 3000', going down to 500' on approaching dropping area. There were no signals out, but as everything else was O.K. I dropped the tank on the strip detailed. An air battle was going on in my vicinity, but was not molested. Landed base 1800hrs."

The next day, F/0 'Gerry' Winter made a similar entry:

> "Set course Nijmegen and ran into heavy rain halfway, so went up to 1000' on instruments. Target clear, so dropped 'jet' [jettisonable] tank on air strip and saw same collected. Returned to base. Landed 1800. No incidents."

S/L Tony Davis, the CO, flew the sortie on the 30th September. His report was laconic, but clear:

> "Flew to target at 3000', coming down to 0' below cloud. Dropped tank on strip and returned low level. No incidents."

The last sortie was flown on 1st October by P/0 Trevor Moody, who encountered heavy flak when approaching from both the south and south-west directions; he decided to return with the messages, rather than risk them falling into the hands of the Germans. So ended an unusual episode in 16 Squadron's varied history.

I was still corresponding with the very knowledgeable Nick Lambrechtsen, and in September 2006 he sent me an aerial photo of Malden, taken in 1949, which showed an airfield, B91, which might have been a simple airstrip in September 1944. This photo had been provided by Jaap Been, a resident of Malden; it raised the question whether this was the airstrip mentioned by the 16 Squadron pilots in the last three message-dropping reports.

Nick had kindly sent me Jaap Been's address, so in May 2007 Hennie Noordhuis and I were able to meet him in his pleasant house in the quiet little town of Malden. Jaap had given up much of his time to guiding veterans and their families round the battle-sites, memorials and cemeteries in and round Nijmegen, Malden and Groesbeek, and we now received the full benefit of his knowledge and experience. The memorials and cemeteries, both British, Canadian and Dutch civilian, bore witness to the fierceness of the fighting and the extent of the casualties incurred in the Allied effort to realise Montgomery's objective of crossing the Rhine at Arnhem and attacking the Ruhr from behind.

Before meeting Jaap, Hennie and I had been to see the great nine-span bridge over the River Maas at Grave, which the 504th Parachute Infantry Regiment (PIR) of the American 82nd Airborne Division

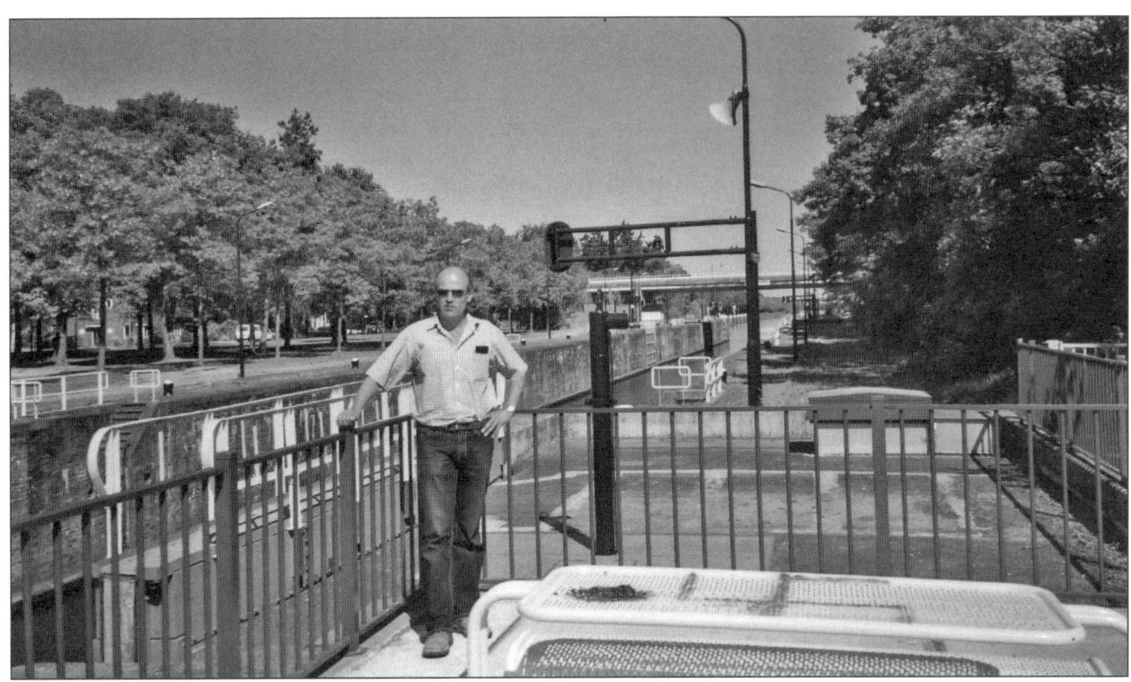

Jaap Been standing at the side of the Heumen Lock on the Maas-Waal Canal

The Nijmegen road-bridge over the River Waal, forms the background to the houses devastated in the fighting.

Photo: Groesbeek Liberation Museum 1944.

had captured on 17th September in a classic airborne action by dropping at both ends simultaneously. Now Jaap Been took us beneath the equally impressive single-span road-bridge over the River Waal at Nijmegen, which the same 504th PIR, aided by the guns of the Guards' tanks, after a dauntless crossing in small wood-and-canvas boats against murderous fire from the opposite bank, had succeeded in capturing undamaged – but to no subsequent avail.

It was a pleasant diversion to visit, near the bridge, the beautiful little 9th-century chapel, remarkably unscathed, built by Charlemagne to complement his impressive cathedral at Aachen, which Jan Bovenmars and I had seen and admired in 1999,

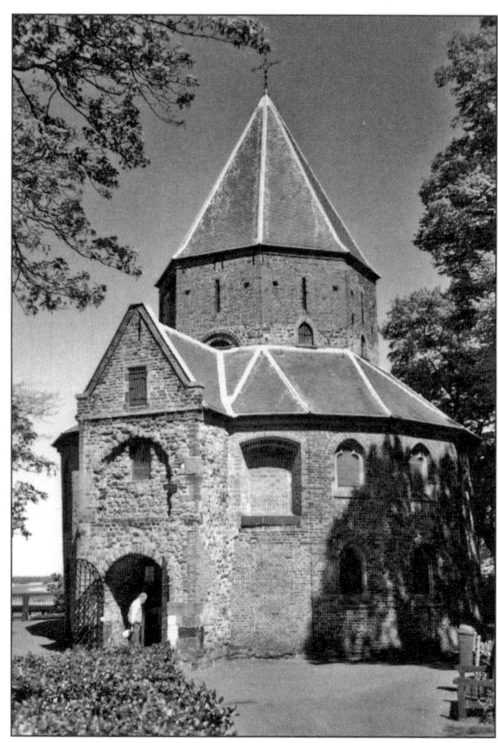

Charlemagne's 9th-century chapel near the Nijmegen road-bridge

After our tour of the battlegrounds round Groesbeek, Malden and Nijmegen, I wanted Jaap to show us Browning's probable HQ in the Primary School in Malden and the site of the nearby airstrip, which I have mentioned earlier. The first was easy: it was still there, but painted white, refurbished and converted into a Day Care Centre for the elderly residents of Malden. The adjacent convent had been demolished several years earlier. On the other hand, the airstrip had disappeared completely in the massive rebuilding of the whole district, so much so that Jaap said there was no point in stopping to try to locate any part of it. This was disappointing; but we said good-bye to Jaap with very deep appreciation of all he had been able to show and tell us in the few hours we were fortunate to spend in his company.

Here the matter of the location of the sites for 16 Squadron's message-dropping activity from 20th September – 1st October 1944 rested until it was resurrected in 2008 by my making belated,, but fairly radical discoveries from an unexpected quarter.

Before writing my 2002 article in "Aeroplane", I had come upon a light-hearted but very enlightening book in my local library called "I Bought a Star" (John Jones Publishing 1999), the personal account of his wartime service by Major Thomas Firbank, MC and Bar. In 1944, he was a G2 on Browning's Staff; this meant he was a Staff Officer at intermediate level, with a fairly wide brief of keeping Browning well-informed and being available for whatever task he directed.

In 2002, I had scanned Firbank's chapter on 'Market Garden' quickly to find out whether he made any reference to our pink Spitfires dropping messages for Browning; but, as he made no mention of any such event, I soon returned the book to the library. Now, however, in January 2008, I felt that he might have left some smaller clues, about the Primary School and the airstrip, which I had missed. I therefore borrowed the book again and subjected the chapter to a closer analysis. What I found surprised and somewhat embarrassed me, as it negatived several of the points I had made in my "Aeroplane" article. I have summarised what he wrote about Browning's HQs and the airstrips during the period covered by 'Market Garden' and added my own comments. Firbank's one weakness was that he did not always give the dates of the events he recorded; I have therefore tried to interpolate these whenever he left them unstated.

In the afternoon of 17th September, Firbank arrived in the third glider of Browning's total of 35, swooping in over the German territory of the Reichswald to land on DZ 'N', close to the small town of Groesbeek. Browning set up his first HQ in a small wood to the north of the DZ, where Firbank joined him, with his jeep and trailer and leading several others. After a night in the wood, on the 18th Browning moved his HQ two miles further north to another wood on the slopes of the Groesbeek Heights, the south-eastern end of the 300ft high ground of Berg-en-Dal (Hill-and-Dale); this was some distance from the Reichswald, from where the Germans were already launching serious attacks on the 82nd Airborne troops holding the dropping- and landing-zones.

On the 19th, Firbank wrote that Browning's men made a small airstrip on a piece of level ground, on which an Auster landed that evening. He said that this was their first physical contact with Dempsey's 2nd Army HQ.

I confirmed the accuracy of Firbank's account by consulting retired Wing Commander C.G.Jefford's wonderfully comprehensive and detailed book, "R.A.F. Squadrons" (Airlife 2001); this lists the seven Auster squadrons spotting for the artillery in NW Europe and available for any other low-level short-range purposes. He states that 662 Squadron was based at Dempsey's HQ from 16th-19th September, after which 658 Squadron replaced it from 20th-22nd. So this first Auster was probably from 662 Squadron.

On 20th September, the day of the capture of the Nijmegen road-bridge, Firbank was told by the Brigadier on the Staff that he should find "more suitable accommodation than a shrubbery" for Browning's HQ and nearer to Nijmegen. Firbank therefore set off in his jeep, together with his adaptable batman Longman (who had already "won" a Studebaker for him), and found some prosperous-looking but deserted houses in an avenue called Sophiaweg (Sophia Road), south-east of the main town. He chose three villas, and also reported a large barracks further up the road towards the west of Berg-en-Dal. That evening, an Operations Room was set up in the house selected by Browning for himself; but bullets from various directions were passing near the barracks, which seemed to be in a no-man's-land between the Americans on the hill and the Germans attacking from the east.

This was a far cry from the Primary School at Malden, which I had hitherto considered was Browning's HQ from 19th September onwards. This is not to deny that, although it was some two miles further south, it might have been used as overflow accommodation when, as recorded by Firbank, more members of Browning's Staff arrived by road with Horrocks's XXX Corps. This may also have led to the story that Browning and Horrocks established their HQs in the Primary School.

Firbank's next five days were overshadowed by the news from Arnhem, culminating in the evacuation of 2,200 Airborne troops over the Rhine on the night of .the 25th, and their reception in a school in Nijmegen on the 26th. Here they slept for 24 hours. Next day, the 27th, Firbank drove the Studebaker to visit them in the school, and learned the fate of many of his friends. Two days later, the 29th, he wrote that the survivors of the 1st Airborne Division were flown home, and were "soon" followed by Corps Headquarters, which would, presumably, have included Browning. Firbank and another G2, Major Dennis Dodge, were left behind to act as liaison officers between the American 82nd and 101st Airborne Divisions and XXX Corps. They moved into the nicest house of the three vacated by Browning's HQ; they each had a jeep, and Firbank also kept the Studebaker; and at their disposal was a flight of Auster aircraft "on a good air-strip close by".

In "Squadrons of the RAF" Jefford has a very useful series of maps, on one of which he places all the wartime airfields and airstrips in north-west Europe. No 65, just south-east of Nijmegen and labelled Berg-en-Dal, is almost certainly the first air-strip described by Firbank. There were, however, a large number of airstrips and airfields situated round Nijmegen, crowding Jefford's map and distorting their true location: No 66 is placed next to the name Nijmegen, while No 64 is located south-east of No 65. I therefore chose the latter as the site of Firbank's second airstrip, close to Sophiaweg. Jefford also gives it the title of B91, and I assumed that this was when it was developed later into an operational airfield. Confirmation of this appears in an excellent photograph of it taken by a 16 Squadron pilot, Lt André

Estaria (Free French), on 16th April 1945, showing the presence of Typhoons and Dakotas. This was reproduced in a booklet of wartime aerial photographs of Holland co-edited by Robert Voskuil and sent to me by him. Robert has worked for many years at the Institute for Aerial Survey and Earth Sciences[1] in Enschede, and collected these photos in "Views of Occupied Holland" as part of an exhibition held at the Agricultural University[2] in Holland in 1980 of special interest to environmentalists. Robert's professional work has led him into also becoming a well-known military historian.

I sent these conclusions to Nick Lambrechtsen in New Zealand. He replied in December 2007 in a long letter, with maps and photographs, to show me that I had got it wrong: Jefford's No. 66 was the airstrip near Sophiaweg, whereas No. 64/B91 was 1½ miles further west and was built as a well-equipped base for aircraft taking part in Operation 'Varsity', the Rhine crossing at Wesel on 24th March 1945.

So it was No. 66 that was Firbank's "good airstrip close by", and it was from here that he took a flight in one of the Austers, flying at tree-top height to Helmond. He wrote that, on their return, as they neared Nijmegen, "a Messerschmitt 262 [jet fighter] took an interest in us. My pilot wove in and out of the roadside trees, and assured me that the German moved too fast to hit us. Nevertheless, I think my conductor was a little upset for, when the time came, he made three attempts to land, and at last finished two-thirds of the way up our ample airstrip and ran into the wood at the far end."

From this part of Firbank's story, we can see that Browning left "soon" after the departure of the Arnhem survivors on the 29th. But how long is "soon"? Trevor Moody flew the final but unsuccessful sortie on 1st October, so it would be reasonable to assume that Browning's Corps HQ did not leave before that date. But as the drops were always timed for about 6.00pm, it is likely that the HQ would not have left until the next day, the 2nd.

From Firbank's account and the pilots' Line Book entries, it should now be possible to decide where the 16 Squadron pilots dropped their message-tanks. Although Browning had moved his HQ to the wood near Berg-en-Dal on 18th September and created a small airstrip there (No.65), neither Mike Wetz, who flew his first sortie on the 20th, nor any of the later pilots up to the 28th mentioned an airstrip. The conclusion must be that they all dropped their tanks on the top end of DZ 'N'. It was only on the 28th that Holden, followed by Winter and Davis, reported dropping their tanks on a "strip" or "airstrip"; this must have been No.66, which was close to Sophiaweg. Its existence was probably known to Firbank by the 20th, but it seems to have taken the 34 Wing Intelligence Officers a week longer before they discovered that it was available as a more appropriate dropping-point than DZ 'N': it was close to Browning's HQ, had a long runway, and was sited alongside an easily identifiable railway-line.

However, it is possible that the need for security may have required that all reports should be deliberately vague or even misleading, and this may have imposed virtual silence on Don Williams until nearly the last moment. It is unfortunate that none of the pilots involved were still alive at the time of my researches to give me more specific information.

I had therefore to rely on their entries in the Line Book and SORB to discover how they carried-out their message-dropping sorties. They flew from Melsbroek to Eindhoven at 3000ft, then veered to the right to fly above the 'corridor' of the narrow roadway to Nijmegen, along which the massive convoys of XXX Corps vehicles were still crawling with frequent halts, once for 24 hours, each time that the Germans succeeded in cutting the highway.

Once the pilots had recognised the dropping-point and seen the signals laid out, they would have come down to 100ft, reduced speed to about 200mph, and flown along the length of the field or airstrip, dropping their tankful of despatches as the target passed under their wing. They would then give the engine full throttle, keeping low until they regained the 'corridor', when they would climb back to 3000ft for the 30-minute trip back to base.

[1] Now the Faculty of Geo-Information and Earth Observation

[2] Now the University of Twente

The 'corridor' offered a slightly safer approach route for the pilots than flying over German-occupied territory, the main danger coming from flak, especially when the Germans were well-established. Thus, on the 22nd, Wetz reported being fired at twice from the airfield at Eindhoven, which they still partially occupied; and, on the next two sorties, Willshaw recorded flak from a wood north of Eindhoven. Burton, as described earlier, was not only attacked by two Me109s on the 26th but, on his way back, encountered concentrated light flak over Veghel, which was inside the 'corridor'.

The actual dropping of the tank was less dangerous for the pilots: flying low and releasing the tank took no more than 15 seconds. A German flak-battery would have had to be on full alert to have heard the sound of an aircraft's engine, spotted the small pink aircraft approaching, identified it as a Spitfire, swung their guns round to aim at it, and actually loosed-off a volley of shells – all in 15 seconds. Only Wetz on his second sortie reported: "Slight inaccurate flak near the dropping-area". The firing would have come, almost certainly, from the Reichswald to the east, or further to the north-east near Wyler: from both these directions the Germans were continually trying to overwhelm the 82nd Airborne troops, gain possession of Berg-en-Dal, and shell or recapture the bridge.

A question-mark, however, is raised by the Line Book entry of Trevor Moody, an experienced pilot, on 1st October:

> "Approached target from the south-west and ran into considerable cross-fire (light A.A.) at 700'. Approached target from the south, but the A.A. was more concentrated. I was then at 100'. I was doubtful as to the origin of the A.A., so returned to base without dropping despatches."

That Trevor should have experienced flak when coming in towards Airstrip No 66 from the south over the 'corridor' is no great surprise; but that he should receive it when approaching from the south-west seems strange, as most of the ground in that direction was in Allied hands. However, Trevor used the British term "AA" rather than the more customary German word "flak", common in 2nd TAF. He expressed his doubts about its source, so this could have been his cryptic way of saying he thought he

The mansion on Sophiaweg, south of Nijmegen, which was probably General Browning's HQ from 20th September – 2nd October 1944.

had been the object of 'friendly fire' – a single low-flying aircraft carrying a drop-tank (= a bomb?) coming close to them might well have appeared suspicious to trigger-happy gunners, both British and American. In this situation, he was wise to give up trying to drop the despatches.

So ended 16 Squadron's photographic missions over the bridges and battle-fields and unusual message-dropping sorties to Browning's HQs – both valuable contributions to Operation 'Market Garden', but overlooked in the bitter recriminations at the failure of Montgomery's enterprise, and in the subsequent public admiration of the Airborne troops – British, American and Polish – for their valour and tenacity.

On 2nd May 2008, I added my personal postscript to this investigation: I persuaded Hennie Noordhuis to drive me to Malden so that I could try to check-up on Firbank's statements about Browning's HQ in Sophiaweg. Because Major Holt, in his distinguished "Battlefield Guide to Operation Market Garden" (Leo Cooper 2001) states that the Marienburg Convent was at the beginning of Sophiaweg, I had assumed that this was the convent next to the former Primary School in Malden. We therefore circled round all the streets near the School, but failed to find Sophiaweg. We then studied Nick Lambrechtsen's map more closely and found "Sophia.." just touching its northern top edge. We had to drive almost two miles towards Nijmegen before we turned right, thankfully, into Sophiaweg.

It is indeed a good-looking avenue, with detached houses in spacious grounds, but we could not find Firbank's three villas close to each other. We did however come upon a handsome mansion, with a big porch and a colonnaded window above it, which I felt would have satisfied Browning's sense of the grandiose – an opinion with which Nick agreed. We drove on further towards Berg-en-Dal, but could find nothing that resembled a barracks. However, I was satisfied with what we had achieved.

As for the airstrip used for the last three drops, we had been shown by Jaap Been in 2007 the site of what we now knew as No 66, but it was totally submerged under intensive post-war housing development, so only its position marked on the map gives evidence of its existence. Perhaps one day someone will find a photograph of it.

As a finale, we moved on through Groesbeek to the village of Breedeweg, to see the simple Memorial erected by the Dutch in 1990 to commemorate the landing of Browning with 35 of the 38 gliders containing his HQ. It consists of a big bronze plaque set in a short length of brick wall. At the top is the emblem of the Airborne Divisions: a shield bearing Pegasus, the winged horse of mythology, flanked by a plan-view of a Horsa glider on each side; beneath the inscription is a larger side-view of a Horsa. In the middle are the following lines in Dutch and English:

The British Airborne Corps Headquarters
under Gen 'Boy' Browning
landed here on 17 Sep 1944
with Horsa gliders as their winged horses
Pilgrim, let Love lend you wings when necessity calls

The British and American Airborne Divisions certainly arrived at Nijmegen and Arnhem on wings, and their coming was indeed a military necessity. But it was the need to rid Europe, and ultimately the world, of Hitler and his grotesque Nazi ideology of domination by his Germanic master-race that lay behind the advance of the self-sacrificing Allies. It was not they who showed love, but those who had lived five years under Occupation by this satanic regime who gave a loving welcome to their Liberators – as I have myself undeservedly experienced.

The Memorial erected in 1990 by the Dutch to commemorate the landing of General Browning and his HQ on LZ 'N' on 17th September 1944.

CHAPTER 40

The Rhine Crossing

Following the debacle of 'Market Garden', the priority for Montgomery was to open-up the great port of Antwerp, to enable supplies and reinforcements to be landed far closer to the front-line than the Mulberry harbours at Arromanches, 400 miles away. The task was given to the Canadian 1st Army, who endured terrible winter conditions and the stubborn resistance of the German 15th Army as they captured the island of Walcheren at the mouth of the River Scheldt and occupied both banks of the 70-mile-long river in an operation that lasted from 3rd October – 8th November and cost 18,000 casualties. The river was finally cleared of mines for the first ships to enter Antwerp on 28th November.

Hitler, meanwhile, had planned a desperate bid through the weakly-held Ardennes Forest to re-capture Brussels and Antwerp and divide the Americans from the British and Canadian armies. The offensive was launched on 16 December and caught the Americans off-guard; however, after strong initial advances, the Germans were held at Bastogne, but not pushed back to their start-line until 28th January. Again, numerous small battles were fought in freezing, muddy conditions, with 80,000 American losses and many more German ones.

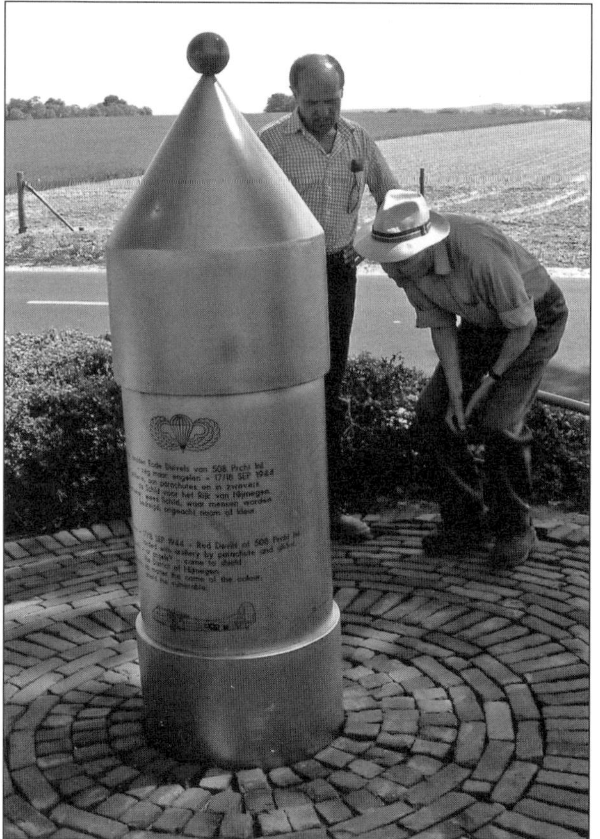

Jaap Been (l) and JT examine the Memorial, resembling an airborne canister, erected by the Dutch in 1990 to commemorate, on one side, the landing of the 508th Parachute Infantry Regiment of the 82nd Airborne Division on 17th/18th September 1944; and, on the other, the launch of Operation 'Veritable', 8th February-10th March 1945, by 300,000 British and Canadian troops to clear the Germans from the area west of the Rhine between Nijmegen and Wesel.

Thereafter, the winter passed in yet more close combat in grim conditions of mud, snow, ice and fog: the British and Canadians participated in Operation 'Veritable' to clear the Germans from Nijmegen south-east-wards between the Rhine and the Maas, starting with difficult fighting in the huge, menacing, dark Reichswald Forest; thereafter they pushed on through Cleve and Goch, eventually reaching the Rhine opposite Wesel on 10th March.

Further south, the American 1st Army, under General Hodges, experienced similar horrible conditions as they cleared the Hochwald Forest and moved on to the flooded countryside north of Aachen. Further south still, Patton's 3rd Army and Patch's 7th Army also fought their way steadily up to the Rhine. Thus, by the beginning of March, the Allies held a front-line of 250 miles, from Arnhem to Strasbourg, along the Rhine, the historic defensive border of the German Fatherland.

From early September 1944 till the end of March 1945, 16 Squadron was involved in regular photographic sorties covering the defences of the Rhine from Arnhem to Venlo, the airfields round Münster that protected this West Wall,

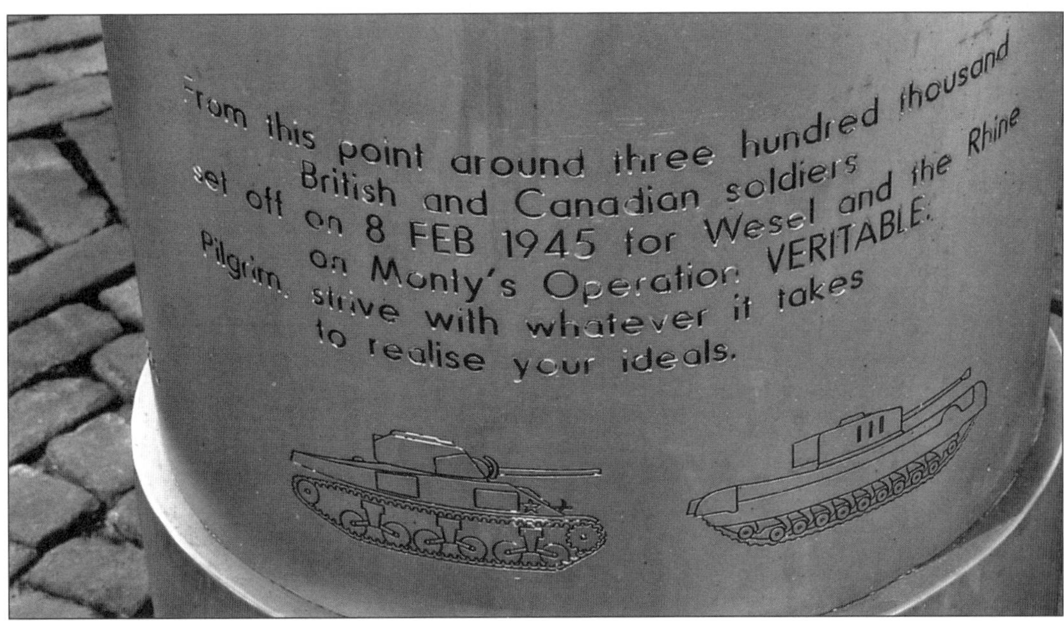

From this point around three hundred thousand
British and Canadian soldiers
set off on 8 FEB 1945 for Wesel and the Rhine
on Monty's Operation VERITABLE.
Pilgrim, strive with whatever it takes
to realise your ideals.

Detail of the Memorial

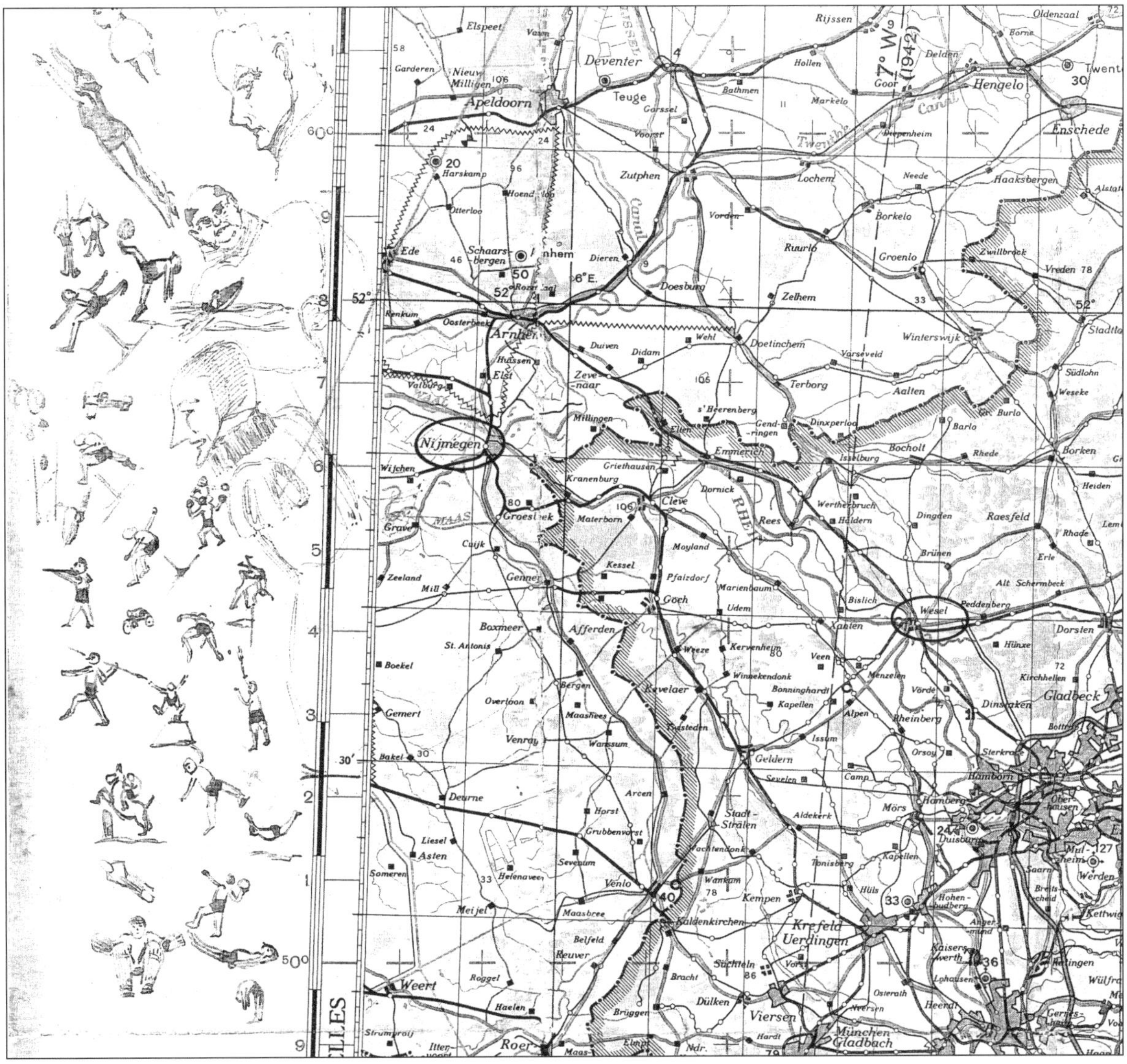

Area between Nijmegen and Wesel (both circled) cleared by 21st Army Group 8th February-10th March 1945 before the Rhine crossing. Photocopy of one of the coloured maps I used in 1944, with my contemporary doodles, which Michael Horsfall packed up with my kit.

and the canal, rail and road systems that supplied it. The Squadron's most significant and unusual sortie was flown jointly by four aircraft along the Rhine on 5th September: two pilots flew at low-level from Arnhem to Dornick, near Cleve, each taking oblique photographs of one bank of the river, while another two did the same from Millingen, a little north of Dornick, up to Wesel. From then on, Wesel featured continually in pilots' reports in the Line Book and SORB. My own entry for my penultimate sortie on 18th November reads:

"Spitfire XI PL905 Up 15.05 Down 15.45 s.36" Viersen-Kempen-Wesel
Took Viersen as ordered, other targets cloud covered. Took further pictures of Viersen and Kempen at intervals but could see no signs of pranging [bombing]. Took other marshalling yards and bridges while hanging around. Landed 15.45. No incidents."

This was fairly typical of many other sorties in this period, a high proportion of which were foiled by the atrocious weather of the autumn and winter of 1944. Sorties usually took in multiple targets, such as the following:

19th November Wesel-Isselburg-Hengelo-Venlo
29th November mapping: Münster-Hannover-Wesel
2nd December radar stations: Osnabruck-Wesel
3rd December Wesel-Velen-Münster-Zwolle
15th December Wesel-Saerbruck
5th January mapping: Boxmeer-Wesel-Brünen-Gennep
14th February Wesel-Gütersloh-Hengelo
14th February Emmerich-Wesel-Gladbeck
16th February Hamm-Neheim-Soest-Lippstadt-Beckum
24th February V1 sites: Zwolle-Almelo-Deventer
9th March Dortmund-Ems Canal Rheine-Wesel-Leeuwarden
24th March Wesel-Münster-Enschede

Looking back with post-war hindsight, we might have guessed that Wesel was going to be a major objective of Montgomery's 21st Army Group but, as I've mentioned earlier, we pilots were not particularly concerned with the significance of the targets we photographed – ignorance would be a line of defence against interrogators if we were captured – and also many other targets besides Wesel received the repeated attentions of our cameras.

With the improved weather of Spring and, with it, the protection now available from the Air Forces, the Allies moved forward. On 7th March, the great city of Cologne, which straddled the Rhine, was surrendered to Hodges' American 1st Army. On the same day, his 29th Armoured Division found the bridge at Remagen, south of Bonn, damaged by the Germans but still standing: tanks, guns and 8000 men crossed the river in the first 24 hours, followed by many more. On 22nd March, the 5th Division of General Patton's Third Army crossed the river at Oppenheim, not far from Frankfurt, with minimum preparations and meeting little initial resistance.

Montgomery, meanwhile, had concentrated a huge force of over 1,000,000 men, comprising 2nd British Army, 1st Canadian Army, and General Simpson's US 9th Army, totalling 25 Divisions and 8 Brigades, for a set-piece crossing of the Rhine at ten points on a 20-mile front; it was centred on Wesel, an industrial town and an important communications centre for the Germans.

The build-up of men and equipment, including hundreds of Buffalo amphibious vehicles and other landing-craft, quantities of bridging material, 1500 tanks, and 3300 guns and rocket-launchers, took ten days; it was concealed from the enemy by a continuous smoke-screen.

The Germans, however, had long realised that the area of Wesel, with the low banks of the Rhine, even though here it was 500 yards wide, would be an attractive crossing-point for the Allies. Forewarned by the smoke, they had moved up extra divisions, albeit totalling only ten, but half of them were veteran Panzer formations and experienced paratroopers. More forbiddingly, remembering the use of Airborne forces in 'Market Garden', they had brought in 800 light and heavy flak-guns, over 100 of which were mobile and stationed in the lanes and woods near the anticipated landing-fields.

On the 23rd March, the artillery and squadrons of Allied fighter-bombers kept up a continuous bombardment of the German gun-positions, flak-batteries and strong-points on the eastern bank; while, further inland, the transport system, towns and bridges were targeted by Allied bombers from bases in England and the Continent.

At 10.00pm, Operation 'Plunder' started when, 10 miles to the north of Wesel, the 51st (Highland) Division of XXX Corps crossed the Rhine and started to fight their way into the town of Rees on the opposite bank, but met with strong resistance from German paratroopers in prepared positions. At the same time, the 1st Commando Brigade landed from Buffalos opposite Wesel and established themselves just inland. At 10.30pm, 250 Lancasters dropped 1200 tons of bombs on Wesel and virtually obliterated it. The Commandos then moved in and occupied the ruins without meeting any strong opposition. At 2.0am on the 24th, 15th (Scottish) Division of XXX Corps crossed from Xanten and Vynen and set up a beach-head between Rees and Wesel. The American 30th and 79th Divisions of XVI Corps of Simpson's 9th Army also crossed at 2.0am at five separate points south of Wesel and met very little opposition at first. This was the general pattern all along the front, but resistance stiffened considerably as the troops moved forward and developed their bridge-heads, while the engineers proceeded with the speedy construction of Bailey bridges, often under fire.

The ruins of Wesel after the bombing by 250 Lancasters at 10.30pm in the night of 23rd March 1945

Photo: A. Berjek "The War on our Doorstep"

At 7.00am on the 24th, the greatest Airborne operation of the war, code-named 'Varsity', got under way when 1795 C-46 Commando and C-47 Dakota troop-carriers, and 1305 Hadrian, Horsa and Hamilcar gliders towed by 1050 Dakota, Stirling and Halifax tugs (a number of Dakotas for the first time pulled two Hadrians at once) brought 21.000 men to seize strategic objectives ahead of the main assault troops and hold them against German counter-attacks.

The huge armada, containing two Airborne Divisions, the American 17th and the British 6th, under the command of the veteran American Airborne General Ridgway, arrived over the Rhine at 10.0am, the paratroops jumping first, just ten minutes before the gliders were released for their landings.

It was then that tragedy struck as, in spite of the initial shelling and bombing, because of early-morning mist and the dust from the bombardment, half the flak-guns had escaped damage and now wreaked havoc on the slow-moving, low-flying troop-carriers, tugs and gliders, and on the men dropping slowly beneath their parachutes. The Americans lost 50 gliders, 44 transports and tugs, and 15 out of 240 Liberators that dropped supplies two hours later; the British had 12 tugs and 32 gliders shot down. Altogether 1100 paratroopers, pilots and aircrews were killed, along with 105 glider pilots: greater losses than were suffered during the landings at Arnhem.

On a hill south of Xanten overlooking the Rhine sat a group of top Allied commanders to witness this last great combined operation of the war. Churchill had arrived the day before and spent the night in a caravan at Montgomery's HQ at Venlo. In Volume VI, "Triumph and Tragedy", of his great six-volume "The Second World War" (Cassell 1954), Churchill himself wrote:

> "Montgomery had arranged for me to witness from a hill-top amid rolling downland the great fly-in,"

But Ken Ford, author of "The Rhine Crossings 1945" (Osprey 2007), includes a photograph of five other main figures above the caption:

> "Prime Minister Winston Churchill watches the airborne fly-in from a vantage point near the Rhine. With the premier, from left to right: Gen Crerar (Commander Canadian First Army), FM Alanbrooke (Chief of the Imperial General Staff), Lt Gen Simmonds (Commander Canadian II Corps) and FM Montgomery (Commander Twenty-First Army Group)."

W.D. and S. Whitaker, in their valuable Canadian-oriented "Rhineland – The Battle to End the War" (Mandarin 1991), add the names of General Simpson (commanding the US 3rd Army), General Brereton (commander of the Allied 1st Airborne Army), and General Ridgway (commanding the Allied XVIII Airborne Corps). General Dempsey (commanding British 2nd Army), and General Horrocks (commander of XXX Corps) are two other names mentioned elsewhere. All these may well have been at the open-air luncheon arranged beside the Rhine for this 'top-brass' gathering.

Looking through field-glasses at the distant Airborne landings, Churchill and his party were appalled to see aircraft and gliders falling out of the sky in flames, some with their Airborne troops still on board, others with the men struggling to get out in time.

Nevertheless, in spite of these horrific scenes and many hundreds of men wounded, the great majority of the Airborne troops reached their objectives: the Americans captured the high ground of the Diersfordt Forest overlooking Wesel from the north, and three bridges over the adjacent River Issel; while the British took the town of Hamminkeln, a little further north, and three other bridges over the Issel.

Once the Germans realised where the various Allied thrusts were heading, they threw in their best units, tanks and guns to stem the tide; but the 12 Bailey bridges over the river enabled an increasing flow of reinforcements of Allied armour, artillery and infantry to be driven across; the German counter-attacks were held and forced back, with many of their soldiers surrendering.

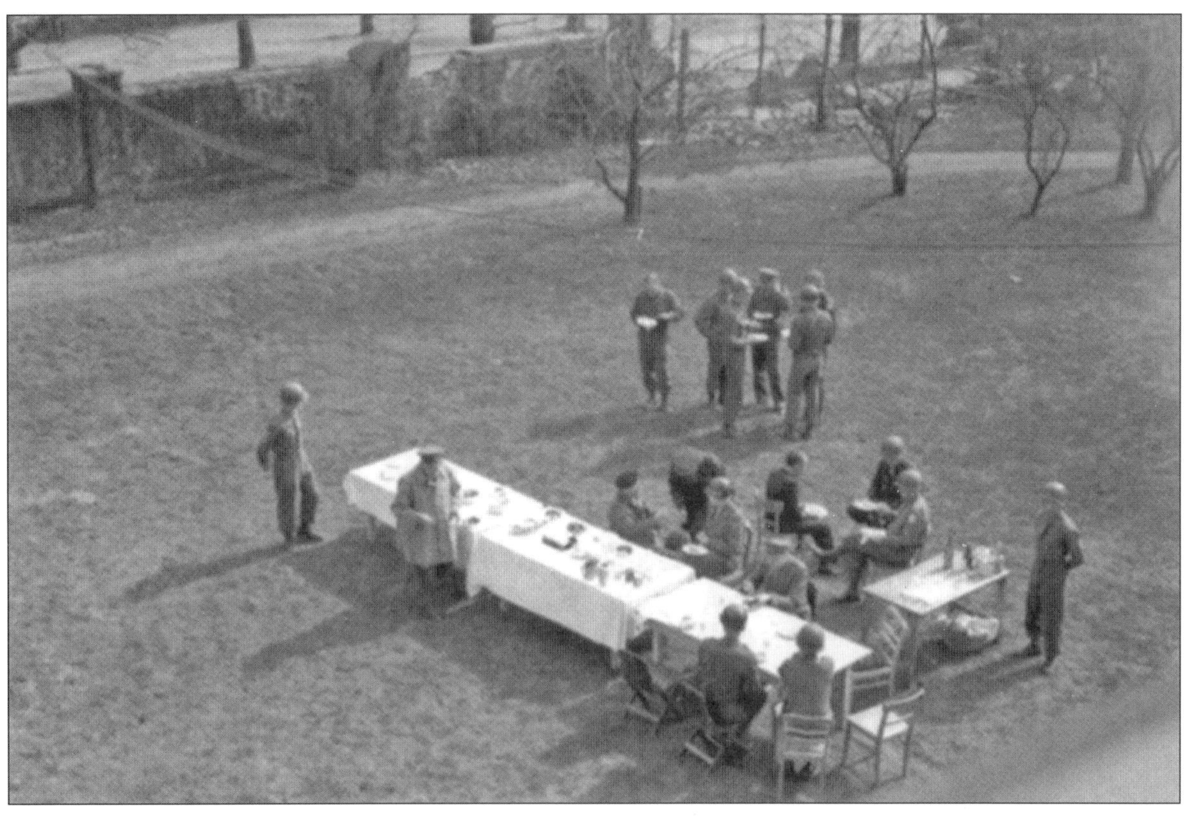

The setting for the buffet lunch for Churchill and the Allied commanders near the Rhine on 24th March 1945

Photo: A. Berjek "The War on our Doorstep"

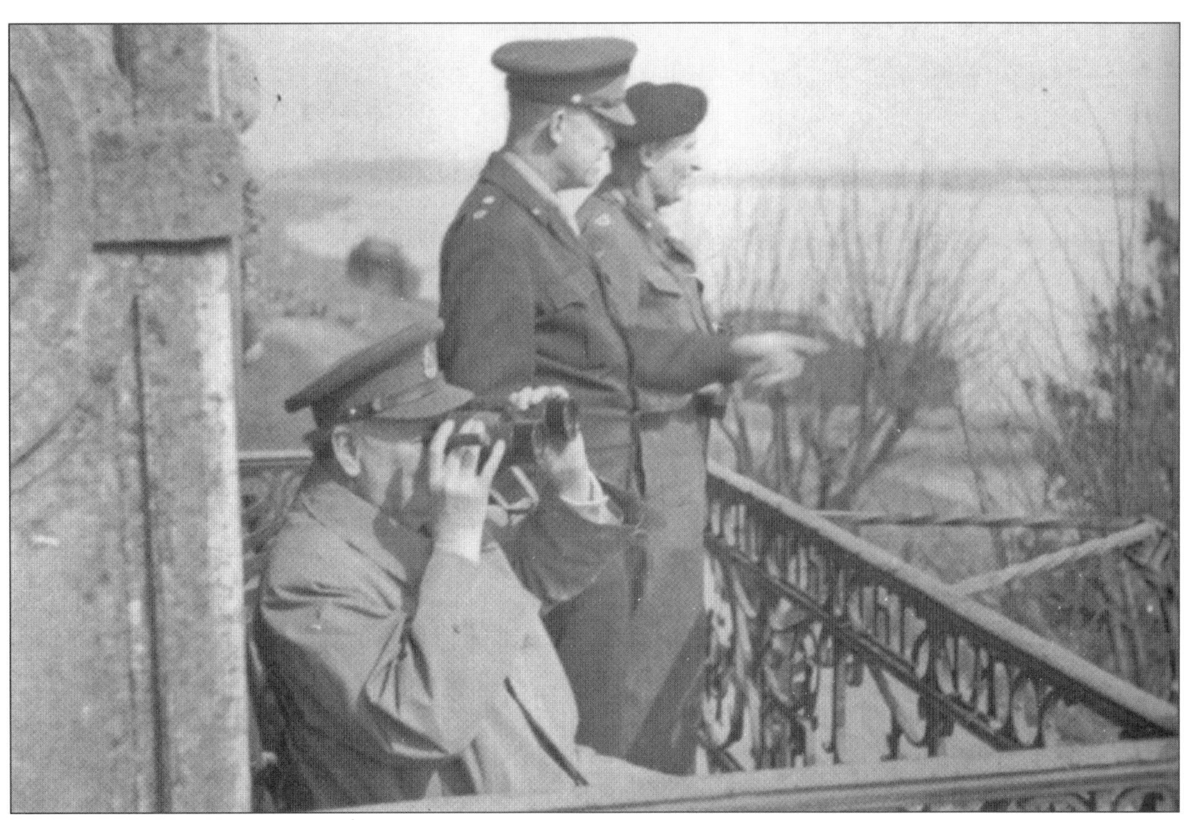

l-r: Churchill, Eisenhower and Montgomery on the balcony of the house overlooking the Rhine on 25th March 1945

Photo: A. Berjek "The War on our Doorstep"

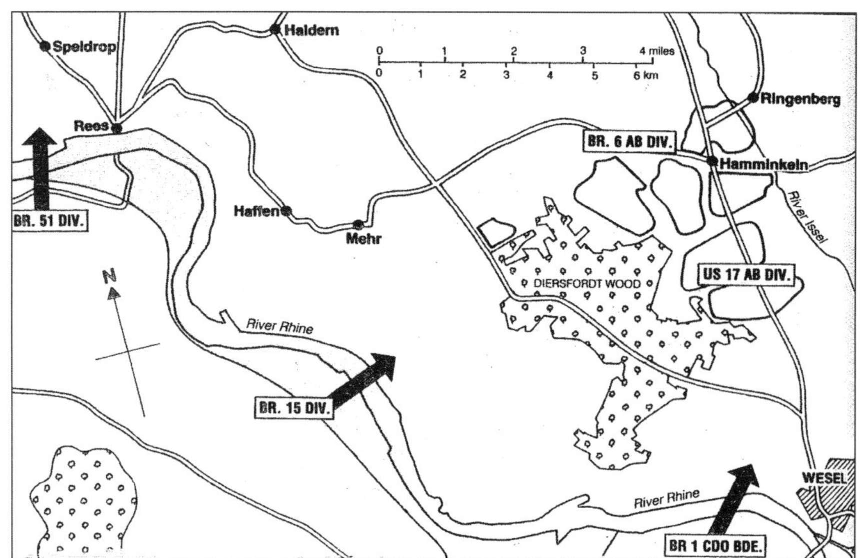

Map of the 15 miles of the Rhine, Rees – Wesel, allocated to 21st Army Group for Operations 'Varsity' and 'Plunder' on 24th March 1945
Map: Robin Neillands "The Conquest of the Reich"

The lessons of Arnhem had clearly been absorbed: the Commandos made contact with some of the British Airbornes within two hours; while, by the end of the day, the Allied ground forces had passed through all the Airbornes' positions and were extending their bridgeheads well beyond the Rhine. By the 28th, all three Armies under Montgomery's command, British, Canadian and American, were well established several miles from the Rhine, ready to break out into the plains of West Germany.

In fact, the success of Operation 'Plunder' in the river-crossings and the subsequent assault on the German defences has made it questionable whether Operation 'Varsity', with its high casualty rate, was really necessary. But Montgomery always liked to have superiority in numbers and equipment over the enemy so that he could almost guarantee victory. The one occasion when he did not adhere to this principle was 'Market Garden', which ended in failure. In 'Plunder' and 'Varsity', he expected the Germans to put up a stronger resistance to the invasion of their Fatherland than they did – and he was taking no chances.

With the Rhine crossings achieved and the Germans surrendering or withdrawing in defeat along the whole river front, the final objective of the Allies was to reach the River Elbe, the boundary agreed with the Russians when Elsenhower accepted their demand to capture Berlin – which he knew would be a hard and expensive nut for the Allies to crack. Devers' 6th US Army Group and 1st Free French Army headed into South Germany, taking Nuremburg and Stuttgart; Patton's 3rd US Army moved into Czecho-Slovakia and Austria; Simpson's 9th US Army returned to Bradley's 12th US Army and, together with Hodge's 1st US Army, they encircled the Ruhr and achieved its surrender, capturing 325,000 prisoners; Montgomery's 21st Army Group advanced into North-West Germany, taking Hamburg on the 17th April; while the Canadian 1st Army veered west into Holland, liberating Arnhem on 15th April, and moving northwards to clear the coastal region.

Because Eisenhower feared that the Germans in Central and Western Holland would open the dykes and flood large parts of the country, causing lasting damage to the future recovery of the Dutch nation, who were already suffering intensely from starvation, this region was left behind as an isolated pocket, which was liberated only when the Germans there and in Denmark, as well as in North-West Germany, surrendered to Montgomery on 5th May.

All this was unknown to me in 1945; so, as Wesel was one of the Allies' focal points in the final stages of the war, it was easy for Hennie and me in 2007 to decide to visit this place about which we knew

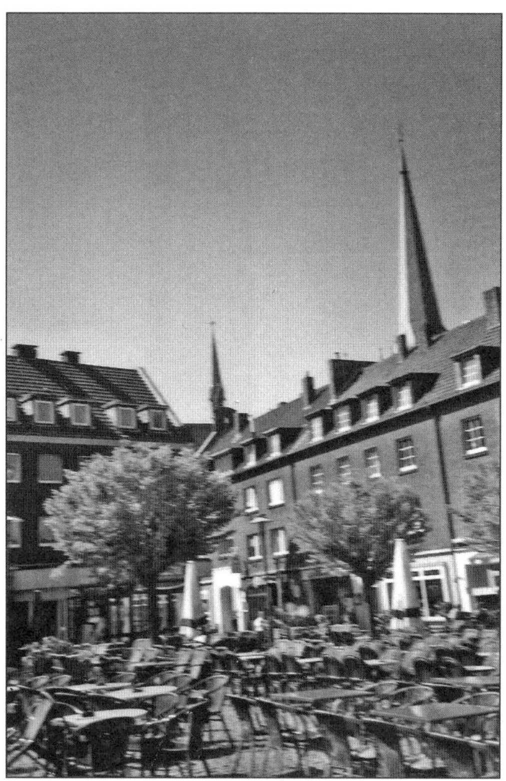

The centre of Wesel in 2007: attractively rebuilt

so little. In this case, the involvement by 16 Squadron was limited to the regular photographic reconnaissance sorties, mentioned earlier, that were flown over the area for the benefit of the Army planners, and later of the formations that undertook the actual Operations 'Plunder' and 'Varsity'.

So, on 2nd May, we set out to drive the 70 miles from Borne to Wesel along a not very interesting route, entering Germany near Bocholt, again with no border control or checks and with the houses looking not very different from those in Holland.

We reached Wesel along a broad avenue attractively lined with trees each side. The whole place had been rebuilt after the devastation of the war, and seemed to us like a new town, although faithfully following the street-plan of the original and restoring or reconstructing the main architectural buildings of the historical town. Like Rheine, it felt fresh and cheerful, and the people looked busy and happy. We had coffee and cake in a pleasant square, surrounded by traditional three- and four-storey commercial houses, with shops at street-level, high-pitched roofs broken by dormer windows, and the spires of churches and old-fashioned halls pointing into the blue sky behind. It was all very peaceful, and made me feel a little sad at what we had destroyed in March 1945 – but the blame lay directly on the head of the demented Hitler.

We had no map of the town and had driven in from the German side of the Rhine: the opposite direction to that taken by Montgomery's forces on 23rd/24th March. We had therefore missed whatever chance there was, 60 years later, of viewing the scenes where the Commandos and the troops

The rural scene on the western bank of the Rhine, with the stumps of the buttresses of the former road-bridge still standing

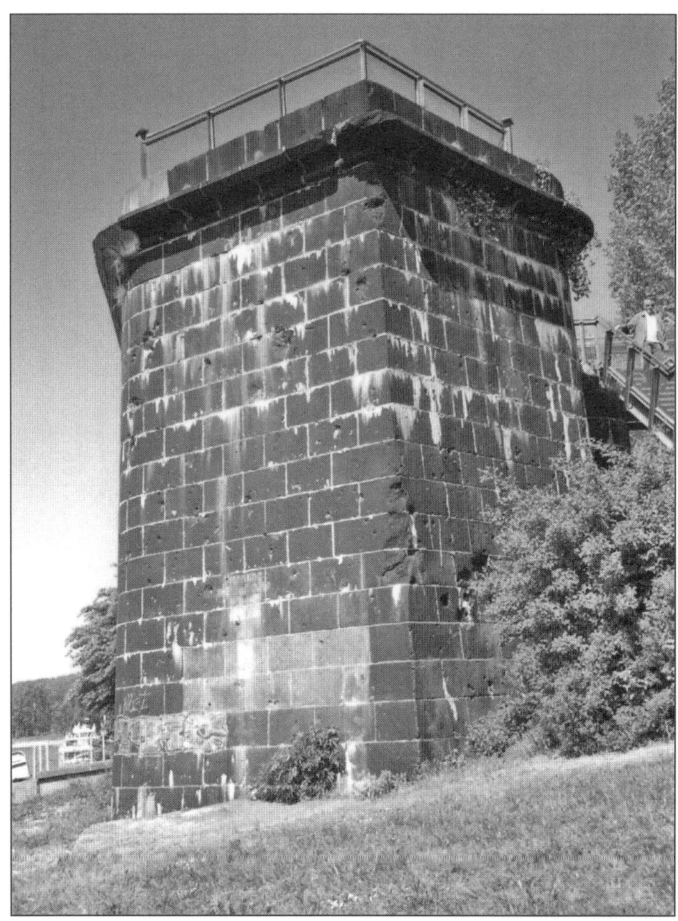

A battle-scarred buttress on the Wesel side made an excellent viewing-point.

A pre-war photograph of the road-bridge over the Rhine into Wesel
Photo: Wesel Town Archive

The same bridge blown up by the Germans after they had retreated to the east side of the Rhine
Photo: A. Berjek "The War on our Doorstep"

of XXX Corps had embarked on their assault craft or driven onto the Bailey bridges before arriving on our side. Our next-best objective was the Rhine itself. Fortunately, we spotted regular sign-posts to the 'Hafen' (harbour, or perhaps marina) and, following these, we came upon an almost country lane, lined with trees, running beside the great river. We followed this as far as we could go and were surprised to pass the entrance to a flying club, with a smart white low-wing monoplane sitting enticingly near the gate. We returned to where several cars were parked beside the river. It was broad and calm, almost placid, except foe the continual passage of the giant barges that made it one of the vital arteries feeding German industries in the Ruhr. The opposite side was purely pastoral, with a low river-bank, green fields with thick hedges and trees, and a few cottages and farm buildings dotted along the skyline. Nothing could be less warlike – or more attractive as a launch-pad for an invading army. The only signs of conflict were the stumps of the stout stone buttresses of the bridge that had carried the roadway over the river into Wesel. This had been blown up by the Germans on 10th March, along with all the other bridges over the Rhine, to prevent its use by the Allies.

One large buttress remained on our side of the river, a huge, blackened stone structure, its surface pitted with shell- and bullet-holes. There was a ladder leading up to a viewing platform on top, which was exactly what we wanted to find. We climbed up to the vantage point – and here I felt a particular thrill, as Churchill, Alan Brooke and Montgomery had done just the same 62 years before, but on the other side of the Rhine.

In "Triumph and Tragedy", Churchill recounted how, on 25th March, he went to meet Eisenhower at Simpson's 9th Army HQ outside Rheinberg, where Eisenhower had gone with Bradley to witness the Rhine crossings of the Americans south of Wesel. Eisenhower took Churchill to a sand-bagged house by the river, with a good view of the opposite bank, apparently unoccupied by any Germans. After Eisenhower had to leave them, Churchill suggested to Montgomery that they should cross the river in a launch moored nearby.

> "Somewhat to my surprise he answered, 'Why not?' ... we started across the river with three or four American commanders and half a dozen armed men. We landed in brilliant sunshine and perfect peace on the German shore, and walked about for half an hour or so unmolested."

So wrote the old warrior, eager to set a symbolic foot on the enemy's homeland.

Eisenhower, however, took a decidedly unromantic view of the adventure. He wrote in his autobiography, "Crusade in Europe" (Heinemann 1948):

> "Had I been present he would never have been permitted to cross the Rhine that day."

He would have been even more upset by the events that followed, as described by Churchill again.

> "As we landed he [Montgomery] said to me, 'Let's go down to the railway bridge at Wesel, where we can see what is going on on the spot.' So we got into his car, and, accompanied by the Americans, who were delighted at the prospect, we went to the big iron-girder railway bridge, which was broken in the middle, but whose twisted iron-work offered good perches. The Germans were replying to our fire, and their shells fell in salvos of four about a mile away. Presently they came nearer. Then one salvo came overhead and plunged in the water on our side of the bridge. The shells seemed to explode on impact with the bottom, and raised great fountains of spray about a hundred yards away. Several other shells fell among the motor-cars which were concealed not far behind us, and it was decided we ought to depart. I clambered down and joined my adventurous host for the two hours' drive back to his headquarters."

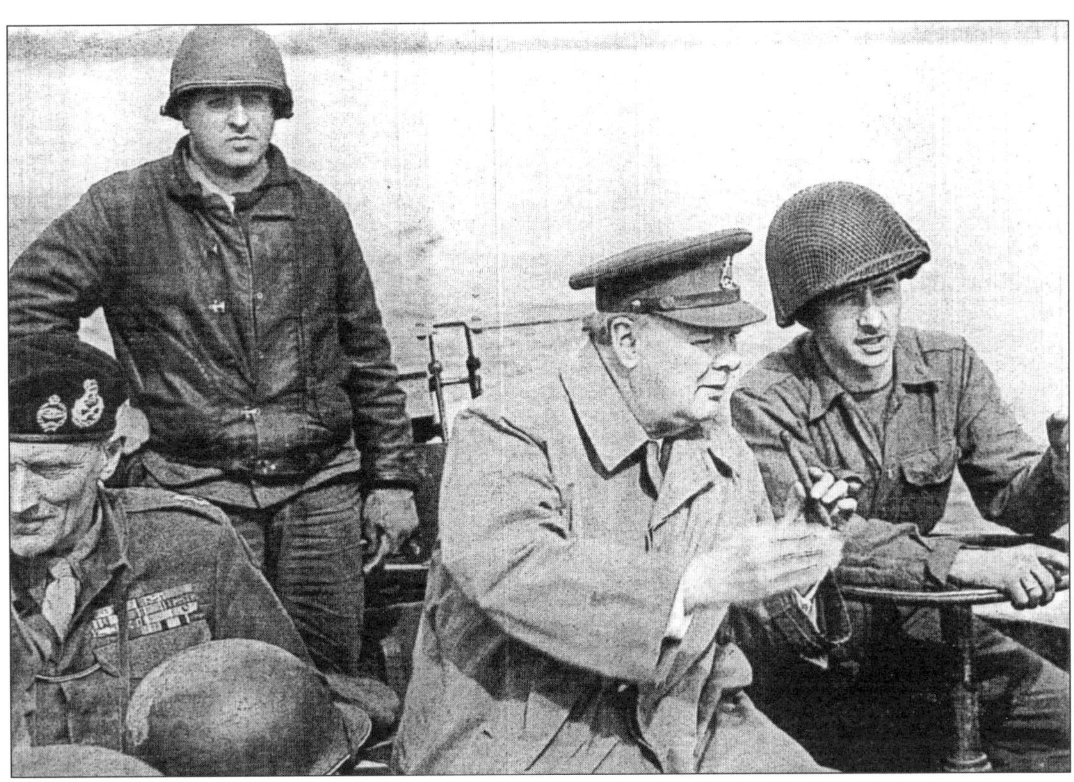

Churchill and Montgomery crossing the Rhine in a launch accompanied by a few American soldiers on the 25th March 1945

Photo: A. Berjek "The War on our Doorstep"

Churchill, Commander Thompson and General Simpson, commanding the 9th US Army, on the wreckage of the Rhine railway-bridge on 25th March 1945

Photo: A. Berjek "The War on our Doorstep"

The battle-scars on our buttress were sufficient evidence that in this case, even for Winston Churchill, discretion was the better part of valour. The twisted ironwork had all long gone, but to find ourselves emulating the great man in gazing across the Rhine on a buttress not far from his railway-bridge was one of the highlights of our visit to Wesel.

The river upstream took a sharp bend to the right so, in case we were missing something, we walked along the bank to look round the curve; but the landscape was still very rural, broken only by a new railway bridge and, further up, two tall industrial chimneys.

We decided we needed a map and information about Wesel, so we returned to the town centre and found the Town Hall, which was usefully sign-posted. Here Hennie telephoned the Archivist of the town, who told him we'd be welcome to pay a visit to his office. This was located in the Citadel, and he gave Hennie directions on how to reach it.

The Citadel proved to be a large fortified redoubt dating from 1681. The military buildings had been restored after the war and converted to form a historical and cultural centre. We drove in through an imposing gateway and stopped first to look into the modern Prussian Museum on our right. Having obtained a town guide from there, but found nothing written in English, we passed a handsome mansion on our left and a long red-brick range, which was an art and music school. Finally, we came to a rather plain entrance, climbed some stairs, and entered a very functional work-room, with a long table in the centre and others round the sides, on which stood television sets and computer screens, while shelves filled the remaining sides, complete with all kinds of books, reports and other archival materials.

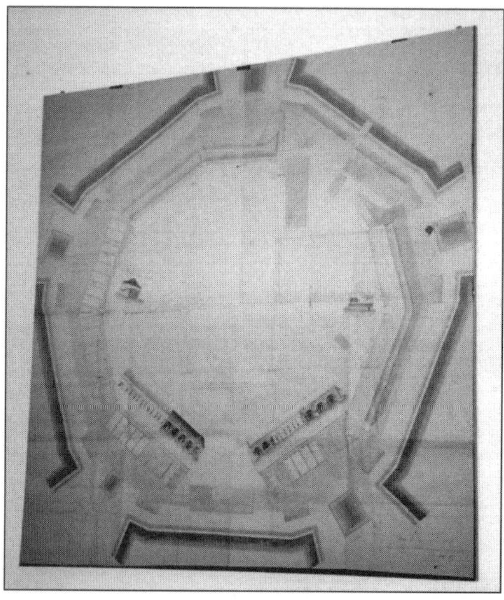

A plan of the 1681 Citadel on the wall of the Town Archive

The Archivist, a large, youngish, friendly man called Martin, greeted us in reasonable English, but preferred to talk to Hennie in German and have him translate important points

Inside the Citadel, the buildings reflect 18th century elegance.

to me. I told him my interest in the crossing of the Rhine in March 1945 and asked him if he had any photographs connected with it. He then produced several albums of fascinating pictures; one, in particular, showed the road-bridge intact before its destruction, a copy of which he kindly made for me. I also bought from him a large volume in German, "The War on our Doorstep", published by the Town Archive in 2004, which was a full description of the Rhine crossings and Airborne landings, with all the photographs that I could wish for. I ventured to ask him what he felt about the war, and received the reassuring all-inclusive answer, *"Hitler was a maniac!"*

The Town Archivist with a group of local Secondary School students working on projects connected with the history of Wesel

At this point, a group of boys and girls, senior pupils of a local Secondary School, arrived to continue work on various projects connected with the history of Wesel; there was plenty of scope for them, as the town was founded in 1241. Martin introduced us to the group, and we had a pleasant exchange in English about what we and they were doing in the work-room.

After spending two hours in his work-place, we expressed our warm gratitude to Martin for his helpfulness and for the liberal attitude to the war that he had revealed in our discussions, We came away much impressed with all we had experienced in Wesel, and not least by the fact that all over the town, including in the courtyard of the Citadel, were full-size models of donkeys, decorated in outrageous colours. They were displayed as the ancient symbol of Wesel, from its original German name of "Esel", which means 'donkey'.

In spite of all the destruction we had unleashed on it in 1945, Wesel in 2007 had proved to be an attractive, flourishing town, and its inhabitants a most likeable people with a fine sense of humour.

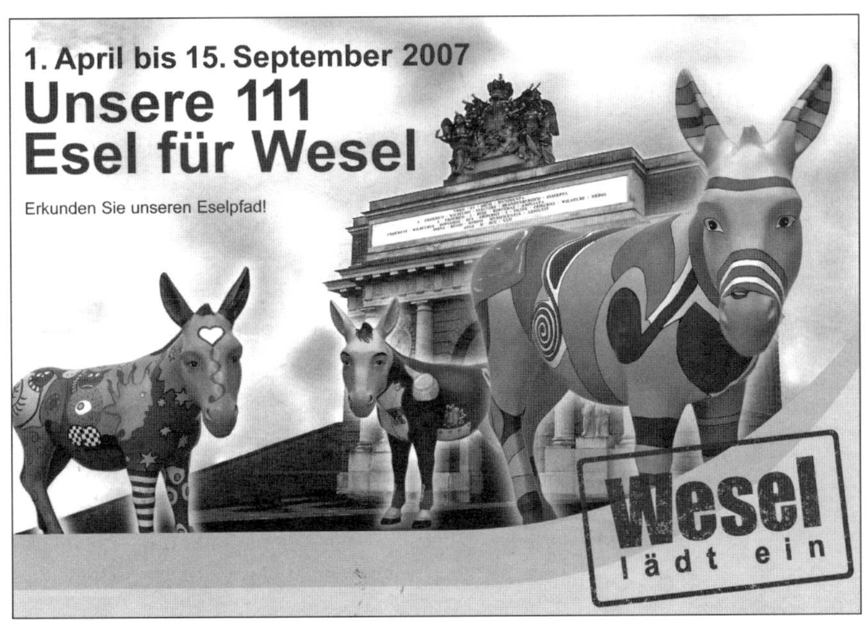

The fantastic Donkeys (Esels) of Wesel (mediaeval name Esel) now the town's proud emblem

CHAPTER 41

Battle for the Twente Canal – the Liberation of Borne

A few days after their successful Rhine crossings round Wesel on 24th March 1945, the Allies broke out of their bridgeheads and began their steady advance across North-West Germany to the River Elbe against varying degrees of opposition: some of it was fanatical, with units obeying Hitler to the last; while others, recognising that the war was lost, put up a token resistance and surrendered, relieved to be doing so to the Allies rather than to the Russians.

XXX Corps set off on 30th March on the left flank of the British 2nd Army, with the 1st Canadian Army on their left; it was heading for Bremen, Hamburg, and the mouth of the Elbe, while the Canadians were aiming at Arnhem, Northern Holland, and the German coast. The Guards Armoured Division was in the lead, followed by the 51st (Highland) Division and the 43rd (Wessex) Division; under Major-General G.I.Thomas, the latter was given the task of clearing the north-east sector of Holland, close to the German border. The Canadian 3rd Division, next to it, concentrated on the sector from Arnhem to Almelo and further north to Groningen. The low-lying centre and west of Holland, as already mentioned, were left alone, as the Germans had threatened to flood them, with immense damage to the Dutch people and their economy for many years to come.

After reaching Anholt, just inside the German border, and moving on to Ruurlo, the British and Canadians were faced with a major obstacle – the Twente Canal. This ran eastwards for 28 miles (45km) from Zutphen, past Lochem, Diepenheim, Goor, Delden and Hengelo, to the western suburbs of Enschede. It was a wide and busy waterway, spanned by at least 17 bridges. As the British and Canadians advanced into this part of Holland, the Germans retreated slowly to the Canal and blew up each bridge (often using aerial bombs as explosives) after they had crossed it. The Canal lay between high banks, behind which they dug themselves in on the far side in positions where the Allies were most likely to try to cross, near the bridges, covering them with machine-guns, mortars and artillery. The Canal became a considerable barrier to the Allies' advance.

I hold a particular grudge against it, as it blocked my path on my first night of running away from my landing-field in 't Hesseler in November 1944 and, on the following night in pouring rain, I tried and failed to swim across it under one of the three bridges that carried roads from Delden over the Canal. Earlier, on my penultimate sortie on 16 Squadron from Melsbroek, in poor visibility, I had made the mistake of confusing it with the Dortmund-Ems Canal that ran past Rheine, which I was meant to be photographing. So I pay particular attention to the Canal in this account.

Seyss-Inquart, the Nazi Reich Commissioner for the Netherlands, had moved his Headquarters to Twickel Castle, a mile north-east of Delden, so causing a larger than usual number of German troops to be stationed in the Goor-Delden-Hengelo area; some of them were veteran paratroopers from the Herman Goering Division, who could be moved up to threatened points and who fought with grim determination; others were boys of only 15-16, members of the Hitler Youth and capable of using weapons with a certain amount of skill; they made up in high morale what they lacked in age and experience.

The 43rd (Wessex) Division consisted of four brigades: the 129th, 130th and 214th Infantry Brigades, and the 8th Armoured Brigade. It also contained the 11th Hussars from the Royal Armoured Corps, and a variety of Divisional units: three Field Artillery Regiments, an Anti-Tank Regiment, a Light Anti-Aircraft Regiment, the 43rd Reconnaissance Regiment, the 4th Corps of the Royal Engineers, the

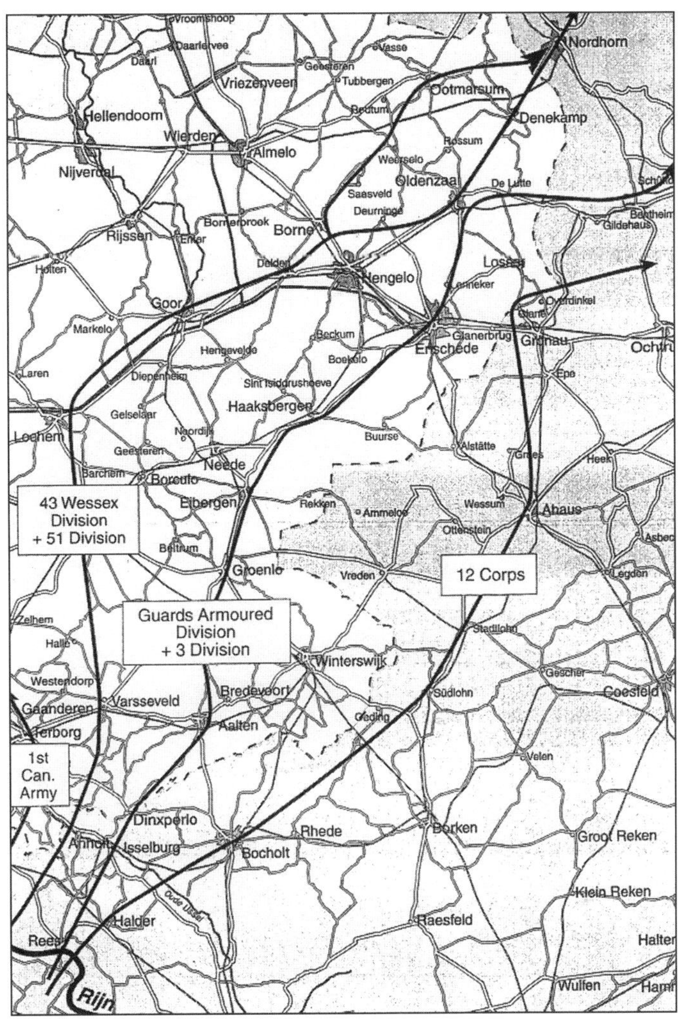

Map showing the general direction of the advance through Holland of the 1st Canadian Army and the 2nd British Army after the Rhine crossing.

Map: Hans Pol "Our Forgotten Liberators"

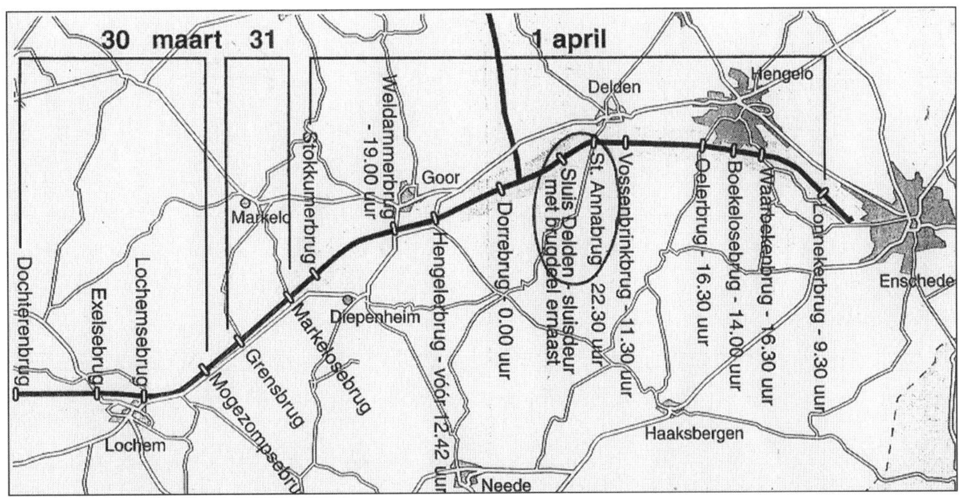

Map showing 17 of the 19 bridges over the Twente Canal between Zutphen and Enschede, all of which were blown up by the Germans. Circled: the Delden lock-bridge (Delden Sluis) and my St Anna bridge.

Map: Hans Pol "Our Forgotten Liberators"

4th Corps of the RASC, three REME Workshops, three Field Ambulances, and three Field Dressing Stations. The 130th Brigade, in particular, consisted of the 7th Battalion of the Royal Hampshire Regiment, and the 4th and 5th Battalions of the Dorset Regiment, who concern us closely later on.

Also involved in the story are the units of the 8th Armoured Brigade, comprising three tank battalions: the 4th/7th Royal Dragoon Guards, the 13th/18th Royal Hussars, and the Nottinghamshire Sherwood Rangers Yeomanry, and the motorised infantry of the 12th Battalion of the King's Royal Rifle Corps (KRRC), supported by the 147th Field Regiment of the Royal Artillery, part of the Essex Yeomanry.

The original battle-plan was for the 43rd (Wessex) Division and the 51st (Highland) Division to cross the Canal at Lochem and advance to Oldenzaal, where they would meet up with the Guards Armoured Division and proceed to Bremen. However, on 1st April, when one brigade of the 43rd arrived at Lochem, they found the bridge had been blown up. They moved further east, while the other two brigades headed for Goor and Hengelo. But when they approached Goor, the bridge there was blown up in front of them. The Canadians on their left, meanwhile, had captured Zutphen and, next day, crossed the Canal at Almen, 4 miles to the east.

Opposing the British, the Germans on the ground several miles in front of the Canal resisted the advance strongly. On the road between Bentelo and Delden stood the inn "Plaat 'n Gerard" ("Place and Prudence"), owned by Mr G.Timmerman; it is now a large and very successful restaurant run by his grandson and my good friend, Henk Timmerman, and re-named "De Rustende Jager" ("The Resting Hunter"). The Germans occupied it and fired on the Wessex brigades until they were driven out. The British then replaced the Germans and it became a Dressing Station. Betsie Timmerman, Henk's aunt, was a girl of 18 and did her best to help tend the wounded, but was distressed by the sight of the young soldiers in agony, one of whom died in her arms. Members of the 147th Field Artillery set up their guns in the surrounding fields and began to shell the Germans near the Canal.

The three bridges close to Delden were: to the west at Wiene, a two-span road-bridge over two locks separated by an island, hence its Dutch name, the Delden Sluis (=locks); in the centre, the St Anna road-bridge, under which I had tried to swim across the Canal; and Vossenbrink, to the east.

In the afternoon of 2nd April, the 12th Battalion of the King's Royal Rifle Corps (KRRC) was ordered to take the Wiene lock-bridge, which had a large hole blown in it, but was thought to be usable if planks were thrown across the gap. 'B' Company, under Major William Deedes, was to head the advance, supported by the tanks of the Sherwood Rangers Yeomanry and by fire from the 147th Field Artillery Regiment, which had moved up from its position near the Bentelo-Delden road.

The first platoon of 'B' Company led the way, with the second close behind, while the third waited in reserve behind the canal-bank. Immediately, the infantry were met with withering fire from four Spandau machine-guns concealed in the woods behind the northern bank. Many men in the two leading platoons were killed or wounded. At the same time, shells from the German mortars fell among the reserve platoon, decimating it. Two Sherman tanks stood up on the south bank and directed their fire hopefully into the woods opposite. Dead and wounded men were lying on the first span and still others were being cut down. It was clear that the frontal attack had failed tragically. Major Deedes' radio had broken down, but he shouted the order to withdraw.

At this point, the commander of the forward platoon, Lt Andrew Burnaby-Atkins, a contemporary of mine at Eton, carrying a Bren gun and a spare magazine, ran ahead of his men, firing from the hip and spraying with bullets whatever Germans he could see. At the same time, Major Deedes dashed forward and threw smoke grenades to cover Burnaby-Atkins and the men while they retreated from the bridge. He went to the bridge and back several times to help bring off the wounded, all the time under

The Wiene lock-bridge, also called the Delden 'sluis'.
This post-war aerial photo show the lock-bridge probably as it was in April 1945, when 12th KRRC tried to capture the wooden bridge in front of the nearest towers. The lock for water-borne traffic lies between the two pairs of towers; these house the electric motors for raising and lowering the massive 'gates' of sheet steel. The writing on the photo refers to the later capture of the lock by the Canadians and the Bailey bridge they threw across the lock to enable their tanks to cross the canal.

Photo: van Ommen

Personalities at the battle of Twente Canal, 2nd April 1944: Major William Deedes (when a Lieutenant) and Lieutenant Andrew Burnaby-Atkins.

Photos: "The Daily Telegraph"

continuous German fire. Altogether, two officers and 20 men were killed, and one officer and 20 more men were wounded: a third of the strength of 'B' Company.

Major Deedes and Lt Burnaby-Atkins were both awarded the Military Cross. Burnaby-Atkins' citation mentioned that, before the attack, he had made a personal reconnaissance of the bridge, dodging about under fire for 20 minutes in order to ascertain the whereabouts and strength of the enemy. It continued by saying that his initiative in returning the German fire had made the withdrawal possible. It ended;

"During the whole of this operation, this officer showed superb coolness and devotion to duty,. His example and complete disregard of his personal safety were an inspiration to all ranks and greatly assisted in keeping the men cool and steady in the most trying conditions."

Major Deedes remained extremely bitter about the waste of lives in mounting a frontal attack on a well-defended German position. He felt keenly the loss of his two 21-year-old officers and of the other men in his Company, who had been with him since D-Day and were now killed in the last five weeks of the war; it affected him for the rest of his life, as he felt responsible by not having spoken out against the attack; he called his MC "a survivor's medal".

After the war, Deedes had a remarkable career: he returned to journalism, but decided to go into politics and was elected to Parliament in 1950 as the Conservative MP for Ashford, in Kent; but he continued to work as a columnist for "The Daily Telegraph". He was made a junior minister by Churchill and Butler, and in 1962 was called to the Cabinet as Minister of Information by Macmillan, until Macmillan resigned in 1964 over the affair of Profumo, who happened to be a school-friend of Deedes. He resumed his work on the "Telegraph" and in 1974 was appointed Editor, a post he held for the next 12 years. Margaret Thatcher created him a Life Peer. He was now 72, but continued to write for the paper as a roving correspondent, his best-known assignment being in 1997 when, at the age of 83, he accompanied Princess Diana to Bosnia to highlight the dangers to ordinary people of landmines left behind when the armies moved on. He went on writing until almost the end of his life: he died in 2007 at the age of 94, having been a journalist for 72 years.

My obsession with the Twente Canal led me to write to Lord Deedes in October 1997 to tell him of my own experiences of the Canal, 't Hesseler, Borne, and Delden, in the war and since then, and asking if he had written anything about the battle for the lock-bridge, in which he had won his MC. I also mentioned that I had been told by the Dutch that the Resistance tried to tell the British of the German positions in and around Delden, but they would not listen; I asked Deedes for his comments on this report.

Lord Deedes sent me a very friendly reply, but was clearly unwilling to provide the details I had asked for. Some extracts from his letter include:

"Dear Taylor,

Thanks for a very interesting letter.

Yes, the Twenthe Canal was one of the last battles my company did. We were a motor battalion with the 8th Armoured Brigade, which did the D-Day job with floating tanks. The Twenthe canal attack was a mess, partly because the lie of the land made it impossible for the tanks to support us. All the officers were killed or wounded excepting Andrew Burnaby Atkins and myself. Andrew died a year or so ago after a long illness.

... I doubt if there is any account of our battle – it was v. small really. We had a lot of losses towards the end, so I left feeling rather mutinous about "unconditional surrender" and all that lark. ... But that is in the past. There had been a moment at Arnhem when they were going to gamble on a squadron of 13/18 Hussars tanks and my motor company racing in from Nijmegen[1] and grabbing it. They called

[1] Operation 'Comet'

it off at the last minute. If we had done it and ended the war before Christmas, we would have saved ourselves a lot of trouble!

The Twenthe job left me with a sour taste, and it only went in my book because the publishers insisted on it. So I don't dwell on it. Andrew got well decorated: he received a Bar to his MC a month later and rightly so, and so became Monty's [Montgomery's] ADC post-war, and through him I came to know Monty well. So I suppose there is a silver lining to most things.

Thanks for writing.

Sincerely,

Bill Deedes"

This letter is fascinating, perhaps more for what it reveals about Arnhem than about the battle for the Delden lock-bridge; but I doubt whether I shall ever learn any more about this small-scale engagement than the little that Lord Deedes added to what I have described earlier.

Meanwhile, the Guards Armoured Division had captured Enschede and the Twente Air Base on 2nd April and moved on to Oldenzaal, leaving Delden, Hengelo and Borne in German hands on their left.

After the failure of the 12th KRRC to cross the canal at Wiene, Major-General Thomas ordered the 12th KRRC, the 4th and 5th Dorsets, the 7th Hampshires, 'A' and 'B' Squadrons of the Sherwood Rangers Yeomanry, 'A' Squadron of the Royal Dragoons, and the 49th Armoured Personnel Carrier (APC) Regiment of the Royal Tank Regiment, to skirt round the eastern end of the Canal by moving to Enschede and then returning north-west to Hengelo and Borne. The rest of the Division would give support to the Canadian 4th Armoured Division, who would cross the Canal opposite Delden.

On 3rd April at 1630hrs, the Lincoln and Welland Regiment of the 10th Canadian Infantry Brigade made a brave crossing of the Canal at two points in small boats; they were well covered by artillery fire and smoke from the 15th Canadian Field Regiment, Royal Canadian Artillery, with further shelling coming from the British 147th Field Regiment, Royal Artillery, near the Hengeio-Borne road. They managed to set up a bridge-head on the opposite bank, which enabled the Engineers to throw a small Bailey bridge across the canal near the blown-up Vossenbrink bridge. The Canadians then advanced further inland and sent patrols into the western half of Delden and occupied the railway station. Next day they linked up with the 12th KRRC, who had penetrated into the town from the east. The Germans retreated and the Engineers were able to place a stronger Bailey bridge, capable of taking heavy tanks and armoured vehicles, over the Canal next to the blown-up St Anna bridge. The 4th Armoured Division was thus able to continue its advance on 4th April to Bornerbroek, Zenderen and Almelo. Here they had a tough battle with the Germans, but drove them out next day, taking many prisoners.

Meanwhile, also on 3rd April, a little further west, the Canadian Lake Superior Regiment and the 22nd Canadian Armoured Regiment, supported by the 15th Canadian Field Regiment, RCA, had forced another boat-crossing of the Canal next to the lock-bridge at Wiene and established a beach-head under cover of heavy artillery fire and smoke against strong German resistance. Here again, the Engineers were able to throw a Bailey bridge over the Canal, which enabled the Lake Superior troops to link up with those of the Lincoln and Welland and advance together eventually to Almelo.

A small but significant question has been asked about these later battles for the Canal: why didn't the British from Enschede by-pass Hengelo and Delden and assist the Canadians by attacking the Germans from the rear? I have seen no answer to this.

The British units that went into Enschede now headed west to Hengelo on 3rd April in two formations: 5th Dorsets and 'A' Squadron of the Sherwood Rangers Yeomanry headed for Hengelo, followed

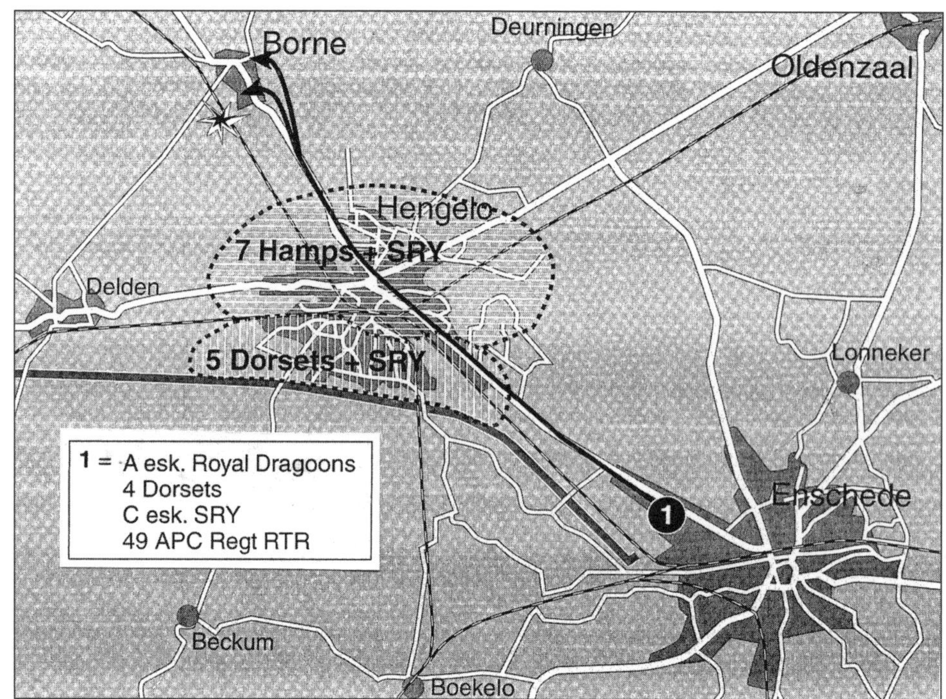

The Liberation of Borne, 4.30pm 3rd April 1945: the route of the 4th Battalion, the Dorset Regiment, from Enschede, assisted by the tanks of 'C' Squadron of the Sherwood Forest Yeomanry.

Map: Hans Pol "Our Forgotten Liberators"

The 4th Dorsets entering Borne, with the tanks in close support.

Photo: A. C. Meyling

Sherman tanks of the Sherwood Forest Yeomanry advancing into Borne.
Photos: A. C. Meyling

A Senior Dutch police officer shepherds a group of cheerful German prisoners in Borne under the guns of a Sherman tank.

Photo: A. C. Meyling

Celebrating the Ending of Five Years of German Occupation:
Sherwood Forest Yeomanry enjoy the moment with the children of Borne.

Photo: Borne Municipal Archive

by 12 KRRC who, however, passed through the town and moved into the woods of Woolde to invest Delden from the east. The tanks of the Sherwood Rangers exchanged shell-fire with the enemy defending Hengelo but, although the Dorsets lost three soldiers in a Bren-gun carrier, they faced little other opposition from the Germans, 200 of whom were taken prisoner. The 8th Armoured Brigade's War Diary recorded:

"With the capture of Hengelo on 3rd, the supply line of V2s from Hannover to Amsterdam was cut off. Woolde and Borne remain. The Canadians took care of the rest of the region."

'C' Squadron Diary stated: "Many RAF escapees were hiding in Hengelo – thanks to the splendidly loyal Dutch – and here we found and freed them." .

Among them would have been Sgt Whittaker, the companion of Peter Thorne when they made their desperate escape from a cattle-truck, which resulted in Peter's sad death. Another person freed was a Jewish girl of 16 hidden in an attic for four years by a non-Jewish Dutch family. There were many other beneficiaries from similar acts of self-sacrifice by ordinary Dutch people who harboured Jews being rounded-up, Dutchmen evading deportation to Germany, and hunted Resistance fighters; everyone rejoiced at returning to a free life, even though it took many years to restore normality.

Hengelo gave the 5th Dorsets and 7th Hampshires a great welcome, with celebrations of their Liberation continuing for the six days that the troops were billeted there, while they rested after their exertions on the battle-field and refitted their vehicles; a dance was even held in the street, illuminated by the light from vehicles' headlights. Another Bailey bridge was thrown across the Canal near Hengelo, next to the blown-up Oeler bridge.

On 9th April, the HQ of the British 130th Brigade moved on to Oldenzaal, but the Canadian 4th Armoured Brigade stayed in Delden, setting-up their HQ in Twickel Castle.

The other formation from Enschede on 3rd April was led by 'A' Recce Squadron of the Royal Dragoons, followed by the tanks of 'C' Squadron of the Sherwood Rangers Yeomanry, and the 4th Battalion of the Dorsets riding in the armoured personnel carriers of 'C' Squadron of the 49th APC of the Royal Tank Regiment. .They turned to the right before Hengelo itself and headed for Borne, four miles away to the north. Everywhere they received a warm welcome from the inhabitants, with Dutch flags flying and people wearing orange rosettes. The weather was comparatively sunny after the persistent rain of the previous three days. Entering Borne at 1600hr, the Dragoons went ahead into the town centre, but found themselves opposed by the Germans and called for help. The tanks of the Sherwood Rangers drove off the enemy – who withdrew steadily out of Borne. 'D' Company of the 4th Dorsets marched in and quickly occupied the south part of the town.

In the northern part Lt. Colonel Roberts, the CO of the 4th Dorsets, called off the artillery support that was available in order to spare the buildings of the town. The 52nd Canadian Grenadier Guards, on their way through Bornerbroek, were detached from the rest of the 4th Canadian Armoured Brigade, and entered Borne from the north. By 2000hr, with the surrender of 12 Germans, Borne was fully liberated, and the 49th APC returned to Hengelo.

The British and Canadians received the same joyous reception from the people as their comrades in Hengelo. The Grotestraat Market in the centre of the town was re-named Dorset Square. The White House, the elegant former home of the Spanjaard family, became the HQ of the 4th Dorsets. They stayed for six days enjoying a well-deserved rest among the grateful population.

On 9th April, they moved on to Lingen, meeting up with the rest of the 130th Brigade, joining the 43rd Wessex Division at Oldenzaal, and then continued their advance to Bremen. On the same day, the 52nd Canadian Grenadier Guards moved their Battalion HQ into the White House, and stayed in Borne till the end of the war and later, not leaving until September 1945.

Further to the west of Holland, the plight of the Dutch people in the cities of Amsterdam, Rotterdam and The Hague was desperate after the Germans had forbidden all transport by train of food when the railway workers went on strike at the urging of the Allies at the time of 'Market Garden'. In the winter of 1944/45 20,000 died of starvation. To try to alleviate their condition, the Allies negotiated with Seyss-Inquart to allow Bomber Command to drop food to the worst-hit districts, unopposed by flak or fighters. On 29th April, Operation 'Manna' started; one squadron, for example, dropped 42 tons of supplies in 20lb cartons, enough to feed one-fifth of the population of The Hague for one day. This, of course, was multiplied a thousand times as many more sorties were flown by many more squadrons. Two days later, thousands of trucks arrived in Holland through France and Belgium, bringing yet more food to the beleaguered population. These deliveries of life-saving food continued until 8th May.

On 3rd May, Hamburg surrendered to the 2nd British Army without a fight; on the same day, the British and the Russians met at the town of Wismar, beside the Elbe. Next day, Field Marshal Montgomery received the surrender of all the German forces in the West in his HQ on Luneburg Heath, close to the river: five representatives of the Commanders-in-Chief of the German Army, Navy and Air Force signed the instrument of surrender; all fighting stopped at 8.0am next day. Three days later, on 7th May, hostilities ceased on all fronts, including the Eastern. In Britain, 8th May 1945 was celebrated as VE-Day, with great joy and relief, but not with wild delight – the suffering and loss of life had been too heavy and the cost to the economy, industry, and living conditions had been too great, not only in Britain but, to a far larger extent, in all the countries occupied by the Germans – a heavy weight round Europe's neck for the next 30 years, further increased by the Cold War with Russia.

Of course, cooped-up behind the wire in Stalag Luft I up on the Baltic, I knew little enough of these stirring events. As the Russians advanced steadily into north-east Germany and along the coast, the Germans announced they were evacuating us from the camp: we were given 24-hours' notice to be ready to march away to the west to escape the Russians, as other POWs were being forced to do. This move was fortunately cancelled when the Russians' advance cut across our route; on the second occasion, the Senior American and British Officers refused to obey the order, on the grounds that it would be impossible to feed, accommodate and protect 15,000 prisoners on the march.

On 30th April, the Germans abandoned the camp – it turned out that the prisoners had agreed not to molest the unarmed administrative staff as they left! This was the day when Hitler committed suicide – but it made no difference to our situation, alone in the midst of a country in chaos. Next day the Russians arrived: every kind of soldier, walking, riding, in horse-drawn landaus, including boys draped in bandoliers, pistols and swords, all swarming over the countryside like wild animals and terrorising the inhabitants. They wanted us to leave the camp and join them in creating mayhem among the German population, in revenge for all the suffering that the Russians had endured at their hands. Many Americans ran off, but the RAF were told they would be court-martialed in Britain if they followed suit: we were safe where we were. On 5th May, we put on our motley uniforms and marched past in front of Marshal Rokossovsky, commander of the Belorussian Army Group. On Sunday 6th May, Wing Commander Hilton arrived by jeep from the British lines 70 miles to the west; he was making a survey of the condition of POWs all over this part of Germany; his driver was a welcome guest in my room, where there was a spare bed. Next day, we were presented with a concert party by a Red Army Choir, who had wonderful voices but, more importantly for many sex-starved ' Kriegies', some of the stage-dancers were girls! The next day was VE-Day in Britain, but we had no share in it – we felt deserted.

The Russians then announced that, as we'd been liberated on the Eastern Front, we would have to be returned to Britain via Odessa, on the Black Sea. They were stalling, playing for time while they negotiated with the Allied Governments that all Russian-born soldiers, including the Cossacks and those who had fought for the Germans, should be returned to Russia. This posed a tragic dilemma: it was almost certain that the two latter categories would be shot or, at best, deported to Siberia; yet our return to

Britain, together with POWs in similar camps, was the bargaining weapon. The move to Odessa did not occur, but we were told that, to leave the Russian Zone, we would each need 12 copies of a passport made out in Russian! Fortunately, the Senior British Officer escaped to the British lines and received assurances that American B-17s would be sent to Barth airfield on 12th May. The Russians were informed but did not dispute this: they watched impassively as the first aircraft landed to take off all the sick prisoners and some others. Next day, we marched informally to the airfield, the B-17s returned, three of us squeezed into the tail-turret of our aircraft, and we were treated to a sight-seeing trip over Hamburg, totally devastated, and other German towns, before landing at Ford Airfield in Sussex.

The first person I saw on the ground was the Station Commander, a Group Captain with a row of medal-ribbons: it was none other than 'Cub' Hartley, the master-cum-Pilot Officer in charge of the Air Section of the OTC at Eton, to whom I used to whisper the words of command before he uttered them! I could not stop to renew our acquaintance of four distant years earlier. So, rather belatedly, ended my war.

Sixty years later, on my annual pilgrimage to 't Hesseler, I was having breakfast quietly by myself in "Jachtlust" ("The Pleasure of Hunting"), my comfortable hotel outside Borne, when a well-dressed middle-aged Dutchman came up to me and said:

"Are you Jimmy Taylor?"

"Yes, I am."

"I'd like you to have this," and he placed a small packet on my table.

I was taken aback, but said:

"May I open it?"

"Yes, of course".

I opened it carefully, and there in tissue-paper was a beautiful tie, dark-blue in colour, and with a recognisable Lancaster bomber embroidered in gold, with a shower of small golden dots falling beneath it. I knew straightaway that this was made in commemoration of Operation 'Manna'.

I looked up at him:

"This is wonderful, but it has nothing to do with me."

"Oh, yes, it has, because you Liberated us."

"But I didn't," I protested. *"I was a prisoner of war and was myself liberated by the Russians."*

"No," he replied. *"You all played your part in our Liberation, and this is my 'Thank you' to you."*

What could I say? I felt very moved; I stood up, shook him warmly by the hand and clapped him on the back.

"Thank you very, very much," I said. *"I shall always treasure this."*

I wanted to ask him many questions, but he just turned and walked away.

Such are the people of Twente. Is it any wonder that my spirits are uplifted and that I am flooded with such a feeling of gratitude that my tears are very close each time that I return?

Note:

I am greatly indebted to Mr Hans J.A.G. Pol and his masterly bi-lingual Dutch-English book "Onze vergeten bevrijders"/ "Our Forgotten Liberators – An investigation into the actions of the British and Canadian units in East Holland, March-April 1945" (Drukkerij Twente Hengelo 1997) for most of the military information in this chapter. JT

CHAPTER 42

Journey's End

My visit to Holland in 2009 was eventful to an extent that I was not expecting, as I considered in 2008 that there was nothing more for me to discover. What I now saw and heard for the first time was almost entirely due to Hennie Noordhuis's understanding of my needs and interests and to his willingness to follow-up leads offered by other people. On this occasion, 1st-5th May 2009, I can link our time-scale to the geography, as we started our researches far from Borne and ended on its outskirts.

Joop Thuring, a Dutch military historian and brother of the well-known Rev G.Thuring, contributor to several Dutch histories of 'Market Garden' in my possession, had seen a copy of my unpublished manuscript "Focus on Arnhem" in the Airborne Museum in Oosterbeek; he had contacted Hennie Noordhuis, had photocopied the whole of Hennie's copy – with my approval when I heard of it – and had told Hennie he would like to meet me. So, on my first morning, Hennie collected me at 8.30 from the "Jachtlust" hotel, and we drove about 80 miles south to join Joop at Volkel Air Base, two miles south-east of Uden, between Eindhoven and Nijmegen. The airfield had been extended by the Germans to become a fully operational base, so it was heavily bombed and put out of action by the Allies just prior to Operation 'Market Garden'. This is why it is rarely mentioned in the histories, even though it was restored and used by the 2nd Tactical Air Force from early October 1944 until 1946, when the RNLAF took it over; it is still a fully-functioning front-line fighter station with F-16 aircraft. Here we met Peter, another historian, and were shown round the very interesting "Typhoon" Museum, which provides extensive coverage of the varied history of the base; I was particularly drawn to the exhibit of a post-war pod for a 'fan' of three cameras, which could be attached to any aircraft, and of another such pod for infra-red imagery – both very different from the cameras and mountings inside our Spitfires.

A 'fan' of three cameras, taking horizon-horizon photos of the ground in a 1975 Orpheus airborne 'pod', which could be attached to a variety of aircraft. In the "Typhoon" Museum at Volkel Air Base.

I try to sort some of Joop Thuring's collection of photographs into their 'line-overlap' sequences.
Photo: Hennie Noordhuis

After he and his wife had given us a good lunch in their pleasant wisteria-covered house, Joop led us out northwards to see a section of the still recognisable "Hell's Highway", up which XXX Corps had struggled to reach Arnhem against continual fierce incursions by the Germans, and over which the 16 Squadron pilots had usually flown on their way to and from their message-dropping sorties. When we stopped by a convent with an outstanding sculptured group on its outside wall, which survived the fighting in 1944, I was surprised to find that the road surface was composed of neatly-cut cobblestones; Joop said they were like the original ones, which must have received very rough treatment from the tanks of XXX Corps.

After going a little further north, we turned left off the Highway to view the site of Keent airstrip, No 67 on Jefford's map, and numbered B82 by the Allied Air Forces. By a nice coincidence, in March Nick Lambrechtsen had sent me from New Zealand a map showing its location due west of Grave, and a long article, with photographs, about its history from its origin in 1928, including the inexplixable failure of 2nd TAF to use it for close-support to our troops during 'Market Garden'; the first instance of its employment in that Operation was when 207 American Dakotas flew from England over two days, 26th/27th September, with reinforcements of soldiers, jeeps, and supplies, and returned with the wounded from the Arnhem survivors and from the battles round the "Highway", Nijmegen and Groesbeek. Seven squadrons of Spitfires and one of Tempests came and went from the strip during October, but it was then deserted until a single Spitfire squadron and an Auster squadron stayed there for two weeks in March-April 1945. After their departure, the airstrip reverted to grassland, and shows no evidence today that it once supported fleets of powerful aircraft and housed their aircrews.

Next day, we came back almost to the same area to visit the excellent "Wings of Liberation" Museum described earlier, as it was publicising a special 'Market Garden' exhibition. However, we were sadly disappointed: the museum had been taken over from the original voluntary body of military enthusiasts by a business-man, who had reduced its size in order to erect money-making buildings, such as a large restaurant and holiday accommodation. Most of the previous exhibits had gone except for a few inside

A section of "Hell's Highway" of 1944 between Uden and Grave; with just room for two-way traffic, it was easily blocked by breakdowns and German attacks on the 20,000 vehicles of XXX Corps trying to reach Arnhem. Note the cobble-stones of this part.

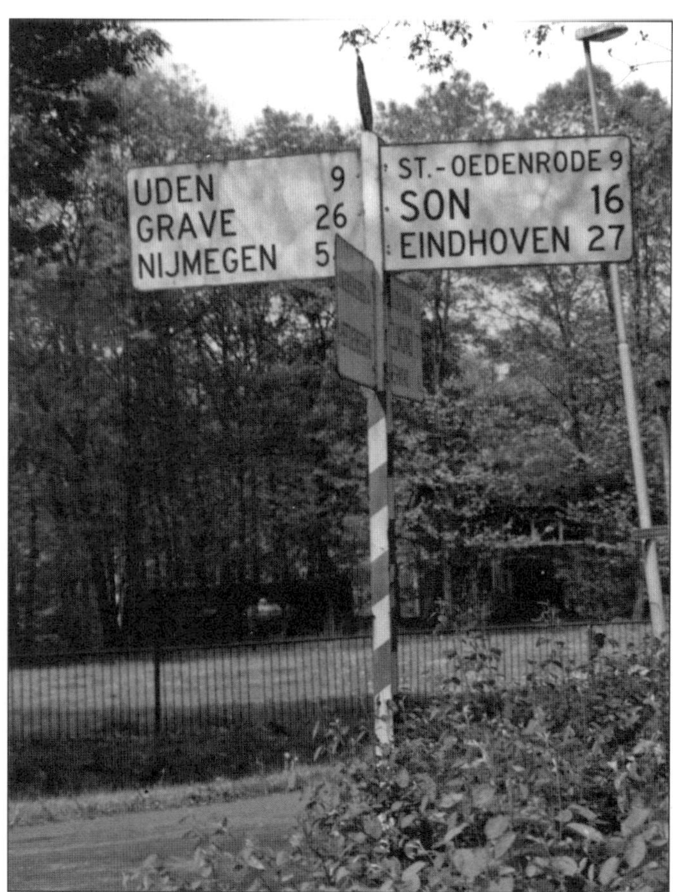

A sign-post giving (from lower right, round to lower left) the names and distances of the principal towns on "Hell's Highway". Now displayed at the "Wings of Liberation" Museum.

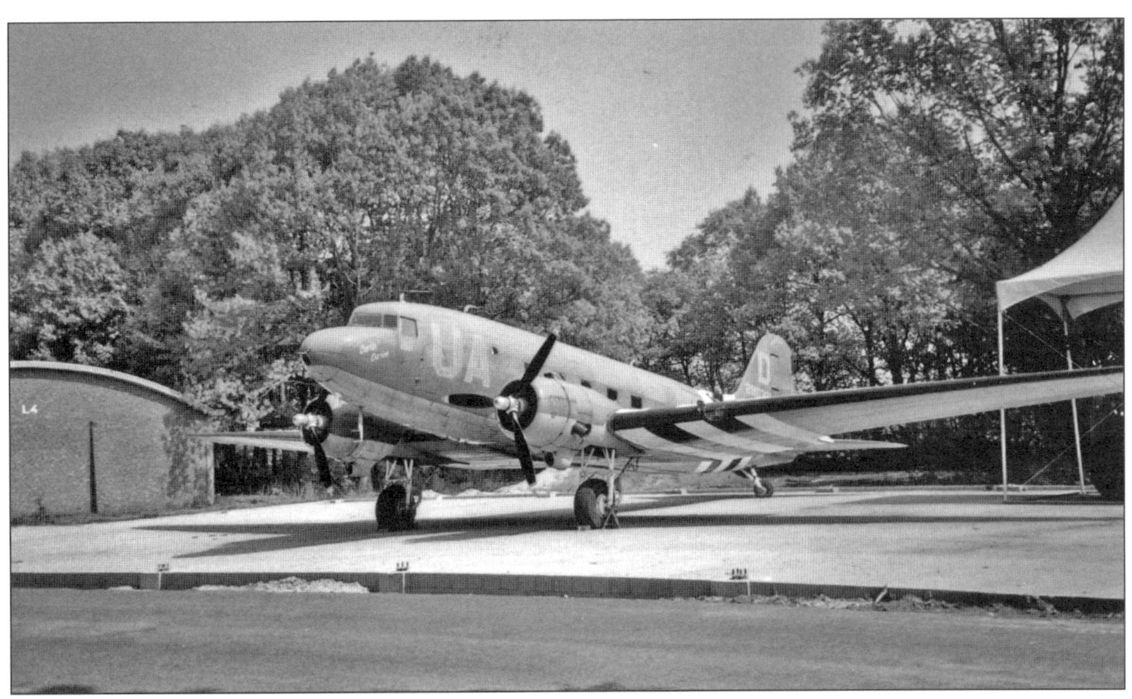

An American Dakota troop-carrier at the "Wings of Liberation" Museum: one of the original exhibits kept by the new owner.

a building devoted to 'Market Garden' but not yet finished. This is a great loss to WW2 veterans, their families, and other interested visitors.

From there we drove to Arnhem, for Hennie to take me to the War Museum, a distinct entity from the Airborne Museum and one I had not yet seen. It is run by helpful volunteers and appeared somewhat cluttered, but the exhibits, displays and large numbers of contemporary photographs gave me a vivid sense of what life in Arnhem during the battle was like from the residents' point of view, and revealed their distress when they were all forcibly evacuated from their homes by the Germans at a few hours' notice in reprisal for their support of the Airborne soldiers. This War Museum, in presenting the civilian view of 'Market Garden', is a valuable complement to the Airborne Museum, with its emphasis on the military aspects of the Battle of Arnhem, in contrast to the unfortunate scaling-down of the "Wings of Liberation" Museum.

A photograph in the Arnhem War Museum of some of the 100,000 inhabitants forced by the Germans to evacuate their homes after the defeat of the 1st British Airborne Division on 26th September 1944.

As I have recounted previously, Marinus Timmerman was a teenager, living with his parents and three brothers and a sister in "The Resting Hunter" restaurant near Bentelo, when my smoke-trailing Spitfire crashed into their nearby field, and he burned his fingers on the hot metal skin. He lived in Arnhem, but had been unwell for some time and sadly died on 24th March this year. We therefore called on Thea, his widow, to express our sympathy at the passing of a good friend, who had often joined us at the restaurant and enjoyed being present at the meetings I held with historians in Arnhem. The following day, we visited his older sister Betsie in her home in Delden, a dear person, now rather frail and much depressed by the death of her favourite brother. I gave her a tin of English "Motoring" sweets, the same gift that I have brought her every year, in the hope that it might help to cheer her up; she died, however, in 2011.

Thea (l) and Marinus Timmerman (r) and Betsie Timmerman, with Hennie Noordhuis, visiting 't Hesseler in 2008.

Earlier that day, Hennie had taken me to Almelo, about ten miles north of Borne. We took a rural route and on the way passed the wooded estate where the very active local Resistance had its HQ until it was betrayed to the Germans in September 1944. They had demolished the house, but on the roadside outside the present entrance gate is a cross, a flag-pole, and a memorial stone inscribed with the names of three members arrested in the house and executed on 23rd September in a wood outside Almelo. In this wood is another memorial to them, which Jan Bovenmars had shown me on a visit there in 2003.

It was strange, really, that we drove only a few miles further to the pleasant town of Almelo, where Hennie took me to see, standing in a tree-lined road, an unpretentious suburban three-storey brick house, which had been the HQ of the local German Security Police, or Gestapo. This was where young Jan Vonk would have been interrogated before being locked-up in Almelo Prison, to be taken out and shot outside Borne Town Hall on the evening of my landing in 't Hesseler on 19th November 1944, "to teach you Dutch not to hide Allied pilots".

The Memorial to three members of the Resistance caught when their HQ, a house surrounded by trees near Zenderen, was raided by the Germans, who demolished the building.

Here also F/0 Gerald Hood, who had been hidden by the Resistance after baling out of his stricken Lancaster on 12th August 1944, would have been questioned after he and his Resistance rescuer Bote van der Val had been betrayed on 13th March 1945; as I have described earlicr, Hood was shot on the 21st, followed by Bote van der Val on the 24th, in the same Wood of Execution that had witnessed the shooting of the three Resistance members on 23rd September, and where memorial stones carry the names of all five victims. These were but some of the atrocities perpetrated by the Almelo Gestapo. This building that looks so innocent is still a symbol of betrayal, inquisition and death – the hallmarks of the German Occupation.

The harmless-looking but dreaded HQ of the Gestapo in Almelo, where all the above men, and also Jan Vonk, were brought, interrogated, and probably tortured, before they were locked in cells until their execution, by a shot in the back of the head, was ordered.

The next day, we went south again to Enschede, where we called-in at the Rijksmuseum Twente to see whether my request that Hanneman's "Father Roeland de Pottere, SJ, 1661" had been re-hung next to his equally fine painting of his Dutch artist-friend in England, Cornelis Jonson, with his wife and young son. I was disappointed to find the portraits were still hanging in separate rooms; but I was pleased to see that other visitors were looking at "Father Roeland" and, I hope, reading on the brass plate alongside it of how it came to be in the Museum.

Hennie had learned that a textile factory was still standing that had been used by the Germans during the war as a temporary cage for Allied prisoners. We had searched Enschede some years earlier

The Memorial gives the names of the three people and dates their execution as 22nd September 1944. There is another Memorial to them in the Wood of Execution where F/O Gerald Hood and his chivalrous helper, Bote van der Wal, were shot similarly in March 1945.

for just such a place, where I had been cooped-up for ten days with about 50 Airborne troops captured in hiding after the Arnhem debacle; but I couldn't recognise either the building, or the sloping street down which we walked for our meals in a simple cafe. Now Hennie drove me into an industrial part of Enschede, with several textile mills still standing, one of which he pointed out as my former prison-camp. My memories had become rather vague after such a long passage of time and, among them, there was no distinctive feature by which to definitely identify this building as the one; but if the local historians and Hennie said that this was the place, I was happy to accept their verdict and glad to have seen it. We could not go in, as everywhere was shut for the Dutch public holiday for the Queen's Birthday and the National Commemoration and Liberation days. As prisoners, we had not been treated badly in it in 1944 and, except for the rats at night, there was nothing against the Geneva Convention in the treatment we received. So my feelings were actually quite positive: of admiration for the discipline of the Airborne NCOs, which they ensured was maintained by the other ranks, and of secret pleasure at my ability to argue for better food and conditions with the German Hauptmann, even though I had little success.

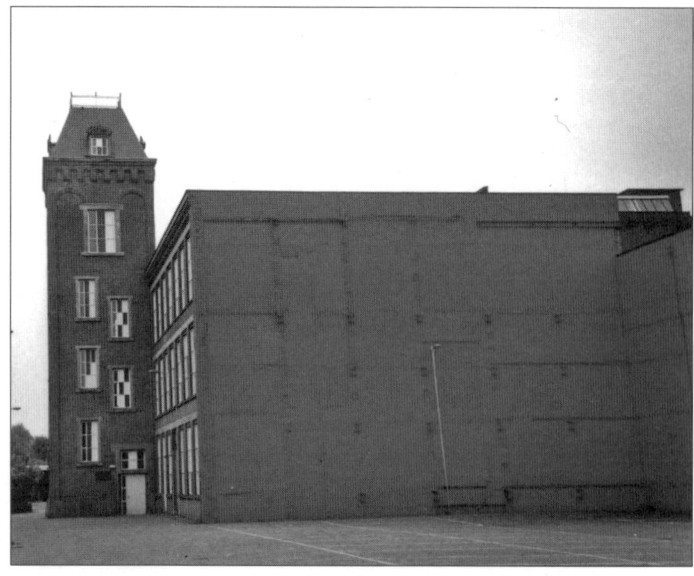

The factory in Enschede used as a POW cage, where I spent from 28th November to 6th December 1944.

On our way to my final objective, the Twente Canal, we stopped beside the Almelo Canal, which joins it at a point between Delden and Goor. It was perhaps this broad junction that I had seen briefly during my parachute descent and which I had thought was a lake in which I might drown – but I had just shut my eyes and gone back into my doze.

The Delden lock-bridge (Sluis) in 2009: the steel gate at each end lifts up between the two towers; the road-bridge crosses behind the towers.

Now we were going to the Twente Canal, not to revisit the St Anna Bridge under which I had tried to swim across the freezing cold water in November 1944, but to have a look at the Delden Sluis, the Dutch name for the lock and bridge over the Canal south of Delden. This a company of the 12th Battalion of the King's Royal Rifle Corps under Major William Deedes had tried, and failed, to capture on 2nd April 1945. What we saw astonished me: a pair of huge brick towers at either end of the lock, each pair supporting between them a massive sheet of steel that was lowered and raised vertically in slots in the towers by invisible machinery. This was totally different from the simple wooden gates, opened horizontally by hand, that are found at each end of the narrow locks in Britain. We were fortunate that a large well-laden barge passed through this Sluis while we were there and we could watch it in operation. The answers to my inquiries all suggested that the two pairs of towers were in existence before and during the war; yet no mention was made of them in a British reconnaissance report on 2nd April which stated that 'a few planks' would cover a hole in the bridge and so enable the troops to cross the Canal. The reports about the battle say nothing about German snipers harassing 12th KRRC from the towers, or of the British guns shelling them; yet a 'Ger(man) sniper' is scribbled on one of the further towers in in the photograph on p.629 in relation to the Canadians' success a few days later.

The better-equipped Canadians later stormed across the Canal in small boats under smoke and strong supporting fire in at least two places, while the British were obliged to follow the Canal eastwards to its terminal in Enschede and drive round this end to head back towards Hengelo. Here the 4th Battalion of the Dorsetshire Regiment, carried in vehicles of the 49th Armoured Personnel Carrier Regiment, and supported by the tanks of C Squadron of the Sherwood Rangers Yeomanry, branched north to liberate Borne on 3rd April.

My last request to Hennie, therefore, was to see this terminal in Enschede. It proved to be a fair-sized harbour equipped with quays and cranes for loading and landing cargoes. It made me realise what an important thoroughfare the Canal provides for the conveyance of industrial and commercial materials and goods between Enschede, Hengelo, Delden, Goor, and smaller places along its 28 miles to Zutphen. It reminded me that on 8th November 1944, I had photographed it in bad visibility

The terminus of the Twente Canal in Enschede.
After 12 KRRC failed to capture the Delden lock-bridge, the 7th Hampshires and 5th Dorsets had to go round the end of the Canal here to reach Hengelo

in mistake for the much longer and better-known Dortmund-Ems Canal, which was not very far away. This was continually bombed and the water drained out by Bomber Command, which interrupted the valuable flow of war materials from the Ruhr industries to the harbours, airfields, and military centres in North-West Germany. I think now that the Twente Canal must have played a similar role, on a much smaller scale, in transporting goods of importance to the Germans from the industrial towns of Enschede and Hengelo to be transhipped at Zutphen. Perhaps we should have given it a little of the treatment we gave its bigger brother.

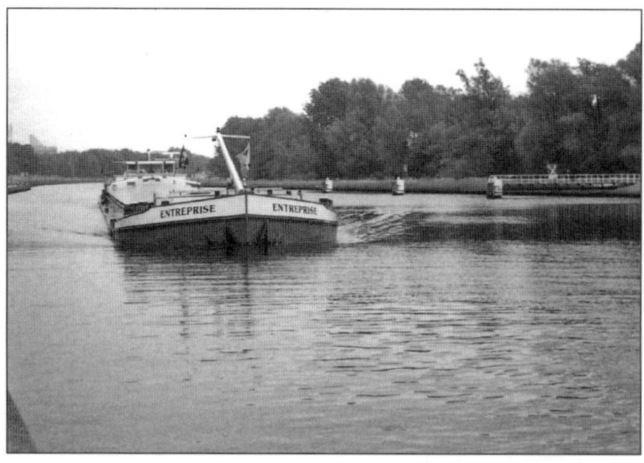

A barge coming from Enschede approaches the lock-gates of 'Delden Sluis'; the central island (as in 1945) is appearing on the right.

As it was, it was a pleasure to stand on the bank of the Canal at the Delden Sluis and salute the skipper of the barge as he steered his large unwieldy craft past us into the close confines of the lock – and to be given a return salute with a smile: he was proud of the job he was doing.

So we returned to Borne: as always, the hub of our excursions to places that had stirred so many memories, joyful and sorrowful, during this visit in May 2009.

Here there were, and a few still are, the families whose friendship has been so heart-warming and invaluable in enabling me to come to terms with the disaster caused by my landing in their midst sixty-five years ago: brothers and sisters of the victims, nephews and nieces, great-nephews and great-nieces – a wonderful community of people united in their loss. Any barrier caused by the differences in our ages is invisible, and the fact that I don't speak Dutch has been no problem, as most of them are fluent English-speakers. In truth, had it not been for the brutality of the occupying Germans, if I had to bale out and land somewhere in Europe in 1944, I could not have found a more kindly place than the scattered hamlet of 't Hesseler

It is equally true that, on coming there in 1991 as a virtual stranger, I could not have chanced on a more dedicated historian, guide, and searcher for the truth, or made a closer, more understanding friend, with a similarly welcoming wife and family, than Hennie Noordhuis. The second half of this book would not have come to life without his long, generous and fertile collaboration.

My indefatigable organisers, collaborators, hosts and friends; Hennie and Joke Noordhuis flying their own Dutch-British flag

CHAPTER 43

Full Circle

In 2008 I felt that my story had come to its logical ending: 16 Squadron had been disbanded; "16 Squadron 1939-1945" was reduced to just four or five known survivors; I had ceased producing "Newsbrief"; and I had finished gliding; only my visits to Holland were still continuing strongly, as evidenced by my activities there in 2009.

After being rebuffed by two reputable aviation publishers, mainly because my manuscript was in typescript and not on the digital disc that publishers now demand, I decided to take it to a self-publisher and, fortunately, found one in Yorkshire. This was York Publishing Services, usefully situated 45 minutes drive away in York itself, and headed by Duncan Beal, with long experience at all levels of the printing and publishing business. He thought that his scanner could produce a satisfactory transfer of my typescript, with perhaps 10% errors but, in fact, it caused lengthy hold-ups until he gave me a new Graphic Designer in the form of Barry Perks, who happened to live in a village even nearer to Leeds and was a maestro on his computer. We developed a very close working relationship, as he agreed to provide whatever I wanted, but I came to rely on his own judgement to such an extent that the finished text, all in digital format ready for printing, came to be virtually a joint production. Barry's empathy with my story was most evident when he joined me in Borne for two days in May 2011, attended the ceremony at the 't Hesseler Memorial, participated in the Silent Walk, visited the main sites connected with my landing, and met many of my friends, including Fred Bakker, who kindly presented me with my portrait in watercolours, which had been under consideration for several years.

Barry's close cooperation brought forward the completion date of the digital version to the autumn of 2011, which meant that a number of events could be included which really brought my story full-circle, linking the distant past to the topical present.

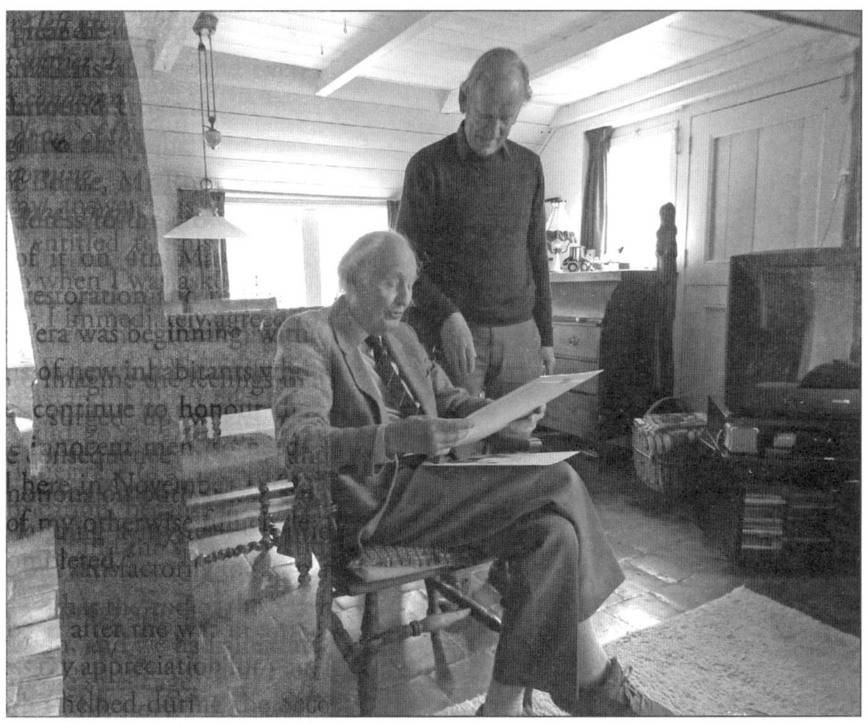

Fred Bakker presents JT with his water-colour portrait.
Photo: Hennie Noordhuis

The starting-point has to be Cheam School, my birthplace and home for 25 years, 12 of them in Cheam village, outside Sutton in Surrey, and the rest in Headley in Hampshire, four miles from Newbury in Berkshire. Here was always a place of warmth, rest, recreation and inspiration.

In my father's time as Headmaster, which was dominated by the 'slump' of the 1930's and the War in the 1940's, the number of boys in the School ranged between 60 and 70. After his retirement in 1947, the increasing prosperity of the country and a series of enlightened Headmasters, who soon became salaried professionals under a Board of Governors, led to a steady increase in the number of pupils, the inclusion of day-boys and then girls, the development of a Pre-Prep, the adoption of a Nursery, and a continuing programme of well-designed new buildings, the latest being an Art, Design and Technology Centre. In 2010, the School numbers reached 400 boys and girls, aged from 3 to 13, with more day-children than boarders. At the same time, both the curriculum and extra-curricular activities were broadened and pupils engaged in ambitious sporting and cultural events in many parts of the world, such as the Cricket XI playing against schools in Kenya and South Africa, and the Choir singing in Notre Dame Cathedral in Paris and at the site of the World Trade Centre in New York.

I have a deep affection for the whole environment of the School, especially the beautiful gardens, although much of the woodlands and the 1½-mile-long drive have been sold-off. Coupled with this is my gratitude for the education I received and the friendships I formed, both with my fellow-pupils and with the teaching and domestic staffs. So it was a very great pleasure in 1985 to join the Committee of the Cheam School Association for former members of the School, whose annual meetings enable me to indulge my nostalgia, keep track of the School's performance, and enjoy the hospitality of the present inspired and energetic Headmaster, Mark Johnson, and his no less creative wife Jane, who teaches Classics and forms a great team with her husband. They live in a delightful house on the edge of the garden, appropriately named Whitehall Lodge, after Whitehall in Cheam village, the original home of the School in 1645 and now a museum and community centre. In 1984 and 2009 I was asked to give a talk to the School as it celebrated the 50th and 75th Anniversaries of my father's saving the School by moving it from Old Cheam to Beenham Court in Headley; and in 2002 I felt very honoured to open Taylor Building, a handsome two-storey complex of classrooms and a library, completing a quadrangle with a central fountain, named in memory of my father.

The Taylor building housing classrooms and the library; the tower encloses a staircase. In the centre of the courtyard behind the nearest shrub is a fountain.
Photo: Mark Johnson, Headmaster

By a remarkable coincidence, when I was visiting Whitehall Lodge under the previous Headmaster, Chris Evers, I happened to see a framed photograph of a pink Spitfire flying low over some countryside. This could only have been a PR Spitfire based at Benson in about 1941 and perhaps flying from St Eval in Cornwall. I asked his wife, Penny, the significance of this photo and she said the pilot was her father, F/Lt Gordon Green! He undertook numerous sorties over German and French ports, such as Heligoland and Brest, whose heavy flak defences caused many PR casualties; this was in the days when the main threat to Britain came from German surface raiders slipping out of harbour to attack the Atlantic convoys on whom our survival depended. Gordon was awarded a DFC and went on to become a respected test-pilot. He married Beryl, Penny's mother, who was in charge of the WAAFs at Benson. I had several lively conversations with her, during one of which she showed me Gordon's wartime log-book. It was a great privilege to meet the family of a pilot who, in the early days, helped to work-out the procedures and tactics of PR, which formed the accepted practices by the time I joined it in 1944.

My relationship with Eton is totally different from that of Cheam, because of the serious damage to my brother Gerald's personality from the constant bullying he was subjected to by his contemporaries in our House. I have no wish to meet any of his tormentors again, so I have never attended any Reunions; I respect the quality of my own education, especially the attention paid to me by my tutors, W.M.M. Milligan and Geoffrey Agnew; but I take little pleasure in my own achievements of becoming Captain of my House, reaching VI Form (the top 12 Oppidans) and being elected to "Pop" (Eton's version of school prefects) – all resulting from many senior boys leaving early to join the Forces. I have never worn my Old Etonian tie.

I hold in much warmer regard the post-war Cambridge University, and especially Trinity College. Of course, I was much older and knew what I wanted from my three years there and I worked hard to achieve it. However, it is the beauty and historic background of the buildings and their setting that have had a lasting effect on me, and I grow fonder with the passing of time. I take every opportunity to return, especially for the Annual Gathering of Alumni at Trinity, when my group of near-contemporaries receives its invitation every ten years. My turn came again on 5th July 2011: there was a wonderful Choral Evensong in the University Church, followed by an outdoor Reception in Nevile's Court, and a splendid Dinner for 240 of us in the candle-lit Great Hall, looked down on by the strutting portrait of the founder Henry VIII above the High Table and by the pictures of eminent Masters and distinguished alumni ranged all round the walls. For me, the high-point was the unaccompanied singing of the College Choir, high up in the gallery at the back of the Hall, while I savoured a selection of the fine wines from the College cellar. I spent the night in an empty study-bedroom on the fifth floor in one of the newer courts of the College, with a wonderful view at sunrise of the spires, turrets, and cupolas of other Cambridge colleges dotting the skyline. On such occasions, I feel very fortunate to have gone up to Cambridge in 1946 and very privileged, 65 years later, to be able to enjoy the pleasures of my association with this pre-eminent seat of learning.

My connection with flying, however, goes much further back. I don't really count as my first flight my experience of flying from Calshot in a Saro London flying-boat when I was about ten years old: I was placed by myself in the fuselage, could hardly see out, and had little idea of what was happening until the noisy landing. Far superior was the flight in 1935 with Sir Alan Cobham's Flying Circus, when my father and all three of us excited children climbed into the cabin of a "Giant Airliner" and headed the stately procession of light aircraft and an autogyro from a field outside Penzance, out to sea over St. Michael's Mount, round the town past Mousehole, and back to the field. This was a joyful occasion with all my senses alert and, no doubt, a factor in all three of us joining the RAF during the War.

Finding Michael Cobham (later Sir Michael) inhabiting the room beneath me in Trinity College in 1948 was an additional bonus and led to my spending a day with him at the works of Flight Refuelling (later Cobham) in Dorset in December 1990. I also stayed over-night in his country-house and enjoyed the company of his wife and daughter. From this visit I became aware of the widespread interests and activities of Michael's enterprising aviation conglomerate and especially of the operation of 21 Dassault Falcons and 16 Hawker Hunters to provide training, through a range of electronic gadgetry, for the RAF and the Royal Navy respectively in simulated offensive and defensive operations at all levels of proficiency.

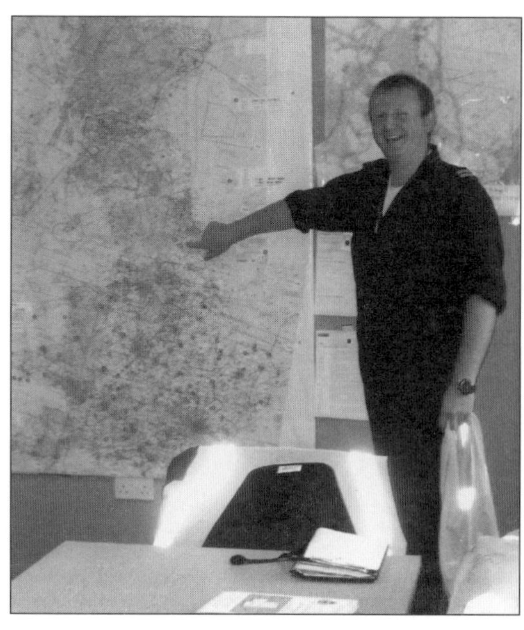
Ben Dorrington, my guide at Cobham, indicates the available zones.

When I discovered in 2009 that two of my former gliding instructors and one of my fellow club-members were all working for Cobham with six Falcons at Teeside Airport near Darlington in County Durham, I felt I had to pay them a visit in order to bring my connection with the Company to a fitting conclusion. On the 3rd August 2011, therefore, I drove to Teesside Airport, which I was surprised to find practically deserted, owing to the major competition from nearby Newcastle Airport. However, it was a delight to see the name "Cobham" written large on one of the hangars, and to meet my friends Bob Spiller, the Chief Engineering Officer; Ben Dorrington, a First Officer on the Falcons; and Keith Wallis, an Electronics Officer, Bob and Keith having done their best to teach me how to glide.

I spent a fascinating day with them: after Bob had shown me a promotional video of the work of Cobham, Ben took me into the Briefing Room and showed me on a wall-map the geographical areas, mainly over the North Sea, where the Falcons carried out their electronic exercises with aircraft of the RAF, and the restricted zones kept open for civil aircraft. He then took me out to one of the Falcons on the flight-line, effectively a former twin-engined executive jet, and explained the manifold purposes of the two main displays facing each of the two pilots, and all the other instruments and switches. Behind, in the cabin, half-filled with two huge 400-litre extra fuel tanks, sat an Electronics Officer waiting to tell me about the working of his instrument panel and all the devices under his control. Ben then took me round the outside of the Falcon, where several missile-shaped pods were hanging on external hard-points; these included an analyser of radar emissions from a hostile airborne aircraft or ground-station; an electronic

The cockpit of a Cobham Falcon, with twin displays for the Captain and 2nd pilot.

jammer for counter-measures; a communications jammer, and a chaff dispenser. By now my head was spinning with all the technical information that I had tried to absorb, and I was glad to return to Bob's office for a sandwich lunch.

One of the electronic pods for threat suppression

In the afternoon, the sortie that Ben would have flown on was cancelled, unfortunately, but I was allowed to sit-in on the briefing of another crew that was scheduled for an exercise with aircraft of No 11 Squadron. The 'Skipper' of the Falcon was a very experienced ex-RAF pilot, as are all the Captains; the First Officer, or 2nd Pilot of the aircraft, was a younger man, who, by Cobham rules, could never become a Skipper – but Ben reckoned that the value of the job was well worth this bar to promotion; the Electronics Officer completed the crew. I couldn't understand much of the 'jargon' they used as they each briefed the others in turn, from notes they had made of the points about the coming encounter for which they were responsible and what action they should take. The serious professional atmosphere of this briefing, in spite of the familiarity of the crew with each other, I found very similar to the briefing for the final flight of 16 Squadron's Jaguar pilots – when they carried-out a simulated attack on Coltishall airfield – which the CO, Wing Commander Guy Stockill, had kindly allowed me to attend. After this, Ben came out with me to the flight-line again to watch the Falcon taxy out and take-off, climbing up to carry-out its planned electronic sortie.

So ended a day that more then fulfilled my expectations and revived my admiration for the Company that Sir Alan had started and his son Michael had developed so successfully. Everything I saw and heard on this visit, and all the people I met, both flying personnel and office workers, reflected a highly efficient organisation; yet, at the same time, I sensed very friendly relations between all the people concerned. Indeed, I felt I was almost back in the Cleveland Gliding Club, with its thread of RAF discipline underlying the informality of the members' dealings with those in authority and with each other. It made for safety in our gliding and, no doubt, is equally effective in Cobham's activities.

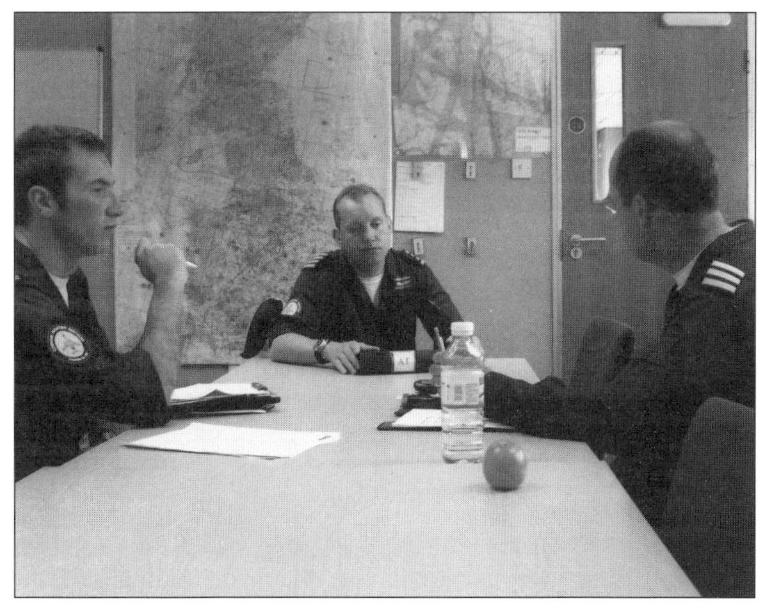
The crew of Falcon G-FRAT at their briefing:
(l-r) First Officer Captain Electronics Officer

I have never been back to the United States, so I can't claim to have completed a relationship that began in 1942 and 1943 with my training and instructing with the USAAF. On the other hand, I have made good friends with Americans outside the USA in connection with some aspect of flying. First, in

Falcon G-FRAT taxies out on its sortie: note the underslung electronic pods.

the crew of the B-17 "Aliquippa", whom I met in Borne at the Reception for the Veterans in the White House: Hubert O'Neill, Walter Sybo, and 'Sarge' Sumpter, and later accompanied them to the Flag-raising and Exhibition in Bentelo.

Second is Spencer Prou, who was a member of the Cleveland Gliding Club during my time and was an Intelligence Officer in the USAF based at Menwith Hill, about 15 miles from Dishforth, one of the two US 'listening posts' in Yorkshire, notable for its 20 or so radar discs housed in white plastic spheres of various sizes, commonly called 'golf-balls'. Spencer was a good glider pilot and was always urging me to go on a 'Buddy' flight with him; but, after my experience with the two veteran RAF pilots on the Instructors' Course at Upavon in 1946, I felt a strong prejudice against this form of two-seater flying, which rather baffled Spencer, as it was normal practice in the USA. After I left the Club in 2007, Spencer was posted to Dubai, where he was employed in assisting in the long-distance sorties of American drones to Afganistan, which I thought was very exciting, but he told me was 'rather boring'!

Spencer ensured that, if I couldn't go to America, America would come to me - in the shape of a beautiful silken 4ft x 2ft "Stars and Stripes", accompanied by a large Certificate saying that this flag had been flown in honour of Flight Lieutenant Jimmy Taylor in a B-1 bomber over Afghanistan in support of Operation 'Enduring Freedom' on 24th August 2008. It gave the names of the four crew: the Commander, the Co-pilot, the Offensive Systems Officer, and the Defensive Systems Officer; the B-1's call-sign, and the bomb-load of 12 GBU-38s and 8 GBU-31s; it was signed by Lt. Col. Kevin 'Trap' Kennedy, CO of the 34th Expeditionary Bomb Squadron, USAF. What a wonderful present from Spencer, literally out of the blue! Unfortunately, we in Britain don't usually have a flagpole in our garden, and it wouldn't be 'done' to fly the "Stars and Stripes" except on special occasions. So it rests on a chair in my dining-room/study, a constant reminder of the great-heartedness of the American people.

My third American I meet in October 2011 after I'd had a lengthy correspondence with him about a mystery connected with Operation 'Market Garden' in September 1944, which has long haunted those who have heard about it. It concerns Major Brian Urquhart, the Intelligence Officer of Lt Gen 'Boy' Browning, OC of the 1st Airborne Corps, the British and American force launched against Arnhem to capture the bridge over the Rhine and the area south of Nijmegen, to clear the 60-mile-long road from

Eindhoven up which it was hoped that XXX Corps would advance to relieve the Airborne troops holding the bridge. In spite of the many obvious drawbacks to the planned Operation, there was a general eagerness to get on with it, as the Germans were thought to be weak and demoralised after their retreat from France and Belgium. Urquhart, however, had word from the Dutch Resistance that tanks of the 9th and 10th SS Panzer Divisions were hiding near woods south-east of Arnhem. Browning dismissed such information, but allowed Urquhart to request a low-level photographic sortie from Benson to reveal whether there was such a threat. The sortie was flown on 12th or 13th September, and Urquhart showed the photos to Browning, who said the tanks were probably broken-down or under repair. When Urquhart protested, Browning sent him to the Medical Officer as suffering from mental strain (Urquhart eventually became Deputy Secretary-General of the United Nations and was given a Knighthood). The photographs disappeared – it is said that Browning tore them up – but several people are convinced that copies existed and could be in some archive or in the possession of one of the officers involved. One of them was Tony Hibbert, at the time the Brigade Major of 1 Parachute Brigade, who recorded in his diary that he saw the photos in Urquhart's caravan office on Moor Park Golf Club at 4.0pm on 12th September, five days before the start of 'Market Garden'.

Michael Cain had been an Intelligence Officer in the US Navy and had always been fascinated by 'Market Garden' ever since, as a boy, reading "A Bridge Too Far" by Cornelius Ryan and seeing the film. He had met Tony Hibbert and learned what he had witnessed, and also looked for evidence of the photographic sortie in our National Archive at Kew, outside London. When he thought that the photos had been taken informally, rather than officially, Mike Mockford, the indefatigable Secretary of the Medmanham Club, with whom Michael had been corresponding, passed the suggestion to me for my opinion. I gave this at some length that, in 16 Squadron, an informal flight would have been impossible. In October 2009, Michael Cain got in touch with me, and I looked through my own archives of the Benson squadrons to try to identify a possible aircraft and pilot concerned. As far as I knew, the search had not progressed any further since then; but at the beginning of October 2011, Michael Cain and his wife Sue, came to see me in Leeds when, if I had found a suitable flagpole, I would have had every reason to fly my pristine "Stars and Stripes"! They spent a good day with us, but the only development in their search was that the photos might have been taken on 6th September 1944.

Later, I sent Michael a copy of one of a series of oblique photos taken on 6th September 1944 by the pilot of a Benson Spitfire fitted with a forward-looking camera as he flew up the Rhine over the bridges of Arnhem.[1] This and Michael's persistence may bring to light further photographs and records, which may lead eventually to the discovery of the 67-year-old controversial pictures. In any case, the search has been for me a final pleasing example of Anglo-American co-operation.

In 2010, much to my surprise and that of the other survivors of "16 Squadron 1939-1945", we heard that the Squadron had been re-formed in 2008 as a Reserve (R) squadron providing the flying component for No 1 Elementary Flying Training School (EFTS) at RAF Cranwell. Here they use Grob Tutors to give their first flight training to potential aircrew cadets at the RAF College, and also navigation training to Weapons

The re-formed 16 (R) Squadron at RAF Cranwell with a Grob Tutor (foreground) and a line of Tutors and a Jaguar.

[1] See the photograph on p.540

The RAF College, Cranwell:
flashback to my flight on 10th September 1993

The Bulldog with JT and the Tornado pilot, who was impressed with my spot-landing ability.

Sharing 16 Squadron's Families Day at RAF Cranwell
r-l: ACM Sir David Cousins Michael Horsfall Jennifer Taylor Annie Horsfall
(behind) Ron Miller (r) and S/L Stephen Foote.

Systems Operators in the adjacent 55(R) Squadron. The Tutor is a side-by-side, low-wing, glass-fibre monoplane, powered by a 180hp Lycoming engine; the 16 Squadron aircraft are owned and serviced by the Vosper Thorneycroft Group, a joint enterprise between the RAF and a private company, typical in the RAF today. This posting is a far cry from the days when the Squadron flew Tornados and Jaguars: but, at least, the Squadron is now back in the air and RAF Cranwell, rubbing shoulders with the RAF College, is one of the most prestigious Stations.

22nd May 2011 was Families Day in the Squadron and the CO, Squadron Leader Stephen Foote, had invited the Members of the 16 Squadron RFC and RAF Association to join in the Day and to hold their Reunion Dinner in the Daedalus Officers' Mess of RAF Cranwell, instead of in the RAF Club in London. This made for a very pleasant day out in the environment of the Squadron, with Jennifer and Jonathan joining me, while Annie and Mickie came with Michael Horsfall, and Ron Miller brought his family; in addition, two former COs of 16 Squadron, Air Chief Marshal Sir David Cousins, KBE, AFC, and Group Captain Ian Travers Smith, DSO, both now retired, came with their wives; other former members and many of the much-reduced present personnel brought their families and friends. We all enjoyed a barbecue lunch and other refreshments out-of-doors on a day blessed with fine weather, while the Tutors were kept busy giving air experience flights to ATC cadets and officials of other local organisations. The Squadron had fairly sparse accommodation in pre-fabricated buildings, but these included a well-visited Museum, with memorabilia displayed from 1915 onwards. However, there was a disappointingly small number of items from WW2 – a situation which would be remedied to some extent when retired Squadron Leader Ray Leach, MBE, finished his History of the Squadron and presented his research material to the Museum.

The Dinner was a grand full-dress affair, with candles and the Squadron silver on the tables and a small orchestra playing in the background. After a sumptuous meal, laced with excellent wine, and the circulation of the port, David Cousins gave a rousing address, hailing the re-emergence of the Squadron, and Stephen Foote told some amusing tales about its life-style in its new situation. I then presented

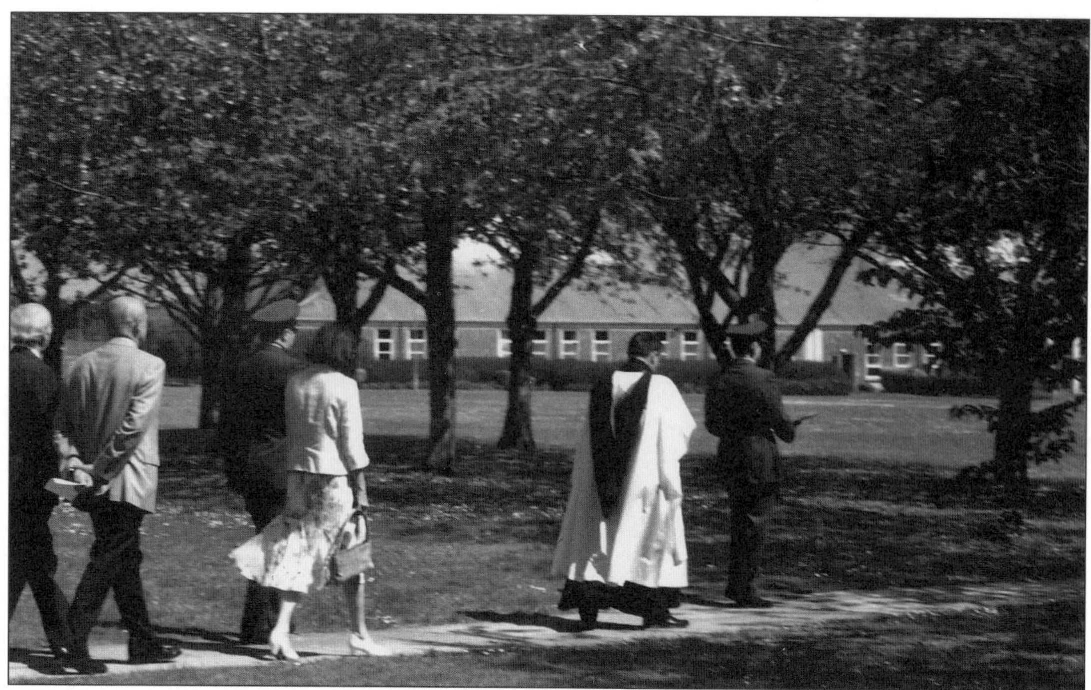

The Chaplain leads the procession behind the 16 Squadron Roll of Honour.

Stephen with the twisted relic of my poor Spitfire, with its polished mount and brass inscription; Wing Commander Guy Stockill had returned it to me when the Squadron disbanded at Coltishall in 2005, and now I said I felt it belonged in its new home, particularly in the Museum, where it would add one more to the number of WW2 exhibits.

Reunion Dinners of this order at the Squadron's base were special occasions: I had been to ones at Laarbruch, Lossiemouth, and Coltishall, and had little doubt that this one at Cranwell would be my last. It was given extra poignancy by a ceremony next morning in one of the College chapels; this was the Dedication by the College chaplain, in the presence of many of the past and present members of the Squadron, of the Roll of Honour, which I had compiled and which had been brought from St Clement Danes, the RAF Church in The Strand, in London. It was carried reverently into the chapel by a young officer and then, after a simple service of Dedication, taken in procession across the lawns to the foyer of the Daedalus Officers' Mess, where it was installed in a glass-topped oak lectern, its pages open so that present-day cadets could see the sacrifice made by too many of their predecessors.

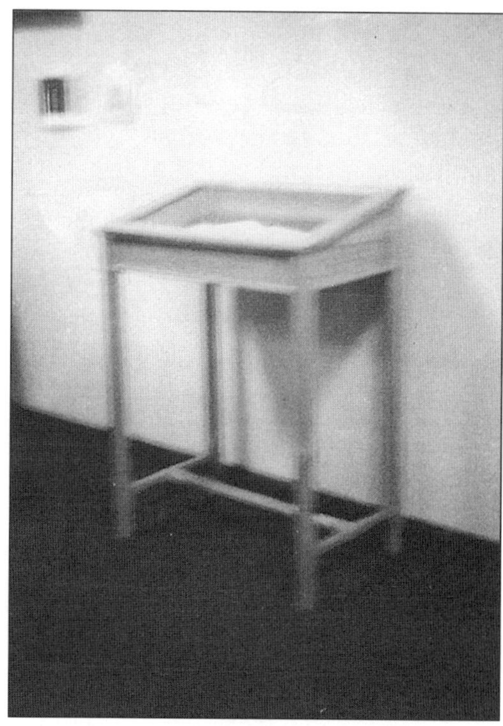

The Roll of Honour in the Daedalus Officer's Mess

Particularly heart-warming for me was the presence of Mrs Penny Crowe, who had asked me if her uncle, F/0 Nigel Davison, who had crashed in Berlin in a Hawker Tempest in 1948 when the Cold War with Russia was at its height, could be added to the names inscribed on the vellum of the Roll. This was a difficult question, but I felt that, as his Tempest would almost certainly have been armed, F/0 Davision was effectively a casualty of war; fortunately, a space was available on the Roll. So Mrs Crowe and her husband had been invited to the Dinner and to the Dedication of the Roll, so that she could visit her uncle's Squadron and see his name included in the sad list of those who had fallen in each of the World Wars and in the Gulf War – and now in the Cold War. I was very pleased to meet Mrs Crowe and to receive her thanks, although it was David Cousins and three Squadron COs who had made the actual inscription possible. Nigel Davison's name was now linked to those of my 16 Squadron friends of 1944 who had 'failed to return'; Jimmy Wallace, 'Gibby' Gibb, John Brodby, 'Jolly' Jolliffe, and Clyde Heath.

The first reunion of my group of "16 Squadron 1939-1945" was held at Duxford Airfield on 19th September 1996. As a result of my telephone call, Squadron Leader Paul Day, AFC, CO of the Battle of Britain Memorial Flight (BBMF), promised to send a Spitfire PRXIX to display at the event; unfortunately, the wind was so strong that day that they could not even take the Spitfire out of its hangar. The following year, again as a result of a telephone call, Paul sent the BBMF Lancaster, a Spitfire XIX, and the Dakota to over-fly our Reunion at RAF Benson on their way to participate in the Air Display in Jersey. In 2000, at our second Reunion at Rolls-Royce's airfield at Hucknall, Paul brought the BBMF Lancaster, Spitfire and Hurricane overhead and they then each performed an individual display before the whole formation gave us a flypast before proceeding, once again, to Jersey – all as a result of a single phone call.

I felt extremely indebted to Paul Day for his unstinted generosity in honouring us so greatly at no cost to ourselves – his real display each time was elsewhere – so when he retired from the RAF in 2009, I was determined to meet him and to thank him in person for being such a good friend to our group and, incidentally, to many other personnel at Benson and hundreds of Rolls-Royce workers at Hucknall, who also saw the displays. Accordingly, we arranged to meet on 3rd September 2010 at RAF Waddington, where 2-seater Spitfire T9 MJ627 was kept, which Paul was flying for its owner at various Air Shows. Not surprisingly at an operational RAF Station, security was tight, but Paul had prepared my way and we drove up to his hangar on the edge of the airfield. He proved to be exactly the kind of man that I had imagined: good-looking, greying-haired, friendly, humorous, and incisive. He had chosen the day deliberately because he was taking the Spitfire to Duxford for a big 16-ship Spitfire formation flypast next day and I could watch him starting-up, taxying-around and taking-off. In fact, I saw the

Two-seater Spitfire T9 MJ627 at RAF Waddington.

first two twice, as he took the aircraft round to a small club-house, for other like-minded enthusiasts, where we had a good talk over a sandwich lunch and I met a number of other interesting flying members. As the time came for his departure, Paul installed one of his two attendant mechanics in the back seat, to service MJ627 before its flight at Duxford. We made our fond farewells and he invited me back any time. He then climbed into the front seat, started-up the Merlin with the help of an external trolley-acc, and taxied away. Unfortunately for me, he took-off on a different runway from the one near the club-house, and I saw no more of this beautifully restored Spitfire. However, I had fulfilled my obligation to Paul for his unforgettable past kindness, and I had made a good friend of a man I had always much admired and who was awarded an OBE when he retired from the BBMF.

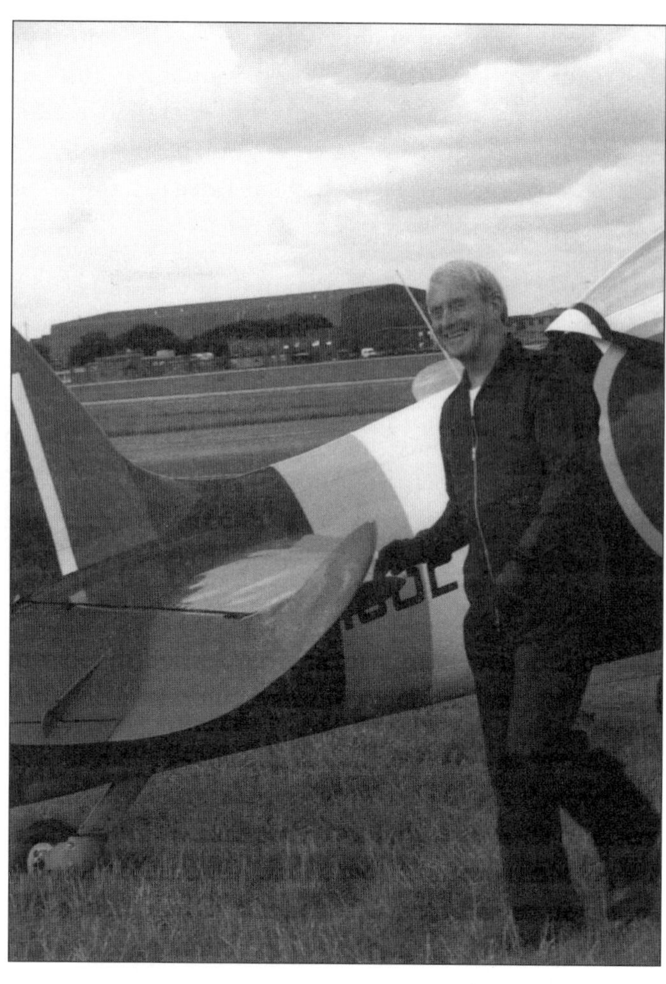

Retired S/Ldr Paul Day tests the controls.

The most unexpected segment of this full-circle occurred in January 2011 when I was invited by a BBC liaison girl to go to North Weald airfield, in Essex, on 3rd March for an interview in connection with a forthcoming programme by BBC2 about the menace of the German V1s and V2s in 1944 and 1945; she agreed to send a taxi to take Margaret and myself there and back. As I had been the first to see the trail of a V2 in flight on 12th September 1944, and had observed what I thought were V2s, but turned-out, in fact, to be V1s being launched from a site near Borne, I felt I was quite an appropriate person to be interviewed. Once again, it was Mike Mockford, of the Medmenham Club, to whom I owed my thanks for suggesting my name to the BBC.

We drove down to North Weald on a freezing cold day and found the producer, Tim Dunn, and his camera crew in "The Squadron", effectively the club-house, canteen, and flight-centre for the many owners of private aeroplanes and restorers of vintage planes and warbirds who occupied hangars and workshops all round this busy civil airfield; Mike Mockford and Christine Hallsall of the Medmenham Club and several other aviation enthusiasts were also present. We moved down to Peter Teichman's Hangar 11, where he kept his Hawker Hurricane, Curtiss P-40, and North American Mustang, as well as 'our' Supermarine Spitfire XI PL965, which flew on operations with 16 Squadron in January – September 1945.

With the doors nearly closed to keep out the cold and the noise, I was interviewed by Tim for 1½ hours, with much contact with the Spitfire, walking round it and climbing up to the cockpit, repeating my words and movements at least twice for the camera and sound-recording. It was then that I realised that the main focus that day was not on the German V-weapons but on the business of photographic reconnaissance, which was essential for taking pictures of the likely launch-sites, and on the photo-interpreters at RAF Medmenham, who were equally important for analysing the photos and identifying the sites, which then became the targets of the fighter-bombers and medium- and heavy-bombers.

When Tim had finished with me, we moved back to "The Squadron" for lunch where I found myself sitting next to Leo Stevenson, an artist and photographer, who happened to have a Dutch mother. We had a suitably deep conversation, which resulted in his sending me copies of the photos he took on this occasion and a print of his painting of PL965 climbing up on a sortie. The flying world is full of interesting people!

In the afternoon, Peter Teichman was scheduled to fly PL965 in company with a helicopter camera-ship, but the weather was unfortunately too cold, grey and cloudy for this to take place. However, with the Spitfire parked outside on the apron, young actors dressed in correct airmen's uniforms and behaving authentically carried out an F52 camera with a 36" lens and busied themselves pretending to insert it through the small hatch on the left side of the fuselage. They did this over and over again for different camera angles before Tim was satisfied, while we were freezing as we watched. I felt sorry for two of the young men and leant on the fuselage while I chatted with them. The photographers began to cluster round, especially when the sun came out for a moment and the actors moved away from me.

By now it was 4.0pm and time for us to leave. We said our good-byes to the many friendly people at the hangar and called-in at the bar-room of "The Squadron" for a wash before our journey home. To my surprise, I found a small middle-aged man had set-up an F52 camera on a vertical stand, complete with a motor, a Type 35 control-box, and all the wiring. He introduced himself as Dr Colin Hall, a photographic enthusiast, with a collection of aerial cameras and other paraphernalia in his house outside Birmingham. He encouraged me to press the "start" button, and immediately there was a whirr and a click, and an exposure was made. I was so thrilled that I pressed it again, with the same nostalgic result. Colin Hall then said that he opened his collection to selected visitors and, when I told him Mike Horsfall lived in his area, he said we'd be very welcome at a later date. When I told Ron Miller, he said he would make every effort to join us in a visit to Colin's tantalising collection. However, I was as disappointed as Colin was when he wrote to tell me that Tim had by-passed his important little exhibit and it did not feature in the subsequent production.

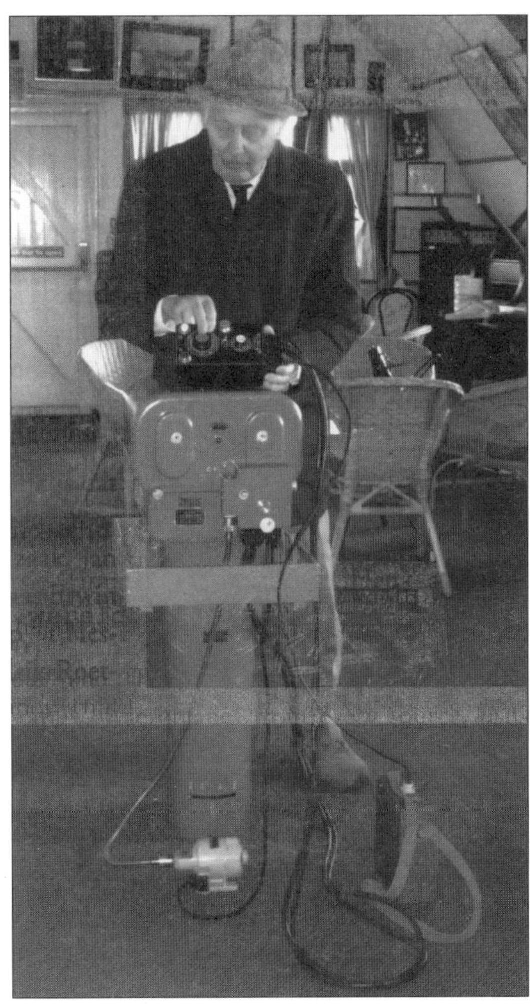

JT operates the Type 35 camera-control on the F52 camera with 36" lens set up by Dr Colin Hall at North Weald.
Photo: Dr Colin Hall

"Operation Crossbow" was screened on BBC2 at 9.0pm on 15th May2011 and shown again a few days later. It turned-out to be an excellent programme, which started with the Germans' achievements in designing and building the jet-propelled V1 and the rocket-powered V2, and the set-back to their time-table by the RAF's discovery and bombing of the research-station at Peenemünde; it then concentrated strongly on the work of the PR squadrons and of the PIs at Medmenham before moving on to the RAF's efforts to destroy the launch-sites in France and Holland, which were not markedly successful; the bombardment was not ended finally until the Allied Armies overran the launch-sites.

I was fortunate in making the opening and closing remarks about the campaign; I was also shown lifting out of their box – for the first time – some of my photos

JT leans against pristine ex-16 Squadron Spitfire X1 PL965 at North Weald during filming of BBC2's "Operation Crossbow".

of Ijmuiden I had taken on 18th September 1944, demonstrating the 60% overlap between successive prints needed for stereoscopic viewing by the PIs, and explaining how, for easy identification, each print was numbered on the accompanying 'plot' of all the exposures taken.

The programme had a considerable effect on viewers of all ages, many of whom wrote-in to the BBC to say that it had opened their eyes to the importance of the work of the PR squadrons and of the PIs, of which they had little previous knowledge.

In my case, the photo of me leaning nonchalantly against the fuselage of PL965 in the sunshine appeared in the "Radio Times" and in several other magazines and newspapers; it was not particularly flattering, but I suppose it symbolises, in the most direct way, that my life and this story have come full-circle, if not from my birth at Cheam School, at least from my first flight in 1935 or from my first take-off in a Spitfire in 1944.

RAF Benson was the home of 1 PRU from January 1941 until the end of the war. As I have mentioned earlier, it spawned other PRUs in all the main theatres of the war, and remained the base for fitting cameras and equipment to PR aircraft and for receiving some aircrew before their posting to other units such as 16 Squadron. On 19th January 1944, I went there to be interviewed for Photographic Reconnaissance and underwent a high-altitude test in a decompression chamber. On 21st May, I ran back there in a panic at the end of my course on Oxfords at Little Rissington as I seemed destined for a Bomber Command OTU; fortunately, F/Lt Cusson's posting to 8 OTU at Dyce came through in time to rescue me, much to the indignation of the CO at Little Rissington. However, I never actually flew from Benson, although I organised a Reunion there in 1997 of "16 Squadron 1939-1945". It was therefore a very pleasant surprise to receive an invitation from the Station Commander, Group Captain Richard Mason, OBE, to attend a Re-Dedication of the Spitfire XI Gate Guardian and a PR veteran's Luncheon, together with my son Jonathan, on 23rd November 2011. The fibre-glass Spitfire had been fully reconditioned and repainted as PL904, the aircraft in which F/Lt Duncan McCuaig, DFC, was shot down and killed over Germany on the final mission of his tour on 28th September 1944. But, more importantly for me, the Re-dedication would also be in commemoration of all the PR aircrew who failed to return which, of course, included those of my friends to whose memory I have dedicated this book.

Group Captain Peter Allan, CO of 16 Squadron 2000-2002, kindly met me at Oxford railway station the day before and drove me to Jonathan's home in Benson village – they live almost next-door to each other. On 23rd, we arrived at the Officers' Mess at 9.30, to find a crowd of people, eventually numbering over 100, drinking coffee and viewing photographs and records of wartime Benson, from the recently-established Archive, laid out for our inspection. I was delighted to see the wedding picture of F/Lt Gordon Green, DFC, and Beryl, the parents of Penny Evers, the wife of the previous headmaster of Cheam School. The rest of the day was most impressive: highly organised, immaculately turned-out, smartly drilled, and with distinguished participants. I give only the highlights here.

We are taken by coach to our seats in the front row with six other veteran PR aircrew under an elongated awning facing the beautiful blue Spitfire, banking slightly as it points upwards in an everlasting climb – the Band of the RAF College Cranwell plays suitable music – we rise as the Standards of the four operational Helicopter Squadrons based at Benson are marched on and the bearers take post in front of the Spitfire – the Station Commander offers us an Official Welcome – the Chaplain-in-Chief of the RAF gives an Address – Mrs Karen Macdonald, daughter of F/Lt McCuaig, reads a poem – we sing a Hymn – the Chaplain-in-Chief declaims the prayers of Dedication and Commemoration – the Band plays the specially-composed "PRU March" – Air Marshal R.F.Garwood, CB, CBE, DFC, Deputy C-in-C Operations, delivers an Address – Wreaths are laid by Mrs Macdonald, the Air Marshal and the Station Commander, while a kilted Piper plays a Lament – we all stand when the Bugler sounds the Last Post, followed by a One Minute's Silence, and then the Reveille – a formation of 3 Pumas flies overhead in Salute – the Band plays the National Anthem – the Squadron Standards are marched off – the Band

One of the four Squadron Standards on parade at the Re-Dedication Ceremony of the Spitfire XI at RAF Benson on 23rd November 2011

Photo: RAF Benson

Salute by Puma helicopters

Photo: RAF Benson

JT tries to persuade Group Captain Richard Mason, OBE, the Station Commander, of the need to locate a comprehensive Photographic Reconnaissance Museum at RAF Benson.

Photo: Jonathan Taylor

parades past the Spitfire and marches off – we return to the Officers' Mess in the coaches that brought us, to drinks and a Buffet Lunch in the Dining Room – Jonathan and I have two Squadron Leaders opposite us and I have a WAAF Squadron Leader on my right – three delightful hosts.

It was indeed a memorable occasion: sad in its commemoration of one pilot in particular and of all PR aircrew in general lost on operations, but an excellent example of the kind of stirring show that an RAF Station, in this case RAF Benson, can put on when necessary. It certainly completed the PR segment of my flying life most effectively for me, and also offered me a moving farewell to my five years in the Royal Air Force.

This ceremony had no suggestion of 't Hesseler in it, yet here also in 2011 there was a feeling of the end of an era. When the new estate behind the Memorial is completed, there will be only the width of a new road to separate the extended Borne from the expanded Hengelo. Aware of this, and of the building of another main road parallel to the simple lane in front of the Memorial, Hennie Noordhuis had it taken down and totally renovated, as the wood had decayed and the mortar had crumbled. The Memorial is now turned round, facing across the new road and relating to the houses that will soon be built there: it will form part of this new community. In addition to my plaque, which had been stolen but was retrieved and has now been renovated, Hennie has designed another, in Dutch, explaining the significance of this Memorial and of the men whose names appear on it, few of whose families still live in what is left of the old 't Hesseler.

This was virtually Hennie's last official action before he retired in July 2011. He can be proud of all he has achieved in Borne and happy, I hope, in what he has done for and with me: but this restored Memorial is also a tribute to his own feelings for the tragic past and his dedication to preserving the memory of it for the future. As it is, the Memorial stands in great beauty, dignity and pathos, on a small rise under the overarching trees; surrounded by a low railing – it looks magnificent. When the new Burgomaster of Borne, Mr Rob Welten, gave the first address to the crowd gathered in front of it on 4th May 2011, welcoming the restoration and re-siting, I felt that a new era was beginning, with new generations of new inhabitants who will, I am sure, continue to honour the memory of the innocent men, so needlessly executed here in November 1944. This segment of my otherwise full circle can never be completed.

The renovated and re-sited Memorial in 't Hesseler

Dutch Voices

Contents

The contents are in Dutch, unless stated otherwise, often with English translations:

"Vlieger vermist"

"De laatste vlucht van H.J.S. Taylor"

"De slachtoffer van de gruweldaden" / "Obituaries of the Victims"

"Requiem voor 't Hesseler 1944" / the English original is in Appendix 'A'

The Burgomaster's Address in English at the Unveiling of JT's Plaque in 1991

Press Reports of the Unveiling

Mr Bruggink's Address in English before returning JT's flying-helmet

Anne Bovenmar's School Project 1992, with an English translation

Press Reports of events in Twente connected with JT's visits 1995-2004, half of them with English translations

Photo of JT's 1998 Dinner Party, with the identities of the guests

HOOFDSTUK 11 VAN "IN VERDRUKKING, VERZET EN VRIJHEID"

VLIEGER VERMIST.

H. Noordhuis

Onuitwisbaar voor velen in onze gemeente, is de herinnering aan de gebeurtenissen op 19 en 25 november 1944 in de buurtschap Het Hesseler, even over de gemeentegrens met Weerselo, door een grenswijziging sedert 1971 Borns grondgebied.

Op zondag 19 november, het liep tegen de middag, stond mevrouw Roetgerink-Hudepohl voor haar huis aan de Mekkelhorstweg water te putten. Boven haar hoofd speelde zich op dat moment een hevig luchtgevecht af tussen een Engelse en Duitse jager.

J.A. Kotte.

J.H. Roetgerink.

J.A. Klaaskate.

H. Smit.

J.G. Boomkamp

H.F. Roetgerink.

Het verloop van het spectaculaire duel met het hoge gieren van de op volle toeren draaiende motoren en het ratelen van de boordwapens, werd door velen in Borne en omgeving gadegeslagen.

In spanning werd de vlucht van de aangeschoten Engelse machine gevolgd, terwijl angstige blikken de hemel afzochten naar een geopende parachute. Dat duurde niet lang, want de piloot was er in geslaagd zijn gehavende toestel te verlaten. Zijn tot ontplooiing gekomen parachute zweefde langzaam naar de aarde en landde op geringe afstand van mevrouw Roetgerink in het weiland van "Knipp'n Mulder", naast het huidige tuincentrum van J. Boomkamp aan de Hesselerweg.

Toegesnelde familieleden van de verbouwereerde vrouw zagen nog juist, hoe de man zich na de landing van zijn parachute, die gedeeltelijk in een boom hing, en zijn vliegenierskap kon ontdoen.

Met handgebaren en een paar woorden Engels maande de onverwachte bezoeker uit het luchtruim hen en de inmiddels snel aangegroeide schare nieuwsgierigen tot zwijgzaamheid en maakte zich vervolgens uit de voeten.

Hij moet daarbij de inmiddels van alle kanten toegesnelde Duitsers zijn gepasseerd.

Met 500 man van een in Borne gelegerd detachement Fallschirmjäger werd onmiddellijk de omgeving afgezet en uitgekamd.

Onder bedreiging met wapens werden omstanders en omwonenden op niet zachtzinnige en brutale wijze ondervraagd.

De zoekactie leverde echter geen bruikbare aanwijzingen, die zouden kunnen leiden tot de aanhouding van de piloot. Dat wekte zo'n grote woede op bij de Duitsers dat werd overgegaan tot willekeurige gijzeling van 6 personen: J.G. Boomkamp, H.F. Roetgerink, J.H. Roetgerink, G.J. Klaaskate, J.A. Kotte en H. Smit.

De eerste drie woonden in de onmiddellijke omgeving van de landingsplaats. Klaaskate, Kotte en Smit waren de piloot tijdens zijn afdaling naar die plaats uit nieuwsgierigheid gevolgd.

Via de marechausseekazerne in Borne, destijds gevestigd in het gemeentehuis, werden de mannen 's middags tegen half vijf door de Feldgendarmerie ten behoeve van de Ortskammandant in Hengelo (O) naar het politiebureau aldaar gebracht.

's Avonds werd op last van de Sicherheitspolizei Enschede nog naar het bureau gebracht, de heer P.A. van Dijk, de 56-jarige vader van gemeenteambtenaar Piet van Dijk, die lid was van de illegaliteit.

De Duitse autoriteiten stelden nog dezelfde dag de gemeente Borne voor het gebeurde aansprakelijk en stelden als ultimatum dat, indien de parachutist niet zou worden gevonden, de gijzelaars de volgende ochtend om zeven uur zouden worden gefusilleerd.

Het protest van burgemeester van den Toren, dat Borne moeilijk aansprakelijk kon worden gesteld voor gebeurtenissen in een andere gemeente, werd door de Sicherheitspolizei Enschede afgedaan met de beschuldiging dat het in Borne een grote "Schweinerei" was en de gemeente vol zat met "terroristen", hulpverleners aan de vijand.

De afdelingscommandant van de Marechaussee Oldenzaal wist van de Feldgendarmerie Hengelo (O) uitstel van executie te bewerkstelligen tot de volgende ochtend tien uur.

De woede van de Duitsers, die de hele middag in touw waren geweest zonder enig resultaat, was tot het kookpunt gestegen. Daarvan werd 's avonds een Bornse jongen het slachtoffer, Jan Vonk. Hij werd naast het gemeentehuis gefusilleerd. Meer daarover kunt u lezen in hoofdstuk 21.

Maandag 20 november 1944

Het begin van een week met grote spanning en onzekerheid voor gegijzelden en hun families. Via marechaussee De Hair, die op het politiebureau in Hengelo (O) werkte en tijdelijk inwoonde bij een familie op Het Hesseler, werden zij over de toestand van hun dierbaren op de hoogte gehouden, en kon hen nog eens

wat worden toegestopt.
Overleg met de Duitsers leidde 's morgens tot uitstel van executie tot 's middags vijf uur.
Duidelijk werd toen ook dat Wilhelm Karl Rudolf Hadler met de zaak was belast, een 46-jarige Untersturmführer van het beruchte Kommando Knop, dat door de snelle opmars van de geallieerden in de septemberdagen van 1944 vanuit Frankrijk in Enschede was terechtgekomen en werd toegevoegd aan de Sicherheitsdienst.
Zijn baas Erwin Knop, nam het commando over van Karl Alfred Schöber, die vanaf 1942 "Postenführer" van de SD Enschede was geweest.
Onder leiding van de afdelingscommandant der Marechaussee Oldenzaal vond 's morgens in het bijzijn van de groepscommandant der Marechaussee in Borne en burgemeester van den Toren een reconstructie van het gebeurde plaats.
Vastgesteld werd, dat de gijzelaars de piloot onmogelijk hebben kunnen zien lopen.
Met die uitleg ging Hadler, die zich aan het eind van de middag met de gevangenen – gezeten in een geblindeerde auto – bij het gemeentehuis meldde, niet akkoord.
Toen hem vervolgens bleek, dat er met het onderzoek ook nog geen enkele vordering was gemaakt, verliet hij woedend de burgemeesterkamer met de woorden: "Dann knallt es".
De burgemeester, die Hadler naliep, probeerde hem in de hal van het gemeentehuis te overtuigen van de onredelijkheid van zijn eis om de verdwenen vlieger uit te leveren en van de onrechtvaardige en onmenselijke voornemens om onschuldige mensen te executeren.
Hadler leek niet voor rede vatbaar. Desondanks bereikte het gemeentebestuur 's avonds het bericht, dat de executie werd uitgesteld tot de volgende dag 's middags om drie uur en dat twee gevangenen, Klaaskate en Kotte waren vrijgelaten.
Waarschijnlijk is dat ook te danken geweest aan burgemeester van den Toren, die Schöber had benaderd om in de kwestie te bemiddelen. Voor de vrijlating eiste Knop een tegenprestatie, de levering van een "terrorist".
Schöber greep deze gelegenheid aan om de vader van Piet van Dijk te arresteren, uit wraak voor de bevrijding van zijn zoon, gemeenteambtenaar en verzetsman, uit het Huis van Bewaring in Almelo op 22 maart 1944. Piet van Dijk was op 13 maart door Schöber op het gemeentehuis aangehouden.
De arrestatie van Van Dijk sr. in zijn woning aan de Almelosestraat in de vooravond van 19 november 1944, leidde een dag later tot de vrijlating van Klaaskate en Kotte.

Mevrouw Roetgerink-Hudepohl aan de Mekkelhorstweg. Rechts op de achtergrond de boom waarin J.H.S. Taylor met zijn parachute terecht kwam.

Dinsdag 21 november 1944
De Duitsers formuleerden een voorwaarde voor vrijlating: er moest worden gemeld in welke richting de vlieger was verdwenen. In verband hiermee organiseerde de burgemeester bijeenkomsten met boeren, die in de omgeving van de landingsplaats woonden, met het gemeentebestuur van Weerselo, met boeren in Deurningen en Borne, respectievelijk in café Bos en de boerderij van Hassels Mönning.
Als gevolg hiervan konden 's middags 3 getuigen worden gehoord, die de piloot hadden gezien: G.H. Leuverink, M. Post en D. Bosman. Twee van hen gaven een bijna gelijkluidend signalement: een slanke gestalte, ca. 1.80 meter lang, donker blond, een overall, vliegerjack en witte trui dragend.
Opvallend was voorts, dat de man enigszins trekkend met zijn been liep. Waarschijnlijk heeft hij dat letsel bij de klap van de landing opgelopen.
Het dienaangaande in het Nederlands en Duits opgemaakte proces-verbaal overtuigde de Feldgendarmerie in Hengelo (O) van de onschuld der gijzelaars, in tegenstelling tot de SD Enschede, die niet verder wilde gaan dan andermaal uitstel van executie te verlenen.
De groeiende competentiestrijd tussen SD en Wehrmacht in deze zaak, leek in het voordeel van de Feldgendarmerie te worden beslecht, toen 's avonds het bericht kwam, dat bij besluit van hogerhand de voorgenomen executie niet zou worden voltrokken.
De vijf gijzelaars moesten echter in hechtenis blijven tot de vermiste man was opgespoord en aangehouden.

Woensdag 22 november 1944
Een gevoel van grote opluchting bij alle betrokkenen door het goede nieuws uit Hengelo (O).
Marie, zuster van de gebroeders Jan en Hendrik Roetgerink fietste 's morgens naar Hengelo (O) om te proberen hen van het nieuws in kennis te stellen.
Hoewel de cellen zich aan de achterkant van het politiebureau bevonden, lukte het haar door middel van gebarentaal het bericht over te brengen.
Hendrik stak, als teken dat hij de boodschap had begrepen, zijn hand door de tralies van zijn cel.
Het zou het laatste levensteken zijn geweest, dat zijn zuster van hem zou krijgen, want op zaterdag 25 november sloegen de Duitsers alle hoop op een goede afloop op een genadeloze wijze de bodem in.
Opnieuw zou blijken dat het woord van de bezetter, zoals zovaak gedurende de oorlog, niets waard was.

De heer P.A. van Dijk, die op 25 november 1944 werd gefusilleerd als represaille voor de bevrijding van zijn zoon Piet uit de gevangenis in Almelo.

Zaterdag 25 november 1944

Tegen het middaguur werd de celdeur van de gebroeders Roetgerink ontgrendeld en werd Jan gesommeerd mee te gaan. In de veronderstelling verkerende dat de Duitsers hem kwamen halen om te worden doodgeschoten, nam hij verslagen afscheid van zijn broer Hendrik en stopte hem nog wat kleine persoonlijke bezittingen toe. Tot zijn grote verbazing en opluchting echter kreeg hij te horen dat hij vrij man was, niet vermoedend welk lot zijn broer Hendrik te wachten stond.

Ook de heer Smit werd die middag op vrije voeten gesteld.

Om half vier maakte Hadler zijn opwachting aan het bureau. Hij was in gezelschap van een commando SS'ers en soldaten van de Wehrmacht. Vòòr zijn komst heeft mevrouw Boomkamp door toedoen van marechaussee De Hair nog even met haar man kunnen praten. Zij waren pas 6 weken getrouwd.

Boomkamp, Roetgerink en Van Dijk werden om half vier uit hun cel gehaald en moesten ieder afzonderlijk plaats nemen in gereedstaande overvalwagens, waarin reeds soldaten van het executiepeloton waren gezeten.

Voorafgegaan door een luxe auto met Hadler van de SD en een functionaris van de Feldgendarmerie, vertrok de stoet even later richting Weerselo.

Om tien over half vier, werd burgemeester van den Toren door de SD van de voorgenomen executie op de hoogte gesteld.

Zijn tegenwerping, dat er een besluit lag dat niet tot terechtstelling zou worden overgegaan, omdat men van de onschuld der gevangenen was overtuigd, werd afgedaan met de opmerking, dat men daar niets mee te maken had. In een laatste alles of niets poging heeft van der Toren toen nog geprobeerd, andere Duitse instanties te bewegen hun invloed aan te wenden de executie tegen te houden. Zowel de Ortskommandant in Hengelo (O), de hoogste Duitse vertegenwoordiger in Borne, alsook de Wehrmachtskommandant in Enschede verklaarden met deze zaak niets van doen te hebben.

De dienstdoende officier bij de SD Enschede verklaarde geen invloed terzake te kunnen aanwenden. Door een gebrekkige telefooncommunicatie lukte het v.d. Toren niet meer "Der Beauftragte" in Zwolle te bereiken.

Het Rijkscommissariaat in Delden, daar gevestigd na "Dolle Dinsdag" in september 1944, distantieerde zich van elke verantwoordelijkheid, maar zegde wel toe met de SD te zullen bellen.

Als resultaat van dat telefoontje werd van den Toren meegedeeld, dat het vonnis reeds was voltrokken, hetgeen werd bewaarheid, toen hij korte tijd later op de plek des onheils arriveerde.

De vliegerbril die piloot Taylor achterliet bij de landingsplaats.

Het uit Hengelo (O) vertrokken konvooi was daar tegen 10 voor vier aangekomen. Uit de eerste wagen stapte Boomkamp, uit de tweede Hendrik Roetgerink en uit de derde van Dijk, alle drie begeleid door een aantal Duitse soldaten.

Inmiddels toegestroomde familie, vrienden en bekenden zagen, dat de Duitsers hun slachtoffers naar een weiland dreven, niet zover van de plek waar de vlieger bijna een week daarvoor was neergekomen. Boomkamp en Roetgerink liepen voorop, steun zoekend bij elkaar in deze laatste minuten.

Zij moesten ook toezien, hoe het in het weiland aangetreden executiepeloton de lichamen van de naast elkaar opgestelde mannen met kogels doorzeefde. Geschokt zagen zij eveneens, op welke weerzinwekkende wijze de onder invloed verkerende Duitse soldaten lallend en zwaaiend "afscheid" namen van hun slachtoffers.

Voor hen moet vergeven wel een haast onmogelijke opgave zijn.

Aannemelijk is, dat Hadler heeft gehandeld in opdracht van zijn chef Knop met goedkeuring van "Der Befehlshaber der Sicherheitspolizei" Dr. Eberhardt Knoop, tevens plaatsvervanger van Rauter. Knoop zetelde ook in de Synagoge in Enschede.

Het is jammer, dat voor een volledige optekening van deze zaak Knop, Hadler en Knoop niet meer gehoord konden worden. Zij werden al kort na de oorlog in Burgsteinfurt door een geallieerde rechtbank tot de strop veroordeeld en opgehangen.

Een deel van onze naspeuringen concentreerden zich op de identiteit van de vlieger en zijn toestel. Dat was niet gemakkelijk, omdat hiervan aanvankelijk geen gegevens bekend waren.

In alle relevante stukken wordt echter gesproken over een Engelse vlieger, terwijl ook ooggetuigen een Engels toestel meenden te hebben herkend.

Een aanknopingspunt vonden we, toen een inwoner uit Hengelo (O) ons de vliegersbril toonde, die hij op de bewuste 19e november 1944 bij de landingsplaats had gevonden.

Nog verrassender was het, dat er op de bevestigingsriemen van de bril een naam was geschreven; J.H.S. Taylor.

Ingeschakelde deskundigen van de Koninklijke Luchtmacht herkenden de bril als een later type jachtvliegersbril van de Amerikaanse Luchtmacht uit de periode 1944-1945. Dikwijls werden er echter ook brillen geruild met de Britten omdat ze aantrekkelijker waren of omdat ze beter pasten, zodat ook weer niet uitgesloten moest worden geacht, dat Engelse jachtvliegers zo'n bril hebben gedragen.

Uit het luchtbeeld van de 19e november 1944, toen 9 toestellen – 6 Typhoons, één Mitchell en 2 Spitfires van de RAF – en een Amerikaans Thunderbolt 390 verloren gingen, kon de oplossing voor ons probleem uiteindelijk worden gedestilleerd.

De aangetroffen naam leidde ons naar de die dag verdwenen Spitfire van het no. 16 squadron van The Royal Air Force. Het toestel, de FR.IX PL 957, werd bestuurd door Harold James Strickland Taylor, en werd nimmer teruggevonden.

Helaas zijn we er (nog) niet in geslaagd de heer Taylor, die in 1946 de RAF heeft verlaten, op te sporen, ondanks de vele inspanningen die Engelse luchtmachtautoriteiten zich de laatste jaren in deze hebben getroost. Ook zijn helpers konden niet worden opgespoord.

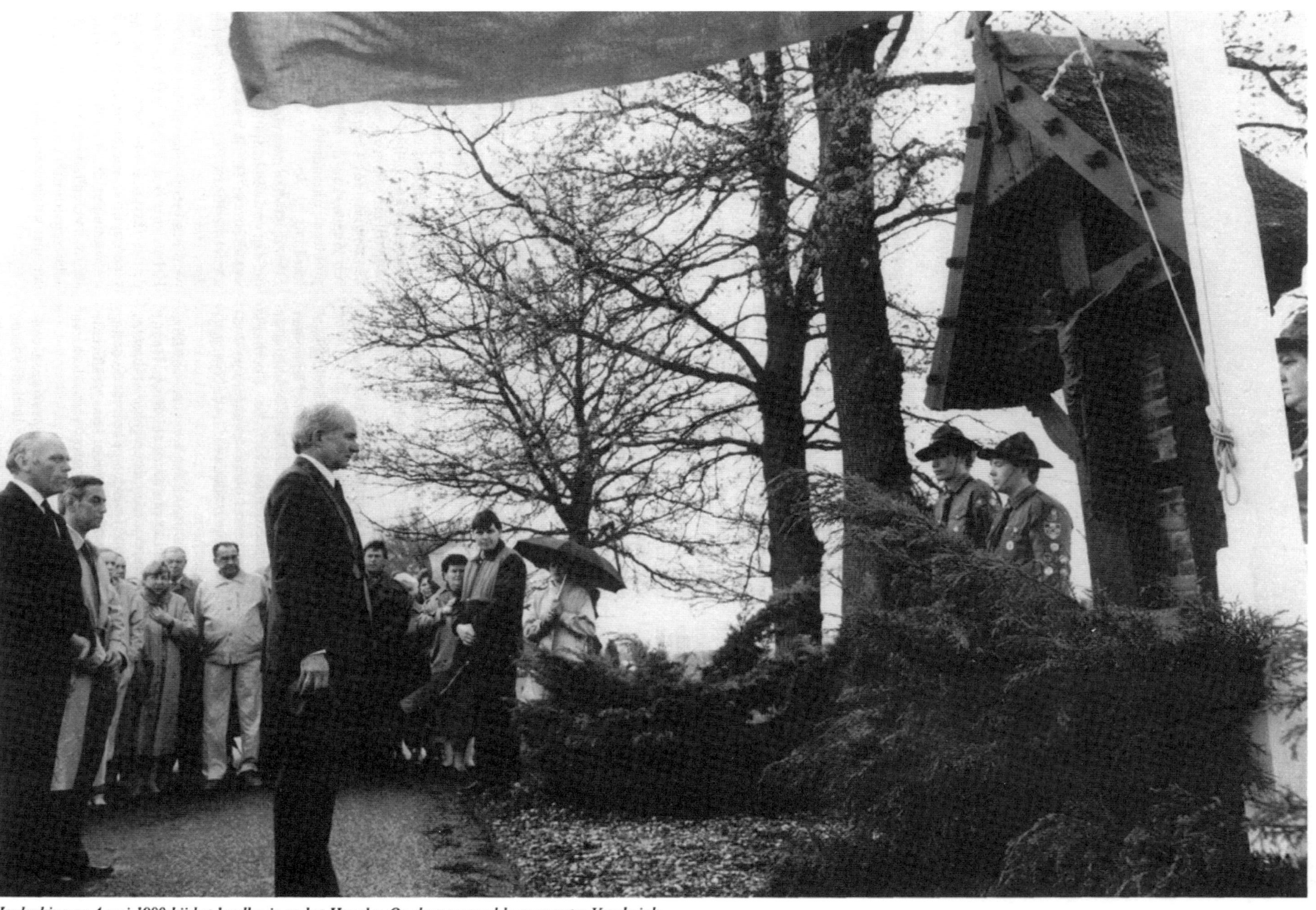

Herdenking op 4 mei 1988 bij het landkruis op het Hesseler. Op de voorgrond burgemeester Vunderink.

The Unveiling of the Memorial to the Victims of the 't Hesseler Tragedy on 4th May 1988.

19-11-1944 28-8-1991

De laatste vlucht van H.J.S. Taylor

The cover of the Dutch translation of 'My Last Flight' distributed to the inhabitants of 't Hesseler in the morning of 28th August 1991

HOOFDSTUK 11A

DE LAATSTE VLUCHT VAN HAROLD JAMES STRICKLAND (JIMMY) TAYLOR

H. Noordhuis

Woensdagavond 28 augustus 1991, het loopt tegen achten.

Onder koraalmuziek en in gezelschap van nabestaanden, gemeentebestuur, officials van de RAF en de vliegbasis Twente, alsmede samengestroomde buurtgenoten, onthult Jimmy Taylor uit Leeds zichtbaar aangedaan een plaquette op het landkruis in de buurtschap 'Het Hesseler'.
Bijna 46 jaar na dato een laatste eerbetoon namens het 16e squadron RAF waartoe hij behoorde, aan J.G. Boomkamp, P.A. van Dijk en H.F. Roetgerink, drie onschuldige mannen die om zijnentwil werden gefusilleerd, vlak bij de plek waar hij op 19 november 1944 was geland en gevlucht om uit handen van de vijand te blijven.
Een dag voor de plechtigheid vraagt journalist Jan ter Haar van de Twentsche Courant hem naar zijn gevoelens, nadat hij medio juni 1990 door mij op de hoogte was gebracht van de trieste gevolgen van zijn vlucht;
"Dat heeft me buitengewoon geschokt en mijn beeld van de oorlog omver gegooid. Tot voor kort keek ik met een zekere voldoening terug op mijn belevenissen als vliegenier. Alles was immers goed verlopen, ik had prima herinneringen, met m'n kameraden veel lol en avonturen beleefd.
Dat spannende jongensboek is voor mij een tragedie geworden. Voor mij is er een zwarte doek over de oorlog geworpen."

De gang van Leeds naar Borne was niet makkelijk. Met name tegen de confrontatie met nabestaanden heeft Taylor het meest opgezien. Alle mogelijke verwijten had hij zich in het hoofd gehaald, die men hem zouden kunnen gaan maken. Hoe anders verliep zijn ontvangst in werkelijkheid; hartverwarmend! Jimmy Taylor heeft tijdens zijn vierdaagse verblijf in Borne eind augustus 1991 zoveel mogelijk nabestaanden bezocht. Onder hen de gebroeders Boomkamp, broers van de omgekomen J.G. Boomkamp en de zuster van de gefusilleerde Roetgerink, Marie Leuveld-Roetgerink.
Tegenover eerder genoemde journalist zegt hij het volgende over die ontmoeting met haar:
"Ik ben haar dankbaar voor haar uitspraak dat ze mij de dood van haar broer niet verwijt. Het is begrijpelijk dat de gemeenschap mij in meer of mindere mate verantwoordelijk acht voor het ombrengen van drie onschuldige mannen. Enerzijds voel ik me ook schuldig omdat, als ik daar niet naar beneden gekomen was, deze mensen wellicht nog steeds zouden leven.
Anderzijds acht ik me onschuldig omdat ik van niets wist, met niemand heb gesproken en me voor iedereen verborgen heb gehouden. Ik kan het één niet zwaarder laten wegen dan het ander. Schuldig en niet schuldig houden elkaar in evenwicht. Het tragische is wel dat ik uiteindelijk op 24 november in Rhenen werd gearresteerd, dus voor de Duitsers boven water was. Maar de executie van de drie is een dag later tòch doorgegaan."

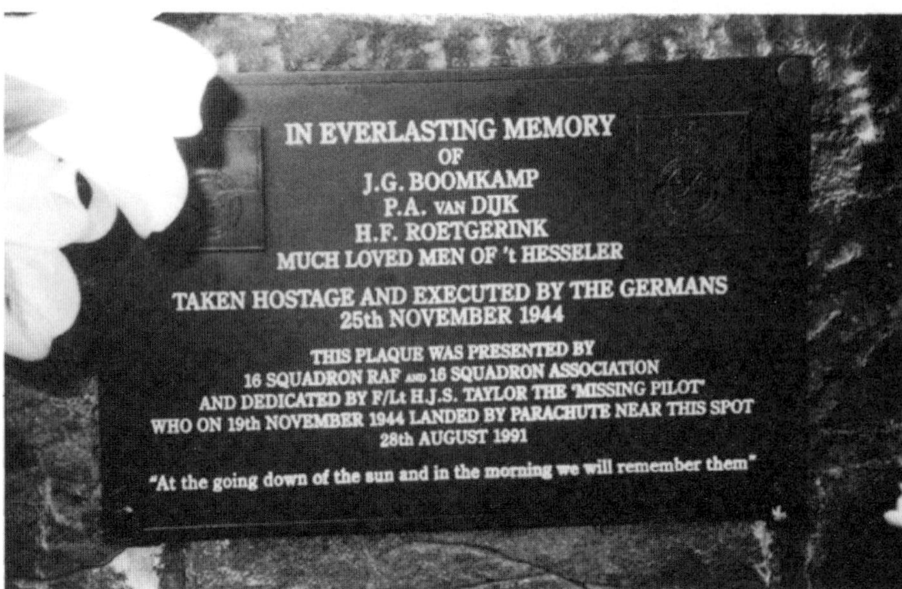
IN EVERLASTING MEMORY
OF
J.G. BOOMKAMP
P.A. VAN DIJK
H.F. ROETGERINK
MUCH LOVED MEN OF 't HESSELER
TAKEN HOSTAGE AND EXECUTED BY THE GERMANS
25th NOVEMBER 1944
THIS PLAQUE WAS PRESENTED BY
16 SQUADRON RAF AND 16 SQUADRON ASSOCIATION
AND DEDICATED BY F/Lt H.J.S. TAYLOR THE 'MISSING PILOT'
WHO ON 19th NOVEMBER 1944 LANDED BY PARACHUTE NEAR THIS SPOT
28th AUGUST 1991
"At the going down of the sun and in the morning we will remember them"

De plaquette op het landkruis in de buurtschap "Het Hesseler", die op 28 augustus 1991 werd onthuld door H.J.S. Taylor namens het 16e squadron RAF.

Jimmy Taylor toont zijn vliegersbril en helm die hem door respectievelijk H.L. ter Borg (R) en A.H.J. Bruggink werden overhandigd.

De vermiste vlieger uit het vorige hoofdstuk is dus terecht. Daarmee kwam tevens een eind aan de jarenlange onzekerheid in de buurtschap. Twijfel of hij nu wel of niet willens en wetens door het Bornse verzet is weggeholpen. Jimmy Taylor heeft het verhaal afgerond. De twijfel is weg. De nabestaanden hebben er vrede mee.
Via een oproep begin juni 1990 in "Air Mail", een RAF magazine, kwam ik uiteindelijk in kontakt met Taylor. Zijn eerste schriftelijke reactie is er één van verbazing; wat wil een ambtenaar uit Borne na ruim 46 jaar (a life-time!) nu nog van hem weten over de 19e november 1944?
Ik besloot, na lang wikken en wegen, hem enige dagen later te bellen, het risico incalculerend dat dit telefoontje 's mans leven op z'n oude dag — 69 was hij toen — ingrijpend zou kunnen veranderen of hem mogelijk een trauma zou kunnen bezorgen. Mijn eerste vermoeden werd bewaarheid, het tweede gelukkig niet.
Na vele briefwisselingen en telefonische discussie over een aantal onjuiste facetten in mijn verhaal "Vlieger vermist", kon ik hem er uiteindelijk van overtuigen dat hij de "missing pilot" was. Zijn vliegersbril en helm hebben daarin een cruciale rol gespeeld.
In een dichterlijke terugblik op die 19e november verzucht Taylor onder meer:
"De dag van afrekening heeft me te pakken gekregen. Had ik maar bij een

van jullie aangeklopt en me bekend gemaakt. Dan had dat het leven van drie onschuldige mensen kunnen sparen. Was ik voor hen maar vindbaar geweest.
Ik moet voor hen nog steeds gevonden worden".

De buurtschap "Het Hesseler" is dankbaar dat het laatste stukje van de puzzel is gelegd. Jimmy Taylor zal voortaan in de harten van de bewoners een bijzondere plaats innemen.

Ondertussen is de zoektocht naar zijn toestel, een Spitfire met registratienummer PR.XI PL 957, onverminderd voortgezet. Naar verwachting zal ook dit mysterie binnenkort kunnen worden opgehelderd.

Tot slot het *verhaal* van Jimmy zelf over het stormachtige verloop van die novemberdagen in '44, waaraan ook de NOS op 25 november 1994, precies 50 jaar na dato, aandacht besteedde in het programma "Van Gewest tot Gewest" onder de veelzeggende titel: "De onwetendheid voorbij".

De NOS-televisie maakt in oktober 1994 een reconstructie van de gebeurtenissen tussen 19 en 25 november 1944.

De laatste vlucht van H.J.S. Taylor 19-24 november 1944

Zondag 19 november 11.00 uur (Britse tijd — mogelijk verschilde deze van de Europese of Nederlandse).

In een Spitfire PRXI van het 16e squadron, steeg ik op van het vliegveld Moelsbroek in Brussel, om foto's te nemen van vliegvelden in het gebied in de omgeving van Rheine in Duitsland.

Halverwege de missie, op iets meer dan 7000 meter hoogte, ('t was niet hoger en dat was waarschijnlijk door vederwolken of de formatie van een condensstreep) begon de motor te proesten en te sputteren: rook en vlammen kwamen uit de uitlaten. De vlammen verdwenen, maar de rook werd steeds dikker en werd daarna gevolgd door zwarte olie. Uiteindelijk raakte de voorruit beroet en kon ik niets meer zien. Nadat ik op allerlei manieren geprobeerd had de motor aan de gang te houden, nam ik de snelheid helemaal terug, draaide om in de richting van Brussel, begon hoogte te verliezen en liet een lange pluim rook achter in het luchtruim. Via de radio riep ik de basis op en vertelde wat er aan de hand was. Ze gaven me de richting aan die ik moest proberen te houden. Ik moest een zweefsnelheid aan zien te houden van ongeveer 225 km per uur. De westenwind, waarvan ik aannam dat die ongeveer 100 km per uur was, (minder naarmate ik lager vloog) maakte dat de feitelijke snelheid waarmee ik vooruit kwam, een stuk lager lag dan die 225 km per uur.

Ongeveer 12.00 uur:
Op ongeveer 3000 meter hoogte was de rook erger geworden en begon ook binnen in de cockpit te komen. Aangezien er een benzinetank van een kleine 400 liter zat tussen de motor en de cockpit, was ik bang dat er zich heel gauw een explosie zou voordoen. Tegelijkertijd viel de radio uit — misschien door brand of omdat ik te laag vloog om nog van enige afstand berichten te kunnen ontvangen. Ik besloot om met m'n parachute uit het vliegtuig te springen. Ik had nog tijd om mijn zuurstofmasker af te doen, de radioverbindingen te verbreken, de kaarten in mijn vlieglaarzen te stoppen en de riemen los te maken waarmee ik aan mijn vliegstoel zat. Ik richtte de neus van het vliegtuig op, draaide haar ondersteboven en viel eruit.

Helaas raakte ik de staart van het toestel, of het toestel draaide en raakte mij. Het leek of ik door midden werd geslagen door een enorme klap tegen mijn middenrif — in ieder geval raakte ik buiten westen. Ik kwam weer net genoeg bij m'n positieven om aan het koord van de parachute te trekken. Ik voelde me zo akelig dat 't me eigenlijk niet kon schelen of de parachute nog open ging of niet, maar toen ik het doek tussen m'n benen voelde fladderen, was ik toch een beetje opgelucht. Vervolgens raakte ik weer buiten westen.

Ik kwam weer bij boven een brede rivier of een kanaal of een meer en dacht

Vliegveld Moelsbroek te Brussel, voorbereidingen voor een verkenningsvlucht.

vagelijk dat ik wel zou kunnen verdrinken. Toen zag ik een man over een weggetje fietsen en ik vond het grappig dat hij mij niet kon zien. Een groen stuk land kwam toen heel snel naderbij en ik herinnerde me het advies: "Benen bij elkaar! Benen bij elkaar!" toen ik op de grond rolde.
Ik lag een poosje op het gras, ik snakte naar adem en telkens als ik ademde deden mijn ribben me pijn. Toen ik helemaal wakker was keek ik op en zag een aantal mannen met lange donkere jassen aan in een kring om me heen staan. Ik wist niet waar ik was, maar dacht dat ik in Duitsland was.- Ik zat nog aan de parachute vast die me over het gras trok. Ik sloeg op het kastje dat de touwen bij elkaar hield en de parachute waaide naar een paar bomen. Alle mannen renden daar naar toe. Ik sprong op, hinkte zo snel ik kon in tegengestelde richting en slaagde erin een bosje te bereiken.

Na enige tijd zag ik enkel mannen met een geweer op de rug over de weg langs het bos fietsen. Ik was er zeker van dat ze het bos spoedig zouden doorzoeken. Ik vond een greppel die dwars door een groot veld liep en daar kroop ik door, totdat ik in het midden van het veld kon zitten, waar ik alles heel goed in de gaten kon houden en iedereen kon zien aankomen zonder dat ze mij zouden kunnen zien. Toen ik er eenmaal zat dacht ik over mijn situatie na: ik was mijn kaarten kwijt, maar ik wist dat ik in zuidwestelijke richting zou moeten trekken om weer in België te komen. Ik was echter bang dat als ik nog in Duitsland zou zijn, ik misschien de hele Maas langs de verkeerde kant zou volgen. Daarom besloot ik om zo lang mogelijk in westelijke richting te gaan, om daarna pas naar het zuiden de Rijn over te steken. De slag om Arnhem had een paar weken ervoor plaats gehad en ik was er niet zeker van of het 21e legeronderdeel de Rijn ergens had bereikt. Ik moest terug, want ik had op woensdag een afspraak met een meisje in Brussel en ik wist dat als ik er niet was, mijn beste vriend uit het eskadron haar in zou pikken. (Ik was er dus niet en hij wel en nu ben ik peetvader van hun eerste kind!).

Ik merkte dat mijn overlevingspakket nog in mijn gevechtsjas zat. Het bevatte een plastic zak voor water, een aantal ontsmettingstabletten, een doosje lucifers, naald en draad, een kompas, een groot aantal Horlicks tabletten en wat repen pure chocola, maar geen geld of kaarten, dat was er misschien uitgevallen. Ik had goed gegeten voor ik was opgestegen en ik rekende dat ik met dit

Klaar voor de volgende missie!

rantsoen en de energie die ik nog over had, 't nog wel een week zou kunnen uithouden.

Ik droeg een heel dik blauw RAF gevechtsuniform dat er op het eerste gezicht onopvallend uitzag. Ik haalde de RAF emblemen er af, bestreek de twee lichtblauwe kapitein-vlieger strepen op mijn schouderkleppen met modder: als ik eventueel gevangen zou worden genomen, dan wilde ik ook dat de Duitsers zouden weten dat ik officier was!

Ik zag angstig dat een boer zijn vee in mijn richting dreef, maar zonder dralen passeerden ze me. Ik bleef tot het donker werd in de sloot liggen en toen werd het erg koud. Ik besloot het erop te wagen en dwars over het land te lopen. Ik vermeed wegen, landweggetjes en huizen. Ik wist dat er spertijd gold in Duitsland en in Nederland en dat 't platteland wemelde van de Duitsers en dat honden blaften. Als schooljongen had ik me voor de slimme duiven verborgen weten te houden als ze 's avonds gingen slapen. Ik was er in geslaagd een paar duiven voor de duivenpastei te schieten en ik was dus vol vertrouwen dat ik uit ieders buurt zou weten te blijven. Zo liep ik eerst naar het westen, vervolgens naar het zuiden naar de Rijn en daarna zou de geluksfactor een grote rol spelen.

Overzicht van de gebeurtenissen:

19 november.
De tocht over de velden ging nogal moeilijk in het donker. Ik raakte vast in het prikkeldraad, viel in een nu eens niet droge sloot. Na verscheidene uren op deze manier langzaam vooruit gekomen te zijn, besloot ik langs landweggetjes te lopen. Deze liepen echter zelden in dezelfde richting. Ik liep toen over een grotere weg maar maakte een lange omweg door het veld, toen ik zag dat ik een dorp (Delden?) naderde. Ik liep naast een grote weg maar vloog de sloot in als er een auto met volle lichten aankwam. Plotseling liep ik op een trottoir, langs etalages (in Goor?) — ik hoorde naderende voetstappen van een patrouille — verstopte me om de hoek en liep weer haastig verder. Ik stak een spoorlijn over, kwam bij een grote brug over een rivier of kanaal. Er stonden wachten op de brug. Ik liep onder de brug door en liep eerst de ene kant langs om een alternatieve overgang te vinden en daarna de andere kant. De rest van de nacht bracht ik onder een boom door.

20 november.
Ik was weer vroeg op, liep zonder succes in beide richtingen langs het water en schuilde in een schuurtje naast tennisvelden (nog steeds in Goor?) en besloot die nacht het water over te zwemmen — 't regende onophoudelijk — kleedde me in het donker onder de brug uit, bond m'n kleren in een bundeltje om m'n nek en probeerde drie keer over te zwemmen. 't Water was ijskoud — de adem stokte me in de keel — ik gaf het op — voelde me half bevroren en ellendig en zou me overgegeven hebben aan iedereen die me een warme maaltijd bij het vuur zou hebben gegeven. Ik bedacht dat de Duitsers dat zeker niet zouden doen. Ik kwam op een boerenerf waar een heleboel aardappels op een lange hoop lagen opgestapeld. Aan het eind van de aardappelhoop stond een schuurtje. Ik ging er binnen en maakte een vuurtje van stro en hout. 't Kon me niks schelen of ze me zouden vinden of niet. Ik droogde m'n natte kleren bij het vuur, pofte een paar aardappelen in het vuur en was twee uur later warm, gevoed en klaar om weer op pad te gaan. Ik liep terug naar de spoorlijn, volgde die naar het westen. De rest van de nacht bleef ik lopen en bij het aanbreken van de dag verstopte ik me in een dennenbos naast de spoorlijn.

21 november.
Gestoord door mensen, die met twee kinderen door het bos liepen. Ik bleef onopgemerkt. De halve nacht bleef ik doorlopen tot ik een grote boogbrug op zag doemen. Ik hoorde de wachten op de brug. Ik schuilde in een spoorwegwagon tot het weer dag werd.

22 november.
Vroeg op. Ik zag een brede rivier of kanaal, verliet de spoorlijn om aan de rechterkant het gebied te verkennen.

Plotseling was ik op een boerenerf waar Duitse soldaten overal paarden aan het wassen waren. Ik mompelde een paar "Morgens" en slenterde door zonder ergens naar te kijken. Ik kwam bij de waterkant — ik liep een eind naar rechts — zag de rivier of het kanaal aan de overkant met een ander water samenkomen. 't Regende en waaide hard.
Ik vond een groot vlot aan de kant. Ik maakte 't los en probeerde naar de overkant te komen. 't Was zwaar en had de wind tegen. Ik liep terug langs de oever — 't was koud en nat — ik vond een kippenhok aan het eind van een diepe tuin. Ik bleef daar tot het donker werd, keerde daarna terug naar het spoorwegemplacement, keek goed naar de treinen, stapte in een wagon en hoopte dat die de brug over zou gaan. Tevergeefs, er kwam geen beweging in. Ik liep zo dicht mogelijk als ik durfde naar de brug en slaagde na ettelijke pogingen in het donker er in me vast te klampen aan een onderstel van een wagon. De wachten schreeuwden toen ze m'n achterwerk over de zijkant van de wagon zagen hangen. Ik liet me vallen toen de trein snelheid begon te krijgen, rolde van de spoordijk, liep verschillende kilometers verder en kwam bij een trein die op een spoordijk stond. Aan het eind van die trein klom ik op een wagen. De trein reed verder. Ik kreeg het zo koud dat ik naar de conducteurswagen ging — ik vond wat broodkorsten en viel in slaap.

23 november.
Heel laat werd ik met daglicht wakker. Ik merkte dat de trein op het goederenemplacement stond en keek naar de bestemmingen op de wagons. Er stond overal Utrecht op en ik maakte daaruit op dat ik dus in Utrecht moest zijn en nu naar het zuiden moest naar de Rijn. Ik liep over de rails, dacht dat het te opvallend zou zijn als ik over de spoordijk zou lopen en kwam bij een grote brug die over een rijweg ging. Naast die weg, op een voetpad, liepen veel mensen in 't blauw. Ik ging er naar beneden en begaf me tussen de mensen. Het bleef voortdurend regenen. Ik ging de rijweg af, rechts een kleinere weg op, kwam op klaarlichte dag in een stadje (Rijsenburg?/Driebergen?) waar Duitse soldaten liepen — ging een boomgaard in — vond een klein schuurtje waarvan de deur met een touwtje dicht zat, maakte 't touwtje los en ging binnen. Ik vond vier krukjes die rond een kacheltje stonden en een mand appelen. Ik was de appelen aan 't opeten toen de deur openging en drie heel verschrikte kinderen hun hoofd om de deur staken. In heel slecht Duits zei ik wat tegen ze en verteld wie ik was. De vader kwam kijken, bood me een kaart aan en een jongensjas. Hij bood me ook een fiets te leen aan en wat voedsel, maar er zaten Duitsers in zijn huis. De kinderen brachten een grote schaal aardappelpuree. Toen 't donker was reden twee kinderen me zo'n honderd meter vóór op een fiets zonder banden en ik volgde op een tweede fiets zonder banden. Toen ik op de fiets wilde klimmen viel ik er met veel lawaai af (het was er een zonder vrijloop) en iedereen was opeens verdwenen! Bij de tweede poging lukte het. Ik reed over de velden waarvan de karresporen hier en daar bedekt waren met sneeuw en ijs. De kinderen brachten me op de weg naar Rhenen. Daar gingen ze weer terug met medeneming van mijn fiets. Rhenen was volgens de vader in Engelse handen. Langzaam liep ik verder.

24 november.
Ik volgde mijn tocht over de weg waar tientallen arbeiders liepen, passeerde een richtingaanwijzer met Doorn erop. Ik kan me niet herinneren dat ik ergens gebouwen zag. Ik dacht aan de Kaiser die hier in ballingschap woonde en zou 't leuk gevonden hebben hem te ontmoeten. Ik besloot dat ik genoeg in deze richting gelopen had en dat het tijd werd dat ik dichter bij de Rijn kwam. Misschien zou ik wel een leegstaand echt Hollands huis vinden waar 't geweckte fruit nog in de kelder stond en kon ik daar de komst van het Britse leger afwachten. Ging uiteindelijk rechtsaf een klein weggetje in. Na enige tijd kwam ik een bord tegen met "Kampfzone" en nog wat waarschuwingen erop. Voor me liep een oud echtpaar dat een kinderwagen met wat bezittingen voortduwde. Ik besloot hen te volgen; zij zouden bij eventuele moeilijkheden het eerst aan de beurt zijn. Ik liep een hoek om en zag Duits afweergeschut aan de kant van de weg opgesteld staan, gericht op de brede vallei van de Rijn met de uiterwaarden aan de andere kant. Zo nu en dan zag ik rookpluimen op de achtergrond (granaten die tussen de Engelsen terecht kwamen?). Het Duitse afweergeschut stond horizontaal maar vuurde niet. Ik liep langzaam verder aangezien soldaten me gezien hadden en ik durfde niet vóór hen, weer om te keren. Er kwamen er verscheidene naar me toe, hielden me tegen en stelden me voor hun plezier wat eenvoudige vragen. Ik antwoordde ruw en ze lieten me gaan. Ik liep door en zocht wanhopig naar een mogelijkheid de weg te verlaten. Een Duitse officier kwam naderbij, hield me staande en vroeg wat ik in de "Kampfzone" deed. Er volgde een lang kruisverhoor. Ik zei dat ik probeerde om naar Rhenen te komen om daar nog wat familiebezittingen op te halen. Hij zei: "Rhenen kaput". Hij liet me gaan en ik volgde het oudere echtpaar vóór mij, maar na 50 meter keek ik om en hij keek ook naar mij om. Toen wist ik dat het spel uit was. Het echtpaar was door een soldaat staande gehouden, hetgeen elk verder gaan blokkeerde. Ik voegde me bij hen en vroeg wat de moeilijkheden waren. Op dat moment voelde ik een hand op mijn schouder en een soldaat op de fiets met een machinepistool om z'n nek zei: "Komm mit mir". Het einde van mijn vrijheid!

31 december - 14 mei 1945;
Stalag Luft 1 POW Camp bij Barthe aan de Oostzee.
Op 1 mei werden we door de Russen bevrijd. Het duurde toen nog twee weken voor we teruggevlogen werden naar de echte vrijheid in Engeland.

Na de bevrijding keerde Taylor terug naar Engeland en bouwde een carrière op in het onderwijs.

Foto gemaakt in krijgsgevangenschap (Stalag Luft 1, kamp bij Barthe aan de Oostzee).

Jimmy Taylor, 50 jaar na dato.

De slachtoffer van de gruweldaad op "Borne" d.d 19 november 1944*

Jan Vonk

Dit relaas is grotendeels overgenomen uit het door Hennie Noordhuis geschreven hoofdstuk over Jan Vonk in het boek "In Verdrukking, Verzet en Vrijheid" ('Noordhuis-ter Braak-Kienhuis'-2e druk, Borne 1995), handelend over de tweede wereldoorlog in Borne en kerkdorpen, aangevuld met enkele persoonlijke details door Hermine Vonk, de jongste zuster van Jan.

Jan Vonk werd geboren in 1920 en was de zoon van een winkelier aan de Grotestraat. Hij was het tweede kind in een gezin met vier kinderen. Het eerste kind, Joanna, werd geboren in 1919 en stierf op 14 februari 2009. Het tweede was Frans, hij werd geboren in 1922 en overleed in 1966. Het jongste kind was Hermine, geboren in 1928.

Jan was een sprankelende jonge man, enthousiast, vrolijk, behulpzaam en ondernemend met veel humor.

Hij was voorbestemd om de winkel van zijn vader in Borne over te nemen, maar wel op zijn eigen manier. Hij had progressieve ideeën, die niet altijd de instemming van zijn vader hadden.

Toen Nederland werd bezet door de Duitsers in mei 1940, sloot Jan zich aan bij het verzet. Als individualist met een drang naar avontuur. Hij werd een soort 'Scarlet Pimpernel' ('Rode Pimpernel')- een avonturen- roman over een 18e eeuwse Batman), hij werkte en dronk samen met de Duitsers, onder voorwendsel hen pistolen afhandig te maken. Bekend zijn onder andere de ontvreemding van pistolen van twee Duitsers, die in café Vaanholt in Hengelo (O) aan het biljarten waren en de diefstal van een wapen uit een Duits militair voertuig bij garage Monninkhof in Oldenzaal.

Dat leidde tot het opgang komen van een geruchtenstroom omtrent zijn persoon: hij zou hebben gecollaboreerd met de Duitsers. Hij werd regelmatig in Duits gezelschap gesignaleerd en ging prat op zijn goede contacten met de plaatselijke Duitse autoriteiten. Vast staat echter, dat hij contacten onder-

Jan Vonk 1920-1944

Photos: Hermine Vonk

* These obituaries are translated into English from p682

hield met mensen uit de illegaliteit. Een van hen was Leendert Immerzeel, een ondergedoken marechaussee, de latere instructeur van de Binnenlandse Strijdkrachten in Olst en omgeving. In diens opdracht stal Jan wapens van Duitsers voor het verzet. Leen was een diep religieus man en een echte vriend van Jan. Hij werd gedood in april 1945, tijdens een actie van de verzetgroep waartoe hij behoorde.

Jan werkte in Rheine, maar kwam door "ziekte" en "blessures " vaak niet opdagen,tot grote wanhoop van zijn moeder. Het lukte hem met zijn paspoort meerdere personen, waaronder een geallieerde vlieger en zijn broer Frans –een student die in Berlijn tewerk was gesteld- uit Duitsland naar Nederland te brengen. Frans vond een schuilplaats in het ouderlijk huis aan de Grotestraat.

Jan kon bluffen, was roekeloos en brutaal als het moest. Dat ondervond ook de heer H. Grote Enzerink uit Vorden, alias "Karel Overijssel", een van de kopstukken van de illegale krant Trouw, toen hij met vijfduizend kranten op zijn fiets staande werd gehouden door een Duitse militair. Door diens aandacht te trekken kon Jan erger voorkomen.

Tijdens een razzia in Almelo op 5 november 1944 werd Jan opgepakt en overgebracht naar het beruchte verblijf van de SD Almelo aan de Bornsestraat, voor menigeen het laatste station voor de dood. De Duitsers vonden bij hem een pistool van Duitse makelij en een vals paspoort. Zijn broer Frans werd dezelfde avond in de ouderlijke woning aan de Grotestraat ook gearresteerd. Bij een confrontatie met zijn broer Jan op de 'Dienststelle' van de SD, zag hij, dat diens gezicht was gezwollen en bebloed. Na een verblijf van een dag in Almelo werd Jan Vonk door de SD Enschede overgenomen. Ook hier werd hij meerdere keren ondervraagd en mishandeld door de Duitsers, die hem als 'terrorist' en 'partisan 'beschouwden.

In de namiddag van de 19e november 1944 werd hij naar Borne overgebracht en naast het gemeentehuis doodgeschoten. De inmiddels gealarmeerde marechaussee Luiken trof het lichaam van Jan Vonk aan onder een boom, een kogel had zijn hart doorboord. Terwijl hij bij de dode neerknielde, stopten er twee Duitse auto's bij het gemeentehuis, waaruit een aantal militairen sprong. Zij overtuigden zich ervan of het slachtoffer wel dood was en schreeuwden de verbouwereerde Luiken toe dat zijn dood een represaille was voor de verdwenen vlieger eerder die dag. Aannemelijk is dat SD chef Schöber, die op 19 november 's avonds met een groot aantal manschappen in Borne was in verband met deze zaak, Jan Vonk heeft laten doodschieten met medeweten van zijn baas Erwin Knop. Bijna een week later zouden er in dezelfde zaak op "'t Hesseler" nog drie slachtoffers vallen; Jan Boomkamp, Hendrik Roetgerink en Piet van Dijk sr.

Een gedenkteken naast het oude gemeentehuis houdt de nagedachtenis aan Jan Vonk levendig.

De slachtoffers van de gruweldaden op "'t Hesseler" d.d 25 november 1944

Johan (Jan) Boomkamp

Ik ben veel dank verschuldigd aan Dirk Boomkamp voor de ontvangen informatie over zijn achterneef Johan (Jan) Boomkamp. Dirk is de zoon van Jan Boomkamp, de zoon van Johan's broer Bernhard. Op mijn verzoek heeft Dirk deze informatie verzameld, mede naar aanleiding van een discussie hierover met zijn vader en met Johan's broer Hendrik, die is getrouwd met Diny. Johan wordt Jan genoemd, de korte versie, zowel op het 'landkruis' als in de hoofdstukken van dit boek, maar ik zal hem hier Johan noemen om hem te onderscheiden van Dirk's vader, de huidige Jan Boomkamp, eigenaar van een bekend tuincentrum in "'t Hesseler", waar Dirk export manager is.

"Johan Boomkamp was een lange, magere en enthousiaste man, die 6 weken na de tragische gebeurtenissen van 25 november 1944, 32 jaar zou zijn geworden. Zijn vader, Dieks Boomkamp en moeder, Siena Engberink, hadden zes kinderen: vijf zonen – Hendrik, Gerard, Bernhard, Herman en Johan. Daarnaast een dochter, Trui

Johan Boomkamp
Photo: Dirk Boomkamp

Johan was een zeer creatief persoon, een natuurliefhebber. Hij had een passie voor de jacht, die overigens wordt gedeeld door de hele Boomkamp familie. Hij was kunstenaar en kon prachtige tekeningen en schilderijen maken van de natuur en van vliegtuigen. Hij studeerde architectuur en bouwkunde aan de ambachtsschool en aanvaardde nadien een baan als product ingenieur bij Dikkers & Co., leverancier van Stork in Hengelo. Creatief als hij was maakte hij een authentiek model van de nieuwe Dikkers fabriek in Hengelo. Hendrik heeft nog een foto waar Johan samen met de directeur van Dikkers op staat.

Toen hij werd gearresteerd was Johan getrouwd met Jo Mol, dochter van een cafébaas aan de Koppelsbrink in Borne. Ze woonden in een huis aan de Deurningerweg 38, dat Johan met trots zelf had gebouwd, gelegen in Hasselo gemeente Weerselo, dat sedert 1971 grondgebied is van de gemeente Borne. Na de dood van Johan betrok Bernhard de woning."

Verder beschreef Dirk hoe Johan één van de gijzelaars werd en waarom hij later door de Duitsers werd geselecteerd om te worden geëxecuteerd.

"Het huis van Johan was ongeveer 100 meter verwijderd van de plek waar u neerkwam. Vanuit een raam zag hij uw parachute in een boom hangen en rende onmiddellijk naar buiten om te zien wat er aan de hand was. Toen hij ter plaatse kwam, hadden zich daar ook al enkele leden van de familie Kotteman en Smit verzameld. Zij werden allen staande gehouden door de Duitsers. Hendrik vertelde me dat hij en zijn broer Herman door de Duitsers werden gesommeerd om te blijven staan ("stehen bleiben"). Toen ze beseften dat Johan was gearresteerd, gingen ze er vandoor zodra ze konden.

De Duitsers dachten dat Johan deel uitmaakte van het verzet. Feitelijk was dat niet zo, maar hij heeft zeker geholpen. Omdat u in de onmiddellijke omgeving van zijn huis neerkwam, was het een koud kunstje voor de Duitsers om de link te leggen tussen u, Johan en het verzet. Ze dachten dat u in handen van het verzet was gevallen en dat Johan daarin een leidende rol speelde om u verder te helpen. Hendrik vertelde ook dat hij de enige was die u heeft zien weglopen door een korenveld. Bijgaand treft u een plattegrond van "'t Hesseler" aan"

Ik ben Dirk erg dankbaar voor deze brief van 7 augustus 2009, die niet alleen een karakterschets van Johan geeft, maar verklaart ook waarom hij een verdachte voor de Duitsers was en waarom zij dachten dat het verzet mij verborgen hield. Een denkbeeld dat, zo bleek, nog lange tijd door een aantal inwoners van "'t Hesseler" werd gedeeld, toen ik voor het eerst terugkwam op 26 augustus 1991.

De plattegrond van Dirk is waardevol, het toont de omvang van tuincentrum Boomkamp in 1989 en bevestigt voor mij tevens dat de plek waar ik landde verder naar het noorden is gelegen dan ik veronderstelde. Dirk heeft op deze plattegrond ook een zwarte pijl getekend, wijzend in oostelijke richting, de richting waarin Hendrik mij heeft zien weglopen. Kennelijk dichter bij de waarheid dan mijn geheugen. In ieder geval kan het landschap in november 1944 enigszins verschillend zijn geweest van dat in 1989, in het bijzonder in relatie tot de omvang van het bos.

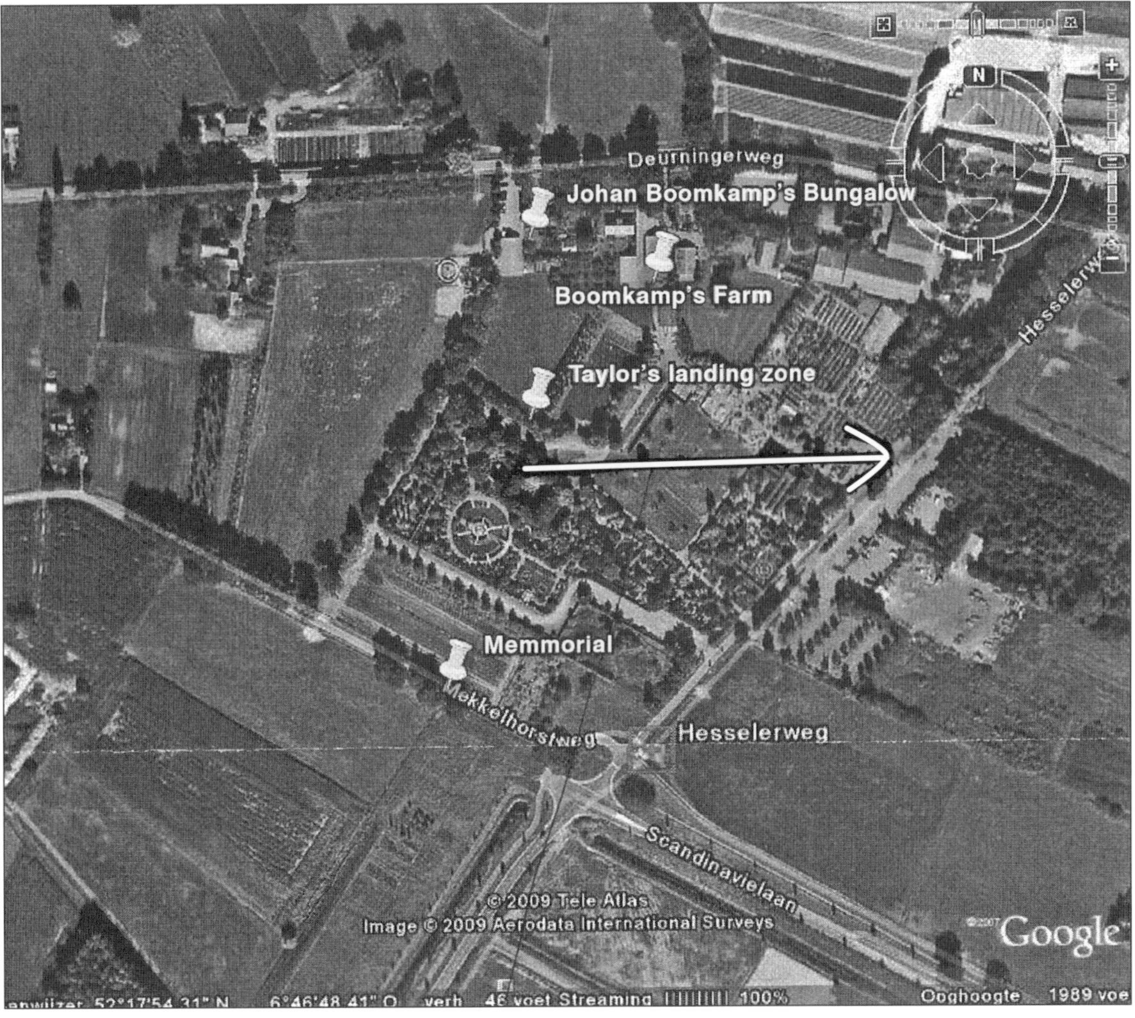

Photo: Google

Hendrik Roetgerink

Mevrouw Riet Sanders-Roetgerink was zo vriendelijk om mij het relaas te zenden van haar oom, Hendrik Roetgerink. Ze is de oudste dochter van mevrouw Roetgerink-Hudepohl en de oudere zuster van Hennie Roetgerink. Mevrouw Marie Leuveld-Roetgerink was de oudere zuster van zowel mevrouw Roetgerink-Hudepohl als Hendrik Roetgerink, één van de slachtoffers op 25 november 1944. Ze stond hem zeer na. Ze was erg aangedaan tijdens de opnamen van de in 1994 door de NOS uitgezonden documentaire "Beyond The Ignorance", ("De Onwetendheid Voorbij")handelend over de gebeurtenissen in de novemberdagen van 1944 en het werd haar teveel toen ze door Ellen van Helsdingen, de producer van het programma, werd geïnterviewd.

Mevrouw Sanders-Roetgerink schreef:

"Hendrik Roetgerink werd geboren op 10 oktober 1915 in de kleine buurtschap "'t Hesseler", bestaande uit verschillende boerderijen aan de rand van de gemeente Borne. Hij was de buurman van Jan Boomkamp en de jongste zoon van een gezin met 6 kinderen. Hun ouders stierven op zeer jonge leeftijd en groeiden als gevolg daarvan op bij een oom en tante.

Hendrik was een rustige en vriendelijke persoon,altijd in voor een praatje met z'n medemens. Zijn passie was voetbal en hij was een fervent supporter van het plaatselijke voetbalteam. Hij mistte nooit een wedstrijd. Hij werkte als boerenknecht op een grote boerderij met veel land vlakbij bij zijn huis. Deze was eigendom van "Erven ten Cate", een fabriek in Borne die tarwe verwerkte tot meel voor verschillende doeleinden.

Hendrik wilde zich graag verder ontwikkelen, maar de economische omstandigheden in de dertiger en veertiger jaren waren ongunstig, de mensen waren al blij als ze hun baan konden behouden. Ook waren er weinig mogelijkheden voor vervolgonderwijs en persoonlijke ontwikkeling. Toen de

Hendrik Roetgerink in 1939
Photo: Riet Sanders-Roetgerink

oorlog was afgelopen probeerde Hendrik aan de slag te komen in de 'licht metaal', een belangrijke economische activiteit in die dagen in Twente. Op die wijze hoopte hij de basis te leggen voor een solide toekomst.

Helaas maakten de gebeurtenissen van 25 november 1944 een abrupt einde aan zijn dromen. Hij was 29 jaar en ongehuwd.

We herinneren ons hem als een goed mens en een fijne oom en houden hem met respect in onze gedachten"

Riet voegde bij dit warme eerbetoon aan haar oom 2 foto's van hem, die op zo moedwillige wijze werd vermoord door de Duitsers. Daarnaast had ze een geruststelling voor mezelf, in verband met mijn aandeel in de tragedie:

"Nu een enkel woord tot u, maar daarom niet minder belangrijk: het is geweldig, dapper en bijzonder, uw komst naar "'t Hesseler" ieder jaar weer. Wees ervan overtuigd, u treft totaal geen schuld. In november 1944, schaarden we ons, mannen, vrouwen en kinderen, nieuwsgierig rond de parachute, toen plotseling de Duitsers verschenen en willekeurig zes mannen meenamen. Dat was een gevolg van de bezetting. En vergeet niet, hun oorlog was bijna een verloren oorlog. Hun gevoelens waren boosaardig en daarom moest er iets gedaan worden om hun kracht te demonstreren, kracht in een gebied van slechts een paar vierkante kilometers. Zowel een domme als vreselijke daad. We weten dat oorlog geen vriendelijke onderneming is onder het genot van een kopje thee, zowel toen als nu niet. Het jaarlijkse moment om samen in uw bijzijn stil te staan bij de gebeurtenissen van toen, doet, ik weet het zeker, onze familie en de bewoners van 't Hesseler" goed, het geeft ons een dankbaar gevoel. We zullen dit nooit vergeten. Wat er ook gebeurt, we zijn u dankbaar"

Wat moet ik nog zeggen na deze grootmoedige woorden? Mijn tranen zijn verbonden met de hare en met die van hen, als ik op 4 mei voor de verzamelde menigte bij het landkruis de ontroerende woorden van Rudyard Kipling uitspreek:

"They shall not grow old,
As we that are left grow old;
Age shall not wither them
Nor the years condemn.
At the going down of the sun,
And in the morning,
We will remember them."

Hendrik Roetgerink op 20-jarige leeftijd
Photo: Riet Sanders-Roetgerink

Piet van Dijk sr.

Helaas heb ik geen reactie ontvangen op mijn brief aan mevrouw van Dijk-Kolkamp, de schoondochter van Piet van Dijk junior, noch van haar zoon, die ook Piet heet.Ik kan dus maar weinig zeggen over Piet van Dijk senior en zijn familie.

Hij was 56 jaar en werkzaam bij Spanjaard.Zijn zoon Piet speelde een vooraanstaande rol in het verzet. Piet junior werd op 13 maart 1944 in het gemeentehuis van Borne gearresteerd door de SD en overgebracht naar het Huis van Bewaring in Almelo. Daaruit werd hij op 22 maart 1944 bevrijd door een verzetsgroep. Deze gebeurtenis zou later voor de familie van Dijk tragische gevolgen hebben, want als represaille werd pa van Dijk, woonachtig aan de Almelosestraat, in de vooravond van 19 november gearresteerd en overgebracht naar Hengelo. Bijna een week later werd hij samen met Johan Boomkamp en Hendrik Roetgerink gefusilleerd. Ze liggen begraven op de begraafplaats in Borne.Hun namen zijn vereeuwigd op het monument (landkruis) aan de Mekkelhorstweg (nu Tuinlaan), evenals op het koperen herinneringsplaatje naast het door mij aan het Rijksmuseum Twente in Enschede geschonken schilderij van "Father Roeland de Pottere, SJ"

Piet van Dijk (sr)

De Gemeentelijke Begraafplaats Grave in Borne

De dood heeft ze niet gescheiden

In terugblik

Uit het voorgaande blijkt dat het de belangrijkste doelstelling van de SD en de Gestapo was om het verzet te breken. Het verzet waarin Jan Vonk alleen opereerde en Piet van Dijk jr. in een verzetsgroep. De Duitsers geloofden dat het verzet mij verborgen hield, reden voor hen om 6 mensen te gijzelen, in de hoop hen te kunnen bewegen mij uit te leveren. In dat geval zou ik gewoon een pion in de onderhandelingen zijn geweest. Of het verzet dat ook daadwerkelijk gedaan zou hebben, is een heikele vraag. Zij waren in oorlog met de Duitsers en leden verliezen, maar zagen ook de dood van vele onschuldige burgers als vergelding voor verzetsacties. Bekend is bijvoorbeeld de aanslag op SS officier Rauter bij de Woeste Hoeve. Ondanks zulke tragedies, die in heel Nederland aan de orde van de dag waren, liet het verzet zich niet afschrikken en zette het de sabotagedaden voort, evenals het voorthelpen van neergekomen geallieerde vliegers.

Mijn persoonlijke mening is dat, als ik mijn toevlucht zou hebben genomen tot het plaatselijke verzet, ze me, tegen de wil van de bewoners van "'t Hesseler", niet aan de Duitsers zouden hebben uitgeleverd. Tegelijk was ik als RAF piloot verplicht om te proberen naar mijn squadron terug te keren, dit in tegenstelling tot wat ik schreef in mijn gedicht in 1990, geëmotioneerd als ik was toen, nadat ik van de executies had vernomen. Ook zou ik, als ik mezelf had aangeven, zoveel gezien en gehoord hebben over de organisatie van het locale verzet, dat ik hun veiligheid in gevaar zou hebben gebracht. Aannemelijk is dat ik voor deze informatie door de Duitsers zou zijn gemarteld. Dus ze konden me niet uitleveren en ik zou het met ze eens zijn geweest.

Gelukkig is dit allemaal hypothetisch, want ik ben nooit in contact geweest met het verzet. Toch zijn het gedachten die me sindsdien steeds weer met ongemak bekruipen.

The Victim of the German Atrocity in Borne on 19th November 1944

Jan Vonk

This account is taken mostly from Hennie Noordhuis's chapter on Jan Vonk in the excellent history of Borne during WW2 entitled "Through Suffering and Resistance to Freedom" by H. Noordhuis, ter Braak and Kienhuis (2nd Edition Borne 1995), with the addition of some personal details supplied, very kindly, by Jan's sister Hermine Vonk in November 2009.

Jan Vonk was born in 1920, the son of a shopkeeper in Grotestraat in Borne; he was the second child in a family of four, the first being Joanna, who was born in 1919 and died on 14th February 2009; the second was Frans 1922-1966, and the youngest was Hermine, born in 1928.

Jan was a sprightly young man, enthusiastic, cheerful, helpful and enterprising, with lots of humour. He was destined to take over his father's shop in Borne, but in his own manner: he had progressive ideas, not always to the liking of his father.

When Holland was occupied by the Germans in May 1940, Jan joined the Resistance, but on his own as an individualist with an urge for adventure. He became a sort of Scarlet Pimpernel, appearing to work and drink alongside the Germans, but actually stealing their pistols and documents and bringing individual Dutchmen out of forced labour in Germany.

This resulted in a steady flow of rumours that he was collaborating with the Germans. Many people said that on their daily rounds they saw him in company with Germans, and he certainly boasted of his good contacts with the German authorities.

There is equally no doubt that he kept in touch with people who were wanted by the Germans and were on the run. One of these was Leen Immerzeel, a military policeman in hiding and later an instructor of the Dutch Home Military Force in Olst and its neighbourhood. On his instructions, Jan stole weapons from the Germans for the Resistance. Leen was a deeply religious man and a real friend to Jan; he was, sadly, killed in action in April 1945 as a member of a Resistance group.

Jan Vonk 1920-1944

Photos: Hermine Vonk

Two examples of Jan's double-dealing with the Germans were his theft of pistols from a couple of Germans who were playing billiards in the Café Vaanholt in Hengelo, and his stealing of a weapon from a German military vehicle in the Monninkhof Garage in Oldenzaal.

Officially, Jan was working in Rheine, 20 miles or so over the border in Germany, but he often claimed that "illness" and "injuries" prevented him from turning up, to the great worry of his mother. His frequent movements enabled him to bring out on false passports several people, including an Allied pilot and his own brother Frans, a student who had been transported to work in Berlin, and who now went into hiding at their home in Grotestraat.

Jan could bluff recklessly and impudently, if necessary. There is the case of Groot Enzerink of Vorden, alias "Karel Overijssel", who was one of the leading lights of the Underground newspaper "Trust". He was carrying 5000 copies of it on his bicycle, when he was stopped by a German soldier. In this critical situation, Jan talked the soldier out of taking any action, thereby saving Groot from an ominous fate.

On 5th November 1944, however, during a scuffle in Almelo, Jan Vonk was picked up and brought to the notorious building of the SD in Bornsestraat, for many the last stop before execution. The Germans found one of their pistols and a false passport on him. His brother Frans was also arrested in the same evening. On meeting Jan at the SD service centre, he saw that his face was swollen and bloody.

After being kept for a day in Almelo, Jan was handed over to the SD of Enschede. Here he was again interrogated several times and tortured by the Germans, who now regarded him as a "terrorist" and "partisan".

On 19th November 1944 (the day of my landing in 't Hesseler), when the Germans could not find me, Jan was brought to Borne and shot outside the Town Hall.

Dutch military policeman Luiken, who had been alerted to the situation, found his body under a tree with a bullet-hole in his heart. While he was kneeling by the dead man, two German cars stopped by the Town Hall and a number of soldiers jumped out and assured themselves that the victim was truly dead.

The horrified Luiken asked one of them, "Why did you kill this innocent boy?" He replied, "To show you what happens if you hide an Allied pilot."

The most likely reason for Jan Vonk's death is that Major Schöber, in charge of the SS in Enschede, was in Borne that evening with a great number of men looking for "the missing pilot" and, with the approval of his superior, Colonel Erwin Knop, had Jan Vonk shot because of his frustration at the lack of any result of the search.

Six days later, the same fate befell the hostages from 't Hesseler: Jan Boomkamp, Hendrik Roetgerink and Piet van Dijk sr.

A Memorial outside the Old Town Hall keeps alive the memory of Jan Vonk, aged 24.

Jan Vonk's Memorial in Borne

The Victims of the German Atrocity in 't Hesseler on 25th November 1944

Johan (Jan) Boomkamp

I am greatly indebted for the following information about Johan (Jan) Boomkamp to his great-nephew, Dirk Boomkamp; he is a son of the present Jan Boomkamp, the son of Johan's brother Bernhard. At my request, Dirk gained it in discussions in the summer of 2009 with his father and with Johan's brother Hendrik, who is married to Diny. Johan is named as Jan, the short form, on the 't Hesseler Memorial and in the chapters of this book, but I will call him Johan here to distinguish him from Dirk's father, the present-day Jan Boomkamp, owner of the well-known Garden Centre in 't Hesseler, where Dirk is the Export Manager.

"Johan Boomkamp was a tall, lean and enthusiastic man, who would have been 32 years old six weeks later. His father, Dieks Boomkamp, and mother, Siena Engberink, had six children: five sons – Hendrik, Gerard, Bernhard, Herman, and Johan – and one daughter, Trui.

Johan Boomkamp
Photo: Dirk Boomkamp

Johan was a very creative person and a lover of nature, with a passion for 'hunting' (= shooting) – which is shared by every member of the Boomkamp family. He was a gifted artist and could make beautiful drawings and paintings from nature as well as of aeroplanes and helicopters. He studied architecture and building engineering at the 'ambachtsschool' (Trade School), and afterwards took a job as a product engineer at Dikkers, a supplier of the Stork Machine Factory in Hengelo. His creativity was so strong that he made a perfect model of the new building that was erected by Dikkers. Hendrik has a small photo of Johan with the director-general of Dikkers.

At the time he was arrested, Johan was married to Jo Mol, who was the daughter of the owner of a café or bar in Koppelsbrink Street in Borne. They lived in a bungalow that Johan had proudly built for himself at No 38 Deurningerweg, in what used to be the Hasselo district of Weerselo, but has been since 1971 part of the municipality of Borne. After Johan was shot by the Germans, Bernhard moved into his house."

Dirk then goes on to describe how Johan became one of the hostages, and why he was later selected by the Germans for execution.

"Johan's house was approximately 100 metres from your landing-field, and from a window he saw your parachute hanging in a tree; he immediately dashed out to see what was going on. When he got there, some members of the Kotteman and Smit families were also there, and they were all stopped by the Germans. Hendrik told me that he and his brother Herman saw the Germans shouting to them, 'Stehen bleiben!" ('Don't move!'). When they realised Johan was being arrested, Herman and Hendrik ran off as soon as they could.

The Germans thought that in the war Johan was part of the Resistance; in fact, he was not part of it, but he certainly helped them. Because you landed very close to his house, it was easy for the Germans to make the link between you, Johan and the Resistance. They thought that you were in the hands of the Resistance and that Johan had a leading role in helping you.

Hendrik also said that he was the only one to see you running away over the young corn-fields.

Enclosed you will find a map of 't Hesseler."

I am immensely grateful to Dirk for this letter, dated 7th August 2009, which not only gives a character-sketch of Johan, but also explains why he was a prime suspect to the Germans and why they thought the Resistance was hiding me, a misconception that was still shared by many of the villagers when I returned to 't Hesseler on 26th August 1991.

Dirk's map is also valuable, as it shows the extent of the Garden Centre in 1989 and reveals that my landing-field was further north than I imagined. Dirk has also drawn a large black[1] arrow pointing eastwards to indicate the direction in which Hendrik says he saw me running, which may be closer to the truth than my memory. In any case, the landscape in November 1944 may have been slightly different from that in 1989, especially in relation to the extent of the woodland.

1989 Map of 't Hesseler, with annotations by Dirk Boomkamp and an arrow pointing east in the direction that witness said I ran away on 19th November 1944.

Photo: Google

[1]Changed to white for better visibility.

Hendrik Roetgerink

Mrs Riet Sanders-Roetgerink very kindly sent me this account of her uncle, Hendrik Roetgerink. She is the eldest daughter of Mrs Roetgerink-Hudepohl, and the elder sister of Hennie Roetgerink (whom I mention in this book). Mrs Marie Leuveld-Roetgerink (also in the book) was the elder sister of both Mrs Roetgerink-Hudepohl and of the victim Hendrik Roetgerink, to whom she was very close. This is why she was much affected by the 1994 TV feature "Beyond The Ignorance" and broke down when she was questioned in her home by the producer, Ellen van Helsdingen. Her son Ger, with his wife Ria and their family, still live in the house at 5 Mekkelhorstweg in 't Hesseler.

Mrs Sanders-Roetgerink wrote:

"Hendrik Roetgerink was born on 10th October 1915 in the small community of 't Hesseler, consisting of several farms near the town of Borne. He was the next-door neighbour of Jan Boomkamp. He was the youngest boy in a family of six children; their parents died at a very early age, so they grew up in the household of an uncle and aunt.

Hendrik was a quiet and friendly person, always glad of contact with his fellow-man. His passion was football and he was an avid supporter of the local soccer team, not missing a single game. He worked as a farmhand on a large farm with abundant land near his house; it belonged to 'Erven ten Gate', which processed wheat into flour in Borne for various purposes.

Hendrik was keen to improve himself, but the economic circumstances in the '30s and '40s were not good, and people were glad if they could hold onto a job; nor was there much opportunity for further education and personal development. Hendrik planned, when the war ended, to get a job in the light-metal industry, which was a major economic activity in the region of Twente in those days. He hoped to get himself an education in this way, paving the way for a solid future.

Hendrik Roetgerink in 1939
Photo: Riet Sanders-Roetgerink

Unfortunately, the sad events of 25th November 1944 ended his dreams abruptly. He was 29 and not yet married.

We remember him as a good person and a fine uncle, and we keep him in our thoughts with due respect."

Riet included with this tender tribute to her uncle, so wantonly murdered by the Germans, two photographs of him. She also added a reassurance for myself for my part in the tragedy:

"Now one important word for you: it is great, brave, and special your coming back to 't Hesseler every year. Be sure, there is no blame on you, not at all. In November 1944, we were standing there, men, women and children, so curious around the parachute. And suddenly the Germans came and took away six men arbitrarily. This was one of the conditions of the Occupation. And don't forget, their war was almost a lost war. Their feelings were grim: that's why something had to be done to demonstrate their power – their power in an area of a few kilometers. A stupid and an awful act – both. We know that war is not a friendly action over a cup of tea. Not in the early days of the war and not at this time.

I'm sure it feels good for our relatives and the inhabitants of 't Hesseler and makes us feel thankful, your coming and standing there with us in silence. We'll never forget this. Whatever may happen, we're thankful to you."

What can I say to these generous words? My tears are joined to hers and theirs as I recite, to those gathered beside the 't Hesseler Memorial to the victims each 4th May, the moving words of Rudyard Kipling:

"They shall not grow old,
As we that are left grow old;
Age shall not wither them
Nor the years condemn.
At the going down of the sun,
And in the morning,
We will remember them."

Hendrik Roetgerink at the age of 20
Photo: Riet Sanders-Roetgerink

Piet van Dijk

Unfortunately, I have received no reply to my letter to Mrs van Dijk-Kolkamp, Piet's daughter-in-law, and to her son, also Piet, so I am unable to offer anything about the elder van Dijk's life and family circumstances.

He was 56 years old and his son, also Piet, was a leading light in the Resistance, who had been caught by the Gestapo and locked-up in their Almelo prison; his Resistance comrades, however, forced an entry into the jail and released him. His father was arrested in Enschede in the evening of 19th November and put into the Hengelo prison together with the other five hostages, and was shot beside two of them. He lies buried with them in a sombre grave in the Borne Municipal Cemetery, and his name is inscribed with theirs on the 't Hesseler Memorial. He is remembered on my plaque on the Memorial and on the brass plate beside the portrait of "Father Roeland de Pottere, SJ" in the Rijksmuseum Twente in Enschede, which may have been his home-town.

Piet van Dijk

The Communal Grave in Borne Cemetery

In Their Death They Were Not Divided

In Retrospect

It is clear from the preceding accounts that the main objective of the German Security Police, or Gestapo, was to overcome the Resistance, of which Jan Vonk was a lone-wolf member, and Piet van Dijk the father of an active member of a group; the Germans' belief that the Resistance was hiding me motivated them to take the seven 't Hesseler hostages, in the hope that this would force the Resistance to hand me over – in which case I was just a pawn in the negotiations. Whether the Resistance would have done so is a delicate question: they were at war with the Germans and suffered many casualties; they also saw the death of many ordinary civilians in reprisal for the Resistance's actions, notably the execution of 100 local people for the wounding of a German officer in a failed Resistance attempt to capture his car. In spite of such tragedies, which were of almost daily occurrence all over Holland, the Resistance were not deterred and continued their acts of sabotage and assisting downed Allied airmen to escape.

My personal opinion is that, if I had found refuge with them, they would not have given me up to the Germans in spite of the pleas of the 't Hesseler villagers for their loved ones. Equally, contrary to what I wrote in my poem in 1990 in my emotional state after hearing my first news of three of the executions, as an RAF pilot I was duty-bound to try to get back to my Squadron. Also, by then, I might have seen and heard too much about the local organisation of the Resistance for them to endanger their own security by giving me up – to be tortured for such information by the Germans. They could not give me up, and I would have agreed with them.

Fortunately, this is all hypothetical, as I was never in touch with the Resistance. Nevertheless, these are thoughts that have rested with me uncomfortably ever since.

"Requiem for 't Hesseler"

translated by Father Paul Begheyn, SJ.

REQUIEM VOOR 'T HESSELER 1944

Nu heeft de Dag van Berekening mij ontdekt;
nu is mij de verschrikkelijke moord op onschuldigen onthuld;
nu is mijn gemoedsrust voorgoed verstoord.

Aan zijden koorden kwam ik neer in een leeg veld.
Ik wist niet dat het een deel was van een land
met aardige en vriendelijke mensen
die toen wreed en gemeen onderdrukt werden
en ernaar verlangden om weer de lucht van vrede in te ademen,
die bereid waren om groot gevaar te trotseren
en te laten zien, dat zij de moed om te leven nog niet hadden
opgegeven.

Verblind liep ik weg
en liet mijn helm, vliegbril en valscherm achter.
Ik verschool me in een bos en vervolgens in een veld
doorsneden met een vriendelijke kinhoge sloot,
totdat het donker werd
en ik stiekem terug kon lopen
naar mijn kameraden bij de Brusselse basis.

Verblind en gemeen
namen de Duitse monsters wraak,
en namen anderen in mijn plaats gevangen:
zij namen hun leven in plaats van het mijne.

Maar ik was een schaduw in de schemering,
ik was in het donker helemaal niet te zien:
niemand kon mij vinden.
Toch moest ik gevonden worden -
O, gevangenen! Hoe konden jullie deze tijd doormaken?

Had ik het maar geweten!
Had ik maar bij een Nederlandse deur aangeklopt om hulp
en verteld over het drama dat een aanvang nam.
Ik zou mijzelf terstond overgegeven hebben :
mijn leven was nooit dat van een ander waard,
en zeker niet van drie anderen.
En in elk geval had het voorkomen kunnen worden,
als we geweten hadden, wat er vier dagen later gebeurde.

Maar ik liep alleen,
struikelde over draden, viel in het water,
kroop om hoeken,
hield me schuil voor koplampen,
hing aan treinen,
viel van vrachtwagens,
schold op de kou en op mijn blaren,
en kwam in de buurt van de Rijn.

Op 24 november valt bitter en noodlottig
de arm van een soldaat op mijn schouder,
het geweer hangt om zijn nek:
'Komm mit mir!'

O, vervloekte Hunnen!
Waarom konden jullie geen verband zien
met de vangst van deze vieze, ongeschoren vlieger,
met de landing, nog geen vijftig mijl verderop
van de piloot uit de lucht,
en waarom konden jullie je handen niet terugtrekken van deze zinloze executie?

En - misschien op datzelfde uur -
voelde hetzelfde veld, dat mij had ontvangen,
andere geweren dodelijke schoten leveren,
en ontving het nog drie martelaren,
drie rechtschapen mannen,
heel walgelijk geveld,
die niets anders gedaan hadden
dan wonen in de buurt
van de plek waar ik geland was.

Nu verheft zich dit droevige monument
om de zinloze slachting van de oorlog te vermelden,
waar een vreemdeling die voorbij vloog
maakte dat in een klap drie levens werden beëindigd
en levenslang verdriet voor drie gezinnen begon.

Zij bereikten hun rust voor hun tijd,
en wij hebben al die tijd om te treuren.

Maar wij zijn niet alleen
en zij zijn niet alleen:
de vrede is gekocht met een afschuwelijk offer.

Jullie - en miljoenen anderen - betaalden die prijs,
waardoor wij, een halve eeuw later, nog steeds vrede hebben.
God zegene het kostbare geschenk, dat jullie ons hebben nagelaten;
wij geven het door aan kinderen van kinderen in de toekomst!

Zo verkondigt dit trotse monument
voor hen, voor ons en voor de hele wereld,
dat jullie, die hier gestorven zijn,
niet liggen in verdoemde vergetelheid,
maar op de weg naar vrijheid
en verlossing voor de mensheid -
toen met behulp van wapengeweld,
thans door broederschap en eenheid
in de vrede, die jullie ons gegeven hebben.

Wij, en ik in het bijzonder,
staan bij jullie in de schuld,
wij zijn jullie dankbaar - voor altijd.

H.J.S.Taylor 18.6.1990

The Burgomaster of Borne (centre) and JT on 28th August 1991 before the Unveiling of the 16 Squadron Plaque on the Memorial to the Victims of the 't Hesseler Tragedy on 25th November 1944

Address by Mr Maarten Vunderink, Burgomaster of Borne, before the Unveiling Ceremony

"46 years ago, in the last months of the war, a British pilot parachuted down here in 't Hesseler. He was lucky to survive and get away, although he was later taken prisoner.

Until this year he never knew where he had landed and that, because he got away, three inhabitants of this neighbourhood were executed by the Germans.

This week he came back.

And now we stand here, together with the relatives of those who died, to commemorate what happened in those last days of the war.

Our thoughts are with the three men who lost their lives, and with their relatives. We realise that they must be in painful memory.

But we also realise that, for the pilot too, this confrontation with the unforeseen effects of the only thing he could do, as any of us would have done under the circumstances, to escape from the enemy, is painful too.

We are grateful for the part he and his squadron played in the liberation of our country, thereby risking their lives.

This Memorial reminds us of the terrible effects of war and of the absolute necessity of preventing it happening again.

Preventing another war was also the task of the Allied Forces in Germany after the war.

16 Squadron of the RAF took part in that too. Their job is finished now, as the risks of another war in Europe have diminished and the Cold War, that followed the Second War War, is coming to an end.

In a few weeks 16 Squadron will fly back to England to be disbanded.

One of their last tasks is to attach their name and the name of the pilot who landed here in 1944 to this stone.

For us and our children to remember what happened here in those last months of the war.

I invite Mr Taylor and the representative of 16 Squadron of the RAF to fulfil this task."

TWENTSCHE COURANT

DONDERDAG 29 AUGUSTUS 1991 · HOOFDREDACTEUR: H.H. MORSINK · LOSSE NUMMERS ƒ 1,30 (ZATERDAG ƒ 1,75) · 144STE JAARGANG NUMMER 204

Piloot Taylor ontmoet nabestaanden gefusilleerden

BORNE – Zichtbaar aangedaan onthulde J. H. S. Taylor, ,The missing pilot', gisteravond een plaquette op het landkruis in de buurtschap 't Hesseler. Na 47 jaar kwam de Engelsman terug op de plek waar hij in de Tweede Wereldoorlog met zijn vliegtuig neerstortte. Om hem heen stonden de nabestaanden van de drie mannen, die destijds om zijnentwil werden gefusilleerd.

Onschuldige mensen, want ze hadden de piloot nooit gezien. Taylor zelf durfde destijds niemand aan te spreken, want hij was er van overtuigd dat hij in Duitsland was neergekomen. De piloot wist te ontkomen, maar viel in Doorn toch in Duitse handen en belandde in een krijgsgevangenenkamp. Na de bevrijding keerde Taylor terug naar Engeland, verliet de RAF en bouwde een carrière op in het onderwijs.

Mede namens het 16e squadron van de RAF wilde Taylor met deze plaquette de laatste eer bewijzen aan de gefusilleerden. „Het doet mij verdriet dat dit is gebeurd en ik voel een diep medelijden met de nabestaanden van deze drie mannen. Ik heb al die jaren niet geweten dat deze mannen vanwege mij zijn doodgeschoten".

Taylor legde samen met zijn echtgenote een krans bij het landkruis, evenals een afgevaardigde van het 16e squadron van de RAF, dat in Laarbruch in Duitsland is gestationeerd. Ook was er een eerbetoon van burgemeester Vunderink en zijn echtgenote, de commandant van de vliegbasis Twenthe en de buurtschap 't Hesseler.

■ De voormalige RAF-piloot H. J. S. Taylor onthult een plaquette bij het landkruis in de buurtschap 't Hesseler, in gezelschap van de nabestaanden van de drie gefusilleerden. FOTO DAAN WILLEMS

Onzekerheid

Jarenlang leefde men in deze buurtschap in onzekerheid. Vele verhalen over de toedracht van het gebeuren op de bewuste zondag 19 november deden de ronde. Zo zou er een luchtgevecht hebben plaatsgehad, waarbij het Engelse vliegtuig zou zijn geraakt. De piloot zou later door verzetsmensen zijn geholpen bij zijn vlucht. In het boek In Verdrukking, Verzet en Vrijheid, geschreven door H. Noordhuis, G. ter Braak en M. Kienhuis, wordt hier uitvoerig op in gegaan.

„Toen we bezig waren met het verzamelen van feiten voor het boek, hebben we diverse keren gesproken met ooggetuigen en familieleden van de gefusilleerden", licht Noordhuis toe. „Aan de hand van deze gegevens hebben we het betreffende hoofdstuk geschreven. Alleen één ding bleef knagen; niemand had ooit iets van die piloot gehoord of gezien.

Op een gegeven mement hebben we een oproep geplaatst in de krant voor materiaal uit de oorlog om een expositie te houden. Daarop reageerde onder meer de heer Ter Borg uit Hengelo. Hij bleek in het bezit van de vliegeniersbril van de piloot en daar stond een naam op. Als kleine jongen was Ter Borg met zijn ouders ondergedoken op 't Hesseler. Op die bewuste zondag hadden ze tijdens een wandeling de bril gevonden".

Met de bril hadden de schrijvers van het boek iets concreets in handen omtrent de vliegenier. Er werd naarstig gespeurd naar een piloot met de naam Taylor, maar dit bleek niet zo eenvoudig. „Telkens liep het spoor dood. Te langen leste hebben we een advertentie geplaatst in een veteranen-magazine en dat had succes. Een vriend van Taylor las de advertentie, knipte hem uit en stuurde hem naar de gezochte piloot", vertelt Noordhuis.

Taylor nam contact op met de Bornenaar. „Dit gebeurde precies twee maanden na het verschijnen van het boek", vervolgt Noordhuis. „Ik vertaalde het hoofdstuk, stuurde het op naar Taylor met de vraag of het hem bekend voorkwam". Taylor antwoordde dat hij onmogelijk de gezochte piloot kon zijn, omdat een aantal facetten van het verhaal niet klopten.

„Er werd melding gemaakt van een luchtgevecht", legt Taylor uit. „Ik was een verkenner en had de opdracht foto's vanuit de lucht te maken, toen plotseling, op onverklaarbare wijze, mijn vliegtuig in brand vloog. Ik was niet in gevecht met een Duits toestel. Ook heb ik tijdens mijn vlucht geen hulp gehad van verzetsstrijders. Bovendien klopte het signalement van de kleding - een jack met witte coltrui - niet. Ik droeg een blauwe overall. Ik was er zeker van dat ik het niet kon zijn".

Maar Noordhuis liet niet los en aan de hand van een reconstructie en de vindplaats van de bril, wist hij Taylor te overtuigen. Deze week was de ‚missing pilot' met zijn echtgenote te gast in Borne, waar hij onder meer een bezoek bracht aan de vliegbasis Twenthe en de nabestaanden van de gefusilleerden. „Daar heb ik het meest tegen op gezien", aldus Taylor. „Ik heb me voor die tijd alle mogelijke verwijten in het hoofd gehaald, die deze mensen mij zouden kunnen gaan maken, maar het was werkelijk hartverwarmend hoe ze mij ontvangen hebben".

Geen schuld

Taylor sprak onder meer met mevrouw Leuveld-Roetgerink. „Het is jouw schuld niet! drukte ze mij op het hart", vervolgt Taylor. „En dat deed me ontzettend goed, want ik voelde me zo schuldig voor de dood van deze mensen". Ook ontmoette hij de gebroeders Boomkamp, broers van de omgekomen G. J. Boomkamp. Zij namen hem mee naar de plek waar hij met zijn parachute was geland. „Bij mijn sprong uit het toestel, had ik de staart geraakt. Hierdoor verloor ik het bewustzijn. In een laatste reflex heb ik mijn parachute geopend en ben zo op 't Hesseler neergekomen.

Toen ik bijkwam stond er een kring van mannen om mij heen in lange zwarte jassen. Ik dacht dat ik in Duitsland was. Ik sloeg op het kastje dat de touwen bij elkaar hield en de parachute waaide naar een paar bomen. Alle mannen renden daar naar toe en ik maakte van de gelegenheid gebruik en vluchtte in tegengestelde richting een bos in. Hier ben ik blijven zitten tot de kust veilig was en van daaruit ben ik beginnen te lopen".

Samen met Noordhuis heeft Taylor zijn vluchtroute nog eens gevolgd. „Na al die jaren is er natuurlijk veel veranderd", vult Noordhuis aan. „Maar aan de hand van Taylors verklaring moet hij in grote lijnen via Delden, Goor, het Twentekanaal, toen met een goederentrein richting Driebergen verder naar Doorn zijn gegaan, waar hij op 24 november, een dag voor de executie van de drie Bornenaren, gevangen werd genomen door de Duitsers".

Al die jaren was Taylor niet op de hoogte van de gebeurtenissen op 't Hesseler. „Het heeft me diep geschokt. Ik heb zelf in de oorlog nooit iemand doodgeschoten, ben nooit in een gevecht verwikkeld geraakt. Dat maakt de schok des te groter. Toch ben ik blij, dat ik nu met de nabestaanden heb kunnen praten".

Vrede

Voor de buurtschap 't Hesseler is het verhaal nu af. Zoals mevrouw Leuveld-Roetgerink het heel treffend uitdrukte: „Jarenlang was er de twijfel of de piloot wel of niet door de ondergrondse is voortgeholpen. Nu het verhaal rond is heb ik er vrede mee".

De twijfel is weg. Taylor heeft het verhaal afgerond. Na de onthulling van de plaquette kreeg Taylor op het gemeentehuis zijn vliegeniersbril en zijn helm terug. Het 16e squadron, waartoe officier Harold James Strickland Taylor behoorde, zal binnenkort worden ontbonden. Het vliegtuig, een Spitfire FR.IX PL 957, waarmee Taylor die dag vloog, is nooit teruggevonden. Noordhuis zal een aanvulling op zijn boek moeten maken om ook zijn verhaal te completeren.

Vandaag vertrekt Taylor voor een laatste bezoek aan zijn squadron in Laarbruch. Van daaruit zal hij terugkeren naar Engeland. De vermiste piloot is terecht.

Headline: "Pilot Taylor meets the relatives of those who were shot"

Oorlogspiloot Taylor spreekt met nabestaanden van wraakactie Duitsers:

'Had ik maar bij jullie in Het Hesseler aangeklopt'

Vervolg van pagina 1

door Jan ter Haar

BORNE - Ze zagen hem naar beneden komen en landen vlakbij de plek waar nu het Tuincentrum Boomkamp aan de Hesselerweg is. De toegesnelden stonden in een kring om hem heen. Voormalig RAF-piloot Harold James Strickland Taylor (69) zegt dat er geen woord gesproken is. Toen hij zijn parachute losmaakte en deze weg waaide, stoof de kring er achteraan. Om het ding te verbergen voor de bezetter? Vanwege de mooie stof? De Engelsman, die niet beter wist dan dat hij in Duitsland was terecht gekomen, maakte in ieder geval dat hij weg kwam en hield zich voor iedereen schuil.

Hij heeft zich 47 jaar lang niet in de streek laten zien, volstrekt onwetend van het feit dat evenzovele jaren de oorlogsherdenking in Het Hesseler, een buurtschap van circa vijftig gezinnen, in het teken stond van de executie van J.G. Boomkamp, P.A. van Dijk en H.F. Roetgerink. Mannen die eruit geplukt waren omdat de buurt niet in staat was de bezetter de schuilplaats van Taylor aan te wijzen. Hoe konden ze ook. De Engelsman hield zich overdag in het struikgewas schuil en verplaatste zich in de duisternis, op zoek naar bevrijd gebied aan de andere kant van de Rijn.

Gisteren deed hij tegenover deze krant opnieuw zijn verhaal over het stormachtige verloop van die novemberdagen in '44.

„Ik was zondag de 19e opgestegen van het vliegveld Moelsbroek in Brussel om foto's te nemen van vliegvelden in de omgeving van Rheine. Op de terugweg begon tegen het middaguur mijn motor te proesten en te sputteren. Uit de uitlaten kwamen vlammen en rook en later dikke olie. De voorruit raakte zwaar beroet. Ik zag geen hand meer voor ogen, besloot uit het toestel te springen, draaide haar ondersteboven en viel eruit.

Ik moet het staartstuk hebben geraakt want ik kreeg een enorme klap tegen mijn borst en ben waarschijnlijk een poosje bewusteloos geweest. Later zag ik een aantal mannen in donkere jassen om me heen staan. Toen ze achter de parachute aan gingen, ben ik in tegenovergestelde richting, al hinkend in een bosje verdwenen. Ik vond een greppel die dwars door een groot veld liep en daar kroop ik door, voortdurend bang om door wie dan ook gezien te worden." Van zijn Spitfire PRXI is nooit een spoor terug gevonden.

Russen

Taylors doel was de andere, geallieerde kant van de Rijn te bereiken. Via sluiptochten langs Delden en Goor, na vergeefse pogingen het Twentekanaal over te zwemmen (de bruggen die hij passeerde waren bewaakt) wist Taylor zich uiteindelijk in Zutphen in een goederentrein te verstoppen. Die bracht hem tot in Utrecht. In Rhenen vlakbij de cruciale rivier liep het uiteindelijk spaak en werd hij voor de Duitsers gearresteerd. Op 1 mei 1945 werd hij als krijgsgevangene in een kamp aan de Oostzee door de Russen bevrijd. Studeerde geschiedenis en doceerde lange jaren Engelse literatuur aan de Universiteit van Leeds. Niets vermoedend van de tragische gevolgen van zijn oorlogsontsnapping indertijd. Een vriend van hem liet hem vorig jaar de oproep zien die via medewerkers van het Bornse gemeentearchief in een Brits blad voor veteranen was afgedrukt. Taylor: „Ik stuurde meteen een brief en werd daarop vanuit Borne opgebeld met een gelukwens dat ik nog in leven was. Tegelijk liet men er op volgen dat drie inwoners als gijzelaars vanwege mij het leven hadden moeten laten. Dat heeft me buitengewoon geschokt en mijn beeld van de oorlog omver gegooid. Tot voor kort keek ik met een zekere voldoening terug op mijn belevenissen als vliegenier. Alles was immers goed verlopen, ik had prima herinneringen, met m'n kameraden veel lol en avonturen beleefd. Dat spannende jongensboek is voor mij een tragedie geworden. Voor mij is er een zwarte doek over de oorlog geworpen."

Schuld

Taylor heeft deze dagen zoveel mogelijk nabestaanden bezocht. Onder hen de zuster van de gefusileerde Roetgerink. „Ik ben haar dankbaar voor haar uitspraak dat ze mij de dood van haar broer niet verwijt. Het is begrijpelijk dat de gemeenschap mij in meer of mindere mate verantwoordelijk acht voor het ombrengen van drie onschuldige mannen. Enerzijds voel ik me ook schuldig omdat, als ik daar niet naar beneden gekomen was, deze mensen wellicht nog

Taylor onthult de RAF-plaquette bij het landkruis ter nagedachtenis van de drie in 1944 gefusileerde mannen. FOTO: VINCENT WILKE

steeds zouden leven. Anderzijds acht ik me onschuldig omdat ik van niets wist, met niemand heb gesproken en me voor iedereen verborgen heb gehouden. Ik kan het een niet zwaarder laten wegen dan het ander. Schuldig en niet schuldig houden elkaar in evenwicht. Het tragische is wel dat ik uiteindelijk op 24 november in Rhenen werd gearresteerd, dus voor de Duitsers boven water was. Maar de executie van de drie is een dag later tòch doorgegaan."

Vergezeld van zijn vrouw bezocht Taylor gisteravond samen met een honderdtal samengestroomde buurtgenoten en andere belangstellenden het monument op het Hesseler en onthulde er onder koraalmuziek de plaquette van zijn RAF-eenheid. Op een ongedwongen bijeenkomst in het gemeentehuis van Borne zou hij later op de aovnd in een dichterlijke terugblik op 19 november 1944 verzuchten: „De dag van de afrekening heeft me te pakken gekregen. Had ik maar bij een van jullie aangeklopt en me bekend gemaakt. Dan had dat het leven van drie onschuldige mensen kunnen sparen. Was ik voor hen maar vindbaar geweest. Ik moet voor hen nog steeds gevonden worden."

Maar de buurt Het Hesseler is dankbaar dat ze het laatste stukje van de puzzel heeft kunnen leggen. Ze sluit de boeken die pas na 47 jaar duidelijkheid kunnen bieden en met de plaquette van de RAF een eervolle en bevredigende afsluiting hebben gekregen.

Plaquette laatste wapenfeit van zestiende Squadron RAF

HET HESSELER - Het 16e Squadron van de RAF, waartoe in 1944 piloot H.J.S. Taylor behoorde, had na de oorlog in Duitsland zijn thuisbasis en opereerde daar in het kader van de geallieerde strijdkrachten. Vanwege de ontspanning na de koude oorlog vliegt het over enkele weken definitief terug naar Engeland om daar te worden ontmanteld.

De onthulling van de plaquette in de buurtschap Het Hesseler betekende gisteravond het laatste wapenfeit van Taylor's vroegere squadron, zo memoreerde Borns burgemeester M. Vunderink. De plechtigheid werd opgeluisterd door koraalmuziek en vond plaats in aanwezigheid van ondermeer officials van de RAF en de Vliegbasis Twenthe.

Headline: "Wartime pilot Taylor meets the relatives of those on whom the Germans took revenge"

Headline: "If I had only knocked on the door of one of you in 't Hesseler"

Mr Bruggink's speech given in English on returning my flying-helmet to me

"Before I give you this cap I should like to take a few minutes to tell you what happened to this cap during the last 47 years.

Herman Bruggink

When I was a little boy of about ten years old, I used to help my father in the garden. Working together he sometimes told me stories about the Second World War. One story that impressed me very much and which I remember very clearly is the one of an English pilot who landed near our home in a place called 't Hesseler.

One day in November 1944, my father saw a parachutist in the distance. He took his bike and rode in the direction he thought the person could have landed. Upon arrival he found the parachute and the airman's cap. Quickly he grabbed this cap and disappeared again. He also told me about the sad consequences of this landing.

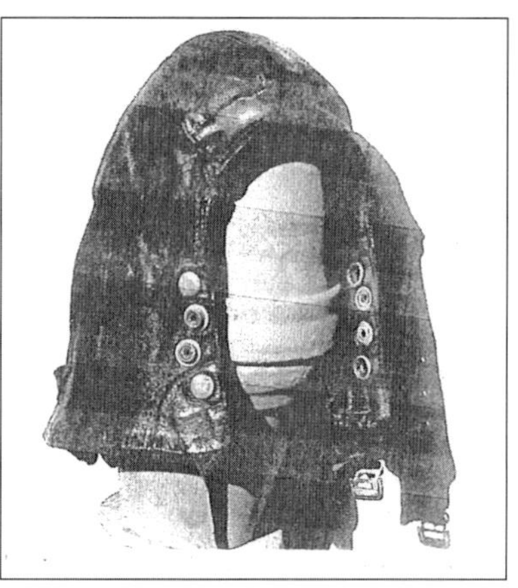

My very well-worn helmet

After the war my father used to wear this cap for many years when he went to work riding his moped. My father died in 1986 and from that time this cap was in the possession of my brother-in-law, who is very interested in collecting Second World War souvenirs.

In 1990 I read in our local newspaper a request for people to place things related to Borne in the Second World War at the disposal of an exhibition. I immediately thought about this cap and contacted Mr Noordhuis, who was organising the exhibition.

Recently he phoned me again and asked me to make the airman's cap available. When I questioned why, he told me that the English pilot who landed at 't Hesseler in those days had been located and would visit Borne.

Of course my answer was "Sure". If there is anyone who is entitled to this cap, then it's you, Mr Taylor. Also when I was asked to hand over this cap to you today, I immediately agreed to do so.

I have tried to imagine the feelings that undoubtedly must have surged up when you heard the story about the consequences of your landing. Your visit awakes emotions on both sides. But with your version of the landing a mystery is unriddled, and I hope it works out satisfactorily for all parties.

Finally, I – born after the war in a free country – I want to express my appreciation for you, Mr Taylor, and all those who helped during the Second World War with our liberation.

Thank you."

Vliegersbril na 50 jaar weer terug

BORNE - De helm en de vliegersbril die de Engelsman H.J.S. Taylor in de Tweede Wereldoorlog bij Borne verloor, heeft hij gisteravond teruggekregen (zie foto). Per parachute redde de Britse piloot zich op 19 november 1944 uit z'n brandende Spitfire-fotoverkenner. Hij landde in de buurtschap Het Hesseler op de gemeentegrens met Weerselo. Daar verdween hij spoorloos voor zowel vriend als vijand. Uit wraak gijzelden de Duitse bezetters zes streekgenoten. Drie van hen werden op 25 november doodgeschoten toen de RAF-piloot niet kon worden teruggevonden.

RAF-piloot H.J.S. Taylor

Zie ook pagina 17

Cutting from the "Twentsche Courant": Headline: "Airman's goggles returned after 50 years"

Primary School Project of Anne Bovenmars, age 11, great-niece of Jan Boomkamp, 15th September 1992

DE 2[E]

WERELD

OORLOG

THE 2nd WORLD WAR

Borne 15-9-92

Hello mr. Jimmy Taylor.

How are you?
We are fine here!
I had prommist you to sent you my project project about the secount world war.
~~Tax~~ That's wh(y) I sent you this letter.
This project is written in Dutch but I hope you like it.
The photo's are from the last evening you were with us.
It whas a pleasant evening. For my grand father (Herman Boomkamp) is also whas a pleasant evening.
May-be you will visit us once aregain

Greetings,
Anne Bovenmars

photo!

Anne,

Inhoud: 7½

Fijn dat je je eigen verhaal hebt verteld. Ik mis wel 't verhaal v/d. piloot over zijn neerstorten en ont-snapping.

Verzorging: 8

Je werk ziet er keurig uit.

Illustratie 8

Plaatjes passen prima bij de tekst.

INHOUD

CONTENTS

INLEIDING

INTRODUCTION

blz. 1 wie is die (piloott x piloot.
1 hongerwinter.

p.1 Who the pilot is.
1 The winter of starvation.

KERN

MAIN SUBJECT

blz. 2 Jimmie Taylor toen.
3 6 mensen.
4 De dodenherdenking.
5 foto en vervolg van 4.

p.2 Jimmy Taylor then.
3 6 months.
4 Remembrance Day.
5 Photo and continuation of 4.

AFSLUITING

CONCLUSION

blz. 6 Mijn mening.

p.6 My opinion.

Inleiding.
Wie is die piloot?
Hongerwinter

Zondagmiddag 19-11-'44:

Jimmy Taylor, hij was het die toen in de spitfire van het 16e squadron vloog om foto's te nemen in het gebied van Rheine. Jimmy Taylor was toen ± 24 jaar. Zuid nederland was al bevrijd, en het noorden kreeg de hongerwinter nog te verduren. Vele mensen gingen er met krakkemikkige fietsen, karretjes en kinderwagens op uit om bij de boeren voedsel te ruilen tegen sieraden en linnengoed. Op het laatst was er ècht niets meer te eten. Zelfs geen ui, bloembol of voederknol.

Kinderen en oude mensen hadden het meest last van de hongerwinter. Ze hadden geen kleding meer en kregen het ijzig koud, werden ziek en vaak stierven ze dan, er was niks meer. Geld, kleren, voedsel, huizen, hout om vuur te maken niks. Niks, niks meer!

Zo gingen de vrouwen en mannen op zoek naar voedsel op het platteland konden ze nog wat krijgen als je geluk had. Als je pech had moest je nog verder lopen op je vermoeide benen.

Jimmy Taylor,
toen

Jimmy Taylor toen † ~~1921-1992~~. Vlak voor zyn laatste vlucht in de spitfire, alles was nog in ~~orde~~. Hy poseerde by een bord van Hitler met de ~~tekst~~; één volk, één ryk, één ~~leider~~. Dit was precies wat Hitler wou, ~~MACHT!~~
Jimmy Taylor steeg op in een Spitfire PRXI van het 16e squadron. Het was 19 november 1944 om 11 uur. De bedoeling was om foto's ~~te maken~~ van vliegvelden in de omgeving van Rheine zo ver is hy helaas niet gekomen.

~~Taylor~~ vertelde by vroeger al Het is nu nog Hy vertelde dat raam hing en van de vlieg-men vliegen mij dat zyn hobby foto's nemen was. wel te zien. hy boven uit z'n dan foto's nam tuigen die over kwa-

Dit is de Spitfire waar hy ~~toen~~ in gevlogen heeft.
←

6 mensen,

J.A. Klaaskate. H. Smit. J.A. Kotte.

deze 3 mensen zijn doodgeschoten.

H.F. Roetgerink. J.H. Roetgerink. G.J. Boomkamp.

Mr Taylor is toen ~~niet~~ goed geland, je kunt wel degenlijk zeggen dat hij is neergestort. De Duitsers hebben direkt de omgeving uitgekamt en doorzocht. De zoekaktie leverde niets op. Uit wraak zijn 3 mensen die toevallig in de buurt waren en 3 mensen die in de buurt wonden gegijzeld, en daarna gefucileerd zijn er 3 dit was echter een grote erge gebeurtenis voor de buurtbewoners.

Elk jaar wordt er nog aan deze gebeurtenis gedacht op 4 mei ~~aan~~ bij het landkruis aan de mekkelhorstweg.

Dit jaar was Taylor er ook bij, en heeft hij een krans gelegd.

De dodenherdenking,
Taylor nu.
4-5-'92 7 uur 's avonds

Op 4 mei 1992 heefd Talor een krans gelegd bij het landkruis aan de Mek-
kelhorstweg. dit is
een jaarlijk- se gebeur-
tenis op 't Hesseler.
Er wordt dan gedacht
aan de 3 personen
die op 19-4-44
zijn dood- geschoten
in de om- geving van
de hesseler- weg en de
deurninger weg.
dit jaar was Tay-
lor er voor het eerst
bij. Hij heeft al wel eens
eerder een krans
gelegd maar dat
was op een dag
van septem ber vorig
jaar. na de
jaargedag tenis is
Talor bij ons op
bezoek geweest.
de 3 broers van G.J. Boomkam waren er ook. We
hebben een stamboekje opgeschreven voor Taylor. Hij
was daar erg in geinteresserd. Dirk heeft ook heel
lang met Talor gepraat over vliegtuigen enz.
Toen hebben we Taylor de vliegtuigjes laten zien die
we van hem opgestuurd hadden gekregen

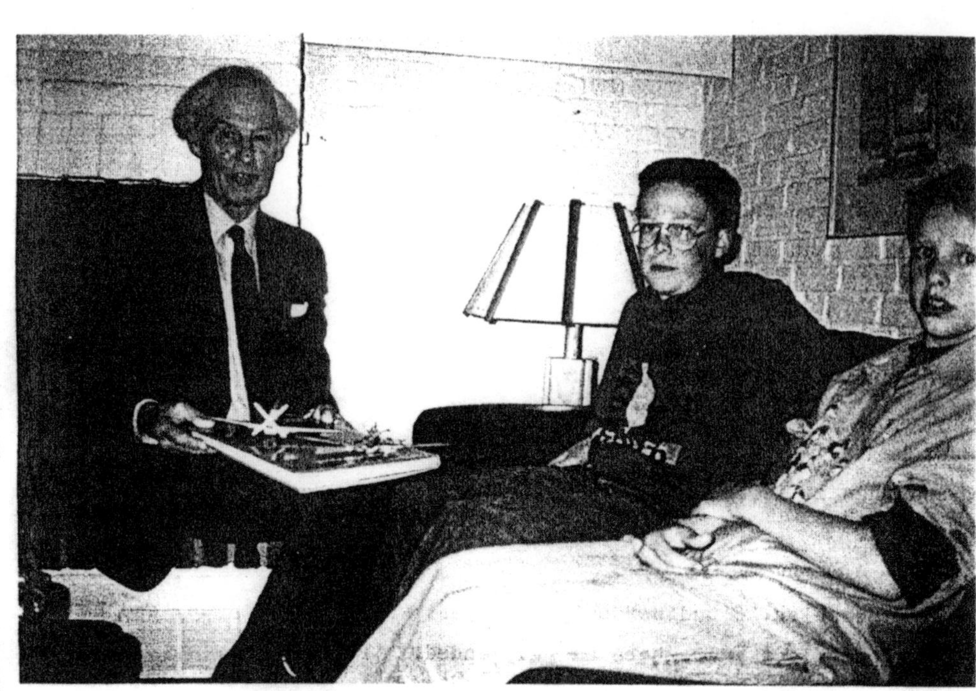

van links naar rechts: H.J.S. Taylor, Dirk Boomkamp en Anne Bouwen mars.

Hij vond dat we de vliegtuigjes goed in elkaar hadden gezet. Daarna heef hij met de 3 opa's gepraat.
En toen is hij weggegaan.

Mijn mening

Iedereen kan er zijn eigen mening over hebben, maar ik vind het heel erg knap van H.J.S. Taylor dat hij nog bij ons op 't Hesseler kan komen.
Ik zou het me goed voor kunnen stellen dat hij hier niet meer kon komen, uit pijn en verdriet.
Het lijkt me heel erg om zoiets als de 2e wereld oorlog te hebben meegemaakt, en dan is het nog dubbelop als er dan ook nog zoiets, als wat er met Taylor is gebeurt, nog bij komt.
Wij op 't hesseler zijn er pas vorig jaar achter gekomen wie die piloot is, en hij is er pas vorig jaar achter-gekomen waar hij geland is. Moet je nagaan!

English translation of Anne Bovenmars' School Project

Introduction

Who is the pilot?
The winter of starvation

Sunday afternoon 19.11.44.

Jimmy Taylor, it was he who flew in a Spitfire of 16 Squadron to take pictures in the area of Rheine. Jimmy Taylor was then +/- 24 years old. The southern part of the Netherlands had already been liberated, but in the north we still had to endure the winter of starvation. Many people went to the farmers with ramshackle bikes, carts and prams to exchange jewellery and linen for food. In the end, there was really nothing more to eat, neither onions, bulbs nor cattlefodder.

Children and old people suffered most in this hungry winter. They had no clothing, were terribly cold, became ill, and often died. There was no money, clothes,food, houses or firewood. Nothing, nothing at all.

So the women and men went into the countryside looking for food. Sometimes they were lucky and could find something. If you were unlucky, you had to keep on walking with tired legs.

Jimmy Taylor

then

For Jimmy Taylor then, 1943-1944, just before his last flight in the Spitfire, everything was still alright. He posed next to a poster of Hitler with the text: "One people, one country, one leader". This was exactly what Hitler wanted - Power!

Jimmy Taylor took off in a Spitfire of 16 Squadron. It was 19th November 1944 at 11 o'clock. The intention was to take photographs of the airfields in the neighbourhood of Rheine. Unfortunately, he didn't get that far.

Taylor told me that in those days his hobby was taking photographs. You can still tell that now. He told me that he used tc lean out of his window and take pictures of the planes that flew overhead.

This is the Spitfire that he was flying then.

6 people

These three people have been shot

Mr Taylor did not land properly then: you could say he crashed. The Germans immediately combed and searched the area. The search revealed nothing. In retaliation, 3 people who happened to be in the area and 3 people who lived in the neighbourhood were taken hostage. Later on, three of them were shot. This was terrible for the people who lived in the area.

Every year we remember this incident on 4th May beside the Crucifix on Mekkelhorstway.

This year Taylor was there too, and he laid a wreath.

Remembrance Day

Taylor now

4.5.92. 7 o'clock in the evening

On 4th May Taylor laid a wreath on the Cross on Mekkelhorstway. This is a yearly event in 't Hesseler. People think then about the 3 people who were shot on 19.11.44 in the neighbourhood of Hesselerway and Deurningerway.

This year, Taylor was there as well, for the first time. He had laid a wreath before, but that was on a day in September last year.

After the Remembrance Day service Taylor visited us; the three brothers of G.J.Boomkamp were there, too. We wrote a family tree for Taylor. He was very interested in this.

Dirk talked a long time to Taylor about planes, etc. Then we showed Taylor the planes he had sent us. He thought that we had assembled the planes very well.

After that he talked to the three grandads. After that he left.

The photo: from left to right: H.J.S.Taylor, Dirk Boomkamp and Anne Bovenmars

My opinion

Everyone can have their own opinion, but I think it is very nice of H.J.S.Taylor that he can still come to us in 't Hesseler.

I can well imagine that he could not come here anymore because of the pain and sorrow.

It must be very bad to have lived through something like the Second World War; and then it is twice as bad when something happens such as Taylor experienced.

We, in 't Hesseler, found out only last year who the pilot was, and he found out only last year where he had landed. Fancy that!

Anne

Contents: 7½ Nice that you have told your own story.
However, I do miss the story about the pilot crashing and escaping.
Presentation: 8 Your work has been presented well.
Illustration: 8 The pictures match the text perfectly.

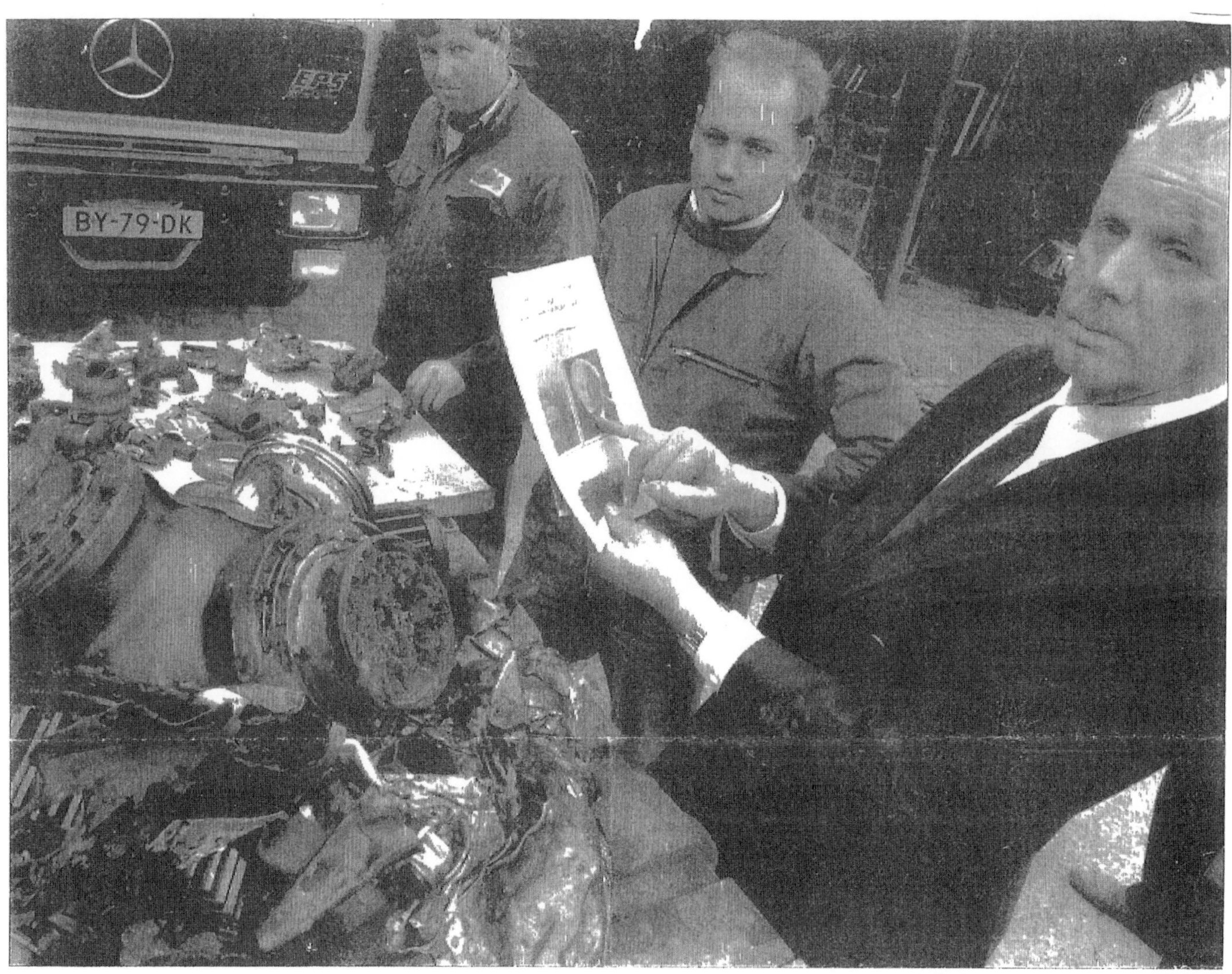

De resten van het oorlogsvliegtuig van Jimmy Taylor worden op dit moment schoongemaakt en geconserveerd. Het is de bedoeling dat ze de komende tijd geëxposeerd worden. Op de foto van links naar rechts: Wim Knoef, Jan Platenkamp en Hennie Egberink (met in zijn handen een foto van Jimmy Taylor. FOTO VINCENT WILKE

Boven Borne neergeschoten vliegtuig neergestort in weiland bij Bentelo

Resten vliegtuig Taylor teruggevonden

BORNE - Na enkele weken speuren en zoeken zijn medewerkers van het museum van de vliegbasis Twenthe er in geslaagd de resten van het vliegtuig van Jimmy Taylor te lokaliseren. Het toestel bleek in een weiland bij Bentelo terecht zijn gekomen. De resten van het toestel worden de komende tijd geëxposeerd in verschillende plaatsen.

Jimmy Taylor was een Engelse piloot die boven Nederland werd neergeschoten door de Duitsers. Hij kon per parachute uit het vliegtuig ontsnappen en landde in de Bornse buurtschap 't Hesseler. Daar werd hij opgevangen door enkele buurtbewoners die hem verstopten voor de Duitsers. Als wraakactie vermoordden de Duitsers daarop vier onschuldige burgers.

Het toestel van Taylor ronkte enige tijd stuurloos verder om vervolgens 'ergens' te pletter te slaan. Tot voorkort was de plek waar het toestel terecht kwam, onbekend.
De opgraving van het toestel is gecoördineerd door Bornenaar H. Noordhuis. Noordhuis, chef interne zaken op het gemeentehuis en nauw betrokken bij de Bornse oorlogsgeschiedenis, kreeg enige tijd geleden een tip over het toestel. „Ik heb daarop mensen van het museum van de vliegbasis Twenthe ingeschakeld. Zij hebben de ervaring en het materiaal om dat toestel op te sporen", vertelt Noordhuis. Ook het Bornse grondverzetbedrijf Egberink verleende zijn medewerking.
Het zoeken naar de resten is zo'n vier weken geleden van start gegaan. „We hebben daar bewust geen ruchtbaarheid aan gegeven omdat we bang waren voor souvenirjagers", aldus Noordhuis.

De opgravingen gebeurden met behulp van van speciale peilapparatuur van de vliegbasis. „Daarmee is ijzer in de bodem te lokaliseren", legt Noordhuis uit. De apparatuur zette de onderzoekers eerst nog op het verkeerde been. „We dachten beet te hebben maar het bleken betonnen palen te zijn, doorvlochten met ijzer", lacht de Bornenaar. Uiteindelijk bracht een tip van een man uit Arnhem die tijdens de oorlog in Bentelo woonde, de speurders op het goede pad. Noordhuis: „We zochten eigenlijk aan de verkeerde kant van een houtwal. Toen we aan de goede kant zochten vonden we spoedig de resten van het vliegtuig van Jimmy Taylor."
De groep trof een grote hoeveelheid resten aan. „Honderden kleine stukken, maar ook hele interessante zaken zoals de propeller van het motorblok dat nog intact was. Ook hebben we naamplaatjes gevonden van onderdelen en stukken stof van de binnenkant van het toestel", aldus Noordhuis.
De resten van het vliegtuig zijn tijdelijk opgeslagen bij de firma Egberink. Daar worden de onderdelen schoongemaakt. Het is de bedoeling dat de resten gebruikt worden bij de herdenkingen van de oorlog. „We willen Taylor die eind april naar Borne komt, natuurlijk ook de resten en plaats waar zijn toestel is terechtgekomen, laten zien. Verder worden enkele onderdelen geëxposeerd op een tentoonstelling in Bentelo.

Uiteindelijk is het de bedoeling dat de spullen naar het museum in Enschede gaan", aldus Noordhuis, „want daar horen dergelijke zaken thuis, en niet ergens in Borne".

Translation on following page

FRAGMENTS OF TAYLOR'S PLANE FOUND
by René Schabos

BORNE – After several weeks of searching, employees of the museum of Twenthe Air Base have succeeded in locating the fragments of Jimmy Taylor's plane. It appears that the machine came to rest in a meadow near Bentelo. In the near future, the fragments of the plane will be exhibited in several places.

Jimmy Taylor was an English pilot who was shot down[1] by the Germans over Holland. He was able to escape from the plane by parachute and landed in the hamlet of 't Hesseler. There he was taken in by some inhabitants, who hid him from the Germans[1]. To take revenge, the Germans murdered four innocent people.

For a while, Taylor's machine flew on out of control and crashed down somewhere. Until quite recently it was not known where the plane had landed.

The excavation of the plane has been coordinated by H.Noordhuis from Borne. Noordhuis, chief of internal affairs at the Town Hall and involved with Borne's war history, recently received a tip-off about the machine. "I enlisted the help of the people of Twenthe Air Base. They have the experience and equipment to find the plane", says Noordhuis. The firm of Egberink also assisted.

"We started searching for the fragments about four weeks ago. We did not publicise this on purpose, because we were afraid of souvenir-hunters", relates Noordhuis.

The excavations took place with the help of special heavy-gauge apparatus from the Air Base. With this it is possible to locate metal in the earth. In the beginning they were on the wrong track: they thought they were successful, but it turned out to be concrete poles reinforced with iron. In the end, a man from Arnhem, who lived in Bentelo during the war, put them on the right path. Noordhuis: "We were looking on the wrong side of a bank. When we started looking on the right side, it wasn't long before we found the fragments of Jimmy Taylor's plane."

The group found a large number of fragments. "Hundreds of small pieces, but also bigger items like the propeller in front of the engine-block, which was still intact. We have also found the name-plates of parts and material from the inside of the plane", according to Noordhuis.

The fragments of the plane are stored temporarily with the Egberink company. There the parts are being cleaned. It is intended that they should be used in conjunction with memorials of the war. "Of course, we want to show Taylor, who is coming to Holland at the end of April, the fragments and the place where his plane landed. Some parts will be exhibited at an exhibition in Bentelo."

"It is the intention that everything shall go eventually to the museum in Enschede", says Noordhuis. "That is where these things belong, and not somewhere in Borne."

Photograph caption

The fragments of Jimmy Taylor's warplane are at this moment being cleaned and preserved.
It is intended that they should be exhibited in the near future. In the photograph from left to right:
Wim Knoef, Jan Platenkamp and Hennie Egberink (with a picture of Jimmy Taylor in his hands).
Foto: Vincent Wilke

[1] There are two mistakes in this account, written before René Schabos interviewed me:
I was not shot down and I was not hidden from the Germans.

RAF-piloot bezoekt plek waar Spitfire in 1944 neerstortte

Verleden laat Jimmy Taylor niet met rust

door René Schabos

BORNE/DELDEN - Stukje bij beetje krijgt hij de stukjes van de puzzel in handen. Letterlijk. Voormalig RAF-piloot Jimmy Taylor graaft met zijn vingers een brokje aluminium uit de zanderige bodem. Door de inwerking van zuurstof is het sterk verweerd. Maar zeker is dat het verwrongen stukje metaal toebehoorde aan zijn Spitfire PL957, die op zondag 19 november 1944 in een weiland achter restaurant De Rustende Jager in Bentelo neerstortte. Drie weken geleden werd de plek opgespoord en gisteravond ging Taylor er, direct na zijn aankomst in Nederland, persoonlijk kijken.

Het verleden laat hem niet met rust. Twee jaren geleden kreeg hij te horen dat na zijn landing aan een parachute in de Bornse buurtschap het Hesseler drie onschuldige burgers door de Duitsers waren vermoord. Omdat de piloot was gevlucht en niemand kon zeggen waar hij zich bevond.

Zevenenveertig jaar lang was hij onwetend van de verschrikkelijke gevolgen van zijn ontsnapping. Totdat Bornenaar Hennie Noordhuis hem wist op te sporen en vertelde wat er was voorgevallen. Sindsdien laat zijn eigen geschiedenis hem niet meer los. Zijn huidige bezoek aan Borne is al het derde in twee jaar. De lach is opgewekt en ontspannen, maar zijn ogen staan serieus als Taylor 's avonds de plek bekijkt waar het toestel is gevonden. Om hem heen verkeren de mensen, die hebben geholpen de plaats te lokaliseren, in een opgewonden stemming.

Taylor doet het vinden van de vliegtuigresten minder: „Ik had geen speciale band met het vliegtuig. We hadden geen eigen toestel. Je nam gewoon de kist die aan de beurt was. Ik nam afscheid van het vliegtuig toen ik er uit sprong.

Fiets

Over wat er daarna mee is gebeurd, heb ik me nooit zo bezig gehouden. Nee, ik ben meer geraakt door de ontmoeting met de mensen die het hebben zien gebeuren. Met hen ben ik door het ongeluk verenigd", zegt hij.

Eén van hen is de tegenwoordig in Almelo woonachtige Joop Roetgerink. Hij woonde aan de Deldenerstraat in Borne toen hij op die zondagmiddag de Spitfire steeds meer hoogte zag verliezen en Taylor aan zijn parachute het vliegtuig verliet. Roetgerink werkte snel zijn middageten naar binnen om vervolgens op zijn fiets te springen en de plek te zoeken waar het wrak was terecht gekomen.

Marinus Timmerman was toen al wezen kijken. De toen 18-jarige zoon van de kastelein van De Rustende Jager was als eerste op de plaats van de crash. „De stukken metaal waren nog gloeiend heet", herinnert hij zich als de dag van gisteren. Het toestel had zich in een houtwal aan de Platenkampweg geboord en was daar grotendeels uit elkaar gespat.

Timmerman werd even later door de voor de Duitsers werkende Landwacht bij het wrak weggestuurd. Die hield ook Joop Roetgerink tegen toen hij de plek had gevonden. „Eentje schoot een paar keer in de lucht, als teken dat ik moest wegwezen. Nou, ik nam geen risico, dat kun je begrijpen".

Puzzel

Allemaal hebben ze hun eigen verhaal, de mannen die elkaar treffen bij de houtwal waar het toestel neerkwam en waar pas drie weken geleden de resten van het wrak werden geïdentificeerd. Want dat er een vliegtuig was neergestort was bekend, maar niet dat het de Spitfire van Taylor was. Dat werd pas duidelijk nadat bij Joop Roetgerink na het zien van een tv-uitzending over de piloot een lichtje was gaan branden.

Taylor is vooral geïnteresseerd in de brokstukken die in een loods in Borne zijn opgeslagen. Ze kunnen hem helpen nog ontbrekende delen van zijn verhaal te vinden. De oud-piloot zoekt vooral naar stukken die voor hem herkenbaar zijn. „Mijn Spitfire was een foto-verkenningstoestel en had daarom een blauwe kleur. Dat kwam niet veel voor. Die kleur heb ik op de brokstukken teruggezien, al was er nog maar een glimp van over".

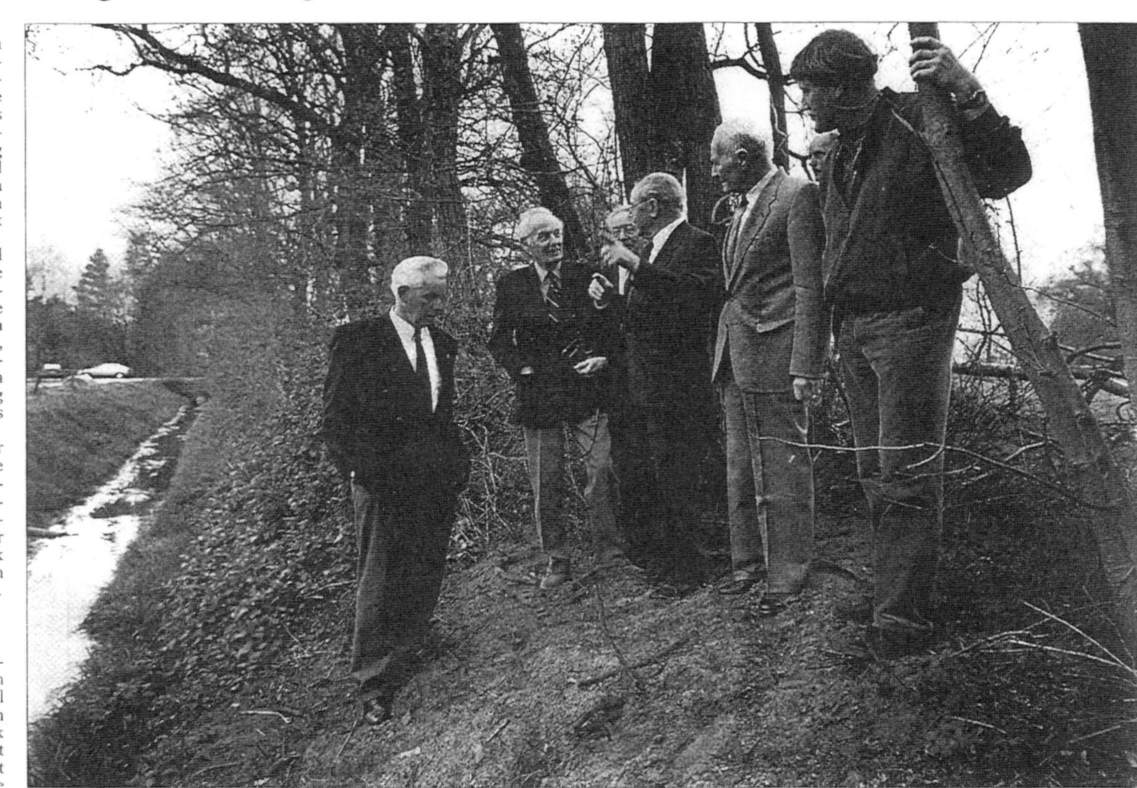

Verenigd door het ongeluk. Vlnr Hennie Egberink, Jimmy Taylor, Marinus Timmerman, Joop Roetgerink en Hennie Noordhuis bij de houtwal waar de resten van de Spitfire zijn gevonden.

FOTO REINIER VAN WILLIGEN

Hij zag ook het tandwielhuis, waaraan de propeller was bevestigd. Delen van de propellerbladen zijn nog aanwezig. Taylor lacht geheimzinnig: „Het was een houten propeller. Maar volgens de mensen van mijn squadron vlogen de Spitfires alleen met metalen propellers. Tja..".

Zelf had hij er nooit op gelet. „Metaal of hout, wat kon het ons schelen". Maar nu houdt het hem in hevige mate bezig. „In een nog niet gepubliceerd boek over een nog vliegende Spitfire, die kort na de mijne uit de fabriek kwam, staat dat de restaurateur zich in 1973 beklaagde over de kwaliteit van de propeller. Hij versplinterde. Metaal verspintert echter niet, dus die was kennelijk van hout".

Storing

Er is meer. Waarom begon de motor van het toestel na de vlucht boven Duits grondgebied plotseling te haperen? „Ik ben niet geraakt door afweergeschut. Het was een motorstoring, misschien als gevolg van slijtage. Het toestel stond bekend als traag en versleten. Ik heb nog met een andere piloot geloot om wie hem zou vliegen. Ik verloor".

Oud-collega's maken soms grapjes dat hij zonder brandstof is komen te zitten. Niet goed opgelet heeft dus. Maar zelf gelooft hij daar niet in. Er is volgens hem wel een andere verklaring. „Voor het maken van foto's moesten we soms lange tijd extreem langzaam vliegen. De motoren konden daar niet goed tegen. Het is bekend dat ze het dan wel eens begaven".

Eén van de zuigers van de Rolls Royce-motor is in Bentelo gevonden. Taylor heeft hem nauwkeurig bestudeerd. „Als de motor is opgeblazen had je het aan de zuiger moeten kunnen zien. Maar hij ziet er normaal uit. Van de andere kant, de motor had 24 zuigers. Misschien was alleen deze ene nog goed..."

From the "Twentsche Courant", 24th April 1995 (translation on following page)

RAF PILOT VISITS SPOT WHERE SPITFIRE CAME DOWN IN 1944
THE PAST DOES NOT LEAVE JIMMY TAYLOR IN PEACE

by René Schabos

BORNE/DELDEN Bit-by-bit he gets the pieces of the puzzle in his hands literally. Former RAF pilot Jimmy Taylor digs a piece of aluminium from the sandy soil with his fingers. It has weathered a lot from oxygenation. One thing is sure: the twisted piece of metal belonged to his Spitfire PL 957[1] that came down on Sunday 19th November 1944 in a meadow behind the restaurant "The Resting Hunter" in Bentelo. The spot was discovered three weeks ago, and Taylor went to have a look at it straight after his arrival in Holland.

The past does not leave him in peace. Two years ago he got to know that, after landing by parachute in the Borne hamlet of 't Hesseler, three innocent people were murdered by the Germans – because the pilot had escaped and nobody could tell them where he was.

For 47 years he did not know the terrible consequences of his escape, until Hennie Noordhuis traced him and told him what had happened. Ever since then his story will not leave him alone. His present visit to Borne is already the third in two years. His laughter is cheerful and relaxed, but his eyes are serious when, in the evening, Taylor looks at the spot where the plane was found. Around him, the people who helped to locate the spot are excited.

Taylor does not feel the same way about the finding of the pieces of the plane: "I had no special ties with the plane. We did not have our own. We simply took the one whose turn it was. I said my good-byes to the plane when I jumped out."

Bicycle

"I never worried about what happened to it afterwards. I am touched by meeting the people who saw it happen. I am united with them through this accident," he said.

One of them is Joop Roetgerink, who now lives in Almelo. He was living on Deldenerstraat in Borne when, on that Sunday afternoon, he saw the Spitfire losing height and Taylor leaving the plane by parachute. Roetgerink finished his lunch quickly and jumped on his bike to find the spot where the wreckage had landed.

Marinus Timmerman had already been to have a look. The then 18-year-old son of the landlord of "The Resting Hunter" was the first person on the site of the crash. "The pieces of metal were still red-hot", he remembers this as if it were yesterday. The machine had plunged on the Platenkampweg Road, and the greater part had exploded there and disintegrated.

Shortly afterwards, Timmerman was told by the Germans to leave the wreck. They also stopped Joop Roetgerink when he had found the site. "They fired a few shots in the air as a warning to leave. As you can understand, I didn't take any risks."

Puzzle

They each have their own tale, the men who meet on the bank where the machine came down and where the pieces of the wreck were identified only three weeks ago. It was known that a plane had crashed, but not that it was Taylor's Spitfire. This only became apparent after Joop Roetgerink realised it after watching a programme on TV.

Taylor is particularly interested in the fragments kept in a shed in Borne. They can help him to find the missing parts of his story. The ex-pilot is looking especially for pieces he can recognise. "My Spitfire was a photo-reconnaissance machine and therefore was a blue colour. This was not very common. I have found that colour on the fragments, but there is only a trace of it left."

[1]Jimmy Taylor's Spitfire was later identified as MB957.

Piloot Jimmy Taylor vindt eindelijk rust

'If I had but known,
I would have given myself up
My life was not worth the life of one Dutchman.
Much less the lives of three'

Door René Schabos

BORNE/LEEDS - Een defecte compressor veroorzaakte naar alle waarschijnlijkheid de motorstoring, die op 19 november 1944 de Spitfire van RAF-piloot Jimmy Taylor in de buurt van Delden deed neerstorten. De Engelsman is dat na een lange speurtocht te weten gekomen van een vroegere specialist van Rolls-Royce, de fabriek waar de vliegtuigmotoren werden gebouwd. Voor Taylor is de ontdekking van groot belang. De gevolgen van de crash waren verschrikkelijk. Omdat de piloot, die zonder hulp kans zag te vluchten, niet kon worden opgespoord, schoten de Duitsers ter vergelding vier inwoners van Borne dood.

'Ik ben blij dat ik ervan vrijgesproken ben schuld te dragen aan het motormankement en aan alle ellende die volgde', schrijft Taylor in zijn publicatie over de nasleep van de tragische gebeurtenis. Het zoeken naar de oorzaak van het neerstorten van de Spitfirne hield hem sinds begin vorig jaar, toen het wrak in een weiland achter restaurant de Rustende Jager werd gevonden, onophoudelijk bezig.

'In feite was het de laatste vraag waarop hij antwoord wilde', zegt de Bornse gemeentearchivaris Hennie Noordhuis. Hij spoorde Taylor eind 1990 op en bracht de Engelsman, die niets van de dramatische gevolgen van de crash wist, op de hoogte van de feiten in zoverre hij die had weten te achterhalen.

'Ik heb daardoor zijn leven op de kop gezet', zegt Noordhuis. 'Het was een dubbeltje op zijn kant. Jimmy had er een trauma aan over kunnen houden, maar het is goed uitgepakt. Hij is hier naar toe gekomen, heeft contact gezocht met de nabestaanden en met veel andere inwoners van Borne en heeft daarbij veel vrienden gemaakt. Hij is een bijzonder sympathiek mens.'

Taylor wilde alles weten en werkte overal aan mee om zijn geschiedenis, waarvan hij bijna een halve eeuw onwetend was geweest, te verwerken. Hij bracht sinds 1990 vaak meerdere bezoeken per jaar aan Borne, de gemeenschap waarbij hij zich naar zijn zeggen meer betrokken voelt dan bij welke plaats in Engeland ook.

Executies

Van Hennie Noordhuis hoorde hij wat na zijn vlucht precies was gebeurd. De executie van de jonge verzetsman Jan Vonk naast de Villa Elisabeth, het toenmalige gemeentehuis, op de avond na zijn landing. En zes dagen later, op 25 november 1944, de executie van Jan Boomkamp, Hendrik Roetgerink en Piet van Dijk in een weiland in de buurtschap 't Hesseler, vlakbij de plek waar Taylor was geland. Uit wraak, omdat de Duitsers ten onrechte veronderstelden dat de Bornse gemeenschap de piloot verborgen hield.

De Engelsman ging in Nederland zelf op zoek naar de route die hem uiteindelijk naar Rhenen leidde. Aan de oever van de Rijn werd hij vijf dagen na zijn landing door de Duitsers opgepakt. Nog had het onheil afgewend kunnen worden. Maar niemand bracht zijn gevangenneming in verband met het neerstorten van een vliegtuig nabij Bentelo. 'Als ze het wel hadden gedaan, dan waren de levens van de drie mensen gered', merkt hij vol spijt op.

Volledig onwetend van het lot dat de gijzelaars in Borne wachtte had Taylor bovendien zijn mond gehouden over zijn militaire actie en de plek waar hij was neergekomen. Als krijgsgevangene hoefde hij volgens de Conventie van Genève slechts zijn naam, rang en nummer bekend te maken.

De gedachte dat hij door zich aan te geven, onschuldige mensen het leven had kunnen redden, was voor hem een schok. 'Als ik het had geweten, had ik mezelf aangegeven. Mijn leven was het niet waard ingeruild te worden tegen het leven van een enkele Nederlander, laat staan tegen dat van drie', schreef hij in 1990 in dichtvorm. Op dat moment was hij zich nog niet bewust dat ook de dood van Jan Vonk met zijn ontsnapping in verband moest worden gebracht.

Jimmy Taylor laat bij een van zijn bezoeken aan Borne de kinderen van de Olthofschool zien hoe hij in '44 met zijn Spitfire naar beneden kwam. FOTO ARCHIEF

'Hij was alles te weten gekomen', zegt Hennie Noordhuis, die met Jimmy Taylor een hechte vriendschapsband kreeg, 'behalve wat precies het neerstorten van het vliegtuig veroorzaakte. Dat was het laatste grote vraagteken. Met enorm veel toewijding is hij daarmee bezig geweest, zoals met alles overigens. Hij heeft iedereen die er maar wat van wist gesproken, heeft alle technische details uitgezocht.'

Jimmy Taylor zegt er lange tijd rekening mee gehouden te hebben dat hij de crash had kunnen voorkomen. Hij vermoedde dat de problemen met de motor waren veroorzaakt doordat hij er lange tijd langzaam mee had gevlogen. Zijn Spitfire deed dienst als fotoverkenningsvliegtuig. Voor het maken van foto's moest het toestel met lage snelheid vliegen.

De piloten wisten dat ze bij een hapering van de motor flink gas moesten geven om de 24 cilinders van de Roll-Royce motor schoon te blazen. Taylor probeerde dat tijdens zijn rampvlucht ook, maar de actie had geen succes. Op een hoogte van 7000 meter walde de cockpit zich met rook en spoot olie op het windscherm. Taylor draaide het toestel op z'n kop en bracht het in een glijvlucht. Op een hoogte van 3000 meter verliet hij het vliegtuig met zijn parachute.

Brokstukken

Drie getuigen herinnerden zich de crash toen zij in november 1994 op de televisie een reportage over de geschiedenis van Jimmy Taylor zagen. Op basis van hun verklaringen kon het wrak van het vliegtuig in maart vorig jaar worden opgespoord, ruim 50 jaar nadat het was neergestort. In een houtwal achter restaurant De Rustende Jager werden tal van kleine stukken verwrongen metaal gevonden, alsmede enkele grotere onderdelen. De grootste stukken, inclusief de motor, waren kort na de crash al door de Duitsers weggehaald.

Taylor had flauwe hoop de oorzaak op basis van de belangrijkste brokstukken te kunnen achterhalen: daaronder waren een in- en uitlaatklep, een bougie en diverse lagers. Met twee zakken vol aluminium keerde hij terug naar Engeland. 'Ik heb hem nog gezegd: daar kom je nooit mee door de douane, maar het is hem gelukt. Die man kan alles', lacht Hennie Noordhuis.

In zijn eigen land begon het echte speurwerk. Taylor riep de hulp in van de Old Flying Machine Company, maar die kon hem niet veel verder helpen. Hij zocht verder en kwam via het oorlogsmuseum in Duxford en een tv-producer, die een film had gemaakt over een nog vliegende Spitfire, in contact met David Birch, een medewerker van de Rolls-Royce Heritage Trust.

Birch op zijn beurt consulteerde Alec Harvey-Bailey, een specialist die tijdens de oorlog nauw betrokken was bij het opsporen van mankementen aan de RR Merlin-vliegtuigmotoren. Taylor: 'Ik vond het verbazingwekkend dat de man, die in de periode 1940-1945 hoofd was van de onderzoekssectie van Rolls-Royce, nog in leven was en bereid om op zijn ziekbed aandacht te schenken aan mijn betrekkelijk onbelangrijke zorgen.'

Afgesloten

Harvey-Bailey opperde dat er drie mogelijke oorzaken waren, maar een motorstoring als gevolg van het langzame vliegen leek hem het meest waarschijnlijk. De uitspraak van de RR-expert was niet bepaald wat Taylor had gehoopt. Ze bevestigde zijn bange vermoeden dat hij het ongeluk zelf had veroorzaakt.

Maar Harvey-Bailey kwam binnen twee weken op zijn oordeel terug. Hij wilde meer weten van Taylor, vooral of de rook uit één of uit alle uitlaten van de motor was gekomen. In dat geval was een defect van de compressor waarschijnlijker.

De onverwachte wending motiveerde Taylor nog dieper in zijn geheugen te graven. Hij kwam er niet helemaal uit, hij had door de positie van de cockpit en de rook niet alles kunnen waarnemen. Maar op basis van wat hij nog wist, kwam de RR- expert tot de conclusie dat een uitgevallen compressor als gevolg van een kapotte kogellager oververhitting en uiteindelijk het uitvallen van de motor zeer waarschijnlijk had veroorzaakt.

Taylor prijst zich diep gelukkig met de ontdekking. 'Ik kon nauwelijks geloven dat ik het geluk had contact te hebben met de enige man in Engeland, en misschien wel in de wereld, die de kennis en autoriteit had een eindoordeel te geven, terwijl het enige beschikbare bewijs mijn eigen onbetrouwbare geheugen was.'

Volgens Hennie Noordhuis is daarmee voor Taylor het onderzoek afgesloten. 'Dit was het laatste stuk. Hij vindt het goed nu. Maar hij blijft naar Borne komen. Hij was hier nog in april en keert in het najaar al weer terug voor de presentatie van het nieuwe Jaarboek Twente, waarvoor hij een bijdrage heeft geschreven. Jimmy vindt het hier geweldig.'

Headline: "Pilot Jimmy Taylor finds peace at last"
He was talking to children in the Olthof Primary School

DE TWENTSCHE COURANT

Tubantia

Zaterdag 3 mei 1997 Jaargang 153, Nummer 105 Losse nummers ƒ 2,00 (Zaterd

Jimmy Taylor ontmoet lid van familie Van Hengstum die hem in 1944 hielp

RAF-piloot in een schuur te Houten

Door **René Schabos**

BORNE/HOUTEN - Drie jongens, kinderen nog, kijken hem verschrikt aan. In het schemerdonker van de schuur doet een RAF-piloot zich tegoed aan een mand appelen. Het schuurtje staat in Houten, in de provincie Utrecht, en het is 23 november 1944. Buiten is het koud en nat. De Engelse vlieger Jimmy Taylor, vier dagen eerder na een motorstoring van zijn Spitfire met zijn parachute geland in de buurtschap 't Hesseler bij Borne, zoekt hongerig en vermoeid een weg naar de geallieerde strijdkrachten aan de overzijde van de Rijn.

De drie broers - Piet, Henk en Ben van Hengstum - zijn bang, maar ook nieuwsgierig en oprecht. Taylor kan ze in zijn beste Duits gerust stellen. Vader Van Hengstum, die even later het schuurtje binnenstapt, is minder onbevangen. 'Ik herinner me hoe achterdochtig hij was. Waarschijnlijk was hij bang dat ik een vermomde Duitse soldaat was. Hij liep natuurlijk een enorm risico. In zijn huis verbleven drie Duitse militairen', zegt Taylor.

De piloot, die zich sinds zijn landing voortdurend schuil heeft gehouden en te voet en in goederenwagons tot in Houten is geraakt, wordt voor het eerst geholpen door Nederlandse burgers. Vader Van Hengstum geeft hem te eten, een fiets, een kaart van Nederland en een jas. Zijn twee zoons, Piet en Ben, krijgen opdracht de Engelsman later op de dag de weg te wijzen naar Rhenen, dat reeds in geal-

maar één onderwerp. 'Hij vroeg me uit Engeland een Greyhoundhond te bezorgen. Als een soort tegenprestatie, geloof ik. Het verzoek bracht me zeer in verlegenheid. Ik wist eigenlijk niet hoe snel ik weg moest komen', zegt de Engelsman.

De behoefte weer contact op te nemen was voor een groot deel verdwenen. Maar het was niet alleen de hond, waarom zijn helper vroeg, die hem de lust ontnam. 'Het was kort na de oorlog. Ik had niet het gevoel in de oorlog iets bijzonders te hebben gedaan. Ik was al lang blij dat ik er ongeschonden uit was gekomen. Bovendien was ik in die jaren een arme student, bezig met overleven. Je keek toen vooral vooruit, niet achteruit.'

Nasleep

Het terugkijken begon pas echt in 1990, het jaar waarin de Bornse gemeente-archivaris Henny Noordhuis hem in Engeland opspoorde en vertelde van de nasleep van zijn parachutelanding bij Borne.

De Almelose verzetsman Jan Vonk was nog dezelfde avond naast Villa Elisabeth geexecuteerd. Zes dagen later, op 25 november 1944, een dag na de aanhouding van Taylor bij Rhenen, werden nog eens drie bewoners van de buurtschap 't Hesseler doodgeschoten. Jan Boomkamp, Hendrik Roetgerink en Piet van Dijk moesten sterven, omdat de Duitsers in Borne veronderstelden dat de bevolking de RAF-piloot nog steeds verborgen hield.

Henny Noordhuis en Jimmy Taylor brachten donderdag een bezoek aan het luchtvaartmuseum in Enschede. Daar is een hoekje over de Engelse piloot en zijn vliegtuig ingericht. FOTO GEORGE NUSME[I]

weiland achter restaurant de Rustende Jager nog wat brokstukken

stum staat, wist hij niet meer te vinden.

Headline: "RAF pilot in a shed in Houten"
Hennie Noordhuis and JT were looking at relics of his Spitfire in the Twente Air Base Museum

Onthulling gedenkbord Mr. Taylor

Tekst van de plaquette: Op 19 november 1944 crashte in achterliggende bomenwal de Spitfire PRXI 1957 van het 16e Squadron RAF, die werd gevlogen door Flight-lieutenant Harold James Strickland (Jimmy) Taylor. Hij had het toestel boven de gemeente Borne verlaten en kon daar na landing aan zijn parachute aan de Duitsers ontkomen. Als gevolg hiervan werden 4 onschuldige burgers gefusilleerd.
V.l.n.r. Burgemeester Van der Vegt, J. Timmerman, Jimmy Taylor en M. Timmerman.

Op zaterdag 3 mei j.l. is nabij De Rustende Jager te Bentelo een gedenkbord onthuld ter herinnering aan het neerstorten van een Spitfire, die gevlogen werd door de RAF-piloot Harold James Strickland (Jimmy) Taylor. Het toestel was op 19 november 1944 boven onze omgeving aan het fotograferen, maar stortte door motorstoring neer op een houtwal achter De Rustende Jager. De piloot moest met zijn parachute het toestel verlaten en is neergekomen in de buurtschap 't Hesseler bij Borne. Daar de Duitsers de piloot niet konden vinden, zijn hiervoor destijds 4 onschuldige burgers gefusilleerd. Op 't Hesseler is hiertoe een gedenkbord geplaatst. Er zijn nog diverse onderdelen van het vliegtuig uit de grond gehaald, welke bewaard worden in het Luchtvaart Museum Twenthe te Enschede. Mr. Taylor is zeer begaan met alles wat rond deze crash is gebeurd en komt elk jaar voor de dodenherdenking naar Borne om de familie van de gefusilleerden en de plek waar het vliegtuig is neergekomen te bezoeken.

Na een korte, passende toespraak van de burgemeester en een even passend antwoord van Mr. Taylor werd een gedenkbord onthuld. Hierna was er onder het genot van een hapje en een glaasje nog een kort samenzijn in De Rustende Jager.

Voor Jimmy Taylor lijkt nu de cirkel rond te zijn over de crash, waar in het verleden al zeer veel over geschreven is.

"Deldens Weekblad" (the weekly paper of Delden), 7th May 1997

Plaquette onthuld voor Jimmy Taylor

BENTELO - Jimmy Taylor, de Britse piloot die in november 1944 in de Bornse buurtschap 't Hesseler aan zijn parachute landde, is zaterdagmiddag geëerd met een plaquette. De onthulling ervan gebeurde in zijn aanwezigheid en op de plek waar zijn Spitfire neerstortte na een motorstoring. Het toestel kwam terecht op een aarden wal aan de Platenkampsweg, ongeveer 200 meter achter café De Rustende Jager in Bentelo. De plaquette is de voormalige piloot aangeboden door de gemeente Ambt Delden en de familie Timmerman van De Rustende Jager.

De tekst op de plaquette luidt: *Op 19 november 1944 crashte in achterliggende bomenwal de spitfire PAXIL957 van het zestiende squadron RAF die werd gevlogen door flight lieutenant Herald James Strickland (Jimmy) Taylor.*

Hij had het toestel boven de gemeente Borne verlaten en kon daarna landend aan zijn parachute aan de Duitsers ontkomen. Als gevolg hiervan werden vier onschuldige burgers gefusilleerd. 3 mei 1997

Headline: "Mr Taylor unveils a commemorative plaque" at the crash-site of his Spitfire

DE TWENTSCHE COURANT
Tubantia

Het weer
Vannacht bewolkt en enige regen bij minimumtemperaturen rond 11 graden. Morgen vooral in de och en maximaal 1

Uw krant
www.tct

999 Jaargang 155, Nummer 105 Losse nummers ƒ 2,50 (Zaterdag ƒ 3,00) - 32

e
19e november 1944
-piloot Jimmy Taylor. 2

Twente
Bouw enorme legbatterij voor Twentse pluimveehouder 'noodzakelijk kwaad'. 6

Binnen & Buitenland
De Schotten gaan kiezen; het nationalisme herleeft. 9

Sport
Finale nationale titel voor drieban
Hengelo ver weg na thuisnederlaa

Het spoor terug van Taylor

RAF-piloot cirkelt na 55 jaar opnieuw boven Borne

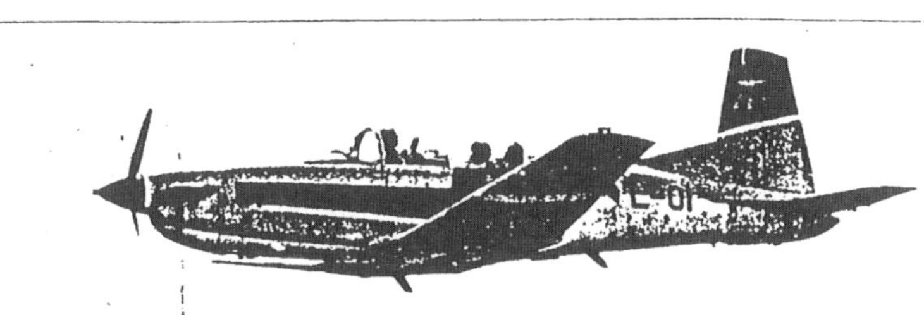

Het lesvliegtuig Pilatus PC-7 lijkt met zijn lange neus enigszins op een Spitfire

Vol zelfvertrouwen stapt voormalig RAF-piloot Jimmy Taylor (76) in de kanariegele Pilatus PC-7, die voor hem gereed staat op de vliegbasis Twenthe. Het is 4 mei. Herdenkingsdag. Ook voor de Brit, die vandaag een bijzondere vlucht maakt boven Borne, Bentelo, Doorn, Rhenen en Elst. Een vlucht die ongetwijfeld herinneringen zal oproepen aan de 19e november 1944. De dag waarop zijn Spitfire, na een defect aan de motor, neerstortte in een houtwal in de buurt van Bentelo. Een crash die - zo blijkt bijna 55 jaar na dato - onuitwisbare sporen heeft achtergelaten.

FOTO'S MARTIJN VAN DE BLAAK

Ready for take-off. De voormalig RAF-piloot is klaar voor zijn herdenkingsvlucht.

hend laat Jimmy Taylor zich de parachute mhangen. 'Ik weet hoe zo'n ding werkt.'

Door Rob Wissink

De zon schijnt, het zicht is uitstekend, alleen de straffe wind baart piloot 'Gorby' enigszins zorgen. De vlieginstructeur van het 131e squadron op vliegbasis Woensdrecht heeft de eer een uurtje boven oost-Nederland te vliegen met Jimmy Taylor. De Engelse oorlogsveteraan mag zich opmaken voor een 'bumpy flight' naar de beroemde bruggen over de Rijn en weer terug.

Taylor veert enthousiast op bij het zien van de kist waarin hij straks omhoog gaat. 'Een Spitfire lookalike!' Gorby knikt. 'De Pilatus is een klein, tweepersoons propellervliegtuig van Zwitserse makelij, dat met zijn lange neus enigszins lijkt op een Engelse Spitfire. Het voornaamste verschil is dat deze kist een neuswiel heeft, terwijl de Spitfire juist bekend staat om zijn staartwiel.'

Taylor, gehuld in een groene vliegeniersoverall, is er helemaal klaar voor.

Alleen de parachute en de helm ontbreken nog. Lachend laat hij zich het valscherm omhangen. 'Ik weet nog hoe het werkt.' Gorby neemt voor alle zekerheid nog wat spelregels door. 'Pas als ik beide handen in de lucht steek, neem jij het stuur over Jimmy.' Dan gaan de duimen omhoog. Ready for take-off. Taylor vergeet terug te zwaaien naar het 'grondpersoneel' en maakt alvast een foto van het instrumentenpaneel.

Op de bewuste zondag 19 november 1944 stijgt Jimmy Taylor op van het vliegveld Moelsbroek in Brussel in een Spitfire PRXI van het 16e squadron. Zijn opdracht luidt: foto's maken van vliegvelden in de omgeving van Rheine in Duitsland. De missie mislukt. Boven Nederland begint de Rolls Royce-motor te sputteren. Rook en vlammen komen uit de uitlaten. Er spuit olie in de cockpit, die hem het zicht ontneemt. Na een lange glijvlucht stort de 'Spit' neer in een weiland in de buurt van Bentelo. Taylor weet zichzelf met behulp van een parachute in veiligheid te brengen. Hij landt ongezien in de buurtschap 't Hesseler, ten oosten van Borne.

De Pilatus cirkelt nu boven die plek. Taylor maakt luchtfoto's. Hij ziet het landkruis. Het herdenkingsmonument ter nagedachtenis van Jan Boomkamp, Hendrik Roetgerink en Piet van Dijk. De drie mannen die op 25 november 1944, zes dagen na zijn parachutelanding, worden geëxecuteerd door de Duitsers. 'Uit wraak, omdat ze vermoeden dat de Bornse gemeenschap een Engelse piloot verborgen houdt. Op de avond na mijn landing wordt om diezelfde reden de jonge verzetsman Jan Vonk geëxecuteerd. Vanavond sta ik weer op de plekken waar het allemaal gebeurde. Ik ben de laatste jaren altijd aanwezig bij de herdenkingsbijeenkomsten in Borne. Mijn aanwezigheid wordt daar zeer op prijs gesteld.'

Taylor heeft tot 1990 nooit iets geweten van de dramatische gevolgen van zijn crash. Hennie Noordhuis, de archivaris van de gemeente Borne, weet hem in dat jaar in Leeds op te sporen en drukt hem met de neus op de feiten. 'Ik heb zijn hele leven op de kop gezet', weet Noordhuis, die inmiddels een goede vriend is van Jimmy Taylor.

Het Twentekanaal glinstert in de zon. In het weiland achter restaurant De Rustende Jager tussen Delden en Bentelo hebben vrienden van Taylor een grote Nederlandse vlag uitgespreid. Een herkenningspunt dat vanuit de lucht gemakkelijk te zien is. 'Dit is de plek waar het wrak van mijn Spitfire begin 1995 is gevonden.'

De ontdekking van het wrak en de restanten van de motor zijn voor de gemoedsrust van Jimmy Taylor heel belangrijk. Experts van Rolls Royce verzekeren hem, na bestudering van de wrakstukken, dat de motorstoring te wijten is aan een kapotte kogellager en niet aan menselijk falen. 'Een hele geruststelling', erkent Taylor, die lang met de gedachte rond liep dat hij de crash had kunnen voorkomen. 'Mijn leven was het niet waard ingeruild te worden tegen het leven van één Nederlander, laat staan dat van vier.'

Arnhem is in zicht. Taylor speurt naar herkenningspunten in het landschap, die hem bekend voorkomen. 'Op 24 november ben ik hier ergens opgepakt door de Duitsers. Het moet ergens tussen Rhenen en Doorn zijn geweest'. Het lijkt op voorhand een onmogelijke opgave om na 55 jaar de juiste plek te vinden. Zelfs vanuit de lucht. 'Je vergeet dat mijn poging om te voet België te bereiken een kwestie van leven of dood was. De dingen die ik destijds heb gezien staan me helderder voor ogen dan gebeurtenissen die ik gisteren heb meegemaakt.'

In 1998 geeft Taylor een feest voor ruimt twintig mensen die hem hebben geholpen met de reconstructie van zijn wonderbaarlijke avontuur in de koude winter van '44. Het boek kan dicht.

Maar nog steeds komen er nieuwe vragen en feiten boven tafel, die hem en Hennie Noordhuis ertoe dwingen hun zoektocht naar de waarheid voort te zetten.

'Ik weet het,' verzucht de sympathieke Engelsman, 'jullie hebben al vaak uit mijn mond kunnen optekenen dat het laatste hoofdstuk van mijn inmiddels 250 pagina's tellende manuscript is voltooid. Vorig jaar was ik daar ook van overtuigd. Maar ik vrees dat er nog een appendix zit aan te komen.'

Issue of "Tubantia" of 5th May 1999 following JT's flight over the Rhine in a Pilatus PC-7 piloted by Captain 'Gorby' Kloosterman
Translation on following page

TAYLOR FOLLOWS THE TRAIL BACK
by Rob Wissink

RAF pilot circles over Borne again after 55 years

RAF pilot Jimmy Taylor (76) self-assuredly gets into the canary yellow PC-7 which is ready for him at the Twenthe air base. It is May 4th. Memorial Day. It is also a memorial day for the British pilot who will fly over Borne, Bentelo, Doorn, Rhenen and Elst today. A flight which will undoubtedly bring back memories of November 19th 1944. The day on which his Spitfire – because of engine trouble – crashed into a wooded bank in the neighbourhood of Bentelo. A crash which is stamped indelibly on his mind as is proved after 55 years from that date.

The sun is shining, the view is excellent, only the stiff wind somewhat worries pilot 'Gorby'. The flying instructor of the 131st Squadron at Woensdrecht air base has the honour to fly for an hour over the eastern part of The Netherlands with Jimmy Taylor. The English war veteran may prepare for a bumpy flight to the famous bridges across the Rhine and back again. Taylor enthusiastically springs to his feet at the sight of the "bus" in which he will climb into the air. "A Spitfire lookalike" 'Gorby' nods. The Pilatus is a small two-seater propeller aircraft – Swiss make – which somewhat resembles an English Spitfire with its protruding nose. The main difference is that the Pilatus has a nose wheel whereas the Spitfire is known for its tail wheel.

Taylor, clad in the green overalls of the airman, is all ready.

The only things missing are the parachute and the helmet. Laughingly he lets himself be helped into his parachute. "I still know how to operate such a thing". For safety's sake 'Gorby' goes over the rules of the game. "Not until I put both my hands into the air, do you take over the steering wheel, Jimmy". Then the thumb goes up. Ready for take-off. Taylor forgets to return the ground crew's waves and starts taking pictures of the instrument panel.

On that particular Sunday of November 19th 1944, Jimmy Taylor takes off from Moelsbroek airfield in Brussels in a Spitfire PRXI of the 16th Squadron. His mission is: photograph the airfields in the environs of Rheine in Germany. His mission fails. Over The Netherlands the Rolls-Royce engine begins to sputter. The exhausts spout smoke and flames. Oil squirts into the cockpit and takes away Jimmy's view. After a long glide down, "The Spit" crashes into a pasture in the neighbourhood of Bentelo. Taylor manages to bring himself to safety by means of a parachute. Without being seen, he lands in the hamlet of 't Hesseler, east of Borne.

The Pilatus now circles over that spot. Taylor makes aerial photographs. He sees the cross on the land. It is the monument in memory of Jan Boomkamp, Hendrik Roetgerink and Piet van Dijk. The three men who were executed by the Germans on November 25th 1944, six days after his landing by parachute. "Out of revenge, because they suspect that an English pilot is kept in a hiding-place by the Borne community. On the evening of my landing, a young member of the Resistance, Jan Vonk, is executed for the same reason. Tonight I'll be on the same spot where it all happened. I have always been present at the memorial services in Borne the last few years. My presence is very much appreciated there"

Until 1990 Taylor never knew of the tragic consequences of his crash. Hennie Noordhuis, the archivist of the municipality of Borne, succeeds in tracing him in Leeds in that year and confronts him with the facts. "I turned his whole life topsy-turvy", says Noordhuis, who is a good friend of Jimmy Taylor's now.

The Twentekanaal lies glistening in the sun. Friends of Taylor's have spread a large Dutch flag in a pasture behind "De Rustende Jager" ("The Resting Huntsman"), a restaurant between Delden and Bentelo. An identifying mark which is easy to see from the air.

"This is the spot where my Spitfire was found in the beginning of 1995". The discovery of the wreck and the remnants of the engine are very important for Jimmy Taylor's peace of mind.

After examining the pieces of the wreckage, experts of Rolls-Royce assure him that the engine trouble had been caused by a broken ball-bearing and not by human failure. "Quite a relief", Taylor acknowledges, as for a long time he had thought that he could have prevented the crash. "My life wasn't worth to be exchanged for one Dutchman's life, let alone for four lives".

Arnhem is in view. Taylor searches for marks in the landscape that he can recognize. "On November 24th I was caught by the Germans. It must have been somewhere between Rhenen and Doorn". From the first it seems to be an impossible job to find the right spot after 55 years. Even from the air. "You forget that my attempt to reach Belgium on foot was a question of life or death. The things I saw in those days are clearer in my mind than events that I experienced yesterday" .

In 1998 Taylor gave a party for more than twenty people who had helped him to reconstruct his strange adventure in the cold winter of 1944. The book can be closed. But again and again new questions and facts come up which compel him and Hennie Noordhuis to keep on searching for the truth. "I know", the sympathetic Englishman sighs, "you have often heard me say that the last chapter of my manuscript of 250 pages was finished. Last year I was quite convinced it was. But I fear there will be an appendix".

Dodenherdenking 4 mei 2000

Velen van u weten waarschijnlijk het landkruis 't Hesselder aan de Mekkelhorstweg wel te staan. Maar weet u ook waarom dit landkruis hier is geplaatst? Hieronder leest u wat hier op 19 en 25 november 1944 is gebeurd.

Op 19 november 1944 was piloot Jimmy Taylor in een Engelse Spitfire PRXI onderweg van Brussel naar Rheine in Duitsland. De opdracht van zijn missie was het maken van foto's van vliegvelden in de omgeving van Rheine. Halverwege deze missie

kreeg hij echter pech en uiteindelijk moest Taylor met zijn parachute uit het vliegtuig springen om zijn leven te redden. Hij kwam neer ten oosten van Borne, in buurtschap 't Hesselder. Enkele nieuwsgierige buurtbewoners kwamen zijn kant op maar Taylor maakte zich snel uit de voeten. Ook de Duitsers kwamen naar de plek waar ze wisten dat de parachute moest zijn geland maar ze vonden geen spoor van de Engelsman, zelfs niet nadat de hele omgeving was afgezet en uitgekamd.

Gijzeling

Er werden 6 willekeurige personen door de Duitsers gevangen genomen. Deze gijzelaars zouden de volgende ochtend worden gefusilleerd als de parachutist niet zou worden gevonden. Uit woede voor de vruchtloze zoekactie werd nog dezelfde avond een Bornse jongen, Jan Vonk, gefu-silleerd.

Door bemiddeling van de burgemeester werd de executie van de gijzelaars enkele malen uitgesteld. Er werden 2 gijzelaars vrijgelaten. Later kwam er toch nog weer een gijzelaar bij. Zelfs toen al was vastgesteld dat deze mensen onschuldig waren, moesten ze in hechtenis blijven totdat de parachutist was gevonden, ook toen er van hogerhand werd bepaald dat er geen executie zou plaatsvinden. Van de piloot werd echter geen spoor meer gevonden.

Executie

Op 25 november werden 2 van de overgebleven 5 gijzelaars vrijgelaten. Geheel tegen de belofte in werden de andere drie mannen, Jan Boomkamp, Piet van Dijk en Hendrik Roetgerink alsnog door de Duitsers geëxecuteerd. Ter nagedachtenis aan deze mensen is landkruis 't Hesselder opgericht.

Herdenking

Buurtvereniging 't Hesselder houdt de herinnering levend door elk jaar op 4 mei een dodenherdenking met kranslegging te organiseren. Net als in voorgaande jaren zullen bij het landkruis 't Hesselder aan de Mekkelhorstweg om 19.00 uur de gevallenen worden herdacht.

Begin jaren '90 bleek dat de piloot Taylor de oorlog heeft overleefd. Hij heeft nooit geweten wat voor de buurtbewoners de gevolgen zijn geweest van zijn ongeluk. Taylor is de laatste jaren dan ook steeds bij de herdenking bij landkruis 't Hesselder aanwezig geweest, wat door de buurvereniging en de nabestaanden natuurlijk erg wordt gewaardeerd.

Het spreekt voor zich dat ook bewoners van onze wijk Slangenbeek van harte welkc zijn om bij deze dodenherdei king en kranslegging aanwez te zijn.

Bezinning

Laat de herdenking een mom van bezinning zijn. Want dat ruim 50 jaar geleden is gebeu en waarvan iedereen zei "dat nooit meer" blijkt toch steeds dichterbij te zijn dan we voor mogelijk hadden gehouden. K bijvoorbeeld maar naar de ge beurtenissen op de Balkan. D afgelopen jaren, of, heel dich bij huis, de recente slachtoffe van het 'zinloze geweld'. Laten we daarom vooral ook onze jeugd betrekken bij het h denken van de slachtoffers en samen met hen stilstaan bij he zinloze van oorlogen en geweld.

Headline: "Commemoration of the Victims, 4th May 2000"

De Twentsche Courant Tubantia

Ex-oorlogsvlieger schenkt museum schilderij

ENSCHEDE - Het Rijksmuseum Twenthe is de trotse eigenaar van een schilderij van de zeventiende-eeuwse Nederlandse schilder Adriaen Hanneman. Het is een gift van de voormalige RAF-piloot Jimmy Taylor die in 1944 in Borne neerstortte.

Oud-RAF-piloot Jimmy Taylor (rechts) met de broer van de in 1944 geëxecuteerde Jan Boomkamp in het Rijksmuseum Twenthe. Tussen hen het schilderij van Adriaen Hanneman, cadeau gedaan door Taylor ter nagedachtenis van vier vermoorde Bornenaren.
(foto CHAREL VAN TENDELOO)

Het geschenk is ter nagedachtenis aan de vier doodgeschoten Bornenaren in het bijzonder, en alle Nederlanders die geleden hebben onder het Duitse juk, verklaarde de 78-jarige Engelsman gistermiddag bij de overdracht. 'Zij stierven omdat ik per ongeluk terecht kwam in 't Hesseler.'

Taylor landde op 19 november 1944 aan zijn parachute in een boom in de Bornse buurtschap. Even daarvoor was zijn Spitfire met motorstoring neergestort in een houtwal achter restaurant De Rustende Jager in Bentelo. Dezelfde avond werd de jonge Bornse verzetsman Jan Vonk opgepakt en doodgeschoten.

De piloot is dan al ongezien ontkomen. Hij wordt op 24 november in de buurt van Rhenen bij Arnhem alsnog door de Duitsers gepakt. Een dag later worden Jan Boomkamp, Hendrik Roetgerink en Piet van Dijk in Borne geëxecuteerd.

De Duitsers in Borne verdenken de plaatselijke bevolking er dan nog steeds van de Engelse piloot schuil te houden. Pas in 1990, als Taylor door de Bornse archivaris Hennie Noordhuis in Leeds wordt getraceerd, hoort de oud-vlieger van het drama in Borne. Sindsdien onderhoudt hij nauwe contacten met de nabestaanden van de vermoorde Bornenaren en andere plaatsgenoten, waaronder Jaap Grootenboer.

Deze was het, die in het op foto's afgebeelde schilderij - dat al generaties eigendom van de familie Taylor was - een meesterwerk zag. Taylor achterhaalde dat het een werk was een Nederlandse schilder die van 1623 tot 1637 in Londen woonde en werkte en daar in aanraking kwam met de hofschilders

Anthoon van Dyck en Cornelis Jansz van Ceulen. Terug in Nederland introduceerde hij de elegante portretstijl van Van Dyck. Het in 1661 door Hanneman geschilderde portret van de pater Jezuïet Roeland te Koppele uit Delft, dat nu in het rijksmuseum hangt, is daar een voorbeeld van.

'Een belangrijke periode in mijn leven is hiermee afgesloten. Het geeft mij veel voldoening dat ik dat op deze manier kan doen', aldus Taylor.

Museumdirectrice Doris Cannegieter toonde zich bijzonder ingenomen met het schilderij. 'Een prachtig doek. Een bijzonderheid ook. Wij zijn een van de weinige musea die een werk van Hanneman in de collectie heeft. Het waarom van deze gift maakt het extra waardevol.'

Het schilderij is vandaag en morgen te zien in de Gobelinzaal van het museum. Daarna wordt het eerst grondig onderzocht door museumrestaurateur Feroza Verberne, alvorens het een definitief plekje krijgt.

Translation overleaf

Wartime Flier Presents Museum with a Picture

The Rijksmuseum Twenthe is the proud owner of a portrait by the 17th-century Dutch artist Adriaen Hanneman. This is the gift of the former RAF pilot Jimmy Taylor, who came down in Borne in 1944.

Enschede – The present is in memory of the four people who were executed in the neighbourhood of Borne, and of all Dutchmen who suffered under the German yoke, explained the 78-year-old Englishman at the presentation yesterday afternoon. "They died because I had the misfortune to land in 't Hesseler."

Taylor landed by parachute in a tree[1] in the neighbourhood of Borne on 19th November 1944. Just before this, his Spitfire came down with engine-failure into a bank among trees behind "The Resting Hunter" restaurant in Bentelo. The same evening, the young Borne Resistance fighter, Jan Vonk, was arrested[2] and shot.

The pilot then ran off without being seen. He was eventually captured by the Germans on 24th November, in the vicinity of Rhenen, not far from Arnhem. Next day, Jan Boomkamp, Hendrik Roetgerink and Piet van Dijk were executed in Borne.

The Germans in Borne thought that the local people were still hiding the English pilot. Only in 1990, when Taylor was traced to Leeds by the local archivist Hennie Noordhuis, did the former flier hear of the tragedy in Borne. Since then, he has made close connections with the relatives of the murdered men of Borne, and with other local people, such as Jaap Grootenboer.

The portrait of the man in the photograph above was in the Taylor family for generations – and reputedly a masterpiece. Taylor discovered it was the work of a Dutch artist who lived and worked in London from 1623 to 1637 and was familiar with the Court painters Anthony Van Dyck and Cornelius Johnson van Ceulen. Returning to the Netherlands, he introduced Van Dyck's elegant style of portrait painting. An example of this is the portrait of Father Roeland, of the Jesuit station at Delft, painted by Hanneman in 1661, which now hangs in the Rijksmuseum.

"A significant period in my life has now been redeemed", said Taylor, "and it gives me great satisfaction that I can do it in this way."

Doris Cannegieter, the Director of the Museum, said she was extremely pleased with the painting, "A splendid canvas. A special one, also. We are one of the few museums that already have a Hanneman in their collection. The circumstances of this gift make it especially valuable."

The picture can be seen today and tomorrow in the Gobelin Room of the Museum. After this, it will be given a thorough examination by Feroza Verbeme, the Museum's restorer, before it is given a definite place.

Photograph caption

Former RAF pilot Jimmy Taylor (right) with Hendrik Boomkamp, the brother of Jan Boomkamp who was executed in 1944, in the Rijksmuseum Twenthe. Between them is the painting by Adriaen Hanneman, a gift from Taylor in memory of the four men of Borne who were murdered.

Photo: Charel van Tendeloo

[1] in fact I landed in a field.

[2] he was already in prison in Almeto

Hendrik Boomkamp (l), brother of the victim Jan Boomkamp, and JT at the presentation of the portrait of "Father Roeland de Pottere, SJ" to the Rijksmuseum Twente on 3rd May 2001.

DE TWENTSCHE COURANT
Tubantia

Hengelo - Borne

'Jongens in bommenwerpers waren echte helden'

Ook de Spitfire van de Britse spionagevlieger Jimmy Taylor stortte neer bij Bentelo. Vlakbij de plek waar momenteel de Stirling wordt geborgen. Taylor, die jaarlijks Borne bezoekt, nam gisteren een kijkje bij de bergingsoperatie.

BENTELO/BORNE - Met interesse bekijkt Jimmy Taylor (83) de zware Stirling-onderdelen bij de bergingsplaats van de bommenwerper. Vliegenier Taylor uit Leeds had zelf de pech dat tijdens een spionagevlucht op 19 november 1944 de Rolls Royce-motor van zijn Spitfire uitviel. Hij sprong en landde aan zijn parachute aan de oostkant van Borne. De Spitfire boorde zich bij Bentelo in de grond. In een weiland achter De Rustende Jager, op een kilometer afstand van de plek waar de Stirling neerstortte.

Deze dinsdagmorgen neemt Taylor een kijkje op de bergingsplaats aan de Suetersweg. De vliegenier heeft zijn onderscheidingen thuis gelaten. 'Wat stellen die stukjes metaal nou voor?' 'De jongens in de bommenwerpers waren de echte helden', zegt Taylor, als hij hoort dat alle zeven bemanningsleden van de bommenwerper zijn omgekomen. De grote vliegtuigen, een makkelijke prooi voor jagers en luchtafweergeschut, waren kwetsbaar in de lucht.

Zelf wilde Taylor nooit in een Stirling vliegen. 'Als piloot ben je dan verantwoordelijk voor het leven van de andere bemanningsleden. Dat trok me niet.'

Over de omgekomen bemanningsleden van de Stirling: 'Vliegtuigen zijn niet bedoeld om in te sterven.'

Als spionagevlieger was Taylor, naar eigen zeggen, een *loner*, die op kilometers hoogte vloog. 'Voor mij was de oorlog een leuk avontuur. Ik heb niemand gedood, in vijf jaar heb ik één lijk gezien.'

Toch heeft de oorlog emotionele sporen nagelaten bij Taylor. Tragische gebeurtenissen in Borne in november 1944 zijn daar de oorzaak van.

Nadat Taylor met zijn parachute in de Bornse buurtschap De Hesseler neerkwam, vluchtte hij het bos in. Om uit de handen van de vijand te blijven. De spionagevlieger, die luchtopnames moest maken van industrieën in Duitsland, had geen flauw idee waar hij zich bevond.

De Duitsers die Taylor per se wilden oppakken, dachten dat leden van het verzet in Borne de Britse vlieger verborgen hielden. Om uitlevering van Taylor te bewerkstelligen werd vervolgens een aantal mannen uit de buurtschap door de Duitsers gegijzeld. Op 25 november zijn drie onschuldige buurtschapbewoners - Jan Boomkamp, Hendrik Roetgerink en Piet van Dijk - gefusilleerd, vlak bij de plek waar Taylor neerkwam.

De Britse piloot hoorde pas 46 jaar later van de tragedie. Bij de berging van de Spitfire in 1991 werd Taylors helm, met naam, gevonden en kon de piloot worden opgespoord. Sindsdien komt Taylor elk jaar naar Borne om herdenkingen bij het monument, dat hij in 1991 zelf onthulde, bij te wonen. De aangrijpende gebeurtenissen veranderden Taylors kijk op de oorlog. De berging van de Stirling, met zware bommen, vindt hij niet zo bijzonder. 'Het verlies van levens is veel belangrijker dan het opgraven van een vliegtuig.'

FOTO WOUTER BORRE

Vliegenier Jimmy Taylor (links) bekijkt met een andere Britse veteraan de opgegraven onderdelen van de Stirling-bommenwerper.

Nieuwe directeur Industrie Museum

HENGELO - Het bestuur van de Stichting Hengelo's Educatief Industrie-Museum (HEIM) heeft sinds zondag een nieuwe adjunct-directeur, A. de Boer. Hij volgt directeur A. Pieterson in de loop van volgend jaar op als directeur na de officiële opening van de nieuwe museumlocatie in de Wilhelminaschool.

De Boer is van 2001 tot 2004 werkzaam geweest als manager publiekstaken en locatiemanager van het Nederlands Instituut voor Scheeps- en Onderwaterarcheologie (NISA) in Lelystad.

Hij wil speciaal aandacht besteden aan 'het behoud en tot leven wekken van de Twentse industrie-historie'.

Verder wil De Boer het museum interessanter en leerzamer maken voor iedereen maar speciaal voor jongeren. Ook wil hij de banden met het bedrijfsleven versterken en instellingen versterken.

Headline: "The young men in the bomber were heroes"
JT visits the excavation site of a Stirling bomber.

DE TWENTSCHE COURANT

Tubantia

Zaterdag 3 mei 2008
Jaargang 163, nummer 104. Prijs € 2,10

20°

Veel hoge sluierbewoking, toch is er ook veel zon. Pagina 22 en www.tubtv.nl

6 Twintigers raken in de ban van de lp

14 Containerterminal wil verdubbelen

38 FC Twente waakt voor verslapping

12 Persvrijheid en China gaan nog niet samen

Binnen- & Buitenland 4 t/m 9 - Opinie 10 en 11 - Economie 14 t/m 17 - Puzzel & Strips 23 - Regio 25 t/m 31 - Stad en Land 34 en 35 - Sport 37 t/m 41 www.tctubantia.nl

3rd May 2008

Taylor met dochter en kleinkind naar Borne

BORNE - Oorlogsveteraan Jimmy Taylor is morgen opnieuw in Borne om bij het landkruis aan de Mekkelhorst de drie Bornenaren te herdenken, die daar op 25 november 1944 door de Duitsers zijn doodgeschoten. Voor het eerst neemt hij zijn dochter Jennifer en kleindochter Dolly mee naar de plek en wandelt hij aansluitend met hen in de stille tocht mee naar het monument voor het oude gemeentehuis.

Het monument aan de Mekkelhorst herinnert aan Jan Boomkamp, Hendrik Roetgerink en Piet van Dijk. De drie mannen werden daar zes dagen nadat Taylor aan zijn parachute neerkwam in de buurtschap Hesseler geëxecuteerd. Hun dood was de wraak van de Duitsers. Die vermoedden dat de Bornse gemeenschap de piloot van het 16e squadron van de RAF verborgen hield, nadat zijn Spitfire bij Bentelo was neergestort. Op de avond na zijn landing werd om diezelfde reden verzetsman Jan Vonk geëxecuteerd. Taylor werd na zijn vlucht op 24 november 1944 in Rhenen door de Duitsers gearresteerd, een dag voor de moordpartij aan de Mekkelhorst Op 28 augustus 1991 keerde hij voor het eerst terug naar Borne om aan de Mekkelhorst het landkruis te onthullen. Sindsdien komt de voormalige piloot elk jaar.

Headline: "Taylor with his daughter and grand-daughter in Borne"

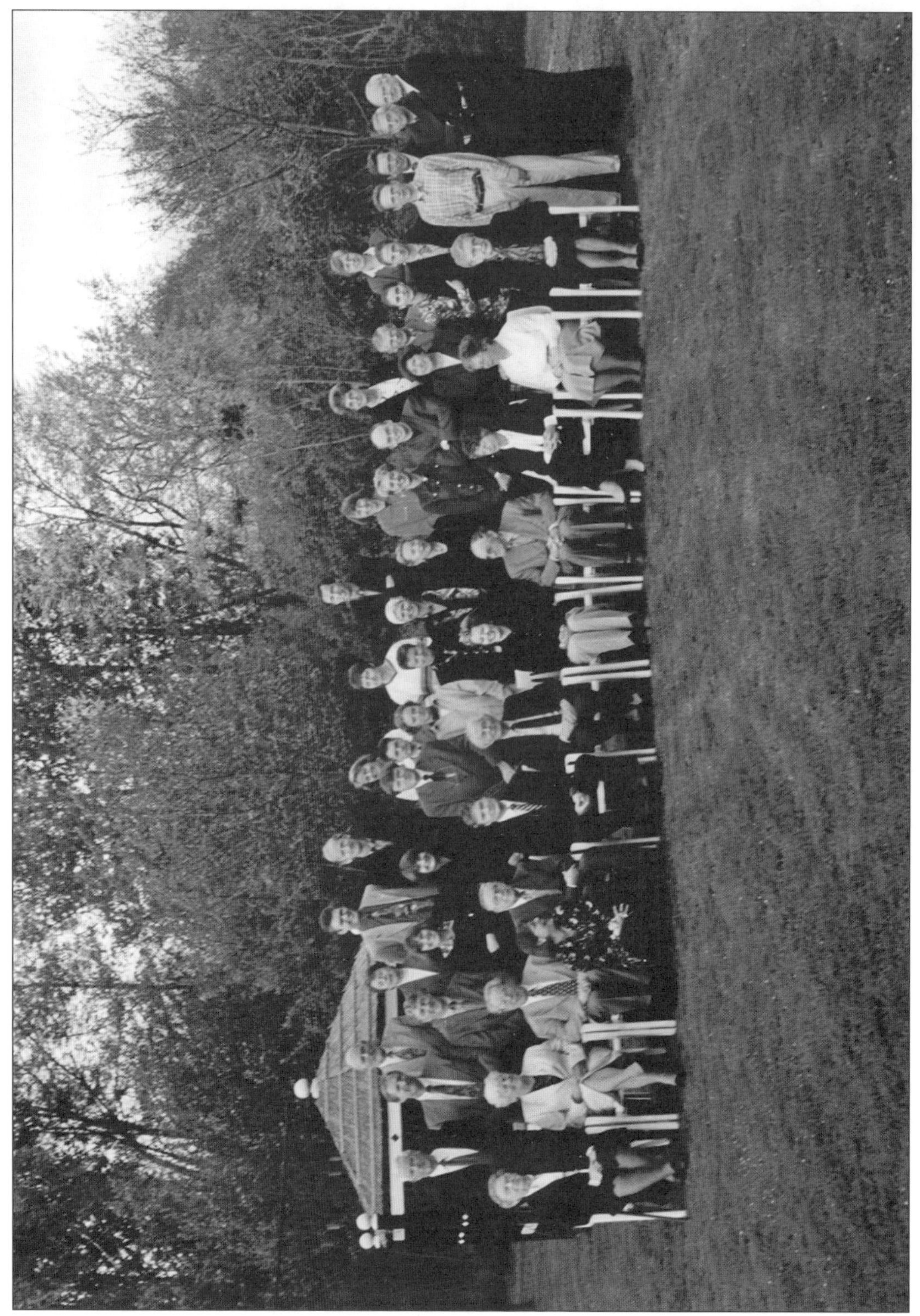

The Guests at my "Thank You" Dinner Party at "The Resting Hunter"
on 3rd May 1998

The Guests at my "Thank You" Dinner Party at "The Resting Hunter" on 3rd May 1998.

[left to right]

Back row:

Joop De Melker Worms (Borne Town Hall) — Thea De Melker Worms — Bert Roberst (Twente Air Base) — Fred Bakker (artist) — Gerite Leuveld (Boomkamp/Roetgerink relative) — Ria Leuveld (Roetgerink relative)

Hans Wools (son-in-law of Bernhard Boomkamp) — Joke Noordhuis — Annie Oude Hilbert — Peggie Breitbarth-van der Stok (art historian and editor)

Middle row:

Hennie Egberink (Spitfire excavator) — Adrie Roding (Twente Air Museum) — Jaap Grootenboer (local historian) — Ine Getkate — Froukje Bakker — Hennie Noordhuis (archivist and identifier of JT as 'the missing pilot' — Herman Bruggink (son of the finder of JT's helmet)

Janneke Bruggink (Olthof School 1995) — Bernadette Bruggink — Josine Wools (daughter of Bernhard Boomkamp) — Jeanette Vunderink — Ellis Schabos — René Schabos (journalist) — Toos de Leeuw

Hennie Oude Hilbert (Twente Air Museum) — Wendy Broekhuizen — Lukas Groen (composer of 'Pro Borne') — Jeroen Liedorp (accompanist) — Henk Timmerman (restauranteur and owner of crash field) — Joke de Leeuw (Chairman of 1995 Liberation Committee) — Maarten Vunderink (former Burgomaster of Borne)

Front row:

Mrs Veenhuis-Weghorst (eye-witness of landing 1944) — Gerda Roetgerink — Jan Timmerman (eye-witness of crash 1944) — Betsy Timmerman — Marinus Timmerman (eye-witness of crash 1944) — Jonathan Taylor (son of JT)

Jimmy Taylor ('the missing pilot' 19th November 1944) — Jennifer Taylor (daughter of JT) — Ben van Hengstum (cycled with JT from Houten 23rd November 1944) — Tinie van Hengstum — Sjaan Timmerman — Betsy Westerink- Timmerman (ear-witness of crash 1944)

The Names of the Guests and their Connections with me

The Epilogue

4th Mays, Days of Commemoration, stretch out beyond my lifetime – endlessly. The War has lost its grip: the Aftermath remains.

We gather at 't Hessler's little crossroads, where erstwhile grassy Borne meets thrusting Hengelo – and England joins the Netherlands.

Old faces grow fewer; young ones grow older; the youngest are brought to shake my hand; the latest leave their new-built homes, curious to learn.

The Burgomaster signs me to start the walk with him. The silver band sends forth its strains, "Abide with Me": it tugs my heart – I can't afford to cry. The crowd falls into line and fills the lane.

We shuffle into place before the fine Memorial: the carven face shows lasting agony. The Ensign flies – the Scouts stand straight – the over-arching trees look down. I grow lamer every year, but the ritual remains the same.

The Burgomaster gives his brief but stark address. The children read their poems in voices hard to hear. We stand in solemn silence for a long Two Minutes. My thoughts flood back to that November day when my Spitfire's broken bearing set off this tragedy. I'm grateful for the interruption of the music of the band.

The Burgomaster lays his wreath. I raise my voice and speak the prescient words of Kipling: "They shall not grow old, as we that are left grow old..." Kind hands display my wreath for me. I bow my head in sorrow and in honour.

Others follow: old and young, families and friends, with wreaths and single flowers. The National Anthem plays – the Scouts salute – the people sing the words in unity.

Again, the Burgomaster beckons me to follow in his steps: the crowd divides to let us through and slowly wander back. Emotion drained, we talk and laugh, so glad to be alive.

We reach the crossroads once again: I greet more friends and welcome new ones, say sorry for forgetfulness: I can't keep track of names.

The close Reunion ends, to my regret. But memories are stirred afresh each year for Boomkamp, Roetgerink, van Dijk, and Vonk, cut down too soon for no necessity – just four, of thousands likewise slain. "Lest We Forget", the call that brings us here.

The Spitfire sits, restored, upon its wheels; my pilot friend invites me to attend; he holds the key to open doors to wonder and delight – I see, I smell, I touch, I hear; I watch a thing of beauty, darting through the heavenly sky, no death within its wings.

Yet I can't forget...

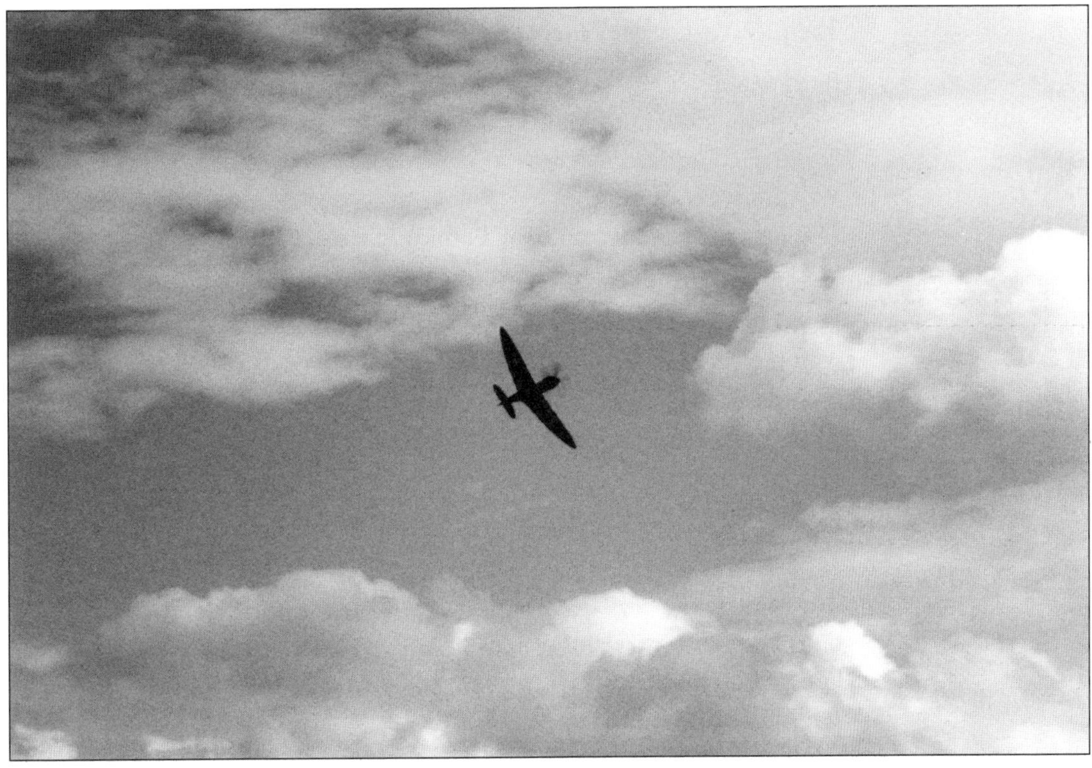

Appendices

APPENDIX A

"Requiem for 't Hesseler"

Now has the Day of Reckoning discovered me;
Now has been revealed to me the awful massacre of the innocents;
Now has my peace of mind been shattered for evermore.

I came down on silken cords into an empty field,
Unknowing that it was part of the homeland
Of a kind and friendly folk,
Then engaged in cruel and evil bondage,
But longing to breathe again the air of freedom
And willing to brave great danger
To show their spirit still unconquered.

Blindly I ran away,
Leaving helmet, goggles, parachute,
Took refuge in a wood and then a field
Sliced kindly by a chin-high ditch,
Till darkness fell
And I could tiptoe back
To my squadron buddies at my Brussels base.

And blindly, but foully, the monster Germans
Took reprisal,
Took hostages against my capture –
Their lives against my life.

But I was a shadow in the twilight,
And in the dark not visible at all:
No man could find me.
Yet I must be found –
Oh, hostages! How could you endure this time?

Had I but known!
Had I but knocked on a Dutch door for help
And been told of the incipient tragedy,
I would have given myself up without a moment's pause:
My life was never worth the life of one,
Much less the lives of three.
And, in any case, it would but have anticipated
What happened four days later.

But I walked alone,
Stumbling into wire and water,
Creeping round corners,
Hiding from headlights,
Clinging to trains,
Rolling off trucks,
Damning the cold and my blisters,
Nearing the Rhine.

24th of November, bitter and fateful:
The soldier's arm fell on my shoulder,
The gun dangling round his neck:
"Komm mit mir!"

Oh cursed Huns'
Why could you not have linked
The capture of this dirty bristled airman
With the landing, not fifty miles away,
Of the pilot from the skies,
And stayed your hand from senseless execution?

And – maybe at that very hour –
The self-same field that had received me
Felt other guns deliver mortal shots
And so received three martyrs,
Three honoured men,
Cut down most vilely
For doing nothing
Except happening to be the neighbours
Of my landing.

Now this sad monument arises
To record the senseless butchery of war,
Whereby a stranger's passing flight
Could cause three lives to end at one fell stroke
And start a lifetime's sorrow for three families.

They reached their rest before their time,
And we have all that time to grieve;
But not alone are we,
And not alone are they:
For peace is bought with ghastly sacrifice.

You – and a million others – paid that price,
And, half a century gone, we still have peace.
God bless the precious gift that you bequeathed to us
And we pass on to future children's children.

So this proud monument proclaims
For them, for us, for all the world to know
That you who died here
Lie not in doomed oblivion,
But on the road to freedom
And salvation for mankind –
Then, by force of arms,
Now, by brotherhood and unity
In the peace you gave us.

We, and most especially I,
Stand in your debt.
We stand in gratitude – for ever.

H.J.S.Taylor, ex-F/Lt 16 Squadron RAF, 18.6.90

At the time of writing this, I had not learned of the death of Jan Vonk, the first victim.

APPENDIX B

Transcript of "Beyond the Ignorance" (translated into English)

Nederlands Broadcasting Company
Programme Series; "From Region to Region"
This Broadcast: "Beyond the Ignorance"

Filmed on location in the Netherlands 15th and 16th November 1994
Broadcast in the Netherlands 25th and 26th November 1994
the 50th Anniversary of the Execution of Three Hostages

1. Bernard, Herman and Hendrik Boomkamp, brothers of Jan Boomkamp, one of the victims, walk along a lane in 't Hesseler, a small hamlet near the town of Borne in north-east Netherlands. They approach the Memorial to the three hostages executed by the Germans on 25th November 1944 after they could not find Jimmy Taylor, 'the missing pilot', who landed in the adjacent field after baling out of his Spitfire on 19th November 1944. With the brothers, in a wheel-chair, is Marie Leuveld-Roetgerink, sister of Hendrik Roetgerink, another victim. Her husband carved the fine Crucifix on the Memorial. [The third victim, Piet van Dijk, was not represented on this occasion. He did not live in 't Hesseler, but was arrested and made hostage by the Germans because his son had recently been freed from prison by the local Resistance, who were a continual thorn in the side of the Germans in Borne.]

2. The Memorial – Jimmy Taylor – the inscription – saluting the victims.

3. Caption: "BEYOND THE IGNORANCE" – Music.

4. Jimmy Taylor reads from his poem:
   "Now has the Day of Reckoning discovered me;
   Now has been revealed to me the awful massacre of the innocents;
   Now has my peace of mind been shattered for evermore."

5. Lukas Groen composing – Lukas Groen and Jimmy Taylor on a train from Arnhem to Utrecht.

   Jimmy Taylor:
   "I met him on the train going back to England, two weeks after I'd unveiled the plaque on this Monument here. I found Lukas sitting opposite me in the compartment, composing music."

6. Lukas Groen:
   "At that time, I wasn't yet composing music at the Conservatory – I did it privately. I think it was his son-in-law who was composing music. He was interested. That's how we got talking about all sorts of things. Just before we ran into Utrecht, he showed me some photographs."

7. Jimmy Taylor:
   "And it occurred to me; as I spoke to Lukas, that it would be a very nice symbol if he could write some music, as a young Dutchman, which represented in musical terms the story of my tragedy – and the hope at the end of it."

8. Music.

9. Jimmy Taylor:
   "I was really an amateur pilot."
   Photos.

"I joined the Air Force because of the war.
The 19th [of November 1944] turned out to be a pretty clear day. My instructions were to take photographs of airfields in the vicinity of Rheine, which is not far from Munster. And it was while I was flying straight and level that the engine suddenly gave a cough and hesitated, and then black smoke started coming out of the exhaust-pipes, and then some flames. And I didn't know where I was. That didn't matter at the moment: the thing was to get out of the aeroplane before it blew me out."

Film of an aircraft in flight – then descending on fire – Music – photo of the landing-field from the air – map of similar area of 't Hesseler – film of parachutist descending – film of trees and branches overhead.

"I looked up and I saw – in my memory, still very clearly – six or eight people standing round me in long black overcoats. And the parachute detached itself, and the wind blew it into a tree, and all these men in their long coats ran away after the parachute.
And I thought, 'This is my chance,' and I ran, or limped away, in the opposite direction, into a wood which I saw about a hundred yards away."

10. Hennie Noordhuis, chief archivist of Borne:
"At that time chaos prevailed, because the Germans thought there was a chance of arresting the man – but it didn't happen. On inquiry, it appeared that no one knew where the man had run to, as no one had seen him. So there was an arbitrary hostage-taking of six persons."

11. Hendrik Boomkamp:
"My brother had to stay where he was, near the parachute, as did the others who were standing there, quite a large group."

    Herman Boomkamp:
    "Some fifteen of them."

12. Interviewer to Marie Leuveld-Roetgerink:
"When did the Germans arrest your two brothers?"

    Marie Leuveld-Roetgerink:
    "That happened when the parachute came down. They arrested a lot of people. We used to take food to them in the evenings.
    At first, we didn't know where they were and the police wouldn't tell us. Then I went to look for them myself, and shouted. They looked out through a window and called out, 'We're captive here.'"

13. Herman Boomkamp:
"If the pilot wasn't found, they would be shot.
The police of Weerselo and Borne did everything they could to find him; but he was nowhere to be found, as he wasn't there anymore."

14. Lukas Groen and the orchestra

    Lukas Groen:
    "It's a strange story, of something that happened during the war: he crashed here – the people were executed – but he ran away.
    It was actually only a very short time that Mr. Taylor had anything to do with Borne – I mean, it was really only one day, and then he was gone.
    Then there is the aftermath of the week in the town and what happened to Taylor. These are two independent stories.
    Then nothing happens for 47 years, and then the two stories come together.
    At that point I come in – and that's the idea I try to use in my music."

15. Music. ‘

    Hennie Noordhuis:
    “Something else happened on that day, 19th November.
    They were busy in Borne all day long, trying to find the pilot.”

    Interviewer:
    “‘They’ are the Germans?”

    Hennie Noordhuis:
    “Yes, ‘they’ are the Germans.
    When they failed to come up with any result, out of sheer rancour they brought a Borne boy from Almelo.
    From a policeman’s account, this boy, Jan Vonk, was brought to Borne in the evening and executed beside the Town Hall.
    The policeman was told, ‘This is what happens if you hide people from us.’”

16. Jimmy Taylor walks along the railway line to Zutphen –

    Jimmy Taylor reads from his poem:
    “Had I but known,
    Had I but knocked on a Dutch door for help
    And been told of the incipient tragedy,
    I would have given myself up without a moment’s pause;
    My life was never worth the life of one,
    Much less the lives of three.
    And, in any case, it would but have anticipated
    What happened four days later.”

17. Hennie Noordhuis:

    “On that day, 25th November, the two Roetgerink brothers, with Boomkamp and Van Dijk, were still in jail in Hengelo.
    In the morning, there was a knock on the door of the cell and one of the Roetgerinks was taken out.
    He thought, ‘This is the end – it’s my turn to be executed.’
    He was quite convinced of this as he came out.
    To his astonishment, he was told he was a free man.
    On his way home, the German cars must have passed him with his brother, Boomkamp and Van Dijk inside.
    Apparently, the Germans had decided that their failure to find the pilot called for reprisals.”

18. Marie Leuveld-Roetgerink:

    “Then the cars appeared, and my nieces came indoors and said, ‘Aunt Marie, there are some cars coming, and in one of them is Uncle Hendrik – and Jan Boomkamp.’
    I went outside, and a German said to me, ‘I should stand next to him, if I were you.’
    It was just a job to him – if he shot more people, it wouldn’t bother him.
    I said to him, ‘That boy hasn’t done anything – why should you shoot him?’
    ‘It’s none of your business’, he replied.
    Then I went back indoors....”

19. The Memorial – the place of execution – photographs of the Victims – the Memorial.

20. Marie Leuveld-Roetgerink :
    “Then we went to the cemetery..’

Photos of the graves.
"...and there they were buried, next to each other: my brother lies in the middle; on one side lies Boomkamp, and old Mr van Dijk on the other."

21. Music and the orchestra.

    Interviewer to Hennie Noordhuis:
    "Have you ever had any doubts about whether it was a good idea to search for the missing pilot?"

    Hennie Noordhuis:
    "What happened was this. I sensed that, among the relatives, there was a belief until two years ago that Taylor had been kept in prison in Borne.
    And I also heard some slight reproaches against the Resistance Movement in Borne: 'If they had handed him over, we should have kept our loved ones.'
    As long as I didn't know the answers to these questions, I thought to myself, 'I need to know the facts.' That's why I decided to bring the case of Taylor to its true conclusion."

22. Jimmy Taylor beside the landing-field.

    Interviewer:
    "Were you glad he found you?"

    Jimmy Taylor:
    "At that time, and between just him and me, I wish he hadn't.
    But I've had such a wonderful welcome in 't Hesseler by the relatives of the victims, and we have such a warm relationship, and I feel I belong :to this little village and these are my family now, that I am very happy to be involved with this community, after the war, after all this has happened.
    But it still fills me with regret that my days of innocence, of ignorance, were destroyed by Hennie's message.
    So I have two feelings."

23. Music – the relatives walk back along the lane from the Memorial with Jimmy Taylor.

24. Credits

    With thanks to:
    Borne Municipality
    Netherlands Railways
    The Air Force Museum

    Camera:
    Hans de Ruiter

    Sound:
    Roelof Dijkman

    Montage:
    Bettie Greidanus

    Producer:
    Ellen van Helsdingen

APPENDIX C

BEVRIJDINGS - COMITÉ BORNE 1945/1995

Dedication

On behalf of all the Veterans of World War Two who came to Borne 29th April-8th May 1995, I should like to congratulate you most warmly, as a member of the Liberation Committee Borne 1945-1995, on the superb programme that you arranged for our benefit.

We were given a wonderful welcome by you and by all the kind people of Borne and its adjacent villages. We received remarkable hospitality from our hosts and hostesses. We were privileged to experience some of the many pleasures of your lives today, both cultural, historical, musical and culinary, and to witness the happiness and maturity of your children, who are fortunate to grow up in the beauty and peacefulness of Borne and its surroundings.

Your Commemoration of the events of 50 years ago brought back to us memories of the dark days of the War - the privation and the fear, the suffering and the sorrow. But it also reminded us of the courage and the fortitude, the comradeship and the self-sacrifice, that were shown by so many Dutch and Allied personnel and which made victory possible.

Peace and freedom were bought at a heavy price. The participation of the children of Borne in your programme showed their awareness of the need to understand and preserve what they have inherited from the Liberation.

For all these reasons, this 50th Anniversary was made unforgettable for us by your work in your Committee - with the blessing, of course, of perfect weather!

It is therefore a very great pleasure and honour for me to record the sincere gratitude of all the Veterans to you, to the Liberation Committee Borne 1945-1995, and to all the generous and friendly people of Borne.

H.J.S.Taylor

ex - 16 Squadron RAF

SECRETARIAAT: GEMEENTEHUIS BORNE, POSTBUS 200, 7622 AE BORNE

JT's expression of gratitude to the members of the Liberation Committee Borne 1945-95 on behalf of all the Veterans

APPENDIX D

Transcript of Alec Harvey-Bailey's recording for David Birch of the Roll-Royce Heritage Trust 7th October 1995

"Dave, this is me Alec, and it is the 7th October.

I've been trying to get my memory into gear to think further about Mr Taylor's Spitfire and the engine-failure he had with it in 1944. You will appreciate that my long-term illness has affected my memory and that it takes me time to get going on these things.

Having read the letters concerned and talked to you, I can say the following things:

The photographs, interesting as though they are from the point of view of the incident, reveal no cause as to the failure.

Secondly, it is a characteristic of the engine problems that different problems can produce similar symptoms to a pilot, and it is not unless one is able to get into an engine and examine it that one can get to the root cause of the trouble. So what I am saying is bound to assume certain things.

First of all, I do not think I was right in assuming that it was ring-gumming. We got ring-gumming where we were using 1800 rpm +71lbs boost, particularly on the 'heavies' for long periods, and it does take time to cause the rings to gum; and, on a thing like a fighter, it is generally possible to detect ring-gumming by increased oil-consumption and the like, possibly increased engine-breathing – and this does not appear to have taken place.

However, the relatively sudden nature of the symptoms that occurred indicates to me that it is more likely to be involved in the supercharger.

The two-stage Merlin in that particular Mark of Spitfire had the conventional rotor-shaft, with a ball-bearing front-bearing location, and a tail-bearing having a floating bronze bush and a floating steel bush running in a fixed bronze bush. This was done to reduce the rubbing speeds, and it was very reliable. But, if one has some other defect in the 'blower', it was possible to increase the oil consumption substantially.

It seems likely, in this case, that there was a defect in the front bearing and we did have a few ball-bearing failures in that position. It is quite a heavy-duty operation, running at high speeds – over 20,000 rpm – and , although the bearing was not short of capacity, we did have the odd failure. The damage was so severe that it was difficult to point to a particular cause, and a lot of our efforts were directed towards improving the standard of bearings.

However, we did go, as a technical change, from a bearing with a cage – a bronze cage, that is – located on the inner race to a ribbon-steel cage spigoted on the balls. We thought the latter bearing offered better lubrication, because the effect of the centrifugal speed of the bearing tended to take the oil diagonally across it, and the spigot location – remote from the oil – tended to be a bit short of oil.

I do not know what the end of the bearing would be in this engine because, to begin with, we did not have a modification, and we had alternate sources of supply before we finally got adequate quantities of the bearing with the steel cage.

This gave us a very good service until after the War; we had a failure on a commercial engine and , as Lovesey (Cyril Lovesey, R-R Chief Development Engineer) had gone onto gas-turbines, we had a Chief

Development Engineer on the Merlin who was rather aged and rather conservative, and he just did not like the steel-cage bearing and went back to the bronze cage, because that was what he was brought-up on, I think. There was no real evidence to make the change at the time.

Other improvements included electrolytic etching of the inner and outer races to inspect for defects in the grinding raw material, and an acid etch of the balls for the same reason.

So it was an item that got a lot of attention, and we did get a very good standard of reliability – apart from the odd casualty, which we never eliminated.

The symptoms described by Mr Taylor, of the engine hiccoughing and loosing revs. all at once and then trying to pick itself up again, are quite symptomatic of supercharger trouble, and the smoke would come, I think, from the tail-bearing, because the tail-bearing would suffer if the front-bearing failed. I do not think I could be more definite than that.

I think it is worth saying that the Company took the service performance of its engines very seriously indeed. I was given charge of the Failure Investigation Section, which was located in the dispersed mill, Longman's Mill in Agard Street (Derby), and I had a team of people working with me; engines that were returned from service with failures attributed to them, either from our service representatives in the field or by 1022 action by the RAF, were sent to Agard Street, where we dismantled the engines and examined them, and sent any failed parts to the laboratory for examination; and – apart from our own expertise, which became considerable – engineers in the Development Department regularly visited us and looked at defective engines that were returned. Every month, we issued a consolidated report on all the engines that we had examined – quite apart from individual investigation reports that were circulated, too, within the Company and also to the MAP (Ministry of Aircraft Production) via the AIB (Accident Investigation Branch), who would also advise the Air Force.

Naturally, in the course of this, we visited stations and talked to personnel, and we had direct communication on issues with the squadrons and the pilots.

Ernest Hives, the Director and General Works Manager, later Lord Hives, who ran his own meetings at least every week and took a great interest in troubles and developments to overcome them, put pressure on everyone to improve the breed and to improve the quality. It so happens that my father (R.W.Harvey-Bailey), who had been Chief Engineer of the Chassis Division immediately before the War – he had joined Royce (Sir Henry Royce) in 1910 and had worked on cars and aero-engines since then (he designed the R-R Eagle and Falcon engines) – became Chief Quality Engineer of the Aero-engine Division, with responsibility for product quality and the investigation of problems. When there was an accident in which the Accident Investigation Branch became involved, the company arranged for a team, if need be, to go out with the RAF and Accident Investigation Branch and examine engines, particularly where there had been 'fatals'.

I say this because, while what I have said about a particular engine has not drawn any satisfactory conclusions, we did take the operation most seriously, and the Firm has always done so – to this day. The practices established on the Merlin during the War years have continued since then, and the investigation of problems is still a key issue with the Company.

So, on that note, I will close.

It has been interesting to think back over those eventful years with the Merlin during the War, and I hope what I have said has been useful.

Goodbye. Alec."

APPENDIX E

Diagram of the Supercharger of Rolls-Royce Merlin and Griffon engines, with annotations by David Birch to show the position of the bearing that broke and caused my engine-failure on 19th November 1944

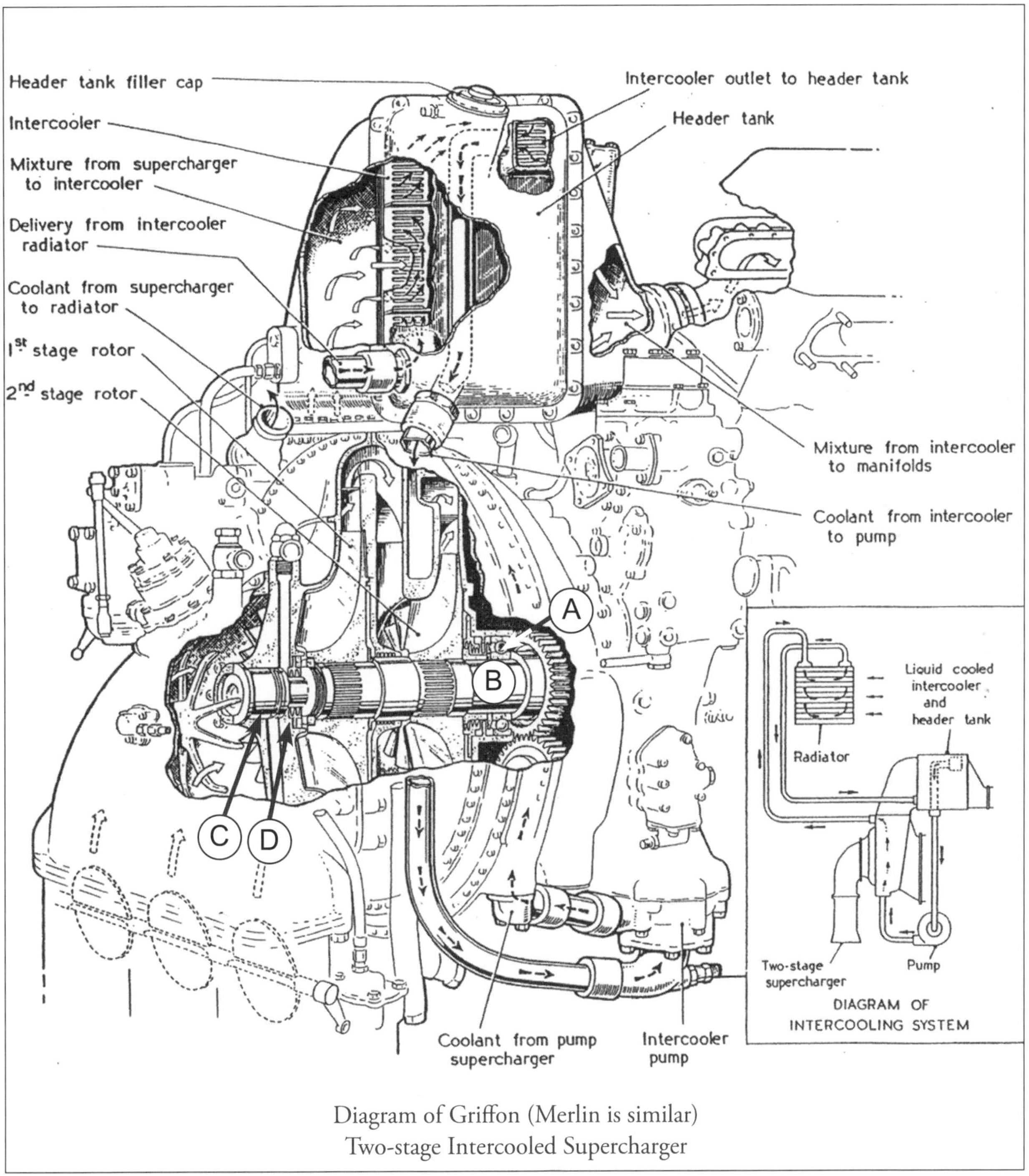

Diagram of Griffon (Merlin is similar)
Two-stage Intercooled Supercharger

When front bearing (ball) fails **A**, the supercharger rotor shaft **B** begins to run erratically and wears the rear bearing (plain) **C** . It also destroys the seating at **D** allowing the rear bearing lubricating oil to enter the supercharger. Result, smoke from exhausts.

APPENDIX F

* entered 18.9.95

Year 1944 Month	Date	Aircraft Type	Aircraft No.	Pilot, or 1st Pilot	2nd Pilot, Pupil or Passenger	Duty (Including Results and Remarks)	S-E Day Dual (1)	S-E Day Pilot (2)	S-E Night Dual (3)	S-E Night Pilot (4)	M-E Day Dual (5)	M-E Day 1st Pilot (6)	M-E Day 2nd Pilot (7)	M-E Night Dual (8)	M-E Night 1st Pilot (9)	M-E Night 2nd Pilot (10)	Pass-enger (11)	Instr/Cloud Flying Dual (12)	Instr/Cloud Flying Pilot (13)	Link Trainer (14)
16 Sqdn.		Northolt *	—	—	—	— Totals Brought Forward	95.15	897.00	2.35	54.50	32.50	33.25	4.00	6.05	14.50		30.35	39.05	26.10	67.05
Aug.	26.	SPITFIRE XI	PL 834 Q834	SELF	—	LOCAL.		1.20												
..	26	..	MB 954 K954	SELF	—	1. A/F: BEACHHEAD: BAYEUX - CAEN 18000'.		2.10												
Aug.	31	SPITFIRE XI	PA 933 J933	SELF	-	2. DUMPS: LILLE - LE CATEAU - VALENCIENNES 25000'.		2.55												
SEPT.	2.	SPITFIRE IX	E 632	SELF	-	PRACTICE: L.L.O. SALISBURY - SWINDON.		1.15												
SEPT	3	SPITFIRE XI	PL 830 PL Q830	SELF	-	BEACHEAD: 'MULBERRYS'. 30,000'.		1.45												
..	..	SPITFIRE XI	PL 795 P795	..	-	3. DUMP: Le CATEAU, A/F: CHIMAY. 5000'.		2.30												
SEPT.	5	WELLINGTON	HZ883	F/o BROADLEY	SELF (pass)	NORTHOLT - A12, FRANCE: LIGNEROLLES.											1.15			
SEPT.	8.	SPITFIRE XI	MB 958 M958	SELF	-	4. VILLAGE S. of NANCY - NO PHOTOS. (First flak) 1200'.		3.30												
SEPT.	9.	SPITFIRE XI	EN 654 F654	SELF	-	A12 - GLISSY A/F, AMIENS.		1.00												
SEPT.	11.	SPITFIRE IX	D	SELF	-	GLISSY - NORTHOLT and RETURN.		1.40												
SEPT.	12th	SPITFIRE XI	MB 957 L957	SELF	-	5. ANTWERP & AREA NORTH MOSAIC 30000'. (First sighting of launching of V2?)		1.50												
SEPT.	14th	SPITFIRE XI	PA 869 T869	SELF	-	6. ROADS N. of BREMEN: CUXHAVEN, WILHELMSHAVEN 24000'.		3.25												
SEPT.	18th	SPITFIRE XI	MB 953 H953	SELF	-	7. IJMUIDEN: COASTAL GUNS 24000'. (150' ceiling on return.)		2.10												
GRAND TOTAL [Cols. (1) to (10)] 1166 Hrs. 20 Mins.						Totals Carried Forward	95.15	922.30	2.35	54.50	32.50	33.25	4.00	6.05	14.50		31.50	39.05	26.10	67.05

Summary for: August. Unit: 16 (P.R.) Sqdn. Date: 3/9/44. Signature: H. Naylor.
Aircraft Types: 1. Spitfire XI 2. 3. 4.
August Ops.: 5.05
Total Ops.: 5.05
O.C. 'B' Flight
C.O. 16 Sqdn.

3.6.08
I have been given a photo of this by Mike Mockford, Sec. of the Medmenham Club.

8th V-2 landed at 0852 at Keston, near Biggin Hill. I was near Ghent when I saw the contrail 20 miles north, from 30000' to about 45000', when the contrail stopped. Corroborated by P/O Cribb. 8th June 1994.
Ref. "Doodlebugs and Rockets" by Bob Ogley 1992

The entries in my Flying Log-Book for my flights in 16 Squadron from 26th August – 19th November 1944

Year 1944 Month	Date	Aircraft Type	Aircraft No.	Pilot, or 1st Pilot	2nd Pilot, Pupil or Passenger	DUTY (Including Results and Remarks)	Single-Engine Day Dual (1)	Single-Engine Day Pilot (2)	Single-Engine Night Dual (3)	Single-Engine Night Pilot (4)	Multi-Engine Day Dual (5)	Multi-Engine Day 1st Pilot (6)	Multi-Engine Day 2nd Pilot (7)	Multi-Engine Night Dual (8)	Multi-Engine Night 1st Pilot (9)	Multi-Engine Night 2nd Pilot (10)	Passenger (11)	Instr/Cloud Flying [Incl. in cols. (1) to (10)] Dual (12)	Instr/Cloud Flying Pilot (13)	Link Trainer (14)
—	—	—	—	—	—	Totals Brought Forward	95.15	922.30	2.35	54.50	32.50	33.25	4.00	6.05	14.50		31.50	39.05	26.10	67.05
Sept.	21st	Spitfire XI	PA 0899	Self	–	8. Road N. of Gardelegen Nr Brunswick 22000'														
						(first encounter with EA:- 22-39000' T.E.)		4.00												
Sept.	22nd	Spitfire IX	V MK 915	Self	–	Amiens – Ford (Bognor!) and return. 1000'.		1.30												
Sept.	23rd	Auster	MT 854	F/Lt. Wales.	F/Lt. Horsfall. Self.	Amiens – St. Omer and return.											2.15			
Sept.	27th	Auster.	MT 864	Self	–	Amiens – Moelsbroek, Brussels.		1.40												
Sept.	29th	Spitfire XI	~~PL 770~~ PA 770	Self	–	9. Brussels: Niensburg, Rotenburg – roads.		3.50												
						Electrical failure landed Florennes.		.25												
[signature]		O.C. 'B' Flt.	F/Lt.	Summary for: September 1944		Aircraft: (1) Spitfire IX		4.25									(7) Sept. ops.			21:15
				Unit: 16 (P.R.) Squadron.		(2) Spitfire XI		24.25									(9) Total ops.			26:45
[signature]			S/Ldr.	Date: 2/10/44.		(3) Auster III		1.40												
		O.C. '16 Sqdn'		Signature: [signature]		(4)		30.30									3.30			
Oct.	1st	Spitfire IX	V MK915	Self (see Alfred Price: "The Spitfire Story" between pp 128-129)	–	Air test.		.20												
Oct.	3rd	Spitfire XI	P PL912 PL 912	Smallwood Self	–	Air test.		.20												
Oct.	5th	Spitfire XI	F ~~PL854~~ PA 854	Smallwood Self	–	10. Mosaic Hook of Holland 5" 32000'. (60% abortive due to haze)		2.20												
Grand Total [Cols. (1) to (10)] 1180 Hrs. 45 Mins.						Totals Carried Forward	95.15	936.55	2.35	54.50	32.50	33.25	4.00	6.05	14.50		34.05	39.05	26.10	67.05

Year 1944 Month	Date	Aircraft Type	Aircraft No.	Pilot, or 1st Pilot	2nd Pilot, Pupil or Passenger	Duty (Including Results and Remarks)	SE Day Dual (1)	SE Day Pilot (2)	SE Night Dual (3)	SE Night Pilot (4)	ME Day Dual (5)	ME Day 1st Pilot (6)	ME Day 2nd Pilot (7)	ME Night Dual (8)	ME Night 1st Pilot (9)	ME Night 2nd Pilot (10)	Passenger (11)	Instr/Cloud Flying [Incl. in cols. (1) to (10)] Dual (12)	Instr/Cloud Pilot (13)	Link Trainer (14)
—	—	—	—	—	—	Totals Brought Forward	95.15	936.55	2.35	54.50	32.50	33.25	4.00	6.05	14.50		34.05	39.05	26.10	67.05
Oct.	12th	Spitfire XI	MB957 L957	Self	—	Air Test.		.50												
Oct.	14th	Spitfire XI	PL851 D851	Self	—	11. 36" Marshalling yards: Utrecht, Amersfoort 3100'. Area Alpen – Homborn in the Ruhr 25500'.		2.00												
Oct.	15th	Spitfire XI	PL830 C830 PL830	Self	—	Brussels – Rouen and Return (abortive)		2.10												
Oct.	16th	Dakota	KG934	F/O Anon	Self	Moelsbroek – Northolt via [illegible] via Antwerp.											2.30			
Oct.	24th	Dakota	693	W/O Anon	Self	Northolt – Moelsbroek via Eindhoven.											2.30			
Oct.	29th	Spitfire XI	MB950 0950*	Self	—	12. Bridges at Venlo and Roermond. 4500'.		1.45												
"	"	" XI	B944 PA944	Self	—	Moelsbroek – Rouen and Return.		2.00												
[signature] F/Lt. O.C. 'B' Flt.				Summary for:	October 1944.	Aircraft: 1. Spitfire XI		11:45									(3)	Oct.	ops.	6:05
				Unit:	16 Sqdn.	2.											(12)	Total	ops.	32:50
[signature] S/Ldr.				Date:	1/11/44.	3.														
C.O. 16 Sqdn.				Signature:	H.J. Taylor F/O.	4.		11:45									5:00			
Nov.	4th	Spitfire XI	PL851 D851	Self	—	13. Frisian Isle – Coastline: 20000'. Deffen – Schillig.		2.15												
Nov.	8th	Spitfire XI	MB950 0950	Self	–	14. "Dortmund-Ems Canal." (Twenthe Canal) 3500'.		1.40												
					Grand Total [Cols. (1) to (10)] 1193 Hrs. 25 Mins.	Totals Carried Forward	96.15	949.25	2.35	54.50	32.50	33.25	4.00	6.05	14.50		39.05	39.05	26.10	67.05

Year 1944 Month	Date	Aircraft Type	Aircraft No.	Pilot, or 1st Pilot	2nd Pilot, Pupil or Passenger	Duty (Including Results and Remarks)	Single-Engine Day Dual (1)	Single-Engine Day Pilot (2)	Single-Engine Night Dual (3)	Single-Engine Night Pilot (4)	Multi-Engine Day Dual (5)	Multi-Engine Day 1st Pilot (6)	Multi-Engine Day 2nd Pilot (7)	Multi-Engine Night Dual (8)	Multi-Engine Night 1st Pilot (9)	Multi-Engine Night 2nd Pilot (10)	Passenger (11)	Instr/Cloud Flying [Incl. in cols. (1) to (10)] Dual (12)	Instr/Cloud Flying Pilot (13)	Link Trainer (14)
—	—	—	—	—	—	— Totals Brought Forward	95.15	949.25	2.35	54.50	32.50	33.25	4.00	6.05	14.50		39.05	39.05	26.10	67.05
Nov.	14th	Spitfire XI	MB957 L957	Self.	—	Brussels - Eindhoven - Brussels.		1.00												
Nov.	15th	Spitfire XI	W PL949 ? PA949 W959 PL913 X913	Self.	—	Air test.		.30												
Nov.	18th	Auster	MT854	F/L Snell	Self.	Circuit.											.20			
"	"	"	MT854	Self	LAC Avon	Air test.		.30												
"	"	Spitfire XI	PL905 S905	Self	—	15. R.R. at Viersen - Kempen - Krefeld - Julken 24000'		2.40												
Nov	19	Spitfire XI	MB957 L957	Self.	—	16. Airfields in Rheine area.					"Missing" from this operation									
		[illegible] F/Lt O.C. A Flight		Summary for November 1944 16 Squadron. 22/11/44		Spitfire		8.35			Operational		4 Sorties.		6.35					
						Auster						Total "	16 "		39.25		.20			
		[signature] S/Ldr C.O. 16 Sqdn																		
1945																				
May	14	Fortress		Capt. Smith	Self & 13 others.	Barthe, Germany - Ford, England.														
June	12	Warwick		F/O Brown	Self & others	Blackbushe - Eindhoven.														
June	13	Mosquito		F/L Pollitt	Self & F/L Horsfall	Eindhoven - Melsbroek.														
				F/L Lord Ossulston + F/L Gavins ?																
June	16	Mosquito		F/Lt. Stitchbury	Self F/L Horsfall A.N. Other.	Melsbroek - Blackbushe.														
				Grand Total [Cols. (1) to (10)] 1198 Hrs. 05 Mins.		Totals Carried Forward	95.15	954.05	2.35	54.50	32.50	33.25	4.00	6.05	14.50		39.25	39.05	26.10	67.05

Bibliography

Early Days

Cobham, Sir Alan — "A Time to Fly"
Shepheard-Walwyn 1978

Flying Training (Chapters 3 – 7)

Currie, Jack — "Wings Over Georgia"
Goodall 1989

Golley, John — "Aircrew Unlimited: the Commonwealth Air Training Plan during World War II"
Patrick Stephens 1993

Hough, Richard — "One Boy's War"
Heinemann 1975
Pen & Sword reprint 2007

34 Wing and 16 Squadron (Chapters 8 – 9)

Rigby, H and Spender, M (possibly) — "34 Wing: an Informal Account"
Unpublished 1945

Smallwood, Hugh — "Spitfire in Blue"
Osprey 1996

The Spitfire (Chapter 9)

Dibbs, John and Holmes, Tony — "Spitfire: Flying Legend"
Osprey 1996

Harvey-Bailey, Alec — "The Merlin in Perspective"
Rolls-Royce Heritage Trust 4th Ed 1995

Matusiak, Wojtek — "Merlin PR Spitfires"
Ventura Publications New Zealand 2007

Morgan, Eric and Shacklady, Edward — "Spitfire: the History"
Key Publishing 1987

Neil, T.F. — "Spitfire from the Cockpit"
Ian Allan 1990

Price, Alfred — "Spitfire: a Complete Fighting History"
Promotional Reprint Company 1997

Smallwood, Hugh — "Spitfire in Blue"
Osprey 1996

Robertson, Bruce — "Spitfire – the Story of a Famous Fighter"
Harleyford 1960

Photographic Reconnaissance (Chapters 10 – 12)

Air Ministry — "Evidence in Camera"
HMSO 1945
Reproduced by the Geo-Information Group 2003

Babington Smith, Constance — "Evidence in Camera"
Chatto and Windus 1958

Brookes, Andrew, J. — "Photo Reconnaissance: the Operational History" Ian Allan 1975

Daglish, Ian — "Operation Goodwood" (many PR photographs) Pen and Sword 2005

Keen, Patricia — "Eyes of the Eighth" Record of the 7th Photo Group of the US 8th Air Force

Nesbit, Roy Conyers — "Eyes of the RAF" Sutton 1996

Powys-Lybbe, Ursula — "The Eye of Intelligence" Kimber 1983

RAF Historical Society — "Photographic Reconnaissance in World War II" RAF Historical Society 1991

Staal, G. and Voskuil, R. — "Een Blik op Beget Nederland" ("A Look at Occupied Holland") (Dutch text) Stadium Generale van de Landbouwhogeschool 1980 (Agricultural University 1980)

Staerck, Chris Ed. — "Allied Photo-Reconnaissance of World War Two" Parkgate 1998

Stanley, Col. Roy, M. USAF — "World War II Photo Intelligence" Sidgwick and Jackson 1982

Royal Air Force

Jefford, Wing Commander C.G. — "Squadrons of the R.A.F." Airlife 2001

Lake, Alan — "Flying Units of the R.A.F." Airlife 1999

Operation 'Market Garden'

Altes, K., Margry, K., Thuring, G. and Voskuil, R. — "September 1944: Operation Market Garden" (Dutch and English text) Fibula-van Dishoeck 1984

Badsey, Stephen — "Operation Market Garden: Arnhem 1944" Osprey 1993

Buckingham, William F. — "Arnhem 1944" Tempus 2002

Buist, L., Reinders, P. and Maasen, G. — "The Royal Air Force at Arnhem" Friends of the Airborne Museum, Oosterbeek 2005

Firbank, Thomas — "I Bought a Star" John Jones 1999

Gregory, Harry and Batchelor, John — "Airborne Warfare 1918-1945" Phoebus 1979

Hagen, Louis — "Arnhem Lift" BCA 1993

Harclerode, Peter — "Arnhem: a Tragedy of Errors" Caxton 2000

Harvey, A.D. — "Arnhem"
Cassell 2001

van Hees, Arie-Jan — "Tugs and Gliders to Arnhem"
van Hees pub. 2000

Holt, Major and Mrs — "Battlefield Guide: Operation Market Garden"
Leo Cooper 2001

Janse, Cor — "Blik Omhoog! 1940 – 1945"
("Look Up! 1940 – 1945")
Drukkerij Tamminga Siegers Duiven Book II 1996

Kershaw, Robert J. — "It Never Snows in September"
Ian Allan 1990

The National Archive — "Battlefront: Operation Market Garden"
Study pack: The National Archive 2000

Neillands, Robin — "The Battle for the Rhine 1944"
Weidenfeld and Nicolson 2005

Parker, John — "The Paras"
Metro 2000

Pitkin Guide — "The Battle for Arnhem"
Jarrold 1998

Powell, Geoffrey — "The Devil's Birthday"
Leo Cooper Rev. Edition 1992

Ryan, Cornelius — "A Bridge Too Far"
Book Club Associates 1974

Saunders, Tim — "Market Garden: Hell's Highway"
Leo Cooper 2001

Saunders, Tim — "Market Garden: Nijmegen"
Leo Cooper 2001

Smith, Claude — "The History of the Glider Pilot Regiment"
Leo Cooper 1992

Steer, Frank — "Market Garden: Arnhem"
Leo Cooper 2002

Steer, Frank — "Market Garden: Arnhem, The Bridge"
Leo Cooper 2003

Thuring, G. et al — "Market Garden: the Waal Crossing"
(Dutch and English text)
Bevrijdingsmuseum 1992
(The Freedom Museum 1992)

Tout, Ken — "In the Shadow of Arnhem"
Sutton 2003

Waddy, John — "A Tour of the Arnhem Battlefields"
Leo Cooper 1999

Prisoner-of-War (Chapter 26)

Clutton-Brock, Oliver — "Footprints on the Sands of Time" RAF Bomber Command POWs and their Camps
Grub Street 2003

The End of the War (Chapter 39)

BBC	"War Report 1944 – 1945" Oxford 1946
Berjek, Alexander	"Krieg vor der Eigenen Haustür" ("War on Our Own Doorstep") (German text) Selbstverlag des Stadtarchivs Wesel (Produced in the Wesel Town Archives) 2004
Churchill, Winston	"The Second World War Vol VI" Cassell 1954
Davies. Norman	"Europe at War 1939 – 1945" Macmillan 2006
Ethell, J. and Price, A.	"The German Jets in Combat" Jane's 1979
Ford, Ken	"The Rhine Crossings 1945" Osprey 2006
Franks, Norman	"The Battle of the Airfields" Kimber 1982
Hastings, Max	"Armageddon: the Battle for Germany 1944 – 45" Macmillan 2004
Neillands, Robin	"The Conquest of the Reich" Orion 1996
Price, Alfred	"The Last Year of the Luftwaffe 1944 – 1945" Arms and Armour 1993
Rekers, Karl	"Das Kriegsende 1945 in Unserer Heimat" ("The End of the War 1945 in Our District" including Rheine) (German text) Druck-Ibbenbüremer Vereinsdruckere GmbH 1998

Twente Canal and Borne (Chapter 40)

Noordhuis, H., Braak, G., . and Kienhuis, M.	"In Verdrukking, Verzet en Vrijheid: Borne, Bornerbroek, Hertme en Zenderen 1940-1945" (Dutch text) ("In Suffering, Resistance, and Freedom 1940-1945") Gemeente Borne 1st Ed. 1990
Pol, H.J.A.G. with Troelstra, H.H.M. and Groot, S.S.S.	"Onze Vergeten Bevrijders Maart-April 1945" ("Our Forgotten Liberators March-April 1945") (Dutch and English text) Drukkerij Twente Hengelo 1999

Acknowledgements

Very many people have contributed to this book, either directly and consciously, or indirectly and unknowingly. I am most grateful to them all and I hope I have acknowledged each of them. With two or three exceptions, I have restricted myself to those who are still living. I offer my apologies to any who may feel they have been left out. There is no priority: the lists are in precise alphabetical order

The staffs of the following national or large-scale institutions have been most helpful; I have pinpointed any individuals that I dealt with.

Institutions in Britain:

The Airborne Forces Museum: Alan Brown; The Air Historical Branch of the Ministry of Defence: Sue Dickinson; The Air Photo Library, Keele (now The Aerial Reconnaissance Archive, Edinburgh); Cobham, Ltd: Ben Dorrington and Bob Spiller; The Commonwealth War Graves Commission: Maureen Annetts; The Defence School of Photography: Dave Humphrey; The Fleet Air Arm Museum; The Imperial War Museum, London: Mary Wilkinson; The Imperial War Museum, Duxford; The Museum of Army Flying; The National Archive (formerly The Public Record Office): Hugh Alexander and Chris Heather; The National Meteorological Archive: M.J.Wood; The RAF Museum, Cosford; The RAF Museum, Hendon: Andrew Renwick and Andrew Whitmarsh; Rolls-Royce Corporate Heritage: Michael Evans and Richard Haigh; Rolls-Royce Heritage Trust: David Birch and Ivor Purkis.

Institutions in Holland:

The Airborne Museum, Oosterbeek: Thomas van Slooten; Bentelo Town Hall: Mr Van Der Vegt; Borne Town Hail: Gees Brekelmans, Joke de Leeuw, Martin and Jeanette Vunderink, Rob Welten, Joop de Melker Worms; The Liberation Museum, Groesbeek: Frank van den Bergh; The Rijksmuseum Twente: Dr Paul Knolle; The University of Emmen; The University of Wageningen: Liesbeth Missal; The War Museum, Arnhem; The Wings of Liberation Museum, Son: Jos Korsten.

Aviation in Britain:

G/C Peter Allan; S/L Dick Cole, RAF (Retd); ACM Sir David Cousins, KCB, AFC, RAF (Retd); S/L Mark Cutmore, RAF; S/L Paul Day, OBE, AFC, RAF (Retd); S/L Peter Fahy, DFC, AFC, RAF (Retd); S/L Stephen Foote, RAF; the late S/L Norman Godfrey, DFC, CdeG, RAF (Retd); W/C Willy Hackett, RAF; the late Mark Hanna; Basil Jackson; the late James Marett; Stuart Marshall; G/C Richard Mason, OBE, RAF: Ron Miller; Steve Naijaim; Terry Potter; Jill Povall; James Prosser; Spencer Prou; Andy Sephton; S/L Derek Smith, RAF (Retd); Tony Smith; G/C Guy Stockill, RAF; A/C Andy Sudlow, MBE, RAF; Peter Teichman.

Aviation in Holland:

Gen. Dick Berlijn, RNLAF (Retd); Capt. Jeroen Kloosterman, RNLAF; Harry van der Meer; Harry Rientjes; Hans Ruijgrok; Capt. Tye Verf, RNLAF (Retd); Col. Vogelpoel, RNLAF.

Historians in Britain:

Peter Arnold; David Campbell; Niall Cherry; Ian Daglish; Lewis Deal, MBE; Chris Goss; Chris Gowing; Dr Colin Hall; F/Sgt Michael Harris, RAF; Reg Harris; Philip Holloway; Chris Horsley; S/L Ray Leach, MBE, RAF (Retd); Keith Miller; W/C Michael Mockford, OBE, RAF (Retd); Mike Nolan; Graham Pitchfork, OBE; Dr Alfred Price; Winston Quested; Robin Rigby; Hugh Smallwood; Leo Stevenson; Geoffrey Teece; Alan Thomas.

Historians in Holland:

Frans Ammerlaan; Jaap Been; Henk Duinhoven, MBE; Bob Gerritsen; Jaap Grootenboer; Arie-Jan van Hees; Cor Jansen; Dr Nick Lambrechtsen; Adrie Roding; Graf Solms; Joop Thuring; Robert Voskuil.

Historians Overseas:

Michael Cain and Sue (USA); Cmdt. Peter Celis, RBAF (Belgium); Luc Cox (Belgium); Tim Coyle (Australia); Joachim Eickhoff (Germany); Dr Thomas Giessmann (Germany); Ronald Hirst (USA); Wojtek Matusiak (Poland); Karl Rekers (Germany); Peter Roberts (Australia); Gerd Schulte (Germany).

Media in Britain:

Sidney Bennett (Channel 4 TV); Ken Delve ("FlyPast"); Tim Dunn (BBC); Simon Garrett (Carlton TV); Tony Holmes (Osprey International); Ron and June Nobes (video); Michael Oakey ("Aeroplane"); Francois Prins ("Wingspan"); Andrew Wise ("RAF News").

Media in Holland:

Hans Bellert (TV Oost); Peggie Breitbarth-van der Stok ("Jaarboek Twente"); Wouter Broke (DotKa); Lukas Groen ("Pro Borne"); Ellen van Helsdingen (NOS TV); David Jonker (DotKa); René Schabos ("Twentsche Courant Tubantia"); Frank Venus (publisher); Rob Wissink ("Twentsche Courant Tubantia"); the Publishers of "Twente Courant Tubantia".

Families and Friends in Britain:

The late Philip Back and June; Nigel Back; Roger Burghall; Lady Catto; Rod Doubble; Chris and Penny Evers; the late Beryl Green; Daphne Greville-Heygate; Brian Hook; Michael and Denise Horsfall, Annie and Mickie; Mark and Jane Johnson; Dick Knight: John Lloyd; Sir Patrick and Lady Moberly; Andrew Moberly; the late Ron Parnell and Eileen; Pat Rowell; Nancy Petrie; Rod Priddle; Helen Ransley; Robin and Clemency Stanes; David and Suzanna Stewart-Monteith; Aileen Taylor; Jennifer Taylor; Jonathan and Amanda Taylor; Peter and Nena Thorley; Susie Watmough; John and Pip Wynne.

Families and Friends in Holland:

Father Dries van den Akker, SJ; Fred and Froukje Bakker; Father Paul Begheyn, SJ; Hendrik and Diny Boomkamp and Maria; Jan and Miny Boomkamp and Dirk; Familie Bosch; Jan and Ria Bovenmars, and Anne, Helen and Bram; Herman and Bernadette Bruggink and Janneke; Mark and Judith Brummelhuis; Mrs van Dijk-Kolkamp; Hennie Egberink; Maarten Haalboom; Ben van Hengstum; Ger and Ria Leuveld; Harry and Gertie Leuveld; Hennie and Joke Noordhuis; Hennie and Ger Roetgerink; Riet Sanders-Roetgerink; the late Betsie Timmerman-Westerink; Henk and Ans Timmerman; Mrs Thea Timmerman; Hermine Vonk; Hans and Josine Wools.

Photo Credits

Ever since I was a small boy I have collected photographs of aeroplanes from every source, usually without a note of their origin and date. While "16 Squadron 1939-1945" was active, I received photographs for "Newsbrief" from the Members' own collections, some of which I copied before returning them. In this book I have credited each photograph to its origin as known to me, usually from the above sources, but some from the public domain. I have not credited my own photographs. I have already mentioned my deep indebtedness to Michael Horsfall and Hennie Noordhuis.

I extend my warm thanks to the following people and institutions whose photographs, diagrams or maps I have used to illustrate this book; their names appear in alphabetical order, and I give the title of the publication if the item appears in it.

Altes, Margry, Thurling and Voskuil: "September 1944"; Peter Arnold; Constance Babington Smith: "Evidence in Camera"; A. Berjek: "The War on Our Doorstep"; Gordon Bellerby, DFC;

David Birch; Dirk Boomkamp; Jan Bovenmars; Borne Municipal Archive; Alan Brown; Charles E. Brown Collection; Cmdt. Peter Celis; "Daily Telegraph"; Lewis Deal; Raeburn Dobson; D. Doornbos; DotKa, Holland; Ray Dutt, AFC; Ethell and Price: "The German Jets in Combat"; Peter Fahy, DFC, AFC; Thomas Giessmann; Norman Godfrey, DFC, CdeG; Groesbeek Liberation Museum 1944; Richard Haigh; Dr Colin Hall; Alec Harvey-Bailey; Ken Holloway; Micheal Horsfall; Basil Jackson; Cor Janse; Mark Johnson; Arthur Kirk-Waring; KLM; Capt. Jeroen ('Gorby') Kloosterman; Dr Nick Lambrechtsen; Harry Leuveld; Eric Martin; A.C. Meyling; Michelin; Ron Miller; Morgan and Shacklady: "Spitfire – the History"; Robin Neillands: "The Conquest of the Reich"; Roy Nesbit: "Eyes of the RAF"; Ron Nobes; Hennie Noordhuis: "In Suffering, Resistance and Freedom"; Michael Oakey: "Aeroplane"; Mr. van Ommen; Ron Parnell, MiD; Douglas Petrie, DFC; Eric Phillips; Graham Pitchfork, OBE; Hans Pol: "Our Forgotten Liberators"; Dr Alfred Price: "Spitfire at War 2", "Supermarine Spitfire"; RAF Benson; RAF Museum, Hendon; Karl Rekers: "The End of the War in our Region"; Hugh Rigby Collection; Bruce Robertson: "Spitfire – the Story of a Famous Fighter"; Rolls-Royce Corporate Heritage; Rolls-Royce Heritage Trust; Wally Rouse; Riet Sanders-Roetgerink; Hugh Smallwood: "Spitfire in Blue"; Chris Staerck: "Allied Photo Reconnaissance in World War II"; Jonathan Taylor; Geoffrey Teece; Betsie Timmerman; Hermine Vonk; Wesel Town Archive; Michael Wetz, DFC.

York Publishing Services:

My special thanks go to Duncan Beal (Managing Director), Barry Perks (my Graphic Designer), and Cathie Poole (Marketing Manager) and all the team at York Publishing Services, who produced this book.

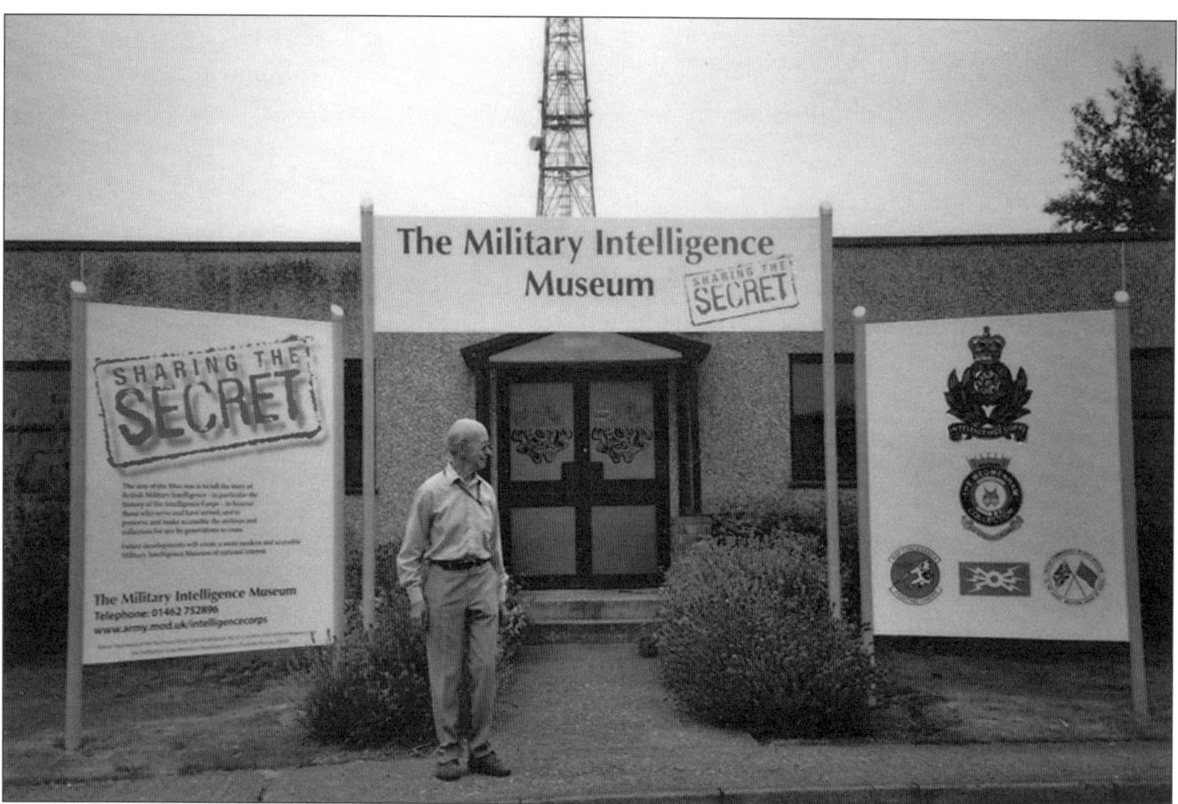

W/C Mike Mockford, OBE, RAF (Retd), tireless Secretary of the Medmenham Club, outside the Medmenham Collection at RAF Chicksands, near Cambridge

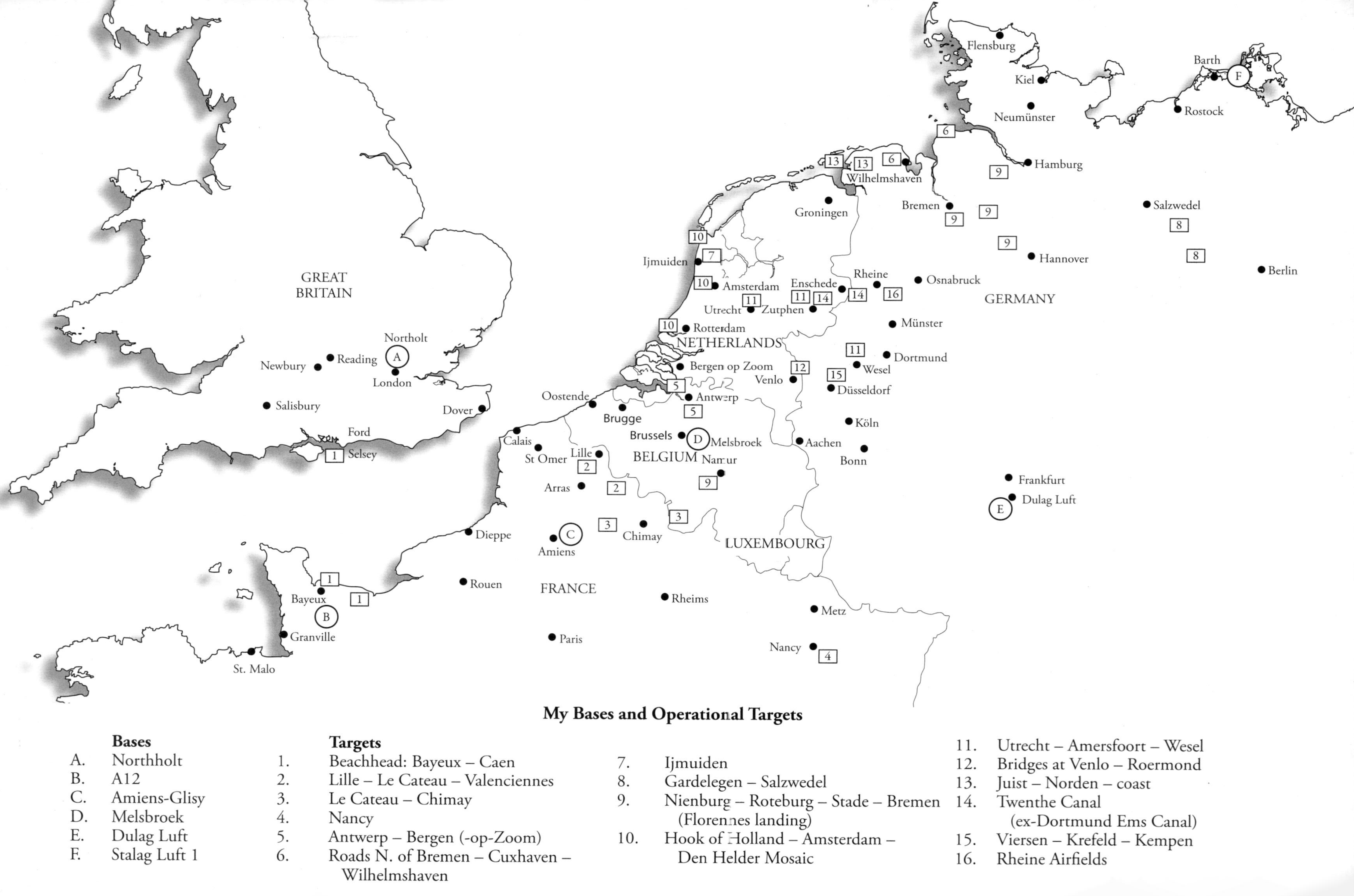

My Bases and Operational Targets

Bases

A. Northholt
B. A12
C. Amiens-Glisy
D. Melsbroek
E. Dulag Luft
F. Stalag Luft 1

Targets

1. Beachhead: Bayeux – Caen
2. Lille – Le Cateau – Valenciennes
3. Le Cateau – Chimay
4. Nancy
5. Antwerp – Bergen (-op-Zoom)
6. Roads N. of Bremen – Cuxhaven – Wilhelmshaven
7. Ijmuiden
8. Gardelegen – Salzwedel
9. Nienburg – Roteburg – Stade – Bremen (Florennes landing)
10. Hook of Holland – Amsterdam – Den Helder Mosaic
11. Utrecht – Amersfoort – Wesel
12. Bridges at Venlo – Roermond
13. Juist – Norden – coast
14. Twenthe Canal (ex-Dortmund Ems Canal)
15. Viersen – Krefeld – Kempen
16. Rheine Airfields